Learning & Memory

SECOND EDITION

MACMILLAN PSYCHOLOGY REFERENCE SERIES

The Macmillan Psychology Reference Series is an on-going collection of single-volume overviews of the disciplines of psychology. Each volume in the series presents a comprehensive and accessible snapshot of a psychology field for general readers, high school seniors, and college freshmen. *Child Development* (2001), the first volume in the series, examines the contemporary issues in the field of child and adolescent development. Each work will feature the latest research in the field along with numerous real-world applications and examples.

Learning
& Memory

SECOND EDITION

John H. Byrne, Editor in Chief

**MACMILLAN
REFERENCE
USA™**

New York • Detroit • San Diego • San Francisco • Cleveland • New Haven, Conn. • Waterville, Maine • London • Munich

Learning and Memory, Second Edition

© 2003 by Macmillan Reference USA.
Macmillan Reference USA is an imprint of
The Gale Group, Inc., a division of Thomson
Learning, Inc.

Macmillan Reference USA™ and Thomson
Learning™ are trademarks used herein under
license.

For more information, contact
Macmillan Reference USA
300 Park Avenue South
New York, NY 10010
Or you can visit our Internet site at
http://www.gale.com

Cover images reproduced by permission of
William T. Greenough and James D. Churchill
(synapses), Photodisc (MRI profile), and Corbis
(brain).

Since this page cannot legibly accommodate all copyright notices, the acknowledg-
ments constitute an extension of the copyright notice.

LIBRARY OF CONGRESS CATALOG-IN-PUBLICATION DATA

Learning & Memory / edited by John H. Byrne. - - 2nd ed.
   p. cm. - - (Macmillan psychology reference series)
        Previous ed. published as: Encyclopedia of learning and memory. New
        York : Macmillan, c1992.
        ISBN 0-02-865619-9
        1. Learning, Psychology of- -Encyclopedias. 2. Memory- -
        Encyclopedias. 3. Learning in animals- -Encyclopedias. 4. Animal
        memory- -Encyclopedias. 5. Neuropsychology- -Encyclopedias. I. Title:
        Learning and memory. II. Byrne, John H. III. Series.

BF318 .E53 2002
153 . 1'03- -dc21   2002008357

Printed in the United States of America
10 9 8 7 6 5 4 3 2 1

CONTENTS

EDITORIAL AND PRODUCTION STAFF

PROJECT EDITOR
Ken Wachsberger

EDITORIAL
Denise Evans
Gretchen Gordon
Bill Kaufman
Gina Misiroglu
Patricia Onorato
Angela Pilchak
Gregory Teague

IMAGING AND MULTIMEDIA
Dean Dauphinais
Mary Grimes
Lezlie Light

PRODUCT DESIGN
Cindy Baldwin

PERMISSIONS
Lori Hines

COMPOSITION
Evi Seoud

MANUFACTURING
Rita Wimberley

INDEXER
Linda K. Fetters

PREFACE

Learning refers to the process of acquiring new information, whereas *memory* refers to the retention of that information so that it can be retrieved at a later time. The topics of learning and memory have intrigued philosophers and writers for centuries, and for good reason. Learning and memory are so central to our daily lives that disruption in these functions can interrupt our most routine activities. For example, consider the extraordinary memory processes that must take place for you to successfully drive from home to work. When you wake up, you need to recall whether or not that day is a workday. When you enter your car, you need to remember the best route to work and any traffic information that you may have heard to expedite your arrival. Next, you have to recall how to drive your car and the complex rules of the road. When you arrive at work, you need to remember the names of your colleagues and draw upon a memory for job-related vocabulary and common past experiences. Most importantly, you need to remember the skills that allow you to perform your job.

The centrality of learning and memory to our daily lives has led to intense analysis by psychologists and neurobiologists for the past century, and it will undoubtedly remain at the forefront of research throughout this new century as well. Learning and memory systems are vast and diverse, yet scientists have determined that memory can be divided into two major types: memory for skills and habits, and memory for facts and events. Moreover, significant progress has been made in understanding the parts of the brain involved in learning and memory as well as in acquiring a basic understanding of the genes, proteins, and signaling molecules that mediate memory acquisition and storage. *Learning and Memory, Second Edition* contains articles that discuss these findings. It also contains biographical sketches of some of the key individuals, now deceased, who have contributed to the current understanding of learning and memory.

Despite the great progress that has been made, many questions remain. Why will we remember exactly where we were on September 11, 2001 for the rest of our lives, but we cannot remember what we had for lunch on this day two weeks ago? Why are we unable to recall events from our infancy? Are there any drugs that can improve our memory? What is Alzheimer's disease and how can it be treated? *Learning and Memory, Second Edition* contains articles on these key aspects of memory. In general, its goal is to provide readers with a comprehensive overview of key topics in learning and memory through brief articles written by selected experts in the field.

All of the entries are original contributions from scholars and researchers, written for a readership of students, teachers, journalists, and members of the educated public. The articles range in length from 800 to 3,000 words. Entries are arranged alphabetically; each is accompanied by a bibliography listing suggestions for further reading. The entries are also linked by a comprehensive set of cross-references that appear at the end of many of the entries. For example, in the entry on infantile amnesia, one finds cross-references to the following entries: CHILDHOOD, DEVELOPMENT OF MEMORY IN; CODING PROCESSES: ORGANIZATION OF MEMORY; EPISODIC MEMORY; EXPERTS' MEMORIES; GUIDE TO THE ANATOMY OF THE BRAIN; NATURAL SETTINGS, MEMORY IN; PROSE RETENTION.

In addition, *blind entries* facilitate access to main articles (for example, "Drugs. *See:* COGNITIVE ENHANCERS; DRUGS AND MEMORY; ELECTROCONVULSIVE THERAPY AND MEMORY LOSS; PHARMACOLOGICAL TREATMENT OF MEMORY DEFICITS."). These blind entries are arranged alphabetically throughout *Learning and Memory* and provide alternate access points to direct the reader to appropriate articles An additional feature is the use of guideposts or series introductions. Where there is a group of related articles on a single topic, a short guidepost is available to orient the reader to the topic. For example, for the area of invertebrate learning, a short introduction presents an overview of the six entries that follow.

This second edition of *Learning and Memory* builds upon the success of the first, which was called *Encyclopedia of Learning and Memory* when it was published by Macmillan in 1992. We are indebted to Larry Squire, the previous editor, for establishing the overall direction and organization of the *Encyclopedia,* which this second edition maintains. This second edition would not have been possible without the tremendous work of the current Editorial Board, who identified the topics and their authors, and reviewed each contribution. Special thanks also go to Jill Lectka, Director of Publishing Operations at Macmillan Reference USA, and Project Editor Ken Wachsberger for supporting the concept of a second edition as well as ensuring that the production schedule was maintained.

John H. Byrne

LIST OF ARTICLES

LIST OF CONTRIBUTORS

Charles I. Abramson
Oklahoma State University
Insect Learning

Marilyn S. Albert
Harvard Medical School
Alzheimer's Disease:
Behavioral Aspects

Brent Alsop
University of Otago, New Zealand
Operant Behavior

Abram Amsel
University of Texas
Hull, Clark L. (1884–1952)

Per O. Andersen
University of Oslo, Norway
Eccles, John (1903–1997)

Andreas Arvanitogiannis
Concordia University, Montreal
Reinforcement or Reward in
Learning: Electrical Self-Stimulation, Brain

Jocelyne B. Bachevalier
University of Texas Medical School at Houston
Sex Differences in Learning

Gregory F. Ball
Johns Hopkins University
Birdsong Learning

Jacques Balthazart
University of Liège, Belgium
Birdsong Learning

Albert Bandura
Stanford University
Observational Learning

Shaowen Bao
University of California, San Francisco
Genetic Substrates of
Memory: Cerebellum

Helen Barbas
Boston University
Guide to the Anatomy of the
Brain: Cerebral Cortex

William B. Barr
New York University School of Medicine
Knowledge Systems and
Material-Specific Memory
Deficits

Andrew G. Barto
University of Massachussetts
Algorithms, Learning
Reinforcement

Barbara H. Basden
California State University, Fresno
Social Memory Processes

Michel Baudry
University of Southern California
Long-Term Potentiation:
Maintenance
Neurotransmitter Systems
and Memory

Mark G. Baxter
Harvard University
Kamin's Blocking Effect:
Neuronal Substrates

Diego E. Berman
Weizmann Institute of Science, Israel
Taste Aversion and
Preference Learning in
Animals

Daniel M. Bernstein
University of Washington, Seattle
Reconstructive Memory

Verner P. Bingman
Bowling Green State University
Migration, Navigation, and
Homing

Robert A. Bjork
UCLA
Interference and Forgetting

Johan J. Bolhuis
Utrecht University, The Netherlands
Imprinting

Robert C. Bolles
University of Washington (ret.)
Learning Theory: A History

Susan E. Brandon
Yale University and American Psychological Association
Sometimes Opponent
Process (SOP) Model, in
Conditioning

Todd S. Braver
Washington University, St. Louis
Working Memory: Humans

Alan S. Brown
Southern Methodist University
Déjà Vu

Thomas H. Brown
Yale University
Long-Term Potentiation:
Amygdala

F. Robert Brush
Purdue University
Active and Passive Avoidance
Learning: Behavioral
Phenomena

Dean V. Buonomano
UCLA
Conditioning, Cellular and
Network Schemes for
Higher-Order Features of
Classical

Rebecca D. Burwell
Brown University
Guide to the Anatomy of the
Brain: Perirhinal Cortex
and Associated Cortical
Areas

John H. Byrne
*University of Texas Medical
School at Houston*
Aplysia: Classical
Conditioning and Operant
Conditioning
Aplysia: Molecular Basis of
Long-Term Sensitization

Thomas J. Carew
University of California, Irvine
Aplysia: Development of
Processes Underlying
Learning
Metaplasticity

Leslie J. Carver
*University of California,
San Diego*
Infancy, Memory in

Claude G. Čech
*University of Louisiana at
Lafayette*
Semantic Memory: Cognitive
Effects

Jason C. K. Chan
Washington University, St. Louis
False Memories

Lu Chen
*University of California, San
Francisco*

Genetic Substrates of
Memory: Cerebellum

James D. Churchill
*University of Illinois at Urbana-
Champaign*
Morphological Basis of
Learning and Memory:
Vertebrates

Patricia Smith Churchland
*University of California, San
Diego*
Aristotle (384–322 B.C.E.)

Anna T. Cianciolo
Yale University
Intelligence and Memory

Len Cleary
*University of Texas Medical
School at Houston*
Morphological Basis of
Learning and Memory:
Invertebrates

Neal Cohen
University of Illinois
Declarative Memory

Thomas S. Collett
*University of Sussex, Brighton,
UK*
Spatial Learning: Animals

Martin A. Conway
University of Durham, UK
Autobiographical Memory

Nelson Cowan
University of Missouri
Modality Effects
Sensory Memory

Fergus I. M. Craik
*Rotman Research Institute of
Baycrest Centre, Toronto*
Aging and Memory in
Humans

Terry J. Crow
*University of Texas Medical
School at Houston*
Invertebrate Learning:
Associative Learning in
Hermissenda

Robert G. Crowder
Yale University (ret.)
Eidetic Imagery

McGeoch, John A.
(1897–1942)

Peter W. Culicover
Ohio State University
Language Learning: Humans

Joel L. Davis
Office of Naval Research
Neurotransmitter Systems
and Memory

Michael Davis
Emory University
Habituation and Sensitization
in Vertebrates
Neural Substrates of Classical
Conditioning: Fear-
Potentiated Startle

Anthony Dickinson
University of Cambridge, UK
Konorski, Jerzy (1903–1973)

John F. Disterhoft
*Northwestern University Medical
School*
Olds, James (1922–1973)

Barbara Anne Dosher
University of California, Irvine
Memory Search

Janet M. Duchek
*Washington University School of
Medicine, St. Louis*
Tip-of-the-Tongue
Phenomenon

M. David Egger
*University of Medicine and
Dentistry of New Jersey*
Habituation and Sensitization
in Vertebrates

Howard Eichenbaum
Boston University
Long-Term Potentiation:
Behavioral

Matthew Hugh Erdelyi
*Brooklyn College and the
Graduate School, City
University of New York*
Freud, Sigmund (1856–1939)

K. Anders Ericsson
Florida State University
Experts' Memories

W. K. Estes
Indiana University
Mathematical Learning
Theory

Michael S. Fanselow
UCLA
Neural Substrates of Classical
Conditioning: Fear
Conditioning, Freezing

Daniel J. Felleman
*University of Texas Medical
School at Houston*
Neocortical Plasticity: Adult
Visual Cortex—Adaptation
and Reorganization

Leif H. Finkel
University of Pennsylvania
Neural Computation:
Neocortex

Thomas M. Fischer
Wayne State University
Metaplasticity

R. Holly Fitch
University of Connecticut, Storrs
Learning Disabilities

William N. Frost
Chicago Medical School
Invertebrate Learning:
Habituation and
Sensitization in Tritonia

John J. Furedy
University of Toronto
Pavlov, Ivan (1849–1936)

Joaquin M. Fuster
UCLA
Prefrontal Cortex and
Memory in

Michael Gabriel
*University of Illinois and
Beckman Institute*
Neural Substrates of
Avoidance Learning

Fred H. Gage
*Salk Institute for Biological
Studies, La Jolla, CA*
Neurogenesis

Bennett G. Galef, Jr.
McMaster University, Ontario
Food Aversion and
Preference Learning in
Humans

John M. Gardiner
University of Sussex, UK
Modality Effects

Alan Gelperin
*Monell Chemical Senses Center,
Philadelphia*
Invertebrate Learning:
Associative Learning in
Limax

Kelly Sullivan Giovanello
*Boston University School of
Medicine*
Amnesia, Organic

Elizabeth L. Glisky
University of Arizona
Rehabilitation of Memory
Disorders

Bill P. Godsil
UCLA
Neural Substrates of Classical
Conditioning: Fear
Conditioning, Freezing

Elkhonon Goldberg
*New York University School of
Medicine*
Knowledge Systems and
Material-Specific Memory
Deficits
Luria, A .R. (1902–1977)

I. Gormezano
University of Iowa (ret.)
Conditioning, Classical and
Instrumental

Gilbert Gottlieb
*University of North Carolina at
Chapel Hill*
Thorndike, Edward
(1874–1949)

Richard H. Granger, Jr.
University of California, Irvine
Neural Computation:
Olfactory Cortex as a Model
for Telencephalic
Processing

Ann M. Graybiel
*Massachusetts Institute of
Technology*
Guide to the Anatomy of the
Brain: Basal Ganglia

John T. Green
Indiana University
Classical Conditioning:
Behavioral Phenomena

Robert L. Greene
Case Western Reserve University
Distributed Practice Effects
Repetition and Learning

William T. Greenough
*University of Illinois at Urbana-
Champaign*
Morphological Basis of
Learning and Memory:
Vertebrates

Howard E. Gruber
*Teachers College, Columbia
University (ret.)*
Piaget, Jean (1896–1980)

Bengt Gustafsson
Göteborg University, Sweden
Long-Term Potentiation:
Overview: Cooperativity and
Associativity

Eric Hanse
Göteborg University, Sweden
Long-Term Potentiation:
Overview: Cooperativity and
Associativity

Gerri Hanten
*Baylor College of Medicine,
Houston*
Head Injury

Kristen M. Harris
Boston University
Guide to the Anatomy of the
Brain: Synapse

Michael E. Hasselmo
Boston University
Guide to the Anatomy of the
Brain: Olfactory Cortex

Harlene Hayne
*University of Otago, New
Zealand*
Amnesia, Infantile

Alice F. Healy
University of Colorado
Serial Organization

Eliot Hearst
University of Arizona
Watson, John B. (1878–1958)

Stephan Heckers
Massachusetts General Hospital
Schizophrenia and Memory

Fred J. Helmstetter
University of Wisconsin,
Milwaukee
Genetic Substrates of
Memory: Amygdala

Stewart Hendry
Johns Hopkins University
Guide to the Anatomy of the
Brain: Cerebral Cortex

Paula Hertel
Trinity University
Emotion, Mood, and
Memory

Peter W. Hickmott
University of California,
Riverside
Neocortical Plasticity:
Somatosensory Cortex

Ernest R. Hilgard
Stanford University (ret.)
Guthrie, Edwin R.
(1886–1959)

Philip N. Hineline
Temple University
Behaviorism

Robert M. Hodapp
UCLA
Mental Retardation
(Intellectual Disabilities)

W. K. Honig
Dalhousie University, Halifax,
Canada (ret.)
Operant Behavior

G. Horn
Cambridge University
Imprinting

James C. Houk
Northwestern University Medical
School
Motor Skill Learning

Masao Ito
Brain Science Institute, RIKEN,
Japan
Long-Term Depression in the
Cerebellum, Hippocampus,
and Neocortex
Neural Computation:
Cerebellum
Vestibulo-Ocular Reflex
(VOR) Plasticity

Bharathi Jagadeesh
University of Washington, Seattle
Primates, Visual Attention in

Marcia K. Johnson
Yale University
Source Monitoring

Robert V. Kail
Purdue University
Children, Development of
Memory in

Gerd Kempermann
Max Delbrück Center for
Molecular Medicine and
Humboldt University, Berlin
Neurogenesis

Howard H. Kendler
University of California, Santa
Barbara (ret.)
Spence, Kenneth
(1907–1967)

John F. Kihlstrom
University of California, Berkeley
Amnesia, Functional
Hypnosis and Memory

Jeansok J. Kim
Yale University
Kamin's Blocking Effect:
Neuronal Substrates

Jeffrey A. Kleim
University of Lethbridge, Alberta,
Canada
Neocortical Plasticity: Motor
Cortex

Barbara J. Knowlton
UCLA
Procedural Learning:
Humans

Bryan E. Kolb
University of Lethbridge, Canada
Harlow, Harry F. (1905–1981)

Yuri Koutcherov
Prince of Wales Medical Research
Institute, Australia
Guide to the Anatomy of the
Brain: Overview

Mark Kritchevsky
University of California, San
Diego
Amnesia, Transient Global

David J. Krupa
Duke University
Localization of Memory
Traces

David Lavond
University of Southern California
Visual Memory, Brightness
and Flux in

Hilde A. E. Lechner
Salk Institute for Biological
Studies, La Jolla, CA
Müller, Georg Elias
(1850–1934)

Joseph E. LeDoux
New York University
Neural Substrates of
Emotional Memory

Harvey Levin
Baylor College of Medicine,
Houston
Head Injury

Seymour Levine
University of California, Davis
Early Experience and
Learning

Derick H. Lindquist
Yale University
Long-Term Potentiation:
Amygdala

Robert S. Lockhart
University of Toronto
Coding Processes: Levels of
Processing
Measurement of Memory

Elizabeth F. Loftus
University of Washington, Seattle
Reconstructive Memory

Jessica M. Logan
Washington University, St. Louis
Tip-of-the-Tongue
Phenomenon

Fred D. Lorenzetti
University of Texas Medical School at Houston
Aplysia: Classical Conditioning and Operant Conditioning

Gary Lynch
University of California, Irvine
Long-Term Potentiation: Maintenance

Colin M. MacLeod
University of Toronto at Scarborough
Individual Differences in Learning and Memory

Steven E. Maier
University of Colorado
Learned Helplessness

Steve Maren
University of Michigan
Learning Theory: Current Status

Marc Marschark
Rochester Institute of Technology
Coding Processes: Imagery

Michael Mauk
University of Texas Medical School at Houston
Guide to the Anatomy of the Brain: Cerebellum

James L. McClelland
Carnegie Mellon University
Parallel Distributed Processing Models of Memory

Mark A. McDaniel
University of New Mexico
Mnemonic Devices
Prose Retention

Kathleen B. McDermott
Washington University, St. Louis
False Memories

Alexander J. McDonald
University of South Carolina School of Medicine
Guide to the Anatomy of the Brain: Amygdala

Brian McElree
New York University
Memory Search

James L. McGaugh
University of California, Irvine
Hormones and Memory

Timothy McNamara
Vanderbilt University
Spatial Memory

Bruce L. McNaughton
University of Arizona
Neural Computation: Hippocampus

Michelle L. Meade
Washington University, St. Louis
Retrieval Processes in Memory

Andrew N. Meltzoff
University of Washington, Seattle
Infancy, Memory in

Randolf Menzel
Freie Universität Berlin
Invertebrate Learning: Associative Learning and Memory Processing in Bees

M-Marsel Mesulam
Feinberg Medical School of Northwestern University
Guide to the Anatomy of the Brain: Basal Forebrain

Peter M. Milner
McGill University, Montreal
Hebb, Donald (1904–1985)

Karen J. Mitchell
Yale University
Source Monitoring

John Moore
University of Massachusetts-Amherst
Discrimination and Generalization

Morris Moscovitch
University of Toronto and Rotman Research Institute, Toronto
Frontal Lobes and Episodic Memory

Edvard I. Moser
Norwegian University of Science and Technology
Place Cells

Neil W. Mulligan
Southern Methodist University
Implicit Memory

Cynthia A. Munro
Johns Hopkins University School of Medicine
Dementia

David J. Murray
Queen's University at Kingston, Canada
Bartlett, Frederic (1886–1969)

Elisabeth A. Murray
National Institute of Mental Health
Primates, Visual Perception and Memory in Nonhuman

Ian Neath
Purdue University
Forgetting

Ulric Neisser
Cornell University
Natural Settings, Memory in

Thomas O. Nelson
University of Maryland, College Park
Metacognition about Memory

Mark G. Packard
Yale University
Multiple-Memory Systems
Place versus Response Learning Revisited in the Brain
Procedural Learning: Animals

Harold Pashler
University of California, San Diego
Attention and Memory

Michael M. Patterson
University of California, San Diego
Spinal Plasticity

George Paxinos
Prince of Wales Medical Research Institute, Australia
Guide to the Anatomy of the Brain: Overview

Steven E. Petersen
Washington University, St. Louis
Neuroimaging

Gregg A. Phares
*University of Texas Medical
School at Houston*
Aplysia: Molecular Basis of
Long-Term Sensitization

Donald A. Powell
*Dorn VA Medical Center and
University of South Carolina*
Neural Substrates of Classical
Conditioning:
Cardiovascular Responses

Donald L. Price
*Johns Hopkins University School
of Medicine*
Alzheimer's Disease: Human
Disease and the Genetically
Engineered Animal Models

Stanley J. Rachman
University of British Columbia
Behavior Therapy
Phobias

Catharine H. Rankin
University of British Columbia
Invertebrate Learning: C. ele-
gans

Donald A. Riley
University of California, Berkeley
Tolman, Edward C.
(1886–1959)

Henry L. Roediger III
Washington University, St. Louis
Retrieval Processes in
Memory

Benno Roozendaal
University of California, Irvine
Hormones and Memory

Gregory M. Rose
*Memory Pharmaceuticals Corp.,
Montvale, NJ*
Cognitive Enhancers
Drugs and Memory
Pharmacological Treatment
of Memory Deficits

Steven P. R. Rose
Open University, UK
Protein Synthesis in Long-
Term Memory in
Vertebrates

Mark R. Rosenzweig
University of California, Berkeley
Tolman, Edward C.
(1886–1959)

Paul Rozin
University of Pennsylvania
Food Aversion and
Preference Learning in
Humans

David C. Rubin
Duke University
Oral Traditions

Duane M. Rumbaugh
Georgia State University
Language Learning:
Nonhuman Primates

Kurt Salzinger
*American Psychological
Association*
Skinner, B. F. (1904–1990)

E. Sue Savage-Rumbaugh
Georgia State University
Language Learning:
Nonhuman Primates

Meghan Saweikis
Purdue University
Children, Development of
Memory in

Daniel L. Schacter
Harvard University
Amnesia, Functional
Semon, Richard (1859–1918)

Glenn E. Schafe
New York University
Neural Substrates of
Emotional Memory

Petra Scheck
*University of Maryland, College
Park*
Metacognition about Memory

Wolfram Schultz
University of Cambridge
Reinforcement or Reward in
Learning: Striatum

Roger W. Schvaneveldt
Arizona State University, East
Coding Processes:
Organization of Memory

James H. Schwartz
Columbia University
Second Messenger Systems

Terrence J. Sejnowski
*Salk Institute for Biological
Studies, San Diego*
Neural Computation:
Approaches to Learning

Matthew L. Shapiro
*Mount Sinai School of Medicine,
New York*
Olton, David (1943–1994)

David F. Sherry
University of Western Ontario
Evolution and Learning
Lorenz, Konrad (1903–1989)

Sara J. Shettleworth
University of Toronto
Foraging

Paul G. Shinkman
*University of North Carolina at
Chapel Hill*
Neocortical Plasticity:
Development of the Visual
System

Jeanne L. Shinskey
University of Denver
Object Concept,
Development of

Tracey J. Shors
*Rutgers University, Picataway,
NJ*
Stress and Memory

Jean-Louis Signoret
Salpetriere Hospital, Paris (ret.)
Ribot, Théodule (1839–1916)

Alcino J. Silva
UCLA
Genetic Substrates of
Memory: Hippocampus
Memory Consolidation:
Molecular and Cellular
Processes

Wolf Singer
*Max Planck Institute for Brain
Research, Frankfurt, Germany*
Oscillations, Synchrony, and
Neuronal Codes

Brian H. Smith
Ohio State University
Insect Learning

E. N. Sokolov
Moscow Lomonosov State University (ret.)
Orienting Reflex Habituation

Peter Somogyi
University of Oxford, UK
Guide to the Anatomy of the Brain: Neuron

Norman E. Spear
Binghamton University
Hunter, Walter S. (1889–1954)

Larry R. Squire
VA Medical Center, San Diego and University of California, San Diego
Electroconvulsive Therapy and Memory Loss
Memory Consolidation: Prolonged Process of Reorganization

Stephan Steidl
University of British Columbia
Invertebrate Learning: C. elegans

Joseph E. Steinmetz
Indiana University
Classical Conditioning: Behavioral Phenomena
Neural Substrates of Classical Conditioning: Discrete Behavioral Responses

Robert J. Sternberg
Yale University
Intelligence and Memory

Robert Stickgold
Harvard Medical School
Sleep and Memory Consolidation

Deborah Suchecki
Universidade Federal de São Paulo
Early Experience and Learning

Rodney A. Swain
University of Wisconsin-Milwaukee
Reinforcement or Reward in Learning: Cerebellum

Larry W. Swanson
University of Southern California
Ramón y Cajal, Santiago (1852–1934)

J. David Sweatt
Baylor College of Medicine, Houston
Long-Term Potentiation: Signal Transduction Mechanisms and Early Events

Jared P. Taglialatela
Georgia State University
Language Learning: Nonhuman Primates

Charles P. Thompson
Kansas State University
Mnemonists

Richard F. Thompson
University of Southern California
Lashley, Karl (1890–1958)

Richard H. Thompson
University of British Columbia
Reinforcement or Reward in Learning: Anatomical Substrates

Sharon L. Thompson-Schill
University of Pennsylvania
Semantic Memory: Neurobiological Perspective

Darold A. Treffert
St. Agnes Hospital, WI
Savant Syndrome

Tim Tully
Cold Spring Harbor Laboratory, NY
Invertebrate Learning: Neurogenetics of Memory in Drosophila

Endel Tulving
Rotman Research Institute of Baycrest Centre, Toronto
Ebbinghaus, Hermann (1850–1909)
Episodic Memory

Almira Vazdarjanova
University of Arizona
Passive (Inhibitory) Avoidance, Fear Learning

Mieke Verfaellie
Boston University School of Medicine and Boston VA Healthcare System
Amnesia, Organic

Indre V. Viskontas
UCLA
Procedural Learning: Humans

Allan R. Wagner
Yale University
Sometimes Opponent Process (SOP) Model, in Conditioning

Michael J. Watkins
Rice University
Memory Span

M. N. Waxham
University of Texas Medical School at Houston
Glutamate Receptors and Their Characterization

Jack C. Waymire
University of Texas Medical School at Houston
Activity-Dependent Regulation of Neurotransmitter Synthesis

Norman M. Weinberger
University of California, Irvine
Neocortical Plasticity: Auditory Cortex

Anthony P. Weiss
Massachusetts General Hospital
Schizophrenia and Memory

James V. Wertsch
Washington University, St. Louis
Collective Memory

Sheldon White
Harvard University
James, William (1842–1910)

Gordon Winocur
*Trent University, Peterborough,
and Rotman Research Institute,
Toronto*
Frontal Lobes and Episodic
Memory

Edward Wisniewski
*University of North Carolina at
Greensboro*
Concepts and Categories,
Learning of

Menno P. Witter
*Vrije Universiteit Medical Center,
Amsterdam*
Guide to the Anatomy of the
Brain: Hippocampus and
Parahippocampal Region

M.C. Wittrock
UCLA
School Learning

Philip C. Wong
*Johns Hopkins University School
of Medicine*
Alzheimer's Disease: Human
Disease and the Genetically
Engineered Animal Models

Diana S. Woodruff-Pak
Temple University
Aging and Memory in
Animals

Anthony A. Wright
*University of Texas Medical
School at Houston*
Comparative Cognition
Working Memory: Animals

Eugene B. Zechmeister
Loyola University
Underwood, Benton
(1915–1994)

ACTIVE AND PASSIVE AVOIDANCE LEARNING: BEHAVIORAL PHENOMENA

Avoidance learning is the behavioral product of an instrumental (operant) training procedure in which a predictable aversive event, typically electric shock, does *not* occur contingent upon the occurrence or nonoccurrence of a specified response by the learning organism. Avoidance training occurs in two forms: active and passive. In the active form, the avoidance contingency depends on the occurrence of a specified response on the part of the organism; in the passive form, the avoidance contingency depends on the *nonoccurrence* (i.e., the suppression) of some specified response. The response to be suppressed may be either spontaneous or learned by virtue of prior reward training. In both forms, however, the avoidance contingency consists of the prevention or omission of a predictable noxious event. Noxious events are defined in terms of the preference relation in which the absence of the event is preferred (measured by choice) to the presence of the event. Usually the noxious event is electric shock, but loud noise, blasts of air, and high and low temperatures have been used.

Avoidance training also utilizes one of two procedures: discrete-trial or free-operant. In the discrete-trial procedure a distinctive stimulus, called a *warning signal* (WS), signals the organism that the occurrence of the aversive event (e.g., electric shock) is imminent. In most experiments the WS-shock interval is five to sixty seconds in duration. In the active form, making the specified response during the WS-shock interval terminates the WS and prevents the occurrence of the shock. In the passive form, suppression of the specified response during the WS-shock interval prevents the occurrence of the shock. In both forms an intertrial interval (ITI) intervenes between successive presentations of the WS, usually in the range of 0.5 to 5.0 minutes.

In the active free-operant procedure there are no discrete trials signaled by WSs. Instead, the avoidance contingency is dependent on time. Specifically, two timers control events: a response-shock (R-S) timer (e.g., set for thirty seconds) and a shock-shock (S-S) timer (e.g., set for five seconds). Training starts with the S-S timer operating. Every time it runs out, it restarts and delivers an inescapable shock of some duration (e.g., 0.5 second). The specified response turns off the S-S timer and starts the R-S timer. Every additional response resets the R-S timer to its full value. If the R-S timer runs out, it presents a shock and starts the S-S timer (Sidman, 1953). This procedure has been used only in the active form. A variation of this procedure eliminates the S-S timer and makes shock termination contingent upon the specified response rather than upon a fixed duration of shock.

In addition, a free-operant passive procedure known as *punishment* simply takes a response, which occurs spontaneously or by virtue of prior reward training, and makes shock or some other aversive event contingent on the occurrence of that response. The response is usually suppressed. This is also called *passive-avoidance training*. It has been used in a proce-

1

dure in which an animal such as a mouse or rat runs from a brightly lighted elevated platform into a dark compartment where it receives a single electric shock. The tendency to enter the dark compartment is innate, and the single punishment results in subsequent long latencies to reenter the dark compartment. This is called one-trial passive-avoidance training, and it has been used extensively in the study of memory because the learning event is fixed in time, which allows analysis and manipulation of temporarily constrained neuropharmacological and endocrine processes associated with learning. Alternatively, a hungry animal may initially be rewarded with food for pressing a lever and subsequently shocked for making that same response. Usually several shocks are required to suppress the lever pressing.

Warner (1932) was the first to use a discrete-trial active-avoidance procedure to study the association span of the white rat (using WS-shock intervals of one to thirty seconds); he used what has become known as a shuttle box, a two-compartment box in which the animal is required to run or jump back and forth between the two compartments to avoid the shock.

These procedures and the behaviors they produce have been of interest to psychologists since the early studies of behaviorism in the United States. John Watson and, especially, Edward Thorndike postulated that learned responses were a product of their consequences. That is, a response occurs, a pleasurable or aversive event ensues, and the response is reinforced (increases) if the event is pleasurable or punished (decreases) if the event is aversive.

Hilgard and Marquis (1940), two early behavioral theorists, had trouble accounting for avoidance learning because it was a product of a procedure where the reinforcing event was the response-contingent *absence* of an event, not the response-contingent *presence* of an event:

> Learning in this [avoidance] situation appears to be based in a real sense on the avoidance of the shock. It differs clearly from other types of instrumental training in which the conditioned response is followed by a definite stimulus change—food or the cessation of shock [reward training (positive reinforcement) or escape training (negative reinforcement)]. In instrumental avoidance training the new response is strengthened in the absence of any such stimulus; indeed, it is strengthened because of the absence of such a stimulus. Absence of stimulation can obviously have an influence on behavior only if there exists some sort of preparation for or expectation of the stimulation. (pp. 58–59)

This theoretical problem was ostensibly solved by Mowrer (1950), supported by Solomon and Wynne (1954) and Rescorla and Solomon (1967), by postulating that Pavlovian conditioning of fear on early escape trials, in which the WS is paired with shock, provided the acquired motivation to terminate the WS (now a conditioned aversive stimulus), thus providing secondary (acquired) negative reinforcement for the escape-from-fear response (i.e., the avoidance response). Others thought that the fear response was instrumentally reinforced by the termination of shock (Miller, 1951), but the upshot was the same: Reduction of fear by termination of the WS, whether acquired by Pavlovian or instrumental means, was the source of the acquired negative reinforcement for the avoidance response. Thus, two processes were postulated: acquisition of fear during escape trials (by Pavlovian or operant conditioning) and acquisition of the instrumental avoidance response, reinforced by fear reduction. This theoretical interpretation was supported by the results of an elegant experiment by Kamin (1956). Additional research in support of two-process theory used a transfer paradigm in which animals were given Pavlovian conditioning in one situation, and the effects of those conditioned stimuli were observed when they were subsequently superimposed on an operant baseline of responding in another situation (Solomon and Turner, 1960). This two-process theory provides the best account of avoidance learning in its various forms.

Some animals of most species learn the avoidance contingency, whether in the active or the passive form, using discrete-trial or free-operant procedures. Dogs are particularly adept at avoidance learning in an active, discrete-trial shuttle-box procedure and typically show strong resistance to extinction (Solomon and Wynne, 1954). In contrast, rats are particularly difficult to train in an active, lever-press, discrete-trial procedure and require special training procedures (Berger and Brush, 1975). Thus, there are important differences among species and response requirements. Additionally, in all forms of avoidance learning—active and passive, discrete-trial and free-operant—there are enormous individual differences. Some individuals of whatever species learn rapidly and well, whereas others do not (Brush, 1966).

In view of these findings it is not surprising that several investigators have genetically selected for differences in avoidance learning. Bignami (1965) reported the first experiment with Wistar albino rats in which the selectively bred phenotypes were good or poor at avoidance learning in a shuttle box. The resulting strains are known as the Roman High Avoidance and Roman Low Avoidance strains (RHA and

RLA, respectively). Training consisted of five daily sessions of fifty trials each. Selection was based on the number of avoidance responses during the first two sessions (many or few) and on good or poor retention from each session to the next. Selection was highly effective because, by the fifth generation, the RHA and RLA animals avoided, respectively, on 68 percent and 20 percent of the trials.

In 1977 Brush reported on the development of the Syracuse High Avoidance and Syracuse Low Avoidance strains (SHA and SLA, respectively). Long-Evans hooded rats were trained for sixty trials in automated shuttle boxes. The data from over twenty generations of selection indicated that shuttle-box avoidance learning is heritable: SHA and SLA animals avoided on 67 percent and 0 percent of the sixty trials of training. Realized heritability (h^2, which can range between 0.0 and 1.0; Falconer, 1960) was estimated to be 0.16 in each strain, a value comparable with that found in other selection studies (Brush, Froehlich, and Sakellaris, 1979).

In 1978 Bammer reported on the first six generations of selective breeding of Sprague-Dawley albino rats for high and low levels of avoidance responding in a shuttle box. The resulting strains are known as the Australian High Avoidance and Australian Low Avoidance strains (AHA and ALA, respectively). Training consisted of fifty trials in one or more daily sessions. Realized heritability over the first five generations of selection was 0.18 and 0.27 for the AHA and ALA strains, respectively.

A unidirectionally selected strain, known as the Tokai High Avoider (THA), was bred in Japan from Wistar stock using a lever-press response and a free-operant procedure (S-S = 5 seconds, R-S = 30 seconds, shock duration = 0.5 second). The selection criterion was an avoidance rate of more than ninety-five percent in the last five of ten daily one-hour training sessions. Selection was successful: THA males and females learn faster and to a higher level of performance than unselected control animals from the original stock.

The fact that so many selective breeding experiments for avoidance behavior have been successful is a clear indicator of the extent to which this kind of behavior is under genetic control. In each experiment the individual variability within each strain becomes less as selection progresses, and it appears not to matter what the details of the training procedures are. For example, SHA animals do better than controls in a free-operant procedure, and THA animals do better than controls in discrete-trial, shuttle-box training. Similarly, AHA animals outperform ALA animals in a discrete-trial avoidance task quite different from the one in which they were selected. Thus, it is clear that avoidance learning is strongly influenced by genetic factors, and many behavioral, physiological, and anatomical correlates of avoidance learning have been identified. Several of those correlates appear to be closely linked, genetically, to the avoidance phenotypes. Researchers are trying to identify the mechanisms by which genes determine avoidance learning. Modern molecular-genetic technology might enable them to identify those genes.

See also: NEURAL SUBSTRATES OF AVOIDANCE LEARNING; PASSIVE (INHIBITORY) AVOIDANCE, FEAR LEARNING

Bibliography

Bammer, G. (1978). Studies on two new strains of rats selectively bred for high or low conditioned avoidance responding. Paper presented at the Annual Meeting of the Australian Society for the Study of Animal Behavior, Brisbane.

Berger, D. F., and Brush, F. R. (1975). Rapid acquisition of discrete-trial lever-press avoidance: Effects of signal-shock interval. *Journal of the Experimental Analysis of Behavior 24,* 227–239.

Bignami, G. (1965). Selection for high rates and low rates of avoidance conditioning in the rat. *Animal Behavior 13,* 221–227.

Brush, F. R. (1966). On the differences between animals that learn and do not learn to avoid electric shock. *Psychonomic Science 5,* 123–124.

—— (1977). Behavioral and endocrine characteristics of rats selectively bred for good and poor avoidance behavior. *Activitas Nervosa Superioris 19,* 254–255.

Brush, F. R., Froehlich, J. C., and Sakellaris, P. C. (1979). Genetic selection for avoidance behavior in the rat. *Behavior Genetics 9,* 309–316.

Falconer, D. S. (1960). *Introduction to quantitative genetics.* London: Oliver and Boyd.

Hilgard, E. R., and Marquis, D. G. (1940). *Conditioning and learning.* New York: Appleton-Century-Crofts.

Kamin, L. J. (1956). The effect of termination of the CS and avoidance of the US on avoidance learning. *Journal of Comparative and Physiological Psychology 49,* 420–424.

Miller, N. E. (1951). Learnable drives and rewards. In S. S. Stevens, ed., *Handbook of experimental psychology.* New York: Wiley.

Mowrer, O. H. (1950). On the dual nature of learning—a reinterpretation of "conditioning" and "problem solving." In Mowrer's *Learning theory and personality dynamics.* New York: Ronald Press.

Rescorla, R. A., and Solomon, R. L. (1967). Two-process learning theory: Relationships between Pavlovian conditioning and instrumental learning. *Psychological Review 74,* 151–182.

Sidman, M. (1953). Two temporal parameters of the maintenance of avoidance behavior by the white rat. *Journal of Comparative and Physiological Psychology 46,* 253–261.

Solomon, R. L., and Turner, L. H. (1960). Discriminative classical conditioning under curare can later control discriminative avoidance responses in the normal state. *Science 132,* 1,499–1,500.

Solomon, R. L., and Wynne, L. C. (1954). Traumatic avoidance learning: The principles of anxiety conservation and partial irreversibility. *Psychological Review 61,* 353–385.

Warner, L. H. (1932). The association span of the white rat. *Journal of Genetic Psychology 39,* 57–89.

F. Robert Brush

ACTIVITY-DEPENDENT REGULATION OF NEUROTRANSMITTER SYNTHESIS

Activity-dependent regulation of neurotransmitter synthesis refers to the ability of some nerve cells to change the amount of neurotransmitter synthesized in response to activity. Study of this regulation is prompted by the belief that it is important not only for maintaining a source of neurotransmitter but also for adaptive changes that take place in certain nerve cells during learning and memory. A basic postulate necessary for neurotransmitter synthesis regulation to be a mechanism for learning and memory is that increased neurotransmitter synthesis acts to increase neurotransmitter secretion and, as a consequence, synaptic strength. It has not been technically possible thus far to demonstrate a causal relationship between activity-dependent regulation of neurotransmitter synthesis and an increase in neurotransmitter secretion. Nonetheless, activity-dependent regulation of neurotransmitter synthesis remains a candidate for the cause of neuroplastic changes that underlie learning, memory, and neuroplasticity. Neurotransmitters that have shown activity-dependent regulation of their biosynthesis are acetylcholine, dopamine, and norepinephrine. This entry reviews the mechanisms of the synthesis of these three neurotransmitters and possible roles of their regulatory mechanisms in learning and memory.

Depending upon both the type of nerve cell and the time scale over which adaptation occurs, the cellular and biochemical mechanisms responsible for activity-dependent regulation of neurotransmitter synthesis vary. The time scale of changes ranges from very rapid changes (seconds), in which covalent modification of enzyme protein structure is involved, to more delayed, longer-term changes (days). The latter involve alterations in genetic expression and turnover of enzymes responsible for neurotransmitter biosynthesis. Catecholamines are regulated at both short- and long-term levels, while acetylcholine is regulated only at a short-term level. The regulatory mechanisms are often similar to cellular and biochemical mechanisms used in nonneural cells to regulate the synthesis of hormones or to regulate the biochemical pathways of intermediary metabolism.

Acetylcholine is the neurotransmitter in the autonomic nervous system, the central nervous system (CNS), and at the neuromuscular junction. Even though acetylcholine has one of the highest rates of turnover of any neurotransmitter, its concentration within nerve tissue fluctuates very little. This is because the precursors for acetylcholine synthesis, acetylcoenzyme A and choline, exist in a steady-state

equilibrium with choline acetyltransferase (CAT), the enzyme that catalyzes acetylcholine synthesis (Jope, 1979). Consequently, acetylcholine synthesis is well below its maximal possible rate. Therefore any change in the concentration of acetylcholine or its precursors produces a change in acetylcholine synthesis. This has been verified by the demonstration that the transport of choline into the cholinergic neuron controls acetylcholine synthesis. For example, choline addition to slices of brain tissue markedly increases the acetylcholine synthesis rate. In addition, increased neuronal activity increases choline uptake (Simon and Kuhar, 1975). This increased uptake occurs in a manner that persists far beyond the period of increased activity. Thus, stimulation of choline uptake is not due merely to a shift in the equilibrium of the CAT-catalyzed reaction; instead, choline uptake is regulated by neural activity per se. This regulation of choline uptake by nerve activity is predicted to maintain the strength of cholinergic synapses and is a candidate to increase the capacity of these synapses to secrete acetylcholine. Despite this evidence for activity-dependent regulation of choline uptake, little is known concerning how this regulation occurs. Thus, the link between nerve activity and choline transport remains unknown.

Catecholamines—dopamine, norepinephrine, and epinephrine—are neurotransmitters in the sympathetic limb of the autonomic nervous system and in several groups of neurons in the CNS. In contrast with the lack of a mechanism linking nerve activity and the regulation of choline uptake, catecholamine-synthesizing cells have several mechanisms in place to regulate catecholamine levels in response to nerve activity, both in peripheral and central nervous systems and at short- and long-term levels. As one review stated, "An intricate scheme has evolved whereby tyrosine hydroxylase activity is modulated by nearly every documented form of regulation" (Kumer and Vrana, 1996). Regulation occurs at the step in catecholamines synthesis where tyrosine is hydroxylated to form L-dopa. The enzyme catalyzing this reaction, tyrosine hydroxylase, is the first of four enzymatic steps in the catecholamine synthesis pathway. Because tyrosine hydroxylase is present in lower concentration than the other enzymes of the synthesis pathway, it restricts the amount of neurotransmitter synthesized. In addition, tyrosine hydroxylase is constitutively inhibited by the binding of a mole of catecholamine to each mole of enzyme. Two interacting mechanisms are important in short-term, nervous-activity regulation of catecholamine synthesis. One mechanism is catecholamine end-product inhibition of tyrosine hydroxylase activity by the catecholamine products of the pathway. The second is modification of tyrosine hydroxylase structure by the placement of phosphate groups on the tyrosine hydroxylase molecule. The latter process, termed phosphorylation, is catalyzed by at least four separate protein kinases (Kumer and Vrana, 1996), which phosphorylate tyrosine hydroxylase on a combination of three serine residues in the N terminal domain of the enzyme. The phosphorylation alters the properties of tyrosine hydroxylase, increasing its catalytic activity. Phosphorylation is commonly used to modify proteins involved in regulation.

The protein kinases that phosphorylate tyrosine hydroxylase are cyclic adenosine monophosphate-dependent protein kinase (PKA), which phosphorylates serine 40; calcium-calmodulin-dependent protein kinase II (CaM KII), which phosphorylates serine 19; and extracellular receptor activated protein kinase (ERK) (Haycock, Ahn, Cobb, and Krebs, 1992), which phosphorylates serine 31. This phosphorylation has three major effects on the enzyme's function; all three changes enhance tyrosine hydroxylase activity and increase catecholamine synthesis. Serine 40 phosphorylation increases the affinity of the enzyme for tetrahydrobiopterin cofactor (the cofactor is normally present below optimal concentrations) and reduces the catecholamine binding and inhibition of tyrosine hydroxylase (Daubner, Lauriano, Haycock, and Fitzpatrick, 1992). Serine 19 phosphorylation causes the enzyme to interact with an activating protein termed 14-3-3 protein (Ichimura et al., 1987; Itagaki et al., 1999). Serine 31 phosphorylation increases the catalytic activity by an as yet undefined mechanism (Haycock, Ahn, Cobb, and Krebs, 1992).

Which of these mechanisms act to regulate the synthesis of catecholamines in response to neural activity, and how may they relate to learning and memory? Although these questions have been difficult to answer, some conclusions are possible. Under circumstances of cell depolarization, such as when a nerve impulse invades the nerve terminal or during cholinergic stimulation at the adrenal medulla, the phosphorylation and activation of tyrosine hydroxylase by Ca/CAM kinase II appear to be responsible for initial activation of tyrosine hydroxylase (Waymire et al., 1988; Waymire and Craviso, 1993) with a later activation through both PKA and ERK. In addition, evidence indicates that the phosphorylation on serine 19 may facilitate the phosphorylation on serine 40 (Bevilaqua et al., 2001). Thus there appears to be a time-dependent hierarchical phosphorylation and activation of tyrosine hydroxylase that occurs in steps to activate catecholamine biosynthesis. Any condition that increases the size of these phosphorylation events is predicted to enhance the synthesis of catecholamines. This may translate into increased neurotransmitter release and synaptic strength.

Catecholamine synthesis is also regulated at a chronic, long-term level in response to persistent or extreme neural activation. In this case the amount of the enzymes in the catecholamine synthetic pathway, and especially tyrosine hydroxylase, is elevated in response to increased synaptic activity. For example, drugs or conditions such as stress that increase the autonomic nerve activity increase the level of tyrosine hydroxylase in peripheral autonomic cells (Thoenen, Mueller, and Axelrod, 1969). Because cutting the innervation to these cells blocks the increase, the influence is thought to be transynaptic. Because a rise in tyrosine hydroxylase mRNA precedes the increase in protein, the mechanism is believed to be increased transcription of the mRNA encoding tyrosine hydroxylase. The observation that drugs that increase CNS neuronal activity also induce increased levels of CNS tyrosine hydroxylase shows that central tyrosine hydroxylase levels are also regulated by neuronal activity. This nerve activity–dependent regulation of tyrosine hydroxylase synthesis is an attractive candidate for learning and memory because the increase in tyrosine hydroxylase level is expected to increase the strength of the activated synapses. Whether or not this is the case is not yet known. Even so, a considerable effort is being carried out to understand as much as possible about transynaptic regulation of tyrosine hydroxylase level because it is likely the best example known of synaptically mediated regulation of protein synthesis.

Among the issues that remain unresolved concerning the mechanism of the long-term regulation of tyrosine hydroxylase is the nature of the intracellular mechanisms responsible for increased transcription. In a model tissue, the adrenal medulla, acetylcholine and pituitary adenylyl cyclase activating polypeptide (PACAP) are each able to modulate tyrosine hydroxylase level. In this tissue either PACAP or acetylcholine stimulates cAMP level and activates PKA. One hypothesis is that PKA migrates to the cell nucleus to regulate the rate of tyrosine hydroxylase transcription by phosphorylating CREB (Cyclic AMP Response Element Binding), a regulatory protein associated with the tyrosine hydroxylase gene (Kurosawa, Guidotti, and Costa, 1976). Unresolved issues in this simple model are 1. whether acetylcholine stimulates a rise in cAMP or 2. whether other transmitters, such as PACAP, are involved. Because neuropeptides are secreted along with acetylcholine at some cholinergic synapses, it has been suggested that these agonists are responsible for long-term regulation of tyrosine hydroxylase level (Wessels-Reiker, Haycock, Howlett, and Strong, 1991). Also, it is not clear whether transcription is regulated solely through PKA. Because several regulatory domains exist in the tyrosine hydroxylase gene, it appears that protein kinases other than the PKA are likely to be involved. In addition it is possible that the rapidly synthesized protein c-Fos may serve as a protein factor regulating tyrosine hydroxylase transcription. An additional question is whether increased transcription is the principal mechanism of regulation. In isolated adrenal medullary chromaffin cells, transcription increases for only a few hours following either acetylcholine of PACAP stimulation, whereas the increase in mRNA occurs over several days and remains elevated long after transcription has subsided. This raises the issue of the stabilization of the tyrosine hydroxylase mRNA as a major component of the synaptic regulation. Indeed, tyrosine hydroxylase mRNA is capable of regulation through stability, as has been demonstrated for its stabilization by elevated oxygen tension (Paulding and Czyzyk-Krzeska, 1999).

The understanding of the activity-dependent regulation of catecholamines is much more complete than for other neurotransmitters, such as acetylcholine. For some neurotransmitter systems—the amino acids and purines, for example—almost nothing is known about their synthesis regulation, so it is not clear whether it is activity-dependent. This is primarily because these compounds are so intimately associated with intermediary metabolism that it is difficult to separate their neurotransmitter-related metabolism from that associated with general cell function. One generalization emerging from the studies of the mechanisms of activity-dependent regulation of catecholamine synthesis is the prominent position protein phosphorylation plays in both short- and long-term regulation. In the future, studies will likely be directed to applying the understanding being gained of the mechanisms regulating catecholamine synthesis to other neurotransmitters. And although it is important to continue to investigate the mechanisms involved in activity-dependent regulation of neurotransmitter synthesis, it is also important to recognize that the role of neurotransmitter synthesis regulation in higher functions, such as learning and memory, is still hypothetical.

See also: PROTEIN SYNTHESIS IN LONG-TERM MEMORY IN VERTEBRATES

Bibliography

Bevilaqua, L. R., Graham, M. E., Dunkley, P. R., Nagy-Felsobuki, E. I., and Dickson, P. W. (2001). Phosphorylation of Ser(19) alters the conformation of tyrosine hydroxylase to increase the rate of phosphorylation of Ser(40). *Journal of Biological Chemistry* 276, 40,411–40,416.

Daubner, S. C., Lauriano, C., Haycock, J. W., and Fitzpatrick, P. F. (1992). Site-directed mutagenesis of serine 40 of rat tyrosine hydroxylase. Effects of dopamine and cAMP-dependent phosphorylation on enzyme activity. *Journal of Biological Chemistry* 267, 12,639–12,646.

Haycock, J. W. (1990). Phosphorylation of tyrosine hydroxylase in situ at serine 8, 19, 31 and 40. *Journal of Biological Chemistry* 265, 11,682–11,691.

Haycock, J. W., Ahn, N. G., Cobb, M. H., and Krebs, E. G. (1992). ERK1 and ERK2, two microtubule-associated protein 2 kinases, mediate the phosphorylation of tyrosine hydroxylase at serine-31 *in situ. Proceedings of the National Academy of Sciences of the United States of America* 89, 2,365–2,369.

Ichimura, T., Isobe, T., Okuyama, T., Yamauchi, T. and Fujisawa, H. (1987). Brain 14-3-3 protein is an activator protein that activates tryptophan 5-monooxygenase and tyrosine 3-monooxygenase in the presence of Ca2+, calmodulin-dependent protein kinase II. *FEBS Letters* 219, 79–82.

Itagaki, C., Isobe, T., Taoka, M., Natsume, T., Nomura, N., Horigome, T., Omata, S., Ichinose, H., Nagatsu, T., Greene, L. A., and Ichimura, T. (1999). Stimulus-coupled interaction of tyrosine hydroxylase with 14-3-3 proteins. *Biochemical Journal* 38, 15,673–15,680.

Jope, R. S. (1997). High affinity choline transport and acetylCoA production in brain and their roles in the regulation of acetylcholine synthesis. *Brain Research Review 1*, 313–344.

Kumer, S. C., and Vrana, K. E. (1996). Intricate regulation of tyrosine hydroxylase activity and gene expression. *Journal of Neurochemistry* 67, 443–462.

Kurosawa, A., Guidotti, A., and Costa, E. (1976). Induction of tyrosine 3-monooxygenase elicited by carbamylcholine in intact and denervated adrenal medulla: Role of protein kinase activation and translocation. *Molecular Pharmacology 12*, 420–432.

Paulding, W. R., and Czyzyk-Krzeska, M. F. (1999). Regulation of tyrosine hydroxylase mRNA stability by protein-binding, pyrimidine-rich sequence in the 3'-untranslated region. *Journal of Biological Chemistry* 274, 2,532–2,538.

Simon, J. R., and Kuhar, M. J. (1975). Impulse-flow regulation of high affinity choline uptake in brain cholinergic nerve terminals. *Nature 255*, 162–163.

Thoenen, H., Mueller, R. A., and Axelrod, J. (1969). Transsynaptic induction of adrenal tyrosine hydroxylase. *Journal of Pharmacology and Experimental Therapeutics* 169, 249–254.

Waymire, J. C., and Craviso, G. L. (1993). Multiple site phosphoryaltion and activation of tyrosine hydroxylase. *Advances in Protein Phosphatases 7*, 495–506.

Waymire, J. C., Johnston, J. P., Hummer-Lickteig, K., Lloyd, A., Vigny, A., and Craviso, G. L. (1988). Phosphorylation of bovine adrenal chromaffin cell tyrosine hydroxylase: Temporal correlation of acetylcholine's effect on site phosphorylation, enzyme activation, and catecholamine synthesis. *Journal of Biological Chemistry 263*, 12,439–12,447.

Wessels-Reiker, M, Haycock, J. W., Howlett, A. C., and Strong, R. (1991). Vasoactive intestinal polypeptide induces tyrosine hydroxylase in PC12 cells. *Journal of Biological Chemistry 266*, 9,347–9,350.

Jack C. Waymire

AGING

See: AGING AND MEMORY IN ANIMALS; AGING AND MEMORY IN HUMANS; ALZHEIMER'S DISEASE: BEHAVIORAL ASPECTS; ALZHEIMER'S DISEASE: HUMAN DISEASE AND THE GENETICALLY ENGINEERED ANIMAL MODELS; PHARMACOLOGICAL TREATMENT OF MEMORY DEFICITS

AGING AND MEMORY IN ANIMALS

The passage of time produces changes in both the behavior and the brains of organisms. A number of useful animal models of learning and memory in normal aging have expanded the knowledge base and extended the prospects for ameliorating learning and memory deficits. Completion of the mapping of the human and mouse genome and the development of transgenic mouse models in the 1990s have accelerated insights about mechanisms of learning, memory, and aging. Since the mid-1990s, mouse models of neuropathology in Alzheimer's disease have become available for behavioral testing. Two features of animal models make them invaluable: First, the life spans of most animals are considerably shorter than the human life span, compressing the time required to observe processes of aging. Second, invasive or high-risk observations and experimental manipulations are feasible with animals but not with humans.

Aging is most typically associated with declines in functioning, both neural and behavioral. However, individual organisms age at different rates. One organism may show a steady decline in functioning, whereas another shows only slight changes over the years. An important goal toward an understanding of aging processes is to determine how changes in neural structures impact behavior. As such, behavioral paradigms that engage well-defined neural substrates are particularly valuable. Two such neurobiologically well-characterized paradigms will be highlighted: eyeblink classical conditioning and spatial learning and memory.

Eyeblink Classical Conditioning

The basic classical conditioning procedure, named the "delay" procedure by Ivan Pavlov, involves repeated trials in which the presentation of an initially neural stimulus, such as a tone (the conditioned stimulus, or CS), is followed after approximately half a second by a stimulus that evokes a reflexive eyelid closure, such as a corneal air puff (the unconditioned stimulus, or US). The CS turns on and remains on while the US is delivered and the two stimuli coterminate. Initially, eye blinks occur only after the US, and the blinks are a reflexive response (the unconditioned response, or UR). Eventually, eye blinks occur after the CS but before the US. This is a learned response (the conditioned response, or CR). Thus, learning is defined as the acquisition of CRs.

Richard F. Thompson suggested that the eyeblink classical conditioning paradigm might be the Rosetta Stone for brain substrates of age-related deficits in learning and memory (Thompson, 1988). Thompson's major point was that eyeblink classical

conditioning is a simple form of learning that can be studied with little modification across a variety of species, including humans. There are at least four advantages to using eyeblink conditioning as an animal model of the effects of aging on learning and memory in humans. First, both animals and humans show age-associated deficits in conditioning, and these can be easily dissociated from age-associated changes in sensory systems (i.e., differences in CS thresholds) or motor systems (differences in UR amplitude). Second, both animals and humans show age-associated changes in the neural substrates critical for eyeblink conditioning, the cerebellum and the hippocampus. Third, age-associated deficits have been artificially induced with drugs in both young animals and young humans. Finally, age-associated deficits can be reversed in normal older animals using cognition-enhancing drugs.

The critical substrate for eyeblink conditioning is the cerebellum. The hippocampus plays a modulatory role in acquisition of CRs. Abnormal functioning of the hippocampus retards the rate of eyeblink conditioning in the delay procedure. In addition, the hippocampus is essential for eyeblink classical conditioning procedures involving greater complexity, such as trace conditioning. In the trace procedure, the CS is presented and then turned off, and a blank period ensues before the onset of the US. The blank period is called the "trace" and is shown in the left panel of Figure 1.

In eyeblink classical conditioning, intervals between the CS and US (called interstimulus intervals, ISIs) of 250 and 750 milliseconds are the most common, with the most rapid conditioning between 250 and 500 milliseconds. The trace procedure extends the ISI in addition to inserting the blank trace period. Thus, it increases difficulty in two ways. Holding the ISI constant at 750 milliseconds, researchers compared the delay and trace procedures in three-month-old and twenty-four-month-old rabbits. There were significant effects of age and procedure (see Figure 1). Older rabbits performed more poorly in both procedures, and both age groups performed more poorly in the trace than in the delay procedure. Comparison of a number of studies testing the delay and trace procedure in older rabbits indicated that age differences in conditioning appeared earlier when the trace procedure was used.

Cerebellar Substrates of Impaired Conditioning in Older Animals

Purkinje cells in the cerebellum integrate CS and US input and show patterns of engagement during eyeblink conditioning. In rabbits, Purkinje cell counts have been carried out using histological techniques after behavioral testing with eyeblink classical condi-

Figure 1

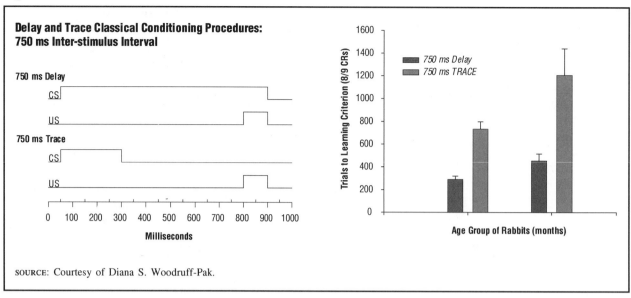

SOURCE: Courtesy of Diana S. Woodruff-Pak.

Left: Delay and trace procedures using same 750 milliseconds ISI (interstimulus intervals). Right: The number of trials it took rabbits to attain a learning criterion of eight conditioned responses in nine consecutive trials. The higher the trials to criterion measure, the slower the animals were to learn. A total of twenty-four young and seventeen old rabbits were tested in either the 750-milliseconds delay or the 750-milliseconds trace (250 milliseconds CS, 500 milliseconds trace) procedure. There were statistically significant differences between the younger and older rabbits, and there were statistically significant differences between the delay and trace procedures. Older rabbits learned more slowly in both the delay and trace procedures, and both younger and older rabbits learned more slowly in the trace than in the delay procedure.

tioning. The correlations between Purkinje cell number and eyeblink classical conditioning in rabbits were high and statistically significant (Woodruff-Pak, Cronholm, and Sheffield, 1990). The fewer Purkinje cells a rabbit had, the longer it took it to acquire CRs. Further analysis demonstrated that this relationship was relatively independent of age because there was a highly significant correlation between Purkinje cell number and conditioning when only young rabbits were included. Mutant mice without Purkinje cells condition slowly and produce fewer CRs, whereas their wild type littermates with Purkinje cells condition normally (Chen et al., 1996). Given the essential role of the cerebellum in the acquisition of CRs, Purkinje cell loss may account for a significant portion of the age-related difference in eyeblink classical conditioning.

Hippocampal Substrates of Impaired Conditioning in Older Animals

There is some evidence of age differences in hippocampal activity during eyeblink conditioning. Neuronal responses were recorded from the dorsal hippocampus of young (three-month-old), middle-aged (twenty-six-to-thirty-three-month-old), and older (thirty-nine-to-fifty-month-old) rabbits during eyeblink conditioning in the 750-millisecond trace procedure shown in Figure 1 (Woodruff-Pak, Lavond,

Logan, and Thompson, 1987). Older rabbits were significantly impaired in acquiring CRs. Furthermore, older rabbits showed significantly less neural activity in the US period than young rabbits by the second session of training. Matthew McEchron and John Disterhoft also reported that older rabbits had less hippocampal responsivity in the US period.

In a series of experiments in young and older rabbits, Disterhoft and McEchron (2000) found that conditioning-related hippocampal pyramidal-cell activity varied across cells and that the different response profiles were differentially affected by aging. Patterns of hippocampal pyramidal cell activation associated with acquisition of trace eyeblink conditioning were different from activity recorded after CRs became asymptotic. Pyramidal-cell activity associated with acquisition was more sensitive to the effects of aging (McEchron, Weible, and Disterhoft, 2001). Various patterns of single-unit pyramidal-cell activity were identified, and three response patterns were different between young and older rabbits that learned and those aged rabbits that did not. The patterns showed significant changes during the first five days of conditioning in the young and aged learners, but the patterns showed no change in the aged nonlearning group. If these cells function to hold important information for consolidation in other neural structures, age-related deficits in conditioning may be ameliorated by enhancing the function of these cells.

Spatial Learning and Memory

Spatial behavioral tests evaluate the ability of the organism to know or to have a representation of its location in the environment and thus to navigate effectively. The intact functioning of the hippocampus is necessary for learning and remembering spatial tasks. In old age, spatial memory is less efficient in humans and animals.

When single cells are recorded in the hippocampus of a behaving rat, firing rate increases when the animal is in a particular place in the environment. These cells have been called "place cells," and the area over which these cells show increased firing rates are called the cells' "place fields." Carol Barnes (2001) described deficits that occur in the development and maintenance of hippocampal place fields in old rats. As rats explore the environment, there is a change in the pattern of hippocampal place-cell discharge that occurs as a consequence of experience. For example, when rats run laps around a track in one direction, there is an expansion of the place fields and a shift in their centers of mass toward the origin of the route. In old rats, there is a striking reduction in this experience-dependent form of plasticity in the old place cells. Barnes suggested that the lack of field broadening observed in old rats might be expected to lead to a loss of precision in the information transmitted as a consequence of experience. Ability to remember routes may also be impaired by this deficit in place-cell field broadening.

Barnes also found that the same memory-impaired old rats that showed deficits in experience-dependent place-field expansion also retrieved inappropriate hippocampal maps on some occasions. Even when these memory-impaired old rats were in familiar environments, they retrieved inappropriate hippocampal maps from time to time. When a young rat is exposed to a familiar environment on one day and then exposed to that environment again a second time later that day, the same place-field map will be recorded from hippocampal place cells on both sessions. Testing old rats in this two-session recording procedure, Barnes and her colleagues (1997) observed a bimodal distribution of responses. For two-thirds of the double-session recordings, the old rats retrieved the same map on both occasions, performing normally as young rats. However, on one-third of the double-session recordings, the old rats exhibited a complete rearrangement of the place-field map between the two sessions. They apparently retrieved the wrong map on one of the sessions. This failure to re-trieve the correct map may explain why old rats are more likely to make behavioral map-retrieval errors. Older organisms, including rats, monkeys, and humans, have a greater tendency to become lost. Altered hippocampal plasticity mechanisms may underlie these changes in cognition that occur during normal aging.

Transgenic Mouse Models of Alzheimer's Disease

Severe memory loss is the most prominent cognitive symptom of Alzheimer's disease (AD), and a fundamental role in the pathogenesis of AD is brain deposition of β-amyloid (Aβ). Mutations in the amyloid precursor protein (APP) and presenilin-1 (PS1) genes are linked to forms of AD that are carried in families and called familial AD. By altering APP metabolism, these mutations result in increased brain levels of Aβ peptide. Transgenic mice harboring mutant forms of the APP and/or PS1 gene associated with AD in humans are valid tools in the study of pathophysiological and behavioral effects of those genes in AD. Due to the relatively short life span of mice (two to three years), a high overexpression of the transgene is necessary to achieve the development of AD-like symptoms in the animals. The first transgenic mouse models of AD were produced in the mid-1990s, and thereafter there were a number of mouse models of AD that developed Aβ-containing plaques in the hippocampus and neocortex, thus modeling human AD.

The hippocampus is engaged in eyeblink classical conditioning and in spatial learning and memory, and both of these behaviors are profoundly impaired in AD. Spatial learning and memory is the behavior most commonly tested in transgenic mouse models of AD, although eyeblink classical conditioning is a useful alternative behavioral measure that has direct parallels and can be tested in humans diagnosed with AD. A frequently used behavioral test for AD mouse models is the Morris water maze, in which mice are placed in a pool of water that is opaque (to hide a platform) and must learn the location of that platform to escape from the water. Impairment in this and other forms of spatial learning and memory are observed in various transgenic mouse models of AD.

Dale Schenk and colleagues (1999) made a remarkable discovery that vaccinations with Aβ peptide can dramatically reduce amyloid deposition in transgenic mouse models of AD. Aβ peptide vaccination prevents spatial learning and memory loss (Morgan et al., 2000). The long-term behavioral results of Aβ peptide vaccinations indicate that the behavioral protection of the vaccinations is task-specific, with preservation of hippocampal-associated spatial-memory tasks most likely to occur (Arendash et al., 2001).

Evidence suggests that normal aging affects mammalian eyeblink conditioning through age-related deficits in the cerebellum and hippocampus. Age-related changes in spatial learning and memory also rely on hippocampal mechanisms. AD exacerbates impairment in learning and memory and profoundly disrupts hippocampal function early in its course. Transgenic models of AD provide a means to test therapeutic interventions, such as vaccination with Aβ peptide, that might protect against the cognitive and neural impairment characteristic of this neurodegenerative disease.

See also: AGING AND MEMORY IN HUMANS

Bibliography

Arendash, G. W., Gordon, M. N., Diamond, D. M., Austin, L. A., Hatcher, J. M., Jantzen, P., DiCarlo, G., Wilcock, D., and Morgan, D. (2001). Behavioral assessment of Alzheimer's transgenic mice following long-term Aβ vaccination: Task specificity and correlations between Aβ deposition and spatial memory. *DNA and Cell Biology 20*, 737–744.

Barnes, C. A. (2001). Plasticity in the aging central nervous system. *International Review of Neurobiology 45*, 339–355.

Barnes, C. A., Suster, M. S., Shen, J., and McNaughton, B. L. (1997). Cognitive map multistability in aged rat hippocampus. *Nature 388*, 272–275.

Chen, L., Bao, S., Lockard, J. M., Kim, J. J., and Thompson, R. F. (1996). Impaired classical eyeblink conditioning in cerebellar lesioned and Purkinje cell degeneration (*pcd*) mutant mice. *Journal of Neuroscience 16*, 2,829–2,838.

Disterhoft, J. F., and McEchron, M. D. (2000). Cellular alterations in hippocampus during acquisition and consolidation of hippocampus-dependent trace eyeblink conditioning. In D. S. Woodruff-Pak and J. E. Steinmetz, eds., *Eyeblink classical conditioning*, Vol. 2: *Animal models*, pp. 313–334. Boston: Kluwer Academic Publishers.

McEchron, M. D., Weible, A. P., and Disterhoft, J. F. (2001). Aging and learning-specific changes in single-neuron activity in CA1 hippocampus during rabbit trace eyeblink conditioning. *Journal of Neurophysiology 86*, 1,839–1,857.

Morgan, D., Diamond, D. M., Gottschall, P. E., Ugen, K. E., Dickey, C., Hardy, J., Duff, K., Jantzen, P., DiCarlo, G., Wilcock, D., Connor, K., Hatcher, J., Hope, C., Gordon, M., and Arendash, G. W. (2000). Aβ peptide vaccination prevents memory loss in an animal model of Alzheimer's disease. *Nature 408*, 982–985.

Schenk, D., Barbour, R., Dunn, W., Gordon, G., Grajeda, H., Guido, T., Hu, K., Huang, J., Johnson-Wood, K., Kahn, K., Kholodenko, D., Lee, M., Liao, Z., Lieberburg, I., Motter, R. Mutter, L., Soriano, F., Shopp, G., Vasquez, N., Vandevert, C., Walker, S., Wogulis, M., Yednock, T., Games, D., and Seubert, P. (1999). Immunization with amyloid-β attenuates Alzheimer-disease-like pathology in the PDAPP mouse. *Nature 400*, 173–177.

Thompson, R. F. (1988). The Rosetta stone for brain substrates of age-related deficits in learning and memory? *Neurobiology of Aging 9*, 547–548.

Woodruff-Pak, D. S., Cronholm, J. F., and Sheffield, J. B. (1990). Purkinje cell number related to rate of eyeblink classical conditioning. *NeuroReport 1*, 165–168.

Woodruff-Pak, D. S., Lavond, D. G., Logan, C. G., and Thompson, R. F. (1987). Classical conditioning in three-, thirty-, and forty-five-month-old rabbits: Behavioral learning and hippocampal unit activity. *Neurobiology of Aging 8*, 101–108.

Diana S. Woodruff-Pak

AGING AND MEMORY IN HUMANS

One of the commonest complaints of older people is that their memory is not what it used to be. The validity of such subjective reports is borne out by the scientific literature: Memory performance does decline as a function of the normal aging process in healthy adults, although the decline is much more evident with some materials and tasks than it is with others. This variability has given researchers useful clues to the specific memory components or processes that are particularly vulnerable to the effects of aging. Some of this work is described below.

Nearly all the studies described use the cross-sectional method of age comparison; that is, a group of young adults (often college students in their early twenties) is compared with a group of older adults (usually community-dwelling volunteers in their sixties and seventies). Additionally, some studies incorporate middle-aged groups of people in their forties and fifties. The cross-sectional method is much more practicable than within-subject longitudinal studies, but it does leave open the possibility that the differences observed between the groups may be attributable to causes other than aging—to differences in education or motivation, for example. Obviously researchers take pains to minimize the possibility of such artifacts, and they do this by matching the groups by educational level, by vocabulary (a rough measure of verbal intelligence), and by other indicators of intelligence and socioeconomic status. Many crucial experimental results take the form of interactions between age and some experimental variable; that is, one condition of the experiment is associated with large age-related differences, whereas another condition is associated with much smaller differences, even though the same subjects are used. The finding of such differential effects makes it harder to argue that group differences are a function, say, of reduced motivation in the older sample.

Like other experimental explorations of individual differences in memory ability, the work on aging has been carried out within various theoretical frameworks and with a view to establishing some theoretical point. In this brief article it is not possible to go into details of theoretical motivation in most cases, but, in summary, four main age-related changes that arguably underlie changes in memory performance are a decline in general processing speed; a decline in processing resources or "attentional energy" (Craik and

Byrd, 1982); an age-related reduction in the efficiency of inhibitory processes; and an impairment in the executive control of cognitive processing. These four theoretical viewpoints, along with supporting evidence, are discussed in Kester, Benjamin, Castel, and Craik (2002); and in Zacks, Hasher, and Li (2000). The present article focuses on empirical work since the 1980s, pointing out the implications for theory where relevant.

Indirect Memory Tests

When we think about memory, it is usually in the sense of the conscious retrieval of a past event or the retrieval of a previously learned fact. However, there are also many cases in which previous events can affect present behavior in the *absence* of conscious awareness of the past event in question. Such cases of "implicit memory" are revealed by indirect memory tests—examples include word-stem completion and word-fragment completion. In word-stem completion, the participant is given the first few letters of a word (e.g., MAR___ or DRA___) and asked to complete the stem with the first word that comes to mind. Word-fragment completion is similar; here the participant is given words with letters missing and is asked to complete them (e.g., M _ _ K _ T or _ R A _ _ R). The general finding in such experiments is that participants can complete the words more readily if they have studied the target words (e.g., MARKET, DRAWER) previously, even though the person may be quite unaware that the words are drawn from the studied list. This phenomenon is known as "priming," and it has typically been found that age differences in tests of priming are much smaller than those found in direct tests (Fleischman and Gabrieli, 1998). A similar discrepancy between direct and indirect tests is found in amnesic patients, who do poorly on explicit or direct tests but comparatively well on implicit or indirect tests. These results are sometimes taken as evidence that encoding processes are therefore intact in elderly individuals and amnesic patients, and that the observed decrements are failures of retrieval. But encoding processes may be somewhat *impaired* in older people and amnesics; they might be sufficient to support later indirect tests, but insufficient to support later direct tests.

Semantic Memory

Semantic memory refers to a person's learned knowledge of facts and concepts. Typically we are unaware of where and when we first learned that Paris is the capital of France, the meaning of *rhinoceros*, and that 7 x 9 = 63; the notion of semantic memory thus stands in contrast to episodic memory, where details of time and place are crucial. There are different views on whether episodic and semantic memory are different "memory systems" or whether they simply exemplify different degrees of abstraction from the original events that gave rise to the encoded knowledge (Craik, 2002). Whatever the resolution of this debate, older adults typically show fewer losses in semantic memory than in episodic memory, provided that the knowledge in question is used on a regular basis. Thus, older people show minimal losses in vocabulary and in knowledge of facts and concepts.

On the other hand, some aspects of semantic memory do appear to decline with age—the ability to learn completely new facts, for example. Even well-learned material can be more difficult to retrieve for older adults, and difficulty in remembering names is possibly *the* most frequent age-related memory complaint. It is unclear, however, whether names show a disproportional impairment with age (Maylor, 1997); a more general statement might be that older adults have sporadic difficulty in retrieving any information that they use infrequently. Having a word or name "on the tip of the tongue" is an experience that occurs more frequently as people grow older, and older adults report less partial information about the target word. In addition, speed of retrieval slows with advancing age, in line with the slowing of many other cognitive processes. In summary, then, whereas the representation of learned knowledge remains reasonably intact into old age, older adults experience occasional difficulty in assessing that knowledge.

Episodic Memory

Episodic memory refers to the ability to recollect specific events, and this form of memory has been extensively studied in the laboratory using tests of recall and recognition. Many such studies have used rather artificial materials—lists of unrelated words, for example. The benefit has been greater experimental control over encoding and retrieval processes, but a possible drawback is that the principles emerging from such studies might not apply to real-life remembering. Work carried out beginning in the 1980s on autobiographical memory has allayed these fears to a large extent, however. In these studies, memory for personally experienced events in the subject's life have shown that real-life memories are affected by the same factors and subject to the same laws as are materials learned in the laboratory. Age-related differences in autobiographical memory have been studied by presenting people of different ages with cue words such a *flag* or *school* and asking participants to generate a personal memory that each word evokes. For adults of all ages, recent memories were generated most often, and the incidence of recollected events declined from the present to the past. One interesting exception to this general trend is that all adults showed a disproportionate "bump" of generated memories from late teenage and early adult years (Rubin, Wetzler, and Nebes, 1986). Presumably this bump reflects the many important career-related and emotionally significant events that occur during this period of our lives.

Episodic memory for events occurring in the last few minutes, hours, or even weeks typically shows large age decrements, and much of the effort of cognitive aging researchers has been directed to understanding the factors underlying this problem. One set of findings points to an age-related decline in the efficiency of retrieval processes. Several investigators have shown larger age differences in tests of free recall (in which participants must recall a list of words or a paragraph of text with no cues or reminders) than in tests of recognition memory (in which participants must pick out the originally studied items from a mixed set of targets and distractors). Details of these experiments are summarized by Kester, Benjamin, Castel, and Craik (2002). The fact that older adults have difficulty recalling studied items but can recognize them suggests that the difficulty lies at the retrieval stage, although recognition is usually the easier test. It seems likely that there are also problems at encoding, however. One piece of evidence supporting the encoding hypothesis is that, when encoding processes are "guided" appropriately by means of questions that emphasize the semantic aspects of the item, age-related differences are often reduced (Craik and Jennings, 1992). One similarity between encoding and retrieval is thus that, when appropriate processes are supported or guided by additional information (e.g., semantic orienting tasks at encoding, retrieval cues or a recognition test at retrieval), age differences are typically reduced. This pattern of findings led Craik (1983) to suggest that, whereas "unsupported" encoding and retrieval processes are often inefficient in older people, possibly due to a reduction in available processing resources, these inefficiencies can be overcome through the "environmental support" provided by the experimental situation or by the context of a person's familiar surroundings.

The conclusion that age-related difficulties in episodic memory are consequences of impaired processing at both encoding and retrieval is supported by findings from studies of functional neuroimaging. Studies using PET (positron emission tomography) and fMRI (functional magnetic resonance imagery) have shown that older adults exhibit less activation of the ventral left prefrontal cortex during memory encoding than do their younger counterparts. Many studies have demonstrated that this left prefrontal region is associated with the processing of semantic information and with good later memory of processed items. Other studies have shown that, whereas young adults activate regions that are predominantly lateralized in the right prefrontal cortex during retrieval, older adults show activations in both right and left prefrontal regions when retrieving information. The additional left-sided activations in older people may reflect the brain's attempt to compensate for the declining efficiency of regions that subserve retrieval in young adulthood. An account of this exciting line of research is provided by Prull, Gabrieli, and Bunge (2000).

One further topic pertaining to episodic memory is the ability to remember the *source* of encoded information, or details of the context in which an event occurred. Everyone has experienced the situation in which a person's face seems very familiar, and yet we cannot say how we know the person. Usually it turns out that we have encountered the familiar person in a very different context from his or her habitual location, leading George Mandler to refer to the experience as "the butcher on the bus" phenomenon. A similar failure of memory for context occurs when we know a fact but cannot recollect whether someone told us the information or whether we read it in the newspaper or heard it on the radio. Older adults are particularly prone to such failures to bind contextual information to the core aspects of the event, or to the item of information (see Kester, Benjamin, Castel, and Craik, 2002, for details). The effects are also seen during the output of information; for example, an older person may be cued by a conversational companion's background to exclaim, "Ah—you will be interested to hear this!" and then proceed to retell the same story that the hapless listener has endured many times previously.

What lies behind the phenomenon of source forgetting? Some researchers have linked the failure to bind contextual details to core features to an inefficiency of frontal lobe function. Other cognitive neuroscientists have suggested that the hippocampus is centrally concerned with such binding functions (Prull, Gabrieli, and Bunge, 2000). At the behavioral level, source forgetting may be viewed as one instance of a general age-related difficulty of association or integration. Naveh-Benjamin (2000) lays out convincing evidence that older adults have particular difficulty remembering the associative links between items of information, although the items themselves may be remembered quite well.

Short-Term and Working Memory

The phrase *short-term memory* has unfortunately been used in a number of slightly different ways, and this can give rise to confusions about findings. Clinicians typically use the phrase to mean recent memory—events that have happened in the last few hours or days—whereas experimental psychologists have used the phrase to refer to information still held in mind, as when we look up a telephone number and rehearse the information until we have dialed it. This latter type of memory (sometimes also referred to as *primary memory*) shows very little decline with age. Similarly, *memory span*—the longest list of digits or words that a person can repeat back accurately—declines only slightly from the twenties to the eighties. If *short-term memory* is used in the first sense, however, it falls into the general category of episodic memory, and substantial age-related decrements are found, as discussed in the previous section.

The term *working memory* has been adopted widely to refer to information held and manipulated in mind. Thus, solving a verbal problem or performing mental arithmetic is considered to involve working memory (WM). In this sense WM incorporates executive processes as well as relatively automatic auxiliary systems such as the articulatory loop and visuo-spatial sketchpad (Baddeley, 1986). With regard to aging, performance relying largely on auxiliary systems holds up well; memory span falls into this category. But when good performance requires executive processes or complex manipulations of information held in mind, then older people typically do less well than their younger counterparts (Craik and Jennings, 1992; Zacks, Hasher, and Li, 2000). It seems possible that this age-related decline reflects the reduced efficiency of frontal lobe processes in older adults (Glisky, Polster, and Routhieaux, 1995).

Older adults often have difficulty dealing with dual-task situations in which they must divide their attention between two simultaneous activities. In one such demonstration Anderson, Craik, and Naveh-Benjamin (1998) found that, when younger and older adults divided their attention between a memory task and an ongoing reaction-time task, memory performance dropped equally for the younger and older groups (relative to performing the memory task on its own) but that performance on the reaction-time task dropped much more for older than for younger adults, especially during the retrieval phase of the memory task. In a similar demonstration, Lindenberger, Marsiske, and Baltes (2000) measured walking accuracy and speed in adults of different ages while they learned a list of words. They found greater dual-task costs in the older group, partly reflecting the increased need for executive processes in word learning but also partly reflecting the older adults' greater need to deploy executive processes to control accurate walking.

Prospective Memory

Prospective memory refers to the situation in which a person intends to carry out some action at a future time and then either performs the action successfully or forgets to perform it. Such situations are common in everyday life, as are failures of prospective memory—forgetting to make a phone call, mail a letter, or to pass on a message, for example. Researchers have made the useful distinction between event-based and time-based prospective memory, the first referring to situations in which the intended action should be cued by an event, such as seeing the letter to be mailed or meeting the colleague for whom the message was intended. On the other hand, time-based prospective actions are cued by times: "I should call home at 3:30 P.M.," for example.

Prospective memory failure generally increases with age. As one example, Mäntylä and Nilsson (1997) reported a study in which participants were asked to remind the experimenter at the end of a testing session that they should sign a form. Successful performance dropped from 61 percent of participants aged thirty-five to forty-five to only 25 percent of participants aged seventy to eighty. Other research demonstrates that older adults do worse on time-based than on event-based, prospective memory tasks, arguably because the former type of task is less well supported by environmental cues (Craik, 1983). Finally, older people do better on real-life prospective memory tasks than on laboratory-based tasks (Kester, Benjamin, Castel, and Craik, 2002). This finding may reflect greater motivation on the part of older adults, or it may reflect their greater use of daily structures and routines.

Summary

Memory performance does decline with age, but the decline is greater in some tasks than in others. Performance is often poor on episodic memory tasks, especially if the person must recall the information without cues. Performance is also comparatively poor on source memory, on prospective memory, and on working memory tasks. On the other hand, memory for general knowledge and for routine activities holds up well with age, as does primary memory for information held briefly in mind. Finally, environmental support from familiar surroundings can be particularly helpful as an aid to remembering in older adults.

See also: AGING AND MEMORY IN ANIMALS; AUTOBIOGRAPHICAL MEMORY; EPISODIC MEMORY; INDIVIDUAL DIFFERENCES IN LEARNING AND MEMORY; TIP-OF-THE-TONGUE PHENOMENON; WORKING MEMORY: HUMANS

Bibliography

Anderson, N. D., Craik, F. I. M., and Naveh-Benjamin, M. (1998). The attentional demands of encoding and retrieval in younger and older adults: 1. Evidence from divided attention costs. *Psychology and Aging 13*, 405–423.

Baddeley, A. D. (1986). *Working memory*. London: Oxford University Press.

Craik, F. I. M. (1983). On the transfer of information from temporary to permanent memory. *Philosophical Transactions of the Royal Society of London, ser. B, 302*, 341–359.

——— (2002). Human memory and aging. In L. Bäckman and C. von Hofsten, eds., *Psychology at the turn of the millennium*, Vol. 1: *Cognitive, biological, and health perspectives*, pp. 261–280. Hove, Sussex, UK: Psychology Press.

Craik, F. I. M., and Byrd, M. (1982). Aging and cognitive deficits: The role of attentional resources. In F. I. M. Craik and S. Trehub, eds., *Aging and cognitive processes*, pp. 191–211. New York: Plenum.

Craik, F. I. M., and Jennings, J. M. (1992). Human memory. In F. I. M. Craik, and T. A. Salthouse, eds., *The handbook of aging and cognition*, pp. 51–110. Hillsdale, NJ: Erlbaum.

Fleischman, D. A., and Gabrieli, J. D. E. (1998). Repetition priming in normal aging and Alzheimer's disease: A review of findings and theories. *Psychology and Aging 13*, 88–119.

Glisky, E. L., Polster, M. R., and Routhieaux, B. C. (1995). Double dissociation between item and source memory. *Neuropsychology 9*, 229–235.

Kester, J. D., Benjamin, A. S., Castel, A. D., and Craik, F. I. M. (2002). Memory in the elderly. In A. Baddeley, B. Wilson, and M. Kopelman, eds., *Handbook of memory disorders*, 2nd edition. London: Wiley.

Lindenberger, U., Marsiske, M., and Baltes, P. B. (2000). Memorizing while walking: Increase in dual-task costs from young adulthood to old age. *Psychology and Aging 15*, 417–436.

Mäntylä, T., and Nilsson, L. G. (1997). Remembering to remember in adulthood: A population-based study on aging and prospective memory. *Aging, Neuropsychology, and Cognition 4*, 81–92.

Maylor, E. A. (1997). Proper name retrieval in old age: Converging evidence against disproportionate impairment. *Aging, Neuropsychology, and Cognition 4*, 211–266.

Naveh-Benjamin, M. (2000). Adult age differences in memory performance: Tests of an associative deficit hypothesis. *Journal of Experimental Psychology: Learning, Memory, and Cognition 26*, 1,170–1,187.

Prull, M. W., Gabrieli, J. D. E., and Bunge, S. A. (2000). Age-related changes in memory: A cognitive neuroscience perspective. In F. I. M. Craik and T. A. Salthouse, eds., *The handbook of aging and cognition*, 2nd edition, pp. 91–153. Mahwah, NJ: Erlbaum.

Rubin, D. C., Wetzler, S. E., and Nebes, R. D. (1986). Autobiographical memory across the adult life-span. In D. C. Rubin, ed., *Autobiographical memory*, pp. 202–221. Cambridge, UK: Cambridge University Press.

Zacks, R. T., Hasher, L., and Li, K. Z. H. (2000). Human memory. In F. I. M. Craik and T. A. Salthouse eds., *The handbook of aging and cognition*, pp. 293–357. Mahwah, NJ: Erlbaum.

Fergus I. M. Craik

ALGORITHMS, LEARNING

Learning algorithms are sets of rules, usually expressed using mathematical equations or computer instructions, that enable a system to improve its performance on the basis of its own experience. Also called learning procedures, methods, or rules, learning algorithms are key components of mathematical models of animal learning and of technological devices engineered to improve their behavior as they operate. Learning algorithms have been studied extensively in artificial intelligence, psychology, computational neuroscience, statistics, and engineering. They are used in many applications in science, industry, and finance that require fitting models to or finding patterns in collections of data or that require learning skills needed to solve specific tasks. Learning algorithms play major roles in artificial neural network systems, where they provide rules for adjusting the strengths, or weights, of connections between network elements. These connections correspond to synapses by which neurons communicate with other neurons and with sensory and motor mechanisms.

Hebbian Learning

In 1949 the psychologist Donald Hebb hypothesized that when a neuron, A, repeatedly and persistently takes part in firing another neuron, B, the synapses by which A stimulates B are strengthened. It then becomes easier for neuron A to fire neuron B. Consequently, any event that stimulates neuron A may also stimulate neuron B and thus become associated with the consequences of B's firing as well as with other events that stimulate B. This is one of the earliest and most influential ideas contributing to neural-network learning algorithms.

Turning this hypothesis into a complete learning algorithm requires precise definitions of the variables involved and how they interact. One of the simplest ways to do this is to consider the situation in which neuron B receives input from other neurons, labeled $1, 2, \ldots, n$, any of which can play the role of neuron A in Hebb's hypothesis. Let $X_B(t)$ be a positive number representing the activity level (the instantaneous rate of firing) of neuron B at time t. Similarly, for $i = 1, 2, \ldots, n$, let $X_i(t)$ represent the activity levels at time t of neurons $1, 2, \ldots, n$ (see Figure l). In representing how the activity of neuron B depends on the activities of the other neurons, the simplest assumption is that $X_B(t)$ is a weighted sum of the activities of the other neurons, where each weight represents the current strength of a synapse. If $W_i(t)$ is the strength at time t of the synapse by which neuron i influences neuron B, this means that

$$X_B(t) = W_1(t)X_1(t) + \ldots + W_n(t)X_n(t). \quad (1)$$

Hebb's hypothesis suggests how the synaptic strengths change over time, depending on the other variables. The extent to which neuron i takes part in firing neuron B at a time t is often represented by the product of the activity levels of neuron B and neuron i: $X_B(t) X_i(t)$. This product is large when the activity levels of both neurons are high, and it is small when the activity level of one or both neurons is close to zero. Thus, if neuron i persistently takes part in firing neuron B, this product will be large for many times t. This leads to a rule for changing synaptic strengths that can be written for each synapse i as:

$$W_i(t + \delta t) = W_i(t) + cX_B(t)X_i(t), \qquad (2)$$

where δt is a small time increment and c is a small positive number. Selecting values for δt and c determines how rapidly the synaptic strengths change. According to Equation 2, at any time, t, when the activity levels of neurons i and B are both greater than zero, $X_B(t)X_i(t)$ is greater than zero, and the synaptic strength $W_i(t)$ increases from time t to time $t + \delta t$. According to Equation 1, this larger synaptic weight means that neuron i's activity will contribute more to the activity of neuron B in the future. Equations 1 and 2 constitute a learning algorithm; both are needed to compute the changes in the synaptic strengths when the values $X_i(t)$, $i = 1, 2, \ldots, n$, are given for each time t. This is the simplest of many learning algorithms based on Hebb's hypothesis, and, despite many shortcomings, it has played an important role in theories of learning in neural networks. Brown et al. (1990) discuss this and many other Hebb-inspired learning algorithms and how well they model synaptic properties actually observed in regions of the brain such as the hippocampus.

Statistical Learning

Other learning algorithms are motivated by a desire to solve problems that occur frequently in a variety of fields. One type of problem that has received much attention, especially in the field of statistics, is that of function fitting. Suppose you observe the inputs and outputs of some system under study and assemble a training set of observations (X^i, Z^i), $i = 1, 2, \ldots, m$, where Z^i is the system's output for input X^i. (The superscripts are used to avoid confusion with the neuron-activity levels used above.) On the basis of these data, you would like to predict what the system's output will be for new inputs. For example, the system might be a medical treatment, with inputs giving features of patients (such as the results of clinical tests) and outputs describing treatment outcome (which can be a quantitative measure or a nonnumeric, or categorical, description, such as recovery /no-recovery). You would like to predict the outcomes of treating new patients.

In statistics, this is known as a regression or a classification problem (for the respective cases of quanti-

Figure 1

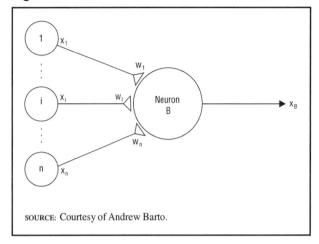

SOURCE: Courtesy of Andrew Barto.

Neurons 1, 2, . . . n provide input to neuron B.

tative and categorical outcomes). Solving it requires finding a rule (mathematically, a function) that best fits the data in the training set (where "best" is precisely defined in some way). The resulting rule is then used to provide the desired predictions. Many methods for solving these problems are formulated as learning algorithms. The training set represents the experience of the learning system, and the rule being learned improves in its ability to provide valid predictions as the data is processed. Learning researchers think of the training set as a set of examples provided by a "teacher," and they call this process learning by example, learning with a teacher, or, most often, supervised learning. Many learning algorithms have been devised for supervised learning problems, and modern research on the theoretical properties of these algorithms is strongly tied to the field of statistics. Hastie et al. (2001) is a good reference for the statistical view of supervised learning algorithms.

Least Mean Square Algorithm

The least mean square (LMS) algorithm is an influential supervised learning algorithm proposed by the electrical engineers Bernard Widrow and Marcian Hoff in 1960. Like the Hebbian algorithm described above, it can be expressed as a rule for changing the synaptic weights of a neuronlike element, but it requires another variable to provide training input to the element. This signal tells the element what its activity should be; it is said to provide the desired outputs or target outputs. During learning, input signals and target outputs are selected from a training set of example input/output pairs. If $Z(t)$ denotes the target output at time t for an element whose actual output is $X(t)$, then $Z(t) - X(t)$ gives the error in the element's output: the discrepancy between what the element's activity should be and what it actually is. The LMS algorithm is an error-correction algorithm because it changes synaptic weights to reduce the sizes of the errors gradually over time.

If we suppose that X(t) is a weighted sum of inputs as given by Equation 1, then the LMS algorithm says that a synaptic weight i changes as follows:

$$W_i(t + \delta t) = W_i(t) + c [Z(t) - X(t)]X_i(t). \quad (3)$$

This means that when the element's output, X(t), is too low, the error is positive and the synaptic weight, $W_i(t)$, increases (assuming both c and $X_i(t)$ are positive). On the other hand, when the element's output is too high, the error is negative, and the weight decreases. In either case, this change in synaptic weight tends to make the element's output more nearly equal to the target output when input element i is active in the future.

The LMS algorithm is closely related to several other error-correction algorithms. The perceptron learning algorithm differs from the LMS algorithm only in using an error that is sensitive to the difference in the signs of the target and actual outputs but is not sensitive to the difference in their sizes. The LMS algorithm is also nearly identical in mathematical form to an influential model of Pavlovian, or classical, conditioning proposed by psychologists Robert Rescorla and Allan Wagner (1972). Instead of changes in synaptic strengths, this model defines changes in behavioral variables called associative strengths that link conditioned stimuli with an unconditioned response. The LMS algorithm is the basis of many models of the cerebellum, where climbing fibers may provide the error signals.

Gradient Descent

Theories of the LMS algorithm and many other learning algorithms depend on viewing the learning process as a search for a set of weights that is best according to some measure of the algorithm's performance. For the LMS algorithm, this measure assigns to each possible set of weights the average, or mean, of the squares of the errors that would result from using that set of weights for all relevant inputs. If we visualize this measure as a surface over "weight space," the error measure for the current weights corresponds to a point on this surface, and the LMS algorithm changes the weights by moving this point down the slope of the surface, thus improving the system's ability to match the target outputs. This is called a gradient-descent algorithm because the direction of steepest slope is given mathematically by the gradient of the error measure. A gradient-descent algorithm

will eventually find a local minimum, meaning a point that is better than all points in the immediate neighborhood, although a better point may exist. When the element's output is a linear function of its weights, as given by Equation 1, all local minima are also global minima, meaning that the error surface does not get any lower than at these points. This means that the LMS algorithm finds a set of weights that produces the least mean-square error over the relevant inputs, thus justifying the algorithm's name.

Error Backpropagation

A generalization of the LMS algorithm known as the error back-propagation algorithm has been influential in artificial neural network research. (Haykin [1999] provides details about this and other network learning algorithms.) In its simplest form, this is a gradient-descent algorithm that applies to networks of neuronlike elements that are connected in multiple layers and that are capable of computing nonlinear functions of the network's input. An error for each element is computed by propagating the error of the network as a whole back through the network in the direction opposite to the flow of element activity. Mathematically, this process computes the gradient of the error surface at the point corresponding to all the current weights in the network. Unlike the linear LMS algorithm, the error back-propagation algorithm is not guaranteed to find a best set of weights because the error surface can have a complex topography with many local minima.

Other Learning Algorithms

A learning algorithm is unsupervised, or self-organizing, if its experience comes from a training set containing inputs but no target outputs. Instead of trying to match target outputs, it tries to recode the inputs according to some built-in principle. For example, some unsupervised learning algorithms recode input signals in order to reduce their complexity while trying to preserve their information content. Often this takes the form of learning how to form clusters of input signals so that signals within a cluster are more similar to one another than they are to signals in other clusters. The Hebbian learning algorithm is most often used for unsupervised clustering in networks where elements compete for the opportunity to represent different inputs.

Reinforcement learning algorithms rely on training input called reward signals, which evaluate the quality of the learning system's behavior without explicitly telling the system what its outputs should be. Reinforcement learning algorithms have to discover how to improve their behavior by trying various outputs and comparing the resulting evaluations. This is a form of trial-and-error learning, which should not be confused with error-correction learning, such as that performed by the LMS algorithm, which requires target outputs. Many reinforcement learning systems use temporal difference (TD) algorithms to learn predictions of the amount of reward a reinforcement learning algorithm will accumulate over an extended period. TD algorithms reduce errors in predictions made at different times by adjusting earlier predictions to be closer to later—and therefore more reliable—predictions. The computer scientists Richard Sutton and Andrew Barto (1998) extensively discuss reinforcement learning and TD algorithms. Physiological experiments by the neuroscientist Wolfram Schultz (1998) reveal intriguing parallels between the behavior of TD algorithms and the activity of dompamine-producing neurons in the brain.

Conclusion

Learning algorithms have been devised for very different purposes: to model hypotheses about neural mechanisms of learning, to model the learning behavior of animals, and to solve important statistical and engineering problems. Despite these different purposes, the resulting algorithms show a remarkable degree of similarity. Perhaps this is not so surprising because animal behavior and its neural basis are nature's solutions to problems that have much in common with those studied by statisticians and engineers.

Bibliography

Brown, T. H., Kairiss, E. W., and Keenan, C. L. (1990). Hebbian synapses: Biophysical mechanisms and algorithms. *Annual Review of Neuroscience 13,* 475–511.

Hastie, T., Tibshirani, R., and Friedman, J. (2001). *The elements of statistical learning.* New York: Springer-Verlag.

Haykin, S. (1999). *Neural networks: A comprehensive foundation.* Upper Saddle River, NJ: Prentice Hall.

Hebb, D. O. (1949). *The organization of behavior.* New York: Wiley.

Rescorla, R. A., and Wagner. A. R. (1972). A theory of Pavlovian conditioning: Variations in the effectiveness of reinforcement and non-reinforcement. In A. H. Black and W. F. Prokasy, eds., *Classical conditioning,* Vol. 2: *Current research and theory,* pp. 64–99. New York: Appleton.

Schultz, W. (1998). Predictive reward signals of dopamine neurons. *Journal of Neurophysiology 80,* 1–27.

Sutton, R. S. and Barto, A. G. (1998). *Reinforcement learning: An introduction.* Cambridge, MA: MIT Press.

Widrow, B., and Hoff, M. E. (1960). Adaptive switching circuits. In *1960 IRE WESCON convention record,* pp. 96–104. New York: IRE. Reprinted in J. A. Anderson and E. Rosenfeld, eds., *Neurocomputing: Foundations of research.* Cambridge, MA: MIT Press, 1988.

Andrew G. Barto

ALZHEIMER'S DISEASE

[*Alzheimer's disease was first described by the German physician Alois Alzheimer in 1906. The disease is associated with a progressive decline in general cognitive function and a specific impairment in the ability to form new memories (anterograde amnesia). Approximately 4 million individuals in the United States suffer from Alzheimer's disease at an estimated cost for treatment and care that exceeds $100 billion per year. Two entries on Alzheimer's disease follow.* BEHAVIORAL ASPECTS *describes the cognitive defects associated with the disease and the ways in which it is diagnosed;* HUMAN DISEASE AND THE GENETICALLY ENGINEERED ANIMAL MODELS *describes recent progress in elucidating the genes and proteins implicated in the disease, the development of an animal model for the disease, and some exciting alternative treatment possibilities. For a discussion of treatments for Alzheimer's disease see* PHARMACOLOGICAL TREATMENTS OF MEMORY DEFECTS.]

BEHAVIORAL ASPECTS

Alzheimer's disease (AD) is the most common cause of dementia in the elderly, affecting 50 percent to 70 percent of dementia patients. Dementia involves impairments in daily functioning related to a progressive decline in two or more areas of mental ability. These mental and functional deficits are traceable to neuritic plaques and neurofibrillary tangles, which cause cell loss in the brain. As the disease progresses, it affects ever larger areas of the brain. Eventually, so many parts of the brain are involved that patients cannot move around normally and feed themselves. They then become susceptible to other potentially fatal diseases such as pneumonia. The disease can last from five to fifteen years. Many drugs are being developed to treat it, but there is no way of preventing the progression of the disease.

When the disease was first described by Alois Alzheimer in 1906, it seemed to affect only persons under the age of sixty-five. In the 1960s, researchers discovered during autopsies that patients whose severe cognitive decline had been attributed to diseases in the blood vessels of the brain (cerebrovascular disease or "hardening of the arteries") in fact exhibited the pathological hallmarks of AD (neurofibrillary tangles and neuritic plaques). The realization that AD affects persons of all ages is, therefore, a recent one. Because of the rarity of the disease among those under sixty—less than 2 percent—it used to be considered an uncommon disorder. Now it is understood that the likelihood of contracting AD increases with age. Among people sixty-five to eighty-five, its prevalence is 5 percent to 15 percent; 30 to 47 percent of those over eighty-five have AD. It is the fourth-leading cause of death among those sixty-five or older.

The earliest symptom of AD in most patients is severe difficulty in learning new information (i.e., anterograde memory impairment), especially increasing forgetfulness about day-to-day events. First, patients may forget a recent event from one week to the next, then from one day to the next, and finally from one minute to the next. AD impairs nearly all aspects of new learning. It is not, for example, limited to information that the patient is trying to learn (i.e., explicit or episodic memory), as is true in some amnesic disorders. Patients also have difficulty with implicit memory—learning information that impinges on consciousness in the absence of any effort at mastering it.

AD does not uniformly impair all implicit memory tasks. The same is true for the ability to learn new general skills (i.e., procedural knowledge). Patients have difficulty on some kinds of skill learning tasks but not others; for example, learning of motor skills is frequently spared. Early in the disease patients' memory for remote events is usually intact. As the disease progresses, however, remote memories also recede, but in reverse chronological order; the most recent memories evaporate first. Only the most severe impairment obliterates memories of earliest childhood.

The rapidity of anterograde memory impairment in AD is dramatic: It occurs after a delay of ten minutes or less after exposure to new information. The best way to reveal this rapid loss of information is to give a patient something new to learn—for example, a story—and to ask him/her to state how much is remembered immediately, and then after a delay. The delay should be less than ten minutes, because after ten minutes most types of patients, and even normal older persons, forget a substantial amount of information. For example, patients with other forms of dementia, such as Pick's disease or Huntington's disease, also have difficulty learning and retaining new information, but if delays last less than ten minutes, their retention is significantly better than that of AD patients. If delays are longer than ten minutes, then normal patients and those with other forms of dementia do not differ significantly from one another.

Two types of changes in the brain are primarily responsible for the severe anterograde memory impairment of AD. The first is damage to the brain regions in the medial temporal lobe that are essential for normal memory, specifically the entorhinal cortex and the hippocampus. Even in very mildly impaired patients, there is approximately a 30-percent neuronal loss in the entorhinal cortex, the primary input path to the hippocampus. There are also declines in the concentration of a number of neurotransmitters, the chemicals that are responsible for the transmission of nerve signals in the brain. One neurotransmitter, acetylcholine, which is important for normal human memory, declines by up to 70 percent in cases of severe impairment. The combination of these structural and chemical changes seems to be responsible for the unique severity of anterograde memory impairment in AD.

The cognitive impairments of AD are not confined to memory. These other difficulties interact with the memory impairment to increase its severity. Early on in the disease the other main area of impairment is the executive functions, which pertain to concept formation, directed attention, and the concurrent manipulation of information. Studies suggest that the early stages of AD present problems with the concurrent manipulation of information and a consequent difficulty with tasks that require simultaneous manipulation of several different components, even when the individual components of the tasks are deeply ingrained (e.g., preparing meals, paying bills, balancing a checkbook, and so on). That is why it sometimes seems as if the patients have difficulty with remote memory early in the disease. However, when the tasks are broken down into their constituent parts, patients can perform them.

Recent evidence suggests that problems with executive function are at least in part the result of pathology in the central portion of the cingulate gyrus. Studies in animals demonstrate that damage to the middle portion of the cingulate alters executive function. Another possible cause of executive-function impairment may be the loss of the corticocortical fibers, which connect different parts of the cortex to one another. The partial degeneration of this intracortical projection system in the early stages of AD could impair the performance that requires the rapid and simultaneous integration of multiple types of information.

The further progression of AD often severs the meaningful associations among words—hence a loss of semantic knowledge or semantic memory. Patients with AD begin to have difficulty with a number of linguistic tasks when they are mildly-to-moderately impaired. These difficulties affect the ability to produce the name of an object when shown the object itself or a picture of the object (confrontation naming). They also affect the ability to produce rapidly a series of words that belong to a particular category, such as vegetables or words starting with the letter s (verbal fluency).

Some researchers argue that AD involves a breakdown in the structure of semantic knowledge and that patients actually lose knowledge they once possessed.

Others argue that semantic knowledge remains intact in mildly and moderately impaired patients but is more difficult to access; thus, when one asks them to intentionally search their semantic memory for information, they have difficulty, but if their semantic knowledge is evaluated indirectly, it appears to be preserved. It has been difficult to resolve this debate because research, although intensive, often yields contradictory findings.

AD is still difficult to diagnose during life. No test can definitively verify the onset of the disease short of examining brain tissue through a biopsy. Researchers have therefore developed a number of conventions to communicate the degree to which patients have been examined and the diagnostic criteria that the patients meet. Patients who have been carefully examined and who meet clinical research criteria but have not had a brain biopsy are said to have probable AD, or probable dementia of the Alzheimer type. Patients who have had dementia during life and in whom results of an examination of brain tissue meet pathological research criteria for the disease are said to have definite AD.

Because novel treatments are under investigation, there has been increasing interest in determining the earliest possible diagnosis of AD. The term *mild cognitive impairment* (MCI) has been developed to describe individuals with evidence of a functional difficulty in daily life that does not warrant a diagnosis of dementia. A large number of individuals with MCI (approximately 15 percent per year) are later diagnosed with AD. Drug trials are underway to see if treating patients with MCI reduces the likelihood that they will be diagnosed with AD.

AD is a common and serious disorder that is caused by damage to the structure and function of the brain. There are several hypotheses concerning the underlying cause of AD, but these remain unproved, and there are no effective treatments. The disease produces a gradual decline in cognitive function. The most common early symptom is a dramatic loss of new information after a brief delay, but AD can impair all aspects of mental ability.

See also: DEMENTIA; PHARMACOLOGICAL TREATMENTS OF MEMORY DEFICITS

Bibliography

Albert, M., and Moss, B. (1999). Early features of Alzheimer's disease. In A. Peters and J. Morrison, eds. *Cerebral Cortex*, Vol. 14, pp. 461–471, New York: Plenum.

Gomez-Isla, T., Price, J., McKeel, D., Morris, J., Growdon, J., and Hyman, B. (1996). Profound loss of layer II entorhinal cortex neurons occurs in very mild Alzheimer's disease. *Journal of Neuroscience* 16, 4,491–4,500.

Katzman, R. and Kawas, C. (1984). The epidemiology of dementia and Alzheimer's disease. In R. D. Terry, R. Katzman, and K. L. Bick, eds., *Alzheimer disease*. New York: Raven.

McKhann, G., Drachman, D., Folstein, M. F., Katzman, R., Price, D., and Stadlan, E. (1984). Clinical diagnosis of Alzheimer's disease. Report of the NINCDS-ADRDA Workgroup under the auspices of Department of Health and Human Services Task Force. *Neurology* 34, 939–944.

Petersen, R., Smith, G., Waring, S., Ivnik, R., Tangalos, E., and Kokmen, E. (1999). Mild cognitive impairment, clinical characterization and outcome. *Archives of Neurology* 56, 303–308.

Marilyn S. Albert

HUMAN DISEASE AND THE GENETICALLY ENGINEERED ANIMAL MODELS

Alzheimer's disease (AD) represents a great challenge for science and medicine because of its prevalence, cost, lack of reliable treatments, and often devastating impact on individuals and caregivers. This age-associated chronic illness involves genetic risk factors, a well-defined clinical syndrome with a progressive course, evidence of dysfunction and/or death of populations of neurons, pathological and biochemical abnormalities, and intra- or extra-cellular protein aggregates (Price, Tanzi, Borchelt, and Sisodia, 1998). Patients become severely disabled and often die of intercurrent illnesses. There are treatments for symptoms but no cure. However, recent research, particularly in animal models, has begun to provide new insights into the mechanisms of Alzheimer's disease and has identified new targets for therapy.

Clinical-Pathological Features of Alzheimer's Disease

In most cases of AD, the initial impairments of memory and cognition appear gradually during the seventh decade. The accuracy of clinical diagnoses improved from 1980 to 2000, and early diagnosis will become increasingly important as mechanism-based treatments become available.

AD involves the brain (and not other organs) and certain neuronal populations are selectively vulnerable. AD results from the selective degeneration of nerve cells in the brain's regions and neural circuits that are critical for memory, cognitive performance, and personality (Albert, 1996). The dysfunction and/or death of these neurons reduces the numbers of generic and transmitter specific-synaptic markers in their target fields; the disruption of synaptic communication in affected regions/circuits can lead to mental impairments and, finally, severe dementia.

AD typically involves intracellular or extracellular protein aggregates in brain. Neurofibrillary tangles (NFTs), inclusions located within cell bodies and proximal dendrites, are composed of poorly soluble paired helical filaments (PHF), which are, in turn, composed principally of hyperphosphorylated isoforms of tau. PHF are also present in dystrophic neurites, the filamentous swellings of distal axons/terminals (usually seen in proximity to Aβ deposits). Perturbations related to hyperphosphorylated tau seem to play a role in disturbances in intracellular transport.

The extracellular aggregates in brain are abnormal accumulations of Aβ, a 4kD β pleated sheet amyloid peptide, derived by β- and γ-secretase cleavages of the amyloid precursor protein (APP). Levels of Aβ are elevated in brain, and Aβ monomers form oligomers and multimers that assemble into protofilaments and then fibrils. Eventually, Aβ fibrils are deposited as the amyloid cores of neuritic or senile plaques, which are complex structures also containing dystrophic neurites, astrocytes, and microglia. Plaques are preferentially localized to the cortex, hippocampus, and amygdala.

The levels and distributions of APP and its cleavage enzymes in neurons lead to the selective appearance of Aβ in brain. It seems that toxic Aβ peptides, particularly oligomers, accumulate near synapses and may impair transsynaptic communication, eventuating in the disruption of synaptic connections between neurons and their targets (other nerve cells). Nerve cells are functionally damaged, changes occur in tau phosphorylation; microtubule stability is compromised; intracellular transport processes are impaired; intracellular PHF appear; and cell geometry is altered, with synapses, axon terminals, and dendrites appearing to be most vulnerable. The neuron is incapable of performing its normal functions for a significant interval before the ensuing demise of the cell.

Mutant Genes/Proteins Implicated in Familial Alzheimer's Disease (FAD)

In some individuals with early onset AD, the illness may be inherited as an autosomal dominant with mutations in three different genes: the APP; PS1; and PS2 (Price, Tanzi, Borchelt, and Sisodia, 1998).

APP

Encoded by a gene on chromosome 21, APP is expressed in many cells and tissues but is particularly abundant in neurons. This type-1 transmembrane protein is cleaved endoproteolytically by an enzyme, β-site APP-cleaving enzyme 1 (BACE1), and by an activity termed "γ-secretase," which, in concert, generate the N- and C-termini of the Aβ peptide, respectively. The levels and distributions of APP and the activities of proamyloidogenic cleavage enzymes, particularly BACE1, in neurons seem to be lead to the formation of Aβ in brain. The formation of Aβ 1-40,42 is precluded by the endoproteolytic cleavage of APP within the Aβ sequence by α-secretase, now

thought to be either tumor necrosis factor (TNF) α converting enzyme (TACE) or a disintegrin and metalloproteinase 10 (ADAM 10), which cut between residues 16 and 17 of Aβ, and by BACE2, a protease sharing features with BACE1, but cleaving APP after residues 19 and 20 of Aβ (i.e., within the Aβ domain). These different endoproteolytic cleavages generate various C-terminal peptides, including the APP intracellular domain (C60), which may play a role in the activation of transcription.

A variety of APP mutations, including APPswe (a double mutation at the N-terminus of Aβ) and APP-717 (near the C-terminus of Aβ), have been reported in cases of FAD. These mutations, strikingly situated near several secretase cleavage sites, are proamyloidogenic, and cells that express mutant APP show aberrant APP processing: the APPswe mutation, which enhances BACE1 cleavage, is associated with elevated levels of Aβ; the APP 717 mutations, which affect γ-secretase activity, lead to a higher secreted fraction of longer, more toxic Aβ peptides (Aβ42) relative to cells that express wild-type APP (Price, Tanzi, Borchelt, and Sisodia, 1998; Citron et al., 1992).

PS1 and PS2

Localized to chromosomes 14 (PS1) and 1 (PS2), respectively, these genes encode highly homologous 43- to 50-kD proteins with multiple transmembrane (TM) domains. Oriented toward cytoplasm are a hydrophilic acidic "loop" region, an N-terminal region, and a C-terminal domain. PS1 is synthesized as an ≈42- to 43-kD polypeptide, but the preponderant PS1-related species that accumulate in vitro and in vivo are ≈27- to 28-kD N-terminal and ≈16- to 17-kD C-terminal derivatives, which accumulate and/or associate in a 1:1 stochiometry and are stable, tightly regulated, and saturable. PS genes are widely expressed at low abundance in the CNS.

PS1 influences APP processing, but it is not clear whether PS1 itself is an aspartyl protease (i.e., γ-secretase), is a cofactor critical for the activity of γ-secretase, or plays a role in trafficking of APP to the proper compartment for γ-secretase cleavage (De Strooper et al., 1998).

The PS1 gene harbors more than fifty different FAD mutations in more than eighty families, whereas only a small number of mutations have been found in PS2-linked families. The vast majority of the abnormalities in PS genes are missense mutations that result in single amino-acid substitutions. However, researchers have found a mutation that deletes exon 9 from PS1 in several different FAD families. The various PS mutations appear to influence γ-secretase activity and increase the generation of the Aβ 42 peptide.

Transgenic Models of Aβ Amyloidogenesis

Some of the lines of mutant APP mice, although they do not reproduce the full phenotype of AD, represent excellent models of Aβ amyloidosis and are of great value for testing causal effects of mutant genes, analyses of pathogenic pathways, determination of the molecules participating in Aβ amyloidogenesis, and identification of therapeutic targets. What follows is a review of selected examples of lines of mice expressing autosomal dominant FAD-linked mutant transgenes.

Mutant APP Mice

Several promoters have been used to drive the expression of an APP minigenes that encode the FAD-linked APP mutants (swe and 717) in strains of mice. The pathology is influenced by the level of transgene product and the specific mutation. The hippocampi and cortices of these mice show elevated levels of Aβ, diffuse Aβ deposits, and plaques consisting of dystrophic neurites displayed around an Aβ core. Astrocytes and microglia are clustered in and around plaques. NFT are not apparent. In some lines of mice there may be mild loss of neurons. Some mice show abnormalities of synapses in hippocampal circuits that precede the deposition of Aβ. In some lines, mice may exhibit learning deficits, problems in object-recognition memory (related to the number of amyloid deposits in specific regions) and impairments of alternation/spatial-reference and working memory (perhaps related to reductions in synaptic densities in the hippocampus).

APPswe/PS1 Mutant Transgenic Mice

Transgenic mice that coexpress A246E HuPS1 and Mouse/Human-APPswe have elevated levels of Aβ in the brain and develop numerous amyloid deposits in the hippocampus and cortex (Borchelt et al., 1997; Borchelt et al., 1996). The Aβ deposits are associated with dystrophic neurites that contain APP, PS1, and BACE1 immunoreactivities; thus, the key participants in amyloidosis appear locally at some of the possible sites of formation of Aβ.

Gene-Targeted Mice Particularly Relevant to AD

APP and APLP2 Null Mice

Homozygous APP-/- mice are viable and fertile, but they appear to have subtle decreases in locomotor activity and forelimb grip strength. The absence of substantial phenotypes in APP-/- mice may be related to the functional redundancy provided by homologous amyloid precursorlike proteins (APLP1 and APlP2), molecules expressed at high levels with developmental and cellular distributions similar to APP.

Consistent with this idea are observations that APLP2-/- mice appear normal but that mice with either both APP and APLP2 targeted alleles or both APLP1 and APLP2 null alleles show significant postnatal lethality.

BACE1-/- Mice

These null mice are viable and healthy, have no obvious phenotype or pathology, and can mate successfully (Cai et al., 2001). In cortical neurons from BACE1 null embryos, there is no cleavage at the +1 and + 11 sites of Aβ (Cai et al., 2001), and the secretion of peptides is abolished even in the presence transfected mutant APP transgenes. Moreover, Aβ peptides are not produced in the brains of BACE1 null mice. These results establish that BACE1 is the neuronal β-secretase required to cleave APP to generate the N-termini of Aβ they further establish that BACE1 is an excellent therapeutic target for drug development for AD.

PS1 and PS2 Null Mice

To examine the roles of PS1 in development, several groups have produced PS1-/- mice (4). Homozygous mutant mice fail to survive beyond the early postnatal period and show severe perturbations in the development of the axial skeleton and ribs (defects in somitogenesis) that resemble a particular Notch1 null phenotype. Because PS1 homologues interact with Notch1, a receptor protein involved in critical cell-fate decisions during development, it is not surprising that cells lacking PS1 show reductions in proteolytic release of the Notch1 intracellular domain (NICD), a cleavage that is thought to be critical for Notch1 signaling. Both wild type and mutant human PS1 transgenes rescue the spectrum of developmental defects in PS1 null mice. These results indicate that the FAD-linked PS1 variants retain sufficient normal function to allow normal mammalian embryonic development. With regard to the role of PS proteins in Aβ biology, mutations in PS genes increase the formation of Aβ42, and ablation of PS1 reduces the secretion of Aβ. Significantly, cells from PS1-/- mice show reductions in the levels of γ-secretase cleavage products and levels of Aβ

Vulnerability of Neurons in Alzheimer's Disease

Among the most challenging mysteries of neurodegenerative diseases is the identification of factors that render neurons susceptible in specific diseases (the principle of selective vulnerability). For example, APP and SOD1 are abundant in many cells. Why, then, do mutations of genes encoding these proteins cause neurological diseases? And why are mutations in APP associated with the development of a dementia syndrome and mutations in SOD1 with an MND phenotype? Recent research has begun to provide exciting new clues concerning the biological basis for vulnerabilities of neurons. AD serves as an illustration. We suggested that the basis for the vulnerabilities of the brain to AD are related to the levels and distributions of APP and its cleavage enzymes in neurons as opposed to other cells (Cai et al., 2001). APP is one of the most abundant proteins in neurons, and available evidence indicates that neurons are the principal source of Aβ. In nerve cell, APP is transported within axons by the fast anterograde system. APP processing can occur at nerve terminals. In the terminal fields of the perforant pathway, BACE1 cleavage generates soluble C-terminally truncated APPs and amyloidogenic C-terminal fragments. Moreover, in mutant APP transgenic mice, APP, BACE1, and PS1, the key proteins in the formation of amyloid, have been seen in swollen neurites in immediate proximity to Aβ deposits. These observations conform to the idea that neurons and their processes, including axon terminals, are one source of the APP that gives rise to Aβ peptide species.

However, the presence of APP in neurons, although necessary, is not sufficient to explain why the brain is particularly vulnerable to Aβ amyloidogenesis whereas other organs, such as the pancreas, are not β. The patterns of APP-cleavage enzymes in different cell populations are of equal importance. The cellular distributions, relative levels, and sites of APP cleavage of BACE1, BACE2, and α-secretase are principal determinants of such vulnerability. Although both BACE1 and BACE2 are expressed ubiquitously, BACE1 mRNA levels are particularly high in the brain and pancreas, whereas the levels of BACE2 mRNA are relatively low in all tissues except the brain, where it is nearly undetectable. As indicated above, Aβ is generated by biochemical pathways involving the endoproteolytic cleavages carried out by BACE1 and by an activity termed "γ-secretase," which generate the N- and C-termini of the Aβ peptide, respectively. Most importantly, BACE1 is the principal β-secretase necessary to cleave APP at the +1 and +11 sites of Aβ in neurons (Cai et al., 2001). In contrast, BACE2 cleaves APP more efficiently at residues +19 and +20 of APP compared to the +1 site of Aβ. Significantly, levels of Aβ1-19 and Aβ1-20 are undetectable in brain. APP can also be cleaved endoproteolytically before residue +17 within the Aβ sequence by "α-secretases," either TACE or ADAM10. These three cleavages within the Aβ domain of APP preclude the formation of Aβ 1- 40,42. Because BACE1 is the principal β-secretase in neurons (Cai et al., 2002) and BACE2 may serve to limit the secretion of Aβ peptides, we suggest that BACE1 is a proamyloidogenic enzyme, wherease BACE2 is an antiamyloidogenic protease, and that the relative levels of BACE1 and BACE2 are major determinants of Aβ amyloidosis. Significantly, γ-secretase, which may be PS1 (or has its activity influenced by PS), is present in a relatively low level in brain and does not form Aβ without BACE1 cleavages.

In this model (Cai et al., 2001), the secretion of Aβ peptides would be highest in neurons/brain as compared to other cell types/organs because neurons express high levels of BACE1 coupled with low expression of BACE2. If the ratio of the level of BACE1 to BACE2 is a critical factor that selectively predisposes the brain to Aβ amyloidosis, AD would likely involve the brain selectively as opposed to other organs. A seemingly contradictory study shows a high level of BACE1 mRNA expression in the pancreas. Since APP is expressed in the pancreas, why do AD and diabetes mellitus not occur together? It now appears that some of the pancreatic BACE1 mRNAs are alternatively spliced to generate a BACE1 isoform that is incapable of cleaving APP. Taken together with the observations that the pancreas possesses low levels of BACE1 and low amounts of BACE1 activity, these results are consistent with the view that a high ratio of BACE1 to BACE2 activity leads to selective vulnerability of neurons and not pancreatic cells to Aβ amyloidosis. To test this hypothesis at the level of specific cell populations, it will be important to define the levels and distributions of BACE1 and BACE2 in specific brain regions, circuits, and neurons using specific BACE1 and 2 antisera and to attempt to correlate these measures with the regional vulnerabilities to Aβ amyloidosis seen in AD.

Treatment in Models of Aβ Amyloidogenesis

Research on model systems relevant to AD illustrates the value of studies of transgenic and gene-targeted mice for experimental treatments. Although they do not model the full phenotype of AD, these mutant mice represent excellent models of Aβ amyloidogenesis and are highly suitable for analyses of pathogenic pathways, determination of the molecular participants in amyloidogenesis, and identification of therapeutic targets. Moreover, they are invaluable for examining the effects of the introduction and/or ablation of specific genes, administration of pharmacological agents (secretase inhibitors), and Aβ vaccination or passive transfer of Aβ antibody. Researchers need to assess the efficacy of anti-Aβ therapies in transgenic mice exhibiting tau pathology.

Bibliography

Albert, M. S. Cognitive and neurobiologic markers of early Alzheimer disease (1996). *Proceedings of the National Academy of Sciences of the United States of America 93*, 13,547–13,551.

Borchelt, D. R., Ratovitski, T., Van Lare, J., Lee, M. K., Gonzales, V. B., Jenkins, N. A., Copeland, N. G., Price, D. L., and Sisodia, S. S. (1997). Accelerated amyloid deposition in the brains of transgenic mice co-expressing mutant presenilin 1 and amyloid precursor proteins. *Neuron 19*, 939–945.

Borchelt, D. R., Thinakaran, G, Eckman, C. B., Lee, M. K., Davenport, F. Ratovitsky, F. Prada, C.-M., Kim, G. Seekins, S., Yager, D., Slunt, H. H., Wang, R., Seeger, M. Levey, A. I., Gandy, S. E., Copeland, N. G., Jenkins, N. A., Price, D. L., Younkin, S. G., and Sisodia, S. S. (1996). Familial Alzheimer's disease-linked presenilin 1 variants elevate Aβ1–42/1–40 ratio in vitro and in vivo. *Neuron 17*, 1,005–1,1013.

Cai, H., Wang, Y., McCarthy, D., Wen, H., Borchelt, D. R., Price, D. L., and Wong, P. C. (2001). BACE1 is the major β-secretase for generation of Aβ peptides by neurons. *Nature Neuroscience 4*, 233–234.

Citron, M., Oltersdorf, T., Haass, C., McConlogue, L., Hung, A. H., Seubert, P., Vigo-Pelfrey, C., Lieberburg, I., and Selkoe, D. J. (1992). Mutation of the β-amyloid precursor protein in familial Alzheimer's disease increases β-protein production. *Nature 360*, 672–674.

De Strooper, B., Saftig, P., Craessaerts, K., Vanderstichele, H., Guhde, G., Annaert, W., Von Figura, K., and Van Leuven, F. (1998). Deficiency of presenilin-1 inhibits the normal cleavage of amyloid precursor protein. *Nature 391*, 387–390.

Price, D. l., Tanzi, R. E., Borchelt, D. R., and Sisodia, S. S. (1998). Alzheimer's disease, genetic studies and transgenic models. *Annual Review of Genetics 32*, 461–493.

Donald L. Price
Sangram S. Sisodia
Revised by Philip C. Wong and Donald L. Price

AMNESIA

See: ALZHEIMER'S DISEASE: BEHAVIORAL ASPECTS; ALZHEIMER'S DISEASE: HUMAN DISEASE AND THE GENETICALLY ENGINEERED ANIMAL MODELS; AMNESIA, FUNCTIONAL; AMNESIA, INFANTILE; AMNESIA, ORGANIC; AMNESIA, TRANSIENT GLOBAL; HEAD INJURY; KNOWLEDGE SYSTEMS AND MATERIAL-SPECIFIC MEMORY DEFICITS; REHABILITATION OF MEMORY DISORDERS

AMNESIA, FUNCTIONAL

Analyses of learning and memory increasingly attempt to take account of clinical and experimental research on victims of amnesia. Most of this literature has focused on pathologies of memory associated with demonstrable brain lesions or the administration of centrally acting drugs. The functional amnesias are a collection of memory disorders instigated by processes that do not result in damage or injury to the brain but that do engender a marked increase in forgetting.

Amnesia in the Dissociative Disorders

One major category of functional amnesia occurs within the context of diagnosable psychopathology, especially the dramatic "Dissociative Disorders" listed in the Diagnostic and Statistical Manual (DSM) (4th edition) of the American Psychiatric Association. In current diagnostic nosology, this category includes a wide variety of syndromes whose common core is an alteration in consciousness affecting memory and identity.

In dissociative amnesia (also known as psychogenic amnesia, limited amnesia), the patient suffers a loss of autobiographical memory for specific past experiences. It sometimes occurs in cases of violent crime (interestingly, affecting either victims or perpetrators), war neurosis, and other types of posttraumatic stress disorder. Unfortunately, many reports of dissociative amnesia are anecdotal and lack independent corroboration of the purported instigating event. Moreover, it is not possible to reliably distinguish genuine cases of psychogenic amnesia from simulated cases.

In dissociative fugue (psychogenic fugue, functional retrograde amnesia), the amnesia covers the whole of the individual's past life and his or her personal identity; there may also be physical relocation (which gives the syndrome its name). The condition may go unnoticed until the patients are asked personal questions that they cannot satisfactorily answer. Recovery typically begins with the patient's recognition of loss of identity. Recovery of identity and memory per se may occur spontaneously or in response to the appearance of a relative or other salient cue. When the fugue is resolved, the patient is typically left with a limited amnesia covering the period of the fugue.

In dissociative identity disorder (multiple-personality disorder), a single individual appears to manifest two or more distinct identities, each alternating in control over conscious experience, thought, and action. Before World War II, the typical case involved only two or three such "ego states"; more recent cases have tended to present more alter egos, leading some to speculate that iatrogenic and sociocultural factors may account for much of the multiple-personality epidemic of the 1980s. In genuine cases, the personalities are separated by an amnesic barrier. The dissociation may be symmetrical, in which each ego state is ignorant of the other(s) or, more commonly, asymmetrical, in which case an ego state may be aware of some of its counterparts but ignorant of others.

In depersonalization the person believes that he or she has changed in some way or is somehow unreal; in derealization the same beliefs are held about one's surroundings. Because these beliefs are objectively inappropriate, these experiences can be construed as disorders of memory: the person fails to recognize some object, self, or situation with which he or she is objectively quite familiar. Episodes of depersonalization and derealization frequently occur in response to stress and in association with anxiety disorders; they may also be induced by psychedelic drugs and occur spontaneously in a substantial proportion of the normal population.

Although dissociative disorders have been of interest at least since the time of Freud and Janet, they rarely have been studied with controlled experimental procedures. For example, little is known about psychogenic amnesia beyond anecdotes. A few cases of fugue and multiple personality have been studied in the laboratory, but we have no idea how representative they are. Nevertheless, the available evidence suggests a pattern of selective memory deficit in some respects resembles that observed in organic amnesia. Thus, psychogenic fugue impairs memory for past experiences and other aspects of self-knowledge but leaves the patient's repertoire of impersonal procedural and semantic knowledge largely intact. Dissociative identity disorder displays a similar pattern.

Nonpathological Amnesias

In other forms of functional amnesia, dramatic forgetting occurs in the ordinary course of everyday living, albeit with no implication of pathology. For example, people commonly fail to remember their dreams and other events of the night's sleep; attempts to demonstrate sleep learning have been almost uniformly unsuccessful. Theoretical accounts of this memory deficit usually revolve around encoding factors. For example, one hypothesis holds that sleep inhibits the higher cortical centers that support perceptual processing.

Another example of nonpathological functional amnesia is the general paucity of memory for infancy and childhood. As with sleep, most theoretical accounts of this developmental amnesia focus on encoding factors. For example, infantile amnesia (covering the first two years of life) may reflect the child's relative inability to encode symbolic and especially linguistic representations of events; even older children may lack the information-processing capacity to encode retrievable memories.

A dramatic form of forgetting known as posthypnotic amnesia occurs in some hypnotized subjects. In some respects, posthypnotic amnesia may serve as a laboratory analogue of the dissociative amnesias seen in the clinic.

Explicit and Implicit Memory

While the functional amnesias by definition impair explicit memory, some anecdotal and experimental evidence suggests that the amnesia may spare implicit memory, or the unconscious influence of past events on subsequent experience, thought, or action. In dissociative identity disorder, for example, both procedural learning and priming effects may transfer between personalities, so that one alter ego is influenced by the experiences of another even though the amnesic barrier prevents conscious recollection. The situation is complicated, however, because not all forms of implicit memory are equally spared. There has been no experimental corroboration of clinical claims that special procedures such as hypnosis and barbiturate narcosis can promote conscious access to the "lost" memories.

Among nonpathological amnesias, the dissociation between explicit and implicit memory is especially well documented in posthypnotic amnesia. Preverbal infants can show long-term retention of new learning in a manner that suggests implicit memory. However, sleep-learning procedures do not appear to leave any traces, even in implicit memory.

Trauma, Repression, and Dissociation

The lack of reliable evidence of brain damage has fostered a tendency to account for functional amnesias in purely psychological terms. Since the nineteenth century, repression and dissociation have been the favored explanations. Repression, as defined by Freud, is the motivated forgetting of material (typically, relating to sexual or aggressive ideas and impulses) that conflicts with physical reality or social sanctions. Dissociation, as discussed by Janet and Prince, is a more adventitious "splitting off" from awareness of a set of percepts, memories, thoughts, or feelings. While Freud argued that repressed contents could be known only by inference (because they were expressed only symbolically, as in dream contents), Janet argued that dissociated contents could be recovered directly, by hypnosis and other means. Given the pervasive influence of Freudian psychoanalysis in twentieth-century discourse, the repression thesis long held sway. There has been a subsequent revival of the concept of dissociation, as indicated by adoption of "Dissociative Disorder" as a category in the DSM. An eclectic combination of Freudian and Jungian theories formed the basis of clinical theories about trauma and memory that emerged in the late twentieth century. These theories, in turn, promoted the 1980s revival of therapeutic strategies based on the recovery and "working through" of traumatic memories.

Paradoxically, the idea that trauma plays a role in amnesia, while a salient aspect of clinical folklore, is not supported by solid empirical evidence. Animal studies indicate that high levels of emotional arousal stimulate the release of stress hormones that activate the amygdala, leading to enhanced memory. A review of more than sixty longitudinal studies of documented trauma survivors yielded not a single instance of amnesia that could not be accounted for by nontraumatic infantile and childhood amnesia or "organic" factors such as intoxication, anoxia, or head injury. Many clinical studies alleging "repression" of trauma also fail to rule out such factors, especially in cases of infantile and childhood amnesia that occur independently of trauma. Others fail to confirm that the ostensibly traumatic event even occurred or misinterpret subjects' failure to disclose their trauma as a failure to remember it.

There are very few corroborated reports of the therapeutic recovery of traumatically lost memories. Most clinicians apparently assume their patients' memories are valid or refrain from challenging them in order to protect the "therapeutic alliance." The techniques of "memory work" used therapeutically to help patients "recover" traumatic memories also increase the risk of memory distortion and confabulation. There is no evidence that either hypnosis or sedation by barbiturate drugs facilitates the recovery of valid traumatic memories. Whenever "recovered" memories are taken as evidence, whether in the clinic or the courtroom, it is critical that they be accompanied by independent, objective, corroborative evidence.

Neuropsychology of Functional Amnesia

Beginning with the discovery of the syphilis spirochete, a major goal of psychiatry has been to transfer syndromes from the functional to the organic category as their neural bases are revealed. It seems likely that neuroscientific research will pinpoint such causal relationships for the dissociative amnesias as well. For example, a recent PET study of dissociative fugue found no sign of the activity in the right posterior frontal and anterior temporal lobes that usually accompanies recollection of emotionally salient personal experiences but did find activation in the left frontal and temporal regions. Although *functional* may eventually prove to be a misnomer, for now the term delineates a class of amnesias in which psychological processes rather than brain insult, injury, or disease are the immediate causes of the memory failure.

See also: AMNESIA, INFANTILE; AMNESIA, ORGANIC; AMNESIA, TRANSIENT GLOBAL; HYPNOSIS AND MEMORY

Bibliography

Bootzin, R. R., Kihlstrom, J. F., and Schacter, D. L. (1990). *Sleep and cognition.* Washington, DC: American Psychological Association.

Eich, E., Macaulay, D., Lowewenstein, R. J., and Dihle, P. H. (1996). Memory, amnesia, and dissociative identity disorder. *Psychological Science 8,* 417–422.

Ellman, S. J., and Antrobus, J. S. (1991). *The mind in sleep: Psychology and psychophysiology.* New York: Wiley.

Howe, M. L. (2000). *The fate of early memories: Developmental science and the retention of childhood experiences.* Washington, DC: American Psychological Association.

Kapur, N. (1999). Syndromes of retrograde amnesia: A conceptual and empirical synthesis. *Psychological Bulletin 125,* 800–825.

Kihlstrom, J. F. (1994). One hundred years of hysteria, *Dissociation: Clinical and theoretical perspectives.* New York: The Guilford Press.

—— (1996). The trauma-memory argument and recovered memory therapy. In K. Pezdek and W. P. Banks, eds.,*The recovered memory/false memory debate.* San Diego: Academic Press.

—— (1997). Suffering from reminiscences: Exhumed memory, implicit memory, and the return of the repressed. In M. A. Conway, ed., *Recovered memories and false memories.* Oxford: Oxford University Press.

—— (2001). Dissociative disorders. In P. B. Sutker and H. E. Adams, eds., *Comprehensive handbook of psychopathology.* New York: Plenum.

Kihlstrom, J. F., and Barnhardt, T. M. (1993). The self-regulation of memory: For better and for worse, with and without hypnosis, In D. M. Wegner and J. W. Pennebaker, eds., *Handbook of mental control.* Englewood Cliffs, NJ: Prentice-Hall.

Kihlstrom, J. F., and Schacter, D. L. (2000). Functional amnesia. In F. Boller and J. Grafman, eds., *Handbook of neuropsychology.* Amsterdam: Elsevier.

Kopelman, M. D. (1995). The assessment of psychogenic amnesia. In A. D. Baddeley, B. A. Wilson, and F. N. Watts, eds., *Handbook of memory disorders.* Chichester, UK: Wiley.

—— (1997). Anomalies of autobiographical memory: Retrograde amnesia, confabulation, delusional memory, psychogenic amnesia, and false memories. In J. D. Read and D. S. Lindsay, eds., *Recollections of trauma: Scientific evidence and clinical practice.* New York: Plenum.

Markowitsch, H. J. (1999). Functional neuroimaging correlates of functional amnesia. *Memory 7,* 561–583.

McNally, R.J. (2002). *Remembering Trauma.,* Cambridge, MA: Harvard University Press.

Piper, A. (1993). "Truth serum" and "recovered memories" of sexual abuse: A review of the evidence. *Journal of Psychiatry and the Law 21,* 447–471.

Piper, A., Pope, H. G., and Borowiecki, B. S. (2000). Custer's last stand: Brown, Schefflin, and Whtfield's latest attempt to salvage "dissociative amnesia." *Journal of Psychiatry and Law 28* 149–213.

Pope, H. G., Oliva, P. S., and Hudson, J. I. (2000). Repressed memories: B. Scientific status. In D. L. Faigman, D. H. Kaye, M. J. Saks, and J. Sanders, eds., *Modern scientific evidence: The law and science of expert testimony.* St. Paul, MN: West Publisher.

Reed, G. (1988). *The psychology of anomalous experience.* Buffalo, NY: Prometheus.

Schacter, D. L. (1986). Amnesia and crime: How much do we really know? *American Psychologist 41,* 286–295.

—— (1987). Implicit memory: History and current status. *Journal of Experimental Psychology: Learning, Memory, and Cognition 13,* 501–518.

—— (2001). *The seven sins of memory: How the mind forgets and remembers.* Boston: Houghton-Mifflin.

Shobe, K. K., and Kihlstrom, J. F. (2002). Interrogative suggestibility and "memory work." In M. L. Eisen, J. Quas, and G. S. Goodman, eds., *Memory and suggestibility in the forensic interview.* Mahwah, NJ: Erlbaum.

Sullivan, M. D. (1990). Organic or functional? Why psychiatry needs a philosophy of mind. *Psychiatric Annals 20,* 271–277.

John F. Kihlstrom
Daniel L. Schacter

AMNESIA, INFANTILE

Do you remember being born? Your first birthday party? Your first day of school? Despite the significance of these early experiences, most adults recall little or nothing about them. The absence of autobiographical memory for events that occurred during infancy and early childhood is commonly referred to as infantile (or childhood) amnesia. Sigmund Freud originally identified the phenomenon of infantile amnesia by asking his patients to describe their earliest personal memories in the course of therapy. On the basis of these patient reports, Freud argued that the period of infantile amnesia extended into the sixth or eighth year of life. Freud's most often-cited explanation of infantile amnesia was highly influenced by his patient population. He believed that memories for our infancy and early childhood were stored in pristine condition, but were actively repressed due to their emotionally and sexually charged content. In fact, one goal of Freud's psychoanalytic process was to "unlock" these hidden memories to allow patients to come to terms with the traumatic thoughts and experiences of their childhood.

Subsequent normative studies of adults' earliest memories have shown that Freud probably overestimated the period of infantile amnesia. There is now general consensus that adults' earliest autobiographical memories are for events that occurred when they were approximately three to four years of age (Bruce, Dolan, and Phillips-Grant, 2000; Dudycha and Dudycha, 1941; Mullen, 1994; Sheingold and Tenney, 1982; Waldfogel, 1948) or even slightly younger (MacDonald, Uesiliana, and Hayne, 2000; Usher and Neisser, 1993). Furthermore, normative studies of adults' earliest memories have failed to provide any empirical evidence in support of Freud's repression model (Pillemer and White, 1989).

Thus, the fundamental question remains: Why is it that we have little or no recollection of events that occurred during our infancy and early childhood? Although repression does not provide an adequate explanation for the phenomenon, empirical studies point to a number of other factors that might account for infantile amnesia (Howe and Courage, 1993).

The Lower Boundary for Long-Term Recall of Early Experiences

Maturation of the Central Nervous System

Maturation of the human brain begins at conception, but continues throughout childhood (and beyond). Although our understanding of the time course of human brain development is not complete, we do know that many of the brain areas that play a role in long-term memory are not fully mature during infancy and early childhood. Thus, although learning occurs rapidly during this phase of development, the ability to retain and use information over a lifetime may be precluded by the immaturity of the brain (Campbell and Spear, 1972).

Maturation of two areas of the brain—in particular, the medial temporal lobe (including the hippocampus) and the frontal cortex—is thought to play a particularly important role in the phenomenon of infantile amnesia (Bachevalier, 1992). Maturation of the hippocampus occurs relatively early in development and may be sufficient to support some of the sophisticated memory skills exhibited by infants; however, maturation of the higher-association areas of the frontal cortex continues well into childhood and may be required for the maintenance and retrieval of memories over the long term (Hayne, Boniface, and Barr, 2000; C. Nelson, 1995).

The Development of Language

When we ask adults to recall their earliest personal memories, we commonly ask them to provide a verbal report of what they can remember—both the instructions they are given ("tell me about your earliest memory") and their response to those instructions require sophisticated language skills. Infants and children, on the other hand, typically express their memories, by necessity, through nonverbal behaviors. Even once they have acquired conversational language skills, children still rely primarily on their nonverbal skills to solve tasks that require memory. Furthermore, the ability to translate early, preverbal experiences into language is extremely limited, if not impossible (Simcock and Hayne, 2002). Although an early preverbal memory may be reflected in some aspect of an adult's behavior (Newcombe, Drummey, Fox, Lie, and Ottinger-Alberts, 2000), he or she will be unable to provide a verbal report of the original experience. In this way, language development is another rate-limiting step in the offset of infantile amnesia.

Beyond the Basic Ingredients: The Emergence of Autobiographical Memory

The basic ingredients for long-term verbal memory are in place by the end of the second year of life.

For example, children as young as two and a half can provide a verbal report of an event that occurred eighteen months earlier (Fivush and Hammond, 1990). Despite this, most adults can recall nothing about events that occurred prior to their third or fourth birthday, and even those memories are few and far between and are significantly less vivid or detailed than events that occurred later in childhood. How can we account for this aspect of infantile amnesia?

A Framework for Organization

Many lines of research have shown that memory is enhanced when the to-be-remembered information can be organized according to some cognitive framework, or schema. Whether the material to be remembered consists of stories, baseball statistics, or lists of words, it is learned and retrieved most effectively by people who can systematically organize the material by relating it to an existing framework of knowledge. Without this kind of schematic organization, recall is only partial and fragmentary, if it occurs at all.

This same principle also applies to the recall of autobiographical information. When we think or talk about our past experiences, for example, we typically recall that information in chunks that reflect milestones in our lives: graduation from high school, attending college, getting married, the birth of our children and grandchildren, and so on. Our schema for these stages in our lives helps us to retrieve individual memories that occurred during each stage. Furthermore, thinking or talking about experiences from a particular stage often reminds us of other events that occurred during the same stage even if those events were greatly separated in time.

Children, on the other hand, do not organize their memories on the basis of milestones that reflect important stages of development or pivotal life events. Because these early experiences are not linked to the same schemata that adults use when they attempt to retrieve them, individual memories become difficult, if not impossible to recall (Pillemer and White, 1989).

Parent-Child Conversations about the Past

Children's emerging ability to organize and recount their life history is shaped through conversations about the past that occur in the context of their family (Fivush and Reese, 1992; Hudson, 1990; K. Nelson, 1993). In the course of reminiscing about mutually experienced events with parents or other significant social partners, children acquire the schema that are necessary to catalog their autobiographical memories. Additionally, conversations about the past allow children the opportunity to practice using another person's language to retrieve their own memory for a particular experience (e.g., "Remember when we went to the zoo last year?"). Furthermore, an adult's account of an event may augment the child's memory for the same experience, yielding a richer, more integrated (and thus more memorable) representation. The frequency and content of these conversations ultimately shape the number and clarity of our earliest recollections (MacDonald, Uesiliana, and Hayne, 2000; Mullen, 1994).

In conclusion, no single explanation of infantile amnesia can account for all of the available data. Instead, it is likely that brain maturation and language acquisition define the lower limit for our earliest recollections, but the number and quality of memories that actually survive will be determined by the way in which those memories have been structured and organized. Conversations about the past during early childhood are a driving force in this process.

See also: CHILDREN, DEVELOPMENT OF MEMORY IN; CODING PROCESSES: ORGANIZATION OF MEMORY; EPISODIC MEMORY; EXPERTS' MEMORIES; GUIDE TO THE ANATOMY OF THE BRAIN; NATURAL SETTINGS, MEMORY IN; PROSE RETENTION

Bibliography

Bachevalier, J. (1992). Cortical versus limbic immaturity: Relationship to infantile amnesia. In M. R. Gunnar and C. A. Nelson, eds., *Developmental behavioral neuroscience,* pp. 129–153. Hillsdale, NJ: Erlbaum.

Bruce, D., Dolan, A., and Phillips-Grant, K. (2000). On the transition from childhood amnesia to the recall of personal memories. *Psychological Science 11,* 360–364.

Campbell, B. A., and Spear, N. E. (1972). Ontogeny of memory. *Psychological Review 79,* 215–236.

Dudycha, G. J., and Dudycha, M. M. (1941). Childhood memories: A review of the literature. *Psychological Review 38,* 668–682.

Fivush, R., and Hammond, N. R. (1990). Autobiographical memory across the preschool years: Towards reconceptualizing childhood amnesia. In R. Fivush and J. A. Hudson, eds., *Knowing and remembering in young children,* pp. 223–248. New York: Cambridge University Press.

Fivush, R., and Reese, E. (1992). The social construction of autobiographical memory. In M. A. Conway, D. C. Rubin, H. Spinnler, and W. A. Wagenaar, eds., *Theoretical perspectives on autobiographical memory,* pp. 115–132. Dordrecht: Kluwer Academic Publishers.

Freud, S. (1960). Three essays on the theory of sexuality: 2. Infantile sexuality. In *The complete psychological writings of Sigmund Freud,* vol. 7, pp. 173–206. London: Hogarth. The original definition of infantile amnesia. First published in 1905.

Hayne, H., Boniface, J., and Barr, R. (2000). The development of declarative memory in human infants: Age-related changes in deferred imitation. *Behavioral Neuroscience 114,* 77–83.

Howe, M., and Courage, M. (1993). On resolving the enigma of infantile amnesia. *Psychological Bulletin 113,* 305–326.

Hudson, J. A. (1990). The emergence of autobiographical memory in mother-child conversation. In R. Fivush and J. A. Hudson, eds., *Knowing and remembering in young children,* pp. 166–196. New York: Cambridge University Press.

MacDonald, S., Uesiliana, K., and Hayne, H. (2000). Cross-cultural and gender differences in childhood amnesia. *Memory 8*, 365–376.

Mullen, M. K. (1994). Earliest recollections of childhood: A demographic analysis. *Cognition 52*, 55–79.

Nelson, C. (1995). The ontogeny of human memory: A cognitive neuroscience perspective. *Developmental Psychology 31*, 723–738.

Nelson, K. (1993). The psychological and social origins of autobiographical memory. *Psychological Science 4*, 7–14.

Newcombe, N. S., Drummey, A. B., Fox, N. A., Lie, E., and Ottinger-Alberts, W. (2000). Remembering early childhood: How much, how, and why (or why not). *Current Directions in Psychological Science 9*, 55–58.

Pillemer, D. B., and White, S. H. (1989). Childhood events recalled by children and adults. In H. W. Reese, ed., *Advances in child development and behavior*, Vol. 21, pp. 297–340. Orlando, FL: Academic Press.

Sheingold, K., and Tenney, Y. J. (1982). Memory for a salient childhood event. In U. Neisser, ed., *Memory observed*, pp. 201–212. San Francisco: Freeman.

Simcock, G., and Hayne, H. (2002). Breaking the barrier? Children fail to translate their preverbal memories into language. *Psychological Science 13*, 225–231.

Usher, J. A., and Neisser, U. (1993). Childhood amnesia and the beginnings of memory for four early life events. *Journal of Experimental Psychology: General 122*, 155–165.

Waldfogel, S. (1948). The frequency and affective character of childhood memories. *Psychological Monographs 62*, 1–39.

Ulric Neisser
Revised by Harlene Hayne

AMNESIA, ORGANIC

Organic amnesia is a neurological disorder characterized by a dense impairment of memory in the context of normal intelligence and other preserved mental abilities. Investigations of patients with this disorder have enhanced the understanding of the psychological processes involved in learning and remembering, as well as the brain organization of human memory.

Much of the current interest in memory and brain function finds its origin in the study of patient H.M., a man who, in 1953, underwent surgery for treatment of refractory seizures (Scoville and Milner, 1957). The surgery involved bilateral resection of a large portion of the medial temporal region, which includes the amygdala, hippocampus, and hippocampal gyrus. Although the surgery was successful in substantially reducing H.M.'s seizures, the procedure produced a pervasive impairment of memory (Milner, Corkin, and Teuber, 1968). Since the time of his surgery at the age of twenty-seven, H.M. has been unable to consciously learn and remember new information (anterograde amnesia). For example, thirty minutes after eating lunch, H.M. cannot recall what he ate for lunch, nor can he recall if in fact he ate lunch at all. He exhibits severe impairment on laboratory tests of word and picture recall, cued-word learning (e.g.,

learning word pairs), and recognition memory. His impairment is global in nature: information received from all sensory modalities is affected, and both verbal and nonverbal (e.g., spatial) memory are impaired. H.M. also evidences deficient recall of remote memories antedating the surgery (retrograde amnesia). For instance, H.M. could not recall the death of a favorite uncle who had died three years prior to the surgery. Moreover, nearly all of his personal memories are from the age of sixteen or earlier (Sagar, Cohen, Corkin, and Growdon, 1985).

Despite the severity of his amnesia, H.M. exhibits normal attention, language, and general intellectual abilities. His performance on tasks of immediate, or working, memory is relatively preserved. That is, he can temporarily store and maintain information over a brief interval, such as that required when rehearsing a telephone number. But if he is distracted or prevented from continually rehearsing the material, the information is forgotten. H.M. exhibits preservation of some long-term memory functions, such as skill and habit learning, where learning is expressed as enhanced task performance. The detailed examination of H.M.'s amnesia has served as a milestone in the quest to elucidate the functional and neuroanatomical basis of memory and has spawned decades of research into the memory processes that are impaired and preserved in amnesia.

Etiologies of Amnesia

Although H.M. still serves as a benchmark for characterizing global amnesia, it has also become clear that the disorder is composed of a number of different patterns of memory loss that may be linked to distinct etiologies and associated patterns of brain damage. Organic amnesia has been associated with a wide range of medical conditions including vascular accidents (i.e., strokes), ischemia (e.g., loss of blood flow to the brain), anoxia (i.e., loss of oxygen to the brain), viral infections, and Wernicke-Korsakoff syndrome. As with H.M., patients with these medical conditions typically show preserved attention, working memory, and general intellectual abilities.

Not all forms of amnesia are permanent. For example, head injury can cause transient and selective memory impairment. Anterograde amnesia following head trauma can last minutes, days, or even weeks. Depending on whether the trauma is mild or severe, patients may completely regain their learning ability or may suffer long-lasting and sometimes permanent impairment. Retrograde amnesia may also occur, and the temporal extent of retrograde amnesia is often correlated with the severity of anterograde amnesia. Quite severe memory problems also occur after electroconvulsive therapy (ECT), a procedure sometimes prescribed for treatment of severe depression. However, ECT-induced amnesia is usually transient, and extensive recovery of memory occurs with time.

The Anatomy of Memory

Analysis of the locus of brain lesions in patients such as H.M. has underscored the importance of the medial temporal region, particularly the hippocampus and adjacent regions, in new learning. Further insight into the prominent role of the hippocampus in memory comes from the study of patient R.B. by Zola-Morgan, Squire, and Amaral (1986). R.B. became amnesic in 1978 when he suffered an ischemic episode during open-heart surgery. Neuropsychological assessment of R.B. revealed moderate level anterograde amnesia alongside mild retrograde amnesia. In 1983, R.B. suffered a fatal cardiac arrest and his brain was brought to autopsy. Examination of his brain revealed that R.B. had sustained discrete bilateral brain damage restricted to a portion of the hippocampus called the CA1 subfield. Several other cases of amnesia resulting from ischemia have come to autopsy since then (Rempel-Clower, Zola, Squire, and Amaral, 1996). These cases have revealed that more extensive damage to the hippocampal formation produces more severe anterograde amnesia, as well as extensive retrograde amnesia for memories predating the brain injury up to fifteen years or more. In many patients, lesions extend beyond the hippocampal formation to include adjacent regions (i.e., entorhinal and perirhinal). This typically leads to dense anterograde and retrograde amnesia. Importantly, comparisons between patients with restricted versus extensive medial temporal lesions suggest that the hippocampal formation and adjacent regions make qualitatively different contributions to memory. It has been suggested that one neural circuit centered in the hippocampus supports recollection (i.e., the conscious or intentional retrieval of past experiences) whereas another neural circuit centered in adjacent perirhinal regions mediates overall feelings of familiarity (i.e., the subjective sense that something was encountered previously) (Aggleton and Brown, 1999; Brown and Aggleton, 2001).

Damage to another region of the brain, the diencephalic midline, can also produce organic amnesia. This brain region includes various midline thalamic nuclei (nuclei are groups of neurons), as well as subthalamic nuclei. These neurons serve as relay groups, sending and receiving projections to numerous parts of the brain, including the medial temporal region. The best-studied cases of amnesia resulting from damage to diencephalic midline structures are patients with Wernicke-Korsakoff syndrome, an amnesic disorder resulting from the convergent effects of chronic alcohol abuse and malnutrition. Studies of postmortem brain tissue by Victor, Adams, and Collins (1989) have revealed bilateral damage involving the dorsomedial nucleus of the thalamus and a subthalamic nucleus called the mamillary bodies. Similar pathology can also occur in nonamnesic alcoholics, but what distinguishes patients with Wernicke-Korsakoff syndrome is that they also show neuronal loss in anterior thalamic nuclei (Harding, Halliday, Caine, and Kril, 2000). Cortical atrophy (i.e., brain-cell loss) and cerebellar damage are also often observed. On neuropsychological tests Wernicke-Korsakoff patients evidence both anterograde amnesia and retrograde amnesia. In addition, these patients may exhibit attention and problem-solving impairments, as well as impaired insight. These additional difficulties may occur as a result of cortical atrophy, especially in prefrontal areas.

Declarative Memory in Amnesia

Globally amnesic patients are severely impaired at consciously and intentionally remembering information. This deficit encompasses the acquisition, long-term retention, and retrieval of both personally experienced events (i.e., episodic memory) and impersonal information (i.e., semantic memory). Collectively, these forms of memory are referred to as *declarative memory*.

Episodic memory enables individuals to remember experiences from their personal past (e.g., remembering what they ate for breakfast this morning). Episodic memories contain a multitude of sources of information including perceptual, conceptual, and emotional components. Episodic memories are not stored in isolation, but are placed within a context of personally relevant information. A pervasive deficit in episodic memory is dramatically exemplified by globally amnesic patients. In the clinic, episodic memory is assessed by tests of recall and recognition. Because these tasks require intentional retrieval of recent experiences, they are referred to as tests of *explicit memory*. Although both recall and recognition require intentional retrieval, their processing demands are not identical. Recognition memory is based on two distinct memory processes: recollection, an effort-dependent process by which information is deliberately brought to mind (e.g., remembering what book you read last night); and familiarity, a facilitation of or fluency in stimulus processing that results from prior experience with that stimulus (e.g., the sense of familiarity when seeing a person on the bus, even though you may not remember when you last saw him or her). By contrast, recall depends largely on recollection. Most globally amnesic patients evidence deficits both on recall and on recognition tests, but their recall performance is typically worse than their recognition performance (Giovanello and Verfaellie, 2001). This finding suggests that recollection may be more severely disrupted in amnesia than is familiarity (Yonelinas et al., 1998).

Whereas episodic memory is concerned with personally experienced events, semantic memory refers to the acquisition and long-term retention of generic factual information. Semantic knowledge encompasses a wide range of information, including facts about the world (e.g., the knowledge that Rome is the capital of Italy), the meanings of words and concepts (e.g., an understanding of the concept *Website*), and the names attached to objects and people (e.g., the knowledge that William Shakespeare wrote *Hamlet*). Studies of H.M. (Gabrieli, Cohen, and Corkin, 1988) and other amnesic patients (Verfaellie, Reiss, and Roth, 1995) suggest that semantic learning is impaired in amnesia. For example, H.M. has been unable to acquire any new vocabulary words that entered the language since his surgery. Other amnesic patients, however, appear able to acquire some new semantic information, and occasionally semantic learning is quite good despite a patient's severe impairment in episodic memory (Verfaellie, 2000). For example, Jon, a young patient who became amnesic following an anoxic episode at birth, has been able to acquire a considerable amount of semantic knowledge, as demonstrated by his ability to attend mainstream schools, despite his pronounced amnesia for day-to-day events, such as remembering conversations or television programs (Baddeley, Vargha-Khadem, and Mishkin, 2001). The degree to which semantic learning is still possible in amnesic patients likely depends on the extent of lesion in the temporal lobe.

Nondeclarative Memory in Amnesia

One of the most striking findings about amnesia is that, despite their severe impairment in conscious, intentional retrieval of information (declarative memory), amnesic patients can acquire several forms of memory normally. These forms of memory are collectively referred to as *nondeclarative memory*. One form of nondeclarative memory is procedural learning, the ability to acquire new perceptual and motor skills on the basis of repeated practice (e.g., learning to ride a bicycle). Studies of H.M. were among the first to establish the preservation of procedural learning in patients with global amnesia. For instance, during one task, H.M. had to learn how to keep a metal stylus in contact with a revolving disc. He learned to adapt his motor movement to the movement of the disc and gradually got better at the task, just like non-amnesic individuals. Strikingly, however, H.M. had no awareness of having practiced the task.

Another form of nondeclarative memory is repetition priming, the facilitation in performance induced by previous exposure to stimuli. A typical priming experiment is composed of a "study" phase followed by a "test" phase. During the study phase, participants are exposed to a list of words or pictures. For example, participants might see a list containing the word *apricot*. During the subsequent test phase, participants are asked to perform a seemingly unrelated task. For example, they may be asked to identify briefly flashed words or to generate as many words as possible when cued with the semantic category "fruit." Priming is measured as the change in accuracy or the bias in task performance induced by recent exposure to task stimuli (e.g., enhanced accuracy at identifying the word *apricot* or enhanced likelihood of generating the word *apricot*), compared to a test condition in which *apricot* did not appear on the prior study list.

Priming in amnesia has been assessed using tasks that require analysis of the perceptual attributes of a stimulus (perceptual priming), such as identification of briefly presented words or pictures and speeded reading of words. Priming has also been assessed using tasks that require analysis of the meaning of a stimulus (conceptual priming), such as category exemplar generation and production of word associates. Amnesic patients show intact priming on both perceptual and conceptual priming tasks, suggesting that these forms of unaware memory do not depend on the medial temporal regions implicated in amnesia. The neural basis of conceptual priming is not well understood, but findings of impaired visual perceptual priming in patients with occipital lesions suggest that perceptual priming is mediated by posterior cortical areas that process modality-specific information (Verfaellie and Keane, 1997).

Remote Memory in Amnesia

Globally amnesic patients evidence deficits in memory for events and for facts predating the onset of their amnesia, although the extent of retrograde memory loss varies from patient to patient. Retrograde amnesia tends to follow Ribot's law, which states that memory for the recent past is more severely affected than memory for the remote past. This pattern of retrograde memory loss provides clues about the mechanisms and time course involved in the storage and retrieval of new memories. Although the medial temporal region plays a critical role in the permanent laying down of information, these brain areas are not the ultimate repositories for new memories. Storage of new memories requires interaction between medial temporal and neocortical (outer brain) regions. The hippocampal formation receives information from a number of neocortical sites and binds together the spatial, perceptual, conceptual, and emotional components of an experience. Subsequent attempts to retrieve this experience cause the hippocampus to reactivate the neocortical sites that contain the information. Reactivation of the neocortical sites leads to a strengthening of the connections between these sites and, over time, allows memories to be retrieved without assistance from the hippocampal formation (Alvarez and Squire, 1994). Consequently, in patients with damage to medial temporal or connected diencephalic structures, information that has not been fully consolidated is vulnerable, whereas fully consolidated older memories can still be retrieved.

Conclusion

Neuropsychological investigations of patients with organic amnesia have contributed greatly to the understanding of memory processes and the brain regions that mediate them. Damage to medial temporal regions or diencephalic midline structures produces a pervasive amnesic disorder in which conscious or declarative memory is severely impaired. In contrast, various forms of nondeclarative memory such as procedural memory and repetition priming are preserved, suggesting that nondeclarative memory is not mediated by the medial temporal region implicated in amnesia. These theoretical advances provide the opportunity for more sophisticated assessment of patients with memory impairments and may lead to the development of new rehabilitation techniques that capitalize on preserved forms of memory.

See also: DECLARATIVE MEMORY;
ELECTROCONVULSIVE THERAPY AND MEMORY
LOSS; EPISODIC MEMORY; IMPLICIT MEMORY;
MEMORY SPAN; PROCEDURAL LEARNING:
HUMANS; RIBOT, THÉODULE; SEMANTIC
MEMORY: COGNITIVE ASPECTS; SEMANTIC
MEMORY: NEUROBIOLOGICAL PERSPECTIVE;
WORKING MEMORY: HUMANS

Bibliography

Aggleton, J. P., and Brown, M. W. (1999). Episodic memory, amnesia, and the hippocampal-anterior thalamic axis. *Behavioral and Brain Sciences* 22, 425–489.

Alvarez, P., and Squire, L. R. (1994). Memory consolidation and the medial temporal lobe: A simple network model. *Proceedings of the National Academy of Sciences of the United States of America 91*, 7,041–7,045.

Baddeley, A., Vargha-Khadem, F., and Mishkin, M. (2001). Preserved recognition in a case of developmental amnesia: Implications for the acquisition of semantic memory? *Journal of Cognitive Neuroscience 13*, 357–369.

Brown, M. W., and Aggleton, J. P. (2001). Recognition memory: What are the roles of the perirhinal cortex and hippocampus? *Nature Review Neuroscience 2*, 51–61.

Gabrieli, J. D. E., Cohen, N. J., and Corkin, S. (1988). The impaired learning of semantic knowledge following bilateral medial temporal-lobe resection. *Brain and Cognition 7*, 525–539.

Giovanello, K. S., and Verfaellie, M. (2001). The relationship between recall and recognition in amnesia: Effects of matching recognition between patients with amnesia and controls. *Neuropsychology 15*, 444–451.

Harding, A., Halliday, G., Caine, D., and Kril, J. (2000). Degeneration of anterior thalamic nuclei differentiates alcoholics with amnesia. *Brain 123* (1), 141–154.

Milner, B., Corkin, S., and Teuber, H.-L. (1968). Further analysis of the hippocampal amnesia syndrome: Fourteen-year follow-up study of H.M. *Neuropsychologia 6*, 215–234.

Rempel-Clower, N. L., Zola, S. M., Squire, L. R., and Amaral, D. G. (1996). Three cases of enduring memory impairment after bilateral damage limited to the hippocampal formation. *Journal of Neuroscience 16*, 5,233–5,255.

Sagar, H. J., Cohen, N. J., Corkin, S., and Growdon, J. H. (1985). Dissociations among processes in remote memory. In D. S. Olton, E. Gamzu, and S. Corkin, eds., *Memory dysfunctions: An integration of animal and human research from preclinical and clinical perspectives*, Vol. 4, pp. 533–535. New York: New York Academy of Sciences.

Scoville, W. B., and Milner, B. (1957). Loss of recent memory after bilateral hippocampal lesions. *Journal of Neurology, Neurosurgery, and Psychiatry 20*, 11–21.

Verfaellie, M. (2000). Semantic learning in amnesia. In *Handbook of neuropsychology, 2nd edition*, Vol. 2: *Memory and its disorders*, ed. L. S. Cermak, pp. 335–354. Amsterdam: Elsevier Science. Verfaellie, M., and Keane, M. M. (1997). The neural basis of aware and unaware forms of memory. *Seminars in Neurology 17*, 75–83.

Verfaellie, M., Reiss, L., and Roth, H. (1995). Knowledge of new English vocabulary in amnesia: An examination of premorbidly acquired semantic memory. *Journal of the International Neuropsychological Society 1*, 443–453.

Victor, M., Adams, R., and Collins, G. (1989). *The Wernicke-Korsakoff syndrome and related neurologic disorders due to alcoholism and malnutrition*. Philadelphia: F. A. Davis.

Yonelinas, A. P., Kroll, N. E., Dobbins, I., Lazzara, M., and Knight, R. T. (1998). Recollection and familiarity deficits in amnesia: Convergence of remember-know, process dissociation, and receiver operating characteristic data. *Neuropsychology 12*, 323–339.

Zola-Morgan, S., Squire, L. R., and Amaral, D. G. (1986). Human amnesia and the medial temporal region: Enduring memory impairment following bilateral lesion limited to the field CA1 of the hippocampus. *Journal of Neuroscience 6*, 2,950–2,967.

Arthur P. Shimamura
Revised by Kelly Sullivan Giovanello and Mieke Verfaellie

AMNESIA, TRANSIENT GLOBAL

Transient global amnesia (TGA) is a benign neurological condition in which the prominent deficit is a temporary organic amnesic syndrome. The episode of TGA is stereotyped. It usually begins suddenly, lasts for at least several hours, and resolves gradually over several hours to a day. Careful examination during an episode of TGA shows that the patient has a relatively isolated amnesic syndrome. Vision, hearing, sensation, strength, and coordination are normal. Language, spatial abilities, and general intellectual function also are normal, and the TGA patient can repeat a list of numbers or words. In contrast, the patient can recall little of any verbal or nonverbal material presented minutes before. The TGA patient often repeats the same question many times because of an inability to remember the answer that was just given. Frequently repeated questions include, "Is there something the matter with me?" and "What's wrong, have I had a stroke?" During TGA the patient has a patchy loss of recall for events dating from several hours to many years before the attack. Older memories are spared, and the patient does not lose personal identity. TGA patients examined carefully after the episode are normal except for an inability to recall the episode.

TGA generally occurs in persons over the age fifty, and 75 percent of patients are fifty to sixty-nine years old. Men and women are affected with nearly equal frequency. The estimated incidence is 5.2 per 100,000 per year for persons of all ages and 23.5 per 100,000 per year for persons older than fifty. A third to a half of TGA attacks are precipitated by physical or psychological stress, including strenuous exertion, sexual intercourse, intense emotion, pain, exposure to intense heat or cold, and minor or major medical procedures. TGA has a recurrence rate of 3 to 5 percent per year for at least five years after the initial episode. However, the patient with TGA does not appear to have an increased risk of developing significant permanent memory deficit or other cognitive dysfunction, and TGA patients have an incidence of subsequent stroke equal to the incidence of a comparable population.

Few laboratory abnormalities are associated with TGA. Blood, urine, and spinal fluid examination, electrocardiogram, electroencephalogram, and brain computerized tomography are normal. Some investigators have noted abnormalities, particularly in one or both medial temporal lobes, on single-photon emission computerized tomography (SPECT) brain scans and on diffusion-weighted magnetic resonance imaging (MRI) brain scans performed during the episode of TGA, which resolve following the episode.

Only a small number of patients have been examined with formal neuropsychological tests during TGA. Of these, eleven were studied with a single battery of memory tests that also had been given to patients with chronic organic amnesia. All of the eleven patients had severe anterograde amnesia (i.e., inability to learn new material) for verbal and nonverbal material, and their test scores were similar to scores obtained by well-studied patients with chronic organic amnesia. The severity of the anterograde amnesia appeared to correlate with the time since onset of TGA. There was no evidence for material-specific, or partial, amnesia—no TGA patient had a significant disparity between the degree of anterograde amnesia for verbal and nonverbal material. The patients also had a temporally graded retrograde amnesia (i.e., inability to recall events that occurred before the onset of amnesia) covering at least twenty years prior to TGA onset. Again, their test scores were similar to the scores of many well-studied patients with chronic organic amnesia. The retrograde amnesia was patchy—all patients were able to recall some events that occurred within the time interval affected by retrograde amnesia. Indeed, during TGA some memories were recalled, albeit incompletely, that were less than one to two months old. The temporally graded retrograde amnesia was similar for both public and personal events. During the episode, TGA patients performed normally on almost all other formal neuropsychological tests.

TGA is likely caused by temporary dysfunction of either bilateral medial temporal lobe structures, including field CA1 of the hippocampus and adjacent, anatomically related, structures; or bilateral medial diencephalic structures, including the dorsomedial nucleus of the thalamus, the mammillothalamic tract, and the mammillary bodies. The exact cause of TGA is not known, although it appears to be a benign condition that requires no medical treatment.

Bibliography

Hodges, J. R. (1998). Unraveling the enigma of transient global amnesia. *Annals of Neurology 43*, 151–153.

Kritchevsky, M. (1987). Transient global amnesia: When memory temporarily disappears. *Postgraduate Medicine 82*, 95–100.

——— (1989). Transient global amnesia. In F. Boller and J. Graffman, eds., *Handbook of neuropsychology*, Vol. 3, pp. 167–182. Amsterdam: Elsevier.

Mark Kritchevsky

AMYGDALA

See: GENETIC SUBSTRATES OF MEMORY: AMYGDALA; GUIDE TO THE ANATOMY OF THE BRAIN; LONG-TERM POTENTIATION: AMYGDALA

ANIMAL COGNITION

See: COMPARATIVE COGNITION

APLYSIA

[*Since the mid-1960s, the marine mollusk* Aplysia *has proved to be an extremely useful model system for gaining insights into the neural and molecular mechanisms of simple forms of memory. Indeed, the pioneering discoveries of Eric Kandel using this animal were recognized by his receipt of the Nobel Prize in physiology or medicine in 2000. A number of characteristics make* Aplysia *well suited to the examination of the molecular, cellular, morphological, and network mechanisms underlying neuronal modifications (plasticity) and learning and memory. The animal has a relatively simple nervous system with large, individually identifiable neurons that are accessible for detailed anatomical, biophysical, biochemical, and molecular studies. Neurons and neural circuits that mediate many behaviors in* Aplysia *have been identified. In several cases, these behaviors have been shown to be modified by learning. Moreover, specific loci within neural circuits where modifications occur during learning have been identified, and aspects of the cellular mechanisms underlying these modifications have been analyzed. The three entries that follow review several aspects of research on* Aplysia. CLASSICAL CONDITIONING AND OPERANT CONDITIONING *describes several of the behaviors of* Aplysia *that exhibit these associative forms of learning and the progress that has been made in examining the underlying mechanisms.* MOLECULAR BASIS OF LONG-TERM SENSITIZATION *describes the elucidation of second-messenger cascades and the roles of specific genes and proteins in the induction and maintenance of this example of nonassociative learning.* DEVELOPMENT OF PROCESSES UNDERLYING LEARNING *describes the ways in which it has been possible to identify and dissociate multiple components of nonassociative learning on both behavioral and cellular levels. For entries on other invertebrates that have proved useful for examining mechanisms of learning and memory, see* INSECT LEARNING, INVERTEBRATE LEARNING, *and* MORPHOLOGICAL BASIS OF LEARNING AND MEMORY: INVERTEBRATES.]

CLASSICAL CONDITIONING AND OPERANT CONDITIONING

The simple nervous system and the relatively large identifiable neurons of the marine mollusk *Aplysia* provide a useful model system in which to examine the cellular mechanisms of two forms of associative learning: classical conditioning and operant (instrumental) conditioning.

Classical Conditioning

Classical conditioning occurs when an animal learns to associate a typically neutral stimulus with a later salient event. If the neutral stimulus precedes the salient event with a fixed latency, then the animal learns that the stimulus can serve as a predictor.

Behavioral Studies

A tactile or electrical stimulus delivered to the siphon results in a reflex withdrawal of the gill and siphon, which presumably serves the defensive role of protecting these sensitive structures from potentially harmful stimuli. The reflex exhibits several simple forms of learning, including habituation, sensitization, and classical conditioning. In studies of aversive classical conditioning, the conditioned stimulus (CS) is a brief, weak tactile stimulus to the siphon, which by itself produces a small siphon withdrawal. The unconditioned stimulus (US) is a short-duration, strong (noxious) electric shock to the tail, which by itself produces a large withdrawal of the siphon (the unconditioned response, UR). After repeated pairings, the ability of the CS to produce siphon withdrawal (the conditioned response, CR) is enhanced beyond that produced by presentations of the US alone (sensitization control) or of explicitly unpaired or random presentations of the CS and the US (Carew, Walters, and Kandel, 1981). The conditioning persists for as long as four days. Thomas J. Carew and colleagues (Carew, Hawkins, and Kandel, 1983) also found that this reflex exhibits differential classical conditioning. Differential classical conditioning can be produced by delivering one CS to the siphon and another to the mantle region. One CS is paired with the US (the CS+) and the other is explicitly unpaired (the CS-). As in the previous studies, the US is an electric shock delivered to the tail. After conditioning, the CS+ will produce more withdrawal than the CS-.

Other behaviors of *Aplysia* can also be classically conditioned. For example, feeding behavior can be classically conditioned with an appetitive protocol (Lechner, Baxter, and Byrne, 2000).

Neural Mechanisms of Aversive Classical Conditioning in Aplysia

A cellular mechanism called activity-dependent neuromodulation contributes to associative learning in *Aplysia* (Hawkins, Abrams, Carew, and Kandel, 1983; Walters and Byrne, 1983; Antonov, Antonova, Kandel, and Hawkins, 2001). A general cellular scheme of activity-dependent neuromodulation is illustrated in Figure 1. Two sensory neurons (SN1 and SN2), which constitute the pathways for the conditioned stimuli (CS+ and CS-), make weak subthreshold connections to a motor neuron. Delivering a reinforcing or unconditioned stimulus (US) alone has two effects. First, the US activates the motor neuron and produces the unconditioned response (UR). Second, the US activates a diffuse modulatory system that nonspecifically enhances transmitter release from all

Figure 1

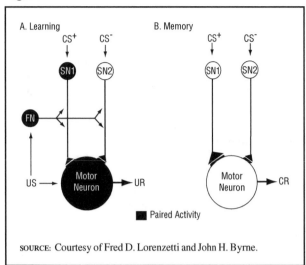

SOURCE: Courtesy of Fred D. Lorenzetti and John H. Byrne.

General model of activity-dependent neuromodulation. A. Learning: Shading indicates paired activity. A motivationally potent reinforcing stimulus (US) activates a motor neuron to produce the unconditioned response (UR) and a facilitatory neuron (FN) or modulatory system that regulates the strength of the connection between sensory neurons (SN1 and SN2) and the motor neuron. Increased spike activity in one sensory neuron (SN1) immediately before the modulatory signal amplifies the degree and duration of the modulatory effects, perhaps through the Ca^{+2} sensitivity of the modulatory evoked second messenger, with possible contributions from the postsynaptic neuron. The unpaired sensory neuron (SN2) does not show an amplification of the modulatory effects. B. Memory: The amplified modulatory effects cause long-term increases in transmitter release and/or excitability of the paired neuron, which in turn strengthens the functional connection between the paired sensory neuron (SN1) and the motor neuron. The associative enhancement of synaptic strength represents the conditioned response (CR).

the sensory neurons. This nonspecific enhancement contributes to sensitization. Temporal specificity, characteristic of associative learning, occurs when there is pairing of the CS (spike activity in SN1) with the US, causing a selective amplification of the modulatory effects in SN1. Unpaired activity does not amplify the effects of the US in SN2. The amplification of the modulatory effects in SN1 leads to an enhancement of the ability of SN1 to activate the motor neuron and produce the CR.

As discussed in the entry "Molecular Basis of Long-Term Sensitization," experimental analyses of sensitization of defensive reflexes in *Aplysia* have shown that the neuromodulator released by the reinforcing stimulus, which is believed to be serotonin, activates the enzyme adenylyl cyclase in the sensory neuron and thereby increases the synthesis of the second messenger cAMP, which activates the cAMP-

dependent protein kinase; the subsequent protein phosphorylation leads to a modulation in several properties of the sensory neurons. These changes in the sensory neuron include modulation of membrane conductances and other processes, which facilitate synaptic transmission. This facilitation results in the increased activation of the motor neuron and, thus, sensitization of the reflex. The pairing specificity of the associative conditioning is due, at least in part, to an increase in the level of cAMP beyond that produced by serotonin alone (Abrams and Kandel, 1988; Ocorr, Walters, and Byrne, 1985). The influx of Ca^{+2} associated with the CS (spike activity) amplifies the US-mediated modulatory effect by interacting with a Ca^{+2}-sensitive component of the adenylyl cyclase (Abrams and Kandel, 1988; Schwartz et al., 1983). A critical role for Ca^{+2}-stimulated cyclase is also suggested by studies of *Drosophila* showing that the adenylyl cyclase of a mutant deficient in associative learning exhibits a loss of Ca^{+2}/calmodulin sensitivity.

There are contributions to the plasticity of the synapse occurring in the motor neuron, as well (Murphy and Glanzman, 1997; Bao, Kandel, and Hawkins, 1998). The postsynaptic membrane of the motor neuron contains NMDA receptors. If these receptors are blocked, then the associative modification of the synapse is disrupted. NMDA receptors require concurrent delivery of glutamate and depolarization in order to allow the entry of calcium. Activity in the sensory neuron (CS) provides the glutamate and the US depolarizes the cell. The subsequent increase in intracellular Ca^{+2} putatively releases a retrograde signal from the postsynaptic cell to the presynaptic terminal. This retrograde signal would then act to further enhance the cAMP cascade in the sensory neuron.

An important conclusion is that this mechanism for associative learning is an elaboration of a process already in place that mediates sensitization, a simpler form of learning. This finding raises the interesting possibility that even more complex forms of learning may use simpler forms as building blocks, an idea that has been suggested by some psychologists for many years but one that until the early years of the twenty-first century has not been testable at the cellular level.

Operant Conditioning

Operant conditioning is a process by which an animal learns the consequences of its own behavior. In an operant-conditioning paradigm, the delivery of a reinforcing stimulus is contingent upon the expression of a designated behavior. The probability of expression of this behavior will then be altered. In other words, the animal learns to associate the behavior with the contingent reinforcement and modifies its behavior accordingly.

Behavioral Studies

Feeding behavior in *Aplysia* has been used to gain insights into the modification of a behavioral response by reinforcement. *Aplysia* feed by protracting a toothed structure called the radula into contact with seaweed. The radula grasps seaweed by closing and retracting. This sequence results in the ingestion of the seaweed. Inedible objects can be rejected if the radula protracts while closed (grasping the object) and then opens as it retracts, releasing the object. Thus, the timing of radula closure determines which behavior will be elicited.

Feeding behavior in *Aplysia* can be modified by pairing feeding with an aversive stimulus. In the presence of food wrapped in a tough plastic net, *Aplysia* bite and attempt to swallow the food. However, netted food cannot be swallowed, and it is rejected. The inability to consume food appears to be an aversive stimulus that modifies feeding behavior, since trained animals do not attempt to bite netted food (Susswein, Schwarz, and Feldman, 1986).

Feeding behavior can also be operantly conditioned with an appetitive stimulus (Brembs et al., 2002). Animals receiving positive reinforcement that is contingent on biting will learn to bite more than animals receiving either reinforcement that is not contingent on their behavior or no reinforcement at all.

Neural Mechanisms of Appetitive Operant Conditioning in Aplysia

The feeding system of *Aplysia* has many advantages. For example, much of the cellular circuitry controlling feeding behavior has been identified. Thus, it is possible for researchers to study neurons with known behavioral significance. One of these neurons, denoted as B51, is implicated in the expression of ingestive behavior. B51 is active predominately during the retraction phase. Furthermore, when B51 is recruited into a pattern, it recruits radula closure motor neurons (see Figure 2).

An in vitro analogue of operant conditioning has been developed using only the isolated buccal ganglia, which is responsible for generating the motor programs involved in feeding (Nargeot, Baxter, and Byrne, 1999a). The ganglion expresses motor patterns that are analogous to feeding behavior. These motor patterns can either be ingestionlike or rejectionlike and the type that will be expressed is not predictable. In the analogue of operant conditioning, motor patterns corresponding to ingestion are selectively reinforced by contingently shocking the esophageal nerve. The esophageal nerve contains dopaminergic processes and is believed to be part of the pathway mediating food reward. The conditioning results in an increase in the likelihood of ingestionlike

Figure 2

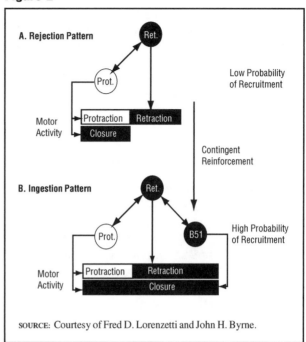

SOURCE: Courtesy of Fred D. Lorenzetti and John H. Byrne.

Model of operant conditioning of feeding in *Aplysia*. The cellular network that mediates feeding behavior is represented by the elements in circles. Motor activity comprising two basic feeding patterns is depicted above. A. At first, the radula protraction-generating element (Prot.) is active, followed by the radula retraction element (Ret.). In the naïve state, neuron B51 has a low probability for recruitment and thus does not take part in the feeding motor program. Radula closure occurs during the protraction phase. Consequently, the pattern elicited is a rejection. B. Neuron B51 now has a higher probability for recruitment following contingent reinforcement. B51 is now active during the motor program, leading to radula closure occurring primarily during the retraction phase. Thus, the pattern elicited will now be an ingestion.

patterns being produced. The contingent reinforcement also results in the modulation of the membrane properties of neuron B51. The input resistance increases and a smaller stimulus is required to elicit electrical activity. Thus, the cell is more likely to be active in the future. This change in the likelihood of B51 activation contributes to the conditioned increase in ingestionlike patterns. Furthermore, these results can be replicated when induced electrical activity in B51 is substituted as the analogue of the behavior, instead of an ingestionlike motor pattern (Nargeot, Baxter, and Byrne, 1999b).

The analogue can be further reduced by removing neuron B51 from the ganglia and placing it in culture (Lorenzetti, Baxter, and Byrne, 2000; Brembs et al., 2002). This single, isolated neuron can be conditioned by contingently reinforcing induced electrical activity (the analogue of behavior) with a direct and temporally discrete application of dopamine (the analogue of reinforcement). After conditioning, the membrane properties of B51 are again modulated such that the cell is more likely to be active in the future. Such a highly reduced preparation is a promising candidate to study the mechanisms of dopamine-mediated reward and the conditioned expression of behavior at the level of the intracellular signaling cascades.

Conclusions

One of the important findings to emerge from recent studies on invertebrates is their capacity to exhibit various forms of associative learning. Of particular significance is the finding that at least some mollusks, such as *Limax*, exhibit higher-order features of classical conditioning, such as second-order conditioning and blocking. Contextual conditioning, conditioned discrimination learning, and contingency effects have been described in *Aplysia* (Colwill, Absher, and Roberts, 1988; Hawkins, Carew, and Kandel, 1986). Such higher-order features can be viewed in a cognitive context, and raise the interesting possibility that other complex behavioral phenomena will be identified as the capabilities of these animals are investigated further.

The possibility of relating cellular changes to complex behavior in invertebrates is encouraged by the progress that has already been made in examining the neural mechanisms of simple forms of nonassociative and associative learning. The results of these analyses of *Aplysia* have shown that: 1. learning involves changes in existing neural circuitry (one does not need the growth of new synapses and the formation of new circuits for learning and short-term memory to occur); 2. learning involves the activation of second messenger systems; 3. the second messengers affect multiple subcellular processes to alter the responsiveness of the neuron (at least one locus for the storage and readout of memory is the alteration of specific membrane currents); and 4. long-term memory requires new protein synthesis, whereas short-term memory does not.

While researchers have made considerable progress in the analysis of simple forms of learning in *Aplysia*, other invertebrates, and vertebrate model systems, there is still no complete mechanistic analysis available for any single example of simple learning. Many of the technical obstacles are being overcome, however, and it is likely that the analyses of several examples of learning will reach completion.

For the near future, major questions to be answered include the following: To what extent are mechanisms for classical and operant conditioning common both within any one species and between different species? What is the relationship between the initial induction of neuronal change (acquisition of learning) and the maintenance of the associative change? What are the relationships among different forms of learning, such as sensitization, classical conditioning, and operant conditioning?

See also: APLYSIA: MOLECULAR BASIS OF LONG-TERM SENSITIZATION; CONDITIONING, CELLULAR AND NETWORK SCHEMES FOR HIGHER-ORDER FEATURES OF; CONDITIONING, CLASSICAL AND INSTRUMENTAL; GLUTAMATE RECEPTORS AND THEIR CHARACTERIZATION; INVERTEBRATE LEARNING: NEUROGENETICS OF MEMORY IN DROSOPHILA; REINFORCEMENT OR REWARD IN LEARNING

Bibliography

Abrams, T. W., and Kandel, E. R. (1988). Is contiguity detection in classical conditioning a system or cellular property? Learning in *Aplysia* suggests a possible site. *Trends in Neurosciences 11*, 128–135.

Antonov, I., Antonova, I., Kandel, E. R., and Hawkins, R. D. (2001). The contribution of activity-dependent synaptic plasticity to classical conditioning in *Aplysia*. *Journal of Neuroscience 21*, 6,413–6,422.

Bao, J. X., Kandel, E. R., and Hawkins, R. D. (1998). Involvement of presynaptic and postsynaptic mechanisms in a cellular analog of classical conditioning at *Aplysia* sensory-motor neuron synapses in isolated cell culture. *Journal of Neuroscience 18*, 458–466.

Brembs, B., Lorenzetti, F. D., Reyes, F. D., Baxter, D. A., and Byrne J. H. (2002). Operant reward learning in *Aplysia*: Neuronal correlates and mechanisms. *Science 296*, 1,706–1,709.

Carew, T. J., Hawkins, R. D., and Kandel, E. R. (1983). Differential classical conditioning of a defensive withdrawal reflex in *Aplysia californica*. *Science 219*, 397–400.

Carew, T. J., Walters, E. T., and Kandel, E. R. (1981). Classical conditioning in a simple withdrawal reflex in *Aplysia californica*. *Journal of Neuroscience 1*, 1,426–1,437.

Colwill, R. M., Absher, R. A., and Roberts, M. L. (1988). Context-US learning in *Aplysia californica*. *Journal of Neuroscience 8*, 4,434–4,439.

Hawkins, R. D., Abrams, T. W., Carew, T. J., and Kandel, E. R. (1983). A cellular mechanism of classical conditioning in *Aplysia*: Activity-dependent amplification of presynaptic facilitation. *Science 219*, 400–405.

Hawkins, R. D., Carew, T. J., and Kandel, E. R. (1986). Effects of interstimulus interval and contingency on classical conditioning of the *Aplysia* siphon withdrawal reflex. *Journal of Neuroscience 6*, 1,095–1,701.

Lechner, H. A., Baxter, D. A., and Byrne, J. H. (2000). Classical conditioning of feeding in *Aplysia*: I. Behavioral analysis. *Journal of Neuroscience 20*, 3,369–3,376.

Lorenzetti, F. D., Baxter, D. A., and Byrne, J. H. (2000). Contingent reinforcement with dopamine modifies the properties of an individual neuron in *Aplysia*. *Society for Neuroscience Abstracts 26*, 1,524.

Murphy, G. G., and Glanzman, D. L. (1997). Mediation of classical conditioning in *Aplysia californica* by long-term potentiation of sensorimotor synapses. *Science 278*, 467–471.

Nargeot, R., Baxter, D. A., and Byrne J. H. (1999a). In vitro analog of operant conditioning in *Aplysia*: I. Contingent reinforcement modifies the functional dynamics of an identified neuron. *Journal of Neuroscience 19*, 2,247–2,260.

——— (1999b). In vitro analog of operant conditioning in *Aplysia*: II. Modifications of the functional dynamics of an identified neuron contribute to motor pattern selection. *Journal of Neuroscience 19*, 2,261–2,272.

Ocorr, K. A., Walters, E. T., and Byrne, J. H. (1985). Associative conditioning analog selectively increases cAMP levels of tail sensory neurons in *Aplysia*. *Proceedings of the National Academy of Sciences of the United States of America 82*, 2,548–2,552.

Schwartz, J. H., Bernier, L., Castellucci, V. F., Polazzolo, M., Saitoh, T., Stapleton, A., and Kandel, E. R. (1983). What molecular steps determine the time course of the memory for short-term sensitization in *Aplysia*? *Cold Spring Harbor Symposium on Quantitative Biology 48*, 811–819.

Susswein, A. J., Schwarz, M., and Feldman, E. (1986). Learned changes of feeding behavior in *Aplysia* in response to edible and inedible foods. *Journal of Neuroscience 6*, 1,513–1,527.

Walters, E. T., and Byrne, J. H. (1983). Associative conditioning of single sensory neurons suggests a cellular mechanism for learning. *Science 219*, 405–408.

John H. Byrne
Revised by Fred D. Lorenzetti and John H. Byrne

DEVELOPMENT OF PROCESSES UNDERLYING LEARNING

In the 1980s exciting progress was made in understanding a variety of developmental processes, ranging from principles governing the birth, differentiation, and migration of nerve cells to the mechanisms underlying the functional assembly of complex neural circuits. In addition to the intrinsic interest in development as a fundamental field of inquiry, the analysis of development has a secondary gain: By affording the experimental opportunity of examining early-emerging processes in functional isolation from later-emerging ones, development can serve as a powerful analytic tool with which to dissect and examine specific behavioral, cellular, and molecular processes as they are expressed and integrated during ontogeny.

A developmental strategy such as that described above has been useful in furthering the analysis of learning and memory in the marine mollusk *Aplysia*, a preparation that has proved to be quite powerful for cellular and molecular studies of several forms of learning. Specifically, using this strategy, it has been possible to identify and dissociate multiple components of nonassociative learning on both behavioral and cellular levels. This type of analysis has also revealed previously unappreciated behavioral and cellular processes in *Aplysia*. Moreover, the developmental dissociation of different components of learning in juvenile *Aplysia* prompted a similar analysis in adult animals, where the same clearly dissociable components of learning were identified. Thus an analysis of the developmental assembly of learning has provided important insights into the final phenotypic expression of learning in the adult.

The Development of *Aplysia*

The life cycle of *Aplysia* can be divided into five phases:

1. an *embryonic* phase (lasting about ten days, from fertilization to hatching)

2. a *planktonic* larval phase (lasting about thirty-five days)

3. a *metamorphic* phase (lasting only two to three days)

4. a *juvenile* phase (lasting at least ninety days)

5. the *adult* phase, defined as the onset of reproductive maturity.

These five phases can be further divided into thirteen discrete stages, each defined by a specific set of morphological criteria (Kriegstein, 1977). In the analysis of learning that will be described here, most work has focused on the juvenile phase of development (stages nine through twelve), since it is during this time that many of the behavioral systems of interest emerge.

Forms of Learning and Developmental Timetables

In adult *Aplysia* the siphon withdrawal reflex exhibits both nonassociative and associative forms of learning. The developmental analysis thus far carried out in *Aplysia* has focused primarily on nonassociative learning in that reflex. The three most common forms of nonassociative learning are habituation, dishabituation, and sensitization. Habituation refers to a decrease in response magnitude occurring as a function of repeated stimulation to a single site; dishabituation describes the facilitation of a habituated response by the presentation of a strong or novel stimulus, usually to another site; sensitization refers to the facilitation of nondecremented responses by a similar strong or novel stimulus. Using a behavioral preparation that permitted quantification of siphon withdrawal throughout juvenile development, Rankin and Carew (1987, 1988) found that these three forms of nonassociative learning emerged according to different developmental timetables. Habituation of siphon withdrawal was present very early (in stage nine) and progressively matured across all juvenile stages in terms of its interstimulus interval (ISI) function: In young animals, extremely short ISIs were necessary to produce habituation, whereas in older animals, progressively longer ISIs could be used to produce habituation. Dishabituation (produced by tail shock)

Figure 1

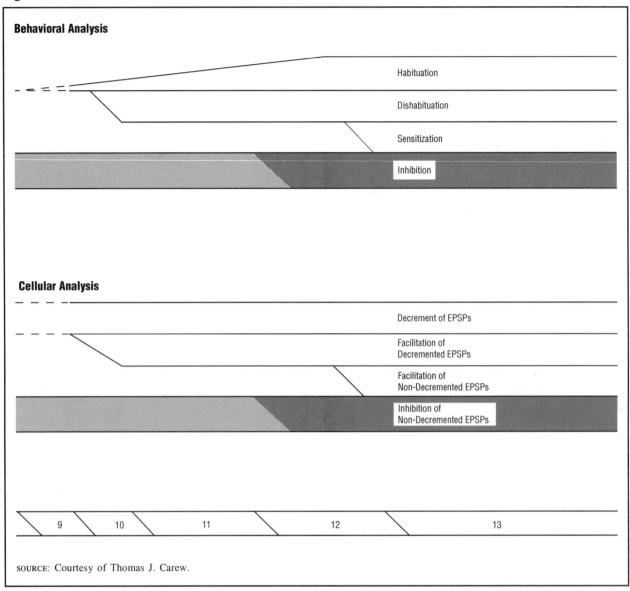

SOURCE: Courtesy of Thomas J. Carew.

Summary of developmental timetables for different forms of learning and their respective cellular analogues. Behavioral analysis: Habituation is present as early as has been examined, in stage 9; dishabituation emerges soon after habituation, in stage 10; sensitization does not emerge until sixty days after dishabituation, in mid to late stage 12. Behavioral inhibition has been measured as early as stage 11 (indicated by shading) but may emerge even earlier. Cellular analysis: The cellular analogue of habituation (homosynaptic decrement of EPSPs in neuron R2) is present in stage 9; the analogue of dishabituation (facilitation of decremented EPSPs in R2) emerges in stage 10; the analogue of sensitization (facilitation of nondecremented EPSPs in R2) emerges between early and mid stage 12. Inhibition of nondecremented EPSPs in R2 has been detected as early as early stage 12 (indicated by shading) but, as with behavioral inhibition, may emerge even earlier. Thus there is a close developmental parallel between the emergence of each behavioral form of learning (as well as behavioral inhibition) and its respective cellular analogue.

emerged soon after habituation, in a distinct and later stage (stage ten). However, sensitization (also produced by tail shock) did not emerge until surprisingly late in juvenile development (stage twelve), at least sixty days after the emergence of dishabituation (see Figure 1).

The observation that dishabituation and sensitization can be developmentally dissociated raises important theoretical questions for a complete explanation of nonassociative learning. For example, until recently a commonly held view was that nonassociative learning could be accounted for by a dual process theory involving two opposing processes: a single decrementing process that gives rise to habituation, and a single facilitatory process that underlies both dishabituation and sensitization (Carew, Castellucci, and Kandel, 1971; Groves and Thompson, 1970). A key prediction of this view is that dishabituation and sensitization should always occur together. However, the developmental dissociation of these processes, together with recent behavioral and cellular evidence in adult *Aplysia,* suggests that a dual-process view is inadequate to account for nonassociative learning in *Aplysia.*

The emergence of sensitization in stage twelve is not confined to the siphon withdrawal reflex in *Aplysia.* Stopfer and Carew (1988) examined another response system, escape locomotion, and found that sensitization in that system also emerges in stage twelve. Thus sensitization is expressed in two different systems, one a graded reflex and the other a centrally programmed cyclical behavior, at the same time in development. This raises the interesting hypothesis that one or more developmental signals may switch on the general process of sensitization in stage twelve, not only in individual response systems but in the whole animal.

Cellular Analogues of Learning and Behavioral Learning

The developmental separation of different learning processes described above provides the opportunity to examine the unique contribution of specific cellular mechanisms to each form of learning. An important step in such a cellular analysis is to show that the cellular analogue of each form of learning can be identified in the central nervous system of juvenile *Aplysia* and that these analogues exhibit a developmental time course parallel to the behavioral expression of the learning. The identified motor neuron can serve as a reliable cellular monitor of plasticity in the afferent input to the siphon-withdrawal reflex.

The developmental emergence of the cellular analogue of habituation (synaptic decrement) and of dishabituation (facilitation of decremented synaptic potentials) was first examined by Rayport and Camardo (1984). They found that synaptic decrement could be observed in neuron R2 as early as stage nine, and that facilitation of depressed synaptic potentials emerged in stage ten. Nolen and Carew (1988) then examined the emergence of the cellular analogue of sensitization (facilitation of nondecremented synaptic potentials) in R2. They found that the analogue of sensitization emerged between early and middle stage twelve, many weeks after the emergence of the analogue of dishabituation. Taken collectively, these

results illustrate two important points. First, the cellular analogue of each form of learning emerges in close temporal register with its respective behavioral form (see Figure 1). Second, just as dishabituation and sensitization can be developmentally dissociated on a behavioral level, so can their cellular analogues be developmentally dissociated.

A Novel Inhibitory Process

When the effects of sensitization training (i.e., the effects of tail shock on nondecremented reflex responses) in different developmental stages were examined, an unexpected effect of tail shock was discovered: Prior to the emergence of sensitization in stage twelve, tail shock had an inhibitory effect on reflex responsiveness (Rankin and Carew, 1988). The properties of this inhibitory process in juvenile *Aplysia* have been studied by Rankin and Carew (1989), who found that tail shock-induced inhibition of siphon withdrawal can be detected in two ways: 1. by reduction of reflex responsiveness; and 2. by the apparent competition of the inhibitory process with the facilitatory process of dishabituation. Specifically, they found that as levels of tail shock were increased, progressively *more* inhibition resulted and, concomitantly, progressively *less* dishabituation was produced, suggesting the hypothesis that the tail shock-induced inhibition could significantly retard the expression of dishabituation in early developmental stages. Finally, as the process of sensitization matured, there was a clear transition from the inhibitory effect of tail shock to reflex facilitation between early and late stage twelve.

In parallel with the behavioral reflection of inhibition described above, Nolen and Carew (1988) identified a clear cellular analogue of this inhibitory process. Specifically, they found that prior to the emergence of the cellular analogue of sensitization in mid to late stage twelve, activation of the pathway from the tail produced significant inhibition of nondecremented synaptic responses in neuron R2 (see Figure 1). As with the behavior, there was a clear transition from inhibition to facilitation in mid to late stage twelve.

The inhibitory process first identified in juvenile *Aplysia* has received considerable attention in the adult. Several laboratories have observed behavioral tail shock-induced inhibition of the siphon withdrawal reflex (Krontiris-Litowitz, Erikson, and Walters, 1987; Mackey et al., 1987; Marcus et al., 1988), and important progress has been made in studying the cellular mechanisms underlying the inhibitory process. For example, Mackey et al. (1987) found that tail shock produced presynaptic inhibition of the transmission from siphon sensory neurons. Wright, Marcus, and Carew (1991) found that polysynaptic input to the siphon motor neurons plays an important role in mediating tail shock-induced inhibition, and Wright and Carew (1990) found that a single identified inhibitory interneuron in the abdominal ganglion, cell L16, can account for most, if not all, of the inhibition of siphon withdrawal following tail shock. Finally, Fitzgerald and Carew (1991) found that serotonin, a known facilitatory neuromodulator in *Aplysia*, can also mimic the inhibitory effects of tail shock. It will be of considerable interest to study the development of these inhibitory mechanisms and examine the way in which they are integrated with facilitatory forms of behavioral plasticity.

Behavioral Dissociation of Dishabituation, Sensitization, and Inhibition in Adults

The developmental studies described above show that dishabituation, sensitization, and a novel inhibitory process, as well as their respective cellular analogues, can each be dissociated in juvenile animals. It is possible, however, that these processes, although separable during ontogeny, are not distinct in the final adult phenotype. Thus an important question arose as to whether the same forms of behavioral plasticity could be identified and separated in adult animals. Marcus et al. (1988) addressed this issue by examining, in adult *Aplysia*, the effects of a wide range of tail-shock intensities, at several times after tail shock, on both habituated and nonhabituated siphon withdrawal responses. They found that dishabituation and sensitization could be clearly dissociated in adult animals in two ways.

First was time of onset. When tested soon (ninety seconds) after tail shock, dishabituation was evident at a variety of stimulus intensities, whereas, in this early test, sensitization was not exhibited at *any* stimulus intensity. In fact, examining nondecremented responses revealed that tail shock produced inhibition of reflex amplitude. Although no sensitization was evident in the ninety-second test, in subsequent tests (twenty to thirty minutes after tail shock) significant sensitization was observed. Thus, dishabituation has an early onset (within ninety seconds), whereas sensitization has a very delayed onset (twenty to thirty minutes) after tail shock. Juvenile *Aplysia* also exhibit delayed-onset sensitization that emerges in early stage twelve, at least thirty days after the emergence of dishabituation.

Second was stimulus intensity. When a range of stimulus intensities to the tail was examined, maximal dishabituation was produced by relatively weak stimuli, whereas maximal sensitization was produced by stronger stimuli. Moreover, the stimulus intensity that was most effective in producing dishabituation produced *no* sensitization, and the intensity that was most effective in producing sensitization produced *no* significant dishabituation. Thus, as in juvenile *Aplysia* (Rankin and Carew, 1989), the processes of dishabituation, sensitization, and inhibition can be behaviorally dissociated in adult animals.

The behavioral observations described above raise important questions about the cellular processes underlying the dissociation of dishabituation and sensitization. One possibility is that these two forms of learning reflect different underlying cellular mechanisms. Alternatively, the same or related mechanisms may be involved in both forms of learning, and the dissociation observed could be due to differential interaction of the inhibitory process with dishabituation and sensitization. Behavioral results alone cannot distinguish between these possibilities. However, progress has been made in elucidating the cellular mechanisms underlying dishabituation and sensitization (Hochner et al., 1986) as well as inhibition (Bellardetti, Kandel, and Siegelbaum, 1987; Mackey et al., 1987; Wright and Carew, 1990; Wright, Marcus, and Carew, 1991). Thus it will be important to determine the degree to which these different cellular processes can account for the behavioral dissociations that are observed in both developing and adult *Aplysia*.

Conclusion

A developmental analysis in *Aplysia* has shown that different forms of learning, as well as their cellular analogues at central synapses, emerge according to very different developmental timetables. These studies have allowed the dissociation of four behavioral processes (see Figure 1): two decrementing (habituation and inhibition) and two facilitatory (dishabituation and sensitization). Whether these dissociations are produced by different facilitatory mechanisms, by differential interactions of inhibition with decremented and nondecremented responses, or by some combination of these alternatives, results suggest that a dual-process view of nonassociative learning, which postulates a single decremental and a single incremental process, requires revision, and that a multiple-process view, which includes the possibility of inhibitory as well as facilitatory interactions, is necessary to account adequately for the mechanisms underlying nonassociative learning.

The developmental studies discussed in this brief review have focused only on nonassociative learning in *Aplysia*, and only on short-term learning, which is retained for a relatively brief time (minutes to hours). However, *Aplysia* is also capable of exhibiting a variety of forms of associative learning. Moreover, in addition to short-term forms, both nonassociative and associative learning in *Aplysia* can exist in long-term forms lasting days to weeks. It will be of interest to examine the development of these additional processes in order to gain insights into theoretically important questions such as the relationships between nonassociative and associative learning and between short-term and long-term memory. As a step in this direction, Carew, Wright, and McCance (1989) have established that long-term memory for sensitization emerges in exactly the same stage as short-term memory, stage twelve. This observation lends support to the notion that short- and long-term memory may be mechanistically interrelated in *Aplysia* (Golet et al., 1986). By analyzing the development of these diverse processes at synaptic, biophysical, and molecular levels, it may be possible to gain unique insights into the substrates underlying learning and memory by examining their developmental assembly.

See also: APLYSIA: CLASSICAL CONDITIONING AND OPERANT CONDITIONING; APLYSIA: MOLECULAR BASIS OF LONG-TERM SENSITIZATION

Bibliography

Bellardetti, F., Kandel, E. R., and Siegelbaum, S. (1987). Neuronal inhibition by the peptide FMRFamide involves opening of S K+ channels. *Nature 325,* 153–156.

Carew, T. J., Castellucci, V. F., and Kandel, E. R. (1971). Analysis of dishabituation and sensitization of the gill withdrawal reflex in *Aplysia. International Journal of Neuroscience 2,* 79–98.

Carew, T. J., Wright, W. G., and McCance, E. F. (1989). Development of long-term memory in *Aplysia:* Long-term sensitization is present when short-term sensitization first emerges. *Society for Neuroscience Abstracts 15,* 1,285.

Fitzgerald, K., and Carew, T. J. (1991). Serotonin mimics tail shock in producing transient inhibition in the siphon withdrawal reflex of *Aplysia. Journal of Neuroscience 11,* 2,510–2,518.

Golet, P., Castellucci, V. F., Schacher, S., and Kandel, E. R. (1986). The long and short of long-term memory—a molecular framework. *Nature 322,* 419–422.

Groves, P. M., and Thompson, R. F. (1970). Habituation: A dual process theory. *Psychological Review 77,* 419–450.

Hochner, B., Klein, M., Schacher, S., and Kandel, E. R. (1986). Additional component in the cellular mechanism of presynaptic facilitation contributes to behavioral dishabituation in *Aplysia. Proceedings of the National Academy of Sciences of the United States of America 83,* 8,794–8,798.

Kriegstein, A. R. (1977). Stages in post-hatching development of *Aplysia californica. Journal of Experimental Zoology 199,* 275–288.

Krontiris-Litowitz, J. K., Erikson, M. T., and Walters, E. T. (1987). Central suppression of defensive reflexes in *Aplysia* by noxious stimulation and by factors released from body wall. *Society for Neuroscience Abstracts 13,* 815.

Mackey, S. L., Glanzman, D. L., Small, S. A., Dyke, A. M., Kandel, E. R., and Hawkins, R. D. (1987). Tail shock produces inhibition as well as sensitization of the siphon-withdrawal reflex of *Aplysia:* Possible behavioral role for presynaptic inhibition mediated by the peptide Phe-Met-Arg-Phe-NH². *Proceedings of the National Academy of Sciences of the United States of America 84,* 8,730–8,734.

Marcus, E. A., Nolen, T. G., Rankin, C. H., and Carew, T. J. (1988). Behavioral dissociation of dishabituation, sensitization, and inhibition in *Aplysia. Science 241,* 210–213.

Nolen, T. G., and Carew, T. J. (1988). A cellular analog of sensitization emerges at the same time in development as behavioral sensitization in *Aplysia. Journal of Neuroscience 8,* 212–222.

Rankin, C. H., and Carew, T. J. (1987). Development of learning and memory in *Aplysia:* II. Habituation and dishabituation. *Journal of Neuroscience 7,* 133–144.

—— (1988). Dishabituation and sensitization emerge as separate processes during development in *Aplysia. Journal of Neuroscience 8,* 197–211.

—— (1989). Developmental analysis in *Aplysia* reveals inhibitory as well as facilitatory effects of tail shock. *Behavior and Neuroscience 103,* 334–344.

Rayport, S. G., and Camardo, J. S. (1984). Differential emergence of cellular mechanisms mediating habituation and sensitization in the developing *Aplysia* nervous system. *Journal of Neuroscience 4,* 2,528–2,532.

Stopfer, M., and Carew, T. J. (1988). Development of sensitization of escape locomotion in *Aplysia. Journal of Neuroscience 8,* 223–230.

Wright, W. G., and Carew, T. J. (1990). Contributions of interneurons to tail-shock induced inhibition of the siphon withdrawal reflex in *Aplysia. Society for Neuroscience Abstracts 16,* 20.

Wright, W. G., Marcus, E. A., and Carew, T. J. (1991). A cellular analysis of inhibition in the siphon withdrawal reflex of *Aplysia. Journal of Neuroscience 11,* 2,498–2,509.

Thomas J. Carew

MOLECULAR BASIS OF LONG-TERM SENSITIZATION

Sensitization is a simple form of nonassociative learning that involves the enhancement of the response to a weak stimulus that occurs after the presentation of a strong or noxious stimulus. Sensitization usually occurs in two forms that differ in their duration and underlying mechanisms. Short-term sensitization lasts seconds to minutes and involves the modification of neuronal membrane properties and synaptic efficacy, often through the alteration of the phosphorylation state of existing proteins. Long-term sensitization lasts from days to weeks, depending on the training protocol. Unlike the short-term version, long-term sensitization requires synthesis of new macromolecules—the inhibition of either gene transcription into mRNA or translation of mRNA into protein blocks long-term sensitization. In its most persistent form, long-term sensitization involves morphological changes and neuronal growth.

The marine mollusk *Aplysia* has proved a useful model for gaining insights into the underlying neural and molecular mechanisms of long-term sensitization. *Aplysia* has a simple nervous system with large, individually identifiable neurons that are accessible for detailed anatomical, biophysical, biochemical, and molecular studies. Researchers have identified many of the neural circuits involved in sensitization of several reflexive withdrawal behaviors and have characterized individual neurons within these circuits. They have also identified specific locations of learning-related modifications in these circuits and have analyzed the underlying cellular mechanisms.

The Siphon Withdrawal Reflexes of *Aplysia*

Sensitization studies in *Aplysia* have focused chiefly on the withdrawal reflexes of the siphon gill and the tail siphon. The gill, the animal's respiratory organ, is in the mantle cavity. The siphon is a fleshy, tubelike extension of the body wall protruding from the mantle cavity. A stimulus delivered to the siphon elicits withdrawal of both the siphon and the gill: This is the siphon-gill withdrawal reflex. Eliciting the tail-siphon withdrawal reflex requires the delivery of a stimulus to the tail, causing withdrawal of both the tail and the siphon. In the wild, sensitization might be induced by an unsuccessful attack by a predator (e. g., pinching or scratching by a crab). In the laboratory, electrical shocks to the body wall are the most common means of sensitizing the animal because it is easier to deliver the same stimulus repeatedly. Long-term sensitization requires prolonged training (multiple shocks delivered over an extended interval—e.g., one to two hours). One training session can sensitize the animal for several days, whereas multiple training sessions repeated over several days can sensitize the animal for weeks.

The afferent signal is carried by mechanosensory neurons. About twenty-four sensory neurons innervate the siphon, and another 200 sensory neurons innervate the body wall (a subset of only about twenty of these innervate the tail). These sensory neurons make excitatory synapses onto motor neurons that cause contractions of muscles in the gill, siphon, and tail. Sensory neuron membrane properties and presynaptic release machinery are the principal sites of plasticity during sensitization. Sensory neurons also synapse with a variety of interneurons. Some interneurons convey sensory information from one body region to the circuits that control other regions. Other interneurons secrete modulatory transmitters such as serotonin that modify the biophysical properties of sensory and motor neurons and the characteristics of neurotransmitter release from the sensory neuron (i.e., heterosynaptic facilitation, discussed in more detail below).

Cellular Correlates of Long-Term Sensitization

One advantage of *Aplysia* for studies on long-term learning is that the nervous system, or portions of it, can be removed for studies in vitro. Studies in reduced preparations derived from sensitized and control animals have shown that changes in the animal's behavior correlate with changes in the properties of both the presynaptic sensory neuron and the postsynaptic motor neuron. Although these are unlikely to be the only sites of plasticity associated with sensitization in the nervous system, changes in the sensory and motor neurons are likely to be important because they occur in the basic circuit of the reflex arc.

Modulation of the Presynaptic Sensory Neuron

The first correlate of long-term sensitization to be described was a decrease in sensory-neuron-membrane potassium current (Scholz and Byrne, 1987). Researchers had found that modulation of the same current for short-term sensitization was sensitive to serotonin (5-hydroxytryptamine, 5-HT) and cyclic adenosine monophosphate (cAMP) treatments. The decrease in membrane current after long-term sensitization training leads to an increase in the number of action potentials elicited for a fixed amount of injected current. Thus, sensory neurons fire more action potentials in response to a given stimulus after sensitization (Cleary, Lee, and Byrne 1998).

Another correlate of long-term sensitization is an increase in synaptic efficacy at the synapses between sensory neurons and motor neurons (Cleary, Lee, and Byrne 1998; Frost, Castellucci, Hawkins, and Kandel, 1985). A major component of this synaptic modulation appears to be due to an increase transmitter release from the presynaptic sensory neurons (Dale, Schacher, and Kandel, 1988), although the nature of this increase is still poorly understood. The prime targets of of modulation are as follows: broadening action potential, increased numbers of release-ready synaptic vesicles, and increased efficiency of the synaptic-release machinery. It is not yet known whether other synapses made by sensory neurons (e.g., onto interneurons) are also enhanced. In addition, postsynaptic mechanisms may also contribute to increased synaptic efficacy (Cleary, Lee, and Byrne 1998; see below).

More extensive training (e.g., four days) produces more persistent sensitization. After four days of training, anatomical studies have revealed remodeling of sensory neuron release sites and the growth of additional axonal and dendritic branches as well as new synaptic contacts that may contribute to increased synaptic efficacy (Bailey and Chen, 1983; Wainwright, Zhang, Byrne, and Cleary, 2002). The recruitment of this growth requires several days of training rather than a single day (Wainwright, Zhang, Byrne, and Cleary, 2002). The down regulation of the

Aplysia neuronal cell adhesion molecule, ApCAM, plays an important role in this growth-associated plasticity (Abel and Kandel, 1998). Sensory neurons reduce their synthesis of new ApCAM protein and internalize ApCAM already present at their plasma membranes. The signal for internalization of ApCAM is phosphorylation by extracellular signal-regulated kinase (ERK, discussed below). The decrease in ApCAM in sensory-neuron axonal membranes may allow the formation of new branches and additional neurotransmitter release sites.

Modulation of the Postsynaptic Neuron

Changes in the properties of the postsynaptic neuron may also contribute to the increase in synaptic efficacy underlying long-term sensitization. After training, there are changes in two motor-neuron membrane properties: an increase in the resting-membrane potential and a decrease in the spike threshold (Cleary et al, 1998). In addition, motor neurons show a protein-synthesis-dependent increased responsiveness to glutamate twenty-four hours after 5-HT treatment (Trudeau and Castellucci, 1995). This result suggests an increase in the number of postsynaptic receptors that accompanies the increase in presynaptic transmitter release. However, blocking this increase in postsynaptic responsiveness does not block long-term facilitation.

Heterosynaptic Modulation

What is the modulatory signal that produces these presynaptic and postsynaptic changes? It seems that the sensory neurons that convey information about the sensitizing stimulus into the central nervous system synapse onto one or more interneurons. These interneurons, in turn, release a modulatory transmitter to produce the changes described above. A growing body of evidence indicates that the transmitter used by these interneurons is serotonin (5-HT) (Byrne and Kandel, 1996). Indeed, 5-HT mimics the many effects of sensitization training: Prolonged or multiple applications of 5-HT are necessary to produce long-term changes in vitro. As an analog of sensitization, 5-HT use has proved invaluable in studies seeking to delineate the cellular mechanisms that underlie long-term sensitization.

In addition to 5-HT, other transmitter molecules may induce long-term sensitization. In the late 1990s, researchers found evidence that a member of the transforming growth factor β family was involved in long-term sensitization (Zhang et al., 1997). Indeed, treatment of *Aplysia* neurons with human transforming growth factor β results in long-term facilitation and increased sensory-neuron excitability (Chin et al.,

1999; Zhang et al., 1997). Furthermore, a scavenger molecule specific for transforming growth factor β blocks long-term facilitation induced by 5-HT treatment. These data suggest that the *Aplysia* homologue of the growth factor may be necessary for the induction or expression of long-term plasticity by acting downstream of 5-HT. Transforming growth factor β activates two protein kinases (PKC and ERK, see below) in *Aplysia* sensory neurons (Chin et al., 2002; Farr, Mathews, Zhu, and Ambron 1999)

Second Messengers and Protein Kinase Cascades

In the early 1980s, researchers found that sensitization training and 5-HT each increased cytoplasmic levels of the intracellular second messenger, cAMP (Bernier, Castellucci, Kandel, and Schwartz, 1982; Ocorr, Tabata, and Byrne, 1986). Regulation of this second messenger is critical for long-term memory in fruit flies, bees, and rodents. In *Aplysia*, injection of cAMP into sensory neurons produces many of the long-term changes previously correlated with sensitization training, including decreased potassium conductance, increased membrane excitability, and neurite growth (O'Leary, Byrne, and Cleary, 1995; Schacher et al., 1988, 1993; Scholz and Byrne, 1988). Indeed, cAMP appears to be sufficient for the induction of several of the major forms of long-term neuronal plasticity associated with sensitization.

The key effector of cAMP for long-term neuronal plasticity is the cAMP-dependent protein kinase (PKA). Inhibition of PKA during the induction and early stages of consolidation of long-term memory blocks synaptic facilitation one day after 5-HT treatment (Abel and Kandel, 1998), and injection of the active catalytic subunit of PKA can induce long-term facilitation in the absence of upstream signaling (Chain et al., 1999). Among the substrates of PKA that are critical for the induction of long-term plasticity are several transcription factors that regulate gene expression. The principal target of PKA is the cAMP/Ca^{2+}-responsive element binding protein (CREB, discussed below), a transcription factor that plays important roles in many forms of long-term memory. In addition, PKA activity persists at least twenty-four hours after sensitization training or treatment with 5-HT (Chain et al., 1999; Müller and Carew, 1998). It is possible, then, that persistent kinase activity is also important for long-term changes.

Although the activation of the cAMP/PKA cascade appears to be sufficient to produce long-term plasticity associated with sensitization, other kinases play important roles in the induction of sensitization. One of the kinases is protein kinase C (PKC). Sensitization training or extended 5-HT treatment results in a prolonged activation of PKC that lasts about two hours after training or treatment. During this period PKC contributes to the regulation of translation and the activation of a transcription factor (C/EBP, see below) that regulates the expression of late genes necessary for long-term sensitization.

Another kinase cascade that plays an essential role in the induction of long-term facilitation is the extracellular signal-regulated kinase (ERK), a member of the mitogen-activated protein kinase family. ERK can be activated by several intracellular cascades. Researchers have yet to pinpoint the one that leads to its activation during sensitization training or by 5-HT treatment. Yet in *Aplysia* sensory neurons cAMP can mediate both the activation of ERK and its translocation to the nucleus. The cAMP cascade appears to be important for activation of ERK during the early stages of long-term sensitization induction. ERK can also be activated by PKC, a cascade that may be important during later stages of induction.

The protein synthesis required for long-term sensitization occurs during a critical period that begins at the onset of training and continues until training ends (Castellucci, Blumenfeld, Goelet, and Kandel, 1989; Levenson et al., 2000). This period corresponds to the time when CREB-dependent transcription occurs.

There is evidence that a second round of protein synthesis occurs during the formation of long-term sensitization. Growth of sensory neurons in response to cAMP injections is blocked by protein-synthesis inhibitor up to seven hours after injection (O'Leary, Byrne, and Cleary, 1995). This second round of protein synthesis may correspond to the gene expression that stabilizes long-term sensitization.

CREB and Memory

As noted above, long-term memory differs from short-term memory chiefly in requiring protein synthesis. During the induction of long-term memory, activated PKA translocates from the sensory neuron cytoplasm into the nucleus, where it phosphorylates the transcriptional activator CREB1 (Abel and Kandel, 1998). CREB1 activates transcription by binding to the DNA of certain genes that contain cAMP/Ca^{2+} responsive element (CRE) sequences in their regulatory domains. Another form of CREB, CREB2, represses transcription of these genes. CREB2 is a substrate of ERK, which also translocates into the nucleus during the induction phase. Thus, expression of CRE-containing genes requires both activation by CREB1 and derepression by CREB2.

Immediate Early Genes

CREB-dependent transcription leads to the expression of immediate early genes. Researchers have identified two of these genes. One is a key component of the ubiquitin-proteosome pathway for the degradation of proteins, *Aplysia* ubiquitin C-terminal hydrolase (ApUCH), and the other is another transcription factor, CCAAT/enhancer binding protein (C/EBP). ApUCH is an enzyme that associates with the proteosome and increases its proteolytic activity. ApUCH is an immediate early gene involved in the induction of long-term sensitization (Abel and Kandel, 1998; Alberini, 1999). CREB activation increases the expression of ApUCH. An important substrate of the proteosome in sensory neurons is the regulatory subunit of PKA. Increased expression of ApUCH results in the proteosome-mediated degradation of a subset of the PKA regulatory subunits (those binding cAMP). As the ratio of the regulatory to catalytic subunits decreases, PKA activity becomes independent of cAMP and is prolonged. Thus, CREB activation leads to degradation of the PKA regulatory subunit and thereby prolongs the activity of the PKA catalytic subunit, which is now independent of cAMP.

C/EBP, the CCAAT/enhancer binding protein, is another transcription factor. In *Aplysia* sensory neurons, C/EBP is an immediate early gene expressed in response to CREB activation (Alberini, 1999). C/EBP can form both homodimers with other C/EBP proteins or heterodimers with other transcription factors to activate transcription of late genes. In order to activate transcription of its target genes, C/EBP must be phosphorylated by ERK. Although the synthesis of a number of proteins are known to be regulated by sensitization, researchers have yet to identify C/EBP target genes in *Aplysia*.

Although there are other sites of neural plasticity, the detailed study of the modifications that occur in sensory neurons and their synapses with motor neurons (i. e., the fundamental reflex arc) during long-term sensitization have led to an understanding of the basic mechanisms that underlie this simple form of learning. Research using the relatively simple nervous system of *Aplysia* has provided insights into memory formation at the cellular, molecular, and biophysical levels. These basic mechanisms appear to form the platform upon which more complex forms of learning (i. e., classical and operant conditioning) develop.

See also: MORPHOLOGICAL BASIS OF LEARNING AND MEMORY: INVERTEBRATES; PROTEIN SYNTHESIS IN LONG-TERM MEMORY IN VERTEBRATES

Bibliography

Abel, T., and Kandel, E. R. (1998). Positive and negative regulatory mechanisms that mediate long-term memory storage. *Brain Research Reviews 26*, 360–378.

Alberini, C. (1999). Genes to remember. *Journal of Experimental Biology 202*, 2,887–2,891.

Bailey, C. H., and Chen, M. (1983). Morphological basis of long-term habituation and sensitization in *Aplysia*. *Science 220*, 91–93.

Bernier, L., Castellucci, V. F., Kandel, E. R,. and Schwartz, J. H. (1982). Facilitatory transmitter causes a selective and prolonged increase in adenosine 3',5'-monophosphate in sensory neurons mediating the gill and siphon withdrawal reflex in *Aplysia*. *Journal of Neuroscience 2*, 1,682–1,691.

Byrne, J. H., and Kandel, E. R. (1996). Presynaptic facilitation revisited: State and time dependence. *Journal of Neuroscience 16*, 425–435.

Castellucci, V. F., Blumenfeld, H., Goelet, P., and Kandel, E. R. (1989). Inhibitor of protein synthesis blocks long-term behavioral sensitization in the isolated gill-withdrawal reflex of *Aplysia*. *Journal of Neurobiology 20*, 1–9.

Chain, D. G., Casadio, A., Schacher, S., Hegde, A. N., Valbrun, M., Yamamoto, N., Goldberg, A. L., Bartsch, D., Kandel, E. R., and Schwartz, J. H. (1999). Mechanisms for generating the autonomous cAMP-dependent protein kinase required for long-term facilitation in *Aplysia*. *Neuron 22*, 147–156.

Chin, J., Angers, A., Cleary, L. J., Eskin, A., and Byrne, J. H. (1999). TGF-β1 in *Aplysia*: Role of long-term changes in the excitability of sensory neurons and distribution of TβR-II-like immunoreactivity. *Learning and Memory 6*, 317–330.

——— (2002). TGF-β1 alters synapsin distribution and modulates synaptic depression in *Aplysia*. *Journal of Neuroscience 22*, RC220.

Cleary, L. J., Lee, W. L., and Byrne, J. H. (1998). Cellular correlates of long-term sensitization in *Aplysia*. *Journal of Neuroscience 18*, 5,988–5,998.

Dale, N., Schacher, S., and Kandel, E. R. (1988). Long-term facilitation in *Aplysia* involves increase in transmitter release. *Science 239*, 282–285.

Farr, M., Mathews, J., Zhu, D. F., and Ambron, R. T. (1999). Inflammation causes a long-term hyperexcitability in the nociceptive sensory neurons of *Aplysia*. *Learning & Memory 6*, 331–340.

Frost, W. N., Castellucci, V. F., Hawkins, R. D., and Kandel, E. R. (1985). Monosynaptic connections made by the sensory neurons of the gill- and siphon-withdrawal reflex in *Aplysia* participate in the storage of long-term memory for sensitization. *Proceedings of the National Academy of Sciences of the United States of America 82*, 8,266–8,269.

Levenson, J., Endo, S., Kategaya, L. S., Fernandez, R. I., Brabham, D. G., Chin, J., Byrne, J. H., and Eskin, A. (2000). Long-term regulation of neuronal high-affinity glutamate and glutamine uptake in *Aplysia*. *Proceedings of the National Academy of Sciences of the United States of America 97*, 12,858–12,863.

Ocorr, K. A., Tabata, A. M., and Byrne, J. H. (1986). Stimuli that produce sensitization lead to an elevation of cyclic AMP levels in tail sensory neurons of *Aplysia*. *Brain Research 371*, 190–192.

O'Leary, F. A., Byrne, J. H., and Cleary, L. J. (1995). Long-term structural remodeling in *Aplysia* sensory neurons requires de novo protein synthesis during a critical time period. *Journal of Neuroscience 15*, 3,519–3,525.

Schacher, S., Castellucci, V. F., and Kandel, E. R. (1988). cAMP evokes long-term facilitation in *Aplysia* sensory neurons that requires new protein synthesis. *Science 240*, 1,667–1,669.

Schacher, S., Kandel, E. R., and Montarolo, P. (1993). cAMP and arachidonic acid simulate long-term structural and functional changes produced by neurotransmitters in *Aplysia* sensory neurons. *Neuron 10*, 1,079–1,088.

Scholz, K. P., and Byrne, J. H. (1987). Long-term sensitization in *Aplysia*: biophysical correlates in tail sensory neurons. *Science 235*, 685–687.

——— (1988). Intracellular injection of cAMP induces a long-term reduction of neuronal K+ currents. *Science 240*, 1,664–1,666.

Trudeau, L.-E., and Castellucci, V.F. (1995). Postsynaptic modifications in long-term facilitation in *Aplysia*: Upregulation of excitatory amino acid receptors. *Journal of Neuroscience 15*, 1,275–1,284.

Wainwright, M. L., Zhang, H., Byrne, J. H., and Cleary, L. J. (2002). Localized neuronal outgrowth induced by long-term sensitization training in *Aplysia*. *Journal of Neuroscience 22*, 4,132–4,141.

Zhang, F., Endo, S., Cleary, L. J., Eskin, A., and Byrne, J. H. (1997). Role of transforming growth factor-β in long-term synaptic facilitation in *Aplysia*. *Science 275*, 1,318–1,320.

Vincent Castellucci
Revised by Gregg A. Phares and John H. Byrne

Aristotle *(The Library of Congress)*

ARISTOTLE (384–322 B.C.E.)

Aristotle was born in northern Greece, in the town of Stagira, in 384 B.C.E. At seventeen, he went to Athens and became a student in Plato's Academy, where he remained for twenty years. Although greatly influenced by Plato and by the pre-Socratic philosophers, especially Empedocles, Aristotle was a highly original thinker and a disciple of no one. In 347 B.C.E. he left Athens and traveled extensively in Asia Minor, becoming tutor to Alexander the Great in 342 B.C.E. Seven years later he returned to Athens and began his own school, the Lyceum. After the death of Alexander the Great in 323 B.C.E., he left Athens, and he died the following year in Khalkís, a few miles north of Athens.

In his main work on memory, *De memoria et reminiscentia*, Aristotle tries to dissect out the central phenomena to be explained, and suggests mechanical explanations of a general sort to account for them. In his scientific works, Aristotle typically seeks the reality behind the appearances, and he expects that the reality may be different from what it seems. This is especially forward-looking in the case of mental phenomena, where subsequent thinkers, such as René Descartes (in the seventeenth century) and Zeno Vendler (in the late twentieth century), insist that mental reality must be exactly as it seems. Aristotle's collection of memory phenomena displays some systematicity, and with characteristic insight, he lights on several basically correct classifications. Nevertheless, to modern eyes some of his collection is a bit of a jumble, and the mechanical explanations tendered are so implausible that they must have been no more than helpful metaphors to him.

Aristotle's relentlessly naturalistic perspective, however, gives him a decidedly modern stamp. That is, he sought physical rather than supernatural or spiritual explanations for memory phenomena, and he well knew the importance of observations even though his own were occasionally mere assumptions. (For example, he thought women had fewer teeth than men.) In the absence of a developed biology, experimental psychology, or neuroscience, he could hardly be expected either to envisage explanations in terms of neuronal connectivity or to know how to penetrate learning phenomena at the behavioral level.

Observations and Explanations

In commenting upon memory and learning phenomena, Aristotle's fundamental distinction is between recalling information to mind and storing information, or, as he puts it, between remembering, which is "the reinstatement in consciousness of something that was there before" (451b6), and memory, "the existence, potentially, in the mind" (452a10), of an earlier perception or conception. In modern parlance, this is the distinction between remembering in the occurrent sense and remembering in the "stored" or dispositional sense. The central problems, in Aristotle's view, are to explain three things: 1. how a per-

ception of a state of affairs can be stored, 2. how it can be brought to mind later, and 3. how it happens that, when it is brought to mind, the relation between the representation and the original state of affairs, now absent, is such that the first is a memory of the second and is known to be such. In contemporary dress, these are the problems of information storage, information retrieval, and the general problem of how representations represent.

Aristotle tries to explain information storage by appeal to the analogy of imprinting soft wax with a seal. He reasons that sense perception is somehow like a picture and that it is the perception picture that stamps its likeness to create a memory. Apparently the perception is stamped on the soul (Aristotle has a physical, not a supernatural, conception of the soul), or at any rate, it is stamped on some sort of physical stuff that can be in causal interaction with it and can take on some of its properties. This helps address the representation problem. The imprint (memory representation) resembles, physically, the perception (perceptual representation), which in turn resembles, physically, that of which it is a perception. So by transitivity of resemblance, there is a correlation between stored representation and original state of affairs. Aristotle's conclusion that there must be a resemblance was taken as axiomatic by most subsequent thinkers, and they searched for the parameters of physical resemblance. Research since the 1970s, especially in computer science and neuroscience, has revealed that representation does not require resemblance in any straightforward sense, a radical departure from earlier theories.

In asking how representations represent, Aristotle identified a truly fundamental problem. Still only partially solved, it remains a central problem, though it is now addressed within the framework of modern psychology, philosophy, neuroscience, and computer science.

Understanding the importance of broad systematicity in a theory, Aristotle tests a theory's strength by seeing how much can be encompassed within its ambit. Thus he claims that the stuff that receives the imprint may have varying degrees of imprintability. Explanations are then forthcoming for one's poor recollection of early childhood and for declining memory in the elderly: In very young children the stuff is too much like running water to take the imprint; in older humans, the stuff hardens and no longer is very impressible. Extending this idea further, Aristotle thinks a related explanation will apply to his observation that those who are "too quick" and those who are "too slow" also have poor memories. Exactly what phenomenon he is addressing here is unclear, and this may be one of those inexplicable Aristotelian "observations" that need a much broadened base of data.

The representation problem, Aristotle notices, has a further dimension. When an image from memory comes to mind, how do we know that it is a memory, rather than a thought or image without relation to bygone events? That is, how does the occurrent presentation carry the information that it is a memory? His answer has two parts. First, sometimes we do get confused, and we think a presentation is a memory when it is not (false memory); and sometimes we have a memory presentation but are unaware that it is a memory. So the system is imperfect. Second, when the system does work, it is because for animals with memory, "the organ whereby they perceive time is also that whereby they remember" (449b30). The idea here is that when perceptions are stored as memories, they are also somehow indexed as to time, so that the imprint bears not only the perception's shape but also its "whenness."

Retrieval appears to require something like an image or an iconic presentation that resembles the original perception. The mechanism of retrieval should, one surmises, have to do with something taking up the stored imprint and re-presenting it, but in fact Aristotle says nothing of this. Instead he discusses the phenomenon of association, noting that events experienced together are often remembered together. He explains associated recollections by saying that the "movement" of a perception causes the "movement" of the memory. He sees, therefore, that part of the theory of storage will include the relations between associated memories, but he neither provides an account of those storage relations nor elaborates on how information is retrieved by the "movements" (451b15–30).

In *Historia animalium* Aristotle suggests that humans and animals differ in that humans alone can remember something at will (488b25), though he also notes in *De memoria et reminiscentia* that recollections can occur without effort. Indeed, he observes that melancholics often have obsessive memories, try though they might to repress them. In the physicalist spirit, he conjectures that melancholics have more moisture around their sense perception center, which is easily set in motion, thus explaining the memory's being presented again and again despite one's will.

Aristotle believed that animals differ in whether they have the capacity to store their perceptions; animals with the capacity to do so have genuine knowledge of their world, whereas animals lacking the capacity merely respond to their current perceptions on the basis of their innate dispositions. The advantage of storing perceptions is that the stored items may come to have systematic relations among themselves, with the result that the animal can recognize different individuals as belonging to the same category. In humans this means, for example, that a pine tree, a yew, and an olive tree may all be recognized as similar despite differences in shape, size, and color. He says that the soul is so constituted that the universal "tree" can be developed from the stored perceptions of individually distinct items. A slug, on the other hand, lacks the capacity to generalize across individuals because it lacks the capacity to store information.

In Aristotle's view, storing information provides the similarity substructure that underpins both scientific categorization and the skilled knowledge displayed by craftsmen who can make many different clay pots or ship's captains who can sail under many different conditions. In modern guise, his idea is that generalization to items that are relevantly similar but incidentally different, both perceptually and behaviorally, requires information storage. Additionally, he regards this capacity as enabling experience, the reason being that experience requires understanding, which in turn requires categorization of perceptions. Consequently, animals such as humans have genuine experience; animals such as slugs do not (*Posterior Analytics*, 99b36;100a5).

Conclusion

Any inclination to feel smug about Aristotle's shortcomings should be tempered by noting that even current classifications of learning phenomena are controversial and tentative, and experimental psychologists are sometimes chided for doing little more than codifying common sense. Nor, of course, should Aristotle himself be blamed for the slavish adoption of his every word by uncritical monks in the Middle Ages. Aristotle the scientist-philosopher was anything but dogmatic. Twentieth-century physical explanations—although not mechanical, but electrical and biochemical—sit well with his abiding naturalism.

For a long period in the history of thought, Aristotle's views on nearly everything were taken as authoritative. His *Metaphysics* probably had the greatest impact; however, the work on memory was not especially influential.

Bibliography

Aristotle (1941). *De anima*, trans. J. A. Smith. In Richard McKeon, ed., *The basic works of Aristotle*. New York: Random House.
——— (1941). *De memoria et reminiscentia*, trans. by J. I. Beare. In Richard McKeon, ed., *The basic works of Aristotle*. New York: Random House.
——— (1941). *Historia animalium*. In Richard McKeon, ed., *The basic works of Aristotle*. New York: Random House.
——— (1975). *Aristotle's Posterior analytics*, trans. J. Barnes. Oxford: Clarendon Press.

Beare, J. I. (1906). *Greek theories of elementary cognition.* Oxford: Clarendon Press.

Churchland, P. S. (2002). *Brain-wise: Studies in neurophilosophy.* Cambridge, MA: MIT Press.

Descartes, R. (1649; reprint 1968). *Les passions de l'âme.* English translation in E. S. Haldane and G. R. T. Ross, trans. (1911), *The philosophical works of Descartes.* Cambridge, UK: Cambridge University Press.

Edel, A. (1982). *Aristotle and his philosophy.* Chapel Hill: University of North Carolina Press.

Kahn, C. H. (1966). Sensation and consciousness in Aristotle's psychology. *Archiv für Geschichte der Philosophie 48,* 43–81.

Ross, W. D. (1923; reprint 1959). *Aristotle.* Cleveland: Meridian Books.

——— (1955). *Aristotle's "Parva naturalia."* Oxford: Oxford University Press.

Sorabji, R. (1972). *Aristotle on memory.* London: Trinity Press.

Patricia Smith Churchland
Georgios Anagnostopoulos
Revised by Patricia Smith Churchland

ATTENTION AND MEMORY

It seems to be a tenet of ordinary common sense that people remember what they attend to and forget what they do not. Not surprisingly, researchers have noted the very close relationship between attention and memory for a very long time, and some empirical evidence for the linkage was offered as far back as the late nineteenth century (Smith, 1895). However, it was only during the twentieth century, with the advent of cognitive psychology and its relatively rich array of methods for studying human information processing over fine time scales, that it became possible to begin to analyze this connection in more detail. To do so, researchers have used taxonomies of memorial and attentional processes that emerge from laboratory studies in each of these areas.

Forms of Attention

The term *attention* as used in everyday language is a diffuse and global term that alludes to both *selectivity* and *capacity limitations.* The potential for selectivity is evident in the fact that of the great multitude of stimuli impinging on the sense organs at any one instant, human beings are usually vividly aware of only a fairly small subset. Capacity limitations are evident whenever people try to attend to more than one stream of inputs, particularly if comprehension or response is required: for example, trying to listen to the radio at the same time as one reads a newspaper. Casual usage seems to imply that attention refers to a single process or substance that accounts for both selectivity and capacity limitations. Thus, people speak of focusing attention on one sensory input or one task, with the result that one does not have enough attention left over for other inputs or other tasks. Ordinary usage also seems to imply that limitations of attention are a key factor restricting one's ability not only to perceive many stimuli at once, but also to perform two tasks at the same time. These commonplace notions from folk psychology may or may not accurately describe humans' information-processing machinery.

Late-twentieth-century research argues that the phenomena of attention are not as unitary as common sense might suggest (Pashler, 1998). This is scarcely surprising given the complexities of the body's underlying neural machinery and of the tasks to which the human brain is adapted. Evidence for distinct attentional mechanisms is seen most clearly in relation to *divided attention:* the performance limitations that arise when a person attempts to process more than one stimulus at a time. On the one hand, there appear to be a set of processing limitations associated with perceptual analysis of inputs in different sense modalities. If a person is confronted with different sensory inputs at the same time, it is more difficult to perceive them when they arrive through the same sense modality rather than through different modalities. This was first demonstrated by A. Treisman and A. Davies (1973), who showed that people were better able to monitor animal names when some of the words to be monitored were presented visually and others auditorily (as compared to both in the same modality). These modality-restricted perceptual capacity limitations are wholly governed by the voluntary direction of selective attention: It is only the stimuli that are attended to that compete for limited resources, not all the stimuli that may be impinging on the senses.

In addition to the perceptual processing limitations tied to particular input modalities, research points to a separate set of limitations that become evident only when a person tries to perform multiple tasks at the same time. These *central* attentional limitations have their locus in the more cognitive stages of processing, especially the planning of actions and the retrieval of information in memory. When two tasks each require mental operations of these types, the processing in the two tasks is normally subject to queuing: selection of a response in one task must be completed before selection of the response in the other task can commence (Pashler and Johnston, 1998). Interestingly, these limitations seem quite indifferent to what modality the information arrives in. If a person must make a speeded response to a tone, for example, this will delay his or her ability to make a rapid response to a concurrently presented color patch. The central interference is also independent of response modalities; for example, if one response is vocal and one manual, the interference is still observed.

When one seeks to understand the relation of attention to memory, it is fruitful to inquire both about the role of modality-specific perceptual attention mechanisms and the role of central attentional mechanisms.

Forms of Memory

Memory, too, appears to be composed of a number of relatively separate functional systems. Several key distinctions have been proposed since the mid-1960s. The most important and well validated of these is the distinction between three broad memory systems that hold information over different time scales (and differ in certain other properties). This analysis, sometimes called the "modal model," postulates separate sensory memory, short-term memory (STM), and long-term memory (LTM) systems. The model arose out of the pioneering work of N. Waugh and D. A. Norman (1965) and M. Glanzer and A. R. Cunitz (1966). Sensory memory systems seem to produce something akin to a brief "literal" persistence of a stimulus for a very short time beyond its actual presentation. This probably reflects continued firing of neurons in sensory pathways after the offset of a stimulus. Short-term (or working) memory refers to a set of very limited-capacity storage mechanisms. It is often assumed to reflect an actively refreshed neural representation in sensory, perceptual, and motor-control areas, perhaps maintained by a reverberative process involving frontal brain structures. Long-term memory, on the other hand, refers to the relatively more permanent set of memory traces that is almost surely encoded by changes in synaptic weights. In addition to the three-part demarcation, many investigators propose a distinction within the realm of long-term memory, distinguishing between so-called explicit memory (underlying conscious recollections, as in recall or recognition tasks) and implicit memory (e.g., changes caused by exposure to a stimulus that modulate later processing without causing conscious recollection).

Attention and Sensory Memory

Sensory memory systems can potentially retain a large amount of detailed sensory information about an input for an extremely short period. For visual inputs, the sensory memory is called *iconic memory*. Iconic memory seems to hold onto inputs for only about 100 to 400 milliseconds, depending on physical properties of the stimulus and the visual input that follows it. Sensory memory for auditory sensations is usually called *echoic memory*, and most investigators agree that

information is normally retained in echoic memory for one to two seconds. Sensory memory systems, while impressive in capacity, do not retain information long enough to be useful for most purposes. If the information is not transferred to short-term and/or long-term memory, it is lost.

Does information get into sensory memory even when a person attempts to ignore it at the time it is presented? For auditory sensory memory, the answer is evidently yes. This is seen, for example, in early observations by Broadbent and others that when people shadow spoken input to one ear, they can, if interrupted, abruptly switch over and (relying on echoic memory) recall the last bit of information presented to the other ear. Daily life offers many examples of the same phenomenon. Although there is little research that directly addresses the question of attentional involvement in iconic memory storage, the data that do exist suggest that even unattended information is briefly represented in this literal memory storage.

Attention and Short-Term Memory

Primary or short-term memory maintains information in an active state, but only so long as it is at least periodically rehearsed or refreshed. While some theorists originally proposed a single unitary STM, it has become clear that there are a number of separate and independent short-term memory systems. One system (sometimes termed the articulatory buffer and familiar to everyone who has ever remembered a phone number for a half minute or so) holds speech-like representations of verbal material. Another kind of STM system holds visual information in a schematic form. There are hints that other independent systems may also exist, holding, for example, nonvisual spatial representations, acoustic imagery, semantic representations, and tactile or kinesthetic patterns. The clearest evidence that different STM systems are indeed independent systems comes from experiments showing that people can hold onto more than one type of information at the same time. For example, people can retain spoken digits and visual materials with little mutual interference. Further clinching the case is the finding that some patients, after suffering brain damage, have lost one form of STM without any loss of the others (Basso, Spinnler, Vallar, and Zanobio, 1982).

Many researchers refer to "working memory" to indicate that information in STM may be actively manipulated or transformed during the time it is retained. Whatever purpose information is put to and whatever term may be used for it, the most notable characteristic of STM storage is limited capacity. For spoken material, a very limited number of words (or perhaps more critically, syllables) can be retained. For visual patterns, even a four-by-four checkerboard grid is enough to overload visual short-term memory. Access time for STM is quite good, however. For example, it appears that the image of a letter can be transferred into visual short-term memory in a matter of a few hundred milliseconds, and the rate for speech is probably not much different. What is the connection between attention and STM storage? Attending to a stimulus is clearly a necessary condition for storing that stimulus in short-term memory. Less clear is whether attending to a stimulus is a sufficient condition. The critical experiment would involve asking whether someone can retain one set of information (A) in STM and then attend to additional information arriving in the same modality (B) without having B overwrite A. Using visual patterns, W. A. Phillips and F. M. Christie (1977) concluded that this may be possible but that the issue requires further study. As for storage of spoken information, attending to irrelevant speech often compromises short-term memory quite considerably, suggesting that mere attention to a new input overwrites the existing contents of STM.

Does the storage and retention of information in STM require *central* attentional mechanisms discussed above? For articulatory STM, the involvement appears to be intermittent rather than continuous (perhaps arising in some initial consolidation in STM, and then later in scheduling periodic rehearsals). A person can retain a phone number, for example, and perform another brief demanding task involving unrelated materials without losing the phone number. However, if the demanding task is initiated immediately after storing some spoken material, memory for this material may suffer (Naveh-Benjamin and Jonides, 1984), and the same can happen when people undertake a continuously demanding task for some sustained period.

The picture that emerges, then, is of short-term memory systems closely tied to perceptual input systems (and corresponding perceptual attention machinery). Central attentional limitations may have some involvement, but it is relatively indirect or intermittent.

Attention and Long-Term Memory

To store information in long-term memory, one need not do anything active to maintain it. Nonetheless, recollecting a memory tends to strengthen its long-term memory representation, often dramatically so; conversely, memories are probably subject to erosion with the mere passage of time. What seems to be most difficult is getting information into LTM, and getting it out (retrieval). Devoting perceptual attention to a stimulus is by no means sufficient for LTM storage (whereas it may be sufficient for STM). A person can see one hundred words exposed one at a time in rapid succession (at a rate of, say, four per second), successfully detecting every word in the list that is an animal name, and at the end he or she will often remember scarcely anything except animal names. Obviously the person attended to all the words in order to determine their semantic category, but the process left no permanent residue.

What does produce memory storage, then? Many studies have concluded that the key factor is *elaboration:* active processing that uncovers connections between a to-be-stored item and other information in long-term store (Craik and Lockhart, 1972). By contrast, mere intention or desire to remember seems relatively unimportant.

Whereas central attentional mechanisms may play only a fairly minor role in the encoding of information into STM, for LTM they appear critical. Nearly every study that has looked at people's ability to form long-term memory traces while performing a concurrent task has found a substantial impairment. This occurs even when there is no discernible similarity between the stimuli to be remembered and those used in the concurrent task: for example, remembering odors while playing a computer game (Perkins and Cook, 1990).

In the late 1990s there was a lively controversy about the role of central attentional mechanisms in retrieval of information from long-term memory. On the one hand, when people are given unlimited time to retrieve materials, a concurrent task often fails to much dent the number of items they can produce (Craik, Govoni, Naveh-Benjamin, and Anderson, 1996). On the other hand, a demanding concurrent task markedly reduces the rate at which information can be retrieved from LTM (Hicks and Marsh, 2000). Furthermore, when an unrelated speeded-choice reaction-time task is performed concurrently with a paired-associate retrieval task, there is evidence that the memory retrieval is completely delayed by central attention to the speeded task (Carrier and Pashler, 1995).

Attention and Implicit Memory

The idea of a separate implicit memory system grew out of data showing amnesics may have a spared ability to form certain kinds of memories: those for which explicit recollection is not required (or at least a subset of such memories). A number of studies reported that formation of implicit memories also does not require limited-capacity attentional resources.

For example, M. E. Smith and M. Oscar-Berman (1990) observed that a concurrent task at the time of word encoding did not reduce the priming effect found for repeated words as tested in a later lexical decision task. However, more recent studies tend to find that there are considerable costs when more demanding secondary tasks are performed at the time of encoding (Mulligan and Hornstein, 2000; Rajaram, Srinivas, and Travers, 2001). Researchers have more to learn about this conflict. It is possible that explicit memory measures are simply more sensitive to impaired storage produced by divided attention, but it is also possible that implicit memory storage reflects mechanisms that are independent of central attentional capacity.

See also: LANGUAGE LEARNING: HUMANS; WORKING MEMORY: ANIMALS; WORKING MEMORY: HUMANS

Bibliography

Basso, A., Spinnler, H., Vallar, G., and Zanobio, M. E. (1982). Left hemisphere damage and selective impairment of auditory verbal short-term memory: A case study. *Neuropsychologia 20,* 263–274.

Broadbent, D. E. (1957). Immediate memory and simultaneous stimuli. *Quarterly Journal of Experimental Psychology 9,* 1–11.

Carrier, L. M., and Pashler, H. (1995). Attentional limits in memory retrieval. *Journal of Experimental Psychology: Learning, Memory, and Cognition 21,* 1,339–1,348.

Craik, F. I. M., Govoni, R., Naveh-Benjamin, M., and Anderson, N. D. (1996). The effects of divided attention on encoding and retrieval processes in human memory. *Journal of Experimental Psychology: General 125,* 159–180.

Craik, F. I. M., and Lockhart, R. S. (1972). Levels of processing: A framework for memory research. *Journal of Verbal Learning and Verbal Behavior 11,* 671–684.

Glanzer, M., and Cunitz, A. R. (1966). Two storage mechanisms in free recall. *Journal of Verbal Learning and Verbal Behavior 5,* 351–360.

Hicks, J. L., and Marsh, R. L. (2000). Toward specifying the attentional demands of recognition memory. *Journal of Experimental Psychology: Learning, Memory, and Cognition 26,* 1,483–1,498.

Mulligan, S., and Hornstein, S. (2000). Attention and perceptual priming in the perceptual identification task. *Journal of Experimental Psychology: Learning, Memory, and Cognition 26,* 626–637.

Naveh-Benjamin, M., and Jonides, J. (1984). Maintenance rehearsal: A two-component analysis. *Journal of Experimental Psychology: Learning, Memory, and Cognition 10,* 369–385.

Pashler, H. E. (1998). *The psychology of attention.* Cambridge, MA: MIT Press.

Pashler, H., and Johnston, J. C. (1998). Attentional limitations in dual-task performance. In H. Pashler, ed., *Attention.* Hove, East Sussex, UK: Psychology Press.

Perkins, J., and Cook, N. M. (1990). Recognition and recall of odours: The effects of suppressing visual and verbal encoding processes. *British Journal of Psychology 81,* 221–226.

Phillips, W. A., and Christie, F. M. (1977). Interference with visualization. *Quarterly Journal of Experimental Psychology 29,* 637–650.

Rajaram, S., Srinivas, K., and Travers, S. (2001). The effects of attention on perceptual implicit memory. *Memory & Cognition 29,* 920–930.

Smith, M. E., and Oscar-Berman, M. (1990). Repetition priming of words and pseudowords in divided attention and in amnesia. *Journal of Experimental Psychology: Learning, Memory, and Cognition 16,* 1,033–1,042.

Smith, W. G. (1895). The relation of attention to memory. *Mind 4,* 47–43.

Treisman, A., and Davies, A. (1973). Dividing attention to ear and eye. In S. Kornblum, ed., *Attention and performance IV.* New York: Academic Press.

Waugh, N., and Norman, D. A. (1965). Primary memory. *Psychological Review 72,* 89–104.

Harold Pashler

ATTENTION DEFICIT DISORDER

See: LEARNING DISABILITIES

AUDITORY MEMORY

See: MODALITY EFFECTS

AUTOBIOGRAPHICAL MEMORY

Autobiographical memory is the psychological history of the self. It consists of memories of personal experiences—episodic memories—and knowledge of the self or autobiographical knowledge: for example, schools we attended, people we had relationships with, places we have lived, places we have worked, and so on (Conway, 2001; Conway and Pleydell-Pearce, 2000; and McAdams, 2001). It is critical for personal identity, forming the basis of the self and binding self-conceptions to reality. Psychiatric illnesses or brain damage can disrupt the connections that bind self to reality through memory, leading to a loss of personal history and the attendant delusions, confabulations, and false beliefs.

The Nature of Autobiographical Memory and Its Relation to Self

Autobiographical knowledge encompasses far more than memory: It includes statements, propositions, declarations, and beliefs about the self, often accompanied by generic and/or specific (mainly visual) images of details of prior experience. Autobiographical knowledge is distinct from sensory perceptual episodic memories, which represent details of actual experience (Conway, 2001). In the formation of an autobiographical memory, autobiographical knowledge becomes linked to episodic memories (Conway and Pleydell-Pearce, 2000). Memory formation leads to recollective experience, a sense or feeling of the self in the past (Tulving, 1985; Wheeler, Stuss, and Tulving, 1997), and attention turns inward to the autobiographical memory and, perhaps, to other episodic memories and autobiographical knowledge. Of course, full autobiographical memory formation does not have to take place, and autobiographical knowledge and episodic memory can be processed independently.

Conway and Pleydell-Pearce (2000) apply the term the *working self* to the control structure that modulates this whole system of autobiographical memory formation—the dynamic combining of autobiographical knowledge with episodic memories. The working self consists of an active goal hierarchy (only parts of which are consciously accessible), models or conceptions of the self, and other forms of self-knowledge that facilitate access to autobiographical knowledge structures. New autobiographical knowledge and episodic memories are formed (encoded) through the working self, which also influences memory construction by controlling input to the knowledge base and by evaluating output (activated autobiographical knowledge). The working self may even exercise inhibitory control over the knowledge base (Conway and Pleydell-Pearce, 2000).

Autobiographical Memory Across the Lifespan

The working self—goal hierarchy and self-conceptions—probably first emerges in some coherent form as the infant develops, in its second year, the capacity for objective and subjective self-awareness in the form of conceptions of "I" and "me." (Howe and Courage, 1997). Children as young as thirty months have detailed autobiographical memories (Fivush, Hadden, and Reese, 1996), although these are not ususaly accessible in adulthood. Undoubtedly the working self and its relation to autobiographical memory changes during childhood and perhaps stabilises into an enduring form only in late adolescence and early adulthood (Erikson, 1950).

These periods of development of the self are reflected in the lifespan-retrieval curve that arises from older adults' (about thirty-five years and older) free or cued recall of autobiographical memories (Franklin and Holding, 1977; Fitzgerald and Lawrence, 1984; Rubin, Wetzler, and Nebes, 1986; Rubin, Rahhal, and Poon, 1998). This technique plots the age of encoding of memories; as shown in Figure 1, the lifespan-retrieval curve consists of three periods: childhood amnesia, (from birth to approximately five years of age), reminiscence bump (from ten to thirty years), and the period of recency (from the present declining back to the period of the reminiscence bump).

There have been many attempted theoretical explanations of childhood amnesia (Pillemer and White, 1989), but most founder on young children's capacity for a wide range of specific episodic memories and detailed autobiographical knowledge (Fivush et al., 1996). Explanations that center on changes in intellect, language, and emotional development fail simply because apparently normal autobiographical memories are typically accessible before the age of five and only after that seem to submerge in a general forgetfulness; it seems unlikely that an increase in general functioning would make unavailable already accessible memories. Hence there is no compelling explanation for this component of the lifespan-retrieval curve, which remains a challenge to autobiographical memory researchers.

The reminiscence bump has also attracted its share of theories (Rubin, Rahhal, and Poon, 1998). One is that this period endures in memory because it is suffused with novel experiences. An alternative explanation holds that although only a small percentage of experiences during the reminiscence bump are novel events, they survive because of their uniqueness in the formation of a person's life circumstances and interests (Fitzgerald, 1988); on this view, it is the high accessibility of memories from this period that accounts for their durability (Conway and Pleydell-Pearce, 2000). Perhaps many memories from the period of the reminiscence bump are of "self-defining" experiences (Fitzgerald, 1988; Singer and Salovey, 1993) and have a powerful effect in binding the working self to a specific reality. But this period, like chlidhood amnesia, has yet to find a definitive explanation for its relation to memory.

The recency component of the lifespan-retrieval curve (see Figure 1) can be simply explained as a period of forgetting: recently encoded memories, whose accessibility is retained for a longer interval, are subject to decay and/or interference and so become progressively less accessible. This is a familiar, often-observed pattern of retention. One might wonder, however, why such memories or salient experiences should be "forgotten" in this way. If older adults are expressly instructed to recall autobiographical memories from this period of forgetting, there are apparently plenty of available memories (Holmes and Conway, 1999). Thus, this seems a matter not of forgetting but rather of bias or preference in access to memories. It may be that the recency portion of the lifespan-retrieval curve reflects a lowering in the self-relevance of memories of recent experiences and hence a lowering in their accessibility rather than complete forgetting.

Figure 1

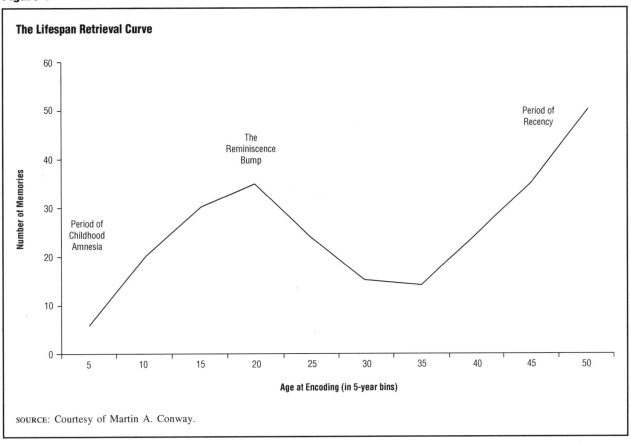

The Lifespan Retrieval Curve

Number of Memories (y-axis)

Period of Childhood Amnesia

The Reminiscence Bump

Period of Recency

Age at Encoding (in 5-year bins)

SOURCE: Courtesy of Martin A. Conway.

Autobiographical Memory and Personality

The working self increases the accessibility of goal-related autobiographical knowledge. Markus (1977) found preferential access to memories of experiences congruent with central self-schema, those that are critical to someone's sense of independence or dependence. McAdams (1982) identified individuals with a strong intimacy motivation or with a distinctive power motivation and found that the intimacy-motivation group recalled peak experiences with a preponderance of intimacy themes compared to individuals who scored lower on this motivation, who showed no memory bias. Similarly, the power-motivation group recalled peak experiences with strong themes of power and satisfaction. Subsequently, McAdams, Diamond, de Aubin, and Mansfield, (1997) examined the influence of the Eriksonian notion of generativity (Erikson, 1963) on the life stories of middle-aged adults. Generativity refers to nurturing and caring for those things, products, and people that have the potential to outlast the self. Those individuals who were judged high in generativity, who had a commitment story, were found to recall a preponderance of events highly related to aspects of gen-

erativity. In contrast, those participants without a prominent commitment story showed no such bias. In a similar way work by Woike and her colleagues has further established the connection between personality and memory (Woike, 1995; Woike, Gershkovich, Piorkowski, and Polo, 1999). Woike and colleagues (1999) investigated groups of individuals classified as "agentic" (concerned with personal power, achievement, and independence) or as "communion" (concerned with relationships, interdependence, and others). Agentic types consistently recalled emotional memories of events that involved issues of agency (mastery, humiliation). In contrast, communal types recalled emotional memories featuring others, often significant others, in acts of love and friendship. These and a range of findings from other studies (McAdams, 2001) all show a that the dominant motives or goals of the self make memories of goal-relevant experiences highly accessible.

Autobiographical Memory in Distress

Brain injury can impair autobiographical memory in various ways (Conway and Fthenaki, 2000). Injuries to regions of the frontal lobes often lead to a clouding or loss of detailed memories. In more extreme cases patients may confabulate, constructing autobiographical knowledge into plausible but false memories. Patients with damage to the temporal lobes and underlying structures in the limbic system, especially the hippocampal formation, may lose the ability to form new memories while retaining access to at least some preinjury memories. Those with damage to posterior regions of the brain, regions involved in visual processing (occipital lobes) may lose the ability to generate visual images of the past and, because of this, become amnesic. Their amnesia occurs because the episodic content of autobiographical memories is predominantly encoded in the form of visual images. When the ability to generate visual images is compromised or lost because of brain damage, then access to specific details of the past held in episodic images is also lost.

In psychiatric illness a common occurrence is that of a severe clouding of autobiographical memory, resulting in overgeneral memories. For instance, in clinical depression patients recall many memories that lack detail and are much more schematic than typical autobiographical memories. Thus, a patient asked to recall specific memories of his father could only recall general events such as "walks in the park after Sunday lunch" but was unable to generate a single specific memory of a single walk (Williams, 1996). Clouded, overgeneral memories have also been observed in schizophrenic patients and in patients suffering from obsessional-compulsive disorder. One possibility is that the complex control processes that modulate memory construction (working self) become attenuated in psychiatric illnesses and so can no longer form fully detailed memories.

Bibliography

Conway, M. A. (2001). Sensory perceptual episodic memory and its context: Autobiographical memory. *Philosophical Transactions of the Royal Society of London 356*, 1,297–1,306.

Conway, M.A., and Fthenaki, A. (2000). Disruption and loss of autobiographical memory. In L. S. Cermak, ed., *Handbook of neuropsychology: Memory and its disorders*. Amsterdam: Elsevier.

Conway, M. A., and Pleydell-Pearce, C. W. (2000). The construction of autobiographical memories in the self memory system. *Psychological Review 107*, 261–288.

Erikson, E.H. (1950). *Childhood and society*. New York: W. W. Norton.

Fitzgerald, J. M. (1988). Vivid memories and the reminiscence phenomenon: The role of a self narrative. *Human Development 31*, 261–273.

Fitzgerald, J. M., and Lawrence, R. (1984). Autobiographical memory across the lifespan. *Journal of Gerontology 39*, 692–698.

Fivush, R., Haden, C., and Reese, E. (1996). Remembering, recounting, and reminiscing: The development of autobiographical memory in social context. In D.C. Rubin, ed., *Remembering our past: Studies in autobiographiocal memory*, pp. 341–359. Cambridge: Cambridge University Press.

Franklin, H. C., and Holding, D. H. (1977). Personal memories at different ages. *Quarterly Journal of Experimental Psychology 29*, 527–532.

Holmes, A., and Conway, M. A. (1999). Generation identity and the reminiscence bump: Memories for public and private events. *Journal of Adult Development 6*, 21–34.

Howe, M. L., and Courage, M. L. (1997). The emergence and early development of autobiographical memory. *Psychological Review 104*, 499–523.

Markus, H. (1977). Self-schemata and processing information about the self. *Journal of Personality and Social Psychology 35*, 63–78.

McAdams, D. P. (1982). Experiences of intimacy and power: Relationships between social motives and autobiographical memory. *Journal of Personality and Social Psychology 42*, 292–302.

—— (2001). The psychology of life stories. *Review of General Psychology 5*, 100–122.

McAdams, D. P., Diamond, A., de Aubin E., and Mansfield, E. (1997). Stories of commitment: The psychosocial construction of generative lives. *Journal of Personality and Social Psychology 72*, 678–694.

Rubin, D. C., Rahhal, T. A., Poon, L. W. (1998). Things learned in early adulthood are remembered best. *Memory & Cognition 26*, 3–19.

Rubin, D. C., Wetzler, S. E., and Nebes, R. D. (1986). Autobiographical memory across the adult lifespan. In D. C. Rubin, ed., *Autobiographical memory*. Cambridge, UK: Cambridge University Press.

Singer, J. A., and Salovey, P. (1993). *The remembered self*. New York: The Free Press.

Tulving, E. (1985). Memory and consciousness. *Canadian Psychologist 26*, 1–12.

Wheeler, M. A., Stuss, D. T., and Tulving, E. (1997). Towards a theory of episodic memory: The frontal lobes and autonoetic consciousness. *Psychological Bulletin 121*, 351–354.

Williams, J. M. G. (1996). Depression and the specificity of autobiographical memory. In D. C. Rubin, ed., *Remembering our past: Studies in autobiographical memory*. Cambridge, UK: Cambridge University Press.

Woike, B. (1995). Most-memorable experiences: Evidence for a link between implicit and explicit motives and social cognitive processes in everyday life. *Journal of Personality and Social Psychology 68*, 1,081–1,091.

Woike, B., Gershkovich, I., Piorkowski, R., and Polo, M. (1999). The role of motives in the content and structure of autobiographical memory. *Journal of Personality and Social Psychology 76*, 600–612.

Martin A. Conway

B

BARTLETT, FREDERIC (1886–1969)

Frederic Charles Bartlett was born on October 20, 1886, in Stow on the Wold, Gloucestershire. He studied literature, logic, and philosophy before becoming a tutor at the University of Cambridge in 1909. At Cambridge, his interests turned to psychology, partly through his acquaintance with James Ward; he was awarded a fellowship at St. John's College in 1913 and obtained a first-class degree in moral sciences in 1914. Cambridge then was in the forefront of the movement to make experimental psychology a recognized branch of science in the British university system; C. S. Myers (1873–1947), a lecturer in experimental psychology there, not only had campaigned for Cambridge to build a laboratory, a wish fulfilled in 1912, but also had helped to found the *British Journal of Psychology* in 1904. Bartlett wrote an account (1937) of the early history of the Cambridge laboratory.

When World War I began in 1914, Myers appointed Bartlett "relief director" of the laboratory. Bartlett instigated research into a variety of topics, including studies of the detection of faint sounds, a project in which he collaborated with Emily Mary Smith, whom he married in 1920, and studies of individual differences in how subjects described pictures. These individual differences, Bartlett believed, reflected above all subjective interests and socially determined interpretations: He ascribed the latter to "conventionalization"; over the next few years he focused on the role of conventionalization in perception but also in the retrieval of memories. Another interest concerned perception and memory performance in people of other cultures, including South Africa, a country he had visited. His discussions of conventionalization leaned heavily on evidence collected in other societies; in the late twentieth century there was a revival of interest in Bartlett's contributions to cross-cultural psychology (Saito, 1999).

In 1922 Myers left Cambridge to head the National Institute for Industrial Psychology, and Bartlett was appointed reader and director of the Cambridge laboratory; two years later he also became editor of the *British Journal of Psychology*, a position he held for twenty-four years. In 1925 he wrote an important paper on the role of the difficult word *feeling* in scientific psychology. In 1931 he was elected to a chair in experimental psychology at Cambridge. During his term as laboratory director, the number of faculty members grew and an increasing number of students graduated in experimental psychology. An indication of the success of the program was that, of the sixteen professorships of psychology in Great Britain in 1957, ten were held by students of Myers and Bartlett. From 1922 to the beginning of World War II, Bartlett continued to study conventionalization and memorizing and wrote three books that show his interest in applied psychology: *Psychology and the Soldier* (1927), which dealt with personnel selection and war neuroses, among other topics; *Psychology and Primitive Culture* (1923), in which he stressed the similarities rather than the differences between people in different societies; and *The Problem of Noise* (1934).

Frederic Bartlett *(Syndics of Cambridge University Library)*

The work for which Bartlett is best known is *Remembering* (1932), an elaboration of his research on conventionalization. In it he describes how he used two experimental paradigms to study memory: the method of repeated reproduction, in which a participant studied a story or a picture and then reproduced it several times over a period of weeks or months; and the method of serial reproduction, in which a participant recalled a story or a picture, then passed this production on to a second participant, who studied it, and so on down a chain of participants. Bartlett observed that the two methods yielded similar results: Recall was not duplicative but represented a reconstruction of the original story or picture based on memories of key details; the reconstruction could be biased by conventionalization and importation.

Given the fact that recall was not simply a duplication of the same pattern over and over again, Bartlett, following the suggestion of his neurologist friend Henry Head, argued that memories were not stored as static traces waiting to be revived; instead they formed parts of large complexes, called schemata, in which individual components could be changed any time there was a retrieval act. He argued that if traces were lifeless entities waiting to be revived, we should always be at the mercy of old habits; but with a schema one could revive individual memories that had been laid down at widely varying periods of time and from them form new combinations. He believed that consciousness had evolved for this purpose, the "looking at" or "turning round on" one's own schemata; the ability to do this was greatly aided by the use of visual images in addition to speech memory.

This insight could not be gained, argued Bartlett, from studies of rote memory along the lines of Hermann Ebbinghaus's experiments; further, the schema theory allowed closer ties to be formed between experimental psychology and social psychology. Schemata, he believed, were linked by "appetites, instincts, interests, and ideals," the first two laid down particularly in childhood, the latter two in later life. At the end of the twentieth century memory researchers still used the word *schema*, though some criticisms had been raised about Bartlett's terms *schema* and *reconstruction* (reviewed in Zangwill, 1972; Zangwill preferred the term *abstraction*).

Bartlett was made a fellow of the Royal Society in 1932, the year *Remembering* was published. His later career was mainly devoted to applied psychology. He was director of the Applied Psychology Unit at Cambridge from 1944 to 1953; he was appointed to the order of Commanders of the British Empire in 1941; and he was knighted in 1948. His best-known work during this period concerned fatigue states following extended periods of skilled work. His book *The Mind at Work and Play* (1951) is unusual in that it was intended for a juvenile audience. In *Thinking* (1958) he discussed the development of the schema theory as an example of scientific thinking. He died on September 30, 1969.

Bibliography

Bartlett, F. C. (1923). *Psychology and primitive culture.* London: Cambridge University Press.
—— (1925). Feeling, imaging, and thinking. *British Journal of Psychology 16,* 16–28.
—— (1927). *Psychology and the soldier.* London: Cambridge University Press.
—— (1932; reprint 1964). *Remembering: A study in experimental and social psychology.* London: Cambridge University Press.
—— (1934). *The problem of noise.* London: Cambridge University Press.
—— (1936). Autobiography. In C. Murchison, ed., *History of psychology in autobiography,* Vol. 3. Worcester, MA: Clark University Press.
—— (1937). Cambridge, England: 1887–1937. *American Journal of Psychology 50,* 97–110.
—— (1951). *The mind at work and play.* London: Allen and Unwin.
—— (1958). *Thinking: An experimental and social study.* London: Allen and Unwin.
Broadbent, D. E. (1970). Obituary of Sir F. C. Bartlett. *Biographical Memoirs of Fellows of the Royal Society 16,* 1–16.
Crampton, C. (1978). *The Cambridge school: The life, works, and influence of James Ward, W. H. R. Rivers, C. S. Myers, and Sir Frederic Bartlett.* Ph.D. diss., University of Edinburgh, Scotland.

Harris, A. D., and Zangwill, O. L. (1973). The writings of Sir Frederic Bartlett, C.B.E., F.R.S.: An annotated handlist. *British Journal of Psychology 64*, 493–510.

Saito, A., ed. (1999). *Bartlett: Culture and cognition*. New York: Routledge.

Zangwill, O. L. (1972). *Remembering* revisited. *Quarterly Journal of Experimental Psychology 24*, 123–138.

David J. Murray

BASAL FOREBRAIN

See: AMNESIA, ORGANIC; GUIDE TO THE ANATOMY OF THE BRAIN

BASAL GANGLIA

See: GUIDE TO THE ANATOMY OF THE BRAIN

BEHAVIORISM

Most generally, behaviorism is a viewpoint that takes psychological phenomena as physical activity rather than as belonging to a special domain of mental events. For a behaviorist, then, psychology is the study of behavior and its physical, mainly environmental, determinants rather than of the nature of experience or of mental process. Behaviorism originated in natural-science traditions of the late nineteenth century, and precursors of its methods and concepts developed at the turn of the century in the work of E. L. Thorndike and Russian physiologist I. P. Pavlov, as well as of several other psychologists and physiologists (Day, 1980; Herrnstein, 1969).

But behaviorism as a distinct viewpoint came to be recognized with the publication of American psychologist John B. Watson's article "Psychology as the Behaviorist Views It" (1913). Identification of behaviorism with the controversial Watson persists despite the fact that it developed into several distinct traditions that bear only a family resemblance to Watson's views and to each other (Malone, 1990; Zuriff, 1985). The leading contemporary behaviorist position derives from the work of B. F. Skinner, which differs from other behaviorisms in its detailed account of verbal functioning and in its inclusion of activities such as thinking and feeling as behavior to be accounted for, while maintaining a primary focus on behavior-environment relations rather than upon processes inferred as underlying those relations.

Behaviorism originated in opposition to an orthodox psychology that attempted to analyze conscious experience by focusing upon reports by observers who were trained to examine their own mental functions through techniques of introspection. Watson boldly rejected this, asserting that behavior, per se, is the proper domain of psychology. For Watson, prediction and control of overt behavior, rather than introspection of mental processes, formed the basis for an objective, scientific psychology. Behavior was to be analyzed into stimulus-response (S-R) units without appeal to hypothetical activities of brain or mind. The units could be of widely varying size, from the relatively molecular eyeblink elicited by a flash of light to the more "molar" shopping trip as response to an empty cupboard. Watson emphasized the continuity between human and nonhuman species, and he stressed the importance of learning, in animals as well as in humans, as the fundamental basis for understanding psychological process.

A neobehaviorism that came to the fore in the 1930s, that of Clark L. Hull and his student Kenneth Spence, dominated until mid-century. Like Watson, Hull described behavior as composed of S-R units, but whereas Watson had presented S-R analyses as adjustable in scale, the Hull-Spence approach focused on molecular building blocks that were described as forming chains of connecting events between environmental stimuli and observed behavior. These mediating events included hypothetical (but presumably physical) stimulus traces, covert responses, and response-produced stimuli. Learned S-R units were called habits. Hull contrived an elaborate theory whose theorems and postulates, presented in geometer's style, were concerned with the formation of habit strength and with the mechanistic conversion of habit strength into overt action. The theory was published as essentially complete in 1943. Although highly touted, it proved ponderous, with numerous terms that were difficult to evaluate; it fell of its own weight within a decade. Nevertheless, Hullian students gained dominant positions within academic psychology, and elements of that approach can be discerned to this day in theorizing that rests on the metaphor of mechanical associative connections. Hull's emphasis on formal hypothesis testing, directed at hypothetical constructs that are anchored to observable events as specified by operational definitions, also survives as a "methodological behaviorism" (Skinner, 1945) that has permeated much of psychology.

A counterpoint to Hull's views in the 1930s and 1940s was provided by Edward C. Tolman, who attempted to include purposive, intentional language within a behavioristic system. He invoked terms like *purpose, expectation,* and *cognition* to capture the larger-scale, goal-oriented "molar" organization of behavior. Tolman asserted that these terms need not imply anything nonphysical or mentalistic; indeed, he employed them in accounting for behavior of laboratory rats as well as of humans. But Tolman undermined such disclaimers by characterizing his view as S-O-R theory, with the "O" denoting a special role for processes within the behaving organism. The learning of complex relationships, often characterized as "cognitive maps," was said to mediate between environment and behavior. Critics of Tolman's account suggested that it left the organism "buried in thought." To the extent that he addressed the sources of action, Tolman placed them within the organism, which tended to link his account with traditional mentalistic explanations of action. Thus it is not surprising that Tolman's inclusion of intentional language never was accepted by the broader behavioristic community.

B. F. Skinner also departed from the S-R behavioral mainstream of the 1930s and 1940s, but in different ways. He rejected mentalistic terms as "misleading fictions" while including the relationships that were Tolman's primary concern. Skinner's first conceptual innovation was to reformulate the reflex; he described this simplest unit of behavior not as stimulus-response connection but as directly observable abstraction, a correlation between classes of stimuli and classes of responses. Then he distanced his theory further from mediational notions of mechanism and associative connection by delineating non-reflexive behavioral units that he called operants. Operants act upon the environment; they are selected by their consequences through processes denoted as *reinforcement, punishment,* and *extinction.* Operants can range from small to large, and are defined by the consequences that shape or maintain them but also by the contexts within which the selecting consequences have occurred. The result is a three-term relationship composed of classes of responses, consequences, and discriminative stimuli.

Operant behavior often is characterized in ordinary language as intentional and purposive, thus having the "molar" characteristics that were Tolman's primary concern. But the traditional appeal to mentalistic intention is replaced by environment-based selection in this account of action, just as in Darwinian biology natural selection replaces divine intention in the account of new species. Learning of new behavior is readily demonstrated by rapidly shaping new patterns through differential reinforcement and through gradual fading of discriminative stimuli. In later work, Skinner (1984) described selectionist principles as applying to behavior patterns at the evolutionary level as well as at the level of cultural practice, giving accounts with close affinity to contemporary work in anthropology (e.g. Lloyd, 1985) and biology (Dawkins, 1982; Smith, 1986).

While his theory also included other principles, Skinner emphasized reinforcement as a basic rela-

tion, examining its properties and its broad implications. Empirically, he asked what would happen if only some occurrences of a response are reinforced; he devised schedules of reinforcement to explore the many ways in which this can happen and their effects on rates, patterning, and persistence of behavior. Contemporary research has extended this to examine issues such as the conditions of self-control and preferences among schedules that are relevant to microeconomics (e.g., Rachlin, 1989) and to biological theories of foraging (e.g., Fantino and Abarca, 1985). Interpretatively, Skinner addressed the functional characteristics of verbal behavior, describing how an individual affects the behavior of others and how others teach the individual's verbal discriminations (Skinner, 1957). His approach initially was not welcomed by linguists, but later developments in linguistics are more congenial to it (Andresen, 1990). The analysis includes activities like thinking, feeling, and even introspecting as behavior to be accounted for rather than as special bases for explaining overt action. It asserts that individuals know their private thoughts and feelings less well than they know external events, because the world cannot as accurately teach individuals to discriminate the former (Skinner, 1963). This provocative position gains independent support from the philosophies of Ryle (Schnaitter, 1985) and Wittgenstein (Day, 1969).

Skinner also addressed ethical and social issues in light of reinforcement-based principles, speculatively in *Walden Two,* a utopian novel that sketches an experimental approach to communal living, and analytically in essays such as "The Ethics of Helping People" (Skinner, 1978), which asserts that human rights properly concern empowerment of effective action rather than access to things or services. Extensive discussions of these and other implications of reinforcement theory are provided by Skinner (1971, 1974), and by Catania and Harnad (1988). Contemporary behavioral research related to language emphasizes relationships between verbal and nonverbal behavior (Cerutti, 1989; Hayes, 1989) and issues such as the nature and origins of symbolic functioning (Sidman, 1986).

Of contemporary approaches, the most distinctly behavioral one is behavior analysis. Extending from Skinner's work, it differs philosophically and conceptually from other behaviorisms as well as from mainstream psychology (Lee, 1988). Its pragmatic contributions have proved effective in such diverse settings as health-maintenance programs concerned with weight control, smoking, and wearing of automobile seat belts; "frequent flier" marketing techniques launched by airlines; techniques for basic research on drug addiction as well as for its treatment; educational techniques of documented effectiveness for handicapped and disadvantaged, as well as for mainstream, children (Becker, 1978; Wolf et al., 1987); and innovative formats for personalized instruction at the college level (Keller, 1977). Contemporary behaviorists are represented by professional organizations that include several thousand researchers, scholars, and practitioners (Thompson, 1988) whose work is represented by more than a score of primarily behavioral journals (Wyatt et al., 1986). Thus, behaviorism has extended well beyond, while continuing an appositional role within, the specialized field where it began.

See also: OPERANT BEHAVIOR; SKINNER, B. F.; TOLMAN, EDWARD C.

Bibliography

Andresen, J. T. (1990). Skinner and Chomsky thirty years later. *Historiographia Linguistica 17*, 145–165.

Becker, W. C. (1978). The national evaluation of follow-through: Behavior theory-based programs come out on top. *Education and Urban Society 10*, 431–458.

Catania, A. C., and Harnad, S. (1988). *The selection of behavior, the operant behaviorism of B. F. Skinner: Comments and consequences.* New York: Cambridge University Press.

Cerutti, D. T. (1989). Discrimination theory of rule-governed behavior. *Journal of the Experimental Analysis of Behavior 51*, 257–276.

Dawkins, R. (1982). *The extended phenotype.* San Francisco: Freeman.

Day, W. F. (1969). On certain similarities between the *Philosophical investigations* of Ludwig Wittgenstein and the operationism of B. F. Skinner. *Journal of the Experimental Analysis of Behavior 12*, 489–506.

—— (1980). The historical antecedents of contemporary behaviorism. In R. W. Rieber and K. Salzinger, eds., *Psychology: Theoretical-historical perspectives*, pp. 203–262. New York: Academic Press.

Fantino, E., and Abarca, N. (1985). Choice, optimal foraging, and the delay–reduction hypothesis. *Behavioral and Brain Sciences 8*, 315-362.

Hayes, S. C., ed. (1989). *Rule-governed behavior: Cognition, contingencies, and instructional control.* New York: Plenum.

Herrnstein, R. J. (1969). Behaviorism. In D. L. Krantz, ed., *Schools of psychology: A symposium*, pp. 51–68. New York: Appleton-Century-Crofts.

Hull, C. L. (1943). *Principles of behavior.* New York: Appleton-Century-Crofts.

Keller, F. S. (1977). *Summers and sabbaticals: Selected papers on psychology and education.* Champaign, IL: Research Press.

Lee, V. (1988). *Beyond behaviorism.* Hillsdale, NJ: Erlbaum.

Lloyd, K. E. (1985). Behavioral anthropology: A review of Marvin Harris's *Cultural materialism. Journal of the Experimental Analysis of Behavior 43*, 279–287.

Malone, J. C. (1990). *Theories of learning: A historical approach.* Belmont, CA: Wadsworth.

Rachlin, H. (1989). *Judgment, decision, and choice: A cognitive/behavioral synthesis.* New York: W. H. Freeman.

Schnaitter, R. (1985). The haunted clockwork: Reflections on Gilbert Ryle's *The concept of mind. Journal of the Experimental Analysis of Behavior 43*, 145–153.

Sidman, M. (1986). Functional analysis of emergent verbal classes. In T. Thompson and M. D. Zeiler, eds., *Analysis and integration of behavioral units*, pp. 213–245. Hillsdale, NJ: Erlbaum.

Skinner, B. F. (1938). *The behavior of organisms: An experimental analysis.* New York: Appleton-Century-Crofts.

—— (1945). The operational analysis of psychological terms. *Psychological Review 52*, 270–277, 291–294.

—— (1948). *Walden two.* New York: Macmillan.

—— (1957). *Verbal behavior.* New York: Appleton-Century-Crofts.

—— (1963). Behaviorism at fifty. *Science 134*, 566–602.

—— (1971). *Beyond freedom and dignity.* New York: Knopf.

—— (1974). *About behaviorism.* New York: Knopf.

—— (1978). *Reflections on behaviorism and society.* Englewood Cliffs, NJ: Prentice-Hall.

—— (1984). Selection by consequences. *Science 213*, 501–504.

Smith, T. L. (1986). Biology as allegory: A review of Elliott Sober's *The nature of selection. Journal of the Experimental Analysis of Behavior 46*, 105–112.

Thompson, T. (1988). Benedictus behavior analysis: B. F. Skinner's magnum opus at fifty. *Contemporary Psychology 33*, 397–402.

Tolman, E. C. (1932). *Purposive behavior in animals and men.* New York: Appleton-Century-Crofts.

Watson, J. B. (1913). Psychology as the behaviorist views it. *Psychological Review 20*, 158–177.

—— (1919). *Psychology from the standpoint of a behaviorist.* Philadelphia: J. B. Lippincott.

Wolf, M. M., Braukmann, C. J., and Ramp, K. A. (1987). Serious delinquent behavior as part of a significantly handicapping condition: Cures and supporting environments. *Journal of Applied Behavior Analysis 20*, 347–359.

Wyatt, W. J., Hawkins, R. P., and Davis, P. (1986). Behaviorism: Are reports of its death exaggerated? *The Behavior Analyst 9*, 101–105.

Zuriff, G. E. (1985). *Behaviorism: A conceptual reconstruction.* New York: Columbia University Press.

Philip N. Hineline

BEHAVIOR THERAPY

Behavior therapy is a term used to describe a number of therapeutic procedures that share certain assumptions about the nature of behavioral and psychological problems and how they can best be overcome. The procedures can be classified into three main groups: fear-reduction procedures, operant conditioning procedures, and aversive techniques.

The major fear-reduction procedures consist of *systematic desensitization*, in which the person is trained to imagine a series of increasingly fearful images while in a state of relaxation; *therapeutic modeling*, in which the person observes and then imitates a therapist model engaging in increasingly close contact with the frightening object or situation; and *flooding*, in which the phobic person is exposed to intensely fearful stimulus situations for prolonged periods. In all of these methods, the phobic person is exposed to the real or imagined fear stimulus repeatedly and/or for prolonged periods, and in all of them attempts to escape from or avoid the fear stimulus are discouraged (*response prevention*). The combination of exposure and response prevention has proved to be a robust and dependable means for reducing fear, and the clinical efficacy of this combination in each of the three forms of fear-reduction procedures has been confirmed in numerous controlled clinical trials (Marks, 1987; O'Leary and Wilson, 1987).

All three methods can be traced back to the work of the Russian physiologist Ivan Petrovich Pavlov on conditioning, and especially to his research on experimental neurosis. In developing the first of the modern methods, systematic desensitization, Wolpe (1958) was influenced by the writings of Pavlov and the modern learning theorists, especially Clark Hull. Having rejected the psychodynamic approach, Wolpe attempted to apply modern learning techniques to psychological problems, particularly those in which anxiety is prominent. After completing a series of animal experiments, he concluded that graded, gradual re-exposures to a fearful stimulus are the best way to weaken or eliminate the fear. He also concluded that the fear-reduction process can be facilitated by the deliberate superimposition on the evoked fear response of a competing incompatible response (such as relaxation imposed on a fear response). Each occasion on which an incompatible response is imposed over the fear response is an instance of reciprocal inhibition. Wolpe argued that repeated instances of such reciprocal inhibition give rise to a relatively permanent form of conditioned inhibition (of fear), and that the therapeutic effects are a direct consequence of the reciprocal inhibition.

Desensitization is the earliest and best-established of the methods, but Wolpe introduced a number of other therapeutic procedures. Most attention, however, has been devoted to desensitization, which has been the subject of considerable experimental work and testing. This research advanced the therapeutic efficacy of these results and gave rise to a fresh view of fear itself.

Additions to and improvements of the clinical techniques were introduced in the early 1970s, and for certain types of anxiety disorders (such as panic disorder, agoraphobia, obsessional disorders, simple phobias), therapeutic modeling replaced desensitization as the method of choice. In most cases, therapeutic modeling and flooding are carried out *in vivo,* an unfortunately chosen term that here means exposure to the fear stimulus rather than to an imagined representation of the stimulus (as in the desensitization procedure). The development of therapeutic modeling, largely the result of Bandura's work (1969), consists of repeated exposures to the fear stimulus. The phobic person first watches and then imitates the approach behavior of a therapeutic model. The method is effective and well accepted by most subjects, clients, and patients. Flooding is seldom the first choice of treatment but can be used in certain cases such as extensive obsessional/compulsive problems. Systematic

desensitization remains useful for numerous problems, especially those in which direct exposure is impractical or unacceptable, as in the treatment of certain sexual disorders and social phobias.

All of the fear-reduction techniques are applications of learning procedures to clinical problems, and, in common with the other forms of behavior therapy, are based on the assumption that most psychological problems can be overcome by the use of conditioning or other learning processes. In the early stages of behavior therapy, it was assumed that most psychological problems are the result of faulty learning (for instance, "Symptoms are unadaptive responses" and "Symptoms are evidence of faulty learning" [Eysenck and Rachman, 1965, p. 12]). Furthermore, it was argued that problems that are the result of faulty learning can be unlearned. In due course, more complex explanations were substituted.

The second form of behavior therapy, consisting of the application of *operant conditioning* ideas and procedures to clinical problems, was engineered in the United States and applied mainly to the psychological problems of children and adults with severe handicaps (e.g., mentally retarded people in or out of institutions and people with chronic and serious psychiatric disturbances, especially chronic schizophrenia). The fear-reduction techniques, developed mainly in Britain, are still used predominantly in dealing with adult neurotic problems, especially anxiety disorders such as obsessional disorders, panic disorders, social phobias, and circumscribed phobias.

The clinical application of operant conditioning later referred to as *reinforcement therapy* was a direct application of Skinnerian ideas, with emphasis on the consequences of behavior. Behavior that is followed by a reward will be strengthened and behavior that is followed by nonreward will be weakened.

The first application consisted of a series of attempts to treat schizophrenic problems in laboratory settings, but only limited success was achieved until the methods were applied, often with considerable ingenuity, to the maladaptive behavior of institutionalized patients with chronic psychiatric disorders (e.g., Ayllon and Azrin, 1968). Notable advances were made by the selective reinforcement of desirable behavior (e.g., self-care, eating) and the withholding of (social) reinforcement after undesirable behavior. Many of these useful advances were later incorporated into an institutional program that Ayllon and Azrin, two pioneers of this work, called the *token economy* (exchangeable tokens having replaced tangible rewards). The fact that the large ambitions of the earlier workers who expected reinforcement therapy to eliminate these psychiatric problems were never achieved does not detract from the contribution that this form of therapy continues to make. It is widely used to modify the maladaptive behavior of retarded children and adults, patients with chronic psychiatric disorders, children with speech or other behavioral deficits, and in educational settings.

Aversion therapy is a direct application of Pavlovian conditioning to appetitive but maladaptive behavior such as the excessive use of alcohol and was originally prompted by the discovery that laboratory animals can develop conditioned nausea reactions to the stimuli that are associated with the administration of drugs that induce nausea. In order to convert the aberrant stimuli (such as inappropriate sexual stimuli or alcohol) into conditioned stimuli for nausea or other unpleasant responses, the alcohol or sexual stimuli are contingently followed by aversive stimulation. The earlier and still most common form of aversion therapy consists of pairing an alcohol-conditioned stimulus with aversive nausea induced by drugs. This form of chemical aversion therapy is used mainly in the treatment of alcoholism; the other technique, *electrical aversion therapy*, in which the aversive stimulus is an electric shock, is used mainly in the treatment of aberrant sexual behavior such as pedophilia. Although aversion therapy appears to make a useful contribution to dealing with alcohol and sexual problems, it is rarely sufficient and nowadays is used as part of a wider therapeutic program that typically includes counseling, group therapy, and family therapy. This insufficiency, the ethical problems involved in the deliberate application of aversive stimuli, and the fact that the precise nature of the conditioning processes involved in aversion therapy is not fully understood have combined to limit its use.

The other two forms of behavior therapy also have their limitations, so clinicians have been receptive to the growing influence of cognitive analyses of psychological and clinical phenomena. Behavior therapy has been expanded to include the influence of cognitive factors, and most practitioners now favor *cognitive behavior therapy*, which combines the original forms of behavior therapy with cognitive analyses of the problem and cognitive procedures for helping to deal with them. Cognitive behavior therapy appears to have achieved most success in the treatment of depression (Beck, 1976; O'Leary and Wilson, 1987).

Bibliography

Ayllon, T., and Azrin, N. (1968). *The token economy.* New York: Appleton.

Bandura, A. (1969). *Principles of behavior modification.* New York: Holt.

Beck, A. (1976). *Cognitive therapy and the emotional disorders.* New York: International University Press.

Eysenck, H., and Rachman, S. (1965). *The causes and cures of narcosis.* London: Routledge and Kegan Paul.

Marks, I. (1987). *Fears, phobias, and rituals.* Oxford: Oxford University Press.

O'Leary, K., and Wilson, G. T. (1987). *Behavior therapy,* 2nd edition. Englewood Cliffs, NJ: Prentice-Hall.

Rachman, S. (1990). *Fear and courage,* 2nd edition. New York: W. H. Freeman.

Wolpe, J. (1958). *Psychotherapy by reciprocal inhibition.* Stanford, CA: Stanford University Press.

Stanley J. Rachman

BIRDSONG LEARNING

Song behavior refers to complex vocalizations used in the context of mate attraction and territorial defense. Birds that produce such sounds are commonly called songbirds. Technically songbirds constitute species in the avian order Passeriformes. This is by far the largest avian order and contains about half of the more than 9,000 living bird species. The songbird order, one of the most recently evolved, includes familiar avian groups such as sparrows, swallows, starlings, canaries, finches, warblers, jays, titmice, crows, wrens, robins, and buntings. This order can be further divided into two suborders, the Oscines (members of the suborder Passeres) and the sub-Oscines (a much smaller group that includes the flycatchers of North America), which appeared earlier in evolutionary history and is thought to be more primitive. All songbirds produce complex vocalizations, but there do appear to be qualitative differences between Oscine species and sub–Oscine species in vocal development and in the neural substrate mediating vocal learning and production.

The Basics of Birdsong

All songbirds have a repertoire of up to twenty or so distinct vocal sounds that they use for communication about danger, food, sex, group movements, and for many other purposes. One can usually make a distinction between a bird's calls, which are usually brief and monosyllabic, and its songs, which are more extended patterns of sound and often tonal and melodic. The decision to classify a vocalization as a song or a call is usually based on the perceived function. The main functions that have been ascribed to song behavior are territory defense (or spacing behavior) and mate attraction, as opposed to calls, which are involved in such functions as signaling danger or food and maintaining flock cohesion. Songs, especially among songbird species in the temperate zone, are usually produced by males. Among tropical species females as well as males often sing. In some species, males and females sing a coordinated song that is known as a duet.

Unlike most calls, songs are learned: They develop abnormally if a young male is reared out of hearing of the sounds of adults (see Figure 1). Among spe-

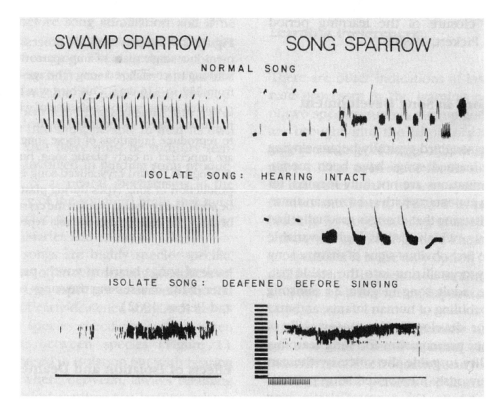

Figure 1. Sound spectrograms of six songs, each about two seconds in duration of male swamp sparrows and song sparrows. Two songs in the top row are typical songs heard in nature, two songs in the middle row were developed by males reared in isolation from adult song, and two songs in the bottom row are songs of males deafened at twenty days of age. Frequencies are marked at 500 hertz intervals. The time marker is 0.5 second. *(Peter Marler)*

cies in the songbird order only the Oscines clearly learn their songs; in the few sub-Oscine species investigated song learning does not appear to occur thus providing a natural comparison between closely related species that vary in one key aspect of their vocal behavior. A common consequence of this dependence on learning among Oscines is the emergence of local song dialects, varying on much the same geographic scale as dialects in human speech. These dialect boundaries have been shown to serve as imperfect barriers for gene flow in species such as the white-crowned sparrow indicating that this intraspecific geographic variation is meaningful (MacDougall-Shackleton and MacDougall-Shackleton, 2001).

Songbirds are unique among animals in the many analogies that can be struck between song learning and the acquisition of human speech (Doupe and Kuhl, 1999). Avian vocal development provides one of the few tractable animal models for studying the behavioral, hormonal, and neural bases of vocal plasticity (Ball and Hulse, 1998). No known nonhuman primate depends upon learning to develop its natural vocal repertoire. Other than humans, cetaceans and perhaps some bats are the only mammals that appear to rely on learning for vocal development. The avian groups known to have learned songs include hummingbirds, parrots, and all Oscine songbirds.

Sensitive Periods and the Timing of Song Learning

There is an underlying pattern in the steps typically required in learning to sing. First is the acquisition phase, when a bird hears songs and commits some to memory. These are stored for a period that varies in duration from species to species—from days to months—until the bird begins to recall songs from memory and starts to produce imitations, sometimes faithful to the original model, sometimes far different. Thus there is a separation in time between the acquisition or sensory phase and the production or sensorimotor phase, ending with the production of crystallized, adult song (Marler, 1997).

There are often sensitive periods for song acquisition, sometimes restricted to a short period early in life, and sometimes extending into adulthood. Even close relatives, such as sparrows and canaries, may differ in this respect. Several species of sparrows have a sensitive period for acquiring songs beginning at about twenty days of age, soon after young males become independent from their parents, and ending four to six weeks later (Nelson, 1997). Such sensitive periods for learning are variable within limits, depending on the strength of song stimulation and the influence of physiological factors, such as hormonal states, that vary with the season. If young are hatched late in the season and singing has already ceased for that year, closure of the sensitive period may be delayed until the following spring. The experimental withholding of stimulation by songs of the birds' own species can also delay closure of the learning (Kroodsma and Pickert, 1980; Baptista and Gaunt, 1997). Species that learn song only during a sensitive period early in ontogeny are known as age-limited learners. Species that continue to learn new songs throughout their lives (such as canaries and European starlings) are referred to as age-independent learners. In addition, there are species that fall in between these extreme cases in terms of song development.

Effects of Isolation and Deafness

Regardless of whether or not they have had the chance to learn, songbirds can always produce some aspects of the normal song of their species. When sparrows are raised in isolation, for example, the note structure and tonal quality of their songs is abnormal, but each species still produces some basic features of normal song "syntax" (see Figure 1). These features are produced irrespective of whether they were represented in any songs a male may have learned.

Insight into the basis of this ability to produce certain normal song features is gained by studying the songs of deaf birds, which are highly abnormal and variable in structure (see Figure 1). This degraded form of singing is observed both if a male becomes deaf before song stimulation and if he is deafened after song stimulation but before the development of singing. There seems to be no internal brain circuitry that makes memorized songs directly available to guide motor development. To transform a memorized song into a produced song, the bird must be able to hear its own voice. One can infer that there are auditory memories for song, involved in guiding song production, conceived of as neural mechanisms in the auditory circuitry of the songbird brain that must vary in their specifications from species to species (Konishi, 1965; Marler, 1997).

The Nature of the Auditory Memory Guiding Song Learning

One aspect of the process of memory formation needed for song learning is that it involves "selective" or "guided" learning. In several sparrow species, for example, species-typical vocalizations appear to be privileged because they are learned preferentially. Such preferences have even been observed for specific subspecies (Nelson, 2000). Another aspect of this memory, strongly advocated by Peter Marler and colleagues, is that the memory encodes species-typical patterns of vocal behavior even before it hears the song of its own species. This idea of an innate specification of species-typical vocalizations would be one way to explain why even in isolated-reared sparrows many species-typical attributes of their vocalizations are still apparent in the abnormal songs produced by these birds. According to this view of song learning, the formation of the auditory memory guiding song learning would result from a memorization by selective activation and attrition of innate circuits rather than from a selective instruction process (Marler, 1997). Researchers have not yet resolved the relative validity of these two opposing models of auditory memory formation.

Song Overproduction, Social Interactions, and Action-Based Learning

The young male songbird typically begins singing sometime after he has memorized learned songs, but the imitations are not fully formed. Instead, the young male starts with subsong, an amorphous, noisy twittering that changes gradually, first into plastic song, which also is highly variable but contains the first obvious signs of mature song structure, finally crystallizing into the stable patterns of mature, adult song (see Figure 2). Subsong resembles the babbling of human infants and may be important for developing the motor skills of singing and other prerequisites for song learning, such as the ability to guide the voice by the ear. Rehearsal of previously memorized song patterns begins in plastic song. Often more plastic song themes are produced than are needed for mature singing (see Figure 3), and many are discarded when song crystallization occurs. Interactions between a male and his neighbors can influence which of the overproduced songs will be selected for crystallization and inclusion into the final repertoire (Nelson, 1997). Songs most similar to the neighbor's songs are retained; those that are different are rejected. It is as if a process akin to operant conditioning influences which songs are selected for later crystallization among those in auditory memory. Marler and Douglas A. Nelson (1993) refer to this process as "action-based" learning to contrast it with "memory-based" learning. The latter refers to cases where crystallized songs are produced in reference to previously formed memories independently of social interactions during the sensorimotor period.

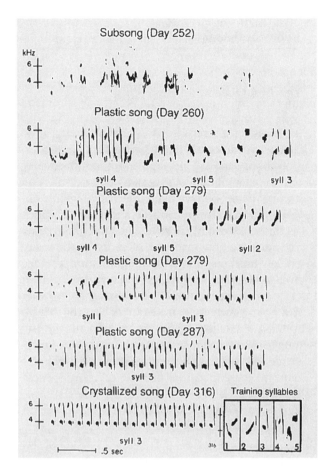

Figure 2. Samples from the process of song development in a single male swamp sparrow ranging from subsong to crystallized song. The age of the bird ranges from 252 to 316 days. This bird was trained with tape-recorded songs, syllables of some of which are indicated in the box insert. As indicated by the labels, early efforts to reproduce imitations of these songs months later are imperfect in early plastic song, but they improve as progress toward crystallized song is made. The overproduction of song types during plastic song can also be seen. The two song types in the crystallized song can also be seen. The two-song type in the crystallized repertoire of this male consisted of syllable types 2 and 3. *(Peter Marler)*

The Song System

A discrete set of brain areas discovered by F. Nottebohm (Nottebohm, 1996), often called the song system, controls song learning and production. The song system suggests a possible location for the neural changes associated with song learning. The song system consists of numerous interconnected nuclei and occupies a relatively large volume of brain (see Figure 4). The brain area nXIIts (the tracheosyringeal portion of the hypoglossal nucleus) contains the motor neurons that control the musculature of the bird's vocal organ, the syrinx. The pathway from Nif (the nucleus interface) through HVc (or high vocal center) to RA (the robust nucleus of the archistriatum) and then to nXIIts constitutes a motor pathway specialized for song production. RA also projects to brainstem areas controlling respiration, which needs to be coordinated with song (Wild, 1997). The anterior forebrain song nuclei lMAN (the lateral part of the magnocellular nucleus of the anterior neostriatum) and area X, as well as the thalamic nucleus that interconnects them, DLM (the medial portion of the dorsolateral nucleus of the thalamus), form a second pathway connecting HVc to RA. All of the song nuclei are present bilaterally, and the thalamic song nucleus Uva (the uvaeform nucleus) forms a connection between the two sides.

The presence of a song system is particularly associated with the learning of song, not just with song production. These brain areas are found only in birds that sing and that learn their song by reference to auditory information. For example, sub-Oscine songbirds that do not learn their vocalizations do not seem to have telencephalic song nuclei such as HVc or RA. The vast majority of vocal learners are Passerine songbirds, but evolutionarily unrelated species that are vocal mimics, such as parrots or hummingbirds, which require conspecific learning to produce their complex vocalizations, are also found to have forebrain structures resembling nuclei in the song system including HVc and RA (Jarvis and Mello, 2000; Jarvis et al., 2000; Gahr, 2000).

A Motor Pathway for Song

Evidence for a specialized motor pathway for song comes from three sources. Behavioral studies show that lesions of HVc, RA, or the hypoglossal nerve cause severe disruption of adult song. Also, electrophysiological recordings in Nif, HVc, and RA of awake birds reveal neurons whose activity is highly correlated with singing (Yu and Margoliash, 1996). These data indicate a hierarchy in motor processing with activity in HVc correlated with syllable production and activity in RA correlated with note production (Yu and Margoliash, 1996). Nif may be the birdsong pattern generator, because section of the tract from Nif to HVc destroys the patterning of song, while lesions of Uva do not (McCasland, 1987). Motor-driven immediate early gene induction also occurs in nuclei such as HVc and RA in that song production is correlated with such induction in deaf birds induced to sing (Jarvis and Nottebohm, 1997).

The song motor commands must ultimately be translated into a pattern of syringeal muscle activation and respiratory control. The output nucleus of the song system, nXIIts, has a map of the muscles of the syrinx: All motor neurons projecting to a particular syringeal muscle are clustered together in discrete

Figure 3

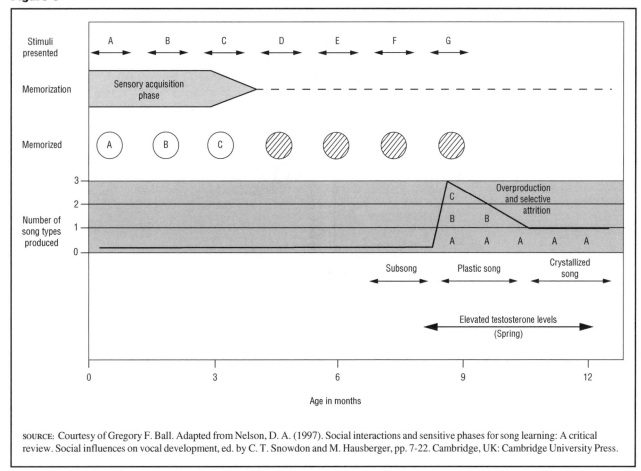

SOURCE: Courtesy of Gregory F. Ball. Adapted from Nelson, D. A. (1997). Social interactions and sensitive phases for song learning: A critical review. Social influences on vocal development, ed. by C. T. Snowdon and M. Hausberger, pp. 7-22. Cambridge, UK: Cambridge University Press.

Diagram illustrating the process of song development in the male swamp sparrow. The horizontal axis represents the bird's age from hatching in months; the successive rows in the vertical axis represent the different processes involved in establishing the adult crystallized song and how these processes were experimentally investigated. A male successively exposed to different song types at various ages (top row, A through G) will only memorize song types presented during the sensory acquisition phase. After a period of subsong during which no song type is recognizable, the bird will start producing during the period of plastic song all song types that were stored in memory. Selective attrition will then take place, in part as a consequence of social interactions with neighbors, and crystallized adult song will then only include one or two selected song types.

zones within the motor nucleus. RA also has zones of premotor neurons that project to the corresponding muscle control area in nXIIts. The dorsal portion of RA does not project to nXIIts but to the dorsomedial nucleus (DM) of the midbrain, an area thought to be involved in vocalization and respiration in all birds, including nonsongbirds (see Figure 4; Vicario, 1991). Neurons in DM then project to nXIIts, suggesting that RA has two parallel and perhaps functionally different inputs to the syringeal motor neurons.

Intrabronchial measurements of both airflow and sound from each syringeal side have clarified how the syrinx functions to produce sound (Suthers, Goller, and Pytte, 1999). The syrinx contains two separate sound sources, each with an independent motor control. There is extensive species variability in how these two separate sources are used to produce a species-typical vocalization. Thus initial claims that control of song production is lateralized similarly to speech production is an oversimplification. It seems that asymmetries in syringeal control when they do occur reflect a peripheral asymmetry rather than a hemispheric specialization, as is the case in humans.

Song-Selective Auditory Pathways and Feedback Mechanisms

Because auditory feedback is used to correct vocal motor output during song learning, there must be a link between the auditory system and the vocal motor pathway. In addition, there must be brain mechanisms for very specific recognition of song and song-like vocalizations. Auditory information is relayed to

Figure 4

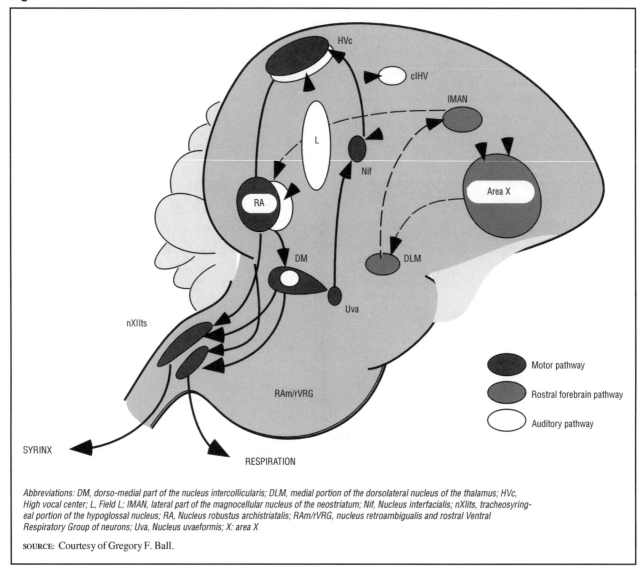

Abbreviations: DM, dorso-medial part of the nucleus intercollicularis; DLM, medial portion of the dorsolateral nucleus of the thalamus; HVc, High vocal center; L, Field L; IMAN, lateral part of the magnocellular nucleus of the neostriatum; Nif, Nucleus interfacialis; nXIIts, tracheosyring-eal portion of the hypoglossal nucleus; RA, Nucleus robustus archistriatalis; RAm/rVRG, nucleus retroambigualis and rostral Ventral Respiratory Group of neurons; Uva, Nucleus uvaeformis; X: area X

SOURCE: Courtesy of Gregory F. Ball.

Schematic representation of the song system in Oscines. The diagram illustrates many of the known nuclei and connections in the song system. Different fill patterns have been used to highlight nuclei that are part of the motor pathway (black), the anterior forebrain pathway mostly involved in song learning (cross-hatching) and the parts of the auditory pathway that convey auditory information to nuclei of the song system (white).

the songbird forebrain as in all other birds, traveling from the cochlear nuclei through the thalamus to the forebrain primary auditory area, Field L. Anatomical experiments show that subdivisions of Field L projects to the vicinity of HVc and RA (Vates, Broome, Mello, and Nottebohm, 1996; see Figure 4). However, electrophysiological investigations also suggest that auditory information gains access to HVc via Nif (Janata and Margoliash, 1999). Field L projects to the caudolateral ventral hyperstriatum (clHV) that in turn projects to Nif (Vates, Broome, Mello, and Nottebohm, 1996). In addition to song-related motor neurons, HVc also contains neurons that respond to

auditory stimuli. Some of these HVc auditory neurons are song-selective: They respond best of all to the bird's own song, even in comparison with very similar songs of conspecifics (Margoliash, 1986). HVc song-selective neurons are also sensitive to temporal order: They are activated more strongly by the bird's own song when the syllables are in the normal sequence than when the identical song components are played out of order or in reverse. This high degree of selectivity in individual neurons provides a possible mechanism for specific recognition of song. Because the bird's own song is learned during development, this song selectivity must also be learned. In fact, studies in young birds have shown that these neurons acquire their specificity during sensorimotor learning.

Lesion studies have shown that the anterior forebrain pathway containing MAN and X (see Figure 4) plays an important role in song learning but is not an essential part of the motor pathway for song in the adult. Lesions of MAN or X have no apparent effect on adult song production, but destruction of either of these areas in young birds results in markedly abnormal song (Bottjer and Johnson, 1997). There are song-selective auditory neurons, similar to those in HVc, in every nucleus in this loop—X, DLM, and MAN. Like the neurons in HVc, these auditory neurons acquire their song selectivity in parallel with song acquisition. If the syrinx is selectively dennervated prior to the sensorimotor phase of song learning, male zebra finches in many cases are unable to match their vocal output to the tutor's song (Solis and Doupe, 2000). In such birds, many neurons in area X exhibited a dual selectivity and responded equally well to the bird's own song and to the tutor song. The degree of selectivity for these stimuli as compared to conspecific song or reversed song was considerably less than in normal adults (Solis and Doupe, 2000).

One possible function of this song-selective auditory pathway is to act as a correction signal provided by auditory feedback for the learning of song and the maintenance of learned song. There is evidence that the delayed auditory feedback can cause a gradual deterioration of adult zebra finch song (Leonardo and Konishi, 1999). Deafening adult male zebra finches also results in a deterioration of song (Nordeen and Nordeen, 1992). However, lesioning a nucleus in the anterior forebrain pathway such as lMAN prevents the deterioration in song resulting from deafening (Brainard and Doupe, 2000). These findings suggest that an active process is required for the maintenance of song and that the anterior forebrain pathway is essential to this process.

The song-selective auditory loop from HVc to the anterior forebrain eventually projects back into the motor pathway through its connection to RA (see Figure 4). This convergence of auditory and motor inputs makes RA a possible site for the auditory guidance of vocal motor development during learning. The NMDA subclass of glutamate receptors is thought to play a role in some forms of synaptic plasticity. NMDA receptor-mediated EPSCs (NMDA-EPSCs) become fast during song development, a transition posited to limit learning. However, manipulations of the sensitive period for song learning by isolating nestling zebra finches delayed NMDA-EPSCs but did not prevent the birds from learning (Livingston, White, and Mooney, 2000). Thus song learning did not require slow NMDA-EPSCs at synapses critical for song development.

The Development of the Song System, Hormonal Effects, and Sex Differences in Brain and Behavior

It is a striking feature of the song system that it continues to develop after hatching, during song learning. Administration of 3H-thymidine can be used to label neurons undergoing their last cell division, or "birthdate." Such birthdating of song nuclei shows that MAN and RA are "born" before hatching, but that there is significant neurogenesis in HVc and X in the first several months after hatching (Alvarez-Buylla and Kirn, 1997). There is also naturally occurring cell death during postnatal development. In male zebra finches, many MAN neurons die around five weeks after hatching. Synaptic connectivity continues to develop at these late stages. The motor projection from HVc reaches its target nucleus RA by postnatal day fifteen, but then "waits" outside RA for about ten days before growing in and completing the circuit (Konishi and Akutagawa, 1985). Interestingly, male zebra finches first begin to sing at the time of ingrowth of HVc axons into RA. Connections from HVc to MAN via X and DLM are present and functional by day fifteen, but topographic features of the projection from lMAN to RA occur at days twenty to twenty-five during the early stages of vocal learning. Timing of this projection is delayed if juvenile birds are deprived of normal conspecific auditory experience (Iyengar and Bottjer, 2002).

Bird song can vary among the sexes. Typically in temperate zone species, male birds sing for courtship and territorial defense, while female birds sing much less or not at all. In the tropics the pattern is quite different: males and females often stay together on territories all year round, and both sexes will sing to defend these territories. The behavioral dimorphism between males and females has a striking correlate in the sexual dimorphism of the song system itself. Initial studies of species the exhibit extreme differences in song behavior: For example, zebra finches and canaries revealed marked male-biased differences between males and females (Nottebohm and Arnold, 1976). Nottebohm and Arnold's discovery provided an opportunity to explore sex differences in the brain in a truly comparative sense. Comparative studies have been employed to understand the function of these sex differences in the brain (see Figure 5). In some songbird species, females sing rarely or not at all, and the brain nuclei that control song are many times larger in volume in males than in females. In other species, males and females sing approximately equally, and the brain nuclei that control song are ap-

Figure 5

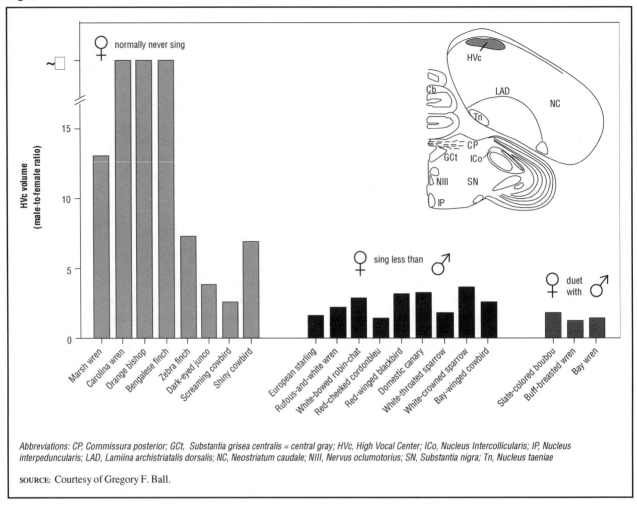

Abbreviations: *CP, Commissura posterior; GCt, Substantia grisea centralis = central gray; HVc, High Vocal Center; ICo, Nucleus Intercollicularis; IP, Nucleus interpeduncularis; LAD, Lamiina archistriatalis dorsalis; NC, Neostriatum caudale; NIII, Nervus oclumotorius; SN, Substantia nigra; Tn, Nucleus taeniae*

SOURCE: Courtesy of Gregory F. Ball.

Interspecific variations in the volumetric sex difference of the song control nucleus HVc in songbirds and their relationship with the sex difference in singing behavior. The figure illustrates the ratio of the HVc volume in males and females in species where the female normally never sings (very large HVC in males compared to females), where females sing but less than males (intermediate ratio of HVc volumes), and where females sing about as often as males (duetting species, ratio of HVc volumes is close to 1). The volume ratio in three species of the first group has been indicated as approximately infinite (≈∞) because HVc cannot be detected in females.

proximately equal between the sexes. Recently statistical methods have been employed control for phylogenetic effects while comparing the coevolution of traits. This analysis indicates that the evolution of sex differences in song has coevolved with the evolution of sex differences in singing behavior in songbird species (Figure 5; MacDougall-Shackleton and Ball, 1999). It is unclear whether these morphological differences related to variation in song are just related to differences in production or if differences in song learning also occur. Sex differences in volume in nuclei such as HVc and RA are associated with differences in cell size and cell number. Other attributes of the phenotype of cells in these nuclei are different in males and females, such as the number of cells expressing androgen receptors.

Steroid hormones influence both singing and the song system. Singing is much increased when androgen levels are high, for instance during the breeding season in the spring. In several songbird species, there is also a seasonal variation in the size of the song nuclei (Tramontin and Brenowitz, 2000). In canaries, where researchers first described this trait, HVc and RA enlarge by approximately 50 percent in the spring (Nottebohm, 1981). These seasonal changes in volume involve changes in cell size and cell number (Tramontin and Brenowitz, 2000). These seasonal morphological changes were initially thought to be related to seasonal changes in song learning but current data support the notion that the changes are more closely related to seasonal changes in song performance (Tramontin and Brenowitz, 2000). In some species, such as canaries and white-crowned sparrows, adult females will respond to the administration of testosterone by beginning to sing and rapidly going through the sensorimotor phase of learning. These injections also induce marked growth of the song nuclei. The effects of testosterone in stimulating these cellular changes in HVc are mediated at least in part via the upregulation of brain-derived neurotrophic factor, or BDNF (Rasika, Alvarez-Buylla, and Nottebohm, 1999). Interestingly, there is also evidence that BDNF is released in HVc in response to singing itself. Thus testosterone can promote morphological changes in HVc by acting directly on cells in that nucleus or by acting elsewhere in the brain (such as the preoptic area) to induce increased singing behavior that results in increased BDNF in HVc (Ball, Riters, and Balthazart, 2002).

The influence of sex steroids on the development of the song system has been extensively studied in zebra finches, where the differences between the male and female song systems are especially pronounced (see Figure 5). Female zebra finches have very small and shrunken song nuclei and, unlike canaries, do not respond with song to testosterone administration in adulthood. If given estrogen early in life, however, female zebra finch chicks develop masculinized song nuclei (Schlinger, 1998). Based on many studies of zebra finches, researchers are clear that this differentiation process that occurs early in ontogeny is not the result of sex differences in gonadal steroid hormone action as is the case in the mammalian brain and in other aspects of sexually dimorphic behaviors in birds (Schlinger, 1998). Rather, it is either the result of estrogen synthesized by the brain acting early in ontogeny to masculinize the system (Holloway and Clayton, 2001) or of sex differences in gene expression in the brain that is triggered independently of the gonad.

Another unusual feature of the songbird brain and avian brains in general is that neurogenesis continues to occur in portions of the periventricular zone in adult birds, and these newly generated neurons migrate out into the forebrain and are incorporated into the neural circuitry. Some of these neurons in HVc project to RA (Alvarez-Buylla and Kirn, 1997). Researchers are not clear, however, what significance this phenomenon has for song learning. The new neurons occur throughout the forebrain, in females as well as males. They are found in one-time learners such as zebra finches as well as in open-ended learners like canaries, and even in nonsongbirds. Nonetheless, this phenomenon suggests that adult birds retain a remarkable ability to generate new neurons as well as a preservation of the cues for axon guidance and neuronal specification in their brains.

Vocal learning early in development during the sensory phase is associated with prominent cellular and synaptic changes. There is a neural reorganization that includes massive synaptogenesis associated with the incorporation of new neurons into the vocal pathways. Behavioral evidence clearly implicates NMDA receptor activation in specific song nuclei as being required for song learning (Basham, Nordeen, and Nordeen, 1996). However, scientists have yet to identify the precise cellular events that occur developmentally that mediate song learning rather than the maturation of the song system.

Conclusion

Bird song is a complex motor behavior that is learned by matching vocal output to an auditory memory. This memory has an innate component but is also modified by experience early in ontogeny. In some species, only songs learned early in life are produced in adulthood. In other species, learning continues throughout adult life. Birds tend to learn more songs than will be used throughout adult life, and these are selected based on social interactions among conspecifics in the area they settle.

A specialized neural circuit has evolved in association with the occurrence of song learning. This circuit contains nuclei primarily involved in motor production or in the auditory feedback needed for the learning and maintenance of song. Neurons within this circuit appear to be feature detectors that exhibit highly selective response to conspecific song. The selectivity of these neurons develops in parallel with song learning. The morphology of the song system varies between males and females in a systematic fashion among different species that reflects species-variability in song behavior. Steroid hormones regulate these sex differences as well as the striking seasonal plasticity in adulthood. Songbirds exhibit adult neurogenesis that contributes to the unusual adult plasticity. Scientists have described cellular changes in synaptogenesis and neuronal incorporation that correlate with song learning. This system will continue to be a valuable model for the investigation of the neurobiology of species-typical learning.

See also: IMPRINTING; NEUROGENESIS

Bibliography

Alvarez-Buylla, A., and Kirn, J. R. (1997). Birth, migration, incorporation, and death of vocal control neurons in adult songbirds. *Journal of Neurobiology 33,* 585–601.

Ball, G. F., and Hulse, S. H. (1998). Bird song. *Am. Psych. 53,* 37–58.

Ball, G. F., Riters, L. V., and Balthazart, J. (2002). Neuroendocrinology of song behavior and avian brain plasticity: Multiple sites of action of sex steroid hormones. *Frontiers in Neuroendocrinology 23,* 137–178.

Baptista, L. F., and Gaunt, S. L. L. (1997). Social interactions and vocal development in birds. In C. T. Snowdon and M. Hausberger, eds., *Social influences on vocal development*. Cambridge, UK: Cambridge University Press.

Basham, M. E., Nordeen, E. J., and Nordeen, K. W. (1996). Blockade of NMDA receptors in the anterior forebrain impairs sensory acquisition in the zebra finch (Poephila guttata). *Neurobiol. Learn. Mem. 66*, 295–304.

Bottjer, S. W., and Johnson, F. (1997). Circuits, hormones, and learning: Vocal behavior in songbirds. *Journal of Neurobiology 33*, 602–618.

Brainard, M. S., and Doupe, A. J. (2000). Interruption of a basal ganglia-forebrain circuit prevents plasticity of learned vocalizations. *Nature 404*, 762–766.

Doupe, A. J., and Kuhl, P. K. (1999). Birdsong and human speech: Common themes and mechanisms. *Annual Review of Neuroscience 22*, 567–631.

Gahr, M. (2000). Neural song control system of hummingbirds: Comparison to swifts, vocal learning (songbirds) and nonlearning (suboscines) passerines, and vocal learning (budgerigars) and nonlearning (dove, owl, gull, quail, chicken) nonpasserines. *Journal of Comparative Neurology 426*, 182–196.

Holloway, C. C., and Clayton, D. E. (2001). Estrogen synthesis in the male brain triggers development of the avian song control pathway in vitro. *Nature Neuroscience 4* (2), 170–175.

Iyengar, S., and Bottjer, S. W. (2002). The role of auditory experience in the formation of neural circuits underlying vocal learning in zebra finches. *Journal of Neuroscience 22* (3), 946–958.

Janata, P, and Margoliash, D. (1999). Gradual emergence of song selectivity in sensorimotor structures of the male zebra finch song system. *Journal of Neuroscience 19*, 5,108–5,118.

Jarvis, E. D., and Mello, C. V. (2000). Molecular mapping of brain areas involved in parrot vocal communication. *Journal of Comparative Neurology 419*, 1–31.

Jarvis, E. D., and Nottebohm, F. (1997). Motor-driven gene expression. *Proceedings of the National Academy of Sciences of the United States of America 94*, 4,097–4,102.

Jarvis, E. D., Ribeiro, S., Da Silva, M. L., Ventura, D., Vielliard, J., and Mello, C. V. (2000). Behaviourally driven gene expression reveals song nuclei in hummingbird brain. *Nature 406*, 628–632.

Konishi, M., and Akutagawa, E. (1985). Neuronal growth, atrophy and death in a sexually dimorphic song nucleus in the zebra finch brain. *Nature 315*, 145–147.

Leonardo, A., and Konishi, M. (1999). Decrystallization of adult birdsong by perturbation of auditory feedback. *Nature 399* (6,735), 466–470.

Livingston, F. S., White, S. A., and Mooney, R. (2000). Slow NMDA-EPSCs at synapses critical for song development are not required for song learning in zebra finches. *Nature Neuroscience 3*, 482–488.

MacDougall-Shackleton, E. A., and MacDougall-Shackleton, S. A. (2001). Cultural and genetic evolution in mountain white-crowned sparrows: Song dialects are associated with population structure. *Evolution 55* (12), 2,568–2,575.

MacDougall-Shackleton, S. A., and Ball, G. F. (1999). Comparative studies of sex differences in the song-control system of songbirds. *Trends in Neuroscience 22*, 432–436.

Margoliash, D. (1986). Preference for autogenous song by auditory neurons in a song system nucleus of the white-crowned sparrow. *Journal of Neuroscience 6*, 1,643–1,661.

Marler, P. (1997). Three models of song learning: Evidence from behavior. *Journal of Neurobiology 33*, 501–516.

Marler, P., and Nelson, D. A. (1993). Action-based learning: A new form of developmental plasticity in bird song. *Netherlands Journal of Zoology 43* (1–2), 91–103.

McCasland, J. S. (1987). Neuronal control of bird song production. *Journal of Neuroscience 7*, 23–39.

Mooney, R., and Konishi, M. (1991). Two distinct inputs to an avian song nucleus activate different glutamate receptor subtypes on individual neurons. *Proceedings of the National Academy of Sciences of the United States of America 88*, 4,075–4,079.

Nelson, D. A. (1997). Social interactions and sensitive phases for song learning: A critical review. In C. T. Snowdon and M. Hausberger, eds., *Social influences on vocal development*. Cambridge, UK: Cambridge University Press.

—— (2000). A preference for own-subspecies' song guides vocal learning in a song bird. *Proceedings of the National Academy of Sciences of the United States of America 97* (24), 13,348–13,353.

Nordeen, K. W., and Nordeen, E. J. (1992). Auditory feedback in necessary for the maintenance of stereotyped song in adult zebra finches. *Behavioral and Neural Biology 57*, 58–66.

Nottebohm, F. (1981). A brain for all seasons: Cyclical anatomical changes in song-control nuclei of the canary brain. *Science 214*, 1,368–1,370.

—— (1996). The King Solomon lectures in neuroethology: A white canary on Mount Acropolis. *Journal of Comparative Neurophysiology A. 179*, 149–156.

Nottebohm, F., and Arnold, A. P. (1976). Sexual dimorphism in the vocal control areas in the song bird brain. *Science 194*, 211–213.

Rasika, S., Alvarez-Buylla, A., and Nottebohm, F. (1999). BDNF mediates the effects of testosterone on the survival of new neurons in an adult brain. *Neuron 22*, 53–62.

Schlinger, B. A. (1998). Sexual differentiation of avian brain and behavior: Current views on gonadal hormone-dependent and independent mechanisms. *Annual Review of Physiology 60*, 407–429.

Solis, M. M., and Doupe, A. J. (2000). Compromised neural selectivity for song in birds with impaired sensorimotor learning. *Neuron 25* (1), 109–121.

Suthers, R. A., Goller, F., and Pytte, C. (1999). The neuromuscular control of birdsong. *Philosophical Transactions of the Royal Society of London [Biol.] 354*, 927–939.

Tramontin, A. D., and Brenowitz, E. A. (2000). Seasonal plasticity in the adult brain. *TINS 23*, 251–258.

Vates, G. E., Broome, B. M., Mello, C. V., and Nottebohm, F. (1996). Auditory pathways of caudal telencephalon and their relation to the song system of adult male zebra finches (Taenopygia guttata). *Journal of Comparative Neurology 366*, 613–642.

Vicario, D. S. (1991). Organization of the zebra finch song control system II: Functional organization of outputs from nucleus Robustus archistriatalis. *Journal of Comparative Neurology 309*, 486–494.

Wild, J. M. (1997). Neural pathways for the control of birdsong production. *Journal of Neurobiology 33*, 653–670.

Yu, A. C., and Margoliash, D. (1996). Temporal hierarchical control of singing in birds. *Science 273*, 1,871–1,875.

Peter R. Marler
Allison J. Doupe
Revised by Gregory F. Ball and Jacques Balthazart

BLOCKING

See: CONDITIONING, CELLULAR AND NETWORK SCHEMES FOR HIGHER-ORDER FEATURES OF; KAMIN'S BLOCKING EFFECT: NEURONAL SUBSTRATES

C

CAJAL, RAMÓN Y SANTIAGO

See: RAMÓN Y CAJAL, SANTIAGO

CATEGORIES

See: CONCEPTS AND CATEGORIES, LEARNING OF

CEREBELLUM

See: GUIDE TO THE ANATOMY OF THE BRAIN; NEURAL COMPUTATION

CEREBRAL NEOCORTEX

See: GUIDE TO THE ANATOMY OF THE BRAIN

CHILDREN, DEVELOPMENT OF MEMORY IN

Memory improves dramatically as children develop. The first section of this entry describes the factors that contribute to improved memory during childhood and adolescence. With this general developmental profile as a backdrop, several special topics in children's memory are discussed in the remainder of the entry.

How Memory Develops During Childhood and Adolescence

Two factors play a critical role in the development of memory during childhood and adolescence: greater use of strategies and greater task-relevant knowledge.

Developmental Change in Use of Memory Strategies

A strategy is any deliberate act that is designed to improve retention. One common strategy is rehearsal, in which people spontaneously repeat (either aloud or silently) information to be remembered. As children grow they are more likely to use strategies to help them remember. Rehearsal, for example, typically emerges at about six or seven years of age. In addition, as children and adolescents develop, they tend to abandon simple but relatively ineffective strategies in favor of complicated but more effective strategies. In the case of rehearsal, school-age children often simply repeat the information exactly as it was presented. In contrast, older children and adolescents are more likely to modify their rehearsal as necessary to fit the nature of the material. Instead of repeating words in the order presented, older children and adolescents may reorganize the words, rehearsing together words that are related semantically.

The general trend for children to use strategies more often and more effectively as they grow apparently reflects parallel developmental changes in children's ability to diagnose memory tasks and to monitor the effectiveness of their chosen strategy. That is,

Figure 1

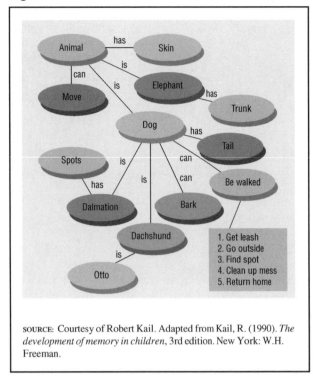

SOURCE: Courtesy of Robert Kail. Adapted from Kail, R. (1990). *The development of memory in children*, 3rd edition. New York: W.H. Freeman.

A representation of a portion of a person's knowledge of animals.

young children often underestimate the difficulty of memory problems, and consequently may underestimate the need for a strategy to remember effectively. Also, young children are less likely than older children to realize that a strategy is not working and should be abandoned for a better strategy (Kail, 1990).

Knowledge and Memory

As children develop, they acquire more and more knowledge of their worlds. Such understanding is an important aid to memory. To explain the impact of knowledge on memory, psychologists represent a person's knowledge as a network like the one shown in Figure 1. This network consists of nodes (the ellipses) linked by different types of associations: *isa* links denote category membership; *can* and *has* denote properties of the node.

Knowledge like that depicted in Figure 1 can aid memory because it provides special codes that simplify memorization. To illustrate, suppose that people were asked to remember a list of words like *collie, terrier, Dalmatian, poodle*. In this case, the category name *dogs* serves as a code for the list. People can recall the category name, then scan memory for words associated with that name and decide if they were presented. Thus, one benefit of children's growing knowledge is that they are more likely to be able to provide a code that reduces the amount of material that must be remembered.

Another way that children's growing knowledge benefits memory is by providing more retrieval cues. Each of the links in Figure 1 provides an alternative way, a cue, to gain access to a word that was presented. Thus, the more links the better. When people are expert in some domain, their knowledge will be linked extensively. If they know little, their knowledge will have relatively few links. Consequently, older children and adolescents will typically have more cues available to recall information than will younger children.

Knowledge is not always beneficial, because it can distort memories. Information to be remembered is often changed so that it conforms to one's existing knowledge or stereotypes. To illustrate, when children hear stories in which superheroes are said to be weak or ugly, they tend to recall the heroes as strong and attractive. Similarly, if asked to remember the actions of boys and girls whose behaviors violate sex-role stereotypes (e.g., a girl sawing wood), children will change the sex of the actor to make it consistent with sex-role knowledge.

Special Topics

The remainder of this entry considers three special topics: origins of memory, children's eyewitness testimony, and working memory.

Origins and Early Development of Memory

Most methods used to study memory in children and adolescents cannot be used with infants because they require speaking or writing. Consequently, the study of infants' memory became possible only after psychologists devised techniques that took advantage of infants' abilities to respond in other ways. One approach is to show a stimulus to an infant; immediately thereafter, the infant is shown the same stimulus with a novel stimulus. Infants typically look longer at the novel stimulus, behavior possible only if they remember the one stimulus from its original presentation. Newborns tested on novelty-preference tasks look longer at novel stimuli, indicating that some form of memory is functional at birth.

In another method used to assess infants' memory, a mobile is placed over an infant's crib and a ribbon connects the infant's leg to the mobile. Infants kick vigorously just a few minutes after their leg is connected to the mobile, demonstrating that they have learned the relation between their kicking and the mobile's movement. To study infant memory, time is allowed to pass, then the infant's leg is reconnected to the mobile. If the infant immediately begins to kick vigorously, then the infant apparently has remembered the relation between his or her kicking and the mobile's movement. If, instead, kicking gradually becomes more vigorous—as if the infant is relearning the relation—then the infant has forgotten the relation.

Research based on techniques like these has demonstrated that by the age of three months infants will remember the link between kicking and the moving mobile for up to fourteen days. That is, when an infant's leg is reconnected to the mobile within fourteen days of the original learning, the infant will kick vigorously, without the need to relearn the relation. When a sufficiently long interval had elapsed such that infants no longer kick (i.e., they apparently have forgotten that kicking moves the mobile), a cue helps infant to remember. If the experimenter moves the mobile for the infant, who is later connected to the mobile with the ribbon, the infant will again kick, apparently signifying that the infant remembers the link between kicking and the moving mobiles. Thus, experiments show that three important features of memory exist as early as two and three months of age: an event from the past is remembered; over time, the event can no longer be recalled; and a cue can serve to dredge up a memory that seems to have been forgotten (Rovee-Collier, 1999).

Both of these memory tasks demonstrate that infants are able to recognize events experienced previously. Other methods are used to assess recall, which refers to retrieving from memory a representation of a past experience that is not currently perceptible (e.g., remembering what one had for dinner yesterday). With older children and adults, recall is usually assessed by having people describe verbally what happened in the past. This method is not appropriate for infants and toddlers with limited language; instead, researchers have relied upon imitation tasks. An experimenter demonstrates novel actions with simple toys; the toys are then presented to children—either immediately or after a delay—and children are encouraged to play with the toys. Accurate imitation of the actions is taken as evidence of recall memory, particularly when children reproduce multiple actions in the correct order.

Research with this method has revealed several important features of early recall memory. First, recall emerges at about nine months: At this age infants can imitate novel events after seeing them modeled once. Second, the amount of information that children can recall immediately—defined as the number of actions from the sequence that are reproduced accurately—increases steadily from two actions at eleven months of age to eight actions at thirty months of age. Third, with development, children can recall events over increasingly large intervals, from four weeks at thirteen months of age to one year at twenty months of age. Fourth, infants and toddlers recall more accurately when they experience events more than once and when they actively participate in the events (e.g., imitate the actions once before the delay).

Children's Eyewitness Testimony

Memory for past events is particularly important when children are asked to provide eyewitness testimony, as they sometimes are in cases of child abuse (Bruck and Ceci, 1999). Although children, even three- to five-year-olds, can remember past events accurately, many commonly used legal procedures can lead children to confuse what actually happened with what others suggest may have happened. This is especially true when interviewers are biased—that is, when interviewers believe they know what happened and use questioning to attempt to confirm these beliefs. The typical result is a highly suggestive interviewing technique that is unlikely to help children recall events accurately. For example, interviewers often ask misleading questions (e.g., ones that imply events happened when they may not have happened) or ask the same question repeatedly (implying that the child's previous answers were wrong); both procedures increase the chances that a child will describe events that never happened.

One particularly controversial practice is the use of anatomically correct dolls to aid children's recall. Many professionals are strong advocates of these dolls, claiming that they improve memory by overcoming children's embarrassment over talking about private events or by overcoming their ignorance of the names of body parts. In fact, research indicates that the use of anatomically correct dolls increases the number of false reports, apparently because the examiner's description of the dolls implicitly encourages children to create stories about body parts.

To improve the reliability of children's testimony, they should not be questioned repeatedly on a single issue and they should be warned that interviewers may sometimes try to trick them (e.g., suggest things that didn't happen). In addition, interviewers should be neutral in their questioning and evaluate alternative explanations of a particular event and who was involved.

Working Memory

Working memory denotes a cognitive structure that includes ongoing information processing as well as the data required for those processes. According to one widely accepted view (Baddeley, 1992), working memory includes a central executive as well as two separate subsystems for storing verbal and spatial information. To measure working memory, investigators often ask people to remember information while concurrently performing other processing tasks. Participants may be asked to read sets of sentences and concurrently remember the last word from each sentence in the set. Testing begins with one or two sentences (hence, participants must remember one or two sentence-ending words) and continues until participants are no longer able to recall the sentence-ending words in the correct sequence. Assessed in this manner, working memory increases substantially during childhood and adolescence.

Researchers have identified the causes and consequences of age-related change in working memory. Regarding the causes, age-related changes in working memory are due primarily to age-related increases in the speed with which children can execute basic cognitive processes. As children develop, their processing speed increases, which allows them to execute the various updating functions of working memory more rapidly. For example, more rapid processing speed results in more rapid rehearsal and more rapid retrieval of items in working memory.

Regarding the consequences, age-related change in working memory contributes to improved reasoning and problem solving during infancy, childhood, and adolescence. That is, in the course of reasoning and solving problems, individuals must remember task elements and coordinate task-relevant operations, which are functions attributable to working memory. Consequently, as the capacity of working memory increases with age, children have more resources available to storing and processing operations during reasoning and problem solving, resulting in improved performance (Kail, 2002). Thus, as children develop, they process information more rapidly, which allows them to use working memory more effectively. This, in turn, produces improved reasoning and problem solving.

Conclusion

Memory improves during childhood and adolescence, due to age-related increases in use of memory strategies and age-related increases in knowledge. Recognition and recall are both evident in the first year of life. Young children can recall past events accurately during legal proceedings, but biased interviewers may alter children's testimony. Working memory increases with age and contributes to age-related improvement in reasoning and problem solving.

See also: AMNESIA, INFANTILE; CODING PROCESSES: ORGANIZATION OF MEMORY; EARLY

EXPERIENCE AND LEARNING; FALSE MEMORIES; INFANCY, MEMORY IN; WORKING MEMORY: HUMANS

Bibliography

Baddeley, A. (1992). Working memory. *Science 255,* 556–559.
Bruck, M. B., and Ceci, S. J. (1999). The suggestibility of children's memory. *Annual Review of Psychology 50,* 419–439.
Kail, R. (1990). *The development of memory in children,* 3rd edition. New York: W. H. Freeman.
——— (2002). Information processing and memory. In M. Bornstein, L. Davidson, C. L. M. Keyes, K. A. Moore, and The Center for Child Well-Being, eds., *Well-being: Positive development across the life course.* Mahwah, NJ: Erlbaum.
Rovee-Collier, C. (1999). The development of infant memory. *Current Directions in Psychological Science 8,* 80–85.

Robert V. Kail
Revised by Robert V. Kail and Meghan Saweikis

CLASSICAL CONDITIONING: BEHAVIORAL PHENOMENA

Classical conditioning involves learning the relations between stimuli. In its simplest form, a neutral stimulus precedes a stimulus (the unconditioned stimulus, or US) that elicits a response (the unconditioned response, or UR). Learning is indexed by the development of a response (the conditioned response, or CR) to the neutral stimulus (which is now a conditioned stimulus, or CS). The interval between the onset of the CS and the onset of the US is called the interstimulus interval (ISI). Stimuli that can become CSs may be discrete or more contextual, and they need not even be external (Bouton, Mineka, and Barlow, 2001). Responses to stimuli (both CRs and URs) may be as simple as an eye blink or more complex, such as approach and withdrawal. Originally thought to be due simply to contiguity between the CS and US, modern conceptions of learning in classical conditioning emphasize that the CS must provide information about the US, and that the CR is both elicited by the CS and anticipates the US.

Excitatory Classical Conditioning

In excitatory procedures, the CS signals that a US will follow. Learning is indexed by the probability, magnitude, and latency of CRs to the CS. In the *delay* procedure, CS onset precedes US onset and the CS remains on when the US is delivered. In the *trace* procedure, CS onset precedes US onset but the CS terminates before the US is delivered, leaving an empty "trace" interval between CS and US. Evidence suggests that CS offset, as well as the CS itself, may elicit CRs in the trace procedure. Kehoe and Weidemann (1999) tested rabbits in eyeblink conditioning using a tone CS and a corneal air puff US in a trace procedure. Typically, longer CS-US intervals slow conditioning relative to shorter CS-US intervals. However, across CS-US intervals of 400 milliseconds to thirty seconds, the learning rate was similar, as long as the interval between CS offset and the US was held constant at 400 milliseconds.

Another procedure for producing excitatory conditioning is the *discrimination* procedure. In simple discrimination conditioning, two CSs that differ along some dimension are used. One CS is always followed by the US (CS+) whereas the other CS is never followed by the US (CS–). Typically, CRs develop to both CSs initially, and then decline to the CS–. This procedure is thought to produce both an excitatory CS (CS+) and an inhibitory CS (CS–, discussed further below). A more complicated type of discrimination is *occasion setting*. In occasion setting, one CS is used. Another stimulus (the occasion setter) signals whether the CS will be paired or unpaired on a particular trial. This occasion setter is not considered a CS because it does not appear to form a direct association with the US. An example of this procedure, in which a contextual stimulus served as the occasion setter, is provided by Rogers and Steinmetz (1998). In that study, a flashing chamber light was the occasion setter. Whenever the flashing chamber light was on, the context was lit and a tone CS was followed by a corneal air puff US. Whenever the flashing chamber light was off, the context was darkened, and the same tone CS was not followed by the US. Rabbits learned CRs when the chamber was lit and suppressed CRs when the chamber was darkened. The light or dark chamber by itself cannot elicit CRs, so it is not a CS. Rather, the state of the context served to modulate the development of CRs to the tone CS.

Inhibitory Classical Conditioning

In inhibitory procedures, the CS signals that a US will not follow. It is important to note that an inhibitory CS, like an excitatory CS, provides information about the US. Thus, a US must be present somewhere in the conditioning situation for inhibitory conditioning to occur. This is in contrast to latent inhibition (discussed under "Stimulus Preexposure," below). The fact that a US must be present somewhere in the conditioning situation means that some other stimulus in the conditioning situation, either discrete or contextual, becomes a conditioned excitor.

A number of procedures are thought to be able to produce inhibitory CSs. The most common procedure was originally used by Ivan Pavlov (1927). In Pavlov's *conditioned inhibition* procedure, two CSs are used. On some trials, one of the CSs is paired with a US (CS1-US trials) and becomes a conditioned excitor. On other trials, the two CSs are presented simultaneously (CS1/CS2-alone trials) and no US is presented. The CS that is never paired with the US (CS2) becomes a conditioned inhibitor. Another common procedure for producing inhibitory CSs is the discrimination procedure, in which one CS (CS+) is followed by the US and the other CS (CS–) is not. In this case, CS+ becomes excitatory and CS– becomes inhibitory.

Because conditioned inhibition involves the suppression of CRs, which renders them unobservable, special tests have been developed to detect conditioned inhibition (Rescorla, 1969). In the retardation test, the potential inhibitory CS, when paired with a US, must take longer to elicit CRs than a new CS in order to be considered a conditioned inhibitor. In the *summation test*, the potential inhibitory CS is presented simultaneously with an excitatory CS. If fewer CRs are observed to this compound than to the excitatory CS alone, the test CS is considered a conditioned inhibitor.

Unlike the widespread acceptance of excitatory associations between a CS and US (but see Gallistel and Gibbon, 2000, for an alternative), inhibitory associations have been controversial (Savastano, Cole, Barnet, and Miller, 1999). The most common view has been that inhibitory associations are simply the opposite of excitatory associations (Rescorla and Wagner, 1972). In this view, a single continuum for association exists, ranging from positive (excitatory) to negative (inhibitory). Other researchers have proposed two separate continuums, one for excitatory associations and the other for inhibitory associations (Pearce and Hall, 1980). These two continuums oppose each other and the presence or absence of CRs is a reflection of this opposition. Finally, Miller and Matzel (1988) have developed a model of classical conditioning in which inhibitory associations do not exist at all, and the presence or suppression of CRs is determined by the inequality of excitatory associations for different stimuli.

Stimulus Preexposure

Exposure to the stimuli by themselves prior to classical conditioning can change the rate at which these stimuli become CSs. The most well-studied example of stimulus preexposure involves preexposure to the CS, or latent inhibition (Lubow and Moore, 1959). In contrast to a new CS, a preexposed CS that is subsequently paired with a US will come to elicit CRs only slowly. Because no US is present during preexposure, the CS does not provide information on either the presence or absence of the US during preexposure and, therefore, forms neither an excitatory nor an inhibitory association. Rather, the preexposed CS is thought to undergo a loss of salience, and is treated as irrelevant.

Schmajuk, Lam, and Gray (1996) developed a detailed neural network model in which latent inhibition is explained by a reduction in the ability to store and retrieve CS-US associations. Preexposure to a CS reduces both attention to and the magnitude of the representation of that CS. During subsequent CS-US pairings, less attention to the CS slows the storage of an excitatory CS-US association and a less intense representation slows the ability of the CS to elicit retrieval of the CS-US association.

Cue Competition

Multiple stimuli may be paired with a US, but not all of them will develop the ability to elicit a CR. Consider two CSs presented simultaneously and followed by a US. If the CSs are similar in salience, each of the CSs will acquire the ability to elicit a CR when presented separately. However, if the CSs differ greatly in salience (for example, a bright light and a soft tone), only one of the two CSs will come to elicit CRs. The more salient CS is said to *overshadow*, or disrupt, the formation of an association between the less salient CS and the US. This phenomenon demonstrates that mere contiguity of a CS and a US is not always enough to produce an association between them.

The insufficiency of contiguity between a CS and a US for learning in classical conditioning was forcefully demonstrated by Kamin (1969). Kamin's procedure, which is known as *blocking*, involves three phases. In phase 1, a CS is paired with a US (CS1-US trials) until it becomes a strong conditioned excitor. In phase 2, the excitatory CS is presented in compound with a new CS, and the entire compound is paired with a US (CS1/CS2-US trials). In phase 3, the two CSs are tested separately (CS1-alone and CS2-alone trials) for the ability to elicit a CR. The typical result is that CRs occur only to the CS used in phase 1 (CS1). This demonstrates that a CS must provide new information about the US in order to form an association with it. Mere contiguity between a CS and a US is not sufficient for classical conditioning.

Contextual cues may contribute to the blocking effect. In essence, it has been proposed that the CS and the context in phase 1 form a combined association with the US and this combined association blocks learning to the other CS in phase 2. Giftakis and Tait (1998) tested rabbits using a tone CS, a flashing light CS, and a periorbital shock US. Rabbits given several sessions of exposure to the context alone between phases 1 and 2, which serves to extinguish any context-US association, showed less blocking than rabbits that did not receive context-alone exposure. In addition, rabbits shifted to a different context between phases 1 and 2 also showed less blocking than rabbits training in the same context in phases 1 and 2.

CR Timing

In classical conditioning, a US elicits a UR and a CS comes to elicit a CR. However, the CR is not just elicited by the CS. In addition, the CR is made in anticipation of the US. In many classical conditioning procedures, such as eyeblink conditioning, this anticipation takes the form of precise timing of the CR to occur just before the onset of the US.

There are several ways to demonstrate timing of CRs. The simplest method is *ISI shift*. In an ISI-shift procedure, training initially occurs at one CS-US interval. When the CS-US interval is lengthened or shortened, the latency of CRs to the CS lengthens or shortens to coincide with the new CS-US interval. Another procedure involves a *dual ISI*. In a dual-ISI procedure, the CS-US interval varies between two values across trials. Typically, this procedure produces a double-peaked CR, with the peaks corresponding to the two CS-US intervals. Finally, timing of CRs can be demonstrated with *ISI discrimination*. In an ISI-discrimination procedure, two CSs that differ along some dimension are used, as in a standard discrimination procedure. However, in contrast to a standard discrimination procedure, each CS is paired with a US, but at a different CS-US interval. Mauk and Ruiz (1992) used tones of different frequencies for the two CSs and a corneal air puff as the US. Rabbits learned a CR to each CS with a latency appropriate to the CS-US interval.

Conclusion

Although classical conditioning involves learning the relations between two stimuli, these relations can be complex. The rate and content of learning in classical conditioning depends upon a number of factors. These include the following: 1. whether the CS is followed by a US or not; 2. how many CSs are present; 3. whether the organism has any previous experience with the CS, the US, or the relationship between the two; and 4. how much time elapses between the delivery of the CS and the delivery of US. In addition, the stimuli used as CSs can be as complex as an entire context. Although the responses examined in laboratory studies of classical conditioning are often simple (such as an eye blink), this is simply a control and measurement issue. Classical conditioning can involve complex learned responses as well, and is believed to play an important role in everyday human behavior.

See also: CONDITIONING, CELLULAR AND NETWORK SCHEMES FOR HIGHER-ORDER FEATURES OF; CONDITIONING, CLASSICAL AND INSTRUMENTAL; DISCRIMINATION AND GENERALIZATION; KAMIN'S BLOCKING EFFECT: NEURONAL SUBSTRATES; NEURAL SUBSTRATES OF CLASSICAL CONDITIONING: DISCRETE BEHAVIORAL RESPONSES

Bibliography

Bouton, M. E., Mineka, S., and Barlow, D. H. (2001). A modern learning theory perspective on the etiology of panic disorder. *Psychological Review* 108, 4–32.

Gallistel, C. R., and Gibbon, J. (2000). Time, rate, and conditioning. *Psychological Review* 107, 289–344.

Giftakis, J. E., and Tait, R. W. (1998). Blocking of the rabbit's classically conditioned nictitating membrane response: Effects of modifications of contextual associative strength. *Learning and Motivation* 29, 23–48.

Kamin, L. J. (1969). Predictability, surprise, attention, and conditioning. In B. A. Campbell and R. M. Church, eds., *Punishment and aversive behavior*, pp. 279–296. New York: Appleton-Century-Crofts.

Kehoe, E. J., and Weidemann, G. (1999). Within-stimulus competition in trace conditioning of the rabbit's nictitating membrane response. *Psychobiology* 27, 72–84.

Lubow, R. E., and Moore, A. U. (1959). Latent inhibition: The effect of nonreinforced preexposure to the conditioned stimulus. *Journal of Comparative and Physiological Psychology* 52, 415–419.

Mauk, M. D., and Ruiz, B. P. (1992). Learning-dependent timing of Pavlovian eyelid responses: Differential conditioning using multiple interstimulus intervals. *Behavioral Neuroscience* 106, 666–681.

Miller, R. R., and Matzel, L. D. (1988). The comparator hypothesis: A response rule for the expression of associations. In G. H. Bower, ed., *The psychology of learning and motivation*, pp. 51–92. San Diego, CA: Academic Press.

Pavlov, I. P. (1927). *Conditioned reflexes*. New York: Dover.

Pearce, J. M., and Hall, G. (1980). A model for Pavlovian learning: Variations in the effectiveness of conditioned but not of unconditioned stimuli. *Psychological Review* 87, 532–552.

Rescorla, R. A. (1969). Pavlovian conditioned inhibition. *Psychological Bulletin* 72, 77–94.

Rescorla, R. A., and Wagner, A. R. (1972). A theory of Pavlovian conditioning: Variations in the effectiveness of reinforcement and nonreinforcement. In A. H. Black and W. F. Prokasy, eds., *Classical conditioning II: Current research and theory*, pp. 64–99. New York: Appleton-Century-Crofts.

Rogers, R. F., and Steinmetz, J. E. (1998). Contextually based conditional discrimination of the rabbit eyeblink response. *Neurobiology of Learning and Memory* 69, 307–319.

Savastano, H. I., Cole, R. P., Barnet, R. C., and Miller, R. R. (1999). Reconsidering conditioned inhibition. *Learning and Motivation* 30, 101–127.

Schmajuk, N. A., Lam, Y-W, and Gray, J. A. (1996). Latent inhibition: A neural network approach. *Journal of Experimental Psychology: Animal Behavior Processes* 22, 321–349.

John T. Green
Joseph E. Steinmetz

CODING PROCESSES

[Coding processes *refers to the ways in which information may be represented in memory. Events in the world strike our senses and may be well perceived, but the mental operations that ensue determine whether the events will be remembered. These mental operations are referred to as coding processes and have been studied in several different ways. Three types of coding processes are discussed in the entries in this section. The first entry is on coding processes that involve mental* **IMAGERY.** *People tend to remember information better if they convert the information to mental pictures while they study it. This technique is frequently used by experts who can memorize huge amounts of information (see* MNEMONISTS) *and by all people who employ effective memory strategies (see* MNEMONIC DEVICES). *In the* **LEVELS OF PROCESSING** *approach, people are directed to think about different aspects of events (attention is directed to superficial properties of events or their meanings) and memory is tested later. The deeper or more meaningful the level of processing, the better the later memory under most circumstances. The final topic in this section is more general, about* **ORGANIZATION OF MEMORY.** *One effective strategy to code information is to organize it in terms of knowledge we already have. The study of memory organization is concerned with both how knowledge is organized and how people use their knowledge to encode new information in memory. The study of coding processes is central to the study of human memory and ramifies through most other topics. For example, whether some bit of information can be retrieved from memory depends on how it was encoded when it was learned (see* RETRIEVAL PROCESSES IN MEMORY).]

IMAGERY

According to Cicero, it was the Greek poet Simonides who first recognized the utility of mental imagery for memory. During a brief absence from a banquet at which the poet recited the entertainment, the roof of the building caved in, mangling the guests so badly that recognition of the bodies was impossible. Simonides (who likely already had developed a fairly good memory in the context of his job) realized that he could remember the faces and clothing of the guests in various locations around the room; thus he was able to identify the corpses for their families. Secondarily, perhaps, the art of memory was born (see Yates, 1966, for full histories).

Image and *imagery* generally are used to refer to those concrete, perceptual, and usually visual modes of thought that appear to represent the physical world relatively directly. These are clearly distinguishable from verbal thought processes, which are arbitrary in the linguistic sense of there being no necessary relationship (other than social agreement) be-

Figure 1

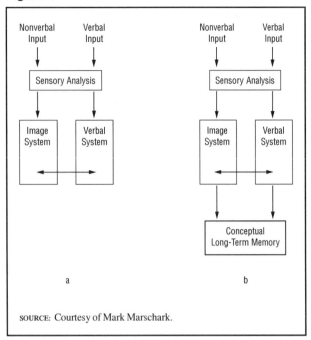

SOURCE: Courtesy of Mark Marschark.

Schematic diagram of the dual coding model and one possible alternative.

tween words and their referents. Mental images of things experienced thus often appear to be fundamentally related to their meanings. It is difficult to think of a pizza without some olfactory or gustatory image or to think of one's mother without experiencing a visual image of her face.

Consistent with subjective impressions, a variety of studies have indicated that visual imagery and visual perception have some similar qualities. Several studies by Shepard and his colleagues, for example, have examined *mental rotation* (Cooper and Shepard, 1973). This paradigm typically involves asking people to judge whether two visually presented stimuli (e.g., letters or three-dimensional shapes) are identical or mirror reflections of each other. Shepard's results have consistently indicated that, in order to decide on the possible identity of the two stimuli, subjects first mentally rotate one of them to the same orientation as the other. This is evidenced by the fact that reaction times to make the identity judgments increase regularly as the angular difference between the two stimuli increases from 0 to 180 degrees and then decreases to 360 degrees (as the rotation can be made "backward").

Kosslyn and his colleagues have demonstrated similar findings in a series of studies on *mental scanning* (Kosslyn, 1973). In this paradigm, subjects memorize several landmarks on a simple map and then are asked to form an image of it. Consistently, the time required for subjects to scan from one location to another on their images is a direct function of the linear distance between the two locations on the original map, thus reflecting the analogue character of mental images. Further studies by Kosslyn, Finke, and others have shown that people can mentally construct two- and three-dimensional figures that have emergent properties not predictable from their component parts. Such findings indicate a perceptionlike quality of mental imagery that has been supported by some neurophysiological evidence (Farah, 1984).

Although the psychological processes underlying these phenomena may not be entirely clear, the utility of mental imagery and pictures to facilitate memory has been recognized for centuries. Simonides's *method of loci*, for example, in which successive items are imaged at specific locations along a familiar route, has long been used for learning ordered lists of unrelated items or remembering a series of points to be made during a speech. Imagery also can be helpful in learning foreign vocabulary, as in forming an image of a cadaver falling from a table for the Italian *cadere* (to fall) or someone harvesting cogs in a field for *cogliere* (to pick or gather). In addition, imagery seems central to the development of thinking and memory in children, and a progression from motor processes to visual images to verbal processes is assumed by most major theories of cognitive development.

In scientific studies of memory, there are several typical findings that indicate an important role of imagery: Words rated as referring to more concrete, highly imageable things are better remembered than words referring to abstract, nonimageable things—the *concreteness effect*; the use of imagery in learning (either by instruction or spontaneously) leads to better memory than nonimaginal strategies—the *imagery effect*; and pictures are better remembered than words—the *picture superiority effect*.

This apparent centrality of mental imagery in thinking and memory has led to several theoretical frameworks for studying human memory and cognition that give images an essential role. The most completely articulated of these, the *dual coding model* of Paivio (1971, 1986), is depicted in Figure 1(a). The model includes a verbal system specialized for dealing with sequential, especially linguistic information and an imagery system specialized for dealing with nonverbal, holistic information. It explicitly entails that concrete experiences generate perceptual memory traces (images) that preserve the structural attributes of the input. Those generated memory representations are assumed to be functionally equivalent to perceptual representations "in the sense that an image of an object generated to its name has the same mnemonic properties as the image evoked by the object itself'' (Paivio, 1986, p. 144). Among other consequences, the storage of information-rich perceptual images is assumed to account for the findings that mental comparisons of things on physical dimensions (such as size) yield similar patterns of response times regardless of whether the objects, their pictures, or their printed names are presented.

The hypothesized existence of separate but interconnected verbal and imaginal systems in the dual coding model explains the concreteness effect in terms of *coding redundancy*: Concrete words usually result in dual verbal and imaginal memory codes (via the intersystem, referential crossover), whereas abstract words usually result in only a single, verbal code. Such redundancy provides two alternative "routes" to the traces for concrete words during recall and provides a "backup" if one code is forgotten. In learning of concrete word pairs (i.e., in *paired-associate learning*), imagery is assumed to provide a means of integrating the meanings of the two words into a single, imaginal unit that can be retrieved later in the context of one of the words as a cue. Integration of this sort is assumed to be unavailable for abstract word pairs, which must be stored as two-unit verbal strings. Finally, pictures are assumed by the dual code model to be better remembered than words in part because images may be inherently more memorable than verbal traces but primarily because pictures are likely to elicit verbal naming (and hence dual memory codes) with a somewhat higher probability than words elicit imagery.

One modified version of the dual coding model is depicted in Figure 1(b). In this alternative, dual verbal and imaginal processing systems are assumed to operate at a level akin to Baddeley's (1986) *working memory*, which has both visual and verbal components. The dual processing systems can account for most of the results concerning verbal processes and image manipulation and inspection. In contrast with the multiple, modality-specific memory codes of the original dual coding model, however, this version assumes that long-term memory involves some more generic, semantic, or propositional code common to both concrete and abstract information (Potter, 1979). Information is retrieved from this conceptual memory and images are constructed in visual working memory. Imagery is still invoked to explain the beneficial effects of imagery instructions, material concreteness, and picture presentation, but the locus of their effects on memory is placed on the *distinctiveness* of imaginally processed items within the encoding and retrieval contexts (Marschark et al., 1987). Inter-item integration is assumed to be possible for abstract as well as concrete materials via conceptual relations.

One difficulty in explaining the effects of imageability on memory is that several other variables co-occur with it. Dimensions such as concreteness and word frequency have been shown to be positively related to rated imagery values, whereas others, such as generality of reference and associative set size, have been shown to be negatively related to it. The effect of imagery can be empirically or statistically separated from all of those other variables, however, and remains a significant predictor of memory when the others are controlled (Paivio, 1986). Exceptions begin to occur only when memory for more complex materials like concrete and abstract texts is considered or when other meaningful contexts make the importance of imaginal processing less essential (Marschark and Cornoldi, 1990).

The precise role of imagery in language comprehension and problem solving remains unclear, although it clearly plays a role in visually and spatially oriented situations, such as route learning and chess playing, which seem to involve *analogue* mental manipulation. Distinguishing imagery from the nature of long-term memory codes highlights the role of individual differences in imagery ability. A variety of standardized and well-documented tests that involve tasks such as mental paper-folding, mental rotation, and mental scanning have provided evidence of large differences between individuals in the vividness, speed, and frequency of image generation. The imagery abilities tapped by these tests generally are not predictive of memory ability even for concrete materials. Nonetheless, it is clear that variability in some imagery abilities can have specific and marked effects in a variety of cognitive domains, including memory. Individuals who have suffered head injuries, for example, typically exhibit deficits in visual-spatial tasks such as finding hidden figures or reconstructing previously presented pictures. They may also fail to exhibit concreteness effects in memory and be particularly slow at making imaginal comparisons (Richardson, 1990). People who score high on tests of image manipulation skill tend to be faster in comparing their images on particular dimensions, although they may be no faster in generating those images in the first place.

Among the more puzzling imagery findings yet to be explained is why people who are totally, congenitally blind still show apparent imagery and concreteness effects (DeBeni and Cornoldi, 1988). These effects appear not to be attributable to tactile knowledge, because they are just as readily obtained when the to-be-remembered items are things for which tactile experience is unlikely (e.g., a moon, a tiger, or a tower). Clearly, imagery is a multidimensional construct that has great theoretical and practical utility but no simple psychological explanation.

Bibliography

Baddeley, A. (1986). *Working memory*. Oxford: Clarendon Press.

Cooper, L. A., and Shepard, R. N. (1973). The time required to prepare for a rotated stimulus. *Memory & Cognition 1*, 246–250.

DeBeni, R., and Cornoldi, C. (1988). Imagery limitations in totally congenitally blind subjects. *Journal of Experimental Psychology: Learning, Memory, and Cognition 14*, 650–655.

Farah, M. J. (1984). The neurological basis of mental imagery: A componential analysis. *Cognition 18*, 245–272.

Kosslyn, S. M. (1973). Scanning visual images: Some structural implications. *Perception and Psychophysics 14*, 90–94.

Marschark, M., and Cornoldi, C. (1990). Imagery and verbal memory. In C. Cornoldi and M. A. McDaniel, eds., *Imagery and cognition*, pp. 133–182. New York: Springer-Verlag.

Marschark, M., Richman, C. L., Yuille, J. C., and Hunt, R. R. (1987). The role of imagery in memory: On shared and distinctive information. *Psychological Bulletin 102*, 28–41.

Paivio, A. (1971; reprint 1979). *Imagery and verbal processes*. Hillsdale, NJ: Erlbaum.

————— (1986). *Mental representations: A dual coding approach*. Oxford: Oxford University Press.

Potter, M. C. (1979). Mundane symbolism: The relations among objects, names, and ideas. In N. R. Smith and M. B. Franklin, eds., *Symbolic functioning in childhood*, pp. 41–65. Hillsdale, NJ: Erlbaum.

Richardson, J. T. E. (1990). Imagery and the brain. In C. Cornoldi and M. A. McDaniel, eds., *Imagery and cognition*, pp. 1–45. New York: Springer-Verlag.

Yates, F. A. (1966). *The art of memory*. Chicago: University of Chicago Press.

Marc Marschark

LEVELS OF PROCESSING

Processing and Recall

The term *levels of processing* was introduced by Craik and Lockhart (1972) to describe the way in which the information contained in a stimulus can be analyzed at levels ranging from surface physical properties to deeper levels involving its meaning. Thus in reading the printed word *clever*, the reader might process orthographic features, such as its being in capital letters, or phonemic features, such as that it rhymes with *ever*, or semantic features, such as that it is a synonym for *skilled*.

The level of processing is a powerful determinant of how well an event will be remembered (Craik and Tulving, 1975). A simple demonstration experiment illustrates this point. Participants in the experiment are presented with a sequence of common words and asked to make one of three possible judgments about each word. For some words participants are asked to make a judgment at the orthographic level, such as whether the word is printed in capital letters; other words require a phonemic-level judgment, such as whether the word rhymes with a certain word; a third set of words requires a judgment involving meaning, such as whether the word is a synonym for a specified word. The assumption is that these three types of judgments require increasingly deep levels of processing. In a subsequent memory test in which participants are asked to recall the words, deeper levels of processing are associated with higher levels of recall: those words that required a semantic-level judgment are recalled best, whereas those requiring orthographic processing yield the lowest recall level.

Craik and Lockhart (1972) proposed the general concept of levels of processing not as a theory of memory but rather as a framework for future research into the relationship between coding processes and memory. Lockhart and Craik have written a retrospective commentary on the significance of this proposal (1990). The basic claim of levels of processing as a research framework is that a thorough understanding of remembering requires a careful analysis of the way in which (and the degree to which) coding processes involve the construction of meaning. According to this view, there is no distinct coding process that can be identified as "committing to memory." Rather, memory coding—the memory trace—is constructed as a byproduct of the everyday mental operations we perform as we interact with our environment and attempt to understand it. One implication of this claim is that a proper account of the relationship between coding processes and memory will involve an understanding of the broader issues of perception and comprehension.

Orienting Tasks

Experimental conditions (orienting tasks) such as those involving judgments of case, rhyme, or synonymity are but three examples of the large number of orienting tasks that have been used in experiments. Other examples are rating a word's pleasantness, deciding how many syllables it has, and whether it is spoken by a male or a female voice. Indeed, we can think of our everyday cognitive activity in terms of a continuous sequence of orienting tasks as our knowledge, goals, and needs interact with the circumstances of the moment. Our goals will influence our orientation toward a stimulus—the specific information that we selectively attend to and analyze. The particular form of the analysis will strongly influence later remembering. In listening to a conversation, for example, our goal may be to comprehend what is being said, but it may also be to infer the speaker's intelligence, mood, or intentions, or the origin of a distinctive accent. When we read a restaurant menu, our goal may involve judgments of taste, preference, cost, or nutritional value. The fundamental principle of levels of processing as a research framework is the claim that since the memory trace is the byproduct of these analyses, the key to predicting subsequent memory performance is a matter of gaining increased understanding of the nature and level of these analyses. Orienting tasks used in experiments—tasks such as judging rhyme or synonymity (meaning)—are the scientist's effort to gain tight control over the processing that a participant applies to a stimulus to evaluate the impact that different processes have on memory.

Incidental versus Intentional Processing

Levels of processing have important implications for the distinction between incidental and intentional processing. Because we do not usually make an intentional effort to commit everyday experiences to memory, much of our normal remembering is incidental. You can probably recall what you were doing exactly twenty-four hours ago even though, at the time, you were not making a conscious effort to commit the activity to memory. This aspect of everyday life can be captured in an experimental setting by using incidental orienting tasks in which participants are not informed that they will receive a subsequent memory test. Participants might perform the judgments believing that the only purpose of the experiment is to see how quickly they can respond. According to the levels of processing approach, such participants should not be disadvantaged relative to those instructed to expect the memory test, provided the level of processing for the two groups is comparable. That is to say, the important determinant of remembering is not the conscious effort of committing something to memory but the level of processing that the orienting task induces. This conclusion is supported by experimental findings. For example, participants who are asked to rate a word for pleasantness as an incidental orienting task perform as well on a subsequent unexpected memory test as those who are given prior warning of the test.

What happens when a researcher exhorts participants in an experiment simply to "try to remember"? Presumably the subjects will process the material in whatever way they think will most effectively support later remembering. A common strategy with verbal material is to rehearse it by silently repeating a word or phrase over and over. Such a strategy is relatively ineffective for long-term remembering, since such repetitive processing typically involves no further analysis of meaning (no deeper-level processing) but consists of maintaining phonemic recollection. Again, the important point is that successful remembering is less a matter of conscious effort than of being led to perform an orienting task that demands deep levels of processing.

Skills and the Material to Be Remembered

Another determinant of the level of processing is the nature of the material to be remembered. Pictures and common words afford the rapid analysis of meaning. Other material, such as proper nouns, can pose greater difficulty. One reason for the common experience of rapidly forgetting names following introductions at a party is that proper nouns do not trigger rapid deep processing. Hence most mnemonic techniques for remembering names are essentially strategies for converting proper names into a visual image that embodies deeper semantic-level processing. Interacting with the nature of the material is a second determinant: the skill of the rememberer. To the nonspeaker of French the letter string *chien* is meaningless, as is a musical score to anyone who has not been trained to read music, or the game position of chess pieces to one who does not play chess. But to the speaker of French, to the trained musician, or to the skilled chess player, the word, the score, and the board position, respectively, afford deep processing and hence better remembering.

Conclusion

Levels of processing is a theoretical framework that claims that memory coding is a byproduct of cognitive and interpretive processes. Memory depends heavily on the degree to which the processing involves the construction and elaboration of meaning. Tasks such as judging case, rhyme, or synonymity provide a clear example of three distinct levels of processing. Depth of processing, however, can vary over a wide range. According to levels of processing as a research framework, research into coding processes seeks to provide a precise account of this variation and its impact on memory. Recent developments of the original idea of levels of processing and critical analyses are discussed in Naveh-Benjamin, Moscovitch, and Roediger (2001).

Bibliography

Craik, F. I. M., and Lockhart, R. S. (1972). Levels of processing: A framework for memory research. *Journal of Verbal Learning and Verbal Behavior 11*, 671–684.

Craik, F. I. M., and Tulving, E. (1975). Depth of processing and the retention of words in episodic memory. *Journal of Experimental Psychology: General 104*, 268–294.

Lockhart, R. S., and Craik, F. I. M. (1990). Levels of processing: A retrospective commentary on a framework for memory research. *Canadian Journal of Psychology 44*, 87–112.

Naveh-Benjamin, M., Moscovitch, M., and Roediger, H. L. III, eds. (2001). *Perspectives on human memory and cognitive aging: Essays in honor of Fergus Craik*. Philadelphia: Psychology Press.

Robert S. Lockhart

ORGANIZATION OF MEMORY

Coding and Organization

Coding refers to the interpretations a person gives to experiences. The significance of experience for memory and action depends on the interpretation of the experience. The same events can be interpreted in dramatically different ways depending on a person's knowledge and expectations. To understand coding we must understand the organization and use of knowledge in interpreting experience. The interrelatedness of ideas is one of the most compelling facts of mental life. In personal memories, a single association with some present event can trigger detailed memories of past experiences. Psychology has developed several ideas about the nature of organization in memory.

We can illustrate the influence of coding by comparing the memories of two people with different degrees of knowledge: in this case, an expert and a nonexpert about cars. They both see the same small red car. The expert identifies it as a Miata; the nonexpert can identify it only as a small red car. Would it surprise you if later the expert was able to state with some confidence that a small red Triumph was not the car seen earlier, while the nonexpert had more difficulty in making this discrimination? Each individual's knowledge influences the coding and thus the memory of the experience.

Human memory imposes organization on our experiences. Tulving (1962) and others have shown that when people learn a list of randomly selected words, they organize the words in recalling the list. As the list is learned, there is more and more consistency in the grouping of the words in recall.

Earlier, Bousfield (1953) showed that subjects recall lists of words as clusters of related words. For example, if the list contained some names of flowers, some names of people, some types of buildings, and so on, then the free recall of these words would group the similar items. This grouping occurs even though the words are presented in random order. Later Bower and his colleagues (Bower, 1970) showed that theories about the structure of memory could predict the organization of material to be learned. Bransford and Johnson (1972) studied passages that are difficult to remember unless people are led to give them appropriate interpretations. Their work is an impressive demonstration of the role of interpretation in remembering.

Organization of Memory

What leads to the organization of memories? Most answers to this question refer to association as at least one fundamental process of organization. Associations derive from the frequent temporal clustering of events. In the early part of the twentieth century, Pavlov (1927) discovered classical conditioning. This discovery led to extensive investigations of the formation and maintenance of associations. Pavlov found that after frequently presenting a neutral stimulus (e.g., a tone) in close proximity to the presentation of food, a dog would salivate at the sound of the tone even in the absence of food. Thus, an association formed between the tone and the food.

Garcia and Koelling (1966) found that some associations are learned more easily than others. Their laboratory rats learned to associate a novel taste with gastrointestinal illness much more easily than they learned the association between a flashing light and gastrointestinal illness. This result suggests that various constraints influence the formation of associations.

Associative Networks

In the direct representation of associations in the form of a network, concepts are shown as nodes and associations are shown by lines (or links) connecting the nodes. Schvaneveldt, Durso, and Dearholt (1989) presented a method of deriving such networks from proximity data such as judgments of relatedness among sets of concepts. Cooke, Durso, and Schvaneveldt (1986) found that networks can predict the way people organize the concepts when they learn a list of words. Goldsmith and Johnson (1990) were able to predict students' grades in a course on experimental methods from the degree of similarity of the students' and the instructor's networks of important concepts.

Semantic Networks and Semantic Features

Semantic networks also use network representations, but they specify more about the relations between concepts by using labeled links (Collins and Quillian, 1969; Meyer and Schvaneveldt, 1976; Quillian, 1969). For example, such a network would show that robin is a member of the class bird with an "isa" link (A robin is a bird). It would also show that a deer has antlers, and so on. Such networks can also support inferences such as concluding that a robin is an animal by retrieving a robin is a bird and a bird is an animal. Semantic networks have been used to explain experimental data from studies in language understanding and category judgments. Such networks are also often a part of computer programs designed to exhibit artificial intelligence (Quillian, 1989). Other theories propose that concepts consist of collections of features that define the concepts (Smith and Medin, 1981). The concept *bird*, for example, might consist of features such as *has wings, flies, lays eggs, has feathers*, and so on. According to feature theories, when people reason about concepts, they retrieve features from memory and use them to draw conclusions.

Schemata

Schemata are general representations of several different items of information together with the specification of the relations among the items (Bartlett, 1932; Minsky, 1975). For example, the schema for a room might specify that it must have a floor, a ceiling, walls, and a door as well as some spatial relations among these. Optionally, it might have additional doors and windows. Scripts are examples of schemata where actions are organized in familiar sequences such as going to a restaurant or visiting the doctor. Schemata invite inferences. Several studies suggest that memory includes inferred information (defaults) in addition to what we actually experience. For example, if we hear the sentence, "Fred drove the nail into the board," we are likely to infer that he used a hammer even though the sentence does not mention a hammer. If someone eats in a restaurant, we assume that he or she paid for the meal.

Chase and Simon (1973) reported a classic demonstration of the power of schemata using memory for the positions of pieces on a chess board. They found that chess masters were no better than novices at reconstructing a board with randomly placed pieces, but the masters were far superior in recalling the positions of pieces from the middle of an actual chess game. Experts presumably have elaborate schemata that can code the positions of the pieces on the board when the positions make sense.

Embodiment and the Need for Representations

In recent years challenges to traditional ideas about the role of mental representations have arisen from researchers in cognitive science. A major concern is that traditional approaches have neglected the constraints imposed on learning and development that stem from the physical body and from the environment. At the extreme, theorists advocating a dynamic systems approach claim that grounding cognition in the interaction of the body and the world obviates the need to propose mental representations that mediate perception and action (Edelman, 1992; Freeman, 1995; Johnson, 1987; Thelen and Smith, 1994; van Gelder, 1997). The grounding of concepts in perception and action helps explain how concepts are learned (Bickard, 2000). Consequently, coding is

constrained by the history and situation of the individual.

Conclusion

Coding is the interpretation of events in light of what we know. Such interpretation can have beneficial consequences, as in the superiority of the memory of chess masters for real board positions. Sometimes interpretation leads to false memories of related information that was not actually experienced (Loftus and Ketcham, 1991). Understanding the memory of an event requires an understanding of the coding that arises from cumulative knowledge. An important question for theory and research concerns the extent to which memory depends on stored representations as opposed to cues available from the body and the environment.

See also: CODING PROCESSES: IMAGERY; CODING PROCESSES: LEVELS OF PROCESSING; FALSE MEMORIES

Bibliography

Bartlett, F. C. (1932). *Remembering: A study in experimental and social psychology.* Cambridge, UK: Cambridge University Press.

Bickard, M. H. (2000). Dynamic representing and representational dynamics. In E. Dietrich and A. Markman, eds., *Cognitive dynamics: Conceptual and representational change in humans and machines.* Mahwah, NJ: Erlbaum.

Bousfield, W. A. (1953). The occurrence of clustering in the recall of randomly arranged associates. *Journal of General Psychology 49,* 229–240.

Bower, G. H. (1970). Organizational factors in memory. *Cognitive Psychology 1,* 18–46.

Bransford, J. D., and Johnson, M. K. (1972). Contextual prerequisites for understanding: Some investigations of comprehension and recall. *Journal of Verbal Learning and Verbal Behavior 11,* 717–726.

Chase, W. G., and Simon, H. A. (1973). Perception in chess. *Cognitive Psychology 4,* 55–81.

Collins, A. M., and Quillian, M. R. (1969). Retrieval time from semantic memory. *Journal of Verbal Learning and Verbal Behavior 8,* 240–247.

Cooke, N. M., Durso, F. T., and Schvaneveldt, R. W. (1986). Recall and measures of memory organization. *Journal of Experimental Psychology: Learning, Memory, and Cognition 12,* 538–549.

Edelman, G. M. (1992). *Bright air, brilliant fire: On the matter of mind.* New York: Basic Books.

Freeman, W. J. (1995). *Societies of brains.* Hillsdale, NJ: Erlbaum.

Garcia, J., and Koelling, R. A. (1966). Relation of cue to consequence in avoidance learning. *Psychonomic Science 4,* 123–124.

Goldsmith, T. E., and Johnson, P. J. (1990). A structural assessment of classroom learning. In R. Schvaneveldt, ed., *Pathfinder associative networks: Studies in knowledge organization.* Norwood, NJ: Ablex.

Johnson, M. (1987). *The body in the mind: The bodily basis of meaning, imagination, and reason.* Chicago: University of Chicago Press.

Loftus, E. F., and Ketcham, K. (1991). *Witness for the defense.* New York: St. Martin's.

Meyer, D. E., and Schvaneveldt, R. W. (1976). Meaning, memory structure, and mental processes. *Science 192,* 27–33.

Minsky, M. (1975). A framework for representing knowledge. In P. Winston, ed., *The psychology of computer vision.* New York: McGraw-Hill.

Pavlov, I. P. (1927). *Conditioned reflexes,* trans. G. V. Anrep. London: Oxford University Press.

Quillian, M. R. (1969). The teachable language comprehender. *Communications of the ACM 12,* 459–476.

Schvaneveldt, R. W., Durso, F. T., and Dearholt, D. W. (1989). Network structures in proximity data. In G. H. Bower, ed., *The psychology of learning and motivation: Advances in research and theory,* Vol. 24. New York: Academic Press.

Smith, E. E., and Medin, D. L. (1981). *Categories and concepts.* Cambridge, MA: Harvard University Press.

Thelen, E., and Smith, L. B. (1994). *A dynamic systems approach to the development of cognition and action.* Cambridge, MA: MIT Press.

Tulving, E. (1962). Subjective organization in free recall of "unrelated" words. *Psychological Review 69,* 344–354.

van Gelder, T. (1997). Dynamics and cognition. In J. Haugland, ed., *Mind design II.* Cambridge, MA: MIT Press.

Roger W. Schvaneveldt

COGNITIVE ENHANCERS

Virtually everyone has occasionally wished that he or she could think faster, had a better memory, or was simply *smarter*. It is possible to improve these facets of cognitive function through practice, but most people are looking for an easier solution. At the beginning of the twenty-first century, the answer is usually imagined to be in the form of a pill.

Cognition has many elements. Key aspects of cognition include sensory perception, attention and concentration, immediate (or working) memory, and long-term memory. More complex and integrated facets of cognition include abstract reasoning and planning. Thus, there are a number of ways for pharmacological treatments to enhance cognition. However, for most people cognitive enhancement is synonymous with having a better long-term memory, so this topic is the primary focus of this entry.

Memory itself is a complex phenomenon that is still not completely understood by the medical and scientific community. Much of the research into understanding memory mechanisms is motivated by the need to develop treatments for memory impairments caused by diseases such as Alzheimer's disease. An important question in the present context is whether treatments that correct memory deficits can also enhance memory in normal healthy individuals. Virtually all drugs that improve memory show an "inverted-U" dose-response relationship: Doses of a compound up to a certain level enhance performance, but at still higher doses the enhancing effect is lost. The argument has been made that cognitive function in normal healthy subjects is at the crest of the inverted-U, while in aged, diseased, or otherwise impaired subjects cognitive function has slipped back onto the rising phase of the dose-response function. In this case, treatments to facilitate cognition in impaired subjects act to restore optimal performance, but the same treatments in normal subjects drive them past the optimal level, resulting in impairment. The inverted-U hypothesis suggests that it is easier to treat memory deficits than to improve normal memory. The results of many studies in animals and humans support this idea.

Still, the possibility of memory enhancement in normal healthy people remains very attractive. A casual search of the Internet leads to hundreds of sites offering memory-boosting aids. In some cases the agents are described only as herbal mixtures, while in others a single compound, or one or more specific components of the blend, is touted. The major constituents of these products are discussed in detail later in this entry. First, this entry reviews some drugs that are known to be able to enhance cognition and memory but are not generally available or usually sold for this purpose.

CNS Stimulants

The common feature of these agents is that they stimulate the central nervous system. Picrotoxin, bicuculline, and strychnine are drugs that block inhibitory systems in the brain, leading to a generalized increase in excitability. Picrotoxin was one of the first agents recognized to be a memory enhancer. All three drugs have been shown in animal studies to improve memory at low doses, but higher doses cause seizures and death. These drugs are too dangerous for experimentation in humans.

Another stimulant drug, amphetamine, has reliably been shown to improve memory in both animals and humans. Amphetamine causes the release of neurotransmitters that promote arousal, including epinephrine and norepinephrine. The resulting increase in attention plays a major role in the memory-enhancing properties of amphetamine. In addition, amphetamine improves memory consolidation, the process that leads to long-term memory storage. The major problems with this drug are that tolerance to its beneficial effects develops quickly, along with side effects that include physical dependence and addiction. These liabilities greatly outweigh amphetamine's utility as a memory enhancer.

Caffeine is the world's most widely used stimulant. It also increases alertness and attention, thereby enhancing cognitive performance. However, caffeine's effects on memory appear to be small. Vasopressin is a pituitary hormone that plays an important role in the body's regulation of water. In addition, vasopressin has been shown to enhance memory in both humans and experimental animals. The precise mechanism is unknown, but since vasopressin affects norepinephrine utilization in the brain researchers believe that increased arousal plays a role.

Cholinergic Agents

The neurotransmitter acetylcholine is known to play an important role in learning and memory. Neurons that contain acetylcholine degenerate in patients with Alzheimer's disease, an illness that is characterized by profound cognitive impairments. In addition, drugs that block the action of acetylcholine in the brain impair cognition in healthy humans and in experimental animals. Researchers have long hypothesized that improving cholinergic system function would be a good way to treat the symptoms of Alzheimer's disease, and this is the primary mechanism of action of drugs that are marketed for this purpose.

Cholinergic function can be enhanced either by preventing the breakdown of the acetylcholine to prolong its action or by directly activating the receptors for neurotransmitter. Physostigmine is an inhibitor of acetylcholinesterase, the enzyme that degrades acetylcholine. Physostigmine and related compounds have been shown to improve memory in normal humans and animals as well as in Alzheimer's disease patients. Activators of either the muscarinic or nicotinic receptor subtypes of cholinergic receptors also improve memory. Nicotine is well recognized as a cognition enhancer, although it is debated whether its effect is mediated by increasing attention or through another mechanism. Drugs that act at muscarinic receptors have also been shown to be effective cognitive enhancers in animal studies. Unfortunately, several muscarinic receptor activators have failed in clinical trials with Alzheimer patients because of side effects. No compound in this class has yet been developed that is safe enough for human use.

Components of "Smart Drugs"

The vast number of concoctions sold over-the-counter to improve memory provides an excellent indication of both the demand and the perceived need for these products. Many of these compounds are extracted from plants or animal tissues and consist of mixtures of ingredients. A major problem with such products is that claims concerning amounts and purity of the supposedly active elements have unusually not been verified by an independent agency. While this lack of oversight could lead to safety problems due to contaminants in the products, a more likely concern is that dosages may not be accurate or consistent. Such unreliability, coupled with the phenome-

non of the inverted-U dosing effect, could explain the inconsistent results of the few formal tests of these agents that have been performed.

Five compounds seem to be most frequently sold as cognition/memory enhancers: huperzine A, vinpocetine, *Ginkgo biloba*, ginseng, and pregnenolone. Huperzine A, an extract derived from a particular type of club moss, is an acetylcholinesterase inhibitor that is far more potent than physostigmine. The acetylcholine plays an important role in the brain circuitry that encodes memories and is used as a neurotransmitter in the peripheral nervous system. Overactivation of these peripheral cholinergic connections can have profound and potentially dangerous consequences. Because of this problem, huperzine A is not a safe drug and should not be used without a physician's supervision.

Vinpocetine is derived from the periwinkle plant, *Cricoceras longiflorus*. It is widely used as a memory enhancer, and has been found to improve memory in healthy people as well as those with impairments caused by aging or disease. It is not clear how vinpocetine works, but there is evidence that vinpocetine enhances blood flow in the brain, which, in turn, provides the basis for observations of increased glucose utilization, a sign of generally increased cerebral activity. In addition, studies have shown that vinpocetine increases the production of norephinephrine, which mediates arousal, and acetylcholine. Vinpocetine is a very safe compound at therapeutic doses.

Extracts from the leaves of the *Ginkgo biloba* tree have been used in traditional Chinese medicine for thousands of years. These extracts consist of many compounds, the behavioral effects of which have yet to be individually characterized. Ginkgo extracts have been widely used as memory enhancers, particularly in the elderly, but studies have shown that ginkgo also improves memory in healthy young people. The primary effect of ginkgo appears to be increased cerebral circulation.

The ginseng plant, *Panax ginseng*, also has a long history of use in traditional Chinese medicine. Extracts from the roots or the entire plant contain over a dozen chemical compounds, collectively termed ginsenosides. Ginsenosides have been used to treat a number of diseases ranging from diabetes to insomnia, and to enhance physical and mental performance. While the memory-enhancing activity of ginseng is not as well documented as that of ginkgo, studies have shown beneficial effects in both young and elderly subjects. Like ginkgo, ginseng also promotes cerebral blood flow, but it also may enhance specific neurotransmitter systems. There is evidence that the combination of ginseng and ginkgo synergistically enhance memory. There are no known major health risks associated with either agent.

Pregnenolone is a neurosteroid, a hormone that is synthesized in the brain from cholesterol. Studies have shown pregnenolone levels decline with aging and are correlated with impaired cognitive performance. In addition, an injection of pregnenolone directly into the brains of aged animals improves memory. Pregnenolone has also been shown to enhance acetylcholine release in the brain. Taken together, these findings have been used to promote the value of taking pregnenolone supplements. While pregnenolone is safe, studies of the compound in humans have yet to provide consistent support for the idea that it is an effective cognitive enhancer.

Conclusion

Enhancing cognitive function remains both a dream and a challenge. There are a number of agents that appear to at least improve memory to some degree, but none of these compounds is so effective that it can be distinguished from the others. What is clear is that some degree of cognitive enhancement is possible even in young healthy people. Maximizing this effect will require systematic research to better understand how pharmacological treatments affect the basic neurobiological mechanisms that are responsible for particular aspects of cognition. A more immediate goal, and probably one that will be more quickly achieved, is to develop treatments to improve the cognitive impairments in aged or diseased individuals.

See also: DRUGS AND MEMORY; PHARMACOLOGICAL TREATMENT OF MEMORY DEFICITS

Bibliography

Born, J., Pietrowsky, R., and Fehm, H. L. (1998). Neuropsychological effects of vasopressin in healthy humans. *Progressive Brain Research 119*, 619–643.

Furey, M. L., Pietrini, P., and Haxby, J. V. (2000). Cholinergic enhancement and increased selectivity of perceptual processing during working memory. *Science 290* (5,500), 2,315–2,319.

Izquierdo, I., and Medina, J. H. (1991). GABAA receptor modulation of memory: The role of endogenous benzodiazepines. *Trends in Pharmacological Science 12* (7), 260–265.

Kennedy, D. O., Scholey, A. B., and Wesnes, K. A. (2000). The dose-dependent cognitive effects of acute administration of Ginkgo biloba to healthy young volunteers. *Psychopharmacology, 151* (4), 416–423.

—— (2001). Dose dependent changes in cognitive performance and mood following acute administration of Ginseng to healthy young volunteers. *Nutritional Neuroscience 4* (5), 295–310.

Kidd, P. M. (1999). A review of nutrients and botanicals in the integrative management of cognitive dysfunction. *Alternative Medicine Review 4* (3), 144–161.

Mattay, V. S. et al. (2000). Effects of dextroamphetamine on cognitive performance and cortical activation. *Neuroimage 12* (3), 268–275.

McGaugh, J. L., and Izquierdo, I. (2000). The contribution of pharmacology to research on the mechanisms of memory formation. *Trends in Pharmacological Science 21* (6), 208–210.

Rees, K., Allen, D., and Lader, M. (1999). The influences of age and caffeine on psychomotor and cognitive function. *Psychopharmacology 145* (2), 181–188.

Soetens, E., Casaer, S., D'Hooge, R., and Hueting, J. E. (1995). Effect of amphetamine on long-term retention of verbal material. *Psychopharmacology 119* (2), 155–162.

Vallee, M., Mayo, W., and Le Moal, M. (2001). Role of pregnenolone, dehydroepiandrosterone and their sulfate esters on learning and memory in cognitive aging. *Brain Resolution Review 37* (1–3), 301–312.

Warburton, D. M. (1995). Effects of caffeine on cognition and mood without caffeine abstinence. *Psychopharmacology 119* (1), 66–70.

Gregory M. Rose

COLLECTIVE MEMORY

Collective memory is a representation of the past that is shared by members of a group, such as a generation or nation-state. The concept is usually traced to writings of the French sociologist Maurice Halbwachs (1887–1945), who argued that remembering is shaped by participation in collective life and that different groups generate different accounts of the past (Halbwachs, 1952).

Collective memory and related notions such as public memory (Bodnar, 1992) have been examined in academic disciplines including anthropology (Cole, 2001), history (Novick, 1999), and sociology (Schudson, 1992). Collective memory is also a part of popular culture discussions about the Vietnam War and the Holocaust. One of the hallmarks of collective memory is that it is tied to identity. Deeply held notions about the past are often the source or pride or shame, and they can give rise to legal, and even armed conflict. For example, the Serbs' collective memory of the Battle of Kosovo in 1389 has often been cited as a factor that made it possible to mobilize against Bosnian Muslims in the twentieth century.

Strong and Distributed Accounts of Collective Memory

Collective memory is often understood in terms of loose analogies with memory in the individual. Many discussions of America's memory about Vietnam, for example, seem to presuppose that America is some sort of a large organism that has intentions, desires, memories, and beliefs just as individuals do, something reflected in assertions such as, "Our memory of Vietnam makes us unwilling to accept combat deaths."

Assumptions about this issue are often not well grounded and as a result have been the object of criticism. For example, one of the fathers of modern memory studies in psychology, Frederic Bartlett (1886–1969), was critical of the "more or less absolute likeness [that] has been drawn between social groups and the human individual" (Bartlett, p. 293), and he warned that collectives do not have some sort of memory in their own right. Bartlett did believe, however, that memory of individuals is fundamentally influenced by the social context in which they function. Indeed, a central point of his argument is that "social organization gives a persistent framework into which all detailed recall must fit, and it very powerfully influences both the manner and the matter of recall" (p. 296). In short, Bartlett accepted the notion of "memory *in* the group, and not memory *of* the group" (p. 294).

Claims about memory "of the group" constitute a "strong version" of collective memory (Wertsch, 2002), and, when made explicit, they have usually been rejected. An alternative that recognizes memory in the group without slipping into questionable assumptions about memory of the group is a "distributed version." From this perspective, memory is viewed as being distributed socially in small group interaction; as well as "instrumentally" (Wertsch, 2002). In the case of social distribution, for example, Mary Sue Weldon (2001) has examined the "collaborative remembering" that occurs when groups of individuals work together to recall information or events from the past.

In the case of instrumental distribution, memory is viewed as involving an active agent and one or more cultural tools such as calendars or other written records. An important transformation of memory in human cognitive evolution occurred with the emergence of "external symbolic storage" (Donald, 1991). This does not mean that such memory somehow resides *in* texts or records, but it does mean that with the rise of new forms of external symbolic storage such as written texts or the Internet the possibilities for remembering undergo fundamental change.

Such change has both psychological and social dimensions. By becoming skilled at using a certain set of cultural tools, new mental habits and "schemata" (Bartlett, 1995) emerge that shape remembering for members of a collective. New forms of collective life also derive from the appearance of novel cultural tools. For example, Benedict Anderson (1991) has tied the development of modern nations and other "imagined communities" to the rise of print media.

Collective versus Individual Memory

Collective memory is widely understood as inherently involving conflict and negotiation in the social sphere (Bodnar, 1992; Wertsch, 2002). Reflecting its ties to identity, it is often assessed in terms of its ability to provide a "usable past," even when this representation comes at the expense of accuracy. In contrast, while recognizing a connection to identity studies of individual memory tend to focus on a criterion of accuracy. This is not to say that psychologists believe memory is fundamentally accurate. Indeed, many studies point to the myriad ways humans can generate incorrect accounts of what actually occurred. The point remains, however, that psychological studies formulate memory largely in terms of its degree of accuracy.

A question that is sometimes asked about collective memory is whether it is anything more than a set of individual memories and hence whether it could be reduced to a personal level. Any attempt to answer this question must say something about the social processes involved in collective memory without falling into a strong version. This is often done by focusing on how narratives and other textual resources for memory are produced, discussed, and understood by members of a collective.

For example, modern states devote major attention to these issues. They produce official accounts of the past through textbooks and other materials used in schools, national commemorations, the media, and other forms of popular culture. In carrying out this project, states seek not only to promulgate their own account but also to control access to alternative accounts. As depicted by George Orwell in his futuristic novel *1984* (1949), such control can be almost total, but in fact every modern state exerts some control over the account of the past presented to its citizens.

This focus on the textual mediation of collective memory raises the question of whether collective memory is really memory at all. What does it mean to say, for example, that a generation of American teenagers remembers World War II when they were born four decades after the event? This might involve memory for textual resources, or perhaps semantic memory, but is it really the kind of episodic memory often assumed?

Such questions provide a reminder of the problems that arise when loose analogies between individual and collective remembering are employed. In order to address them, one must again turn to the instrumental distribution of collective memory, and in the end it may be more appropriate to discuss this in terms of knowledge about a set of shared textual resources rather than memory per se. What is striking about collective memory, however, is the ways in which it goes beyond what would normally be described as knowledge or semantic memory. This is so first because of the social conflict and control involved in producing the textual resources, and second because much more than neutral knowledge is involved. When discussing highly charged historical events, it is very easy to slip into heated discussions about what "really happened" and deny others' accounts in such a way that narrative texts become emotionally powerful tools of collective identity and memory.

One of the ways that studies of individual and collective memory have overlapped concerns generational differences. Martin A. Conway (1997) and others have examined the "reminiscence bump" that exists for members of a generation for events that occurred when they were between fifteen and twenty-five years of age. Research suggests that such events provide the foundation for a generation's lifelong collective memory. Providing another hint about the close tie between identity and collective memory, Conway argues that the reminiscence bump and its power to shape a generation are inherently tied to processes of identity development in young adulthood.

Collective Remembering versus History

Notions of collective memory and history often overlap. In both cases, the events involved are likely to have occurred before the lifetime of the individuals or group doing the remembering, and in both cases there is a tendency to assert that the account being presented is true. Furthermore, both rely on narrative as a cultural tool. Despite such shared properties, it is possible, indeed essential, to distinguish between them.

Among the properties of collective memory that tend to distinguish it from history are the following:

1. it reflects a single, subjective, committed perspective of a collective, whereas analytic history strives to be objective and distance itself from any particular perspective;

2. collective memory leaves little room for doubt or ambiguity about events and the motivations of actors (Novick, 1999), whereas analytic history strives to take into account multiple, complex factors;

3. collective memory presupposes an unchanging essence of a group across time, whereas analytic history focuses on the transformations that collectives undergo.

These three properties of collective memory characterize, for example, the highly charged dispute between China and Japan over whether events in 1937 constitute the "rape of Nanking" (Chang, 1997) or the "incident in Nanking" (as mentioned in some Japanese textbooks).

A final property that characterizes collective remembering is that it tends to be heavily shaped by "schemata" (Bartlett, 1995), "implicit theories" (Ross, 1989), or other simplifying and organizing frameworks. Such frameworks also shape individual memory and history, but in the case of collective memory they take on a particularly important role due to the processes of conflict and negotiation involved. What is shared in collective memory is often little more than a "schematic narrative template" (Wertsch, 2002) in which detailed information, especially contradictory information, is distorted, simplified, and ignored; this schema stands in contrast to what are at least the aspirations of analytic history. It is for this reason that collective memory often appears to be impervious to new information that might challenge it.

Bibliography

Anderson, B. (1991). *Imagined communities: Reflections on the origin and spread of nationalism.* London: Verso.

Bartlett, F. C. (1932; reprint 1995). *Remembering: A study in experimental and social psychology.* Cambridge, UK: Cambridge University Press.

Bodnar, J. (1992). *Remaking America: Public memory, commemoration, and patriotism in the twentieth century.* Princeton, NJ: Princeton University Press.

Chang, I. (1997). *The rape of Nanking: The forgotten holocaust of World War II.* New York: Basic Books.

Cole, J. (2001). *Forget colonialism? Sacrifice and the art of memory in Madagascar.* Berkeley: University of California Press.

Conway, M. A. (1997). The inventory of experience: Memory and identity. In J. W. Pennebaker, D. Paez, and B. Rimé, eds., *Collective memory of political events: Social psychological perspectives.* Mahwah, NJ: Erlbaum.

Donald, M. (1991). *Origins of the modern mind: Three stages in the evolution of culture and cognition.* Cambridge, MA: Harvard University Press.

Halbwachs, M. (1952; reprint 1992). *On collective memory,* ed. and trans. Lewis A. Coser. Chicago: University of Chicago Press.

Novick, P. (1999). *The Holocaust in American life.* Boston: Houghton Mifflin.

Ross, M. (1989). Relation of implicit theories to the construction of personal histories. *Psychological Review* 96 (2), 341–357.

Schudson, M. (1992). *Watergate in American memory: How we remember, forget, and reconstruct the past.* New York: Basic Books.

Weldon, M. S. (2001). Remembering as a social process. In D. L. Medin, ed., *The psychology of learning and motivation.* San Diego, CA: Academic Press.

Wertsch, J. V. (2002). *Voices of collective remembering.* New York: Cambridge University Press.

James V. Wertsch

COMPARATIVE COGNITION

Comparative cognition is the comparison of how animals (including humans) process and interact with the world. What sets animal cognition apart from the behavioristic tradition of stimulus-response (S-R) learning is the recognition that (mental) processes in-

Figure 1

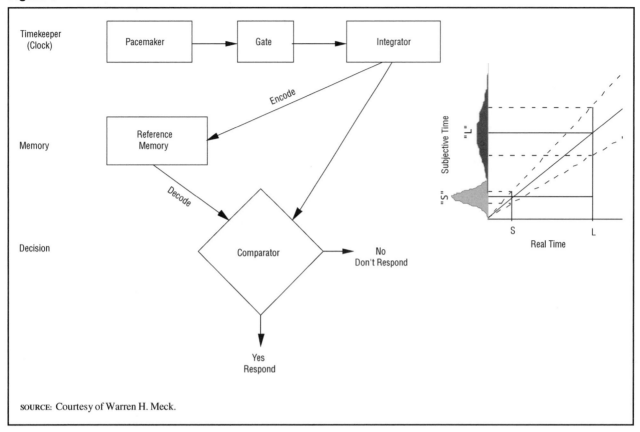

SOURCE: Courtesy of Warren H. Meck.

An information-processing model of temporal processing representative of scalar timing theory.

tervene between the stimulus and response. Some animal-cognitive procedures may be complex (e.g., "feeling of knowing" experiments by Hampton, 2001). But even "simple" Pavlovian conditioning procedures can deal with cognitive processes: for example, taste-aversion conditioning to the "image" of an expected type of food (e.g., Holland, 1990), or higher-order and backward fear conditioning to a neutral stimulus never paired with shock (Cole, Barnet, and Miller, 1995). Techniques developed in the late twentieth century to study cognitive processes have produced exciting revelations about how animals perceive, learn, remember, navigate, communicate, time, and count. This entry highlights some of these developments.

Interval Timing

A tremendous amount of information has accumulated since the 1980s about the interval-timing mechanisms of rats, pigeons, and primates. In a popular "peak" procedure, a stimulus cue is presented and after a fixed elapsed time the next response is rewarded. On some trials, reward is omitted and responding increases to a peak rate and then de-

creases. The peak indicates maximum expectancy of reward. Interval timing typically displays the scalar property—variability (spread) increases proportionally with time. The interval-timing theory receiving the most attention is shown in Figure 1. It includes a clock (pacemaker), a switch (gate) to an accumulator (integrator), reference memory for the expected time, and a comparator for the reference time versus accumulated time to see if "time's up." Converging evidence has been accumulating for each of these hypothetical processes. One example is that drug manipulations of the clock produce abrupt changes in peak time (see Figure 2) with gradual compensation by storage of new accumulator values in reference memory, whereas drug manipulations of the memory produce gradual changes (see Figure 3) due to distorted intervals accumulating in reference memory (Meck, 1996).

Numerosity: A Scale of Numbers

Learning a number scale is fundamental to mathematics. Evidence indicates that rhesus monkeys can learn a number scale (Brannon and Terrace, 1998, 2000). Monkeys touched randomly placed areas on a

Figure 2

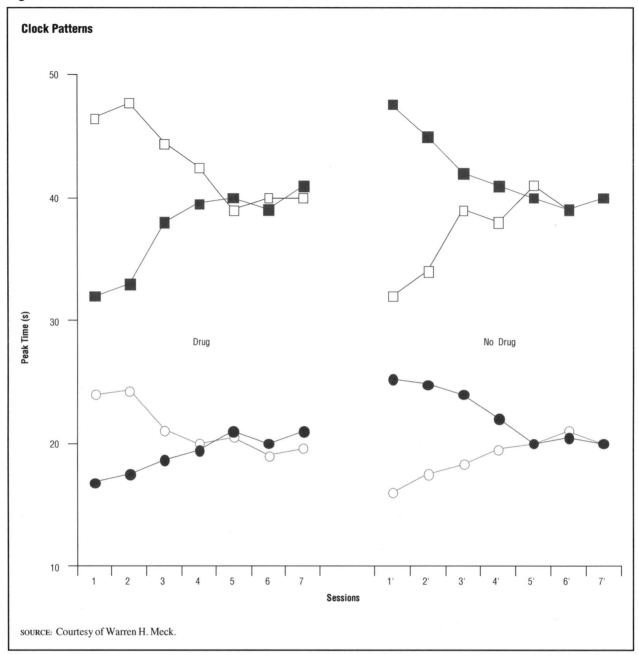

Mean peak times from four different groups of rats (n=10/group) initially trained on either a 40-s (squares) or 20-s (circles) PI-timing procedure and tested under the influence of dopaminergic drugs that affect clock speed (left panel) or after the removal of the drugs (right panel). The closed symbols represent rats treated with methamphetamine (1.5 mg/kg i.p.), and the open symbols represent rats treated with haloperidol (0.12 mg/kg i.p.).

computer screen in order: first the area containing one object, then two, then three, and finally four objects. Objects varied in size, shape, or color and combinations of these dimensions within and across trials. The most remarkable result was that this training spontaneously generalized to larger novel numbers of five to nine objects beyond the range of training numbers.

Landmark Navigation and Cognitive Maps

Clark's nutcrackers apparently use directional bearings from several landmarks to "fix" the location of seed caches (Kamil and Jones, 2000; Kamil and Cheng, 2001). Nutcrackers were more accurate using multiple bearings than any single bearing with a distance measure along the bearing line. This remarkable finding came from manipulating the

Figure 3

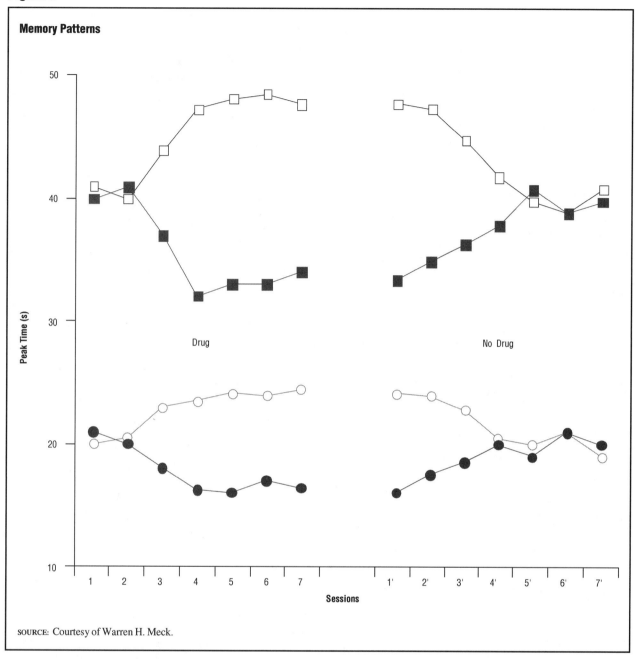

Mean peak times from four different groups of rats (n=10/group) initially trained on either a 40-s (squares) or 20-s (circles) PI-timing procedure and tested under the influence of cholinergic drugs that affect memory-storage speed (left panel) or after the removal of the drugs (right panel). The closed symbols represent rats treated with physostigmine (0.01 mg/kg i.p.) and the open symbols represent rats treated with atropine (0.05 mg/kg i.p.).

goal site in relationship to geometrical properties of fixed landmarks rather than manipulating the landmarks themselves. Landmarks seem to function as a configural whole, not as independent elements. Young children, but not older children or adults, use similar geometric navigation strategies (Hermer-Vazquez, Moffet, Munkholm, 2001). The issue of cognitive maps, however, is complex and is more than configural-landmark navigation (Shettleworth, 1998).

Abstract Concepts

Researchers have long debated which species are capable of abstract concept learning. Abstract concepts are rules (same versus different, identity matching) that transcend the training stimuli. Novel stimuli are used to test for abstract concept learning. Pigeons (like humans, apes, dolphins, and monkeys) are capable of learning abstract concepts. One study showed matching-to-sample (MTS) concept learning by pigeons (Wright, 1997). In MTS, a sample stimulus is followed by two choice stimuli, one of which is correct and matches the sample. Pigeons required to respond to (peck) the sample twenty times before getting the choice stimuli learned the concept fully (as opposed to partially). Other pigeons required to respond fewer times (e.g., once) did not learn the concept at all, and instead learned the configural pattern of each display (sample plus choice stimuli).

Pigeons are also capable of learning a same/different (S/D) abstract concept. In S/D, subjects identify stimuli as same or different. Pigeons most rapidly learn S/D (and the S/D concept partially) with large 384 element arrays and contrasting target regions on different trials (Cook, Katz, and Cavoto, 1997), or with sixteen-element arrays that are composed of all different or all same elements (Young, Wasserman, and Garner, 1997). But when the number of elements in these tasks is reduced to two (minimum number), performance falls to chance. Nevertheless, pigeons are capable of learning a S/D task when trained with two stimuli from the beginning and attain full S/D concept learning when the training set is expanded to 128 to 512 pictures. Rhesus monkeys attained full S/D concept learning with somewhat smaller set sizes than pigeons, and chimpanzees remarkably learned an S/D concept with only two training stimuli (Oden, Thompson, and Premack, 1988).

Equally remarkable is the S/D concept learning by a parrot, Alex, with stimuli that varied along three dimensions (Pepperberg, 1987). Alex responded with the English words "color," "shape," or "mah-mah" (matter). When Alex was presented with a red wooden triangle and a green rawhide triangle, for example, and asked, "What's same?" he typically said, "Shape." When presented with a red wooden square and a blue wooden square and asked, "What's different?" he typically said, "Color." Alex's novel object transfer performance was 85 percent correct. What makes this experiment so remarkable was that Alex had no way of telling which dimension (color, shape, or matter) would be questioned and whether he would be asked, "What's same?" or "What's different?"

Abstract Concepts Based on Categories

Research developments have shown that monkeys could learn an S/D concept with food versus non-food categories (Bovet and Vauclair, 2001). Baboons were given experience with the items and then pres-

ented with pairs of them (behind a window). They were required to pull one of two ropes to indicate whether they were of the same or different categories (food versus nonfood). Novel item transfer was better than 80 percent correct. Rhesus monkeys have also showed category matching (Neiworth and Wright, 1994).

Relations Between Relations: Analogical Reasoning

If abstract concept learning is higher order, then analogical reasoning is higher-higher order. The Miller's Analogies Test is a test of relations between relations. A recent MTS study showed that baboons could learn a relation between relations (Fagot, Wasserman, and Young, 2001). Baboons saw a brief sixteen-icon sample, which was then replaced by two sixteen-icon choice displays. Neither choice display had any icons in common with the sample. The baboons successfully learned and transferred this performance to novel stimuli, which could not be based on stimulus identity or functional categories. It is difficult to escape the conclusion that this behavior is based on a relation between relations. A similar conclusion came from a study on rhesus monkey music perception (Wright et al., 2000). Six-note tonal (childhood songs, tonal algorithm) musical passages, separated by one or two octaves were judged "same" better than 80 percent of the time. Tonal passages form a relation (tune), and thus this octave generalization (no common frequencies) is a relation between relations.

Great apes are particularly remarkable in their ability to form relations between relations. Chimpanzees with no relations-between-relations training "spontaneously" performed correct analogical choices without reward (Thompson, Oden, and Boysen, 1997). If anything could be more remarkable, Sarah, a highly trained chimpanzee arranged four out of five "scattered" geometric forms in the unique analogical relationship (and set aside the distractor) without explicit training (Thompson and Oden, 2000).

Episodic Memory

Episodic memory is memory for a particular event and is related to the issue of consciousness in animals. Recent experiments show that scrub jays have episodic memory (Clayton and Dickinson, 1998; Clayton and Dickinson, 1999; Emery and Clayton, 2001). In one experiment, jays cached wax worms and peanuts in separate and distinctive halves of two distinctive sand-filled ice cube trays (two-by-seven arrays). After four hours, the jays recovered the more desirable wax worms first from one tray. After 124 hours, they recovered the peanuts first from the other tray. In pretraining, they had learned that the wax worms deteriorated after 124 hours. Reversal of their earlier preference for wax worms means that they remembered what (peanuts versus wax worms), when (four versus 124 hours), and where (which tray side) the foods were stored. Cache recovery by Clark's nutcrackers in the forest must also be episodic memory because they use different cache sites each year and overcome potential proactive interference (i.e., confusions) from previous years' sites. Thus, they too know what, when, and where.

Feeling of Knowing: Metacognition

Exciting research developments with monkeys indicate that they "know when they remember" (Hampton, 2001). This ability in humans indicates conscious cognition and is closely aligned with the issue of consciousness and recognition of "self." In a MTS experiment, rhesus monkeys saw a sample (clip-art image), touched the sample, had a retention delay, and then decided whether or not to take a memory test. If they chose to take the memory test, four choices were presented on the four corners of the monitor and reward for the correct choice was highly desired peanuts. If they declined to take the test, they (automatically) received a less preferred pellet. The monkeys were more accurate when they chose to take the test than when they were required to take the test, and this difference increased with delay. An important aspect of this study was requiring the monkeys to monitor their memory before the test was presented. It is difficult to escape the conclusion that these monkeys know when they remember. Pigeons do not show this choice-test advantage (Inman and Shettleworth, 1999), and thus may lack metacognition.

Directions for Future Research

Animals have cognitive abilities that were previously thought to be uniquely human. Other qualitative differences may disappear as procedures better fit the predispositions of species being tested (Clayton and Dickinson, 1999). But there are issues other than finding human cognitive abilities in animals and these issues continue to revolve around what is meant by "comparative" and "cognition."

The Comparative Issue

Criticisms of comparative cognition have been that they are not comparative (Shettleworth, 1993). However, researchers have seen species comparisons in interval timing, landmark navigation, abstract concept learning, analogical reasoning, and metacognition. A problem with proving qualitative differences is that one can never be sure that some other test con-

ditions would not show this ability. The study of quantitative differences encounters the same difficulty. Some argue that comparisons should be among closely related species to study cognitive evolution (Cambell and Hodos, 1991) or environmentally specialized cognitive behavior (Sherry and Schacter, 1987). But even testing closely related species (e.g., Clark's nutcrackers, Mexican jays, pinyon jays, and scrub jays) in the same task does not ensure that quantitative differences represent cognitive differences, as opposed to the task fitting the predispositions of some of the species better. Nevertheless, testing the species in a variety of tasks and varying critical parameters can converge on persuasive evidence for quantitative differences (Olson, Kamil, Balda, and Nims, 1995).

A more overarching goal would seem to understand the mechanisms and processes involved; in short, how cognition works. Any thorough understanding will need evidence from at least three domains: conditions (i.e., natural context) best suited to express this cognitive ability; laboratory tests that manipulate critical parameters over a substantial range; and neurobiology and neural circuitry that mediates this behavior. One can begin in any domain, but will need regular input from the other domains—a sort of cumulative upward spiral and a revisit of issues as evidence accumulates. Ultimately, quantitative differences (e.g., interval timing [Church, Meck, and Gibbon, 1994]) and even qualitative differences (e.g., serial-order learning [Terrace, Chen, and Newman, 1995]; memory rehearsal [Cook, Wright, and Sands, 1991]) should be shown to be individual points of comparison along much larger functional relationships revealed by parametric studies and quantitative models.

The Cognitive Issue

Issues associated with the cognition part of comparative cognition mainly revolve around the strength of evidence for private events (cognitive processes) between the stimulus and response. There will certainly be skeptics of the feeling-of-knowing experiments with animals (Hampton, 2001), but this is only the tip of the iceberg. It gets only better (or worse depending on one's persuasion) with experiments on beliefs, intentions, wants, desires, altruism, concept of self, and knowledge about another's beliefs and intentions—the so-called "theory of mind" experiments (Povinelli, 2001; Tomasello and Call, 1997). These investigations have stimulated a great deal of enthusiasm among scientists. Continued growth and acceptance will likely depend on parametric studies (i.e., manipulating critical variables over a substantial range) and converging evidence from several experiments like the blue jay and wax-worm studies. Furthermore, researchers will need to show that their findings cannot be accounted for by simpler associative learning principles involving observable stimuli and responses, like behavior-based theories timing (Killeen and Fetterman, 1988; Machado, 1997) as opposed to scalar-timing theory (see Figure 1). A wide variety of learning, cognitive, and memory phenomena can be accounted for by careful parametric experimentation coupled with powerful mathematical models to reveal underlying processes (Gallistel and Gibbon, 2000; White and Wixted, 1999). Any time we are tempted to get too heady over some new animal-cognitive phenomenon, we might reflect on the exuberance originally generated by ape-language studies, and recall the instructive (if not tongue-in-cheek) S-R conditioning demonstrations of the pigeon's (cognitive) concepts of insight, symbolic communication, and self conducted by Epstein, Skinner, and their collaborators (1981).

Bibliography

Bovet, D., and Vauclair, J. (2001). Judgment of conceptual identity in monkeys. *Psychonomic Bulletin & Review 8,* 470–475.

Brannon, E. M., and Terrace, H. S. (1998). Ordering of the numerosities 1 to 9 by monkeys. *Science 282,* 746–749.

——— (2000). Representation of the numerosities 1–9 by rhesus macaques (Macaca mulatta). *Journal of Experimental Psychology: Animal Behavior Processes 26,* 31–49.

Campbell, C. B. G., and Hodos, W. (1991). The scala naturae revisited: Evolutionary scales and anagenesis in comparative psychology. *Journal of Comparative Psychology 105,* 211–221.

Church, R. M., Meck, W. H., and Gibbon, J. (1994). Application of scalar timing theory to individual trials. *Journal of Experimental Psychology: Animal Behavior Processes 20,* 135–155.

Clayton, N. S., and Dickinson, A. (1998). Episodic-like memory during cache recovery by scrub jays. *Nature 395,* 272–274.

——— (1999). Memory for the content of caches by scrub jays (Aphelocoma coerulescens). *Journal of Experimental Psychology: Animal Behavior Processes 25,* 82–91.

Cole, R. P., Barnet, R. C., and Miller, R. R. (1995). Temporal encoding in trace conditioning. *Animal Learning and Behavior 23,* 144–153.

Cook, R. G., Katz, J. S., and Cavoto, B. R. (1997). Pigeon same-different concept learning with multiple stimulus classes. *Journal of Experimental Psychology: Animal Behavior Processes 23,* 417–433.

Cook, R. G., Wright, A. A., and Sands, S. F. (1991). Interstimulus interval and viewing time effects in monkey list memory. *Animal Learning and Behavior 19,* 153–163.

Emery, N. J., and Clayton, N. S. (2001). It takes a thief to know a thief: Effects of social context on prospective caching strategies in scrub jays. *Nature 414,* 443–446.

Epstein, R., Lanza, R. P., and Skinner, B. F. (1981). "Self-awareness" in the pigeon. *Science 212,* 695–696.

Fagot, J., Wasserman, E. A., and Young, M. E. (2001). Discriminating the relation between relations: The role of entropy in abstract conceptualization by baboons (Papio papio) and humans (Homo sapiens). *Journal of Experimental Psychology: Animal Behavior Processes 27,* 316–328.

Gallistel, C. R., and Gibbon, J. (2000). Time, rate, and conditioning. *Psychological Review 107,* 289–344.

Hampton, R. R. (2001). Rhesus monkeys know when they remember. *Proceeding of the National Academy of Sciences of the United States of America 98,* 5,359–5,362.

Hermer-Vazquez, L. Moffet, A., and Munkholm, P. (2001). Language, space, and the development of cognitive flexibility in humans: The case of two spatial memory tasks. *Cognition 79,* 263–299.

Holland, P. C. (1990). Event representation in Pavlovian conditioning: Image and action. *Cognition 37,* 105–131.

Inman, A., and Shettleworth, S. J. (1999). Detecting metamemory in nonverbal subjects: A test with pigeons. *Journal of Experimental Psychology: Animal Behavior Processes 25,* 389–395.

Kamil, A. C., and Cheng, K. (2001). Way-finding and landmarks: The multiple-bearings hypothesis. *Journal of Experimental Biology 204,* 103–113.

Kamil, A. C., and Jones, J. E. (2000). Geometric rule learning by Clark's nutcrackers (Nucifraga columbiana). *Journal of Experimental Psychology: Animal Behavior Processes 26,* 439–453.

Katz, J. S., Wright, A. A., and Bachevalier, J. (2002). Same/different concept learning in Rhesus monkeys. *Journal of Experimental Psychology: Animal Behavior Processes 28.*

Killeen, P. R., and Fetterman, J. G. A behavioral theory of timing. *Psychological Review 95,* 274–295.

Machado, A. (1997). Learning the temporal dynamics of behavior. *Psychological Review 104,* 241–265.

Meck, W. H. (1996). Neuropharmacology of timing and time perception. *Cognitive Brain Research 3,* 227–242.

Neiworth, J. J., and Wright, A. A. (1994). Monkeys (Macaca mulatta) learn category matching in a nonidentical same-different task. *Journal of Experimental Psychology: Animal Behavior Processes 20,* 429–435.

Oden, D. L., Thompson, R. K., and Premack, D. (1988). Spontaneous transfer of matching by infant chimpanzees (Pan troglodytes). *Journal of Experimental Psychology: Animal Behavior Processes 14,* 140–145.

Olson, D. J., Kamil, A. C., Balda, R. P., and Nims, P. J. (1995). Performance of four seed-caching corvid species in operant tests of nonspatial and spatial memory. *Journal of Comparative Psychology 109,* 173–181.

Pepperberg, I. M. (1987). Acquisition of the same/different concept by an African Grey parrot (Psittacus erithacus): Learning with respect to categories of color, shape, and material. *Animal Learning and Behavior 15,* 423–432.

Povinelli, D. J. (2001). On the possibilities of detecting intentions prior to understanding them. In B. F. Malle, L. J. Moses, and D. A. Baldwin, eds., *Intentions and intentionality: Foundations of social cognition.* Cambridge, MA: MIT Press.

Sherry, D. F., and Schacter, D. L. (1987). The evolution of multiple memory systems. *Psychological Review 94,* 439–454.

Shettleworth, S. J. (1993). Where is the comparison in comparative cognition? Alternative research programs. *Psychological Science 4,* 179–184.

——— (1998). *Cognition, evolution, and behavior.* New York: Oxford University.

Terrace, H. S., Chen, S., and Newman, A. B. (1995). Serial learning with a wild card by pigeons (Columba livia): Effect of list length. *Journal of Comparative Psychology 109,* 1,162–1,172.

Thompson, R. K. R., and Oden, D. L. (2000). Categorical perception and conceptual judgments by nonhuman primates: The paleological monkey and the analogical ape. *Cognitive Science 24,* 363–396.

Thompson, R. K. R., Oden, D. L., and Boysen, S. T. (1997). Language-naïve chimpanzees (Pan troglodytes) judge relations between relations in a conceptual matching-to-sample task. *Journal of Experimental Psychology: Animal Behavior Processes 23,* 31–43.

Tomasello, M., and Call, J. (1997). *Primate cognition.* New York: Oxford University Press.

White, K. G., and Wixted, J. T. (1999). Psychophysics of remembering. *Journal of the Experimental Analysis of Behavior 71,* 91–113.

Wright, A. A. (1997). Concept learning and learning strategies. *Psychological Science 8*, 119–123.

Wright, A. A., Rivera, J. J., Hulse, S. H., Shyan, M., and Neiworth, J. J[GU2]. (2000). Music perception and octave generalization in rhesus monkeys. *Journal of Experimental Psychology: General 129*, 291–307.

Young, M. E., Wasserman, E. A., and Garner, K. L. (1997). Effects of number of items on the pigeon's discrimination of same from different visual displays. *Journal of Experimental Psychology: Animal Behavior Processes 23*, 491–501.

Anthony A. Wright

CONCEPTS AND CATEGORIES, LEARNING OF

Concepts are a fundamental aspect of intelligent behavior. Traditionally, a concept has been viewed as a mental representation that picks out a group of equivalent items or a category. For example, every person has a concept of *dog* and can use that concept to pick out a category of things that one would call *dogs*. Some of the most fundamental questions about the mind include the following: *What* do human concepts consist of (i.e, what is their structure)? *How* are they are acquired? *Why* do humans have concepts (i.e, What functions do they have)?

What Do Human Concepts Consist Of?

An early, popular view of concepts was the classical view. For a variety of reasons this approach was unsatisfactory and gave way to the probabilistic view. These views are described and compared below.

Classical versus Probabilistic View

The classical view argues that concepts are structured around defining features (Bruner, Goodnow, and Austin, 1956). Defining features are features that are singly necessary and jointly sufficient to define the concept. For example, the concept *bachelor* has the defining features *human*, *unmarried*, and *male*.

However, the classical view appears to have a number of serious problems. First, if concepts have defining features, then one ought to be able to specify what they are. But many common concepts, such as *game* or *chair*, seem to have no defining features. Instead, instances of these concepts have characteristic features that are neither necessary nor sufficient for category membership (e.g., *has four legs* and *has a back* for *chairs*). Second, not all instances of a concept are equally good examples of that concept. For example, people judge robins to be better examples of the concept *bird* than ostriches. If both robins and ostriches have the defining features of birds, then why should robins be considered better examples of birds than ostriches? These and other problems (Smith and Medin, 1981) have led to a shift in attention from the classical view to the probabilistic view.

The probabilistic view argues that most concepts are organized around properties that are only characteristic or typical of a category (rather than defining). One specific account of the probabilistic view assumes that a concept is a summary representation or prototype that indicates what is, on the average, true of a category (e.g., the bird prototype would include features such as *flies* and *sings* because the properties are true of most though not all birds). The prototype view readily handles goodness-of-example effects; the more similar an item is to the prototype, the more typical it will be of the category. For example, robins would be more similar to the bird prototype than are ostriches because they have more features that are generally true of birds. Thus, they would be better examples of birds.

However, the prototype view also has problems. Prototype representations alone are not rich enough to capture people's knowledge about a category. For example, people are sensitive to the number of instances in a category (e.g., there are many more houses than igloos), the variability of features (e.g., the size of quarters varies less than the size of pizzas), and the correlations between features (e.g., wooden spoons tend to be big whereas metal spoons tend to be small [Medin, 1989]). To overcome such difficulties, researchers have suggested that instead of (or in addition to) a prototype people may simply store memory instances or examples of the category and reason with them (Brooks, 1978). Thus, according to the exemplar view, for instance, the concept of a chair would include memory traces of particular chairs and their associated features.

The Theory View

Another approach to concepts is the theory view. As described below, this approach developed as a reaction to certain limitations of the classical and probabilistic approaches. In particular, the classical and probabilistic views failed to take into account people's background knowledge or theories of the world.

The shift from the classical view to the probabilistic view was motivated by a detailed analysis of natural object categories. Associated with this analysis is the view that concepts or mental representations of categories closely mirror the structure afforded by properties of category members. It seems almost a tautology that if the structure of examples does not have defining features then the corresponding mental representations cannot conform to the classical view. Similarly, a probabilistic category structure suggests a probabilistic concept representation. In brief, researchers assume that mental representations are determined by the structure of examples in the world.

However, the classical and probabilistic views tend to ignore the role of the learner in their accounts of concepts. According to the theory view, learners also impose structure on their concepts. That is, concepts are based on a learner's general knowledge and theories of the world together with information provided by the environment (Carey, 1985; Murphy and Medin, 1985; Rips, 1989). For example, Susan Carey showed that children's biological theories influence their patterns of inductions at a very early age. To illustrate, a mechanical monkey is rated by both children and adults to be more similar to a human being than is a worm, yet even young children infer that worms rather than toy monkeys have a spleen after being told that people have a spleen, *a round and green [thing] . . . in the person's body*. In this example, the feature *has a spleen*, which is more consistent with a child's background knowledge or "theory" about animate things than inanimate things.

Theories themselves may be anchored by how well their predictions receive support from the world. Gregory Murphy and Douglas Medin (1985) suggest that the relation between concept and examples is like that between theory and data. Thus, concepts would not necessarily consist of features that are also in examples; rather, the constituents of examples would only need to *support* more abstract constituents of concepts (Wisniewski and Medin, 1994). For example, one may infer that a man is drunk because one sees him jump into a pool fully clothed. If one does so, it is probably not because the feature *jumps into pools, clothed* is listed with the concept *drunk*. Rather, it is because part of one's concept of *drunk* involves a theory of impaired judgment that serves to explain the man's behavior.

How Are Concepts Acquired?

Young children probably enter the world with few preexisting concepts. Instead, they must acquire or form concepts from experiences (e.g., form a concept of dog from existing experiences with dogs). As described below, the classical, probabilistic, and theory views of concepts propose different ways in which concepts are acquired.

According to the classical view, the process of concept formation is one of discovering necessary and sufficient attributes by observing which attributes occur in all members and only in members of the category. Research associated with the classical view has been directed at investigating hypothesis testing strategies, with each hypothesis being a guess as to which features are part of the definition (Levine, 1971).

In contrast, according to the probabilistic view, concept learning occurs by averaging values of members (Posner and Keele, 1968), by attending to features commonly shared by members and discarding features varying among members (Elio and Anderson, 1981), or by noting the most common value on each dimension. The basic idea behind these models can be traced to Galton's "composite photograph" theory (Galton, 1879). Galton superimposed several faces to make a composite photograph in which common properties were accentuated and variant properties were attenuated. Such a process is assumed in prototype theories. On the other hand, exemplar models assume category instances are stored but generally have not specified detailed learning mechanisms (see Kruschke, 1992, for an exception). These views assume that the learner begins with features of the entities and then learns which features are important for the concept. However, research conducted in the 1990s suggests that an important part of concept learning is learning to identify the features themselves (Schyns, Goldstone, Thibaut, 1998).

The theory-based view of concepts takes a different perspective on concept formation. Several researchers have proposed that humans may be born with a naive physics and a naive biology or psychology (Carey, 1985; Keil, 1989; Spelke, 1990) that act as initial theories to organize conceptual knowledge. A major implication of the theory-based view is that concept learning involves integrating new examples with prior knowledge. In particular, prior knowledge may influence the identification of features and, in turn, information about examples may modify a person's prior knowledge (Wisniewski and Medin, 1994).

Taking the theory-based view, a group of researchers in artificial intelligence (an area in computer science the goal of which is to develop computers to do intelligent things) have developed models of concept formation called explanation-based learning (Mitchell, Keller, and Kedar-Cabelli, 1986; DeJong and Mooney, 1986). These models suggest that the most important aspect of concept learning is to explain why a given example is an instance of the concept. Construction of the explanation is carried out by causally connecting known concepts. For example, suppose a computer is to learn a concept *cup* and it already knows such concepts as *liftable, handle, liquid container,* and *stable*. Seeing an object that can be lifted, has a handle, contains liquid, and is stable, the system uses its background knowledge to construct an explanation about why one can drink from this object. Then it generalizes this explanation to develop its concept of *cup*.

Learning by analogy is another form of theory or knowledge-driven learning in which a known similar concept is modified. For example, one can learn about the internal structure of atoms by applying one's knowledge of solar system (e.g., electrons revolve around the nucleus as planets revolve around the sun [Gentner, 1989]). One can also discover new features through analogy or metaphors (e.g., given *a smile is like a magnet*, one can learn that a smile attracts).

The Why of Concept Learning

There are many reasons why humans have concepts. They allow people to classify things (e.g., recognize that something is snake) and to make important predictions or inferences (e.g., that snake may be poisonous). John Anderson (1990) has developed a theory of concepts that emphasizes this prediction function. Other functions include explanation (e.g., the concept *introvert* might help to explain why some person did not attend a party), reasoning (deriving knowledge from the stored information), communication, and conceptual combination (e.g., from the concepts *glass* and *elephant* one might construct the combined concept *glass elephant*). Many approaches to concept learning have focused only on the classification function. However, functions of concepts interact such that it is important to study multiple functions together. For example, Brian Ross (1997) found that the diagnosis (classification) of a disease was importantly influenced by features that were relevant to its treatment (Malt et al., 1999; Markman and Makin, 1998, for other examples of interactions). Researchers have begun to appreciate and investigate the variety of functions that concepts have.

See also: SEMANTIC MEMORY: COGNITIVE ASPECTS; SEMANTIC MEMORY: NEUROBIOLOGICAL PERSPECTIVE

Bibliography

Anderson, J. R. (1990). *The adaptive characteristic of thought.* Hillsdale, NJ: Erlbaum.

Brooks, L. R. (1978). Non-analytic concept formation and memory for instances. In E. Rosch and B. Lloyd, eds., *Cognition and categorization.* Hillsdale, NJ: Erlbaum.

Bruner, J. S., Goodnow, J. J., and Austin, G. A. (1956). *A study of thinking.* New York: Wiley.

Carey, S. (1985). *Conceptual change in childhood.* Cambridge, MA: MIT Press.

DeJong, G. F., and Mooney, R. J. (1986). Explanation-based learning: An alternative view. *Machine Learning 1,* (2) 145–176.

Elio, R., and Anderson, J. R. (1981). The effects of category generalizations and instance similarity on schema abstraction. *Journal of Experimental Psychology: Human Learning and Memory 7,* 397–417.

Galton, F. (1879). Composite portraits, made by combining those of many different persons into a single, resultant figure. *Journal of the Anthropological Institute 8,* 132–144.

Gentner, D. (1989). The mechanisms of analogical learning. In S. Vosniadou and A. Ortony, eds., *Similarity and analogical reasoning.* Cambridge, UK: Cambridge University Press.

Keil, F. C. (1989). *Concepts, kinds, and cognitive development.* Cambridge, MA: MIT Press.

Kruschke, J. K. (1992). ALCOVE: An exemplar-based connectionist model of category learning. *Psychological Review 99,* 22–44.

Levine, M. (1971). Hypothesis theory and non-learning despite ideal S-R reinforcement contingencies. *Psychological Review 45,* 626–632.

Malt, B. C., Sloman, S. A., Gennari, S., Shi, M., and Wang, Y. (1999). Knowing versus naming: Similarity and the linguistic categorization of artifacts. *Journal of Memory and Language 40,* 230–262.

Markman, A. B., and Makin, V. S. (1998). Referential communication and category acquisition. *Journal of Experimental Psychology: General 127,* 331–354.

Medin, D. L. (1989). Concepts and conceptual structure. *American Psychologist 12,* 1,469–1,481.

Mitchell, T. M., Keller, R. M., and Kedar-Cabelli, S. T. (1986). Explanation-based generalization: A unifying view. *Machine Learning 1,* 47–80.

Murphy, G. L., and Medin, D. L. (1985). The role of theories in conceptual coherence. *Psychological Review 92,* 289–316.

Posner, M. L., and Keele, S. W. (1968). On the genesis of abstract ideas. *Journal of Experimental Psychology 77,* 353–363.

Rips, L. J. (1989). Similarity, typicality, and categorization. In S. Vosniadou and A. Ortony, eds., *Similarity and analogical reasoning.* Cambridge, UK: Cambridge University Press.

Ross, B. H. (1997). The use of categories affect classification. *Journal of Memory and Language 37,* 240–267.

Schyns, P. G., Goldstone, R. L., and Thibaut, J. P. (1998). The development of features in object concepts. *Behavioral and Brain Sciences 21,* 1–54.

Smith, E. E., and Medin, D. L. (1981). *Categories and concepts.* Cambridge, MA: Harvard University Press.

Spelke, E. S. (1990). Principles of object perception. *Cognitive Science 14,* 29–56.

Wisniewski, E. J., and Medin, D. L. (1994). On the interaction of theory and data in concept learning. *Cognitive Science 18,* 221–281.

Douglas L. Medin
Wou-Kyoung Ahn
Revised by Edward Wisniewski

CONDITIONING

[*A survey of the forms of learning called conditioning will be found under* CONDITIONING, CLASSICAL AND INSTRUMENTAL. *The following articles discuss specific aspects of the classical conditioning paradigm in greater detail:*

CLASSICAL CONDITIONING: BEHAVIORAL PHENOMENA
CONDITIONING, CELLULAR AND NETWORK SCHEMES FOR HIGHER-ORDER FEATURES OF CLASSICAL
NEURAL SUBSTRATES OF CLASSICAL CONDITIONING

A particular type of instrumental conditioning is more closely examined under OPERANT BEHAVIOR.]

CONDITIONING, CELLULAR AND NETWORK SCHEMES FOR HIGHER-ORDER FEATURES OF CLASSICAL

Experimental work on invertebrates and vertebrates has begun to allow the analysis of the neural mechanisms underlying second-order conditioning, blocking, and contingency. Here we look at the experimental and theoretical data that provide a cellular- and network-level description of higher-order forms of classical conditioning.

Experimental Models of Higher-Order Forms of Classical Conditioning

The development of neural analogs of habituation, sensitization, and classical conditioning have greatly enhanced the understanding of the neural mechanisms responsible for these forms of learning. A logical extension of these studies is to develop neural analogs of higher-order forms of classical conditioning. Research has shown that because many higher-order forms of conditioning are present in invertebrates, these preparations may lead to the establishment of neural analogs of higher-order conditioning. Moreover, recent research in vertebrates has also begun to examine the neural mechanisms of higher-order conditioning.

Second-Order Conditioning

In second-order conditioning, a CS produces a conditioned response not by direct pairing with the US but by pairing with another CS that has previously been paired with the US. The training protocol for second-order conditioning proceeds in two phases. During Phase I, CS1 is paired with the US (resulting in CS1+). During Phase II, a novel CS2 is paired with CS1+. The defining feature of second-order conditioning is that a conditioned stimulus (CS1+) functions as a reinforcing stimulus for the conditioning of a second conditioned stimulus (CS2).

Second-order conditioning has been demonstrated in various invertebrate (e.g., Menzel, 1981; Sahley et al., 1982) and vertebrate preparations (Rescorla, 1980). It has also been observed in the gill-withdrawal reflex in a reduced preparation in *Aplysia* (Hawkins et al., 1998). In this preparation the mantle organs are isolated together with the abdominal ganglia. Tactile and electrical stimulation of the siphon and gill can be used as CSs and US. In this study extinction of CS1 resulted in extinction of CS2, suggesting the formation of a direct association between both conditioned stimuli. Indeed an important question regarding the underlying mechanisms of second-order conditioning is whether CS1+ essentially takes over the system

generally activated by the US or whether qualitatively different associations are formed between the CSs. The notion that the same associative forms of synaptic plasticity are involved in both the formation of the CS1-US and CS2-CS1 associations has been corroborated by studies in rat fear conditioning that have shown that the same manipulation that blocks first-order conditioning also blocks second-order conditioning without blocking the conditioned response (Gewirtz and Davis, 1997). It was shown that infusion of an NMDA antagonist (which blocks associative synaptic plasticity) into the amygdala prevented second-order conditioning. This finding supports the notion that second-order conditioning relies on the same forms of synaptic plasticity as classical conditioning.

Blocking

Blocking, along with contingency, establishes that pairing of a CS with a US is not sufficient to produce conditioning. Blocking shows that it is important that the CS contains novel information about the US. A typical blocking protocol (Kamin, 1968) consists of two phases. First CS1 is paired with the US. In Phase II a compound stimulus CS1+/CS2 is paired with the US. In the case of complete blocking, CS2 does not undergo any conditioning. The argument is that even though it was explicitly paired with the US, CS2 does not provide any information that was not already predicted by CS1+.

Blocking has been described in many vertebrates, in the snail *Limax* (Sahley et al., 1982) and in bees (Smith and Cobey, 1994). A critical question regarding the mechanisms underlying blocking is, How does preconditioning of CS1 prevent or "block" the conditioning of CS2, even though CS2 is paired with the US? One study on eyeblink conditioning in rabbits has suggested that blocking relies on active inhibition of the US pathway (Kim et al., 1998). Eyeblink conditioning relies on the cerebellum. It was shown that complex spikes in Purkinje cells of the cerebellum (which represent activity in the inferior olive) are elicited by the CS-US pairing in naïve animals but not by CS-US presentations in trained animals. Since inferior olive activity seems to mediate the US, these studies suggest that the US pathway is actively inhibited during Phase II of a blocking protocol. The active suppression of the US response seems to be mediated by the inhibition in the inferior olive produced by the cerebellar output (representing CS1+). Indeed, blocking of this inhibition during Phase II of training prevented blocking—that is, it allowed CS2 to undergo conditioning. This manipulation did not prevent first-order conditioning to the CS1 in a separate group of control animals. These experiments suggest that first-order conditioning not only results in the production of a CR but also causes active inhibition of the US pathway; they also suggest that this negative-feedback loop is involved in blocking (see below).

Contingency

Rescorla (1968) suggested that it is not just the number of CS-US pairings but also the correlation between the CS and the US, or the ability of the CS to predict the US, that determines the occurrence of conditioning. He demonstrated that if one group of animals was presented with ten CS-US pairings, and one group was trained with ten extra USs in addition to the ten CS-US pairings (i.e., the probability of a US given a CS equals .5), the latter group displayed less conditioning. Despite both groups having received an equal number of CS-US pairings, the group that received the additional US presentations exhibited less conditioning.

In most invertebrate (Abramson and Bitterman, 1986; Farley, 1987) and vertebrate preparations in which it has been examined, contingency has been observed. However, it is important to distinguish between the different protocols used to study contingency. The extra US presentations can take place before (US preexposure), interspersed with, or after (US postexposure) the CS-US pairings. In *Aplysia* it has been shown that extra US presentations interspersed with training decreases conditioning (Hawkins et al., 1986). Understanding the mechanisms underlying contingency requires a determination of whether both US pre- and postexposures decrease conditioning. This is because both US pre- and postexposure effects are difficult to explain with the same mechanism. For example, Hawkins and Kandel (1984) suggested that contingency could result from habituation of the US pathway; this phenomenon, however, would not account for postexposure effects. Thus, it is possible that what is often thought of as a single higher-order form of conditioning may actually reflect multiple mechanisms.

Theoretical Models of Higher-Order Forms of Conditioning

Some researchers have proposed numerous mechanistic models that address both the cellular and network mechanisms underlying higher-order forms of conditioning (Hawkins and Kandel, 1984; Gluck and Thompson, 1987; Buonomano et al., 1990). Many of these models share common conceptual features that we will examine with respect to a model of second-order conditioning and blocking originally developed in the context of the *Aplysia* siphon-withdrawal reflex (Buonomano et al., 1990).

Figure 1

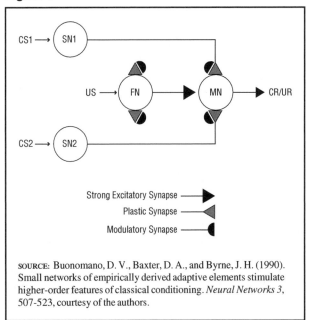

SOURCE: Buonomano, D. V., Baxter, D. A., and Byrne, J. H. (1990). Small networks of empirically derived adaptive elements stimulate higher-order features of classical conditioning. *Neural Networks 3*, 507-523, courtesy of the authors.

Schematic circuit of a model which exhibits second-order conditioning and blocking. Conditioned stimuli (CS) activate sensory neurons (SN). In the naïve state the SNs make weak synapses unto both the motor neuron (MN) and the facilitatory neuron (FN). These synapses can be potentiated by activity-dependent plasticity: Synapses undergo potentiation if they are coactive with the (FN). A key element of the model is that plasticity is occurring in parallel at two sites: SN→MN and SN→FN. It is this feature that allows a previously conditioned stimulus to function as a US.

Consider two CS pathways, CS1 and CS2, each represented by a sensory neuron (SN1 and SN2), a US pathway represented modulatory or facilitatory neuron (FN), and a single output unit that generates both the CR and UR, represented by a motor neuron (MN). An important aspect of the network is that the CS neurons not only connect to the MN but also to the FN (see Figure 1). During first-order conditioning in which the SN1 and FN are paired (for example with a 100-ms interval), the facilitatory neuron will produce associative plasticity at both the SN1→MN and SN1→FN synapse.

Second-Order Conditioning

It is easy to see how this circuit is intrinsically able to account for second-order conditioning. Since plasticity is also occurring at the SN1→FN synapse, CS1 can take over the FN and become a US. When CS2 and CS1 are paired, CS1 will activate the FN and result in conditioning of CS2. In this model, second-order conditioning results directly from associative synaptic plasticity occurring at two synapses. Plasticity at the SN1→MN synapse is responsible for the generation of the conditioned response, whereas plasticity at the SN1→FN synapses accounts for second-order conditioning. One important prediction of this type of model is that it should be possible to block second-order conditioning without interfering with first-order conditioning by specifically blocking plasticity at the SN1→FN synapse.

Blocking

Like second-order conditioning, blocking could arise from the ability of a previously conditioned CS1+ (SN1+) to "take control" of the FN. As in second-order conditioning, during Phase I of training, the synaptic strength of SN1 would increase and become strong enough to activate the FN. There are two consequences of this CS1-induced activity in the FN that would contribute to blocking. Note that if SN1+ effectively activates the FN (and activity in the FN undergoes rapid depression), during the Phase II of blocking in which CS1+/CS2 are paired with the US, two important things happen: First, the FN will be activated approximately simultaneously with the onset of CS1+/CS2, essentially resulting in a 0-ms interstimulus interval that should not result in conditioning of CS2. Second, since the FN undergoes depression, the output of the FN in response to a US that followed CS1/CS2 would be small or zero and would not support associative conditioning of SN2. One subtle aspect of blocking pertains to the question of extinction of CS1+: if CS2 does not undergo conditioning because the US in ineffective, why doesn't CS1+ undergo extinction? Plasticity in the *Aplysia* sensory neurons predicts that the effective interstimulus interval function of plasticity will be state-dependent. That is, while a nonconditioned SN may not exhibit plasticity with a 0-ms ISI, a conditioned SN can exhibit plasticity at 0 ms and thus prevent extinction of CS1+ during Phase II of blocking.

Therefore, in this model, although CS2 would be paired with the US during Phase II of training, prior conditioning of CS1 would block associative enhancement of SN2. Thus, blocking could be supported by activity-dependent neuromodulation (the mechanism of classical conditioning) in combination with accommodation or synaptic depression.

Conclusion

The results of both empirical and theoretical studies indicate that at least two factors determine the ability of neural circuits to support various features of learning: the learning rules or forms of synaptic plasticity and the connectivity of the circuitry in which those forms of plasticity are embedded. Therefore,

complex forms of learning may differ from simple forms of learning in either the form(s) of cellular plasticity involved and/or in the circuitry. However, the studies described above indicate that when the same forms of synaptic plasticity responsible for simpler forms of associative learning are embedded in more complex networks, more complex forms of learning may emerge, including blocking and second-order conditioning.

See also: APLYSIA: CLASSICAL CONDITIONING AND OPERANT CONDITIONING; INVERTEBRATE LEARNING: ASSOCIATIVE LEARNING AND MEMORY PROCESSING IN BEES; INVERTEBRATE LEARNING: ASSOCIATIVE LEARNING IN LIMAX

Bibliography

Buonomano, D. V., Baxter, D. A., and Byrne, J. H. (1990). Small networks of empirically derived adaptive elements simulate higher-order features of classical conditioning. *Neural Networks 3*, 507–523.

Gewirtz, J. C., and Davis, M., (1997) Second-order fear conditioning prevented by blocking NMDA receptors in amygdala. *Nature 368*, 471–474.

Gluck, M. A., and Thompson, R. F. (1987). Modeling the neural substrates of associative learning and memory, A computational approach. *Psychological Review 94*, 176–191.

Hawkins, R. D., Carew, T. J., and Kandel, E. R. (1986). Effects of interstimulus interval and contingency on classical conditioning of the *Aplysia* siphon withdrawal reflex. *Journal of Neuroscience 6*, 1,695–1,701.

Hawkins, R. D., Cohen, T. E., Greene, W., and Kandel, E. R. (1998). Classical conditioning, differential conditioning, and second-order conditioning in the *Aplysia* gill-withdrawal reflex in a simplified mangle organ preparation. *Behavioral Neuroscience 112*, 636–645.

Hawkins, R. D., and Kandel, E. R. (1984). Is there a cell-biological alphabet for simple forms of learning? *Psychological Review 91*, 376–391.

Kim, J. J., Krupa, D. J., and Thompson, R. F. (1988). Inhibitory cerebello-olivary projections and blocking effect in classical conditioning. *Science 279*, 570–573.

Rescorla, R. A. (1968). Probability of shock in the presence and absence of CS in fear conditioning. *Journal of Comparative and Physiological Psychology 66*, 1–5.

—— (1980). *Pavlovian second-order conditioning, studies in associative learning.* New York: Erlbaum.

Smith, B. H., and Boey, S. (1994). The olfactory memory of the honeybee Apis mellifera II Blocking between odorants in binary mixtures. *Journal of Experimental Biology 195*, 91–108.

Jennifer L. Raymond
John H. Byrne
Revised by Dean V. Buonomano

CONDITIONING, CLASSICAL AND INSTRUMENTAL

Classical (Pavlovian) and instrumental (Thorndikian) conditioning are the two most widely employed paradigms for studying simple, associative learning resulting from the organism's exposure to the temporal conjunction of two or more events. The fully specified classical conditioning paradigm consists of a set of operations involving an *unconditioned stimulus* (US) reliably producing an *unconditioned response* (UR) and a *conditioned stimulus* (CS) initially shown not to produce a response resembling the UR. The CS and US are then presented repeatedly to the organism in a specified order and temporal spacing, and a response similar to the UR develops to the CS that is called the *conditioned response* (CR); that is, *CS-CR* functions are obtained. Control over the temporal conjunction of the CS, US, and UR makes classical conditioning preparations ideal vehicles for studying associative learning because they can uniquely specify stimulus antecedents to the target response. Various temporal arrangements of the CS and US give rise to different forms of classical conditioning (e.g., *delay, trace, simultaneous*). Classical conditioning is called *classical reward* conditioning if the US is a positive stimulus and *classical defense* conditioning if it is negative stimulus. The positive or negative designation depends on the independent demonstration of the organism's performing instrumental responses necessary to obtain the US or to remove itself from the US, respectively. What distinguishes classical from instrumental conditioning is that presentation or omission of the US is independent of CR occurrence; and the definition of a CR is restricted to a target response selected from among those effector systems elicited as URs by the US. Adherence to both components of the definition of classical conditioning avoids common confusions and ambiguities with other associative learning paradigms commonly designated as "classical conditioning."

Stimulus-Stimulus Paradigms

The designation "classical conditioning" has been applied to paradigms meeting only the requirement that CS and US be administered independent of the target response, ignoring selection of the UR. As a consequence, the term "classical conditioning" has been extended from Russian physiologist Ivan Petrovich Pavlov's *CS-CR* to stimulus—stimulus (*S-S*) conditioning paradigms involving principally conditioned stimulus-instrumental response (*CS-IR*) and *autoshaping* procedures. The *CS-IR* paradigms include *conditioned suppression* and other *classical-instrumental transfer* procedures in which the stimulus-stimulus pairings of classical conditioning are conducted with a CS and a biologically significant event (e.g., shock) but without measurement of a UR or CR. The CS is then presented during ongoing instrumental behavior and its facilitory or disruptive effect on responding is measured; therefore, CS-IR functions

are obtained. Autoshaping consists of response-independent presentations of a lighted manipulandum (e.g., lighted key) as a CS and activation of a food magazine as the US; the target response is contact with the manipulandum (e.g., key pecking). Key pecking is not an instrumental response, nor is it a UR appearing in the constellation of URs to food in the mouth (Woodruff and Williams, 1976). Hence, acquisition of a response in an effector system not elicited by the US qualifies autoshaping as a "new" associative learning paradigm.

Some *discriminative approach* procedures have been designated as "Pavlovian" simply because an explicit cue (CS) is presented and food or water, designated the US, is made available at a fixed time following CS onset (e.g., Holland and Rescorla, 1975) and the approach behavior, by definition instrumental to receipt of the reinforcing event, has been erroneously designated a CR. At present, the preceding paradigms are widely employed in the study of associative learning, but whether they will converge with the empirical laws of CS-CR paradigms has yet to be determined systematically. The S-S and discriminative approach paradigms lack the capability of CS-CR paradigms to exercise absolute control over the timing and sequencing of stimulus events; and to identify the stimulus antecedents to the target response from the outset of training. In addition, with CS-IR and discriminative approach procedures, the target response is instrumentally conditioned. Consequently, these paradigms might be expected to be even less likely to display convergence with the empirical laws of CS-CR paradigms. In any event, despite the greater technical demands of measuring URs and CRs in CS-CR research, their methodological characteristics favor their use in the study of associative learning.

Biological Substrates

The CS-CR paradigms are ideally suited for the study of the biological substrates of associative learning because the target response is defined anatomically by a set of movements or secretions. The UCS's elicitation of the UCR permits identification of the target response's final common neural pathway(s) outside the conditioning situation and, thereby, affords the opportunity to observe changes in its activity from the start of conditioning (Thompson, 1976). In contrast, S-S contingency and discriminative approach paradigms are inherently unsuitable for studying the biological basis of learning. First, in CS-IR paradigms, changes in the instrumental target response are not the consequences of its participation in the learning process. Rather, the changes are the result of interactions of hypothetical (unobserved) CRs with the CS that are governed by prior CS-US pairings. As a consequence, any neural analysis of learning that is directed at changes in the target response is pointless. Second, since the target response in the discriminative approach paradigm is outcome-defined, a wide variety of different body movements can yield the required outcome. Therefore, it is virtually impossible to identify a final common pathway for the movements that make up the response.

Control Methodology

The associative nature of a conditioning preparation has come to be determined by the contiguous occurrence of the CS and US and a set of control operations intended to estimate the contribution of other possible processes to responding. All response systems show some level of baseline activity, often raised by UCS presentations, which can produce an accidental coincidence of the CS and target response. Moreover, the likelihood of a target response to the CS may be systematically affected by *alpha responses*, which are URs to the CS in the same effector system as the target response; and *pseudo-conditioned* and *sensitized* responses established on the basis of prior US-alone presentations. A detailing of the latency, duration, amplitude, and course of habituation of the alpha response with a control group given CS-alone presentations can provide a basis for eliminating alphas from consideration as a CR, since they are usually of a shorter latency than CRs. Hence, if a sufficiently long CS-US interval is employed, both alphas and CRs can be observed in the interval and scored accordingly (Gormezano, 1966; Gormezano et al., 1983).

The reinstatement or augmentation of alphas to the CS through US-alone or CS-US pairings is referred to as *sensitization*. After eliminating alphas from consideration, the contribution of *pseudo-CRs* to CR measurement can be assessed by presentations of the US one or more times prior to CS presentations. The procedure frequently results in responses to the CS, labeled pseudo-CRs, which are treated separately from CRs because of their occurrence in the absence of CS-US pairings. However, the US-alone procedure precludes trial-by-trial assessment of pseudo-CRs for comparison with CRs. Accordingly, a single *unpaired control* procedure has evolved in which CS-alone and US-alone trials are presented randomly the same number of times as the paired CS-US group, but at variable CS-US intervals exceeding those effective for CR acquisition. Under the unpaired control, responses on CS trials (excluding alphas) provide a summative measure of pseudo-CRs and baseline responses.

Use of the unpaired control is based on associative assumptions that temporal contiguity of the CS and US is necessary for CR acquisition; and responding produced by the unpaired control is nonassociative, since the randomized sequencing of CSs and USs at exceedingly long, random intervals prevents any CS-US contiguity effects. However, associative theory and its unpaired control methodology have been challenged by a *contingency hypothesis* (Prokasy, 1965; Rescorla, 1967), which asserts that associative learning in classical conditioning can be viewed as determined by the statistical relationship between the CS and US. The hypothesis assumes that if US probability is greater in the presence of the CS than in its absence, a *positive contingency* prevails and *excitatory* associative effects would accrue to the CS; conversely, if US probability is higher in the absence than in the presence of the CS, the *negative contingency* would yield *inhibitory* associative effects. Moreover, the contingency hypothesis assumes the unpaired control's perfectly negative contingency would lead the CS to acquire inhibitory associative effects. Hence, Rescorla (1967) proposed a *truly random control* to provide an associatively neutral condition for assessing excitatory and inhibitory conditioning.

Rescorla (1967) specified the truly random control as involving independent programming of the CS and US or equal US probabilities in the presence and absence of the CS. However, delineating pairing/ unpairing cannot be determined a priori but only empirically. CS-US pairing is specified by the CS-US intervals demonstrated to produce CR acquisition for a specific preparation, while "explicitly unpaired" denotes the use of stimulus intervals outside the effective CS-US intervals. Consequently, in the absence of an empirically derived metric (i.e., effective CS-US conditioning intervals) to designate paired and unpaired conditions, it is virtually impossible to program an associatively neutral truly random control or predictable excitatory or inhibitory conditioning groups. Rescorla, seeking to validate the truly random control, reported that its CS had no effect upon avoidance conditioning (Rescorla, 1966) or upon responding in a CS-IR study where shock-US probability in the presence and absence of the CS were equal (Rescorla, 1968). However, these findings were challenged by CS-IR studies revealing that trial number and frequency of chance CS-US pairings under a truly random control could substantially affect (excitatory) conditioning (Gormezano and Kehoe, 1975). Subsequently, Rescorla (1972) disavowed the contingency hypothesis and truly random control and reverted to the use of the unpaired control. Nevertheless, the truly random control is still widely employed despite the detailing of additional methodological limitations (Papini and Bitterman, 1990; Wasserman, 1989).

Instrumental Conditioning

Instrumental conditioning procedures are all characterized by a contingent relationship between the organism's response and a stimulus. Typically, if the stimulus increases, decreases, or leaves unaffected the probability of the response, it is identified as positive, negative, or neutral, respectively. Although such labeling appears to be circular, Edward Thorndike's (1913) characterizations of stimuli as "satisfying" (positive) and "annoying" (negative) were not circular because they were specified by behavior changes independent of the target response. Noncircularity can also be achieved by demonstrating transitivity of stimulus effects on the target response to other (new) responses.

A positive or negative contingency between the target response and reinforcing stimulus gives rise to a variety of instrumental conditioning paradigms. The five most extensively studied are *reward, punishment, omission, escape,* and *avoidance,* which derive from responses producing a positive (reward) or a negative (punishment) stimulus; preventing a positive (omission) or negative (avoidance) stimulus from occurring; and terminating a negative stimulus (escape). Woods (1974), employing a classification schema that includes *operant conditioning* and presence or absence of a discriminative stimulus, enumerated sixteen instrumental conditioning paradigms. However, despite repeated attempts at conceptual clarification, the operant remains devoid of causal stimulus antecedents (Coleman, 1981) and, consequently, it cannot be employed to study associative learning. The operant is applicable only to the study of performance variables affecting postasymptotic or steady-state responding. Aside from the study of discrimination learning processes, *discriminative instrumental conditioning* paradigms are widely employed to assess the effects of concurrent classical conditioning of "fear" or "incentive motivation" to the discriminative stimulus upon the instrumental target response.

Control Methodology

Any occurrence of the target response without prior conjunction with the reinforcing stimulus is designated a *nonassociative* response attributable to 1. base rate; 2. independent presentations of the reinforcing stimulus; and 3. presentations of the reinforcing stimulus independent of the target response. Implementing controls for the first two factors are self-evident, and achieving a control for the third factor has been essentially limited to the *yoked-control* design. In the design, pairs of subjects are selected and one of them is randomly designated the experimental and the other the control subject. During conditioning, when the experimental subject performs the target response, the contingent event is received by both subjects. Therefore, both members of the pair receive the same number and temporal distribution of stimulus events; the only difference is that the experimental but not the control subject always receives the reinforcing event after execution of the target response, while the yoked partner receives the reinforcing event independent of execution of the response.

Thus, the yoked-control design appears to be admirably suited to test the (null) hypothesis that the temporal relationship between the response and subsequent stimulus event is irrelevant to the observed behavior change. Unfortunately, the design confounds within-subject sources of random error with the treatment effect: Control of stimulus events by experimental subjects can allow for systematic differences in the number of experimental subjects that are more affected by the stimulus event than their yoked partners. The possibility of such confounding has rendered the results of yoked-control designs necessarily ambiguous. As a consequence, a means for assessing the contribution of the third nonassociative factor to instrumental conditioning has not yet been achieved.

See also: OPERANT BEHAVIOR; PAVLOV, IVAN; THORNDIKE, EDWARD

Bibliography

Coleman, S. R. (1981). Historical context and systematic functions of the concept of the operant. *Behaviorism 9,* 207–226.

Gormezano, I. (1966). Classical conditioning. In J. B. Sidowski, ed., *Experimental methods and instrumentation in psychology.* New York: McGraw-Hill.

Gormezano, I., and Kehoe, E. J. (1975). Classical conditioning: Some methodological-conceptual issues. In W. K. Estes, ed., *Handbook of learning and cognitive processes,* Vol. 2: *Conditioning and behavior theory.* Hillsdale, NJ: Erlbaum.

Gormezano, I., Kehoe, E. J., and Marshall, B. S. (1983). Twenty years of classical conditioning research with the rabbit. In J. M. Sprague and A. N. Epstein, eds., *Progress in psychobiology and physiological psychology,* Vol. 10. New York: Academic Press.

Holland, P. C., and Rescorla, R. A. (1975). Second-order conditioning with food unconditioned stimulus. *Journal of Comparative and Physiological Psychology 88,* 459–467.

Papini, M. R., and Bitterman, M. E. (1990). The role of contingency in classical conditioning. *Psychological Review 97,* 396–403.

Prokasy, W. F. (1965). Classical eyelid conditioning. Experimenter operations, task demands, and response shaping. In W. F. Prokasy, ed., *Classical conditioning: A symposium.* New York: Appleton-Century-Crofts.

Rescorla, R. A. (1966). Predictability and number of pairings in Pavlovian fear conditioning. *Psychonomic Science 4,* 383–384.

—— (1967). Pavlovian conditioning and its proper control procedures. *Psychological Review 74,* 71–80.

—— (1968). Probability of shock in the presence and absence of CS in fear conditioning. *Journal of Comparative and Physiological Psychology 66,* 1–5.

—— (1972). Informational variables in Pavlovian conditioning. In G. H. Bower and J. T. Spence, eds., *Psychology of Learning and Motivation.* New York: Academic Press.

Thompson, R. F. (1976). The search for the engram. *American Psychologist 31*, 209–227.

Thorndike, E. L. (1913). *Educational psychology*. New York: Teachers College, Columbia University.

Wasserman, E. A. (1989). Pavlovian conditioning: Is contiguity irrelevant? *American Psychologist 44*, 1,550–1,551.

Woodruff, G., and Williams, D. R. (1976). The associative relation underlying autoshaping in the pigeon. *Journal of the Experimental Analysis of Behavior 26*, 1–13.

Woods, P. J. (1974). A taxonomy of instrumental conditioning. *American Psychologist 29*, 584–597.

I. Gormezano

CONSOLIDATION

See: AMNESIA, ORGANIC; ELECTROCONVULSIVE THERAPY AND MEMORY LOSS; KAMIN'S BLOCKING EFFECT: NEURONAL SUBSTRATES; MEMORY CONSOLIDATION: MOLECULAR AND CELLULAR PROCESSES; MEMORY CONSOLIDATION: PROLONGED PROCESS OF REORGANIZATION

D

DECLARATIVE MEMORY

Memory is the process or processes by which the brain enables us to represent experience and permits experience to shape us. Rather than a unitary capacity supported by a single set of processes, however, there are different forms of memory, supported by multiple, functionally, and anatomically distinct memory systems. The form of memory upon which we seem to depend most in the activities of everyday life and about which we can most readily reflect is declarative memory.

Declarative and Procedural Memory

There are various proposed taxonomies of memory, each offering a different account of the divisions among the memory systems of the brain. Most such accounts distinguish between declarative memory and procedural memory (Cohen and Squire, 1980; Cohen, 1984). Declarative memory supports the on-demand accumulation, storage, and retrieval of new data about facts and events—the information that we capture from our experiences through our representations of it. In contrast, procedural memory supports the shaping of behavioral repertoires acquired through experience. Declarative memory differs from procedural memory in being a relational memory system.

The Nature of Declarative Memory

Declarative memory supports representations of relationships among the constituent elements of an experience. It also supports representations of relationships among various events, providing the larger record of one's experience. It provides the critical means for rapidly representing events, those one-time arbitrary or accidental concurrences of people, places, and things, and the spatial, temporal, and interactional relations among them.

Moreover, declarative memory enables one to learn arbitrary, nonderivable associations through experience—for example, learning the names connected with people's faces, or their addresses and telephone numbers. Declarative memory thereby provides for representations of relations beyond the province of events, encompassing the relations among the facts that constitute our knowledge of the world. This point leads to a further critical distinction: between episodic memory, which contains autobiographical records of personally experienced events, and semantic memory, consisting of world knowledge stored outside of personal contexts (Tulving, 1972). As fundamentally relational, capturing the relations among many different elements of knowledge, both episodic and semantic memory are supported by the declarative memory system.

A second critical property of declarative memory is representational flexibility (Cohen, 1984; Cohen and Eichenbaum, 1993). Declarative memories can be activated by all manner of external sensory or even purely internal inputs, regardless of the current context. And they can be accessed by any number of different brain processors, not only the ones involved in initially acquiring the memories. Once accessed, they

105

can be manipulated and used flexibly to guide performance under an enormous range of testing conditions, including those differing significantly from the circumstances of original learning. In this manner, declarative memory serves as the relational database on which so much of cognitive processing and behavioral performance depends. Among the brain systems that access and manipulate the declarative-memory database are the frontal-lobe systems that support cognitively mediated and consciously aware processes, including conscious introspection and verbal reports of the contents of one's memories.

Deficit of Declarative Memory in Amnesia

Amnesia is a devastating memory impairment following damage to the hippocampal system. Patients with hippocampal amnesia typically have a combination of anterograde amnesia, an impairment in acquiring new memory, and retrograde amnesia, loss of memories preceding the trauma. The deficits seem confined to the domain of declarative memory (Cohen and Squire, 1980; Cohen, 1984; Ryan, Althoff, Whitlow, and Cohen, 2000). Thus, amnesic patients show marked impairment in tasks or situations in which performance depends on learning the relations among items, especially items associated only arbitrarily or accidentally. For example, such patients have great difficulty in remembering the events of daily life. The amnesic patient H.M., who has been studied fifty years, since undergoing a surgical resection of medial temporal lobe structures (Scoville and Milner, 1957; Corkin, 1984), exhibits marked impairment on various tests of memory for public events that occurred after the onset of amnesia and can barely recall any personal events since the time of his surgery (Sagar, Cohen, Corkin, and Growdon, 1985).

Formal laboratory testing confirms the deficit in memory for relations. Paired-associate learning is especially useful in diagnosing amnesia; in this procedure, in which one must learn a set of arbitrarily paired words, amnesic patients show severe impairment, as they do on most list-based recall or recognition-memory tasks, in which they are asked to commit to memory a set of common words, faces, or visual objects presented in a study list and then to report (in recall tests) or to judge (in recognition tests) which items appeared on that particular study list. Because such common stimuli are familiar from a lifetime of previous experience, remembering of specific study items requires the linkage of their identity to this particular study list or learning experience, thereby calling on declarative memory.

Amnesic patients are usually impaired on explicit or direct tests of memory (Graf and Schacter, 1985; Schacter, 1987; Richardson-Klavehn and Bjork, 1988), in which performance depends on using the test item to permit conscious recollection of some specific prior learning experience and then inspecting the contents. A successful outcome requires recall of the relation between the items to be tested and the study list or study experience.

The deficit in amnesia is evident in all manner of relations, whether verbal or nonverbal, spatial or nonspatial, or episodic or semantic. As regards the last, hippocampal amnesia typically affects both personal and public events (Sagar, Cohen, Corkin, and Growdon, 1985; Zola-Morgan, Cohen, and Squire, 1984); it includes not only autobiographical but also world knowledge. One example is the profound deficit shown by the patient H.M. in learning new vocabulary (word-definition relations) that has entered the language since the onset of his amnesia (Gabrieli, Cohen, and Corkin, 1988).

Despite profound and pervasive impairment of memory, amnesic patients show impressive preserved learning and memory abilities. Such patients can learn motor, perceptual, and cognitive skills even though they are unable to remember the experiences during which they acquired the skills. For example, amnesic patients were able to learn to read mirror-reversed text in training extended over several days; and they retained the skill after three months despite marked impairment in recollecting the training experiences or recognizing the words on which they were actually trained (Cohen and Squire, 1980). Preserved memory is characteristic of performance that can be based on tuning of skills in particular domains, built up of incremental improvements in performance with each exposure, and expressed in a repetition of the original learning situation—successful performance in this case does not require the flexible, relational representations of declarative memory (Cohen, 1984; Schacter, 1987; Gabrieli, 1998; Eichenbaum and Cohen, 2001).

Declarative Memory and Consciousness

Declarative memory is critical for conscious introspection and conscious recollection. But this system does not mediate any particular aspect of conscious processing; rather, it provides the flexible access to information about relations among people, places, objects, and actions—the relational database—that undergirds conscious recollection and introspective reports. This view accounts for the amnesic deficits in memory for relations, even those do not enter into the conscious awareness of normal subjects (Ryan, Althoff, Whitlow, and Cohen, 2000; Chun and Phelps, 1999). It also underscores the affinities between human and animal models of amnesia. Hippocampal amnesia in rodents and nonhuman primates produces the same dissociation among memory capacities that are typical of human amnesia. Such animals show impairments in learning and remembering spatial relations among environmental cues, configurations of multiple perceptually independent cues, contextual or conditional relations, and comparisons among temporally discontinuous events—all of which require a relational form of memory. Yet the same animals can show normal learning and remembering of a large variety of conditioning, discrimination, and skill tasks, none of which require a relational form of memory but rather only gradual, incremental changes in bias or reactivity to individual items with repeated exposure.

Brain Mechanisms of Declarative Memory

The critical role of the hippocampal system in declarative memory is evident in the phenomenology of amnesia. Neurophysiological and neuroimaging studies of the hippocampal system also demonstrate its association with memory for relations. Hippocampal neurons encode various relationships among significant elements of an experience, firing preferentially for particular conjunctions of the elements in studies of freely behaving rodents (Wood, Dudchenko, and Eichenbaum, 1999; Eichenbaum et al., 2000). In functional neuroimaging studies of humans, hippocampal system activation arises whenever the task engages memory for the relations among items (Henke, Buck, Weber, and Wieser, 1997; Cohen et al., 1999).

Amnesia indicates that the hippocampal system must interact with other brain systems to effect declarative memory. Retrograde amnesia in cases of hippocampal amnesia can extend backward over variable lengths of time, but it is never total; the storage of long-term memory is never completely lost. Hence the hippocampal system cannot be the repository, or permanent storage site, of all long-term memory. Instead, the reciprocal connections of the hippocampal system with all the higher-order cortical processors allow it to mediate storage in interaction with neocortical sites. After the various cortical processors identify the constituent elements of the event or experience, the hippocampal system binds together the multiple elements into long-term declarative memory representations that capture the relations among the elements, with the individual elements or attributes represented in distributed fashion in the relevant cortical processors. Thus, the interaction of the hippocampal system with neocortical processors and storage sites mediates the relational memory binding that allows the formation of declarative memory. Such

memories are then flexibly accessible to various cortical processors in supporting cognitive processing and behavioral performance.

See also: AMNESIA, FUNCTIONAL; AMNESIA, INFANTILE; AMNESIA, ORGANIC; AMNESIA, TRANSIENT GLOBAL; EPISODIC MEMORY; GUIDE TO THE ANATOMY OF THE BRAIN; SEMANTIC MEMORY: COGNITIVE ASPECTS; SEMANTIC MEMORY: NEUROBIOLOGICAL PERSPECTIVE

Bibliography

Chun, M. M., and Phelps, E. A. (1999). Memory deficits for implicit contextual information in amnesic subjects with hippocampal damage. *Nature Neuroscience 2*, 844–847.

Cohen, N. J. (1984). Preserved learning capacity in amnesia: Evidence for multiple memory systems. In N. Butters and L. R. Squire, eds., *The neuropsychology of memory.* New York: Guilford Press, pp. 83–103.

Cohen, N. J., and Eichenbaum, H. (1993). *Memory, amnesia and the hippocampal system.* Cambridge, MA: MIT Press.

Cohen, N. J., Ryan, J., Hunt, C., Romine, L., Wszalek, T., and Nash, C. (1999). Hippocampal system and declarative memory (relational) memory: Summarizing the data from functional neuroimaging studies. *Hippocampus 9*, 83–98.

Cohen, N. J., and Squire, L. R. (1980). Preserved learning and retention of a pattern-analyzing skill in amnesia: Dissociation of knowing how and knowing that. *Science 210*, 207–210.

Corkin, S. (1984). Lasting consequences of bilateral medial temporal lobectomy: Clinical course and experimental findings in H.M. *Seminars in Neurology 4*, 249–259.

Eichenbaum, H., and Cohen, N. J. (2001). *From conditioning to conscious recollection: Memory systems of the brain.* NY: Oxford University Press.

Eichenbaum, H., Dudchenko, P., Wood, E., Shapiro, M., and Tanila, H. (1999). The hippocampus, memory, and place cells: Is it spatial memory or a memory space? *Neuron 23*, 209–226.

Gabrieli, J. D. E. (1998). Cognitive neuroscience of human memory. *Annual Review of Psychology 49*, 87–115.

Gabrieli, J. D. E., Cohen, N. J., and Corkin, S. (1988). The impaired learning of semantic knowledge following bilateral medial temporal-lobe resection. *Brain and Cognition, 7*, 157–177.

Graf, P., and Schacter, D. L. (1985). Implicit and explicit memory for new associations in normal and amnesic subjects. *Journal of Experimental Psychology: Learning, Memory, and Cognition 11*, 501–518.

Henke, K., Buck, A., Weber, B., and Wieser, H. G. (1997). Human hippocampus establishes associations in memory. *Hippocampus 7*, 249–256.

Richardson-Klavehn, A., and Bjork, R. A. (1988). Measures of memory. *Annual Review of Psychology 39*, 475–543.

Ryan, J. D., Althoff, R. R., Whitlow, S., and Cohen, N. J. (2000). Amnesia is a deficit in relational memory. *Psychological Science 11*, 454–461.

Sagar, H. J., Cohen, N. J., Corkin, S., and Growdon, J. M. (1985). Dissociations among processes in remote memory. *Annals of the New York Academy of Sciences 444*, 533–535.

Schacter, D. L. (1987). Implicit memory: History and current status. *Journal of Experimental Psychology: Learning, Memory, and Cognition 13*, 501–518.

Scoville, W. B., and Milner, B. (1957). Loss of recent memory after bilateral hippocampal lesions. *Journal of Neurology Neurosurgery and Psychiatry 20*, 11–21.

Tulving, E. (1972). Episodic and semantic memory. In E. Tulving and W. Donaldson, eds., *Organization of Memory.* New York: Academic Press, 382–403.

Wood, E. R., Dudchenko, P. A., and Eichenbaum, H. (1999). The global record of memory in hippocampal neuronal activity. *Nature 397,* 613–616.

Zola-Morgan, S., Cohen, N. J., and Squire, L. R. (1983). Recall of remote episodic memory in amnesia. *Neuropsychologia 21,* 487–500.

Neal J. Cohen

DÉJÀ VU

Déjà vu is a memory phenomenon widely experienced by the general public and is often cited in the popular literature. While the experience was described in the scientific literature as early as the mid-1800s, researchers used a variety of different terms to describe the experience (e.g., paramnesia) until the middle of the twentieth century. A standard definition of déjà vu used today was provided by Neppe (1983, p. 3): "any subjectively inappropriate impression of familiarity of a present experience with an undefined past."

Survey research indicates that between half to two-thirds of individuals have had a déjà vu experience, although this estimate varies considerably (30 to 97 percent) across three dozen investigations. Of those who experience déjà vu, nearly all have had more than one, and most experience one or more each year. A déjà vu experience is typically triggered by a visual scene, lasts for a few seconds, and is associated with mild stress, anxiety, or fatigue. The primary psychological reaction is surprise, and the time sense seems to slow down.

The incidence of déjà vu decreases systematically with age, and this is probably due to an increase in societal awareness across recent years. For example, Gallup and Newport (1991) found that belief in déjà vu nearly doubled between 1978 and 1990. There may be a decrease in reports of déjà vu with age because older adults grew up in a time when belief in déjà vu was not as widely accepted as it is today.

Déjà vu appears to be more common in better-educated and better-traveled individuals; there is no evidence of gender differences. Déjà vu also occurs in the aura preceding a seizure in some temporal lobe epileptics (TLEs). This trend motivated research to determine whether déjà vu is a potential diagnostic tool in seizure activity, epilepsy, and brain pathology. Accumulating evidence, however, does not support such speculation.

Explanations of Déjà Vu

Interpretations of déjà have varied from the parapsychological (a telepathic reversion to a previous lifetime) to the psychodynamic (the mind neutralizes an emotional situation by displacing it into the past). These theses are thoroughly discussed by Sno and Linszen (1990) and Neppe (1983). We will examine several possible scientific interpretations.

Neurological Explanations

For more than a century, researchers have suggested that a déjà vu experience reflects a neurological dysfunction. Since déjà vu is part of the preseizure aura in some TLEs, it seems reasonable that déjà vu in nonepileptics may result from small temporal lobe seizures. Another interpretation is that the déjà vu experience results from a momentary delay in neuronal transmission from the perceptual organ to the higher processing centers of the brain. This slight (several millisecond) increase in the normal time taken to transmit the message because of a synaptic dysfunction may lead to a misinterpretation of the information as being old.

Another neurological interpretation involves two pathways rather than one. In the visual system, information is received in the cortex first from the primary and then a secondary pathway. When the normally brief delay between the two tracks lengthens, the usually seamless integration of the two messages is disrupted and experienced as two separate messages. A variation on this position is that the primary rather than the secondary neuronal path is inordinately slowed, resulting in a reversal of the normal sequence of messages. We routinely interpret information from the primary pathway as our initial perception, so when the secondary pathway arrives slightly before the primary pathway, the information from the primary pathway feels familiar because a "memory" match already exists—it was established moments before.

Memory Explanations

It is possible that the individual experienced the present situation not directly but through a magazine, movie, TV show, or dream. Considerable research suggests that source confusions are routine and that déjà vu may reflect a match with a "memory" created by media or imagination. Another memory perspective is that the type of cognitive processing is being duplicated rather than the actual memory. Retrieval success often depends upon the correspondence between the way information is processed during input and retrieval. If the cognitive processing of new information follows a set of mental procedures similar to those of a prior experience, an unexpected sense of familiarity may result.

Another memory perspective is that one aspect of the present setting is objectively familiar, but conscious recognition fails when the object appears in a different context. The familiarity elicited by the unidentified object is then overgeneralized to the entire setting. On a visit to a friend's home for the first time, for example, the grandfather clock in the corner is identical to one in your aunt's home. The implicit familiarity of this object is not connected to the "old" object but instead misattributed to the objectively new setting.

Finally, the present setting may evoke a sense of déjà vu because of a familiar organization of the elements in a scene. It is not the grandfather clock in the living room of your friend's new home that is familiar but rather that the room's layout: a sofa to the right of the love seat, with a stairway to the left and a grandfather clock against the back wall, the same as in your aunt's house.

Attentional Explanations

An ongoing perceptual experience may occasionally be divided into separate perceptions through distraction or inattention. In this explanation, first proposed by Titchener in 1924, a brief initial perception under diminished attention is followed immediately by a second perception under full attention. The second impression matches the "ignored" first glance taken moments earlier, giving rise to the feeling that the current experience duplicates something experienced before. As you walk into a new hotel lobby talking on your cell phone, you process the scene without full attention. When you hang up, you perceive the situation with full awareness and get the feeling that you have been here before. Recent research on inattentional blindness by Mack and Rock (1998) suggests that individuals often miss clearly visible objects if they are focused on something else, even when the unattended object is directly in front of them.

Dual-Processing Explanations

Routine cognitive experience may often involve the operation of two separate but interactive processes. While both processes usually operate in concert, occasionally they might shift out of synchrony, or one process might occur in the absence of the other. For example, retrieval and familiarity usually operate in an independent but coordinated manner, with recall accompanied by familiarity. When retrieval is activated without familiarity, a familiar setting seems momentarily unfamiliar (jamais vu). Conversely, when familiarity is activated in the absence of retrieval, déjà vu is the result. Another interpretation is that memory encoding and retrieval usually operate independently of each other. We experience a new situation; then we encode it into memory. However, if both encoding and retrieval are simultaneously activated, this spurious familiarity results in déjà vu.

Finally, we may have two different varieties of consciousness: One processes information from the environment, whereas the other monitors our inner, mental world. Déjà vu may occur when normal consciousness is diminished by distraction, fatigue, or seizure, forcing reliance on the internal consciousness operating from internally generated images, resulting in a misreading of a new experience as old.

In summary, déjà vu is experienced by most people on an average of once per year. Its incidence decreases with age, increases with education, and is more common under stress or fatigue. Likely explanations include neurological dysfunction (seizure, synaptic slowdown), implicit familiarity of objects, divided attention followed by full perception, and/or alteration in the normal function of two cognitive processes.

Bibliography

Gallup, G. H., and Newport, F. (1991). Belief in paranormal phenomena among adult Americans. *The Skeptical Inquirer 15*, 137–146.

Mack, A., and Rock, I. (1998). *Inattentional blindness.* Cambridge, MA: MIT Press.

Neppe, V. M. (1983). *The psychology of déjà vu: Have I been here before?* Johannesburg: Witwatersrand University Press.

Sno, H. N., and Linszen, D. H. (1990). The déjà vu experience: Remembrance of things past? *American Journal of Psychiatry 147*, 1,587–1,595.

Titchener, E. B. (1924). *A beginner's psychology.* New York: Macmillan

Alan S. Brown

DEMENTIA

The term *dementia* describes a decline of previously acquired intellectual, or cognitive, skills. Memory loss is the primary symptom of dementia, but other cognitive symptoms exist as well. A diagnosis of dementia requires an impairment in memory and at least one other cognitive domain (American Psychiatric Association, 1994). This can include an impairment in comprehending or expressing language, sustaining attention, orientation (knowing where one is and the date and time), visual perception, visual construction, or executive (planning and organizing) skills. In addition to cognitive deficits, dementia is often associated with behavioral and/or psychiatric changes such as poor judgment (for example, spending money recklessly or dressing inappropriately), delusions (false beliefs), or hallucinations (seeing, feeling, or hearing things that are not actually there). Disinhibition, exemplified by the use of inappropriate language (i.e., swearing), the telling of off-color jokes, or acting overly familiar with others, can also occur. Mood symptoms, such as depression, apathy, or increased irritability, can accompany dementia as well.

Dementia is not a disease, but a syndrome that has many causes, including head injury, vitamin deficiency, hydrocephalus, epilepsy, depression, medication effects, and toxic exposure. In addition, there are a number of diseases that can cause dementia. These include Alzheimer's disease, vascular disease, HIV infection, multiple sclerosis, Parkinson's disease, Huntington's disease, Lewy body disease, and others. Depending on the cause of dementia, its onset may be gradual or sudden, and its course may be progressive, stable, or reversible.

Pathophysiology of Dementia

The pathology associated with dementia varies, depending on the cause of dementia. The term *neurodegenerative* is used to describe dementia caused by diseases that lead to the progressive death of nerve cells (neurons) in the brain. Some diseases are associated with the development of abnormalities within or around neurons that interfere with communication between brain cells and/or cause cell death. For example, the amyloid plaques (insoluble deposits of a type of protein found between neurons) and neurofibrillary tangles (abnormal collections of twisted threads found within neurons) associated with Alzheimer's disease (AD) are found primarily in the cerebral cortex (outer covering of the brain), hippocampus, and entorhinal cortex. Parkinson's disease, in contrast, is associated with Lewy bodies (accumulations of neurofilamentous material located within neurons) in the substantia nigra and locus ceruleus (Kish, Shannak, and Horneykiewicz, 1988). Pick bodies (a common neuropathological finding in frontotemporal dementia) are concentrated primarily in the frontal and/or temporal cortex of the brain (McKhann et al., 2001).

Cerebrovascular disease causes dementia by disrupting blood flow to brain cells and is not considered to be neurodegenerative. If blood vessels in the brain are blocked (e.g., by cholesterol), blood flow is constricted. Such an event, called *ischemia*, results in oxygen deprivation, which can cause neuron death. *Vascular dementia* is the term used to refer to dementia caused by multiple vascular accidents, such as small strokes (in which case it is sometimes referred to as multiinfarct dementia), or a single stroke. Whether numerous small vessel changes can cause dementia is unclear, but with sufficient accumulation these changes have been associated with significant cognitive changes (Boone et al., 1992). There are, of course, many other mechanisms leading to death of brain tissue and dementia, but these examples explain some of the ways dementia can be caused.

Dementia, Delirium, Senility, or Mental Retardation?

Dementia is diagnosed only in the absence of delirium. Like dementia, delirium is associated with memory loss, but it is also associated with disorientation, confusion, and alterations in consciousness that fluctuate throughout the day. Unlike dementia, delirium typically begins suddenly and is usually the result of a treatable cause such as illness or the effects of medications.

Dementia and advancing age often co-occur because the biggest risk factor for the development of dementia is advancing age. Dementia is not, however, an inevitable consequence of aging. The term *senility* has been incorrectly applied to memory impairment that accompanies old age. Senility actually refers only to the age of onset of dementia; the term *senile dementia* is sometimes used to refer to dementia that occurs after age sixty-five. The term *presenile dementia*, in contrast, signifies dementia whose onset is prior to age sixty-five.

Mental retardation differs from dementia in that it describes intellectual and adaptive functioning that has developed subnormally. Thus, functioning has not declined from a previously higher level, as is the case with dementia. It is possible, however, for someone with mental retardation to acquire dementia. The most common example of this occurs in people with Down's syndrome, most of whom will develop AD by the time they are in their fifties (Mann, 1993).

Memory Functioning in Dementia

Due to similarities in the clinical presentation of patients with disorders affecting primarily subcortical structures, which differs from that observed in dementia caused by cortical damage, the terms *cortical dementia* and *subcortical dementia* are often used. A cortical pattern of cognitive deficits is characterized by an inability to perform purposeful motor movements (apraxia), language disturbance (aphasia), memory impairment (amnesia), and difficulty with object recognition (agnosia). The most common disease causing cortical dementia is AD. Subcortical dementia, in contrast, has many more causes, such as Huntington's disease (HD) or Parkinson's disease (PD), and is characterized by slowed mentation (bradyphrenia), forgetfulness, motor abnormalities, impaired planning and judgment (so-called "executive" dysfunction), and mood changes such as depression or apathy (Cummings and Benson, 1984). Memory performance also differs between cortical and subcortical dementia (see Table 1).

Short-Term Memory

Short-term, or *working*, *memory* refers to information that is stored for only a few seconds, such as when one repeats a list of numbers immediately after hearing them. This skill does not reliably differentiate patients with cortical from those with subcortical dementia, as both have been shown to perform as well as normal control subjects in repeating digits forwards, and deficits in their ability to repeat digits in reverse order (Calderon et al., 2001; Redondo Verge, Brown, and Chacon Pena., 2001). Patients with Lewy body dementia, however, are impaired on both portions of this task (Calderon et al., 2001).

Long-Term Memory

Long-term, or *secondary*, *memory* refers to memory for information that must be recalled after some period of time, such as after few minutes or after many years. *Semantic memory*, a type of long-term memory relating to meanings of words and their relationships, is typically impaired in patients with cortical dementia. Perhaps the most impressive example of this deficit is observed in patients with fronto-temporal dementia (FTD), who can have very severe language impairment, such as word-finding difficulty, inability to appreciate syntax, and/or impaired language comprehension, with relative sparing of other cognitive abilities (Mesulam, 2000). The word-finding difficulty observed in AD is also an example of the impaired semantic memory seen among patients with cortical dementia. Semantic memory is not typically impaired in patients with subcortical dementia.

Another type of long-term memory, *episodic memory*, concerns memory for events. Patients with AD are typically severely impaired in their ability to recall recent events, but are much better able to recall events that occurred many years ago (Dorrego et al., 1999). Patients with HD, however, have been found to exhibit a "flat" gradient of remote memory, with equal impairment for all previous years (Albert, Butters, and Brandt, 1981). Whether this is the case for patients with other types of subcortical dementia (e.g., PD) has not been consistently shown (Fama et al., 2000).

Long-term memory has been further divided into explicit and implicit memory. *Explicit memory* (sometimes used interchangeably with the term *declarative memory*) is typically more severely impaired in cortical than subcortical dementia. Both types of dementia cause an impairment in this ability to recall information (e.g. a list of words, a story, or simple line drawings) that was presented earlier. Provided with cues, however, such as the category from which the words belong, or a recognition (e.g. multiple choice or yes/no) paradigm, the performance of those with cortical

Table 1

Memory Functioning in Cortical and Subcortical Dementia		
Memory type	Cortical dementia	Subcortical dementia
Short-term/ working memory	Mildly impaired	Impaired
Semantic	Impaired	Normal
Episodic	Impaired; remote memories much better than memory for recent events	Moderately impaired; "flat" gradient of recall across past decades
Explicit (Declarative) Free recall	Impaired	Mildly/frankly impaired
Recognition	Impaired	Mildly impaired or normal
Implicit (Procedural)	Normal	Impaired

SOURCE: Courtesy of Cynthia Munro.

dementia is not improved. Patients with subcortical dementia, however, benefit from cues, and might even perform as well as normal healthy adults. This difference is thought to demonstrate that cortical dementia causes an inability to encode new information, whereas subcortical dementia causes a deficit in retrieving information. Tests of *implicit* (or *procedural*) *memory* (memory that occurs without conscious awareness, such as the learning of motor movements) elicit the opposite pattern. That is, subcortical dementia produces impairment on tests of implicit memory, such as a mirror-tracing task, whereas patients with cortical dementia improve as much as normal healthy adults with practice, even if they have no recollection of having performed the task previously (Butters, Heindel, and Salmon, 1990).

Recent Developments in Dementia Research

New Drug Treatments

In 1996, the Food and Drug Administration approved the first drug (tacrine) to treat the memory impairment that results from AD. The drug works by increasing the amount of a particular chemical, called a neurotransmitter, in the brain. This neurotransmitter, called acetylcholine, is related to memory functioning, and is depleted in the brains of people with AD. Since approval of the first drug to treat AD, three new drugs with similar mechanisms of action have also been approved. Another development in clinical trials research for memory disorders has been the investigation of over-the-counter herbs such as *Ginkgo biloba* and the antioxidant vitamin E.

Refining Diagnostic Criteria for Types of Dementia

Because dementia-causing disorders can be difficult to diagnose during life, and because of new developments in neuropathological techniques, criteria for dementing disorders are evolving. To achieve consistency, experts in these disorders meet to establish a consensus regarding the features that distinguish a particular disorder from others. From 1984 to 1999, fourteen consensus guidelines concerning dementing disorders were published (Beck et al., 2000). Examples of these include Lewy body dementia (McKeith et al., 1997) and FTD (McKhann et al., 2001).

Mild Cognitive Impairment

Sometimes patients do not meet criteria for dementia because they have a mild impairment in memory but in no other cognitive domain, and their everyday functioning is not impaired. Scientists have introduced the term *mild cognitive impairment* (MCI) to describe this syndrome, and in 2001 consensus criteria for MCI were published (Petersen et al., 2001). This disorder has received a great deal of attention because, in many cases, it is considered to be a harbinger of AD (Morris et al., 2001). Because of the availability of new drug treatments for the memory impairment caused by AD, there is a great deal of interest in diagnosing this disease before it has progressed to dementia.

Conclusion

Burgeoning interest in dementia research in the late twentieth century has led to better understanding of its neuropathological underpinnings, treatments for its memory impairments, and refinements in the diagnostic criteria for the disorders causing it. The importance of early diagnosis of neurodegenerative disorders has led to an increasing efforts to identify very mild, objective memory problems. Thus, characterization of memory functioning continues to be an essential aspect for the diagnosis of dementia syndromes.

See also: ALZHEIMER'S DISEASE: BEHAVIORAL ASPECTS; ALZHEIMER'S DISEASE: HUMAN DISEASE AND THE GENETICALLY ENGINEERED ANIMAL MODELS; COGNITIVE ENHANCERS; PHARMACOLOGICAL TREATMENT OF MEMORY DEFICITS

Bibliography

Albert, M. S., Butters, N., and Brandt, J. (1981). Patterns of remote memory in amnesic and demented patients. *Archives of Neurology 38,* 495–500.

American Psychiatric Association (1994). *Diagnostic and Statistical Manual of Mental Disorders,* 4th edition. Washington, DC: American Psychiatric Association.

Beck, C., Cody, M., Souder, E., Zhang, M., and Small, G. W. (2000). Dementia diagnostic guidelines: Methodologies, results, and implementation costs. *Journal of the American Geriatrics Society 48,* 1,195–1,203.

Boone, K. B., Miller, B. L., Lesser, I. M., Mehringer, C. M., Hill-Guttierrez, E., Goldberg, M. A., and Berman, N. G. (1992). Neuropsychological correlates of white-matter lesions in healthy elderly subjects: A threshold effect. *Archives of Neurology 49,* 549–554.

Butters, N., Heindel, W. C., and Salmon, D. P. (1990). Dissociation of implicit memory in dementia: Neurological implications. *Bulletin of the Psychonomic Society 28,* 359–366.

Calderon, J., Perry, R. J., Erzinclioglu, S. W., Berrios, G. E., Dening, T. R., and Hodges, J. R. (2001). Perception, attention, and working memory are disproportionately impaired in dementia with Lewy bodies compared with Alzheimer's disease. *Journal of Neurology, Neurosurgery, and Psychiatry 70,* 157–164.

Cummings, J. L., and Benson, D. F. (1984). Subcortical dementia: Review of an emerging concept. *Archives of Neurology 41,* 874–879.

Dorrego, M. F., Sabe, L., Cuerva, A. G., Kuzis, G., Tiberti, C., Boller, F., and Starkstein, S. E. (1999). Remote memory in Alzheimer's disease. *Journal of Neuropsychiatry and Clinical Neurosciences 11,* 490–497.

Fama, R., Sullivan, E. V., Shear, P. K., Stein, M., Yesavage, J. A., Tinklenberg, J. R., Pfefferbaum, A. (2000). Extent, pattern, and correlates of remote memory impairment in Alzheimer's disease and Parkinson's disease. *Neuropsychology 14,* 265–276.

Kish, S. J., Shannak, K., and Horneykiewicz, O. (1988). Uneven pattern of dopamine loss in the striatum of patients with idiopathic Parkinson's disease: Pathophysiologic and clinical implications. *New England Journal of Medicine 318,* 876–880.

Mann, D. M. A. (1993). Association between Alzheimer disease and Down syndrome: Neuropathological observations. In J. M. Berg, H. Karlinsky, and A. J. Holland, eds., *Alzheimer disease, Down syndrome and their relationship.* Oxford: Oxford University Press.

McKeith, I. G. et al. (1997). Dementia with Lewy bodies: Trying to define a disease. *Neurology 47,* 1,113–1,124.

McKhann, G. M., Albert, M. S., Grossman, M., Miller, B., Dickson, D., and Trojanowski, J. Q. (2001). Clinical and pathological diagnosis of frontotemporal dementia. Report of the work group on frontotemporal dementia and Pick's disease. *Archives of Neurology 58,* 1,803–1,809.

Mesulam, M. (2000). Aging, Alzheimer's disease, and dementia: Clinical and neurobiological perspectives. In *Principles of Behavioral and Cognitive Neurology,* 2nd edition. New York: Oxford University Press.

Morris, J. C., Storandt, M., Miller, J. P., McKell, D. W., Price, J. L., Rubin, E. H., and Berg, L. (2001). Mild cognitive impairment represents early-stage Alzheimer disease. *Archives of Neurology 58,* 397–405.

Petersen, R. C., Stevens, J. C., Banguli, M., Tangalos, E. G., Cummings, J. L., and DeKosky, S. (2001). Practice parameter: Early detection of dementia: Mild cognitive impairment (an evidenced-based review). *Neurology 56,* 1,133–1,142.

Redondo Verge, L., Brown, R. G., and Chacon Pena, J. R. (2001). Executive dysfunction in Huntington's disease. *Reviews in Neurology 32,* 923–929.

Jason Brandt
Ralph H. B. Benedict
Revised by Cynthia A. Munro

See also: APLYSIA: DEVELOPMENT OF PROCESSES UNDERLYING LEARNING; CHILDREN, DEVELOPMENT OF MEMORY IN; EARLY

EXPERIENCE AND MEMORY; LANGUAGE
LEARNING; SCHOOL LEARNING

DIENCEPHALON

See: AMNESIA, ORGANIC

DISCRIMINATION AND GENERALIZATION

The decade of the 1990s witnessed acceleration in the convergence of theoretical and experimental studies of discrimination and generalization from the domains of classical conditioning and instrumental (operant) learning. *Classical conditioning* refers to the establishment of behavioral adaptations (conditioned responses; CRs) by the methods of Pavlov. *Instrumental learning* is a general term for goal-seeking behavior, and operant conditioning refers to reinforcement learning by the methods of Skinner. The term *discrimination* refers to the capacity of organisms to learn different modes of behavior depending on signals or cues from the environment about the imminence or accessibility of reinforcement. *Generalization* refers to stimulus generalization, the capacity for signals or cues that are different from those used for establishing learned behavior to evoke this behavior. *Stimulus generalization* in classical conditioning refers to the capacity of a stimulus other than the conditioned stimulus to evoke a CR. In operant conditioning, one set of stimuli, an occasion setter (OS), might evoke the behavior controlled by another OS, depending on their shared features or similarity. Skinner coined the term *occasion setter* to refer to signals or cues that predict reinforcement. In recent years, the term *occasion setting* has been extended to encompass both classical and operant forms of behavioral learning. As a consequence of this mixing, the terminology and paradigms used in occasion setting research borrow from the two domains. The mixture of the two domains has led to a healthy integration of methods and ideas (Schmajuk and Holland, 1998).

The convergence of ideas about discriminations and generalization from classical and operant conditioning began during the late 1960s, when the principles of stimulus control enunciated by operant-conditioning studies involving pigeons were found to extend to eyeblink conditioning in rabbits (Moore, 1972). Specifically, generalization along an auditory frequency dimension shares many of the same characteristics as visual wavelength generalization in pigeons. Conditioned stimulus preexposure (latent inhibition) also generalizes along an auditory frequency dimension, with gradients forming an inverted V shape (Siegel, 1972). Latent inhibition refers to retarded classical conditioning as a result of preexposure to the CS. Inverted-V-shape generalization gradients have also been observed with tonal stimuli trained with Pavlov's conditioned inhibition procedure (Mis, Lumia, and Moore, 1972). Inverted-V generalization gradients have been observed in pigeon operant tasks (Hearst, 1969).

Paradigms for Occasion Setting

Occasion setters are stimulus *features*, such as the presence of a light or tone, that serve as discriminative stimuli. For example, the presence of a light might signal that operant responses will be reinforced. The absence of this light would signal that operant responses are not reinforced. In general, a *feature-positive* paradigm is one in which the OS signals reinforcement; a *feature-negative* paradigm is one in which the OS signals the absence of reinforcement. The presence of a light or tone might signal reinforcement, whereas its absence signals nonreinforcement. In classical conditioning a feature-positive occasion-setting task would involve adding a feature to the CS. For example, if the CS is a tone, the addition of a light sets the occasion for reinforcement, whereas the tone alone would not signal reinforcement. A feature-negative task would be one in which the light, instead of signaling reinforcement when presented with the tone, would signal its absences. If the occasion setter overlaps the CS and signals the reinforcement, it can result in a more robust CR than would otherwise be the case. By contrast, if OS overlaps the CS and signals the *absence* of the US, it can inhibit the CR. This feature-negative discrimination recognizing the absence of an OS as a signal of the absence of the US is a relatively difficult discrimination for animals to master. In fact, a classical conditioning situation like this is called a *conditioned inhibition paradigm,* and research has shown that this is relatively difficult discrimination for animals to master.

Pattern Learning

The relative difficulty in learning feature-negative discrimination as compared with feature-positive discrimination learning extends also to the paradigms of positive and negative patterning. Demonstrations of patterning in both classical and operant conditioning tasks involve two signaling stimuli, A and B, which could be occasion setters, and three types of trials. In positive patterning, the trial types are AB+, A–, and B–. Animals readily learn to respond more vigorously to the reinforced stimulus

Figure 1

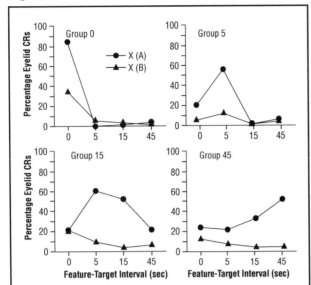

SOURCE: From a figure in "The Effect of Feature-Target Intervals in Conditional Discriminations on Acquisitions and Expression of Conditional Nicitating Membrane and Heart-Rate Responses in the Rabbit," by E. J. Kehol, N. Palmer, G. Weidemann, and M. Macrae (2000). *Animal Learning and Behavior*, 28, p. 80–91. Reproduced by permission of Psychonomic Society Publications.

Percentage of conditioned eyeblink responses in rabbits to the target CS (X) in the presence of feature positive (A) and feature negative (B) occasion setters as a function of the A→X and B→X intervals (0, 5, 15, 45 seconds) used in training.

compound, AB, and to inhibit responses to A– and B–, where (+) denotes a reinforced trial and (–) denotes a nonreinforced trial. In negative patterning, the trial types are AB–, A+, and B+. In order to behave appropriately in a negative-patterning task, the animal must somehow learn that responding to the stimulus compound AB must be suppressed. This can happen only if the compound stimulus has unique features that are subsets of neither A nor B (Pearce and Bouton, 2001). That is, the compound has a configural component that is shared by neither A nor B.

The general difficulty in learning a negative-patterning discrimination suggests that this configural component is often overshadowed by the nonconfigural aspects of A and B, each of which in isolation drives a tendency to respond by virtue of their association with reinforcement. At the same time, some negative-patterning tasks can be mastered comparatively easily, suggesting that the compound AB forms a unique pattern that, although similar to A and B, nevertheless is treated as a whole, thereby allowing the animal to master the discrimination.

Perceptual Learning

Exposure to discriminative stimuli enhances subsequent discrimination learning, an effect known as *perceptual learning* (Hall, 1991). The phenomenon of perceptual learning might seem to contradict the idea that exposure to stimuli retards later learning, as in latent inhibition. But latent inhibition can actually account for perceptual learning, if we assume that pre-exposed discriminatory stimuli share features in common. Latent inhibition develops to shared and unshared features alike, but the common features lose associability more rapidly than the unshared features. Animals learn to ignore the shared features, allowing the unshared features to dominate subsequent discrimination learning and thereby facilitating performance (McLaren and Mackintosh, 2000).

Not only do the shared features undergo more latent inhibition than the unshared features, the unshared features also can become mutually inhibitory through mechanisms of Pavlovian conditioned inhibition, provided the two stimuli are alternated during the preexposure phase (Dwyer, Bennett, and Mackintosh, 2001). The unique aspect of one preexposed stimulus can actively suppress associations with the unique aspect of the other preexposed stimulus, and vice versa. Thus, any tendency for one stimulus to elicit a representation of the other is reduced, and this promotes perceptual learning.

Acquired Distinctiveness

Acquired distinctiveness refers to enhanced discrimination learning to stimuli or stimulus dimensions that had been used in a prior discrimination task. Unlike perceptual learning, however, acquired distinctiveness appears to entail more than latent inhibition of shared stimulus features and mutual inhibition of unique features. The additional ingredient is correlation with reinforcement. The nature of this correlation remains in question. George and Pearce (1999) have argued that acquired distinctiveness stems from prior learning about the relevance of the stimuli for solving problems based on the same class of reinforcers. The relevance-to-reinforcement account of acquired distinctiveness does not imply that prior learning about the lack of correlation of the stimuli for reinforcement impedes discrimination learning.

Time Discrimination

Temporal control of behavior is one of the signature features of operant conditioning methods, and instances of temporal discrimination and generalization for duration has been well documented in operant conditioning tasks in animals and humans (e.g.,

Wearden and Bray, 2001). Similar instances of temporal control of behavior occur in classical conditioning (Gallistel and Gibbon, 2000; Kehoe and Macrae, 2002). Conditioned-response timing depends on the CS-US interval(s) used in training. Conditioned responses are timed so that they achieve maximal amplitude at the anticipated time(s) of the US, and this occurs whether the CS is defined operationally as the onset or the offset of a stimulus (e.g., Kehoe, Schreurs, Macrae, and Gormezano, 1995). In classical conditioning the timing of conditioned responses becomes more variable as the CS-US interval increases (Gallistel and Gibbon, 2000; White, Kehoe, Choi, and Moore, 2000). Temporal discriminative control of classically conditioned responses also occur in occasion setting (Kehoe, Palmer, Weiderman, and Macrae, 2000; see Figure 1).

See also: CLASSICAL CONDITIONING: BEHAVIORAL PHENOMENA

Bibliography

Dwyer, D. W., Bennett, C. H., and Mackintosh, N. J. (2001). Evidence for inhibitory associations between the unique elements of two compound flavors. *Quarterly Journal of Experimental Psychology 54B*, 97–107.

Gallistel, C. R., and Gibbon, J. (2000). Time, rate, and conditioning. *Psychological Review 107*, 289–344.

George, D. N., and Pearce, J. M. (1999). Acquired distinctiveness is controlled by stimulus relevance and not correlation with reward. *Journal of Experimental Psychology: Animal Behavior Processes 25*, 363–373.

Hall, G. (1991). *Perceptual and associative learning*. Oxford: Clarendon Press.

Hearst, E. (1969). Excitation, inhibition, and discrimination learning. In N. J. Mackintosh and W. K. Honig, eds., *Fundamental issues in associative learning*, pp. 1–41. Halifax: Dalhousie University Press.

Kehoe, E. J., and Macrae, M. (2002). Fundamental behavioral and findings in classical conditioning. In J. W. Moore, ed., *A neuroscientist's guide to classical conditioning*, pp. 171–231. New York: Springer.

Kehoe, E. J., Palmer, N., Weiderman, G., and Macrae, M. (2000). The effect of feature target intervals in conditioned discriminations on acquisition and expression of conditioned nictitating membrane and heart-rate responses in the rabbit. *Animal Learning and Behavior 28*, 80–91.

Kehoe, E. J., Schreurs, B. G., Macrae, M, and Gormezano, I. (1995). Effects of modulating tone frequency, intensity, and duration on the classically conditioned nictitating membrane response. *Psychobiology 23*, 103–115.

McLaren, I. P. L., and Mackintosh, N. J. (2000). An elemental model of associative learning: Latent inhibition and perceptual learning. *Animal Learning and Behavior 28*, 211–246.

Mis, F. W., Lumia, A. W., and Moore, J. W. (1972). Inhibitory control of the classically conditioned nictitating membrane response of the rabbit. *Behavior Research Methods and Instrumentation 4*, 297–299.

Moore, J. W. (1972). Stimulus control: Studies of auditory generalization in rabbits. In A. H. Black and W. P. Prokasy, eds., *Classical conditioning II: Current research and theory*, pp. 206–230. New York: Appleton-Century-Crofts.

Pearce, J. M., and Bouton, M. E. (2001). Theories of associative learning in animals. *Annual Review of Psychology 52*, 111–139.

Schmajuk, N. A., and Holland, P. C., eds. (1998). *Occasion setting*. Washington, DC: American Psychological Association.

Siegel, S. (1972). Latent inhibition and eyelid conditioning. In A. H. Black and W. P. Prokasy, eds., *Classical conditioning II: Current research and theory*, pp. 231–247. New York: Appleton-Century-Crofts.

Weardon, J. H., and Bray, S. (2001). Scalar timing without reference memory? Episodic temporal generalization and bisection in humans. *Quarterly Journal of Experimental Psychology 54B*, 289–309.

White, N. E., Kehoe, E. J., Choi, J-S, and Moore, J. W. (2000). Coefficient of variation in timing of the classically conditioned eyeblink in rabbits. *Animal Learning and Behavior 28*, 520–524.

David R. Thomas
Revised by John W. Moore

DISTRIBUTED PRACTICE EFFECTS

Learning and memory are generally improved by repetition. However, not all repetitions are equally beneficial. The effectiveness of repetitions depends in part on their temporal distribution. A piece of information studied on several occasions widely spaced apart in time will be remembered better than a similar fact studied on several occasions close in time.

The advantage of distributed repetitions over spaced repetitions has long been known. Hermann Ebbinghaus discussed distributed practice effects in his classic 1885 monograph on memory. He noted that "with any considerable number of repetitions a suitable distribution of them over a space of time is decidedly more advantageous than the massing of them at a single time" (p. 89). Similarly, Jost (1897) formulated the advantage of distributed over massed repetitions as one of his laws of memory. In subsequent decades, distribution of repetition became an important manipulation in the study of learning and memory. Because many different procedures were used and many conflicting results were found, the overall pattern was long unclear, and investigators, such as Underwood (1961), sometimes despaired of being able to find consistent advantages for distributed practice over massed practice.

Among researchers on human memory, an important breakthrough was the research of Arthur Melton (1967), who used a procedure that became standard for many subsequent investigators. Participants saw a list of words presented one at a time. Some words were shown once on the list, while others were shown twice. Of the words that were shown twice, some were repeated in massed fashion; that is, they were presented twice in a row. Other words were repeated in spaced or distributed fashion; that is, they had their occurrences separated by one or more intervening words. After presentation of the list was complete, participants were asked to recall the items in any order. Melton found that the probability of recall for repeated items increased as a positive function of the number of intervening items between presentations. This advantage for distributed repetitions over massed repetitions is often called the spacing effect; the fact that memory for spaced items may improve somewhat as the distribution between repetitions is increased further is sometimes called the lag effect.

Are massed presentations ever more effective than distributed repetitions? Glenberg (1976) presented evidence that massed presentations may be superior if memory is only required for a very short interval. When the memory test is given almost immediately after the last presentation, massed repetitions may lead to superior memory than spaced repetitions. Evidently, the benefit one obtains from having multiple study episodes right before the test can sometimes be greater than the advantage usually gained from distributed rehearsal. Therefore, cramming may be a reasonably effective study strategy if one is sure that the test will occur as soon as the cramming is finished. However, distributed practice consistently results in better long-term retention.

Importance of Distributed-Practice Effects

One reason why the effects of distributed practice on memory are seen by many researchers as important is that they have wide generality. One can find these effects in many different subject populations, including nonhuman animals (Davis, 1970), human infants (Cornell, 1980), children (Toppino, 1991), and the elderly (Balota, Duchek, and Paullin, 1989; Benjamin and Craik, 2001). These effects are found on all sorts of memory tests and on a wide variety of different materials.

Distributed practice can also be used to improve learning and retention of meaningful material. For example, Rea and Modigliani (1985) showed that distributed practice facilitates memory for spelling and multiplication facts. Reder and Anderson (1982) found that distributed practice leads to improved memory for information from textbooks, relative to massed practice. Dempster (1987) showed that learning of the definitions of uncommon English words benefited from distributed practice. Bahrick and Phelps (1987) demonstrated that retention of Spanish vocabulary words over an eight-year period was greatly affected by distribution of practice. In short, distribution of practice seems to be as important in the mastery of classroom material as it is in the memorization of lists in a laboratory. Dempster (1988) called for educators to be more sensitive to the importance of this variable for classroom instruction, as distributing practice may improve retention without requiring additional time and resources.

Study-Phase Retrieval Accounts

Many different theories have been used to explain distributed-practice effects. Although the details of these theories vary, contemporary accounts can generally be grouped into three separate approaches. One such approach emphasizes the importance of study-phase retrieval (Braun and Rubin, 1998). This approach assumes that one way in which repetition helps to improve memory is by reminding the learner of earlier encounters with the studied information. For example, if a particular word occurs twice on a list, the second presentation may remind the learner of the first presentation. The learner may then think about the first presentation again, and this retrieval and added rehearsal would make the first presentation particularly memorable. To explain why the distribution of repetitions affects memory, one must add on the assumption that this reminding process benefits memory only if sufficient time has passed to guarantee that the first presentation is not already being consciously rehearsed.

It is reasonable that an encounter with a stimulus may serve as a reminder of earlier encounters. However, at least one critical claim of this approach is unsupported. A study-phase retrieval account predicts that memory for the first occurrence of a repeated item is affected by distribution of practice. Although it is difficult to distinguish between memory for the first occurrence and memory for the second occurrence of a repeated item, what little evidence researchers have suggests that it is memory for the second occurrence, not the first, that is affected by distribution of practice (Hintzman, Block, and Summers, 1973). Although a study-phase retrieval process may contribute to effects of distributed practice, there is little direct evidence in favor of this approach.

Deficient-Processing Accounts

An alternative approach to explaining distributed-practice effects is to claim that learners do not process the second occurrence of an item as fully when it is repeated in massed fashion as when it is repeated in spaced fashion. That is, the second occurrence of a massed repetition is not given as much attention or rehearsal as the second occurrence of a spaced repetition.

Zechmeister and Shaughnessy (1980) suggested that deficient processing of massed items may reflect rehearsal strategies on the part of learners. For example, in the case of people memorizing a list of words, the participants do not just rehearse each item as it is presented; rather, they presumably divide their rehearsal between the current item and previous items. The amount of rehearsal that a person devotes to an item presumably depends on how difficult the item appears to be. Zechmeister and Shaughnessy found that participants overestimate the extent to which they would remember massed repetitions. Because people may mistakenly believe that massed items will be easy to remember, they may not devote as much rehearsal and attention to them as they do to spaced items. Indeed, when participants are asked to rehearse aloud or to pace themselves through a list, massed repetitions seem to receive less rehearsal than distributed repetitions.

Another version of this approach (advocated by Hintzman, 1974) attributes distributed-practice effects to deficient processing of the second occurrence of massed repetitions but views this as a result of an automatic, unconscious process, not as the result of a deliberate strategy. This type of account has the advantage of being applicable to subject populations, such as human infants, that show distributed-practice effects but that presumably do not employ conscious rehearsal strategies.

Encoding-Variability Accounts

Encoding-variability accounts of distributed-processing effects assume that spacing between repetitions facilitates memory by increasing the likelihood that each occurrence of a repeated item is stored in a very different way in memory. This sort of approach may best be explained by way of an analogy. Imagine that a business office is very disorganized, and that workers often have difficulty finding papers they need. If they have an important document that they want to be able to find at a later time, it would make sense for them to make multiple copies of it. However, it would be wise for them to keep each of the copies in different places and filed in different ways; this would increase the probability that they would find at least one copy when they need it. Encoding-variability accounts assume that distributed practice increases the probability that different occurrences of a repeated item will be stored in memory in different ways, thereby increasing the probability that a person would be able to retrieve at least one occurrence.

Different theorists have approached encoding variability in different ways. Landauer (1976) argued that distribution of practice directly influenced the location of memories of specific occurrences. Other theorists, such as Gartman and Johnson (1972) and Glenberg (1979), have emphasized that distribution of practice may increase the probability that a repeated item will be interpreted or analyzed differently at each occurrence. What these approaches have in common is the assumption that repeated items are remembered better if they are studied differently at each occurrence and that distributed rehearsal increases the probability that variability in study will occur.

Multiprocess Accounts

It seems increasingly likely that there will be no single explanation for why distributed practice improves memory. Rather, there are several reasons why distributed repetitions are more effective than massed repetitions, and all three of the major approaches (study-phase retrieval, deficient processing, encoding variability) may apply under some circumstances. Greene (1989) and Russo, Parkin, Taylor, and Wilks (1998) have offered multiprocess accounts that combine these approaches. The nature of the subject population, the stimulus material, and the experimental procedure all seem to determine the nature of the processes that underlie the advantage for distributed practice.

Although the theoretical explanation for the effects of distributed practice is likely to be complex, there is no question that these effects are powerful and of wide generality. The fact that distributed practice leads to superior retention than massed practice needs to be taken into account by both experimenters and educators.

See also: REPETITION AND LEARNING

Bibliography

Bahrick, H. P., and Phelps, E. (1987). Retention of Spanish vocabulary over 8 years. *Journal of Experimental Psychology: Learning, Memory, and Cognition 13,* 344–349.

Balota, D. A., Duchek, J. M., and Paullin, R. (1989). Age-related differences in the impact of spacing, lag, and retention interval. *Psychology and Aging 4,* 3–9.

Benjamin, A. S., and Craik, F. I. M. (2001). Parallel effects of aging and time pressure on memory for source: Evidence from the spacing effect. *Memory & Cognition 29,* 691–697.

Braun, K., and Rubin, D. C. (1998). The spacing effect depends on an encoding deficit, retrieval, and time in working memory: Evidence from once-presented words. *Memory 6,* 37–65.

Cornell, E. H. (1980). Distributed study facilitates infants' delayed recognition accuracy. *Memory & Cognition 8,* 539–542.

Davis, M. (1970). Effects of interstimulus interval length and variability on startle-response habituation in the rat. *Journal of Comparative and Physiological Psychology 78,* 260–267.

Dempster, F. N. (1987). Effects of variable encoding and spaced presentations on vocabulary learning. *Journal of Educational Psychology 79,* 162–170.

—— (1988). The spacing effect: A case study in the failure to apply the results of psychological research. *American Psychologist 43,* 627–634.

Ebbinghaus, H. (1885; reprint 1964). *Memory: A contribution to experimental psychology.* New York: Dover.

Gartman, L. F., and Johnson, N. F. (1972). Massed versus distributed repetition of homographs: A test of the differential-encoding hypothesis. *Journal of Verbal Learning and Verbal Behavior 11,* 801–808.

Glenberg, A. M. (1976). Monotonic and nonmonotonic lag effects in paired-associate and recognition memory paradigms. *Journal of Verbal Learning and Verbal Behavior 15*, 1–15.

—— (1979). Component-levels theory of the effects of spacing of repetitions on recall and recognition. *Memory & Cognition 7*, 95–112.

Greene, R. L. (1989). Spacing effects in memory: Evidence for a two-process account. *Journal of Experimental Psychology: Learning, Memory, and Cognition 15*, 371–377.

Hintzman, D. L. (1974). Theoretical implications of the spacing effect. In R. L. Solso, ed., *Theories in cognitive psychology: The Loyola symposium*. Hillsdale, NJ: Erlbaum.

Hintzman, D. L., Block, R. A., and Summers, J. J. (1973). Modality tags and memory for repetitions: Locus of the spacing effect. *Journal of Verbal Learning and Verbal Behavior 12*, 229–238.

Jost, A. (1897). Die Assoziationsfestigkeit in Abhangigkeit von der Verteilung der Wiederholungen. *Zeitschrift fur Psychologie 14*, 436–472.

Landauer, T. K. (1976). Memory without organization: Properties of a model with random storage and undirected retrieval. *Cognitive Psychology 7*, 495–531.

Melton, A. W. (1967). Repetition and retrieval from memory. *Science 158*, 532.

Rea, C. P., and Modigliani, V. (1985). The effect of expanded versus massed practice on the retention of multiplication facts and spelling lists. *Human Learning 4*, 11–18.

Reder, L. M., and Anderson, J. R. (1982). Effects of spacing and embellishment on memory for the main points of a text. *Memory & Cognition 10*, 97–102.

Russo, R., Parkin, A. J., Taylor, S. R., and Wilks, J. (1998). Revising current two-process accounts of spacing effects in memory. *Journal of Experimental Psychology: Learning, Memory, and Cognition 24*, 161–172.

Toppino, T. C. (1991). The spacing effect in young children's free recall: Support for automatic-process explanations. *Memory & Cognition 19*, 159–167.

Underwood, B. J. (1961). Ten years of massed practice on distributed practice. *Psychological Review 4*, 229–247.

Zechmeister, E. B., and Shaughnessy, J. J. (1980). When you know that you know and when you think that you know but you don't. *Bulletin of the Psychonomic Society 15*, 41–44.

Arthur M. Glenberg
Revised by Robert L. Greene

DRUGS

See: COGNITIVE ENHANCERS; DRUGS AND
MEMORY; ELECTROCONVULSIVE THERAPY
AND MEMORY LOSS; PHARMACOLOGICAL
TREATMENT OF MEMORY DEFICITS

DRUGS AND MEMORY

The psychopharmacological approach to the study of memory involves a systematic examination of the behavioral changes that occur following the administration of psychoactive drugs. This approach complements neuropsychological research in its neurobiological approach to the study of learning and memory. Most psychoactive drugs produce reversible effects in the central nervous system, allowing subjects to be used as their own controls. The ability to evaluate memory performance in both a drugged and an undrugged state is particularly useful in human studies, where the number of subjects can be limited. An additional advantage of this approach is that using the same subjects as both the control and experimental groups (within-subjects design) is a much more powerful way to detect small drug effects. Using a within-subjects experimental design is particularly useful for evaluating memory, because there can be substantial differences in baseline performance among individuals.

Studies of the effects of drugs on memory are valuable for several reasons. First, it is important to know whether a drug that is being used to relieve a particular condition can affect (usually impair) memory as a side effect (see Table 1). For example, agents that block the effect of acetylcholine, a neurotransmitter long known to modulate memory, are frequently used as part of the treatment for the movement disorders of Parkinson's disease. At high doses, anticholinergic drugs produce profound memory impairments. Second, experimental studies using drugs with defined mechanisms of action have helped to define the involvement of specific neurochemical systems in memory. One example is the class of drugs called benzodiazepines. These drugs facilitate the effects of the inhibitory neurotransmitter GABA (gamma-aminobutyric acid) and impair memory. Unfortunately, not all agents that affect memory act discretely. Ethanol (alcohol) impairs memory by an unknown mechanism that appears to involve actions on several neurotransmitter systems and on nerve-cell membranes. Third, studies with drugs offer the possibility of helping to better define different types of memory. Fourth, drug studies offer the hope of developing treatments for diseases with symptoms of memory impairment, such as Alzheimer's disease.

Characteristics of Memory

There are several distinct memory systems in the brain. One useful classification scheme divides long-term memory into declarative (explicit) and nondeclarative (implicit) categories. Declarative memory involves the conscious recall of facts or events (e.g., remembering a name), whereas nondeclarative memory is not conscious and is usually expressed through performance (e.g., riding a bicycle). Subtypes of memory within each of these systems rely on different brain regions and therefore involve different sets of neural connections and combinations of chemical neurotransmitters and second-messenger systems. In addition to distinctions based on neuroanatomy, there are separate processes governing short-term and long-term memory. This diversity implies that there are a number of sites where drugs can modulate memory and that different drugs should influence different types of memory.

There are at least three components of memory: acquisition, consolidation, and retention or retrieval. Each can be affected by drugs. The most frequently documented effects of drugs on learning and memory pertain to acquisition. In such studies researchers administer the drug before training begins. Arousal and attention influence acquisition, so sedatives usually impair memory, whereas stimulants usually enhance it. Mood and motivation also affect acquisition; agents that reduce either usually impair memory. At the most basic level, drugs can impair acquisition by interfering with sensory perception—blurring vision, for example. Possible drug effects on peripheral functions must be controlled for in experimental studies, especially when animals are used as subjects.

Administering the agent after training helps to disentangle the memory-altering properties of drugs from their effects on sensory or motor functions. This is the protocol used to study the effects of drugs on memory consolidation. If the drug has been metabolically eliminated by the time memory is tested, then posttraining treatments affect only consolidation, not acquisition or retention. Studies of consolidation in animals have provided valuable information about the biochemical mechanisms of memory formation and the intervals during which learning activates these mechanisms.

The research on drug effects on retrieval is not as extensive as that on acquisition or consolidation. Perhaps the best-known example of drug-induced alterations in retrieval comes from the literature on state-dependency. *State-dependent retrieval* refers to the ability of subjects to retrieve information better when they are in the same state as they were when the material was acquired. For example, if material was learned under the influence of a drug such as alcohol, retrieval under sober conditions is often worse than if the subject is again intoxicated. Some such effects hinge on the nature of the retrieval test, and not all results appear to depend on the state of the subject.

Drugs That Impair Memory

Many chemical compounds are known to impair memory; only a general overview of these agents is possible here. The initial question is whether a given compound can be considered a drug. At one end of the spectrum are commonly available agents that normally have another use. For example, sniffing the organic solvents (e.g., toluene) in glue will impair memory. At the other extreme are arcane chemical

Table 1

Types of Drugs That Affect Memory

Category	Example	Effect on memory	Mechanism
Neurotoxin	Domoic acid	Impairs	Destroys hippocampal neurons
Alters Neurotransmitter Levels/Release/ Activity	MDMA (Ecstasy)	Impairs	Lowers serotonin levels
	Amphetamine	Enhances	Releases norepinephrine
	Physostigmine	Enhances	Prevents breakdown of acetylcholine
Affects Neurotransmitter Receptors	Scopolamine	Impairs	Blocks cholinergic receptors
	Diazepam (Valium)	Impairs	Enhances effect of GABA
	Pentobarbital	Impairs	Enhances effect of GABA
	Dizocipline (MK-801)	Impairs	Blocks noradrenergic receptors
	Propranolol	Impairs	Blocks glutamatergic NMDA receptors
	Picrotoxin	Enhances	Blocks GABA receptors
	Nicotine	Enhances	Activates nicotinic cholinergic receptors
Affects Other Processes	Ethanol (Alcohol)	Impairs	Disrupts brain neurotransmission
	Cycloheximide	Impairs	Disrupts protein synthesis
	Ginkgo biloba	Enhances	Improves cerebral blood flow

SOURCE: Courtesy of Gregory M. Rose.

structures used only in scientific research. Most compounds mentioned here either have a role as medicines or are well known among scientists who study the neuropharmacology of memory.

The most pernicious drug-induced impairment of memory is the destruction of neurons in brain regions involved in memory formation. For example, domoic acid destroys neurons in the hippocampus, an area that is critical for the formation of long-term declarative memories. Other agents act by severely depleting levels of neurotransmitters in pathways that modulate memory. One example of this phenomenon is the recreational drug Ecstasy (MDMA), which impairs memory by reducing serotonin levels. While the effects of these types of treatments are long lasting, the memory impacts of most drugs are reversible.

Many drugs that impair memory act as neurotransmitter receptors. Usually they reduce the function of a particular neurotransmitter. For example, scopolamine blocks the receptor for acetylcholine, propranol blocks a class of receptors for norepinephrine, and dizocipline (MK-801) blocks a subtype of glutamate receptors. Sedative drugs are the exception: Benzodiazepines (e.g., diazepam [Valium]) and barbiturates enhance the action of GABA, the primary inhibitory neurotransmitter in the brain, thus disrupting memory.

Long-term memory formation requires activation of certain enzymes such as protein kinases (e.g, PKC, PKA, CaMKII). This activation is controlled by several different neurotransmitters and can be affected by drugs that act at any of their receptors. Also, specific inhibitors of protein kinases impair memory. An important consequence of protein kinase activation is the initiation of new protein synthesis. Inhibitors of protein synthesis (e.g., cycloheximide or anisomycin) can disrupt long-term memory formation.

A given drug seldom uniformly impairs all types of memory. For example, ethanol and the benzodiazepine drugs affect mainly long-term memory, leaving short-term memory relatively unaffected. These drugs also preferentially disrupt declarative memory while leaving nondeclarative memory relatively intact.

There has been considerable interest in the possibility of using drugs in normal subjects to model clinical amnesias such as Korsakoff's syndrome or Alzheimer's disease. Knowledge of the neuropharmacology of a drug that would model a particular amnesic syndrome might suggest useful treatment strategies. The specific impairments seen in normal subjects treated with alcohol resemble those of patients with Korsakoff's syndrome, and it has been suggested that scopolamine mimics some of the features of the cognitive impairments seen in dementia patients. However, no drug treatment has been described that completely mimics the pattern of memory disruption induced by a specific disease.

Drugs That Enhance Memory

More drugs hinder memory than help it, so there is a lively interest in discovering memory-enhancing drugs, especially because many neurological diseases impair memory. Also, some memory loss occurs in old age even in healthy people. Finally, nearly everyone would like to have a better memory. An important unanswered question is whether enhancing "normal" memory is a reasonable possibility.

In general, the agents that enhance memory act in the opposite way from drugs that impair memory.

For example, picrotoxin reduces the inhibitory effect of GABA receptors, while amphetamine causes the release of norepinephrine. Acetylcholinesterase inhibitors increase the effect of acetylcholine and are used to treat the memory deficits of Alzheimer's disease. All of these drugs are effective memory enhancers, but they all have have serious side effects.

Drugs can influence many aspects of brain function, including learning and memory. Most drugs adversely affect memory, although some can enhance it. There is an increasing need to develop safe and effective drugs to treat memory problems caused by aging or disease.

Bibliography

Castellano, C., Cabib, S., and Puglisi-Allegra, S. (1996). Psychopharmacology of memory modulation: Evidence for multiple interaction among neurotransmitters and hormones. *Behavioral Brain Research 77*, 1–21.

Castellano, C., Cestari, V., and Ciamei, A. (2001). NMDA receptors and learning and memory processes. *Current Drug Targets 2*, 273–283.

Davis, H. P., and Squire, L. R. (1984). Protein synthesis and memory: A review. *Psychology Bulletin 96*, 518–559.

Duka, T. T., Curran, H. V. H., Rusted, J. M. J., and Weingartner, H. J. H. (1996). Perspectives on cognitive psychopharmacology research. *Behavioral Pharmacology 7*, 401–410.

Ellis, K. A., and Nathan, P. J. (2001). The pharmacology of human working memory. *International Journal of Neuropsychopharmacology 4*, 299–313.

Farr, S. A., Flood, J. F., and Morley, J. E. (2000). The effect of cholinergic, GABAergic, serotonergic, and glutamatergic receptor modulation on posttrial memory processing in the hippocampus. *Neurobiology of Learning and Memory 73*, 150–167.

Lister, R. G., and Weingartner, H. J. (1987). Neuropharmacological strategies for understanding psychobiological determinants of cognition. *Human Neurobiology 6*, 119–127.

McGaugh, J. L., and Izquierdo, I. (2000). The contribution of pharmacology to research on the mechanisms of memory formation. *Trends in Pharmacological Science 21*, 208–210.

Squire, L. R., and Zola, S. M. (1996). Structure and function of declarative and nondeclarative memory systems. *Proceedings of the National Academy of Sciences of the United States of America 93*, 13,515–13,522.

Sutherland, R. J., Hoesing, J. M., and Whishaw, I. Q. (1990). Domoic acid, an environmental toxin, produces hippocampal damage and severe memory impairment. *Neuroscience Letters 120*, 221–223.

Richard G. Lister
Herbert J. Weingartner
Revised by Gregory M. Rose

DYSLEXIA

See: LEARNING DISABILITIES

E

EARLY EXPERIENCE AND LEARNING

The brain of the developing organism is a unique and dynamic system. During the prenatal and postnatal periods the brain differs dramatically from that of the adult. For example, it contains more synapses early in development than it does at any other stage in life (Purves and Lichtman, 1980). Receptors for a number of neuropeptides (e.g., oxytocin) are found in higher concentrations early in development than later in life (Shapiro and Insel, 1989). In certain brain areas (e.g., the suprachiasmatic nucleus of the hypothalamus), glucocorticoid receptors are found in high concentrations only during early ontogeny (Van Eekelen et al., 1987). These are but a few examples that attest to the differences in the brain during development. For the most part, scientists have not determined the functional significance of these neuronal features of the newborn brain.

One of the critical aspects of the developing brain is its plasticity. Both physiological and environmental stimuli have been shown to profoundly, and often permanently, influence the functional capacities of the organism (Levine and Mullins, 1966). Neonatal disturbance of the normal hormonal milieu leads to some of the best-known cases of permanent alterations of function induced by early manipulations of physiological events. Neonatal exposure to heterotypical gonadal hormones, for example, results in a permanently altered reproductive physiology and behavior. Both over- and underexposure to thyroid hormone during early development cause changes in the brain that produce learning disabilities.

The purpose of this entry is to illustrate the effects of alterations in early environments on learning capacity in the adult organism. Several areas of investigation have demonstrated the importance of early experience for later behavior, using a number of different models to examine this issue. Thus, deprivation of visual experience early in development has been shown to markedly affect adult vision; this also affects the animal's behavior (Hyvarinen and Hyvarinen, 1979). There is an extensive research on the effects of "enriched environments" on subsequent learning ability (Rosenzweig, 1984). This entry examines the role of early handling as a model of infantile stimulation on learning in the adult.

In 1956 S. Levine and colleagues reported that neonatal manipulations have profound effects on later behavior. In essence, their study showed that neonatal handling (i.e., removing rat pups from their mother for a few minutes and returning them to their mother), or electric shock during the same period, markedly improved the animals' capacity to learn a conditioned avoidance response when tested as adults. This procedure involves placing the animal in a two-compartment chamber. Both sides of the chamber contain grid floors that can be electrified. The animal is presented with a signal, the conditioned stimulus, which is followed after a brief time by an electric shock. The animal is required to cross from the electrified side of the chamber to the safe side. If it crosses within the interval between the onset of the signal and the onset of shock, it avoids the shock (conditioned avoidance). However, if the animal fails to cross during this interval and the shock is delivered, this response is considered an escape response.

Researchers conducted a number of studies following their initial observations that demonstrated these marked differences between handled and nonhandled pups. In order to verify whether the effects of early handling were age-dependent, early-handled pups were compared with nonhandled pups and with animals that were handled after weaning. Pups manipulated as infants were found to show avoidance learning superior to that of nonhandled pups. Postweaning-handled animals were more similar to nonhandled rats.

Although experiments showed that early handling improved avoidance learning, the underlying causes of this improvement remained to be determined. One possible explanation for these findings is that emotional reactivity was modified as a function of these early experiences. The more efficient avoidance learning may therefore be a consequence of reduced arousal levels. Increasing the shock levels during avoidance conditioning results in an inverted U-shaped function with regard to acquisition of the conditioned avoidance response. Thus, acquisition is improved by very low levels of shock but impaired by very high levels.

There are numerous reports that early handling reduces emotional reactivity (Whimbey and Denenberg, 1967). This reduced reactivity is demonstrable using both behavioral and physiological indices. Activity levels and defecation in the open field differ between handled and nonhandled subjects. Handled animals explore more actively (i.e., show less freezing), defecate less in the open field, are less neophobic (Weinberg, Smotherman, and Levine, 1978), and are less reactive to human handling as adults (Ader, 1965). One of the more sensitive physiological indices of arousal is the activation of the hypothalamic-pituitary-adrenal (HPA) system (Hennessy and Levine, 1978). Following stress, nonhandled animals show plasma corticosterone (the primary glucocorticoid secreted by the rodent) elevations that are both larger and more persistent than those found in animals handled during infancy (Levine et al., 1967).

These differences in emotionality are consistently found using a variety of different testing paradigms. However, the effects of early handling on avoidance conditioning appear to vary when the parameters are different from those used in the original studies. Both R. Ader (1965) and J. Weinberg and S. Levine (1977) failed to find differences in conditioned avoidance response, although differences in emotional reactivity were clearly present. The question of whether early handling influences associative learning therefore still remained unanswered.

In order to address the issue of the effects of early handling on learning, V. H. Denenberg and J. R. C. Morton (1962) studied the effect of early handling on the ability of rats to learn tasks that did not involve noxious stimuli. These investigators examined the interaction between early handling and environmental enrichment on the ability of adult rats to solve a Hebb-Williams maze. After weaning handled and nonhandled rats were reared in a neutral, restricted, or enriched environment. The animals were then required to solve a sequence of twelve test problems. The results indicated that the animals' ability to learn the maze was affected by the postweaning, but not by the pre-weaning, manipulation. Thus, rats reared in an enriched environment made significantly fewer errors than those reared in neutral or restricted environments. Based on these results, it was concluded that pre-weaning handling affected emotional processes but not learning ability.

In 1972 R. Wong attempted to clarify the issue of whether early handling directly affects associative learning or whether the improvement in learning is due mainly to differences in emotional reactivity. An experiment was conducted that presumably could discriminate these two processes. Thus, subjects were trained to reach a criterion of stable performance on a positive reinforcement task (food) and then punished with an aversive stimulus (shock) for making the reinforced response. Comparisons could then be made in terms of the degree of response suppression following the presentation of the aversive event; and the rate of recovery after removal of the aversive stimulus. Wong argued that if handled animals showed greater response suppression and a slower recovery than nonhandled animals, this would indicate a direct effect of handling on learning. If the contrary occurred, it could be assumed that the primary influence on the behavior was attributable to differences in emotionality. Animals were trained to alternate goal boxes in a T-maze to obtain food. Once the criterion had been reached, they were given a shock in the goal box where they had obtained positive reinforcement (S+ box). Testing began one day after the punished trial. The animals were placed in the maze and received food only in the S+ box. During the acquisition phase the handled group made more correct responses (alternations) than the nonhandled group, indicating superior learning on a positive reinforcement task. Following the shock exposure handled rats made fewer choices to the food reward box (S+) than nonhandled animals, suggesting that handled animals had superior associative learning.

Decades later A. Tang (2001) investigated the role of exposure to novelty on hippocampal dependent learning. Neonatal rats were exposed for three minutes daily to a nonhome environment and compared with littermate controls that remained in the home cage for the period with the mother removed. The novelty exposed rats showed more rapid acquisition as juveniles and greater retention in adulthood in a spatial learning task. Further, these animals also showed greater retention in an odor discrimination task.

In many of the studies described above, learning was investigated using behavioral situations in which an aversive motivational component was present, making it difficult to dismiss entirely the effects of emotional reactivity on learning. Latent inhibition, a behavioral paradigm that avoids some of these problems, has been used to examine the relationship between handling and learning. This paradigm was described in the context of classical conditioning. Ivan Pavlov was the first to demonstrate that repeated exposure to a conditioned stimulus (CS), prior to pairing this stimulus with an unconditioned stimulus (UCS), impairs the rate of conditioning that subsequently occurs (Pavlov, 1927). Thus, repeated exposure to a stimulus that is not followed by meaningful consequences renders this stimulus ineffective for subsequent learning.

I. Weiner, Schnabel, Lubor, and Feldon (1985) employed the latent inhibition paradigm to study the question of early handling and learning. The experiment was conducted in two phases. During the first phase (preexposure) members of one group were placed in a shuttle box and presented with sixty five-second tones. Members of the second group were placed in the shuttle box for an equivalent time without exposure to the tones. In the second phase the animals were presented with one hundred tone (CS) and shock (UCS) pairings and the number of conditioned avoidance responses was recorded. The results showed that nonpreexposed handled animals exhibited better avoidance learning than nonhandled rats, thus replicating earlier findings. However, preexposed handled animals performed more poorly than non-pre-exposed handled rats. The findings were to some extent sex-dependent: Whereas preexposed handled males and females and preexposed nonhandled females exhibited the latent inhibition (i.e., performed more poorly than nonpreexposed animals), the nonhandled males did not show any effect of preexposure on the conditioned avoidance response.

In a further study, latent inhibition was investigated using a conditioned emotional response (CER) to test the influence of early handling (Weiner, Feldon, and Ziv-Harris,1987). The CER procedure was conducted in three phases: 1. pre-exposure; 2. acquisition, in which the pre-exposed tone was paired with shock; and 3. testing, during which latent inhibition was indexed by the animals' suppression of licking during tone presentation. As in the previous experiment, latent inhibition was observed in the handled males and females and in nonhandled females, but not in the nonhandled males. Based on both of these studies, the conclusion was that early handling exerts a beneficial influence on learning capacity in the adult animal.

Only a very limited literature has attempted to examine the neural substrates of the early handling phenomenon. Michael Meaney and his colleagues (1988) studied the long-term influence of early handling on the neuroendocrine regulation of the HPA system. These researchers reported a long-term down regulation of glucocorticoid receptors (GR) in the hippocampus of nonhandled, but not of handled, aged animals. They further reported that spatial learning, a hippocampus-dependent process, is significantly improved in aged animals that had undergone early handling. However, the aged nonhandled animals appeared to have suffered hippocampal cell loss. The differences in spatial learning may thus be due to the prevention of this cell loss by early handling. However, given the results presented by Tang, it would appear that the influence of early experiences on hippocampal dependent learning is evident throughout the life span. These studies do demonstrate the long-term consequences of early handling for at least one aspect of neural regulation. Although the implications of this down regulation of GRs for learning have not been extensively investigated, there is some evidence that administering specific GR antagonists interferes with the acquisition of a spatial learning task (Oitzl, and de Kloet, 1992). Other aspects of the HPA system also seem to be involved in learning and memory (van Wimersma Greidanus, 1982).

Conclusion

There are many examples in the literature of long-term consequences of manipulations during infancy that affect learning and memory. However, most of these studies have utilized toxic agents resulting in permanent and irreversible morphological and physiological changes in the central nervous system that are later reflected as impairments in the adult organism's ability to learn (Grimm, 1987). Environmental enrichment and early handling constitute examples of subtle environmental manipulations that cause permanent alterations in adult function that facilitate rather than impair adult learning abilities.

See also: CHILDREN, DEVELOPMENT OF MEMORY IN; EMOTION, MOOD, AND MEMORY

Bibliography

Ader, R. (1965). Effects of early experience and differential housing on behavior and susceptibility to gastric erosions in the rat. *Journal of Comparative and Physiological Psychology 60,* 233–238.

Denenberg, V. H. (1969). Open-field behavior in the rat: What does it mean? *Annals of the New York Academy of Sciences 159,* 852–859.

Denenberg, V. H., and Morton, J. R. C. (1962). Effects of preweaning and postweaning manipulations upon problem-solving behavior. *Journal of Comparative and Physiological Psychology 55,* 1,096–1,098.

Grimm, V. E. (1987). Effects of teratogenic exposure on the developing brain: Research strategies and possible mechanisms. *Developmental and Pharmacology Therapeutics 10,* 328–345.

Hennessy, M. B., and Levine, S. (1978). Sensitive pituitary-adrenal responsiveness to varying intensities of psychological stimulation. *Physiology and Behavior 21,* 295–297.

Hyvarinen, J., and Hyvarinen, L. (1979). Blindness and modification of association by early binocular deprivation in monkeys. *Child Care and Health Development 5,* 385–387.

Levine, S., Chevalier, J. A., and Korchin, S. (1956). The effects of early shock and handling on later avoidance. *Journal of Personality 24,* 475–493.

Levine, S., Haltmeyer, G. C., Karas, G. G., and Denenberg, V. H. (1967). Physiological and behavioral effects of infantile stimulation. *Physiology and Behavior 2,* 55–59.

Levine, S., and Mullins, R. F. (1966). Hormonal influences on brain organization in infant rats. *Science 152,* 1,585–1,592.

Meaney, M. J., Aitken, D. H., van Berkel, C., Bhatnagar, S., and Sapolsky, R. M. (1988). Effects of neonatal handling on age-related impairments associated with the hippocampus. *Science 239,* 766–768.

Oitzl, M. S., and de Kloet, E. R. (1992). Selective corticosteroid antagonists modulate specific aspects of spatial orientation learning. *Behavior Neuroscience 106,* 62–71.

Pavlov, I. P. (1927). *Conditioned reflexes,* trans. G. V. Arenp. London: Oxford University Press.

Purves, D., and Lichtman, J. W. (1980). Elimination of synapses in the developing nervous system. *Science 210,* 153–157.

Rosenzweig, M. R. (1984). Experience, memory, and the brain. *American Psychologist 39,* 365–376.

Shapiro, L. E., and Insel, T. R. (1989). Ontogeny of oxytocin receptors in the rat forebrain: A quantitative study. *Synapse 4,* 259–266.

Tang, A. (2001) Neonatal exposure to a novel environment enhances hippocampal-dependent memory function during infancy and adulthood. *Learning and Memory 8,* 257–264.

Van Eekelen, J. A. M., Rosenfeld, P., Levine, S., Westphal, H. M., and de Kloet, E. R. (1987). Post-natal disappearance of glucocorticoid receptor immunoreactivity in the suprachiasmatic nucleus of the rat. *Neuroscience Research Communications 1,* 129–133.

van Wimersma Greidanus, T. B. (1982). Disturbed behavior and memory in the Brattleboro rat. *Annals of the New York Academy of Sciences 394,* 655–662.

Weinberg, J., and Levine, S. (1977). Early handling influences on behavioral and physiological responses during active avoidance. *Developmental Psychobiology 10,* 161–169.

Weinberg, J., Smotherman, W. P., and Levine, S. (1978). Early handling effects on neophobia and conditioned taste aversion. *Physiology and Behavior 20,* 589–596.

Weiner, I., Feldon, J., and Ziv-Harris, D. (1987). Early handling and latent inhibition in the conditioned suppression paradigm. *Developmental Psychobiology 20,* 233–240.

Weiner, I., Schnabel, I., Lubow, R. E., and Feldon, J. (1985). The effects of early handling on latent inhibition in male and female rats. *Developmental Psychobiology 18,* 291–297.

Whimbey, A. E., and Denenberg, V. H. (1967). Experimental programming of life histories: The factor structure underlying experimentally created individual differences. *Behavior 29,* 296–314.

Wong, R. (1972). Infantile handling and associative processes of rats. *British Journal of Psychology 63,* 101–108.

Seymour Levine
Deborah Suchecki

EBBINGHAUS, HERMANN (1850–1909)

Hermann Ebbinghaus was the founder of the experimental psychology of memory. He laid the foundation for the scientific study of memory in a monograph titled *Über das Gedächtnis* (1885), translated into English in 1913 under the title *Memory: A Contribution to Experimental Psychology.*

Life

Ebbinghaus was born on January 23, 1850, at Barmen, near Bonn, Germany. His father was a well-to-do merchant. He studied languages and philosophy at the University of Bonn. He served in the army during the Franco-Prussian War of 1870–1871, and upon returning to the university completed his doctoral dissertation in 1873. He then spent some five years traveling in France and England. He began his research on memory at Berlin in 1878, spending more than a year on the initial set of experiments. Upon completing these studies he became a private lecturer at the University of Berlin in 1880, and he continued his studies of memory. He repeated many of the original experiments from 1879–1880 in 1883–1884 and added new ones. He published the report on both series in his 1885 monograph.

Ebbinghaus's life after he published his epoch-making study was active and productive. He was appointed a professor at the University of Berlin in 1886, remaining there until 1894, when he moved to the University of Breslau. He stayed at Breslau for eleven years and then accepted an appointment at the University of Halle. Over the years he became a prominent and respected member of the new scientific discipline of experimental psychology. A major source of his renown lay in his textbook of general psychology, *Grundzüge der Psychologie* (1897), which became the most widely read psychology text in Germany. Ebbinghaus died of pneumonia at Halle on February 26, 1909.

Ebbinghaus's Approach to Memory

Before Ebbinghaus, the study of memory consisted of philosophical armchair speculation concerning remembering and forgetting in everyday life, and clinical observations of patients with memory disorders. The philosophical approach of the day is reflected in William James's *Principles of Psychology* (1890);. the clinical approach is illustrated by the work of Théodule Ribot. Both lines of thought produced many insights into the nature and workings of normal and impaired memory. However, there were also curious gaps; not surprisingly, the contemporary thinkers were unaware of many of them. One widely held view, for instance, maintained that memory could not be studied by strict scientific methods. Although methods of science had been applied to the "lower" mental processes, such as sensation and perception, under the general rubric of psychophysics, the "higher" mental processes such as memory were regarded as being beyond the pale of such methods. Another tacit idea of the time was that remembering and forgetting occur in an all-or-nothing fashion: A person either does or does not remember a fact, a thought, a name, and the like. The possibility that nonrecoverable mental contents could exist at different levels of strength was discussed neither by philosophers nor by students of memory pathology.

Ebbinghaus's work changed all that. In his now-classic monograph he introduced the general approach to the study and measurement of learning and memory by psychological means, outlined the appropriate methodology, and reported a number of experiments illustrating the power of his methods.

The general strategy that Ebbinghaus adopted can be summarized in terms of three simple principles for the scientific study of mental processes that are not directly observable. These principles are as valid today as they were when Ebbinghaus first made use of them. First, it is necessary to find a way of converting the unobservable mental processes into observable behavior. Second, it is necessary to be able to measure this observable behavior reliably. Third, it is necessary to show that the behavior thus quantified varies systematically with other variables and experimental conditions.

The unobservable mental processes that Ebbinghaus wanted to study and measure were associations between ideas. Like almost all of his contemporaries, he assumed that memory reflects the existence of associations between ideas. He also thought that learning consists of the acquisition of associations, whereas forgetting reflects their loss. Ebbinghaus decided that the study of the acquisition and loss of associations would best be undertaken in a situation in

Hermann Ebbinghaus *(Corbis-Bettmann)*

which the associations to be learned were initially nonexistent. To that end he invented the nonsense syllable as a basic idea unit to be used in experiments on memory. A nonsense syllable is a meaningless single syllable consisting of two consonants separated by a vowel or a diphthong (e.g., WEZ, SIF). A single "lesson" to be learned and remembered consisted of a series of randomly chosen syllables. It was natural to imagine that no associations existed between and among the members of the series. The learning of a "lesson" (committing the series to memory) therefore would involve the formation and strengthening of associations between its constituent syllables. The process of learning could be captured by observing and measuring some behavior that could be assumed to be closely correlated with changes in the associations.

Methods and Results

In all his experiments Ebbinghaus was his sole subject. In numerous studies, in which he varied the conditions of learning and retention, he would learn and then test himself with a large number of different series of syllables. He would learn a given series by first reading and then repeating the sequence of syllables aloud to the beating of a metronome, at the rate of two and a half syllables per second, until he could produce the series faultlessly. The amount of effort required to master the series provided measures of both original learning and subsequent retention (or forgetting, the opposite of retention). Ebbinghaus adopted the number of readings, or the amount of time required for the learning of the series, as the measure of learning. Some time later he would relearn the same series, using the same method of reading and repeating the syllables. The comparison of initial learning and relearning scores provided a measure of what Ebbinghaus called *savings*. Ebbinghaus took savings to represent a measure of retention of the original learning.

Using these methods of measurement of memory, Ebbinghaus investigated a number of basic phenomena of learning and retention. The results of his experiments, concerning things such as the relation between the length of the series and the difficulty of learning it, the effects of the original overlearning of a series on its subsequent relearning, the advantages of distributed over massed practice, and the shape of the forgetting curve, turned out to be highly regular and lawful. Ebbinghaus exercised meticulous care in carrying out his experiments. Among other things, he went to great trouble in performing large numbers of replications of individual experiments. The resulting regularity and lawfulness of his findings greatly impressed other scientists.

In one particularly ingenious set of experiments Ebbinghaus measured and compared three kinds of associations: forward associations between adjacent members of a series, backward associations, and remote associations. In order to measure remote associations he would initially learn a series of syllables in a particular order, and subsequently relearn various series systematically derived from the original one. In these derived series the originally learned syllables were separated by a certain number of other syllables. For instance, if the original series is symbolized by A B C D E F . . . ("..." designating other syllables), then the derived series "skipping one syllable" would consist of A C E . . . B D F . . . , and the derived series "skipping two syllables" would consist of A D . . . B E . . . C F . . . Ebbinghaus found that the savings in learning these derived series varied systematically with the remoteness of the members of the derived series from one another in the originally learned series. These data suggested that in the course of learning a series of syllables, associations are formed not only between immediately adjacent syllables but also among remote ones, the strength of the remote associations between any two members of a series varying directly with the degree of their remoteness in the original series.

Influence

Ebbinghaus's work proved to be highly influential for a number of reasons. Despite the pioneering nature of his work, he did just about everything right by the standards of science. He replaced philosophical discussions about memory and its phenomena with tightly controlled experimental demonstrations of how memory could be measured and how memory performance could be found to be related to and determined by various independent variables. He discussed the sources of error and the problems of unreliability of measurement. He explained and demonstrated how one could measure fine gradations in mental processes that until then were thought to be scientifically intractable. He showed how the "higher" mental processes seemed to obey the same general kinds of laws that governed the "lower" processes. He explicitly and forcefully pointed out the intimate connection that exists between learning and memory, a realization that has guided the study of memory ever since. Like many other novel ideas introduced by Ebbinghaus, the connection between learning and memory is obvious in our day, but it had been overlooked by most thinkers before Ebbinghaus. Perhaps the most important innovation introduced by Ebbinghaus was his adoption of the basic study-and-test paradigm in which a subject learns some previously unknown material and is subsequently tested for retention of the studied material. The study-test paradigm contrasted sharply with the then current philosophical practice of discussing problems and phenomena of memory from the vantage point of existing associations.

Three features of Ebbinghaus's groundbreaking work that are most frequently mentioned in textbooks—his invention of the nonsense syllable; his serial learning task; and his adoption of the savings method as a measure of strength of associations—have had little direct influence on succeeding generations of memory researchers, who even shortly after 1885 rapidly adopted other methods and techniques of studying and measuring memory. Nonsense syllables turned out to vary greatly in meaningfulness and thus lost the advantage of their homogeneity. The serial learning task did not allow independent manipulation or assessment of stimulus and response functions in learning and retention. And the originally ingenious savings method was replaced with more direct methods of measuring retention and forgetting.

Ebbinghaus's most momentous single achievement consisted in his convincing demonstration that it is possible to reliably measure aspects of complex mental processes that are not directly observable. Almost as important were his general orientation and approach and his attitude and spirit in the matter of applying the methods of science to the study of the human mind. These were embraced by his contemporaries and have continued to inspire and guide the thinking of succeeding generations of students of psychology interested in learning and memory.

Ebbinghaus's pioneering role in the founding of the field of research on human learning and memory is universally acknowledged. *Über das Gedächtnis* represented a remarkable achievement of a great scientist, one that has left an indelible stamp on the study of one of the most fascinating problems of the human brain (or mind).

Bibliography

Ebbinghaus, Hermann (1885). *Über das Gedächtnis: Untersuchungen zur experimentellen Psychologie.* Leipzig: Duncker and Humblot. Trans. (1913) H. A. Ruger and C. E. Bussenius, *Memory: A contribution to experimental psychology.* New York: Teachers College, Columbia University. Reprint (1964), New York: Dover.
——— (1897). *Grundzüge der Psychologie.* Leipzig: Veit.
Hoffman, R. R., Bringmann, W., Bamberg, M., and Klein, R. (1987). Some historical observations on Ebbinghaus. In D. S. Gorfein and R. R. Hoffman, eds., *Memory and learning: The Ebbinghaus centennial conference.* Hillsdale, NJ: Erlbaum.
Postman, L. (1968). Hermann Ebbinghaus. *American Psychologist 23,* 149–157.
Roediger, H. L. (1985). Remembering Ebbinghaus. *Contemporary Psychology 30,* 519–523.
Slamecka, N. J. (1985). Ebbinghaus: Some associations. *Journal of Experimental Psychology: Learning Memory, and Cognition 11,* 414–435.

Endel Tulving

John Eccles *(Sven Landgren)*

as an undergraduate. In 1927, he began working with Charles Sherrington, Nobelist and pioneer of neurophysiology. Together they discovered the dual-fiber composition of the ventral spinal nerve roots and established the time course of the *central excitatory state* and the contrasting *central inhibitory state*, excitability changes induced in spinal motoneurones by an impulse volley arriving from the same or the antagonistic muscle nerve, respectively. In 1929, Eccles received a D. Phil. degree from Oxford for a thesis on excitation and inhibition.

ECCLES, JOHN (1903–1997)

The Australian-born scientist John Carew Eccles was a pioneer in neuroscience, discovering the elementary synaptic processes of the central nervous system known as excitatory and inhibitory postsynaptic potentials (EPSPs and IPSPs). He was particularly eager to understand how synaptic changes could serve learning and memory processes. He was awarded the Nobel Prize in physiology or medicine in 1963 for his pioneering analysis of central synaptic transmission.

Education

Eccles was born on January 27,1903, in Melbourne, Australia. His parents, Mary and William Eccles, were both schoolteachers and strongly supported his academic interests. Although he was highly interested in mathematics, he eventually decided to study medicine and entered Melbourne University at the age of seventeen. After finishing his medical course with top marks in 1925, he won a Rhodes Scholarship and entered Magdalen College, Oxford,

Eccles's Main Scientific Discovery

Eccles's major scientific achievement was the identification of the membrane potential changes underlying synaptic transmission in the central nervous system. These studies began at Oxford with analyses of simpler synaptic systems such as the cat nictitating membrane, the cervical sympathetic ganglia, and the neuromuscular junction and continued with spinal cord and supraspinal synapses. In 1937, Eccles moved to Sydney, where he set up a physiological laboratory in the Sydney Hospital and where he and W. J. O'Connor (1939) discovered and named the endplate potential, the immediate electrical muscle cell response to the nerve impulse. In the early 1940s Eccles was joined by two distinguished scholars, Bernard Katz and Stephen Kuffler, who came to Australia as refugees fleeing Nazi Germany and Nazi occupation of Austria, respectively. Together they analyzed the properties of the end-plate potential (Eccles, Katz, and Kuffler, 1941, 1942), and Kuffler made his classical report on the effect of curare (Kuffler, 1942).

The Electrical-Chemical Synaptic Transmission Controversy

Between 1933 and 1938, Eccles made a set of studies on synaptic transmission through the cervical sympathetic ganglion and identified a fast and a slower type of transmission. A pharmacological analysis led him to conclude that, although the slower variety of synaptic transmissions were chemically mediated by acetylcholine (ACh), faster transmissions were likely to be electrically mediated. This interpretation challenged the view of Henry Dale and colleagues (1936), who had hypothetized that all phases were due to ACh. Dale won the 1936 Nobel Prize for the codiscovery with Otto Loewi of acetylcholine as transmitter in the nervous system. Although the scientific debate was intense and lasted for several years, it never damaged the lifelong friendship between Eccles and Dale. Prompted by his friend the philosopher Karl Popper, whom he first met in New Zealand in 1946, and influenced by his demand for testability of the ideas and with falsification as an admirable scientific goal, Eccles in 1949 restated his hypothesis that neuromuscular and autonomous synapses are operated chemically, but transmission in the central nervous system is likely to be electrically mediated.

Discovery of EPSPs and IPSPs in Motoneurones

The introduction of new technology allowed researchers (Fatt and Katz, 1951) to clarify the situation at the neuromuscular synapse, and the issue of the spinal cord mechanism was resolved when Eccles and two younger colleagues, Lawrence Brock and Jack Coombs, working at Otago University in Dunedin, New Zealand (where Eccles had moved in 1946), succeeded in impaling cat motoneurones with glass micropipettes and recording the transmembrane responses to stimulation of various nerves (Brock, Coombs, and Eccles, 1952). A cathode follower and amplifier designed by Coombs allowed the use of high-impedance electrodes that helped identify these processes and were fundamental to the researchers' success. When activating the afferent nerve, the motoneurone response was a depolarizing signal (see Figure 1), which Eccles called the *excitatory postsynaptic potential* (EPSP). Conversely, stimulation of a nerve from an antagonistic muscle inhibited the motoneuron, signaled by a hyperpolarizing response, the *inhibitory postsynaptic potential* (IPSP). Injection of ions via the impaling microelectrode showed that the IPSP depended upon the chloride and potassium ion gradients across the membrane. For these discoveries, Eccles was awarded the Nobel Prize in physiology or medicine for 1963, shared with Alan Hodgkin and Andrew Huxley.

In 1951, Eccles suddenly came to the conclusion that his former position regarding synaptic transmission in the spinal cord was untenable and that the situation was mediated by a chemical transmitter, just as at peripheral synapses. Two convincing observations resulted. First, there was invariably a distinct time delay between the arrival of the afferent nerve impulse and the onset of the postsynaptic response; the electrical hypothesis required simultaneity. Second, the polarity of responses at excitatory and inhibitory synapses was reversed in spite of similar presynaptic action potentials in the two cases. Eccles suggested that the EPSP and IPSP were mediated by two different chemical mediators. The new results were discussed in detail in the first five chapters of his Waynflete Lectures, *The Neurophysiological Basis of Mind* (1953), delivered at Magdalen College, Oxford, in 1952. (A further three chapters discussed synaptic plasticity, the cerebral cortex, learning, memory, and the mind-brain problem.)

During his term at Otago University, Eccles successfully reorganized and modernized the physiology and biochemistry program, but his teaching burden was considerable. In 1953, he accepted a newly established chair of physiology at the John Curtin School of Medical Research in Canberra, Australia, and there he proceeded to set up a modern and efficient neurophysiological laboratory. Joined by scientific colleagues from Australia and abroad, Eccles continued to use intracellular recording to analyze reflex circuits. He also made a set of significant discoveries on synaptic plasticity—for example, that posttetanic potentiation (PTP) is associated with an enhanced EPSP amplitude to a standard test stimulus and, with Arthur Buller and Rosamund Eccles (his daughter), that motoneuronal type controls motor unit contraction speed, a remarkable case of neuronal plasticity. In 1955 he was invited to give the Herter lectures at Johns Hopkins University, printed as *The Physiology of Nerve Cells* (1957), a small book that had tremendous influence.

Eccles and his colleagues analyzed a newly reported form of spinal inhibition reported by Frank and Fuortes in 1957 and found that it was due to reduced transmitter release from the presynaptic terminals of the test fibers, a finding they described as *presynaptic inhibition*. Their pharmacological analysis pointed to gamma-amino-butyric acid (GABA) as the mediating agent. In other collaborations, Eccles made a series of valuable discoveries about pre- and postsynaptic inhibition in the dorsal column nuclei, recurrent inhibition in the thalamus, hippocampal basket cell inhibition, and cerebellar organization. The largest impact of Eccles's studies of supraspinal neurons came from his work on the cerebellum, supported by the neuro-

Figure 1

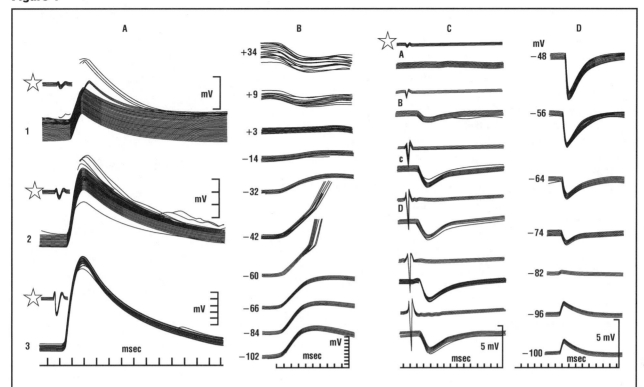

SOURCE: Courtesy of Paul Fatt. A and B are adapted from Coombs, J. S., Eccles, J. C., and Fatt, P. (1955). Excitatory synaptic action in motoneurones *The Journal of Physiology* (London) *130*, 374–395; C from Coombs, J. S., Eccles, J.C., and Fatt, P. (1955). The inhibitory suppression of reflex discharges from motoneurones. *The Journal of Physiology* (London) *130*, 396–413; and D from Coombs, J.S., Eccles, J. C. and Fatt, P. (1955). The specific ionic conductances and the ionic movements across the motoneuronal membrane that produce the inhibitory post-synaptic potential. *The Journal of Physiology* (London) *130*, 326–373.

Properties of EPSP and IPSPs. A. superimposed records of excitatory postsynaptic potentials (EPSPs) from a biceps-semitendinosus motoneuron in response to increasing number of afferent fiber impulses from muscle spindles of its own muscle. Insets (stars) show the signals of the impulses in the afferent nerve as they enter the spinal cord. B. an EPSP recorded at various artificially set levels of the membrane potential (small numbers). The reversal around zero indicates that several ion currents (mostly sodium currents) are responsible. C. inhibitory postsynaptic potentials (IPSPs, lower traces in each pair) in response to increasingly strong impulse volleys from an antagonistic muscle nerve (upper traces in each pair). D. the reversal of the IPSP at potentials negative to about -80 mV, suggesting that chloride ions are involved since the chloride equilibrium potential is at this level.

histologist János Szentágothai of Budapest and by findings made by Masao Ito of Tokyo, who found that cerebellar Purkinje cells were monosynaptic inhibitory on target neurons in intracerebellar and vestibular nuclei. In the influential book *Cerebellum as a Neuronal Machine* (1967), Eccles, Ito, and Szentágothai characterized all neuronal elements and their properties and produced a detailed chart of the cerebellum and.

The Mind and the Brain

In the last chapter of *The Neurophysiological Basis of Mind* (1953), Eccles gave a first account, largely in pictorial form, of a possible site of interaction between the mind and the physical machinery of the brain, concentrating on models for perception and will in motor tasks. From his adolescence, Eccles had been strongly interested in the mind-brain problem, and he returned to the subject throughout his life, in particular after 1975. Although he met considerable opposition from other neuroscientists, he proposed a set of models for illustrating an interaction between the mind and cortical neuronal activity. His writings reveal him as a dualist, with ideas similar but not identical to those of René Descartes, maintaining that our mental processes are not identical to the associated physical nervous activity. He incessantly strived to improve and clarify his mind-brain proposals; above all, he wanted to design situations where a dualistic influence on the brain, a separate effect of the mind, could be experimentally tested. His book *The Self and Its*

Brain (1977), coauthored with Karl Popper, achieved a wide readership and considerable influence.

A Magnificent Leader

A major factor in Eccles's success was his ability as a team builder and a leader. He demanded much of his colleagues, but he was generous and rewarding to those who engaged themselves fully in the research. Although his enthusiasm and excitement were infectious, he insisted upon controlled experiments and repeatability of observations to avoid false results. His main ambition was to acquire insight in the problems and phenomena under investigation and not merely a description. He combined wide knowledge and a tremendous working capacity (more than 550 scientific articles) with a keen demand for further understanding, the whole coupled to a humility toward the magnitude of the challenge of understanding the brain.

See also: GUIDE TO THE ANATOMY OF THE BRAIN: SYNAPSE; NEUROTRANSMITTER SYSTEMS AND MEMORY

Bibliography

Brock, L. G., Coombs, J. S., and Eccles, J. C. (1952). The nature of the monosynaptic excitatory and inhibitory processes in the spinal cord. *Proceedings of the Royal Society of London*, Series B, *Biological Sciences 140*, 170–176.

Coombs, J. S., Eccles, J. C., and Fatt, P. (1955a). Excitatory synaptic action in motoneurones. *Journal of Physiology (London) 130*, 374–395.

—— (1955b). The inhibitory suppression of reflex discharges from motoneurones. *Journal of Physiology (London) 130*, 396–413.

—— (1955c). The specific ionic conductances and the ionic movements across the motoneuronal membrane that produce the inhibitory post-synaptic potential. *Journal of Physiology 130*, 326–373.

Dale, H. H., Feldberg, W. and Vogt, M. (1936). Release of acetylcholine at voluntary motor nerve endings. *Journal of Physiology (London) 86*, 353–380.

Eccles, J. C. (1949). A review and restatement of the electrical hypotheses of synaptic excitatory and inhibitory action. *Archives des sciences physiologiques (Paris) 3*, 567–584.

—— (1953). *The neurophysiological basis of mind: The principles of neurophysiology*. Oxford: Clarendon Press.

—— (1957). *The physiology of nerve cells*. Baltimore: Johns Hopkins Press.

Eccles, J. C., Ito, M., and Szenthágothai, J. (1967). *The cerebellum as a neuronal machine*. Berlin: Springer.

Eccles, J. C., Katz, B., and Kuffler, S. W. (1941). Nature of the end-plate potential in curarized muscle. *Journal of Neurophysiology 4*, 362–387.

—— (1942). Effect of eserine on neuro-muscular transmission. *Journal of Neurophysiology 5*, 211–230.

Eccles, J. C., and O'Connor, W. J. (1939) Responses which nerve impulses evoke in mammalian striated muscle. *Journal of Physiology (London) 97*, 44–102.

Fatt, P., and Katz, B. (1951). An analysis of the end-plate potential recorded with an intracellular electrode. *Journal of Physiology 115*, 320–369.

Frank, K., and Fuortes, M. G. F. (1957). Presynaptic and postsynaptic inhibition of monosynaptic reflexes. *Federeation Proceedings 16*, 39–40.

Kuffler, S. W. (1942). Electrical potential changes at an isolated nerve-muscle junction. *Journal of Neurophysiology 5*, 18–26.

Popper, K. R., and Eccles, J. C. (1977) *The self and its brain*. Berlin: Springer.

Per O. Andersen

ECOLOGICAL MEMORY

See: NATURAL SETTINGS, MEMORY IN

EIDETIC IMAGERY

Nothing captures better the popular belief in "photographic memory" than the term *eidetic imagery*, although the latter hardly supports the exaggerated claims made for the former capacity. Photographic memory is the general claim that people can "still see in front of them" things that were experienced in the past. Eidetic imagery, on the other hand, is more closely tied to objective experimental criteria.

A generation of German investigations of eidetic imagery in the early years of the twentieth century (Woodworth, 1938, p. 45) was largely ignored at midcentury when American psychology was dominated by theoretical behaviorism and had, at best, no use for the concept of imagery. The silence was broken in 1964 by publication of a paper by R. N. Haber and R. B. Haber (see also later summaries in Haber, 1979, and accompanying commentaries). Their report launched modern research on eidetic imagery and largely sustained conclusions from the continental work of a generation earlier.

Haber and Haber (1964) studied 150 elementary-school children in a standardized testing situation. The children were shown a set of four coherent pictures for thirty seconds apiece and interviewed immediately after each as to what they "saw" on a blank easel in the same location as the picture had been. Eight measures were collected, such as whether they saw an image, how long it lasted, whether the image description used positive coloration (rather than complementary colors, as in afterimages), and whether it was described in the present tense. Although more than half the children (84/150) reported at least some kind of imagery for the presented picture, there was considerable variability in scores on these eight measures: In particular, a group of twelve children was easily distinguished from the other seventy-two who had indicated some imagery. These twelve children were discontinuous with their classmates in the presence of positive coloration, duration of the images, use of the present tense to describe images, and visual scanning (of the blank surface) during the interview after each picture. For example, positive coloration was an average of 90 percent in the group of twelve but an average of only 34 percent in the remaining seventy-two children. In visual scanning (eye movements across the blank easel where the eidetic image was "projected"), the difference was even larger (100 percent versus 2 percent). Thus, the incidence of eidetic skill in the original survey was 8 percent (12/150). A survey using similar criteria by Paivio and Cohen (1979), on 242 second- and third-grade children, gave excellent agreement on the incidence of eidetic imagery in normal schoolchildren—8.6 percent (21/242).

In subsequent work (Leask et al., 1969) the "fusion method" was used to identify eidetic imagers. This method presents two individually meaningless pictures successively. After display of the first, the second picture is presented on the same surface, with the subject instructed to superimpose his or her image of the first picture upon the second. The pictures are designed so that this superposition yields a meaningful picture. Children identified by the criteria above to be possessors of eidetic imagery could perform this task, whereas normal children could not.

Age

Giray and colleagues (1976) examined 280 children, twenty at every age from five- to eighteen-years old, using the Habers's (Haber and Haber, 1964) criteria. Fifteen children (5.6 percent) were identified as eidetic, but a clear relation to age emerged: Nine of these fifteen were either five- or six-years old, and only a single subject was over ten. The decline in eidetic skills with age is well documented (Haber, 1979; Leask et al., 1969; Richardson and Harris, 1986); they are apparently virtually absent among adults.

Recent evidence (Giray et al., 1985; Zelhart et al., 1985) suggests that the eidetic skill increases in geriatric populations and that the true relation between age and the incidence of eidetic imagery should be U-shaped. This possibility places the interpretation of high eidetic skill among young children in a different light: These young individuals might be especially likely to show eidetic imagery not because of their age but because of the functional level of their brains.

Brain Damage

The suggestion that eidetic imagery varies inversely with age (up to the college years) indicated that it might be a marker for retarded development *within* any age group. Although Haber (1979) had

been unimpressed with the evidence favoring such a view, the many peer commentaries following his article demonstrate that the point is at least controversial. Leask and colleagues (1969) showed no evidence for mental retardation among their eidetic children, but they did observe more minor visual defects (wearing glasses) among the eidetic than among the noneidetic children. Siipola and Hayden (1965) tested mentally retarded children and found incidence rates of about fifty percent, a strikingly higher figure than among the comparable nonretarded population. Furthermore, eidetic imagery was a marker, among these children, for "organic" as opposed to "familial" diagnoses of retardation. Other investigators (Gummerman et al., 1972; Richardson and Cant, 1970; Symmes, 1971) have, however, reported many fewer cases among retardates of all types. But Giray and colleagues (1976) found even a higher incidence (78.5 percent of fourteen cases) in hydrocephalic children and only a "normal" rate (5 percent to 10 percent) among children with other forms of mental retardation. The force of these tantalizing observations is not yet clear.

Cross-Cultural Approaches

In the context of eidetic imagery as a developmentally primitive information storage mode, Doob (1966) supposed that primitive, illiterate societies might show a higher incidence of it, even among adults. An initial report did, as expected from this reasoning, show a high incidence using the Habers' criteria among the Ibo of Nigeria. However, Doob's further research was disappointing: He had expected that within the Ibo population, the incidence of eidetic imagery would be greater in truly remote, agrarian settlements than in more modern, urbanized population centers, but this was not the case.

Conclusion

The most important conclusion about eidetic imagery is that it is a genuine phenomenon, capable of objective measurement and study. Moreover, the skill has been distinguished from such related phenomena as iconic memory, sensory afterimages, and extremely accurate memory (but see Gray and Gummerman, 1975, for reservations on this last point). Eidetic imagery is characteristic of a minority of young children and is probably related to some forms of brain disorders. It is rather certainly not the agency for good memory of detail, as the Habers (1964) showed originally. Thus, systematic work on eidetic imagery indicates that it shares practically nothing with the popular concept of photographic memory. The apparent absence of eidetic imagery among adults and the fact that it is not predictive of particularly good memory for detail make it a poor basis for claims of photographic memory.

See also: CODING PROCESSES: IMAGERY

Bibliography

Doob, L. W. (1966). Eidetic imagery: A crosscultural will-o'-the-wisp? *Journal of Psychology 63,* 13–34.

Giray, E. F., Altkin, W. M., and Barclay, A. G. (1976). Frequency of eidetic imagery among hydrocephalic children. *Perceptual and Motor Skills 43,* 187–194.

Giray, E. F., Altkin, W. M., Vaught, G. M., and Roodin, P. A. (1976). The incidence of eidetic imagery as a function of age. *Child Development 47,* 1,107–1,210.

——— (1985). A life span approach to the study of eidetic imagery. *Journal of Mental Imagery 9,* 21–32.

Gray, C. R., and Gummerman, K. (1975). The enigmatic eidetic image: A critical examination of methods, data, and theories. *Psychological Bulletin 82,* 383–407.

Gummerman, K., Gray, C. R., and Wilson, J. M. (1972). An attempt to assess eidetic imagery objectively. *Bulletin of the Psychonomic Society 28,* 115–118.

Haber, R. N. (1979). Twenty years of haunting eidetic imagery: Where's the ghost? *Behavioral and Brain Sciences 2,* 583–629.

Haber, R. N., and Haber, R. B. (1964). Eidetic imagery: I. Frequency. *Perceptual and Motor Skills 19,* 131–138.

Leask, J., Haber, R. N., and Haber, R. B. (1969). Eidetic imagery in children: II. Longitudinal and experimental results. *Psychological Monograph Supplements 3* (3) (whole no. 35).

Paivio, A., and Cohen, M. (1979). Eidetic imagery and cognitive abilities. *Journal of Mental Imagery 3,* 53–64.

Richardson, A., and Cant, R. (1970). Eidetic imagery and brain damage. *Australian Journal of Psychology 22,* 47–54.

Richardson, A., and Harris, L. J. (1986). Age trends in eidetikers. *Journal of Genetic Psychology 147,* 303–308.

Siipola, E. M., and Hayden, S. D. (1965). Exploring eidetic imagery among the retarded. *Perceptual and Motor Skills 21,* 275–286.

Symmes, J. S. (1971). Visual imagery in brain injured children. *Perceptual and Motor Skills 21,* 507–514.

Woodworth, R. S. (1938). *Experimental psychology.* New York: Holt.

Zelhart, P. F., Markley, R. B., and Bieker, L. (1985). Eidetic imagery in elderly persons. *Perceptual and Motor Skills 60,* 445–446.

Robert G. Crowder

ELECTROCONVULSIVE THERAPY AND MEMORY LOSS

Electroconvulsive therapy (ECT) was developed in the 1930s as an alternative to psychiatric treatments that depended on inducing a convulsion. More recently, ECT has been reviewed and evaluated by scientific groups in several countries, and has been found to be a safe and effective treatment for severe and disabling depression. The therapeutic effect is caused by a brain seizure, not a convulsion visible in the limbs. In contemporary practice, ECT is administered in conjunction with a short-acting general anesthetic and a muscle relaxant. As a result, the seizure is most easily detected by recording brain waves during treatment. ECT can be either *bilateral,* in which case one electrode is applied to each side of the head, or *unilateral,* in which case two electrodes are applied to the right side of the head. The benefit of ECT is evaluated by considering both its effectiveness for treating depression and the adverse effects of treatment. The most prominent of the adverse effects is impaired memory. The extent of the memory impairment varies depending on how ECT is administered. Memory impairment is greater after bilateral ECT than after unilateral ECT, and it is greater when ECT is administered using machines that deliver sine-wave current rather than brief pulses of current.

Studies of the memory impairment associated with ECT suggest that memory is affected only temporarily. After a course of treatment, which typically involves six to twelve treatments given over a period of two to four weeks, the ability to learn new material is reduced and access to some memories that were formed prior to ECT is lost. *Anterograde amnesia* refers to the difficulty that patients have in remembering events that occur after treatment begins. This difficulty persists for many weeks after treatment, gradually resolving as the capacity for new learning recovers. *Retrograde amnesia,* the loss of memories acquired prior to treatment, can initially involve memories acquired many years earlier. Access to these memories gradually recovers as time passes after treatment.

It should be emphasized that memory for the period surrounding the treatment does not recover after ECT. For example, when patients were asked three years after treatment to identify what past time periods they had difficulty remembering, the average patient reported difficulty remembering the time during ECT, the two months after treatment, and the six months prior to treatment. Thus, except for this lacuna around the time of ECT, formal memory testing suggests that patients eventually recover their capacity for learning and memory. At the same time, absence of evidence for a lasting memory problem is not the same as proving that no such problem exists. It is possible that more sensitive tests could be developed that would detect persisting impairment. It is always difficult to prove that something does not exist. However, memory tests sensitive enough to show differences between the memory abilities of healthy forty-year-olds and healthy fifty-year-olds (some decline in memory ability does occur with normal aging) do not detect lasting memory problems in patients who have received ECT.

In contrast with the findings from memory tests, it is noteworthy that some patients do report, even long after ECT, that their memory is not as good as it used to be. Although it is possible that the patients have a degree of sensitivity about their own memory problems beyond what can be detected by memory tests, there are a number of other possibilities. One possibility is that, having recovered gradually from a period of rather severe and easily documented memory impairment, it is difficult for a person to know when memory abilities have recovered to what they should be. People who lead active lives use their memories many times each day to recall past events and previously acquired knowledge. It is commonplace for recall to be incomplete or inaccurate, especially for information that lies at the fringes of our stored knowledge, such as information that was encountered only once or material that was not fully attended to when it was first encountered. Sometimes memory fails altogether. If someone has had ECT, how can he or she know whether any particular failure of memory is normal or whether it might be due to ECT? To the extent that ECT does lead many patients to doubt the integrity of their own memories, it is possible that this effect of treatment could be attenuated or eliminated by sympathetic and informed counseling during the period immediately following ECT.

Bibliography

American Psychiatric Association (1990). *The practice of ECT: Recommendations for treatment, training and privileging.* Washington, DC: American Psychiatric Association.

Consensus Conference (1985). Electroconvulsive therapy. *Journal of the American Medical Association 251,* 2,103–2,108.

D'Elia, G., Ottosson, J. O., and Stromgren, L. S. (1983). Present practice of electroconvulsive therapy in Scandinavia. *Archives of General Psychiatry 40,* 577–581.

Fink, M. (1979). *Convulsive therapy: Theory and practice,* pp. 203–204. New York: Raven Press.

Malitz, S., and Sackeim, H., eds. (1986). *Electroconvulsive therapy: Clinical and basic research issues. Annals of the New York Academy of Sciences 462.*

Royal College of Psychiatrists. (1989). *The practical administration of electroconvulsive therapy (ECT).* London: Gaskell.

Larry R. Squire

EMOTIONAL MEMORY

See: NEURAL SUBSTRATES OF EMOTIONAL MEMORY

EMOTION, MOOD, AND MEMORY

The ways in which we attend, learn, and remember are related to our transitory moods and to our enduring emotional states. Intuitively appealing to the self-reflective person, this claim has been verified by experimental and clinical psychologists in both laboratory and naturalistic studies. In some studies, psychologists measure differences in emotional states and determine whether those differences are associated with differences in the ways that the participants perform cognitive tasks. These studies usually focus on unpleasant emotions and moods, such as depression and anxiety. In other studies, psychologists attempt to induce either unpleasant or pleasant moods in the participants (perhaps by having them listen to different types of music) and then examine how performance is affected by these manipulations. Both types of research have tried to answer two major questions about the interaction of mood and memory: Do people remember events that are emotionally consistent with their moods better than other events? Do depressed and anxious moods hinder performance on neutral cognitive tasks?

Mood-Congruent Memory

People remember episodes and materials that are consistent with their moods more often than they remember other occurrences; this phenomenon is known as mood-congruent memory (MCM). MCM can sometimes be attributed to the ways that people initially interpret the events to be remembered because interpretations tend to be mood-congruent. A clear example of mood-congruent interpretation can be seen in research conducted by Michael Eysenck and his colleagues (1987): Anxious participants, more often than nonanxious participants, spelled spoken homophones (such as *die* and *dye*) to coincide with the more threatening concept. Andrew Mathews and his associates (1989) found similar mood-congruent interpretation on a test of implicit memory. In this test, the participants were shown the first three letters of words and were asked to complete them to form the first word that came to mind. The anxious subjects completed with threat-related words that they had seen in an earlier task more often than other types of previously seen and unseen words; nonanxious subjects did not show this bias. As they occur in both initial encounters and later indirect tests of memory, these biased interpretations occur automatically or without any intent to focus on mood related meaning.

On more direct tests of memory, such as tests of explicit recall, anxious people do not always remember anxiety-related material better than other material, perhaps because they turn their attention away from anxiety-provoking stimuli, once they are conceived. Research concerned with depressed and sad states, however, shows more consistent evidence of MCM for both autobiographical and experimentally controlled events. A thorough review of MCM is provided in *Cognitive Psychology and Emotional Disorders* (Williams, Watts, MacLeod, and Mathews, 1997), which also describes variations and exceptions to the basic findings. One variation is that depressed moods are often associated with a reduction in the recall of positively toned events instead of an increase in the recall of negative events. More exceptional is the finding that temporarily sad students have shown evidence of mood-incongruent recall (better recall for positive material), which Parrott and Sabini (1990) have interpreted as an outcome of the students' elaborative processing of positive material, in attempt to improve their moods.

To the extent that MCM is observed in depression, it reflects enduring concerns with negative events and at the same time plays an important role in maintaining depressed mood. Sonja Lyubormirsky and her colleagues (1998) found that ruminations by students in depressed moods increased their recall of negative events. Moreover, just as they tend to remember fewer positive episodes from the past, depressed people also tend to expect fewer positive events to occur in the future (MacLeod, 1999).

Mood-Related Impairments in Memory for Emotionally Neutral Events

Because depressed and anxious people ruminate about self concerns, it not hard to imagine that they devote less attention to the emotionally neutral events of everyday experience. Some routine cognitive acts require little attention for successful performance; the cognitive processes involved are relatively automatic, which means that they are well practiced and can occur simultaneously with other cognitive processes, even rumination about personal concerns. Other tasks require a more laborious and deliberate focus of attention if good performance is to be achieved. In short, cognitive tasks vary in the degree to which focused attention is required for good performance. This is true of procedures that are performed during initial exposure or learning and tasks that are devised to reveal memory for past events.

At the time of initial learning, for example, reading a long list of unrelated words requires little effort by fluent readers, but organizing them in ways that will be useful during later attempts to remember them clearly requires more deliberate focus. Similarly, tests of memory for those words vary in the degree of focused attention that they require. Rereading the same words is one index of memory (in that the previously read words can be read faster than new words). This type of implicit-memory test involves procedures that are relatively automatic. In contrast, trying to recall the words on the list is a deliberate task that can benefit from a great deal of attention and the use of special strategies.

The learning and memory tasks that benefit from focused attention are the tasks that present difficulties to depressed and anxious people; they perform less well than do people who are not mood-impaired.

Weingartner and his colleagues (1981), for example, discovered that clinically depressed patients could learn lists of words organized into simple categories as well as could other people, but when the same word lists were disorganized, the depressed patients learned less well. When people approach these types of learning tasks by providing their own organization or by using other elaborative strategies, they later enjoy benefits on tests of deliberate memory. In contrast, depressed people use fewer self-initiated procedures and suffer the memory-related consequences.

Similar conclusions can be reached in examining different types of memory tests. Hertel and Hardin (1990), for example, found that depressed college students performed as well as other students when the test of memory did not explicitly focus attention on the past event (i.e., the spelling of homophones that indirectly revealed memory for their prior exposure). When the test required such explicit focus, however, depressed students did not spontaneously use strategies for recognition that characterized the performance of the other students. Similarly, in tests of autobiographical memory, depressed patients' recall is often inappropriately general. They respond to instructions to recall prior specific events when given cues (e.g., *happy*) by citing categories of events instead of particular episodes (e.g., *going to baseball games*, instead of *the time my dad took me to see the Yankees for my birthday*; Healy and Williams, 1999).

Why do mood-impaired people experience impaired attention and corresponding memory deficits? Some researchers (e.g., Weingartner et al., 1981) have proposed that the deficits result from a fundamental depletion of resources, possibly associated with biochemical changes. Alternatively or in addition, the difficulties might indirectly reflect mood-impaired people's enduring and ruminative concern with mood-related aspects of their experience—aspects that are often irrelevant to the task at hand. These task-irrelevant thoughts can distract attention when participants are left to their own devices (e.g., when they are told to learn a list of words). Yet when learning or memory tasks are devised in ways that constrain attention to task materials, specify appropriate strategies, or distract from personal concerns, mood-impaired people may perform as well as others (Hertel, 2000).

Memory for emotionally neutral events might also benefit from the correspondence of mood at the time of the test to the mood at the time of initial learning. The advantage of a similar mood state on both occasions has been called mood-dependent memory (MDM) and is similar to other state-dependent memory effects, such as those obtained with alcohol. MDM also has much in common with MCM: Remembering mood-congruent events is often a matter of being in the same mood at the test as when those events were encountered previously. However, MDM is properly demonstrated with emotionally neutral materials to be learned and recalled. When the materials are not inherently related to mood—when MCM is not involved—attempts to demonstrate MDM often do not succeed. A consistent emotional state by itself is not a strong basis for retrieving memories, particularly when other more obvious cues are available. However, Eric Eich (1995) provides evidence that MDM is a robust phenomenon when, like mood, the events to be remembered and the cues for retrieving them arise from the individual rememberer, instead of being provided by others.

In conclusion, the most inclusive framework for describing mood, emotion, and memory is one that emphasizes the nature and content of ongoing thoughts. In all but the most transitory mood states, the extent to which people think about their personal concerns is also the extent to which they remember emotionally consistent experiences and fail to remember experiences unrelated to their mood states.

See also: ATTENTION AND MEMORY; IMPLICIT MEMORY

Bibliography

Eich, E. (1995). Searching for mood dependent memory. *Psychological Science 6*, 67–75.

Eysenck, M. W., MacLeod, C., and Mathews, A. (1987). Cognitive functioning in anxiety. *Psychological Research 49*, 189–195.

Healy, H., and Williams, J. M. G. (1999). Autobiographical memory. In T. Dalgleish and M. J. Power, eds., *Handbook of cognition and emotion.* New York: Wiley.

Hertel, P. T. (2000). The cognitive-initiative account of depression-related impairments in memory. In D. Medin, ed., *The psychology of learning and motivation*, Vol. 39. New York: Academic Press.

Hertel, P. T., and Hardin, T. S. (1990). Remembering with and without awareness in a depressed mood: Evidence for deficits in initiative. *Journal of Experimental Psychology: General 119*, 45–59.

Lyubormirsky, S., Caldwell, N. D., and Nolen-Hoeksema, S. (1998). Effects of ruminative and distracting responses to depressed mood on retrieval of autobiographical memories. *Journal of Personality and Social Psychology 75*, 166–177.

MacLeod, A. K. (1999). Prospective cognitions. In T. Dalgleish and M. J. Power, eds., *Handbook of cognition and emotion.* New York: Wiley.

Mathews, A., Mogg, K., May, J., and Eysenck, M. (1989). Implicit and explicit memory bias in anxiety. *Journal of Abnormal Psychology 98*, 236–240.

Parrott, W. G., and Sabini, J. (1990). Mood and memory under natural conditions: Evidence for mood incongruent recall. *Journal of Personality and Social Psychology 59*, 321–336.

Weingartner, H., Cohen, R. M., Murphy, D. L., Martello, J., and Gerdt, C. (1981). Cognitive processes in depression. *Archives of General Psychiatry 38*, 42–47.

Williams, J. M. G., Watts, F. N., MacLeod, C., and Mathews, A. (1997). *Cognitive psychology and emotional disorders.* New York: Wiley.

Paula Hertel

ENGRAM

See: LOCALIZATION OF MEMORY TRACES

EPISODIC MEMORY

Psychologists have been studying memory experimentally since Hermann Ebbinghaus's (1885) groundbreaking work more than a hundred years ago, but only in the late twentieth century were questions raised about exactly what has been and is being studied in memory experiments. As a result of the pursuit of these questions it became widely if not universally accepted that there exist different kinds of memory. Episodic memory is one of these kinds.

The term *episodic memory* is used in several senses. One of these has to do with episodic memory as a particular class of laboratory tasks or experiments (Lockhart, 2000); another concerns episodic memory as a kind of mental capacity, or a neurocognitive system (Schacter and Tulving, 1994), that allows people to remember past experiences. Although closely related, the two senses (episodic tasks and the episodic system) should not be confused. This entry will consider the two senses in turn.

Episodic Memory Tasks

Episodic memory in the first sense manifests itself when a person remembers some information acquired on a particular occasion. Such situations occur frequently in real life where something happens at one time (Time 1) and the individual who witnessed the happening remembers it at a later time (Time 2). In the laboratory these situations are formalized as "tasks." A prototypical laboratory task of episodic memory consists of 1. an original study experience during which individual items, such as words, are encoded and stored by the learner (Time 1), and 2. a subsequent test during which some aspect of the experience is retrieved (Time 2). Episodic memory tasks are sometimes also referred to as explicit memory tasks.

Many variables affect performance on episodic memory tasks. They include ability differences among subjects, the type of information presented for study, the amount of time and effort devoted to learning, subjects' previous knowledge of the to-be-learned material, the length of the retention interval between study and test, and other such obvious factors. One important determinant of the rememberer's performance in episodic tasks includes the way he or she thinks about the material to be remembered as it is studied, the so-called encoding operations. or coding processes. Also important are the conditions under which retrieval (recovery of stored information) occurs or is attempted, and especially critical is the relation between encoding and retrieval conditions (Tulving, 1983). Performance on episodic memory tasks can be measured in a variety of ways—free or non-cued recall, cued recall, free choice or forced choice recognition, frequency judgment, and recency judgment, among others (Lockhart, 2000). Episodic memory tasks in which both study and test (encoding and retrieval) occur under fixed constant conditions are referred to as episodic memory tests and are widely used for the purpose of psychometric assessment of individuals' episodic memory abilities. The information that women outstrip men in episodic memory (Herlitz, Nilsson, and Bäckman, 1997) and that the earliest cognitive impairment in the functional development of Alzheimer's disease is episodic memory (Hodges, 2000), among other findings, is based on observations gleaned from episodic memory tests.

Episodic Memory System

The second sense of the term *episodic memory* is that of a hypothetical neurocognitive system that differs from the other major memory systems for which evidence exists (Schacter and Tulving, 1994). These other systems include semantic memory, procedural memory, short-term memory (also known as *working memory*), and the perceptual representation system that subserves perceptual priming (also known as *implicit memory*). Episodic memory is most closely related to semantic memory, and the two are usually regarded as subcategories of declarative memory. (Another closely related concept is autobiographical memory, which refers to recollection and knowledge of significant events from and facts about one's life.) The postulation of the existence of separable memory systems is part of the enterprise of the classification of natural phenomena of memory. Classification is a necessary prerequisite for the study of memory mechanisms and processes.

The ability of an individual to consciously recollect personally experienced past events, that is, to become aware again at Time 2 of some aspect or some part of a previous experience at Time 1, is possible only by virtue of an intact brain system specialized for that purpose, namely the episodic memory system. On the other hand, the ability to think about the world, and everything in it, which exists or is imag-

ined as existing beyond immediate perception, depends on the integrity of the semantic memory system and does not require episodic memory (Tulving, 2001).

The defining features of episodic memory (system) are self, subjective time, and a special phenomenal awareness of remembering, familiar to all, that is referred to as autonoetic consciousness (Tulving, 2001). Episodic memory is unique among other memory systems in that it alone allows the individual to "mentally travel" through time, to remember the past and to think about the future. The evidence in support of a separable episodic system steadily increases. One source of relevant observations is the study of brain-damaged patients suffering from amnesia. Some brain-damaged patients who suffer from a severe memory disorder and are severely impaired in or completely lack episodic memory are nevertheless capable of acquiring, even if laboriously, new factual (semantic) knowledge (Hayman, MacDonald, and Tulving, 1992; Kitchener, Hodges, and McCarthy, 1998). This kind of dissociation between failure of remembering personally experienced events and success of learning new facts implies that the neural substrate of episodic and other kinds of memories are at least partially distinct. A related category of relevant evidence is source amnesia: Individuals with impaired or frail memories, such as amnesic patients and elderly people, can recall recently learned facts better than they can recollect the episode in the course of which they learned these facts (Shimamura and Squire, 1987).

A second major source of evidence is electrophysiological recording and functional neuroimaging of brain activity that is correlated with memory processes. When episodic and semantic memory retrieval are compared, the findings show not only similarities in brain activity but also differences (Dalla Barba et al., 1998; Nyberg, 1999; Tulving et al., 1994).

Relation Between Tasks and System

The two senses of episodic memory (task and system) are related but they cannot be equated. The main reason for this assertion lies in the fact that episodic tasks do not usually tap an individual's (autonoetic) awareness of self-centered experiences of the past but rather require only that the learner reproduce or otherwise indicate his or her knowledge of the semantic contents of the learning episode. Episodic memory of course can, and usually does, greatly contribute to this knowledge but it is not necessary for it. Putting it differently, episodic task performance does not only depend on the episodic system but can be supported by nonepisodic systems as well. In the extreme case, individuals without or with severely impaired episodic memory system are capable of dealing satisfactorily with many episodic memory tasks. In the laboratory, when the rememberer has been exposed to a set of study items at Time 1 and is then given a recognition test at Time 2, the rememberer's performance is influenced both by recollection of what happened at Time 1 (episodic system) and by feelings that certain test items are familiar (other systems). An extensive and rapidly expanding literature exists on the distinction between (episodic) "remembering" and (nonepisodic) "knowing" as indicants of processes involved in episodic tasks (Gardiner and Richardson-Klavehn, 2000). The feelings of familiarity enable neurological patients and other organisms whose episodic memory system is absent or severely impaired to make correct discriminations between previously encountered and previously nonencountered test items in an episodic recognition task (Vargha-Khadem et al., 1997).

See also: AMNESIA, ORGANIC; CODING PROCESSES: IMAGERY; CODING PROCESSES: LEVELS OF PROCESSING; CODING PROCESSES: ORGANIZATION OF MEMORY; DECLARATIVE MEMORY; FRONTAL LOBES AND EPISODIC MEMORY; IMPLICIT MEMORY; WORKING MEMORY: HUMANS

Bibliography

Dalla Barba, G., Parlato, V., Jobert, A., Samson, Y, Pappata, S. (1998). Cortical networks implicated in semantic and episodic memory: Common or unique? *Cortex 34,* 547–561.

Ebbinghaus, H. (1885). *Über das Gedächtnis.* Leipzig: Duncker and Humblot.

Gardiner, J. M., and Richardson-Klavehn, A. (2000). Remembering and knowing. In E. Tulving and F. I. M. Craik, eds., *The Oxford handbook of memory,* pp. 229–244. New York: Oxford University Press.

Hayman, C. A. G., MacDonald, C. A., and Tulving, E. (1993). The role of repetition and associative interference in new semantic learning in amnesia. *Journal of Cognitive Neuroscience 5,* 375–389.

Herlitz, A., Nilsson, L.-G., and Bäckman, L. (1997). Gender differences in episodic memory. *Memory & Cognition 25,* 801–811.

Hodges, J. R. (2000). Memory in the dementias. In E. Tulving and F. I. M. Craik, eds., *The Oxford handbook of memory,* pp. 441–459. New York: Oxford University Press.

Kitchener, E. G., Hodges, J. R., and McCarthy, R. (1998). Acquisition of post-morbid vocabulary and semantic facts in the absence of episodic memory. *Brain 121,* 1,313–1,327.

Lockhart. R. S. (2000). Methods of memory research. In E. Tulving and F. I. M. Craik, eds., *The Oxford handbook of memory,* pp. 45–57. New York: Oxford University Press.

Nyberg, L. (1999). Imaging episodic memory: Implications for cognitive theories and phenomena. *Memory 7,* 585–597.

Schacter, D. L., and Tulving, E. (1994). What are the memory systems of 1994? In D. L. Schacter and E. Tulving, eds., *Memory systems 1994,* pp. 1–38. Cambridge, MA: MIT Press.

Shimamura, A. P., and Squire, L. R. (1987). A neuropsychological study of fact memory and source amnesia. *Journal of Experimental Psychology: Learning, Memory, and Cognition 13,* 464–473.

Tulving, E. (1983). *Elements of episodic memory.* New York: Oxford University Press.

—— (2001). Episodic memory and common sense: How far apart? *Philosophical Transactions of the Royal Society of London, ser. B, 356,* 1,505–1,515.

Tulving, E., Kapur, S., Craik, F. I. M., Moscovitsch, M., and Houle, S. (1994) Hemispheric encoding/retrieval asymmetry in episodic memory: Positron emission tomography findings. *Proceedings of the National Academy of Sciences of the United States of America 91,* 2,016–2,020.

Vargha-Khadem, F., Gadian, D. G., Watkins, K. E., Connelly, A., Van Paesschen, W., Mishkin, M. (1997). Differential effects of early hippocampal pathology on episodic and semantic memory. *Science 277,* 376–380.

Endel Tulving

EVERYDAY MEMORY

See: NATURAL SETTINGS, MEMORY IN

EVOLUTION AND LEARNING

Learning is a biological adaptation, and like any other adaptation is the outcome of evolution by natural selection. Because it is acted on by natural selection, learning in different species of animals exhibits both descent with modification and specialized adaptations. Many properties of learning, like the formation of associations, are widely shared among animals. The molecular mechanisms of learning are also remarkably similar among animals as different as sea slugs, honeybees, and rats. But, in addition, learning exhibits specialized adaptations, modifications of learning which differ between species. Evolutionary adaptation in learning is usually investigated using comparative methods to examine similarities or differences among animals in how or what they learn. Learning can also have a reciprocal effect on the process of evolution. Animals can learn to exploit new habitats and new resources within their habitat and thus change the selective pressures they are exposed to. Learning can even have an evolutionary impact that extends beyond the animal itself and affects other animals and plants it interacts with.

There are two basic requirements for evolution of a trait like learning by natural selection. First, the trait must be at least partly heritable: Genotypic variation must produce phenotypic variation in the trait. Second, variation in the trait must have an effect on reproductive success. Learning meets both of these requirements.

Genetic Variation in Learning

Some of the clearest evidence for genetic variation in learning comes from studies of learning mutations in the fruit fly *Drosophila* (Waddell and Quinn, 2001). Fruit flies are good learners, and can readily learn to avoid an odor that has been associated with electric shock. Mutation of single genes in the *Drosophila* genome can be induced with chemicals, and some of these mutations have dramatic effects on learning. Mutations in genes with whimsical names like *rutabaga* and *dunce* make fruit flies unable to learn an association between odor and shock, or cause them to quickly forget what they have learned. These particular genes code for components of the intracellular signaling system that transforms neural activity into more long-lasting changes in neurons that record experience. The *rutabaga* and *dunce* genes code for enzymes that increase and decrease, respectively, the intracellular concentration of cAMP (cyclic AMP), an intracellular second messenger that responds to neurotransmitter signals received by a neuron. Other learning mutations have been discovered that affect different aspects of the learning process, like *volado*, a gene that affects cell adhesion and influences communication between neurons. These mutations can reveal a great deal about the molecular mechanisms of learning and help unravel the neuroanatomy of learning by pinpointing sites in the brain where expression of the gene makes a difference in learning. But learning mutations are also important discoveries for understanding evolution. They show that changes in genes (in some cases substitution of a single nucleotide) can affect the properties of learning. The phenotypic effects of genetic variation of this kind provide the raw material on which natural selection can act.

Learning and Reproductive Success

Learning contributes directly and indirectly to reproductive success in many ways. Bumblebees learn how to obtain nectar from flowers. Colonial swallows learn to recognize their young, and young herring gulls learn to recognize their parents. Most animals must learn what is edible and what is not; others learn migration routes, how to identify predators, how to defend a territory, and how to attract a mate. In all of these cases, any heritable variant in learning that makes the animal slightly more successful at the task will make it more successful at reproducing itself, and hence more likely to pass on the variant in learning to its offspring. As a consequence of the action of natural selection on learning, learning can differ between species and possess specialized adaptive properties that make learning more effective. Learned food aversions illustrate this kind of specialization. Animals sometimes eat food that makes them ill, either because the food is contaminated or because the plant or animal they have eaten produces toxins to

discourage predation. Animals can clearly benefit from learning which foods are edible and which are not, but the natural situation presents them with a problem. Toxic food may not have its effect for several hours after it was eaten. Animals usually have great difficulty learning that two events are related if more than a few minutes separates them in time. Experiments in the laboratory show that rats can associate illness with food even if the food was eaten several hours previously. Rats may require only a single experience with the food to form a strong aversion to it. Furthermore, rats associate the taste and odor of food, not its appearance, with illness. Selectivity in what is learned and the ability to associate events separated in time are distinctive features of taste-aversion learning.

Songbirds exhibit specialized learning in the way they acquire their songs. The songs that male Passerine birds use to advertise territory ownership and to attract a mate are learned. The song-learning system possesses a number of unusual features. Most birds learn only the songs of their own species, even if they are experimentally exposed to songs of other species for an equal period. In addition, the young of many birds have a "sensitive period" during which they learn songs most readily. Songs are not learned by singing them. Instead, songs heard during the sensitive period are remembered until they are first sung many months later, when the breeding season begins. Finally, there are specialized nuclei in the avian brain that are responsible for acquisition and production of song. Restrictions on what is learned, a sensitive period, separation in time of learning and performance, and specialized neural structures make the song learning system different from other kinds of learning, but effective for memorizing and performing species typical songs.

Comparative Methods

Comparative methods that have been used to examine adaptation and evolutionary change in animal physiology and anatomy can also be used to examine the evolution of learning. The clearest way to see the effect of evolution on the process of learning is by comparing the ways in which different species of animals learn. Closely related animals that share most of their evolutionary history but differ in some aspects of their current behavior or ecology may differ in how they learn. Comparisons of learning in closely related animals can thus reveal adaptive modifications of learning that are the result of recent selection. Another approach is to compare animals that are not closely related but share some current aspect of behavior or ecology. Similarities in learning between such animals occur not because of a shared evolutionary history but because they have been exposed to similar selective pressures. If such animals show similarities in how they learn or what they can learn it is likely to be the result of convergent evolution. These animals have independently evolved similar learning capacities because they have been exposed to similar selective pressures. Both kinds of comparison have been used to identify the selective pressures that can influence learning and to illuminate how evolutionary change in learning can occur.

Learning in food-storing birds illustrates how these comparative methods can be used. Some species of birds, notably chickadees, nuthatches, and jays, store food. They make hundreds to thousands of food caches and return between several days and many months later to collect and consume the food they have hidden. Caches are widely scattered and contain only a few food items each. Remarkably, these birds remember precisely where they have placed each cache. Some birds in the jay family, the *Corvidae*, store a great deal of food and some store little or none. Comparisons among these closely related species of birds have shown that reliance on stored food is associated with the level of performance on spatial tasks. Ecological dependence on food storing has selected for enhanced spatial ability. Food storing evolved independently in jays and in the chickadee family, the *Paridae*. Food-storing chickadees and food-storing jays both possess enhanced spatial abilities as an evolutionary consequence of their shared reliance on stored food.

Learning and Evolution of the Brain

Evolutionary change in learning requires evolutionary change in the neural apparatus of learning. Evidence for evolutionary modification of learning comes not only from observing differences between species in learning itself, but also from examining differences between species in brain areas that are important for learning. The song control nuclei of species of birds with large song repertoires are larger than the nuclei of birds with small repertoires. An increase in the size of neural structures that participate in learning has been found for a number of other kinds of learning.

The avian hippocampus plays an important role in memory, as it does in mammals, and the hippocampus of food-storing birds is over twice the size of the hippocampus of closely related birds that do not store food (Sherry, 1998). Comparative studies of this kind show that adaptive evolutionary change occurs in brain regions involved in learning. A further example illustrates that such adaptive change can occur within a species. Most voles (rodents in the family *Cricetidae*) are polygynous: One male has several mates. Male home ranges are larger than female home ranges, and the home range of a polygynous male may encompass the home ranges of several females. Some species of vole, however, are monogamous, and male and female home ranges are of equal size in these species. Laboratory experiments have found that males of polygynous species perform better on spatial memory problems than do females, but in monogamous species males and females perform equally well. The sex difference in spatial ability in polygynous species is an adaptation to their breeding system and to the sex difference in home range size. As with food-storing birds, the consequences of natural selection for learning ability can be seen in the brain. Lucia Jacobs and colleagues (1990) found that the hippocampus of male polygynous voles is larger than that of females, whereas in monogamous voles there is no sex difference in the size of the hippocampus.

The Effect of Learning on Evolution

Evolutionary change occurs in learning, but learning can, in turn, affect the course of evolution. Many species of animals do things that are culturally determined. Behaviors that are traditional within a population of animals are learned from other members of the group, either directly or simply by associating with other group members. Migration routes, learned songs, and food preferences can all be transmitted culturally. Naive birds can learn to recognize predators by participating in mobbing attacks on animals that other members of the social group treat as predators. The effect of such culturally transmitted behavior on biological evolution is not fully understood, though it is clear that learned behavior can consistently expose animals to new environments and new sources of natural selection.

Learning can also have evolutionary effects that extend beyond the animal that does the learning. There is awe-inspiring diversity in protective mimicry among insects. The monarch butterfly contains toxins that make predators ill. The viceroy is a palatable butterfly that mimics the monarch butterfly in appearance so closely that birds that have tasted a monarch avoid both monarchs and viceroys. Many similar model and mimic systems are found in insects. Some syrphid flies have evolved to closely resemble bees and wasps in their appearance, posture, and behavior. They possess the distinctive black and yellow banding pattern found on many bees and wasps, at rest they hold their forelegs in front of their head to resemble wasp antennae, and their seasonal period of activity coincides with that of their bee and wasp models. These mimicry systems have evolved because the animals that would normally prey on the mimetic insects—primarily birds—learn to avoid the toxic, bad tasting, or stinging model and because of its similar appearance, also avoid the mimic. Without learning by potential predators, there would be no mimicry.

As they gather nectar, insects such as honeybees, bumblebees, flies, and wasps carry pollen from one flower to another and serve as the sole means of fertilization for many flowering plants. Among some pollinators, such as bumblebees, different individuals from the same colony learn a preference to visit one kind of flower over others, a phenomenon remarked on by Charles Darwin and known as constancy. Pollinators are probably constant because visiting the same kind of flower makes it easier for them to recognize the flower and extract its nectar. This behavior also affects the flowers, and indeed flowers have probably evolved to promote constancy because it increases the likelihood that pollen will be transferred to another flower of the same species. Constancy can also have a further evolutionary effect (Jones, 2001). Constancy by pollinators may promote speciation in flowering plants by increasing assortative mating, the tendency of similar members of a population to mate with each other. If a population of flowering plants exhibits variation in the appearance or structure of its flowers, constancy by pollinators will result in preferential mating between flowers with the same structure and appearance, leading ultimately to the formation of new species.

Conclusion

Because genetic variation can produce variation in the mechanisms of learning, and because learning makes important contributions to the ability of animals to reproduce themselves, learning evolves by natural selection. Many properties of learning are shared among animals by virtue of their common descent. The formation of associations and some molecular mechanisms of learning are remarkably similar across a wide range of animals. Evolutionary change in learning has also produced specialized adaptations of learning. Food-aversion learning, song learning, and cache retrieval in food-storing birds provide examples of such adaptive specialization. The effects of evolutionary change in learning can also be observed in brain areas that play important parts in learning. Not only has evolution affected learning, but learning can affect evolution, both by exposing animals to selective pressures they would not otherwise encounter and by causing evolutionary change in the animals and plants with which they interact.

See also: BIRDSONG LEARNING; GUIDE TO THE ANATOMY OF THE BRAIN: HIPPOCAMPUS AND PARAHIPPOCAMPAL REGION; PROTEIN SYNTHESIS IN LONG-TERM MEMORY IN VERTEBRATES; SEX DIFFERENCES IN LEARNING; SPATIAL LEARNING: ANIMALS; TASTE AVERSION AND PREFERENCE LEARNING IN ANIMALS

Bibliography

Jacobs, L. F., Gaulin, S. J. C., Sherry, D. F., and Hoffman, G. E. (1990). Evolution of spatial cognition: Sex-specific patterns of spatial behavior predict hippocampal size. *Proceedings of the National Academy of Sciences of the United States of America 87,* 6,349–6,352.

Jones, K. N. (2001). Pollinator-induced assortative mating: causes and consequences. In L. Chittka and J. D. Thomson, eds., *Cognitive Ecology of Pollination.* Cambridge, UK: Cambridge University Press.

Sherry, D. F. (1998). The ecology and neurobiology of spatial memory. In R. Dukas, ed., *Cognitive Ecology.* Chicago: University of Chicago Press.

Waddell, S., and Quinn, W. G. (2001). Flies, genes, and learning. *Annual Review of Neuroscience 24,* 1,283–1,309.

David F. Sherry

EXPERTS' MEMORIES

An expert is "one who has acquired special skill in or knowledge about a particular subject through professional training and practical experience" (Webster's, 1976, p. 800). By that definition, experts will have a greater body of knowledge about their domain of expertise than other individuals. More remarkable is the experts' accurate memory for new experiences in their domain. Some athletes can discuss minute details of individual plays from games played years ago. Expert chess players can readily recall chess positions from their matches in recent tournaments.

Early in the twentieth century many believed that experts were innately gifted with a superior memory. Numerous anecdotes attested to such amazing powers of recollection. For example, Mozart was supposed to be able to reproduce a presented piece of music after hearing it a single time. Later research, however, cast doubt on the hypothesis of superior innate memory in experts and has demonstrated that experts' remarkable recall is limited to their specialties and arises from acquired skills and knowledge.

The Specificity of Experts' Superior Memory

The most influential research on experts' memories focused initially on chess masters' superior recall of board positions (Chase and Simon, 1973). Chess players ranging from beginners to international masters were shown a position from an actual chess game (such as the one illustrated in panel A of Figure 1) for a brief time (normally five seconds) and then asked to

Figure 1

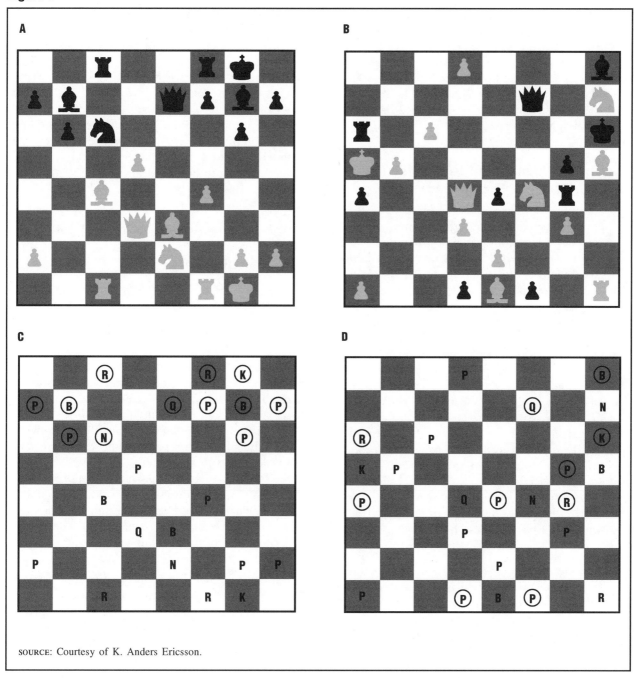

SOURCE: Courtesy of K. Anders Ericsson.

Standard diagrams of an actual chess position (Panel A) and a chessboard with randomly arranged pieces (Panel B). A nonstandard representation of the same information using the first letter of the names of the pieces is shown in Panels C and D.

recall the location of all the chess pieces. The ability to recall increased as a function of chess skill. Beginners at chess were able to recall the correct location of about four pieces, whereas international-level players recalled nearly all of the more than twenty pieces.

To rule out the innateness of the chess masters' superior visual memory, Chase and Simon had chess players recall chessboards with randomly placed

pieces (as illustrated in Panel B of Figure 1). With briefly presented random chessboards, players at all levels of skill had roughly the same poor recall performance and were able to recall the correct location of only three to five pieces on the average—a performance comparable to that of chess beginners for actual positions from chess games. Further, Chase and Simon showed that when an actual chess position was shown using an unfamiliar notation (see Panel C in

Figure 1), the chess expert was able to display a similar level of superior memory performance after a brief period of adjustment. This result implies that the superior memory of experts is not innate but rather a function of learned skills. Since Chase and Simon's classic study, other investigators have arrived at similar findings for experts in other fields such as computer programming, basketball, and dance (Ericsson, Patel, and Kintsch, 2000).

The Role of Meaningful Relations in Superior Memory Performance

Without the expertise of a master, it is nearly impossible to grasp the meaningful relations between chess pieces perceived by the expert in panels A and C of Figure 1. If, on the other hand, the availability of knowledge providing meaning to a stimulus is critical to superior memory, it should be possible to demonstrate the same effect in a domain where all adults are proficient, such as language. Human adults are able to recall verbatim meaningful sentences of twenty or more words after a brief presentation (Chase and Ericsson, 1982). An example of such a sentence would be, "The woman in front of him was eating peanuts that smelled so good that he could barely contain his hunger." If the words of the sentence are randomly rearranged in a manner analogous to that used in Chase and Simon's procedure for generating random chessboards, accurate verbatim recall drops to around six words. An example of a random rearrangement of the above sentence would be, "Was smelled front that that his the peanuts he good hunger eating barely woman of so in could that him contain."

For random lists of words, the recall of subjects is limited by the small number of words they can keep rehearsing, and once they stop rehearsal, the words are quickly forgotten. In contrast, once meaningful sentences are understood, their meaning is well retained in long-term memory. For example, during normal comprehension of a text, the essential information in each sentence is efficiently stored in memory so it can be integrated with related information presented later in the text (Ericsson and Kintsch, 1995).

Stimuli from an unfamiliar domain of expertise, such as diagrams of chess positions and medical terms, are about as meaningless to most adults as random lists of words and digits. Recent studies have shown that memory for meaningless information can be dramatically improved through training by actively seeking out meaningful associations for the meaningless material. For example, the sequence 671945 can be remembered as 67 being the retirement age and 1945 being the year of the end of World War II. Through extended training individuals can acquire memory skills allowing them to increase their memory of briefly presented lists of numbers from an initial level of seven digits to over eighty random digits. Hence, it is possible for regular college students to attain exceptional memory performance after 50 to 200 hours of practice. Laboratory studies of individuals with exceptional memory performance for numbers, names, and pictures reveal that they rely on acquired memory skills that often involve some kind of mnemonics (Ericsson and Lehmann, 1996; Wilding and Valentine, 1997).

How Superior Memory of Experts Mediates Their Superior Performance on Representative Tasks

The primary goal for all experts is to excel at the demands of their fields. For example, chess experts need to find the best moves to win chess matches, and medical experts have to diagnose sick patients in order to give them the best treatment. Unlike the memory experts who attempt to improve their memory performance by acquiring mnemonic techniques through extended practice, chess experts and medical doctors do not deliberately train their memory. Their superior memory ability must thus be a byproduct of their improved performance on representative tasks (Vicente and Wang, 1988). Furthermore, experts appear to store task-relevant information in memory when they normally perform representative tasks in their domain, because, if they are unexpectedly asked to recall information about a performed task, their memory is typically far superior to that of less skilled individuals.

In fact, experts' incidental memory of the relevant information is frequently so good that instructing them to intentionally memorize the information does not reliably improve their memory. For example, when chess experts analyze a position to find the best move, their memory of the position is just as good whether they were informed about an upcoming memory test or not. As part of performing the representative task of selecting the best move, the experts encode the important features of the presented information and store them in an accessible form in memory. In contrast, when subjects, after training based on mnemonics and knowledge unrelated to chess, attain a recall performance comparable with that of the chess experts, they still lack the ability to extract the information important for selecting the best move. Hence, the remarkable characteristic of expert memory is not just the amount recalled, which can often be matched by training, but the rapid extraction and storage of important patterns and relevant information that allows superior execution of the representative task (Ericsson, Patel, and Kintsch, 2000).

An analysis of expert performance shows that it is not sufficient to have merely stored the knowledge in memory; it is also critical that the relevant knowledge be well organized and easily retrievable. In fact, the principal challenge of expertise is to acquire and organize the vast body of domain knowledge (Chi, Feltovich, and Glaser, 1981) such that all relevant prior knowledge can be immediately accessed to guide action in encountered situations. For example, with his or her superior organization of knowledge, a chess expert can rapidly perceive a promising move, or a medical expert can rapidly notice an inconsistency in a suggested diagnosis.

Efficient and reliable storage of relevant information in memory is especially important to experts when they engage in planning and complex reasoning that mediate their superior performance. During planning experts have to mentally compare many alternative sequences of actions, storing a great deal of information in working memory. Consequently, beginning chess players do not generate long plans, and it takes years of chess study before chess experts are able to plan long sequences of future moves reliably (Charness, 1989). Chess masters eventually improve their memory skills for planning so much that they are even able to play chess without seeing the chessboard (blindfold chess). Analyses of the superior ability to plan suggest that experts acquire memory skills that allow them to rely on long-term memory for storage of generated information (Ericsson and Kintsch, 1995). Research on expertise is making it increasingly clear that the vast knowledge of experts has to be well organized and supplemented with special memory skills so as to support memory-demanding planning, design, and reasoning.

Further research has revealed the complex and intricate structure of expert performance and its asso-ciated memory skills. These skills are not attained automatically with experience but require engagement in deliberate practice that is often designed by teachers. Even the most talented individuals have spent around ten years of intense preparation before attaining a world-class level of performance in many domains such as sports, chess, and arts (Ericsson, 1996).

See also: NATURAL SETTINGS, MEMORY IN

Bibliography

Charness, N. (1989). Expertise in chess and bridge. In D. Klahr and K. Kotovsky, eds., *Complex information processing: The impact of Herbert A. Simon.* Hillsdale, NJ: Erlbaum.

Chase, W. G., and Ericsson, K. A. (1982). Skill and working memory. In G. H. Bower, ed., *The psychology of learning and motivation,* Vol. 16. New York: Academic Press.

Chase, W. G., and Simon, H. A. (1973). The mind's eye in chess. In W. G. Chase, ed., *Visual information processing.* New York: Academic Press.

Chi, M. T. H., Feltovich, P. J., and Glaser, R. (1981). Categorization and representation of physics problems by experts and novices. *Cognitive Science 5,* 121–152.

Ericsson, K. A., ed. (1996). *The road to excellence: The acquisition of expert performance in the arts and sciences, sports, and games.* Mahwah, NJ: Erlbaum.

Ericsson, K. A., and Kintsch, W. (1995). Long-term working memory. *Psychological Review 102,* 211–245.

Ericsson, K. A., and Lehmann, A. C. (1996). Expert and exceptional performance: Evidence on maximal adaptations on task constraints. *Annual Review of Psychology 47,* 273–305.

Ericsson, K. A., Patel, V. L., and Kintsch, W. (2000). How experts' adaptations to representative task demands account for the expertise effect in memory recall: Comment on Vicente and Wang (1998). *Psychological Review 107,* 578–592.

Webster's Third New International Dictionary (1976). Springfield, MA: Merriam.

Wilding, J., and Valentine, E. (1997). *Superior memory.* Hove, UK: Psychology Press.

K. Anders Ericsson

EXPLICIT MEMORY

See: DECLARATIVE MEMORY

F

FALSE MEMORIES

False memories may be full-blown memories of events that were never experienced or (perhaps more commonly) memories that are distorted (i.e., the event one is remembering actually occurred, but it did not occur in the way that is being recalled). Even though memory can foster an illusion of reliving an experience, it is actually a reconstruction and hence subject to departures from objective facts. This entry focuses on false episodic memories, or inaccurate memories of episodes in one's past, which can be distinguished from false semantic memories, which include inaccurate knowledge (e.g., erroneously believing that the capital of Russia is St. Petersburg).

For example, when conveying anecdotes in casual social interactions, people sometimes embellish them to make them more interesting, often spicing them with fresh details in subsequent retellings to assure the desired pungency. Although innocent in intent, such embellishments can actually alter the teller's own memory of the event. Even though the raconteur might be fully aware of the fictional enhancements at the time, he or she may in time come to think of them as actual components of the original event (Tversky and Marsh, 2000).

We distinguish here between two broad classes of episodic false memories: those that arise from internal processes (e.g., the example regarding embellishments) and those that arise from external events (e.g., from hearing other peoples' erroneous accounts of an event). In the former case, people's own thoughts, as-

sociations, or inferences cause them to misremember the past, whereas in the latter case, the false memories arise from someone else's overt suggestion or misleading statements.

False Memories Arising from Internal Processes

In everyday conversation, listeners often make inferences that stretch the meaning of the speaker's explicit words. For example, if a colleague told you that his infant had "stayed awake all night," you might infer that the baby had cried. Such inferences often insinuate themselves into memory. Indeed, when asked later, one might be likely to recall the statement as having been "the infant cried all night" (Brewer, 1977; Bransford and Franks, 1971).

The literature on the role of schemas (or general world knowledge) on memory also sheds light on the influence that inferences can have on memory. This work is rooted in studies by Bartlett (1932), who demonstrated that when English students were presented with an American Indian folktale that they found difficult to comprehend, the flaws in their memories of the folktale often betrayed British cultural influences.

More recent experimental investigations into internally generated false memories include studies in which people are given short lists of about fifteen related words to remember (e.g., *bed, rest, awake, tired, dream*). When given an immediate free recall test after such a list (and told to recall every word that is remembered in any order but without guessing), people

145

often recall *sleep,* a related (but not presented) word (Roediger and McDermott, 1995). This approach, which allows the rapid implanting of numerous mini false memories, enables researchers to manipulate various independent and subject variables in order to observe their effects on false recall (and false recognition) probabilities (Roediger and McDermott, 2000). This work shows not only that people recall and recognize the nonpresented, related words but that they also claim to remember the precise moment of presentation of these (nonpresented) words. In addition, the forgetting function for the related, nonpresented words is less steep than the forgetting function for studied words.

Another recent line of research has investigated the role that imagination can play in distorting memory. The mere act of imagining an event can inflate the probability that a person will come to have a full-blown recollection of the (nonexistent) prior event. This phenomenon has been dubbed imagination inflation (Garry, Manning, and Loftus, 1996; Goff and Roediger, 1998).

Not only can imagining an event that did not previously occur create memories for that event, but also describing an event that did indeed occur can color memory for that event. For example, if expert wine tasters describe a wine they just sampled, it does not change their memory for the wine; if, however, intermediate-level wine tasters attempt to describe the wine just enjoyed, the descriptions skew their later memory of the wine (Melcher and Schooler, 1996). This interference from attempting to verbalize an experience that is not readily amenable to accurate verbal description has been termed "verbal overshadowing" by Jonathan Schooler.

False Memories Arising from External Factors

Some of the best-known false memory work can be considered adaptations of the classic studies of retroactive interference, in which a subsequent event can interfere with memory for a similar, prior event (McGeoch, 1932). In its more modern manifestation, subjects might be presented with a slide show or videotape depicting a car crash and later be exposed to misleading information about this event either through a narrative, suggestive questions, or both. In a classic study by Loftus and Palmer (1974), such a crash was followed by a questionnaire asking people a series of questions about the crash. The critical manipulation was a single verb in one of the questions: *contacted, hit, bumped, collided,* or *smashed.* That is, people were asked, "How fast were the cars going when they ___ into each other?" Speed estimates varied markedly as a function of the verb used; when the more dramatic verb *smashed* was invoked, the average estimated speed was forty-one miles per hour, whereas the verb *contacted* elicited an average estimate of only thirty-two miles per hour. Even more amazing was that the wording of this single question influenced peoples' memories even a week later when they were asked, "Did you see any broken glass?" Subjects were more likely to erroneously recollect broken glass if they had encountered the verb *smashed* a week earlier (relative to the verb *hit*).

Work within this tradition is often referred to as the misleading-information paradigm or sometimes the eyewitness-memory paradigm. Similar findings with respect to the role of intervening suggestions on peoples' memories have been demonstrated for police lineups among other domains. Elizabeth Loftus combined this procedure with the imagination-inflation procedures in a case study in which she created a full-blown memory of being lost in a shopping mall in a teenage boy (Chris) who was never actually lost in a mall (Loftus, 1993). Loftus prompted the false memory by having Chris's brother suggest the incident to Chris, complete with specific details. Two weeks after the initial description of the nonevent, Chris was able to "recall" minute details from this incident, including the balding head and the kind of eyeglasses worn by the man who rescued him. Ira Hyman and his colleagues have performed systematic studies of this type and explored individual differences among people that influence the likelihood of such false memories (Hyman and Billings, 1998).

Processes That Give Rise to False Memories

Many theoretical perspectives have been applied to the study of false memories. We focus here primarily on the Source Monitoring Framework, which has been espoused by Marcia Johnson and her colleagues (Johnson, Hastroudi, and Lindsay, 1993; Johnson and Raye, 1981). Accurate memory requires disentangling recollection of events from speculations, inferences, and imaginings. Achieving the seemingly simple goal is easier in theory than in practice. Simply asking people to focus carefully on whether something was experienced or only imagined or thought and to be sure to recall only what overtly occurred (and not what they inferred or thought) is not sufficient to avoid false memories and may even exacerbate them in some situations (Hicks and Marsh, 2001). Telling people before an encoding phase that they might be misled and that they should encode the information carefully so as not to confuse their thoughts with the overt event may aid them somewhat but is by no means sufficient to eliminate later false memories. Some research has shown that, relative to young adults, old adults have more difficulties in monitoring the retrieval process in order to avoid false memories.

Practical Implications

The fallibility of memory has become a contentious subject not only in psychological theory, but also as a result of its practical implications in the legal system, where the reliability of eyewitness accounts has come increasingly into question. Several conclusions can be safely reached from this research, however. Perhaps the most important point is that a full-blown, vivid recollection of a prior event is not diagnostic of its prior occurrence; it is perfectly possible to vividly recollect an event that was only previously imagined or thought about. The stories we tell ourselves and others color our memory for the object of the story. In this vein, retrieval has been described as a double-edged sword: It helps us remember what occurred previously (the testing effect), but it also can distort memory. Simple instructions to try to avoid false memories are often insufficient to do so.

Finally, memory's reconstructive nature might be considered a cognitive asset rather than a drawback. Most of our misguided recollections are fairly harmless, and many inferences about another's conversational intent are probably correct—in the foregoing example, the baby probably was crying all night. Only in the high-stakes atmosphere of, say, the courtroom or the police lineup does it become critical to disentangle the wheat of accurate memory from the chaff of imagination, inference, conjecture, and embellishment.

See also: RECONSTRUCTIVE MEMORY

Bibliography

Bartlett, F. C. (1932). *Remembering: A study in experimental and social psychology.* New York: Macmillan.

Bransford, J. D., and Franks, J. J. (1971). The abstraction of linguistic ideas. *Cognitive Psychology 2,* 331–350.

Brewer, W. F. (1977). Memory for the pragmatic implications of sentences. *Memory & Cognition 5,* 673–678.

Garry, M., Manning, C. G., and Loftus, E. F. (1996). Imagination inflation: Imagining a childhood event inflates confidences that it occurred. *Psychonomic Bulletin & Review 3,* 208–214.

Goff, L. M., and Roediger, H. L., III. (1998). Imagination inflation for action events: Repeated imaginings lead to illusory recollections. *Memory & Cognition 26,* 20–33.

Hicks, J. L., and Marsh, R. L. (2001). False recognition occurs more frequently during source identification than during old-new recognition. *Journal of Experimental Psychology: Learning, Memory, and Cognition 27,* 375–383.

Hyman, I. E., and Billings, F. J. (1998). Individual differences and the creation of false childhood memories. *Memory 6,* 1–20.

Johnson, M. K., Hashtroudi, S., and Lindsay, D. S. (1993). Source monitoring. *Psychological Bulletin 114,* 3–28.

Johnson, M. K., and Raye, C. L. (1981). Reality monitoring. *Psychological Review 88,* 67–85.

Loftus, E. F. (1993). The reality of repressed memories. *American Psychologist 48,* 518–537.

Loftus, E. F., and Palmer, J. C. (1974). Reconstruction of automobile destruction: An example of the interaction between language and memory. *Journal of Verbal Learning and Verbal Behavior 13,* 585–589.

McGeoch, J. A. (1932). Forgetting and the law of disuse. *Psychological Review 39,* 352–370.

Melcher, J. M., and Schooler, J. W. (1996). The misremembrance of wines past: Verbal and perceptual expertise differentially mediate verbal overshadowing of taste memory. *Journal of Memory and Language 35,* 231–245.

Roediger, H. L., and McDermott, K. B. (1995). Creating false memories: Remembering words not presented in lists. *Journal of Experimental Psychology: Learning, Memory, and Cognition 21,* 803–814.

——— (2000). Tricks of memory. *Current Directions in Psychological Science 9,* 123–127.

Tversky, B., and Marsh, E. (2000). Biased retellings of events yield biased memories. *Cognitive Psychology 40,* 1–38.

Kathleen B. McDermott
Jason C. K. Chan

FOOD AVERSION AND PREFERENCE LEARNING IN HUMANS

To survive, animals must select, from among myriad nonnutritive and toxic items they could ingest, those few that are both nutritious and relatively toxin-free. Humans are, of course, animals, and many of the behavioral processes that guide the food choices of other animals influence humans' food choices as well. However, diet selection by humans is unusual in at least two ways. First, most human knowledge about foods comes secondhand, either directly or indirectly from others. Second, the feeding environment of humans living today in the developed world is dramatically different from that in which humans evolved their abilities to choose foods. We experience food excess, rather than food shortage, extraordinary variety in available foods, rather than restricted food choices, and we are exposed to foods with artificially enhanced palatability. Consequently, our evolved mechanisms of food choice, selected for in widely different circumstances, may sometimes prove maladaptive in the modern world.

Dietary Specialists and Dietary Generalists

Solving the problem of diet selection is relatively simple for animals that eat only one food. Such animals tend to evolve sense organs that identify the chemical signature of whatever species they find edible. For the tobacco hornworm, as its name implies, leaves of the tobacco plant are food, and the worm's taste receptors are particularly sensitive to chemicals found in tobacco leaves.

For dietary generalists—animals that, like humans, compose a diet consisting of many different foods—there is no chemical signature that allows discrimination of food from nonfood items. Dietary generalist have inherent sensory-affective systems biasing them to ingest substances with certain tastes or smells; at birth, human infants like the taste of sugar and reject the bitter of quinine and the sour of lemons. However, dietary generalists still must learn which specific items to ingest and which to avoid eating.

Learning to eat nutritious foods while avoiding toxic or worthless potential foods is especially difficult because effects of toxins and nutrients often occur long after their ingestion. Consequently, many animals, humans included, have evolved a special type of conditioning, called *taste-aversion learning* (discussed below as a type of evaluative conditioning), allowing them to bridge the temporal gap between ingesting an item and experiencing consequences of its ingestion.

Human Food Rejection and Acceptance

Humans reject potential foods for one or more of four reasons. They may find a food distasteful, rejecting it because it has undesirable sensory properties. Alternatively, a food may be rejected because it is perceived as dangerous, for instance, as causing illness such as allergic reaction. A potential food may also be rejected because it is viewed as inappropriate, as, for example, is dirt. Last, some foods may not be eaten because they seem disgusting, as with rotting meat, which is viewed as disgusting by members of some cultures, but not others.

There are only two categories of accepted items: those that taste good and, like diet soda, are consumed because of their sensory properties, and those consumed because they are believed to produce positive consequences, as are health foods, and medicines. Many accepted items have both properties.

Effects of Exposure and Conditioning

Generally, previous exposure of either humans or other animals to a food without obvious positive or negative consequences ("mere" exposure) tends to increase liking for that food. On the other hand, a great deal of exposure to a food in a brief period can produce a temporary decline in liking labeled *sensory-specific satiety*. Too much of even a good thing can produce temporary avoidance of it.

A further means of changing response to food preference involves a form of classical conditioning called *evaluative conditioning*, of which taste-aversion learning is one example. In evaluative conditioning, affective response to a stimulus (a conditioned stimulus, or CS) is changed as a result of pairing with either a liked or disliked stimulus (an unconditioned stimulus, or UCS). In the case of taste-aversion learning, if an animal such as a rat or a human eats a relatively unfamiliar food and, within a few hours, becomes nauseous, the sick individual will develop a distaste for the smell and taste of the food ingestion of which preceded illness. Such taste-aversion learning, reflecting a change in affective response to a food, can seem irrational, occurring even if the sick individual "knows" that the food did not cause the nausea (for example, the nausea might clearly be a symptom of the flu).

Taste-aversion learning differs from situations in which ingestion of a food is followed by negative effects other than nausea: for example, hives or respiratory distress. In the latter case, people can learn that a potential food is dangerous and should not be eaten. However, the taste of the food does not become unpleasant, and the victim of an allergic reaction may continue to want to eat the food causing distress, but will avoid doing so from fear of the consequences. For example, a person who eats shrimp and becomes nauseated tends thereafter to dislike shrimp and may find even the smell of shrimp distasteful, whereas someone who experiences respiratory distress after eating shrimp will avoid eating shrimp but may still like their taste and smell. Nausea serves as a special UCS that, when paired with a food, even once and with a lengthy delay between CS and US, often produces distaste.

In humans as in other animals, enhancement of liking for a neutral flavor can occur if it is paired with a desirable flavor, and pairing a neutral flavor with introduction of nutrients into the stomach also can increase liking for the previously neutral flavor. However, pairings of flavors with calories or good tastes usually has modest effects in comparison with pairings of flavors with nausea.

Social Influences on Human Food Choices

In humans, social forces account for many food preferences and aversions. Approval or disapproval of foods by respected others seems to influence one's own response to those foods, though the way in which such change occurs is not well understood. The process of change could be cognitive, could involve social learning, or could be a form of as-yet unexplored social, classical conditioning. In the last case, displays of pleasure, displeasure, or disgust by another could become associated with a flavor, changing affective response to it.

We do know that children show increased liking for foods associated with positive displays by significant others and that such socially induced changes in food preference can last for months. Changes in affective response to foods seem to occur when children do not feel forced or "bribed" to consume a food: when children are rewarded for eating a food, they do not tend to like it more. However, when the same food is either used as a reward or is seen to be enjoyed by others, it does become liked more. Social factors are almost surely also involved in the development of disgust responses, as when children observe negative responses of their parents to finding half a worm in a half-eaten apple or to body wastes. However, this process has not been investigated.

A distinctive feature of the human diet is that many foods that are liked by some humans have sensory properties that are inherently aversive to both other humans and other animals. Members of many cultures like bitter substances such as coffee, quinine water, and tobacco as well as irritants such as chili pepper and horseradish, substances that animals, infant humans, and adults from some other cultures find aversive. Such preferences may be learned in social settings, although we do not really know how.

Humans clearly differ from all other animals in the importance of *cuisine* (defined here as a system for selecting, processing, combining, and flavoring foods that incorporates the nutritional wisdom of past generations) in their food selection. Although social learning affects food choices of nonhuman animals (for example, after an "observer" rat interacts with a "demonstrator" rat that has eaten a food, the observer prefers the food its demonstrator ate), social influences on food choice are neither as pervasive nor as long lasting in nonhuman animals as in humans.

Young humans are also probably the only animals explicitly taught what to eat and what to avoid eating, although some evidence suggests that chimpanzees may have rudimentary abilities to instruct their young about foods. Still, only humans learn socially to give foods emotional, social, and moral values, and only humans learn about nutritive values, appropriate times for ingestion, and means of preparation of foods in a manner perhaps best described as social-cognitive, just as they learn about other aspects of the physical environment.

Conclusion

Unfortunately, not enough is yet known about the development of food preferences in the human species to give much helpful advice to parents wishing to modify a child's food choices. Indeed, one of the most surprising facts known about human food choices is that there is little similarity between food preferences of parents and their mature children. Important as

teaching, social learning, and cuisine may be in shaping human food choices, other factors, as yet poorly understood, play a major role in shaping the dietary repertoires of humans.

See also: TASTE AVERSION AND PREFERENCE LEARNING IN ANIMALS

Bibliography

Birch, L. L., Fisher, J. O., and Grimm-Thomas, K. (1996). The development of children's eating habits. In H. J. H. Macfie and H. L. Meiselman, eds., *Food choice, acceptance and consumption*, pp. 161–206. Glasgow: Blackie Academic and Professional.

Booth, D. A. (1994). *Psychology of nutrition*. London: Taylor and Francis.

Capaldi, E. D., ed. (1996). *Why we eat what we eat: The psychology of eating*. Washington, DC: American Psychological Association.

De Hower, J., Thomas, S., and Baeyens, F. (2001). Associative learning of likes and dislikes: A review of twenty-five years of research on human evaluative conditioning. *Psychological Bulletin 127*, 853–869.

Galef, B. G., Jr. (1996). Food selection: Problems in understanding how we choose foods to eat. *Neuroscience and Biobehavioral Reviews 20*, 67–73.

——— (1996). Social enhancement of food preferences in Norway rats: A brief review. In C. M. Heyes and B. G. Galef Jr., eds., *Social learning in animals: The roots of culture*, pp. 49–64. San Diego: Academic Press.

Garcia, J., Hankins, W. G., and Rusiniak, K. W. (1974). Behavioral regulation of the milieu internal in man and rat. *Science 185*, 824–831.

Macfie, H. J. H., and Meiselman, H. L. (1996). *Food choice, acceptance, and consumption*. Glasgow: Blackie Academic and Professional.

Rozin, P. (1999). Food is fundamental, fun, frightening, and far reaching. *Social Research 66*, 9–30.

Rozin, P., and Shulkin, J. (1990). Food selection. In E. M. Stricker, ed., *Handbook of behavioral neurobiology*, Vol. 10: *Neurobiology of food and fluid intake*, pp. 297–328. New York: Plenum Press.

Paul Rozin
Revised by Bennett G. Galef Jr. and Paul Rozin

FORAGING

Foraging, the search for food, is a fundamental part of behavior. All animals, from the simplest invertebrates to primates, have to take in food. Because appropriate food may be more abundant at some times and places than others, an animal that can learn about the characteristics of its food supply is likely to be able to forage more efficiently than one that cannot learn. Indeed, the need for efficient foraging creates a strong selection pressure for the evolution of learning and memory.

Since the late twentieth century, the study of foraging behavior has been guided by *optimal foraging theory*, a body of mathematical models specifying how animals should behave so as to maximize foraging efficiency. After briefly introducing this framework, this entry describes some of the ways in which animals use learning and memory in foraging.

Optimal Foraging Theory

Optimal foraging theory is a topic in behavioral ecology, the field of biology dealing with how behavior contributes to an animal's reproductive success or fitness. Many aspects of foraging can be understood by assuming that animals have evolved to maximize the rate at which they take in energy while foraging. An animal that can forage efficiently will have more time for other important activities like finding a mate or defending a territory. If the economics of a particular foraging situation are understood well enough, it is possible to make a mathematical model that specifies what the animal should do in order to maximize its energy intake while foraging. Stephens and Krebs (1986) describe this approach in detail. However, some examples are easy to understand intuitively without any mathematics.

Consider a small bird in the spring collecting food to bring back to the young in its nest. To feed the hungry nestlings it must spend a good part of the day searching for food and carrying it back home. How far should it travel and how much should it collect on each trip? It might seem obvious that the bird should load up as much as it can each time, but this suggestion overlooks the fact that as the bird loads its beak with food like grubs or caterpillars, increasing the load becomes harder and harder. In addition, more energy is needed to fly back to the nest with more prey items. On the other hand, if the bird has had to fly some distance from the nest in order to find suitable prey, it is worth its while to collect as many items as possible. This informal argument suggests that there should be a direct relationship between the size of the bird's load and the distance it has traveled: Bigger loads should be collected when the bird is farther from the nest.

Kacelnik and Cuthill (1987) studied this problem of central-place foraging with starlings nesting around a farm. They trained the birds to visit a feeder and collect mealworms that the experimenter dropped down a pipe. By placing the feeder at different distances from the starlings' nests while keeping constant the rate of dropping mealworms, Kacelnik and Cuthill were able to obtain clear evidence of the predicted relationship. With further experiments in both the field and the laboratory they were able to account for many details of what the birds learn and remember.

Implicit in this example are a number of uses of learning and memory. To return straight home with its prey, a starling had to learn the location of its nest.

On each trip it had to remember where it was in relation to the nest. The birds also had to learn how often worms were available at the experimental feeder and how valuable they were.

Prey Selection

An animal encountering a potential prey item may accept it or go on searching for alternative prey. What it should do to maximize its rate of energy intake can be understood intuitively. If it can expect to find a bigger or more quickly consumed item soon enough, the forager should reject the item at hand and go on searching; otherwise it should take the encountered item. To select prey as efficiently as they do, animals must learn about their value and their abundance and adjust their behavior as the environment changes. Many of the studies of prey selection and other aspects of foraging reviewed by Shettleworth (1998) have emphasized how the learning mechanisms animals use in foraging are the same as those revealed in experiments on operant conditioning.

Learning to Find Cryptic Prey

Many animals that are potential prey for other animals have evolved to look like their surroundings so they are hard for predators to see. For example, moths may be speckled black and gray like the bark of the trees where they rest, and caterpillars that live on green plants may be green. In turn, predators have evolved the ability to learn how to discriminate such cryptic prey from their backgrounds. Laboratory studies using bluejays, chicks, and pigeons searching for grains or for images on slides under controlled conditions have provided evidence that predators may form a specific search image for, or "learn to see," cryptic prey. When a bird encounters several cryptic prey items in a row, it becomes better at detecting them. It may be paying more attention to subtle details that differentiate the prey items from their background, or it may be learning to search more slowly when prey are difficult to detect. Both kinds of learning probably contribute to improving foraging efficiency. Using a computerized "virtual ecology" in which bluejays search for moths, Kamil and Bond (2001) have shown how the birds' learning can contribute to the evolution of one prey type rather than another.

Learning about Patches of Food

Not only do animals have to detect and capture prey efficiently, they have to learn where prey can be found. Food generally occurs in patches. For example, a freshly watered lawn is a good place for a robin to look for worms, but lawns may be separated by roads and sidewalks that do not provide good foraging for a robin. Clearly, it is best to be in the patch with the most abundant prey—foraging in the freshly watered lawn with worms close to the surface is preferable to foraging in the dried-up lawn next door. An efficient forager needs good spatial learning abilities so it can navigate from one part of the environment to another. Information about location of suitable foraging areas and the density of prey in each has to be constantly updated as the environment changes. Thus animals should sample the environment, sometimes exploring new patches or patches that were not good the last time they were tried, in order to discover whether they have changed for the better.

One aspect of patch choice that has been studied extensively is how animals should respond to depletion of foraging patches. In our example, as the robin hops around the lawn finding worms, its own foraging activity (and perhaps that of other birds) reduces the density of worms in the patch. Some are eaten and others burrow down into the soil at the birds' approach. When should the robin leave this patch and look for another? The foraging theorist's answer to this question takes into account several factors other than the average density of prey in the current patch. These factors include the density of prey in other patches, how far away the patches are, and whether prey are constant or variable in size or frequency. Experiments reviewed by Shettleworth (1998) have shown how animals learn about and respond to all these variables.

Some Special Problems for Foragers: Nectar-Feeding and Food-Storing

Learning where to search for prey and detecting and selecting it once a suitable patch is found are problems for virtually any forager. Some animals also face special problems that may require specialized learning and memory abilities. One set of problems, related to the patch-depletion problem just discussed, is faced by bees, bats, and hummingbirds that suck nectar from flowers. A flower that has been depleted of nectar produces more nectar at a rate that depends on factors like what kind of flower it is. The efficient forager will time its visits so as to return at long enough intervals to find the flower full, but not so long that some other forager will have depleted the flower. One way to ensure this is to travel a fixed route among a number of plants. Some nectar-feeding animals do forage in this way. For example, Gould (1982) describes how bees learn the features of flowers and the times and places at which nectar can be found. As reviewed by Shettleworth (1998), an exqui-

site sensitivity to times of day and time intervals between foraging opportunities is evident in the foraging behavior of many other species.

Another specialized foraging problem requiring memory is faced by some birds that spend the winter in a harsh climate. To have enough to eat at such times, birds such as chickadees, nuthatches, and jays store food when it is abundant. The Clark's nutcracker, a bird of the American Southwest, buries thousands of pine seeds in the late summer and recovers them up to six months later. Because each cache is in a different place, the birds must use memory to recover the food. Experiments in the laboratory with nutcrackers and chickadees, described by VanderWall (1990), have shown that these birds can indeed remember the locations of their stores and do not need to use other cues. Some research reviewed by Shettleworth (1998) suggests that they have evolved a better spatial memory than birds that do not store food. This suggestion is supported by evidence that relative to body size, food-storing birds have a larger hippocampus (the brain area necessary for spatial memory) than other birds.

Conclusion

Considering what and how animals must learn and remember to forage efficiently is one of the best illustrations of how observations and theories about behavior in the wild have been integrated with the study of animals' cognitive processes. This analysis is at the core of cognitive ecology, a growing interdisciplinary area of animal behavior research discussed by Healy and Braithwaite (2001).

See also: EVOLUTION AND LEARNING; OPERANT BEHAVIOR; SPATIAL LEARNING: ANIMALS

Bibliography

Gould, J. L. (1982). *Ethology.* New York: W. W. Norton.

Healy, S. D., and Braithwaite, V. (2001). Cognitive ecology: A field of substance? *Trends in Ecology and Evolution 15*, 22–26.

Kacelnik, A., and Cuthill, I. C. (1987). Starlings and optimal foraging theory: Modelling in a fractal world. In A. C. Kamil, J. R. Krebs, and H. R. Pulliam, eds., *Foraging behavior*, pp. 303–333. New York: Plenum Press.

Kamil, A. C., and Bond, A. B. (2001). The evolution of virtual ecology. In L. A. Dugatkin, ed., *Model systems in behavioral ecology*, pp. 288–310. Princeton, NJ: Princeton University Press.

Shettleworth, S. J. (1998). *Cognition, evolution, and behavior.* New York: Oxford University Press.

Stephens, D. W., and Krebs, J. R. (1986). *Foraging theory.* Princeton, NJ: Princeton University Press.

VanderWall, S. B. (1990). *Food hoarding in animals.* Chicago: University of Chicago Press.

Sara J. Shettleworth

Table 1

Retroactive and Proactive Inhibition

	Retroactive Inhibition				Proactive Inhibition			
	Learn	Learn	Recall	Result	Learn	Learn	Recall	Result
Control Group	List 1	None	List 1	Better	None	List 2	List 2	Better
Experimental Group	List 1	List 2	List 1	Worse	List 1	List 2	List 2	Worse

SOURCE: Courtesy of Ian Neath.

FORGETTING

It is a common experience to forget what one has learned. Usually, forgetfulness increases with with the length of the retention interval, the time elapsed since the material was last studied or thought about. A graph of the amount remembered (as measured by tests of recall or recognition or relearning) as a function of increasing retention intervals produces a forgetting curve, the slope of which represents the overall rate of forgetting. The first forgetting curve was published in 1885 by Hermann Ebbinghaus, the pioneer in the scientific study of memory. His curve showed the now-familiar monotonic and negatively accelerated form, where the momentary rate of forgetting decreases over time.

Trace Decay

Perhaps the earliest and simplest attempt to account for forgetting was the idea of trace decay, which postulated that memorizing something lays down a neurochemical imprint or record in the brain, called a memory trace or engram, whose later reactivation is responsible for remembering. This trace was assumed to fade away spontaneously over time if it was not refreshed by some reacquaintance with the learned material; hence forgetting would ensue. With very few exceptions (noted below), trace-decay theory has been abandoned. This is not only because the hypothetical memory trace has never been identified but also because of subsequent research that undermined the thesis: for example, the findings that forgetting is influenced by other activities taking place both before and after the original learning and that forgetting is also greatly affected by the kinds of cues given at the time of test. Providing different retrieval cues in situations where the trace was supposed to have decayed often results in successful recall of the supposedly forgotten material (Capaldi and Neath, 1995); in many instances memory performance can improve with the passage of time (Bjork, 2001). Thus,

although forgetting takes place over time, it is probably not because of some inexorable, autonomous fading of a memory trace.

Forgetting is attributed to decay in only two areas of memory research: pro forma decay parameters in abstract mathematical models of memory and the invocation of an unspecified decay process in certain accounts of short-term memory. The former can be seen as mathematical conveniences rather than as strong theoretical statements. The latter suffer from two major problems: ambiguity in the explication of the decay process (i.e., it is unclear exactly what aspect of memory is decaying, what parts of the memory remain) and the reevaluation of the data supporting such assertions. In principle, decay can be empirically demonstrated if one rules out alternative, better-established causes of forgetting, such as interference. When this is done, the evidence for decay is not appreciable; in the words of Cowan, Saults, and Nugent (2001), "no clear evidence of decay has emerged in, lo, these many years."

Interference

One theoretical approach to forgetting that has inspired an enormous amount of experimental effort over several decades is interference theory. As the name implies, it focuses upon forgetting caused by interference. Among its beginnings was the influential demonstration by Jenkins and Dallenbach (1924) that the forgetting of a list of verbal items was markedly reduced if subjects passed the retention interval in sleep rather than in their usual waking activities. This result suggested that the experiences of daily life somehow interfered with the memory of the original material. Eventually, interest narrowed upon other learning experiences as the sources of that interference.

The empirical cornerstones of interference theory are to be found in two kinds of laboratory-produced forgetting. These are schematized in Table

1, and each defines a source of interference by comparing the memory performance of one experimental group, which acquires two lists in succession, with that of a control group, which acquires only one. Retroactive inhibition is the forgetting of the first set of materials, which is caused by the subsequent learning of a second set during the retention interval. Proactive inhibition is the forgetting of the second set, which is caused by the prior learning of a first set. It may seem strange that a preceding list would reduce the memory for a subsequently acquired one, but it can, especially when a retention interval precedes testing. Interference theory construes retroactive and proactive inhibition to be the basic models for its approach to forgetting, inside or outside of the laboratory. It is the task of the theory to devise an experimentally testable description of the processes of retroactive and proactive inhibition.

Whenever two sets of materials are acquired in succession, two processes can impair memory of them. One is the dynamic competition of responses for emergence at the time of the test. To the extent that both sets of materials are activated, a response from the first list may be blocked from consciousness by a stronger competing response from the second list, or vice versa. Two competing responses of equal strength may even block each other. This process is set into motion by the demands of the memory test, and it reduces performances on both lists compared with the single-list control condition. The other process, which takes place during the learning of the second list, consists of the temporary suppression of the contents of the first list, to the extent that they conflict with new response requirements. For example, if the first set of materials contains an A-B association and the second set requires an A-C association, then A-B may be suppressed. With both factors taken into consideration, the memory situation immediately after second-list acquisition is that of a suppressed first list competing against a dominant second list. This correctly predicts that retroactive inhibition will be much stronger than proactive inhibition. Another important observation to be explained is that with a delayed memory test, proactive inhibition increases in magnitude. This fact is incorporated by postulating a gradual dissipation of first-list suppression, wherein the list regains its strength and competes more effectively, producing increased interference. This implies that a suppressed set of materials should be better recalled after some time has passed, which is the opposite of forgetting. Such an effect has been experimentally verified.

Table 2

| | | Proportion of Items Correctly Recalled as a Function of the Presence or Absence of Various Types of Cues at Encoding and Retrieval | | |

Proportion of Items Correctly Recalled as a Function of the Presence or Absence of Various Types of Cues at Encoding and Retrieval

		Retrieval Cue		
		None	Weak	Strong
Encoding Cue	None	0.49	0.43	0.68
	Weak	0.30	0.82	0.23

SOURCE: Courtesy of Ian Neath.

Cue-Dependency Theory

Cue-dependency theory is an alternative approach to forgetting. Although quite different from interference theory, it supplements rather supplants it. Cue-dependency stresses the importance of the reminders, or retrieval cues, that operate at the time of test. It emphasizes that the act of remembering requires not only the stored products of original learning but also an appropriate testing environment in which to make contact with that learning. The successful interaction of stored information and retrieval information produces recollection. Forgetting is proportional to the inadquate accessibility of retrieval cues. Remembering depends on the interaction between the conditions at encoding and the conditions at retrieval.

An experiment reported by Thomson and Tulving (1970) emphasizes the importance of the encoding/retrieval. The researchers asked subjects to recall the target words from a list they were shown. At encoding the target word was sometimes presented by itself, and sometimes with a weak cue. At retrieval there were three cue conditions: Sometimes, no retrieval cue was given, sometimes a weak cue was given, and sometimes a strong cue was given. The terms *strong cue* and *weak cue* refer to a cue's ability to elicit a target. For example, if you were asked to respond with the first word that popped into your head when you heard *bloom,* you are very likely to respond with *flower.* So *bloom* is a strong cue for *flower.* In contrast, you are likely to respond with *flower* only about 1 percent of the time to the weak cue *bloom.* The results, shown as the probability of recalling the correct target word, are displayed in Table 2.

When there was no cue at encoding, the weak and strong cues at retrieval functioned as expected: More target items were reported when given a strong cue (0.68) than when given a weak cue (0.43). However, when there was a weak cue at encoding, the weak cue at retrieval elicited the target word more than 80 percent of the time, whereas the strong cue elicited the target word barely 20 percent of the time.

What matters is the extent to which the conditions at retrieval uniquely specify the target information. Thus, if you study in the presence of a particular odor (say, freshly baked chocolate-chip cookies) but are tested in the absence of that odor, your ability to remember is impaired. A change in mood, environment, or pharmacological state can result in similar decrements. Most of the things you have memorized were not accompanied by the smell of chocolate-chip cookies; having the odor at retrieval provides a cue that greatly narrows down the possible items to be recalled. According to this view, the way to overcome forgetting is to envision what cues will be uniquely available at the time the information is going to be needed. Once those cues are identified, then the material can be encoded with reference to those cues.

Normal Forgetting

Are there any conditions of original learning that influence the rate of forgetting of a single set of materials learned in the laboratory? Curiously, normal forgetting rates appear to be independent of the materials memorized. They also seem impervious to the levels of processing (superficial versus meaningful) employed at study. There is little evidence that they yield to deliberate mnemonic strategies. There is even serious doubt about whether the degree of original learning has any effect upon the rate of loss. The present picture suggests a remarkable resistance to experimental manipulation. Surely no theory or model of memory can be expected to account satisfactorily for normal forgetting short of resolution of this question.

Bibliography

Bjork, R. A. (2001). Recency and recovery in human memory. In H. L. Roediger III, J. S. Nairne, I. Neath, and A. M. Surprenant, eds., *The nature of remembering: Essays in honor of Robert G. Crowder.* Washington, DC: American Psychological Association.

Capaldi, E. J., and Neath, I. (1995). Remembering and forgetting as context discrimination. *Learning and Memory 2,* 107–132.

Cowan, N., Saults, S., and Nugent, L. (2001). The ravages of absolute and relative amounts of time on memory. In H. L. Roediger III, J. S. Nairne, I. Neath, and A. M. Surprenant, eds., *The nature of remembering: Essays in honor of Robert G. Crowder.* Washington, DC: American Psychological Association.

Ebbinghaus, H. (1885/1913; 1964). *Memory: A contribution to experimental psychology,* trans. H. A. Ruger and C. E. Bussenius. New York: Dover.

Jenkins, J. G., and Dallenbach, K. M. (1924). Obliviscence during sleep and waking. *American Journal of Psychology 35,* 605–612.

McGeoch, J. A. (1932). Forgetting and the law of disuse. *Psychological Review 39,* 352–370.

Neath, I. (1998). *Human memory: An introduction to research, data, and theory.* Pacific Grove, CA: Brooks/Cole.

Postman, L., and Underwood, B. J. (1973). Critical issues in interference theory. *Memory & Cognition 1,* 19–40.

Slamecka, N. J. (1985). Ebbinghaus: Some associations. *Journal of Experimental Psychology: Learning, Memory, and Cognition 11,* 414–435.

Slamecka, N. J., and McElree, B. (1983). Normal forgetting of verbal lists as a function of their degree of learning. *Journal of Experimental Psychology: Learning, Memory, and Cognition 9,* 384–397.

Thomson, D. M., and Tulving, E. (1970). Associative encoding and retrieval: Weak and strong cues. *Journal of Experimental Psychology 86,* 255–262.

Underwood, B.J. (1957). Interference and forgetting. *Psychological Review 64,* 49–60.

Norman J. Slamecka
Revised by Ian Neath

FREUD, SIGMUND (1856–1939)

Sigmund Freud was the founder of psychoanalysis, a system of psychological therapy and personality theory that remains one of the most influential and controversial in psychology. Born in 1856 in Freiberg, Moravia (then a province of the Austro-Hungarian Empire and today a part of Czechoslovakia), he was the first son of Jakob Freud, a wool merchant, and of Amalie Nathansohn Freud, Jakob's third wife.

Freud's background was Jewish, a fact that figured importantly in his life and work, although he himself was an atheist—in his words, "a Godless Jew"—and was to write withering critiques of religion, which he considered a "psychological narcotic" (see, e.g., Freud, 1927, 1930).

Notwithstanding his birthplace, Freud for all intents and purposes was a Viennese. His family moved to Vienna when he was four, and he remained there until about a year before his death, when he fled Nazi Austria to settle with his family in London. His four sisters, who stayed behind, perished in the Holocaust. In 1886 Freud married Martha Bernays. They had three sons and three daughters, the youngest of whom, Anna, became a prominent figure in the psychoanalytic movement.

Freud, a heavy cigar smoker, tried several times to give up his "vice" but found that he could not write without smoking. He was found to have cancer of the mouth in 1923 and endured more than thirty operations before his death in 1939. He remained a prolific writer until the end, leaving some two dozen volumes of psychological works.

Education and Early Career

For the last six of his eight years in gymnasium (the European version of academic high school), Freud was at the top of his class. He claimed to have a photographic memory, and he possessed a powerful, brilliant writing style. In 1930 he received the Goethe prize, a literary award. He had less of a bent for the hard sciences and mathematics. After an initial inclination toward a career in law or politics, Freud decided upon the natural sciences and at seventeen enrolled in the medical school of the University of Vienna, where he conducted research in anatomy and physiology.

After some dawdling, Freud obtained his M.D. degree in 1881, at the age of twenty-five. He hoped to remain a research scientist at the university, but, realizing that he was not apt to receive a permanent university appointment (there were no likely openings soon, and his Jewish background also worked against him), he reluctantly opted for medical practice, training at the Vienna General Hospital (1882–1885) and, after a stint as an army doctor, assuming the directorship of the neurological department of a hospital for children while he established a private practice. In this period Freud published some papers on neurology, among them articles on children's paralyses, and a book on aphasia (1891). He also experimented on himself with the then exotic drug cocaine. Enthusiastic over its enhancing effects on energy and creativity, he was soon urging the drug upon his fiancée and family members. This cocaine phase came to an abrupt end when a friend of his (whom he was trying to wean from heroin addiction with cocaine) overdosed and died. The episode may have hurt Freud's medical reputation in Vienna although it did, indirectly, lead to the successful use of cocaine as a local anesthetic in ophthalmology.

In 1885, while at the Vienna General Hospital, Freud won a four-month grant to study with the world's preeminent neurologist, Jean Charcot, in Paris, who at the time was pursuing research on hysteria and hypnosis. Four years later Freud also visited the great center of hypnotic research and therapy, headed by Hippolyte Bernheim, at Nancy, France. Freud was much taken by demonstrations there of posthypnotic suggestion with amnesia, in which subjects carried out hypnotic suggestions after awakening from their trance without being aware of the reason for their actions. Beyond their therapeutic import, Freud saw such demonstrations as laboratory confirmations of the power of the unconscious to affect behavior.

The Birth of Psychoanalysis

Because of Freud's background in neurology, his colleagues tended to refer patients to him who suffered from neurological symptoms such as paralysis, tic, or amnesia. Clearly, however, many of these pa-

Sigmund Freud *(World Health Organization/Washington, DC)*

tients were not actually afflicted with organic disorders but were suffering from psychological conditions that mimicked neurological symptoms. Such patients were often referred to as "neurotics" or "hysterics." Psychoanalysis was born in the effort to devise psychological treatment for these psychological afflictions.

An important partner in Freud's early psychotherapeutic research was his older friend and mentor, Josef Breuer, an eminent Viennese physician. Breuer had experimented with hypnotic suggestion therapy, a technique in which the hysteric patient, under hypnosis, is given the suggestion that his or her symptoms will disappear. With his famous patient Anna O., Breuer varied the procedure and stumbled on a striking phenomenon: When Anna was able to recollect and report the painful events that had brought about her symptoms, the symptoms permanently disappeared. The procedure, which Anna O. referred to as the "talking cure," was more formally designated by Breuer as the cathartic technique. Freud experimented with and extended the hypnotic and cathartic techniques, and in 1895 he and Breuer published what may be considered the founding work in psychoanalysis, *Studies on Hysteria.*

The central idea of the *Studies* was that "hysterics suffer mainly from reminiscences"—memories of disturbing events from the past that are not accessible to their consciousness but are expressed in the recondite dialect of body language as hysterical symptoms. The cathartic strategy was to recover the pathogenic idea and its associated effect into awareness. Freud gradually dropped hypnosis as his hypermnesic (memory-enhancing) agent, though he retained the couch on which hypnotized patients reclined. Eventually he adopted psychoanalysis's free-association technique, in which the patient is committed to the "basic rule" of saying anything that comes to mind, without censorship. Freud, an ardent determinist, believed that the superficially haphazard approach would willy-nilly lead back to the pathogenic trauma or conflict. He found that the problem-causing mental contents often originated in childhood sexual and aggressive feelings, especially those arising from the "Oedipus complex" around the age of five or six, when, Freud claimed, the child develops overtly erotic desires for the parent of the opposite sex and hateful feelings toward the parent of the same sex.

A prominent yield of the free-association procedure, considered within psychoanalysis a "microscope" of the mind, was that the basic rule was psychologically impossible to honor. Freud came to realize that certain thoughts and wishes were too disturbing to communicate even to oneself. This inward dishonesty led to the fundamental concept of defense mechanisms, psychological processes deployed to distort or exclude from consciousness thoughts and desires that are too anxiety producing. Ultimately (*The Ego and the Id*, 1923), Freud viewed the mind as divided into three often-conflicting subsystems: an executive, reality-oriented component, the ego; a primitive, passion-controlled subsystem, the id; and a moral subsystem, the superego.

Attempting a Scientific Understanding of Psychological Processes

In addition to the publication of *Studies on Hysteria*, the year 1895 was a watershed in another way. Freud feverishly attempted to create a neurological model of basic psychological processes—"Psychology for Neurologists"—but by the end of the year concluded that the effort was failure and withheld the text from publication. In effect he abandoned neurology and became a full-fledged psychologist. His followers published the manuscript posthumously under the title *Project for a Scientific Psychology*. Convoluted and often impenetrable, the one-hundred-page monograph does contain some remarkably prescient neurological intuitions about learning and memory, among them the notion that the neurological basis of

learning and memory is the selective facilitation and inhibition of the flow of excitation across the "contact barriers"—synapses, in modern parlance—between neurons, resulting in the gradual differentiation of functional neural units or systems within broader neural networks. Freud's speculative neuropsychology foreshadowed many key notions in contemporary neuroscience, including today's influential "parallel distributed processing" models of learning, perception, and memory.

Freud is well known, and much criticized, for his theory of infantile sexuality, which holds that children are sexual creatures who, in the first years of life, go through "psychosexual" developmental stages (oral, anal, and phallic) that presage adult sexuality (the genital stage), reached at puberty after a period of sexual latency. Problems during the early sexual stages (e.g., traumas, deprivation) result in developmental arrests—fixations—that produce distinctive adult "character types": the oral (associated with traits such as dependency, passivity, propensity for smoking), anal (e.g., fussy orderliness, stinginess, sadism), and phallic (e.g., seductiveness, impotence). It might be noted that Freud had no direct clinical experience with children nor any research involvement with them. Modern scientific evaluations (e.g., Fisher and Greenberg, 1996) suggest that the cluster of traits defining "oral" or "anal" character do exist but that the notion that developmental events cause these types has little support. Thus, the typology may have some validity but the etiology does not.

In 1900, following a self-analysis initiated in 1895, Freud published his seminal *Interpretation of Dreams*. If free associations were a microscope of the mind, dreams to Freud were the "royal road" to the unconscious. During sleep, defenses are weakened and the primitive drives and primitive modes of cognition—primary process thinking—come to the fore. Like any complex mental product, dreams have multiple levels of meaning. The surface meaning, which Freud called the manifest content, often makes no sense; the deep or latent content, which requires interpretation, carries the important meaning. In dreams, the latent content is often unconscious to the subject. Thus, like a hysteric symptom, a dream involves a meaningful communication of which the patient may not be aware.

Dream analysis, along with the free-association method, became an integral feature of psychoanalytic therapy. To these, later on, was added the analysis of transference. Freud found that in the course of therapy, patients developed passionate feelings for the therapist of both a loving and a hating character. Because these were not realistically warranted, Freud took the transference manifestations to be reenactments of past significant relations, especially between the patient and his or her parents. The "transference neurosis," then, was a profound form of remembering, involving not conscious recollection but reliving of problematic themes from the past. The goal of psychoanalysis was always in some sense "the education of consciousness." Through self-knowledge, the patient was thought to gain mastery over the irrational determinants of his or her pathological symptoms and behavior.

Freud always insisted on the scientific status of his creation, although his practices were often unscientific. Disagreements with his colleagues—figures such as Josef Breuer, Carl Gustav Jung, Alfred Adler—led to personal and professional ruptures. Freud did not engage in any true experimental research, and the empirical anchoring of his "science" was clinical observation, which often amounted to all-too-fallible interpretation. Probably for this reason, more than resistance to supposedly unpalatable claims (such as the doctrine of infantile sexuality), mainstream scientific psychology has maintained a suspicious, ambivalent stance toward psychoanalysis. Nevertheless, for all his great flaws, Freud had his great insights, among them the concept of unconscious mental activity; the notion of remembering without awareness through behavior and other indirect channels; the meaningfulness of dreams; the therapeutic value of talking and of the interpersonal relation in therapy; and the pervasiveness of biased, often defensive, reconstructions of memory. In the century after they were proposed, these themes emerged as mainstream notions in modern psychology.

Freud is a towering but transitional figure in scientific psychology—a sort of Moses, who achieved great things but was not himself destined to reach the promised land.

See also: GUIDE TO THE ANATOMY OF THE BRAIN; PARALLEL DISTRIBUTED PROCESSING MODELS OF MEMORY

Bibliography

Breuer, J., and Freud, S. (1895; reprint 1955). *Studies on hysteria*, trans. A. Strachey and J. Strachey. In J. Strachey, ed., *The standard edition of the complete psychological works of Sigmund Freud*, Vol. 2. London: Hogarth Press.
Fisher, S., and Greenberg, R. P. (1996). *Freud scientifically reappraised: Testing the theories and therapy*. New York: Wiley.
Freud, S. (1891). *On aphasia*. New York: International Universities Press, 1953.
—— (1895; reprint 1966). *Project for a scientific psychology*. In J. A. Strachey, ed., *The standard edition of the complete psychological works of Sigmund Freud*, Vol. 1. London: Hogarth Press.
—— (1900; reprint 1953). *The interpretation of dreams*. In J. A. Strachey, ed., *The standard edition of the complete psychological works of Sigmund Freud*, Vols. 4 and 5. London: Hogarth Press.
—— (1914; reprint 1958). *Remembering, repeating, and working through: Further recommendations . . . of psychoanalysis II*, J. Rivi-
ere and J. Strachey, trans. In J. Strachey, ed., *The standard edition of the complete psychological works of Sigmund Freud*, Vol. 12. London: Hogarth Press.
—— (1917). *A general introduction to psychoanalysis*, J. Riviere, trans. New York: Liveright.
—— (1923; reprint 1961). *The ego and the id*, J. Riviere and J. Strachey, trans. In J. Strachey, ed., *The standard edition of the complete psychological works of Sigmund Freud*, Vol. 19. London: Hogarth Press.
—— (1926; reprint 1959). *Inhibitions, symptoms, and anxiety*, A. Strachey and J. Strachey, trans. In J. Strachey, ed., *The standard edition of the complete psychological works of Sigmund Freud*, Vol. 20. London: Hogarth Press.
—— (1927; reprint 1961). *The future of an illusion*, W. D. Robson-Scott and J. Strachey, trans. In J. Strachey, ed., *The standard edition of the complete psychological works of Sigmund Freud*, Vol. 21. London: Hogarth Press.
—— (1930; reprint 1961). *Civilization and its discontents*, J. Riviere and J. Strachey, trans. In J. Strachey, ed., *The standard edition of the complete psychological works of Sigmund Freud*, Vol. 21. London: Hogarth Press.

Matthew Hugh Erdelyi

FRONTAL LOBES AND EPISODIC MEMORY

The idea that the frontal lobes are implicated in memory has a long and controversial history (Luria, 1980; Teuber, 1964). Damage to the frontal lobes can produce memory impairment and sometimes even severe memory loss, but it has proved difficult to specify the nature of the disorder. The scholarly consensus now holds that frontal-lobe damage does not lead to memory deficits in consolidation, storage, and retention of newly acquired information (Petrides, 2000; Moscovitch and Winocur, 2002). Such disorders, which in their most extreme form lead to a profound global amnesia, are associated with damage to the medial temporal lobes, particularly the hippocampus and related structures, and to midline thalamic nuclei (Milner, 1966).

Working-with-Memory

Memory loss following frontal-lobe lesions, on the other hand, involves organizational or strategic aspects of memory that are necessary for devising strategies for encoding, for guiding search at retrieval, for monitoring and verifying memory output, for placing retrieved memories in their proper spatial and temporal contexts, and for using mnemonic information to direct thought and plan future actions. In other words, the frontal lobe's memory functions are consistent with its functions in other domains. It helps organize the raw material that is made available by other structures so that thought and behavior can be goal-directed. If the hippocampus and its related structures can be considered raw memory structures,

Figure 1

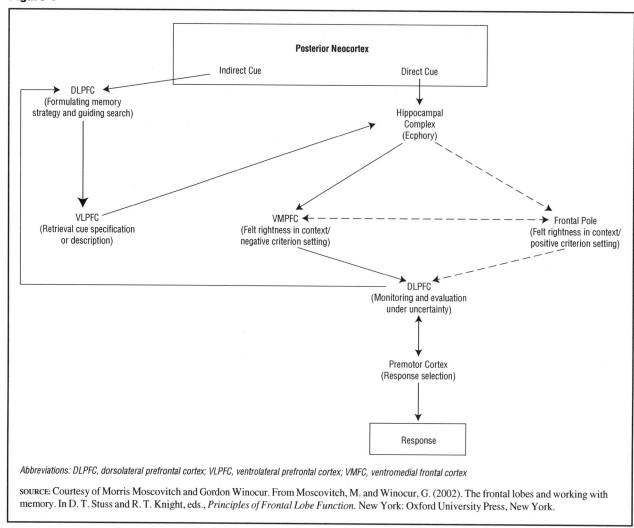

Abbreviations: DLPFC, dorsolateral prefrontal cortex; VLPFC, ventrolateral prefrontal cortex; VMFC, ventromedial frontal cortex

SOURCE: Courtesy of Morris Moscovitch and Gordon Winocur. From Moscovitch, M. and Winocur, G. (2002). The frontal lobes and working with memory. In D. T. Stuss and R. T. Knight, eds., *Principles of Frontal Lobe Function*. New York: Oxford University Press, New York.

The sequence of frontal and medial temporal lobe activation during retrieval of episodic memories to a direct or indirect cue.

then the frontal lobes are working-with-memory structures that operate on the input and output of the hippocampal circuit (see Figure 1). We prefer the descriptive term *working-with-memory* to the more theoretically loaded terms *working memory* or *executive function* favored by others (Baddeley, 1986; Goldman-Rakic, 1987; Smith and Jonides, 1998; Stuss and Knight, 2002); this term captures the essence of frontal-lobe contribution to memory but does not commit the user to endorse a working-memory theory that may be flawed or inappropriate (Moscovitch and Winocur, 1992).

Review of Lesions Studies and Memory Tasks

One can best appreciate the contribution of the frontal lobes to memory by comparing the effects of frontal damage on various memory tests with effects of damage to the hippocampus and midline thalamic nuclei. Recognition and recall of isolated random words or pictures are typically normal in patients with frontal lesions but impaired in patients with hippocampal or diencephalic damage (Mayes, 1988; Milner, Petrides, and Smith, 1985). Recall of categorized lists or of logical stories, however, is impaired in frontal patients, presumably because they cannot take advantage of the organizational structure inherent in that material (Incissa della Rochetta, 1986). Deficits may also occur in free recall if normal performance depends on strategic search or retrieval (Janowsky, Shimamura, Kritchevsky, and Squire, 1989; Wheeler, Stuss, and Tulving, 1995; Moscovitch and Winocur, 1995, 2002).

In contrast with memory for target items or facts that can be elicited by cues directly associated with them, memory for spatiotemporal context often requires strategic search. Consider introspectively the difference in the processes involved in answering these two questions: *Have you seen* Gone with the Wind? *What did you do two weekends ago?* The first elicits an immediate, automatic reply; the second typically initiates a labored, strategic search. As expected, memory for spatiotemporal context, but not for targets, is impaired after frontal lesions, whereas the reverse is true after hippocampal or midline diencephalic lesions.

Memory for temporal order is poor in frontal patients when it is tested by asking patients to judge the relative recency of a pair of items or to arrange a set of items in the order in which they were presented (Milner, Petrides, and Smith, 1985; Shimamura, Janowsky, and Squire, 1990). The deficit also extends to remote memories that were acquired long before the lesion occured. Defective memory for sources of facts they had learned has also been observed in patients with frontal lesions or frontal dysfunction. They erroneously ascribe the factual information to an incorrect source on tests of source recall and source recognition (Schacter, Harbluk, and McLachlan, 1984; Janowsky, Shimamura, and Squire, 1989b). On the other hand, hippocampal or diencephalic damage leads to deficient memory for targets or facts at long delays but not for their temporal order or for sources at delays in which the facts can be remembered. In other words, their memory for temporal order is no more impaired than, and may be superior to, their memory for facts (Milner, Petrides, and Smith, 1985; Shimamura, Janowsky, and Squire, 1990).

Poor memory for spatiotemporal context that results from impaired strategic processes may also underlie the frontal patient's deficits on a variety of other tests, such as delayed alternation, delayed response, and delayed match-to-sample with a small, repeated set of items (Freedman and Oscar-Berman, 1986; Prisko, 1963; Milner, Petrides, and Smith, 1985). On delayed response, after a short delay the subject must choose one of the items that had been designated as the target. On delayed alternation, the designated target alternates on every trial. In delayed match-to-sample, the subject chooses from a small set of items the one that matches a target that was inspected earlier. On all these tests, frontal patients fail not because they cannot remember the target but because they cannot segregate the current trial (keep the spatiotemporal context distinct) from preceding ones.

Impaired performance by frontal patients on self-ordered pointing tests may have a similar cause (Petrides and Milner, 1982). In these tests, subjects are required to point to one of a set of words, line drawings, or designs that appear on a sheet of paper. On

each subsequent trial, new sheets are presented with the same items arranged differently, and the subject is required to point to a different item each time. There are as many trials as there are items. Apart from remembering the items and keeping spatiotemporal context distinct, subjects performing this test need to monitor their responses and use their memory of them to plan future actions. Monitoring and planning are both prototypical frontal functions that are applied to memory and may be impaired by frontal lesions. Another way to interpret these results is to say that the test requires monitoring information that is held in working memory (Petrides, 2000).

Impaired estimation of frequency of occurrence is also associated with frontal lesions (Smith and Milner, 1988). In one test of this association, items are repeated a number of times and the subject's task is to estimate the number of repetitions. It is not clear whether the deficit on this test is a symptom of a general deficit in cognitive estimation that accompanies frontal damage (Shallice and Evans, 1978) or whether it also results from a failure to search memory strategically.

Although the formation and retrieval of new associations are not dependent on the frontal lobes, learning conditional associations is (Petrides and Milner, 1982). The difference between the two tests highlights the distinction between memories elicited directly by cues associated with them, a process that involves the hippocampus, and memories for which additional extra-cue, strategic processes are necessary and involve the frontal lobes. In learning new associations, a single cue such as a light is paired with a unique response such as an arm movement, which it eventually elicits. In conditional associative learning, all cues and potential responses are present in the situation and typically resemble one another. For example, a set of six lights is presented, each of which needs to be associated with one of six movements that the subject has mastered. The cue, one of the lights, does not elicit the response, the designated movement, but only provides the occasion for the subject to select from among potential responses the one that is appropriate for one particular cue, another one for another cue, and so on. That is, the subject must determine which light is associated with which movement. Response selection and monitoring, both strategic frontal functions, are key elements of this task. Patients with frontal lesions have difficulty learning only conditional associations, whereas patients with hippocampal lesions have difficulty forming new associations.

Less consistent effects of frontal lesions are found on other memory tests, such as release from proactive inhibition (PI) and "feeling-of-knowing" judgments.

In release from PI, four different lists of words from the same semantic category are presented, followed by a list from a different category. Recall, which is tested after each list, declines from the first to the fourth list as PI builds up, but recall recovers to baseline levels on the fifth trial. Release from PI occurs at retrieval. It is not surprising, therefore, that deficits in release from PI have been reported in patients with frontal lesions (Moscovitch, 1982); these are most reliable, however, when a severe memory disorder accompanies frontal dysfunction (Freedman and Cermak, 1986; Janowsky, Shimamura, Kritchevsky, and Squire, 1989).

"Feeling of knowing" is an aspect of metamemory, the knowledge about one's own memory. It refers to a person's belief that he or she would know the correct answer to a memory question. In testing the accuracy of feeling-of-knowing judgments, Janowsky, Shimamura, and Squire (1989a) gave subjects a cued recall test for information they had learned earlier. For those items they failed to recall, subjects were asked to rate their feeling of knowing, their likelihood of recognizing the correct answer among a number of alternatives. Because this metamemory test involves goal-directed search and monitoring, it was expected that patients with frontal lesions would perform poorly on it. Although some deficits were found, the impairment, as in release from PI, was most reliable and far-reaching in patients who had severe memory problems in addition to frontal dysfunction (Shimamura, Janowsky, and Squire, 1990).

Defective performance on memory tests sensitive to frontal lesions is noted in people with neurological conditions associated with frontal dysfunction—that is, with signs of impaired frontal functions though there is no evidence of direct frontal damage. Among those are patients with Parkinson's and Huntington's diseases, the neuropathology of which affects basal ganglia structures that are part of the "complex loop" that connects them to the frontal lobes (Brown and Marsden, 1990; Saint-Cyr, Taylor, and Lang, 1988) and that may be needed for maintaining dopamine levels in the prefrontal cortex. Declines in performance on frontal-sensitive tests also occur in the elderly, presumably because their frontal lobes deteriorate with age (Moscovitch and Winocur, 1992), and in patients with schizophrenia, both because of frontal deterioration and impaired dopamine function.

Even normal young adults may show deficits on frontal tests under conditions that deplete cognitive resources. Because frontal functions are strategic—which implies that voluntary, often conscious, control is an integral part of them—they demand substantial cognitive, attentional resources if they are to operate effectively (Moscovitch and Umilta, 1990). In contrast, the operations of the hippocampus can be run off relatively automatically once the appropriate input is received. Experiments reported in the literature suggest that general interference at the time of retrieval affects primarily performance on tests that are sensitive to frontal function, such as word fluency, recall of categorized lists, and list differentiation. A series of experiments designed to test this hypothesis further has confirmed that a sequential, finger-tapping encoding-and-retrieval task interfered with performance on frontal-sensitive tests, such as recall of categorized lists, release from PI, and phonemic fluency (Moscovitch, 1994). Similar divided-attention effects are observed on tests of source, but not item memory (Moscovitch, Fernandes, and Troyer, 2002). To affect memory on nonfrontal tests such as free recall and recognition of lists of random word the interference at retrieval must be material-specific in the sense that the interfering task consists of material that is similar to that of the target, memory task. In such cases, it is believed that the locus of interference is for access to representational systems in posterior neocortex (Moscovitch et al., 2002).

All the memory tests mentioned so far are explicit tests that require conscious recollection of the past for successful performance. In contrast, on implicit tests, memory is inferred from the effects of experience or practice on performance without requiring the individual to refer to the past. Since the frontal lobes are working-with-memory structures, they should be implicated on tests of implicit memory. Indeed, frontal lesions or dysfunctions lead to impaired performance on those tests that are not simply stimulus-driven but require strategic search or application of organized rules or procedures. Thus, patients with frontal lesions or dysfunction have difficulty mastering the Tower of Hanoi, a cognitive puzzle whose solution depends on the application of a sequential, iterative rule (Owen et al., 1990; Shallice, 1982; St. Cyr, Taylor, and Lang, 1988). Frontal patients may also be impaired on other implicit tests, such as learning to read geometrically transformed script and completing word stems after being exposed to target words (Winocur, Moscovitch, and Stuss, 1996; Nyberg, Winocur, and Moscovitch, 1997). The results suggest that the frontal lobes are implicated on implicit tests that have a selection or generative component, but not on tests that are purely perceptually driven (Gabrieli et al., 1999). The extent of frontal involvement on implicit tests is still uncertain. A great deal of work on amnesic patients with hippocampal or diencephalic lesions shows that their performance on a variety of implicit tests appears mostly unscathed, suggesting that these structures are involved only with conscious recollection (Moscovitch, 1982; Moscovitch and Umilta, 1991).

Many of the features of frontal-lobe memory disorders are observable in an especially severe and striking form in confabulating patients with aneurysms or infarcts of the anterior communicating artery. Admittedly, the lesions that typically affect the ventromedial and orbital regions of the frontal lobes also involve other structures in the basal forebrain such as the anterior cingulate, the septum, and the anterior hypothalamus. Nonetheless, the memory symptoms displayed by these patients indicate frontal rather than hippocampal circuit damage. When tested formally, their recognition on tests that do not involve strategic search is relatively well preserved, a result that distinguishes them from amnesic patients with hippocampal damage. However, their ability to search memory and to place events in a proper spatiotemporal context is nearly lost. That loss likely accounts for their tendency to confabulate or make up patently false, often contradictory, and occasionally bizarre or fantastic stories.

For example, one patient who had been in the hospital for months claimed he was still at his office. When asked to account for the beds in his room, he suggested that they were brought in to deal with an epidemic. When such patients confabulate, they do not intentionally lie but inadvertently combine true memories whose spatiotemporal context they have lost. According to Schnider and his collaborators (1996; 2000), such temporal confusion is due to difficulty suppressing information that no longer is relevant and focusing on that which is. It is as if the nonfrontal memory system, in response to situational cues, spews out loosely associated memories in a quasi-ordered fashion. Lacking intact frontal lobes, these patients cannot evaluate this output or impose a sensible organization on it. Their memory deficits, therefore, are not restricted to recently acquired memories but extend to remote, personal memories and even to historical information on events that occurred before they were born (Moscovitch and Melo, 1997). Their memory is intact only for events and activities, such as their job routines, that are stored as self-organized and self-contained schemata that depend little on supervision by the frontal lobes for their operation (Moscovitch, 1989).

Localization Within the Prefrontal Cortex: Evidence from Lesions and Neuroimaging

Though we have paid little attention so far to localization within the frontal lobes, we do not wish to leave the reader with the impression that the prefrontal cortex is a homogeneous structure; on the contrary, it is a heterogeneous structure consisting of a number of distinct areas with unique projections to and from other brain regions, and with different phylogenetic and ontogenetic histories (Pandya and Barnes, 1986; Petrides and Pandya, 1994). Two large subdivisions of the prefrontal cortex, the orbital and dorsolateral regions, have different functions (Milner, Petrides, and Smith, 1985), one more emotional and motivational and the other more cognitive. Structural and functional neuroimaging has allowed the discernment of specialized functions of even smaller regions within these subdivisions (Goldman-Rakic, 1987, 2002; Petrides, 2000, 2002). Indeed, there is now evidence for regional specialization for many of the functions that contribute to performance on the various tests of frontal function.

Brodmann areas 6 and 8 (premotor cortex) are implicated in response selection and inhibition, a key feature of conditional associative learning, and retrieval from remote memory (Moscovitch and Winocur, 2002). Areas 46/9 (dorsolateral prefrontal cortex) is for manipulating and operating on information held in working memory or retrieved from long-term memory, as on tests of self-ordered pointing, where monitoring is a crucial component. This region is also important for initiating effective retrieval strategies and monitoring the outcome of implementing them (i.e. retrieval output). The ventrolateral prefrontal cortex, area 47, is important for specifying the cues needed for retrieval (Fletcher and Hensen, 2001). Perhaps it is for this reason that the extent of activation of this area at encoding can predict subsequent memory performance (Wagner et al., 1998) and therefore plays a role in simple recognition (Petrides, 2000). This region also comes into play on tests of conceptual priming, with less activation for material that has been primed (Schacter and Buckner, 1998). The ventromedial prefrontal cortex is important for inhibiting or preventing the expression or behavioral impact of activated memories that are anomalous within a given context. The region is a context-dependent criterion-setting device that determines which memories are relevant—the felt rightness of a memory. The function of area 10 in the frontal pole is much debated, with some investigators believing that it is crucial for allowing one to experience memories as part of oneself and tying them inextricably to conscious, coherent recollection of one's past (Tulving, 2002). Others, however, believe that the role of area 10 is to maintain elaborate retrieval goals and strategies (Fletcher and Hensen, 2001). Still others think it may operate in concert with the verntromedial cortex to endorse memories that are appropriate within a given context. The possible sequential interaction of the regions with each other is displayed in Figure 1.

In addition to regional specificity, there is also lateralization of function within the frontal lobes:

Some regions show material specificity with greater left-hemisphere involvement for verbal material and right-hemisphere involvement for spatial material (Milner, Petrides, and Smith., 1985; Petrides, 2000; Kelley et al., 1998). Over and above the material specificity, Tulving and his colleagues (1994) noted a hemispheric encoding/retrieval asymmetry (HERA) in PET studies, with the greater frontal activation on the left during encoding and on the right during retrieval. This pattern has since been observed in numerous functional neuroimaging studies using different techniques (Cabeza and Nyberg, 2000); it cuts across material type in some regions of prefrontal cortex. The reason for this asymmetry is unknown; nor is it clear whether such asymmetries are needed for successful encoding and retrieval. Researchers have debated which aspects of retrieval are associated with right frontal activation: retrieval mode (the establishment of a memory "set" and perhaps setting memory goals and strategies), monitoring (the determination of whether a target item was studied), retrieval success (the accuracy of recall and recognition of items), retrieval task or domain (memory for source or for items), and retrieval effort (how difficult the retrieval task is) (Buckner and Wheeler, 2001; Holding and Rugg, 2000). It seems that as memory retrieval requires more effort, either because the task is more difficult or reflective (Johnson, 2000) or because cognitive resources are limited (as in aging, Cabeza, 2001), both frontal regions are recruited, and the asymmetry is diminished.

Conclusion

Although there has been some progress in identifying the frontal components implicated in encoding and retrieval and isolating them functionally and anatomically, discrepancies and controversies persist in efforts to understand how the different regions interact with one another to yield organized, seamless performance. Future research should also help in deciding between two opposing views of frontal function that have dominated recent theories. One view holds that a common function underlies the operation of all regions in the frontal lobes but that the function expresses itself in diverse ways determined by each region's unique anatomical connections. The other view does not assume a functional link among various regions but argues for true functional independence among them along domain specific lines (Moscovitch and Umlita, 1990; Goldman Rakic, 2002; Petrides, 2002; Stuss and Knight, 2002). The view that prevails will determine our conception of the mechanisms underlying memory, consciousness, and volitional behavior.

See also: EPISODIC MEMORY; METACOGNITION ABOUT MEMORY; WORKING MEMORY: ANIMALS; WORKING MEMORY: HUMANS

Bibliography

Baddeley, A. D. (1986). *Working memory.* Oxford: Oxford University Press.

Brown, R. G., and Marden, C. D. (1990). Cognitive function in Parkinson's disease: From description to theory. *Trends in Neurosciences 13,* 21–29.

Buckner, R. L. and Wheeler, M. E. (2001). The cognitive neuroscience of remembering. *Nature Reviews: Neuroscience 2,* 624–634.

Cabeza, R., Mangels, J., Nyberg, L., Habib, R., Houle, S., McIntosh, A. R. et al. (1997). Brain regions differentially involved in remembering what and when: a PET study. *Neuron, 19,* 863–870.

Cabeza, R., and Nyberg, L. (2000). Imaging cognition II: an empirical review of 275 PET and fMRI studies. *Journal of Cognitive Neuroscience 12,* 1–47.

DeLuca, J. (2000) A cognitive neuroscience perspective on confabulation. *Neuro-psychoanalysis 2,* 119–132.

Fletcher, P. C., and Henson, R. N. A. (2001). Frontal lobes and human memory. Insights from functional neuroimaging. *Brain 124,* 849–881.

Freedman, M., and Cermak, L. S. (1986). Semantic encoding deficits in frontal lobe disease and amnesia. *Brain and Cognition 5,* 108–114.

Freedman, M., and Oscar–Berman, M. (1986). Bilateral frontal lobe disease and selective delayed response deficits in humans. *Behavioral Neuroscience 100,* 337–342.

Gabrieli, J. D. E., Vaidya, C. J., Stone, M., Francis, W. S., Thompson-Schill, S. L., Fleischman, D. A., Tinklenberg, J. R., Yesavage, J. A., and Wilson, R. S. (1999). Convergent behavioral and neuropsychological evidence for a distinction between identification and production forms of repetition priming. *Journal of Experimental Psychology: General 128,* 479–498.

Goldman–Rakic, P. S. (1987). Circuitry of primate prefrontal cortex and regulation of behavior by representational memory. In F. Plum, ed., *Handbook of physiology: The nervous system,* Vol. 5. Bethesda, MD: American Physiological Society.

—— (2002). The prefrontal cortex: from molecule to mind. In D. T. Stuss and R. T. Knight, eds, *Principles of frontal lobe function.* New York: Oxford University Press.

Incissa della Rochetta, A. I. (1986). Classification and recall of pictures after unilateral frontal or temporal lobectomy. *Cortex 22,* 189–211.

Janowsky, J. S., Shimamura, A. P., Kritchevsky, M., and Squire, L. R. (1989). Cognitive impairment following frontal lobe damage and its relevance to human amnesia. *Behavioral Neuroscience 103,* 548–560.

Janowsky, J. S., Shimamura, A. P., and Squire, L. R. (1989a). Memory and metamemory: Comparison between patients with frontal lobe lesions and amnesic patients. *Psychobiology 17,* 3–11.

—— (1989b). Source memory impairment in patients with frontal lobe lesions. *Neuropsychologia 27,* 1,043–1,056.

Kelley, W. M. et al. (1998) Hemispheric specialization in human dorsal frontal cortex and medial temporal lobe for verbal and nonverbal encoding. *Neuron 20,* 927-936.

Kolb, B., and Whishaw, I. Q. (1990). *Fundamentals of human neuropsychology,* 3rd edition. New York: Freeman.

Kopelman, M. D. (1999). Varieties of false memory. *Cognitive Neuropsychology 16,* 197–214.

Luria, A. R. (1980). *Higher cortical functions in man.* New York: Basic Books.

Mayes, A. R. (1988). *Human organic memory disorders.* Cambridge, UK: Cambridge University Press.

Milner, B. (1966). Amnesia following operation on the temporal lobe. In C. W. M. Whitty and O. L. Zangwill, eds., *Amnesia.* London: Butterworth.

Milner, B., Petrides, M., and Smith, M. L. (1985). Frontal lobes and the temporal organization of memory. *Human Neurobiology 4,* 137–142.

Moscovitch, M. (1982). Multiple dissociations of function in amnesia. In L. S. Cermak, ed., *Human memory and amnesia.* Hillsdale, NJ: Erlbaum.

——— (1989). Confabulation and the frontal system: Strategic versus associative retrieval in neuropsychological theories of memory. In H. L. Roediger and F. I. M. Craik, eds., *Varieties of memory and consciousness: Essays in honor of Endel Tulving.* Hillsdale, NJ: Erlbaum.

——— (1994). Interference at retrieval from long-term memory: The influence of frontal and temporal lobes. *Neuropsychology 4,* 525–534.

Moscovitch, M., Fernandes, M., and Troyer, A. (2002). Working-with-memory and Cognitive Resources: A component-process account of divided attention and memory. In M. Naveh-Benjamin, M. Moscovitch, and H. L. Roediger, eds., *Essays in Honour of Fergus I. M. Craik.* New York: Psychology Press.

Moscovitch, M., and Melo, B. (1997). Strategic retrieval and the frontal lobes: Evidence from confabulation and amnesia. *Neuropsychologia 35,* 1,017–1,034.

Moscovitch, M., and Umilta, C. (1990). Modularity and neuropsychology: Implications for the organization of attention and memory in normal and brain-damaged people. In M. E. Schwartz, ed., *Modular processes in dementia.* Cambridge, MA: MIT/Bradford.

——— (1991). Conscious and nonconscious aspects of memory: A neuropsychological framework of modules and central systems. In H. J. Weingartner and R. G. Lister. eds., *Perspectives in cognitive neuroscience.* Oxford: Oxford University Press.

Moscovitch, M., and Winocur, G. (1992). The neuropsychology of memory in the elderly: The hippocampus and frontal lobes. In T. Salthouse and F. I. M. Craik, eds., *The handbook of cognition and aging.* New York: Academic Press.

——— (1995). Frontal lobes, memory and aging. In J. Grafman and K. Holyoak, eds., Structure and function of human prefrontal cortex. *Annals of the New York Academy of Sciences 769,* 119–150.

——— (2002). The frontal lobes ad working with memory. In D. T. Stuss and R. T. Knight, eds., *Principles of frontal lobe function.* New York: Oxford University Press.

Nolde, S. F., Johnson, M. K., and Raye, C. L. (1998). The role of prefrontal cortex during tests of episodic retrieval. *Trends in Cognitive Science 2,* 399–406.

Nyberg, L., Winocur, G., and Moscovitch, M. (1997) Correlation between frontal-lobe functions and explicit and implicit stem completion in health elderly. *Neuropsychologia 11,* 70–76.

Owen, A. M., Downes, J. J., Sahakian, B. J., Polkeg, C. E., and Robbins, T. W. (1990). Planning and spatial working memory following frontal lobe lesions in man. *Neuropsychologia 28,* 1,021–1,034.

Pandya, D., and Barnes, C. I. (1986). Architecture and connections of the frontal lobes. In E. Perleman, ed., *The frontal lobes revisited.* New York: IRBN Press.

Petrides, M. (1989). Frontal lobes and memory. In F. Boller and J. Grafman, eds., *Handbook of neuropsychology,* Vol. 3. Amsterdam: Elsevier.

——— (2000). The role of the mid-dorsolateral prefrontal cortex in working memory. *Experimental Brain Research 133,* 44–54.

Petrides, M., and Milner, B. (1982). Deficits on subject-ordered tasks after frontal and temporal-lobe lesions in man. *Neuropsychologia 20,* 249–262.

Petrides, M., and Pandya, D. (2002). Association pathways of the prefrontal cortex and functional observations. In D. T. Stuss and R. T. Knight, eds., *Principles of frontal lobe function.* New York: Oxford University Press.

Rugg, M. D. and Wilding,. L. (2000) Retrieval processing and episodic memory. *Trends in Cognitive Science 4,* 108–115.

Saint-Cyr, J. A., Taylor, A., and Lang, A. (1988). Procedural learning and neostriatal dysfunction in man. *Brain 111,* 941–959.

Schacter, D. L., Harbluk, J. L., and McLachlan, D. R. (1984). Retrieval without recollection: An experimental analysis of source amnesia. *Journal of Verbal Learning and Verbal Behavior 23,* 593–611.

Schnider, A., and Ptak, R. (1999). Spontaneous confabulators fail to suppress currently irrelevant memory traces. *Nature Neuroscience,* 677–681.

Schnider, A., von Daniken, C., Gutbrod, K. (1996). The mechanisms of spontaneous and provoked confabulations. *Brain 119,* 1,365–1,375.

Shallice, T. (1982). Specific impairments of planning. *Philosophical Transactions of the Royal Society of London B298,* 199–209.

Shallice, T., and Evans, M. D. (1978). The involvement of the frontal lobes in cognitive estimation. *Cortex 14,* 294–303.

Shimamura, A. P., Janowsky, J. S., and Squire, L. R. (1990). Memory for temporal order in patients with frontal lobe lesions and patients with amnesia. *Neuropsychologia 28,* 803–813.

Smith, M. L., and Milner, B. (1988). Estimation of frequency of occurrence of abstract designs after frontal or temporal lobectomy. *Neuropsychologia 26,* 297–306.

Stuss, D. T., and Benson, D. F. (1986). *The frontal lobes.* New York: Raven Press.

Stuss, D. T., and Knight, R. T., eds. (2002) *Principles of frontal lobe function.* New York: Oxford University Press.

Teuber, H.-L., (1964). The riddle of frontal lobe function in man. In J. M. Warren and K. Akert, eds., *The frontal granular cortex and behavior.* New York: McGraw-Hill.

Tulving, E., Kapur, S., Craik, F. I. M., Moscovitch, M., and Houle, S. (1994). Hemispheric encoding/retrieval asymmetry in episodic: Positron emission tomography findings. *Proceedings of the National Academy of Sciences of the United States of America 91,* 2,016–2,020.

Wagner, A. D., Schacter, D. L., Rotte, M., Koutstaal, W., Maril, A., Dale, A. M., Rosen, B. R., and Buckner, R. L. (1998). Building memories: Remembering and forgetting of verbal experiences as predicted by brain activity. *Science 281,* 1,188–1,191.

Wheeler, M. A., Stuss, D. T., and Tulving, E. (1995). Frontal lobe damage produces episodic memory impairment. *Journal of the International Neuropsychological Society 1,* 525–536.

Winocur, G., Moscovitch, M., and Stuss, D. T. (1996) A neuropsychological investigation of explicit and implicit memory in institutionalized and community-dwelling old people. *Neuropsychology 10,* 57–65.

Morris Moscovitch
Gordon Winocur

FUGUE STATE

See: AMNESIA, FUNCTIONAL

G

GENERALIZATION

See: DISCRIMINATION AND GENERALIZATION

GENES AND MEMORY

See: APLYSIA: MOLECULAR BASIS OF LONG-TERM
SENSITIZATION; GENETIC SUBSTRATES OF
MEMORY; PROTEIN SYNTHESIS IN LONG-
TERM MEMORY IN VERTEBRATES

GENETIC SUBSTRATES OF MEMORY

*[The understanding of biological substrates of learning and
memory has been greatly facilitated by the application of the
techniques of molecular biology and genetics. Studies done
in the 1960s argued that longer-term memory processes required protein synthesis (i.e., required certain genes to increase or alter their expression of proteins). Technology developed in the 1990s has made it possible to "knock out" or
"knock in" specific genes experimentally, as well as to make
use of naturally occurring mutants. This work has involved
both invertebrates (e.g., the fruit fly and C. elegans) and
vertebrates, mostly mice. Learning is a particularly interesting aspect of behavior to manipulate genetically since memory involves changes in behavior as a result of experiences in
the environment. As with language in humans, the ability
to learn and the mechanisms of memory storage are largely
determined genetically, but what is learned depends almost
entirely on experience.*

The first article in this series focuses on the **AMYGDALA**
and fear conditioning (see NEURAL SUBSTRATES OF
CLASSICAL CONDITIONING: FEAR CONDITIONING,
FREEZING). *Induction of fear conditioning alters the expression of immediate early genes in the amygdala, and
blocking gene expression in the amygdala prevents long-
term fear memory. Using viral vector gene-transfer technology, increasing the expression of the transcriptional activator CREB (Cyclic AMP Response Element Binding) in the
amygdala enhances fear memory, whereas decreasing CREB
expression in the amygdala impairs fear memory.*

*Genetic approaches have provided much new informa-
tion concerning the* **CEREBELLAR** *substrates of classical eyeblink condition (see* NEURAL SUBSTRATES OF CLASSICAL
CONDITIONING: DISCRETE BEHAVIORAL RESPONSES).
*The Purkinje cell degeneration (pcd) mutant mouse loses all
Purkinje neurons in the cerebellar cortex within four weeks
after birth. These animals are able to learn eyeblink conditioning, but the learning is slower and to a lower degree
than normal, and it slows extinction. Lesions of the interpositus nucleus in the pcd mouse completely prevent learning.
So both cerebellar cortex and interpositus are involved but
the basic association seems to be formed in the interpositus.
Mutant and knock-out mice that are deficient in cerebellar
long-term depression (LTD) are also much impaired in
learning and in adaptive timing of the CR, indicating an
important modulatory role of the cerebellar cortex.*

The third article, on the **HIPPOCAMPUS**, *is written by
a pioneer in this new field, Alcino Silva. The first studies to
use genetics to manipulate plasticity and learning in mammals (mice) targeted kinases (calcium-calmodulin dependent
kinase II) and the tyrosine kinase Fyn. These studies showed
that disruption of hippocampal-synaptic plasticity (i.e., long-
term potentiation, LTP) resulted in hippocampal-dependent*

learning deficits. Recent approaches involve targeted, selective, temporally controlled expression of normal or altered genes, an extraordinarily promising technology.]

AMYGDALA

Scientists believe that the amygdala plays a critical role in the ability to learn and remember certain types of information. Converging evidence from studies using humans as well as a variety of laboratory species support the idea that the amygdala, together with a network of closely interconnected brain regions, allows people to store long-term memories for events that are emotionally important and to respond appropriately to stimuli in the environment that signal threat. The ability to store long-term memories of this type is likely due to experience-dependent changes in gene expression within amygdala neurons. Many scientists and clinicians believe that understanding the functions of the amygdala may be the key to the treatment and prevention of human anxiety disorders and other psychiatric problems.

Scientific knowledge about how the amygdala works comes largely from the development and widespread use of Pavlovian fear-conditioning with rodents as a model system throughout the late 1980s and 1990s. In a typical fear-conditioning experiment, a rat is placed in a distinctive observation chamber where a simple signal such as a flashing light or a tone (the conditional stimulus, or CS) is repeatedly activated prior to delivery of a mild electric shock to the animal's feet. The rat will learn that the signal predicts shock and will display species-appropriate fear behaviors when presented with the CS alone after training. The animal will also learn to fear the apparatus, or context, in which the training took place. This relatively simple form of learning is rapidly acquired, easy to observe in the laboratory, retained indefinitely, and completely disrupted in animals with significant damage to the amygdala (Davis, 2000; LeDoux, 2000; Maren, 2001).

Fear conditioning experiments have shown that discrete anatomical regions within the amygdala may play selective roles in the learning process. The lateral nucleus and closely related cell groups within the basolateral region of the amygdala receive direct and indirect synaptic input from sensory systems that detect and process stimuli in the animal's environment. On the other hand, the central nucleus of the amygdala appears to play a key role in the expression of behavioral and physiological reactions to fear-provoking stimuli through its extensive connections with the brain stem. The amygdala is important for learning about new danger signals in the environment as well as for producing the appropriate behav-

ioral reactions to those signals (Helmstetter and Bellgowan, 1994). Changes in gene expression within amygdala neurons may accompany both learning and response performance in fear conditioning.

Learning Can Alter Gene Expression in the Amygdala

A number of studies have been able to show that exposure to the training procedures used in Pavlovian fear conditioning will selectively alter the expression of messenger RNA (mRNA) or protein in the amygdala. Immediate early genes (IEGs) tend to be minimally expressed in quiescent cells but are often rapidly and dramatically activated when cells are stimulated by synaptic inputs. Many IEGs encode transcription factors that ultimately regulate other gene products expressed later after stimulation. In one of the first studies of gene expression during fear conditioning, Serge Campeau and colleagues (1991) showed that the amount of mRNA coding *c-fos* in the amygdala was elevated by exposing rats either to foot shock itself, or to an environment that had been previously paired with foot shock. Therefore, the time-dependent storage of new memory following the shock experience as well as the neuronal activity in the amygdala provoked by exposure to a fear-producing stimulus may increase production of FOS protein. Subsequent experiments have continued to shed light on this and related phenomena. Several different aspects of the fear conditioning procedure appear to activate *c-fos* transcription and the level of expression of FOS protein correlates with how well animals learn during fear conditioning (Radulovic, Kammermeir, and Spiess, 1998).

J. B. Rosen and colleagues (1998) reported that while mRNA for *c-fos* was elevated in the amygdala in animals that learned fear conditioning as well as in control subjects that did not learn, another IEG, "early growth response gene 1" (*egr*-1), showed a pattern of message expression in the lateral nucleus of the amygdala that was specific to learning. *Egr*-1 mRNA is selectively expressed in the amygdala between fifteen and thirty minutes after learning and only in the region of the amygdala likely to undergo critical synaptic plasticity during the formation of memory. Importantly, simple retrieval of fear memory and performance of fear responses do not alter *egr*-1 expression supporting the idea that this IEG, unlike *c-fos*, may play a selective role in the formation of long-term memory (Mackani and Rosen, 2000).

Alterations in gene expression in the amygdala are not restricted to IEGs nor are they solely related to the initial storage of information. Cyclic AMP responsive-element binding protein (CREB) is a tran-

Figure 1

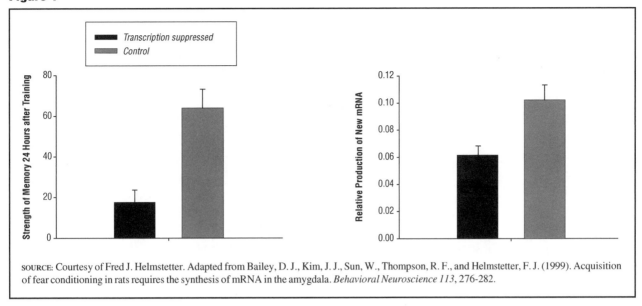

SOURCE: Courtesy of Fred J. Helmstetter. Adapted from Bailey, D. J., Kim, J. J., Sun, W., Thompson, R. F., and Helmstetter, F. J. (1999). Acquisition of fear conditioning in rats requires the synthesis of mRNA in the amygdala. *Behavioral Neuroscience 113*, 276-282.

Rats treated with a drug that reduces the formation of new mRNA in the amygdala fail to remember their experiences during fear conditioning.

scription factor that plays a key role in memory formation in a number of species (Silva, Kogan, Frankland, and Kida, 1998). In mice exposed to a simple fear-conditioning protocol, levels of phosphorylated CREB (pCREB) in the amygdala were elevated in trained animals relative to controls during the memory consolidation period after conditioning (Stancui, Radulovic, and Speiss, 2001). Increased phosphorylation and thus activity of CREB is also seen in the amygdala when rats retrieve memories learned in fear conditioning that have already been stored (Hall, Thomas, and Everitt, 2001). Retrieval and/or emotional responding also causes cells in the central nucleus to increase production of mRNA for the neuropeptide enkephalin (Petrovich, Scicli, Thompson, and Swanson, 2000).

Manipulating Gene Expression in the Amygdala Can Affect Learning

Demonstrating that cells in the amygdala express a different quantity or a unique pattern of gene products while animals are learning is an important step toward understanding the mechanisms of long-term memory. However, one can see that just because a particular protein or mRNA appears to change when subjects learn, it does not necessarily follow that this gene product is essential for formation of the memory. In order to know if something is required for memory formation, one must be able to manipulate it directly.

D. J. Bailey and colleagues (1999) took a first step in this direction by asking a more general question. They tested whether or not the general ability of cells in the amygdala to synthesize new mRNA is critical for the formation of long-term memory in fear conditioning. Actinomycin-D, a drug that selectivity prevents cells from copying information from DNA in the nucleus onto new mRNA molecules (transcription), was microinjected into the amygdala of rats prior to training with foot shock. Twenty-four hours after training the animals were returned to the laboratory and tested for memory of what was learned the day before. The results of this experiment are summarized in Figure 1. Suppressing transcription of new mRNA in the amygdala greatly disrupted the rats' ability to remember what happened during training. This experiment was one of the first direct sources of evidence that mRNA synthesis, and by implication the synthesis of new protein, is required in the amygdala during the acquisition of fear learning.

Several other studies have supported the idea that the synthesis of new proteins in the amygdala is critical for memory formation. The molecular events occurring during the period directly after training when long-term memories are consolidated are of particular interest. Blocking the translation of mRNA into new protein in the amygdala during this post-training period prevents long-term retention of fear conditioning, as does selective disruption of the activity of the enzyme protein kinase A (PKA) (Schafe et al., 2000). In taste-aversion learning, where animals associate a specific taste with illness, pretraining amygdala injections of antisense oligodeoxynucleotides (ODNs) that selectively prevent the translation of *c-fos* mRNA into protein prevent the formation of taste-aversion memory (Lamprecht and Dudai, 1996).

Studies in which mRNA transcription or protein translation is globally affected within amygdala neurons are somewhat limited given their lack of specificity. Suppression of specific proteins with antisense ODNs has several advantages but also suffers from important limitations. One of the most exciting recent technical advances in this area involves the use of viral-vector gene-transfer technology to selectively introduce and promote the expression of target gene products within restricted brain regions. For example, S. A. Josselyn and colleagues (2001) were able to cause the selective overexpression of CREB in rat amygdala neurons prior to training in fear conditioning. Rats that had significantly more CREB being expressed actually showed better memory than control animals. This type of evidence, when coupled with the variety of experiments showing that down regulation of CREB impairs memory, makes a very convincing case for the role of this particular transcription factor in memory formation.

Conclusion

Neuroscientists are developing a clear picture of how the amygdala contributes to memory at the circuit and neural systems level. Comparatively little is known about the molecular events taking place within amygdala neurons as an organism learns. Several gene products have been identified that undergo changes in expression that appear to be related to learning. In some cases, direct manipulation of these proteins can have an effect on the formation of memory. As interest in this area increases and the technology available to scientists improves, new genes that are involved in amygdala-dependent memory phenomena will continue to be described.

See also: EMOTION, MOOD, AND MEMORY; GENETIC SUBSTRATES OF MEMORY: CEREBELLUM; GENETIC SUBSTRATES OF MEMORY: HIPPOCAMPUS; GUIDE TO THE ANATOMY OF THE BRAIN: AMYGDALA; HORMONES AND MEMORY; LONG-TERM POTENTIATION: AMYGDALA; NEURAL SUBSTRATES OF CLASSICAL CONDITIONING: FEAR CONDITIONING, FREEZING; NEURAL SUBSTRATES OF CLASSICAL CONDITIONING: FEAR-POTENTIATED STARTLE; NEURAL SUBSTRATES OF EMOTIONAL MEMORY; PROTEIN SYNTHESIS IN LONG-TERM MEMORY IN VERTEBRATES; TASTE AVERSION AND PREFERENCE LEARNING IN ANIMALS

Bibliography

Bailey, D. J., Kim, J. J., Sun, W., Thompson, R. F., and Helmstetter, F. J. (1999). Acquisition of fear conditioning in rats requires the synthesis of mRNA in the amygdala. *Behavioral Neuroscience 113*, 276–282.

Campeau, S., Hayward, D., Hope, B. T., Rosen, J. B., Nestler, E. J., and Davis, M. (1991). Induction of the *c-fos* proto-oncogene in rat amygdala during unconditioned and conditioned fear. *Brain Research 565*, 349–352.

Davis, M. (2000). The role of the amygdala in conditioned and unconditioned fear and anxiety. In J. P. Aggleton, ed., *The amygdala: A functional analysis*. New York: Oxford University Press.

Hall, J., Thomas, K. L., and Everitt, B. J. (2001). Fear memory retrieval induces CREB phosphorylation and Fos expression within the amygdala. *European Journal of Neuroscience 13* (7), 1,453–1,458.

Helmstetter, F. J., and Bellgowan, P. S. (1994). Effects of muscimol applied to the basolateral amygdala on acquisition and expression of contextual fear conditioning in rats. *Behavioral Neuroscience 108*, 1,005–1,009.

Josselyn, S. A., Shi, C., Carlezon, W. A., Neve, R. L., Nestler, E. J., and Davis, M. (2001). Long-term memory is facilitated by cAMP response element-binding protein overexpression in the amygdala. *Journal of Neuroscience 21*, 2,404–2,412.

Lamprecht, R., and Dudai, Y. (1996). Transient expression of *c-fos* in rat amygdala during training is required for encoding conditioned taste aversion memory. *Learning and Memory 3*, 31–41.

LeDoux, J. E. (2000). Emotion circuits in the brain. *Annual Review of Neuroscience 23*, 155–184.

Malkani, S., and Rosen, J. B. (2000). Specific induction of early growth response gene 1 in the lateral nucleus of the amygdala following contextual fear conditioning in rats. *Neuroscience 97*, 693–702.

Maren, S. (2001). Neurobiology of Pavlovian fear conditioning. *Annual Review of Neuroscience 24*, 897–931.

Petrovich, G. D, Scicli, A. P., Thompson, R. F., and Swanson, L. W. (2000). Associative fear conditioning of enkephalin mRNA levels in central amygdalar neurons. *Behavioral Neuroscience 114*, 681–686.

Radulovic, J., Kammermeier, J., and Spiess, J. (1998). Relationship between fos production and classical fear conditioning: Effects of novelty, latent inhibition, and unconditioned stimulus preexposure. *Journal of Neuroscience 18*, 7,452–7,461.

Rosen, J. B., Fanselow, M. S., Young, S. L., Sitcoske, M., and Maren, S. (1998). Immediate-early gene expression in the amygdala following footshock stress and contextual fear conditioning. *Brain Research 796*, 132–142.

Schafe, G. E., Atkins, C. M., Swank, M. W., Bauer, E. P., Sweatt, J. D., and LeDoux, J. E. (2000). Activation of ERK/MAP kinase in the amygdala is required for memory consolidation of Pavlovian fear conditioning. *Journal of Neuroscience 20* (21), 8,177–8,187.

Silva, A. J., Kogan, J. H., Frankland, P. W., and Kida, S. (1998). CREB and memory. *Annual Review of Neuroscience 21*, 127–148.

Stanciu, M., Radulovic, J., and Spiess, J. (2001). Phosphorylated cAMP response element binding protein in the mouse brain after fear conditioning: relationship to Fos production. *Molecular Brain Research 94*, 15–24.

Fred J. Helmstetter

CEREBELLUM

The cerebellum has been traditionally regarded as a part of the motor system, mainly because of clinical and experimental observations that humans and animals with cerebellar damage are impaired in coordinated movement. Early theoretical consideration indicated that the unique and stereotyped cellular organization of the cerebellar cortex could also function as a learning machine (Albus, 1971; Marr, 1969). The cerebellar-learning hypotheses inspired broad experimental investigations. In 1982, Masao Ito and colleagues discovered that conjoint activation of the mossy fiber and climbing fiber led to long-lasting depression of the Purkinje-cell responses to mossy fiber activation, known as cerebellar long-term depression (LTD). Behavioral studies also indicate that the cerebellum is involved in several forms of motor learning, including classical eyeblink conditioning and adaptation of vestibulo-ocular reflex. In the 1990s, considerable progress was made in understanding the cellular and molecular mechanisms underlying cerebellum-dependent learning and memory. A number of spontaneous mouse mutants with relatively specific cerebellar deficits proved useful in dissecting the cerebellar circuitry involved in learning. Studies of gene knockout mice provided much insight into the molecular and cellular basis of learning and memory.

Classical Eyeblink Conditioning

Classical eyeblink conditioning is a form of motor learning, in which animals learn to associate an innocuous stimulus to a noxious one and to respond adaptively. For example, a naive animal will blink to a mild eyelid electrical shock but not to a brief tone. If the tone (serving as a conditioned stimulus, CS) is repeatedly paired with the eyelid shock (serving as an unconditioned stimulus, US), the animal will gradually learn to respond by eye blink to the tone. Richard F. Thompson and colleagues, among others, have characterized the brain circuitry involved in this learning. In essence, conditioned stimulus information is conveyed through mossy fibers, and unconditioned stimulus information is conveyed through climbing fibers. These converge in the cerebellum, where learning occurs and memory is stored (Thompson et al., 1996).

Cerebellar Cortex

Both the cerebellar cortex and the deep nuclei receive mossy fiber and climbing fiber projections and therefore are potentially capable of supporting learning and memory of the conditioned eyeblink response. The relative importance of the cortex and the deep nuclei in classical eyeblink conditioning is unclear, partly because it is virtually impossible to lesion the entire cerebellar cortex without damaging the deep nuclei. Lu Chen and colleagues (1996) examined classical eyeblink conditioning in Purkinje-cell degeneration (*pcd*) mutant mice to dissect the components of the cerebellar circuitry that are crucial for learning. These *pcd* mutant mice are born with Purkinje cells, but gradually lose all of them during the first four weeks of postnatal development. Other neural degenerations occur much later, allowing a time window to examine behavioral consequences associated with the loss of Purkinje cells. Because the Purkinje cells are the only output neurons in the cerebellar cortex, *pcd* mice are functionally equivalent to animals with complete cortical lesions. Classical delay (i.e., the US follows and overlays with the CS) eyeblink conditioning was impaired in the *pcd* mice in three aspects: the learning was slower; the maximal level of learning was lower; and the learned responses occurred earlier and were hence maladaptive. The low level of residual learning in *pcd* mice was completely abolished by lesions of the cerebellar deep nuclei, indicating the learned eyeblink response is stored in both the cerebellar cortex and the deep nuclei (Chen, Bao, and Thomson, 1999).

The Conditioned-Stimulus Pathway

The *stargazer* is another mutant with deficient cerebellar cortical circuit. The gene coding for stargazin, a protein that targets a-amino-3-hydroxy-5-methylisoxazoleproprionic acid (AMPA) receptors to their synaptic locations, is truncated in this mutant. The mutation results in a loss of AMPA receptors at the cerebellar mossy fiber–granule cell synapses, thereby disrupting the conditioned-stimulus pathway to the cerebellar cortex (Chen et al., 2000). This AMPA receptor defect is observed only in the cerebellar granule cells, possibly because in other neurons the loss of stargazing is compensated for by expression of functionally similar proteins. These stargazer mutant mice were impaired in classical eyeblink conditioning in similar ways to the *pcd* mutant mice, showing slower and reduced learning and disrupted response timing (Qiao et al., 1998). Further, the mutant mice performed normally in classical fear conditioning with a tone CS and a foot-shock US, a task that does not involve the cerebellum.

The Unconditioned-Stimulus Pathway

In early stages of rodent postnatal development, each Purkinje cell is innervated by several climbing fibers. By the end of third postnatal week, all but one of the climbing fibers are eliminated. In some mutants, a large portion of their Purkinje cells remain innervated by more than one climbing fiber even in adulthood. These mutants provide useful tools to study roles of climbing fibers as the US pathway in eyeblink conditioning.

For example, in the adult mutant mice deficient in the γ isoform of protein kinase C (PKCγ), 30 percent of the Purkinje cells are innervated by multiple climbing fibers. Other cerebellar physiological properties examined are all normal in this mutant. Multiple climbing fiber innervation presumably enhances US input (i.e., the teaching signal) to the cortex. In agreement with this view, PKCγ mutant mice showed facilitated eyeblink learning (Chen et al., 1995). Whereas wild-type mice attained maximal level of learning in five days, the mutant mice reached the same level in only two days. In addition, the learned eyeblink responses in the PKCγ mutant mice were more resistant to extinction by presentations of CS alone.

Cerebellar Long-Term Depression

Conjoint activation of the mossy parallel fiber and the climbing fiber induces long-term depression of the parallel fiber–Purkinje cell synaptic transmission, which is considered a cellular mechanism for some forms of motor learning such as classical eyeblink conditioning. Cerebellar LTD probably reduces Purkinje-cell responses, resulting in increased activity in the deep cerebellar nuclei, which may code for the learned responses. Testing the role of cerebellar LTD in motor learning had been hindered by the lack of pharmacological agents that specifically block cerebellar LTD and by the difficulty in applying the agents to the entire cerebellar cortex. The advent of modern molecular biology made it possible to completely remove specific proteins from a mouse by deleting the corresponding genes from the mouse genome. Using this powerful technique, a number of gene knockout mice with deficient cerebellar LTD were generated, including the mice lacking mGluR1 (type 1 metabotropic glutamate receptor), GFAP (glial fibrillary acidic protein), GluRδ2 (glutamate receptor δ2 subunit) or PLCβ4 (phospholipase C β4 isoform). Behavioral examinations indicated that they were all impaired in classical eyeblink conditioning (Aiba et al., 1994; Kishimoto et al., 2001; Miyata et al., 2001; Shibuki et al., 1996).

Mutation of a gene may have widespread effects in the brain, making any results difficult to interpret. In that respect, results obtained in GluRδ2 knockout mice are particularly informative, because GluRδ2 is expressed only in the dendritic spines of the Purkinje cells. Impairments in both cerebellar LTD and eyeblink learning suggest that cerebellar LTD is involved in learning conditioned eyeblink responses.

Vestibulo-Ocular Reflex Adaptation

Vestibulo-ocular reflex (VOR) adaptation is another form of motor learning that depends on an intact cerebellum. An animal normally moves its eyes opposite in direction to its head turn to keep visual images steady on the retina. This reflex is guided by vestibular inputs (hence called vestibulo-ocular reflex) and is present even in complete darkness. If an erroneous motion of images on retina is artificially introduced, for example, by fitting spectacles on the eyes or by moving the visual scene, the animal learns to adjust the amplitude of VOR to compensate for the error. Cerebellar LTD has been hypothesized as a molecular mechanism for this VOR adaptation.

Chris I. De Zeeuw and colleagues (1998) examined cerebellar LTD and VOR adaptation in L7-PKCI transgenic mice in which the protein kinase C (PKC) inhibitor is artificially expressed in the cerebellar Purkinje cells under the control of L7 promoter. Protein kinase C, required for cerebellar LTD, has several isoforms coded by separate genes. Knockout of the γ isoform did not impair cerebellar LTD (see discussion above on PKCγ knockout mice), possibly due to compensatory expression of other isoforms of the kinase. In L7-PKCI mice, expression of a selective inhibitor to a broad range of PKC isoforms virtually blocked LTD induction. These L7-PKCI mice showed normal VOR. When subjected to visuo-vestibular training, in which the visual scene was rotated in addition to the head turn, the wild-type mice learned to adapt their VOR. In contrast, L7-PKCI exhibited no VOR adaptation. These results suggest that cerebellar LTD is a mechanism for VOR adaptation.

Complex Motor-Skill Learning

In addition to classical eyeblink conditioning and VOR adaptation, the learning of more complex motor skills has also been examined in many mutant mice with what is know as the rotorod test. Typically, a mouse is placed on either a stationary rod or a rod that rotates at a certain speed, and the time it remains on the rod is measured to assess motor-skill learning. Impaired motor-skill learning has been observed in various mutant mice with cerebellar deficits including altered Purkinje-cell excitability, altered short-term synaptic plasticity, impaired cerebellar long-term potentiation, impaired cerebellar LTD, and multiple climbing fiber innervation.

Mutant mice with deficient cerebellar LTD are generally impaired in learning complex motor skills, with the exception of the GFAP knockout mice. As mentioned before, the GFAP knockout mice showed deficient cerebellar LTD and impaired eyeblink conditioning. However, they learned to stay on the rotating rod as well as normal mice, suggesting that there may be other forms of cerebellar plasticity supporting motor-skill learning.

Chong Chen and colleagues (1995) proposed that multiple climbing fiber innervation of the Purkinje cells disrupts learning of component movement and, hence, learning of complex motor skills. This notion is supported by numerous studies but has been challenged by De Zeeuw and colleagues (1998). These investigators reported normal rotorod performance and multiple climbing fiber innervations in the L7-PKCI transgenic mice.

Conclusion

Impaired motor learning in the cerebellum-specific mutants such as the GluRδ2 knockout and the L7-PKCI transgenic mice provides convincing evidence that the cerebellum is a learning machine. Deficient cerebellar LTD and motor learning have been observed in vastly different mutants, suggesting a causal link between cerebellar LTD and motor learning. In addition to cerebellar LTD, other forms of synaptic plasticity may also be involved in cerebellum-dependent learning. The cerebellum may also be involved in spatial learning (Goodlett, Hamre, and West, 1992). Further studies using cerebellum-specific mutant mice should help illuminate some other aspects of this question.

See also: GENETIC SUBSTRATES OF MEMORY: AMYGDALA; GENETIC SUBSTRATES OF MEMORY: HIPPOCAMPUS; GLUTAMATE RECEPTORS AND THEIR CHARACTERIZATION; LOCALIZATION OF MEMORY TRACES; LONG-TERM DEPRESSION IN THE CEREBELLUM, HIPPOCAMPUS, AND NEOCORTEX; NEURAL COMPUTATION: CEREBELLUM; NEURAL SUBSTRATES OF CLASSICAL CONDITIONING: DISCRETE BEHAVIORAL RESPONSES; REINFORCEMENT; VESTIBULO-OCULAR REFLEX (VOR) PLASTICITY

Bibliography

Aiba, A., Kano, M., Chen, C., Stanton, M. E., Fox, G. D., Herrup, K., Zwingman, T. A., and Tonegawa, S. (1994). Deficient cerebellar long-term depression and impaired motor learning in mGluR1 mutant mice. *Cell* 79 (2), 377–388.

Albus, J. S. (1971). A theory of cerebellar function. *Mathematical Bioscience* 10, 25–61.

Chen, L., Bao, S., Lockard, J. M., Kim, J. K., and Thompson, R. F. (1996). Impaired classical eyeblink conditioning in cerebellar-lesioned and Purkinje cell degeneration (*pcd*) mutant mice. *Journal of Neuroscience* 16 (8), 2,829–2,838.

Chen, L., Bao, S., and Thompson, R. F. (1999). Bilateral lesions of the interpositus nucleus completely prevent eyeblink conditioning in Purkinje cell-degeneration mutant mice. *Behavioral Neuroscience* 113 (1), 204–210.

Chen, L., Chetkovich, D. M., Petralia, R. S., Sweeney, N. T., Kawasaki, Y., Wenthold, R. J., Bredt, D. S., and Nicoll, R. A. (2000). Stargazin regulates synaptic targeting of AMPA receptors by two distinct mechanisms. *Nature* 408 (6,815), 936–943.

Chen, C., Kano, M., Abeliovich, A., Chen, L., Bao, S., Kim, J. J., Hashimoto, K., Thompson, R. F., and Tonegawa, S. (1995). Impaired motor coordination correlates with persistent multiple climbing fiber innervation in PKC gamma mutant mice. *Cell* 83 (7), 1,233–1,242.

De Zeeuw, C. I., Hansel, C., Bian, F., Koekkoek, S. K., van Alphen, A. M., Linden, D. J., and Oberdick, J. (1998). Expression of a protein kinase C inhibitor in Purkinje cells blocks cerebellar LTD and adaptation of the vestibulo-ocular reflex. *Neuron* 20 (3), 495–508.

Goodlett, C. R., Hamre, K. M., and West, J. R. (1992). Dissociation of spatial navigation and visual guidance performance in Purkinje cell degeneration (*pcd*) mutant mice. *Behavioral Brain Research* 47 (2), 129–141.

Kishimoto, Y., Kawahara, S., Fujimichi, R., Mori, H., Mishina, M., and Kirino, Y. (2001). Impairment of eyeblink conditioning in GluRdelta2-mutant mice depends on the temporal overlap between conditioned and unconditioned stimuli. *European Journal of Neuroscience* 14 (9), 1,515–1,521.

Marr, D. (1969). A theory of cerebellar cortex. *Journal of Physiology* 202 (2), 437–470.

Miyata, M., Kim, H. T., Hashimoto, K., Lee, T. K., Cho, S. Y., Jiang, H., Wu, Y., Jun, K., Wu, D., Kano, M., and Shin, H. S. (2001). Deficient long-term synaptic depression in the rostral cerebellum correlated with impaired motor learning in phospholipase C beta4 mutant mice. *European Journal of Neuroscience* 13 (10), 1,945–1,954.

Qiao, X., Chen, L., Gao, H., Bao, S., Hefti, F., Thompson, R. F., and Knusel, B. (1998). Cerebellar brain-derived neurotrophic factor-TrkB defect associated with impairment of eyeblink conditioning in Stargazer mutant mice. *Journal of Neuroscience* 18 (17), 6,990–6,999.

Shibuki, K., Gomi, H., Chen, L., Bao, S., Kim, J. J., Wakatsuki, H., Fujisaki, T., Fujimoto, K., Katoh, A., Ikeda, T., Chen, C., Thompson, R. F., and Itohara, S. (1996). Deficient cerebellar long-term depression, impaired eyeblink conditioning, and normal motor coordination in GFAP mutant mice. *Neuron* 16 (3), 587–599.

Thompson, R. F., Bao, S., Chen, L., Cipriano, B., Grethe, J. S., Kim, J. J., Thompson, J. K., Tracy, J., Weninger, M. S., and Krupa, D. J. (1996). In J. D. Schmahmann, ed., *Associative learning. The Cerebellum and Cognition,* 151–189. Academic Press, New York.

Shaowen Bao
Lu Chen

HIPPOCAMPUS

The identification and manipulation of genes (genetics) has influenced the study of most biological phenomena, including hippocampal learning and memory. The first studies to use genetics to manipulate plasticity and learning in mammals targeted the α-calcium calmodulin-dependent kinase II (αCaMKII) (Silva, Paylor, Wehner, and Tonegawa, 1992a; Silva, Stevens, Tonegawa, and Tang, 1992b) and the tyrosine kinase Fyn (Grant et al., 1992). The results showed that genetic manipulations that disrupt hippocampal synaptic plasticity result in hippocampal-dependent learning deficits. These studies were also influential in starting the new field of molecular and cellular cognition, which combines genetics, neurophysiology, and behavioral neuroscience. What have we learned so far about the hippocampus from this new field, and how successful has this general approach been?

The hippocampus plays a key role in learning and memory. Patients with hippocampal lesions are unable to store new conscious memories, with more severe impairments in recent memories than in remote ones. Hippocampal lesions spare other cognitive functions, including intelligence, attention, and emotion. Together with parallel animal experiments, studies of the hippocampus established that memory is separate from other cognitive abilities and that the hippocampus has a prominent role in early stages of memory consolidation (Eichenbaum, 2001).

Nearly twenty years after the publication of the first hippocampal lesion studies, Bliss, Lomo and colleagues discovered long-term potentiation or LTP in the hippocampus, a form of synaptic plasticity that strongly suggests a role in learning and memory. Moreover, computer simulations (parallel neuronetworks) implementing abstractions of LTP-like mechanisms process information in ways that are reminiscent of human and animal learning, suggesting that synaptic phenomena like LTP could be mediating learning and memory. But is LTP a necessary component of learning and memory mediated by the hippocampus?

Pharmacological inhibitors of the N-Methyl-D-Aspartate receptor (NMDAR) were used in the earliest attempts to answer this question. The NMDAR seems to be a coincidence detector. The receptor regulates a calcium channel that is normally blocked by magnesium; binding of glutamate and postsynaptic depolarization remove the magnesium block of the channel, allowing calcium to enter the synapse and induce LTP. NMDAR antagonists impair hippocampal LTP and cause severe deficits in hippocampal-dependent spatial learning tasks (Morris, Anderson, Lynch, and Baudry, 1986). However, NMDAR blockers have a number of other behavioral effects, such as sensimotor deficits, that complicated the interpretation of those studies. When the first NMDAR studies were published, there were few other pharmacological manipulations that could be used to investigate the possible role of LTP in learning. Fortunately, transgenetic manipulations (transgenics, knock outs, knock ins, and so on) provided the means to modify or delete any one of the molecular components known to be involved in LTP (i.e. CaMKII).

αCaMKII, TP, and Learning

αCaMKII is a member of a family of serine/threonine kinases activated by calmodulin loaded with calcium. The αCaMKII is expressed in postnatal forebrain structures such as the hippocampus and cortex. Studies with pharmacological inhibitors demonstrated that the CaMKII family of kinases was involved in the induction of LTP. These kinases, particularly the α and the β, can potentiate synaptic transmission by a variety of mechanisms, including the phosphorylation of glutamate receptors (Lisman and McIntyre, 2001). Transgenetic studies showed that both a null mutation of αCaMKII (Silva, Stevens, Tonegawa, and Tang, 1992b; Silva, Paylor, Wehner, and Tonegawa, 1992a) and a transgenic overexpression of a constitutively active form of this kinase (αCaMKIIT286D) (Bach et al., 1995; Mayford, Wang, Kandel, and O'Dell, 1995) altered hippocampal LTP and hippocampal-dependent learning. Later studies showed that a point-mutation that substituted threonine at position 286 for alanine (T286A) and prevented the autophosphorylation of αCaMKII at threonine 286 impaired hippocampal LTP and learning (Giese, Fedorov, Filipkowski, and Silva, 1998). αCaMKII, however, affects activity-dependent structural plasticity; hence the learning abnormalities described for these three mutants could be due to deficits in later stages of hippocampal development.

To address this problem, the tetracycline-controlled transactivator system (tTA) was used to regulate the expression of a constitutive active form of αCaMKII that disrupts LTP and learning (αCaMKIIT286D) (Mayford et al., 1996). With this system it was possible to repress the mutant αCaMKIIT286D transgene during development and simply lift the repression at appropriate experimental times. These inducible studies confirmed the importance of αCaMKII function for hippocampal LTP and learning (Mayford et al., 1996). However, αCaMKII has a wide substrate specificity that is normally restricted by the localization of the enzyme. Thus, it is possible that the higher levels of constitutively active kinase in the inducible transgenic mice may have led to the phosphorylation of proteins that are not normally phosphorylated by this kinase. Consequently, the learning deficits in these tTA-αCaMKIIT286D mutants could be an artifact of the overexpression of this constitutively active kinase.

To circumvent this problem, researchers used a new approach that combines pharmacology and genetics to test the role of αCaMKII in LTP and learning (Ohno et al., 2001). This pharmacogenetic strategy takes advantage of synergisms between pharmacological and genetic manipulations. For example, unlike the homozygous T286A mutation of αCaMKII described above, the heterozygous mutation (T286A hets) does not affect hippocampal-dependent learning. Similarly, although 10 mg/kg of CPP (NMDAR blocker) injected intraperitoneally thirty minutes before training blocks contextual learning (hippocampal-dependent), 5 mg/kg of this drug does not. This same low dose, however, can reveal a contextual learning deficit in the T286A heterozygotes, thus making a compelling connection between kinase activity and contextual learning (Ohno et al., 2001). Although each of the experiments presented above suffers from specific technical limitations, taken together the results presented demonstrate that the activation of αCaMKII is critical for LTP and for hippocampal-dependent learning. This convergence of information is critical for every major finding described here.

Detecting Coincidences with the NMDAR

Learning is heavily dependent on the generation of associations between previously unrelated phenomena. As described above, the molecular properties of the NMDAR suggest that this receptor may have a role in these associations. A number of transgenetic NMDAR manipulations affect both hippocampal synaptic plasticity and learning. A deletion of the NMDAR epsilon subunit and a point mutation of the glycine site in the NMDAR1 subunit (glycine binding potentiates receptor function) disrupt hippocampal LTP and learning. Remarkably, a Cre-mediated deletion of the NMDAR1 subunit restricted to hippocampal CA1 pyramidal neurons also disrupts CA1 LTP and hippocampal-dependent learning (Tsien et al., 1996), indicating that NMDAR function in this hippocampal subregion is critical for learning. The bacterial phage Cre-recombinase can delete any genomic segment flanked by its recognition sites (LoxP). Thus, any gene flanked by LoxP sites can be deleted from any region or cell type expressing Cre-recombinase. This strategy could be used to delete any gene from anywhere in the brain. Specific brain regions or cell types can even be targeted by using virus vectors expressing Cre-recombinase.

The Many Roads of Plasticity and Learning

Aside from NMDAR-dependent activation of αCaMKII, there are many other signaling pathways that are critical for both synaptic plasticity and learning. For example, the ERK signaling pathways are also involved in plasticity and learning (Sweatt, 2001)). Inhibitors of MEK, a kinase that activates ERK, disrupt LTP and learning; both the induction of LTP and training activate ERK. Mutations of genes thought to modulate ERK signaling, including Ras, the neurofibromin GTPase Activating Protein, the guanine-nucleotide-releasing-factor (GRF), and the B-Raf kinase disrupt hippocampal LTP and learning and memory.

The cAMP-signaling pathway is also involved in hippocampal learning and memory. A number of studies indicated that a balance between the activities of cAMP-dependent protein kinase A (PKA) and the phosphatases PP1 and calcineurin gate the stability of both synaptic changes and memory. For example, transgenic mice expressing R(AB), an inhibitory form of the regulatory subunit of PKA, show unstable LTP and memory (Abel et al., 1997). Transgenic expression of a constitutively active form of calcineurin, a Ca/CaM-dependent Ser/Thr phosphatase, also results in unstable LTP and memory. Importantly, repression of this calcineurin transgene, under the control of the tTA system, reverses the long-term memory deficits of the mutants, demonstrating that these effects are not due to the developmental expression of the transgene (Mansuy et al., 1998a).

Inducible overexpression of calcineurin with a modified tetracycline system (rtTa) also resulted in unstable LTP and memory (Mansuy et al., 1998b). The rtTA system was also used to overexpress a COOH-terminal autoinhibitory domain that represses calcineurin function (rtTA-CN inhibitor mice). Inducible overexpression of this inhibitory domain enhances early and late phases of CA1 LTP as well as short- and long-term memory (Malleret et al., 2001). The studies described above indicate that calcineurin and PKA play a critical role in one of the mechanisms that gate the stability of plasticity and memory. But what are the molecular mechanisms responsible for the stability of synaptic changes and memory?

Transcription, Translation, and Memory

A large body of work in a number of organisms and memory systems have demonstrated a universal requirement for transcription and translation in long-term memory (Davis and Squire, 1984)). Moreover, pioneering studies in *Aplysia* showed the involvement of the transcription factor cAMP Responsive Element Binding protein (CREB) in the stability of synaptic changes. This transcription factor is activated by a number of signaling pathways, including ERK and the cAMP cascades (see above). Interestingly, a null mutation of the CREB α and δ isoforms (CREBαδ-), which disrupted the stability of hippocampal LTP, also impaired memory (but not learning) tested in a wide range of tasks, suggesting that CREB-dependent transcription was required for long-term memory. Injection of a herpes simplex virus carrying a CREB gene into the amygdala, a structure with a well-characterized role in fear conditioning, enhanced this form of learning. These and many other studies have shown that CREB has a universal role in memory (Silva, Kogan, Frankland, and Kida, 1998).

There is extensive evidence that cAMP-dependent signaling can activate CREB (Silva, Kogan, Frankland, and Kida, 1998). Indeed, deleting both calcium/calmodulin induced adenylate cyclases (1 and 8) blocks the maintenance but not the induction of CA1 LTP and disrupts hippocampal long-term memory. A drug that activates adenyl cyclases turns on CREB and rescues the LTP and memory deficits of this double mutant (Wong et al., 1999). Another protein that can activate CREB is calcium/calmodulin kinase IV (CaMKIV). Experiments with a dominant-negative form of CaMKIV (dnCaMKIV) expressed in the postnatal forebrain showed that this transgene affected late but not early stages of CA1 LTP. Similarly, behavioral experiments revealed specific long-term memory deficits in both spatial learning and contextual fear conditioning. CREB activation was impaired by the dnCaMKIV mutation, indicating that this kinase may activate CREB during learning (Kang et al., 2001).

CREB seems to regulate the expression of Zif268, a transcription factor whose expression is triggered by LTP and learning. Strikingly, studies of a Zif268 null-mutant mouse showed that this transcription factor is needed for the stability of hippocampal plasticity and memory (Jones et al., 2001). These results suggest that Zif268 is downstream of CREB and that this transcriptional cascade is critical for memory.

A key facet of the experiments summarized above is that short-term memory is normal in the mutant mice, demonstrating that the processes required for learning (sensory processing, motivation, and so on) are unaffected in these mice, thus simplifying the interpretation of the results.

Enhancing LTP and Learning

Remarkably, molecular manipulations that enhance LTP often also enhance learning and memory. For example, the mutation of the nociceptin receptor, which mediates the inhibition of adenylyl cyclase, facilitates hippocampal LTP and spatial learning and memory (Manabe et al., 1998). Presumably, during learning the nociceptin receptor mutants generate higher levels of cAMP than controls. This cAMP increase enhances LTP, resulting in faster learning.

A transgenic Tissue Plasminogen Activator (TPA) also enhances LTP and learning, whereas a null mutation of this gene impairs them. TPA is an extracellular protease that seems to be involved in synaptic remodeling triggered by plasticity and learning. Therefore, loss of TPA impairs this remodeling and disrupts hippocampal LTP and learning, whereas overexpressing TPA facilitates both synaptic and behavioral plasticity (Madani et al., 1999). Just like the overexpression of TPA, the transgenic overexpression of the NMDAR subunit 2B, which appears to lengthen the opening time of the NMDAR, also enhances LTP and learning (Tang et al., 1999).

The overexpression of the presynaptic Growth Associated Protein 43, the mutation of a telencephalon-specific cell adhesion molecule, the transgenic inhibition of Calcineurin, and the mutation of Rin 1 (a ras effector) all facilitate LTP and learning. Nevertheless, not all manipulations that enhance LTP improve learning or memory. For example, LTP enhancements that disrupt basic associativity mechanisms do not quicken learning.

Disconnections Between LTP and Learning

There are cases where hippocampal LTP seems to be disrupted with no apparent effect on learning and memory. For example, the deletion of the Glutamate Receptor 1 (GluR1) leads to deficits in CA1 LTP but not in spatial learning. Similarly, the deletion of the Thy-1 gene also spared spatial learning but disrupted LTP in the dentate gyrus. The interconnections between biological phenomena such as LTP and learning are almost always more complex than expected. For example, in vivo recordings revealed LTP in the Thy-1 mutants, and tests with more physiological LTP-inducing protocols demonstrated that the GluR1 mutants can express robust levels of LTP. Nevertheless, it is possible that glutamate receptors are not essential for the expression of all synaptic-specific changes underlying learning and memory. Perhaps other classes of channels (i.e., potassium channels) can also mediate these changes and therefore support learning in mutants with deficits in GluR LTP.

There have also been studies of the impact of some of the mutations described above in hippocampal circuit function. For example, hippocampal circuits represent spatial information. Recordings in behaving rats and mice have demonstrated that hippocampal pyramidal cells fire in a place-specific manner (place fields). Remarkably, a number of manipulations that disrupted hippocampal LTP did not block these spatial representations but impaired their stability. Thus, stable synaptic changes may be crucial for the stability of circuit representations of information in the brain. This possibility also implies that mechanisms other than synaptic plasticity are responsible for generating these representations. Undoubtedly, transgenetic approaches will also have a role in revealing the nature and function of these mechanisms.

The molecular and cellular cognitive studies summarized above provide compelling evidence that the mechanisms responsible for the induction and stability of synaptic changes have a critical role in the acquisition and storage of information in the hippocampus. Because many of the same molecular mechanisms are present throughout the brain, they might have a universal role in learning and memory in other structures. Nevertheless, there is also evidence for important differences between the molecular mechanisms underlying learning in different brain structures (e.g., the amygdala and hippocampus). The findings and ideas immerging from these studies could be the foundation stone for understanding the molecular and cellular processes that underlie our thoughts, fears, desires, and dreams.

See also: GLUTAMATE RECEPTORS AND THEIR CHARACTERIZATION; LONG-TERM POTENTIATION; PROTEIN SYNTHESIS IN LONG-TERM MEMORY IN VERTEBRATES; SECOND MESSENGER SYSTEMS

Bibliography

Abel, T., Nguyen, P. V., Barad, M., Deuel, T. A., Kandel, E. R., and Bourtchouladze, R. (1997). Genetic demonstration of a role for PKA in the late phase of LTP and in hippocampus-based long-term memory. *Cell 88*, 615–626.

Bach, M. E., Hawkins, R. D., Osman, M., Kandel, E. R., and Mayford, M. (1995). Impairment of spatial but not contextual memory in CaMKII mutant mice with a selective loss of hippocampal LTP in the range of the theta frequency. *Cell 81*, 905–915.

Davis, H. P., and Squire, L. R. (1984). Protein synthesis and memory. *Psychology Bulletin 96*, 518–559.

Eichenbaum, H. (2001). The hippocampus and declarative memory: Cognitive mechanisms and neural codes. *Behavioral Brain Research 127*, 199–207.

Giese, K. P., Fedorov, N. B., Filipkowski, R. K., and Silva, A. J. (1998). Autophosphorylation at Thr286 of the alpha calcium-calmodulin kinase II in LTP and learning. *Science 279*, 870–873.

Grant, S. G., O'Dell, T. J., Karl, K. A., Stein, P. L., Soriano, P., and Kandel, E. R. (1992). Impaired long-term potentiation, spatial learning, and hippocampal development in *fyn* mutant mice. *Science 258*, 1,903–1,910.

Jones, M. W., Errington, M. L., French, P. J., Fine, A., Bliss, T. V., Garel, S., Charnay, P., Bozon, B., Laroche, S., and Davis, S. (2001). A requirement for the immediate early gene Zif268 in the expression of late LTP and long-term memories. *Nature Neuroscience 4*, 289–296.

Kang, H., Sun, L. D., Atkins, C. M., Soderling, T. R., Wilson, M. A., and Tonegawa, S. (2001). An important role of neural activity-dependent CaMKIV signaling in the consolidation of long-term memory. *Cell 106*, 771–783.

Lisman, J. E., and McIntyre, C. C. (2001). Synaptic plasticity: A molecular memory switch. *Current Biology 11*, R788–791.

Madani, R., Hulo, S., Toni, N., Madani, H., Steimer, T., Muller, D., and Vassalli, J. (1999). Enhanced hippocampal long-term potentiation and learning by increased neuronal expression of tissue-type plasminogen activator in transgenic mice. *EMBO Journal 18*, 3,007–3,012.

Malleret, G., Haditsch, U., Genoux, D., Jones, M. W., Bliss, T. V., Vanhoose, A. M., Weitlauf, C., Kandel, E. R., Winder, D. G., and Mansuy, I. M. (2001). Inducible and reversible enhancement of learning, memory, and long-term potentiation by genetic inhibition of calcineurin. *Cell 104*, 675–686.

Manabe, T., Noda, Y., Mamiya, T., Katagiri, H., Houtani, T., Nishi, M., Noda, T., Takahashi, T., Sugimoto, T., Nabeshima, T., and Takeshima, H. (1998). Facilitation of long-term potentiation and memory in mice lacking nociceptin receptors. *Nature 394*, 577–581.

Mansuy, I. M., Mayford, M., Jacob, B., Kandel, E. R., and Bach, M. E. (1998a). Restricted and regulated overexpression reveals calcineurin as a key component in the transition from short-term to long-term memory. *Cell 92*, 39–49.

Mansuy, I. M., Winder, D. G., Moallem, T. M., Osman, M., Mayford, M., Hawkins, R. D., and Kandel, E. R. (1998b). Inducible and reversible gene expression with the rtTA system for the study of memory. *Neuron 21*, 257–265.

Mayford, M., Bach, M. E., Huang, Y. Y., Wang, L., Hawkins, R. D., and Kandel, E. R. (1996). Control of memory formation through regulated expression of a CaMKII transgene. *Science 274*, 1,678–1,683.

Mayford, M., Wang, J., Kandel, E. R., and O'Dell, T. J. (1995). CaMKII regulates the frequency-response function of hippocampal synapses for the production of both LTD and LTP. *Cell 81*, 891–904.

Morris, R. G. M., Anderson, E., Lynch, G. S., and Baudry, M. (1986). Selective impairment of learning and blockade of long-term potentiation by an N-methyl-D-asparate receptor antagonist, AP5. *Nature 319*, 774–776.

Ohno, M., Frankland, P. W., Chen, A. P., Costa, R. M., and Silva, A. J. (2001). Inducible, pharmacogenetic approaches to the study of learning and memory. *Nature Neuroscience 4*, 1,238–1,243.

Silva, A. J., Kogan, J. H., Frankland, P. W., and Kida, S. (1998). CREB and memory. *Annual Review of Neuroscience 21*, 127–148.

Silva, A. J., Paylor, R., Wehner, J. M., and Tonegawa, S. (1992a). Impaired spatial learning in alpha-calcium-calmodulin kinase II mutant mice. *Science 25*, 206–211.

Silva, A. J., Stevens, C. F., Tonegawa, S., and Wang, Y. (1992b). Deficient hippocampal long-term potentiation in alpha-calcium-calmodulin kinase II mutant mice. *Science 257*, 201–206.

Sweatt, J. D. (2001). The neuronal MAP kinase cascade: A biochemical signal integration system subserving synaptic plasticity and memory. *Journal of Neurochemistry 76*, 1–10.

Tang, Y. P., Shimizu, E., Dube, G. R., Rampon, C., Kerchner, G. A., Zhuo, M., Liu, G., and Tsien, J. Z. (1999). Genetic enhancement of learning and memory in mice. *Nature 401*, 63–69.

Tsien, J. Z., Chen, D. F., Gerber, D., Tom, C., Mercer, E. H., Anderson, D. J., Mayford, M., Kandel, E. R., and Tonegawa, S. (1996). Subregion- and cell type-restricted gene knockout in mouse brain. *Cell 87*, 1,317–1,326.

Wong, S. T., Athos, J., Figueroa, X. A., Pineda, V. V., Schaefer, M. L., Chavkin, C. C., Muglia, L. J., and Storm, D. R. (1999). Calcium-stimulated adenylyl cyclase activity is critical for hippocampus-dependent long-term memory and late phase LTP. *Neuron 23*, 787–798.

Alcino J. Silva

GLUTAMATE RECEPTORS AND THEIR CHARACTERIZATION

The amino acids L-glutamate and L-aspartate are the major excitatory neurotransmitters in the mammalian central nervous system (CNS). Some subtleties aside, glutamate is considered the predominant excitatory neurotransmitter and for simplicity the receptors that bind excitatory amino acids will be referred to as glutamate receptors, or GluRs. Glutamate mediates its effects by interacting with receptors that can be distinguished by pharmacological, physiological, anatomical, molecular, and genetic criteria. The interaction of glutamate with its receptors underlies many normal physiological processes, from rapid synaptic signaling and information transfer to longer-lasting changes in synaptic efficacy that are thought to be the cellular basis of learning and memory. In addition, neurotransmission mediated by glutamate and its receptors is implicated in a variety of CNS pathologies, including epilepsy, cell death due to excitotoxicity and ischemia, and Alzheimer's disease. This entry will review the general characteristics of GluRs, including pharmacological specificity, ion selectivity, and modulation by other compounds.

Glutamate Receptor Classes

Glutamate receptors can be divided into two major classes. One class is termed *ionotropic*, because glutamate binding causes a conformational change in the receptor that directly opens a gate, permitting ion passage in and out of the cell. The channel and the glutamate-binding site are part of a single multisubunit macromolecule found in the plasma membrane. Three pharmacologically distinct glutamate receptor subclasses of this ionotropic type are distinguished, named after their selective agonists: the N-methyl-D-aspartate (NMDA), 2-amino-3-hydroxy-5-methyl-4-isoxazolepropionate (AMPA), and kainate (KA) receptors. The AMPA and KA subclasses are frequently referred to as non-NMDA receptors.

A second class of glutamate receptors is characterized by their capacity to couple to second-messenger generating systems via guanine nucleotide-binding protein activation (G-proteins) and are termed the *metabotropic glutamate receptors* (mGluRs). The binding of glutamate to these mGluRs induces secondary changes that are mediated by intracellular molecules distinct from the receptor itself. One such mGluR is coupled to the phosphoinositide (PI) second messenger system and is named after its selective agonist, trans-1-amino-1,3-cyclopentanedicarboxylic acid (trans-ACPD). A second is named after its selective agonist, l-2-amino-4-phosphonobutanoic acid (L-AP4) and exists in the retina, whereas a distinct L-AP4-sensitive receptor type has been described in select CNS pathways.

Non-NMDA Receptors

Non-NMDA receptors mediate the rapid on-off type of synaptic signaling that underlies the fast excit-

atory postsynaptic potential (EPSP) at glutamatergic synapses. Binding of glutamate to these receptors opens a channel that is permeable to Na^+ and K^+ (and in some instances Ca^{2+}), inducing the depolarizing currents characteristic of these receptors. GluRs can desensitize rapidly, limiting the time the channel spends in the open state. This desensitization helps in truncating the duration of the EPSP at excitatory synapses.

The nonendogenous agonists AMPA and quisqualate (QA), and other structurally related compounds, selectively activate the AMPA receptor subclass. A series of quinoxaline derivatives (6-cyano-7-nitroquinoxaline-2,3-dione [CNQX]; 6,7-dinitroquinoxaline-2, 3-dione [DNQX]; and 6-nitro-7-sulfamoyl-benzo (f)quinoxaline-2,3-dione [NBQX]) are the most selective known AMPA/QA antagonists, but they can also act as KA antagonists.

KA has been shown to be both a potent excitant and a potent excitotoxin. The case for a KA receptor that is distinct from AMPA/QA receptors initially stemmed from pharmacological studies in which KA responses were inhibited by select antagonists more potently than were AMPA/QA or NMDA responses, and from anatomical studies in which KA and AMPA/QA receptors displayed distinct anatomical localizations. However, even considering the quinoxaline antagonists, accurate distinction of KA from AMPA/QA receptors remains difficult because of their similar pharmacological profiles. Localization of AMPA/QA and KA receptors by autoradiographic techniques demonstrates a differential distribution of these two types. For example, [³H]AMPA-binding sites are concentrated in the hippocampal CA1 region, outer cortical layers, lateral septum, and the molecular layer of the cerebellum, whereas [³H]KA-binding sites are concentrated in the hippocampal mossy fibers, deep cortical layers, and the granule cell layer of the cerebellum.

Advances in molecular genetic techniques have led to the identification of a series of complementary DNA (cDNA) clones that encode a family of GluRs. Thus, injection of messenger RNA derived from these cDNA sequences into *Xenopus* oocytes results in electrophysiological responses to glutamate, KA, QA, and AMPA, but not to NMDA or AP-4. The non-NMDA receptor family is composed of at least seven separate genes (GluR1–GluR7) in the rat, and the proteins expressed from these genes each have an approximate molecular weight of 100 kilodaltons. GluR1–GluR4 are the predominant forms expressed in the brain, and the mature form of the receptor appears to be a tetrameric complex of approximately 600 kilodaltons composed of different combinations of the GluR subunits. Two genes (KA-1 and KA-2) have also been identified that encode proteins that represent the high-affinity KA binding site in the brain. KA-1 and KA-2 do not form functional receptors themselves. They must combine with other GluR subunits to produce an ionotropic glutamate receptor. Such structural complexity helps to explain the difficulty in distinguishing AMPA/QA from KA responses using pharmacological approaches. In addition, the capacity to mix different subunits (and their splice variants) provides for a large number of possible GluR phenotypes when analyzed using either pharmacological or electrophysiological techniques.

The GluR family is evolutionarily divergent from other ionotropic receptors (e.g., nicotinic AchR). Ionotropic receptors all have four membrane-spanning domains; however, the GluR family is unique in that the second membrane-spanning segment (TM2) forms a kink in the membrane, exiting back into the cytoplasm instead of traversing the bilayer and exiting into the extracellular space. This kink in TM2 is analogous to a pore (P) forming element in K^+ channels and forms the structure of the GluR responsible for determining ion permeation. GluRs are permeant to Na^+ and K^+ although certain GluR variants can also be significantly permeable to Ca^{++}.

NMDA Receptors

The NMDA receptor is pharmacologically and functionally more complex than AMPA/QA and KA receptors. For example, binding of glutamate to the NMDA receptor will open the ion channel only if the membrane is depolarized and if glycine is present. Because NMDA receptors open as a function of the extent of membrane depolarization, they are described as voltage-dependent and are thus sensitive to postsynaptic activity. Therefore, the NMDA receptor complex provides an example of a conditional logic gate where Hebb-like conditions are realized at a single synapse. Furthermore, the ion channel is significantly permeable to Ca^{++} in addition to Na^+ and K^+, resulting in a significant influx of Ca^{++} that induces a variety of secondary Ca^{++}-activated processes. These processes include 1. the induction of long-term potentiation (LTP), which is regarded as a cellular model of memory analogous to Hebb-type synaptic plasticity; 2. learning and memory in animal models; 3. the pathophysiology of epilepsy; and 4. some forms of excitotoxicity.

The NMDA receptor appears to be regulated by a variety of endogenous and exogenous compounds that act at distinct binding sites to modify the function of the receptor. The first of these binding sites is the transmitter recognition site, which binds L-glutamate (or L-aspartate), the synthetic ligand NMDA, and other agonists. Glutamate-binding can be selectively and competitively antagonized by a series of compounds, including D-2-amino-5-phosphonopentanoate (D-AP5) and 3-(2-carboxypiperazin-4-yl)propyl-1-phosphate (CPP). Second is the glycine-binding site, which must be occupied in order for the channel to be opened by glutamate binding to its recognition site. The pharmacology of the NMDA glycine site is distinct from that of the inhibitory glycine receptor in the spinal cord and brain stem, in that the NMDA receptor glycine site is insensitive to strychnine but is antagonized by kynurenate, 7-chlorokynurenate, and other compounds. Although this site may always be saturated in vivo, glycine is often referred to as a cotransmitter. Third is a site within the ion channel that binds Mg^{++}. Binding of Mg^{++} at this site blocks current flow through the channel when the membrane is at hyperpolarized potentials. This block is removed under depolarizing conditions, providing the molecular basis for the NMDA receptors' voltage dependence. Fourth is a site within the ion channel that binds phencyclidine (PCP), dibenzocyclohepteneimine (MK-801), and other compounds, causing blockage of ion flow through the channel. Binding of these compounds is permitted only when the ion channel is in the open state and the compounds are, therefore, referred to as open channel blockers. Finally, a variety of other molecules have been shown to be modulators of the NMDA receptor. For example, spermine and spermidine increase MK-801 binding to the NMDA complex and NMDA-evoked currents in cell culture and *Xenopus* oocyte preparations. Additionally, Zn^{++} and H^+ have been shown to modulate NMDA receptor currents in a number of preparations.

Localization of NMDA receptors by autoradiographic techniques demonstrates an anatomical distribution that in general parallels the distribution of AMPA/QA receptors, further supporting the idea that these two receptors work in concert in many synapses. Thus, NMDA receptors are found in the CA1 region of the hippocampus, throughout the cortex (particularly in outer cortical layers), and in striatum. However, specific localization of binding shows a different distribution of NMDA agonist- and antagonist-preferring binding sites, suggesting that subpopulations of NMDA receptors exist in different brain areas.

The NMDA receptor has been successfully isolated and characterized, and several distinct subunits of this receptor complex have been cloned. NMDAR1 was the original isolate, and various NMDAR2A–2D subunits coassemble with NMDAR1 to form functional receptors. Anatomical gene-mapping studies have confirmed that subpopulations of NMDA receptors exist in different brain regions. As with the non-NMDA receptors, numerous pharmacological and electrophysiological phenotypes are possible through the mixing of different subunits. The TM2 segment of the NMDARs is responsible for determining the ion permeation properties of the channel and forms a kink in the membrane analogous to that described for the GluRs above.

G-Protein-Coupled Glutamate Receptors

The G-protein coupled receptors (GPCRs) that bind glutamate and other excitatory amino acids are referred to as the *metabotropic glutamate receptors,* or mGluRs. They are similar in general structure to other GPCRs in having seven transmembrane spanning domains; however, they are divergent enough to be considered to have originated from a separate evolutionary-derived receptor family. In fact, sequence homology between the mGluR family and other GPCRs is minimal except for the GABAB receptor. The mGluR family is heterogeneous in size, ranging from 854 to 1,179 amino acids. The ligand-binding site for mGluRs resides in the large N-terminal extracellular domain. Additionally, the mGluRs exist as functional dimers in the membrane in contrast to the single subunit form of most GPCRs. These significant structural distinctions support the idea that the mGluRs evolved separately from the other GPCRs. The third intracellular loop, thought to be the major determinant responsible for G-protein coupling of the mGluRs, is relatively small, whereas the C-terminal domain is quite large. The coupling between mGluRs and their respective G proteins may occur through unique determinants that exist in the large C-terminal domain.

Eight different mGluRs can be subdivided into subgroups on the basis of sequence homologies and their capacity to couple to specific enzyme systems. For example, both mGluR1 and mGluR5 activate a G protein coupled to phospholipase C. mGluR1 activation can also lead to the production of cAMP and of arachidonic acid by coupling to G proteins that activate adenylate cyclase and phospholipase A2, respectively. The subtype mGluR5 seems more specific, activating predominantly the G-protein-activated phospholipase C.

Distinctions between the mGluR subtypes can also be made pharmacologically. One group, mGluR2, 3, and 8, favors the agonist trans-ACPD for activation, whereas a second group, including mGluR4, 6, and 7, favors AP-4 for activation. The subtypes mGluR2 and mGluR4 can be further distinguished pharmacologically by using the agonist 2-(carboxycyclopropyl)glycine, which is more potent at activating mGluR2 receptors.

The mGluRs are widespread in the nervous system and are found both pre- and postsynaptically. Presynaptically, they serve as autoreceptors and appear to participate in the inhibition of neurotransmitter release. Their postsynaptic roles appear to be varied and depend on the specific G protein to which they are coupled. Activation of mGluR1 has been implicated in long-term synaptic plasticity at many sites in the brain, including long-term potentiation in the hippocampus.

Conclusion

More than one receptor subclass may be present in any given excitatory synapse. The function of glutamatergic synapses depends on the combination of the above-mentioned receptor subtypes at a given synapse (e.g., non-NMDA, NMDA, both non-NMDA and NMDA, and mGluR, among others). Working in concert these receptors yield a complex synaptic response that depends on the number and location of individual receptors. Because these subtypes clearly serve distinct functions, the capacity to manipulate individual receptor molecules is critical to understanding the role of a subtype in a normal physiological event or in the etiology of a given glutamate-linked disease. The advent of more potent and selective drugs for each receptor subclass will allow for more precise experimental and clinical manipulation of these receptors. Similarly, molecular genetic approaches to analyzing both the structure and the function of these receptors has revealed a wealth of information, and further analysis of their genes and gene products will have far-reaching implications for the basic science of glutamate receptors and for a variety of glutamate-linked human diseases.

See also: GUIDE TO THE ANATOMY OF THE BRAIN: SYNAPSE; HEBB, DONALD; LONG-TERM POTENTIATION; NEUROTRANSMITTER SYSTEMS AND MEMORY; SECOND MESSENGER SYSTEMS

Bibliography

Boulter, J., Hollmann, M., O'Shea-Greenfield, A., Hartley, M., Deneris, E., Maron, C., and Heinemann, S. (1990). Molecular cloning and functional expression of glutamate receptor subunit genes. *Science* 249, 1,033–1,037.

Cotman, C. W., Monaghan, D. T., Ottersen, O. P., and Storm-Mathisen, J. (1987). Anatomical organization of excitatory amino acid receptors and their pathways. *Trends in Neurosciences* 10, 273–280.

Hollmann, M., and Heinemann, S. (1994). Cloned glutamate receptors. *Annual Review of Neuroscience* 17, 31–108.

Keinanen, K., Wisden, W., Sommer, B., Werner, P., Herb, A., Verdoorn, T. A., Sakmann, B., and Seeburg, P. H. (1990). A family of AMPA-selective glutamate receptors. *Science* 249, 556–560.

Masu, M., Tanabe, Y., Tsuchida, K., Shigemoto, R., and Nakanishi, S. (1991). Sequence and expression of a metabotropic glutamate receptor. *Nature* 349, 760–765.

Nakanishi, S. (1994). Metabotropic glutamate receptors: Synaptic transmission, modulation, and plasticity. *Neuron 13*, 1,031–1,037.

Nakanishi, N., Shneider, N. A., and Axel, R. (1990). A family of glutamate receptor genes: Evidence for the formation of heteromultimeric receptors with distinct channel properties. *Neuron 5*, 569–581.

Rosenmund, C., Stern-Bach, Y., and Stevens, C. F. (1998). The tetrameric structure of a glutamate receptor channel. *Science 280*, 1,596–1,599.

Sommer, B., Kohler, M., Sprengel, R., and Seeburg, P. H. (1991). RNA editing in brain controls a determinant of ion flow in glutamate-gated channels. *Cell 67*, 11–19.

Watkins, J. C., Krogsgaard-Larsen, P., and Honore, T. (1990). Structure activity relationships in the development of excitatory amino acid receptor agonists and competitive antagonists. *Trends in Pharmacological Sciences 11*, 25–33.

Waxham, M. N. (1998). Ionotropic and metabotropic receptors. In F. E. Bloom, S. L. Landis, J. L. Roberts, L. R. Squire, and M. J. Zigmond, eds., *Fundamental neuroscience*, pp. 235–267. New York: Academic Press.

C. W. Cotman
E. R. Whittemore
Revised by M. N. Waxham

GUIDE TO THE ANATOMY OF THE BRAIN

[In the brain, as in other complex systems, function follows form. Therefore, an understanding of learning and memory is critically dependent on a complete description of the anatomical organization of brain systems that support memory. Brain organization is composed at many levels, from cellular morphology to synapse types and their patterns of connection, to the cytoarchitecture of cortical and subcortical areas and the organization of neuronal types and input/output patterns, to major pathways and hierarchies of information processing. These levels of brain organization are surveyed in the OVERVIEW section that follows.

The fundamental alteration in plasticity that underlies memory occurs at the level of cellular anatomy and, in particular, synaptic structure. Therefore two sections of this guide provide a summary of our current knowledge about the structure of NEURONS and SYNAPSES. The section on neurons considers the major components of neurons and focuses on the cellular elements where plasticity occurs, specifically in the dendrites and synapses. This section also considers different neuron types and nature of connectivity patterns that form the circuitry in which plasticity exerts its effects on function. The section on synapses reviews the components of synapses and functionally distinct types of synapses. This section focuses on dendritic spines as the likely sites of plasticity that supports memory.

In other sections, this guide focuses on brain areas that play prominent roles in learning and memory. One area is the vast expanse of the CEREBRAL CORTEX. The cerebral cortex includes several functionally specific, hierarchically organized, areas and pathways that subserve specific perceptual, motor, emotional, and cognitive information processing functions. At the same time, these cortical areas are also the storehouses of memories for the specific information processed in those dedicated pathways. Therefore, understanding the functional organization of the cerebral cortex holds the key to characterizing the nature of the brain's representation of our accumulation of knowledge. The OLFACTORY CORTEX is a part of the cerebral cortex that is simpler in its architecture than other cortical areas, and has served as a model system for anatomical and physiological studies and for the development of computational models of combined perceptual and memory processing.

The remaining sections consider a set of brain areas that are nodal points within brain pathways that support specific kinds of memory, or modulate memory. The PERIRHINAL CORTEX and HIPPOCAMPUS are major components of the brain system that mediates "declarative memory," our capacity for conscious recollection of facts and events. The AMYGDALA is a major component of a system for "emotional memory," the system that mediates assignments of affective value to otherwise neutral stimuli and initiates automatic responses to stimuli of acquired emotional significance. The BASAL GANGLIA and CEREBELLUM are major components of distinct subsystems that mediate "procedural memory," the acquisition of skills, habits, and conditioned motor responses. The BASAL FOREBRAIN plays a major role within the modulatory pathways that regulate attentional mechanisms that influence memory processing. The amygdala also plays a role in the modulation of memory processing in emotional circumstances. Thus each area plays a distinctive role in memory processing. In real life, they act in parallel to mediate the impact of experience on the brain's information-processing systems. This guide provides the reader with the anatomical framework in which these brain areas make their individual contributions to memory.]

OVERVIEW

The adult human brain weights about 1,400 grams, the heaviest of any species relative to total body weight. This perhaps most impressive human organ appears to be responsible for our intellectual superiority over other species—although, paradoxically, human intelligence is not strongly correlated to brain size.

The modern discipline of neuroanatomy has developed over the past 400 years through the descriptive studies of workers such as Vesalius, Willis, Retzius, Purkinje, Brodmann, Campbell, Ramón y Cajal, and Golgi. Rather than answering a pedestrian question—What does it look like?—the main objective of studying anatomy of the brain is to create physiologically and psychologically meaningful structural inferences. The capacity and the choice of visualization methods define the level of differentiation of the brain structure from gross features to a single neuron.

In actuality, the anatomy of the brain proceeds on four levels, depending on the aim of the description. At the most superficial level, based on the evolutionary and embryonic development, the brain can be divided into the forebrain, the midbrain, and the hindbrain. In development, neurons, which consitute these subdivisions, multiply, develop distinct appearance and aggregate into groups forming nuclei, layers, or areas of the brain. This cellular level of brain anatomy, called cytoarchitectonic, differentiates cell types and their location. Further differentiating brain structures are the biochemical properties of neurons, which permit classification of different cell groups into chemically coded systems. At the most sophisticated level of resolution development are cytoarchitecture and chemoarchitecture, along with information about cellular connections and aspects of neuronal functioning. These eclectic criteria of structural classification provide the most meaningful structural references within the general scope of brain and bodily function.

Gross Anatomy

In early embryonic development the brain has rather simple gross features and is composed of just three vesicles, the hindbrain, the midbrain, and the forebrain. These soon subdivide to give place to more complicated arrangement of four vesicles: rhombencephalon (parallelogram-brain), mesencephalon (middle-brain), diencephalon (between-brain) and telencephalon (end-brain) (many neuroanatomists still use Greek to name newly discovered structures). Progressive development gives the brain a sophisticated form, which is traditionally segmented into numerous smaller structures on the basis of gross anatomical features. For example, the frontally positioned forebrain gives rise to two voluminous hemispheres of the cerebral cortex (brain "bark") separated from each other by the longitudinal fissure. The surface of the cortex is convoluted into folds known as gyri, which are separated by groves known as sulci. The cortex enfolds numerous subcortical neuronal structures, such as thalamus (the main relay for neural input to the cortex), hypothalamus (the neuro-hormonal regulatory center that keeps the rest of the body alive), hippocampus, and amygdala (structures implicated in emotional behavior, learning, and memory), caudate, putamen, and globus pallidus (major parts of the so-called basal ganglia, which seem to play a role in learning and control of movement). Other obvious gross features of the forebrain include cerebral ventricles (a network of fluid-filled cavities) and prominent fiber tracts such as the exter-

nal capsule, which interconnects the cortex with subcortical structures and spinal cord, and the corpus collosum, which connects two cortical hemispheres.

The midbrain in mammals is a much smaller structure than the forebrain. Topographically the midbrain is a caudal continuation of the thalamus and the hypothalamus. Two major gross features of the midbrain are the upper tectum (the roof) and the lower tegmentum (the covering). (Latin terminology is still prominent in neuronatomy alongside the Greek.) The tectum also features two swellings on each side of the midline: the superior and the inferior colliculi, which harbor major visual and auditory pathways, respectively. Another prominent feature of the midbrain is the cerebral aqueduct, a canal connecting ventricular systems of the forebrain and the hindbrain.

The most caudal part of the brain, the hindbrain, is composed of three major parts: the pons (bridges), the cerebellum (small brain) and the medulla oblongata (long brain). In neuroanatomy the medulla, pons, and midbrain are often collectively refered to as the brain stem. The pons are positioned immediately caudally to the midbrain and appear as a large protuberance (a bridge) on the ventral surface of the brain. Dorsally the pons are covered by the tegmentum pontis, which is a caudal continuation of the mesencephalic tegmentum. The cerebellum is positioned on the posterior surface of the brain and connected to it by three pars of cerebellar peduncules (pillars). In gross terms the cerebellum features two lateral hemispheres abutting the middle structure called the vermis (worm). Finally, the medulla is the most posterior part of the brain, immediately succeeded by the spinal cord. Superficially, it resembles the spinal cord with the major exception of the presence of bilateral inferior olives on its ventro-lateral surface and the floor of the fourth ventricular cavity on its dorsal surface.

Cytoarchitecture

The brain of humans and the head ganglion of mosquitoes are both made up of two general types of cells: neurons and glial cells. Although glial cells are the most numerous cells in the brain—they outnumber neurons by about twenty-five to one—it is neuronal activity that is associated with brain function. Neurons show greater diversity in shape and size than any other type of cell in the body. In contrast to other cells in the body, neurons can generate and relay electrical impulses—"action potentials." In order to transmit action potentials over great distances, neurons have extended processes—axons that, for some spinal motor neurons of large mammals, may have lengths on the order of meters.

Since neurons usually do not communicate by direct contact—each neuron operates as an independent unit—they have evolved highly specialized points of interaction: synapses. Synapses are essentially clefts between neurons. They are asymmetrically flanked by structures that release specialized chemicals neurotransmitters from one presynaptic neuron in response to the presence of action potentials. The response of the recipient—the postsynaptic neuron—is determined by highly specific detectors: receptors. The structure of the synapse allows information to flow in one direction only. Throughout the nervous system different neurons utilize a multiplicity of both neurotransmitters.

Staining cellular ribosomes with a Nissl substance stain allows light microscopic visualization of the cellular morphology of the brain. This process reveals that neurons within the various parts of the brain look different and are not evenly distributed—they are, rather, grouped into structures, which make up the cytoarchitectonic plan of the brain. The form, size, and position of neurons in the cerebral cortex reveal the layered organization of this structure. Studies have demonstrated differences in cytoarchitectonic organization of neuronal layers in different parts of the cortical mantle. These differences lead to the differentiation of fifty-two cortical areas in the frequently used cortical map of Brodmann.

Subcortical structures demonstrate even greater cytoarchitectonic diversity. In small areas of the thalamus and hypothalamus, neurons are grouped into numerous nuclei, areas, and zones with distinct morphological characteristics and topographical positions. The hypothalamus, for example, contains over forty nuclei and areas on either side of the third ventricle with distinct cytoarchitectonic characteristics. Cytoarchitectonic differentiation can go even further: The paraventricular nucleus of the hypothalamus is composed of ten subnuclei of specific neuronal types and topographical positions. These subnuclei also differ in function. Reflecting back onto brain areas identified by their gross anatomical features, most of them show complicated cytoarchitectonic organization. Several cytoarchitectonically distinct nuclei have been identified in the amygdala, whereas the layered organization of neurons in the hippocampus shows only four distinct areas. Cytoarchitecture has revealed an internal and an external component of the globus pallidus and has shown that neurons in the putamen are organized in patch-matrix compartments.

There are several neuronal groups in the midbrain, the best known of which is the substantia nigra (black substance), a complex, compartmentalized structure whose cells die in Parkinson's disease. Neurons of the superior and inferior colliculi are orga-

nized in layers, while the tegmentum contains nuclei of the oculomotor and trochlear cranial nerves responsible for eye movement and pupil constriction. The periaqueductal gray, another distinct cellular structure of the midbrain, is composed of neurons surrounding the cerebral aqueduct and appears to play a role in the regulation of blood pressure.

The cytoarchitecture of the pons also features several cranial nerve nuclei, raphe nuclei, and a dispersed area called the reticular formation, which is, however, not confined to pons but is spread throughout the entire brain stem. The cytoarchitecture of the cerebellum resembles the citoarchitecture of the forebrain in also having a cortex with a layered arrangement of cells and several subcortical nuclei.

In contrast to the diverse cytoarchitecture of the cerebral cortex, that of the cerebellar cortex is very homogeneous. Although topographically the medulla can be viewed as a dorsal extension of the spinal cord, the cytoarchitecture of the medulla differs radically from that of the spinal cord and embodies a tightly packed amalgam of dispersed areas, compact nuclei, and fiber tracts. The medulla contains nuclei of several cranial nerves, including the nucleus of the hypoglossal nerve and a complex of nuclei of the vagus nerve. In fact, many medullary nuclei boast complex compartmental cytoarchitecture; the nucleus of the solitary tract, for example, is composed of nine cytoarchitectonically distinct sunuclei.

Glial cells are the most numerous cells in the central nervous system. They are less complex than neurons, and they show less structural diversity. Unlike neurons, they retain the ability to divide, a facility they use in their participation in the reaction of nervous tissue to injury. There are two types of glial cells in the CNS: oligodendrocytes and astrocytes. The peripheral nervous system contains a related cell type, the Schwann cell, which is crucial to the formation and maintenance of the myelin sheaths of peripheral nerves. Within the brain, glial cells are involved with structural and metabolic maintenance of neuronal function and the blood-brain barrier. During the fetal and postnatal development, glial cells play a role in axon guidance and the correct arrangement of neural patterns.

An overview of the cellular anatomy of the brain would be incomplete without reference to the ependymal cells lining the cerebral ventricles, the meningeal membranes surrounding and physically supporting the brain, and the network of blood vessels that form the vascular supply to the brain. Unlike neurons and glial cells, these elements are not exclusive to the nervous system. They share many common structural and functional features with other support cells found throughout the body.

Chemoarchitecture

For most of the twentieth century, the understanding of human neuroanatomy was gleaned mainly from cytoarchitectonic observations. The most widely used maps of the human cortex were produced by Brodmann in 1909 on the basis of Nissl substance and myelin staining, while the most detailed neuroanatomical description of the human hypothalamus was published by Brockhaus in 1942 and was also based on early cytoarchitectonic techniques. The main shortcoming of early neuroanatomical techniques was their distance from the mechanisms underlying human brain function. One of the most exciting developments in neuroanatomy was the identification of chemical coding for individual neural pathways and the proliferation of chemoarchitectonic techniques, which allow almost unlimited scope in the classification of neuronal groups. Chemoarchitecture establishes a bridge between structural and functional characteristics of neuronal populations in the brain. Chemical neuroanatomy has been used to establish the organizational plan of brain regions in experimental animals and to infer their human homologies. It has also been useful in identifying chemically specified connections in animals. Finally, it has helped to derive hypotheses on the function of brain pathways and nuclei. Chemical neuroanatomy has developed as a branch of the structural brain mapping methodology that was previously based largely on cytoarchitectonic consideration of cell shape, size, and density. The insubordination of chemically specified neurons to classic cytoarchitectonic boundaries required a more meaningful delineation of the brain, one that incorporates the information about the distribution of neuroactive substances, connectivity, and function. In this respect, chemical neuroanatomy opened a new dimension in neuroscience and allowed greater precision, resolution, and reliability in differentiating cell groups and brain areas.

Studies using chemical neuroanatomy were first carried out in rats to facilitate logistical and technical applications. It was not until the 1980s that the chemoarchitectonic techniques of histochemistry and immunohistochemistry became sensitive enough to allow their full application to human brain tissue. Thus, it became increasingly possible to reveal the distribution of some of the important neurotransmitters, receptors, and enzymes of in the human brain and then make cross-species comparisons. An advantage of chemoarchitecture is that each chemical substance offers a different window on the organization of the central nervous system, with successive stains revealing more of the areas of interest. There are, of course, significant species differences, and any given substance may have inconsistent distributions in otherwise homologous nuclei and areas. Nevertheless, in terms of overall value, chemoarchitectonic delineations have become a preferred method in comparative neuroscience. Naturally, the neuroactive profile of neurons offers grounds for determining the organization of neuronal groups within a species and for comparing them across species. For example, dopamine, norepinephrine, epinephrine and γ-aminobutyric acid (GABA) are neuroactive chemical compounds that can characterize neuronal subgroups. However, the term *chemoarchitecture* implies the use of chemical compounds for differentiation between neuronal populations. These compounds are not only neurotransmitters but can also be enzymes, receptors, peptides, and molecules related to neuronal metabolism—calcium-binding proteins, for example.

Catecholamines are a family of functionally important neurotransmitters. The application of the tyrosine hydroxylase enzyme immunohistochemistry allowed the identification of fifteen groups of catecholaminergic neurons in the mammalian brain. These cell groups were not confined to traditional cytoarchitectonic boundaries and sequentially were termed A1 to A16 (there is no A3 cell group), extending throughout the mammalian brain from the medulla to olfactory bulbs. In the human, as in the rat, the majority (A1–A2 and A4–A10) of catecholaminergic neuronal groups were found in the brain stem, where, for example, tyrosine hydroxylase immunostaining has been used to delineate the intermediate reticular zone. Four prominent tyrosine hydroxylase positive catecholaminergic cell groups (A11–A15) are located in the hypothalamus and one (A16) in the substantia innominata of the ventral forebrain. The later cell group is thought to be homologous to the rat's catecholaminergic cell group in the olfactory bulb. Subsequent work has shown that cell groups such as the A1 and C1 catecholaminergic neurons are critical for autonomic control in experimental animals and also that these cell groups are strikingly similar in rats and humans. A number of studies used multiple markers to confirm a high degree of conservation in the chemical identity of brain-stem neurons among rats, monkeys, and humans.

Neuropeptides are largely neuron-specific chemical compounds that, depending on the neuropeptide, are characteristic of specific neuronal subgroups. For example, vasopressin is characteristic of large cells in the lateral magnocellular subnucleus of the paraventricular hypothalamic nucleus. The corticotropin-releasing factor (or hormone CRF) is a neuroendocrine peptide in the cortex, basal telencephalon, brain stem, and hypothalamus. The distribution of CRF is very specific. In neuroanatomy CRF distribution has been used in the human brain to distinguish the subcompartmental organization of specific nuclei in the medulla and hypothalamus. In the paraventricular hypothalamic nucleus, for example, CRF neurons are confined to the parvicellular compartment, whereas the neurons that contain oxytocin are found primarily in the dorsal compartment. Applying these two markers to the same brain allowed researchers to distinguish between these subcompartments, which otherwise appear to be amalgamated, and also allowed the establishment of subcompartmental homologies between the paraventricular nucleus in rats and humans.

As an example of a distinct receptor distribution, the NK3 receptor (a component of Neuromedin K peptide circuitry) in the human hypothalamus was found in neurons of the paraventricular nucleus, specifically in the parvicellular and posterior subnuclei, thus distinguishing these structural subcompartments. Another prominent population of NK3-containing cells in the human hypothalamus was found in the perifornical nucleus, distinguishing it from the rest of the lateral hypothalamic area. The neuromedin K circuitry in experimental animals seems to play an important role in blood-pressure regulation; in cross-species comparison there were marked similarities in the distribution of NK3 in the human and rat hypothalamus.

Functional Systems

The anatomy of functional systems reflects, first of all, the neural basis of specific neural functions. At the systems level we can introduce a functional aspect to structural neuroanatomy. By this means we can begin to address which regions are involved with which function and determine those aspects of cellular and regional anatomy that contribute to specialized functions. For example, in the visual system the sensory part is made up of a sensory transducer (the retina) and a sensory nerve (the optic nerve). After some initial processing, these components transmit visual information into two structures in the thalamus and midbrain (the lateral geniculate nucleus and then the superior colliculus) for further processing. Visual information is then projected to the visual regions of the neocortex (in the occipital lobes) for final assessment. Cellular and regional neuroanatomy can tell us the detailed structure of each component, but at the systems level we want to know how the components interact: which neurotransmitters are used in which connections, which cells receive which type of information, and what routes are used between the various structures.

It is important to study the connections between neuronal groups. There are various techniques that reveal neuronal connections, including axonal degeneration, anterograde and retrograde tracing, various dyes, and even virus tracing, which enables researchers to trace not just one affiliation but an entire functional pathway. Techniques such as the tensor MRI (magnetic resonance imaging) allow the identification of projection and their direction in the living brain. Combined with cytoarchitecture tracing techniques, such advances have enabled researchers to make meaningful conclusions about the neural circuitry underlying specific functions.

Conclusion

Many of the pioneer neurophysiologists (e.g., David Ferrier, Charles Sherrington) who provided the seminal experimental observations of the functions of the nervous system appreciated the contributions that neuroanatomy made to the interpretation of their findings. Since the same strategy is still a prerequisite for the neuroscience of today, a great deal of current research concentrates on describing the direction and the biochemical and molecular composition of the neurons connecting different neural systems.

The complicated array of cell groups and fiber pathways in the brain form an incestuous web rather than a hierarchy; however, the connecting threads can be teased apart thanks to advances in neuroanatomical methods that allow a cellular level of resolution.

Bibliography

Mai, J. K., Assheuer, J., and Paxinos, G. (1997). *Atlas of the human brain.* San Diego: Academic Press.

Nolte, G. (2002). *The human brain: An introduction to its functional anatomy.* St. Louis: Mosby.

Paxinos, G. (1990). *The human nervous system.* San Diego: Academic Press.

Alan G. Watts
Revised by Yuri Koutcherov and George Paxinos

AMYGDALA

The amygdala, a complex of several nuclei located in the anteromedial part of the temporal lobe, was named in the nineteenth century for its supposed resemblance to an almond (Latin, *amygdalum*) embedded in the temporal lobe. This portion of the brain is involved in a wide range of functions, including emotion, biologically based behaviors, attention, memory, and learning. It exhibits pathological and pathophysiological changes in several important neurological and psychiatric diseases, including temporal lobe epilepsy, Alzheimer's disease, schizophrenia, anxiety disorders, and depression.

Figure 1

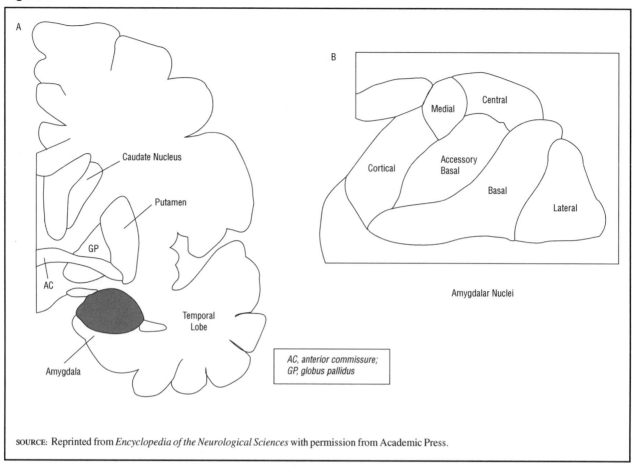

AC, anterior commissure;
GP, globus pallidus

SOURCE: Reprinted from *Encyclopedia of the Neurological Sciences* with permission from Academic Press.

A. Drawing of a coronal section through the human brain at the level of the amygdala (only the right half of the brain is shown; the amygdala is actually found on both sides of the brain). Note that the amygdala (gray) is located in the anteromedial part of the temporal lobe. B. Enlargement of the amygdala at the level shown in A, illustrating the locations of the main amygdalar nuclei.

Investigations in the 1990s demonstrated that the human amygdala is critical for the recognition of the emotional significance of auditory, visual, and olfactory stimuli, including complex stimuli such as facial expressions, vocal intonation, and expressive body movements. These findings came from studies of patients who had the amygdalar region surgically removed to control epilepsy, patients who have a rare disease (Urbach-Wiethe disease) that exhibits selective destruction of the amygdala, and normal individuals who were studied using function magnetic resonance imaging (fMRI). The human amygdala is also important for learning conditioned emotional responses (usually fear) to sensory stimuli and events. These findings agree with numerous animal studies that have shown that the amygdala is essential for classical Pavlovian fear conditioning to simple sensory cues and to complex sensory representations such as the context in which an emotional event has occurred. Additional investigations in humans and animals have demonstrated that the release of noradrenaline in the amygdala is essential for the formation and recall of memories involving emotional events.

Intrinsic Structure

The amygdaloid complex consists of cortical areas on the medial surface of the temporal lobe and several deep nuclei (see Figure 1). Traditionally, two major amygdalar nuclear groups were recognized: a superficial "corticomedial" group (which included the cortical, medial, and central nuclei) and a deeper "basolateral" group (which included the lateral, basal, and accessory basal nuclei). However, studies in the 1980s and 1990s indicated that the central and medial nuclei exhibit anatomical characteristics that are different from those of the remainder of the corticomedial group. Therefore, in this entry the amygdalar nuclei will be divided into three main groups: the basolateral nuclear group; cortical nuclear group; and centromedial nuclear group. In addition, attenuated portions of the centromedial nuclear group extend forward to become continuous with a brain region called the bed nucleus of the stria terminalis, which is located in the septal region adjacent to the anterior commissure. The term *extended amygdala* has been used to designate the centromedial group and its forward extensions, including the bed nucleus.

Extensive connections operate within and between the amygdaloid nuclei. The major axonal systems between nuclei arise in the lateral, basal, and accessory basal nuclei and terminate in successively more dorsomedial parts of the amygdala. In contrast, only moderate projections exist in the opposite direction.

Neurons

The cell types in the basolateral and cortical nuclear groups are similar to each other. Most of the neurons in both groups are termed *pyramidal cells* because they resemble the pyramidal neurons in the cerebral cortex. They have large pyramidal-shaped cell bodies and dendrites that exhibit a dense covering of dendritic spines. The pyramidal cells are the main projection neurons of these nuclear groups (i.e., their axons project out of the amygdala and allow the amygdala to activate other brain regions). Pyramidal cells are thought to utilize the amino acid glutamate as an excitatory neurotransmitter. The remaining cell types in the basolateral and cortical nuclear groups are nonpyramidal neurons. These cells are morphologically heterogeneous and have dendrites that lack spines. The axons of these cells establish synaptic contacts with neighboring amygdalar neurons but do not extend beyond the amygdala (i.e., they are interneurons). They utilize gamma-aminobutyric acid (GABA) as an inhibitory neurotransmitter.

Unlike the nuclei of the basolateral and cortical nuclear groups, the cell types of the centromedial group do not resemble those of the cerebral cortex. Neurons in the lateral portions of the centromedial amygdala resemble the medium-sized spiny neurons of the adjacent caudate and putamen. Most of the neurons in the centromedial nuclear group contain neuropeptides, GABA, or both. Neurons in the more rostral parts of the extended amygdala (e.g., the bed nucleus of the stria terminalis) are similar to the cell types found in the central and medial amygdalar nuclei.

Functional Anatomy

Bilateral damage to the amygdaloid nuclei in monkeys produces the Kluver-Bucy syndrome, in which the animal is unable to appreciate the emotional and behavioral significance of sensory stimuli (psychic blindness). As a result, monkeys with amygdalar lesions exhibit a lack of appropriate emotional and social behavior, including a loss of fear and aggressiveness. In fact, the amygdala is thought to form an essential link between brain regions that process sensory information (such as the cerebral cortex and thalamus) and brain regions responsible for eliciting emotional and motivational responses (such as the hypothalamus, brain stem, and striatum). For this reason the amygdala has been called the "sensory gateway to the emotions."

The amygdala has extensive connections with the olfactory cortex and with sensory association areas in the cerebral cortex (see Figure 2A). The cortical and medial nuclei receive olfactory information from the olfactory cortex and olfactory bulb. The amygdala also receives visual and auditory information from the temporal lobe, somatosensory and viscerosensory information from the insular lobe, and polysensory information from the prefrontal cortex and hippocampal region. These nonolfactory inputs primarily target the basolateral and, to a lesser extent, the centromedial amygdala. The basolateral but not the centromedial, amygdalar nuclei have reciprocal projections back to these same cortical regions. The latter projections may be important for attention to emotionally and behaviorally significant stimuli and for the storage of emotional memories.

The amygdala also has connections with a variety of subcortical regions (see Figure 2B). Projections from the thalamus to the amygdala, which arise mainly from the midline and intralaminar thalamic nuclei and terminate primarily in the basolateral and central amygdalar nuclei, convey auditory, somatosensory, viscerosensory, and visual information to the amygdala. Amygdalothalamic projections are more limited and consist of projections from the central nucleus to the midline thalamic nuclei and from the basolateral amygdala to the mediodorsal thalamic nucleus.

Extensive reciprocal connections operate between the medial portions of the preoptic-hypothalamic region and the amygdala, particularly the medial amygdalar nucleus, the cortical nuclei, and medial portions of the basolateral amygdala. Consistent with these connections, stimulation and lesion studies in experimental animals have shown that the amygdala is involved in behavior related to biological drives and motivation, including arousal, orienting, and sleep; fight or flight; feeding and drinking; and social, reproductive, and maternal behavior. In humans these behaviors are often associated with emotional feelings (e.g., fear with flight, anger and rage with fighting and defensive behavior). In each of these emotional states the amygdala generates a coordinated response consisting of autonomic, endocrine,

Figure 2

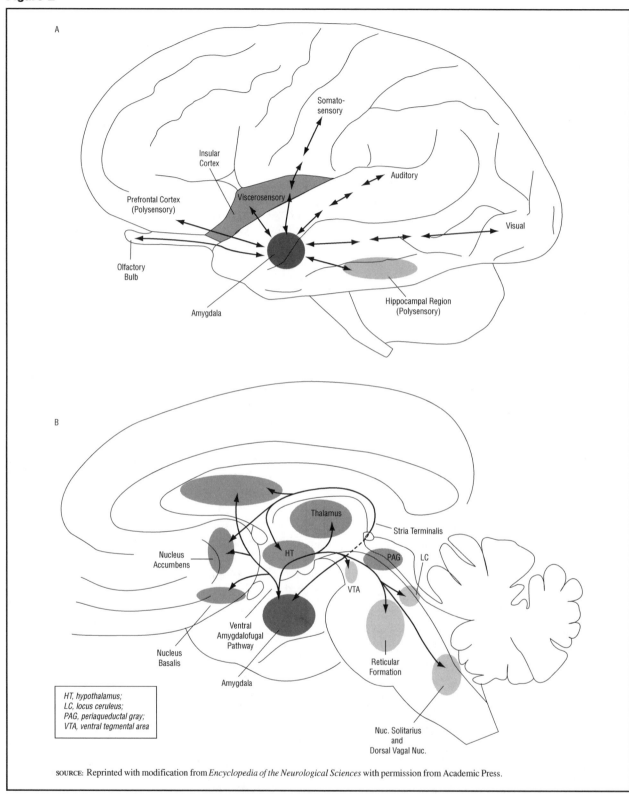

SOURCE: Reprinted with modification from *Encyclopedia of the Neurological Sciences* with permission from Academic Press.

A. Drawing of a lateral view of the human brain illustrating the anatomy of the main cortical pathways conveying sensory information to the amygdala. Note that somatosensory, auditory, and visual information is transmitted to the amygdala over polysynaptic cortical pathways; only higher order cortical areas involved in processing the most complex sensory information in these modalities have projections to the amygdala. B. Drawing of a medial view of the human brain illustrating the connections of the amygdala with subcortical brain regions. All connections are reciprocal except those to the caudate and nucleus accumbens, which do not have projections back to the amygdala.

and behavioral components by way of its projections to various subcortical regions, especially the hypothalamus. The endocrine responses produced by amygdalar stimulation are due to its activation of hypothalamic areas that control the secretion of hormones by the pituitary gland.

Another significant subcortical target of the amygdala that is important for producing behavioral responses is the striatum (caudate, putamen, and nucleus accumbens). This projection originates mainly in the basolateral nuclear group and terminates primarily in the ventral and medial portions of the striatum, including the nucleus accumbens. Lesion studies indicate that the projections of the basolateral amygdala to the striatum are important for controlling behavior related to the reinforcing properties of sensory stimuli.

The central nucleus is the main amygdalar region exhibiting connections with the brain stem and basal forebrain. Among these targets are several areas involved in visceral function, including the parabrachial nucleus, dorsal vagal nucleus, and nucleus solitarius. In addition, the central nucleus innervates several brain regions that give rise to neurotransmitter-specific fiber systems that target the amygdala and other forebrain areas. These regions include the locus ceruleus (noradrenergic), substantia nigra and ventral tegmental area (dopaminergic), raphe nuclei (serotonergic), and the nucleus basalis (cholinergic). The latter region is also innervated by portions of the basolateral nuclear group. These transmitter-specific systems are activated in particular behavioral states, particularly during stress, and can modulate amygdalar activities related to emotion, attention, and memory.

Conclusion

The amygdala is an anatomically complex region of the brain that contains many distinct nuclei. Each nucleus is characterized by distinctive connections with specific brain areas. By way of these connections the amygdala generates a variety of behaviors related to basic biological drives and motivation. The amygdala also appears to be critical for the formation of emotional memories.

See also: EMOTION, MOOD, AND MEMORY; GENETIC SUBSTRATES OF MEMORY: AMYGDALA; LONG-TERM POTENTIATION: AMYGDALA; NEURAL SUBSTRATES OF CLASSICAL CONDITIONING: FEAR CONDITIONING, FREEZING; NEURAL SUBSTRATES OF CLASSICAL CONDITIONING: FEAR-POTENTIATED STARTLE; NEURAL SUBSTRATES OF EMOTIONAL MEMORY; PASSIVE (INHIBITORY) AVOIDANCE, FEAR LEARNING; REINFORCEMENT OR REWARD IN LEARNING: STRIATUM

Bibliography

Aggleton, J. P., ed. (1992). *The amygdala: Neurobiological aspects of emotion, memory, and mental dysfunction*. New York: Wiley-Liss.
——— (2000). *The amygdala: A functional analysis*. Oxford: Oxford University Press.
Alheid, G. F., de Olmos, J. S., and Beltramino, C. A. (1995). Amygdala and extended amygdala. In George Paxinos, ed., *The rat nervous system*, pp. 495–578. Orlando, FL: Academic Press.
Gloor, P. (1997). *The temporal lobe and limbic system*. New York: Oxford University Press.
LeDoux, J. (1996). *The emotional brain*. New York: Simon and Schuster.
McDonald, A. J. (1998). Cortical pathways to the mammalian amygdala. *Progress in Neurobiology* 55, 257–331.
Price, J. L., Russchen, F. T., and Amaral, D. G. (1987). The limbic region. Part 2: The amygdaloid complex. In A. Björklund, T. Hökfelt, and L.W Swanson, eds., *Handbook of chemical neuroanatomy*, Vol. 5, pp. 279–388. Amsterdam: Elsevier.

Joseph L. Price
Revised by Alexander J. McDonald

BASAL FOREBRAIN

The septal area, the diagonal band nuclei, and the nucleus basalis of the substantia innominata are components of the basal forebrain. These structures lack a true cortical organization but can be said to have a "corticoid" architecture because of their location on the surface of the cerebral hemispheres (Mesulam, 2000). The basal forebrain projects to many different regions, using excitatory amino acids, GABA, and acetylcholine as the transmitters. Its single most important output is a cholinergic projection directed to the hippocampus, amygdala, and all other parts of the cerebral cortex (see Figure 1). The projections from the septal and diagonal band nuclei to the hippocampus travel in the fornix. In the human brain, the massive projections from the nucleus basalis to the cerebral cortex travel in the external and extreme capsules, the uncinate fasciculus, and the cingulum (Selden et al., 1998).

The medial septal nucleus of the primate brain is an inconspicuous structure containing relatively small neurons. Less than half of the medial septal neurons are cholinergic and correspond to the Ch1 sector of the basal forebrain. A second group of somewhat larger cholinergic neurons is embedded within the vertical nucleus of the diagonal band of Broca, a nucleus that is usually considered a component of the septal complex. Approximately three-quarters of the neurons of the vertical limb nucleus are cholinergic and constitute the Ch2 sector. The substantia innominata (or the subcommissural gray) is a complex region composed of the ventral globus pallidus, the nucleus basalis of Meynert, and the horizontal nucleus of the

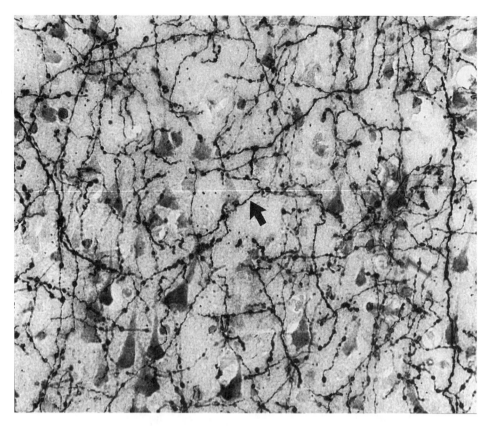

Figure 1. Inferotemporal visual association cortex of the human brain processed for acetylcholinesterase histochemistry shows a dense plexus of cholinergic axons (arrow) coming from the basal forebrain. *(M-Marsel Mesulam)*

diagonal band. A small percentage (a tenth or less) of the neurons in the horizontal limb nucleus are cholinergic and constitute the Ch3 sector. These neurons tend to be hypochromic on Nissl stains and are shaped like a spindle.

The most conspicuous group of cholinergic neurons in the primate brain is found within the nucleus basalis of Meynert. Approximately 90 percent of the larger neurons in the nucleus basalis of the monkey and human brain are cholinergic and constitute the Ch4 sector (see Figure 2). In the human brain, each hemisphere may contain approximately 200,000 nucleus basalis neurons, about 90 percent of which belong to Ch4 (Arendt, Bigl, Tennstedt, and Arendt, 1985). The anteroposterior extent of the human Ch4 complex is 1.5 to 2 centimeters. In addition to the cholinergic neurons within the cytoarchitectonic confines of the nucleus basalis, there are interstitial cholinergic neurons embedded within the anterior commissure, the ansa peduncularis, the ansa lenticularis, and the internal capsule (Mesulam and Geula, 1988). These neurons can be considered part of the Ch4 complex on the basis of morphological, cytochemical, and hodological criteria.

Gorry (1963) pointed out that the nucleus basalis displays a progressive evolutionary trend, becoming more and more extensive and differentiated in more highly evolved species, especially in primates and cetaceans. Observations of the brains of turtles, mice, rats, squirrel monkeys, rhesus monkeys, and humans are consistent with this general view. There are considerable interspecies differences in the organization of these cholinergic pathways. The rodent cerebral cortex contains intrinsic cholinergic interneurons whereas the primate does not, making it entirely dependent on afferents from the basal forebrain for its cholinergic innervation. Furthermore, the Ch4 neurons of the primate express calbindin, whereas those of the rodent do not.

The Ch4–nucleus basalis complex displays a partial overlap with surrounding cell groups of the preoptic area, hypothalamus, striatum, diagonal band of Broca, amygdala, and globus pallidus. There is no strict delineation between nuclear aggregates and passing fiber tracts. As noted above, many Ch4 neurons are embedded within the internal capsule, the diagonal bands of Broca, the anterior commissure, the ansa peduncularis (inferior thalamic peduncle), and the ansa lenticularis. In fact, previous designa-

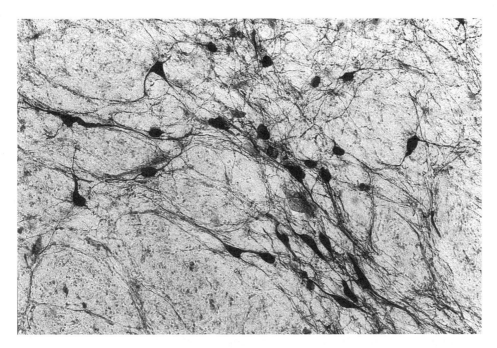

Figure 2.   Choline acetyltransferase immunohistochemistry in the human brain shows cholinergic Ch4 neurons. *(M-Marsel Mesulam)*

tions for the nucleus basalis included "nucleus of the ansa peduncularis" and "nucleus of the ansa lenticularis." The physiological implication of this intimate association with fiber bundles is unknown. In addition to this open nuclear structure, the neurons of Ch4 are of variable shape and have an isodendritic morphology with overlapping dendritic fields. These characteristics, also present in the nuclei of the brain-stem reticular formation, have led to the suggestion that the Ch4 complex could be conceptualized as a telencephalic extension of the brain-stem reticular core (Ramon-Moliner and Nauta, 1966).

Studies using monkeys (based on the concurrent demonstration of perikaryal cholinergic markers and retrograde transport) have shown that each group of cholinergic cells projects widely but also with some degree of topographical specificity. According to these studies, Ch1 and Ch2 collectively provide the major source of cholinergic input for the hippocampal formation, Ch3 provides the major cholinergic input to the olfactory bulb, and Ch4 provides the major cholinergic innervation for the amygdala and all neocortical regions. The primate Ch4 can be divided into anteromedial (Ch4am), anterolateral (Ch4al), intermediate (Ch4i), and posterior (Ch4p) subsectors. Each cortical area receives its cholinergic input primarily (but not exclusively) from a specific subsector of Ch4. For example, Ch4am is the major source of cholinergic innervation for the cingulate gyrus and adjacent medial cortical areas; the Ch4al subsector is the major source of cortical innervation for the amyg-

dala and the frontoparietal operculum; the Ch4i subsectors provide the major cholinergic innervation for peristriate, inferotemporal, and lateral frontoparietal cortex; and the Ch4p subsector provides the major source of cholinergic innervation for the superior temporal gyrus and the temporopolar area. Not all cortical areas receive an equal density of cholinergic fibers. There is a much more intense cholinergic innervation in limbic and paralimbic areas than in association and primary sensory-motor areas. Cholinergic drugs may therefore be expected to have their greatest impact on limbic and paralimbic areas.

Limbic and cortical areas of the primate brain contain several different types of postsynaptic muscarinic and nicotinic receptors. The dominant species is the pirenzepine-sensitive m1 subtype of muscarinic receptor. The regional distribution of this receptor subtype shows a relatively good agreement with the regional distribution of presynaptic cholinergic fibers (Mash, White, and Mesulam, 1988). Electron microscopic examinations of immmunostained tissue shows that incoming cholinergic fibers make traditional synaptic contact predominantly on dendritic spines of cortical pyramidal neurons (Smiley, Morrell, and Mesulam, 1997). At m1 muscarinic receptor sites, the acetylcholine that is released by cortical cholinergic fibers reduces the potassium conductance of the postsynaptic membrane and promotes the activation of cholinoceptive neurons by other excitatory inputs (Krnjevic, 1981). These physiological properties have led to the designation of acetylcholine as an excitatory neuromodulator.

The cholinergic Ch4 neurons receive cholinergic, glutamatergic, GABAergic, noradrenergic, serotonergic, and dopaminergic inputs (Záborszky, Cullinan, and Luine, 1993; Smiley, Morrell, and Mesulam, 1999). All cortical areas receive cholinergic input, but only limbic and paralimbic areas send substantial neural projections back to the nucleus basalis–Ch4 complex (Mesulam and Mufson, 1984). This anatomical arrangement indicates that most cortical areas have no direct feedback control over the cholinergic innervation that they receive, whereas limbic and paralimbic areas have powerful feedback control over the cholinergic input that they receive and over the cholinergic input directed to other parts of cortex. The Ch4 complex may thus act as a cholinergic relay for rapidly shifting cortical activation in a way that reflects the emotional-motivational state encoded by the limbic system. A restricted corticofugal control of widely distributed corticopetal pathways appears to be a feature common to other transmitter-specific systems (e.g., monoaminergic) that are also implicated in setting global behavioral states.

Single-unit studies indicate that neurons in the nucleus basalis of the rhesus monkey are sensitive to sensory information that signals the delivery of reward (Wilson and Rolls, 1990). Cholinergic projections may thus help to enhance the cortical impact of motivationally relevant events. Such an effect would influence both selective attention and learning. Experiments in various animal models are consistent with this dual role of cortical cholinergic innervation (Berger-Sweeney et al., 1994; Sarter and Bruno, 2000; Voytko et al., 1994). Cholinergic projections from the basal forebrain also influence learning-induced physiological and structural plasticity within the cerebral cortex (Kilgard and Merzenich, 1998).

The vast majority of Ch4 neurons express the p75 NGF receptor (NGFr). These neurons are dependent on NGF retrogradely transported from the cerebral cortex for survival. This makes them particularly vulnerable to cortical diseases such as Alzheimer's disease (AD). The few NGFr-negative Ch4 neurons selectively project to the amygdala and adjacent structures (Heckers and Mesulam, 1994). There is an age-related loss of calbindin in human Ch4 neurons (Wu, Mesulam, and Geula, 1997). This may contribute to their vulnerability to neurofibrillary degeneration in AD. Neurofibrillary tangles in Ch4 and a severe loss of cortical cholinergic innervation are hallmarks of AD neuropathology. Cholinesterase-inhibiting drugs are used to treat AD, with the aim of reversing some of this cholinergic depletion.

See also: ALZHEIMER'S DISEASE: HUMAN DISEASE AND THE GENETICALLY ENGINEERED ANIMAL MODELS; COGNITIVE ENHANCERS; NEOCORTICAL PLASTICITY: AUDITORY CORTEX; PHARMACOLOGICAL TREATMENT OF MEMORY DEFICITS

Bibliography

Arendt, T., Bigl, V., Tennstedt, A., and Arendt, A. (1985). Neuronal loss in different parts of the nucleus basalis is related to neuritic plaque formation in cortical target areas in Alzheimer's disease. *Neuroscience 14*, 1–14.

Berger-Sweeney, J., Heckers, S., Mesulam, M-M, Wiley, R. G., Lappi, D. A., and Sharma, M. (1994). Differential effects upon spatial navigation of immunotoxin-induced cholinergic lesions of the medial septal area and nucleus basalis magnocellularis. *Journal of Neuroscience 14*, 4,507–4,519.

Gorry, J. D. (1963). Studies on the comparative anatomy of the ganglion basale of Meynert. *Acta Anatomica 55*, 51–104.

Heckers, S., and Mesulam M-M. (1994). Two types of cholinergic projections to the rat amygdala. *Neuroscience 60*, 383–397.

Kilgard, M. P., and Merzenich, M. M. (1998). Cortical map reorganization enabled by nucleus basalis activity. *Science 279*, 1,714–1,718.

Krnjevic, K. (1981). Cellular mechanisms of cholinergic arousal. *Behavioral and Brain Sciences 4*, 484–485.

Mash, D. C., White, W. F., and Mesulam, M-M. (1988). Distribution of muscarinic receptor subtypes within architectonic subregions of the primate cerebral cortex. *Journal of Comparative Neurology 278*, 265–274.

Mesulam, M-M. (2000). Behavioral neuroanatomy: Large-scale networks, association cortex, frontal syndromes, the limbic system, and hemispheric specialization. In M-M Mesulam, ed., *Principles of behavioral and cognitive neurology*, 1–120. New York: Oxford University Press.

Mesulam, M-M., and Geula, C. (1988). Nucleus basalis (Ch4) and cortical cholinergic innervation in the human brain: Observations based on the distribution of acetylcholinesterase and choline acetyltransferase. *Journal of Comparative Neurology 275*, 216–240.

Mesulam, M-M., and Mufson, E. J. (1984). Neural inputs into the nucleus basalis of the substantia innominata (Ch4) in the rhesus monkey. *Brain 107*, 253–274.

Ramon-Moliner, E., and Nauta, W. J. H. (1966). The isodendritic core of the brain. *Journal of Comparative Neurology 126*, 311–336.

Sarter, M., and Bruno, J. P. (2000). Cortical cholinergic inputs mediating arousal, attentional processing, and dreaming: Differential afferent regulation of the basal forebrain by telencephalic and brainstem afferents. *Neuroscience 95*, 933–952.

Selden, N. R., Gitelman, D. R., Salamon-Murayama, N., Parrish, T. B., and Mesulam, M-M. (1998). Trajectories of cholinergic pathways within the cerebral hemispheres of the human brain. *Brain 121*, 2,249–2,257.

Smiley, J. F., Morrell, F., and Mesulam, M-M. (1997). Cholinergic synapses in human cerebral cortex: An ultrastructural study in serial sections. *Experimental Neurology 144*, 361–368.

Smiley, J. F., Subramanian, M., and Mesulam, M-M. (1999) Monoaminergic-cholinergic interactions in the primate basal forebrain. *Neuroscience 93*, 817–829.

Voytko, M.L., Olton, D. S., Richardson, R. T., Gorman, L. K., Tobin, J. R., and Price, D. L. (1994). Basal forebrain lesions in monkeys disrupt attention but not learning and memory. *Journal of Neuroscience 14*, 167–186.

Wilson, F. A. W., and Rolls, E. T. (1990). Neuronal responses related to novelty and familiarity of visual stimuli in the substantia innominata, diagonal band of Broca and periventricular region of the primate basal forebrain. *Experimental Brain Research 80*, 104–120.

Wu, C.-K, Mesulam, M-M., and Geula, C. (1997). Age-related loss of calbindin from basal forebrain cholinergic neurons. *NeuroReport 8*, 2,209–2,213.

Záborszky, L., Cullinan, W. E., and Luine, V. N. (1993). Catecholaminergic-cholinergic interaction in the basal forebrain. *Progress in Brain Research 98*, 31–49.

M-Marsel Mesulam

BASAL GANGLIA

The basal ganglia are subcortical nuclei that are highly developed in primates and are strongly interconnected with the neocortex. They are major components of the telencephalon (endbrain) in mammals and lie beneath the cerebral cortex, which forms the outer sheet of the endbrain. The basal ganglia include two well-known parts of the extrapyramidal motor system (the striatum and the pallidum). Technically, the amygdala is also part of the basal ganglia, but, as a functional system quite different from the striatopallidal complex, falls outside the scope of this article.

The basal ganglia are involved in motor and psychomotor control and are therefore a central focus for studies of Parkinson's disease and Huntington's disease, motor disorders involving reduced movement capacity (Parkinson's disease) or too much movement (Huntington's disease). It is recognized that the basal ganglia can affect neuropsychiatric and cognitive functions and that basal ganglia dysfunction thus may contribute to neuropsychiatric disorders. Examples of neuropsychiatric disorders involving the basal ganglia include obsessive-compulsive disorder and Tourette's syndrome.

The basal ganglia are part of cortico-basal ganglia circuits receiving inputs from the neocortex (and thalamus), processing that information, interacting with modulatory loop-circuits, and passing the processed information on to the frontal neocortex (via the thalamus) and to brainstem targets such as the superior colliculus and the reticular formation (see Figure 1). Nearly the entire cortex projects to the striatum, which is considered the main input site of the basal ganglia. The striatum, in turn, projects to the pallidum (globus pallidus), which gives rise to the main basal ganglia outflow to the thalamus and other sites. A remarkable characteristic of these basal ganglia connections is that they are inhibitory. The striatum inhibits the pallidum, and the pallidum inhibits the thalamus. This means that activation of the striatum can release the thalamus and other output targets (see Figure 1).

This double-inhibition circuit is considered to be critical to the release of movements and complex ac-

Figure 1

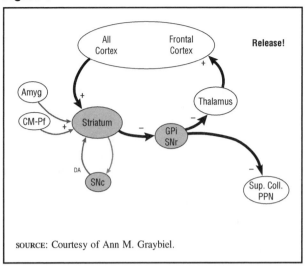

SOURCE: Courtesy of Ann M. Graybiel.

Schematic information flow diagram showing the basic release circuit of the basal ganglia. Darker shading, main elements of the basal ganglia. Many neocortical areas project to the striatum, which also receives input from the amygdala (Amyg), the intralaminar thalamus (CM-Pf), and the substantia nigra pars compacta (SNc), which provides dopamine (DA) to the striatum. There is a double inhibitory pathway from the striatum to the internal pallidum (GPi) and substantia nigra pars reticulata (SNr) and then on to the thalamus. Thus excitatory input coming from the cortex excites the thalamocortical projection of the system, releasing it from chronic inhibition by the GPi/SNr. Other outputs of the system are shown leading downstream to the superior colliculus (Supp. Coll.) and the pendunculopontine nucleus (PPN). Note in Figure 2 how this basic circuit, the *direct pathway* of the basal ganglia, is paired with the *indirect pathway*.

tions, probably including cognitive actions. An important aspect of the circuit is that most of the striatal neurons that project to the pallidum (projection neurons) fire action potentials phasically at low rates. But pallidal neurons fire tonically (nearly continuously) at high rates. These physiological findings suggest that the basal ganglia tonically inhibit their targets (e.g., the thalamus) but that when the striatum becomes active, this tonic inhibition is briefly (phasically) released. Because the inputs to the striatum are excitatory, the general circuit plan involves cortical excitation of the striatum, leading through the double inhibition to release of the thalamus. This release from inhibition (known as disinhibition) is considered to underlie the movement release-inhibition functions of the basal ganglia.

The striatum and pallidum act in close cooperation with two other nuclei, the substantia nigra and the subthalamic nucleus. The substantia nigra lies in the midbrain and attains a very large size in the human brain. The substantia nigra has two parts, one of which is called the pars reticulata and is very much like the pallidum. The nigral pars reticulata is, judging by its anatomy, likely to be a differentiated extra part of the pallidum displaced caudally into the midbrain. Like the pallidum, the pars reticulata of the substantia nigra receives input from the striatum and projects strongly to the thalamus. An important difference from the pallidum is that the nigral pars reticulata also projects to the superior colliculus, a structure involved in controlling eye movements (especially saccadic eye movements). The second part of the substantia nigra is the pars compacta. Its neurons synthesize the neurotransmitter dopamine, and they give rise to the dopamine-containing nigrostriatal tract, which innervates the striatum and releases dopamine there. In Parkinson's disease, these neurons degenerate, leading to a loss of dopamine in the striatum.

The second nucleus closely associated with the striatum and pallidum is the subthalamic nucleus. This nucleus (named for the fact that it lies in the territory underneath the thalamus) is a key regulator of the release-inhibition functions of the basal ganglia (see Figure 2). It receives inhibitory input from the pallidum's so-called external segment and sends excitatory output back to the pallidum. It thus is disinhibited when the striatum is phasically activated, and it excites the pallidum's internal segment. This subthalamic loop or indirect pathway opposes the action of the direct pathway from striatum to internal pallidum to thalamus (see Figure 2).

The striatum, as the input side of the basal ganglia and as the first stage of the main pathways leading out from the basal ganglia, sets up important functional subdivisions of the basal ganglia and its circuits. The striatum has three anatomical subdivisions that roughly correspond to functional parts: the caudate nucleus, the putamen, and the ventral striatum. The caudate nucleus makes up the largest part of the striatum at anterior levels and receives strong inputs from the frontal cortex and some other areas of association cortex. The putamen is the large, laterally placed nucleus of the striatum and receives most of the input from sensorimotor and association cortex. The ventral striatum—which, as its name implies, lies at the base of the striatum—receives inputs related to the limbic system (including inputs from the hippocampal formation and amygdala).

All three of these large subdivisions of the striatum project to corresponding parts of the pallidum and substantia nigra. There is considerable evidence that these pathways are fairly distinct from one another, so that the functional channels set up in the striatum are maintained in the pallidum and substantia nigra and, in their outflow pathways, to the rest of the brain. This is true also for the dopamine-containing

Figure 2

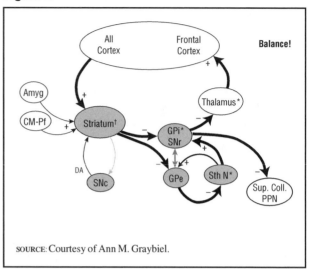

SOURCE: Courtesy of Ann M. Graybiel.

Schematic flow diagram showing the balance between the direct and indirect pathways of the basal ganglia. The movement release pathway (shown as black in Figure 1) is called the direct pathway, and the opposing pathway is called the indirect pathway (shown here). When the two are in balance, the system is at equilibrium. When the direct pathway is more active, the thalamus is disinhibited, but when the indirect pathway is more active, the thalamus is inhibited. Asterisks indicate focal sites for neurosurgical intervention in Parkinson's disease therapy. Dagger indicates site for dopamine replenishment or dopamine receptor activation used in Parkinson's disease therapy and site of primary neurodegeneration in Huntington's disease. Plus signs indicate excitatory (glutamatergic) connections; minus signs indicate inhibitory (GABAergi) connections.

projections from the midbrain to the striatum. For example, medial to the nigra substantia pars compacta, in and near the midline of the midbrain, there are other dopamine-containing neurons that form the ventral tegmental area. This region innervates the ventral striatum and is part of reward circuits of the brain, mediating reward-based behaviors and some forms of drug addiction (e.g., to cocaine and amphetamine).

These functional subdivisions are differentially affected in the major disorders associated with basal ganglia dysfunction. The dorsal striatum (caudate nucleus and putamen) are abnormal in Parkinson's disease and Huntington's disease. The most severe motor disturbances in these disorders are associated with loss of dopamine (Parkinson's disease) or neurons (Huntington's disease) in the putamen, which receives inputs from sensory and motor cortex. Cognitive-affective disturbances in these disorders are associated with loss of function in the caudate nucleus, which receives inputs from frontal areas of the association cortex. Neuropsychiatric disorders ranging from obsessive-compulsive disorder to depression are also associated with abnormal function of the caudate nucleus. Dysfunction of the ventral striatum is suspected in some psychiatric disorders, including schizophrenia. The ventral tegmental area, which projects to the ventral striatum, is largely spared in Parkinson's disease. The anatomical organization of basal-ganglia pathways suggests that the cortically directed outflow of the basal ganglia mainly targets executive areas of the neocortex, including motor, premotor, or prefrontal cortex. The breadth of frontal cortex affected may also help to account for the broad functional influences of the basal ganglia suggested by clinical evidence.

Some disorders affecting the basal ganglia are associated with major changes in neurotransmitter systems in basal-ganglia circuits. Drugs affecting these systems include not only levodopa, given to Parkinson's patients as a replacement therapy for the lost dopamine, but also agents with powerful effects on mental activity and behavior, including antipsychotics such as haloperidol (a dopamine receptor antagonist) and psychoactive drugs such as marijuana. This large range also conforms to evidence that the basal ganglia mediate cognitive-affective as well as motor functions.

The basal ganglia are implicated not only in the continuing control of action but also in the learning mechanisms that underlie the development of the near-automatic behaviors that we think of as habits and rituals. Studies of these learning functions of the basal ganglia suggest that the anatomical circuits summarized here are actually highly dynamic networks. Recordings from behaving animals suggest that the activity patterns of neurons in the striatum undergo major changes as the animals become conditioned or learn new procedures. A teaching signal for the striatal neurons is thought to come from the dopamine-containing neurons of the substantia nigra. This new evidence suggests that the very nuclei disabled in disorders such as Parkinson's disease and Huntington's disease normally help to modify cortico-basal ganglia circuits as a result of experience, so that habits and procedures can be learned and produced as whole sequences or chunks. Such automatized behaviors are fundamentally important in freeing the brain to react to new events in the environment and to carry out many cognitive functions. The basal ganglia, then, may provide a base for cognitive activity as well as for motor activity.

See also: REINFORCEMENT OR REWARD IN
LEARNING: ANATOMICAL SUBSTRATES;
REINFORCEMENT OR REWARD IN LEARNING:
STRIATUM

Bibliography

Graybiel. A. M. (1997). The basal ganglia and cognitive pattern generators. *Schizophrenia Bulletin 23*, 459–469.

Graybiel, A. M., Aosaki, T., Flaherty, A. W., and Kimura, M. (1994). The basal ganglia and adaptive motor control. *Science 265*, 1,826–1,831.

Graybiel A. M., and Penney J. B. (1999). Chemical architecture of the basal ganglia. In F. E. Bloom, A. Björklund, and T. Hökfelt, eds., *Handbook of chemical neuroanatomy*. Amsterdam: Elsevier.

Graybiel, A. M., and Rauch, S. L. (2000). Toward a neurobiology of obsessive-compulsive disorder. *Neuron 28*, 343–347.

Hikosaka O., Miyashita K., Miyachi S., Sakai K., and Lu, X. (1998). Differential roles of the frontal cortex, basal ganglia, and cerebellum in visuomotor sequence learning. *Neurobiology of Learning and Memory 70* 137–149.

Leckman, J. F., and Riddle, M. A. (2000). Tourette's syndrome: When habit-forming systems form habits of their own? *Neuron 28*, 349–354.

Mink, J. W. (1996). The basal ganglia: Focused selection and inhibition of competing motor programs. *Progressive Neurobiology 50*, 381–425.

Salmon, D. P., and Butters, N. (1995). Neurobiology of skill and habit learning. *Current Opinion in Neurobiology 5*, 184–190.

White, N. M. (1997). Mnemonic functions of the basal ganglia. *Current Opinion in Neurobiology 7*, 164–169.

Wichmann T., and DeLong, M. R. (1996). Functional and pathophysiological models of the basal ganglia. *Current Opinion in Neurobiology 6*, 751–758.

Ann M. Graybiel

CEREBELLUM

That cerebellum's importance as a component of the motor system is clearly indicated by its anatomy and by the effects of lesions or pathology. Abnormal development of or injury to the cerebellum results in severe impairment of the ability to produce accurate and coordinated movements. Normal, everyday movements become uncoordinated and clumsy, hobbled by errors in direction, rate, amplitude, sequence, and precision. Depending on which portions of the cerebellum are damaged, these impairments can include abnormal voluntary movements of the limbs (e.g., reaching movements that miss the target), abnormal eye movements (e.g., saccades that miss the target), or abnormal vestibular (balance) reflexes and postural adjustments (e.g., patients struggling simply to stand without falling over).

How the neurons and synapses of the cerebellum contribute to accurate and coordinated movements has been the subject of much research and debate. The anatomy of the cerebellum indicates that some sort of sensory-motor integration is taking place. There is also evidence that the cerebellum contributes not only to the learning of and adaptation to movements based on experience, but also to the proper timing of movements. These various ideas about cerebellar function are all related to a relatively simple

Figure 1

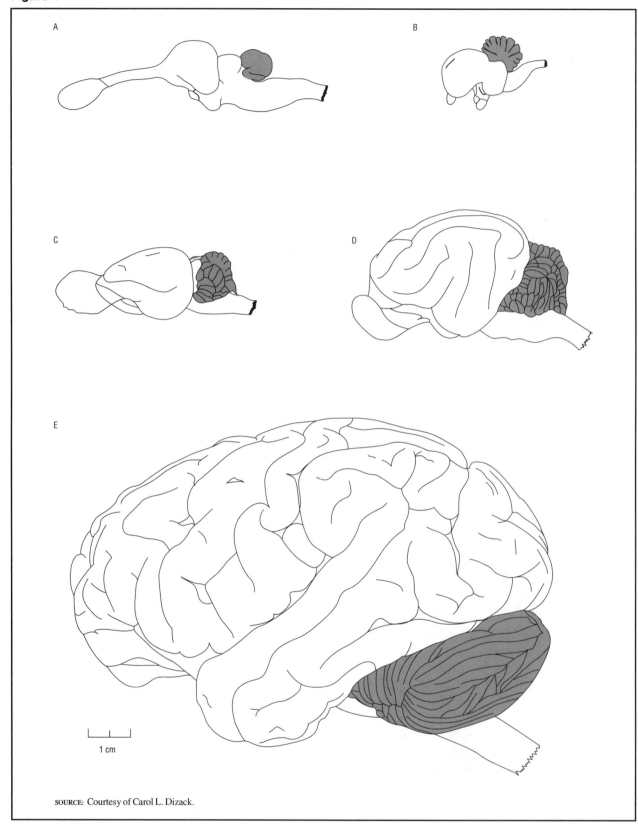

SOURCE: Courtesy of Carol L. Dizack.

The cerebellum (in gray) varies widely in relative size, shape, and folding pattern in different animals: A. alligator; B. pigeon; C. opossum; D. domestic cat; E. chimpanzee. All brains are viewed from the left side and are drawn to the same scale. In the larger animals (cat and chimp), the cerebral cortex extends backward over the top of the cerebellum, concealing its greater size and complexity.

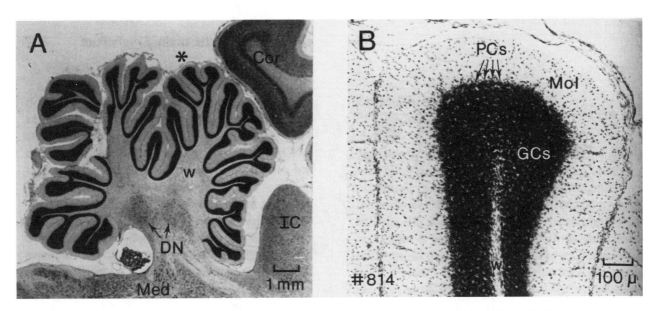

Figure 2. Stained 30-micron section through the whole cerebellum (A) and through a single fold or folium (B) of a domestic cat. In A the front of the brain is to the right, where cerebral cortex (Cor) overlies a portion of the cerebellum and an auditory center (inferior colliculus, IC) protrudes up in front of the cerebellum at the anterior part of the medulla (Med) of the brainstem. The asterisk (*) in A indicates the folium that is enlarged in B. In B, the molecular layer consists mostly of parallel fibers as well as the dendrites (not stained) of Purkinje, Golgi, basket, and stellate cells. The large Purkinje cells lie in a row just above the densely packed tiny granule cells. Magnification of each photograph is indicated by the scale bars. Abbreviations: DN, deep cerebellar nuclei; GC, granule cells; Mol, molecular layer; PC, Purkinje cells; W, white matter (axons). *(T. P. Stewart and Carol L. Dizack)*

function that the cerebellum performs. It uses sensory information in a particular way (feedforward) to contribute to the accuracy of movements. Understanding what this means and how the cerebellum accomplishes this task requires a basic appreciation of the anatomy and connectivity of the cerebellum.

All vertebrates have a cerebellum (see Figure 1). It lies behind the forebrain and on top of the hindbrain. If you grab the back of your neck (fairly high), your hand surrounds the cerebellum. It is a small, smooth protuberance in most fish, amphibians, and reptiles, but in birds and mammals the surface of the cerebellum is folded into a complex arrangement of thin, elongated folia. The size, shape, and complexity of the cerebellum vary widely in different mammals; those that have more complex behavioral repertoires that are modifiable by learning are likely to have a larger and more convoluted cerebellum.

Figure 2 illustrates some of the unique anatomical features of the cerebellum. A stained section just lateral to the midline reveals the highly folded cerebellar cortex (each fold is a folia), which consists of a three-layer sheet of neurons. The cerebellar cortex is about one millimeter thick in all mammals. Near the base of the cerebellum are several clusters of neurons that make up the cerebellar deep nuclei, which provide the output of the cerebellum. The white matter beneath the cortex and around the deep nuclei con-

sists of numerous axons, providing connections between the cortex, deep nuclei, and other parts of the central nervous system.

All ideas about cerebellar function stem from its unique connectivity or wiring diagram. Although the cerebellum contains a great many neurons, there are only seven types of neurons in the cerebellar cortex that are interconnected in highly organized and specific ways (see Figure 3). Thus, the wiring diagram of the cerebellum lends itself to accessible depiction of the sort shown in Figure 4. Neurons of the deep nuclei provide the output of the cerebellum; they project to the motor nuclei such as the red nucleus and vestibular nuclei, and to the VL region of thalamus, which projects mostly to motor regions of cerebral cortex. The Purkinje cells are the sole output of the cerebellar cortex; they inhibit neurons of the deep nuclei. Mossy fibers represent one type of input to the cerebellum. They project directly to the deep nucleus neurons and to the cerebellar cortex. In the cortex, they branch diffusely to contact numerous granule and Golgi cells. In turn, the granule cell axons, the parallel fibers, make excitatory connections onto many Purkinje cells. Despite its many subtleties, the main properties of the cerebellum's wiring diagram are relatively simple. Output via the deep nucleus neurons is influenced by two parallel pathways: the direct excitatory pathway from mossy fibers and the more complex inhibitory pathway from the Purkinje

Figure 3

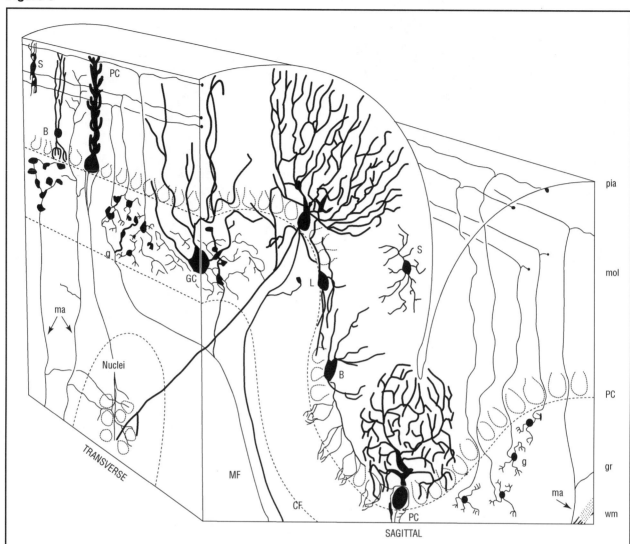

Abbreviations: PC, Purkinje cell and Purkinje cell layer; B, basket cell; g, granule cell; S, stellate cell; GC, Golgi cell; L, cell of Lugaro; ma, monoamine axons; mol, molecular layer; gr, region of granule-cell layer; wm, white matter; pia, pia-arachnoid layer covering the cerebellar surface; MF, mossy-fiber input from brain-stem sources projecting into the granule cell layer; CF, climbing fiber input from the inferior olivary nucleus of the brain stem to a Purkinje cell. "Transverse" means a cross section and "Sagittal" means the plane from front to back.

SOURCE: Adaption of a figure in "Cerebellar Dentate Nucleus: Organization, Cytology, and Transmitters," by S. L. Palay and V. Chan–Palay. From *Cerebellar Cortex: Cytology and Organization*. Springer–Verlag GmbH & Co. KG. Reproduced by permission of the publisher.

Schematic drawing of the major cell and axon types and their connections in a portion of cerebellar cortex. Connections to the deep nuclei (Nuclei) are also shown.

cells. A simple numeric ratio illustrates the relative complexity of these pathways. For every deep-nucleus output neuron there are about 2 million parallel fiber synapses onto the Purkinje cells.

A second type of input to the cerebellum, the climbing fibers, are quite different from the mossy fibers. Climbing fibers project to the cerebellar cortex and contact only a few Purkinje cells. There are also weak collateral projections to the deep nuclei. Whereas each Purkinje cell has around 100,000 inputs from different granule cells, it gets input from only one climbing fiber. The climbing fiber branches profusely, "climbs" over the dendrites of the Purkinje cell, and makes numerous synapses. This spatially distributed input is so powerful that each action potential in the climbing fiber produces an all-or-none response in the Purkinje cell, which, in part, involves the wide-

Figure 4

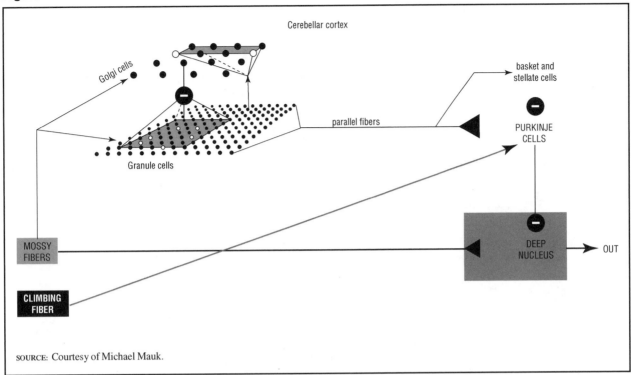

SOURCE: Courtesy of Michael Mauk.

A schematic representation of the synaptic organization or wiring diagram of the cerebellum. Cells in the deep nuclei provide the output of the cerebellum. These neurons are controlled by excitatory mossy fiber inputs and inhibitory input from the Purkinje cells of the cerebellar cortex. The mossy fiber inputs to the cerebellar cortex excite both granule and Golgi cells. The granule cells provide excitatory input to the Purkinje cells via their axons, which are called parallel fibers. Climbing fiber inputs to the cerebellum project primarily to the Purkinje cells.

spread influx of calcium into the Purkinje cell. This calcium influx is important for the synaptic changes that mediate the learning in the cerebellum.

In 1969 David Marr published a theory of cerebellum that proposed that the wiring diagram described above is well suited to adapt movements via learning. There are three main components of Marr's theory:

- The mossy fiber/granule cell inputs encode what is happening for the Purkinje cells. Mossy fibers convey all sorts of sensory information, especially the position of the body, and information about motor commands from the cerebral cortex. Thus, each combination of motor commands and sensory input would produce a unique pattern of mossy-fiber activity and an even more complex pattern of granule-cell activity. These different patterns would allow Purkinje cells to respond differently under various circumstances.
- Climbing fibers, in contrast, seem to convey signals indicating that a movement should be different from each other.
- Marr then suggested that these climbing-fiber signals would alter the strength of the granule cell

to Purkinje synapses that were active at that time. In this way the movement could be different next time, and this learning would be specific for the combination of circumstances encoded by that particular pattern of granule-cell activity.

The basic tenets of this theory have been supported by a wide variety of experimental evidence. There are several well-characterized examples of motor learning that require the cerebellum, and plasticity in the cerebellum controlled by climbing fibers has been firmly established. Results from eyelid-conditioning experiments provide a straightforward example. This simple example of motor learning involves training an animal by repeatedly presenting a relatively neutral stimulus like a tone paired with a reinforcing stimulus like a puff of air in the eye (see Figure 5A). Initially, the eyelids do not move during the tone, but with repeated training, the tone elicits a learned closure of the eyelids. Lesion, stimulation, and recording experiments have shown that the tone-activated mossy-fiber inputs to the cerebellum, the puff activates climbing-fiber inputs, and output from a cerebellar deep nucleus is responsible for the expression of the learned responses (see Figure 5B).

Figure 5

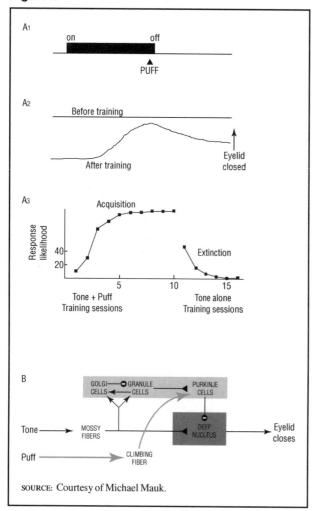

SOURCE: Courtesy of Michael Mauk.

The relationship of Pavlovian eyelid conditioning and the cerebellum. A₁. A schematic representation of a typical eyelid conditioning training trial. A neutral stimulus such as a tone is paired with a reinforcing stimulus such as a puff of air directed at the eye. A₂. Example eyelid responses from a conditioning experiment. For each trace, eyelid closure is indicated by upward deflection. Before training presentation of the tone has no consistent effect on the eyelids. After training the tone elicits a robust and well-timed conditioned eyelid closure. A₃. Example learning curves for eyelid conditioning. Training with the tone paired with the puff gradually increases the likelihood that the tone will elicit a conditioned eyelid response. This process is called acquisition. Extinction of the conditioned responses occurs when training consists of presentation of the tone alone, without the puff. In extinction training, the tone gradually loses its ability to elicit the conditioned eyelid response. B. A schematic representation of the way in which eyelid conditioning engages the cerebellum. Conditioned stimuli such as a tone are conveyed to the cerebellum via activation of mossy fibers, whereas presentation of the reinforcing unconditioned stimulus is conveyed to the cerebellum via activation of climbing fibers. Output of the cerebellum via one of the deep nuclei (anterior interpositus in the case of eyelid responses) drives the expression of the conditioned response.

Eyelid-conditioning experiments also reveal the temporal specificity or timing component of this cerebellar learning. The eyelids do not close at the onset of the tone (as they do for the puff); instead, the responses are delayed to peak at the time the puff is presented, optimizing the adaptive, protective nature of the response.

Figure 6 illustrates the sequence of events believed to occur during cerebellar learning—for example, eyelid conditioning. The tone activates a certain subset of mossy fibers, which, in turn, activate a subset of the granule cells. All these tone-activated mossy fibers may excite the deep nucleus neurons; eyelid responses are absent in part because the Purkinje cells are spontaneously active, and their inhibition of the nucleus cells prevents a response. Since the puff activates climbing fibers, the synapses made by the tone-activated granule cells onto the Purkinje cells are modified—they are made weaker. Eventually, the Purkinje cells learn to decrease activity during the tone, which releases the deep nucleus cells from inhibition and contributes to the expression of the conditioned responses. Learning seems to involve changes in the deep nuclei as well, which also contribute to the ability of the tone to excite the deep-nucleus neurons and produce a learned conditioned response.

Although such results are a clear illustration, the cerebellum did not evolve to mediate eyelid conditioning. Rather, such experiments reveal the basic capacity of the cerebellum for learning and reveal the basic properties of this learning. From such revelations the purpose of the cerebellum's capacity to learn becomes clearer. It is exactly the type of learning required to permit sensory input to improve the accuracy of movements. Making accurate movement necessarily requires input from sensory systems; this input is revealed by the severe motor impairments that result from sensory impairments like large-fiber neuropathies, wherein information about the position of the body does not reach the brain.

In principle, sensory input can be used in two ways to guide movements. One is via feedback, whereby a movement command is initiated; then sensory input is used during the execution of the movement to make the corrections required for proper performance. Feedback can be very effective and requires no learning, but it is slow. For this reason feedback cannot be used for most of our movements. The other alternative is feedforward. In this mode, sensory input is used at the beginning of a movement (when the motor command is issued) to guess what muscle forces will produce the proper movement. It can be schematized in this way: Given this command and the present sensory input, and based on previous experi-

Figure 6

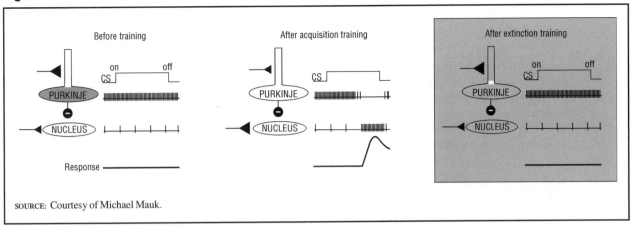

SOURCE: Courtesy of Michael Mauk.

A schematic representation of the cerebellar learning thought to occur during eyelid conditioning. Each cartoon depicts typical activity of a Purkinje cell, a deep nucleus cell, and the corresponding eyelid response that would be expected. Also, the strength of the granule to Purkinje synapses and the mossy fiber to deep nucleus synapses (those activated by the tone) are depicted by the relative size of the triangles. Before training (left panel), the granule-to-Purkinje synapses are relatively strong, and the mossy fiber-to-nucleus synapses are relatively weak. Thus, presenting a tone has little effect on the spontaneous activity of the Purkinje cell and provides little excitatory input to the deep nucleus cells. The result is little change in the activity of the nucleus cell. After acquisition training (center panel), the tone-activated granule-to-Purkinje synapses are weaker so that presenting the tone causes a decrease or cessation of Purkinje cell activity. The mossy fiber-to-nucleus synapses may also be strong. The combination of decreased inhibition and increased excitation increases the deep nucleus cell activity and elicits a conditioned response. After tone-alone extinction training (right panel) the granule-Purkinje synapses have strengthened, and the spontaneous Purkinje cell activity does not decrease during the tone. Since the deep nucleus neurons are strongly inhibited during the tone by the Purkinje cells, the conditioned responses are suppressed.

ence, here are the forces that are likely to produce an accurate movement.

Notice that "based on previous experience" means learning. Indeed, it means the type of learning where errors in performance (like those that the climbing fibers convey) make changes so that later, given a similar situation (like those that the mossy fibers convey), performance will improve. If you reach for an object and miss, cerebellar learning makes adjustments so that the next time your hand naturally arrives at the right spot. The cerebellum is constantly using this type of learning to make small adjustments so that our movements remain accurate. We can see, then, that the inaccurate and uncoordinated movements arising from damage to the cerebellum reflect performance without the benefit of the cerebellum's reservoir of previous experience.

See also: GENETIC SUBSTRATES OF MEMORY: CEREBELLUM; LONG-TERM DEPRESSION IN THE CEREBELLUM, HIPPOCAMPUS, AND NEOCORTEX; NEURAL COMPUTATION: CEREBELLUM; NEURAL SUBSTRATES OF CLASSICAL CONDITIONING: DISCRETE BEHAVIORAL RESPONSES; VESTIBULO-OCULAR REFLEX (VOR) PLASTICITY

Bibliography

Bloedel, J. R., Dichgans, J., and Precht, W., eds. (1985). *Cerebellar functions.* New York: Springer-Verlag.

Chan-Palay, V. (1977). *Cerebellar dentate nucleus: Organization, cytology and transmitters.* New York: Springer-Verlag.

Glickstein, M., Yeo, C., and Stein, J., eds. (1987). *Cerebellum and neuronal plasticity.* New York: Plenum Press.

Ito, M. (1984). *The cerebellum and neural control.* New York: Raven Press.

Linden D. J., and Connor, J. A. (1995). Long-term synaptic depression. *Annual Review of Neuroscience 18,* 319–57.

Marr, D. (1969). A theory of cerebellar cortex. *Journal of Physiology 202,* 437–470.

Mauk, M. D., and Donegan, N. H. (1997). A model of Pavlovian eyelid conditioning based on the synaptic organization of the cerebellum. *Learning and Memory 4,* 130–158.

Mauk, M. D., Medina, J. F, Nores, W. L. and Ohyama, T. (2000). Cerebellar function: Coordination, learning or timing? *Current Biology 10,* R522–R525.

Medina, J. F., Garcia, K. S., Nores, W. L., Taylor, N. M., and Mauk, M. D. (2000). Timing mechanisms in the cerebellum: Testing predictions of a large scale computer simulation. *Journal of Neuroscience 20,* 5,516–5,525.

Medina, J. F., and Mauk, M. D. (2000). Computer simulation of cerebellar information processing. *Nature Neuroscience 3,* 1,205–1,211.

Palay, S. L., and Chan-Palay, V. (1974). *Cerebellar cortex: Cytology and organization.* New York: Springer-Verlag.

Raymond, J., Lisberger, S.G., and Mauk, M. D. (1996). The cerebellum: A neuronal learning machine? *Science 272,* 1,126–1,132.

Thach, W. T., Goodkin, J. P., and Keating, J. G. (1992). Cerebellum and the adaptive coordination of movement. *Annual Review of Neuroscience 15,* 403–442.

W. I. Welker
Revised by Michael Mauk

Figure 1

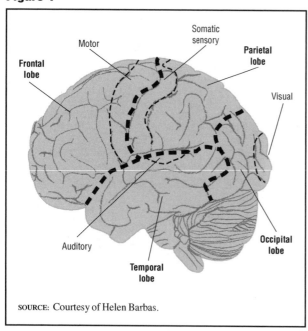

SOURCE: Courtesy of Helen Barbas.

The division of the cortex of the human brain into lobes (thick dashed lines) and into the primary sensory and motor areas (thin dotted lines). The gray lines show the numerous sulci of the cortex.

CEREBRAL CORTEX

The cerebral cortex is the large overgrowth of the mammalian forebrain. It is best developed in primates and especially in humans, where it makes up a thin sheet, about 3 mm thick and 1600 cm² in area, folded into intricate convolutions to fit in the skull. Most of the cortex is buried in the banks and depths of elongated crevices called sulci. At a gross level the cerebral cortex is divided into four lobes. In the human brain the frontal lobe is located behind the forehead and above the eyes; the occipital lobe is found at the back of the head. Between them are the parietal lobe, near the top of the head, and the temporal lobe, along the sides of the head, behind the ears (see Figure 1). These lobes are easiest to locate in the brains of humans and other primates, where the sulci divide the cortex into lobes, and the lobes into smaller units, called lobules.

Even at the gross level of lobes, each region of anatomy in the cerebral cortex entails a distinct physiology. Thus, within the frontal lobes there are motor regions devoted to the planning and execution of movements; within the parietal lobe, regions devoted to the sense of touch; within the occipital lobe, regions devoted to vision; and, within the temporal lobe, regions devoted to the sense of hearing (see Figure 1). Each lobe also includes regions, neither sensory nor motor, called association regions, which further analyze sensory information or combine information from two or more senses or from several brain regions. For example, in the frontal lobe there is a region called the prefrontal cortex, which is important for planning and keeping track of sequential tasks such as cooking an elaborate meal or remembering driving directions long enough to get to a destination. Specialized parts of the prefrontal cortex behind the eyes are associated with control of social behavior, sorting appropriate and inappropriate responses demanded by various situations (Damasio, 1994; Fuster, 1997).

The cerebral cortex of the human is highly specialized. For example, one region at the junction of the frontal and temporal lobes, Broca's area, coordinates the movements of the mouth and tongue to produce speech ("motor speech"), while a second region at the junction of the parietal and temporal lobes, Wernicke's area, is necessary for understanding the meaning of spoken and written words ("sensory speech"). Humans with damage in Broca's area are unable to articulate grammatically correct speech, while those with damage in Wernicke's area are capable of fluent, though nonsensical, speech (Geschwind, 1979).

All cortical lobes are further divided into anatomically and physiologically distinct areas. Each cortical area is defined by the unique organization and physiology of the cells within it and by the set of connections the area has with other parts of the brain. There are nearly one hundred known cortical areas, which are usually designated by a numbering scheme, or code. For example, the primary area of cortex devoted to vision is designated area 17, or V1 (visual area 1), and the primary area for movement is area 4, or M1 (see Figure 1).

The cells of the cortex make up the outer gray matter of the brain, and their axons leave the cortex and connect with other cortical areas and other parts of the brain. The cortex also receives information from other brain regions. The white matter just beneath the cortex is made up of axons entering or leaving the cortex. These connections render the cortex a massive communication system. For example, there is two-way communication between the cortex and a region beneath the cortex, the thalamus (Steriade, Jones, and McCormick, 1997). This reciprocal link is very precise, so that one area of the cortex communicates mainly with one or two of the many groups of cells, or nuclei, in the thalamus. In addition, each cortical area on one side of the brain has some connections with its reciprocal area and a few neighboring areas on the opposite side. The connections to the opposite side are made by axons of cortical cells, which form bundles called the corpus callosum and the anterior commissure. The corpus callosum is a major highway linking most of the cortical areas between the two brain halves, or hemispheres. The anterior commissure is a smaller pathway, connecting mostly temporal areas across the hemispheres.

There are other connections between cortical areas on the same side of the brain. Each of the precise connections with the thalamus, opposite cortex, and cortex on the same side contributes to the unique physiological characteristics of a cortical area. More widespread connections that go to all areas of cortex come from cells beneath the cortex and use the chemicals dopamine, norepinephrine, serotonin, acetylcholine, or histamine as neurotransmitters. These widespread connections appear responsible for setting the overall level of activity in the cortex (Foote and Morrison, 1987; Kandel et al., 2000).

A typical area of the cerebral cortex is divided horizontally into six layers. The cells in each layer have similar structure and connections and are segregated from cells in other layers with different properties (see Figure 2, top left panel). Superimposed on the horizontal organization is a vertical grouping of cells across layers, forming cortical columns, or modules. The key to the cortical column is that the cells within a single column are interconnected such that all its cells exhibit common physiological properties, while cells in neighboring columns exhibit different properties. Columns or modules of cells with similar properties are the fundamental units of organization and function in the cerebral cortex and are found throughout the cortex, including areas involved in vision, hearing, movement, or high-order cognitive processes and memory (Mountcastle, 1998). For example, in the visual area of the primate cortex, cells that analyze signals from one eye make up one set of columns, each 0.5 to 1.0 millimeter wide, and these interdigitate with a second set of columns containing cells that analyze signals from the other eye. Thus, cells in different columns are dominated by one eye or the other (Hubel and Wiesel, 1977).

The correlation of function with structure prevails among single cells as well. There are two general categories of cells in the cortex. One, called a pyramidal cell, has a triangular cell body and is excitatory (see Figure 2, top panels). Pyramidal cells are the principal source of axons that leave an area of cortex, carrying information to other cortical areas or to regions outside the cortex. The second category includes cells with a rounded cell body; called nonpyramidal, they play a role in local communication.

Nonpyramidal cells are a heterogeneous group and include one or two types of excitatory cells and many types of inhibitory cells. The latter have differ-

Figure 2

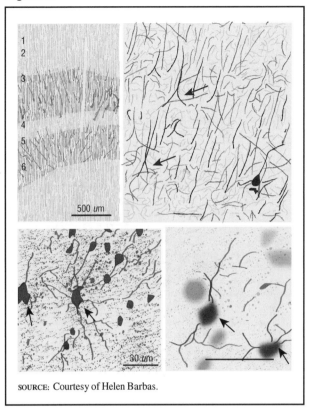

SOURCE: Courtesy of Helen Barbas.

Layers and cell types of the cerebral cortex. (Top, left) Photograph of a thin section through the prefrontal cortex of a nonhuman primate showing the horizontal division of the cortex into six layers. This section was stained to show mostly pyramidal cells in layers 3, 5 and 6; the rest of the neurons in this section are unstained and consequently invisible. (Top, right) Pyramidal cells from the top left section are magnified to show their triangular shape. (Bottom panels) Nonpyramidal cells in the cortex are a heterogeneous group. The panels show photographs of nonpyramidal inhibitory neurons in the cortex (arrows). The scale for the top left panel is 0.5 millimeters (500 micrometers), and at the bottom the scales are 30 micrometers.

ent shapes and colorful names, such as chandelier cells, basket cells, and double-bouquet cells (see Figure 2, bottom panels). Inhibitory cells, which use gamma-aminobutyric acid (GABA) as a neurotransmitter, are important in controlling the activity of other neurons in the cortex (Somogyi et al, 1998). Excitatory cells in the cortex use glutamate as a neurotransmitter. From these excitatory and inhibitory cells and the interconnections they give rise to physiological properties that are unique to the cerebral cortex (Peters and Jones, 1984).

Although extraordinarily complex, the cerebral cortex has a general plan of organization. The great diversity of function of the cerebral cortex is built up from the physiology of single cells to progressively larger compartments that link neurons within modules, layers, areas, and lobes.

Bibliography

Damasio, A. (1994). *Descartes's error: Emotion, reason, and the human brain.* New York: G. P. Putnam's Sons.

Foote, S. L., and Morrison, J. H. (1987). Extrathalamic modulation of cortical function. *Annual Review of Neuroscience 10,* 67–95.

Fuster, J. (1997). *The prefrontal cortex: Anatomy, physiology, and neuropsychology of the frontal lobe.* 3rd edition. New York: Lippincott, Williams, and Wilkins.

Geschwind, N. (1979). Specializations of the human brain. *Scientific American 241,* 180–199.

Hubel, D. H., and Wiesel, T. N. (1977). Ferrier Lecture: Functional architecture of macaque monkey visual cortex. *Proceedings of the Royal Society of London B 198,* 1–59.

Kandel, E. R., Schwartz, J. H., and Jessel, T. M. (2000). *Principles of neural science.* New York: McGraw-Hill.

Mountcastle, V. B. (1998). *Perceptual neuroscience: The cerebral cortex.* Cambridge: Harvard University Press.

Peters, A., and Jones, E. G., eds. (1984). *Cerebral cortex,* Vol. 1: *Cellular components of the cerebral cortex.* New York: Plenum.

Somogyi, P., Tamas, G., Lujan, R. and Buhl, E. (1998). Salient features of synaptic organization in the cerebral cortex. *Brain Research Reviews 26,* 113–135.

Steriade, M., Jones, E. G., and McCormick, D. A. (1997). *Thalamus—organization and function,* Vol. 1: *Organization and function.* Oxford: Elsevier.

Stewart Hendry
Revised by Helen Barbas and Stewart Hendry

HIPPOCAMPUS AND PARAHIPPOCAMPAL REGION

The hippocampus is part of the cerebral cortex. It is closely linked to a restricted number of related cortical areas, which are collectively referred to as the parahippocampal region. Both the hippocampus and parahippocampal region are reciprocally connected with a wide variety of higher order association cortices representing all sensory domains. From this recently emerged perspective it comes as no surprise that scientific conjectures about the functions of the (para)hippocampal network emphasize an important role in higher order cognitive functions, specifically learning and memory processes. The (para)hippocampal structures also have strong functional links with subcortical structures that researchers believe play a role in the selection of behavior in favor of either survival of the individual or of the species.

General Features of the (Para)Hippocampus

In order to describe any feature of a structure, either morphological or connectional, one needs to have a nomenclature. It is inevitable that opinions about nomenclature differ, so for the purposes of this essay differences in numbers of principal layers have been selected as the major criterion. All fields of the hippocampus exhibit a characteristic three-layered appearance. The parahippocampal region, in contrast to the hippocampus, comprises cortical regions, which show more than three, generally five or six, layers. The hippocampus consists of three major subdivisions: the dentate gyrus, the Ammon's horn (fields CA1, CA2, and CA3), and the subiculum. Note that some authors distinguish a prosubiculum from the subiculum proper. Also, readers may find texts in which reference is made to the subicular complex, consisting of (pro)subiculum, presubiculum, and parasubiculum. Based on connectional arguments as well as the criterion chosen for this discussion (number of layers), it is preferred to consider the presubiculum and parasubiculum as functionally different from the subiculum.

In all species the parahippocampal region comprises five main regions: the pre- and parasubiculum, the perirhinal and entorhinal cortices, and a fifth area that in primates is commonly referred to as the parahippocampal cortex. In nonprimates, the most likely homologue for the latter area is the so-called postrhinal cortex. Different researchers have subdivided each of these five regions in a variety of different ways.

All fields of the (para)hippocampus can be easily appreciated as longitudinal strips of cortex, neatly aligned one next to the other, beginning at the dentate gyrus on one end and the most outside portion of the parahippocampal region, in effect the perirhinal field, at the other end. The precise orientation and curvature of this entire cortical structure and thus its overall position in the brain may vary between different species. In species with a clearly developed temporal lobe (humans and monkeys, for example), the hippocampus is more ventrally and anteriorly located; in contrast, the rat's hippocampus looks more like a c-shaped structure positioned in the caudal third of the hemisphere. However, such difference in position does not alter the major characteristics and the topological relations between the hippocampus and the parahippocampal structures. Nor does it influence the fact that the most anterior/ventral portion of the hippocampus has a close spatial relationship with the amygdala.

Wiring of the (Para)Hippocampus

Most detailed information about the connectivity of the system comes from anatomical tracing studies in the rat, although for some pathways relevant detailed information has been collected in other species as well. Overall, the connectivity is rather conservative, such that a general non-species-specific description may suffice. Moreover, this "conserved" connectional organization does allow making inferences concerning the overall organization of the human (para)hippocampus. The hippocampus has two major pathways through which is connected to the rest of the brain. The first pathway makes use of the parahippocampal connectivity and predominantly mediates the connections with the cortex. The second pathway, which mainly, but not exclusively, links the hippocampus to subcortical structures, makes use of the fornix.

The Parahippocampal-Cortical System

The famous Spanish anatomist Ramón y Cajal, who provided one of the most detailed and earliest descriptions of the (para)hippocampal system, emphasized the so-called trisynaptic circuit, comprising an exclusive unidirectional pathway from the entorhinal cortex to the distal dendrites of the granular (simple pyramidal) cells in the dentate gyrus, which, in turn, give rise to the mossy fiber pathway to the proximal part of the apical dendrites of CA3 pyramidal cells. These CA3 neurons finally convey their output by way of the Schaffer axon collaterals to the apical and basal dendrites of pyramidal cells in CA1. The trisynatic circuit was once thought to be organized in restricted planes perpendicular to the longitudinal axis of the hippocampus, such that the structure as a whole was considered as a series of repetitive circuits, so-called lamellae, stacked together along the long axis. This proposal has stimulated functional analysis of the network using isolated brain slices containing these lamellar circuits. However, it also emphasized the relative isolation of the trisynaptic circuitry, which contrast to the notion that the hippocampal trisynaptic circuit has to be part of a larger neural system in order to function. Added details emphasize the overall longitudinal connectivity as an integral feature of the trisynaptic organization. Moreover, the entorhinal cortex is a complex cortical structure in itself that, in addition, has strong reciprocal connections with widespread association cortices, largely mediated by its neighboring parahippocampal fields. Finally, the subiculum has been added on a crucial position within this circuit.

Neurons in entorhinal layers II and III, which are the main recipients of the extensive cortical inputs, give rise to the already mentioned input to the hippocampus, the so-called perforant pathway. This name is derived from the traditional descriptions by Ramón y Cajal, who noted that fibers from the entorhinal cortex perforate the pyramidal-cell layer of the subiculum to gain access to the dentate gyrus molecular layer. The perforant pathway harbors two different projection systems. Layer II cells distribute their axons to most, if not all of the dentate gyrus, as origi-

nally described, but also to CA3. Cells in one particular subdivision of the entorhinal cortex, generally referred to as lateral entorhinal cortex, distribute their axons exclusively to the most distal portions of the dendrites of dentate and CA3 cells. The other subdivision, referred to as medial entorhinal cortex, sends its projection to the middle portions of the apical dendrite. This routing results in a specific laminar termination, such that each neuron receives both pathways but on different segment of its apical dendrite. The second pathway, which attracted more experimental attention only in the late twentieth century, originates from layer III cells and distributes to CA1 and the subiculum. In contrast to the laminar pattern as described for the lateral and medial layer II components, axons of layer III cells target only restricted groups of the available neurons in CA1 and the subiculum. This targeting results in an organization such that the lateral entorhinal cortex disseminates its output only to the neurons clustered around the CA1-subiculum border, whereas the medial entorhinal cortex selectively innervates CA1 neurons close to the border with CA2/CA3 and subiculum neurons, which are close to the border with the presubiculum.

CA1 neurons project to the subiculum and, by doing so, add a fourth synapse to the originally defined trisynaptic circuit. These projections, which are again almost entirely unidirectional, show an interesting topographical organization along the transverse axis, which is reminiscent of that of the entorhinal terminal distribution. Neurons in CA1, close to the border with the subiculum, are connected to subicular neurons, which are similarly close to that border; these two connected populations are thus most likely innervated by entorhinal inputs from the lateral entorhinal cortex. In contrast, CA1 neurons closer to the border with CA3 will distribute their axons to subicular neurons close to the border with the presubiculum; these two connected populations thus most likely receive medial entorhinal inputs.

The lateral and medial entorhinal cortex may process functionally different types of information. The main cortical input of the lateral entorhinal cortex originates from the perirhinal cortex and olfactory cortices, whereas the medial entorhinal cortex receives strong inputs from the presubiculum as well as from the parahippocampal or postrhinal cortex. In view of the aforementioned anatomical organization researchers have suggested that in the hippocampus these two functionally different input streams converge at the level of the dentate gyrus and CA3, whereas they are kept more or less separate at the level of CA1 and the subiculum. This connectional differentiation taken in conjunction with the overall differences in intrinsic wiring between, for example, CA3 and CA1 suggests that the (para)hippocampal system harbors two systems that may be related to different memory processes.

Both CA1 and the subiculum constitute the major output structures of the hippocampus. They distribute strong projections back to the entorhinal cortex, mainly to its deep layers. The overall topographical organization of this projection is in register with that of the perforant pathway, such that a particular portion of the entorhinal cortex, projecting to restricted populations of neurons in CA1 and the subiculum, receive a return projection originating from these same neuronal groups in CA1 and the subiculum. This striking reciprocity, taken in conjunction with the aforementioned overall intrinsic hippocampal organization, may have important functional implications that researchers do not yet fully understand.

The Fornix

The fornix is a major fiber bundle that connects the hippocampus to the hypothalamus, in particular the mammillary bodies. The fornix originates from CA1 and subiculum, although parahippocampal cortices, in particular the pre- and parasubiculum and, to a much lesser extent, the entorhinal cortex, contribute fibers. On its way to the mammillary bodies, the fornix also issues fibers to the septal complex, the ventral striatum, and the amygdala. The fornix also carries the fibers from CA1 and subiculum targeting parts of the prefrontal cortex. The fornix is not a pure output pathway since projections from the septal complex to the hippocampus and in part to the entorhinal cortex travel by way of the fornix. These septal afferents provide the (para)hippocampus with most of its cholinergic inputs. The fornix also forms one of the input routes for the noradrenergic, serotonergic, and dopaminergic innervation. Additional aminergic fibers enter the parahippocampal region through a ventral route. Finally, the commissural connections between the left and right hippocampi also partially travel by way of the fornix.

The hippocampal connection to the mammillary bodies is part of the traditionally described limbic or Papez circuit, which includes the mammillo-thalamic tract connecting the mammillary bodies to the anterior complex of the thalamus, which in turn project to large portions of the limbic cortex, including anterior and posterior cingulate cortex, and pre- and parasubiculum. All these structures, in turn, provide input to the hippocampus, either directly, or indirectly by way of the entorhinal cortex.

Conclusion

The (para)hippocampus may be viewed as a cortical system with bidirectional connections with almost all of the multimodal associational domains of the cerebral cortex as well as a number of subcortical structures reportedly involved in motivation and selection of appropriate behaviors. Therefore, the (para)hippocampus may be at the crossroad of the cognitive and the affective side of behavior. Most functionally oriented research unfortunately addresses either of those sides, whereas a combined analysis of both is rare.

Bibliography

Amaral, D. G., and Witter, M. P. (1995). Hippocampal formation. In G. Paxinos, ed., *The rat nervous system*. San Diego, CA: Academic Press.

Burwell, R. D. (2000). The parahippocampal region: Corticocortical connectivity. *Annals of the New York Academy of Sciences 911*, 25–42.

Ramón y Cajal, S. (1911). *Histologie du Système Nerveux de l'Homme et des Vertebrés*. Maloine, Paris

Witter, M. P., Wouterlood, F. G., Naber, P. A., and van Haeften, T. (2000). Anatomical organization of the parahippocampal-hippocampal network. *Annals of the New York Academy of Sciences 911*, 1–24.

Larry W. Swanson
Revised by Menno P. Witter

NEURON

Cells of the central nervous system are divided into two categories, *neurons* and *glial cells*. The following entry deals with the characteristics of neurons in the vertebrate central nervous system. Neurons are independent morphological, trophic, and functional entities; they develop from the neural plate of the ectoderm. They differ from glial cells in their ability to generate propagated *action potentials* (spikes), in the release of neuroactive substances called *neurotransmitters,* and in their ability to communicate with other cells through specialized membrane junctions called *synapses*. A long debate in the first half of the twentieth century pitted those who maintained that the brain was a continuous reticulum of fibers against those who proposed that elements of the nervous system were discrete cells (for a historical account see Peters, Palay, and Webster, 1991). The first electron microscopic studies decisively resolved the issue by showing that each neuron is delineated by a continuous *plasma membrane* and is separated from other cells by a gap. However, like other cells of the body, neurons in some parts of the nervous system are interconnected through continuous cytoplasmic bridges organized into *gap junctions* that are permeable to ions and small molecules.

Neurons are polarized cells receiving information at certain locations on their plasma membrane and releasing neurotransmitters to other cells, usually from other sites (Kandel and Schwartz, 1985; Peters, Palay, and Webster, 1991; Shepherd, 1990). They emit several processes originating from the *cell body* or *soma*. One (occasionally two or three) of the processes is an *axon* propagating the action potential to the transmitter-releasing nerve terminals. The other processes are called *dendrites* and are usually shorter and branch less frequently than the axon. The shape and three-dimensional distribution of the processes are characteristic of each category of neuron and reflect their connections with other cells and the neuron's place in the neuronal network. The general arrangement is that information arrives through afferent (i.e., inward-transmitting) synapses on the dendritic processes and the cell body, and is transmitted to other cells through axonal enlargements, also called *boutons*, present on the axonal arborization. However, significant exceptions to this rule occur in some parts of the brain. Neurons in invertebrates usually have only one process originating from the cell body that gives rise to branches, all of which both receive and give information and are involved in different operations.

The Soma

The soma has a diameter of five to fifty microns and contains the nucleus and the usual cell organelles present in most cells, with great similarity to those present in secretory cells. This is in line with the observation that most neurons secrete proteins and peptides in addition to small transmitter molecules. For example, the rough endoplasmic reticulum (ER), the site of protein synthesis, is often highly developed and is organized into parallel lamellae forming large *Nissl bodies*. The *Golgi apparatus* is similarly highly developed and often extends into the proximal dendritic processes, which also contain ER and ribosomes. The axons are usually devoid of ribosomes and, together with the nerve terminals, lack the ability for significant protein synthesis. Thus the neuron is also a polarized biochemical machine where protein and other components synthesized in the cell body are transported through the axon to the nerve terminals.

The transport of molecules and organelles between the processes and the soma is bidirectional and is supported by the cytoskeleton, which also maintains the shape of the processes (Kandel and Schwartz, 1985). The cytoskeleton consists of *microtubules* (polymers of *tubulin* dimers, external diameter twenty-five to twenty-eight nanometers); *neurofilaments* (polymers of *cytokeratins*, diameter ten nanometers); and *microfilaments* (polymers of *actin*, diameter five to seven nanometers).

In addition to rough ER, many neurons are rich in smooth ER that is involved in intracellular Ca_2+ storage and release. Cysternae of the ER are often closely aligned with the plasma membrane of both the soma and dendrites forming *subsurface cysternae*.

Lysosomes are found in all neurons. Secondary lysosomes accumulate throughout the life of the cell and coalesce into *lipofuscin granules* showing characteristic distribution for each neuronal type.

The Dendrites

The dendrites are rarely longer than one millimeter and can be as short as ten to fifty microns with a diameter of three to 0.05 microns, tapering toward their tip and decreasing in diameter at branching points. The main difference between them and the axon is that dendrites lack the morphologically distinct initial segment at their origin from the soma. With the exception of peripheral sensory neurons, all neurons have dendrites. They are generally postsynaptic to axon terminals; from scores to tens of thousands of synapses converge on the dendritic tree of a single neuron.

In some parts of the nervous system, most prominently in the retina (amacrine cells), the olfactory bulb, the thalamus, the substantia gelatinosa of the brain stem and spinal cord, and the superior colliculus, dendrites of some classes of cells can be both pre- and postsynaptic. In these cases the dendrite at the presynaptic site contains synaptic vesicles and presynaptic membrane specialization as well as near-by postsynaptic membrane specializations at synapses received by the neuron. Often these combined pre- and postsynaptic sites are located on protrusions, grapelike clusters or gemmules, isolating the formations from each other on the same cell, and providing a basis for independent action. Synapses between two dendrites can be reciprocal, each partner receiving as well as giving synapses to the other at closely located sites.

Dendrites have various short postsynaptic extrusions, the best-known of them being *dendritic spines* (see Figure 1). Spines are particularly prominent and numerous on cortical pyramidal and spiny stellate cells, on Purkinje cells, and on the spiny neurons of the neostriatum. Spines frequently contain a specialized organelle, the spine apparatus, consisting of parallel membrane saccules and continuous with the smooth ER of the dendritic shaft. The spine apparatus is thought to be involved in Ca^{2+} sequestration. Spines usually receive excitatory synaptic input and occasionally an additional inhibitory input. Numer-

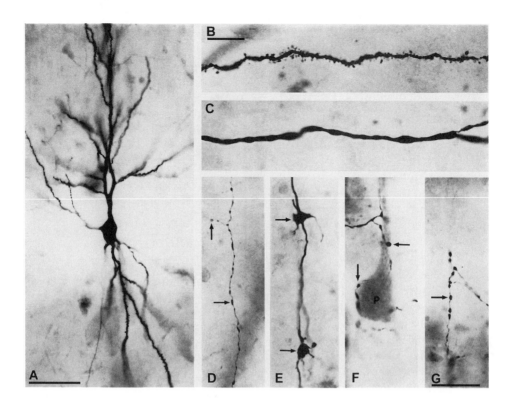

Figure 1. Parts of different neurons in the rat hippocampus shown in light microscopic photographs. The hippocampal formation is involved in memory formation. All cells were marked by intracellular injection of a marker molecule through a fine glass micropipette. The marker was transported to all the processes of the living cells. A. Pyramidal cell in the CA1 region emitting dendrites into two different layers toward the top and bottom of the picture; the two sets of dendrites sample different inputs coming from different sources. The light band in the middle contains the cell bodies of many more unmarked pyramidal cells. The rightmost dendrite is shown at higher magnification (rotated) in B, illustrating the large number of dendritic spines typical of these cells. C. Another type of cell, the basket cell, which has its cell body and dendrites in the same layers as the pyramidal cells, has smooth dendrites. Such dendrites have integrative properties different from spiny dendrites. D-G. Terminal axonal segments of four different neuronal types, showing the differences in transmitter-releasing terminals (arrows) reflecting the specializations in synaptic connections. D. Axon collateral of a CA1 pyramidal cell similar to that shown in A. E. Two terminals of a mossy fiber originating from a granule cell in the dentate gyrus and making synapses with the apical dendrites of hippocampal pyramidal cells (not marked). F. Terminals of a cell (P), seen as a pale silhouette. G. The vertically aligned boutons of a chandelier cell form multiple synaptic contacts with the axon initial segment (not marked) of a pyramidal cell. Basket and chandelier cells release the inhibitory neurotransmitter GABA, but to different parts of the same postsynaptic cell. The pyramidal and granule cell terminals release the excitatory amino acid glutamate. Scales: A, 50 microns; B and C, 10 microns; D-G, 20 microns. *(Peter Somogyi)*

ous theories have been put forward for the role of spines. Of these, the formation of a biochemical compartment, semi-independent from the dendritic shaft and from other spines, seems the most attractive. The integrative properties of dendrites are determined by 1. their shape; 2. their intrinsic membrane properties, underlined by the presence and distribution of different *ion channels*; and 3. the location of synaptic inputs and their relationship to other inputs (for more detail, see Shepherd, 1990).

In addition to receiving and sometimes giving synaptic junctions, dendrites can also be connected to other dendrites and nerve terminals through small cytoplasmic bridges forming gap junctions. Gap junctions are sites of electrotonic transmission because they are permeable to ions and can facilitate the synchronization of neurons.

The Axon

Most neurons have axons; the few exceptions are retinal amacrine cells and granule cells of the olfactory bulb (Shepherd, 1990). Axons usually originate from the soma, rarely from a major dendrite, and

Figure 2

dendrites

cell body

main axon

100 μm

SOURCE: Courtesy of Peter Somogyi based on data in Somogyi, P., Freund, T. F., Hodgson, A. J., Somogyi, J., Beroukas, D., and Chubb, I. W. (1985). Identified axo-axonic cells are immunoreactive for GABA in the hippocampus and visual cortex of the cat. *Brain Research 332*, 143–149.

Tracing of the processes of a local circuit inhibitory neuron, the *chandelier cell*, from the hippocampus of the cat. The terminals of this cell make synapses exclusively with the axon initial segment of pyramidal cells; therefore, the axon is localized mainly to the layer of pyramidal cell bodies enclosed by broken lines. Each vertically oriented terminal axon segment targets one initial segment; thus from this partial reconstruction it can be established that this single chandelier cell makes synapses with at least 320 pyramidal cell dendrites, so the cell has access to all the information pryamidal cells receive. The cell was visualized by Golgi impregnation.

Figure 3

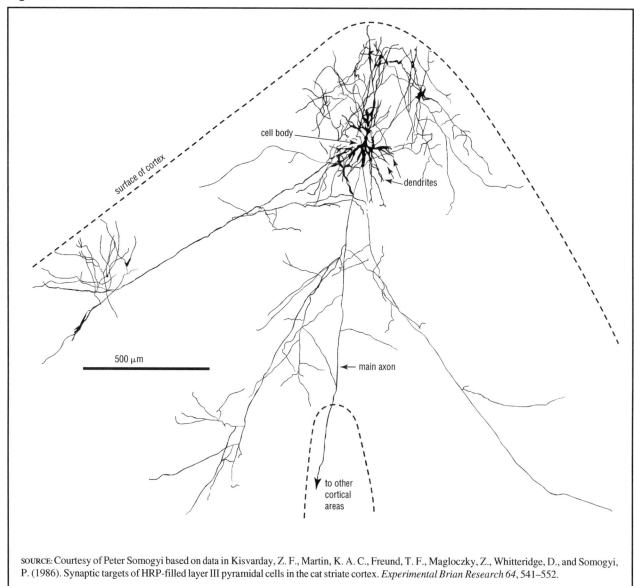

cell body

surface of cortex

dendrites

500 μm

main axon

to other
cortical
areas

SOURCE: Courtesy of Peter Somogyi based on data in Kisvarday, Z. F., Martin, K. A. C., Freund, T. F., Magloczky, Z., Whitteridge, D., and Somogyi, P. (1986). Synaptic targets of HRP-filled layer III pyramidal cells in the cat striate cortex. *Experimental Brian Research 64*, 541–552.

Tracing of the processes of a *pyramidal cell* in the visual cortex of the cat. The cell body is in the superficial layer and emits dendrites reaching a few hundred microns. The main axon descends to the white matter (lower broken line) and proceeds to innervate other cortical areas. On its way through the gray matter, it gives rise to several axon collaterals traveling for several millimeters within the same cortical area and addressing groups of cells with local ramifications while ignoring other groups of cells. The axon also richly supplies neurons in the vicinity of the cell body. Such selective connections enable effective coordination of neurons with similar properties. Having both a local axon arborization and a distant one gives the neuron both a local circuit role and a role in connecting different areas of the brain. The call was visualized by the intracellular injection of a marker molecule.

begin with the axon hillock. A specialized trilaminar inner coat of the membrane, recognizable with the electron microscope, identifies the *axon initial segment,* which has the highest density of voltage-sensitive sodium channels. It is thought to be the site of the generation of the propagated-action potential. A similar membrane undercoating is found in the axon at *nodes of Ranvier* between myelin segments. The other unique feature of the initial seg-

ment is the presence of interconnected microtubules organized into fascicles. In some regions of the brain the axon initial segment can receive numerous synapses. Such synapses are provided by the *chandelier cell,* a specialized inhibitory neuron unique to the cortex, which makes synapses exclusively on the axon initial segment of pyramidal and spiny stellate neurons (see Figure 2). Most axons emit several collaterals along their course, addressing particular brain areas or groups of cells in the same brain area (see Figure 3).

Myelin Sheath

The axons of neurons in the brain can be myelinated for part or for the whole of their course, or can be completely unmyelinated (Peters, Palay, and Webster, 1991). Some types of neurons, such as corticospinal cells and Purkinje cells, always have myelinated axons. The myelin is segmented, and each segment is formed by the plasma membrane of an *oligodendroglial cell*. Segments are interrupted by nodes of Ranvier, where axon collaterals often originate. The axons may acquire myelin for part of their course as they traverse a particularly heavily myelinated part of the brain. Axons may contain synaptic vesicles at nodes of Ranvier, and they may be presynaptic to neighboring dendrites.

Nerve Terminals

The terminal axon arborizations are characteristic of each cell type. The transmitter-releasing sites are bulbs or varicose enlargements having a diameter usually of 0.5 to three microns; they may have a position on the end of axon branches as *boutons terminaux*, or may be varicosities along the axon forming *boutons en passant* (see Figure 1D–G). Many terminal boutons sit on the ends of short stalks branching off from main axon collaterals (see Figure 1D, vertical arrow). Specialized formations of nerve terminals evolved, such as large mossy fiber terminals providing multiple localized input to the same target (see Figure 1E), and climbing fibers providing multiple synapses distributed over the postsynaptic dendritic tree of the same target dendrite or cell. Boutons form *synaptic junctions*. Boutons are usually only presynaptic to other cells, but terminals of a few cell types, most prominently the primary sensory afferents in the brain stem and spinal cord, may receive synapses and are postsynaptic to inhibitory terminals. One bouton may make synaptic junctions with only one postsynaptic element or may provide input to up to about ten different postsynaptic targets originating from about the same number of individual neurons. In some cases almost every bouton of the same axon establishes synapses with a different cell, providing a large degree of divergence in information transfer. Cortical cells, for example, may make synapses with thousands of other cortical neurons in a given area (see Figure 3).

The boutons contain *synaptic vesicles*, which are membrane-delineated discrete structures. The morphology of the vesicles is characteristic of cell types and to some degree correlates with the chemistry of their neurotransmitter content. The two most common families of vesicles are the *small clear vesicles* with a diameter of thirty to fifty nanometers and the *large granulated vesicles* with a fine electron dense core and a diameter of about eighty to two hundred nanometers. Boutons are also rich in mitochondria.

The synaptic vesicle-containing varicosities of some neurons do not establish morphologically recognizable synaptic junctions at all of their boutons. This applies in particular to neurons that use monoamines as transmitters.

Analysis of Neuronal Circuits

Connectivity patterns of morphologically identified neurons can be traced via the transport of marker molecules through the processes (Heimer and Zaborszky, 1989). The active transport in the living cell can be exploited by introducing suitable tracers into the neuron that are carried to the dendritic and axonal processes (see Figures 1 and 3). Tracer molecules can be introduced directly into the cell or into the surrounding extracellular space from which the cell can take them up by an active process. It is also possible to label the processes of neurons that have been fixed with chemical agents (see Figure 2). The visualization of processes makes it possible to identify the connections of particular types of neurons in the same area of the brain or among different brain regions. The morphological appearance of neurons reflects their patterns of connections. In many cases synapses from a given source terminate on certain parts of the neuron because the operation that the given input provides is best carried out in that part of the cell (see Figures 1E–G, and 2). Homologous parts of numerous postsynaptic cells in a given area of the brain tend to align with inputs arriving at that part of the cell, and this leads to the development of laminated structures. For example, axons originating from the CA3 region of the hippocampus terminate mainly on the main *apical dendrites* of pyramidal cells in the CA1 region, and the local recurrent collaterals of pyramidal cells in the CA1 sector address the *basal dendritic* region of the pyramidal cells (see Figure 1A). The separation of inputs and the minimum amount of axon necessary to achieve addressing is ensured by the alignment of pyramidal cells.

The terminals of some neurons are all localized in the same brain area where the cell body is located. These cells play a role in the local processing of information and are called *local circuit neurons* (see Figure 2). Other cells connect different brain regions or supply the periphery with their axons; these are called *projection neurons*. Many projection neurons also have axon collaterals within the same brain area where the cell is located, and thus play both a local circuit and a projection role (see Figure 3). Accurate knowledge of the connectivity, especially in quantitative terms, is a prerequisite of establishing the operations taking place in real neural networks.

See also: NEUROTRANSMITTER SYSTEMS AND MEMORY

Bibliography

Heimer, L., and Zaborszky, L., eds. (1989). *Neuroanatomical tract-tracing methods*, Vol. 2: *Recent progress.* New York: Plenum Press.

Kandel, E. R., and Schwartz, J. H., eds. (1985). *Principles of neural science*, 2nd edition, New York: Elsevier.

Kisvarday, Z. F., Martin, K. A. C., Freund, T. F., Magloczky, Z., Whitteridge, D., and Somogyi, P. (1986). Synaptic targets of HRP-filled layer III pyramidal cells in the cat striate cortex. *Experimental Brain Research 64*, 541–552.

Peters, A., Palay, S. L., and Webster, H. deF., eds. (1991). *The fine structure of the nervous system, neurons and their supporting cells*, 3rd edition. New York: Oxford University Press.

Shepherd, G. M., ed. (1990). *The synaptic organization of the brain*, 3rd edition. New York: Oxford University Press.

Somogyi, P., Freund, T. F., Hodgson, A. J., Somogyi, J., Beroukas, D., and Chubb, I. W. (1985). Identified axo-axonic cells are immunoreactive for GABA in the hippocampus and visual cortex of the cat. *Brain Research 332*, 143–149.

Peter Somogyi

OLFACTORY CORTEX

The olfactory cortex is the only part of the vertebrate forebrain to receive a direct sensory input. Present in even the most primitive fish, it retains its place and form throughout the vertebrate series, suggesting that it is a core element in the basic plan of the vertebrate forebrain. Since olfaction is the dominant sensory modality in most vertebrate species, an understanding of olfactory cortical mechanisms can yield insight into basic behavioral patterns underlying much of mammalian and primate behavior. The olfactory system is also one of the first sensory systems to differentiate and become functional during fetal life.

Overall Structure

An understanding of the olfactory cortex requires a clear view of its place in the olfactory pathway. This pathway and its constituent neurons were first revealed by the use of the Golgi stain in the later part of the nineteenth century. The pathway consists of three main parts (see Figure 1). First is the olfactory sensory epithelium in the nose, containing the olfactory sensory neurons, which transduce the stimulating odor molecules into impulses that are sent over their axons in the olfactory nerve to the olfactory bulb, the second main structure of the olfactory pathway. Here the axons extend synapses onto the den-drites of relay neurons, the large mitral cells and smaller tufted cells. These cells interact with interneurons in the olfactory bulb and send the processed information by means of impulse discharges in their axons in the lateral olfactory tract (LOT) on the ventrolateral surface of the brain. The axons give rise to numerous collaterals, which terminate in the third main region, the olfactory cortex, to make synapses on the dendrites of cortical pyramidal neurons.

The olfactory cortex is the area of cortex in the vertebrate forebrain that receives direct input form the olfactory bulb. In most mammals there are several areas of this cortex: The main region is the piriform cortex (PC) (meaning "pear-shaped"—it was originally termed "prepyriform" and sometimes spelled "pyriform"). In most mammalian brains it extends over much of the ventrolateral surface of the brain dorsal to the LOT, as shown in Figure 2. The piriform cortex sends its output axons to several areas. One target area is the mediodorsal nucleus of the thalamus, which has connections to the prefrontal areas of the neocortex. This pathway is believed to be involved in conscious perception of odors. Depending on the species, the piriform cortex also sends fibers to other cortical areas, such as the insula, where odor information may be combined with taste information to give the overall perception of flavor. Subcortical connections are made to parts of the limbic system, including the hypothalamus, hippocampus, and basal ganglia.

The other olfactory cortical areas include the following: The anterior olfactory nucleus (AON) is a major station for integrating activity of the olfactory bulb with that of olfactory cortical areas on both sides of the brain via connections through the anterior commissure. The olfactory tubercle (OT) in rodents lies medial to the LOT; it is notable for receiving a heavy input of dopaminergic axons from the midbrain. Because of the implication of dopamine systems in various types of mental disorders (depression, sleep disturbances, schizophrenia), the olfactory tubercle has been studied intensively in rodents for its possible role in these types of disorders. Another target for olfactory input is the amygdala. The accessory olfactory bulb (AOB) receives input from the vomeronasal organ in the nose about chemical signals involved in mating in many vertebrate species and projects to the corticomedial nuclei within the amygdalar complex; these, in turn, project to the hypothalamus, where they presumably activate some of the behavioral patterns in mating. Finally, there is the lateral entorhinal cortex (LEC), a major region for multimodal integration of olfactory, visual, auditory, and somatosensory inputs; the output of this region is carried in fibers of the perforant pathway to the hippocampus, which is a critical region for storage

Figure 1

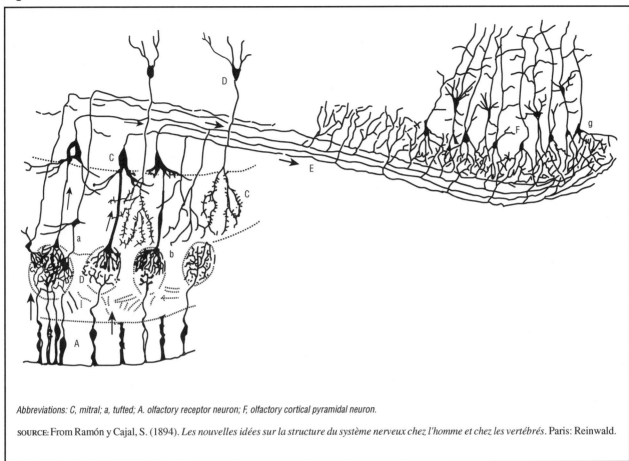

Abbreviations: *C, mitral; a, tufted; A. olfactory receptor neuron; F, olfactory cortical pyramidal neuron.*

SOURCE: From Ramón y Cajal, S. (1894). *Les nouvelles idées sur la structure du système nerveux chez l'homme et chez les vertébrés*. Paris: Reinwald.

The main types of neurons and their connections in the olfactory pathway in the mammal.

and retrieval of information of behavioral significance.

Human Olfactory Cortical Areas

The regions of the rodent brain described above are similar in the brains of other mammals and some lower primates; in higher primates, including humans, there are a number of differences. In the monkey brain, the olfactory pathway appears much reduced in relative terms compared with the large forebrain, seemingly reflecting the reduced importance of the sense of smell. However, absolute numbers of neurons or fibers are not a reliable guide to the behavioral importance of a particular system; for example, the LOT contains many more fibers than the auditory nerve, yet no one would say that hearing is unimportant in human life.

As a result of the overgrowth of the forebrain in primates, the olfactory pathway is limited to the ventral surface of the brain. The olfactory bulbs give rise to a long LOT, which divides into three roots as it enters the brain. The lateral root goes to a cortical area at the junction of the frontal and temporal cortexes, which seems to be the homologue of the piriform cortex. From here there are connections to the prefrontal cortex, called the orbital cortex because it is on the surface of the brain facing the orbit of the eye. The medial root dives into a small area that, being pockmarked with many penetrating blood vessels, is called the perforated substance, a homologue of the olfactory tubercle. The medial root includes fibers that project toward or into the hypothalamus, from which there is a projection to the orbital cortex complementary to that from the piriform cortex. There are thus several routes over which information can be processed, through different olfactory cortical regions, to both cortical and subcortical regions.

The Basic Cortical Circuit

The main regions and pathways described above are like cities and motor routes on a map. An understanding of the basis of information processing requires an analysis of the structures within each region.

Figure 2

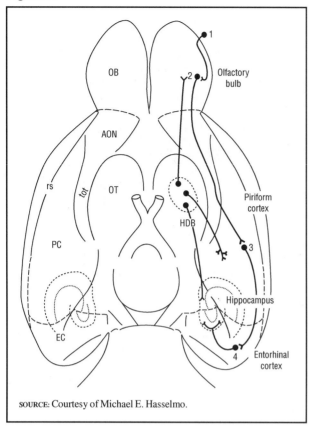

SOURCE: Courtesy of Michael E. Hasselmo.

Schematic drawing of the ventral surface of the rat brain showing components of the olfactory system. Receptor cells activated in the olfactory epithelium (1) project into the olfactory bulb (OB, 2). Principal neurons of the olfactory bulb project along the lateral olfactory tract (lot) into the piriform cortex (PC, 3). Pyramidal cells of the piriform cortex project to entorhinal cortex (EC, 4). Other structures receiving olfactory projections include the anterior olfactory nucleus (AON) and the olfactory tubercle (OT). Cholinergic innervation of these structures arises from the horizontal limb of the diagonal band (HDB). Rs = rhinal sulcus.

A traditional way to characterize the organization of the olfactory cortex is by its layers. The olfactory cortex is the prototypical three-layer cortex, consisting of an outer molecular layer of incoming fibers and apical dendrites; a middle layer of pyramidal cell bodies; and an inner plexiform or polymorphic layer of basal dendrites, fibers, and interneurons. It shares this three-layer organization with the hippocampus and contrasts with the six-layer construction of the neocortex.

Researchers have clarified the synaptic circuits of these cortical regions. A basic circuit is made up of the minimum types of input fibers, output neurons, intrinsic neurons, and their connections sufficient to represent the most important information-processing

functions of a given region. For the olfactory cortex, the main input elements are the fibers from the LOT, which make excitatory synapses on the spines of the distal dendrites of the pyramidal neurons. The main output elements are the pyramidal neurons, each consisting of apical and basal dendrites, receiving excitatory synapses on their dendritic spines and inhibitory synapses on their dendritic shafts and cell bodies. The main intrinsic elements are two types of interneurons that make the inhibitory connections onto the pyramidal neurons. There are two main types of intrinsic circuits: a reexcitatory feedback circuit through long axon collaterals of the pyramidal neurons and inhibitory circuits for feedforward and feedback inhibition of the pyramidal neurons.

This basic circuit not only summarizes the main anatomical circuits within the piriform cortex but also, with minor variations, applies to the other olfactory cortical areas; moreover, it is similar to the other circuits: those of the hippocampus; the neocortex, particularly its superficial layers; and the "canonical circuit" proposed by some researchers for the neocortex. Thus, the basic circuit for the olfactory cortex is a useful model for correlating the general properties of all types of forebrain cortices.

Researchers seek to characterize the functional properties of each type of cortical element and synaptic circuit and to identify the stages of expression of different circuit components and types of excitatory, inhibitory, and modulatory neurotransmitters. Through such studies they seek correlations with the developing behavior of the fetus and the neonate. Studies of plasticity have indicated that the properties of the excitatory synapses made by the sensory input fibers from the LOT are different from those of the intrinsic reexcitatory collateral system; the latter give evidence of n-methyl-D-aspartate (NMDA) receptors and are thus strong candidates for mediating the long-term potentiation in the piriform cortex. Computational networks based on the basic circuit model suggest that sensory inputs and reexcitatory feedback interact over extensive areas of the olfactory cortex to provide a distributed parallel system; such analyses shed light on the mechanisms of odor discrimination and may constitute a model for related types of pattern recognition by other cortical systems. In particular, the excitatory feedback between pyramidal cells within the piriform cortex may mediate autoassociative memory function. During initial encoding, synaptic modification of these recurrent connections in the piriform cortex could store associations between neurons activated by a given odor stimulus. Subsequent encounters with similar stimuli could activate a subset of these neurons, and activity could spread across the modified connections to complete the previously encoded pattern of activity. This pattern completion could serve as a retrieval of the previously encoded memory for the odor. Further knowledge of the structural organization of the olfactory cortex should provide a better basis for understanding these and other important aspects of olfactory function and behavior.

Bibliography

Haberly, L. B. (1990). Olfactory cortex. In G. M. Shepherd, ed., *The synaptic organization of the brain*. New York: Oxford University Press.

Ramón y Cajal, S. (1894). *Les nouvelles idées sur la structure du système nerveux chez l'homme et chez les vertébrés*. Paris: Reinwald.

Shepherd, G. M. (1989). A basic circuit for cortical organization. In M. C. Gazzaniga, ed., *Perspectives on memory research*. Cambridge, MA: MIT Press.

Shepherd, G. M., and Stewart, W. B. (1985). The chemical senses: Taste and smell. In M. Swash and C. Kennard, eds., *Scientific basis of clinical neurology*. London: Churchill Livingstone.

Gordon M. Shepherd
Revised by Michael E. Hasselmo

PERIRHINAL CORTEX AND ASSOCIATED CORTICAL AREAS

Research on learning and memory has confirmed that the structures within the hippocampal formation, including the dentate gyrus, Ammon's horn, and the subiculum play an important role in certain kinds of memory. Memory functions are also subserved by nearby cortical regions that are closely interconnected with the hippocampal formation. These regions, called the parahippocampal region, include the perirhinal, parahippocampal, and entorhinal cortices together with the parasubiculum and the presubiculum (The postrhinal cortex in the rat brain is analogous to the primate parahippocampal cortex [Burwell and Amaral, 1998a]). Of these regions, the perirhinal cortex has received the most emphasis from researchers on memory. However, the individual structures within the parahippocampal region are so strongly interconnected with one another and with the hippocampal structures that it is difficult to discuss one without addressing the others. With interest in all of these regions on the rise, it is likely that future research will identify roles for each in memory functions.

In the basic scheme of cortico-hippocampal circuitry, highly processed cortical input reaches the entorhinal cortex though projections from the perirhinal and parahippocampal cortices. The entorhinal cortex projects primarily to the dentate gyrus, the input structure of the hippocampal formation. The output structure of the hippocampal formation, the subiculum, projects back to the entorhinal cortex directly and indirectly through the presubiculum and

parasubiculum. This basic circuitry, however, is augmented by additional pathways. Each parahippocampal structure, including the perirhinal cortex, is interconnected with at least two hippocampal-formation structures. Moreover, all parts of the parahippocampal region are highly interconnected with cortical and subcortical regions.

Cortical Connections

The cortical afferentation of the perirhinal cortex is consistent with a role in higher-level visual perception, such as the identification of objects based on complex features such as size, shape, color, and pattern. Most of its input arises from sensory associational regions. In primates the input is weighted toward higher-order visual areas. The perirhinal cortex also receives substantial input from polymodal associational regions; a large proportion arises from its neighbor, the parahippocampal cortex, and other temporal regions. The rest arises roughly equally from prefrontal, frontal, and insular regions. In the primate brain there is no input to perirhinal cortex from the retrosplenial cortex, a structure that may play a role in visuospatial functions. The connectivity of the parahippocampal cortex suggests a role in visuo-spatial functions. A large input to the parahippocampal cortex arises in the cingulate and retrosplenial cortices, and the projections are reciprocal. There is also substantial input from the posterior parietal cortex, a region that seems to contribute to visuospatial attention. The parahippocampal cortex is not solely a visual region, however; one of its subdivisions is connected with unimodal auditory regions. The region is also connected with the orbital frontal cortex.

The perirhinal and parahippocampal cortices provide the major cortical input to the entorhinal cortex. The connections are organized such that the perirhinal cortex projects to rostral portions of the entorhinal cortex and the parahippocampal cortex projects to caudal portions. The entorhinal cortex also receives direct cortical input arising in the piriform cortex, frontal and prefrontal regions, the insular cortex, the inferior and temporal gyrus, and the retrosplenial cortex.

The presubiculum and parasubiculum are reciprocally connected with the entorhinal cortex, but they are also interconnected with several neocortical regions. Input to the presubiculum includes the dorsolateral prefrontal cortex, superior and inferior temporal gyrus, cingulate and retrosplenial cortex, and parietal cortex. The parasubiculum appears to receive input from the inferior temporal gyrus and dorsolateral prefrontal cortex.

Subcortical Connections

With the advent of modern neuroanatomical tract tracing methods, subcortical connectivity has become particularly useful in the attempt to understand brain functions. Perirhinal subcortical connections are extensive and include structures within the basal ganglia, claustrum, and thalamus, including the pulvinar and mediaodorsal nucleus, basal forebrain, and amygdala. There are extensive and sometimes reciprocal perirhinal conections with basal-forebrain structures, including the medial septum, the diagonal band of Broca, and the substantia innominata.

The perirhinal connections with the amygdala have received much interest because of a possible role in emotional memory. The perirhinal cortex is most strongly interconnected with the deep amygdaloid nuclei, including the lateral, basal, and accessory basal nuclei. The perirhinal cortex connections with subdivisions of the amygdala are stronger than those with any other region in temporal cortex, including the parahippocampal cortex.

The parahippocampal cortex, like the perirhinal cortex, is widely connected with subcortical structures. These include the basal ganglia, particularly the head, body, and tail of the caudate nucleus, the nucleus accumbens, and the ventral putamen; septal regions, including the medial septum, the diagonal band of Broca, and the substantia innominata; and several thalamic nuclei, including the medial pulvinar, the medial dorsal, and the lateral dorsal. The parahippocampal cortex is also connected with the amydala, particularly the basal nucleus.

Not to be overshadowed, the entorhinal cortex also receives direct input from multiple subcortical regions, including the basal forebrain, claustrum, amygdala, thalamus, hypothalamus, and brain stem. The input from the claustrum, especially the ventral, visual portion is relatively strong. Most of the subcortical structures that project to the entorhinal cortex also project to fields of the hippocampal formation.

The entorhinal cortex projects to the lateral, basal, and accessory basal nuclei of the amygdala and the periramygdaloid cortex. All parts of the entorhinal cortex receive amygdalar input, but the rostral subfields, those most strongly interconnected with the perirhinal cortex, are more strongly interconnected with the amygdala than the caudal subfields. The major thalamic input arises in midline nuclei, particularly the nucleus reunions.

The presubiculum and parasubiculum also receive direct input from the lateral, basal, and basomedial nuclei of the amygdala. Other subcortical connections include the laterodorsal thalamic nucleus, the midline thalamic nuclei, the ventral tegmental area, and the dorsal raphe nucleus.

Hippocampal Connections

The entorhinal cortex provides the major input to the hippocampal formation through the perforant pathway. To summarize the projection, all regions of the entorhinal cortex project to the outer two-thirds of the molecular layer of the dentate gyrus. The region also projects to fields CA3, CA2, and CA1 of the hippocampus proper (Ammon's horn) and to the subiculum. The projections to the dentate gyrus, CA3, and CA2 originate in layer II of the entorhinal cortex, whereas the projections to CA1 and the subiculum originate in layer III. The entorhinal projections to the CA1 and subiculum exhibit a certain topography such that the rostral and caudal entorhinal cortex project to different parts of CA1 and the subiculum.

The dentate gyrus and field CA3 do not receive direct cortical input from regions other than the entorhinal cortex. However, the situation is different for CA1 and the subiculum. Both receive input from entorhinal cortex, but they also receive direct input from the perirhinal and parahippocampal cortices. The perirhinal and parahippocampal cortices do not provide any direct input to the dentate gyrus. The subiculum projects to the entorhinal cortex directly and indirectly through the presubiculum and the parasubiculum. It appears that at least the presubiculum-entorhinal projection is reciprocal, but there is no conclusive evidence for that hypothesis.

Conclusion

Highly processed sensory and sensory associational input terminates in the perirhinal and parahippocampal cortices. Further processing occurs in these regions, and they, in turn, provide the primary cortical input to the entorhinal cortex. Via the perforant pathway, the entorhinal cortex projects mainly to the dentate gyrus of the hippocampal formation. The output structure of the hippocampus, the subiculum, is reciprocally connected with the entorhinal cortex. The subiculum also projects indirectly to the entorhinal cortex through the presubiculum and parasubiculum. Although a primary source of cortical input to the hippocampal formation is from the perirhinal cortex through an entorhinal cortical projection, an important principle of cortico-hippocampal circuitry is that all other parahippocampal regions also project directly to one or more structures in the hippocampal formation. Moreover, all structures within the parahippocampal have extensive cortical and subcortical connections. Thus the connections between the parahippocampal region and the hippocampal formation include multiple parallel and redundant pathways.

See also: GUIDE TO THE ANATOMY OF THE BRAIN: CEREBRAL CORTEX; GUIDE TO THE ANATOMY OF THE BRAIN: HIPPOCAMPUS AND PARAHIPPOCAMPAL REGION

Bibliography

Aggleton, J. P., Vann, S. D., Oswald, C. J., and Good, M. (2000). Identifying cortical inputs to the rat hippocampus that subserve allocentric spatial processes: A simple problem with a complex answer. *Hippocampus 10* (4), 466–474.

Amaral, D. G., and Witter, M. P. (1995). Hippocampal formation. In G. Paxinos, ed., *The rat nervous system,*. 2nd edition. San Diego: Academic Press.

Baleydier, C., and Mauguiere, F. (1985). Anatomical evidence for medial pulvinar connections with the posterior cingulate cortex, the retrosplenial area, and the posterior parahippocampal gyrus in monkeys. *Journal of Comparative Neurology 232*, 219–228.

Burwell, R. D. (2001). The perirhinal and postrhinal cortices of the rat: Borders and cytoarchitecture. *Journal of Comparative Neurology 437*, 17–41.

Burwell, R. D., and Amaral, D. G. (1998a). Cortical afferents of the perirhinal, postrhinal, and entorhinal cortices. *Journal of Comparative Neurology 398*, 179–205.

———— (1998b). The perirhinal and postrhinal cortices of the rat: Interconnectivity and connections with the entorhinal cortex. *Journal of Comparative Neurology 391*, 293–321.

Insausti, R., Amaral, D. G., and Cowan, M. W. (1987a). The entorhinal cortex of the monkey: II. Cortical afferents. *Journal of Comparative Neurology 264*, 356–395.

———— (1987b). The entorhinal cortex of the monkey: III. Subcortical afferents. *Journal of Comparative Neurology 264*, 396–408.

Naber, P. A., Witter, M. P., and Lopez da Silva, F. H. (1999). Perirhinal cortex input to the hippocampus in the rat: Evidence for parallel pathways, both direct and indirect. A combined physiological and anatomical study. *European Journal of Neuroscience 11*, 4,119–4,133.

———— (2001). Evidence for a direct projection from the postrhinal cortex to the subiculum in the rat. *Hippocampus 11*, 105–117.

Pikkarainen, M., and Pitkanen, A. (2001). Projections from the lateral, basal, and accessory basal nuclei of the amygdala to the perirhinal and postrhinal cortices in rat. *Cerebral Cortex 11*, 1,064–1,082.

Saunders, R. C., and Rosene, D. L. (1988). A comparison of the efferents of the amygdala and the hippocampal formation in the rhesus monkey: I. Convergence in the entorhinal, prorhinal, and perirhinal cortices. *Journal of Comparative Neurology 271*, 153–184.

Shi, C. J., and Cassell, M. D. (1999). Perirhinal cortex projections to the amygdaloid complex and hippocampal formation in the rat. *Journal of Comparative Neurology 406*, 299–328.

Stefanacci, L., Suzuki, W. A., and Amaral, D. G. (1996). Organization of connections between the amygdaloid complex and the perirhinal and parahippocampal cortices in macaque monkeys. *Journal of Comparative Neurology 375*, 552–582.

Suzuki, W. A., and Amaral, D. G. (1990). Cortical inputs to the CA1 field of the monkey hippocampus originate from the perirhinal and parahippocampal cortex but not from area TE. *Neuroscience Letters 115*, 43–48.

van Groen, T., and Wyss, J. M. (1990). The connections of presubiculum and parasubiculum in the rat. *Brain Research 518*, 227–243.

van Hoesen, G. W., Rosene, D. L., and Mesulam, M. M. (1979). Subicular input from temporal cortex in the rhesus monkey. *Science 205*, 608–610.

Witter, M. P., and Amaral, D. G. (1991). Entorhinal cortex of the monkey: V. Projections to the dentate gyrus, hippocampas, and subicular complex. *Journal of Comparative Neurology 307*, 437–459.

Witter, M. P., Groenewegen, H. J., Lopes de Silva, F. H., and Lohman, A. H. M. (1989). Functional organization of the extrinsic and intrinsic circuitry of the parahippocampal region. *Progressive Neurobiology 33*, 161–253.

Witter, M. P., Naber, P. A., and Lopes da Silva, F. (1999). Perirhinal cortex does not project to the dentate gyrus. *Hippocampus 9*, 605–606.

Witter, M. P., Naber, P. A., van Haeften, T., Machielsen, W. C., Rombouts, S. A., Barkhof, F., Scheltens, P., and Lopes da Silva, F. H. (2000). Cortico-hippocampal communication by way of parallel parahippocampal-subicular pathways. *Hippocampus 10*, 398–410.

Rebecca D. Burwell

SYNAPSE

Neurons give rise to processes known as dendrites and axons that form a complex network of interconnections throughout the brain at specialized sites called *synapses.* Around the turn of the nineteenth century, the Italian physician Camillo Golgi (1873) developed a silver staining technique that revealed the full extent of dendritic and axonal arbors. From these images, he proposed the "reticular theory" suggesting that the neurons are not discrete cells, but instead are continuous with each other and form a syncytium. The renowned Spanish neuroscientist Santiago Ramón y Cajal (1891) used Golgi's method to reveal individual neurons in the brain and spinal cord during development and after a variety of experimental manipulations. These experiments led Cajal to conclude that neurons were discrete cells with axons ending on dendrites of different cells, a theory referred to as the "neuron doctrine." The term *synapse* is derived from the Greek word meaning "to clasp" and was first used by Sir Charles Sherrington (1897) in reference to Cajal's findings to indicate the point of contact between the axons and dendrites. Electron microscopy resolved the controversy in the 1950s by showing that a gap, the synaptic cleft, which is about twenty nanometers wide, separates the presynaptic axon from the postsynaptic dendrite, in favor of the neuron doctrine (Peters et al., 1991; Cowan et al., 2001). Scientists widely acknowledge that communication between neurons via signals at synapses provides an important cellular basis for perception, behavior, learning, and memory.

Synapses are characterized presynaptically by an axon that contains membrane bound vesicles and postsynaptically by a thickening in the membrane referred to as the postsynaptic density (see Figure 1). Excitatory synapses contain round vesicles in the presynaptic bouton (swelling in the axon) and an asymmetric postsynaptic density along the inside of the postsynaptic membrane (see Figure 1a, b). Depend-

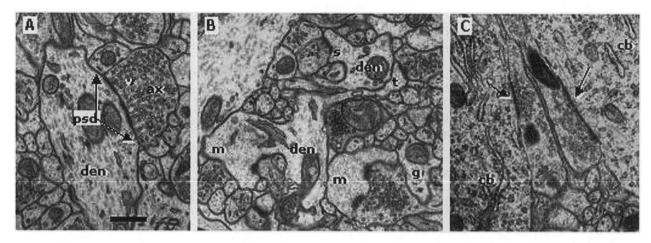

Figure 1. Synapses between neurons in the central nervous system. A. Asymmetric excitatory synapse from an axon (ax) containing presynaptic vesicles (v) onto a dendritic shaft (den, arrows indicate psd). B. Longitudinal section through dendritic spines of varying shapes, mushroom (m), thin (t), stubby (s). A small glial process (g) is visible at the lower left. C. Two symmetric, inhibitory synapses (arrows) on neuronal cell bodies (cb). Scale bar = 0.5 microns. *(Kristen M. Harris)*

ing on the particular synapse, the presynaptic bouton may contain as few as three or as many as 5,000 or more of the synaptic vesicles each having diameters of approximately twenty to sixty nanometers. The other primary organelles in the presynaptic bouton include mitochondria (for production of ATP); smooth endoplasmic reticulum (to store and release calcium); and organelles involved in the recycling of the vesicular membrane called endosomes. The postsynaptic dendrite also contains these organelles in the vicinity of synapses. The internal structure is held together by cytoskeletal elements composed primarily of actin filaments and their linking proteins, and a few microtubules that provide transport of molecules and organelles to and from the cell body. The pre- and postsynaptic elements are held together by adhesion molecules that span the synaptic cleft.

The presynaptic vesicles of excitatory synapses contain the neurotransmitter glutamate, visualized by antibody labeling of the molecule in the vesicles, or special electrodes that detect glutamate released from the synapses. When an action potential arrives at the synapse, one or more vesicles fuse with the presynaptic membrane, and the contents of the vesicle are released into the synaptic cleft. Glutamate released in this way activates receptors located in the postsynaptic membrane, resulting in a variety of signals to the postsynaptic neuron. Activation of the AMPAergic glutamate receptors causes the postsynaptic membrane to become depolarized. This relieves the magnesium blockade of the calcium channel associated with a second important glutamate receptor, the NMDA receptor. When the NMDA receptor is both activated by glutamate and the postsynaptic membrane is depolarized, calcium enters the postsynaptic

neuron through the channels associated with the NMDA receptor. A variety of calcium-dependent signaling molecules are tethered in the postsynaptic membrane and comprise the heavily stained postsynaptic density. Depending on the strength of synaptic activation and the amount of calcium entering the dendrite, the signaling molecules will trigger second messenger cascades that result in temporary changes in synaptic strength through activation of phosphorylation events, or more permanent changes in synaptic strength via the synthesis and insertion of more synaptic proteins thereby enlarging the synapse.

Inhibitory synapses are distinguished morphologically from excitatory synapses by the presence of symmetric pre- and postsynaptic thickenings that are not as wide as the postsynaptic density of excitatory synapses (see Figure 1c). The presynaptic vesicles of inhibitory synapses are typically smaller and are less uniform in shape, often appearing somewhat flattened. These synapses contain glycine or GABA as their primary neurotransmitter, and when they are activated they typically reduce the level of activity at the neuron. These synapses also have a specific set of signaling molecules tethered to their densities, such that depending on the degree of activation their strength can also be modified.

In addition to the excitatory and inhibitory synapses some synapses are modulatory, containing neuropeptides and hormones that act to modify the strength of the excitatory or inhibitory synaptic input. These neuromodulatory substances, along with growth factors, are often found co-localized in the same presynaptic boutons that form excitatory or inhibitory synapses. Their release also depends on the rate or intensity of presynaptic activation. In addition, there are electrical synapses (often called gap junctions) that form very close appositions between neurons such that channels in the adjacent membranes are aligned and current passes directly between the cells, without the need for a chemical neurotransmitter. If one of the two neurons that are coupled via electrical synapses is depolarized by chemical synaptic transmission at other synapses along its dendrites, then the current generated will also depolarize the coupled cell.

The third important partner at a synapse is the glial cell process (see Figure 1b). Astrocytic glia form long processes that end in numerous tiny projections. Some of these processes form end feet on the blood capillaries of the brain and through these end feet pass glucose and other substances from the blood. The glia store the glucose in the form of glycogen and provide the neuron with glucose or lactate as a form of energy to make ATP. Neurons usually do not store their own glucose, and hence are dependent on the glia for this metabolic energy. Glia also extend tiny processes to surround or partially surround synapses. In some brain regions, such as the cerebellar cortex, nearly all of the synapses are completely ensheathed with the astrocytic glia. In other brain regions, such as hippocampus and cortex, the glial processes end at the edge of the synaptic cleft, but rarely completely surround the synapse. Glia are critical for regulating ionic conditions in the extracellular milieu. If, for example, a glutamatergic neuron fires rapidly, it is the glia that remove the potassium that is extruded into the extracellular space, and also the glia that take up the excess glutamate that is released during neuronal firing. The glutamate stimulates the glia to break down glycogen and provide glucose or lactate to the neuron to replenish its energy. Removal of glutamate and potassium returns the neuron's environment to its normal resting state, thereby readying the neuron to respond to the next activation.

Synapses occur in many different locations on the neurons. The majority of excitatory synapses are distributed along the dendrites and are located up to one millimeter away from the cell body. More than 90 percent of the neurons in the brain have tiny protrusions called dendritic spines emanating from the postsynaptic surface (see Figure 1b). Most of the excitatory synapses are located on these dendritic spines and the neurons are referred to as spiny or sparsely spiny neurons depending on the number of dendritic spines they have. Nonspiny neurons comprise about 1 percent to 10 percent of the neurons in a particular brain region and these often have excitatory synapses distributed directly onto the dendritic shaft. Most inhibitory synapses are located on the neuronal cell body. The axon leaves the neuron from the cell body

at a specialized site called the axonal hillock and travels millimeters to meters to make synapses with different neurons. Therefore, inhibitory synapses located between the excitatory inputs on the dendrites and the output axon can dampen the total amount of excitation and prevent the neuron from firing too rapidly. In this way, the inhibitory synapses serve to put the "brakes" on rapidly firing neurons before their activity can spread to other cells and cause a seizure. Neuromodulatory synapses are also widely distributed along the dendrites and cell bodies, but usually at a lower frequency than the excitatory and inhibitory inputs. Gap junctions also occur at a lower density and it remains to be determined whether all neurons are coupled in this way to one or more other neurons or the surrounding glia.

The remainder of this section focuses on the structure and function of dendritic spines because many scientists agree that the dendritic spines are crucial elements for learning and memory. Dendritic spines vary greatly in their structure. Some spines are short and stubby. Other spines, called thin or sessile spines, are short or long with a constricted neck and a slightly enlarged head. Yet other spines have a constricted neck with a very large head and are referred to as "mushroom" spines. Spines range in length from about 0.3 to 2 μm; volume from 0.01 to 0.6 μm^3; and in synapse area from 0.03 to 0.5 μm^2, both within and across brain regions. There is a near perfect correlation between the number of presynaptic vesicles and the size of the synapse on a spine head, as well as the spine's volume, suggesting that larger spines have greater synaptic activity at them. The full range in spine diversity can be found along a single short segment of dendrite suggesting that each spine has a unique history of activation.

Like other excitatory synapses, spines contain a postsynaptic density. Some spines contain smooth endoplasmic reticulum (SER) in proportion with their volume, presumably to regulate internal calcium. Due to the very small volume of some spines, they appear not to need SER and cytoplasmic calcium buffers are sufficient. Spine cytoskeleton is primarily made up of actin, and microtubules are not found in the spine compartment, though they run extensively in the neighboring dendritic shaft beneath the spines.

The constricted spine neck imparts several important properties (Harris and Kater, 1994). In most brain regions the spine necks are just long and thin enough to elevate the postsynaptic response to activation of the glutamatergic synapse during synaptic transmission without choking off the signal to the parent dendrite. This elevation in postsynaptic potential facilitates the opening of the voltage-dependent channels on the spine head, such as the calcium channel associated with the NMDA glutamatergic receptor discussed above. The spine necks are also constricted enough to concentrate and compartmentalize the calcium and possibly other signaling molecules in the head near to the specific synapses that were activated. In this way, only those synapses will be modified during particular patterns of activity that lead to elevated or depressed synaptic responses underlying different forms of learning and memory. In addition, by concentrating the calcium in the spine head, spines protect the neuron from excitotoxicity by isolating the calcium near the synapse and away from the rest of the neuron where high concentrations would damage key structural elements, such as microtubules, in the dendrite.

Neurons are born without spines. As an animal matures, more dendritic spines are acquired. Dendritic spine number is affected by experience, such that an enriched environment results in more dendritic spines along the dendrite, compared to animals raised in an impoverished environment. Animals given extensive training also have more dendritic spines. An open question among scientists is whether learning, memory, and other experiences induce the formation of new spines and synapses, or if instead experience preserves spines from an ongoing production and loss of spines and synapses.

See also: APLYSIA: MOLECULAR BASIS OF LONG-TERM SENSITIZATION; GLUTAMATE RECEPTORS AND THEIR CHARACTERIZATION; GUIDE TO THE ANATOMY OF THE BRAIN: NEURON; LONG-TERM POTENTIATION: SIGNAL TRANSDUCTION MECHANISMS AND EARLY EVENTS; MORPHOLOGICAL BASIS OF LEARNING AND MEMORY: INVERTEBRATES; MORPHOLOGICAL BASIS OF LEARNING AND MEMORY: VERTEBRATES; NEUROTRANSMITTER SYSTEMS AND MEMORY

Bibliography

Cowan, W. M., Sudhof, T. C., and Stevens, C. F. (2001). *Synapses.* Baltimore, MD: The Johns Hopkins University Press.

Harris, K. M., and Kater, S. B. (1994). Dendritic spines: Cellular specializations imparting both stability and flexibility to synaptic function. *Annual Review of Neuroscience 17,* 341–371.

Peters, A., Palay, S. L., and Webster, H. deF. (1991). *The fine structure of the nervous system: The neurons and supporting cells,* 3rd edition. New York: Oxford University Press.

Thomas H. McNeill
Jonathan R. Day
Revised by Kristen M. Harris

GUTHRIE, EDWIN R. (1886–1959)

Edwin Ray Guthrie, a distinguished psychologist, spent most of his professional career at the University of Washington, where he served as an instructor in philosophy from 1914 to 1918 and as an assistant professor for a year before he joined the department of psychology as an assistant professor. He was promoted to associate professor in 1925 and was made a professor in 1928. During World War II he served in Washington, DC, as chief (civilian) consultant to the overseas branch of the general staff in 1941, and as chief psychologist of the overseas branch of the Office of War Information in 1942. Upon his return to the University of Washington, he was named dean of the graduate school from 1943 until he reached retirement age in 1951. He was honored by having a campus building named for him while he was still alive. Among his other honors was an honorary LLD. from his alma mater, the University of Nebraska, where he had received his A.B. in 1907, his A.M. in 1910, and his Ph.D. in 1912 (under Edgar A. Singer, a philosopher whom he much admired and whose views continued to influence his thinking). In 1945, the year he received the LLD, Guthrie was elected president of the American Psychological Association. In 1958, the year before his death, he received the Gold Medal of the American Psychological Foundation, awarded for "outstanding lifetime contribution to psychology."

Guthrie was born December 9, 1886, in Lincoln, Nebraska, the eldest of five children of Edwin R. Guthrie and Harriett Pickett Guthrie. His father, the son of a clergyman, managed a piano store; his mother, the daughter of a newspaperman, taught elementary school prior to her marriage. In 1920 Edwin married Helen Macdonald, who helped him translate Pierre Janet's *Principles of Psychotherapy* (1924). Their son, Peter M. Guthrie (b. 1926), followed in his father's footsteps and became a professor of psychology (and department head) at Carleton College.

Although Guthrie had already published two short philosophical papers in the *Midwest Quarterly*, his first major publication was his Ph.D. dissertation on Bertrand Russell, which appeared as a monograph (Guthrie, 1915). Once he became a psychologist, he published chiefly in outlets for psychology, although some aspects of his psychological work appeared in *Journal of Philosophy* (e.g., Guthrie, 1924) and in a collection of philosophical essays (Guthrie, 1942). In other words, he never forgot his affiliation with philosophy. Because of his primary interest in learning and motivation, he had a scientific interest in education (Guthrie, 1945, 1949, 1959a; Guthrie and Powers, 1950).

Guthrie's philosophy mentor, Edgar Singer, had written an article titled "Mind as an Observable Object" (Singer, 1911). His point of view prepared Guthrie for a behaviorist orientation prior to American psychologist John B. Watson's announcement of behaviorism (Watson, 1913). It was not too surprising, therefore, that his early text *General Psychology in Terms of Behavior,* written in collaboration with Stevenson Smith, his senior colleague and friend at the University of Washington (Smith and Guthrie, 1921), should have stressed behavior and introduced to a wider audience the type of conditioning as an interpretation of learning that was carried on particularly by Guthrie (e.g., Guthrie, 1930, 1960). At least among later students at the University of Washington, the theory was known as Guthrie's, whatever role Smith may have played earlier.

Guthrie's students became imprinted with this theory, and its influence upon them is recalled to this day. Guthrie developed his theory through a charming writing style, with an emphasis upon convincing examples rather than experimental demonstration. The most convincing experimental demonstration took place many years after the theory was first announced (Guthrie and Horton, 1946), and eleven years after the first edition of his *Psychology of Learning* (1935).

Much of American psychology had long emphasized learning as a fundamental psychological process. What humans are competent to do or learn may be considered a combination of what one is born with and the capacities that develop as a matter of natural growth processes. Children learn to crawl before they learn to walk, and healthy children require little instruction to achieve this skill. Other things they have to learn with assistance. While there is doubtless some natural tendency to babble and hence to speak, in order to speak the artificial language that their home environment demands, children obviously have to learn the words that they hear and gradually to understand and talk in sentences. So the problem for the psychology of learning is how they acquire speech, reading, writing, and arithmetic. These cannot be entirely inborn, although one child may have more potential—that is, may be brighter—than another and hence a more accomplished learner.

One of the early and persistent theories of learning was known as the doctrine of association: that one word (or one idea) became associated with another, just as the name becomes associated with the object named or a skilled action becomes associated with the task performed, as when a hammer is used to pound a nail. There developed theories of how such associations came about. One widespread theory assumed that there were three laws of association: the laws of similarity, contrast, and contiguity. These are familiar enough. Many animals are four-footed, so the child easily learns to group a cat, a dog, and a cow as animals through their similarities. At first the class is nar-

Edwin Guthrie *(Psychology Archives, University of Akron)*

row, and the first lamb observed may be thought to be a different kind of dog. But associations get to be corrected, both by discrimination and by generalization over a wider range. A fish and a duck do not at first seem to be like other animals—at least they do not have four feet—but they are alive and breathe and move about, and similarities such as these permit them eventually to be included as animals.

The law of contrast operates in a corresponding way, and the child soon learns that day contrasts with night, up with down, and large with small. Thus the contrasting pairs become associated, and one may suggest the other: day-night, up-down, large-small, and many other such pairs.

The third law of association in this scheme is that things that occur together—that is, in contiguity—become associated. Hence a color name may suggest an object often of that color—a red apple or a red tomato, or the contiguity may be more emphasized, as in an orange orange, where name and object are kept together.

Another idea that entered into early learning theory was that the consequences of an act, either pleasurable or painful, would affect the associations formed, as in "The burned child fears the fire" or "Nothing succeeds like success."

This kind of theory was further extended by assuming that a child would develop certain preferences (hence activities to be enjoyed) and also some annoyances (to be avoided). These were elaborated into theories of motivation—how one's goals affect what one does, and how they are tied to theories of learning based on the sensible notions that humans learn what affords pleasure by satisfying their own wants, and that one hesitates to learn tasks that lead to results that one dislikes.

The Russian scientist Ivan Pavlov introduced the idea of a *conditioned reflex* (CR). The standard experiment was to present a *conditioned stimulus* (CS) to a dog—say the turning on of a light. This was indifferent to the dog in that it did not start the flow of saliva, which was to become the *conditioned reflex* (CR). Following the CS, the flow of saliva was produced as an unconditioned reflex (UR) by a natural *unconditioned stimulus* (US), such as some meat powder in a dish accessible to the dog and attached to an apparatus designed to measure the flow of saliva. After the two stimuli, CS and US, were repeated several times, the CS would yield the original UR as a newly learned CR. It is easy to see that the CR can also be described as a form of associative learning, but the experimental setting in which it was achieved gave rather good controls over some circumstances favorable to learning.

It soon became clear that all that gets conditioned is *not* simple reflexes, such as the salivary reflex to food in the mouth, and many psychologists began talking about conditioned responses instead of conditioned reflexes (Hilgard and Marquis, 1940). This is where Guthrie came in. He had some disagreements with Pavlov, and offered his own interpretation of conditioning.

Guthrie proposed to reduce the laws of association (and the other theories of learning) to a single law of association by contiguity. He pointed out that similarity and contrast were effective only because of their occurrence together, and then interpreted the other theories of motivated learning and of conditioned response by his one principle appropriate to all instances of learning: "A combination of stimuli which has accompanied a movement will on its recurrence tend to be followed by that movement." (Note that Guthrie does not limit the stimulating condition to a single stimulus [S], nor the movement to a precise reflex as a response [R].) A slight revision was introduced later, to give some credit to attentive processes. Guthrie suggested that his basic law might alternatively be stated as follows: "What is being noticed becomes a signal for what is being done" (Guthrie, 1959b).

A second statement is needed before his theory can be understood: "A stimulus pattern gains its full associative strength on its first pairing with a response." This is a remarkably parsimonious basic theory. Guthrie elaborated it to explain many puzzling problems of learning and forgetting.

Learning with repetition leads to the usual "learning curve" because a skilled response becomes conditioned to a variety of cues, so that as learning proceeds, the proportion of cues—internal and external—that have become conditioned, each on a single trial, increases the probability that the intended responses will occur, but a limit is approached as nearly all the cues become conditioned.

Guthrie gave a cogent analogy of how the probability model works. He told of an artist whose meager income derived sporadically from the sale of his pictures. In order not to live beyond his means, he converted his cash to dimes that he scattered about the messy floor of his studio. When he needed money for a meal, he could at first easily find enough dimes; but as the dimes became used up, it was harder and harder to find more than enough for a very modest meal. The difficulty became greater and greater as the dimes were used up, but by diligent searching he could find enough to keep him going until he made another sale.

Much later, Estes (1950) developed a stimulus-sampling mathematical theory of learning that followed much the same logic of one-trial learning leading to higher achievement as stimuli were assimilated to response, but again approaching an asymptote after most available stimuli had been used up.

Guthrie's theory was given a more formal statement by his student V. W. Voeks (1950), and in the area of learning theory and experimentation others of his students have shown the direct influence of what they learned from him (e.g., Sheffield, 1961).

See also: REPETITION AND LEARNING

Bibliography

Estes, W. K. (1950). Toward a statistical theory of learning. *Psychological Review* 57, 94–107.

Guthrie, E. R. (1915). *The paradoxes of Mr. Russell: With a brief account of their history.* Lancaster, PA: New Era Printing.

—— (1924). Purpose and mechanism in psychology. *Journal of Philosophy* 21, 673–682.

—— (1930). Conditioning as a principle of learning. *Psychological Review* 37, 412–428.

—— (1942). Conditioning: A theory of learning in terms of stimulus, response, and association. *Yearbook, National Society for the Study of Education* 41 (part 2), 17–60.

—— (1945). The evaluation of faculty service. *Bulletin, American Association of University Professors* 31, 255–262.

—— (1949). The evaluation of teaching. *Educational Record* 30, 109–115.

—— (1959a). *The state university: Its function and its future.* Seattle: University of Washington Press.

———— (1959b). Association by contiguity. In S. Koch, ed., *Psychology: A study of a science,* Vol. 2, pp. 158–195. New York: McGraw-Hill.

———— (1935; reprint 1960). *The psychology of learning,* rev. edition. Gloucester, MA: Smith.

Guthrie, E. R., and Horton, G. P. (1946). *Cats in a puzzle box.* New York: Rinehart.

Guthrie, E. R., and Powers, F. F. (1950). *Educational psychology.* New York: Ronald Press.

Hilgard, E. R., and Marquis, D. G. (1940). *Conditioning and learning.* New York: Appleton-Century.

Janet, P. (1924). *Principles of psychotherapy,* trans. H. M. Guthrie and E. R. Guthrie. New York: Macmillan.

Sheffield, F. D. (1961). Theoretical considerations in the learning of complex sequential tasks from demonstration and practice. In A. A. Lumsdaine, ed., *Student expectations in programmed instruction,* pp. 13–32. Washington, DC: National Academy of Sciences/National Research Council.

Singer, E. A. (1911). Mind as an observable object. *Journal of Philosophy, Psychology and Scientific Method 8,* 180–186.

Smith, S., and Guthrie, E. R. (1921). *General psychology in terms of behavior.* New York: Appleton.

Voeks, V. W. (1950). Formalization and clarification of a theory of learning. *Journal of Psychology 30,* 341–362.

Watson, J. B. (1913). Psychology as the behaviorist views it. *Psychological Review 20,* 158–177.

Ernest R. Hilgard

H

HABITUATION AND SENSITIZATION IN VERTEBRATES

When a ringing bell is presented to a cat, it may evoke a turning of the head toward the sound source. If that same stimulus is repeated over and over again, the probability and magnitude of this orienting response decrease. This phenomenon is called *habituation*. If a mouse now runs in front of the cat and then the bell is rung again, the cat may reorient to the bell. This phenomenon is called *dishabituation*. By recording electrical activity in the first central synapse in the auditory system or using another stimulus that elicits an orienting response of the same size, it can be shown that habituation cannot be explained by either sensory adaptation or muscle fatigue (Thompson and Spencer, 1966). Thus, even though the original response no longer occurs, the stimulus still evokes the same electrical activity in early auditory structures as it did before and the original response can be fully elicited by a different stimulus or the same stimulus following dishabituation (e.g., the bell after the mouse ran by). Hence, the decrement in response strength must result from a synaptic change somewhere within the nervous system, and this change is specific to the stimulus that was presented repetitively.

Habituation has been the subject of a great deal of empirical investigation because practically every organism displays habituation, even those with very primitive nervous systems (Harris, 1943). In reviewing this literature, Thompson and Spencer (1966, pp. 18–19) enumerated nine parametric features of habituation and dishabituation that can be seen in a variety of organisms:

1. Given that a particular stimulus elicits a response, repeated applications of the stimulus result in decreased response (habituation). The decrease is usually a negative exponential function of the number of stimulus presentations.

2. If the stimulus is withheld, the response tends to recover over time (spontaneous recovery).

3. If repeated series of habituation training and spontaneous recovery are given, habituation becomes successively more rapid (this might be called potentiation of habituation).

4. Other things being equal, the more rapid the frequency of stimulation, the more rapid and/or more pronounced is habituation.

5. The weaker the stimulus, the more rapid and/or more pronounced is habituation. Strong stimuli may yield no significant habituation.

6. The effects of habituation training may proceed beyond the zero or asymptotic response level (i.e., additional habituation training given after the response has disappeared or reached asymptote will result in slower recovery).

7. Habituation of response to a given stimulus exhibits stimulus generalization to other stimuli.

8. Presentation of another (usually strong) stimulus results in recovery of the habituated response (dishabituation).

9. Upon repeated application of the dishabituatory stimulus, the amount of dishabituation produced habituates (this might be called habituation of dishabituation).

Thompson and Spencer's extremely influential review gave investigators working in diverse areas an explicit operational definition of habituation against which to test plasticity (change in response output with experience) in their particular preparations. In addition, it led to the general belief that habituation might be mediated by a single, fundamental mechanism inherent to most organisms across the phylogenetic scale.

Other experiments indicated, however, that the way in which one interrogates an animal can determine these parametric relationships. For example, the probability or amplitude of response is generally larger, the higher the intensity of the eliciting stimulus. It is not surprising, therefore, that it takes longer to reach a low level of response with intense, as opposed to weak, stimulus intensities. However, if the effects of prior exposure to strong and weak stimuli are subsequently evaluated, when all animals are tested with a common stimulus intensity, the magnitude of response change is actually greater following strong, as opposed to weak, stimuli (Davis and Wagner, 1968). Similarly, the probability of response is generally lower the shorter the interval from an immediately prior stimulus. This leads to a rapid rate of response decrement when stimuli are presented at short, rather than long, interstimulus intervals. However, when animals are subsequently tested under conditions where the interstimulus interval is *identical* for all animals, prior exposure with long interstimulus intervals actually produces a greater decrease in response strength (Davis, 1970). On the one hand, habituation (i.e., the change in response during stimulus repetition) seems to be greater with weak stimuli presented at short intervals (Thompson and Spencer, 1966); but on the other hand, habituation (i.e., the change in response strength following stimulus repetition) seems to be greater with strong stimuli presented at long intervals (Davis, 1970; Davis and Wagner, 1968).

These disparities illustrate how the term *habituation* has been used to denote the empirical observation of response decrement with stimulus repetition as well as a theoretical construct to describe the underlying process that accounts for the observed response decrement. However, the two terms may not be isomorphic, so that it is just as necessary to apply a distinction between performance and learning within the study of habituation as it is with other forms of learning such as classical and instrumental conditioning.

The Dual-Process Theory of Habituation

On the basis of the observation that dishabituation appeared to result from a facilitating effect superimposed on the habituation process (Humphrey, 1933; Sharpless and Jasper, 1956; Thompson and Spencer, 1966) and of some unusual results when stimulus intensity was used to study habituation (Davis and Wagner, 1969), Groves and Thompson (1970) proposed that novel and especially intense stimuli activate two hypothetical processes: habituation, which decreases response strength; and sensitization, which increases response strength. The final response output is then the net result of these two opposing influences. With strong stimuli, the underlying habituation process may be masked by a competing sensitization process that tends to decrease the rate of response decrement during stimulus repetition. However, because sensitization may not last as long as habituation, subsequent test sessions may be used to evaluate the effects of prior habituation, somewhat less contaminated by sensitization (e.g., Davis, 1972). The Groves and Thompson dual-process theory received wide empirical support and provided a fundamental theoretical base upon which to study the neural mechanisms of response change during iterative stimulus presentation, in both invertebrates and simple mammalian systems.

Mechanisms of Habituation and Sensitization in Vertebrates

Because of the ubiquity of habituation, many believe it is the simplest form of learning. The most definitive analysis of the cellular mechanisms of habituation and sensitization has been done in invertebrates. In vertebrates, the cellular mechanisms of habituation and sensitization are poorly understood. In broad terms, habituation could be mediated by some neural process intrinsic to the neural pathway in the reflex circuit under study or by activation of other neural circuits extrinsic to, but impinging on, the reflex pathway. Much of the literature on humans has assumed the latter mechanism, probably because of the influential theory of E. N. Sokolov (1960), who proposed a brain comparator process whereby higher brain centers form a neuronal model of incoming stimuli and actively inhibit response output when subsequent stimuli match the neuronal model.

Many animal experiments have attempted to prevent habituation by making lesions of brain areas extrinsic to the reflex circuits under study, or by giving drugs that might prevent these systems from inhibiting the reflex pathway. On balance, however, there are very few behavioral experiments that clearly show that habituation within a single test session is actually prevented by lesions or drugs. When effects are reported, they generally result from a change in overall response levels that does not affect the slope of response decrement (provided the manipulations do not push the initial response levels to the ceiling or floor of the response scale and that measures such as percent decrement or trials to criterion, which depend heavily on changes in overall response level, are not used). Moreover, when effects on the slope of the response decrement curve are found, it is not clear whether this is due to a change in the underlying process of habituation or of sensitization. It has thus been extremely difficult to study in whole organisms how various manipulations affect the process of habituation, since the change in behavioral output may well be the product of two underlying processes, which cannot be distinguished with a single measure.

Habituation and Sensitization in the Spinal Cord

As illustrated by the landmark studies of Spencer, Thompson, and Neilson (1966a, 1966b), the most definitive work on the mechanism of habituation and sensitization in vertebrates has been done in the spinal cord, because this is one of the few places where the underlying neural circuitry of the reflexes being studied is reasonably well understood. Habituation and sensitization have been investigated in centrally projecting sensory fibers and in the interneurons and motoneurons to which they project. The reflexes most studied include the monosynaptic stretch reflex, the oligosynaptic plantar cushion reflex (Egger, 1978; Egger, Bishop, and Cone, 1976); the polysynaptic flexion reflex in the cat (Mendell, 1984); and the lateral column-motoneuron pathway in the frog (Farel, Glanzman, and Thompson, 1973). Mammalian monosynaptic stretch reflexes (activated by primary afferents from muscle spindles that project directly to motoneurons) typically do not demonstrate marked habituation or sensitization, in contrast to reflexes involving interneurons, which typically do. Current evidence indicates that habituation and sensitization are mediated by synaptic changes intrinsic to interneurons within the reflex pathways being studied (depression or facilitation of transmitter release). To date, there is no direct evidence that interneuronal networks extrinsic to the reflex pathway account for habituation and sensitization by actively inhibiting or facilitating transmission (Mendell, 1984), although such mechanisms cannot be entirely ruled out.

Habituation and Sensitization of the Startle Reflex

In complex mammalian systems habituation and sensitization of the acoustic startle reflex have been studied by eliciting startlelike responses at different points along the neural pathway believed to mediate the very-short-latency (eight milliseconds) startle reflex in rats, with a high level of background noise used to sensitize startle (Davis et al., 1982). Startle elicited by electrical stimulation in the early part of the pathway was increased by the noise but then decreased with repeated elicitations. Startle elicited by stimulation of the part of the pathway that projected directly to the spinal cord was also increased by noise but did *not* decrease with stimulus repetition. In humans, the R1 component of the eyeblink reflex (latency = ten milliseconds), elicited by electrical stimulation of the facial nerve, which is mediated by a disynaptic circuit, shows a net increase in response amplitude with stimulus repetition. However, the R2 component (latency = twenty-five to forty milliseconds) elicited by the same stimulus, which involves a polysynaptic pathway, shows a net decrease in response strength (Sanes and Ison, 1983). Taken together, the data suggest that sensitization tends to act on the motor side of reflex arcs, whereas habituation tends to act on earlier parts of the circuitry. This suggestion is consistent with data from Thompson and Spencer (1966) on spinal preparations.

The best evidence for extrinsic control of habituation and sensitization has been gathered by looking at between-session or long-term habituation of the startle reflex. Leaton and Supple (1986) have shown that lesions of the cerebellar vermis, which is not part of the acoustic startle pathway, significantly attenuate the decrease in startle amplitude seen across daily test sessions without affecting the rate of response decrement within test sessions. This blockade of long-term habituation was observed with two different stimulus intensities and cannot be explained by ceiling or floor effects caused by the cerebellar lesions. This effect has been replicated when the lesion was made before habituation training, but not when the lesion was made afterward (Lopiano, DeSperati, and Montarolo, 1990). Hence, the cerebellar vermis appears to be necessary for the acquisition but not the retention of long-term habituation. In contrast, lesions of the mesencephalic reticular formation, which again is not itself part of the acoustic startle pathway, block both the acquisition (Jordan and Leaton, 1982) and the expression (Jordan, 1989) of long-term habituation. In other studies Borszcz, Cranney, and Leaton (1989) have shown that loud startle stimuli produce sensitization that can best be described as fear of the experimental context in which startle is measured. Reintroducing animals into this context produces a good deal of freezing, a reliable index of fear. Fear of the context elevates startle on subsequent test sessions, leading to a reduction in the amount of long-term response decrement. Treatments such as lesions of the ventral central gray matter (Borszcz, Cranney, and Leaton, 1989) that are known to reduce freezing, and treatments such as lesions of the amygdala or drugs such as diazepam, which reduce fear in many situations, facilitate the degree of long-term response decrement, presumably by blocking sensitization and hence allowing long-term habituation to be revealed. Taken together, these data provide some of the best evidence that extrinsic systems may be involved in both long-term habituation and sensitization of the startle reflex elicited by intense auditory stimuli.

Conclusion

Because habituation could be observed at all levels of the phylogenetic scale, there was great hope that its analysis would lead to fundamental insights into the neural mechanisms of learning and memory. Moreover, because habituation was such a basic mechanism, deficits in habituation might allow one to understand complex cognitive disturbances such as schizophrenia or mental retardation. These hopes have stimulated a great deal of research. Curiously, however, insights gained from this experience have not been as profound as anticipated. In the only systems where habituation could be analyzed at the cellular level (e.g., invertebrates and short-term spinal preparations), the decrease in response output seemed to result from a relatively short-term decrease in transmitter release. However, the actual cellular mechanism that mediates this effect is still unknown. Long-term habituation seems to be a more interesting phenomenon with respect to learning and memory, yet it has been much more difficult to study. Theories that seek to account for enduring, long-term habituation (Wagner, 1976) or sensitization (Borszcz, Cranney, and Leaton, 1989) inevitably appeal to an associative process, that of classical conditioning. As a result, research on the neural mechanisms of habituation and sensitization has been largely replaced by research on the neural mechanisms of classical conditioning.

See also: APLYSIA: DEVELOPMENT OF PROCESSES UNDERLYING LEARNING; APLYSIA: MOLECULAR BASIS OF LONG-TERM SENSITIZATION; INVERTEBRATE LEARNING: C. ELEGANS; INVERTEBRATE LEARNING: HABITUATION AND SENSITIZATION IN TRITONIA; ORIENTING REFLEX HABITUATION

Bibliography

Borszcz, G. S., Cranney, J., and Leaton, R. N. (1989). Influence of long-term sensitization on long-term habituation of the acoustic startle response in rats: Central gray lesions, pre-exposure, and extinction. *Journal of Experimental Psychology and Animal Behavior Processes 15,* 54–64.

Davis, M. (1970). Effects of interstimulus interval length and variability on startle response habituation in the rat. *Journal of Comparative Physiology and Psychology 72,* 177–192.

—— (1972). Differential rates of decay of sensitization and habituation of the startle response in the rat. *Journal of Comparative Physiology and Psychology 78,* 260–267.

Davis, M., Parisi, T., Gendelman, D. S., Tischler, M. D., and Kehne, J. H. (1982). Habituation and sensitization of "startle" responses elicited electrically from the brainstem. *Science 218,* 688–690.

Davis, M., and Wagner, A. R. (1968). Startle responsiveness following habituation to different intensities of tone. *Psychonomic Science 12,* 337–338.

—— (1969). Habituation of the startle response under an incremental sequence of stimulus intensities. *Journal of Comparative Physiology and Psychology 67,* 486–492.

Egger, M. D. (1978). Sensitization and habituation of dorsal horn cells in cats. *Journal of Physiology 279,* 153–166.

Egger, M. D., Bishop, J. W., and Cone, C. H. (1976). Sensitization and habituation of the plantar cushion reflex in cats. *Brain Research 103,* 215–228.

Farel, P. B., Glanzman, D. L., and Thompson, R. L. (1973). Habituation of a monosynaptic response in vertebrate central nervous system: Lateral column-motoneuron pathway in isolated frog spinal cord. *Journal of Neurophysiology 36,* 1,117–1,130.

Groves, P. M., and Thompson, R. F. (1970). Habituation: A dual process theory. *Psychological Review 77,* 419–450.

Harris, J. D. (1943). Habituatory response decrement in the intact organism. *Psychological Bulletin 40,* 385–422.

Humphrey, G. (1933). *The nature of learning.* New York: Harcourt, Brace.

Jordan, W. P. (1989). Mesencephalic reticular formation lesions made after habituation training abolish long-term habituation of the acoustic startle response. *Behavioral Neuroscience 4,* 805–815.

Jordan, W. P., and Leaton, R. N. (1983). Habituation of the acoustic startle response in rats after lesions in the mesencephalic reticular formation or in the inferior colliculus. *Behavioral Neuroscience 97,* 710–724.

Leaton, R. N., and Supple, W. F. (1986). Cerebellar vermis: Essential for long-term habituation of the acoustic startle response. *Science 232,* 513–515.

Lopiano, L., DeSperati, C., and Montarolo, P. G. (1990). Long-term habituation of the acoustic startle response: Role of the cerebellar vermis. *Neuroscience 35,* 79–84.

Mendell, L. M. (1984). Modifiability of spinal synapses. *Physiological Review 64,* 260–324.

Sanes, J. N., and Ison, J. R. (1983). Habituation and sensitization of components of the human eyeblink reflex. *Behavioral Neuroscience 97,* 833–836.

Sharpless, S., and Jasper, H. (1956). Habituation of the arousal reaction. *Brain 79,* 655–682.

Sokolov, E. N. (1960). Neuronal models and the orienting reflex. In M. A. B. Brazier, ed., *The central nervous system and behavior: III.* New York: Josiah Macy Foundation.

Spencer, W. A., Thompson, R. F., and Neilson, D. R. (1966a). Response decrement of the flexion reflex in the acute spinal cat and transient restoration by strong stimuli. *Journal of Neurophysiology 29,* 221–239.

—— (1966b). Alterations in responsiveness of ascending and reflex pathways activated by iterated cutaneous afferent volleys. *Journal of Neurophysiology 29*, 240–252.

Thompson, R. F., and Spencer, W. A. (1966). Habituation: a model phenomenon for the study of the neuronal substrates of behavior. *Psychological Review 73*, 16–43.

Wagner, A. R. (1976). Priming in STM: An information processing mechanism for self-generated or retrieval-generated depression. In T. N. Tighe and R. L. Leaton, eds., *Habituation: Perspectives from child development, animal behavior, and neurophysiology.* Hillsdale, NJ: Erlbaum.

Michael Davis
M. David Egger

Harry F. Harlow *(Harlow Primate Laboratory, University of Wisconsin)*

HARLOW, HARRY (1905–1981)

Harry F. Harlow was born in Fairview, Iowa, on October 31, 1905, and died on December 6, 1981. He attended Reed College in 1923 before transferring to Stanford, where he received his Ph.D. in 1930 under the supervision of C. P. Stone. Harlow's first appointment was at the University of Wisconsin, where he later established the Wisconsin Primate Laboratory. Except for the period from 1949 to 1951, when he was chief psychologist for the U.S. Army, he remained at Wisconsin until his formal retirement in 1974, when he moved to the University of Arizona. Harlow's research, characterized by imaginative methods of studying cognition and motivation, led to important discoveries. He was elected president of the American Psychological Association and received its Distinguished Scientific Contribution Award. He also received awards from the Society for Research in Child Development and was recipient of the Kittay International Scientific Foundation Award, the Gold Medal Award of the American Psychological Foundation, and the U.S. National Medal of Science.

Harlow was primarily interested in the cortical localization of intellectual functions such as learning and memory, and decided to work with primates because of their obvious cognitive capacities. As he approached this problem, he was convinced that the contemporary learning systems were fundamentally limited because they were based upon inadequate information, and he set out to collect such information from his monkeys in a systematic manner. One of the most important innovations that Harlow introduced was the study of transfer of training. Although there was a long history in the study of this general issue, previous workers had studied interproblem learning over a narrow range of problems in which subjects were trained to mastery on a given problem before being shifted to new ones. Harlow departed radically from this approach by training animals on individual problems for a small number of trials before shifting to new problems. He showed that on the initial train-ing trials animals worked largely by trial and error, but at some point they began to catch on to a general principle that could be used to successfully solve problems in a single trial; that is, the animals had learned how to learn, a process that he called the development of a "learning set." This simple observation was important for theoretical reasons, but it had another important impact: It could be used to study the organization of cortical processes related to learning and memory. This represented another major breakthrough, and this type of behavioral analysis still represents a major tool in studies of neural mechanisms underlying learning and memory processes.

Harlow was convinced that many of the shortcomings of the contemporary theoretical systems were due to the paucity of data on the ontogenetic development of learning, perception, and motivation. In an effort to determine how and when different learning and perceptual processes developed, he and his colleagues began a major program in which infant monkeys were separated from their mothers at birth and then studied intensively over the ensuing years. While the contributions of these experiments go far beyond the questions of learning and memory, it was clear from these studies that there were major maturational changes in the performance of monkeys on different learning tests. These changes could not be accounted for by traditional learning theories and thus led to a new field of inquiry in learning and memory research.

Finally, Harlow was a major advocate of the use of the comparative method in studies of learning and memory: "Basically the problems of generalization of behavioral data between species are simple—one cannot generalize, but one must. If the competent do not wish to generalize, the incompetent will fill the field"

(Harlow, Gluck, and Suomi, 1972). The comparative studies of Harlow and those that followed were based upon the concepts related to learning sets, which led in turn to major advances in the understanding of the phylogenetic changes in learning and memory abilities.

Harlow thus made a unique and long-lasting contribution not only to the way in which learning and memory are now studied but also to the development of psychological theory of learning and memory. His work helped shape the nature of the questions that are now being addressed.

See also: COMPARATIVE COGNITION

Bibliography

Harlow, H. F. (1956). Learning set and error factor theory. In S. Koch, ed., *Psychology: A study of a science*, Vol. 2, pp. 492–537. New York: McGraw-Hill.

Harlow, H. F., Gluck, J. P., and Suomi, S. J. (1972). Generalization of behavioral data between nonhuman and human animals. *American Psychologist 27*, 709–716.

Sears, R. R. (1982). Harry Frederick Harlow (1905–1981). *American Psychologist 37*, 1,280–1,281.

Bryan E. Kolb

HEAD INJURY

Closed head injuries (CHI; nonpenetrating head injury produced by sudden acceleration/deceleration, as in motor vehicle crashes) often cause memory impairments. Both retrograde amnesia (RA) and difficulty in learning and retaining new information (anterograde amnesia) can result from CHI. Posttraumatic amnesia (PTA) refers to the symptom complex of anterograde amnesia, disorientation, and attentional disturbance during the initial stage of recovery, but dissociations can occur in some patients. Even after the abatement of PTA and RA, half of severe CHI victims suffer from residual impairments. (Russell, 1971).

The pathophysiologic contribution to residual memory disturbance is difficult to isolate because of the heterogeneity of many injuries associated with CHI, including primary and secondary causes of brain damage and confounding comorbidities such as alcohol abuse. However, several pathophysiologic features of CHI, including the Glasgow Coma Scale score (GCS) and duration of coma have been linked to memory deficit. Proximity of the sphenoidal ridges and bony protrusions on the base of the skull to the frontal cortex and the anterior temporal lobes makes these areas particularly vulnerable to diffuse CHI, often with superimposed focal lesions (Adams, 1975). Further, magnetic resonance spectroscopy (MRS)

studies of persons after CHI reveal that neuroaxonal cellular damage to the frontal lobes may be present even within normal-appearing white matter (Garnett et al., 2000), a finding consistent with the weak correlation between visible structural damage revealed by conventional imaging techniques and performance on neuropsychological tests (Wilson et al., 1988).

Posttraumatic versus Retrograde

In contrast with the duration of PTA, which may exceed a week after severe CHI, memory loss associated with RA typically substantially resolves during the early stages of recovery. RA can initially extend backward several months from the time of injury but eventually shrinks to encompass only the minutes or seconds immediately before the injury. (Russell, 1971). During early recovery, RA frequently manifests backward displacement of temporal orientation far into the past (High, Levin, and Gary, 1990).

Residual Memory Disorders

The possible link between localized traumatic focal lesion and memory disorder is complicated by variation across patients in type and size of lesion. Nonetheless, recent research relating to specific memory deficits after CHI indicates that certain types of memory disorders are a more likely consequence than others, possibly reflecting the greater probability of frontal and temporal lobe damage after CHI.

Verbal and Nonverbal Learning

Adults and children who have had severe CHI and are in the postacute stages of injury are likely to show deficits in immediate and delayed. Many studies have found that individuals with severe CHI suffer from recognition impairment on tests of nonverbal memory that use abstract, nonverbalizable stimuli, drawings of nameable objects, and unfamiliar faces. Although deficient initial learning is common, accelerated forgetting has also occurred in a subgroup of CHI patients. Although most studies of verbal recall report reduction of memory span or other errors of omission after CHI, persons with severe CHI have frequent commission errors, including a high incidence of intrusions and perseverations.

Long-Term Memory, Semantic Knowledge

Although patients with CHI may have normal semantic knowledge, access to it is often slowed or difficult and may be qualitatively different than that of uninjured persons (Haut, 1991). CHI seems to cause impairment of the ability to use semantic information to facilitate recall in children and adults (Levin and

Goldstein, 1986). Naming impairments, especially in relation to familiar people, sometimes coexists with accurate and specific semantic knowledge of the people that could not be named (Sunderland, Harris, and Baddeley, 1983). Impaired naming of familiar objects is also frequently present following CHI in adults (Levin, Grossman, and Kelly, 1977). For example, Levin, Grossman, and Kelly (1977) found impaired object naming in 40 percent of the fifty patients they studied in whom PTA had resolved.

Procedural Memory

Most procedural memory studies have focused on the acquisition of the knowledge to perform actions, rather than the systematic testing of loss or preservation of knowledge. Most studies have shown intact procedural learning, even when conjoined with impaired verbal learning (Timmerman and Brouwer, 1999).

Implicit Memory

Although studies directly comparing conscious learning (explicit tests of memory) to learning without conscious awareness (implicit tests of memory) in CHI patients are relatively sparse, findings suggest that implicit memory is more resistant to impairment after CHI than is explicit memory in both adults (Glisky, 1993) and children.

Prospective Memory

There has been little research on prospective memory—the intention to remember in the future—after CHI. Self-reports indicate that adult CHI patients report impaired prospective memory as opposed to uninjured adults. In studies using experimental tasks to investigate prospective memory in adults after CHI, impairments have been reported after short delay (Shum, Valentine, and Cutmore, 1999) but not long delay. Children with severe CHI also suffer impairment on experimental tasks of prospective memory.

Conclusion

Most studies of persons with CHI using verbal and nonverbal learning paradigms have found that learning impairment is a likely consequence of serious head injury. The magnitude of the impairment is related to the severity of the injury as determined by the GCS (Levin, Goldstein, High, and Eisenberg, 1988).

Bibliography

Adams, J. H. (1975). The neuropathology of head injury. In P. J. Binken and G. W. Bruyn, eds., *Handbook of clinical neurology*, Vol. 23. New York: Elsevier.

Garnett, M. R., Blamire, A. M., Rajagopalan, B., Styles, P., and Cadoux-Hudson, T. A. D. (2000). Evidence for cellular damage in normal-appearing white matter correlates with injury severity in patients following traumatic brain injury. A magnetic resonance spectroscopy study. *Brain 123*, 1,403–1,409.

Glisky, E. (1993). Computer-assisted instructions for patients with traumatic brain injury: Teaching of domain specific knowledge. *Journal of Head Trauma Rehabilitation 7*, 1–12.

Haut, M. W., Petros, T. V., Frank, R. G., and Haut, J. S. (1991). Speed of processing within semantic memory following severe closed-head injury. *Brain and Cognition 17*, 31–41.

High, W. H. J., Levin, H. S., and Gary, H. E. J. (1990). Recovery of orientation and memory following closed-head injury. *Journal of Clinical and Experimental Neuropsychology 12*, 703–714.

Levin, H. S. (1989). Memory deficit after closed head injury. *Journal of Clinical and Experimental Neuropsychology 12*, 129–153.

Levin, H. S., and Goldstein, F. C. (1986). Organization of verbal memory after severe closed-head injury. *Journal of Clinical and Experimental Neuropsychology 8*, 643–656.

Levin, H. S., Goldstein, F. C., High, W. H. J., and Eisenberg, H. M. (1988). Automatic and effortful processing after severe closed-head injury. *Brain and Cognition 7*, 283–297.

Levin, H. S., Grossman, R. G., and Kelly, P. J. (1977). Aphasic disorder in patients with closed head injury. *Journal of Neurology, Neurosurgery and Psychiatry 39*, 1,062–1,070.

Russell, W. R. (1971). *The traumatic amnesias.* New York: Oxford University Press.

Shum, D., Valentine, M., and Cutmore, T. (1999). Performance of individuals with severe long-term traumatic brain injury on time-, event-, and activity-based prospective memory tasks. *Journal of Clinical and Experimental Neuropsychology 21*, 49–58.

Sunderland, A., Harris, D., and Baddeley, A. D. (1983). Do laboratory tests predict everyday memory? A neuropsychological study. *Journal of Verbal Learning and Verbal Behavior 22*, 341–357.

Timmerman, M. E., and Brouwer, W. H. (1999). Slow information processing after very severe closed-head injury: Impaired access to declarative knowledge and intact application and acquisition of procedural knowledge. *Neuropsychologia 37*, 467–478.

Wilson, J. T., Wiedmann, K. D., Hadley, D. M., Condon, B., Teasdale, G., and Brooks, D. N. (1988). Early and late magnetic resonance imaging and neuropsychological outcome after head injury. *Journal of Neurology, Neurosurgery and Psychiatry 51*, 391–396.

Harvey S. Levin
Revised by Gerri Hanten and Harvey S. Levin

HEBB, DONALD (1904–1985)

Donald Olding Hebb was born July 22, 1904, in the small community of Chester Basin on the Atlantic coast of Nova Scotia, Canada. Both his parents were physicians; his two brothers followed in their footsteps, and his sister Catherine became a well-known neurophysiologist after receiving her medical degree. Donald, however, was the family's nonconformist: he wanted to be a novelist, and in 1925 he graduated from Dalhousie University with a degree in English. He spent the next two years teaching and traveling. Hebb never completed his novel, but he was an excellent writer (his classical work on the neurological

Donald Hebb *(Peter M. Milner)*

bases of behavior, *The Organization of Behavior*, 1949, is eminently readable), and he taught numerous students how to communicate clearly.

Early Career

In 1927, having become interested in the work of Sigmund Freud, Hebb enrolled as a part-time graduate student in psychology at McGill University. He supported himself by teaching and soon was appointed principal of a local elementary school. He experimented with teaching methods in his school, and at McGill he developed an interest in the "nature-nurture" question.

Around this time, newly married, Hebb almost decided to make a career in education, but illness and tragedy diverted his course. He was immobilized by tuberculosis of the hip for more than a year, and during his illness he wrote a theoretical master's thesis, "Conditioned and Unconditioned Reflexes and Inhibition," which his university examiners rated cum laude. In this thesis he speculates about a phenome-

non that later became known as the *Hebb synapse*, stating that "the discharge of one neuron into another is increased by the discharge of the second neuron." Hebb further proposes that: "An excited neuron tends to decrease its discharge to inactive neurons," an idea that he apparently considered too audacious to include in the famous neurophysiological postulate that appears in his 1949 book, *The Organization of Behavior*. Boris Babkin, a McGill physiologist and former student of Pavlov, read Hebb's thesis, and when Hebb was mobile again, Babkin encouraged him to embark on a conditioning experiment. This type of research soon palled, however, and after his wife was killed in a motor accident, Hebb decided to leave Montreal. He was offered an assistantship at Yale University, but Babkin recommended that he apply to study with Karl Lashley in Chicago. Hebb took his advice, a crucial step in his career, and was accepted.

Karl Lashley as Mentor and Colleague

At the University of Chicago, Hebb came under the influence of L. L. Thurstone, C. Judson Herrick, Nathaniel Kleitman, Wolfgang Köhler, and, of course, Lashley himself. Lashley believed that the goal of psychology was to discover how the brain determines behavior, so the questions he asked were different from those arising at the time in mainstream behaviorism.

After a year Lashley moved to Harvard University and Hebb went with him, completing his experiments on the effect of dark-rearing on rat visual perception. After receiving his doctorate, Hebb remained at Harvard for a year and then received a fellowship to study Wilder Penfield's patients at the newly established Montreal Neurological Institute. A major project was to determine the effect of frontal-lobe removal on measures of intelligence. Hebb found that extensive damage to that area had a negligible effect on standard intelligence test scores, which pleased Penfield and posed an enduring problem for Hebb. Another finding was that large right-temporal-lobe ablations impaired visual perception.

At the end of his two-year fellowship, Hebb went to Queen's University, in Kingston, Ontario. There he lectured and experimented with rats to follow up his work at the Neurological Institute. He devised a rat intelligence test (Hebb and Williams, 1946) that he considered analogous to the tests used on human patients and, on the basis of his experiments, concluded that early experience had a significant effect on intelligence. Hebb developed this theme and used it to explain the lack of effect of large frontal-lobe lesions in adults (Hebb, 1942).

In 1942 Lashley was appointed director of the Yerkes Laboratories of Primate Biology in Orange

Park, Florida, and he invited Hebb to join the staff. The opportunity to work with Lashley again easily outweighed Hebb's doubts as to the suitability of chimpanzees as experimental subjects, and he seized the opportunity. Lashley intended to develop tests of learning and problem solving while Hebb worked on tests of temperament and emotionality. The effects of brain lesions on these tests would then be studied. In fact no operations were performed until after Hebb left five years later, largely because Lashley's experience with rats did not adequately prepare him for a battle of wits with chimpanzees. In the meantime Hebb made some interesting discoveries about the causes of fear, and he accumulated a fund of chimpanzee anecdotes that enlivened his writing and lectures for the next forty years. But it was the time he spent pondering the neurophysiology of thought and intelligence, and discussing his ideas with Lashley and other members of the staff, that Hebb valued most. In 1944 a paper by Lorente de Nó on neuronal loops and recurrent circuits came to Hebb's attention and restructured his conception of the brain. Strangely, although many psychological phenomena, such as attention, cried out for explanations in terms of feedback from central to peripheral brain areas, and neurophysiologists had known about recurrent circuits for some time, the idea of one-way sensory-to-motor paths remained deeply ingrained among psychologists. The only feedback route envisaged was via the effects of responses on sensory input.

One of the most important questions raised by Lashley in his monograph *Brain Mechanisms and Intelligence* (1929) was why the connections established during learning could not be localized by brain lesions. Another topic that must have been discussed at length by Lashley's circle was stimulus generalization. Why, for example, is learned recognition not disturbed by a change in the size of a visual stimulus? Hebb thought that Lorente de Nó's neural loops would provide answers to many long-standing problems concerning the nature of the representation of objects in the brain.

A Neural Model of the "Idea"

The theory that finally emerged (Hebb, 1949) was, in keeping with the views of the day, strongly empiricist. Hebb postulated that initially random connections between cortical cells become organized by sensory input into densely interconnected groups that he called *cell assemblies*. Hebb's answer to Lashley's localization problem was that the cells of each assembly are dispersed over a large area of the cortex so that enough interconnected cells survive all but the largest lesions, ensuring that objects continue to be represented. Hebb explained generalization by stipu-

lating that during the initial investigations of an object, many different sensory patterns contribute inputs that are incorporated into, or closely linked to, a single cell assembly representing the object. The dense intrinsic connections ensure that the whole assembly fires when only partial input is presented.

Cell assemblies that are active successively acquire connections with each other, which explains expectancy and the association of ideas. In effect, Hebb developed a neural model of the "idea," rescuing it from the obloquy of mentalism under which it had languished for almost half a century. Many psychologists were chafing under the constraints and dogmas of behaviorism, and they received Hebb's liberating ideas with enthusiasm. Hebb presented psychologists with an alternative to the mind-body dichotomy that had forced behaviorists to outlaw many important psychological phenomena.

The establishment of cell assemblies and the connections between them requires neural plasticity. The mechanism Hebb proposed was that if an axon terminal and its postsynaptic neuron were active at about the same time, the effectiveness of the synapse would increase. This model of synaptic change is now known as the Hebb synapse, and in the years since his death it may be that Hebb has come to be viewed as a neurophysiologist. If so, this is a pity; Hebb's attempt to explain how the brain represents the outside world, in which the Hebb synapse played a role, was a more original contribution than the Hebb synapse itself and, by illustrating the power of neurological models, was of more far-reaching influence.

Although Hebb made no attempt to test a computer or mathematical model of his conception of the cell assembly, a not very successful attempt to do so was made by Rochester, Holland, Haibt, and Duda (1956) at IBM shortly after *The Organization of Behavior* was published. The cell-assembly idea has influenced all subsequent neural-network models of learning, from the *perceptron* (Rosenblatt, 1962) to the *parallel distributed processing* models of Rumelhart and McClelland (1986). Although Hebb's neural network was a paper and pencil model that he showed little inclination to computerize, its pioneering quality should make Hebb nerve nets would be a more fitting memorial to his name than Hebb synapses.

Later Career

Hebb returned to the McGill department of psychology in 1947 and became chairman a year later. He studied the effects of rearing environment in rats and dogs, obtaining results that were influential in shaping programs for providing more stimulating surroundings for disadvantaged infants. Later he measured effects of prolonged sensory deprivation on human subjects and probed the cell assembly hypothesis more directly by studying the patterns of breakdown of perception at reduced contrast, as when an image is held fixed on the retina.

Hebb was elected president of the Canadian Psychological Association in 1952 and of the American Psychological Association in 1960. In 1966 he was made a fellow of the Royal Society, and in 1979 a foreign associate of the National Academy of Sciences (USA). He was chancellor of McGill University from 1970 to 1974. Hebb retired to his birthplace in 1977 and died there in August 1985.

See also: PARALLEL DISTRIBUTED PROCESSING MODELS OF MEMORY

Bibliography

Hebb, D. O. (1932). Conditioned and unconditioned reflexes and inhibition. Master's thesis, McGill University.

—— (1942). The effect of early and late brain injury upon test scores, and the nature of normal adult intelligence. *Proceedings of the American Philosophical Society* 85, 275–292.

—— (1949). *The organization of behavior.* New York: Wiley.

—— (1980). D. O. Hebb. In G. Lindzey, ed, *A history of psychology in autobiography*, Vol. 7, pp. 273–303. San Francisco: Freeman.

Hebb, D. O., and Williams, K. (1946). A method of rating animal intelligence. *Journal of General Psychology* 34, 59–65.

Orbach, J. (1998). *The neuropsychological theories of Lashley and Hebb.* Lanham, MD: University Press of America.

Rochester, N., Holland, J. H., Haibt, L. H., and Duda, W. L. (1956). Tests on a cell assembly theory of action of the brain, using a large digital computer. *IRE Transactions. Information Theory* IT-2, 80–93.

Rosenblatt, F. (1962). *Principles of neurodynamics: Perceptrons and the theory of brain mechanisms.* Washington, DC: Spartan Books.

Rumelhart, D. E., and McClelland, J. L. (1986). *Parallel distributed processing*, Vol. 1: *Foundations.* Cambridge, MA: MIT Press.

Peter M. Milner

HORMONES AND MEMORY

Hormones influence many physiological systems involved in regulating adaptation to environmental changes. In addition to their many other influences, hormones serve an adaptive role in regulating the neurobiological processes underlying memory formation and other cognitive processes. Extensive evidence indicates that, in laboratory animals, hormones administered shortly after training influence the retention of recently acquired information. Although many hormones either enhance or impair long-term retention when administered after training, the effects of hormones normally released by mildly stressful stimulation have been studied most extensively. The findings suggest that endogenous hormones released by emotionally arousing training experiences influence long-term memory by modulating memory consolidation processes. In addition to such acute effects, hormones may also have more sustained effects on cognition through neurotrophic and neuroprotective actions.

Epinephrine

The adrenergic catecholamine epinephrine is released into the blood from the adrenal medulla following arousing or stressful stimulation. Systemic injections of epinephrine administered after training produce dose-dependent effects on subsequent retention: Low doses enhance retention, whereas high doses impair retention. As epinephrine passes the blood-brain barrier poorly, epinephrine's effects on memory appear to be initiated by the activation of peripheral adrenoceptors. The finding that drugs that selectively block peripheral β-adrenoceptors (when administered systemically) prevent the memory-enhancing effects of epinephrine supports this conclusion. Epinephrine acts on receptors in the liver to initiate the release of glucose. Evidence that glucose can enhance memory suggests that glycogenolysis may play a role in mediating epinephrine influences on memory. Epinephrine also stimulates the release of the arousal-related neuromodulator norepinephrine in the brain by activating β-adrenoceptors located on vagal afferents terminating on brain-stem noradrenergic cell groups in the nucleus of the solitary tract and locus coeruleus. Noradrenergic projections originating in these nuclei innervate forebrain structures involved in learning and memory. Extensive evidence indicates that the memory-enhancing effects of epinephrine involve the release of norepinephrine and activation of β-adrenoceptors within a specific brain region, the basolateral nucleus of the amygdaloid complex. Microinfusions of β-adrenoceptor antagonists into this brain region block the memory-modulating effects of peripherally administered epinephrine and microinfusions of norepinephrine into this nucleus after training enhance memory. Norepinephrine also enhances memory consolidation when administered to other brain regions, including the nucleus of the solitary tract and the hippocampus.

Glucocorticoids

Glucocorticoids (corticosterone in the rat, cortisol in humans), which is a class of steroid stress hormones released from the adrenal cortex, also influence long-term memory consolidation. Glucocorticoid hormones freely enter the brain and bind to two intracellular types of adrenal steroid receptors, glucocorticoid receptors and mineralocorticoid receptors. The low-affinity glucocorticoid receptors are involved in mediating glucocorticoid effects on memory consolidation. Glucocorticoids act through intracellular and intranuclear receptors and can affect gene transcription by direct binding of receptor homodimers to DNA. Glucocorticoids may also affect memory consolidation through transactivation or protein-protein interactions with other transcription factors or effector systems. Administration of low doses of glucocorticoids enhances memory consolidation and glucocorticoid antagonists impair consolidation. Memory-modulating effects are induced by systemic injections of glucocorticoid receptor agonists and antagonists as well as by infusions administered into several brain regions, including the nucleus of the solitary tract, the basolateral amygdala, or the hippocampus. Glucocorticoid-induced memory-modulating effects require concurrent noradrenergic activation within the amygdala. Glucocorticoid effects on memory consolidation are, thus, conditional, that is, their actions require coactivation of other transmitter systems. Glucocorticoid effects on memory are not restricted to influences on consolidation. Glucocorticoids generally impair short-term memory in experimental animals and human subjects, and, when administered shortly before retention testing, glucocorticoids also impair retrieval of long-term memory for spatial-contextual and declarative information. These effects are temporary and dissipate within several hours after stress exposure or hormone injection. Prolonged exposure to high levels of glucocorticoids due to chronic stress tends to induce prolonged impairment of cognitive functioning.

ACTH and CRH

The peptide hormone adrenocorticotropin (ACTH) is secreted from the anterior pituitary. Early studies investigating the influence of hormones on learning and memory reported that hypophysectomy produced impairment of learning and memory and that the impairment was attenuated by injections of ACTH. Many subsequent experiments using animals with intact pituitary glands found that memory is enhanced by low doses of ACTH and impaired by high doses. Evidence that retention is affected by fragments of the ACTH peptide that do not induce the release of glucocorticoids from the adrenal cortex indicates that ACTH effects on memory are not mediated by glucocorticoids. The corticotropin-releasing hormone (CRH), another peptide hormone released into the blood and brain after arousing or stressful stimulation, enhances memory consolidation when administered shortly after training, an effect that does not require release of glucocorticoids. The involvement of extra-hypothalamic CRH in memory and related cognitive functions has been found in experiments with both animal and human subjects. Local infusions

of CRH into the hippocampus, the amygdala, or the bed nucleus of the stria terminalis affect memory consolidation by interacting with noradrenergic mechanisms.

Vasopressin and Oxytocin

Vasopressin and oxytocin are synthesized in the hypothalamus and are released in the brain and into the cerebrospinal fluid and general circulation (via the posterior pituitary). The possibility that vasopressin may influence learning and memory was suggested by findings that lesions of the posterior pituitary affected the extinction of an avoidance response and that the effect was attenuated by injections of an extract of pituitary tissue containing vasopressin. Subsequent research has provided extensive evidence that memory is enhanced by vasopressin administered immediately after training. Although some evidence suggests that the effects of vasopressin on memory may be mediated, at least in part, by peripheral effects, including alterations in blood pressure, other evidence indicates that central actions of vasopressin influence memory consolidation. Peptide metabolites of vasopressin that do not affect blood pressure have highly potent effects on memory. Additionally, administration of a vasopressin antagonist into the cerebral ventricles blocks the memory-enhancing effect of peripherally administered vasopressin without altering vasopressin effects on blood pressure. Memory is also enhanced by low doses of vasopressin administered directly into a number of brain regions, including the hippocampus. Evidence that lesions of the dorsal adrenergic bundle block the memory-enhancing effect of vasopressin indicates that, as with other hormonal effects of memory, nonadrenergic activation may be required. Although the effects of oxytocin have been less extensively examined, oxytocin may either impair or enhance memory, depending on the experimental training conditions.

Opioid Peptides

Research findings indicating that the opiate drug morphine impairs memory when injected after training suggest that endogenous opioid peptides may play a role in the regulation of memory consolidation. The endogenous opioid peptide β-endorphin is released within the brain and is also released from the anterior pituitary into the blood along with ACTH. Enkephalins are released from the adrenal medulla, together with epinephrine. Experimental findings indicating that effects of these opioid peptides on memory are similar to those of morphine suggest that endogenously released opioid peptides regulate memory consolidation. Studies of the effects of opiate antagonists provide additional support for this view: Opiate antagonists enhance retention when administered after training. As with other hormones, opioid peptide influences on memory involve the amygdala. Injections of opiate agonists and antagonists administered directly into the amygdala after training produce effects on memory highly comparable to those produced by systemic injections. Such effects also involve interactions with the noradrenergic system: β-adrenoceptor antagonists injected into the amygdala block the memory-enhancing effects of the opiate antagonist naloxone. Such findings agree with the evidence that opioid peptides inhibit the release of norepinephrine in the amygdala and other brain regions. Memory can also be influenced by a number of peptide hormones, including substance P, neuropeptide Y, somatostatin, prolactin, and cholecystokinin (CCK) that are not generally thought to be stress related.

Gonadal Hormones

Gonadal hormones generally have more sustained effects on cognitive functioning, but acute effects on memory consolidation have also been reported. For example, testosterone and estradiol, major gonadal steroid hormones, have neurotrophic and neuroprotective actions on the brain. A decline in cognitive function (particularly spatial memory) can be found in postmenopausal women and estrogen-replacement therapy may attenuate the deficits. Estrogens also appear to have a protective effect against the neurodegenerative and memory-impairing effects of excessive glucocorticoids.

Interactions Among Hormonal Systems

There are many interactions among hormones as well as interactions among hormones and transmitter systems in modulating memory consolidation. For example, the effects of epinephrine on memory are influenced by glucocorticoids. The memory-enhancing effects of epinephrine are blocked by metyrapone, a drug that prevents the synthesis and release of glucocorticoids. Furthermore, vasopressin is ineffective in influencing memory consolidation in adrenal demedullated animals. Opioid peptides modulate memory consolidation through influences on central noradrenergic and cholinergic systems. Naloxone effects on memory are blocked by the (-adrenoceptor antagonist propranolol as well as by the muscarinic cholinergic antagonist atropine. Additionally, the muscarinic cholinergic agonist oxytremorine and the acetylcholinesterase inhibitor physostigmine attenuate the memory-impairing effects of β-endorphin. Thus, several hormonal systems known to have important roles in enabling adaptation to stressful con-

ditions also serve a highly adaptive role of influencing memory by interacting with neuromodulatory systems in brain regions involved in regulating memory consolidation.

See also: STRESS AND MEMORY

Bibliography

Bohus, B. (1994). Humoral modulation of learning and memory processes: Physiological significance of brain and peripheral mechanisms. In J. Delacour, ed., *The memory system of the brain*, pp. 337–364, Singapore: World Scientific.

De Wied, D. (1991). The effects of neurohypophyseal hormones and related peptides on learning and memory processes. In R. C. A. Frederickson, J. L. McGaugh, and D. L. Felten, eds., *Peripheral signaling of the brain*, pp. 335–350. Toronto: Hogrefe and Huber.

Koob, G. F. (1987). Neuropeptides and memory. In L. L. Iversen and S. H. Snyder, eds., *Handbook of psychopharmacology*, Vol. 19: *Behavioral pharmacology, and update*, pp. 531–573. New York: Plenum.

McEwen, B. S. (2000). Stress, sex, and the structural and functional plasticity of the hippocampus. In M. S. Gazzaniga, ed., *The new cognitive neurosciences*, 2nd edition, pp. 171–198. Cambridge, MA: MIT Press.

McGaugh, J. L., Roozendaal, B., and Cahill, L. (2000). Modulation of memory storage by stress hormones and the amygdaloid complex. In M. S. Gazzaniga, ed., *The new cognitive neurosciences*, 2nd edition, pp. 1,081–1,098. Cambridge, MA: MIT Press.

Roozendaal, B. (2000). Glucocorticoids and the regulation of memory consolidation. *Psychoneuroendocrinology 25*, pp. 213–238.

James L. McGaugh
Revised by James L. McGaugh and Benno Roozendaal

HULL, CLARK L. (1884–1952)

Clark Leonard Hull was born in Akron, New York, on May 24, 1884, and died in New Haven, Connecticut, on May 10, 1952. He earned his bachelor's degree from the University of Michigan in 1913, his master's degree in 1915, and a Ph.D. in experimental psychology in 1918 from the University of Wisconsin. His graduate work was done primarily under the direction of Joseph Jastrow, Daniel Starch, and Vivian A. C. Henmon.

Hull recorded some of his earliest career plans in his Idea Books. "It seems," he wrote, "that the greatest need in the science at present is to create an *experimental* and a *scientific* knowledge of higher mental processes" (Ammons, 1962, p. 814). He planned to become the "supreme authority" in the psychology of abstraction, concept formation, and, possibly, reasoning—to "both know the literature and create the literature on the subject." His doctoral dissertation, *Quantitative Aspects of the Evolution of Concepts,* was published in *Psychological Monographs* (1920).

Hull was afflicted with a variety of health problems, and his relatively late entry into the field was another threat to his long-range goal. In 1930, at the age of forty-six, he wrote, "Sometimes I have been depressed and discouraged in my hope to achieve a major contribution to the theory of knowledge by the fact of my age. Recently, however, the examination of the ages at which several of the great critics have produced their best works has shown that I have by no means reason to be depressed" (Ammons, 1962, p. 836). The list included English philosopher Thomas Hobbes, sixty-three; Dutch philosopher Baruch Spinoza, forty-five; German philosopher and mathematician Gottfried Wilhelm von Leibnitz, sixty-eight; English philosopher John Locke, fifty-eight; and German philosopher Immanuel Kant, fifty-seven. (He could have added that Russian scientist Ivan Pavlov was fifty-six years old when he first proposed the principle of the conditioned reflex.)

Hull was elected to the American Academy of Arts and Sciences in 1935, to the National Academy of Sciences in 1936, and to the presidency of the American Psychological Association 1935. He received the Warren Medal of the Society of Experimental Psychologists in 1945. A measure of his influence is that during the decade spanning 1941 to 1950 approximately 40 percent of all experimental articles published in the *Journal of Experimental Psychology* and the *Journal of Comparative and Physiological Psychology* included references to his work (Spence, 1952). Today Hull is best remembered for one theoretical publication on learning theory, *Principles of Behavior* (1943). However, a case has been made that the twenty-one theoretical articles he published in the *Psychological Review* between 1929 and 1950, the earliest of which introduced the Pavlovian construct the *fractional anticipatory goal response* (r_G-s_G), represent at least as important a contribution to learning theory. (For an extensive account of Hull's work and influence, see Amsel and Rashotte, 1984.)

After receiving his doctorate, Hull stayed in the psychology department at the University of Wisconsin, where he became director of the laboratory in 1925. During these years, his projects included the effects of tobacco smoking on mental and motor efficiency; the definitive books of the time in aptitude testing and hypnosis; and, as forerunners of the computer age, a logic machine that automatically computed correlations, and a robot that learned.

For Hull, Pavlov's conditioning identified the principle by which an event in one subsystem could come to influence functioning in remote parts of such machines, and Edward Thorndike's law of effect, the principle whereby originally random movements could be selected and be linked as responses to specific stimulus patterns (trial-and-error learning and the principle of the habit-family hierarchy). The design

Clark L. Hull *(Psychology Archives, University of Akron)*

of a machine that learned, he thought, should allow for common reactions to stimuli with sensory similarity (generalization); for the learning of common reactions to stimuli with quite different sensory qualities (discrimination); and for the possibility of differential responding to minute differences in stimulus pattern (afferent neural interaction). These became central principles in his papers and in his later formal writings (Hull, 1943, 1952).

In 1929, Hull accepted the position of research professor of psychology at the Institute of Psychology (later the Institute of Human Relations) at Yale University, where he remained for the rest of his career. When he arrived at Yale, at the age of forty-five, he made this entry in his Idea Books, which seems prophetic in the light of the computer age:

Just as the correlation machine has been intimately associated with the testing program, so it appears that the design and construction of automatic physical machines will be intimately associated with my attempts to work out my program involving the higher mental processes. . . . I am pretty certain to be criticized and called a trifle insane at the very least. But whatever genius I have quite evidently lies in this direction. I can do no less than make the best of it—let the tendency, have free rein and go as far as it possibly can. . . . It may lead to real insight into the higher mental processes. . . . It may [on the other hand] possibly serve as the final *reductio ad absurdum* of a mechanistic psychology. If it does, well and good. But even if this should take place, it may at the same time result in such a development in psychic machines displaying an utterly new and different order of automaticity that mechanical engineering of automatic machines will be revolutionized to a degree similar to the introduction of steam engines and electricity. (Ammons, 1962, pp. 828–829)

As research professor at Yale, Hull had no formal teaching assignment, but he engaged in graduate instruction through a weekly seminar that attracted students and faculty of the institute for discussion of a variety of issues in behavior theory.

By Hull's own account, the Institute of Human Relations was a loose organization of behavioral scientists from various fields, mainly psychologists, sociologists, and cultural anthropologists. However, the conceptual framework for the unified contribution it provided was Hull's theoretical system, and it seems fairly clear, in retrospect, that this conceptual framework was an amalgam of influences from English naturalist Charles Darwin, Pavlov, and Austrian neurologist Sigmund Freud. Their influences, filtered through Hull's own, are evident in several important publications written by members of the institute, all of which featured stimulus-response analyses of complex learning. Books in this genre include *Frustration and Aggression* (Dollard et al., 1939), *Social Learning and Imitation* (Miller and Dollard, 1941), and *Personality and Psychotherapy* (Dollard and Miller, 1950).

Even before going to Yale, Hull had planned to prepare a magnum opus on the scientific (mechanistic) analysis of higher mental processes. The earliest titles he considered for his work, listed in his Idea Books in 1928 (Ammons, 1962, pp. 824–825), indicate this intended focus and the mechanistic emphasis: Mechanisms of Thought, Mechanisms of Mind, Mental Mechanisms, Mechanisms of Mental Life, Psychology from the Standpoint of a Mechanist.

Hull's plan was to invert the direction taken by the great philosophers—David Hume, Locke, Kant, and Hobbes—who had attempted to construct a theory of knowledge, thought, and reason on the basis of conscious experience but who, in Hull's eyes, had failed. He planned to attack the same problem using the opposite strategy. He wrote, "I shall start with action—habit—and proceed to deduce all the rest, including conscious experience, from action, i.e., habit" (Ammons, 1962, p. 837).

To carry out this task, Hull planned a three-volume work. The first volume was intended mainly to present a set of formal axioms that constituted a logical system from which hypotheses about mammalian adaptive behavior could be deduced. Completed in Hull's fifty-eighth year, this volume appeared in 1943 and was titled *Principles of Behavior: An Introduction to Behavior Theory*. The orientation of the second volume, based on the principles set down in the first, was toward specific instances of more complex adaptive behavior, such as maze learning and problem solving. Completed in Hull's sixty-eighth year, it appeared shortly after his death in 1952 and was titled *A Behavior System: An Introduction to Behavior Theory Concerning the Individual Organism*. The third volume, which Hull thought would be the most important, was to have applied the system to some elementary phenomena of social mammalian behavior. It was never completed.

The basic formal structure of the theorizing in Hull's *Principles*, as revised in *Essentials of Behavior* (1951), was an intervening variable approach borrowed from Edward Tolman (1938). It involved antecedent, manipulable environmental conditions (independent variables), consequent behavioral conditions (dependent variables), and a bridge of lower- and higher-level constructs connecting the two (the intervening variables). Hull's final version of the theory is summarized in the first chapter of *A Behavior System* as a set of postulates and corollaries, most of which are restated in mathematical form. Examples are Postulate II, relating the strength of an intervening variable, the "molar stimulus trace" S^1, to the independent variables, the physical stimulus (S), as a power function of time since the beginning of the stimulus; and Postulates XIV, XV, and XVI, in which the momentary effective reaction potential $_sE_R$, which already takes into account the behavioral oscillation $_sO_R$ and the threshold for responding $_sL_R$, is related to four response measures—response latency, response amplitude, response frequency, and resistance to experimental extinction—by negatively accelerated functions in the first, third, and fourth cases, and by a linear function in the second. This is the nature of Hull's formal theorizing.

These later, more formal portions of Hull's theorizing were not taken up after his death except by Kenneth Spence (1954, 1956) and a few of Spence's students (Grice, 1968; Logan, 1960). One reason was the advent of the *cognitive revolution* in psychology, which was for the most part a reaction against B. F. Skinner's behaviorism, but also against Hull's stimulus-response associationism, his hypothetico-deductive version of it in particular (Amsel, 1989). Many thought that such a formal Newtonian treatment was both too general in scope and premature. However, more recent mathematical models of associative learning, greatly influenced by Hull but more restricted in explanatory scope (Rescorla and Wagner, 1972), remain influential. Still very important in learning theory is the general approach, taken from Hull's earlier work, of employing hypothetical constructs derived from Pavlovian conditioning in the explanation of instrumental behavior. Hull (1931) regarded this work as stimulus-response analyses of "goal attraction" and "directing ideas," and called the mechanism the *fractional anticipatory goal response* (r_G-s_G). An extensive treatment of such a mechanism in appetitive learning occurs in frustration theory (Amsel, 1962).

The similarity of Hull's theorizing in the 1930s and 1940s to recent computer-generated models of learning and memory has been noted by Hintzman (1992) in an article with the subtitle "Was the Cognitive Revolution a Mistake?" Hintzman, himself a product of the cognitive revolution, asserts that "Key ideas of the cognitive revolution, including cognitive organization and the computer metaphor, have been largely abandoned; and basic concepts from the era of behaviorism and functionalism, such as association, inhibition, similarity, unconscious learning, and transfer, have reemerged." He points particularly to the similarity of "Hullian theories of fifty years ago" to connectionist and production-system models of more recent cognitivists. Much the same can be said about the approaches to theory based on neural networks that often depend on what is called the Hebbian synapse. The proposition here is that the efficiency of cell A in firing cell B is increased as a function of a growth process that takes place at the synapse between cell A and cell B. As a principle of association, this is not greatly removed from Hull's reinforcement postulate. In short, it appears that a part of Hull's lasting contribution will be to modern theories of the neurobiology of learning and memory, an ironic outcome considering the criticisms Hull suffered for what was called his "neurologizing."

See also: HEBB, DONALD

Bibliography

Ammons, R. B. (1962). Psychology of the scientist: IV. Passages from the Idea Books of Clark L. Hull. *Perceptual and Motor Skills 15*, 807–882.

Amsel, A. (1962). Frustrative nonreward in partial reinforcement and discrimination learning: Some recent history and theoretical extension. *Psychological Review 69*, 306–328.

—— (1989). *Behaviorism, neobehaviorism, and cognitivism in learning theory.* Hillsdale, NJ: Erlbaum.

Amsel, A., and Rashotte, M. E. (1984). *Mechanisms of adaptive behavior: Clark L. Hull's theoretical papers with commentary.* New York: Columbia University Press.

Dollard, J., and Miller, N. E. (1950). *Personality and psychotherapy.* New York: McGraw-Hill.

Dollard, J., Doob, L. W., Miller, N. E., Mowrer, O. H., and Sears, R. R. (1939). *Frustration and aggression.* New Haven: Yale University Press.

Grice, G. R. (1968). Stimulus intensity in response evocation. *Psychological Review 75*, 359–373.

Hintzman, D. L. (1992). Twenty-five years of learning and memory: Was the cognitive revolution a mistake? In D. E. Meyer and S. Kornblum, eds., *Attention and performance XIV.* Hillsdale, NJ: Erlbaum.

Hull, C. L. (1920). *Quantitative aspects of the evolution of concepts. Psychological monographs 28*, whole no. 123.

—— (1931). Goal attraction and directing ideas conceived as habit phenomena. *Psychological Review 38*, 487–506.

—— (1943). *Principles of behavior: An introduction to behavior theory.* New York: Appleton-Century-Crofts.

—— (1951). *Essentials of behavior.* New Haven: Yale University Press.

—— (1952). *A behavior system: An introduction to behavior theory concerning the individual organism.* New Haven: Yale University Press.

Logan, F. A. (1960). *Incentive.* New Haven: Yale University Press.

—— (1979). Hybrid theory of operant conditioning. *Psychological Review 86*, 507–541.

Miller, N. E., and Dollard, J. (1941). *Social learning and imitation.* New Haven: Yale University Press.

Rescorla, R. A., and Wagner, A. R. (1972). A theory of Pavlovian conditioning: Variations in the effectiveness of reinforcement and nonreinforcement. In A. H. Black and W. F. Prokasy, eds., *Classical conditioning II: Current research and theory.* New York: Appleton-Century-Crofts.

Spence, K. W. (1952). Clark Leonard Hull: 1884–1952. *American Journal of Psychology 65*, 639–646.

—— (1954). The relation of response latency and speed to the intervening variables and N in S-R theory. *Psychological Review 61*, 209–216.

—— (1956). *Behavior theory and conditioning.* New Haven: Yale University Press.

Tolman, E. C. (1938). The determiners of behavior at a choice point. *Psychological Review 45*, 1–41.

Abram Amsel

HUNTER, WALTER S. (1889–1954)

Scientists studying learning and memory know Walter Samuel Hunter best for his analytical application of a device for assessing short-term retention, the delayed-response task. But his contributions to psychology were much more broad, and deep, than that. He was an influential and moderating force in the behaviorist movement; his thoughts and experiments included topics that remain issues of mainstream interest, such as the nature of an animal's representation for memory, consciousness, and genetic influences on intellectual achievement; and he was a significant applied psychologist with the military.

When Hunter was born, in 1889, it had been about a century since his Scotch-Irish ancestors had

Walter S. Hunter *(Brown University Archives)*

come to the United States. Born in Decatur, Illinois, within a year of the births of U.S. president Dwight D. Eisenhower (1953 to 1961), French soldier Charles de Gaulle, German dictator Adolf Hitler, English motion-picture actor Charles Chaplin, and English poet and critic T. S. Eliot, Hunter spent his early adolescence working on his father's farm near Fort Worth, Texas. His intellectual interests emerged early. In the first stages of his adolescence he purchased and read English naturalist Charles Darwin's groundbreaking *Origin of Species* and *Descent of Man,* and by age fifteen he had developed an active interest in a career in electrical engineering (Hunt, 1956). He attended Polytechnic College at Fort Worth with this objective in mind, but psychology attracted his attention through his reading of American psychologist and philosopher William James's textbooks, and he transferred to the University of Texas in 1908 to study this field (Hunt, 1956).

After graduating from the University of Texas in 1910, he pursued his graduate work at the University of Chicago. Within only two years he completed his doctorate and returned as an instructor to the University of Texas. But these two years at Chicago must have been a concentrated experience indeed, in view of two particularly substantial outcomes. First, his

thinking as a scientist was shaped by two of his professors, James Angell and Harvey Carr, who were among the leading functionalists of the day. Their influence undoubtedly helped form Hunter's favorable view of behaviorism, which had close links to functionalism (an orientation that emphasized the relationships between environmental or task variables and learning, rather than theories of how hypothetical processes determine the occurrence of learning). In addition, Angell had directed the Ph.D. dissertation of John Watson at the University of Chicago a few years earlier. He undoubtedly maintained sufficient contact with Watson to transmit the latter's ideas to his own students. It is likely that in this way, Hunter was exposed early to the notions set forth by Watson in his *Psychological Review* paper mapping out the elements of behaviorism just one year after Hunter received his Ph.D.

Undeterred by a teaching load of four courses per semester, Hunter was productive in his research at the University of Texas, and after four years was appointed professor and head of the department of psychology at the University of Kansas (at age twenty-seven). Soon afterward, World War I required that Hunter work in the military service. As a psychological examiner he helped illustrate the predictive value of simply administered psychological tests, and in World War II he served as one of the military's leading administrators of such testing. In 1925 Hunter became the first G. Stanley Hall Professor of Genetic Psychology at Clark, and in 1936 he was named head of the department at Brown University, where he remained until his death in 1954 (Carmichael, 1954). Hunter worked influentially in the editing of several journals (*Psychological Bulletin, Comparative Psychology Monographs, Behavior Monographs,* and *Journal of Animal Behavior*), and he created *Psychological Abstracts* and edited it for twenty years. His several and diverse honors included membership in the National Research Council and the National Academy of Sciences, posts as president of several professional research societies, including the American Psychological Association, and receipt of the U.S. President's Medal for Merit for his service as chairman of the Applied Psychology Panel of the National Defense Research Council during World War II (Schlosberg, 1954).

Hunter's scientific contributions are equally impressive and diverse, including his study of visual afterimages, auditory discriminations, and issues of social psychology, consciousness, and thinking, but his most lasting contributions dealt with the topic that pervaded his writing in all other respects: memory. This is despite the fact that Hunter himself assiduously avoided reference to "memories" or a "memory process" in animals. To describe how a horse seemed to remember the route home, Hunter preferred instead the concept of "sensory recognition," which, he felt, avoided attributing ideation to animals.

Hunter's Ph.D. thesis was intended to test the animal's behavior in the absence of an eliciting stimulus, the sort of circumstance that might be thought to require a memory system of some sort. He chose a test of retention that had been tried out by two of Carr's students, Haugh and Reed. Whatever its origin, Hunter adapted the delayed-response task in a fashion sufficiently convincing to persuade others to use it as the dominant task for short-term retention over the next fifty years, until delayed matching-to-sample came to be more effectively applied through the use of computers.

In his first version of this task Hunter trained hungry animals initially to obtain food by entering the lighted door of three possible doors (in a later version, no light was used and only the location of the door indicated the reward site). After the animal had perfected this discrimination, Hunter began trials in which the light was shown in the same way but turned off before the animal was allowed to choose a door. For the animal to reach this point required hundreds of training trials. Yet, because responding was permitted only in the absence of the stimulus, at specified intervals after taking it away, reliable correct responding hardly could be caused by sensory recognition; there were no sensory events to be recognized. So long as he could discount "overt orienting attitudes" of the sort that a hunting dog might use when indicating the location of a bird in the field, accurate choice could apparently be attributed to control by an internal representational response, or some other form of ideation. Hunter reasoned that the efficiency of ideation could be compared across various species of animals or even between animals and humans by increasing the interval between the offset of the light and the opportunity to respond.

Hunter estimated the longest retention interval that each of his subjects could tolerate before retention no longer was significant. For rats he estimated this to be about ten seconds, for raccoons twenty-five seconds, for dogs five minutes, for his thirteen-month-old daughter Thayer about twenty-four seconds, for two-and-a-half-year old children fifty seconds, and for a six-year-old child twenty minutes. Hunter judged that the rats were solving the problem by using the overt orienting attitudes of the pointer, but this did not seem necessary for the raccoons and children, so Hunter entertained the possibility that "sensory thought" might be involved for these subjects. He supposed that the critical stimulus—the position of the light or the location of the exit holding

the reward—might be represented within the animal as an intraorganic cue, probably of a kinesthetic nature.

Hunter's research stimulated a number of studies by other scientists directed at one of two issues of phylogeny: which animals can perform such a delayed response task without the use of physical orientation and thus reveal a capacity for internal ideation of the "sensory thought" type suggested by Hunter; and how animals are ordered phylogenetically in terms of their capacity for such ideation, which was presumed to be tapped by the degree to which correct responding occurred after a long delay interval. Hunter later argued that correct performance of the double alternation task also could reveal a capacity for ideation. Hunter made substantial contributions to psychology throughout his forty-two years in the field. His ideas in a variety of areas within psychology were influential, but it can be argued that none of his subsequent experiments had the impact of his Ph.D. thesis.

Some intriguing paradoxes of Hunter's career have been described by Hunt (1956) and are paraphrased here. Despite Hunter's success in avoiding serving in university administration, for which he was frequently sought, he was obviously a successful administrator, as indicated by the strength of the department he built at Brown and his work in the military. Despite his sympathy with and support of behaviorism, some of his most important research seemed more clearly understandable in terms of the use of symbolic processes by animals. Although he was one of the most influential experimental psychologists of the first half of the twentieth century, he spent the last ten years of his life focusing on psychology's applications. Finally, Hunt notes two paradoxes of Hunter's personal life: Despite a high rate of professional productivity, Hunter always seemed relaxed and with time to spare; and, despite his emphasis on being impersonal and objective as a scientist, he was warm in his relationships with others.

Hunter's primary contribution to the field of learning and memory was to implement two tasks, the delayed response and the double alternation task, which provided a metric for discussing animal memory in an objective fashion and a forum for considering the use of representation in memory by animals.

See also: DISCRIMINATION AND GENERALIZATION

Bibliography

Carmichael, H. (1954). Walter Samuel Hunter: 1889–1954. *American Journal of Psychology 67*, 732–734.
Hunt, J. McV. (1956). Walter Samuel Hunter. *Psychological Review 63*, 213–217.
Schlosberg, H. (1954). Walter S. Hunter: Pioneer objectivist in psychology. *Science 120*, 441–442.

Tinklepaugh, O. L. (1928). An experimental study of representative factors in monkeys. *Journal of Comparative Psychology 8,* 197.

Norman E. Spear

HYPNOSIS AND MEMORY

Hypnosis is a social interaction in which one person, called the subject, acts on suggestions from another person, called the hypnotist, for imaginative experiences involving alterations in cognition and voluntary action. Among those individuals who are most highly hypnotizable, these alterations in consciousness can be associated with subjective conviction bordering on delusion, and an experience of involuntariness bordering on compulsion.

Posthypnotic Amnesia

Upon termination of hypnosis, some subjects find themselves unable to remember the events and experiences that transpired while they were hypnotized. This posthypnotic amnesia does not occur unless it has been specifically suggested to the subject, and the memories are not restored when hypnosis is merely reinduced. Moreover, amnesia can be suggested for events that occurred outside of hypnosis. Thus, posthypnotic amnesia is not a form of state-dependent memory. However, it is temporary: Upon administration of a prearranged cue, the amnesia is reversed and the formerly amnesic subject is able to remember the events perfectly well. Reversibility marks posthypnotic amnesia as a disruption of memory retrieval, as opposed to encoding or storage, somewhat like the temporary retrograde amnesias observed in individuals who have suffered concussive blows to the head. The difference is that posthypnotic amnesia is a functional amnesia—an abnormal amount of forgetting that is attributable to psychological factors rather than to brain insult, injury, or disease. Posthypnotic amnesia may serve as a laboratory model of the functional amnesias associated with hysteria and dissociation, such as psychogenic (dissociative) amnesia, fugue, and multiple-personality disorder (dissociative identity disorder).

Posthypnotic amnesia impairs conscious recollection, or explicit memory, while leaving implicit memory unimpaired. Evidence for spared implicit memory is provided by studies of savings in relearning, proactive and retroactive interference, preserved skill learning during hypnosis, source amnesia for factual information learned during hypnosis, repetition priming in word-stem completion, and semantic priming on free association and category generation tasks. In contrast to the explicit-implicit dissociation observed in other forms of amnesia, however, the items in question were deeply processed at the time of encoding. Moreover, posthypnotic amnesia is the only form of amnesia where implicit memories can be restored to explicit recollection, following administration of the prearranged reversibility cue.

Hypnotic Agnosia

In contrast to posthypnotic amnesia, which is a disruption in episodic memory, hypnotic agnosia is best construed as a disruption in semantic or procedural memory—that is, in the subject's ability to access generic, context-free, declarative, and procedural knowledge. For example, subjects who receive suggestions that a particular digit will disappear from their number systems have difficulty when asked to perform additions in which the offending digit appeared in the problem, intermediate step, or solution. Similarly, subjects who are told that certain words are meaningless show no priming when these words are presented for free associations. In contrast to posthypnotic amnesia, hypnotic agnosia has not been subject to much experimental investigation.

Hypnotic Hypermnesia

A great deal of popular interest in hypnosis stems from its reputation as a means of transcending normal limits on human performance. While subjects who receive suggestions for performance enhancement often have the impression that their performance has in fact improved, this impression appears to be illusory. This conclusion holds for learning and memory as it does for strength and endurance. For example, the induction of hypnosis and suggestions for enhanced memory add little or nothing to the hypermnesia that often occurs on repeated test trials in the normal waking state.

Although there is little or no evidence that hypnosis enhances accurate recollection, hypnosis does appear to increase false recollection, or illusory memories. On recognition tests, for example, hypnosis increases the frequency of false alarms and confidence levels attached to items endorsed by subjects without increasing the accuracy of recognition itself. Moreover, perhaps by virtue of their increased suggestibility, hypnotized subjects may be more vulnerable to postevent misinformation effects. It seems likely that the suggestive atmosphere of hypnosis interacts with the reconstructive nature of memory retrieval to create, or enhance, an illusion of remembering.

Hypnotic Age Regression

The role of illusory experience in hypnosis is dramatically revealed in the phenomenon of age regression. While age-regressed subjects may genuinely believe that they are children again, and behave in a childlike manner, they do not grow smaller in the chair. In terms of psychological changes, there are at least three different facets of age regression that bear on questions of hypnosis and memory. First is *ablation*: To what extent does an age-regressed person lose access to the fund of knowledge and repertoire of skills characteristic of his or her chronological age? This is really a question about both amnesia and agnosia, because the loss of access extends to semantic and procedural knowledge as well as episodic memory. The question of ablation is generally coupled to the conceptually distinct question of *reinstatement*: To what extent does an age-regressed adult return to "archaic" modes of cognitive and emotional functioning characteristic of the suggested age? Finally, there is the question of *revivification*: Can the imagined experience of returning to childhood, perhaps coupled with specific suggestions for hypermnesia, enhance memory for childhood events?

Unfortunately for those who would like to use hypnosis as a shortcut in developmental research, studies employing a wide variety of experimental paradigms—including the Babinski reflex, a characteristic of infancy, various illusions that show developmental trends, memory tests, and a host of tasks derived from the developmental theories of Heinz Werner and Jean Piaget, not to mention psychoanalysis—have yielded nothing by way of replicable evidence of either ablation or reinstatement. Positive findings either have not replicated or have proved to be artifacts of the demand characteristics of the testing situation. Age-regressed adults may have the subjectively compelling experience of being children again, and they may appear to behave in a childlike manner, but what observers see is an imaginative reconstruction of childhood—not a reversion to the genuine article.

Although age regression does not yield a faithful reproduction of childlike mental functioning, the subjectively convincing experience of being a child might produce revivification, the third issue in age-regression research, in a manner analogous to state- or context-dependent memory. As with hypnotic hypermnesia, however, there is no convincing evidence that revivification actually occurs. The few studies that have attempted to corroborate the memories reported by age-regressed subjects did yield results favorable to hypnosis. However, these studies suffer from serious methodological flaws that render their positive findings suspect. There may be some memory enhancement produced by hypnotic age regression, as would be expected with any reinstatement of context, but age regression is a product of the imagination. As with hypnotic hypermnesia, any accurate memory

produced during age regression is likely to be blended with a great deal of false recall, and the ultimate test is whether the procedure reliably enhances memory.

Hypnotic Recovery of Memory in the Court and the Clinic

Some proponents of clinical hypnosis have criticized studies, such as those described in this entry, on the grounds that they test memories that are devoid of affect and personal meaning in the sterile confines of the experimental laboratory. They have suggested that different results might be obtained with more lifelike materials and settings. However, this claim rests on an evidentiary base that is almost entirely anecdotal and uncorroborated. Testimonials are no substitute for evidence. One carefully controlled in vivo study staged a mock organized-crime execution in front of an introductory criminal justice class (after first insuring that none of the police officers in attendance were carrying their service weapons). Although a standard forensic interview technique produced an increase in correct responses compared to controls, chiefly by reducing the incidence of response omissions, hypnosis added nothing to the experiment. In another controlled but lifelike study, in which subjects viewed police training films, a nonhypnotic "cognitive interview" increased the number of correct memory reports; however, when hypnosis was added to the experiment, performance went down somewhat. Although police investigators still sometimes turn to hypnosis in an attempt to enhance the memories of witnesses and victims, most jurisdictions in the United States hold that no special credence should be placed on hypnotically refreshed memory is of uncertain reliability, and some states prohibit testimony based on such memories.

Despite the conclusions of laboratory research and the courts, some clinical practitioners continue to use hypnosis to recover "repressed" or "dissociated" memories of incest, sexual abuse, or other forms of trauma, and hypnosis has even been used to recover memories of prenatal experiences and of alien abductions. However, there is little evidence that genuine amnesia occurs in these situations: The chief effect of emotional arousal is to increase, rather than diminish, memory. Moreover, there is no reason to think that hypnosis can overcome the effects of infantile or childhood amnesia. Most important, the "memories" recovered in recovered-memory therapy are rarely subjected to independent confirmation, so it cannot be determined to what extent they are distorted or illusory. In the clinic as in the courtroom, uncorroborated memory reports are useless as evidence about the historical past. In fact, there is almost no evidence supporting either the validity of the trauma-memory argument or the efficacy of recovered memory therapy.

Conclusion

Although hypnosis appears to be incapable of enhancing memory, hypnotic procedures can impair memory in at least two different ways. First, by means of suggestions for posthypnotic amnesia, hypnosis can impair explicit memory for the events and experiences that transpired during hypnosis—although, as with many other forms of amnesia, it appears to spare implicit memory. The mechanism for this amnesia appears to be a division of consciousness, such that the subject is unaware of events that would otherwise be memorable. Hypnosis appears incapable of expanding awareness, so as to enable subjects to remember things that would otherwise remain forgotten. However, the social context of hypnosis, including widely shared (though false) beliefs about its capacity for memory enhancement (with or without age regression), and the suggestive context in which hypnosis occurs in the first place, renders the hypnotized subject vulnerable to various kinds of distortions in memory. Because the risks of distortion vastly outweigh the chances of obtaining any useful information, forensic investigators and clinical practitioners should avoid hypnosis as a technique for enhancing recollection.

Bibliography

Hilgard, E. R. (1965). *Hypnotic susceptibility*. New York: Harcourt, Brace, and World.

Kihlstrom, J. F. (1979). Hypnosis and psychopathology: Retrospect and prospect. *Journal of Abnormal Psychology 88* (5), 459–473.

——— (1985). Posthypnotic amnesia and the dissociation of memory. *Psychology of Learning and Motivation 19*, 131–178.

——— (1997). Hypnosis, memory and amnesia. *Philosophical Transactions of the Royal Society: Biological Sciences 352*, 1,727–1,732.

——— (1998). Exhumed memory: In S.J. Lynn and K. M. McConkey, eds., *Truth in memory*. New York: The Guilford Press.

——— (1998). Hypnosis and the psychological unconscious. In H. S. Friedman, ed., *Encyclopedia of mental health*, Vol. 2. San Diego, CA: Academic Press.

Kihlstrom, J. F., and Barnhardt, T. M. (1993). The self-regulation of memory: For better and for worse, with and without hypnosis. In D. M. Wegner and J. W. Pennebaker, eds., *Handbook of mental control*. Englewood Cliffs, NJ: Prentice-Hall.

Kihlstrom, J. F., and Eich, E. (1994). Altering states of consciousness. In D. Druckman and R. A. Bjork, eds., *Learning, remembering, and believing: Enhancing performance*. Washington, DC: National Academy Press.

Kihlstrom, J. F., and Schacter, D. L. (2000). Functional amnesia. In F. Boller and J. Grafman, eds., *Handbook of neuropsychology*, 2nd edition, Vol. 2. Amsterdam: Elsevier.

Nash, M. (1987). What, if anything, is regressed about hypnotic age regression? *Psychological Bulletin 102*, 42–52.

——— (2001). The truth and the hype of hypnosis. *Scientific American* (July), 47–55.

Schacter, D. L. (1987). Implicit memory: History and current status. *Journal of Experimental Psychology: Learning, Memory, and Cognition 13*, 501–518.

R. Edward Geiselman
Revised by John F. Kihlstrom

I

IMPLANTED MEMORIES

See: FALSE MEMORIES; HYPNOSIS AND MEMORY

IMPLICIT MEMORY

Psychological investigations of human memory have traditionally been concerned with conscious recollection or explicit memory for specific facts and episodes. Since the 1980s, however, there has been growing interest among the scientific community in a nonconscious form of memory, referred to as *implicit memory* (Roediger and McDermott, 1993; Schacter, 1987; Toth, 2000). Implicit memory does not require any explicit recollection of specific episodes. Recent experimental investigations have revealed dramatic differences between implicit and explicit memory, and these differences have had a major impact on psychological theories of the processes and systems involved in human memory.

To understand the nature and significance of implicit memory, it is necessary first to consider the types of experimental paradigms that are used to assess both explicit and implicit memory. In a traditional explicit memory paradigm, there are three main phases: a study episode in which people are exposed to a set of target materials, such as a list of words or a set of pictures; a retention interval, which typically lasts for several minutes or hours, during which people perform tasks unrelated to the study phase; and a memory test in which people are asked to think back to the study phase and either produce the target materials (recall) or discriminate the targets from items that were not presented during the study phase (recognition).

The typical implicit memory experiment includes a study phase and a retention interval that are similar to those used in studies of explicit memory. The critical difference between implicit and explicit memory experiments is observed during the test phase. Instead of being asked to try to remember previously studied items, people are simply instructed to perform a perceptual or cognitive task, such as identifying a word from a brief exposure or rating how much they like a face or an object; no reference is made to the prior study episode. However, some of the test items represent previously exposed target items—that is, words, faces, or objects that have been presented during the study episode; other test items represent novel or nonstudied words, faces, or objects that have not been presented during the study phase. Implicit memory for a previously studied item is inferred when it can be shown that subjects' task performance is influenced by prior exposure to studied items.

The hallmark of implicit memory is a facilitation of performance that is attributable to information acquired during a specific episode on a test that does not require conscious recollection of the episode. This facilitation of performance is often referred to as direct or repetition priming. Examples of tests used to assess priming include stem or fragment completion tasks, in which people are asked to complete word stems or fragments (e.g., *tab*) with the first word that comes to mind (e.g., *table*), and priming is inferred from an enhanced tendency to complete the stems with previously studied words relative to non-studied words; and perceptual identification tasks, in which people try to identify a word or object from a brief (e.g., fifty milliseconds) perceptual exposure, and priming is indicated by more accurate identification of recently studied items than of new, nonstudied items.

Although it has been studied quite extensively, priming is not the only type of implicit memory. For instance, tasks in which people learn motor or cognitive skills may involve implicit memory, in the sense that skill acquisition does not require explicit recollection of a specific previous episode but does depend on information acquired during such episodes. Similarly, tasks in which people are required to make various kinds of cognitive judgments, such as judging whether a name is famous or how much they like a face, can be influenced by implicit memory, in the sense that the cognitive judgment may be altered by information acquired during a study episode, even in the absence of conscious recollection of the episode.

Dissociations Between Implicit and Explicit Memory

One of the most fascinating aspects of implicit memory is that it can be separated or dissociated from explicit memory—that is, there are various experimental manipulations that affect implicit and explicit memory differently, and there are populations of people for whom explicit memory is impaired while implicit memory is spared.

Population Dissociations

Perhaps the most dramatic dissociation between implicit and explicit memory has been provided by studies of brain-damaged patients with organic amnesia. Amnesic patients are characterized by a severe impairment of explicit memory for recent events, although intelligence, perception, and language are relatively normal. Lesions to either medial temporal or diencephalic brain regions typically produce this memory deficit. In contrast, a number of studies have demonstrated that amnesic patients show intact implicit memory. For example, researchers have found repeatedly that amnesic patients show just as much priming as do normal subjects on stem completion and similar tasks, despite their inability to remember explicitly the target items or the study episode in which the items were encountered (Shimamura, 1993). In addition, it has been demonstrated that amnesic patients often show normal or near-normal learning of motor and perceptual skills, and that their

cognitive judgments can be biased by information acquired during specific episodes that the amnesic patient cannot remember explicitly (Mayes, 2000).

Researchers have reported several other population dissociations. For instance, healthy older adults generally show worse explicit memory than younger adults. However, older adults often produce the same amount of priming on implicit tests (Zacks, Hasher, and Li, 2000). Similarly, patients with depression or schizophrenia have deficits in explicit remembering (compared to healthy control subjects) but produce intact priming.

Pharmacological Dissociations

The administration of certain drugs (e.g., benzodiazepines, a class of drugs used in anesthesia and to treat anxiety) produce similar dissociations between implicit and explicit memory. Scientists have long known that these drugs produce a temporary form of amnesia that wears off as the drug is metabolized. However, recent research indicates that these effects are restricted to explicit memory. In a typical study, one group of subjects is administered a dose of a benzodiazepine and another group is given a placebo, after which both groups are presented with study materials. Some time later, memory is tested. Compared to the placebo group, the group given the drug exhibits poor explicit memory for the studied materials. In contrast, the two group produce equivalent performance on implicit tests, such as stem and fragment completion. Thus, drug-induced amnesia produces the same type of dissociation as that produced by organic amnesia: It affects conscious recollection but appears to have little or no effect on nonconscious influences of memory (Curran, 2000).

Functional Dissociations

Experimental manipulations also produce dissociations between implicit and explicit memory, providing insight into functional differences between these forms of memory. For example, researchers have observed one important dissociation in experiments that have compared the effects of semantic and nonsemantic study tasks on implicit and explicit memory. Research has well established that performance on explicit recall and recognition tests is higher following semantic, rather than nonsemantic, study of an item; researchers have called this the levels of processing effect. For example, when subjects perform a semantic encoding task during the study phase of an experiment (e.g., rate the pleasantness of a word or provide a definition of the word), subsequent probability of explicitly remembering the word is much higher than if subjects perform a nonsemantic encoding task during the study phase (e.g., count the number of vowels and consonants in the word). In contrast, however, research has shown that the magnitude of priming on a stem completion task or perceptual identification task is less affected, or even unaffected, by the same manipulation: Priming effects do not differ significantly following semantic and nonsemantic encoding (Roediger and McDermott, 1993).

Conversely, the similarity between the physical (or perceptual) features of the stimuli as presented at the time of study and test has a strong effect on many implicit memory tests but little or no effect on many explicit tests. An example is the effect of study modality. If some of words on a study list are presented visually and some are presented aurally, later explicit memory for the words is typically unaffected. However, when memory is tested with the implicit tests of stem and fragment completion, study modality has a large impact; visually presented words leading to more priming than the aurally presented words. Presenting study items as pictures versus words produces similar matching effects on implicit memory, in which words produce more priming on word-based implicit tests (e.g., stem and fragment completion) and pictures produce more priming on implicit tests which use pictorial cues (such as picture fragment completion).

The foregoing is only a partial list of dissociations between implicit and explicit memory. In addition, similarities between implicit and explicit memory have also been observed; this is to be expected, because both are forms of memory and hence presumably share some common characteristics. However, the differences between the two are most revealing theoretically and have led to a variety of proposals concerning the nature of implicit memory.

Theoretical Accounts of Implicit Memory

Some explanations of implicit memory focus heavily on the sorts of dissociations described above and emphasize differences between implicit and explicit memory. Other explanations seek to elucidate common principles that may underlie both implicit and explicit memory phenomena.

Activation View

An early theoretical view held that implicit memory is attributable to the temporary activation of pre-existing units or nodes in memory: Exposure to a word or object automatically activates a memory representation of it, and this activation subsides rapidly. Although able to accommodate some experimental results, this general idea has difficulty accounting for other important results. First, priming can be surprisingly long-lived under certain conditions lasting weeks and months. Second, priming has been observed following exposure to unfamiliar materials, such as nonsense words or novel patterns and objects, that do not have any preexisting representation in memory as a unit. Third, priming often shows perceptual specificity (e.g., effects of study modality), which seems incompatible with the idea that priming is attributable to abstract, amodal representations of words and concepts.

Multiple Memory Systems

Neuropsychological and neuroscientific analyses have proposed multiple memory systems for implicit and explicit memory. Because amnesia is typically associated with damage to the hippocampus and medial temporal lobes, scientists believe that these parts of the brain are necessary for explicit memory. Initially, theories differentiated between two memory systems (e.g., declarative versus procedural, episodic versus semantic) to account for explicit and implicit memory, respectively. However, as evidence for dissociable forms of implicit memory mounted, the number of proposed systems has increased. A 2000 version of this theory proposes four: episodic memory, semantic memory, the perceptual representation system (PRS), and procedural memory (Schacter, Wagner, and Butter, 2000). Episodic memory stores information about episodes from one's personal past, enabling the experience of recollection. Semantic memory stores general knowledge about the world, including facts, conceptual information, and vocabulary. The PRS is a perceptual memory systems that processes information about the form and structure of words and objects independently of their semantic content. Finally, procedural memory represents knowledge of cognitive and motor skills. Explicit memory is assumed to be a product of the episodic memory system, whereas various forms of implicit memory are produced by the other systems.

Population and pharmacological dissociations argue for the existence of multiple memory systems in the brain. For example, amnesia produces deficits on explicit memory but typically not on verbal implicit memory tests (such as stem and fragment completion) or on tests of skill learning, indicating that amnesia damages the episodic memory system but not the other systems. Even stronger support for the multiple-memory-systems view comes from reports of double dissociations, dissociations in which two different patient groups (with damage to different parts of the brain) exhibit complementary dissociative patterns on implicit and explicit memory tests. For example, amnesic patients (with damage to medial-temporal regions of the brain) have disrupted memory on explicit tests but not on implicit tests, as noted. The opposite dissociation occurs in patients with occipital-lobe lesions, who exhibit preserved explicit memory coupled with deficits in implicit memory for visual-perceptual information (Gabrieli et al., 1995). This provides strong support for the view that brain systems mediating performance on these two types of tests differ. Similar dissociative patterns support distinctions among the other imputed memory systems (Schacter et al., 2000).

Transfer-Appropriate Processing

Although population and pharmacological dissociations provide strong support for distinct memory systems, functional dissociations have often been interpreted in terms of the divergent processing requirements of different memory tests within a single memory system. The general idea is that dissociations between implicit and explicit memory are special cases of the general principles of transfer-appropriate processing and encoding specificity, which hold that memory performance is best when encoding and retrieval processes match. Specifically, it is held that most standard explicit memory tests require a good deal of conceptual processing: semantically based, subject-initiated attempts to recollect the study episode. By contrast, performance on such implicit memory tests as word completion and perceptual identification is held to be largely dependent on perceptual, or data-driven, processing—processing that is determined largely by the physical characteristics of test cues. It thus follows that explicit memory—but not priming—should benefit from semantic study processing (which researchers believe support conceptually driven processing) more than from nonsemantic study processing, whereas priming should be strongly dependent on matching of surface features between study and test (Jacoby, 1983; Roediger and McDermott, 1993). However, it is possible to devise implicit tests that entail conceptual processing, and the transfer-appropriate processing view has led to predictions and corresponding demonstrations of dissociations *between* implicit tests, by contrasting implicit tasks that draw primarily on perceptual processing with implicit tasks that draw primarily on conceptual processing.

The transfer-appropriate processing view is parsimonious and has enjoyed great success in accounting for functional dissociations between explicit and implicit tests, and among implicit tests of different types (i.e., perceptual and conceptual). Thus, the distinction between perceptual and conceptual processing is likely an important aspect of any explanation of implicit memory phenomena. However, it does not provide a complete account because it does not naturally account for population and pharmacological dissociations. In particular, it has been generally found that both organic and drug-induced amnesia disrupt performance on explicit tests (whether conceptual or perceptual) but produce normal levels of priming on conceptual as well as perceptual implicit tests. Likewise, older and younger adults generally produce equivalent levels of conceptual and perceptual priming, even though older adults perform worse on tests of explicit memory. These dissociations are difficult to explain in terms of perceptual versus conceptual processing.

Component-Processes Approach and Evidence from Neuroimaging

The complementary successes of multiple memory systems view and the transfer-appropriate processing approach has produced the view that emphasizes multiple forms of priming and attempts to articulate the component processes that mediate performance on various memory tasks (Foster and Jelicic, 1999). Neuroimaging techniques, such as positron emission tomography (PET) and functional magnetic resonance imaging (fMRI), play a critical role in supplementing traditional approaches. These techniques attempt to determine neural regions involved in explicit and implicit memory tests. One result is the substantial degree of overlap in the active brain regions during explicit and implicit retrieval tasks. Despite this overlap, there are important differences in the patterns of brain activation. In particular, explicit retrieval relies heavily on anterior frontal (especially right prefrontal) lobe as well as the medial-temporal regions, including the hippocampus. Scientists believe the activity in frontal lobe reflects an explicit retrieval mode in which the individual intentionally tries to retrieve information about past events and is generally oriented toward the past. They believe the medial temporal activity contributes to the recollective experience itself when a memory is successfully retrieved (Nyberg and Cabeza, 2000). Another finding is that priming on implicit tests is often associated with decreased activity in certain regions of the brain, which may reflect a reduction in processing demands when a stimulus is processed a second time (Schacter and Badgaiyan, 2001). The brain areas involved depend on whether the implicit test is perceptual or conceptual. Perceptual tests, such as stem or fragment completion, produce decreased processing in visual cortex (in the posterior occipital lobe). In contrast, conceptual implicit tests produce decreased activity in the inferior frontal lobe and the mid-temporal lobe. In general, these results indicate that the same neural substrates required for the initial (perceptual or conceptual) processing are reengaged at the time of test and exhibit the effects of the initial processing by their subsequent reduced activity.

See also: AMNESIA, ORGANIC; CODING PROCESSES:
    LEVELS OF PROCESSING; DECLARATIVE
    MEMORY; EPISODIC MEMORY; FRONTAL LOBES

AND EPISODIC MEMORY; GUIDE TO THE
ANATOMY OF THE BRAIN; MOTOR SKILL
LEARNING; PREFRONTAL CORTEX AND MEMORY
IN PRIMATES; SEMANTIC MEMORY: COGNITIVE
ASPECTS; SEMANTIC MEMORY:
NEUROBIOLOGICAL PERSPECTIVE

Bibliography

Curran, H. V. (2000). Psychopharmacological approaches to human memory. In M. S. Gazzaniga, ed., *The new cognitive neurosciences*, 2nd edition. Cambridge, MA: MIT Press.

Foster, J. K., and Jelicic, M., eds. (1999). *Memory: Systems, process, or function?* New York: Oxford University Press.

Gabrieli, J. D. E. et al. (1995). Double dissociation between memory systems underlying explicit and implicit memory in the human brain. *Psychological Science 6*, 76–82.

Jacoby, L. L. (1983). Remembering the data: Analyzing interactive processes in reading. *Journal of Verbal Learning and Verbal Behavior 22*, 485–508.

Mayes, A. R. (2000). Selective memory disorders. In E. Tulving and F. I. M. Craik, eds., *The Oxford handbook of memory*. New York: Oxford University Press.

Nyberg, L., and Cabeza, R. (2000). Brain imaging of memory. In E. Tulving and F. I. M. Craik, eds., *The Oxford handbook of memory*. New York: Oxford University Press.

Roediger, H. L., and McDermott, K. B. (1993). Implicit memory in normal human subjects. In F. Boller and J. Grafman, eds., *Handbook of neuropsychology*. Amsterdam: Elsevier.

Schacter, D. L. (1987). Implicit memory: History and current status. *Journal of Experimental Psychology: Learning, Memory, and Cognition 13*, 501–518.

Schacter, D. L., and Badgaiyan, R. D. (2001). Neuroimaging of priming: New perspectives on implicit and explicit memory. *Current Directions in Psychological Science 10*, 1–4.

Schacter, D. L., Wagner, A. D., and Buckner, R. L. (2000). Memory systems of 1999. In E. Tulving and F. I. M. Craik, eds., *The Oxford handbook of memory*. New York: Oxford University Press.

Shimamura, A. P. (1993). Neuropsychological analyses of implicit memory: History, methodology, and theoretical interpretations. In P. Graf and M. E. J. Masson, eds., *Implicit memory: New directions in cognition, development, and neuropsychology*. Hillsdale, NJ: Erlbaum.

Toth, J. P. (2000). Nonconscious forms of human memory. In E. Tulving and F. I. M. Craik, eds., *The Oxford handbook of memory*. New York: Oxford University Press.

Zacks, R. T., Hasher, L., and Li, K. Z. H. (2000). Human memory. In F. I. M. Craik and T. A. Salthouse, eds., *The handbook of aging and cognition*, 2nd edition. Mahwah, NJ: Erlbaum.

Daniel L. Schacter
Revised by Neil W. Mulligan

IMPRINTING

Imprinting is the learning process through which the social preferences of animals of certain species become restricted to a particular object or class of objects. A distinction is made between filial and sexual imprinting. *Filial imprinting* is involved in the formation, in young animals, of an attachment to, and a preference for, the parent, parent surrogate, or siblings. *Sexual imprinting* is involved in the formation of mating preferences that are expressed in later life.

The phenomenon of filial imprinting was described as early as 1518 by Sir Thomas More in his *Utopia*. However, imprinting was investigated experimentally much later, by D. A. Spalding in 1873 and by Oscar Heinroth in 1911. Konrad Lorenz, who gave the phenomenon its name, subsequently provided a detailed description of imprinting in a number of bird species in an influential work published in 1935.

Filial Imprinting

Although filial imprinting may occur in mammals (Sluckin, 1972), it has been studied mostly in precocial birds such as ducklings and chicks. These birds can move about shortly after hatching, and they approach and follow an object to which they are exposed. In a natural situation the first object the young bird encounters usually is its mother. In the absence of the mother, inanimate mother surrogates are effective in eliciting filial behavior (Bateson, 1966; Horn, 1985; Sluckin, 1972). When the chick or duckling is close to an appropriate object, it will attempt to snuggle up to it, frequently emitting soft twitters. Initially the young bird approaches a wide range of objects, though some are more attractive to it than others. After the bird has been exposed to one object long enough, it remains close to this object and may run away from novel ones. If the familiar object is removed, the bird becomes restless and emits shrill calls. When given a choice between the familiar stimulus and a novel one, the bird shows a preference for the familiar stimulus. Thus, filial imprinting refers to the acquisition of a social preference and not just an increase in following (Sluckin, 1972).

Conditions for Imprinting

To study visual imprinting in the laboratory, chicks or ducklings may be hatched in darkness and exposed for a period of one to two hours to a conspicuous object when they are about twenty-four hours old. The animals are then returned to a dark incubator and kept there until their preferences are tested by exposing them to the familiar object and a novel object. A widely used measure of filial preference is approach to the familiar object relative to approach to a novel object. Another measure takes advantage of the fact that an imprinted chick emits distress calls in the presence of a novel object and does not do so, or does so less frequently, in the presence of the familiar.

The effectiveness of imprinting stimuli varies. For example, young ducklings approach and follow objects larger than a matchbox, but peck at smaller objects. For chicks, red and blue objects are more effective imprinting stimuli than yellow and green objects.

Movement, brightness, contrast, and sound all enhance the attractiveness of an imprinting stimulus.

Imprinting and Learning

Filial imprinting has been regarded as different from other forms of learning because it proceeds without any obvious reinforcement such as food or warmth (Bolhuis, De Vos, and Kruijt, 1990). However, an imprinting object may itself be a reinforcer, that is, a stimulus that an animal finds rewarding. Just as a rat learns to press a pedal to receive a reward of food, so a visually naive chick learns to press a pedal to see an imprinting object. When chicks are exposed to two imprinting stimuli simultaneously, they learn more about the individual stimuli than when they are exposed to the stimuli sequentially, or to only one stimulus. This so-called within-event learning has also been found in conditioning paradigms in rats and humans (Bolhuis and Honey, 1998). The ability to learn and remember the characteristics of objects to which an animal is exposed may be a common form of learning.

Reversibility and Sensitive Periods

Imprinting was thought to be irreversible and to occur during a *sensitive period* (or *critical period*). Numerous studies have demonstrated that filial preferences can in fact be reversed when the original object is removed and the animal is exposed to a novel object. Evidence suggests that there is a difference between the memory of the first stimulus and that of subsequent stimuli to which the animal is exposed. Under certain circumstances the preference for the first object may return (Bolhuis, 1991). The ability to form filial attachments has been shown to depend on both developmental age and time since hatching. The ability to imprint is related to the development of the animal's sensorimotor abilities. The sensitive period is brought to an end by the learning experience (imprinting) itself: Once the bird has formed a preference for a particular object, it avoids novel objects. Consequently it tends not to be exposed to them for long and so may learn little about them. When the bird is left in its cage, it may form an attachment to features of its rearing environment. Rearing the bird in a visually impoverished environment (in darkness or deprived of patterned light) extends the period during which it forms an attachment to a conspicuous object (Bateson, 1966). The sensitive period pertains to filial attachment and may relate to the link formed between the (neural) representation of the imprinted object and approach behavior. Although the formation of this link may have a sensitive period, there is no reason to suppose that the learning and recognition processes have one.

Auditory Imprinting

In the natural context auditory stimuli play an important role in the formation of filial preferences (Gottlieb, 1971). Auditory preferences may be formed in the same way as visual preferences (i.e., learning as a result of exposure). However, preferences resulting from exposure to an auditory stimulus only, whether before or after the birds have hatched, are relatively weak and short-lived. Such preferences can be strengthened when the young bird is simultaneously exposed to an auditory stimulus and a visual stimulus during auditory training, just as exposure to auditory stimuli can improve visual imprinting.

Sexual Imprinting

It might seem that one of the consequences of filial imprinting would be the determination of adult sexual preferences, but research suggests that filial imprinting and sexual imprinting are two separate (although perhaps partially overlapping) processes. Not only is the time of expression of the preferences different, but so is the period during which experience affects preferences. Sexual preferences continue to be affected by experience up to the time of mating. Furthermore, filial preferences may be formed after a relatively short period of exposure to an object. In contrast, sexual preferences develop as the result of a long period of exposure to and social interaction with the parents as well as the siblings. Normally, sexual imprinting ensures that the bird will mate with a member of its own strain or species. When the young bird is cross-fostered—that is, reared with adults of a different species—it develops a sexual preference for the foster species. In Japanese quail (*Coturnix coturnix japonica*) and domestic chickens (*Gallus gallus domesticus*), mating preferences are for individual members of the opposite sex that are different, but not too different, from individuals with which the young bird was reared (Bateson, 1978).

Predispositions

Research shows that filial preferences are formed not only as a result of learning through exposure but that they are also influenced by a specific predisposition (Bolhuis, 1991; Horn, 1985; Johnson and Bolhuis, 2000). This predisposition may be measured in the laboratory by giving chicks a choice between a rotating stuffed jungle fowl and (for instance) a rotating red box. Under some conditions the two stimuli are equally attractive. But if the young chick is given a certain amount of nonspecific experience, such as being handled and allowed to run, the chick prefers the fowl to the box when tested twenty-four hours later. In order to be effective, this nonspecific experience must occur within a sensitive period (about twenty to forty hours after hatching). It appears that the "target" stimuli of the predisposition are in the head and neck region but are not species-specific. Once the predisposition has developed, it does not function as a filter that prevents the chick from learning about objects that do not resemble conspecifics; such chicks can learn about other objects by being exposed to them. Thus, it is likely that the mechanisms underlying the predisposition and those underlying learning influence behavior independently.

Neural Mechanisms of Filial Imprinting

The neural basis of the recognition memory underlying filial imprinting has been studied most extensively in the domestic chick (Horn, 1985, 1998, 2000). When dark-reared chicks are trained by exposing them to an imprinting object for approximately one to two hours, metabolic changes occur in the dorsal part of the cerebral hemispheres. Specifically, there is an increase in the incorporation of radioactively tagged uracil into RNA in this brain region of trained chicks compared with control chicks (dark-reared chicks or chicks that have merely been exposed to overhead light). Several reasons support the idea that the biochemical changes are related to learning rather than to various side effects of training (e.g., to differences in movement, excitement, sensory stimulation between the trained chicks and their controls): when visual input is restricted to one hemisphere, incorporation of radioactive uracil into RNA is higher in the trained than in the untrained hemisphere; the amount incorporated is related to how much the chicks learn and not to various other measures of behavior; the increase is not related to short-term effects of sensory stimulation.

Neural Changes Localized to Specific Brain Regions

Imprinting leads to changes in the incorporation of radioactive uracil into RNA in a restricted brain region, the intermediate and medial part of the hyperstriatum ventrale (IMHV), a sheet of cells in the cerebral hemispheres (see Figure 1). Further evidence that the region is crucially involved in learning is the following: destruction of IMHV before training prevents imprinting; if the region is destroyed immediately after training, chicks do not prefer the training object, though for chicks with lesions of IMHV an imprinting object still elicits approach behavior but the chicks appear incapable of learning its characteristics; it is possible to bias chicks' preferences by delivering trains of short pulses of electric current to IMHV through electrodes that have been implanted into the

Figure 1

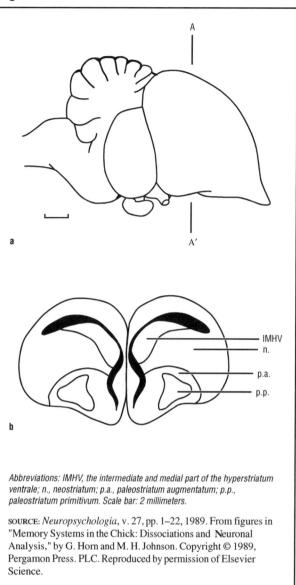

Abbreviations: IMHV, the intermediate and medial part of the hyperstriatum ventrale; n., neostriatum; p.a., paleostriatum augmentatum; p.p., paleostriatum primitivum. Scale bar: 2 millimeters.

SOURCE: *Neuropsychologia*, v. 27, pp. 1–22, 1989. From figures in "Memory Systems in the Chick: Dissociations and Neuronal Analysis," by G. Horn and M. H. Johnson. Copyright © 1989, Pergamon Press. PLC. Reproduced by permission of Elsevier Science.

Outline drawing of the chick brain. The vertical lines AA' above and below the drawing of the lateral aspect a indicate the plane of the transverse section outline b of the brain. IMHV extends approximately 2.5 millimeters from front to back of the cerebral hemisphere.

region. At the end of the period of electrical stimulation, the chicks were shown two lights, one flashing at the rate of 4.5 per second and the other at 1.5 per second. If the IMHV region had been stimulated at 4.5 trains per second, the chicks preferred the light flashing at this frequency. In contrast, chicks that had received electrical stimulation of IMHV at the rate of 1.5 trains per second preferred the light flashing at this rate. Electrical stimulation of two visual receiving areas of the forebrain did not influence the chicks' preferences. Taken together, these results strongly suggest that the IMHV region is involved in the recognition memory of imprinting, probably storing information.

Neuronal Mechanisms of Memory

Imprinting leads to changes in the structure of synapses in IMHV, in particular to an increase in the area of thickened membrane on the postsynaptic side of certain synapses. This area of membrane is known as the postsynaptic density. The changes are restricted to synapses on the spines of dendrites (axospinous synapses) and are found in the left but not in the right IMHV. Certain spine synapses in the mammalian brain are excitatory and possess, in the postsynaptic density, receptors for the excitatory neurotransmitter l-glutamate. The increased area of the postsynaptic density of axospinous synapses seems to imply that imprinting leads to an increase in the number of receptors for l-glutamate: After chicks have been trained, there is an increase in the number of a certain type of receptors for l-glutamate in the left IMHV, but not in the right. The increased number of receptors is related to the amount the chicks have learned about the imprinting object. One consequence of this change may be that, after training, the release of a given amount of l-glutamate from a presynaptic ending may exert a greater excitatory action on the postsynaptic cell than before training. That is, as many hypotheses have suggested, learning leads to an increased efficacy of synaptic transmission.

The particular l-glutamate receptors shown to be affected by imprinting are those of the N-methyl-D-aspartate (NMDA) variety. In mammals, these receptors are involved in other forms of synaptic plasticity. Thus the cellular mechanisms of synaptic plasticity may be similar in diverse systems though the functions of the synaptic change may be different: In circuits involved in learning, the synaptic changes may play a part in information storage. In other systems, these changes may be a response to either physical damage or physiological dysfunction. Exposure to an imprinting stimulus for approximately two hours leads to a trebling in the proportion of neurons in IMHV responding to the imprinting stimulus compared with the proportion responding before training. Some neurons in IMHV respond in a highly selective way to the imprinted stimulus and so critically have the properties of neurons postulated by Donald Hebb (1949) as forming part of a memory trace. The increase in responsiveness does not develop linearly but, remarkably, develops in contrasting phases during and in the hours that follow training. These findings challenge models of memory based on synaptic strengthening to asymptote (Horn, Nicol, and Brown, 2001).

Cerebral Asymmetry and Imprinting

Studies in which the left or right IMHV region has been surgically damaged suggest that, in accordance with the data on synaptic changes, the left IMHV functions as a long-term store. During the first day after imprinting, however, another memory system, referred to as S', is established outside IMHV. S' is formed under the influence of the right IMHV: If this region is absent, S' is not formed. The right IMHV perhaps transfers information to S', a possibility that implies a dynamic element to memory formation. Electrophysiological evidence (Horn, Nicol, and Brown, 2001) demonstrates that imprinting leads to changes in neuronal responsiveness in the right IMHV that are similar to those in the left. These results are puzzling because various morphological and biochemical measures indicate differences in the effect of learning on the two brain regions. To reconcile these findings it has been suggested that both regions are similarly affected by learning, but that other functions of the right IMHV (e.g., in the formation of S') bring about additional structural and biochemical changes that obscure these effects (Horn, 1998). The right and left IMHV regions are not directly interconnected, so it is likely that they and S' are independent stores working in parallel. Thus, even in the case of the recognition memory of imprinting, more than one memory system is formed. Further evidence that several memory systems exist in the young chick is that chicks with lesions of IMHV (placed before S' has been formed), while being severely impaired in their ability to imprint, are nevertheless able to learn certain other tasks. Multiple memory systems therefore not only are found in mammalian brains but also may be a fundamental part of the design of the vertebrate brain.

On the basis of its connections and developmental history IMHV has been compared to the prefrontal and cingulate areas of the primate cerebral cortex (Horn, 1985). Evidence from humans suggests that these regions play an important role in the organization of memory (Janowsky, Shimamura, and Squire, 1989; Tulving et al., 1994).

See also: BIRDSONG LEARNING; GLUTAMATE
RECEPTORS AND THEIR CHARACTERIZATION;
REINFORCEMENT

Bibliography

Bateson, P. P. G. (1966). The characteristics and context of imprinting. *Biological Reviews 41,* 177–220.
—— (1978). Sexual imprinting and optimal outbreeding. *Nature 273,* 659–660.
Bolhuis, J. J. (1991). Mechanisms of avian imprinting: A review. *Biological Reviews 66,* 303–345.
Bolhuis, J. J., De Vos, G. J., and Kruijt, J. P. (1990). Filial imprinting and associative learning. *Quarterly Journal of Experimental Psychology 42B,* 313–329.

Bolhuis, J. J., and Honey, R. C. (1998). Imprinting, learning, and development: From behaviour to brain and back. *Trends in Neurosciences 21,* 306–311.

Gottlieb, G. (1971). *Development of species identification in birds.* Chicago: University of Chicago Press.

Heinroth, O. (1911). Beiträge zur Biologie, namentlich Ethologie und Psychologie der Anatiden. In *Verhandlungen des 5,* 589–702. Berlin: Internationaler Ornithologischer Kongress.

Hebb, D. O. (1949). *The organization of behavior.* New York: Wiley.

Horn, G. (1985). *Memory, imprinting, and the brain.* Oxford: Clarendon Press.

—— (1998). Visual imprinting and the neural mechanisms of recognition memory. *Trends in Neurosciences 21,* 300–305.

—— (2000). In memory. In J. J. Bolhuis, ed., *Brain, perception, Memory: Advances in cognitive neuroscience.* Oxford: Oxford University Press.

Horn, G., Nicol, A. U., and Brown, M. W. (2001). Tracking memory's trace. *Proceedings of the National Academy of Sciences of the United States of America 98,* 5,282–5,287.

Janowsky, J. S., Shimamura, A. P., and Squire, L. R. (1989). Source and impairment in patients with frontal lobe lesions. *Neuropsychologia 27,* 1,043–1,056.

Johnson, M. H., and Bolhuis, J. J. (2000). Predispositions in perceptual and cognitive development. In J. J. Bolhuis, ed., *Brain, perception, memory. Advances in cognitive neuroscience.* Oxford: Oxford University Press.

Lorenz, K. (1935). Der Kumpan in der Umwelt des Vogels. *Journal für Ornithologie 83,* 137–213, 289–413.

Sluckin, W. (1972). *Imprinting and early learning.* London: Methuen.

Spalding, D. A. (1873). Instinct, with original observations on young animals. *Macmillan's Magazine 27,* 282–293.

Tulving, E., Kapur, S., Markowitsch, H. J., Craik, F. I. M., Habib, R. and Houle, S. (1994). Neuroanatomical correlates of retrieval in episodic memory: Auditory sentence recognition. *Proceedings of the National Academy of Sciences of the United States of America 91,* 2,012–2,015.

Johan J. Bolhuis
G. Horn

INDIVIDUAL DIFFERENCES IN LEARNING AND MEMORY

Individual differences in learning and memory abilities have fascinated people since they began thinking about how their minds work. In discussing his wax metaphor of memory, Plato (1953) noted that memories made of "pure and clear [wax] . . . easily learn and easily retain," whereas those made of "muddy and of impure wax [have] . . . a corresponding defect in the mind." Plato realized that people differ in what they learn and remember and in how well they do both. This is certainly true at the extremes, but how relevant is it over the normal range of memory abilities?

The psychological research supports four main conclusions about individual differences in learning and memory (Bors and MacLeod, 1996). First, people differ in what they know, their knowledge base. Second, people differ in their working memory capacity, the ability to hold information in consciously accessible memory. Third, people possess and invoke differ-

ent strategies for learning. Fourth, people differ in the retrieval efficiency with which they can summon information from more permanent, long-term memory. To these can be added one "negative conclusion": There do not appear to be consistent sex differences in learning and memory ability, although women and men may choose to learn different information (which affects their knowledge base). This entry examines these four main conclusions in more detail.

Knowledge Differences

Standard intelligence tests (Wechsler, 1945, 1958) measure two aspects of memory, the first being general knowledge and vocabulary. People differ in their breadth and depth of knowledge. Consider the "paradox of the expert": A simple theory might claim that forgetting is caused by interference among related concepts in memory. This would imply that someone who knows more about a topic should be more subject to forgetting in that domain. But if this were true, how would one ever become an expert in a domain? One resolution is that people integrate their knowledge so that related ideas are joined, supporting rather than competing with each other (Smith, Adams, and Schorr, 1978).

Indeed, those with high knowledge learn and retain new facts in that domain more easily than do those with low knowledge (Voss, Vesonder, and Spilich, 1980). Furthermore, experts seem especially superior in remembering the important information. Popular memory metaphors of libraries or warehouses do not fit comfortably here. Instead, think of memory as a scaffolding: The more memories that are attached to the structure, the more places there are to attach new memories. The scaffolding may even guide people to where it would be best to attach each new memory.

People differ not only in what they know and how much they know, but also in how that knowledge is organized (Coltheart and Evans, 1981). Because retrieval relies heavily on the association between facts and ideas, organization influences how people retrieve their knowledge. An individual who has two facts directly connected in memory should be able to get from one to the other more quickly than someone who must go through multiple "way stations." Part of coming to understand a domain better is reorganizing one's knowledge more appropriately.

Each person is unique in part because of what he or she knows, both in terms of autobiographical knowledge and general world knowledge. Thus, content of memories is one major source of individual differences. The other three differences all relate more to how people acquire, store, transform, and use that knowledge—that is, the cognitive processes.

Capacity Differences

Probably the best known individual differences dimension in learning and memory is that of the capacity of conscious, working memory. This is the other aspect of memory that is directly measured in standard intelligence tests: memory span (Dempster, 1981). Individuals have a sharp limitation on how much they can consciously think about and retain at one time. Even in the normal range of intelligence, not everyone's span is the same. What causes these differences? There seem to be two main mechanisms underlying working memory span—the ability to identify the specific elements to be held and the ability to retain their order (Humphreys et al., 1983). Speed of scanning through the information held in working memory does not seem to differ reliably across individuals (Hunt, 1978), although speed is affected by age (Salthouse, 1996).

It is tempting to view span differences as irrelevant to the "real world." After all, how often do people listen to a string of items and then repeat them back? In fact, holding information in working memory is something people do constantly and rely upon heavily. Meredyth Daneman and Patricia Carpenter (1980; Hannon and Daneman, 2001; Miyake, 2001) showed that span differences have powerful implications for how successfully people read. Those with larger spans in reading (or in listening) show better comprehension of what they read: They can hold previous sentences in mind more easily, and thus assemble the overall meaning more effectively. This has led Marcel Just and Carpenter (1992) to a theory of comprehension based on working memory capacity.

Individual differences in working memory capacity do not influence only language. These effects are also apparent in spatial processing (Shah and Miyake, 1996) and in enumeration (Tuholski, Engle, and Baylis, 2001). Human ability to acquire and execute skills (Ackerman, 1987) is also a function of working memory capacity (Perlow, Jattuso, and Moore, 1997). Individual differences in working memory and attention, in fact, appear to be intimately linked (Kane, Bleckley, Conway, and Engle, 2001).

Learning Strategy Differences

There are many different ways to learn, from rote repetition to complex mnemonics. All learning involves recoding: Information must be transformed from its perceived form into a form suitable for remembering. It is well established that people differ in their speed and in their efficiency of recoding (Gagné, 1967). But people also differ in their learning styles, in which processes they use, and in when they use them (Sternberg and Zhang, 2001).

Studies of learning style suggest that, at a global level, learners emphasize either overall comprehension or specific detail, appearing to be either conclusion oriented or description oriented (Schmeck, 1983). Those who emphasize overall comprehension engage in deeper processing; those concerned with specific detail focus more on surface processing. Ordinarily such a strategic difference favors those who undertake deeper processing. Thus, note taking in a classroom induces deeper processing and better retention of important information.

Another illustration is individual differences in reported imagery ability (Richardson, 1999). People vary in whether they use more language-based or picture-based strategies to learn and remember. Indeed, research suggests that visual memory can be quite independent of verbal memory. People who recognize faces or pictures well will not necessarily remember what they read better than will people with poorer visual memory. Yet the widely held belief that some people learn best visually and others learn best auditorily has not been strongly supported experimentally. One can make sense of this by realizing that verbal skills need not be auditory.

There are many other techniques and strategies for learning. Thus it seems quite reasonable to suppose that different individuals learn most effectively using different strategies. However, evidence to support this intuition has been notoriously difficult to obtain. Usually a strategy that improves one person's learning also improves another person's learning. What may differ, then, are the choices that people make, a metacognitive issue as Christian Schunn and Lynne Reder (2001) argue, relating successful choice to working memory capacity. How people select optimal process(es) from their repertoire for a particular learning situation may be one of the most critical differences of all.

Retrieval Speed Differences

Retrieval time for information in working memory is not a reliable source of individual differences. Given the sharp capacity limitation, the small content of working memory is easily searched. But the same is not true of long-term memory, where all of a person's knowledge is stored. If the average person knows upward of 10 billion facts, as some scientists speculate, how can he or she find any one of them quickly? Even searching at the impossibly fast rate of 1 millisecond per fact, it would take months to find any single fact.

Extensive research (Hunt, 1978) has shown that different people retrieve information from long-term memory at different rates. Consider a very simple retrieval: It takes longer to determine whether two letters have the same name for *Aa* than for *aa* or *AA*. Presumably this is because long-term memory access is required only for *Aa*, where the two are not physically identical. On average, this retrieval time is about 80 milliseconds, but high-ability individuals are faster than low-ability individuals by about 30 milliseconds or more. A naive critic might say, "But this is a tiny difference." Consider reading, however. If one were to lose 30 milliseconds for every letter read in this entry, this time would quickly add up. And that is just for such highly learned facts as the letters of the alphabet; the problem must be vastly greater for more complex and unfamiliar types of knowledge. If the elementary processes are not executed as efficiently by one individual as by another, the cost for learning and memory as a whole can be large. Indeed, it is quite clear that working memory capacity also affects retrieval from long-term memory (Rosen and Engle, 1997).

Conclusion

The goal of this brief sketch has been to localize four of the more crucial individual differences in learning and memory and to provide some of the evidence for these differences. Of course, there are many other differences in how people learn and remember, but these are usually more isolated and less characteristic of the memory system as a whole. Scientists hope to find ways of recognizing these differences in educational systems around the world in order to realize the full potential of learning skills.

See also: AMNESIA, FUNCTIONAL; AMNESIA, ORGANIC; CODING PROCESSES: IMAGERY; CODING PROCESSES: LEVELS OF PROCESSING; CODING PROCESSES: ORGANIZATION OF MEMORY; EPISODIC MEMORY; EXPERTS' MEMORIES; INTERFERENCE AND FORGETTING; MEMORY SPAN; METACOGNITION ABOUT MEMORY; MNEMONISTS; SEMANTIC MEMORY: COGNITIVE ASPECTS; SEMANTIC MEMORY: NEUROBIOLOGICAL PERSPECTIVE

Bibliography

Ackerman, P. L. (1987). Individual differences in skill learning: An integration of psychometric and information processing perspectives. *Psychological Bulletin 102*, 3–27.

Bors, D. A., and MacLeod, C. M. (1996). Individual differences in memory. In E. L. Bjork and R. A. Bjork, eds., *Handbook of perception and cognition*, Vol. 10: *Memory*. San Diego, CA: Academic Press.

Coltheart, V., and Evans, J. S. B. T. (1981). An investigation of semantic memory in individuals. *Memory & Cognition 9*, 524–532.

Daneman, M., and Carpenter, P. A. (1980). Individual differences in working memory and reading. *Journal of Verbal Learning and Verbal Behavior 19*, 450–466.

Dempster, F. N. (1981). Memory span: Sources of individual and developmental differences. *Psychological Bulletin 89*, 63–100.

Gagné, R. M., ed. (1967). *Learning and individual differences*. Columbus, OH: Charles E. Merrill.

Hannon, B., and Daneman, M. (2001). A new tool for measuring and understanding individual differences in the component processes of reading comprehension. *Journal of Educational Psychology 93*, 103–128.

Humphreys, M. S., Lynch, M. J., Revelle, W., and Hall, J. W. (1983). Individual differences in short-term memory. In R. F. Dillon and R. R. Schmeck, eds., *Individual differences in cognition*, Vol. 1. New York: Academic Press.

Hunt, E. (1978). Mechanics of verbal ability. *Psychological Review 85*, 109–130.

Just, M. A., and Carpenter, P. A. (1992). A capacity theory of comprehension: Individual differences in working memory. *Psychological Review 99*, 122–149.

Kane, M. J., Bleckley, M. K., Conway, A. R. A., and Engle, R. W. (2001). A controlled-attention view of working-memory capacity. *Journal of Experimental Psychology: General 130*, 169–183.

Miyake, A. (2001). Individual differences in working memory: Introduction to the special section. *Journal of Experimental Psychology: General 130*, 163–168.

Perlow, R., Jattuso, M., and Moore, D. D. W. (1997). Role of verbal working memory in complex skill acquisition. *Human Performance 10*, 283–302.

Plato. (1953). *The dialogues of Plato*, 4th edition, trans. B. Jowett. Oxford, UK: Clarendon Press.

Richardson, John T. E. (1999). *Imagery*. Hove, UK: Psychology Press.

Rosen, V. M., and Engle, R. W. (1997). The role of working memory capacity in retrieval. *Journal of Experimental Psychology: General 126*, 211–227.

Salthouse, T. A. (1996). The processing-speed theory of adult age differences in cognition. *Psychological Review 103*, 403–428.

Schmeck, R. R. (1983). Learning styles of college students. In R. F. Dillon and R. R. Schmeck, eds., *Individual differences in cognition*, Vol. 1. New York: Academic Press.

Schunn, C. D., and Reder, L. M. (2001). Another source of individual differences: Strategy adaptivity to changing rates of success. *Journal of Experimental Psychology: General 130*, 59–76.

Shah, P., and Miyake, A. (1996). The separability of working memory resources for spatial thinking and language processing: An individual differences approach. *Journal of Experimental Psychology: General 125*, 4–27.

Smith, E. E., Adams, N., and Schorr, D. (1978). Fact retrieval and the paradox of interference. *Cognitive Psychology 10*, 438–464.

Sternberg, R. J., and Zhang, L., eds. (2001). *Perspectives on thinking, learning, and cognitive styles*. Mahwah, NJ: Erlbaum.

Tuholski, S. W., Engle, R. W., and Baylis, G. C. (2001). Individual differences in working memory capacity and enumeration. *Memory & Cognition 29*, 484–492.

Voss, J. F., Vesonder, G. T., and Spilich, G. J. (1980). Text generation and recall by high-knowledge and low-knowledge individuals. *Journal of Verbal Learning and Verbal Behavior 19*, 651–667.

Wechsler, D. (1945). *Wechsler memory scale*. San Antonio, TX: The Psychological Corporation.

——— (1958). *The measurement and appraisal of adult intelligence*, 4th edition. Baltimore, MD: Williams and Wilkins.

Colin M. MacLeod

INFANCY, MEMORY IN

According to classic developmental theory, infants operate in the present, without thoughts of the past or anticipations of the future. Adults cannot remember events from infancy, a fact sometimes cited to corroborate the notion that memories are not formed during the preverbal period. However, experimental studies conducted in the late twentieth century demonstrate that young infants have more robust memories than heretofore believed. Indeed, modern theorists focus on the different types of memory infants might have. Infants seem to remember particular things under certain conditions and not others; they may also have privileged memory for biologically relevant signals such as faces and speech sounds.

Techniques for Investigating Infant Memory

Three experimental procedures have been developed to probe infant preverbal memory: visual preference tests; conditioning procedures; and deferred imitation. Each approach measures a different type of nonverbal memory. A fourth technique, object permanence, can also be used and it is only briefly mentioned in this entry because it is reviewed elsewhere in the encyclopedia.

Infant Visual Recognition Memory

The procedures used to evaluate infant visual recognition rely on infants' curiosity for exploring novel visual patterns (Bremner, 1994). Infants are shown a visual pattern for a certain length of time. A delay is imposed, and then they are presented with the old visual pattern and a new one. If infants devote more looking time to the new pattern than to the old one, this is taken as evidence that they have memory of the previously exposed target. Two specific techniques use this underlying principle: the *habituation-dishabituation* technique and the *paired-comparison* technique. For habituation-dishabituation, infants are repeatedly exposed to the initial target until they become bored with it (habituated). The new pattern is then introduced, and if looking time increases significantly (dishabituation), this shows that the infants recognize the pattern as being different from the one in memory. For the paired-comparison technique, infants are initially shown two identical patterns side by side for a certain familiarization period. It is not required that the infants habituate, only that they visually examine the display (usually thirty seconds to two minutes). Then a delay is imposed, and two patterns (the old one and a new one) are again presented. The index of memory is their preference for the novel pattern.

Advances in technology allow researchers new ways of looking at the brain basis of memory in infants. Event-related potentials (ERP) can be used to examine the neural correlates of recognition memory and attention in infants (Nelson, 1995). Typically, one of two approaches is used. In one case, infants are habituated or familiarized with a stimulus. Brain activity is then measured by recording electroencephalogram (EEG) signals in response to a series of trials in which either the habituated stimulus or a novel stimulus is presented. Brain measures record whether infants discriminate between the new and the old stimulus. In a second type of study, infants are shown stimuli that are familiar: for example, their mother's face or a familiar toy, and brain activity to these remembered stimuli is measured and compared to novel stimuli (de Haan and Nelson, 1999). The first approach provides brain measures of memory for well-controlled, briefly exposed stimuli; the second approach measures brain reactions to naturally occurring stimuli that have been frequently seen.

Age-Related Findings. Initially, studies of visual recognition memory reported no memory in infants younger than about ten to twelve weeks of age. However, researchers soon discovered that if the length of time infants studied the to-be-remembered stimuli was increased (up to five minutes) and the patterns were made very different from one another, even newborn infants could retain information in the visual recognition paradigm, at least for delays of a few seconds. Research then shifted to the effect of study time on memory; and the length of retention interval that can be tolerated by infants.

Study Time (Length of the "Encoding" Phase). Infants require shorter study times to demonstrate the novelty preference (the measure of memory) when the choice stimuli are vastly different than when the stimuli are similar. This idea was illustrated in a study by Joseph Fagan (1990) using the paired-comparison technique. He tested five-month-old infants using pairs of patterns that were graded in the degree to which they were discriminable from one another. The results showed that when the easiest pair was used, infants needed only about five seconds of study time to demonstrate the novelty preference; when the pair of medium discriminability was used, they needed about twenty seconds; and when the least discriminable pair was used, they required about thirty seconds. Thus, infants, like students studying for an exam, seem to need relatively more time to study material if they are asked to remember subtle distinctions.

Length of Retention Interval. Fagan showed visual patterns to five-month-olds and then imposed delays of three hours and one, two, seven, and fourteen days. The results revealed that infants could recognize which target they had previously seen even after the fourteen-day delay. What makes babies forget? Results from a variety of studies show that young infants will forget if they are shown highly related material during the retention interval. For example, if infants study photographs of faces and then are shown other face photographs during the retention interval, their subsequent memory performance will be poorer. The two factors that lead to maximum interference are stimuli that closely resemble the to-be-remembered material; and interfering presented soon after the initial exposure. This is reminiscent of adult memory, inasmuch as interference with remembering a telephone number is maximized by hearing other numbers soon after the initial information is delivered.

Another factor that influences the length of infant retention is the temporal spacing of the initial studying time. In one study, two groups of infants were given the same length of time to study a face photograph (twenty seconds). However, for one group this study time was massed, meaning it consisted of four five-second intervals with only a few seconds separating each interval. For the other group this experience was distributed, meaning there were much longer pauses between the four five-second intervals. Both groups demonstrated immediate recognition memory; however, only the group that received the distributed exposure remembered over long delays. This effect of distributed study is also a well-documented aspect of adult memory.

Conditioning Techniques

The second approach to evaluating infant memory was developed by Carolyn Rovee-Collier (1997). It involves training infants to produce a foot-kick response to a mobile hanging in their cribs. The mobile is often attached by a ribbon to one of the infant's ankles, so that the frequency and intensity of the movement mimics that of the infant (known as conjugate reinforcement). Infants as young as two to three months rapidly learn the contingency, doubling or tripling their baseline rates during the nine-minute training period. Once the infant has learned the response, a delay period can be inserted between the initial training period and the reintroduction of the mobile into the crib. Memory for the learned response is indexed by an increase in kicking over baseline rates, even after this delay interval.

Age-Related Findings. With this technique, Rovee-Collier and colleagues discovered a steady increase in the duration over which infants retain responses from two to eighteen months of age. Whereas the youngest infants tested in this paradigm remembered the response contingency for one day to one week, eighteen-month-olds remembered for thirteen weeks or longer.

Retrieving Infant Memories That Were Once Forgotten. One remarkable discovery made using this conditioning technique is that infants can be reminded about a past event that they have forgotten (Rovee-Collier, Hayne, and Colombo, 2001). This reminder stirs (reactivates) a previously inaccessible memory. Rovee-Collier's classic demonstration involved three-month-old infants who had forgotten the learned response after two weeks. These infants were then exposed to a brief reminder (the mobile, which was being moved surreptitiously by the experimenter). Then the infant was given another twenty-four-hour delay; finally, the stationary mobile was reintroduced to assess memory. Infants administered the reminder had their memories "reactivated" and kicked vigorously when the mobile was reintroduced. Control infants who were not given the reminder did not show any memory under the same circumstance.

Memory Specificity and the Importance of Context. In the first six months of life, infants are extremely sensitive to the context in which a behavior is acquired and show better memory if the test occurs in the same context as the learning episode. In one study, six-month-olds were given foot-kick training in a specially decorated crib (the context). As long as these infants were tested in the same context as the original training, they remembered to kick, even after a fourteen-day delay. However, if the crib decoration changed, the infants could not access their memories, even after a one-day delay (Rovee-Collier, 1997).

Deferred Imitation

The third procedure for testing infant memory is deferred imitation, that is, imitation after a delay (Barr and Hayne, 2000; Meltzoff and Moore, 1998). This technique capitalizes on the fact that preverbal infants enjoy imitating the actions of adults. To test memory, the infant is shown the to-be-imitated event, and then a delay is inserted before the infant is allowed to demonstrate the response. Memory is indexed by accurate reproduction of the target behavior after the delay. Control groups are tested to ensure that the production of the target behavior would not have occurred spontaneously in infants not exposed to the initial modeling.

Age-Related Findings. Classic developmental theories, such as those of the Swiss psychologist Jean Piaget, had supposed that imitation from memory was a cognitive achievement that first emerged at about eighteen months of age. Empirical research revised this classic view by showing that infants can perform deferred imitation as early as nine months of age (Meltzoff, 1988).

Imitative Learning and Length of Retention Interval. Scientists have been interested in infants learning novel material through observation. Andrew

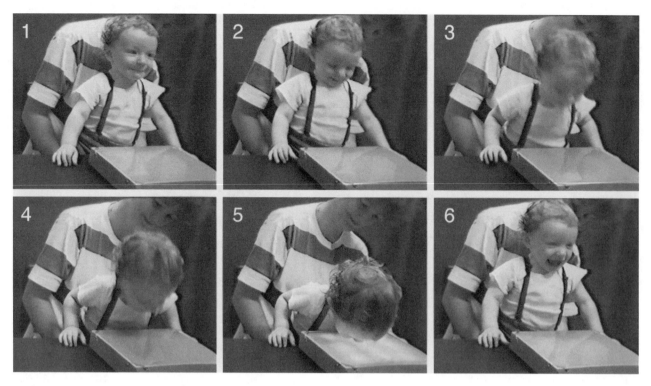

Figure 1. A fourteen-month-old infant imitating the novel act of head touching. Infants often react to successful imitation with a smile, as illustrated in panel 6. *(Andrew N. Meltzoff)*

Meltzoff (1990) showed infants a novel act that had not occurred in the baseline behavior of infants, and tested their memory for this act after a one-week delay. The act consisted of bending forward from the waist and tapping the top surface of a box with the top of one's forehead. Even after a one-week delay, 67 percent of fourteen-month-olds bent forward from the waist and touched their head to the panel (see Figure 1). Leslie Carver and Patricia Bauer (2001) found that ten-month-olds were able to retain at least some information about to-be-imitated events for delays of up to six months. Jean Mandler (1990) assessed memory for temporal order by presenting a sequence of behaviors that could be performed in one order or another. Both the sixteen- and twenty-month-olds showed immediate memory for the temporal order of these arbitrary sequences; the groups differed, however, on their long-term memory performance. The twenty-month-olds still showed memory for temporal order after a two-week delay, whereas the sixteen-month-olds were at chance levels. Long-term memory for arbitrarily sequenced events may develop toward the second half of the second year, and perhaps is aided by the emergence of language during this time.

Combined Brain and Imitation Measures. Carver, Bauer, and Nelson (2000) tested nine-month-olds for deferred imitation of ordered sequences of actions. About half of the infants recalled the events after a delay of one month. Event-related potentials (ERP) were mea-

sured during the delay interval to pictures of toys. Brain electrical responses mapped onto individual differences in behavior: Infants who successfully performed deferred imitation showed recognition memory as measured by ERP patterns during the delay interval; infants who did not imitate showed no recognition memory as measured by ERP. These results, and others, suggested that there are changes in the organization of brain systems involved in memory near the end of the first year of life, and that these changes can be observed in measures of individual differences in both brain and behavior.

Real-World Implications. Infants remember what they see on television. In one study infants were shown how to manipulate a new toy by an experimenter who appeared on television. The infants were not allowed to handle the real toy, but the next day the real toy was presented on the table. The results showed that infants accurately imitated the television-presented actions they had seen one day earlier. Another study examined whether fourteen-month-olds could remember actions performed by other infants. A "tutor infant" was taught how to perform a series of particular acts. This tutor infant was then brought to day-care centers where he demonstrated the acts to "naive infants." After a forty-eight-hour delay, the naive infants were visited at their homes by a researcher who laid out the toys on the floor. The results showed that the infants imitated what they had seen their peer do two days earlier. A general implication of this work is that imitation and memory are robust enough to play a significant role in the social and personality development of the preverbal infant (Meltzoff and Moore, 1998).

Conclusion and a Look to the Future

Multiple Memory Systems in Infants

The three techniques used to explore infant memory complement each other but do not address precisely the same aspects of infant memory. The distinctions are important for theory.

Recognition Versus Recall. In deferred imitation, infants go beyond the regulation of attention; they do more than react to the "newness" of a pattern. They must produce an absent act without seeing it and without having previously imitated it. Deferred imitation taps something more than visual recognition memory and provides a measure of recall memory prior to the acquisition of language.

Imitative Learning Versus Conditioning. Like deferred imitation, the conditioned foot-kick technique goes beyond visual recognition memory because the infants do more than recognize the familiar mobile; they also retrieve from memory what to do (kick). However, the conditioning procedure and the deferred imitation task differ in the type of information retained. Deferred imitation is based not on an incrementally learned procedure (as in the case of conditioned foot kicks) but on the performance of an act that was simply perceived during a brief previous episode. The deferred imitation test does not involve any motor practice during acquisition of the to-be-remembered event (no immediate imitation is allowed). The two tests also differ because the link between the stimulus and the infant's response is not forged through conditioning in deferred imitation. These distinctions are relevant for theories of memory and its development. Cognitive scientists and neuroscientists have made a distinction in different types of memory systems, particularly between procedural and declarative memory systems. One hypothesis is that deferred imitation provides a technique for exploring a primitive form of declarative memory, which researchers believe is mediated by the medial temporal lobe.

Relations Between Infant Memory and Childhood IQ

Do scores on infant memory tests predict later cognitive performance? Empirical work demonstrates that infants who perform better on tests of memory between two to nine months of age score higher on IQ (intelligence quotient) tests given later in childhood (McCall and Carriger, 1993; Rose and Feld-man, 1997). There is a (heated) social policy debate as to whether tests of early memory should be advertised as "infant intelligence tests." This debate should not mask the scientific discovery that there is continuity between the mental performance of infants, as measured by their performance on tests of memory, and childhood IQ scores.

Early and Rapid Memory Formation for Biologically Relevant Signals

Newborn infants are predisposed to encode and remember biologically important signals such as facial and speech signals. Newborn infants, with only a few hours of exposure to the mother, look longer at their own mother's face than at a stranger's face. Newborns also choose to listen to the voice of their own mother than to that of a strange female talker, suggesting that perhaps the sound of the mothers voice is learned prenatally. Finally, recent discoveries show that young infants respond differently to native- as opposed to foreign-language speech sounds. For example, Patricia Kuhl and colleagues (2001) showed that six-month-old Swedish infants have committed Swedish but not English speech sounds to memory, whereas American infants have done the opposite, demonstrating that infants are listening to the ambient sounds in the environment and remembering them even before they can talk.

Infantile Amnesia Revisited

Research indicates that infants have far more robust and complex memories than classic theories predicted. The puzzling phenomenon of infantile amnesia becomes more of a mystery when considered in light of this modern infancy research, because it can no longer be thought that infants do not form memories or that they are confined to sensorimotor skill routines during the preverbal period (Meltzoff, 1995). It is possible that the amnesia adults experience about their own infancy is due to the extreme mismatch between the cognitive, emotional, and physical context of the initial learning and that of the adult. It is sometimes reported that adults can gain access to "lost" childhood memories by immersing themselves in unique situations they have not encountered since childhood. Alternatively, the fact that adults use a linguistic code may shroud their memories of the preverbal period.

See also: AMNESIA, INFANTILE; CHILDREN, DEVELOPMENT OF MEMORY IN; DISTRIBUTED PRACTICE EFFECTS; INTERFERENCE AND FORGETTING; LANGUAGE LEARNING: HUMANS; OBJECT CONCEPT, DEVELOPMENT OF; REINFORCEMENT

Bibliography

Barr, R., and Hayne, H. (2000). Age-related changes in imitation: Implications for memory development. In C. Rovee-Collier, L. P. Lipsitt, and H. Hayne, eds., *Progress in infancy research.* Mahwah, NJ: Ablex.

Bremner, J. G. (1994). *Infancy,* 2nd edition. Cambridge, MA: Blackwell.

Carver, L. J., and Bauer, P. J. (2001). The dawning of a past: The emergence of long-term explicit memory in infancy. *Journal of Experimental Psychology: General 130,* 726–745.

Carver, L. J., Bauer, P. J., and Nelson, C. A. (2000). Associations between infant brain activity and recall memory. *Developmental Science 3,* 234–246.

de Haan, M., and Nelson, C. A. (1999). Brain activity differentiates face and object processing in 6-month-old infants. *Developmental Psychology 35,* 1,113–1,121.

Fagan, J. F., III. (1990). The paired-comparison paradigm and infant intelligence. In A. Diamond, ed., *Annals of the New York Academy of Sciences,* Vol. 608: *The development and neural bases of higher cognitive functions.* New York: The New York Academy of Sciences.

Kuhl, P. K., Tsao, F. M., Liu, H. M., Zhang, Y., and de Boer, B. (2001). Language/culture/mind/brain: Progress at the margins between disciplines. In A. R. Damasio et al., eds., *Unity of knowledge: The convergence of natural and human science.* New York: The New York Academy of Sciences.

Mandler, J. M. (1990). Recall of events of preverbal children. In A. Diamond, ed., *Annals of the New York Academy of Sciences,* Vol. 608: *The development and neural bases of higher cognitive functions.* New York: The New York Academy of Sciences.

McCall, R. B., and Carriger, M. S. (1993). A meta-analysis of infant habituation and recognition memory performance as predictors of later IQ. *Child Development 64,* 57–79.

Meltzoff, A. N. (1988). Infant imitation and memory: Nine-month-olds in immediate and deferred tests. *Child Development 59,* 217–225.

—— (1990). Towards a developmental cognitive science: The implications of cross-modal matching and imitation for the development of representation and memory in infancy. In A. Diamond, ed., *Annals of the New York Academy of Sciences,* Vol. 608: *The development and neural bases of higher cognitive functions.* New York: The New York Academy of Sciences.

—— (1995). What infant memory tells us about infantile amnesia: Long-term recall and deferred imitation. *Journal of Experimental Child Psychology 59,* 497–515.

Meltzoff, A. N., and Moore, M. K. (1998). Object representation, identity, and the paradox of early permanence: Steps toward a new framework. *Infant Behavior and Development 21,* 201–235.

Nelson, C. A. (1995). The ontogeny of human memory: A cognitive neuroscience perspective. *Developmental Psychology 31,* 723–738.

Rose, S. A., and Feldman, J. F. (1997). Memory and speed: Their role in the relation of infant information processing to later IQ. *Child Development 68,* 630–641.

Rovee-Collier, C. (1997). Dissociations in infant memory: Rethinking the development of implicit and explicit memory. *Psychological Review 104,* 467–498.

Rovee-Collier, C., Hayne, H., and Colombo, M. (2001). *The development of implicit and explicit memory.* Philadelphia: John Benjamins Publishing Co.

Andrew N. Meltzoff
Revised by Andrew N. Meltzoff and Leslie J. Carver

INSECT LEARNING

Why study learning in insects? What can it contribute to a general knowledge of how learning takes place in a wide variety of animals? There are many potential answers to these questions. This review will focus on the general contribution that can be made to systematic understanding of how learning has evolved and is controlled in a wide variety of vertebrate and invertebrate species. Any systematic study must begin with a well-defined phylogenetic lineage. Insects are in the phylum Arthropoda, which contains animals that have jointed exoskeletons (e.g., insects, ticks, crabs, lobsters, spiders). With at least 2 million extant species (some estimates range as high as 30 to 50 million), the arthropod class Insecta comprises the most diverse group of multicellular organisms (Borror, Triplehorn, and Johnson, 1989). Insects have adapted to a wide array of living conditions, ranging from most terrestrial to many aquatic environments. The diverse insect species found in these environments must solve the basic problems inherent in locating resources such as food or mates and avoiding predatory or environmental threats. The learning abilities observed in any laboratory situation probably evolved to solve these problems.

Because of this species and habitat diversity, insects provide an excellent means of testing patterns of phylogenetic emergence of different learning mechanisms. The appropriateness of using cognitive explanations, the lack of generally agreed upon operational definitions, the need for learning taxonomies, and a recognition of individual differences in performance are all relevant issues in the study of invertebrate learning. One must also carefully distinguish phylogenetically homologous traits from analogous ones. *Homology* refers to traits that arise from a common ancestral condition. Researchers must always consider rigorous criteria for any proposed homology between behaviors of different groups of invertebrates and/or vertebrates (Wenzel, 1992). A monophyletic group of animals that possesses homologous traits is a clade, and the process of modification of those traits is cladogenesis.

Through a comparison of traits that may appear dissimilar and thus unrelated in several closely related, extant species, it is possible to obtain a picture of which traits are ancestral (plesiomorphic) and which are derived. For example, are nonassociative learning mechanisms homologous to associative mechanisms? That is, did ancestral species possess the ability to modify behavior through habituation and sensitization prior to the ability to express associative conditioning? Were changes in the evolution of learning abilities gradual, adaptive alterations or the result of rapid, discontinuous changes resulting from dramatic reorganization of neural tissue (Wyers, Peeke, and Herz, 1973)? Through a study of insect species whose phylogenies with respect to other characteristics (e.g., morphological, physiological) are known, such hypotheses can be tested.

Analogous traits are physically similar but have been derived from very different ancestral conditions. For example, the expression of operant conditioning of leg movement in an insect might be analogous to operant conditioning of leg movement in a vertebrate. Insect legs and vertebrate legs are not homologous structures, but both enable animals to move throughout their environment and thus the rules for operant conditioning of each may be similar. Analogous traits associated with complex learning abilities arise through convergent evolution, perhaps because of similar environmental problems that require one or more ways to modify behavior based on experience. This description of analogous learning abilities in terms of degrees of complexity is anagenesis (Demarest, 1983). A comparative study of potentially analogous learning mechanisms in such phylogenetically diverse groups as insects and vertebrates allows the testing of hypotheses about the conditions that give rise to analogous learning abilities. Thus learning abilities studied in insects have an important value for deriving hypotheses that are testable in vertebrates. Even if learning traits do not have a common phylogenetic origin, working out mechanisms in one species can generate conceptual advances in understanding a similar learning ability in another species.

No single study can be designed to investigate all of these issues. In the long run this approach must make extensive use of several species that are chosen to appropriately test defined phylogenetic hypotheses (Wenzel, 1992). What follows, then, is not a comprehensive review of the invertebrate learning literature but rather a highlighting of significant studies.

Orthoptera

The order Orthoptera comprises cockroaches, grasshoppers, and locusts. Horridge (1962) published results of an experiment in which headless cockroaches and locusts learned to keep one leg raised to terminate a series of electric shocks. This experiment generated considerable interest because it was one of the first to suggest that an insect can be used to explore the physiology of learning and memory. Subsequently, leg-position learning, or the Horridge paradigm, has demonstrated learning in a wide variety of experimental situations, ranging from intact animals to a single ganglion. This latter information demonstrated that learning need not be confined to a single area of the central nervous system (e.g., the

brain) but can be distributed throughout several stimulus and motor processing pathways in a nervous system.

The Horridge paradigm also brought into focus the adequacy of the yoked-control design in separating learning from nonassociative effects. In the original Horridge experiment, learning was inferred from a difference in the number of shocks received by experimental subjects and by their yoked controls. The experimental subjects were shocked contingent on leg position; control subjects were yoked in such a way that they received a shock whenever the experimental subjects did, but independent of their own behavior. The yoked paradigm has been extensively criticized in the literature. Church (1964), for instance, pointed out that because of the nature of the yoked paradigm, random differences in inherent responsiveness will lead to artifactual learning in the population.

To answer such criticisms, a new experimental design was developed for training leg position in the locust (Forman, 1984). Rather than simply requiring the animal to raise a leg to terminate a series of shocks, Forman required his locust to maintain a particular range of leg movements arbitrarily selected by the experimenter. After a few minutes of training, the animal learns to shift its leg position to an angle that terminates aversive heat to the head or produces access to food. Locusts can also be trained to manipulate leg position to produce heat to the head in a cold environment. The task can be made more complex by narrowing or shifting the range of leg movement necessary to control the heat stimulus. The Forman experiment is important because it represents the first significant improvement in the Horridge paradigm; both the response and the reinforcer are arbitrary, and learning can be identified in an individual animal. This procedure has the additional advantage of eliminating shock as the aversive stimulus.

The rationale for developing the Forman paradigm is to obtain data on the cellular mechanisms underlying operant behavior. By using electromyograms and intracellular techniques, the motor neurons involved in learning have been found and characterized. Forman and Zill (1984), for example, identified three separate motor strategies utilized by the locusts during training ("kicking," changes in muscle tonus, and tonic slow excitor motor neuron activity). Each of these strategies can be selectively trained. An exciting application of the technique and a fine example of the comparative method is an analysis of the similarities and differences in response strategies between locusts and the weta, a primitive New Zealand insect related to the locust (Hoyle and Field, 1983).

Diptera

The order Diptera comprises all flies. Fly species that have been extensively used in studies of learning include *Phormia regina* (blowflies) and *Drosophila melanogaster* (fruit flies). Research interest in flies was generated by the extreme ease of maintaining populations under controlled mating conditions over generations that cover only weeks rather than years. Controlled breeding experiments have characterized the behavioral, genetic, and biochemical bases of different learning mechanisms.

Some of the first comprehensive studies of learning behavior in flies began with the pioneering work of Dethier and colleagues (1990), which worked out in considerable detail the stimulus control of feeding reflexes in *Phormia regina*. They described a procedure in which the tarsal (leg) receptors that mediate sucrose taste sensation were stimulated to elicit extension of a subject's proboscis (the sucking mouthparts) through which it feeds on the sucrose-water droplet. They found that prior exposure to sucrose greatly increased the probability that a fly would extend its proboscis to the presentation of water alone. The motivational state that was modulated by the sucrose exposure was termed central excitatory state (CES), which describes a nonassociative (sensitization) modification of the probability of proboscis extension to a neutral stimulus (water). CES can be characterized by at least three factors: There is a decay over time between the sensitizing and test stimuli; increased sucrose concentrations lead to increases in CES; food deprivation leads to increased levels of CES for any given sucrose concentration.

Tully and Hirsch's studies (Tully, 1984) have documented genetic bases for CES effects in *P. regina*, and other studies extended the results on the genetic basis for CES effects to *D. melanogaster* (Vargo and Hirsch, 1986). Bidirectional selection for high and low CES lines in *P. regina* has shown that the response to selection is rapid and may reach asymptotic levels in one or a few generations. Hybridization of the different lines indicated that one major gene segregated in the selected lines was responsible for producing most of the variability in CES effect. Selection for CES effects in *D. melanogaster* has shown a slightly different genetic basis. Sometimes a low but not a high line was produced, or vice versa. These data indicate that several genes may be involved in regulating CES in fruit flies. Further studies have shown that genes reside on at least two chromosomes; heritable cytoplasmic factors may also be involved (Vargo and Hirsch, 1986).

Theories of anagenesis predict that as metazoan life becomes physically more complex, more complex learning abilities will emerge (Demarest, 1983). Thus associative learning mechanisms may be mechanistically related to simpler nonassociative processes. Accordingly, learning studies with both *P. regina* and *D. melanogaster* have focused on developing associative conditioning paradigms and testing for genetic correlates with nonassociative processes. By associating either a saline or a water conditioned stimulus (CS) with sucrose, *P. regina* can learn to extend their proboscises to the CS (Nelson, 1971). Tully, Zawistowski, and Hirsch (1982) selected for high and low learning lines of blowflies. These lines showed a positive correlation between CES levels and asymptotic levels of learning performance. Therefore, CES and associative conditioning appear to have at least some common genetic bases, which might include pleiotropic genetic effects.

Aversive conditioning has been widely used to select large numbers of *D. melanogaster* in order to rapidly isolate mutant strains that show deficiencies in learning and/or memory (Dudai, 1983). The procedure involves exposing flies sequentially to two odors while they walk across a metal grid (Tully and Quinn, 1985). While they are exposed to one odor, they receive shocks through the grid. Flies are then presented with a sequence of new "collection" tubes that contain either the odor paired with shock (S+) or the odor that was not paired with shock (S-). The response measure is the number of flies that enter a new tube that contains the S+ odor versus the number that enter a tube containing the S- odor. Over several runs, decreased entries into the tube with the S+ odor relative to the tube with the S- odor indicate learning.

Hymenoptera

The order Hymenoptera contains a diverse group of insects commonly referred to as sawflies, ants, wasps, and bees. Hymenopterans such as ants and honeybees have been widely used to document learning abilities related directly to learning problems in the animal's natural environment. Furthermore, experiments with ants and bees in laboratory learning paradigms have demonstrated that these abilities conform to standard definitions of learning. But an ant's or a bee's learning ability may be less complex and/or less generalizable to new situations than that of animals with larger, more elaborate nervous systems (Demarest, 1983). Indeed, the crucial question is how complex these abilities are and to what natural situations they can be applied.

Learning in ants was first brought into the laboratory by Fielde (1901), who reported that ants can successfully negotiate a simple maze. Schnierla (1946) described the chemical, visual, and kinesthetic cues used by ants in solving a more complex maze. DeCarlo and Abramson (1989) used a different procedure to extend vertebrate learning paradigms to ants. They demonstrated an ant's ability to choose one compartment of a two-compartment chamber based on rates of stimulus delivery.

The honeybee (*Apis mellifera*) is an ideal species with which to research similar questions. On warm, sunny days worker bees regularly depart from the colony on foraging trips during which they collect resources (e.g., nectar, pollen, water) crucial for survival and reproduction of the colony. A large number of studies have documented the abilities of freely flying honeybees to learn the relationships of visual, tactile, and olfactory cues to appetitive and aversive stimuli (Menzel, 1990; Bitterman, 1996). For example, forager bees learn the association of nectar, which for most conditioning studies is replaced with a sucrose-water mixture and floral color, shape, odor, and the time of day that floral rewards are available. Other work has documented the honeybee's ability to learn compounds of stimuli. The unconditioned stimulus-preexposure effect and latent inhibition have also been studied. For studies of aversive learning, Abramson (1986) has demonstrated the ability of freely flying bees to use certain stimuli as a means of avoiding exposure to an aversive-shock stimulus. The learned avoidance ability of the honeybee may have evolved as a means to cope with bitter and even toxic nectars found in some flowers.

Proboscis-extension conditioning of honeybees is a common technique for studying learning under easily controllable stimulation variables (Menzel 1990). Honeybees restrained individually in harnesses can be readily conditioned to extend their proboscises upon presentation of a floral odor. After one or a few pairings of an odor-conditioned stimulus with a sucrose unconditioned stimulus, 40 to 90 percent of the subjects will extend their proboscises (conditioned response) to the odor alone. Enhancement of a background rate of proboscis extension to odor is specific to situations in which the CS precedes the US (forward pairing) and is sensitive to latency of onset of odor relative to sucrose. Proboscis-extension conditioning has been used to study a variety of phenomena in honeybees, such as sensory discrimination (Smith and Menzel, 1989a); control of motor systems (Smith and Menzel, 1989b); memory consolidation (Menzel, 1990). More recent work has extended to restrained bees Abramson's (1986) study of aversive conditioning in freely flying bees. The majority of subjects that received a shock contingent upon their response to sucrose in the context of a particular odor learned to withhold proboscis extension to sucrose in order to avoid shock (Smith, Abramson, and Tobin, 1991).

The question whether bees and ants have a cognitive map has generated controversy. That is, have they learned a "mental analogy of a topographic map, i.e., an internal representation of the geometric relations among noticeable points in the animal's environment" (Wehner and Menzel, 1990, p. 403)? Evidence to date points to a vector-based navigation system combined with memory matching of relative positions of landmarks (Cartwright and Collett, 1987) rather than to a more complex topographic representation.

New Developments in Invertebrate Learning

Later research in insect learning has emphasized one species of insect: the honeybee (Bitterman, 1996). This work emphasizes the type of research program into learning mechanisms that ought to be taken up on a much wider array of species.

Blocking

Kamin (1968) conditioned rats to one stimulus (A) and followed that with conditioning to a second stimulus that was a compound of the first with a novel stimulus (AX). When finally tested with X, subjects typically revealed that they had learned less about X than subjects in appropriate control groups. This "blocking" phenomenon went on to spawn a tremendous volume of both theoretical and empirical research. Most research on vertebrates has emphasize blocking between cues from different stimulus modalities (e.g., compounds of one visual and one acoustic cue). Recently, blocking has been investigated in a series of studies in honeybees (Smith 1997). In contrast to vertebrates, blocking is more evident in compounds made of the same stimulus modality (mixtures of two olfactory or two visual cues), although intermodal blocking has been identified for some stimulus compounds (Couvillon, Campos, Bass, and Bitterman, 2001). Whether this stimulus specificity represents a fundamental difference between vertebrates and invertebrates must await further study.

CS Preexposure

Unreinforced exposure to a conditioned stimulus leads to retardation of learning about that CS when it is subsequently paired with reinforcement in a way that would normally result in robust conditioned responding. This mechanism has also been referred to as "latent inhibition." Abramson and Bitterman (1986) initially reported a CS-preexposure effect in free-flying honeybees. Studies of odor preexposure have revealed the effect in laboratory studies in honeybees (Chandra, Hunt, and Smith, 2001). These latter studies highlight the importance of recognition of individual difference in expression of a preexposure effect. Individual honeybees differ in the extent that they exhibit the effect, and both studies were successful in demonstrating that individual differences have a genetic basis. This latter finding indicates that individual differences are most likely not an artifact of the approach, and they may point in future studies to an ecological meaning for individual differences. Chandra, Hunt, and Smith (2001) isolated segments of chromosomal DNA that presumably house genes that influence this trait.

Risk Sensitivity and Choice Behavior

Two studies have revealed risk sensitivity in honeybees (Shafir, Wiegmann, Smith, and Real 1999; Shapiro, Couvillon, and Bitterman, 2001). When two different conditioned stimuli are reinforced at the same mean rate but the reinforcement differs in variance, animals may prefer the less variable option (risk aversion), the more variable option (risk prone), or neither (risk insensitive). Under normal conditions honeybees are risk-averse. As with CS preexposure, individuals differ in their degree of risk sensitivity. This behavior resembles risk sensitivity in vertebrates. But a model that incorporates associationist concepts can account for risk sensitivity in honeybees (Shapiro, Couvillon, and Bitterman, 2001). So more cognitive interpretations of this phenomenon need not be invoked. More recently, Shafir, Waite, and Smith (2002) have shown that honeybees violate basic properties of rational choice because the choice between two options for reward depends on available alternatives. Their relative preference between two options changes with the introduction of a third, relatively unattractive option.

Matching-to-Sample

Honeybees master more abstract relationships among cues, such as "sameness" or "difference" (Giurfa et al., 2001). Honeybees can be conditioned to respond to a cue based on whether or not it matched a sample cue to which animals were recently exposed. This rule can also be used in a more general sense: once the rule is learned in one stimulus modality. it can apply to cues from a different modality. Risk sensitivity and matching-to-sample may yet prove to be fruitful for pursuit of more cognitive manifestations of invertebrate learning.

Comparative Analysis of Learning in Africanized Honeybees

Another recent development in learning of honeybees is the study of the Africanized honeybee. Studies have examined conditioning to various stimuli, extinction (both unpaired and CS only), conditioned inhibition, color and odor discrimination, and learning in day-old bees. The results suggestion a subspecies difference between European and Africanized honeybees. In addition to work on basic phenomena, experiments on practical applications of conditioning methodology are illustrated with studies demonstrating the effects of insecticides on learning and the reaction of Africanized bees to consumer products (Abramson, Aquino, Silva, and Price, 1997; Abramson, Aquino, Ramalho, and Price, 1999; Abramson, Aquino, and Stone, 1999).

The Development of a Social Insect Model of Alcoholism

Honeybees are also a model for studies of alcoholism in humans. Honeybees have much to recommend them for such studies, including a language and social structure. Studies have shown that bees will self-administer ethanol and that locomotion and learning is impaired in a dose-dependent manner (Abramson et al., 2000).

See also: EVOLUTION AND LEARNING; INVERTEBRATE LEARNING: ASSOCIATIVE LEARNING AND MEMORY PROCESSING IN BEES; INVERTEBRATE LEARNING: NEUROGENETICS OF MEMORY IN DROSOPHILA; OPERANT BEHAVIOR; PAVLOV, IVAN; SPATIAL LEARNING: ANIMALS

Bibliography

Abramson, C. I. (1986). Aversive conditioning in honeybees (*Apis mellifera*). *Journal of Comparative Psychology 100*, 108–116.

Abramson, C. I., Aquino, I. S., Ramalho, F. S., and Price, J. M. (1999). Effect of insecticides on learning in the Africanized honey bee (*Apis mellifera* L.). *Archives of Environmental Contamination and Toxicology 37*, 529–535.

Abramson, C.I., Aquino, I. S., Silva, M. C., and Price, J. M. (1997). Learning in the Africanized honey bee: *Apis mellifera* L. *Physiology and Behavior 62*, 657–674.

Abramson, C. I., Aquino, I. S. and Stone, S. M. (1999). Failure to find proboscis conditioning in one-day old Africanized honeybees (*Apis mellifera* L.) and in adult Uruçu honeybees (*Melipona scutellaris*). *International Journal of Comparative Psychology 12*, 242–262

Abramson, C. I., and Bitterman, M. E. (1986). Latent inhibition in honeybees. *Animal Learning and Behavior 14*, 184–189.

Abramson, C. I, Stone, S. M., Ortez, R. A., Luccardi, A., Vann, K. L., Hanig, K. D. and Rice, J. (2000). The development of an ethanol model using social insects I: Behavior studies of the Honey Bee (*Apis mellifera* L.). *Alcoholism: Clinical and Experimental Research 24*, 1,153–1,166.

Bitterman, M.E. (1996). Comparative analysis of learning in honeybees. *Animal Learning and Behavior 24*, 123–141.

Borror, D. J., Triplehorn, C. A., and Johnson, N. F. (1989). *An introduction to the study of insects*, 6th edition. Philadelphia: Saunders College Publishing.

Cartwright, B. A., and Collett, T. S. (1987). Landmark maps for honeybees. *Biological Cybernetics 57*, 85–93.

Chandra, S. B. C., Hunt, G., and Smith, B. H. (2001) Quantitative trait loci associated with reversal learning and latent inhibition in honeybees (*Apis mellifera*) *Behavior Genetics 31*, 275–285.

Church, R. M. (1964). Systematic effect of random error in the yoked control design. *Psychological Bulletin 62*, 122–131.

Couvillon, P. A., Arakaki, L., and Bitterman, M. E. (1997). Intra-modal blocking in honeybees. *Animal Learning and Behavior* 25, 277–282.

Couvillon, P. A., Campos, A. C., Bass, T. D., and Bitterman, M. E. (2001). Intermodal blocking in honeybees. *Quarterly Journal of Experimental Psychology B. 54*, 369–381.

DeCarlo, L. T., and Abramson, C. I. (1989). Time allocation in the carpenter ant (*Camponotus herculeanus*). *Journal of Comparative Psychology 103*, 389–400.

DeJianne, D., McGuire, T. R., and Pruzan-Hotchkiss, A. (1985). Conditioned suppression of proboscis extension in *Drosophila melanogaster*. *Journal of Comparative Physiology and Psychology 99*, 74–80.

Demarest, J. (1983). The ideas of change, progress, and continuity in the comparative psychology of learning. In D. W. Rajecki, ed., *Comparing behavior: Studying man studying animals*. Hillsdale, NJ: Erlbaum.

Dethier, V. G. (1990). Chemosensory physiology in an age of transition. *Annual Review of Neuroscience 13*, 1–13.

Dudai, Y. (1983). Mutations affect storage and use of memory differentially in *Drosophila*. *Proceedings of the National Academy of Sciences of the United States of America 80*, 5,445–5,448.

Fielde, A. (1901). A further study of an ant. *Proceedings of the National Academy of Sciences of the United States of America 53*, 521–544.

Forman, R. R. (1984). Leg position learning by an insect. I. A heat avoidance learning paradigm. *Journal of Neurobiology 15*, 127–140.

Forman, R. R., and Zill, S. N. (1984). Leg position learning by an insect. II. Motor strategies underlying learned leg extension. *Journal of Neurobiology 15*, 221–237.

Giurfa, M., Zhang, S., Jenett, A., Menzel, R., and Srinivasan, M.V. (2001). The concepts of "sameness" and "difference" in an insect. *Nature 410*, 930–933.

Horridge, G. A. (1962). Learning of leg position by headless insects. *Nature 193*, 697–698.

Hoyle, G., and Field, L. H. (1983). Elicitation and abrupt termination of behaviorally significant catchlike tension in a primitive insect. *Journal of Neurobiology 14*, 299–312.

Kamin, L. J. (1968). Attention-like processes in classical conditioning. In Jones, M.R., ed., *Miami symposium on predictability of behavior: Aversive stimulation*. Coral Gables, FL: Miami University Press.

Menzel, R. (1990). Learning, memory, and "cognition" in honeybees. In R. P. Kesner and D. S. Olton, eds., *Neurobiology of comparative cognition*. Hillsdale, NJ: Erlbaum.

Nelson, M. C. (1971). Classical conditioning in the blowfly (*Phormia regina*): Associative and excitatory factors. *Journal of Comparative Physiology and Psychology 77*, 353–368.

Schnierla, T. C. (1946). Ant learning as a problem in comparative psychology. In P. Harriman, ed., *Twentieth-century psychology*. New York: Philosophical Library.

Shafir, S., Waite, T. A., and Smith, B. H. (2002). Context-dependent violations of rational choice in honeybees (*Apis mellifera*) and gray jays (*Perisoreus canadensis*). *Behavioral Ecology Sociobiology 51*, 180–187.

Shafir, S., Wiegmann, D. D., Smith, B. H., and Real, L. A. (1999). Risk-sensitivity of harnessed honeybees to variability in volume of reward. *Animal Behaviour, 57*, 1,055–1,061.

Shapiro, M. S., Couvillon, P. A., and Bitterman, M. E. (2001). Quantitative tests of an associative theory of risk-sensitivity in honeybees. *Journal of Experimental Biology 204*, 565–573.

Smith, B. H. (1997). An analysis of blocking in binary odorant mixtures: An increase but not a decrease in intensity of reinforcement produces unblocking. *Behavioral Neuroscience 11*, 57–69.

Smith, B. H., Abramson, C. I., and Tobin, T. R. (1992). Conditional withholding of proboscis extension in honeybees (*Apis mel-lifera*) during discriminative punishment. *Journal of Comparative Psychology 105*, 345–356.

Smith, B. H., and Menzel, R. (1989a). The use of electromyogram recordings to quantify odor discrimination in the honeybee. *Journal of Insect Physiology 35*, 369–375.

——— (1989b). An analysis of variability in the feeding motor program of the honey bee: The role of learning in releasing a modal action pattern. *Ethology 82*, 68–81.

Tully, T. (1984). *Drosophila* learning: Behavior and biochemistry. *Behavior Genetics 14*, 527–557.

Tully, T., and Quinn, W. G. (1985). Classical conditioning and retention in normal and mutant *Drosophila melanogaster*. *Journal of Comparative Physiology 157*, 263–277.

Tully, T., Zawistowski, S., and Hirsch, J. (1982). Behavior-genetic analysis of *Phormia regina*: III. A phenotypic correlation between the central excitatory state (CES) and conditioning remains in replicate F2 generations of hybrid crosses. *Behavior Genetics 12*, 181–191.

Vargo, M., and Hirsch, J (1986). Biometrical and chromosome analyses of lines of *Drosophila melanogaster* selected for central excitation. *Heredity 56*, 19–24.

Wehner, R., and Menzel, R. (1990). Do insects have cognitive maps? *Annual Review of Neuroscience 13*, 403–404.

Wenzel, J. W. (1992). Behavioral homology and phylogeny. *Annual Review Entomology 23*, 361–381.

Wyers, E. J., Peeke, H. V. S., and Herz, M. J. (1973). Behavioral habituation in invertebrates. In H. V. S. Peeke and M. J. Herz, eds., *Habituation*, Vol. 1. New York: Academic Press.

Brian H. Smith
Charles I. Abramson

INSTRUMENTAL CONDITIONING

See: APLYSIA: CLASSICAL CONDITIONING AND OPERANT CONDITIONING; OPERANT BEHAVIOR

INTELLECTUAL DISABILITIES

See: MENTAL RETARDATION (INTELLECTUAL DISABILITIES)

INTELLIGENCE AND MEMORY

Memory plays an important role in intelligent behavior. Modern assessments of cognitive functioning, such as the Wechsler Adult Intelligence Scale (WAIS-III), include memory tests among other essential measure of mental capability. Modern information-processing conceptions of memory, however, represent a distinct change from the information-reservoir conceptions of memory put forth by earlier researchers such as Richard Atkinson and Richard Shiffrin (1968). This change, a consequence of the shift from using storage metaphors for memory to using computer processing metaphors, has revolutionized scientific understanding of memory and its link to intelligence.

Figure 1

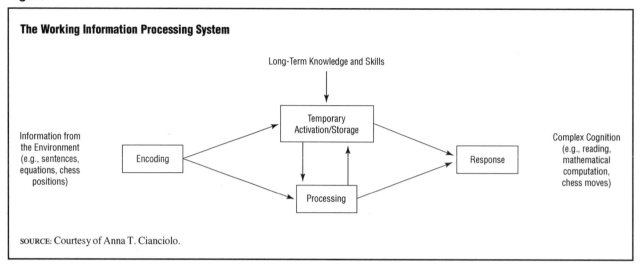

The Working Information Processing System

SOURCE: Courtesy of Anna T. Cianciolo.

Memory as Information Processing

In their edited volume, Akira Miyake and Priti Shah (1999) integrated the work of leading memory theorists into a consensus definition of memory, which dispenses with the notion of a biochemical filing cabinet in the brain and proposes a multifaceted, working information-processing system whose function is to aid in complex cognition. As illustrated in Figure 1, the limitations of this information-processing system can be attributed to multiple factors: such as the encoding of novel information, the simultaneous storage and processing of information, and the retrieval of information stored long term. The concept of working memory is not new but was first put forth by Alan Baddeley and Graham Hitch in 1974. However, much hard work since the 1970s has extended Baddeley and Hitch's initial work to develop a more precise characterization of this system, its limitations, and its relationship to intelligent behavior.

Measures of working memory have shown a strong and consistent relationship with measures of intelligence and complex cognitive processing. Though numerous experimental findings demonstrate this link, those of Patrick Kyllonen and his colleagues, Raymond Christal and Deborah Stephens, have been especially illuminating. Seeking to provide an information-processing explanation for intelligence, Kyllonen and his colleagues developed and tested his model of intelligent performance, which posited that mental functioning depends on four cognitive sources: working memory, processing speed, declarative knowledge, and procedural knowledge. They found that of the four sources, working memory showed the strongest relations to skill acquisition and performance on intelligence tests (Kyllonen, 1996; Kyllonen and Stephens, 1990). Kyllonen discovered a high correlation between measures of working memory and tests of reasoning, even concluding that working memory and general intelligence amount to the same thing (Kyllonen, 2002).

Other work has been geared toward determining more precisely what accounts for the relationship between working memory and cognitive functioning. Researchers have focused on the encoding, processing, and retrieval aspects of the working memory system.

The Role of Encoding

Encoding involves transforming perceptual information from the environment into initial input for the information-processing system (see Figure 1). Limitations in receiving information from the environment have implications for later information processing and, ultimately, intelligent behavior.

Christopher Jarrold, Alan Baddeley, and Alexa Hewes (2000) examined the relative amount of immediate recall, near-immediate recall, and short-term recall in children of varying levels of retardation. They briefly presented the children with three spoken words, each of which was associated with one of three horizontal positions on a computer screen such that the first word spoken was associated with the leftmost position. They then highlighted one of the three positions and asked the children to recall the word that had been associated with that position. Recalling the word associated with the leftmost position, spoken earliest, required short-term recall, the middle position, near-immediate recall, and the rightmost position, immediate recall.

These researchers were interested in determining whether failure to rehearse to-be-remembered information could account for memory deficits in children with Down's syndrome. They discovered, however, that differences in short-term recall associated with intellectual ability occurred despite the fact that none of the children used rehearsal as a memory aid. Further, these memory differences occurred only during short-term recall, in which children with Down's syndrome demonstrated memory deficits that the other children did not; all of the children had equally poor near-immediate recall and equally good immediate recall. Jarrold, Baddeley, and Hewes suggested that one possible explanation for these results could be encoding limitation—even though their perceptual processing was equivalent, children with Down's syndrome could not transform environmental information into system input (i.e., memory traces) as efficiently as the other children with lesser intelligence deficits could.

This conclusion mirrors that of Norman Ellis and Darlene Meador (1985), who investigated mnemonic strategies and short-term recall deficits in retarded children. They presented children with an experimental stimulus and then, after a delay, presented a probe stimulus. They asked the children to compare the probe stimulus with their memory of the experimental stimulus and indicate whether they matched. As expected, recognition accuracy on this task decreased as IQ decreased. More important, rates of forgetting across different levels of IQ were equivalent on this task, even with the precluding of mnemonic strategies. Performance differences correlated with IQ differences with the simultaneous presentation of experimental and probe stimuli, even at retention intervals of twenty seconds.

The Role of Processing

As illustrated in Figure 1, after encoding, information must remain temporarily active during its support of cognitive activity. Limitations in simultaneously storing and processing information have implications for complex cognition because the active maintenance and processing of information in working memory plays an important role in intelligent behavior. There are, however, differing views on the nature of limitations in this aspect of the working-memory system, whether it is task-specific or task-independent.

Meredyth Daneman and her colleagues, Patricia Carpenter and Brenda Hannon, have tested the hypothesis that the efficiency of task-specific processing is the critical link between working memory and complex cognition. This work and related research helped to develop several working-memory tests, each with a storage and processing aspect (see Figure 2). The critical difference between these tests is the type of processing required in each. The reading-span test requires verbal processing specific to reading in addition to verbal storage. The individual must read a set of sentences and, after finishing reading all of the sentences in the set, recall the last word of each sentence. The speaking-span test is similar in calling for the remembering of a set of target words but calls for the presentation of the target words first; the individual must remember the words while using each of them to orally generate a sentence, a task that requires verbal fluency. The operation-span test, created by Marilyn Turner and Randall Engle (1989), requires mathematical processing: After completing a set of simple mathematical operations, the individual must recall the word associated with each one.

Findings from research using these memory tests suggest that the correlation between memory and task performance depends on the degree of similarity between the type of processing required by the task and the memory test. Daneman (1991) found, for example, that speaking-span scores showed a stronger relation to a measure of oral fluency than did reading-span scores. Conversely, reading-span scores showed a stronger relation to oral reading skills than did speaking-span scores. Daneman and Hannon (2001) demonstrated that operation-span scores showed a relatively weaker correlation to reading comprehension than did reading-span scores.

Not all research agrees with the conclusion the processes on memory tests must be task-specific. In contrast, Engle his colleagues have repeatedly demonstrated that the relationship between memory and cognition is not mediated by efficient task-specific processing. Engle, Kane, and Tuholski (1999) described a series of studies in which task-specific processing efficiency was statistically or experimentally controlled but in which the relationship between working memory and performance on various tests was not eliminated. In one study, the mathematical processing demands of the operation span test were equated across individuals. The mathematical ability of each participant was determined, and the difficulty of the operations administered in the operation span test was tailored to ability level. Controlling for individual differences in mathematical ability failed to reduce the strong correlation between performance on the memory test and reading comprehension.

The operation span test required the allocation of attention to both completing mathematical operations and remembering target words, but equating mathematical ability did not reduce the correlation between working memory and complex cognition.

Figure 2

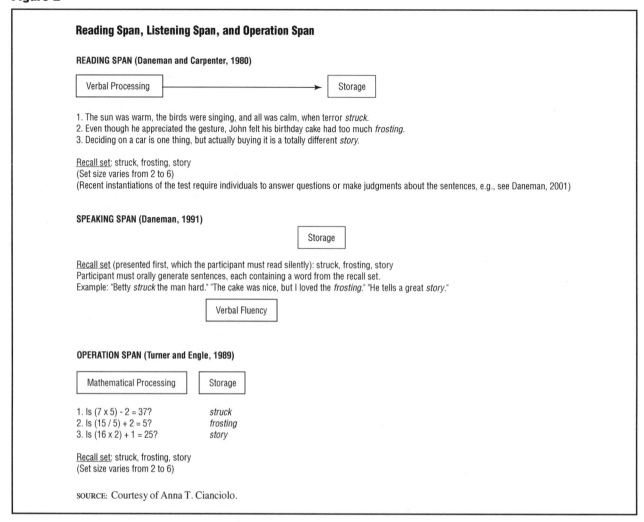

Reading Span, Listening Span, and Operation Span

READING SPAN (Daneman and Carpenter, 1980)

Verbal Processing ———————————→ Storage

1. The sun was warm, the birds were singing, and all was calm, when terror *struck.*
2. Even though he appreciated the gesture, John felt his birthday cake had too much *frosting.*
3. Deciding on a car is one thing, but actually buying it is a totally different *story.*

<u>Recall set</u>: struck, frosting, story
(Set size varies from 2 to 6)
(Recent instantiations of the test require individuals to answer questions or make judgments about the sentences, e.g., see Daneman, 2001)

SPEAKING SPAN (Daneman, 1991)

Storage

<u>Recall set</u> (presented first, which the participant must read silently): struck, frosting, story
Participant must orally generate sentences, each containing a word from the recall set.
Example: "Betty *struck* the man hard." "The cake was nice, but I loved the *frosting.*" "He tells a great *story.*"

Verbal Fluency

OPERATION SPAN (Turner and Engle, 1989)

Mathematical Processing   Storage

1. Is (7 x 5) - 2 = 37?   *struck*
2. Is (15 / 5) + 2 = 5?   *frosting*
3. Is (16 x 2) + 1 = 25?   *story*

<u>Recall set</u>: struck, frosting, story
(Set size varies from 2 to 6)

SOURCE: Courtesy of Anna T. Cianciolo.

Engle and his colleagues argued, therefore, that domain-free controlled attention is the essence of working-memory limitations and drives the relationship between measures of working memory and measures of intelligence. They claimed that controlled attention activates information, either from the immediate environment or from long-term memory, and maintains that information in memory while it is being processed, particularly in the face of distraction. Tuholski, Engle, and Baylis (2001) found that performance on the operation span test could predict distractibility on a computerized counting task, indicating the role of controlled attention in reducing the impact of distraction.

Regardless of disagreement over the nature of working-memory limitations, the work of both Daneman and her colleagues and Engle and his colleagues clearly indicates that the storage aspect of memory alone does not account for its strong relationship to complex cognition. Daneman and Carpenter (1980) found that performance on the reading span test correlated substantially with verbal Scholastic Assessment Test (SAT) scores and reading comprehension, whereas a test of verbal storage—memorizing a list of words—showed only moderate correlations with SAT scores and reading comprehension. Consistent with these findings, Engle and his colleagues (1999) used structural equation modeling techniques to demonstrate that working memory had a stronger correlation with general reasoning than did short-term storage. They also showed that working-memory measures were better predictors of verbal and quantitative SAT scores than was short-term storage.

The Role of Knowledge and Skills

An emerging interest in understanding everyday cognitive functioning has turned the focus of some researchers to the role of long-term knowledge and skills in the memory system. These researchers are wary of experimental results based on performance on simple laboratory tasks such as simple mental calculations. They argue that, in typical college student samples, such tasks highlight working memory demands at the expense of acquired knowledge and experience, which is a critical aspect of everyday functioning. Instead, they study how highly developed skills and knowledge influence memory performance.

Anders Ericsson and Peter Delaney (1999) proposed that the functioning of the working-memory system during highly skilled performance is determined by specialized encoding and retrieval mechanisms formed over extended periods of practice. They claimed that individuals use these mechanisms to encode information from the environment into long-term memory to enable efficient and extensive retrieval of this information later on. These mechanisms allow the individual to demonstrate an unexpectedly large skill-specific memory capacity because of the ready availability of information relevant to that skill that readily available in long-term memory.

Ericsson and Delaney found support for their theory in the verbalizations of memory experts, people who, through training, have developed above-average memory skills. These verbal reports indicated that memory experts use existing knowledge to encode information into larger chunks for later retrieval. For example, to memorize a very large string of digits, one expert reported encoding the digits as mile running times and retrieving the digit string as groups of digits rather than as individual numbers. When digits were presented in such a way that they could not be associated with existing knowledge (e.g., they would make nonsensical running times), there was no expansion of memory. In addition, Ericsson and Delaney reported that chess experts not only encoded individual chess pieces according to meaningful configurations but also developed retrieval structures associated with locations on the chessboard.

Although memory assessment is still a critical aspect of commercial intelligence tests, such as the WAIS-III and its companion Wechsler Memory Scale (WMS), memory testing has changed. In contrast to the WAIS-R, the WAIS-III no longer features digit span as a mandatory test, but it does feature several additional tests of working memory. Also consistent with the findings of recent research, the WMS features tests of immediate, delayed, and working memory. Instead of reflecting a static storage capacity, the memory aspect of modern intelligence tests now reflects the dynamic functioning of a complex, multifaceted information-processing system. Such changes in memory and intelligence testing indicate growing understanding of the critical role of information processing in complex cognition.

Bibliography

Atkinson, R. C., and Shiffrin, R. M. (1968). Working memory. In G. H. Bower, ed., *The psychology of learning and motivation: Advances in research and theory*, Vol 2. New York: Academic Press.

Baddeley, A. D., and Carpenter, P. A. (1980). Individual differences in working memory and reading. *Journal of Verbal Learning and Verbal Behavior 19*, 450–466.

Baddeley, A. D., and Hannon, B. (2001). Using working memory theory to investigate the construct validity of multiple-choice reading comprehension tests such as the SAT. *Journal of Experimental Psychology: General 130*, 208–223.

Baddeley, A. D., and Hitch, G. (1974). Working memory. In G. H. Bower, ed., *The psychology of learning and motivation: Advances in research and theory*, Vol. 2. New York: Academic Press.

Baddeley, A. D., and Logie, R. H. (1999). Working memory: The multiple-component model. In A. Miyake and P. Shah, eds., *Models of working memory: Mechanisms of active maintenance and executive control.* Cambridge, UK: Cambridge University Press.

Daneman, M. (1991). Working memory as a predictor of verbal fluency. *Journal of Psycholinguistic Research 20*, 445–464.

Ellis, N., and Meador, D. M. (1985). Forgetting in retarded and nonretarded persons under conditions of minimal strategy use. *Intelligence 9*, 87–96.

Engle, R. W., Kane, M. J., and Tuholski, S. W. (1999). Individual differences in working memory capacity and what they tell us about controlled attention, general fluid intelligence, and functions of the prefrontal cortex. In A. Miyake and P. Shah, eds., *Models of working memory: Mechanisms of active maintenance and executive control.* Cambridge, UK: Cambridge University Press.

Engle, R. W., Tuholski, S. W., Laughlin, J. E., and Conway, A. R. A. (1999). Working memory, short-term memory and general fluid intelligence: A latent variable approach. *Journal of Experimental Psychology: General 128*, 309–331.

Ericsson, K. A., and Delaney, P. F. (1999). Long-term working memory as an alternative to capacity models of working memory in everyday skilled performance. In A. Miyake and P. Shah, eds., *Models of working memory: Mechanisms of active maintenance and executive control.* Cambridge, UK: Cambridge University Press.

Jarrold, C., Baddeley, A. D., and Hewes, A. K. (2000). Verbal short-term memory deficits in Down Syndrome: A consequence of problems in rehearsal? *Journal of Child Psychology and Psychiatry and Allied Disciplines 41*, 223–244.

Kyllonen, P. C. (1996). Is working memory capacity Spearman's g? In I. Dennis and P. Tapsfield, eds., *Human abilities: Their nature and measurement.* Mahwah, NJ: Erlbaum.

——— (2002). 'g:' knowledge, speed, strategies, or working-memory capacity? A systems perspective. In R. J. Sternberg and E. L. Grigorenko, eds., *The general factor of intelligence: How general is it?* Mahwah, NJ: Erlbaum.

Kyllonen, P. C., and Stephens, D. L. (1990). Cognitive abilities as determinants of success in acquiring logic skill. *Learning and Individual Differences 2*, 29–160.

Miyake, A., and Shah, P. (1999). Toward unified theories of working memory. In A. Miyake and P. Shah, eds., *Models of working memory: Mechanisms of active maintenance and executive control.* Cambridge, UK: Cambridge University Press.

Tuholski, S. W., Engle, R. W., and Baylis, G. C. (2001). Individual differences in working memory capacity and enumeration. *Memory & Cognition 29*, 484–492.

Turner, M. L., and Engle, R. W. (1989). Is working memory capacity task dependent? *Journal of Memory and Language 28,* 127–154.

Anna T. Cianciolo
Robert J. Sternberg

INTERFERENCE AND FORGETTING

Human long-term memory is characterized by a nearly limitless storage capacity. At any time, however, much of the information that exists in long-term memories (names, numbers, facts, procedures, events, and so forth) is not recallable. Why do people forget information that was once recallable? Because access to information in memory is subject to interference from competing information in memory. Before characterizing such interference processes in more detail, it is necessary to introduce some terminology.

The first concept is *transfer.* After some early point in life, people rarely, if ever, learn anything that is entirely new. Rather, people bring to any "new" learning of knowledge or skills an accumulation of related knowledge, skills, and habits from the past. Such prior learning influences the qualitative and quantitative character of the new learning process. Such transfer effects may be positive or negative, depending on whether prior experiences facilitate or impair the new learning process.

The second concept is *retroactive interference.* Whereas transfer refers to the effect of earlier learning on later learning, retroaction refers the impact of interpolated (intervening) learning experiences on one's memory for something teamed earlier. Once again, such effects may be positive or negative (retroactive facilitation and interference, respectively), depending on the similarity of the original and interpolated learning tasks. It is the negative case—where retroactive interference causes forgetting—that applies to this discussion. Thus, if one's ability to recall the maiden name of a woman friend is impaired by virtue of having learned her married name, one is suffering from retroactive interference.

The third concept is *proactive interference.* Something learned earlier may also impair one's ability to recall something learned more recently. If, for example, one is less able to recall a woman friend's married name by virtue of having learned her maiden name at an earlier time, one is suffering from proactive interference.

A Brief History of Research on Forgetting

Rigorous research on the possible causes of forgetting dates back to the turn of the twentieth century when two German researchers, Georg Elias Müller and A. Pilzecker, first demonstrated retroactive interference under controlled conditions. The history of that research interests contemporary scientists, partly because it is a case where intuition proved a poor guide to theorizing.

Early Theories That Proved Inadequate

Consolidation. Müller and Pilzecker (1900) found that subjects' memory for a series of nonsense syllables (consonant-vowel-consonant nonword syllables, such as DAX) was impaired by subsequent activity, such as learning a new series of nonsense syllables (compared with a condition where subjects simply rested for a similar period of time). They put forward a perseveration-consolidation hypothesis to explain their results. They argued that the changes in the nervous system that result in true learning are not complete by the end of training—that activity in the brain perseverates after learning, and that during that perseveration the memory traces corresponding to learning are consolidated. A subsequent activity, particularly if demanding and close in time to the original learning task, can disrupt the perseveration process, resulting in retroactive interference.

The consolidation idea seems plausible, especially given the evidence that certain traumas, such as electroconvulsive shock or a head injury, can produce retrograde amnesia (loss of memory for events occurring just prior to the injury), and that a period of sleep after a learning session produces less forgetting than does a comparable period of waking activity. The consolidation hypothesis proved unsatisfactory, however, because it does not provide an account for a variety of empirical phenomena. Long after the perseveration-consolidation process should be complete, for example, interpolated learning still produces substantial retroactive interference. Other problematic findings are that increasing the intensity of an unrelated interpolated activity results in little or no increase in forgetting, whereas increasing intertask similarity does play an important role in forgetting. A final blow for the theory is that it cannot explain proactive interference.

Decay. An explanation of forgetting that seems particularly plausible was put forth by Edward Thorndike (1914) as his so-called law of disuse. The thrust of his "law" is straightforward: Unless a person continues to access and use the memory representations corresponding to skills and information, those representations decay. Learning processes create memory representations; practice maintains those representations; but they fade with disuse.

The decay theory seems in general agreement with the average person's introspections as to how memories are formed and lost, but it proved entirely inadequate as a theory of forgetting. Thorndike's law was thoroughly discredited in a devastating critique by John McGeoch (1932). Among the problems with the theory are that forgetting is a function not simply of disuse across some retention interval but also of the nature of the activity in that interval, particularly its similarity to what is being remembered; information appears not to be lost from memory in some absolute sense, as implied by the theory, but, rather, becomes nonrecallable except under special circumstances; and it does not account for proactive interference.

The Emergence of Interference Theory

As an alternative to the consolidation and decay ideas, McGeoch (1932, 1942) put forth the initial version of what came to be called interference theory. That theoretical framework, as modified and refined over subsequent decades, constitutes the most significant and systematic theoretical formulation in the field of human learning and memory.

Reproductive Inhibition. McGeoch argued that human memory is fundamentally associative—that recall is guided by cues or stimuli to which items in memory are associated. As a consequence of a given individual's various experiences, however, multiple items in memory (responses) may become associated to the same cue. The recall of a given target response to a given cue, then, can suffer competition from other responses associated to that cue. Such competition, according to McGeoch, produces forgetting through reproductive inhibition: Recall of the target response is blocked or inhibited by the retrieval of other responses associated to that cue. Those other responses may have been learned before or after the response in question (proactive and retroactive interference, respectively), and such interference should be a function of intertask similarity across learning episodes.

Another factor in forgetting, according to McGeoch, is that the stimulus conditions existing at the time recall is tested will differ from the conditions that existed during training. Such differences are likely to increase as the interval from training to test grows longer; and to the degree the stimulus conditions at test do differ they will become less effective as cues for the response that was the target of training.

Unlearning and Spontaneous Recovery. In a pivotal study, Arthur W. Melton and J. M. Irwin (1940) took issue with McGeoch's analysis of retroactive interference. In their experiment, subjects learned two similar lists of verbal items and then were asked to relearn the first list. They found that the retroactive interference caused by the second list was, as predicted, an increasing function of the number of learning trials on the second list, but that the frequency of overt intrusions of second-list items during the relearning of the first list actually decreased with high levels of training on the second list. They argued that response competition could not, therefore, be the sole factor contributing to retroactive interference, because such intrusions are a straightforward measure of such competition. They proposed a second factor: unlearning of first-list responses during second-list learning. Their idea, which must have seemed somewhat bizarre, is analogous to a basic result in the animal-learning literature: Learned responses are gradually extinguished when no longer reinforced by a reward of some kind. From that perspective, intrusions of first-list responses during second-list learning constitute unreinforced errors.

As if the unlearning idea were not strange enough by itself, it had an additional counterintuitive implication: If unlearning is analogous to experimental extinction, then—as in animal-learning research—the unlearned responses should show spontaneous recovery over time. That is, the unlearned responses should recover—become more available in memory—as time passes following the retroactive learning episode. Such an implication seems to violate a law or first principle of memory—namely, that items in memory become less available with time. However unintuitive the unlearning/spontaneous recovery idea may seem, research carried out over the twenty years or so following the Melton and Irwin (1940) paper provided unambiguous support for the basic idea (see Barnes and Underwood, 1959; Briggs, 1954; Underwood, 1957).

By the late 1960s the basic interplay of proactive and retroactive interference had become clear. The dynamics of that interplay are summarized in the next section of this entry. More complete versions of the history and final state of "classical" research on interference and forgetting are available in Roberta Klatzky (1980), Gordon Bower and E. Hilgard (1981), Robert Crowder (1976), and Leo Postman (1971).

The Dynamics of Interference and Forgetting

Figure 1 summarizes the dynamics of interference and forgetting. Assume that the original learning episode involves learning to associate each member, B, of a set of responses with a particular member, A, of a set of stimuli. Assume further that the new (interpolated) learning episode involves associating each member, D, of a different set of responses with a particular member, A', of a set of stimuli that may vary from being only generally similar to the A stimuli to being essentially identical. At the time memory is tested, assume that a given member of stimulus set A or A' is presented as a cue for the associated B or D response.

Figure 1

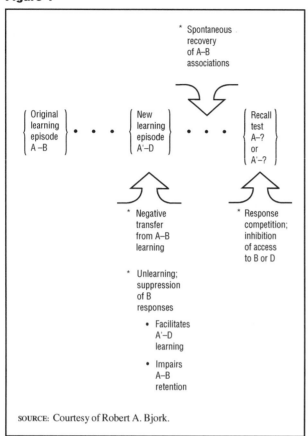

* Spontaneous recovery of A–B associations

Original learning episode A –B   · · ·   New learning episode A'–D   · · ·   Recall test A–? or A'–?

* Negative transfer from A–B learning

* Response competition; inhibition of access to B or D

* Unlearning; suppression of B responses

• Facilitates A'–D learning

• Impairs A–B retention

SOURCE: Courtesy of Robert A. Bjork.

Summary of the processes underlying proactive and retroactive interference; A-B and A'-D denote associative learning tasks in which A and A' are similar or identical stimuli and B and D are different responses.

The A-B, A'-D notation is meant to be interpreted quite broadly. A given stimulus might be a person's face and the response that person's name, for example, and the number of A-B and A'-D pairings to be learned might vary from one of each to some large number (as in the case of a grade-school teacher learning the names of the students in each year's class). In certain cases the stimulus might actually correspond to a configuration of stimuli and the response might be a coordinated set of verbal or motor responses (A-B and A'-D, e.g., could refer to learning to operate two different automobiles, the first in the United States and the second in England). The time course of the A-B and A'-D learning episodes might vary from brief to very extended (as would be the case if A-B denotes learning to label objects in a first language and A'-D denotes learning to label those same objects in a second language).

Unlearning

During the new learning episode (A'-D), competing responses from the original learning episode (A-B) are gradually suppressed or extinguished. Such suppression facilitates A'-D learning by reducing the negative transfer from competing B responses, but it also impairs any subsequent efforts to recall B responses. On the basis of a considerable body of research (particularly McGovern, 1964; Postman et al., 1968), it appears that—depending on the relationship of the stimulus-response pairings in the two learning episodes—one or more of three distinct types of unlearning may take place. Forward associations (from A to B) can be unlearned (which facilitates A'-D learning), backward associations (from B to A) can be unlearned (which would, for example, facilitate C-B learning, where C denotes stimuli that are not similar to A), and the entire set of B responses can be suppressed (which would aid A'-D or C-D learning).

Spontaneous Recovery

During the retention interval following A'-D learning (typically filled with other real-world activities on the part of the learner) the A-B associations that were suppressed during A'-D learning gradually recover in strength. Any other preexperimental associations to a given A or A' stimulus that may have been learned prior to A-B or A'-D learning will recover in strength as well.

Thus, at the end of A'-D learning, the D responses will be highly accessible in memory and the B responses will be relatively inaccessible (the exact ratio of B and D strengths will depend, of course, on the initial levels of A-B and A'-D learning, and on the overlap of the A and A' stimuli). As the retention interval from the end of A'-D learning increases, however, the pattern changes: The D responses become less recallable as the interval increases, and the B responses become relatively or absolutely more recallable. Whether the B responses themselves become more recallable in absolute terms appears to depend on whether those responses are also in competition with other (recovering) responses learned prior to the A-B episode. If a given A-B association is itself subject to proactive interference from one or more prior associations (A-E, A-F, and so forth), recall of the B response will tend to decrease, not increase, as the retention interval increases.

As the B responses (and any other prior associations to a given A' stimulus) recover, recall of the D responses will suffer increasing proactive interference. One implication of such recovery is that the rate of forgetting of D responses after A'-D training should be a function of the number of preceding similar lists a subject has learned. In an analysis of the results of many experiments reported in the literature, Underwood (1957) found striking support for that prediction.

Response Competition

At the time a given A or A' stimulus is presented as a cue for recall of the appropriate B or D response learned earlier, that target response will be in competition with any other responses associated to that stimulus. The impact of that competition is to inhibit access to the target response in memory. In general, recall of a given target response will decrease as the number and strength of competing responses increases. That generalization, in more modern terms, is the cue-overload principle (Watkins and Watkins, 1975). In the analysis of such response competition, however, an important distinction is relevant. It is the functional stimulus, not the nominal stimulus, that cues the retrieval of items in memory. Thus, A and A' may be nominally identical or highly similar stimuli, but if the learning episodes involving those stimuli differ substantially—in terms of the environmental, temporal, or social context, or even in terms of the learner's emotional or physical state—the functional encoding of those stimuli may differ markedly. Thus, any stimulus, together with the context in which it is embedded, offers the learner a variety of aspects that may be "sampled" (Estes, 1955) or attended to, and that process determines the functional encoding of a given stimulus.

Consistent with the foregoing analysis, the degree to which different learning episodes result in later response competition depends on how discriminable—on one basis or another—those episodes are from each other at the time of test. The more such episodes are separated from each other temporally, for example, the less they will interfere with each other (Underwood and Ekstrand, 1967).

Retrieval as a Memory Modifier

The results of research conducted in the late twentieth century add to the body of research. There is abundant evidence that the recall process alters the relative accessibility of items in memory. The act of recall is itself a learning event in the sense that an item recalled in response to a given cue becomes more recallable in the future. One consequence of such response-produced strengthening of future access to recalled items, however, is that other items associated with that cue may become less recallable. That is, the recall process can alter the pattern of relative access strengths across the set of items associated to a given cue.

Output Interference and Part-List Cuing

Consistent with the foregoing argument, there is evidence that recall is a "self-limiting process" (Roediger, 1978). Attempts to recall the members of a category or list of items occasion difficulty in recall-ing all the items in that set that exist in memory because the early items recalled impede the recall of subsequent items; having been recalled, the early items become more accessible in memory and block access to yet-to-be-recalled items.

Similar dynamics are probably at work in the inhibitory consequences of part-list cuing. When some members of a list or category of items are presented to subjects as cues to aid their recall of the remaining items, the recall of those remaining items is typically hindered rather than helped. Such inhibitory effects, considered an "enigma" in memory research (Nickerson, 1984), are at least in part a consequence of the cued items becoming too available in memory.

Retrieval-Induced Forgetting

The negative consequences of retrieval have been examined more explicitly via a retrieval-practice paradigm introduced by M. C. Anderson, R. A. Bjork, and E. L. Bjork (1994). The procedure includes an initial study phase, during which a number of category-exemplar pairs (such as Fruit-*Orange*) are presented. Typically, about forty-eight pairs are presented, which might be composed, for instance, of six exemplars of each of eight categories. There is then a retrieval-practice phase, during which participants are cued to recall, in response to cues such as Fruit-*Or____*, half of the exemplars of half of the studied categories multiple times. Finally, after a retention interval of twenty minutes or so, a surprise test is administered during which participants are presented each of the category names and asked to recall all of the exemplars they can remember having been paired with that name during the study phase.

Not surprisingly, the practiced members of practiced categories are recalled better on the final test than are corresponding unpracticed members of unpracticed categories. In contrast, the unpracticed members of practiced categories are actually recalled worse than are corresponding unpracticed members of unpracticed categories. That is, there seems to be retrieval-induced forgetting of exemplars that are in the same category as the practiced exemplars, but are not themselves practiced.

The findings obtained with various versions of the retrieval-practice paradigm suggest that retrieval-induced forgetting is a consequence of suppression of not-to-be-recalled exemplars during the retrieval-practice phase. Thus, correctly recalling "Orange" in response to a cue such as Fruit-*Or____* requires not only selecting from among the studied items the fruit that fits "*Or____*," but also not recalling (suppressing) other studied exemplars in the fruit category, such as "Banana." M. C. Anderson and B. A. Spellman (1995) have suggested that such selection-suppression processes are simiar to those known to categorize human attention and that retrieving targeted information from memory requires a type of conceptually focused attention, one consequence of which is retrieval-induced forgetting of unselected items.

Conclusion

Interference and transfer are fundamental to human learning, memory, and performance. After a period of almost twenty years, from roughly 1970 to 1990, during which research on interference and forgetting was not a dominant theme in experimental psychology, there has been a resurgence of interest in such phenomena. Several contributing factors in that resurgence can be mentioned. First, there is renewed evidence of and appreciation for the role inhibitory processes play in human cognition. Second, in certain applied fields, such as research on memory factors in advertising and witness testimony, there is a need to understand how successive inputs to memory compete and interact. In research on witness memory, for example, an issue of intense concern is how memory representations are modified by misleading postevent information. Third, among researchers who are working to implement and test various types of mathematical and computer models of human memory there is a growing realization that any plausible model must account for the basic patterns of proactive and retroactive interference (Mensink and Raaijmakers, 1988).

Forgetting is not simply a failure or weakness of the memory system. In terms of the overrall functioning of the system, there must be some means of restricting what is retrieved in response to a given cue: Information that is out of date or inappropriate needs to be suppressed, segregated, or eliminated. During the attempt to recall one's home phone number, or where one left the car, for example, it is not useful to retrieve one's prior home phone number, or where one left the car yesterday or a week ago. In short, in terms of speed and accuracy of the recall process, one does not want everything that exists in one's memory to be accessible, especially given the essentially unlimited capacity of human memory.

There are clearly some adaptive functions of the interference mechanisms that underlie forgetting. As a person continues to learn and continues to use new information, for example, access to the out-of-date information it replaces is inhibited. Such retrieval inhibition has several advantages over the kind of destructive updating of memory characteristic of computers (Bjork, 1989). Because the old information is inhibited, it tends not to interfere with the recall of the new information, but because that informa-

tion still exists in memory—in contrast to overwritten items in a computer's memory—it tends to be recognizable and readily relearned should the need arise. Finally, should one stop using the new information (e.g., how to drive in Britain), there will be some recovery of the old information (e.g., how to drive in the United States), which will often be adaptive as well.

In general, it appears that differences in accessibility across the vast number of items in memory acts as a kind of filter. The information and skills most readily accessible in human memories will tend to be those people have been using in the recent past. On a statistical basis, those are the same skills and knowledge people will tend to need in the near future

See also: FORGETTING; MCGEOCH, JOHN A.; MEMORY CONSOLIDATION: PROLONGED PROCESS OF REORGANIZATION; MÜLLER, GEORG ELIAS; RECONSTRUCTIVE MEMORY; THORNDIKE, EDWARD

Bibliography

Anderson, M. C., Bjork, R. A., and Bjork, E. L. (1994). Remembering can cause forgetting: Retrieval dynamics in long-term memory. *Journal of Experimental Psychology: Learning, Memory, and Cognition 20,* 1,063–1,087.

Anderson, M. C., and Spellman, B. A. (1995). On the status of inhibitory mechanisms in cognition: Memory retrieval as a model case. *Psychological Review 102,* 68–100.

Barnes, J. M., and Underwood, B. J. (1959). Fate of first-list associations in transfer theory. *Journal of Experimental Psychology 58,* 97–105.

Bjork, R. A. (1989). Retrieval inhibition as an adaptive mechanism in human memory. In H. L. Roediger and F. I. M. Craik, eds., *Varieties of memory and consciousness: Essays in honour of Endel Tulving.* Hillsdale, NJ: Erlbaum.

Bower, G. H., and Hilgard, E. R. (1981). *Theories of learning,* 5th edition. Englewood Cliffs, NJ: Prentice-Hall.

Briggs, G. E. (1954). Acquisition, extinction and recovery functions in retroactive inhibition. *Journal of Experimental Psychology 47,* 285–293.

Crowder, R. G. (1976). *Principles of learning and memory.* Hillsdale, NJ: Erlbaum.

Estes, W. K. (1955). Statistical theory of spontaneous recovery and regression. *Psychological Review 62,* 145–154.

Klatzky, R. L. (1980). *Human memory: Structures and processes,* 2nd edition. San Francisco: Freeman.

McGeoch, J. A. (1932). Forgetting and the law of disuse. *Psychological Review 39,* 352–370.

—— (1942). *The psychology of human learning.* New York: Longmans, Green.

McGovern, J. B. (1964). Extinction of associations in four transfer paradigms. *Psychological Monographs 78* (16, whole no. 593).

Melton, A. W., and Irwin, J. M. (1940). The influence of degree of interpolated learning on retroactive inhibition and the overt transfer of specific responses. *American Journal of Psychology 53,* 173–203.

Mensink, G. J., and Raaijmakers, J. G. W. (1988). A model for interference and forgetting. *Psychological Review 93,* 434–455.

Müller, G. E., and Pilzecker, A. (1900). Experimentelle Beiträge zur Lehre von Gedächtnis. *Zeitschrift für Psychologie 1,* 1–300.

Nickerson, R. S. (1984). Retrieval inhibition from partlist cuing: A persisting enigma in memory research. *Memory & Cognition 12,* 531–552.

Postman, L. (1971). Transfer, interference, and forgetting. In J. W. Kling and L. A. Riggs, eds., *Woodworth and Schlosberg's experimental psychology*, 3rd edition. New York: Holt, Rinehart and Winston.

Postman, L., Stark, K., and Fraser, J. (1968). Temporal changes in interference. *Journal of Verbal Learning and Verbal Behavior 7*, 672–694.

Roediger, H. L. (1978). Recall as a self-limiting process. *Memory & Cognition 6*, 54–63.

Thorndike, E. L. (1914). *The psychology of learning*. New York: Teachers College Press.

Underwood, B. J. (1957). Interference and forgetting. *Psychological Review 64*, 49–60.

Underwood, B. J., and Ekstrand, B. R. (1967). Studies of distributed practice: XXIV: Differentiation and proactive inhibition. *Journal of Experimental Psychology 74*, 574–580.

Watkins, O. C., and Watkins, M. J. (1975). Buildup of proactive inhibition as a cue-overload effect. *Journal of Experimental Psychology: Human Learning and Memory 104*, 442–452.

Robert A. Bjork

INVERTEBRATE LEARNING

[*Invertebrates are particularly useful for analyzing the neural and molecular events underlying learning and memory. The nervous systems of many invertebrates contain only several thousand cells (compared with the billions of cells in the vertebrate nervous system). Despite the small number of cells, an invertebrate ganglion can control a variety of behaviors. A given behavior may, therefore, be mediated by 100 or fewer neurons, and this small size of the circuit makes complete description easier. Moreover, many neurons are relatively large and can be repeatedly identified as unique individuals, permitting one to examine the functional properties to a specific behavior mediated by the cell. Changes in cellular properties that occur when a behavior is modified by learning can then be related to specific changes in behavior. Molecular and biophysical events underlying the changes in cellular properties can then be determined. This approach has been particularly successful with the bee and the mollusks* Aplysia, Hermissenda, Limax, *and* Tritonia.

Invertebrates are also excellent subjects for a genetic dissection of behavior and learning and memory. Two animals that have been particularly useful are the fruit fly Drosophila *and the worm* C. elegans. *The basic strategy is to alter the genotype with a mutagen and to test for specific defects in the ability of the animals to learn or remember. The role of individual biochemical processes and genes then can be related to specific aspects of learning and memory.*

The entries that follow discuss each of these invertebrates except APLYSIA, *which is the subject of a separate section. For additional information on insect species, see* INSECT LEARNING.]

ASSOCIATIVE LEARNING AND MEMORY PROCESSING IN BEES

The social life of the honeybee colony forms the ecological framework for the individual animal's behavior and is crucial for each bee's survival, because an individual bee cannot exist on its own (Frisch, 1967; Lindauer, 1967).

Associative Learning

The study of learning and memory formation in bees under natural conditions has focused on latent learning during navigation and on operant learning in the context of food collection. In the laboratory it has focused on appetitive classical conditioning. Bees departing from the hive perform observatory learning flights (Capaldi et al., 2000), and establish a map-like spatial memory for their colony's location relative to landmarks within the framework of their sun compass system (Menzel et al., 2000). When a searching bee discovers a nectar- or pollen-producing flower, it quickly learns to associate the surrounding visual and olfactory signals with the reward. It learns olfactory stimuli (e.g., floral odorants) and colors very quickly (within one or a few learning trials). Patterns need more learning trials. Whereas latent learning during navigational tasks may not require a rewarding stimulus, reward learning is a forward-associative process because signals perceived before the reward are associated, whereas those perceived during the reward or during the departure flight are associated less effectively or not at all.

Research on various operant learning phenomena (e.g. reversal and multireversal learning, overlearning, inhibitory learning, context-dependent learning, and reward schedule learning) has found performances similar to those in mammals (Couvillon and Bitterman, 1988; Menzel, 1990). Multiple experience with varying signals but one constant feature (e.g., different kinds of symmetrical patterns) leads to the formation of a concept (the concept of symmetry) that allows the bee to choose new patterns with the same feature as learned targets (Giurfa, Eichmann, and Menzel, 1996). Bees also develop a concept of sameness and difference when they are trained in delayed matching-to-sample tasks, in which they are required to respond to a matching stimulus or a nonmatching stimulus (Giurfa et al., 2001). They also transfer the learned rules to new stimuli of the same or a different sensory modality. Thus, not only can bees learn specific objects and their physical parameters, but they also extract rules and apply them to novel situations.

Classical Conditioning

Classical conditioning of reflexes is a convenient way to study the behavioral and neural mechanisms of associative learning. In the honeybee, the proboscis-extension reflex (PER) to a sucrose stimulus at the antennae is a reliable reflex in the context of feeding. A hungry bee will reflexively extend its proboscis (tongue) when the antennae are touched with a drop of sucrose solution. An odor (conditioned stimulus, CS) presented shortly before the sucrose reward (unconditioned stimulus, US) will be associated with the reward, even under conditions in which the animal is harnessed in a tube or is being prepared for physiological studies (Menzel and Müller, 1996). The associative nature of PER conditioning to odors has been established by demonstrating that only forward-pairing of CS-US sequences is effective. Unpaired CS and US presentations or CS- or US-only presentations do not lead to learning, and in differential conditioning (one odor CS+ paired with US, the other CS- unpaired), bees respond only to the CS+ and not to CS- (Menzel, 1990). The predictive value of the CS depends on the reliability with which it is causally related to the US. In differential conditioning, the reversal to the initially unpaired stimulus CS- is slower after more frequent unreinforced preexposures than after fewer preexposures. The same applies for US-only preexposures in an otherwise reinforced context, indicating that the absence of an expected US leads to inhibitory learning. If naive animals are stimulated with a compound of two odors and one of them is later associated with sucrose reward, the animals will also respond the second odor of the compound, even though this odor was not explicitly experienced during a learning trial (Müller et al., 2000). This form of learning (sensory preconditioning) indicates stimulus associations between equally evaluated stimuli and thus transcends the classical associative paradigm.

The role of reinforcement in the formation of an association is an essential question in learning theories: Are associations formed only by close contiguity between the CS and US? The blocking phenomenon indicates that this is not the case: If a novel CS appears together with a learned stimulus, this novel stimulus will be learned to a lesser extent or not at all (Kamin, 1968). The blocking paradigm is central to most current models of associative learning, and the phenomenon is explained either by the assumption of a competition between the two CSs (the already learned one and the novel one) for attention (Mackintosh, 1975) or for a limitation of reinforcing function that depends on the expectation or prediction of reinforcement (Rescorla and Wagner, 1972). Since attention, expectation and prediction are cognitive faculties, it is argued that cognitive capacities need to be introduced in theories about associative learning. It is thus interesting from a comparative point of view whether the bee with its tiny brain shows the blocking phenomenon. This question cannot yet be definitively answered. Blocking is found in some studies (Smith and Cobey, 1994; Thorn and Smith, 1997), but not in others (Gerber and Ullrich, 1999). Blocking across sensory modalities was also not seen in training free-flying bees (Bitterman, 1996; Funayama, Couvillon, and Bitterman, 1996). Second-order conditioning is another procedure that tests whether associative learning requires contiguity between CS and US. In a positive outcome of second-order conditioning one argues that a CS can acquire the potential of a US. This has been demonstrated for olfactory PER conditioning (Menzel, 1990).

Rules of elementary associative learning assume that in learning a compound stimulus, animals learn the associations between the reinforcer and the compound elements separately (Rescorla and Wagner, 1972). Contrary to this assumption, configural learning theories assume that, in learning a compound, animals build a new entity made from the conjunction of compound elements and that a connection is made between this new configuration and the reinforcer (Rudy and Sutherland, 1992). The different processing strategies underlying elementary and configural olfactory learning were studied by the negative patterning discrimination. In negative patterning two single stimuli are reinforced (A+, B +), while the compound is not (AB-). Solving this problem—responding less to the compound than to the single elements—can be explained only by taking configural associations into account. Otherwise, summation of the elementary associative strengths in the compound should result in stronger response to the compound than to the elements. Honeybees can solve negative patterning discrimination in olfactory conditioning of the PER (Deisig, Lachnit, Hellstern, and Giurfa, 2001). The fact that bees solve negative patterning discrimination in olfactory conditioning and in color/odor tasks (Couvillon and Bitterman, 1988) shows that linear associations between single stimuli and the reinforcer are not the only ones underlying associative learning in honeybees (Giurfa et. al, 2001).

Memory Dynamics and Memory Localization

Memory is an animal's capacity to retain acquired information and to use it for future behavior. In the context of association theory, memory is the potential of a conditioned stimulus to activate an established associative link. Some researchers, however, view learning as acquiring information rather than responses, in which case memory would be a dynamic and self-

Figure 1

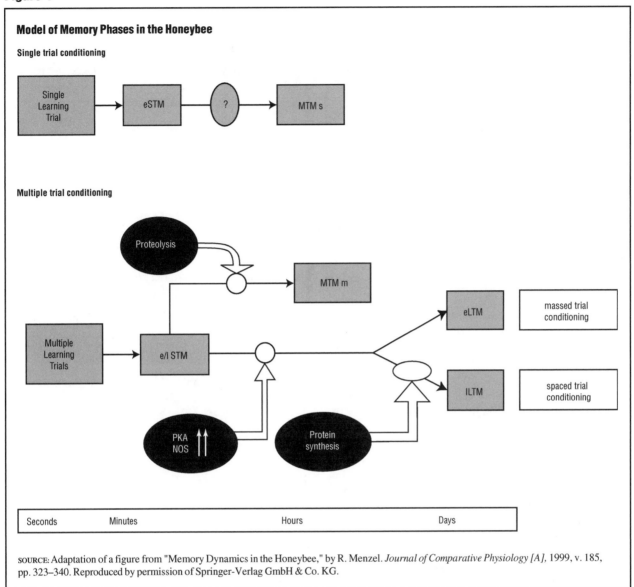

Model of Memory Phases in the Honeybee

Single trial conditioning

Multiple trial conditioning

SOURCE: Adaptation of a figure from "Memory Dynamics in the Honeybee," by R. Menzel. *Journal of Comparative Physiology [A]*, 1999, v. 185, pp. 323–340. Reproduced by permission of Springer-Verlag GmbH & Co. KG.

A single learning trial leads to an early form of short-term memory (eSTM) that is accompanied by a short enhancement of PKA and PKC activity. Consolidation to mid-term memory after a single trial (MTMs) is a time-dependent process lasting several minutes. The molecular and cellular events related to the transition from eSTM to MTMs are unknown (see ?). MTMs decays after several hours but retention is still significant after one day, indicating that even a single trial can induce longer-lasting forms of memory to a low degree. Multiple learning trials lead to a succession of four memory phases that are arranged partially sequentially and partially in parallel. Early and late STM (e/lSTM) are not separable, because consolidation is strongly facilitated by trial repetition, high retention rates within the acquisition process, and strong resistance to extinction and reversal trials even immediately after conditioning. e/lSTM is accompanied by stronger and longer-lasting PKA activation and an activation of NO synthase (NOS). Both cellular responses are required for the transition to LTM, but may not be necessary for MTM formation. Transition to MTM after multiple trials (MTMm) is accompanied by constitutive activation of PKM via a proteolytic pathway that is essential for MTMm formation. Blocking proteolysis, however, does not inhibit the transition to the two forms of long-term memory (LTM), indicating parallel pathways from STM to MTM and LTM. Inhibition of protein synthesis interferes only with the formation of lLTM. Massed conditioning leads predominantly to eLTM, spaced conditioning to lLTM.

organizing process of information storage. Support for such a cognitive interpretation of memory in the honeybee comes from the fact that olfactory memory formation is not identical to the process of acquisition. Memory needs time to develop and proceeds through phases that differ in their susceptibility to interfering events, their content, and their neural and cellular substrates (Menzel, 1999; Menzel and Müller, 1996; see Figure 1).

The memory trace for olfactory cues is distributed and involves two of the three convergence sites between the olfactory pathway and the reward pathway. The reward pathway was identified by Hammer (1993) and assigned to a single identified neuron, the VUM_{mx1} neuron. Two of the three convergence sites—antennal lobes and mushroom bodies—are, respectively, the primary and secondary processing regions in the olfactory pathway, and each of these two neuropils establishes its own memory trace independently of the other (Hammer and Menzel, 1998). The two traces are, however, different at least with respect to their dynamics, and are likely to store different information.

Researchers have made progress in unraveling the neural correlates of memory for the antennal lobe by visualizing the changes in odor coding as a consequence of olfactory conditioning (Faber, Joerges, and Menzel, 1999). The antennal lobe is organized into glomeruli; odors are coded as specific spatial-activation patterns of the glomeruli. These patterns can be imaged using calcium-sensitive fluorescent dyes. As a result of conditioning, the neural representation of a trained odor becomes more pronounced and more distinct from nonrewarded odors, but its general features do not change, indicating that learning at this level intensifies the neural code of the learned signal but does not create a new representation. It is unclear what specifies the odor-induced activity patterns as those of a learned odor, because a stronger stimulus also induces a more pronounced and distinct activity pattern, but bees have no trouble distinguishing between a strong nonlearned odor and a weak learned odor.

A stable, lifelong memory is formed even after only a few learning trials as the result of sequential steps of memory processing. Five memory stages are distinguishable on the basis of their respective temporal dynamics and their physiological and biochemical properties. The cellular and neural machinery underlying the memory stages is basically similar to those known for other model systems (*Aplysia:* Botzer, Markovich, and Susswien, 1998; Müller and Carew, 1998; *Drosophila:* Dubnau and Tully, 1998; *Chick:* Rose, 1991), although each model system has its own temporal dynamics. This indicates that the cellular and molecular machinery underlying the processing of associative memory follows general rules but is flexible enough to adapt to the particular timing required under natural conditions. Some researchers argue that the timing of memory stages in the honeybee reflects an adaptation to the requirements during for-

aging at distributed and unreliable food sources (e.g., flowers; Menzel, 1999; Giurfa et al., 2001).

Conclusion

The honeybee provides a model system for the study of neural substrates of low and intermediate levels of cognitive faculties. Neural analysis is supported by robust forms of associative learning that occur even under conditions when intracellular recordings or optophysiological measurements of single or multiple neuron activities are performed. The functional organization of the brain with a considerable number of uniquely identifiable neurons is also advantageous for relating cognitive functions to neural events in circumscribed circuits. Biochemical analyses of the role of protein kinases (e.g., PKA, PKC) and enzymes (e.g., NO synthase) relate directly to behavioral phenomena such as memory stages. Associative processes in the bee brain are not restricted to elementary forms but reflect configural processing and context-dependent associations. Thus the bee brain may serve as a model for the study of cognitive processes at an intermediate level of complexity.

See also: CONDITIONING, CELLULAR AND NETWORK SCHEMES FOR HIGHER-ORDER FEATURES OF; CONDITIONING, CLASSICAL AND INSTRUMENTAL; INSECT LEARNING; KAMIN'S BLOCKING EFFECT: NEURONAL SUBSTRATES; SECOND MESSENGER SYSTEMS

Bibliography

Bitterman, M. E. (1996). Comparative analysis of learning in honeybees. *Animal Learning Behavior 24,* 123–141.

Botzer, D., Markovich, S., and Susswein, A. J. (1998). Multiple memory processes following training that a food is inedible in *Aplysia. Learning and Memory 5,* 204–219.

Capaldi, E. A., Smith, A. D., Osborne, J. L., Fahrbach, S. E., Farris, S. M., Reynolds, D. R., Edwards, A. S., Martin, A., Robinson, G. E., Poppy, G. M., and Riley, J. R. (2000). Ontogeny of orientation flight in the honeybee revealed by harmonic radar. *Nature 403,* 537–540.

Couvillon, P.A., and Bitterman, M. E. (1988). Compound-component and conditional discrimination of colors and odors by honeybees: Further tests of a continuity model. *Animal Learning and Behavior 16,* 67–74.

Deisig, N., Lachnit, H., Hellstern, F., and Giurfa, M. (2001). Configural olfactory learning in honeybees: Negative and positive patterning discrimination. *Learning and Memory 8,* 70–78.

Dubnau, J., and Tully, T. (1998). Gene discovery in *Drosophila,* new insights for learning and memory. *Annual Review of Neuroscience 21,* 407–444.

Faber, T., Joerges, J., and Menzel, R. (1999). Associative learning modifies neural representations of odors in the insect brain. *Nature Neuroscience 2,* 74–78.

Funayama, E. S., Couvillon, P. A., and Bitterman, M. E. (1996). Compound conditioning in honeybees, blocking tests of the independence assumption. *Animal Learning and Behavior 23,* 429–437.

Gerber, B., and Ullrich, J. (1999). No evidence for olfactory blocking in honeybee classical conditioning. *Journal of Experimental Biology 202,* 1,839–1,854.

Giurfa, M., Eichmann, B., and Menzel, R. (1996). Symmetry perception in an insect. *Nature 382*, 458–461.

Giurfa, M., Zhang, S., Jenett, A., Menzel, R., and Srinivasan, M. V. (2001). The concepts of "sameness" and "difference" in an insect. *Nature 410*, 930–933.

Hammer, M. (1993). An identified neuron mediates the unconditioned stimulus in associative olfactory learning in honeybees. *Nature 366*, 59–63.

Hammer, M., and Menzel, R. (1998). Multiple sites of associative odor learning as revealed by local brain microinjections of octopamine in honeybees. *Learning and Memory 5*, 146–156.

Kamin, L. J. (1968). Attentionlike processes in classical conditioning. In M. R. Jones, ed., *Miami symposium on predictability, behavior and aversive stimulation*. pp. 9–32. Miami, FL: University of Miami Press.

Mackintosh, N. J. (1975). A theory of attention: Variations in the associability of stimuli with reinforcement. *Psychology Review 82*, 276–298.

Menzel, R. (1990). Learning, memory, and "cognition" in honey bees. In R. P. Kesner and D. S. Olton, eds., *Neurobiology of comparative cognition*. Hillsdale, NJ: Erlbaum.

——— (1999). Memory dynamics in the honeybee. *Journal of Comparative Physiology[A] 185*, 323–340.

Menzel, R., Brandt, R., Gumbert, A., Komischke. B., and Kunze, J. (2000). Two spatial memories for honeybee navigation. *Proceedings of the Royal Society of London B 267*, 961–968.

Menzel, R., and Giurfa, M. (2001). Cognitive architecture of a mini-brain: The honeybee. *Trends in Cognitive Sciences 5*, 62–71.

Menzel, R., and Müller, U. (1996). Learning and memory in honeybees: From behavior to neural substrates. *Annual Review of Neuroscience 19*, 379–404.

Müller, D., Gerber, B., Hellstern, F., Hammer, M., and Menzel, R. (2000). Sensory preconditioning in honeybees. *Journal of Experimental Biology 203*, 1,351–1,364.

Müller, U., and Carew, T. J. (1998). Serotonin induces temporally and mechanistically distinct phases of persistent PKA activity in *Aplysia* sensory neurons. *Neuron 21*, 1,423–1,434.

Rescorla, R.A., and Wagner, A. R. (1972). A theory of classical conditioning: Variations in the effectiveness of reinforcement and non-reinforcement. In A. H. Black A.H. and W. F. Prokasy, eds., *Classical conditioning II: Current research and theory*. New York: Appleton-Century-Crofts.

Rose, S. P. R. (1991). How chicks make memories: The cellular cascade from c-fos to dendritic remodelling. *Trends in Neurosciences 14*, 390–397.

Rudy, J. W., and Sutherland, R. J. (1992). Configural and elemental associations and the memory coherence problem. *Journal of Cognitive Neuroscience 4*, 208–216.

Smith, B. H., and Cobey, S. (1994). The olfactory memory of the honey bee, *Apis mellifera*. II: Blocking between odorants in binary mixtures. *Journal of Experimental Biology 195*, 91–108.

Thorn, R. S., and Smith, B. H. (1997). The olfactory memory of the honeybee *Apis mellifera*, III. Bilateral sensory input is necessary for induction and expression of olfactory blocking. *Journal of Experimental Biology 200*, 2,045–2,055.

Randolf Menzel

ASSOCIATIVE LEARNING IN HERMISSENDA

Few features of conscious experience have captured the human imagination more than the proclivity of animals to learn and to retain the consequences of experience in memory. Learning not only provides for the adaptation of organisms to changing environmental demands, but also, and more important, for the persistence of learning—that is, long-term memory—which provides us with a history of human experience. In spite of the widespread interest in learning and memory, their basic mechanisms remain among the least thoroughly understood areas of physiology.

An attractive experimental approach to this problem at a fundamental level is the analysis of learning and memory in the less-complex central nervous system of invertebrates. One animal that has contributed to the physiology of learning and memory is the nudibranch mollusk *Hermissenda crassicornis*, whose behavior can be modified by a Pavlovian conditioning procedure. The *Hermissenda* central nervous system is relatively simple, consisting of many identifiable neurons that can be studied in detail using biochemical, biophysical, and molecular techniques. An additional advantage is that the two sensory structures and their central pathways supporting the conditioned stimulus (CS) and unconditioned stimulus (US) are totally intact in the isolated central nervous system. This attractive feature facilitates the search for cellular correlates of learning that have been identified and have been the focus of biochemical and molecular analyses.

Pavlovian Conditioning

Pavlovian conditioning of *Hermissenda* involves changes in light-elicited locomotion and foot length (conditioned responses, CRs) produced by stimulation of the visual and vestibular systems with their adequate stimuli (Crow and Alkon, 1978; Lederhendler, Gart, and Alkon, 1986). The Pavlovian conditioning procedure consists of pairing light, the conditioned stimulus (CS), with high-speed rotation, the unconditioned stimulus (US). As shown in Figure 1, after conditioning, the CS suppresses normal light-elicited locomotion and elicits foot shortening. Retention of conditioned behavior persists for several days to weeks depending upon the number of conditioning trials used in initial acquisition (Alkon, 1989; Crow and Alkon, 1978). Pavlovian conditioning in *Hermissenda* exhibits CS specificity and is dependent upon the association of the two sensory stimuli involving both contiguity and contingency. Crow and Offenbach (1983) showed that conditioned animals exhibit suppressed locomotor behavior in the presence of the CS; however, their locomotor behavior in the dark was not significantly changed. Nonassociative contributions to behavior are expressed in the initial trials of the conditioning session and the decrement rapidly following the termination of multitrial conditioning.

In addition to multiple-trial conditioning of suppression of light-elicited locomotion and foot contraction, one-trial conditioning also modifies light-elicited locomotion (Crow and Forrester, 1986). Pairing the CS with the direct application of one of the transmitters of the US pathway (serotonin 5-HT, nominal US) to the exposed nervous system of otherwise intact *Hermissenda* produces suppression of light-elicited locomotion when the animals are tested twenty-four hours following the one conditioning trial. One-trial conditioning also produces enhanced excitability of type-B photoreceptors (see Figure 1), a component of the CS pathway that expresses cellular plasticity produced by multitrial Pavlovian conditioning (discussed further below).

Cellular and Synaptic Plasticity Associated with Pavlovian Conditioning

An essential step in the analysis of Pavlovian conditioning is the search for the loci in the animal's nervous system where memories of the associative experience are stored. Crow and Alkon (1980) identified the primary sensory neurons (photoreceptors) of the pathway mediating the CS as one site for memory storage. Intrinsic modifications of cellular and synaptic plasticity in classically conditioned animals involve both enhanced excitability and synaptic facilitation of connections between sensory neurons in the pathway mediating the CS (Alkon, 1989; Crow and Alkon, 1980; Frysztak and Crow, 1994). Enhanced excitability in identified photoreceptors of conditioned *Hermissenda* is expressed by a significant increase in spike activity elicited by the CS or extrinsic current, an increase in the input resistance, an alteration in the amplitude of light-elicited generator potentials, decreased spike frequency accommodation, and a reduction in the peak amplitude of voltage-dependent (I_A, I_{Ca}) and Ca^{2+}-dependent ($I_{K,Ca}$) currents (Alkon et al., 1985; for reviews, see Alkon, 1989; Crow, 1988; Sahley and Crow, 1998). Enhanced excitability, expressed by an increase in both the amplitude of CS-elicited generator potentials and the number of action potentials elicited by the CS, may be a major contributor to changes in the duration and amplitude of CS-elicited complex postsynaptic potentials (PSPs) and enhanced CS-elicited spike activity observed in postsynaptic targets. However, changes in the strength of synaptic connections between identified type-B photoreceptors and other components of the CS pathway have also been detected following conditioning (Frysztak and Crow, 1994).

Facilitation of the amplitude of unitary inhibitory postsynaptic potentials (IPSPs) elicited by single spikes in identified type-B photoreceptors are detected in type-A photoreceptors and type-I_ii interneurons

of conditioned animals (see Figure 1). Facilitation of type-I_e interneuron EPSPs (excitatory postsynaptic potentials) elicited by lateral type-B spikes is also observed following conditioning. Studies of the signal transduction pathways responsible for the modification of diverse K^+ currents of type-B photoreceptors of conditioned animals have identified several second messenger systems. Both protein kinase C (PKC) (Farley and Auerbach, 1986; Crow et al., 1991) and extracellular signal-regulated protein kinase (ERK) (Crow et al., 1998) contribute to modifications of excitability and synaptic efficacy of conditioned *Hermissenda*. A second site of cellular plasticity in conditioned animals is the type-A photoreceptor. Lateral type-A photoreceptors of conditioned animals exhibit an increase in CS-elicited spike frequency, a decrease in generator potential amplitude, and enhanced excitability and decreased spike frequency accommodation to extrinsic current (Frysztak and Crow, 1993). Taken collectively, the evidence for localization of cellular changes in the CS pathway indicates that multiple sites of cellular and synaptic plasticity involving changes in both excitability and synaptic strength exist in the photoreceptors and interneurons of conditioned animals (see Figure 1). Anatomical studies of type-B photoreceptors indicate the existence of spatially segregated compartments (Alkon, 1989). Phototransduction occurs in the soma-rhabdomeric compartment, spike generation in the distal axon, and synaptic interactions in the axon terminal regions within the cerebropleural neuropil. Therefore, a decrease in K^+ conductances of type-B photoreceptors could contribute both directly and indirectly to enhanced excitability by increasing the amplitude of CS-elicited generator potentials and increasing CS-elicited spike activity in the spike-generating zone by modification of conductance that influence the interspike interval.

Mechanisms of Memory Consolidation Underlying Pavlovian Conditioning

Studies of memory have identified components of memory consolidation that can be differentiated based upon the contribution of signal transduction pathways, protein synthesis, and gene induction (for review, see DeZazzo and Tully, 1995). An analysis of one-trial conditioning in *Hermissenda* has provided insights into the mechanisms of different stages of memory consolidation. One-trial conditioning produces long-term suppression of light-elicited locomotion (Crow and Forrester, 1986) and short-term and long-term enhancement of excitability in sensory neurons of the CS pathway (Crow and Forrester, 1991, 1993). Short-term and long-term enhanced excitability appear to be independent, parallel process-

Figure 1

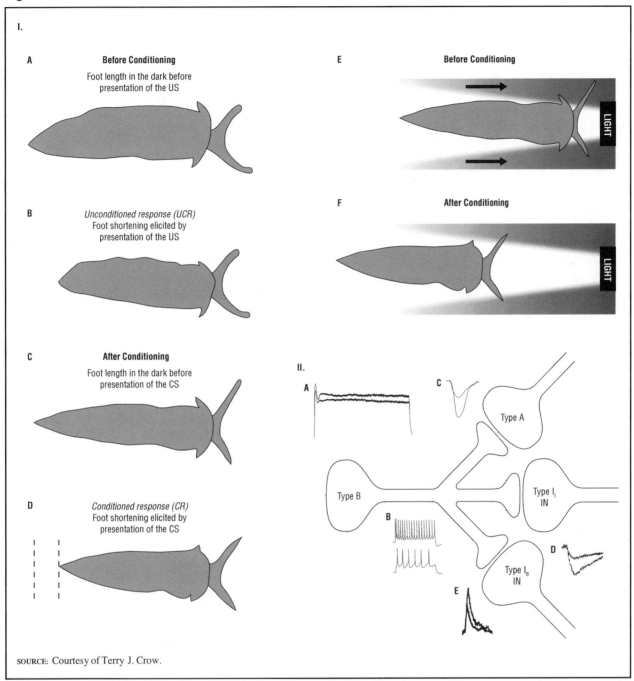

SOURCE: Courtesy of Terry J. Crow.

I. Pavlovian-conditioned foot-shortening and conditioned suppression of light-elicited locomotion of Hermissenda. A. Foot length in the dark before presentation of the unconditioned stimulus (US). B. The unconditioned response (UCR) elicited by rotation (US) of the animal in the dark. C. Foot length in the dark after Pavlovian conditioning before presentation of the light (CS). D. Conditioned response (CR), foot-shortening elicited by presentation of the CS. The area indicated between the dashed lines in D represents the magnitude of foot-shortening elicited by the CS after conditioning. E. Light-elicited locomotion towards a light source assessed before conditioning. F. Suppression of light-elicited locomotion detected after Pavlovian conditioning. Pseudorandom or random presentations of the CS and US do not result in the development of suppression of either light-elicited locomotion or CS-elicited foot shortening. II. Components of the CS pathway that express plasticity in conditioned Hermissenda. A. The CS elicits a larger amplitude generator potential (upper trace) recorded from type B photoreceptors as compared to pseudorandom controls (lower trace). B. An extrinsic current pulse elicits more action potentials in type B photoreceptors from conditioned preparations as compared to pseudorandom controls. C. Conditioning results in facilitation of the synaptic connections between type B photoreceptors and type A photoreceptors and type B photoreceptors and type Ii and Ie interneurons D. E. as compared to control animals that received pseudorandom presentations of the CS and US.

es, because long-term enhanced excitability can be expressed in the absence of prior short-term enhanced excitability (Crow and Forrester, 1993). Moreover, enhanced excitability in type-B photoreceptors follows a biphasic pattern in its development following one-trial conditioning. Excitability reaches a peak three hours after one-trial conditioning, declines toward baseline control levels five to six hours after conditioning, and is followed by an increase to a stable plateau at sixteen to twenty-four hours post-conditioning. In addition, one-trial conditioning produces an intermediate stage of memory that depends on translation but not transcription, whereas long-term memory for enhanced excitability depends upon both translation and transcription (Crow and Forrester, 1990; Crow, Xue-Bian, and Siddiqi, 1999).

Associated with intermediate memory is the phosphorylation of a 24 kDa protein (CSP24). A one-trial conditioning procedure that only produces short-term memory does not result in the increased phosphorylation of CSP24 (Crow and Xue-Bian, 2000). Therefore, the regulation of this phosphoprotein by one-trial conditioning is associated with experimental conditions that produce intermediate and long-term memory. The protein-synthesis inhibitor anisomycin, present during the intermediate phase of memory, blocked the increased phosphorylation of CSP24 but did not block the increased phosphorylation of other proteins associated with one-trial conditioning (Crow, Xue-Bian, and Siddiqi, 1999). Experiments examining ^{35}S-methionine labeling of CSP24 during the intermediate phase of memory showed similar labeling of CSP24 for the conditioned group and unpaired controls. However, both conditioned and unpaired groups were greater than unstimulated controls with respect to ^{35}S-methionine labeling of CSP24. Therefore the requirement for protein synthesis is necessary but not sufficient for long-term associative memory, or it may reflect an indirect involvement in phosphorylation due to changes in the synthesis of protein kinases in signal transduction pathways or phosphatase inhibitors. Experiments where CSP24 was excised from multiple two-dimensional gels and subjected to reverse phase HPLC (high pressure liquid chromatography) and automated sequence analysis showed that the sequenced peptides exhibited a homology to the β-thymosin family of actin-binding proteins (Crow and Xue-Bian, 2000). All known vertebrate and invertebrate β-thymosins bind actin monomers (Nachimias, 1993). Cytoskeletal-related proteins such as CSP24 thus may contribute to long-term structural remodeling in the CS pathway by regulating the turnover of actin filaments during the intermediate-term transition period between short- and long-term memory.

Conclusion

One-trial and multi-trial Pavlovian conditioning produce changes in both synaptic efficacy and cellular excitability in several identified neurons of the pathway supporting the CS. Activation of PKC and ERK is produced by both one-trial and multi-trial Pavlovian conditioning of *Hermissenda*. Enhanced cellular excitability expressed by CS-elicited spike activity or extrinsic current results from the reduction in several K+ conductances in type-B photoreceptors of conditioned animals. Studies of memory formation in *Hermissenda* have shown that intermediate and long-term memory produced by one-trial conditioning involves the synthesis and phosphorylation of cellular proteins. One protein, CSP24, a β-thymosin-like protein associated with intermediate memory, is regulated by conditioning and may contribute to reorganization of the actin cytoskeleton underlying structural remodeling supporting long-term memory.

See also: SECOND MESSENGER SYSTEMS

Bibliography

Alkon, D. L. (1989). Memory storage and neural systems. *Scientific American 261* (1), 42–50.

Alkon, D. L., Sakakibara, M, Forman, R., Harrigan. J., Lederhendler, I., and Farley, J. (1985). Reduction of two voltage-dependent K+ currents mediates retention of a learned association. *Behavioral and Neural Biology 44*, 278–300.

Crow, T. (1988). Cellular and molecular analysis of associative learning and memory in *Hermissenda*. *Trends in Neurosciences 11*, 136–142.

Crow, T., and Alkon, D. L. (1978). Retention of an associative behavioral change in *Hermissenda*. *Science 201*, 1,239–1,241.

—— (1980). Associative behavioral modification in *Hermissenda*: Cellular correlates. *Science 209*, 412–414

Crow, T., and Forrester, J. (1986). Light paired with serotonin mimics the effects of conditioning on phototactic behavior in *Hermissenda*. *Proceedings of the National Academy of Sciences of the United States of America 83*, 7,975–7,978.

—— (1990). Inhibition of protein synthesis blocks long-term enhancement of generator potentials produced by one-trial in vivo conditioning in *Hermissenda*. *Proceedings of the National Academy of Sciences of the United States of America 87*, 4,490–4,494.

—— (1991). Light paired with serotonin in vivo produces both short- and long-term enhancement of generator potentials of identified B-photoreceptors in *Hermissenda*. *Journal of Neuroscience 11*, 608–617.

—— (1993). Down-regulation of protein kinase C and kinase inhibitors dissociate short- and long-term enhancement produced by one-trial conditioning of *Hermissenda*. *Journal of Neurophysiology 69*, 636–641.

Crow, T., Forrester, J., Williams, M., Waxham, N., and Neary, J. (1991). Down regulation of protein kinase C blocks 5-HT-induced enhancement in *Hermissenda* B photoreceptors. *Neuroscience Letters 121*, 107–110.

Crow, T., and Offenbach, N. (1983). Modification of the initiation of locomotion in *Hermissenda*: Behavioral analysis. *Brain Research 271*, 301–310.

Crow, T. J., and Xue-Bian, J. J. (2000). Identification of a 24 kDa phosphorylation associated with an intermediate stage of memory in *Hermissenda*. *Journal of Neuroscience 20* (10), RC74, 1–5.

Crow, T., Xue-Bian, J. J., and Siddiqi, V. (1999). A protein synthesis-dependent and mRNA synthesis-independent intermediate phase of memory in *Hermissenda*. *Journal of Neurophysiology 82* (1), 495–500.

Crow, T., Xue-Bian, J. J., Siddiqi, V., Kang, Y., and Neary, J. T. (1998). Phosphorylation of mitogen-activated protein kinase by one-trial and multi-trial classical conditioning. *Journal of Neuroscience 18* (9), 3,480–3,487.

DeZazzo, J., and Tully, T. (1995). Dissection of memory formation from behavioral pharmacology to molecular genetics. *Trends in Neuroscience 18*, 212–218.

Farley, J., and Auerbach, S. (1986). Protein kinase C activation induces conductance changes in *Hermissenda* photoreceptors like those seen in associative learning. *Nature 319*, 220–223.

Frysztak, R. J., and Crow, T. (1993). Differential expression of correlates of classical conditioning in identified medial and lateral type-A photoreceptors of *Hermissenda*. *Journal of Neuroscience 13* (7), 2,889–2,897.

——— (1994). Enhancement of type-B- and type-A photoreceptor inhibitory synaptic connections in conditioned *Hermissenda*. *Journal of Neuroscience 14* (3), 1,245–1,250.

Lederhendler, I., Gart, S., and Alkon, D. L. (1986). Classical conditioning of *Hermissenda*: Origin of a new response. *Journal of Neuroscience 6*, 1,325–1,331.

Nachmias, V. T. (1993). Small actin-binding proteins: the β-thymosin family. *Current Opinion in Cell Biology 5*, 56–62.

Sahley, C., and Crow, T. (1998). Invertebrate learning: Current perspectives. In J. Martinez and R. Kesner, eds., *Neurobiology of Learning and Memory*, pp. 171–209. New York: Academic Press.

Terry J. Crow

ASSOCIATIVE LEARNING IN LIMAX

Given the goal of understanding the cellular basis of associative learning (Kandel, 2001), comparative physiology seeks to identify a brain donor with highly developed associative learning and a nervous system well suited to biophysical analysis. Early work made clear that the central neurons and networks of gastropod mollusks were particularly favorable for the cellular analysis of synaptic plasticity and behavioral control. With this background we chose to explore the odor-learning ability of the terrestrial gastropod mollusk *Limax maximus*, which has large central neurons that are useful for studies of calcium transients during single-action potentials (Chang et al., 1974), neural control of heart rate (MacKay and Gelperin, 1972), cellular analysis of [³H]-2-deoxyglucose uptake (Sejnowski et al., 1980), neural control of feeding motor programs (Prior and Gelperin, 1977; Delaney and Gelperin, 1990c), and serotonergic modulation of feeding motor programs (Gelperin, 1981).

Learning cued by olfactory stimuli was chosen because olfactory systems in a wide variety of species can modify their input-output functions, linking odors to behaviors in ways that depend on previous olfactory experience. Synaptic plasticity and learning are essential components of olfactory information processing from mollusks to mammals (Hudson, 1999). Plasticity can be induced by passive exposure to odors or by arranging stimulus contingencies in which odors predict the presence or absence of other stimuli or rewards (Sahley, 1990; Eichenbaum, 1998; Slotnick et al., 2000). The ample evidence of plasticity in olfactory processing systems over wide phyletic boundaries suggested that *Limax* would be a good candidate for behavioral assessment of odor learning. I will emphasize here recent work in the *Limax* odor-learning system and related work on olfactory learning in closely related species— *Helix*, for example—which has appeared since my previous review (Gelperin, 1992).

Limax is an odor-dominated species dependent on olfaction for finding food, mates, and homesites (Gelperin, 1974). Associative learning about odor cues is rapid (Gelperin, 1975; Teyke, 1995) and shows several higher-order contingencies such as compound conditioning, second-order conditioning, and blocking (Sahley, 1990; Sekiguchi et al., 1991; Yamada et al., 1992; Sekiguchi et al., 1994; Suzuki et al., 1994; Sekiguchi et al., 1997). Appetitive conditioning can modify feeding behavior so that previously aversive odors become attractive (Sahley et al., 1992; Gelperin, 1999). The reliable and robust nature of odor conditioning in *Limax*, combined with the complex nature of the logic operations performed during odor conditioning (Gelperin et al., 1986) prompted an exploration of the central circuits for odor processing.

Central Olfactory Centers

Primary and second-order input from olfactory receptors projects to a distinctive integrative center, the procerebral (PC) lobe of the cerebral ganglion (Chase, 2000), where some 10^5 interneurons process olfactory inputs (Ratté and Chase, 1997, 2000) and may store odor memories (Kimura et al., 1998a; Nakaya et al., 2001). Our initial search for the central site of odor learning therefore focused on the PC lobe, which has oscillatory dynamics of its local field potential (LFP) (Gelperin and Tank, 1990; Kawahara et al., 1997) and propagates activity waves along its apical-basal axis (Delaney et al., 1994).

Because odor-memory coding in the PC lobe depends on the dynamics of wave propagation, it is important to understand the mechanism of wave initiation and propagation. The PC lobe contains a small (1–2 percent) population of bursting inhibitory neurons (Watanabe, 1998) that seem to couple to each other by electrical and excitatory chemical synapses (Ermentrout et al., 2001). Two-photon laser-scanning microscopy has discerned two populations of inhibitory-bursting neurons, differing in the speed and direction of propagation of calcium-based action potentials in their neurites (Wang et al., 2001). The bursting inhibitory neurons produce chloride-mediated inhibitory synaptic potentials in the major population of nonbursting neurons (Watanabe et al., 1999). The population of bursting inhibitory neurons shows a gradient of excitability from the apex to the base of the PC, such that bursting occurs first in the most apical bursting neurons and then, because of excitatory coupling between bursting neurons, propagates along the apical-basal axis to the base of the PC lobe, where the activity wave ends. The gradient of excitability is shown by taking a series of transverse slices of the PC lobe along the apical-basal axis and measuring the frequency of spontaneous oscillations of the LFP in each slice. The most apical slice oscillates fastest, the most basal slice oscillates slowest, and the intermediate slices have intermediate oscillation frequencies, depending on their apical-basal position.

There is evidence of the apical-basal activity wave in two-site LFP measurements made simultaneously in apical and basal recording sites (Ermentrout et al., 1998; Gelperin et al., 2001) or in optical recordings where voltage-sensitive or calcium-sensitive dyes stain PC neurons. Sequential images of the PC lobe based on the calcium or voltage signals show the initiation of the activity wave at the apex and its propagation to the base (Kleinfeld et al., 1994; Toda et al., 2000; Nikitin and Balaban, 2001b). The LFP signal at a particular site along the apical-basal axis is produced by the simultaneous generation of a 5–7-mV inhibitory synaptic potential in a large number of nonbursting neurons by synaptic divergence from the local bursting neurons. The oscillatory nature of the LFP derives from the periodic nature of the activity wave in the bursting neurons propagating past a particular recording site along the apical-basal axis. Oscillatory dynamics is a universal feature of olfactory analyzers in mollusks, arthropods, and vertebrates (Tank et al., 1994; Gelperin, 1999; Laurent, 1999) and may contribute an essential temporal component to the odor code.

Odor-Memory Storage in the Procerebral Lobe

Learning-dependent labeling of a band of nonbursting PC neurons after one-trial odor conditioning provides some of the most direct evidence that odor memories are stored in the PC lobe (Kimura et al., 1998a; Gelperin, 1999). The learning-dependent labeling has been demonstrated as a consequence of both aversive and appetitive one-trial odor conditioning. The slug is given a single training trial with odor as a positive or negative conditioned stimulus, and then, twenty minutes after the conditioning trial, the animal receives an injection of with Lucifer yellow (LY) into the blood space. The hour-long interval that begins twenty minutes after the conditioning trial is when the short-term memory of odor conditioning is converted to a long-term form (Sekiguchi et al., 1991; Sekiguchi et al., 1994; Sekiguchi et al., 1997). The LY in the PC neuron somata after conditioning is contained in membrane-bound vesicles, as in the original reports of "activity-dependent" LY labeling in fly retina (Wilcox and Franceschini, 1984), perhaps because of an activity-dependent pinocytotic process. The causal coupling between electrical, synaptic, or biochemical events in the labeled neurons and pinocytotic uptake of LY is unknown.

The striking feature of the learning-dependent labeling in the *Limax* PC lobe is that various control procedures, such as odor presentation alone, which do not allow learning to occur, do not lead to LY labeling (Kimura et al., 1998a). If two odors are used as separate conditioned stimuli during training in the sequential aversive training trials, two LY-labeled bands appear in one PC lobe (Kimura et al., 1998a). The unilateral nature of the learning-dependent labeling was completely unexpected, but is also occurs in the replication and extension of the original work. (Gelperin, 1999) The existence of crossed inhibition between the right and left odor-processing circuits, demonstrated in an in vitro nose-brain preparation (Teyke et al., 2000), may explain why only one PC lobe is the dominant site of odor-memory storage.

The second major indication that the PC lobe is the likely site of odor-memory storage is that one-trial odor conditioning selectively activates a small set of genes in PC lobe neurons (Nakaya et al., 2001). Brain tissue from 200 *Limax* given one-trial odor conditioning was obtained, and differential mRNA expression was compared between this collection of learned brain and tissue from 200 brains of control animals given odor stimulation (CS) and an aversive unconditioned stimulus (US) with a CS-US delay too long to permit learning to occur (Gelperin, 1975). A gene coding for a twenty-three amino-acid peptide was identified, cloned, and sequenced and the deduced peptide was constructed for antibody production. The level of expression of the learning-activated gene was clearly enhanced selectively in neurons of the PC lobe in trained slugs relative to control slugs (Nakaya et al., 2001). The peptide is secreted to extracellular space and may play a role in stabilizing synapses, as suggested by recent work on cellular consequences of learning in *Drosophila* (Connolly and Tully, 1998).

Modulation of Procerebral Lobe Dynamics

The PC lobe has both intrinsic and extrinsic synaptic modulation using twenty-one known and putative neurotransmitters (Gelperin, 1999), notably nitric oxide (NO) (Gelperin, 1999), carbon monoxide (Gelperin et al., 2000), acetylcholine (Watanabe et al., 2001), dopamine (Gelperin et al., 1993; Rhines et al., 1993), serotonin (Yamane, 1989; Inoue, 2001), and glutamate (Watanabe et al., 1999), along with numerous small peptides such as FMRFamide and small cardioactive peptide B (Yamane and Gelperin, 1987; Cooke and Gelperin, 1988). It is therefore not surprising that recordings of PC lobe LFP in vivo using implanted fine-wire electrodes reveal a much richer range of activity than the isolated brain in vitro (Cooke and Gelperin, 2001). There are periods in vivo during which the 0.5–1.0 Hz oscillation of the PC LFP in vitro is recorded, but during other periods the diversity of LFP waveforms makes clear that the PC lobe has modes of activity in vivo not predicted from recordings in vitro.

The maintenance of LFP oscillations and therefore wave propagation is dependent on synthesis of NO in the Limax PC lobe. If NO synthesis is blocked in the terrestrial snail Helix by injecting a substituted arginine that blocks the activity of NO synthase, odor learning is blocked (Teyke, 1996). It is tempting to speculate that the dose of NO synthase blocker that blocks oscillatory dynamics in the PC lobe is also the dose that produces the odor-learning deficit. The Limax PC lobe stains intensely for nitric oxide synthase (Cooke et al., 1994; Gelperin et al., 2001). NO may set the level of bursting by the bursting neurons in the PC and hence determine the frequency of LFP oscillation and perhaps the rate of wave propagation (Inoue, 2001).

The use of olfactory nerve (ON) shock as a substitute for odor stimulation makes it is clear that odor inputs to the PC lobe have a phase-dependent effect on the bursting neurons (Inoue et al., 2000). Excitatory postsynaptic potentials (EPSPs) are recorded with short latency after ON shock in nonbursting neurons, while EPSPs with longer and variable latency are recorded in bursting neurons after ON shock. This procedure suggests a monosynaptic connection from fibers in the ON onto nonbursting PC neurons and an excitatory connection from nonbursting neurons onto bursting neurons. This direct excitation of nonbursting neurons by ON input is consistent with the known anatomy of the ON projection into the PC lobe as the ON fibers fill the neuropil of the PC lobe but do not project to the layer of neuronal somata (Gelperin and Flores, 1997; Kawahara et al., 1997). The neurites of the bursting PC neurons are confined to the layer of neuronal somata (Watanabe, 1998), so the bursting neurons cannot receive direct synaptic input from olfactory afferents. The demonstration that odor inputs can alter the frequency of the PC LFP (Gervais et al., 1996) must be due to odor inputs onto nonbursting neurons having indirect excitatory effects on bursting neurons.

Model of Odor Memory Formation

The current model of odor-memory band formation in the Limax PC lobe is summarized in Figure 1. The odor-memory bands have a bandlike shape because of the interaction of the wave front of the propagating-activity wave with the region of the PC most strongly driven by the odor used as the conditioned stimulus. The confluence of the activity wave-front and sensory drive from the odor produces a short-term memory of the odor. Behavioral evidence for the existence of a short-term odor memory comes from the finding that a brief odor stimulus can be given, and then, after tens of minutes, the delivery of unconditioned stimulus can still result in CS-US pairing (Gelperin, 1975). This long-delay or trace-conditioning aspect of odor conditioning is typical. The short-term odor memory is subsequently converted to a long-term odor memory because of the action of a modulatory transmitter liberated on the PC neurons storing the short-term memory as a consequence of application of the US.

We have elaborated the model to suggest that if two odors are learned, then the spacing of the two bands representing the odors will depend on the similarity of the two odors (see Figure 1). If the two odors are very similar (odor A and odor A'), then the odor-memory bands representing odor A and odor A' will be at the minimum interband spacing consistent with the ability to access the two memory bands individually and uniquely. If odor A is learned, if its odor memory band is formed, and then if wave propagation is blocked by blocking NO, then the brain will report that odor A' is the same as odor A (see Figure 1C). This result has been obtained with the isolated Limax nose-brain preparation (Teyke and Gelperin, 1999), whereas in honeybee blocking the oscillatory dynamics of the antennal lobe with picrotoxin produced the behavioral result that the bee could not discriminate between two similar odors but could discriminate between two very different odors (Stopfer et al., 1997). Blockade of NO synthase activity in honeybee antennal lobe impairs olfactory discrmination (Hosler et al., 2000).

PC Lobe Inputs and Outputs

Researchers have identified the nature of the behavioral modifications occurring during Helix food-

Figure 1

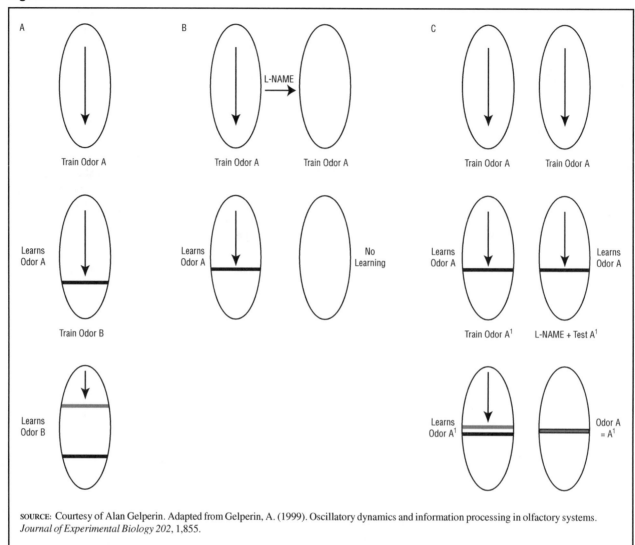

SOURCE: Courtesy of Alan Gelperin. Adapted from Gelperin, A. (1999). Oscillatory dynamics and information processing in olfactory systems. *Journal of Experimental Biology 202*, 1,855.

Diagram of a possible relationship between waves, odor memory bands, and odor discrimination. A. Forming odor memories for two dissimilar odors leads to two well-separated odor memory bands. B. Blocking of oscillations and waves in the procerebral lobe blocks odor learning. C. Learning two similar odors (A and A[1]) leads to the formation of two closely spaced odor memory bands. After learning odor A, if oscillations and waves are blocked, odor A[1] is not discriminated from odor A. Arrows signify the propagated activity wave. L-NAME, N_ω-nitro-L-arginine methyl ester.

odor conditioning and some of the motor pathways expressing the learned alteration in odor response (Peschel et al., 1996; Friedrich and Teyke, 1998). The same motor-output pathway that expresses odor learning in the *Helix*, the peritentacular nerves controlling the superior tentacle muscles, also expresses the modified motor output attributable to odor learning in the *Limax* (Teyke and Gelperin, 1999). Researchers have identified a neuron in the metacerebral lobe of the *Limax* PC lobe with a neurite in the PC lobe (Shimozone et al., 2001) that shows membrane potentials oscillations arising from input in the PC lobe. This neuron may convey PC-processed olfactory information to other chemointegrative sites in the cerebral ganglion, such as feeding command neurons.

The PC lobe receives inputs from other regions of the cerebral ganglion and from the tentacular ganglia adjacent to the olfactory receptor epithelia of the superior and inferior noses. The tentacular ganglia appear to have an oscillatory component to their LFP that is modulated by odor stimulation (Ito et al., 2001). The PC lobes contain neurites of neurons located in other parts of the cerebral ganglia (Ratté and Chase, 1997, 2000; Shimozone et al., 2001) and in the buccal (Gelperin and Flores, 1997) and pedal (Chase and Tolloczko, 1989) ganglia that provide the pathways for integrating olfactory information with other inputs to make behavioral decisions. Activation of the PC-connected buccal neurons can reset the PC LFP oscillation, whereas the pedal cells are activated by PC stimulation but cannot reset the LFP oscillation by their activity. The PC LFP oscillation can also be modulated by electrical stimulation of the digits of the tentacular ganglia (Ito et al., 1999), a result that may be due to the FMRFamide contained in some of the primary sensory neurons projecting through the tentacular ganglia to the PC lobe (Suzuki et al., 1997).

Imaging Odor Memories

A number of imaging studies have attempted to clarify the nature of odor responses in the PC lobe (Kleinfeld et al., 1994; Inoue et al., 1998; Toda et al., 2000; Nikitin and Balaban, 2001a), particularly after odor conditioning (Kimura et al., 1998c; Nikitin and Balaban, 2000). Initial studies on naïve preparations showed that odor stimulation led to a collapse of the apical-basal phase gradient for a few cycles after odor stimulation (Kleinfeld et al., 1994). Imaging studies of PC lobe dynamics after one-trial odor conditioning have provided evidence for regional localization of odor excitation (Kimura et al., 1998c). Recordings of PC lobe LFP oscillations after odor training also indicate regional localization of baseline shifts in response to application of conditioned odors (Kimura et al., 1998b). It would be interesting to know if the region of localized excitation to a conditioned odor corresponds to the region of learning-dependent LY labeling in the same slug.

Summary

The olfactory-processing system of the *Limax* displays many of the design features of other species, including receptor turnover (Chase and Rieling, 1986), central neurogenesis (Zakharov et al., 1998), oscillatory dynamics of central-processing centers (Gelperin, 1999), rapid and long-lasting learning (Delaney and Gelperin, 1986), extensive local-feedback synapses (Zs.-Nagy and Sakharov, 1970; Ratté and Chase, 2000), glomerular processing of some inputs (Chase and Tolloczko, 1986), nitric-oxide-dependent synaptic plasticity (Teyke, 1996), memory-dependent alterations in early-processing stages (Nakaya et al., 2001), and several dozen neurotransmitters and neuromodulators involved in experience-dependent circuit reconfiguration (Gelperin, 1999). The comparative approach has produced evidence that molluscan model systems can yield principles of synaptic plasticity and associative learning (Kandel, 2001). Future work in the *Limax* will extend this foundation, for example, by clarifying how the biochemical substrates

governing the transition from short-term memory to long-term memory (Burrell and Sahley, 2001; Sutton et al., 2001) are modified (Yin and Tully, 1996; Dubnau and Tully, 1998) to produce an odor-memory system wherein one-trial learning is the normal condition. Also, the learning-activated gene in the PC lobe has significant homology with gene sequences in zebrafish, mouse, and human, providing further support for the idea that molluscan model systems implement synaptic plasticity mechanisms of relevance to mammalian systems.

Bibliography

Burrell, B. D., and Sahley, C. L. (2001). *Learning in simple systems. Current Opinion in Neurobiology* 11, 757–764.

Chang J. J., Gelperin, A., and Johnson, F. H. (1974). Intracellularly injected aequorin detects trans-membrane calcium flux during action potentials in an identified neuron from the terrestrial slug, *Limax maximus. Brain Research* 77, 431–442.

Chase R (2000). Structure and function in the cerebral ganglion. *Microscopic Research Techniques* 49, 511–520.

Chase, R., and Rieling, J. (1986). Autoradiographic evidence for receptor cell renewal in the olfactory epithelium of a snail. *Brain Research 384*, 232–239.

Chase R., and Tolloczko, B. (1986). Synaptic glomeruli in the olfactory system of a snail. *Cell Tissue Research 246*, 567–573.

——— (1989). Interganglionic dendrites constitute an output pathway from the procerebrum of the snail *Achatina fulica. Journal of Comparative Neurology 283*, 143–152.

Connolly, J.B., and Tully, T. (1998). Integrins, a role for adhesion molecules in olfactory memory. *Current Biology 8*, R386–R389.

Cooke, I., and Gelperin, A. (1988). Distribution of FMRFamide-like immunoreactivity in the nervous system of the slug *Limax maximus. Cell Tissue Research 253*, 69–76.

Cooke, I. R. C., Edwards, S.L., and Anderson, C. R. (1994). The distribution of NADPH-diaphorase activity and immunoreactivity to nitric oxide synthase in the nervous system of the pulmonate mollusc *Helix aspersa. Cell Tissue Research 277*, 565–572.

Cooke, I. R. C., and Gelperin, A. (2001). In vivo recordings of spontaneous and odor-modulated dynamics in the *Limax* olfactory lobe. *Journal of Neurobiology 46*, 126–141.

Delaney, K., and Gelperin, A. (1986). Post-ingestive food-aversion learning to amino acid deficient diets by the terrestrial slug *Limax maximus. Journal of Comparative Physiology A 159*, 281–295.

——— (1990). Cerebral interneurons controlling fictive feeding in *Limax maximus*. III. Integration of sensory inputs. *Journal of Comparative Physiology A 166*, 327–343.

Delaney, K. R., Gelperin, A., Fee, M. S., Flores, J. A., Gervais, R., Tank, D.W., and Kleinfeld, D. (1994). Waves and stimulus-modulated dynamics in an oscillating olfactory network. *Proceedings of the National Academy of Sciences of the United States of America 91*, 669–673.

Dubnau J., and Tully, T. (1998). Gene discovery in *Drosophila:* New insights for learning and memory. *Annual Review of Neuroscience 21*, 407–444.

Eichenbaum, H. (1998). *Using olfaction to study memory. Annual of the New York Academy of Science 855*, 657–669.

Ermentrout, B., Flores, J., and Gelperin, A. (1998). Minimal model of oscillations and waves in the *Limax* olfactory lobe with tests of the model's predictive power. *Journal of Neurophysiology 79*, 2,677–2,689.

——— (2001). Model for olfactory discrimination and learning in *Limax* procerebrum incorporating oscillatory dynamics and wave propagation. *Journal of Neurophysiology 85*, 1,444–1,452.

Friedrich, A., and Teyke, T. (1998). Identification of stimuli and input pathways mediating food–attraction conditioning in the snail, *Helix. Journal of Comparative Physiology A 183*, 247–254.

Gelperin, A. (1974). Olfactory basis of homing behavior in the giant garden slug, *Limax maximus. Proceedings of the National Academy of Science of the United States of America 71*, 966–970.

——— (1975). Rapid food-aversion learning by a terrestrial mollusk. *Science 189*, 567–570.

——— (1981). Synaptic modulation by identified serotonergic neurons. In B. Jacobs and A. Gelperin, eds., *Serotonin Neurotransmission and Behavior*. Cambridge, MA: MIT Press.

——— (1992). Associative learning in *Limax*. In L. Squire, ed., *Encyclopedia of learning and memory*. New York: Macmillan.

——— (1999). Oscillatory dynamics and information processing in olfactory systems. *Journal of Experimental Biology 202*, 1,855–1,864.

Gelperin, A., and Flores, J. (1997). Vital staining from dye-coated microprobes identifies new olfactory interneurons for optical and electrical recording. *Journal of Neuroscience Methods 72*, 97–108.

Gelperin, A., Flores, J., Raccuia-Behling, F., and Cooke, I. R. C. (2000). Nitric oxide and carbon monoxide modulate oscillations of olfactory interneurons in a terrestrial mollusc. *Journal of Neurophysiology 83*, 116–127.

Gelperin, A., Hopfield, J. J., and Tank, D. W. (1986). The logic of *Limax* learning. In A. I. Selverston, ed., *Model neural networks and behavior*. New York: Plenum Press.

Gelperin, A., Kao, J. P. Y., and Cooke, I. R. C. (2001). Gaseous oxides and olfactory computation. *American Zoology 41*, 332–345.

Gelperin, A., Rhines, L., Flores, J., and Tank, D. (1993). Coherent network oscillations by olfactory interneurons: Modulation by endogenous amines. *Journal of Neurophysiology 69*, 1,930–1,939.

Gelperin, A., and Tank, D. W. (1990). Odor-modulated collective network oscillations of olfactory interneurons in a terrestrial mollusc. *Nature 345*, 437–440.

Gervais, R., Kleinfeld, D., Delaney, K. R., and Gelperin, A. (1996). Central and reflex neuronal responses elicited by odor in a terrestrial mollusc. *Journal of Neurophysiology 76*, 1,327–1,339.

Hosler, J. S., Buxton, K. L, and Smith, B. H. (2000). Impairment of olfactory discrimination by blockade of GABA and nitric oxide activity in the honeybee antennal lobes. *Behavioral Neuroscience 114*, 514–525.

Hudson, R. (1999). From molecule to mind, the role of experience in shaping olfactory function. *Journal of Comparative Physiology A 185*, 297–304.

Inoue, T., Kawahara, S., Toda, S., Watanabe, S., and Kirino, Y. (1998). Selective optical recording of the neural activity in the olfactory center of land slug using a calcium indicator dye. *Bioimages 6*, 59–67.

Inoue, T., Watanabe, S., Kawahara, S., and Kirino, Y. (2000). Phase-dependent filtering of sensory information in the oscillatory olfactory center of a terrestrial mollusk. *Journal of Neurophysiology 84*, 1,112–1,115.

Ito, I., Kimura, T., and Ito, E. (2001). Odor responses and spontaneous oscillatory activity in tentacular nerves of the terrestrial slug, *Limax marginatus. Neuroscience Letters 304*, 1,455–1,148.

Ito, I., Kimura, T., Suzuki, H., Sekiguchi, T., and Ito, E. (1999). Effects of electrical stimulation of the tentacular digit of a slug upon the frequency of electrical oscillations in the procerebral lobe. *Brain Research 815*, 121–125.

Kandel, E. R. (2001). The molecular biology of memory storage, a dialogue between genes and synapses. *Science 294*, 1,030–1,038.

Kawahara S., Toda, S., Suzuki, Y., Watanabe, S., and Kirino, Y. (1997). Comparative study on neural oscillation in the procerebrum of the terrestrial slugs Incilaria bilineata and *Limax marginatus. Journal of Experimental Biology 200*, 1,851–1,861.

Kimura, T., Suzuki, H., Kono, E., and Sekiguchi, T. (1998a). Mapping of interneurons that contribute to food aversion conditioning in the slug brain. *Learning and Memory 4*, 376–388.

Kimura T., Toda, S., Sekiguchi, T., Kawahara, S., and Kirino, Y. (1998c). Optical recording analysis of olfactory response of the procerebral lobe in the slug brain. *Learning and Memory 4*, 289–400.

Kimura, T., Toda, S., Sekiguchi, T., and Kirino, Y. (1998b). Behavioral modulation induced by food odor aversive conditioning and its influence on the olfactory responses of an oscillatory brain network in the slug *Limax marginatus. Learning and Memory 4*, 365–375.

Kleinfeld, D., Delaney, K. R, Fee, M. S., Flores, J. A., Tank, D. W., and Gelperin, A. (1994). Dynamics of propagating waves in the olfactory network of a terrestrial mollusc: An electrical and optical study. *Journal of Neurophysiology 72*, 1,402–1,419.

Laurent, G. (1999). A systems perspective on early olfactory coding. *Science 286*, 723–728.

MacKay, A., and Gelperin, A. (1972). Pharmacology and reflex responsiveness of the heart of the giant garden slug, *Limax maximus. Comparative Biochemistry and Physiology 43A*, 877–896.

Nakaya, T., Kawahara, S., Watanabe, S., Lee, D.-S., Suzuki, T., Kirino, Y. (2001). Identification and expression of a novel gene in odour-taste associative learning in the terrestrial slug. *Genes to Cells 6*, 43–56.

Nikitin, E. S., and Balaban, P. M (2000). Optical recording of odor-evoked responses in the olfactory brain of the naïve and aversively trained terrestrial snails. *Learning and Memory 7*, 422–432.

——— (2001a). Optical recording of responses to odor in olfactory structures of the nervolus system in the terrestrial mollusk *Helix. Neuroscience and Behavioral Physiology 31*, 21–30.

——— (2001b). Optical recording of responses to odor in olfactory structures of the nervous system in the terrestrial mollusk *Helix. Neuroscience and Behavioral Physiology 31*, 21–30.

Peschel, M., Straub, V., and Teyke, T. (1996). Consequences of food–attraction conditioning in *Helix*, A behavioral and electrophysiological study. *Journal of Comparative Physiology A 178*, 317–327.

Prior, D., and Gelperin, A. (1977). Autoactive molluscan neuron, Reflex function and synaptic modulation during feeding in the terrestrial slug *Limax maximus. Journal of Comparative Physiology 114*, 217–232.

Ratté, S., and Chase, R. (1997). Morphology of interneurons in the procerebrum of the snail *Helix aspersa. Journal of Compartive Neurology 384*, 359–372.

——— (2000). Synapse distribution of olfactory interneurons in the procerebrum of the snail *Helix aspersa. Journal of Comparative Neurology 417*, 366–384.

Rhines, L., Sokolove, P., Flores, J., Tank, D. W., and Gelperin, A. (1993). Cultured olfactory interneurons from *Limax maximus*, Optical and electrophysiological studies of transmitter-evoked responses. *Journal of Neurophysiology 69*, 1,940–1,947.

Sahley, C. L. (1990). The behavioral analysis of associative learning in the terrestrial mollusc *Limax maximus*, The importance of interevent relationships. In S. Hanson and C. Olson, eds., *Connectionist modeling and brain function: The developing interface*. Cambridge, MA: MIT Press.

Sahley, C. L., Martin, K. A., and Gelperin, A. (1992). Odors can induce feeding motor responses in the terrestrial mollusc *Limax maximus. Behavioral Neuroscience 106*, 563–568.

Sejnowski, T. J., Reingold, S. C., Kelley, D. B., and Gelperin, A. (1980). Localization of [³H]-2-deoxyglucose in single molluscan neurones. *Nature* 287, 449–451.

Sekiguchi, T., Yamada, A., and Suzuki, H. (1997). Reactivation-dependent changes in memory states in the terrestrial slug *Limax flavus*. *Learning and Memory 4*, 356–364.

Sekiguchi, T., Yamada, A., Suzuki, H., and Mizukami, A. (1991). Temporal analysis of the retention of a food-aversion conditioning in *Limax flavus*. *Zoological Science (Tokyo) 8*, 103–111.

Sekiguchi, T., Suzuki, H., Yamada, A., and Mizukami, A. (1994). Cooling-induced retrograde amnesia reflexes Pavlovian conditioning associations in *Limax flavus*. *Neuroscience Research 18*, 267–275.

Shimozone, S., Watanabe, S., Inoue, T., and Kirino, Y. (2001). Identification and characterization of an output neuron from the oscillatory molluscan olfactory network. *Brain Research 921*, 98–105.

Slotnick, B., Hanford, L., Hodos, W. (2000). Can rats acquire an olfactory learning set? *Journal of the Experimental Psychology of Animal Behavioral Process 26*, 399–415.

Stopfer, M., Bhagavan, S., Smith, B. H., and Laurent, G. (1997). Impaired odour discrimination on desynchronization of odour-encoding neural assemblies. *Nature 390*, 70–74.

Suttona, M.A., Masters, S. E., Bagnall, M. W., and Carew, T. J. (2001). Molecular mechanisms underlying a unique intermediate phase of memory in *Aplysia*. *Neuron 31*, 143–154.

Suzuki, H., Kimura,T., Sekiguchi. T., and Mizukami, A. (1997). FMRFamide-like-immunoreactive primary sensory neurons in the olfactory system of the terrestrial mollusc, *Limax marginatus*. *Cell Tissue Research 289*, 339–345.

Suzuki, H., Sekiguchi, T., Yamada, A., and Mizukami, A. (1994). Sensory preconditioning in the terrestrial mollusk, *Limax flavus*. *Zoological Science 11*, 121–125.

Tank, D. W., Gelperin, A., and Kleinfeld, D. (1994). Odors, oscillations, and waves, Does it all compute? *Science 265*, 1,819–1,820.

Teyke, T. (1995). Food-attraction conditioning in the Roman snail, *Helix pomatia*. *Journal of Comparative Physiology A 177*, 409–414.

——— (1996). Nitric oxide, but not serotonin, is involved in acquisition of food-attraction conditioning in the snail *Helix pomatia*. *Neuroscience Letters 206*, 29–32.

Teyke, T., and Gelperin, A. (1999). Olfactory oscillations augment odor discrimination not odor identification by *Limax* CNS. *NeuroReport 10*, 1,061–1,068.

Teyke, T., Wang, J. W., and Gelperin, A. (2000). Lateralized memory storage and crossed inhibition during odor processing by *Limax*. *Journal of Comparative Physiology A 186*, 269–278.

Toda, S., Kawahara, S., and Kirino, Y. (2000). Image analysis of olfactory responses in the procerebrum of the terrestrial slug *Limax marginatus*. *Journal of Experimental Biology 203*, 2,895–2,905.

Wang, J. W., Flores, J., Gelperin, A., and Denk, W. (2001). Initiation and propagation of calcium-dependent action potentials in a coupled network of olfactory interneurons. *Journal of Neurophysiology 85*, 977–985.

Watanabe S., Kawahara, S., and Kirino, Y. (1999). Glutamate induces Cl⁻ and K⁺ currents in the olfactory interneurons of a terrestrial slug. *Journal of Comparative Physiology A 184*, 553–562.

Watanabe, S., Inoue, T., Murakami, M., Inokuma, Y., Kawahara, S., and Kirino, Y. (2001). Modulation of oscillatory neural activities by cholinergic activation of interneurons in the olfactory center of a terrestrial slug. *Brain Research 896*, 30–35.

Wilcox, M., and Franceschini, N. (1984). Illumination induces dye incorporation in photoreceptor cells. *Science 225*, 851–854.

Yamada, A., Sekiguchi, T., Suzuki, H., and Mizukami, A. (1992). Behavioral analysis of internal memory states using cooling-induced retrograde amnesia in *Limax flavus*. *Journal of Neuroscience 12*, 729–735.

Yamane, T., and Gelperin, A. (1987). Aminergic and peptidergic amplification of intracellular cyclic AMP levels in a molluscan neural network. *Cell Molecular Neurobiology 7*, 291–301.

Yin, J., and Tully, T. (1996). CREB and the formation of long-term memory. *Current Opinion in Neurobiology 6*, 264–268.

Zakharov, I. S., Hayes, N. L., Ierusalimsky, V. N., Nowakowski, R. S., and Balaban, P. M. (1998). Postembryonic neuronogenesis in the procerebrum of the terrestrial snail, *Helix lucorum*. *Journal of Neurobiology 35*, 271–276.

Zs.-Nagy, I., and Sakharov, D. A. (1970). The fine structure of the procerebrum of pulmonate molluscs, *Helix and Limax*. *Tissue Cell 2*, 399–411.

Alan Gelperin

C. ELEGANS

Simple invertebrate organisms have provided a wealth of information concerning the molecular and cellular basis of learning and memory. Research conducted in one such simple system, the nematode *Caenorhabditis elegans* (*C. elegans*), has made several important contributions to the field.

Advantages of *Caenorhabditis elegans* as a Model System

C. elegans is a small (about one millimeter), hermaphroditic, soil-dwelling nematode (see Figure 1). In the laboratory, *C. elegans* spends its short life (about twenty days) swimming on agar-filled petri dishes laying eggs and feeding on *E. coli* bacteria. Its hermaphroditic mode of reproduction makes the maintenance of strains easy, thus allowing for large quantities of inexpensive, readily available animals for testing. Its nervous system is simple, consisting of 302 neurons with 5,000 electrical and 10,000 chemical synapses, all of which have been identified and mapped at the electron microscope level (White, Southgate, and Durbin, 1988; White, Southgate, Thomson, and Brenner, 1986). Complete developmental lineages of all cells are also known. Furthermore, the worm is transparent, so that with the appropriate microscopic power, its simple nervous system is easily visible. Single neurons can be easily ablated with a laser, while leaving the rest of the nervous system intact. Such an approach can elucidate the role of specific neurons in behavioral processes.

Consistent with the simplicity of its nervous system, the *C. elegans* genome is small and has been fully sequenced, with 8 x 107 nucleotide pairs arranged on six haploid chromosomes. Both classic genetic techniques and modern genetic engineering have produced a large number of mutant strains, which have provided the opportunity for investigating the role of single genes in behavioral processes. Worms are able

Figure 1

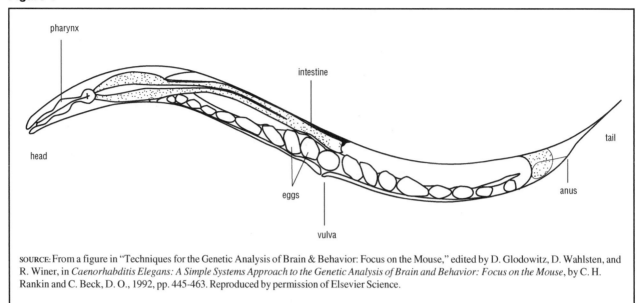

SOURCE: From a figure in "Techniques for the Genetic Analysis of Brain & Behavior: Focus on the Mouse," edited by D. Glodowitz, D. Wahlsten, and R. Winer, in *Caenorhabditis Elegans: A Simple Systems Approach to the Genetic Analysis of Brain and Behavior: Focus on the Mouse*, by C. H. Rankin and C. Beck, D. O., 1992, pp. 445-463. Reproduced by permission of Elsevier Science.

Schematic drawing of the nematode *Caenorhabditis elegans*. The adult worm is approximately one millimeter long and forty micrometers wide.

to survive freezing, and thus mutant strains, once acquired, can be maintained indefinitely.

The behavioral repertoire of *C. elegans* is complex enough to offer a number of interesting behaviors to study. In the laboratory worms move forward along the surface of agar-filled petri dishes, using rhythmic, coordinated contractions of dorsal and ventral muscle groups, resulting in smooth sinusoidal waves of forward locomotion. Worms will respond to a variety of stimuli by changing direction and by swimming backward. Stimuli that produce reversals include touch, heat probes, some chemical compounds, and vibrations caused by the force of a mechanical tapper applied to the side of the dish. The response to a mechanical tap has been termed the tap withdrawal response (TWR) by Rankin, Beck, and Chiba (1990) and has proved to be important for studies of both short- and long-term memory. Using laser ablation techniques, Wicks and Rankin (1995) determined that the TWR consists of six sensory neurons, ten interneurons, and approximately sixty-nine motor neurons.

Short-Term Memory

The simplest forms of learning are habituation, dishabituation, and sensitization. These are nonassociative forms of learning. *Habituation* is a decrease in the rate or amplitude or both, of responding due to repeated stimulus presentation (Groves and Thompson, 1970). *Dishabituation* is the facilitation of a decre-

mented or habituated response following presentation of a novel, usually aversive, stimulus. *Sensitization* is the facilitation of a nondecremented response resulting from presentation of an aversive stimulus. The TWR of *C. elegans* shows each of these three nonassociative types of learning (Rankin, Beck, and Chiba, 1990).

The response habituation observed in the TWR with repeated presentation of the tap stimulus is not due to fatigue of the system, because presentation of a novel stimulus to a habituated animal immediately causes a return of the behavior to prehabituation levels—that is, dishabituation (Rankin, Beck, and Chiba, 1990). Consistent with the rules of habituation outlined by Groves and Thompson (1970), the rate of habituation of the TWR in *C. elegans* is sensitive to the frequency of stimulation. In wild-type worms habituation occurs more rapidly at short interstimulus intervals (ISIs) (i.e., intervals of two or ten seconds) compared to long ISIs (i.e., intervals of sixty seconds); subsequent recovery from habituation is also affected by ISI, with animals recovering more rapidly from habituation with short ISIs than with long ISIs (Rankin and Broster, 1992; see Figure 2). Thus short-term memory for habituation training lasts less than fifteen minutes when trained with short ISIs and can last for one to two hours when trained with long ISIs.

As *C. elegans* follows the generally agreed upon rules of habituation, it provides an effective model in which to study the role of genes underlying habitua-

Figure 2

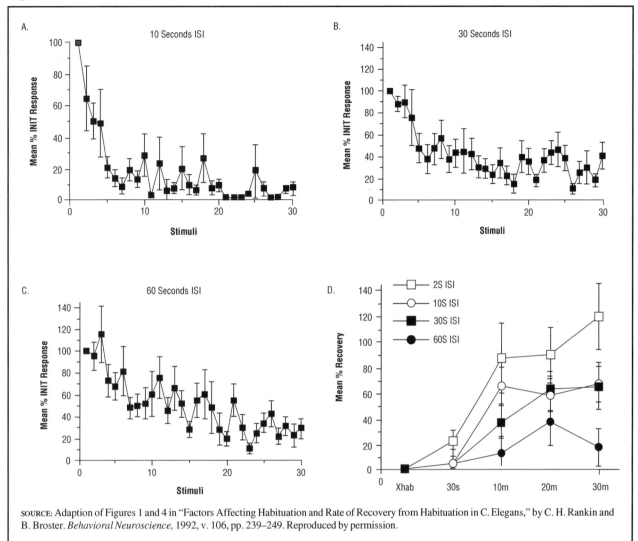

SOURCE: Adaption of Figures 1 and 4 in "Factors Affecting Habituation and Rate of Recovery from Habituation in C. Elegans," by C. H. Rankin and B. Broster. *Behavioral Neuroscience*, 1992, v. 106, pp. 239–249. Reproduced by permission.

A. Habituation of response amplitude expressed as a percentage of initial (INIT) response (± SE) for thirty stimuli delivered at a ten-second ISI (n = 20). B. Habituation of response amplitude expressed as a percentage of initial (INIT) response (± SE) for thirty stimuli delivered at a thirty-second ISI (n = 20). C. Habituation of response amplitude expressed as a percentage of initial (INIT) response (± SE) for thirty stimuli delivered at a sixty-second ISI (n = 20). D. Spontaneous recovery (n = 10 per group) for habituation following sixty stimuli delivered at two-, ten-, thirty-, and sixty-second ISIs measured at thirty seconds and ten, twenty, and thirty minutes after habituation training. Recovery is shown as an increase in percent initial response magnitude from the habituated level (determined for each ISI by subtracting the mean of the last three responses of habituation training for that ISI from itself and from each of the recovery points). Recovery is more rapid following habituation at short ISIs (two or ten seconds) than following long ISIs (sixty seconds).

tion. There are mutant strains of worms that show differences in short-term habituation, one of which is *eat-4*. Studies of *eat-4* and its mammalian homologues suggest that it regulates the amount of glutamate in neuron terminals (Bellocchio, Reimer, Fremeau, and Edwards, 2000; Lee et al., 1999). The *eat-4* gene product is expressed on the sensory neurons of the TWR circuit (Lee et al., 1999). Rankin and Wicks (2000) showed that while responding normally to a single tap, and displaying the usual pattern of ISI-dependent habituation, *eat-4* worms had more rapid overall rates of habituation with depressed asymptotic levels compared to wild-type worms. Furthermore, their recovery from habituation was slower compared to wild-type worms. Rankin and Wicks (2000) hypothesized that with repeated stimulation glutamate becomes rapidly depleted, resulting in more rapid response decrements in *eat-4*. However, the fact that the usual effects of ISI on the rate of habituation were preserved in *eat-4* indicates that it is more than simple neurotransmitter depletion underlying habituation. The *eat-4* strain did *not* show dishabituation. Since dishabituation does not occur in the *eat-4* strain, dishabituation does require the presence of an intact *eat-4* gene product. The cellular processes underlying habituation and dishabituation are likely not the same, and each involves *eat-4* to a different extent.

Associative Learning

Although for many years researchers believed that the response decrements seen in habituation were due solely to repeated stimulus presentation, it has now been demonstrated that organisms can make associations during habituation training that affect future performance. The most common of such associations is context conditioning, where some aspect of the training environment is encoded by the organism, which then influences future responses to the original training stimulus. Thus the long-held view that habituation is a purely nonassociative form of learning may not be warranted. Rankin (2000) showed that *C. elegans* is capable of context conditioning during habituation training. Worms were habituated to thirty-tap stimuli in the presence or absence of a distinctive chemosensory cue (sodium acetate). When tested an hour later, worms trained in the presence of sodium acetate showed greater retention of training when tested in the presence of sodium acetate than when tested on plain agar plates. Placing worms on sodium acetate plates for the hour between training and testing produced extinction of the context effect.

Classical conditioning has also been demonstrated in *C. elegans* using both appetitive and aversive conditioning paradigms. Conditioned worms showed clear postconditioning preferences for distinctive tastes that were paired with food during training (Wen et al., 1997). Similarly, in an aversive-conditioning paradigm, worms learned to avoid tastes that were paired with an aversive stimulus during training. Similar results have been obtained using olfactory rather than taste cues, where worms learned to avoid a previously attractive odor after it was paired with an aversive acetic acid solution (Morrison, Wen, Runciman, and van der Kooy, 1999). Two mutant strains of worms, *lrn-1* and *lrn-2*, were generated that were not able to form taste or olfactory associations.

Long-Term Memory

C. elegans is also capable of retention of habituation training for at least twenty-four hours. This phenomenon, *long-term habituation*, has been used as an effective model for the study of long-term memory (defined as retention for twenty-four hours or more). Distributed or spaced habituation training of the

TWR (three to four blocks of twenty stimuli each at a sixty-second ISI, separated by one-hour periods) resulted in retention of the habituated response twenty-four hours later when tested with a series of twenty taps (Beck and Rankin, 1997; Rose, Chen, Kaun, and Rankin, 2001). This effect was observed only when a sixty-second ISI was used during training (i.e., it was not seen with a ten-second ISI) and when a distributed training procedure was used. Consistent with what has been observed in other species, such as *Aplysia* and *Drosophila*, massed training (one block of sixty taps), with either a ten-second or a sixty-second ISI, did not produce long-term habituation in *C. elegans*. In addition, Beck and Rankin (1995) showed that long-term habituation was protein-synthesis dependent. When worms were exposed to as few as fifteen minutes of heat shock, which disrupts protein synthesis, during the early part of the rest period in a distributed-training paradigm, long-term memory was significantly reduced, suggesting that the time immediately after training is most vulnerable to heat shock and thus may be a critical phase in the formation of long-term memory. Heat shock applied during the one-hour rest period did not, however, have any effect on the accumulation of short-term habituation seen over successive blocks of training, suggesting that short- and long-term memory recruit different cellular and molecular processes.

As with short-term memory, *C. elegans* also provides an effective model with which to study the role of genes underlying long-term memory for habituation training. For example, *glr-1*, a gene coding for a homologue of mammalian kainate/AMPA-type glutamate receptor, has been identified and cloned in *C. elegans*. Worms missing functional *glr-1* showed no long-term retention of habituation training twenty-four hours later (Rose, Chen, Kaun, and Rankin, 2001). These results suggest that stimulation of kainate/AMPA-type glutamate receptors on the interneurons is required for long-term habituation to tap. The same mutation has also been shown to prevent olfactory associative learning (Morrison and van der Kooy, 2001).

Conclusion

C. elegans has proved to be a useful model system for the study of learning and memory processes. Unlike other animals used in this area of research, *C. elegans* is an inexpensive, easily obtained and maintained organism, with a large amount of information available about its nervous system and genome. Knowledge of the neural circuitry underlying behavior combined with knowledge of the genome has allowed for the investigation of genetic factors involved in both short-term and long-term memory. That is, if a certain gene is expressed on a component of a neural circuit known to underlie a behavior, then that gene is a prime candidate for playing a role in either the behavior itself or its plasticity. This kind of an approach has proved fruitful in *C. elegans* by elucidating the importance in learning and memory of glutamate, a neurotransmitter that has also been determined to play a major role in mammalian learning and memory processes. The fact that the same results are obtained in *C. elegans* attests to its validity as a model system. The rules of habituation outlined by Groves and Thompson (1970) apply to *C. elegans*, making it an appropriate model system for the study of short-term memory as well. Research using *C. elegans* has made it clear that habituation is not a unitary process but is rather a set of processes, differentially recruited by short and long ISIs that cannot be neatly tucked away into the category of "simple," nonassociative learning.

Bibliography

Beck, C. D. O., and Rankin, C. H. (1992). *Caenorhabditis elegans*: A simple systems approach to the genetics of behavior. In D. Goldowitz, D. Wahlstein, and R. E. Wimer, eds., *Techniques for the genetic analysis of brain and behavior: Focus on the mouse*, 445–463. Amsterdam: Elsevier.

—— (1995). Heat-shock disrupts long-term memory consolidation in *Caenorhabditis elegans*. *Learning and Memory 2*, 161–177.

—— (1997). Long-term habituation is produced by distributed training at long ISIs and not by massed training or short ISIs in *Caenorhabditis elegans*. *Animal Learning and Behavior 25* (4), 446–457.

Bellocchio, E. E., Reimer, R. J., Fremeau, R. T., and Edwards, R. H. (2000). Uptake of glutamate into synaptic vesicles by an inorganic phosphate transporter. *Science 289*, 957–960.

Groves, P. M., and Thompson, R. F. (1970). Habituation: A dual-process theory. *Psychological Reviews 77*, 419–450.

Lee, R. Y. N., Sawin, E. R., Chalfie, M., Horvitz, H. R., and Avery, L. (1999). *Eat-4*, a homolog of a mammalian sodium-dependent inorganic phosphate co-transporter, is necessary for glutamatergic neurotransmission in *Caenorhabditis elegans*. *Journal of Neuroscience 19*, 159–167.

Morrison, G. E., and van der Kooy, D. (2001). A mutation in the AMPA-type glutamate receptor, *glr-1*, blocks olfactory associative and nonassociative learning in *Caenorhabditis elegans*. *Behavioral Neuroscience 115* (3), 640–649.

Morrison, G. E., Wen, J. Y. M., Runciman, S., and van der Kooy, D. (1999). Olfactory associative learning in *Caenorhabditis elegans* is impaired in lrn-1 and lrn-2 mutants. *Behavioral Neuroscience 113* (2), 358–367.

Rankin, C. H. (2000). Context conditioning in habituation in the nematode *Caenorhabditis elegans*. *Behavioral Neuroscience 114*, 496–505.

Rankin, C. H., Beck, C. D. O., and Chiba, C. M. (1990). *Caenorhabditis elegans*: A new model system for the study of learning and memory. *Behavioral Brain Research 37*, 89–92.

Rankin, C. H., and Broster, B. S. (1992). Factors affecting habituation in the nematode *Caenorhabditis elegans*. *Behavioral Neuroscience 106*, 239–242.

Rankin, C. H., and Wicks, S. R. (2000). Mutations of the *Caenorhabditis elegans* brain-specific inorganic phosphate transporter *eat-4* affect habituation of the tap-withdrawal response without affecting the response itself. *Journal of Neuroscience 20*, 4,337–4,344.

Rose, J., Chen, S., Kaun, K., and Rankin, C. H. (2001). Glutamate and AMPA-receptor function are necessary for long-term memory in *C. elegans*. *Society for Neuroscience Abstracts 27*, 45.

Wen, J. Y. M., Kumar, N., Morrison, G., Rambaldini, G., Runciman, S., Rousseau, J., and van der Kooy, D. (1997). Mutations that prevent associative learning in *C. elegans*. *Behavioral Neuroscience 111* (2), 354–368.

White, J. E., Southgate, E., and Durbin, R. (1988). Appendix 2: Neuroanatomy. In W. B. Wood, ed., *The nematode* Caenorhabditis elegans, pp. 433–455. Cold Spring Harbor, NY: Cold Spring Harbor Laboratory Press.

White, J. E., Southgate, E., Thompson, J. N., and Brenner, S. (1986). The structure of the nervous system of the nematode *Caenorhabditis elegans*. *Philosophical Transactions of the Royal Society of London. Series B: Biological Sciences 314*, 1–340.

Wicks, S. R., and Rankin, C. H. (1995). Integration of mechanosensory stimuli in *Caenorhabditis elegans*. *Journal of Neuroscience 15*, 2,434–2,444.

Stephan Steidl
Catharine H. Rankin

HABITUATION AND SENSITIZATION IN TRITONIA

Studies of learning in both vertebrates and invertebrates indicate that individual memories are stored in the brain as distributed sets of cellular and synaptic modifications. Most research in this area has focused on characterizing the detailed mechanisms underlying specific sites of learning-related plasticity, such as presynaptic facilitation at sensory to motor neuron synapses in the marine mollusc *Aplysia* and long-term potentiation at synapses in the vertebrate hippocampus. However, the fragmented nature of memory storage raises additional issues at a network, rather than synaptic, level. For example, how is the information represented by a given memory organized across the different sites of plasticity encoding it—do different sites store the same information redundantly, or does each encode a unique component of the total acquired information? If different memories overlap in the brain, as seems likely, how do they avoid interfering with one another? Such network-level issues of memory storage have been investigated in the marine mollusc *Tritonia diomedea*, an organism well suited to both cellular and network studies of learning and memory.

When touched by the tube feet of its highly mobile seastar predators, *Tritonia* responds with vigorous alternating ventral and dorsal body flexions that propel it away to safety. The neural circuit underlying this response is known in detail and consists of identified afferent neurons, command interneurons, central pattern generator (CPG) interneurons, and efferent flexion neurons. A key advantage for cellular studies of learning is that the neural program underlying the swim behavior can be readily elicited in the isolated brain preparation, where the neurons and synapses storing memory can be easily identified and studied.

Studies of behavioral plasticity in *Tritonia* have focused on two universal forms of nonassociative learning: habituation and sensitization. *Sensitization* refers to the increase in responsiveness that follows a single, unexpected, and therefore potentially dangerous stimulus. *Habituation* refers to the gradual decrease in responsiveness that occurs in response to repetitive innocuous stimuli. In *Tritonia*, a single swim stimulus produces a period of sensitization, during which test swims have a lower threshold, faster onset latency, and higher cycle number (Frost, Brandon, and Mongeluzi, 1998). On the other hand, repeatedly eliciting the escape swim leads to habituation, characterized by swims with fewer cycles, a higher threshold, and a longer cycle period (Frost, Brown, and Getting, 1996).

Evidence suggests that the multiple, habituation-related behavioral changes are encoded by distributed sites of plasticity in the swim circuit. First, habituation is accompanied by a progressive drop in the number of incoming afferent neuron action potentials per stimulus. In addition, the synaptic connections made by the afferent neurons progressively decrease in strength with repeated stimulation. Bypassing the afferent neurons with repeated intracellular stimulation of the swim-command neurons still results in a progressive decrement of the number of cycles per swim motor program, implicating the involvement of interneuronal sites of plasticity. This is further supported by the finding that habituation produced by stimulating one sensory neuron population also leads to habituation of swims elicited by previously unstimulated sensory populations (Frost et al., 1996).

The memory for sensitization also appears to be encoded by multiple circuit modifications. Sensitizing stimuli produce a long-lasting enhancement of the excitability and synaptic strength of CPG neuron C2. An important effect of this enhancement is to strengthen a positive feedback connection from C2 to the command neurons that drive the swim motor program. Sensitizing stimuli also cause prolonged tonic firing of the CPG's Dorsal Swim Interneurons. These serotonergic cells participate in generating the swim motor program and also appear responsible for the neuromodulatory enhancement of C2 excitability and synaptic strength observed in sensitization (Katz, Getting, and Frost, 1994; Katz and Frost, 1997).

Scientists are just beginning to understand how the information represented by habituation and sensitization is organized in the *Tritonia* circuitry. After ten stimulus trials animals often display both forms of learning simultaneously—habituation of swim cycle number and sensitization of swim onset latency (Mongeluzi and Frost, 2000). That these two components of the different memories can coexist without conflict suggests that they involve different anatomical loci in the swim circuit. Other swim features modified in sensitization—cycle number and threshold—reverse direction during habituation training, suggesting that the underlying circuit modifications may be located at the same sites for both forms of learning. Studies since the 1990s have sought to determine the behavioral role (information content) of each site of learning-related plasticity.

See also: APLYSIA: MOLECULAR BASIS OF LONG-TERM SENSITIZATION; INVERTEBRATE LEARNING: C. ELEGANS; ORIENTING REFLEX HABITUATION; VESTIBULO-OCULAR REFLEX (VOR) PLASTICITY

Bibliography

Frost, W. N., Brandon, C. L., Mongeluzi, D. L. (1998). Sensitization of the *Tritonia* escape swim. *Neurobiology of Learning and Memory 69*, 126–135.

Frost, W. N., Brown, G., Getting, P. A. (1996). Parametric features of habituation of swim cycle number in the marine mollusc *Tritonia diomedea*. *Neurobiology of Learning and Memory 65*, 125–134.

Katz, P. S., Frost, W. N. (1997). Removal of spike frequency adaptation via neuromodulation intrinsic to the *Tritonia* escape swim central pattern generator. *Journal of Neuroscience 17*, 7,703–7,713.

Katz, P. S., Getting, P. A., Frost, W. N. (1994). Dynamic neuromodulation of synaptic strength intrinsic to a central pattern generator circuit. *Nature 367*, 729–731.

Mongeluzi, D. L., Frost, W. N. (2000). Dishabituation of the *Tritonia* escape swim. *Learning and Memory 7*, 43–47.

William N. Frost

NEUROGENETICS OF MEMORY IN DROSOPHILA

Neurogenetic analysis of memory seeks to identify genes involved in behavioral plasticity, to characterize the cells and neuroanatomies in which they are expressed, and to define the biochemistries and cell biologies in which they participate. From the study of *Drosophila* (fruit flies) beginning in the 1970s, two fundamental notions became apparent. First, a complex circuitry, consisting of sensory inputs, central processing, and motor outputs from thousands of neurons, likely is required. In addition, hundreds to thousands of genes likely participate in the neuronal-synaptic plasticity underlying behavioral plasticity. Hence, a vertical integration of function, from gene to behavior, will entail five primary levels of experimental analysis: molecular-genetic, gene network computation, neurophysiological, neural network computation, and behavioral. Second, molecular biological work across the animal kingdom has revealed a remarkable degree of evolutionary conservation, from basic phenomenology of cell biology during development to behavioral biology of sleep and senescence. Thus, a horizontal integration of gene action from lower organisms to humans appears the rule rather than the exception. Given the economy of scale (short generation time, inexpensive rearing costs), extant experimental tools, and a knowledge base of *Drosophila* genetics that goes back to the nineteenth century, this model system will continue to yield valuable information on the neurobiological basis of plasticity. Moreover, functional insights gained from flies will inform the mammalian condition directly, thereby allowing discovery of genetic and pharmacological therapies for various forms of cognitive dysfunction in humans.

Behavioral Plasticity

In the final quarter of the twentieth century, a plethora of behavioral learning tasks were developed for *Drosophila* (Connolly and Tully, 1998). Nonassociative tasks exist for the landing response, cleaning reflex, proboscis extension response, and odor avoidance response. Associative tasks include conditioned task aversion, courtship conditioning, operant conditioning to visual cues in a flight simulator, and olfactory discriminative conditioning. The last task, in particular, has proved valuable. Because initial conditioned avoidance levels are robust and memory retention can last more than a week, this learning task has been used extensively to identify and characterize single-gene mutations (see below). Careful analyses of the learning/memory defects in these mutants has suggested that olfactory memory formation occurs in five genetically distinct phases: acquisition or learning (LRN), short-term memory (STM), middle-term memory (MTM), anesthesia-resistant memory (ARM), and long-term memory (LTM) (Tully et al., 1996; Tully, Preat, Boynton, and Del Vecchio, 1994). Processing through these memory phases seems to occur sequentially from LRN to STM to MTM, at which point memory is processed independently (in parallel) into ARM and LTM. These temporal stages of memory processing likely reflect a combination of neural activity in different anatomic sites and biochemical activity within each.

Genetics

Three mutageneses have been conducted to screen for behavioral mutants with learning/memory defects. All have used an odor-avoidance procedure (Boynton and Tully, 1992; Dudai et al., 1976). The first screen, in Seymour Benzer's laboratory at the California Institute of Technology, yielded *dunce*, the first experimentally induced mutant gene that produced deficient learning. The second screen, in W. G. Quinn's laboratory at Princeton University, produced the "vegetable" mutants, *rutabaga*, *radish*, *turnip*, and *cabbage*, which also showed no odor-avoidance learning (Aceves-Pina et al., 1983). A modification of this behavioral screen also yielded the *amnesiac* mutant, which showed normal learning but defective memory retention thereafter (Quinn, Sziber, and Booker, 1979). The third screen, in T. Tully's laboratory at Brandeis University, looked for performance defects three hours after Pavlovian training and yielded the mutants *latheo*, *linotte*, *nalyot*, and *golovan* (Tully et al., 1996).

Anatomical experiments (see below) have revealed that olfactory memory formation involves the mushroom body structures, neuropillar structures in the central brain thought to integrate sensory input. Accordingly, another screen for memory mutants was accomplished by looking first for "enhancer trap" strains that expressed a beta-galactosidase reporter gene preferentially in mushroom bodies and then by screening for behavioral defects in olfactory memory. Mutants of *dunce* and *rutabaga* were reisolated with this approach, which also yielded the mutants *PKA-C1*, *leonardo*, and *Volado* (Roman and Davis, 2001).

Biochemistry

Early biochemical experiments (see Aceves-Pina et al., 1983) and subsequent molecular cloning (see Dubnau and Tully, 1998) have established that *dunce* encodes a cAMP (Cyclic adenosine monophosphate)-specific phosphodiesterase (PDE), *rutabaga* encodes a calcium-sensitive adenylyl cyclase (AC), and *amnesiac* encodes a neuropeptide similar to vertebrate PACAP (pituitary adenylyl cyclase activating peptide). Three reverse-genetic experiments, focusing on additional components of this pathway, have strengthened this notion: 1. Mutations targeted to the regulatory subunit of PKA (*PKA-RI*) produced flies with olfactory learning defects. 2. Overexpression of a dominant-negative mutation of the stimulatory G protein subunit (G_s) in transgenic flies produced olfactory learning defects. 3. Overexpression of a repressor isoform of the CREB (cAMP response element binding protein) transcription factor in transgenic flies blocked olfactory long-term memory. Together, these behavior-genetic experiments strongly support the notion that cAMP signaling is central to olfactory memory formation in *Drosophila*. These data also are consistent with behavioral, electrophysiological, and cellular experiments in *Aplysia* (Bailey, Bartsch, and Kandel, 1996) and in mice (Wong et al., 1999), suggesting that cAMP signaling is part of an evolutionarily conserved molecular mechanism underlying synaptic and behavioral plasticity.

The MAP (mitogen-activated protein) kinase signaling pathway also may be involved. Molecular cloning of *leonardo* revealed it to be a mutation of the *14-3-3* gene, which, among other tasks, regulates the function of Ras/Raf, two of several proteins involved in GTP (guanine triphosphate) exchange. The *Volado* mutation has been shown to reside in a gene encoding α-integrin, a cell surface adhesion molecule. This general class of molecule often activates the MAP kinase pathway via interactions with receptor tyrosine kinases, though such a connection has not yet been made for *Volado*.

Mysteries remain and puzzles present themselves. The mutants *radish*, *turnip*, and *cabbage* have yet to be cloned. The *linotte* mutation resides either in the receptor tyrosine kinase, *derailed*, or in a novel neighboring transcript. The *nalyot* mutation lies in the *Adf1* transcription factor; *golovan* is in the neurogenetic locus, *extra machrochaetea*. Exactly how these molecular-genetic components fit into the cell biology of olfactory memory is not yet clear. Curiously, the *latheo* mutation has been shown to disrupt *ORC3*, which encodes a protein subunit of the Origin Recognition Complex involved in DNA replication during cell proliferation. Surprisingly, the protein *LAT* also is expressed in synapses of terminally differentiated neurons, thereby suggesting a completely novel function for this protein outside of the nucleus of dividing cells. Although such genetic pleiotropy is not unusual, this observation nevertheless emphasizes how genetic screens can break the bondage of hypothesis-driven research. These "dangling mutants" presage an ultimate understanding of a more complicated and complete genetic basis of memory.

Physiology

Gaining electrophysiological access to neurons in the adult central nervous system that subserve olfactory memory has been challenging. Thus, initial physiological characterizations of memory mutants relied on neural circuitries underlying other behaviors. Corfas and Dudai (1990), for instance, found that habituation of the (bristle) cleaning reflex in *dunce* and *rutabaga* mutants was abnormal, but this behavioral effect resulted from opposite physiological defects in the underlying sensory neurons. Sensory fatigue was accelerated in *dunce* mutants, while it was retarded in *rutabaga* mutants. Research by Engel and Wu (1996) began to characterize normal and mutant electrophysiological responses in the giant-fiber neurons, which contribute to habituation of the jump response.

Much insight on a role for memory genes in synaptic plasticity has come from studies of the larval

neuromuscular junction (NMJ). In short, all memory mutants known to date produce distinct defects in synaptic structure or function, or both, at the NMJ (Saitoe and Tully, 2000). Increases in neural activity or in cAMP levels lead to increases in the number of synaptic boutons onto muscles (structure) and to increased excitability of synaptic transmission (function). *Adf1* (*nalyot*) or *fasII* (another cell adhesion molecule) appear involved in changes of synaptic structure but not function, while *dCREB2* regulates synaptic function but not structure (Davis, Schuster, and Goodman, 1996; DeZazzo et al., 2000). Thus, a genetic dissection of this form of developmental plasticity is under way.

Anatomy

Early electrophysiological and lesion experiments in bees identified a distinct anatomical region of the insect brain, the mushroom body, to be involved in associative processes (Menzel et al., 1991). In *Drosophila*, mutants with structural defects in specific adult brain anatomies were identified by M. Heisenberg's laboratory in Wurzburg, and those with abnormal mushroom bodies also displayed olfactory learning defects (Heisenberg, Borst, Wagner, and Byers, 1985). Four subsequent experiments clearly established mushroom bodies as a neural substrate of adult olfactory memory:

1. Chemical ablation of mushroom body neurons completely abolishes olfactory learning (de Belle and Heisenberg, 1994);

2. Overexpression of a dominant-negative G_s protein specifically in mushroom bodies completely abolishes olfactory learning (Connolly et al., 1996);

3. Transgenic expression of RUTABAGA (the protein encoded by the *rutabaga* gene) in mushroom bodies specifically rescues the learning defect of *rutabaga* mutants (Zars, Wolf, Davis, and Heisenberg, 2000); and

4. Structural mutants with lesions restricted to the alpha lobes (axonal projections from intrinsic mushroom body neurons) specifically abolish long-term memory (Pascual and Preat, 2001).

Together, these observations suggest that olfactory learning and memory depend, at least in part, on the activity of mushroom body neurons. Though these neurons remain largely inaccessible to classic electrophysiological investigations (but see Wright and Zhong, 1995), less invasive imaging techniques are revealing some of their cellular properties in response to experience (Rosay, Armstrong, Wang, and Kaiser, 2001; Wang et al., 2001).

The primary strength of neurogenetic analysis of memory in *Drosophila* lies in the discovery of genes. Behavioral screens for memory mutants enable this discovery process without any preconceived (and naive) assumptions about the underlying biochemical or anatomical substrates. To this end, yet another behavioral screen by Tully and coworkers at Cold Spring Harbor laboratory has discovered fifty-seven new mutants, defining forty-seven new genes. DNA microarrays also have been used to identify more than one thousand candidate memory genes (CMGs), which are transcriptionally regulated in normal flies during olfactory long-term memory formation. Significant genetic overlap exists between these two experimental approaches. As outlined above for the first few (*dunce, rutabaga, latheo*), these genes become an experimental "common currency" with which to investigate mechanisms of plasticity at several biological levels of organization (biochemical, physiological, anatomical, and so forth) and across many animal models. Combined, these data will reveal in more detail the molecular and cellular mechanisms by which memories form. In humans, various types of heritable mental retardation will become associated with homologues of these "memory genes" and the neurobiological pathways in which they participate (Oike et al., 1999; Petrij et al., 1995; Zhang et al., 2001). Ultimately, these mammalian homologues will become targets of drug discovery, thereby yielding viable therapies for those who suffer from cognitive dysfunction (Scott et al., 2002).

See also: APLYSIA: CLASSICAL CONDITIONING AND OPERANT CONDITIONING; GENETIC SUBSTRATES OF MEMORY: HIPPOCAMPUS; INSECT LEARNING; INVERTEBRATE LEARNING: ASSOCIATIVE LEARNING AND MEMORY PROCESSING IN BEES; INVERTEBRATE LEARNING: C. ELEGANS; SECOND MESSENGER SYSTEMS

Bibliography

Aceves-Pina, E. O., Booker, R., Duerr, J. S., Livingstone, M. S., Quinn, W. G., Smith, R. F., Sziber, P. P., Tempel, B. L., and Tully, T. P. (1983). Learning and memory in *Drosophila*, studied with mutants. *Cold Spring Harbor Symposia on Quantitative Biology 48*, 831–839.

Bailey, C. H., Bartsch, D., and Kandel, E. R. (1996). Toward a molecular definition of long-term memory storage. *Proceedings of the National Academy of Sciences of the United States of America 93*, 13,445–13,452.

Boynton, S., and Tully, T. (1992). *latheo*, a new gene involved in associative learning and memory in *Drosophila melanogaster* identified from P element mutagenesis. *Genetics 131*, 655–672.

Connolly, J. B., Roberts, I. J., Armstrong, J. D., Kaiser, K. M. F., Tully, T., and O'Kane, C. J. (1996). Associative learning disrupted by impaired G$_s$ signaling in *Drosophila* mushroom bodies. *Science 274*, 2,104–2,107.

Connolly, J. B., and Tully, T. (1998). Behaviour, learning, and memory. In D. B. Roberts, ed., Drosophila: *A practical approach*, 2nd edition, pp. 265–318. Oxford, UK: Oxford University Press.

Corfas, G., and Dudai, Y. (1990). Adaptation and fatigue of a mechanosensory neuron in wild-type *Drosophila* and in memory mutants. *Journal of Neuroscience 10*, 491–499.

Davis, G. W., Schuster, C. M., and Goodman, C. S. (1996). Genetic dissection of structural and functional components of synaptic plasticity, Part 3: CREB is necessary for presynaptic functional plasticity. *Neuron 17* (4), 669–679.

de Belle, J. S., and Heisenberg, M. (1994). Associative odor learning in *Drosophila* abolished by chemical ablation of mushroom bodies. *Science 263*, 692–695.

DeZazzo, J., Sandstrom, D., deBelle, S., Velinzon, K., Smith, P., Grady, L., DelVecchio, M., Ramaswami, M., and Tully, T. (2000). *nalyot*, a mutation of the *Drosophila* myb-related *Adf1* transcription factor, disrupts synapse formation and olfactory memory. *Neuron 27*, 145–158.

Dubnau, J., and Tully, T. (1998). Gene discovery in *Drosophila*: New insights for learning and memory. *Annual Review of Neuroscience 21*, 407–444.

Dudai, Y., Jan, Y.-N., Byers, D., Quinn, W., and Benzer, S. (1976). *dunce*: A mutant of *Drosophila melanogaster* deficient in learning. *Proceedings of the National Academy of Sciences of the United States of America 73*, 1,684–1,688.

Engel, J. E., and Wu, C. F. (1996). Altered habituation of an identified escape circuit in *Drosophila* memory mutants. *Journal of Neuroscience 16*, 3,486–3,499.

Heisenberg, M., Borst, A., Wagner, S., and Byers, D. (1985). *Drosophila* mushroom body mutants are deficient in olfactory learning. *Journal of Neurogenetics 2*, 1–30.

Menzel, R., Hammer, M., Braun, G., Mauelshagen, J., and Sugawa, M. (1991). Neurobiology of learning and memory in honeybees. In R. C. Fisher, ed., *The behavior and physiology of bees*, pp. 323–353. London: CAB International.

Oike, Y., Hata, A., Mamiya, T., Kaname, T., Noda, Y., Suzuki, M., Yasue, H., Nabeshima, T., Araki, K., and Yamamura, K. (1999). Truncated CBP protein leads to classical Rubinstein-Taybi syndrome phenotypes in mice: Implications for a dominant-negative mechanism. *Human Molecular Genetics 8*, 387–396.

Pascual, A., and Preat, T. (2001). Localization of long-term memory within the *Drosophila* mushroom body. *Science 294*, 1,115–1,117.

Petrij, F., Giles, R., Dauwerse, H., Saris, J., Hennekam, R., Masuno, M., Tommerup, N., van Ommen, G.-J. B., Goodman, R., Peters, D., and Breuning, M. (1995). Rubinstein-Taybi syndrome caused by mutations in the transcriptional co-activator CBP. *Nature 376*, 348–351.

Quinn, W., Sziber, P. P., and Booker, R. (1979). The *Drosophila* memory mutant *amnesiac*. *Nature 277*, 212–214.

Roman, G., and Davis, R. L. (2001). Molecular biology and anatomy of *Drosophila* olfactory associative learning. *Bioessays 23*, 571–581.

Rosay, P., Armstrong, J. D., Wang, Z., and Kaiser, K. (2001). Synchronized neural activity in the *Drosophila* memory centers and its modulation by *amnesiac*. *Neuron 30*, 759–770.

Saitoe, M., and Tully, T. (2000). Making connections between synaptic and behavioral plasticity in *Drosophila*. In J. McEachern and C. Shaw, eds., *Toward a theory of neuroplasticity*, pp. 193-220. New York: Psychology Press.

Scott, R., Bourtchuladze, R., Gossweiler, S., Dubnau, J., and Tully, T. (2002). CREB and the discovery of cognitive enhancers. *Journal of Molecular Neuroscience.*

Tully, T., Bolwig, G., Christensen, J., Connolly, J., DelVecchio, M., DeZazzo, J., Dubnau, J., Pinto, S., Regulski, M., Svedberg, B., and Velinzon, K. (1996). A return to genetic dissection of memory in *Drosophila*, *Cold Spring Harbor Symposium on Quantitative Biology 61*, 207–218.

Tully, T., Preat, T., Boynton, S. C., and Del Vecchio, M. (1994). Genetic dissection of consolidated memory in *Drosophila*. *Cell 79*, 35–47.

Wang, Y., Wright, N. J., Guo, H., Xie, Z., Svoboda, K., Malinow, R., Smith, D. P., and Zhong, Y. (2001). Genetic manipulation of the odor-evoked distributed neural activity in the *Drosophila* mushroom body. *Neuron 29*, 267–276.

Wong, S., Athos, J., Figueroa, X., Pineda, V., Schaefer, M., Chavkin, C., Muglia, L., and Storm, D. (1999). Calcium-stimulated adenylyl cyclase activity is critical for hippocampus-dependent long-term memory and late phase LTP. *Neuron 23*, 787–798.

Wright, N. J. D., and Zhong, Y. (1995). Characterization of K+ currents and the cAMP-dependent modulation in cultured *Drosophila* mushroom body neurons identified by *lacZ* expression. *Journal of Neuroscience 15*, 1,025–1,034.

Zars, T., Wolf, R., Davis, R., and Heisenberg, M. (2000). Tissue-specific expression of a type I adenylyl cyclase rescues the rutabaga mutant memory defect: in search of the engram. *Learning and Memory 7*, 18–31.

Zhang, Y. Q., Bailey, A. M., Matthies, H. J., Renden, R. B., Smith, M. A., Speese, S. D., Rubin, G. M., and Broadie, K. (2001). *Drosophila* fragile X-related gene regulates the MAP1B homolog Futsch to control synaptic structure and function. *Cell 107*, 591–603.

Yadin Dudai
Revised by Tim Tully

J

JAMES, WILLIAM (1842–1910)

The American philosopher and psychologist William James was one of the most important American intellectuals of his era, making key contributions to the development of both philosophical pragmatism and psychological theory.

James was born in New York City in 1842, the oldest of five children (his brother Henry became a famous novelist). His father was a man of leisure who gave his children an unusual and rich education based on large amounts of travel and instruction in Europe. Young William set out to be an artist, apprenticing with William Morris Hunt for a year, but then turned toward science. He entered Harvard's Lawrence Scientific School in 1861 and worked with Charles William Eliot in chemistry and Jeffries Wyman in comparative anatomy. He then entered Harvard Medical School, took a year off to go with Louis Agassiz on an expedition to the Amazon, and eventually received his M.D. in 1869.

James never practiced medicine but pursued an academic career at Harvard. In 1872 he was appointed instructor in physiology and anatomy. He became assistant professor of philosophy in 1880 and full professor in 1885. In 1889 he was named professor of psychology, returning to philosophy in 1892 when Hugo Münsterberg came from Germany to take charge of Harvard's psychological laboratory. James retired in 1907 and spent his last years writing out his systematic philosophy.

Like most people of his time, James saw psychology as part of philosophy, an empirical approach toward philosophical questions. Findings in science and medicine stimulated a vision of a physiological psychology in James, spurred by the writings of people like Wilhelm Wundt, Ivan Sechenov, John Hughlings Jackson, Henry Maudsley, and Theodor Meynert. His varied academic appointments reflected his early efforts to establish a "new psychology" in philosophy and then, skeptical about much of the "normal science" that began growing up around him, to seek a more meaningful inquiry into psychic life through spiritualism and the study of exceptional mental states.

The culmination of James's first was his 1890 *Principles of Psychology*, an enormously popular and influential work that brought some people into "new psychology" and induced many others to accept it as a possibility. The two volumes are a delight to read today, brimming with life, ideas, and insights.

James defines psychology as "the Science of Mental Life, both of phenomena and their conditions" (p. 1). His book explores the psyche using a mixture of introspective, physiological, medical, comparative, and experimental observations. The first six chapters are given to "the physiological preliminaries," a psychobiology of mind. "Both the anatomy and the detailed physiology of the brain are achievements of the present generation, or rather we may say (beginning with Meynert) the last twenty years" (p. 14). James sets forth a picture of a hierarchically organized brain and mind, one that remains today, with amplifica-

William James *(Archive Photos, Inc.)*

tions and amendments, a framing conception of contemporary neuropsychology. There are levels of behavioral organization: first reflexes and automatisms, then instincts, then habits, and then, finally, voluntary and planned activity. Lower levels are more mechanical and sense-driven; higher centers are the seat of spontaneity and intellectual control. "In all ages the man whose determinations are swayed by reference to the most distant ends has been held to possess the highest intelligence" (p. 23).

In Chapter 7, James turns to psychological inquiry, which, he says, uses three methods: introspection, experiment, and the comparative approach. Introspection is the foundation, "what we have to remember first and foremost and always" (p. 185). The experimental method had been developed in Germany. "[It] taxes patience to the utmost, and could hardly have arisen in a country whose natives could be *bored*" (p. 192). Experimental psychology explores psychophysics, sensation and perception, attention span, and rote memory. The comparative method is loosest, "wild work," and includes psychological observa-

tions of the behavior of animals, mental patients, children, and people of other cultures, and inferences about the mind drawn from artifacts such as human languages, customs, and social and political institutions.

James's discussions of learning and memory are not well integrated. His discussion of learning rests largely on comparative observations, whereas he approaches memory introspectively. His book appeared only five years after Hermann Ebbinghaus launched the systematic study of human memory. James discusses Ebbinghaus's work in his chapter on memory, but the discussion is clearly an appendage. An integrated, fully elaborated discussion of human learning and memory began to emerge five years after James published his book.

A Parliamentary Theory of Learning

Like all evolutionary writers, James addresses the problem of the instinctual and the learned in the organization of human activity. Contrary to most writers, he argues that humans have many instincts and that they play a large role in the behavior of higher organisms.

> Nature [in the lower wild animals] has made them act *always* in the manner which would be *oftenest* right. There are more worms unattached to hooks than impaled upon them; therefore, on the whole, says Nature to her fishy children, bite at *every* worm and take your chances. But as her children get higher, and their lives more precious, she reduces the risks. . . . *Nature implants contrary impulses to act on many classes of things,* and leaves it to slight alterations in the conditions of the individual case to decide which impulse shall carry the day. (pp. 1,012–1,013)

The proliferation of instincts in the higher animals leads to the beginnings of deliberation and choice. In higher animals, instincts do not remain fixed action patterns. Once an instinct is exercised, it produces consequences, and anticipations of those consequences henceforth accompany instinctive impulses. The experienced organism faces ever more new situations, armed with a number of impulses; the organism is not a slave to any one instinct; and there are rational anticipations of the consequences various actions might bring. James's parliamentary theory of the inner competition among impulses and their anticipated consequences foreshadows twentieth-century behaviorism. Edward L. Thorndike, James's student, was the bridging figure. His connectionism built the parliamentary theory into a logic of response choice in problem-solving situations; that connectionism, in turn, has influenced all subsequent learning theories.

Optimal human development, James argues, implies the fruition of as many instinctive tendencies as possible. After attributing to humans a large set of instincts (more, he says, than any animal), James writes,

> In a perfectly-rounded development every one of these instincts would start a habit towards certain objects and inhibit a habit towards others. Usually this is the case; but, in the one-sided development of civilized life, it happens that the timely age goes by in a sort of starvation of objects, and the individual then grows up with gaps in his psychic constitution which future experiences can never fill. Compare the accomplished gentleman with the poor artisan or tradesman of a city: during the adolescence of the former, objects appropriate to his growing interests, bodily and mental, were offered as fast as his interests awoke, and, as a consequence, he is armed and equipped at every angle to meet the world. . . . Over the city poor boy's youth no such golden opportunities were hung, and in his manhood no desires for most of them exist. Fortunate it is for him if gaps are the only anomalies his instinctive life presents; perversions are too often the fruit of his unnatural bringing-up. (pp. 1,056–1,057)

Memories as Beliefs

James approaches the phenomena of human memory introspectively, though his conception of the presenting phenomena of mental life differs radically from that of previous psychological writings. Beginning with John Locke, and continuing through the research programs of nineteenth-century brass-instruments laboratories, psychologists repeatedly asserted that human experience begins with simple sensations and ideas. James argues that this is false to experience. "Simple" sensations and ideas are, in fact, abstractions contrived from experience. What presents itself to the mind is an always dynamic, often inchoate, moving flow—a fluidity that in the *Principles* he calls the "stream of consciousness" and in later writings he calls "pure experience." Redefining the mental life with which the psychologist must deal, James at once sets aside the traditional denizens of that mental life—sensations, ideas, faculties. In return, he has the obligation and the opportunity to ask in a very wide-open way where in the fluidity one may locate the conventional chapter headings: Attention,

Conception, Discrimination and Comparison, Memory, and so on.

In older writings, memories are referred to as returns or reinstatements of experiences of the past; James, looking at mental life with a fresh eye, argues there must be more to the experience of a memory than that. "Memory," he says, "is the knowledge of an event, or fact, of which meantime we have not been thinking, *with the additional consciousness that we have thought or experienced it before*" (p. 610). It is not enough to see or hear something that one has seen or heard before. There must be some aspect of the experience that says the event has occurred before, not in just any past but in the person's past. "It must have that 'warmth and intimacy' which were so often spoken of in the chapter on the self, as characterizing all experiences 'appropriated by the thinker as his own.'" James concludes that a memory is far more than an image or copy of a fact in the mind, that it is in fact a very complex representation with objective, personal, and metacognitive components. What we usually refer to as memory, James argues, is a form of belief.

James's analyses of habit, as we have seen, had an immediate and large influence on the development of psychology in subsequent decades. His discussions of memory and other cognitive phenomena were out of step with the elementistic introspectionism of his time. It seems very likely that contemporary cognitive psychology—in particular, the study of personal, narrative memories—is picking up the thread of William James's thought.

Bibliography

Bjork, D. W. (1983). *The compromised scientist: William James in the development of American psychology.* New York: Columbia University Press.

Feinstein, H. M. (1984). *Becoming William James.* Ithaca: Cornell University Press.

James, W. (1890). *The principles of psychology.* 2 vols. Reprinted (1981) in F. H. Burkhardt, F. Bowers, and I. K. Skrupskelis, eds,. *The works of William James.* Cambridge, MA: Harvard University Press.

——— (1899). *Talks to teachers on psychology: And to students on some of life's ideals.* New York: Holt.

——— (1902). *The varieties of religious experience: A study in human nature.* New York: Longmans.

——— (1983). *Essays in psychology.* Vol. 13 in F. H. Burkhardt, F. Bowers, and I. K. Skrupskelis, eds., *The works of William James.* Cambridge, MA: Harvard University Press.

Myers, Gerald E. (1986). *William James: His life and thought.* New Haven: Yale University Press.

Perry, R. B. (1935). *The thought and character of William James, as revealed in unpublished correspondence and notes, together with his published writings.* 2 vols. Boston: Little, Brown.

Taylor, E. (1983). *William James on exceptional mental states: The 1896 Lowell lectures.* New York: Scribner's.

Sheldon H. White

K

KAMIN'S BLOCKING EFFECT: NEURONAL SUBSTRATES

Blocking is a classical conditioning phenomenon that has profoundly influenced thinking about associative learning. This article will discuss the key characteristics of blocking and the role it may play in several mammalian brain systems in regulating particular types of learning.

Introduction and Significance

Classical or Pavlovian conditioning is an elementary form of associative learning—systematically described by a Russian physiologist Ivan Pavlov in the early twentieth century—that is considered an essential building block for complex learning. Typically, classical conditioning occurs when an initially neutral stimulus (conditional stimulus, CS) is paired in close temporal proximity (or contiguously) with a biologically significant stimulus (unconditional stimulus, US) that elicits an unlearned, reflexive behavior (unconditional response, UR). Through CS-US association formation, the animal acquires a behavior (conditional response, CR) to the CS that typically resembles the UR (but not always), precedes the US in onset time, and reaches a maximum magnitude at about the time of US onset.

Although the temporal arrangement between the CS and the US was thought to be the critical feature of classical conditioning, three separate studies in the late 1960s revealed that the informational, rather than temporal, relationship between the CS and US is the essential determinant of classical conditioning (Kamin, 1968; Rescorla, 1968; Wagner et al., 1968) and profoundly shaped subsequent thinking about associative learning. One of the three findings was the phenomenon of blocking, discovered by Leon Kamin. In a typical blocking experiment (see Table 1), one CS (denoted *A*) is first extensively paired with a US (A–US). Then a second CS (denoted *B*) undergoes compound conditioning with *A* and the same US (AB–US). Later, when *B* is tested, almost no (or very little) conditioning has accrued to *B*. However, if *A* was previously not (or weakly) conditioned with the US, then *B* (as well as *A*) accrues substantial associative strength during the compound conditioning phase. Thus, conditioning to *B* during the compound (AB–US) conditioning is inversely proportional to the magnitude of previous conditioning to *A*, and it is not *B*'s temporal relationship with the US that determines whether or not conditioning will develop to *B*.

It was originally suggested that if a US is already fully predicted by one stimulus and if the addition of a new stimulus provides no new significant information about the US, then the US will not activate or support the learning process responsible for establishing a new CS-US association (Kamin, 1968, 1969). Since its discovery, blocking has become the cornerstone of all modern learning theories (see Rescorla and Wagner, 1972; Mackintosh, 1975; Pearce and Hall 1980; Wagner, 1981; Sutton and Barto, 1990) and has been considered as an instance of cognitive

301

Table 1

Kamin's Blocking Paradigm			
Group	Phase I	Phase II	Test
Control	—	AB-US	B → CR
Experimental	A-US	AB-US	B → no CR

SOURCE: Courtesy of Jeansok Kim. Adapted from Kamin, L. J. (1968). Attention-like processes in classical conditioning. *Miami symposium. Predictability, behavior, and aversive stimulation*, ed. M. R. Jones. Miami: University of Miami Press.

processing in classical conditioning (Thompson et al., 1998).

Theoretical Aspects

Robert Rescorla and Allan Wagner (1972) proposed a simple learning equation based on "US processing"

$$\delta Vn = \kappa(\lambda - \sigma Vi)$$

that elegantly describes the blocking effect; where κ is a learning constant; λ is the maximum associative strength conditionable with a given US; σVi is the sum of associative strengths between all CS elements present and the US; and δVn is the change in the associative strength of a particular CS on trial n. In essence, the associative strength between the CS-US is driven by "errors" between the expected US and the actual US. According to this equation, blocking occurs when the associative strength acquired by a CS (A) that was paired with a US (Phase I; A-US) reaches the λ value. Then, when a new CS (B) is introduced during the compound conditioning (Phase II; AB-US), stimulus A already fully predicts the US and has acquired all of its associative strength, because

$$V_A = \lambda.$$

Hence, the stimulus B will not accrue any associative strength, because

$$\delta V_B = \lambda - (V_A + V_B) = 0$$

because

$$V_A = \lambda.$$

Other learning theories based on CS processing rather than US processing can also effectively accommodate blocking by postulating that the absence of surprising events on a trial (e.g., in the presence of a well-predicted reinforcer) reduces the associability (the ability to enter into new associations) of CSs present on that trial (Mackintosh, 1975; Pearce and Hall, 1980). In this view, blocking occurs because stimulus B rapidly loses associability because no surprising events occur after the compound CS presentation. Conditioning to B is blocked because its associability is reduced (rapidly to zero) and thus it does not enter into associations with the US, not because of any loss of effectiveness of the US as a reinforcer.

The US and CS processing theories, however, make somewhat different predictions regarding blocking; for example, whereas the Rescorla-Wagner model predicts one trial blocking, theories based on CS processing do not; conversely, CS-processing models can account for the disruption of blocking ("unblocking") when the magnitude of the reinforcer is decreased simultaneously with the addition of an element to the CS (Dickinson et al., 1976; Holland and Gallagher, 1993), a phenomenon that causes difficulty for the Rescorla-Wagner model.

Progress in identifying neural circuits subserving particular learning phenomena has yielded insight into the neural basis of this phenomenon. We will briefly discuss the involvement of the cerebellum, amygdala, midbrain dopamine neurons, and septohippocampal systems in blocking.

Cerebellum and Eyeblink Conditioning

In eyeblink conditioning the animals learn to respond with eyelid closure to a CS (tone or light) that has been contingently paired with a US (e.g., airpuff to the eye). The anatomically rooted neural circuit underlying eyeblink conditioning (Kim and Thompson 1997) is remarkably similar to the US processing view of the Rescorla-Wagner model (see Figure 1).

Briefly, the CS pathway consists of excitatory mossy-fiber projections from the pontine nuclei to the cerebellum, whereas the US pathway consists of excitatory climbing-fiber projections from the inferior olive to the cerebellum. The cerebellum, in turn, sends monosynaptic γ-aminobutyric acid (GABA)-containing projections to the inferior olive. As GABA neurotransmitters generally exert inhibitory influences, it is conceivable that this cerebello-olivary pathway serves a negative feedback function and thus "gates" the inferior olive activity. Consistent with this view, neurons in the inferior olive show evoked neural activity to the airpuff US during the initial stage of CS-US training (before the animal exhibits any CRs), but not when the animals perform CRs during CS-US trials (Sears and Steinmetz, 1991; Hesslow and Ivarsson, 1996).

If the cerebello-olivary GABAergic projection serves a negative-feedback function in regulating the

US information from reaching the cerebellum (where the CS-US association is thought to take place), then this can explain the blocking effect in eyeblink conditioning in the following manner: According to Figure 1, blocking will occur when a CS (e.g., auditory CS_A) acquires sufficient associative strength to activate the cerebellum, which then inhibits the inferior olive (via the GABA-containing cerebello-olivary pathway) from US activation. Because the input representing the US can no longer reach the cerebellum, it cannot support conditioning to a new CS (e.g., visual CS_B). Consistent with this view, a study found that pharmacological blockade of the cerebello-olivary activity (by infusing a GABA antagonist directly into the inferior olive) during the compound tone/light-airpuff conditioning—thereby disinhibiting inferior olive neurons—prevented blocking (Kim et al., 1998).

Amygdala and Fear Conditioning

Fear conditioning typically involves pairing a tone (or light) CS with a nociceptive shock US. After few CS-US pairings, the CS not only becomes capable of activating fear responses but also acquires the ability to inhibit/decrease sensitivity to nociceptive stimuli (e.g., foot shock) via a conditioned analgesic response (involving partly endogenous opioids) (Chance, 1980; MacLennan et al., 1980). Because the amygdala has been implicated as the locus of fear conditioning and sends projections to hypothalamus and brainstem nuclei that mediate various fear responses (LeDoux, 1997), some researchers believe that as fear conditioning proceeds, the ability of the nociceptive US to support fear conditioning diminishes as a function of the CS ability to elicit conditioned analgesia via the amygdala (see Figure 2). Consistent with this notion, systemic administration of the opioid antagonist naloxone during compound fear conditioning (phase II, blocking procedure) attenuated blocking (Fanselow and Bolles, 1979; Fanselow, 1998). It is possible that naloxone, by opposing the conditioned opioid analgesia response to the first CS, prevented the CS-associated decline in the nociceptive US's ability to support fear conditioning to the second CS (during compound conditioning). However, the locus of naloxone's effects on blocking is not known, and further research is necessary to determine whether the US-evoked responses in the amygdala decrease as a function of fear conditioning.

Striatum and Dopaminergic Midbrain Neurons

Other brain structures may employ a negative-feedback mechanism similar to that of the cerebellum to regulate the US or "reinforcing" input (Graybiel et

Figure 1

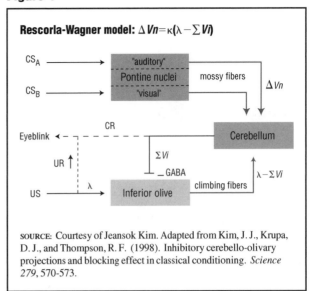

Rescorla-Wagner model: $\Delta Vn = \kappa(\lambda - \sum Vi)$

SOURCE: Courtesy of Jeansok Kim. Adapted from Kim, J. J., Krupa, D. J., and Thompson, R. F. (1998). Inhibitory cerebello-olivary projections and blocking effect in classical conditioning. *Science* 279, 570-573.

The Rescorla-Wagner equation has been mapped onto a simplified eyeblink conditioning circuit to illustrate how one form of blocking might occur in the mammalian brain.

al., 1994; Schultz et al., 1993). For example, some researchers report that many dopamine neurons in the substantia nigra (SN) and the ventral tegmental area (VTA) show phasic responses to the delivery of liquid reward in monkeys undergoing a spatial delayed-response task (Schultz et al., 1993). However, once learning is established (i.e., the animal learns that a light cue predicts the reward), the delivery of the reward no longer elicits phasic responses in dopaminergic neurons. Such negative-feedback circuits in the brain may well provide the neuronal instantiation of behavioral phenomena of blocking.

Indeed, when examined in a blocking paradigm, dopamine neurons did not fire in response to the blocked element of a compound stimulus but did fire to one element of a compound control stimulus (Waelti et al., 2001). These neurons seem to enable blocking phenomena in more complex forms of associative learning that involve appetitive stimuli and more complex motor responses and that depend on forebrain structures by conveying a "prediction error" signal that enables the formation of associations (Schultz and Dickinson, 2000). On a neural level, this system is analogous to that in the cerebellum (see Figure 1), replacing the inferior olive with the SN/VTA and the cerebellum with the basal ganglia and neocortex (which receive dopaminergic input from the SN/VTA). These findings are also consistent with reports of disrupted blocking after manipulations of the dopamine system (Crider et al., 1982, 1986).

Figure 2

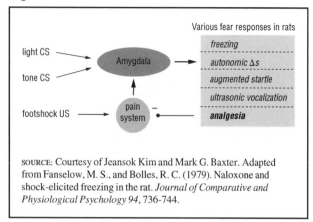

SOURCE: Courtesy of Jeansok Kim and Mark G. Baxter. Adapted from Fanselow, M. S., and Bolles, R. C. (1979). Naloxone and shock-elicited freezing in the rat. *Journal of Comparative and Physiological Psychology 94*, 736-744.

A simple model of fear conditioning illustrating how the regulation of US processing may account for blocking. A CS-evoked conditioned analgesia response is hypothesize to dampen sensitivity/reactivity to nociceptive US, thereby inhibiting or decreasing the reinforcer's ability to support further conditioning.

Septohippocampal System

The hippocampus appears to play a role in the capacity to reduce the associability of a CS (Han, Gallagher, and Holland, 1995; Kaye and Pearce, 1987; Solomon and Moore, 1975; Honey and Good, 1993; Gallo and Cándido, 1995; Reilly, Harley, and Revusky, 1993); moreover, this function of the hippocampus appears to depend on the integrity of its cholinergic input (Baxter et al., 1997). Based on the view that the blocking effect results from variations in processing of the US, one would not expect the hippocampal damage to affect blocking, and some experiments have found just that (Garrud et al., 1984). In contrast, CS-processing theories of blocking propose that the associability of the added element of the compound CS is reduced because the reinforcer is already well predicted. On this view, damage to the hippocampus (or its cholinergic input) should eliminate this reduction in associability and, by extension, the blocking effect. In support of this view, several investigators have reported that lesions of the hippocampus reduced or eliminated blocking (Gallo and Cándido, 1995; Rickert et al., 1978; Rickert et al., 1981; Solomon 1977). These variations in the effectiveness of hippocampal system damage on blocking are consistent with the view that blocking has diverse origins (Holland, 1988) and may reflect different contributions of CS and US processing systems in different conditioning situations.

Experiments in an appetitive Pavlovian conditioning paradigm suggested that a blocking paradigm produces both CS- and US-processing mecha-

nisms. Baxter et al. (1999) examined blocking in rats with selective removal of medial septal cholinergic neurons. These lesions remove hippocampal cholinergic input and impair reductions in CS associability in several different learning paradigms (Baxter et al., 1997). Although lesioned rats showed a normal blocking effect when tested in an extinction test with the added cue B, learning about B was facilitated relative to controls in subsequent savings tests, in which B alone was paired with reinforcement or served as a conditioned inhibitor. These findings suggested that although B did undergo a loss of associability as a consequence of the blocking procedure, this loss of associability was not necessary for blocking of learning about B to occur.

Conclusion

Functionally, blocking (or other similar processes) may play an important role in how animals process and attend to information in their environments. Because animals are constantly bombarded by numerous stimuli, it benefits them respond selectively to those stimuli that reliably predict biologically significant events. Other stimuli that provide no new useful information should be disregarded (or filtered), otherwise animals would be constantly forming unnecessary associations with various stimuli in their surroundings, thus inviting information overload. Indeed, malfunctioning selective attention mechanisms in the brain may contribute to psychopathological conditions such as schizophrenia (Bender et al., 2001). The behavioral phenomenon of blocking, which appears to use heuristic negative-feedback attentional processes, may circumvent such redundant learning.

See also: CONDITIONING, CELLULAR AND NETWORK SCHEMES FOR HIGHER-ORDER FEATURES OF; LEARNING THEORY: CURRENT STATUS; REINFORCEMENT OR REWARD IN LEARNING: CEREBELLUM; REINFORCEMENT OR REWARD IN LEARNING: STRIATUM

Bibliography

Baxter, M. G., Gallagher, M., and Holland, P. C. (1999). Blocking can occur without losses in attention in rats with selective lesions of hippocampal cholinergic input. *Behavioral Neuroscience 113*, 881–890.

Baxter, M. G., Holland, P. C., and Gallagher, M. (1997). Disruption of decrements in conditioned stimulus processing by selective removal of hippocampal cholinergic input. *Journal of Neuroscience 17*, 5,230–5,236.

Bender, S., Muller, B., Oades, R. D., and Sartory, G. (2001). Conditioned blocking and schizophrenia: A replication and study of the role of symptoms, age, onset-age of psychosis and illness-duration. *Schizophrenia Research 49*, 157–170.

Chance, W. T. (1980). Autoanalgesia: opiate and nonopiate mechanisms. *Neuroscience and Biobehavioral Reviews 4*, 55–67.

Crider, A., Blockel, L., and Solomon, P. R. (1986). A selective attention deficit in the rat following induced dopamine receptor supersensitivity. *Behavioral Neuroscience 100*, 315–319.

Crider, A., Solomon, P. R., and McMahon, M. A. (1982). Disruption of selective attention in the rat following chronic d-amphetamine administration: relationship to schizophrenic attention disorder. *Biological Psychiatry 17*, 351–361.

Dickinson, A., Hall, G., and Mackintosh, N. J. (1976). Surprise and the attenuation of blocking. *Journal of Experimental Psychology: Animal Behavior Processes 2*, 313–322.

Fanselow, M. S. (1998). Pavlovian conditioning, negative feedback, and blocking: Mechanisms that regulate associative formation. *Neuron 20*, 625–627.

Fanselow, M. S., and Bolles, R. C. (1979). Naloxone and shock-elicited freezing in the rat. *Journal of Comparative and Physiological Psychology 94*, 736–744.

Gallo, M., and Cándido, A. (1995). Dorsal hippocampal lesions impair blocking but not latent inhibition of taste aversion learning in rats. *Behavioral Neuroscience 109*, 413–425.

Garrud, P., Rawlins, J. N. P., Mackintosh, N. J., Goodall, G., Cotton, M. M., and Feldon, J. (1984). Successful overshadowing and blocking in hippocampectomized rats. *Behavioural Brain Research 12*, 39–53.

Graybiel, A. M., Aosaki, T., Flaherty, A. W., and Kimura, M. (1994). The basal ganglia and adaptive motor control. *Science 265*, 1,826–1,831.

Han, J.–S., Gallagher, M., and Holland, P. C. (1995). Hippocampal lesions disrupt decrements but not increments in conditioned stimulus processing. *Journal of Neuroscience 15*, 7,323–7,329.

Hesslow, G., and Ivarsson, M. (1996). Inhibition of the inferior olive during conditioned responses in the decerebrate ferret. *Experimental Brain Research 110*, 36–46.

Holland, P. C. (1988). Excitation and inhibition in unblocking. *Journal of Experimental Psychology: Animal Behavior Processes 14*, 261–279.

Holland, P. C., and Gallagher, M. (1993). Effects of amygdala central nucleus lesions on blocking and unblocking. *Behavioral Neuroscience 107*, 235–245.

Honey, R. C., and Good, M. (1993). Selective hippocampal lesions abolish the contextual specificity of latent inhibition and conditioning. *Behavioral Neuroscience 107*, 23–33.

Kamin, L. J. (1968). Attention-like processes in classical conditioning. In M. R. Jones, ed., *Miami Symposium. Predictability, Behavior and Aversive Stimulation*. Miami: University of Miami Press.

——— (1969). Predictability, surprise, attention, and conditioning. In B. A. Campbell and R. M. Church, eds., *Punishment and Aversive Behavior*. New York: Appleton-Century-Crofts.

Kaye, H., and Pearce, J. M. (1987). Hippocampal lesions attenuate latent inhibition of a CS and of a neutral stimulus. *Psychobiology 15*, 293–299.

Kim, J. J., Krupa, D. J., and Thompson, R. F. (1998). Inhibitory cerebello–olivary projections and blocking effect in classical conditioning. *Science 279*, 570–573.

Kim, J. J., and Thompson, R. F. (1997). Cerebellar circuits and synaptic mechanisms involved in classical eyeblink conditioning. *Trends in Neuroscience 4*, 177–181.

LeDoux, J. E. (1997). *The Emotional Brain*. New York: Simon and Schuster.

Mackintosh, N. J. (1975). A theory of attention: Variations in the associability of stimuli with reinforcement. *Psychological Review 82*, 276–298.

MacLennan, A. J., Jackson, R. L., and Maier, S. F. (1980). Conditioned analgesia in the rat. *Bulletin of the Psychonomic Society 15*, 387–390.

Pavlov, I. P. (1927). *Conditioned Reflexes*. London: Oxford University Press.

Pearce, J. M., and Hall, G. (1980). A model for Pavlovian learning: Variations in the effectiveness of conditioned but not of unconditioned stimuli. *Psychological Review 87*, 532–552.

Reilly, S., Harley, C., and Revusky, S. (1993). Ibotenate lesions of the hippocampus enhance latent inhibition in conditioned taste aversion and increase resistance to extinction in conditioned taste preference. *Behavioral Neuroscience 107*, 996–1,004.

Rescorla, R. A. (1968). Probability of shock in the presence and absence of CS in fear conditioning. *Journal of Comparative and Physiological Psychology 66*, 1–5.

Rescorla, R. A., and Wagner, A. R. (1972). A theory of Pavlovian conditioning: Variations in the effectiveness of reinforcement and nonreinforcement. In A. H. Black and W. F. Prokasy, eds., *Classical conditioning: II. Current research and theory*. New York: Appleton-Century-Crofts.

Rickert, E. J., Bennett, T. L., Lane, P., and French, J. (1978). Hippocampectomy and the attenuation of blocking. *Behavioral Biology 22*, 147–160.

Rickert, E. J., Lorden, J. F., Dawson Jr., R., and Smyly, E. (1981). Limbic lesions and the blocking effect. *Physiology and Behavior 26*, 601–606.

Schultz, W., Apicella, P., and Ljungberg, T. (1993). Responses of monkey dopamine neurons to reward and conditioned stimuli during successive steps of learning a delayed response task. *Journal of Neuroscience 13*, 900–913.

Schultz, W., and Dickinson, A. (2000). Neuronal coding of prediction errors. *Annual Review of Neuroscience 23*, 473–500.

Sears, L. L., and Steinmetz, J. E. (1991). Dorsal accessory inferior olive activity diminishes during acquisition of the rabbit classically conditioned eyelid response. *Brain Research 545*, 114–122.

Solomon, P. R. (1977). Role of the hippocampus in blocking and conditioned inhibition of the rabbit's nictitating membrane response. *Journal of Comparative and Physiological Psychology 91*, 407–417.

Solomon, P. R., and Moore, J. W. (1975). Latent inhibition and stimulus generalization of the classically conditioned nictitating membrane response in rabbits (*Oryctolagus cuniculus*) following dorsal hippocampal ablation. *Journal of Comparative and Physiological Psychology 89*, 1,192–1,203.

Sutton, R. S., and Barto, A. G. (1990). Time-derivative models of Pavlovian reinforcement. In M. Gabriel and J. Moore, eds., *Learning and computational neuroscience*. Cambridge, MA: MIT Press.

Thompson, R. F., Thompson, J. K., Kim, J. J., Krupa, D. J., and Shinkman, P. G. (1998). The nature of reinforcement in cerebellar learning. *Neurobiology of Learning and Memory 70*, 150–176.

Wagner, A. R. (1981). SOP: a model of automatic memory processing in animal behavior. In N. E. Spear and R. R. Miller, eds., *Information processing in animals: Memory mechanisms*. Hillsdale, NJ: Erlbaum.

Wagner, A. R., Logan, F. A., Haberlandt, K., and Price, T. (1968). Stimulus selection in animal discrimination learning. *Journal of Experimental Psychology 76*, 171–180.

Waelti, P., Dickinson, A., and Schultz, W. (2001). Dopamine responses comply with basic assumptions of formal learning theory. *Nature 412*, 43–48.

Jeansok J. Kim
Mark G. Baxter

KNOWLEDGE SYSTEMS AND MATERIAL-SPECIFIC MEMORY DEFICITS

The face of cognitive neuroscience has changed drastically since the mid–twentieth century. In the past, lesions were the only basis for inference regarding the functional neuroanatomy of normal cognition. Today the tools of cognitive neuroscience include various methods of neuroimaging, both structural and functional, in normal subjects.

Classifications of Memory Systems

The structure of knowledge representation in the brain is elucidated by the studies of specific dissociations of knowledge loss in brain disease. The question whether there is one memory store or several is of the foremost interest. Studies of amnesias are particularly illuminating in this respect. In most amnesic syndromes, skills are better preserved than facts. Within the declarative domain, context-free information is usually better preserved than context-dependent information. Generic information is better preserved than singular information. Generally, the patient's ability to give a conscious account of previously acquired knowledge is more likely to be impaired than the ability to benefit from this knowledge in various behavioral situations. These observations have been interpreted to indicate the neuropsychological reality of the distinctions between procedural knowledge (skills) and declarative knowledge (facts) (Cohen and Squire, 1980), semantic memory (for general facts) and episodic memory (for personal facts) (Tulving, 1983; Kinsbourne and Wood, 1975), generic knowledge (referring to large classes of equivalent objects) and singular knowledge (referring to unique entities), and explicit knowledge (demonstrated through conscious reports) and implicit knowledge (demonstrated through behavioral gains) (Schacter, 1987; Tulving and Schacter, 1990).

While the phenomenal distinctness of these knowledge categories is widely accepted, consensus is lacking as to whether these knowledge types are mediated by neurally distinct stores, or by different processing demands. Robustness and uniformity of the dissociations are often mentioned as the arguments in favor of separate stores (Schacter, 1985). An alternative hypothesis is that the difference between procedural and declarative, semantic and episodic, generic and singular, and explicit and implicit knowledge types reflects different degrees of accessibility of engrams that are part of the same store. This position suggests that the differences between components of the above dichotomies are quantitative rather than qualitative, and are discrete approximations of continuous variations in the degree of engram accessibility.

Recent studies using PET (positron emission tomography) and fMRI (functional magnetic imaging) methodology have further elucidated the neuroanatomical distinctiveness of these systems. There is evidence to indicate that many aspects of semantic memory processing involve regions of the left lateral prefrontal cortex and the anterior temporal cortex. Some findings converge to suggest that this system is organized hierarchically along the posterior to anterior axis (Martin and Chao, 2001). Functional imaging studies of episodic memory have not provided support for the view that these processes are mediated primarily by the medial temporal lobe memory system (Bookheimer, 1996). Researchers have suggested that encoding and retrieval of episodic information might be related more to the functions of the left and right prefrontal cortex respectively (Tulving et al., 1994), although this view is not consistent with the bulk of information obtained from lesion studies and may be too simplistic to account for the complex nature of these processes.

Modality-Specificity of Knowledge Systems

Two additional types of knowledge-base dissociations have been described: sensory modalities and by semantic categories. Modality-specific knowledge loss is exemplified by associative agnosias and modality-specific aphasias. In associative agnosias, the subject loses the ability to identify objects as members of generic categories (Warrington, 1975; Goldberg, 1990). The deficit may be isolated, in that it may be present without sensory or language impairment, and without dementia. Most important in the context of this analysis, the deficit is modality-specific, and at least three types of associative agnosias have been identified: visual object agnosia (McCarthy and Warrington, 1986), pure astereognosis (Hecaen and Albert, 1978), and auditory associative agnosia (Vignolo, 1982).

In each of these agnosias, the ability to interpret object meaning is impaired with respect to a distinct input modality. A patient can see that a watch is round and flat but does not recognize it as a watch in visual object agnosia; a patient can feel that it has a smooth, glassy surface and a small bump on the side, but does not recognize it as a watch in pure astereognosis; and a patient can hear it tick but does not recognize it as a watch in auditory associative agnosia. The knowledge-base impairment in associative agnosias is evident both in patients' inability to correctly name the object and in their inability to signal its correct meaning through nonverbal means, such as pantomime. However, successful object identification, both verbal and nonverbal, will be accomplished in each of these three conditions with reliance on other sensory modalities. The existence of modality-specific associative agnosias has led to the hypothesis that the nonverbal knowledge base is dimensionalized at least in part by sensory modalities (Warrington, 1975; Goldberg, 1990; Damasio, 1990; Shallice, 1987). This hypothesis is strengthened by the presence of double dissociations between any two types of associative agnosia.

In modality-specific aphasias, the patient can correctly identify the object meaning through nonverbal means (e.g., pantomime) but cannot come up with a correct name (Beauvois, 1982). However, the name is easily retrieved when the patient is allowed to resort to other sensory input modalities. The existence of sense-specific aphasias further supports the notion of modality-specific knowledge stores, by suggesting that each of them has a separate access to an amodal lexical store (Beauvois, 1982).

Modality-specific associative agnosias are distinct not only phenomenally but also neuroanatomically. Each type of agnosia has a distinct cortical territory that is consistent across patients. This observation lends further support to the notion of multiple, neurally distinct, modality-specific knowledge stores. It has been suggested that the modality-specific associative agnosias are all linked predominantly to the left hemisphere (Warrington, 1975; Goldberg, 1990). If this assertion is true, then the left hemisphere emerges as the repository of multiple knowledge systems, verbal and nonverbal alike. It has been further suggested that the neocortical functional organization within the posterior portion of a hemisphere is characterized by continuous, gradiental distributions of cognitive functions. The geometry of the cognitive gradients is determined by the sensory cortices (Goldberg, 1989). This position is consistent with the notion that representations are dimensionalized in terms of sensory modalities. Functional neuroimaging studies in normal subjects have further supported the notion of the distributed nature of mental representations. Information from both PET and fMRI have demonstrated that information about objects and their features may be represented in the same neural systems that are active during their perception (Martin, 2001).

Category-Specific Knowledge Representation

Category-specific knowledge loss has also been reported (Damasio, 1990; Warrington and Shallice, 1990; Hart, Berndt, and Caramazza, 1985). In the lexical domain, this pertains to the double dissociation of comprehension and naming of object names and action names (Goodglass, Klein, Carey, and Jones, 1966; Miceli, Silveri, Villa, and Caramazza, 1984). Further fractionation of noun loss has also been reported (Warrington and Shallice, 1990; Hart, Berndt, and Caramazza, 1985; McKenna and Warrington, 1980).

Category-specific knowledge loss also may manifest itself as a selective inability to describe objects or elicit their mental images (Warrington and Shallice, 1984), or as selective agnosia for certain categories of objects but not for others (Nielsen, 1946). The most common and consistent observation of category-specific knowledge loss is that the knowledge of living objects or foods is more impaired than the knowledge of inanimate objects (Vignolo, 1982; Goldberg, 1989; Hart, Berndt, and Caramazza, 1985; Goodglass et al., 1986). However, researchers have also reported the opposite pattern (Warrington and McCarthy, 1983, 1987).

To account for the overwhelming unidirectionality of dissociation, with most studies reporting greater preservation of knowledge about inanimate than living things, and very few reporting the opposite pattern, it has been proposed that the difference may reflect inherently greater perceptual similarities, and therefore confusability, within the living domain than within the inanimate domain (Riddoch, Humphreys, Coltheart, and Funnell, 1988). Alternatively, it has been proposed that the category-specific knowledge loss may reflect different patterns of relative salience of different sensory modalities for different categories (Goldberg, 1989; Warrington and McCarthy, 1987). The latter helps to explain category-specific double dissociations. It also interrelates category- and sense-specific aspects of mental representations.

The inanimate objects used in most studies are in fact human-made objects or tools. Therefore, it is difficult to know which of the two distinctions, living versus inanimate or human-made versus natural, best captures the observed differences. The latter distinction emphasizes the secondary nature of category-specific aspects relative to modality-specific aspects of knowledge representations. This is because human-made tools have mandatory somatosensory and motor representations in the brain that are absent for most natural objects or foods. Therefore, tools are encoded with reliance on more sensory dimensions compared with most natural objects, which would make the corresponding engrams more robust.

In considering the more esoteric types of category-specific knowledge loss or knowledge preservation (Hart, Berndt, and Caramazza, 1985; Yamadori and Albert, 1973; McKenna and Warrington, 1978), one must also take into account the possible premorbid idiosyncrasies of individual lexical strengths and weaknesses. This may be a potent source of artifact in analyzing postmorbid performance.

Finally, combined category- and modality-specific knowledge loss has been reported in a patient who had a selective loss of living things but not objects in the verbal but not visual domain (McCarthy and Warrington, 1988). Elizabeth Warrington and Tim Shallice (1984) conclude that knowledge is organized along both sensory and category dimensions.

Knowledge of the object's superordinate category is well preserved in modality-specific, category-specific, and combined knowledge loss (Warrington, 1975; McCarthy and Warrington, 1988). This pervasive observation has lent support to the hypothesis that knowledge about things is hierarchic. Researchers have proposed that the access to a specific category member invariably begins with accessing a superordinate category (Warrington, 1975). While this may be true in some cases, the observation of the relative preservation of superordinate knowledge does not in itself necessitate this conclusion. In fact, a different route of object identification has also been proposed, from the basic category to superordinate and subordinate categories (Rosch, 1978).

Researchers have evoked both degraded-store (Warrington and Shallice, 1984) and impaired-access (Humphreys, Riddoch, and Quinlan, 1988) hypotheses to account for category- and modality-specific memory loss. They have suggested that a degraded store is characterized by the uniformity of responses across recall trials, and impaired access by their variability (Warrington and Shallice, 1984; Cermak and O'Connor, 1983; Shallice, 1988). The possible neuroanatomical basis for this distinction may be related to whether the critical lesion affects neocortical sites where representations are distributed, thus resulting in degraded store, or subcortical structures involved in various aspects of activation and arousal, thus resulting in impaired access.

Functional neuroimaging studies in normal subjects also point to the segregation of the neural systems involved in category-specific knowledge. Investigators have shown that specific regions of the ventral temporal cortex respond differentially to processing of various categories (Chao, Haxby, and Martin, 1999). There have been some indications that dissociations in the pattern of activation follow the distinction between animate and inanimate categories (Caramazza and Shelton, 1998); however research findings in the late 1990s and early 2000s have failed to find evidence that these category distinctions exist at the neural level (Devlin et al., 2002).

See also: CONCEPTS AND CATEGORIES, LEARNING OF; MODALITY EFFECTS

Bibliography

Beauvois, M. F. (1982). Optic aphasia: A process of interaction between vision and language. *Philosophical Transactions of the Royal Society (London) B298,* 35–47.

Bookheimer, S. Y. (1996). Functional MRI applications in clinical epilepsy. *Neuroimage 4,* S139–146.

Caramazza, A., and Shelton, J. R. (1998). Domain-specific knowledge systems in the brain: The animate inanimate distinction. *Journal of Cognitive Neuroscience 10,* 1–34.

Cermak, L. S., and O'Connor, M. (1983). The retrieval capacity of a patient with amnesia due to encephalitis. *Neuropsychologia 21,* 213–234.

Chao, L. L., Haxby, J. V., and Martin, A. (1999). Attribute-based neural substrates in temporal cortex for perceiving and knowing about objects. *Nature Neuroscience 2,* 913–919.

Cohen, N. J., and Squire, L. R. (1980). Preserved learning and retention of pattern-analyzing skill in amnesia: Dissociation of "knowing how" and "knowing that." *Science 210,* 207–209.

Damasio, A. R. (1990). Category related recognition defects as a clue to the neural substrates of knowledge. *Trends in Neurosciences 13,* 95–98.

Devlin, J. T., Russell, R. P. Davis, R. H., Price, C. J., Moss, H. E., Fadili, M. J., and Tyler, L. K. (2002). Is there an anatomical basis for category-specificity? Semantic memory studies in PET and fMRI. *Neuropsychologia 40,* 54–75.

Goldberg, E. (1989). Gradiental approach to the neocortical functional organization. *Journal of Clinical and Experimental Neuropsychology 11,* 489–517.

—— (1990). Associative agnosias and the functions of the left hemisphere. *Journal of Clinical and Experimental Neuropsychology 12,* 467–484.

Goodglass, H., Klein, B., Carey, P., and Jones, K. (1966). Specific semantic word categories in aphasia. *Cortex 2,* 74–89.

Goodglass, H., Wingfield, A., Hyde, M. R., and Theurkauf, J. (1986). Category-specific dissociation in naming and recognition by aphasic patients. *Cortex 22,* 87–102.

Hart, J., Berndt, R. S., and Caramazza, A. (1985). Category-specific naming deficit following cerebral infarction. *Nature 316,* 439–440.

Hecaen, H., and Albert, M. L. (1978). *Human neuropsychology.* New York: Wiley.

Humphreys, G. W., Riddoch, M. J., and Quinlan, P. T. (1988). Cascade processes in picture identification. *Cognitive Neuropsychology 5,* 67–103.

Kinsbourne, M., and Wood, F. (1975). Short-term memory processes and the amnestic syndrome. In D. Deutsch and J. A. Deutsch, eds., *Short-term memory.* New York: Academic Press.

Martin, A. (2001). Functional neuroimaging of semantic memory. In R. Cabaza and A. Kingstone, eds., *Functional imaging of semantic memory.* Cambridge, MA: MIT Press.

McCarthy, R. A., and Warrington, E. K. (1986). Visual associative agnosia: A clinico-anatomical study of a single case. *Journal of Neurology, Neurosurgery and Psychiatry 49,* 1,233–1,240.

—— (1988). Evidence for modality-specific meaning systems in the brain. *Nature 334,* 428–430.

McKenna, P., and Warrington, E. K. (1978). Category-specific naming preservation: A single case study. *Journal of Neurology, Neurosurgery and Psychiatry 41,* 571–574.

—— (1980). Testing for nominal dysphasia. *Journal of Neurology, Neurosurgery and Psychiatry 43,* 781–788.

Miceli, G., Silveri, M. C., Villa, G., and Caramazza, A. (1984). On the basis for the agrammatic's difficulty in producing main verbs. *Cortex 20,* 207–220.

Nielsen, J. M. (1946). *Agnosia, apraxia, aphasia: Their value in cerebral localization,* 2nd edition. New York: Hoeber.

Riddoch, M. J., Humphreys, G. W., Coltheart, M., and Funnell, E. (1988). Semantic systems or system? Neuropsychological evidence re-examined. *Cognitive Neuropsychology 5*, 3–25.

Rosch, E. (1978). Principles of categorization. In E. Rosch and B. B. Lloyd, eds., *Principles of categorization*. Hillsdale, NJ: Erlbaum.

Schacter, D. L. (1985). Multiple forms of memory in humans and animals. In N. M. Weinberger, J. L. McGaugh, and G. Lynch, eds., *Memory systems of the brain*. New York: Guilford Press.

—— (1987). Implicit memory: History and current status. *Journal of Experimental Psychology: Learning, Memory, and Cognition 13*, 501–518.

Shallice, T. (1987). Impairments of semantic processing: Multiple dissociations. In M. Coltheart, G. Santori, and R. J. Job, eds., *The cognitive neuropsychology of language*. Hillsdale, NJ: Erlbaum.

—— (1988). *From neuropsychology to mental structure*. Cambridge, MA: Cambridge University Press.

Tulving, E. (1983). *Elements of episodic memory*. Oxford: Oxford University Press.

Tulving, E., Kapur, S., Craik, F. I. M., Moscovitch, M., and Houle, S. (1994). Hemispheric encoding/retrieval asymmetry in episodic memory: Positron emission tomography findings. *Proceedings of the National Academy of Sciences of the United States of America 91*, 2,016–2,020.

Tulving, E., and Schacter, D. L. (1990). Priming and human memory systems. *Science 247*, 301–306.

Vignolo, L. A. (1982). Auditory agnosia. *Philosophical Transactions of the Royal Society (London) B298*, 16–33.

Warrington, E. K. (1975). The selective impairment of semantic memory. *Quarterly Journal of Experimental Psychology 27*, 635–657.

Warrington, E. K., and McCarthy, R. A. (1983). Category specific access dysphasia. *Brain 106*, 859–878.

—— (1987). Categories of knowledge: Further fractionations and an attempted integration. *Brain 110*, 1,273–1,296.

Warrington, E. K., and Shallice, T. (1984). Category specific semantic impairments. *Brain 107*, 829–853.

Yamadori, A., and Albert, M. L. (1973). Word category aphasia. *Cortex 9*, 112–125.

Elkhonon Goldberg
William B. Barr

KONORSKI, JERZY (1903–1973)

Although Jerzy Konorski always regarded himself as a neurophysiologist, his empirical and theoretical legacy has been in psychology. Like those of the Russian scientist Ivan Pavlov, Konorski's theories, although expressed in terms of speculative physiology, were largely based on behavioral experiments and are readily recast into psychological concepts. And it is in this form that his ideas have come to exert a preeminent influence over the contemporary study of associative learning through conditioning.

Konorski was born in the Polish city of Lódz. From his earliest student days, he was fascinated by brain function, and while studying medicine at Warsaw University, he came into contact with Pavlov's work. Although inspired by Pavlov's ideas, he doubted that Pavlovian mechanisms could explain all forms

Jerzy Konorski *(Nencki Institute)*

of acquired behavior, especially instrumental or operant conditioning. Along with a fellow student, Stephan Miller, he set up a makeshift conditioning laboratory to investigate whether instrumental and classical (Pavlovian) conditioning obey the same principles of reinforcement. On the basis of this work, Miller and Konorski (1969) published the first statement of the distinction between the two forms of conditioning in 1928, while they were still students. The existence and importance of this distinction was not realized in the West until Konorski and Miller entered into a published debate with B. F. Skinner on the matter in the next decade.

Their subsequent work on instrumental conditioning, conducted in Pavlov's laboratory between 1931 and 1933, and subsequently at the Nencki Institute of Experimental Biology in Warsaw, was unknown in the West before World War II. Their studies of both modulatory and conditioned reinforcing effects of Pavlovian stimuli on instrumental conditioning led them to a two-process theory that was not approximated in the West until the 1960s. Their analysis of avoidance conditioning still stands.

Ignorance of Konorski and Miller's work before World War II is understandable, for the presentation of this research in English had to await the publication of Konorski's monograph *Conditioned Reflexes and Neuron Organization* (1948). The neglect of this volume is less comprehensible, however, for in it Konorski presented the first detailed connectionist account of conditioning within the framework of a Sherringtonian conception of the central nervous system. Aside from its pioneering a connectionist approach to learning, two aspects of Konorski's 1948 theory deserve special mention. The first is his treatment of conditioned inhibition. Although inhibitory processes were studied intensively in Pavlov's laboratory, their importance was not recognized in the West until the 1960s. When research on this topic finally got under way in the West, Konorski's conception of an inhibitory connection was incorporated into current theories of conditioning.

The second notable feature of Konorski's theory, which has not yet received due recognition, is the rules that he outlined for changing connection weights. Konorski (1948, p. 106) suggested that a positive increment in an excitatory connection weight occurs when activity in an input element is paired with a rise in activity in the receptor element. Correspondingly, inhibitory connections are strengthened when input element activity is paired with a fall in the activation of the receptor element. The importance of these suggestions is that they provide a way of implementing in connectionist terms the error-correcting learning rules (e.g., the Rescorla-Wagner rule) that have come to dominate current theories of associative learning.

When Konorski returned to Poland immediately after World War II, he was instrumental in reestablishing the Nencki Institute, first as the head of the Department of Neurophysiology and later as its director. His enthusiasm and dedication to behavioral neuroscience are clear from the recollections of some of his students, published in his memorial issue of the institute's journal, *Acta neurobiologiae experimentalis* (Zernicki, 1974), which contains a full bibliography. Unfortunately, his research activity was constrained at that time by the promulgation of Pavlovian orthodoxy in the later years of Russian dictator Joseph Stalin's reign, because his 1948 monograph was regarded as a revisionist text.

Stalin's death eventually loosened these intellectual shackles and allowed Konorski to establish contacts with American researchers. These contacts had a profound influence on him and culminated in the publication of *Integrative Activity of the Brain* (1967). The scope of this book was ambitious, attempting to describe the brain mechanisms subserving not just learning and conditioning but also perception, cognition, motivation, and emotion—indeed, the overall integration of these functions. Although replete with many interesting and perceptive ideas, this volume is less satisfactory than the first book. Its theoretical substance is too dependent upon the neuroscientific theories and claims of the time, many of which have suffered at the hands of subsequent research. Moreover, its scope precluded one of the most elegant and impressive features of the earlier book, the attempt to achieve a detailed concordance between theory and data.

When Konorski died in 1973, Western psychology had just begun to appreciate his legacy. His influence on research in conditioning and associative learning rivals that of Pavlov and the neobehaviorists (see Dickinson and Boakes, 1979).

See also: CONDITIONING, CLASSICAL AND INSTRUMENTAL

Bibliography

Dickinson, A., and Boakes, R. A., eds. (1979). *Mechanisms of learning and motivation: A memorial volume to Jerzy Konorski.* Hillsdale, NJ: Erlbaum.

Konorski, J. (1948). *Conditioned reflexes and neuron organization.* Cambridge, MA: Cambridge University Press.

——— (1967). *Integrative activity of the brain: An interdisciplinary approach.* Chicago: University of Chicago Press.

Miller, S., and Konorski, J. (1969). On a particular form of conditioned reflex. *Journal of the experimental analysis of behavior 12,* 187–189. English translation by B. F. Skinner from the original French publication (1928).

Zernicki, B., ed. (1974). *Acta neurobiologiae experimentalis 34* (6).

Anthony Dickinson

L

LANGUAGE

See: LANGUAGE LEARNING: HUMANS; LANGUAGE
LEARNING: NONHUMAN PRIMATES

LANGUAGE LEARNING: HUMANS

An understanding of language learning presupposes
clarification of what knowledge of language consists
of, what mechanisms are available for language learning, and what the course of language development is.
There are two broad types of knowledge of language:
grammatical knowledge, the nature of which is largely
biologically determined; and experiential knowledge,
which arises mostly from the learner's encounter with
the world (O'Grady, Archibald, Aronoff, and Rees-
Miller, 2001).

Grammatical knowledge bears on rule-governed
phenomena susceptible of a precise formal description. A formal description of a language is called a
grammar of the language. Typically, grammar consists of phonology (sound patterns), morphology
(structure of words), syntax (structure of phrases and
sentences), and semantics (meanings of words,
phrases, and sentences). Experiential knowledge of
language consists in part of the specific meanings and
pronunciations of the individual words of a language.
Such knowledge is more or less idiosyncratic; it must
be acquired item by item and cannot be predicted by
general rules. For example, the fact that the word *pig*
is pronounced a certain way and refers to a certain

type of animal is something that we must learn
through experience. The totality of this knowledge
constitutes the lexicon of a language.

Pragmatics concerns the relationships among the
language, the speaker, and the speaker's knowledge
of the real world. People employ knowledge of the
world to infer the communicative intentions and expectations of other speakers and hearers (Bach and
Harnish, 1979). For example, when someone asks,
"What are you eating?" we might use our knowledge
of the world to infer that they might be asking to
share what we are eating. Our language may also encode aspects of the social relationships between
speakers, knowledge of which is acquired through experience. For example, both an imperative sentence
(e.g., "Give me a piece of pizza") and a question (e.g.,
"Could you give me a piece of pizza?") can be used
to ask the hearer to do something. But it is part of the
knowledge of how English is used that the imperative
is much more direct and in many circumstances will
be viewed as insufficiently polite.

Paralleling the distinction between grammatical
and experiential knowledge of language are two
broad areas of study: development of knowledge of
formal structure of language (development of grammar) and language development (development of
word meanings and of the use of language to communicate ideas and intentions and to interact socially in
other ways). This article focuses on the study of the relationship between the theory of grammar of natural
language and the development of grammar, since it
is this aspect of language learning that is least likely

to prove to be merely a special case of a more general theory of knowledge acquisition.

Universal Grammar

The most influential (and controversial) view of the development of grammar is called universal grammar, or UG (Chomsky, 1975). The UG theory claims that linguistic knowledge consists of an inborn, universal, skeletal protolanguage, the details of which are elaborated in the course of learning. (A similar view has been proposed for the development of certain birdsong systems.). On this view, innate knowledge of language has two basic components: a catalog of the fixed, universal set of possible grammatical categories along with a set of universal constraints on how these categories may combine to form phrases and sentences, and a fixed set of specific, universal grammatical principles that determine in detail the shapeliness of linguistic phrasal structures. Typically, each constraint and principle may allow for some very limited range of variation.

The grammatical categories are assumed to be the familiar lexical categories of noun (e.g., *pig*), verb (e.g., *imagine*), adjective (e.g., *tall*), and preposition (e.g., *about*), and so on, and a set of functional categories whose members have formal grammatical functions and limited meaning (such as *that* in the sentence, "I think that it is raining") and grammatical inflection such as tense, case, and agreement.

Here is an example of a constrained phrasal structure that allows for limited variation between languages. It is known that in natural languages there is a privileged relationship between the verb and its direct object such that the two form, or are constituents of, a verb phrase (VP) (e.g., "read the book"). The verb and the direct object can thus be said to be sisters within VP. A native speaker of English knows that in a VP, the verb (V) normally precedes its sister, the direct object noun phrase (NP). On the basis of this knowledge, the native speaker judges that "*the book read" is not a valid VP of English. (The asterisk indicates that a string of words does not constitute a grammatical sequence in the language.) But in a language such as Japanese, the proper order is the reverse of that in English: [VP=NP V]. (Constituents within square brackets are sisters.)

On the UG approach to this phenomenon, language learners do not have to learn what the sisters in VP may be; they already know that the sisters in VP are V and NP. What learners do learn about their language is the proper order of the sisters inside VP. Learners of English learn that V precedes NP in VP, while learners of Japanese learn that V follows NP in VP.

Let us turn now to an example of a universal grammatical principle. Consider first the following sentences:

1a. [$_S$ [$_{NP}$ George] [$_{VP}$ loves himself]].
1b. [$_S$ [$_{NP}$ *George's mother] [$_{VP}$ loves himself]].
1c. [$_S$ [$_{NP}$ *Himself] [$_{VP}$ loves George]].

If two constituents, A and B, are sisters, then A is said to c-command B and all of the constituents of B. The subject NP *George* in (1a) is a sister of VP, and hence the NP *George* c-commands *loves* and *himself*. The c-command relation is illustrated in the tree diagram in Figure 1, corresponding to the sentence (1a), where the NP *George* c-commands the circled constituents. Sisters are represented as branches from the same node.

Sentences (1a) to (1c) show that a reflexive must be c-commanded by its antecedent. (This principle is part of what is called the binding theory.) In (1a), the antecedent *George* and the VP *loves himself* are sisters in S; thus *George* c-commands *himself*. In contrast, George does not c-command *himself* in (1b) or (1c). Again, the UG claim is that the knowledge of this principle is not acquired through experience but is part of the linguistic endowment of the language learner.

Support for the Theory of Universal Grammar

Why is the UG view plausible? There are several reasons. Language apparently is learned almost entirely through exposure to examples of speech in a natural setting. That is, there is little or no explicit language instruction, and what instruction does take place is not in general perceived as such by learners. The spoken language to which the learner is exposed is not structured in the form of organized "language lessons" designed to reveal certain important properties of the language. Hence the learner is not systematically provided with information about what is grammatical and what is ungrammatical. In fact, while much of the speech encountered by learners is grammatical, much is not, yet all learners acquire the correct grammar of the language or languages that they are exposed to. Many utterances are incomplete, which also constitutes a potentially confounding input to the learner (Newport, Gleitman, and Gleitman, 1977). There is little if any explicit correction by adults of learner's errors, especially grammatical errors (Brown and Hanlon, 1970; Wexler and Culicover, 1980). In fact, it is not clear that the learner would know what the correction is about, even if such correction occurred (Pinker, 1989).

In spite of all this, children make remarkably few errors in their acquisition of a grammar, and they have essentially completed the task within the first three years of life. The implication is that in order for learning to be accomplished so rapidly and under such unfavorable circumstances, much of what the learner knows in the end must be known from the outset. There is also experimental evidence that certain aspects of children's knowledge of language are in place at the earliest stages of language use, before experience could have determined the form of this knowledge. For example, Crain and McKee (1985) have shown that children exhibit correct knowledge of aspects of the binding theory as early as age two (Crain, 1991).

Further, there is the "argument from the poverty of the stimulus," which says that much of our linguistic knowledge could not be based on experience, since the crucial evidence for acquiring this knowledge does not exist in the discourse around us. One example is the binding theory outlined above. A very different example involves sentences that contain relative clauses such as

2. John knows [NP the man [S that loves Susan]].

When a noun phrase is questioned in English, it must be located at the beginning of the sentence. Thus, if we replace *Susan* in "John said that the man loves Susan" with a question word like *who*, we have a sentence like "Who does John say that the man loves—." The dash indicates the original position of the moved *who*.

Strikingly, it is impossible to perform the same sort of replacement on a noun phrase when the noun phrase is situated within a relative clause, as in

3. *Who does John know [NP the man [S that loves—]].

The question naturally arises as to how we know that this sentence is ungrammatical. The literature on language development provides no evidence that there is any stage at which children learning English treat (3) as grammatical. There is no evidence that children produce systematic errors of the form given in (3), and hence no evidence that children are explicitly corrected for producing such ungrammatical sentences. There is no evidence that children are instructed as to the ungrammaticality of (3). Thus, the claim of the UG approach is that the environment of the learner simply does not provide evidence, in the form of either instruction or correction, on the basis of which the ungrammaticality of (3) could be determined. The UG approach claims that what is going on here is that there is a universal, inborn principle of language that prevents interrogatives (and other types of phrases) from moving out of a relative clause, among other structures. This principle is called subjacency (Chomsky, 1973).

Figure 1

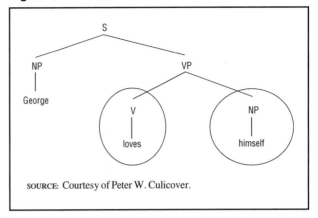

SOURCE: Courtesy of Peter W. Culicover.

The c-command relation illustrated in this tree diagram, corresponding to the sentence (1a) (see text), where the NP George c-commands the circled constituents. Sisters are represented as branches from the same node.

Finally, there are formal learnability considerations that support the UG view. Without severe constraints on rules, formal systems that have the essential properties of natural languages are not learnable under plausible definitions of what the input to the learner is, and of what constitutes "learning" (Wexler and Culicover, 1980). It is posited that the learner is exposed to examples of utterances in context from some language L and must acquire the grammar of L, call it G(L). Only if the learner has available a highly restricted set of possible hypotheses consistent with experience can the learner's hypothesis about the grammar to be learned converge rapidly to G(L). On this approach, universal principles such as the binding theory and subjacency exist precisely because they restrict the range of hypotheses available to the learner so that such rapid convergence is possible.

At the same time, there is substantial evidence that not all grammatical knowledge is available to the learner at the earliest stages of development. Whether this is because the learner simply lacks this knowledge and acquires it gradually (in contrast to the strong UG view) or whether it is wired into the learner but not fully accessible is an open question. This issue is often referred to as continuity (Pinker, 1984). In contrast to continuity, Tomasello (2000), among others, has argued that learners first acquire specific forms and sequences and generalize to rules relatively late in their linguistic development.

Let us turn briefly to the problem of acquiring knowledge of the lexicon. For every word, the learner must learn at least the following:

- The meaning of the word—For a noun (e.g., *book, grandfather, happiness*) the meaning is tied intimately to its reference; for a verb (e.g., *read, eat, think, see*) the meaning is tied to a class of events or states of affairs (Dowty, 1979; Jackendoff, 1990);

- The category of the word (e.g., noun, verb, adjective);

- The conceptual structure of the word—Word meanings are composed of subtle and effectively arbitrary components (e.g., the difference between *hop* and *skip*, between *kill, murder,* and *assassinate,* or the difference between *broil* and *roast*). But some meaning components appear to have a privileged status in being intimately tied to the structure of sentences in which they appear. Whether the subject of a verb is a causal agent (*John* in "John read the book" versus *the bomb* in "The bomb exploded") is a more fundamental component of its meaning than is the manner of locomotion (e.g., *hop* and *skip*) (Jackendoff, 1990).

In acquiring the category and the conceptual structure of a word, the learner learns to link the word appropriately to the syntactic structures in which the word is used. Experiments on lexical development suggest that acquisition of the linguistic properties of a word proceeds very rapidly; between the ages of one and a half and six years, a learner acquires about 14,000 words, which works out to about nine words a day (Carey, 1977). Learning is "bootstrapped" by generalization of the conceptual structure of the word with that of words with similar meanings and grammatical functions (Pinker, 1989; Gleitman, 1990).

On the other hand, to acquire the meaning of a word, the learner must be able to link the word with the world. Full understanding of the word in a strict sense thus depends crucially on the learner's ability to interpret the fine detail of perceptual, cognitive, and social experience correctly. Experiments on the acquisition of word meanings show that this aspect of lexical development, not unexpectedly, is tightly yoked to perceptual, cognitive, and social development (Slobin, 1985; De Villiers and De Villiers, 1978; Bates, Bretherton, and Snyder, 1988).

In summary, then, two major types of linguistic knowledge are acquired in the course of language learning. The grammar of the language is acquired through a process in which the learner starts with a universal set of structures and constraints, and through experience fixes aspects of the grammar that the theory of grammar allows to vary from language to language. There is considerable debate as to how much knowledge of language the learner begins with and how much is acquired through experience. In addition to linguistic structure, the learner acquires a vast array of knowledge of the semantic and phonological properties of individual words and expressions, and learns how to use language to convey complex meanings.

Bibliography

Bach, K., and Harnish, R. M. (1979). *Linguistic communication and speech acts.* Cambridge, MA: MIT Press.

Bates, E., Bretherton, I., and Snyder, L. (1988). *From first words to grammar.* Cambridge. UK: Cambridge University Press.

Brown, R., and Hanlon, C. (1970). Derivational complexity and the order of acquisition in child speech. In J. R. Hayes, ed., *Cognition and the development of language.* New York: Wiley.

Carey, S. (1977). The child as word learner. In M. Halle, J. Bresnan, and G. A. Miller, eds., *Linguistic theory and psychological reality.* Cambridge, MA: MIT Press.

Chomsky, N. (1973). Conditions on transformations. In S. Anderson and P. Kiparsky, eds., *Festschrift for Morris Halle.* New York: Holt, Rinehart, and Winston.

—— (1975). *Reflections on language.* New York: Pantheon.

Crain, S. R. (1991). Language acquisition in the absence of experience. *Brain and Behavioral Sciences 14,* 597–612.

Crain, S. R., and McKee, C. (1985). Acquisition of structural restrictions on anaphora. In *Proceedings of the Northeastern Linguistics Society 16,* 94–110.

De Villiers, J. G., and De Villiers, P. A. (1978). *Language acquisition.* Cambridge, MA: Harvard University Press.

Dowty, D. R. (1979). *Word meaning and Montague grammar.* Dordrecht, The Netherlands: D. Reidel.

Gleitman, L. R. (1990). The structural sources of verb meanings. *Language Acquisition 1,* 3–55.

Jackendoff, R. S. (1990). *Semantic structures.* Cambridge, MA: MIT Press.

Marler, P., and Sherman, V. (1983). Song structure without auditory feedback: Emendations of the auditory template hypothesis. *Journal of Neuroscience 3,* 517–531.

Newport, E. L., Gleitman, H., and Gleitman, L. R. (1977). Mother I'd rather do it myself: Some effects and non-effects of maternal speech style. In C. E. Snow and C. A. Ferguson, eds., *Talking to children.* Cambridge, UK: Cambridge University Press.

O'Grady, W., Archibald, J., Aronoff, M., and Rees-Miller, J. (2001). *Contemporary linguistics.* Boston/New York: Bedford/St. Martin's.

Pinker, S. (1984). *Language learnability and language development.* Cambridge, MA.: Harvard University Press

—— (1989). *Learnability and cognition: The acquisition of argument structure.* Cambridge, MA: MIT Press.

Slobin, D. I., ed. (1985). *The crosslinguistic study of language acquisition.* Hillsdale, NJ: Erlbaum.

Tomasello, M. J. (2000). Do young children have adult syntax? *Cognition 74,* 209–253.

Wexler, K., and Culicover, P. W. (1980). *Formal principles of language acquisition.* Cambridge, MA: MIT Press.

Peter W. Culicover

LANGUAGE LEARNING: NONHUMAN PRIMATES

Guided by modern evolutionary theory, scientists have been able to explicate the origin of the morphology of the human body. However, the evolution of the human mind has yet to be so satisfactorily accounted for. Comparative psychology has already succeeded in providing evidence to help clarify the biobehavioral origins of human language and symbolic competence through studies of our nearest living relatives—the Pongidae (chimpanzee, *Pan*; orangutan, *Pongo*; and gorilla, *Gorilla*). These great apes are substantially more like humans than are the lesser apes, monkeys, or any other mammals. The similarities between human and chimpanzee DNA exceed 98 percent. Genetic relatedness enhances the probability that life forms will have similar psychology as well as appearance. Consequently, we might reasonably expect to find linguistic and cognitive competencies in the ape that are similar to those observed in humans.

Early Studies

Speculation that apes might be capable of language began in the nineteenth century. Early in the twentieth century, occasional studies were undertaken to determine whether or not this might be true, but none succeeded. Efforts were renewed in the mid-1960s, with studies by the Gardners (Gardner and Gardner, 1969; Gardner, Gardner, and van Cantfort, 1989) and by Premack (1971, 1976). The Gardners used American Sign Language, and Premack used plastic tokens of different shapes and colors to function as words, with the aim of establishing two-way communication and an experimental analysis of language functions, respectively. Their chimpanzees, Washoe and Sarah, learned relatively large numbers of signs and tokens and, seemingly, their appropriate use.

Project LANA

In 1971, the LANA Project was initiated by Rumbaugh and his colleagues. A computer-based research system provided Lana, a chimpanzee, with a keyboard that held 125 keys, each embossed with a distinctive geometric symbol called a lexigram (see Figure 1). Lexigrams functioned as words, and their concatenation was computer-monitored for correctness. The computer could activate a bank of devices, some of which delivered various foods and drinks, movies, slides, and music. Lana readily learned her lexigrams in order to request things and to give the names and colors of objects. Tests revealed that she saw Munsel color chips in a manner that resembles the way humans see them, an observation reaffirmed by Matsuzawa (1985) in Japan with the chimpanzee Ai.

Within limits, Lana demonstrated her ability to modify her sentences so as to achieve ends other than the specific ones for which they were designated, such as using them to attract attention to malfunctioning food vendors and to the devices that produced slides and music. A cucumber was innovatively called "banana which-is green," an overly ripe banana was called "banana which-is black," and an orange was called "apple which-is orange (colored)." Comprehensive analyses clearly indicated that Lana's productions could not be satisfactorily attributed either to rotely learned sequences or to imitation. Project LANA contributed what was perhaps the first successful application of a computer to a system for communicative research. Romski, Sevcik, and Pate (1988) have demonstrated that keyboards similar to the one developed for LANA augment the communicative effectiveness of children with language deficits. Project LANA also affirmed the ability of the chimpanzee to learn large numbers of symbols, to use them in prescribed sequences, to alter use of those sequences creatively, and to use symbols so as to facilitate perceptions of sameness and difference between items when one was presented visually and the other by touch.

Other Language-Learning Projects with Chimpanzees

Terrace (1979) began Project Nim in the early 1970s. The chimpanzee Nim learned signs, but Terrace concluded that Nim's signs—and also those of the Gardners' Washoe—were predominantly partial or complete imitations of the human researchers working with these apeshad recently signed. (As noted, imitation was not an issue in the LANA Project because the project was carried out using a computer to monitor and record Lana's lexigram utterances.)

Also in the 1970s, Miles (1990) began Project Chantek. Chantek, an orangutan, was taught manual signs; Miles concluded that Chantek's signing was not confounded by or due to his imitation of human signers, as Terrace had claimed to be the case with Nim and Washoe.

Research of the mid- and late 1970s by Savage-Rumbaugh and Rumbaugh with two chimpanzees named Sherman and Austin used a variation of Lana's keyboard. These chimpanzees demonstrated their abilities to classify lexigrams, each of which represented a specific food or tool, through the use of two other lexigrams, glossed as *food* and *tool*, embedded among more than one hundred other keys on their keyboard. This ability to categorize lexigrams was strong evidence that each symbol did, in fact, represent an item to the apes and that they could use these representations, on trial-1 tests in controlled conditions, to classify almost without error the symbols of their working vocabulary.

Figure 1.   Lana (*Pan troglodytes*) works at her computer-monitored keyboard (upper left); Kanzi (*Pan paniscus*) gestures to a lexigram on his keyboard (upper right); Kanzi listens to spoken words through headphones and is asked to select the appropriate lexigram or picture of an array presented in a test booklet—the experimenter knows neither when nor what word Kanzi hears (lower left); Panbanisha (*Pan paniscus*) vocalizes while participating in a communicative interaction with a researcher (lower right). *(Georgia State University Language Research Center)*

Studies with Bonobos

Research by Savage-Rumbaugh with the bonobo (*Pan paniscus*), a species apart from the common chimpanzee (*P. troglodytes*), was the first to demonstrate the chimpanzee's ability to learn the meanings of symbols spontaneously. The bonobo came to comprehend the meanings of lexigrams, and even human speech, *prior* to developing competence in use of the keyboard. All previous apes had been able to "talk" (e.g., produce signs, use tokens, use lexigrams) as a result of specific training programs, but their comprehension skills were either deferred or never assessed. For the first time, a model of language learning in the ape tracked or paralleled the course of language acquisition in the normal child. Early experience from birth has been critical for such observational learning of language to occur in the bonobo. The common chimpanzee also benefits similarly from such rearing, though possibly to a lesser degree than

does the bonobo (Brakke and Savage-Rumbaugh, 1995a; Brakke and Savage-Rumbaugh, 1995b).

One bonobo, Kanzi, responded appropriately to about three-fourths of more than seven hundred novel requests presented to him verbally under controlled test conditions to preclude cuing. His performance was generally comparable with that of a two-year-old girl whose mental age was two and a half years. Neither Kanzi nor the girl had the benefit of people modeling the requests, nor had they been trained to do what was requested of them. The conclusion is, then, that they comprehended the syntax of the novel requests conveyed by normal human speech.

Kanzi not only comprehends single spoken utterances, he also participates in linguistically mediated communicative interactions with humans in which both Kanzi and his human counterparts employ a variety of communicative modalities concomitantly (e.g., lexigram use, gesture, vocalization, speech). These exchanges share characteristics with human conversations, as Kanzi participates in turn taking, responds to commands, and makes requests of his own. Taglialatela and Savage-Rumbaugh (2001) have reported that during these conversations, Kanzi produces acoustically distinct vocal utterances that vary with the semantic context in which they are produced.

Conclusion

Language competence rests fundamentally in an individual's ability to comprehend, process, and produce meaningful utterances. Chimpanzees can come to acquire and use human language if raised in an environment that permits the emergence of these abilities. It is no longer reasonable to insist that the potential for language is unique to the human species—and reason, according to Descartes, should be humans' strongest suit.

See also: COMPARATIVE COGNITION; LANGUAGE LEARNING: HUMANS

Bibliography

Brakke, K. E., and Savage-Rumbaugh, E. S. (1995a). The development of language skills in bonobo and chimpanzee, Part 1: Comprehension. *Language and Communication 15*, 121–148.

——— (1995b). The development of language skills in bonobo and chimpanzee, Part 2: Production. *Language and Communication 16*, 361–380.

Gardner, B. T., and Gardner, R. A. (1969). Teaching sign language to a chimpanzee. *Science 162*, 664–672.

Gardner, R. A., Gardner, B. T., and van Cantfort, T. E. (1989). *Teaching sign language to chimpanzees.* Albany: State University of New York Press.

Greenfield, P. M., and Savage-Rumbaugh, E. S. (1990). Grammatical combination in *Pan paniscus*: Processes of learning and invention in the evolution and development of language. In S. T. Parker and K. R. Gibson, eds., *"Language" and intelligence in monkeys and apes: Comparative developmental perspectives*, pp. 540–578. New York: Cambridge University Press.

Matsuzawa, T. (1985). Color naming and classification in a chimpanzee (*Pan troglodytes*). *Journal of Human Evolution 14*, 283–291.

Miles, H. L. W. (1990). The cognitive foundations for reference in a signing orangutan. In S. T. Parker and K. R. Gibson, eds., *"Language" and intelligence in monkeys and apes: Comparative developmental perspectives*, pp. 511–539. New York: Cambridge University Press.

Premack, D. (1971). On the assessment of language competence in the chimpanzee. In A. M. Schrier and F. Stollnitz, eds., *Behavior of nonhuman primates*, Vol. 4, 186–228. New York: Academic Press.

——— (1976). *Language and intelligence in ape and man.* Hillsdale, NJ: Erlbaum.

Romski, M. A., Sevcik, R. A., and Pate, J. L. (1988). The establishment of symbolic communication in persons with mental retardation. *Journal of Speech and Hearing Disorders 53*, 94–107.

Rumbaugh, D. M. (1977). *Language learning by a chimpanzee: The Lana Project.* New York: Academic Press.

Savage-Rumbaugh, E. S. (1986). *Ape language: From conditioned response to symbol.* NewYork: Columbia University Press.

Karl Lashley (*UPI/Corbis-Bettman*)

Taglialatela, J. P., and Savage-Rumbaugh, S. (2001). Bonobo cognition: Expectations, explications, and conversations. Paper presented at the 109th convention of the American Psychological Association. San Francisco, CA.

Terrace, H. S. (1979). *Nim.* New York: Knopf.

Duane M. Rumbaugh
E. Sue Savage-Rumbaugh
Revised by Duane M. Rumbaugh, E. Sue Savage-Rumbaugh, and Jared P. Taglialatela

LASHLEY, KARL (1890–1958)

Karl Spencer Lashley pioneered the study of brain mechanisms of learning and memory. He was born in 1890 in Davis, West Virginia, and entered the University of West Virginia at the age of fifteen. As a freshman he signed up for a class in zoology under the distinguished neurologist John Black Johnston, and within a few weeks he "knew that I had found my life work." After graduation in 1910, he obtained a teaching fellowship at the University of Pittsburgh and received his M.S. degree there. Lashley then went to Johns Hopkins University to study for his doctorate in zoology under Herbert S. Jennings. He elected a minor in psychology with John B. Watson, the founder of behaviorism. His work with Watson convinced him to make his career in psychology. This was the critical time in Lashley's development as a scientist. In his own words:

> In 1914, John Watson called attention to a seminar in the French edition of Bechterev's book on the conditioned reflex. In that winter the seminar was devoted to the translation and discussion of the book. In the spring I served as an unpaid assistant and we constructed apparatus and did experiments, repeating a number of Pavlov's experiments. Our whole program was then disrupted by the move to the lab in Meyer's Clinic. There were no adequate animal quarters there. Watson started work with infants as the next best material available. I tagged along for awhile but disliked the babies and found me a rat lab in another building. We accumulated a considerable amount of experimental material on the conditioned reflex that was never published. Watson sought the basis of a systematic psychology and was not greatly concerned with the reaction itself (letter from K. S. Lashley to Ernest Hilgard, ca. 1930; reprinted with the permission of Professor Hilgard).

The conditioned reflex formed the basis of Watson's behaviorism. Lashley, on the other hand, became interested in the physiology of the reaction and the attempt to trace conditioned reflex paths through the central nervous system. Over the next several years Lashley collaborated with Shepherd Franz, who was then at St. Elizabeth's Hospital in Washington, DC. Their research, examining effects of lesions of the frontal cortex on learning abilities in the rat, was the foundation of his major work, *Brain Mechanisms and Intelligence* (1929). In 1920 Lashley accepted an assistant professorship at the University of Minnesota and began in earnest his search for the memory trace. He was made full professor at Minnesota in 1924, and in 1926 moved to the University of Chicago, where he became a professor in 1929. In this same year he was president of the American Psychological Association and published his monograph *Brain Mechanisms and Intelligence*. In 1935 Lashley accepted a professorship at Harvard University, and in 1937 he was appointed research professor of neuropsychology with nominal teaching duties, which made it possible for him to accept the directorship of the Yerkes Laboratories of Primate Biology in Orange Park, Florida, in 1942. He held both these positions, spending only a few weeks a year at Harvard (he was not fond of formal teaching), until his death in 1958.

Lashley devoted many years to an analysis of brain mechanisms of learning, using the lesion-behavior method that he developed and elaborated

from the work with Franz. During this period, Lashley's theoretical view of learning was heavily influenced by two widely held notions: localization of function in neurology and behaviorism in psychology.

Localization of function, the notion that each psychological "trait" or function has a specific locus of representation, a particular place, in the brain, was perhaps the major intellectual issue concerning brain organization at the beginning of the twentieth century. An extreme form of the idea of localization, known as *phrenology*, was popular early in the nineteenth century. The field of neurology then moved away from that position, though the discovery of a speech center began to move the pendulum back. Work in the last three decades of the nineteenth century identified the general locations of the motor, visual, and auditory regions of the cerebral cortex. Localization of function appeared to be winning the day.

In Watson's behaviorism, the learning of a particular response was held to involve the formation of a particular set of connections, a series set. Consequently, Lashley argued, it should be possible to localize the place in the cerebral cortex where that learned change in brain organization, the *engram* (memory trace), was stored. It was generally believed at the time, consistent with Ivan Pavlov's view, that learning was coded in the cerebral cortex. Thus, behaviorism and localization of function were consistent; they supported the notion of an elaborate and complex switchboard on which specific and localized changes occurred in the cerebral cortex when specific habits were learned.

Lashley systematically set about finding the places in the cerebral cortex where learning occurred—the engrams—in an extensive series of studies culminating in his 1929 monograph. In this research he used mazes of differing difficulty and made lesions of varying sizes in different regions of the cerebral cortex of the rat. The results profoundly altered Lashley's view of brain organization and had an extraordinary impact on the young field of physiological psychology: the locus of the lesion was unimportant; the size was critically important, particularly for the difficult mazes. These findings led to Lashley's notions of *equipotentiality* (locus not important) and *mass action* (size critical).

Subsequently, Lashley focused on a detailed analysis of the role of the cerebral cortex in vision and in visual discrimination learning and memory. But his interests and research also included classic work on the cytoarchitectonics (microscopic structure) of the cerebral cortex; a brilliant analysis of the problem of serial order in human language and thought; and a penetrating analysis of the biological substrates of motivation. Lashley, more than any other scientist, shaped and developed the field of physiological psychology.

It is fitting to close this biographical entry with Lashley's own summing up of his search for the memory trace, written in 1950:

> This series of experiments has yielded a good bit of information about what and where the memory trace is not. It has discovered nothing directly of the real nature of the memory trace. I sometimes feel, in reviewing the evidence of the localization of the memory trace, that the necessary conclusion is that learning is just not possible. It is difficult to conceive of a mechanism that can satisfy the conditions set for it. Nevertheless, in spite of such evidence against it, learning sometimes does occur.

See also: LOCALIZATION OF MEMORY TRACES

Bibliography

Lashley, K. S. (1929). *Brain mechanisms and intelligence: A quantitative study of injuries to the brain.* Chicago: University of Chicago Press.

—— (1935). The mechanism of vision, Part 12: Nervous structures concerned in the acquisition and retention of habits based on reactions to light. *Comparative Psychology Monographs 11,* 43–79.

—— (1950). In search of the engram. *Society of Experimental Biology, Symposium 4,* 454–482.

Orbach, J., ed. (1982). *Neuropsychology after Lashley.* Hillsdale, NJ: Erlbaum.

Richard F. Thompson

LEARNED HELPLESSNESS

The term *learned helplessness* is used to refer to any behavioral or physiological consequence of exposure to an aversive event that is produced not by the event itself but by the organism's *lack of behavioral control* over the event. By *behavioral control* is meant the organism's ability to alter the onset, termination, duration, intensity, or temporal pattern of the event. If the event (e.g., a loud noise, a painful electric shock, an attack by another animal or person) can be altered by some behavioral response, then the organism has some control over the event. If there is nothing that the organism can do to change the event, then the event is uncontrollable.

This concept has been studied using an experimental paradigm called the *triadic design.* Here one subject, say a rat, is given control over the event, say a mild electric shock, delivered to the rat's tail. The rat is exposed to a number of shocks, and performing some behavioral response, say pushing a lever with its paws, terminates each of the shocks. This rat thus has control over the termination of each shock. A second rat is placed in a similar apparatus, but this rat does not have control. Each shock begins for this rat at the same instant as it does for the rat with control, but for this second rat pushing the lever has no consequence. Each shock terminates whenever the rat with control presses the lever. Thus both rats receive identical shocks, but one has behavioral control and the other does not. A third rat is merely placed in the apparatus and receives no shock. Subsequent behavior and physiological functioning can be examined, and it is possible to determine which changes are caused by the stressor per se (here the animals with and without control would be identical and differ from the non-shocked controls), and which are a function of the controllability of the stressor (here the animals with and without control would differ).

Use of this sort of experimental design has revealed that many of the consequences that are normally thought to be produced by stressors actually are determined by the controllability/uncontrollability of the stressor rather than by mere exposure to the stressor. Three kinds of behavioral changes follow exposure to stressors, but only if they are uncontrollable.

The first type is *cognitive changes.* A particularly important consequence of exposure to uncontrollable aversive events has come to be called the *learned helplessness effect.* This refers to the fact that organisms ranging from fish to humans fail to learn to escape and avoid aversive events such as electric shocks, loud noises, and cold water after an initial exposure to aversive events that are uncontrollable (Overmier and Seligman, 1967). A great deal of research has been conducted to determine why this learning deficit occurs, and it has been found that at least part of the reason is cognitive. Uncontrollable aversive events interfere with some of the information-processing steps required to learn relationships between behavior and outcomes (Maier, 1989).

The second type is *motivational changes.* The motivation to obtain many of the reinforcers that are normally important for that organism is undermined. For example, a rat that is exposed to uncontrollable shock (but not to equal amounts of controllable shock) does not later compete for food, becomes inactive, and shows decreased sexual and maternal behavior.

The third type is *emotional changes.* Uncontrollable aversive events lead to increases in aspects of emotionality such as fear and anxiety. Physiological indicants of stress such as ulcer formation and blood pressure increases are similarly influenced by the controllability/uncontrollability dimension.

A considerable amount of research has been devoted to uncovering the behavioral and physiological mechanisms that produce these learned helplessness effects. This fact is at least in part attributable to the resemblance between the consequences of uncontrollable stressors in animals and human depression. Indeed, what is now known about the substrates of learned helplessness is remarkably similar to what is thought to underlie human depression (Weiss and Simson, 1986).

Bibliography

Maier, S. F. (1989). Learned helplessness: Event co-variation and cognitive changes. In S. B. Klein and R. R. Mowrer, eds., *Contemporary learning theories*, pp. 73–109. Hillsdale, NJ: Erlbaum.

Overmier, J. B., and Seligman, M. E. P. (1967). Effects of inescapable shock upon subsequent escape and avoidance behavior. *Journal of Comparative Physiology and Psychology 63*, 23–33.

Weiss, J. M., and Simson, P. G. (1986). Depression in an animal model: Focus on the locus coeruleus. In R. Porter, G. Bock, and S. Clark, eds., *Antidepressants and receptor function*, pp. 191–216. New York: Wiley.

Steven F. Maier

LEARNING CURVE

See: REPETITION AND LEARNING

LEARNING DISABILITIES

An individual is said to have a *learning disability* if he or she has difficulty using or understanding written or spoken language (including academic subjects such as reading, writing, and mathematics) in a way that is inconsistent with overall intelligence quotient (IQ). Individuals with low IQ in all areas (for example, in cases of mental retardation) are excluded from the diagnosis. Environmental factors such as deprivation are also excluded (because learning disabilities are defined as congenital rather than acquired problems), as are physical disabilities that might cause secondary learning problems (for example, hearing and vision deficits, epilepsy, or attention deficit and hyperactivity disorder [ADHD]). Although learning disabilities can be concurrent with other physical disabilities (i.e., blind or deaf children can also be learning disabled), it is generally established that the physical disability is not inherently the *cause* of the learning disability. ADHD has a high concurrence with learning disabilities, but clinicians usually try to establish that attention deficits (not typically considered under the scope of learning disabilities) are not the direct cause of the learning problems. A child who exhibits difficulties with language may be diagnosed with a learning disability (for example, with specific lan-

guage impairment, or SLI), even before entering school, but typically a diagnosis emerges in the context of an academic setting, for example when a child has unexpected difficulties with reading (called specific reading impairment, or dyslexia). There is significant overlap between preschool SLI and school-age dyslexic populations (Stark and Tallal, 1988).

Learning Disabilities from a Behavioral Perspective

The long-standing assumption that learning disabilities reflect subtle anomalies in the brain is reflected in early terms such as *minimal brain damage* and *minimal brain dysfunction*. Although an emergent body of research has shown that learning-disabled populations exhibit neural anomalies, the field remains at a point where behavioral data are used to make an evaluation or clinical diagnosis, and neural features of these behaviorally identified populations are then studied to discern differences from normal controls. A diagnosis of specific reading impairment (or dyslexia) may someday be confirmed or even routinely screened (like vision testing) via neuroimaging. Moreover, neurological diagnosis of learning disorders may alter their very definitions (e.g., it may become possible to diagnose neural anomalies associated with dyslexia prior to behavioral expression of the disorder, possibly even in infancy; see Leppänen and Lyytinen, 1997; Leppänen, Pihko, Eklund, and Lyytinen, 1999; Molfese and Molfese, 1997; Pihko et al., 1999). This dependence on behavioral criteria is reflected in debate over whether traditional health insurance should cover treatment for learning disorders (Tallal, 1988).

Diagnostic dependence on behavioral criteria is associated with other intrinsic pitfalls, including those inherent to the definition of abnormal behavior. This pivotal issue forms the focus of controversy surrounding learning disabilities (e.g., assertions of gender and ethnic bias in school curricula, and over-referral of boys for special education due to boys' more "active" behavior). One objective way that behavior can be quantified is by comparison to a norm derived from sample population data, allowing clinicians to use a standard curve to set cutoff criteria to define when an individual is "significantly impaired" relative to their peers for a specific function. Academic performance in a school setting may also be compared to age-appropriate norms in a more general way by schoolteachers who refer potentially learning disabled children for further testing. Learning disabilities are also defined by comparison of a child's own scores or performance in a specific area relative to their overall intelligence, entailing use of a "discrepancy criteria."

Even with the use of such criteria, clinicians and educators may disagree over the definition of what constitutes "disabled"—for example, whether a child is simply part of the lower tail of a normal curve (e.g., is a poor reader) or whether that child functions distinctly differently from the norm and thus has a clinically defined disorder (e.g., specific reading impairment or dyslexia; see Shaywitz et al., 1992). Moreover, individual cases are sometimes difficult to capture within the parameters of standard behavioral definitions. For example, if a child demonstrates generally superior academic performance but performs only at an average level in one specific area such as reading, is he or she reading impaired? Such a child is unlikely to be referred, at any rate, for special education services. Similarly, if a child demonstrates general intelligence well below the mean, but performs even worse in one specific area (e.g., reading) than would be predicted by nonverbal IQ, is this child mentally retarded, or reading impaired, or both? Confusion surrounding such unresolved issues is fueled by educational dictates that define the aid and curricula a child may receive depending on clinical diagnosis, and also fueled by social controversies surrounding the labeling of children. (These issues are not addressed in this entry, but see Wong, 1986, or Woody, 1989, for review.) Finally, the definition of learning disabilities is weighted to some degree by a standard academic curricula that does not tend to focus on deficiencies in art, music, or sports but, rather, only in reading, writing, and math.

The populations of children who receive special education services at school are distinct but overlapping: Some children are in SE due to lagging academic performance, whereas others in SE classes have been clinically diagnosed as learning disabled. SE encompasses a heterogeneous population of students exhibiting general cognitive delays and deficits, social-environmental deprivation, psychological problems, and concurrent disabilities such as ADHD. This entry focuses on children identified as learning disabled through relatively rigorous clinical diagnosis—that is, language, reading, or mathematically impaired children performing below levels predicted by their overall intelligence in one of these specific academic areas.

Neurobiological Correlates of Learning Disabilities

Advances in neuroimaging and gene linkage technology have expanded research possibilities for noninvasive study of clinical populations, but characteristics of various learning disabilities have yet to be isolated and defined. Reasons for these limitations include:

1. Heterogeneity of subject criteria. If the population under study is not homogeneous, biological data from this sample will be difficult to interpret. Also, when different researchers use different behavioral criteria, cross-study comparisons will show inconsistencies.

2. Heterogeneity of disorders. Even where careful attention to consistent behavioral criteria is applied, diverse underlying etiologies can produce the same behavioral profile. Conversely, behavioral profiles (even within a relatively specific subtype of a disorder) can show large individual differences.

3. Difficulties inherent to the study of children. Although modern magnetic resonance imaging (MRI) techniques are considered noninvasive, they are stressful and time consuming, and parents will not always consent to participation of their affected children. Although studies can be conducted using adults affected since childhood, the data obtained from such studies may not accurately reflect anomalies that characterize early disruption of brain development. Moreover, retrospective diagnosis of childhood disorders frequently relies on memory (e.g., a patient is asked, "Did you have difficulty reading as a young child?") and hence can be unreliable.

Despite these hindrances, research has uncovered important neurological and genetic features that seem to be associated with specific developmental learning disorders. Such studies have shown that learning disabled children do not exhibit focal damage to specific regions of the brain, with all other systems and functions spared intact. Although localized damage can indeed occur via localized hemorrhage, trauma, or tumor (and can lead to subsequent learning disabilities) these types of injuries comprise acquired rather than congenital disabilities. For example, language deficits caused by an acquired lesion of the left hemisphere are classified as acquired aphasia, rather than developmental language impairment (Tallal, 1987), which is considered congenital. This distinction relies on the notion of "inherent" versus "imposed" neural damage (although most diagnoses accept brain damage of prematurity within the scope of congenital disabilities). Research suggests that some learning disabled children may, in fact, exhibit evidence of relatively focal (i.e., narrowly circumscribed) brain damage of unknown cause from very early (i.e., prenatal) periods of neurodevelopment (e.g., see Galaburda, 1992; Galaburda et al., 1985). This early focal injury—particularly if it occurs during critical neural events such as neuromigration (cortical neurons migrating to cortical layer locations)—may disrupt neurodevelopment, with deleterious behavioral consequences. Unlike damage to a relatively static adult brain, focal damage that occurs during the formation of neural circuitry exerts widely distributed effects on brain organization (see Aicardi, 1994; Galaburda, 1992; Kolb and Fantie, 1989). Some children with learning disabilities appear to have experienced such subtle injuries to the brain or interference with development of the brain during critical periods of growth, resulting in pervasive reorganization of brain systems.

Specific Language Impairment (SLI) and Dyslexia

SLI and dyslexia are the two most frequently studied forms of learning disability. Longitudinal studies suggest that a large majority of children with SLI overcome the most noticeable aspects of language delays of early childhood (e.g., they do eventually learn to talk) but that underlying components of their disorder appear to be expressed more visibly in other areas, for example as the child attempts to use phonological systems to learn to read (see Leonard, 1998, for review). Consequently, studies on the neurophysiology of SLI (which typically comprises a childhood population) are difficult to separate from studies of dyslexia (which frequently is studied in adults).

Some functional deficits in children with SLI may arise from basic sensory integration deficits, reflecting in turn dysfunctional neural processing of rapidly changing sensory information. For example, research has shown that language-impaired children exhibit severe deficits in the ability to perform auditory discriminations of information that changes rapidly in time. Although this deficit is profoundly evident when children with SLI are asked to discriminate speech stimuli characterized by brief and rapidly changing acoustic spectra (e.g., consonant-vowel syllables), deficits are also observed on nonlingual tasks such as tone-sequence discrimination (Tallal and Piercy, 1973). Such rapid auditory processing deficits may disrupt phonological processing and speech perception, leading to developmental impairment of language skills acquisition (Tallal, Miller, and Fitch, 1993). Although a neurophysiological basis for sensory processing deficits in language-impaired children has not been identified, evidence has shown cellular anomalies in the visual and auditory divisions of the thalamus (lateral geniculate and medial geniculate nucleus; LGN and MGN) of dyslexic brains.

Specifically, Livingstone, Rosen, Drislane, and Galaburda (1991) found that the magnocellular component of the visual system, which is responsible for processing fast, low-contrast information, appears to be impaired in dyslexics. Using evoked potential measurements taken from the scalp, the electrophysiologic response to visual stimuli designed to activate the magnocellular subsystem was found to be significantly slower in dyslexic as compared to control subjects. Consistent with this functional data, postmortem studies of several dyslexic brains demonstrated that the magnocellular neurons of the lateral geniculate nucleus (the visual thalamic nucleus, which relays visual information to the cortex) were smaller in dyslexic than in control brains. The authors speculate that electrophysiological and anatomical evidence of a visual processing disturbance could reflect interference with normal reading (see also Lovegrove, Garzia, and Nicholson, 1990; Slaghuis, Lovegrove, and Freestun, 1992). A subsequent postmortem study of the same dyslexic brains studied by Livingstone, Galaburda, Menard, and Rosen (1994) found that there were more small neurons and fewer large neurons in the left medial geniculate nucleus (MGN) of dyslexics as compared to controls. This finding may relate to the behavioral and electrophysiological evidence of disrupted auditory processing in both SLI and dyslexic individuals, which may in turn give rise to the phonological processing deficits observed in these patients (see Tallal, Miller, and Fitch,, 1993, for review).

These findings may further relate to evidence of neuropathologic lesions in dyslexic brains (Benton, 1964; Cohen, Campbell, and Yaghamai, 1989; Galaburda and Kemper, 1979; Galaburda et al., 1985; Humphreys et al., 1991; reviewed in Galaburda, 1992). Specifically, researchers have used postmortem analysis to show evidence of cerebrocortical microdysgenesis consisting of neuronal ectopias in neocortical layer I, subjacent laminar dysplasia, focal microgyria, and microvascular anomalies. These abnormalities tend to be located in prefrontal and perisylvian regions, and they usually involve the left more than the right hemisphere. Evidence from animal models suggests that focal cortical damage during the period of cortical neuromigration induces the formation of cortical cellular anomalies, as well as structural anomalies at the thalamic level, much like those seen in dyslexic brains. Moreover, these anomalies are associated with auditory processing deficits strikingly similar those seen in language-impaired children (Clark, Rosen, Tallal, and Fitch, 2000a, 2000b; Fitch et al., 1994; Fitch, Brown, Tallal, and Rosen, 1997; Herman et al., 1997).

On a more global level, studies of both language impairment and dyslexia have focused heavily on regions of the brain known to be involved in language processing, particularly left-hemisphere regions of temporal, parietal, and frontal cortex such as Wernicke's area and Broca's area. In most normal subjects, the planum temporale (which lies on the superior surface of the temporal lobe and encompasses a portion of Wernicke's area) is larger on the left as compared to the right side of the brain (Geschwind and Levitsky, 1968; Kulynch, Vladar, Jones, and Weinberger, 1994; Teszner, Tzavaras, Gruner, and Hécaen, 1972; Wada, Clarke, and Hamm, 1975; Witelson and Pallie, 1973). Such findings are consistent with left-hemisphere specialization for language processing found in behavioral studies, neuroimaging studies, and studies of the behavioral effects of lateralized lesions. In one of the few studies of neuropathology underlying specific language impairment, Jernigan, Hesselink, Sowell, and Tallal (1991) used MRI techniques to examine a sample of SLI children and showed that the volume of the posterior perisylvian region (which includes the planum temporale) was reduced bilaterally in language-impaired children (markedly so in the left hemisphere; see also Plante, Swisher, Vance, and Rapcsak, 1991). Asymmetries in the inferoanterior and superoposterior cerebral regions showed significant differences between control and impaired children. Neurological studies of dyslexia have also consistently reported anomalous asymmetry of the planum temporale (Dalby, Elbro, and Stodkilde-Jorgensen, 1998; Galaburda et al., 1985; Haslam, Dalby, Johns, and Rademaker, 1981; Hier, LeMay, Rosenberger, and Perlo, 1978; Humphreys et al., 1991; Hynd and Semrud-Clikeman, 1989; Hynd et al., 1990; Hynde, Marshall, and Semrud-Clikeman, 1991; Jancke, Schlaug, Huang, and Steinmetz, 1994; Kushch et al., 1993; Larsen, Hoien, Lundberg, and Odegaard, 1990; Leonard et al., 1993; Rosenberger and Hier, 1980; Rumsey et al., 1986; Schultz et al., 1994). These anatomical anomalies are consistent with evidence of activational differences in the cortex of dyslexics during the performance of reading-related tasks (e.g., Demb, Boynton, and Heeger, 1998; Shaywitz et al., 1998). Atypical asymmetries (along with language difficulties) also occur in the parents and siblings of children with language disabilities (Plante, 1991).

Evidence of structural left hemisphere anomalies in dyslexics is further consistent with data showing anomalous EEG recording from left-hemisphere language regions of dyslexics, as well as anomalous recordings from anterior frontal regions (Duffy and McAnulty, 1990), anomalies in regional cerebral activity in frontal and occipital areas of dyslexics as measured during reading tasks (Gross-Glenn et al., 1991; Shaywitz et al., 1998), and electrophysiological anomalies of cerebral lateralization in learning-disabled children (Mattson, Sheer, and Fletcher, 1992). Significant differences in electrophysiological responses to acoustic stimuli (including tones and speech) have also been reported in studies of both dyslexic and language-impaired individuals (e.g., Brunswick and Rip-

pon, 1994; Byring and Järvilehto, 1985; Dawson, Finley, Phillips, and Lewy, 1989; Jirsa and Clontz, 1990; Kraus et al., 1996; Lincoln, Courchesne, Harms, and Allen, 1995; Neville, Coffey, Holcomb, and Talall, 1993; Pinkerton, Watson, and McClelland, 1989; Tonnquist-Uhlen, Borg, Persson, and Spens, 1996; Wood, Flowers, Buchsbaum, and Tallal, 1991), supporting the existence of an auditory processing deficit in these groups as discussed above.

Conclusion

Learning disabilities are characterized by unexpected difficulties with language, reading, or math that are inconsistent with IQ, or ability in other areas, or both. These problems remain after other known causes for learning problems have been excluded. The neurobiological basis for these disorders remains elusive but appears to involve very early neurodevelopmental disruption leading to distributed processing deficits in the brain. These disruptions appear to leave some higher processing systems intact while causing severe deficits in other systems (e.g., rapid sensory processing). Nevertheless, learning disabilities encompass a wide range of subtypes of disorders, with large individual variability in behavioral expression, and they appear to reflect a heterogeneity of neural anomalies of varied origin, ranging from genetic factors to early focal injury. Improved neuroimaging technology should allow scientists to create more precise neurobehavioral templates of disruption characterizing various subtypes of learning disability, providing in turn more reliable and consistent diagnostic tools for the assessment and remediation of learning disabilities.

Bibliography

Aicardi, J. (1994). The place of neuronal migration abnormalities in child neurology. *Canadian Journal of Neurological Sciences 21*, 185–193.

Benton, A. L. (1964). Developmental aphasia and brain damage. *Cortex 1*, 40–52.

Brunswick, N., and Rippon, G. (1994). Auditory event-related potentials, dichotic listening performance, and handedness as indices of lateralisation in dyslexic and normal readers. *International Journal of Psychophysiology 18* (3), 265–275.

Byring, R., and Järvilehto, T. (1985). Auditory and visual evoked potentials of schoolboys with spelling disabilities. *Developmental Medicine and Child Neurology 27*, 141–148.

Clark, M., Rosen, G., Tallal, P., and Fitch, R. H. (2000a). Impaired processing of complex auditory stimuli in rats with induced cerebrocortical microgyria. *Journal of Cognitive Neuroscience 12* (5), 828–839.

——— (2000b). Impaired two-tone processing at rapid rates in male rats with induced microgyria. *Brain Research 871*, 94–97.

Cohen, M., Campbell, R., and Yaghamai, F. (1989). Neuropathological anomalies in developmental dysphasia. *Annals of Neurology 25*, 567–570.

Dalby, M. A., Elbro, C., and Stodkilde-Jorgensen, H. (1998). Temporal lobe asymmetry and dyslexia: An in vivo study using MRI. *Brain and Language 62*, 51–69.

Dawson, G., Finley, C., Phillips, S., and Lewy, A. (1989). A comparison of hemispheric asymmetries in speech-related brain potentials of autistic and dysphasic children. *Brain and Language* 37 (1), 26–41.

Demb, J. B., Boynton, G. M., and Heeger, D. J. (1998). Functional magnetic resonance imaging of early visual pathways in dyslexia. *Journal of Neuroscience 18*, 6,939–6,951.

Duffy, F. H., and McAnulty, G. (1990). Neuropsychological heterogeneity and the definition of dyslexia: Preliminary evidence for plasticity. *Neuropsychologica 28*, 555–571.

Fitch, R. H., Brown, C., Tallal, P., and Rosen, G. (1997). Effects of sex and MK-801 on auditory processing deficits associated with developmental microgyric lesions in rats. *Behavioral Neuroscience 111*, 404–412.

Fitch, R. H., Tallal, P., Brown, C., Galaburda, A., and Rosen, G. (1994). Induced microgyria and auditory temporal processing in rats: A model for language impairment? *Cerebral Cortex 4*, 260–270.

Galaburda, A. M. (1992). Neurology of developmental dyslexia. *Current Opinion in Neurology and Neurosurgery 5* (1), 71–76.

Galaburda, A. M., and Kemper, T. L. (1979). Cytoarchitectonic abnormalities in developmental dyslexia: A case study. *Annals of Neurology 6*, 94–100.

Galaburda, A. M., Menard, M. T., and Rosen, G. D. (1994). Evidence for aberrant auditory anatomy in developmental dyslexia. *Proceedings of the National Academy of Sciences of the United States of America 91*, 8,010–8,013.

Galaburda, A. M., Sherman, G. F., Rosen, G. D., Aboitiz, F., and Geschwind, N. (1985). Developmental dyslexia: Four consecutive cases with cortical anomalies. *Annals of Neurology 18*, 222–233.

Geschwind, N., and Levitsky, W. (1968). Human brain: Left-right asymmetries in temporal speech region. *Science 161*, 186–187.

Gross-Glenn, K, Duara, R, Barker, W. W., Lowenstein, D, Chang, J. Y., Yoshii, F., Apicella, A. M., Pascal, S., Boothe, T., Sevush, S., Jallad, B. J., Novoa, L., and Lubs, H. A. (1991). Positron emission tomographic studies during serial word reading by normal and dyslexic adults. *Journal of Clinical and Experimental Neuropsychology 13*, 531–544.

Haslam, R. H. A., Dalby, J. T., Johns, R. D., and Rademaker, A. W. (1981). Cerebral asymmetry in developmental dyslexia. *Archives of Neurology 38*, 679–682.

Herman, A., Galaburda, A., Fitch, R. H., Carter, A. R., and Rosen, G. (1997). Cerebral microgyria, thalamic cell size, and auditory temporal processing in male and female rats. *Cerebral Cortex 7*, 453–464.

Hier, D. B., LeMay, M., Rosenberger, P. B., and Perlo, V. P. (1978). Developmental dyslexia. *Archives of Neurology 35*, 90–92.

Humphreys, P., Rosen, G. D., Press, D. M., Sherman, G. F., and Galaburda, A. M. (1991). Freezing lesions of the newborn rat brain: A model for cerebrocortical microgyria. *Journal of Neuropathology and Experimental Neuroloy 50*, 145–160.

Hynd, G. W., Marshall, R. M., and Semrud-Clikeman, M. (1991). Developmental dyslexia, neurolinguistic theory, and deviations in brain morphology. *Reading and Writing 3*, 345–362.

Hynd, G. W., and Semrud-Clikeman, M. (1989). Dyslexia and brain morphology. *Psychological Bulletin 106*, 447–482.

Hynd, G. W., Semrud-Clikeman, M., Lorys, A. R., Novey, E. S., and Eliopulos, D. (1990). Brain morphology in developmental dyslexia and attention deficit disorder/hyperactivity. *Archives of Neurology 47*, 919–926.

Jancke, L., Schlaug, G., Huang, Y., and Steinmetz, H. (1994). Asymmetry of the planum temporale. *NeuroReport 5*, 1,161–1,163.

Jernigan, T. L., Hesselink, J. R., Sowell, E., and Tallal, P. (1991). Cerebral structure on magnetic resonance imaging in language- and learning-impaired children. *Archives of Neurology 48*, 539–545.

Jirsa, R. E., and Clontz, K. B. (1990). Long latency auditory event-related potentials from children with auditory processing disorders. *Ear and Hearing 11* (3), 222–232.

Kolb, B., and Fantie, B. (1989). Development of children's brain and behavior. In C. R. Reynolds and J. Fletcher-Janzen, eds., *Handbook of child clinical neuropsychology,* pp. 17–40. New York: Plenum Press.

Kraus, N., McGee, T. J., Carrell, T. D., Zecker, S. G., Nicol, T. G., and Koch, D. B. (1996). Auditory neurophysiologic responses and discrimination deficits in children with learning problems. *Science 273*, 971–973.

Kulynych, J. J., Vladar, K., Jones, D. W., and Weinberger, D. R. (1994). Gender differences in the normal lateralization of the supratemporal cortex: MRI surface-rendering morphometry of Heschl's gyrus and the planum temporale. *Cerebral Cortex 4*, 107–118.

Kushch, A., Gross-Glenn, K., Jallad, B., Lubs, H., Rabin, M., Feldman, E., and Duara, R. (1993). Temporal lobe surface area measurements on MRI in normal and dyslexic readers. *Neuropsychologia 31*, 811–821.

Larsen, J., Hoien, T., Lundberg, I., and Odegaard, H. (1990). MRI evaluation of the size and symmetry of the planum temporale in adolescents with developmental dyslexia. *Brain and Language 39*, 289–301.

Leonard, C., Voeller, K. K. S., Lombardino, L. J., Morris, M. K., Hynd, G. W., Alexander, A. W., Andersen, H. G., Garofalakis, M., Honeyman, J. C., Mao, J., Agee, O. F., and Staab, E. V. (1993). Anomalous cerebral structure in dyslexia revealed with magnetic resonance imaging. *Archives of Neurology 50*, 461–469.

Leonard, L. B. (1998). *Children with specific language impairment.* Cambridge, MA: MIT Press.

Leppänen, P. H. T., and Lyytinen, H. (1997). Auditory event-related potentials in the study of developmental language-related disorders. *Audiology and Neuro-Otology 2*, 308–340.

Leppänen, P. H. T., Pihko, E., Eklund, K. M., and Lyytinen, H. (1999). Cortical responses of infants with and without a genetic risk for dyslexia, Part 2: Group effects. *NeuroReport 10*, 969–973.

Lincoln, A. J., Courchesne, E., Harms, L., and Allen, M. (1995). Sensory modulation of auditory stimuli in children with autism and receptive developmental language disorder: Event-related brain potential evidence. *Journal of Autism and Developmental Disorders 25* (5), 521–539.

Livingstone, M. S., Rosen, G. D., Drislane, F. W., and Galaburda, A. M. (1991). Physiological and anatomical evidence for a magnocellular defect in developmental dyslexia. *Proceedings of the National Academy of Sciences of the United States of America 88*, 7,943–7,947.

Lovegrove, W., Garzia, R., and Nicholson, S. (1990). Experimental evidence for a transient system deficit in specific reading disability. *Journal of the American Optometric Association 2*, 137–146.

Mattson, A. J., Sheer, D. E., and Fletcher, J. M. (1992). Electrophysiological evidence of lateralized disturbances in children with learning disabilities. *Journal of Clinical and Experimental Neuropsychology 14*, 707–716.

Molfese, D. L., and Molfese, V. J. (1997). Discrimination of language skills at five years of age using event-related potentials recorded at birth. *Developmental Neuropsychology 13*, 135–156.

Neville, H., Coffey, S., Holcomb, P., and Tallal, P. (1993). The neurobiology of sensory and language processing in language impaired children. *Journal of Cognitive Neuroscience 5*, 235–253.

Pihko, E., Leppänen, P. H. T., Eklund, K. M., Cheour, M., Guttorm, T. K., and Lyytinen, H. (1999). Cortical responses of infants with and without a genetic risk for dyslexia, Part 1: Age effects. *NeuroReport 10*, 901–905.

Pinkerton, F., Watson, D. R., and McClelland, R. J. (1989). A neurophysiological study of children with reading, writing, and spelling difficulties. *Developmental Medicine and Child Neurology 31*, 569–581.

Plante, E. (1991). MRI findings in the parents and siblings of specifically language-impaired boys. *Brain and Language 41*, 67–80.

Plante, E., Swisher, L., Vance, R., and Rapcsak, S. (1991). MRI findings in boys with specific language impairment. *Brain and Language 41*, 52–66.

Rosenberger, P. B., and Hier, D. B. (1980). Cerebral asymmetry and verbal intellectual deficits. *Annals of Neurology 8*, 300–304.

Rumsey, J. M., Dorwart, R., Vermess, M., Denckla, M. B., Kruesi, M. J. P., and Rapoport, J. L. (1986). Magnetic resonance imaging of brain asymmetry in severe developmental dyslexia. *Archives of Neurology 43*, 1,045–1,046.

Schultz, R. T., Cho, N. K., Staib, L. H., Kier, L. E., Fletcher, J. M., Shaywitz, S. E., Shankweiler, D. P., Katz, L., Gore, J. C., Duncan, J. S., and Shaywitz, B. A. (1994). Brain morphology in normal and dyslexic children: The influence of sex and age. *Annals of Neurology 35*, 732–742.

Shaywitz, S. E., Escobar, M. D., Shaywitz, B. A., Fletcher, J. M., and Makuch, R. (1992). Evidence that dyslexia may represent the lower tail of a normal distribution of reading ability. *New England Journal of Medicine 326*, 145–150.

Shaywitz, S. E., Shaywitz, B. A., Pugh, K., Fulbright, R., Constable, R., Mencl, W., Shankweiler, D., Liberman, A., Skudlarski, P., Fletcher, J., Katz, L., Marchione, K., Lacadie, C., Gatenby, C., and Gore, J. (1998). Functional disruption in the organization of the brain for reading in dyslexia. *Proceedings of the National Academy of Sciences of the United States of America 95*, 2,636–2,641.

Slaghuis, W. L., Lovegrove, W. J., and Freestun, J. (1992). Letter recognition in peripheral vision and metacontrast masking in dyslexic and normal readers. *Clinical Vision Sciences 7*, 53–65.

Stark, R. E., and Tallal, P. (1988). The children with specific language impairment. In R. J. McCauley, ed., *Children: Neuropsychological Studies*. Boston: College Hill Press.

Tallal, P. (1987). Dysphasia, developmental. In G. Adelman, ed., *Encyclopedia of Neuroscience*, Vol. 1, 351–353. Boston: Birkhauser Press.

—— (1988). Speech before the US Congress on clinical definitions of developmental disability.

Tallal, P., Miller, S., and Fitch, R. H. (1993). Neurobiological basis of speech: A case for the preeminence of temporal processing. In P. Tallal, A. M. Galaburda, R. Llinas, and C. von Euler, eds., *Temporal information processing in the nervous system, with special reference to dyslexia and dysphasia*, pp. 27–47. New York: New York Academy of Sciences.

Tallal, P., and Piercy, M. (1973). Defects of non-verbal auditory perception in children with developmental aphasia. *Nature 241*, 468–469.

Teszner, D., Tzavaras, A., Gruner, J., and Hécaen, H. (1972). L'asymétrie droite-gauche du planum temporale: A propos de l'étude anatomique de 100 cervaeux. *Revue Neurologique 126*, 444–449.

Tonnquist-Uhlen, I., Borg, E., Persson, H. E., and Spens, K. E. (1996). Topography of auditory evoked cortical potentials in children with severe language impairment: The N1 component. *Electroencephalography and Clinical Neurophysiology 100*, 250–260.

Wada, J. A., Clarke, R., and Hamm, A. (1975). Cerebral hemispheric asymmetry in humans. *Archives of Neurology 32*, 239–246.

Witelson, S. F., and Pallie, W. (1973). Left hemisphere specialization for language in the newborn: Neuroanatomical evidence of asymmetry. *Brain 96*, 641–646.

Wong, B. Y. L. (1986). Problems and issues in the definition of learning disabilities. In J. R. Torgesen and B. Y. L. Wong, eds., *Psychological and educational perpectives on learning disabilities*, 3–26. Orlando, FL: Academic Press.

Wood, F., Flowers, L., Buchsbaum, M., and Tallal, P. (1991). Investigation of abnormal left temporal functioning in dyslexia through rCBF, auditory evoked potentials, and positron emission tomography. *Reading and Writing 3* (3–4), 379–393.

Woody, R. H. (1989). Public policy and legal issues for clinical child psychology. In C. R. Reynolds and J. Fletcher-Janzen, eds., *Handbook of child clinical neuropsychology*, 573–584. New York: Plenum Press.

Chris Chase
Paula A. Tallal
Elena Plante
Revised by R. Holly Fitch

LEARNING THEORY: A HISTORY

Even before psychology became an experimental science in the 1890s, learning was an important part of it. But there came a time in the 1910s when psychologists started to become fascinated by learning concepts and learning theories. The 1930s and 1940s are sometimes called the golden age of learning theory; that was when learning was the heart and soul of psychology. And then gradually the gold began to lose its glitter. The theorists did not seem able to settle their differences of opinion, psychologists began to think that the differences were only a matter of opinion with little empirical significance, and there emerged a growing distaste for the great debates over fundamental issues. In the 1960s new procedures and new phenomena were discovered that led psychologists away from the basic issues that the learning theorists had debated. Learning remains an important part of psychology, but the issues are quite different from the classical ones, and there is little theorizing in the grand style that characterized the golden age.

British empiricism culminated with the fourth edition of Alexander Bain's *The Senses and the Intellect* (1894). Everything psychological about humans is based on experience and is due to learning, he said. Bain argued that through association, sensations are linked with each other and with responses. He argued further that sensations can arouse ideas, and that when one's ideas of pleasure and pain are aroused, they are particularly likely to produce responses. At the same time, Morgan (1894) reported a number of rather casual learning experiments, interpreting his results very much as Bain had. Morgan had the same reliance upon associationist theory, empiricist philosophy, and the pleasure-pain principle. The difference was that Bain was a philosopher who thought about human knowledge, whereas Morgan was a naturalist who conducted research with animals. Looking back, it appears that Morgan's orientation was compelling because learning theory turned to the study of animals rather than of human learning, and to experimental studies rather than philosophical speculation.

Edward Thorndike

The first systematic experimental study with animals was Edward Thorndike's (1898) puzzle-box experiment. Thorndike simply measured the time it took a cat to pull a string that opened the door of the box so that it could go out and eat. He was struck by the fact that the time scores decreased steadily and smoothly over trials; he never found a sudden improvement in performance. He therefore concluded that the cat was not learning anything about ideas but must be acquiring some sort of direct connection between the stimulus (S) that was present and the response (R) of pulling the string. It must be a direct neural connection between S and R. Thus, at the outset of learning experiments and learning theory, there was a strong commitment to the S-R concept of learning. One attraction of this approach was that it minimized all mentalist concepts; it took the mind out of the picture. It was "scientific."

Thorndike (1911) introduced what he called the Law of Effect, what we now call the law of Reinforcement. Whether an S-R connection is strengthened on a particular trial depends, he argued, upon the environmental effect of the response. If the effect is positive, such as providing the hungry cat with food, then the connection gets stronger. Bain had a similar principle; he said the association will get stronger if the response produces pleasure. But pleasure is a mental concept, and so it had to go. Thorndike's version preserved the reinforcement mechanism but got rid of the mind and everything in it. It also took the control of the organism's behavior away from the organism and put it in the environment. The cat's behavior was totally controlled by the stimuli in the situation and the food.

John B. Watson

John B. Watson (1914) called Thorndike's approach behaviorism; it was the ultimate mechanistic psychology. Everything remotely related to the mind was discarded. Even Thorndike's reinforcement mechanism was tainted because a positive effect looked too much like pleasure. In Watson's psychology just the stimulus and response occurring together would create a connection between them. Everything was habit, or what was called learning by contiguity.

Thus began two long lines of theorists—the contiguity people and the reinforcement people. Watson also discarded all motivation concepts; hunger became just an internal stimulus, and emotion just a set of fixed responses to certain kinds of stimuli. Watson's behaviorism was appealing because it was so mechanistic and so conceptually simple. At the same time, Watson suggested that to understand anything and everything psychological, one had to start with learning. The description of the fear conditioning of Little Albert (Watson and Rayner, 1920) stated that that is how our personalities take shape. The message, which was believed by many, if not all, psychologists, was that wherever one wanted to go in the field, one had to start with learning theory.

There was, however, one problem that would be significant historically: In order to deal with certain cognitive-looking phenomena, Watson introduced some miniature responses, responses so small that they were basically unobservable. When individuals first learn to read, they read out loud. As they become practiced enough to read silently, they still move our lips. Ultimately nothing seems to move. But no, Watson asserted, there are still tiny responses in the mouth and throat. And it is the feedback from these small responses that mediates and controls what looks like intelligent or speech-related behavior. So Watson's learning theory, which was so elegantly simple, objective, and scientific, was obliged to hypothesize unobservable little responses.

Edwin Guthrie

Edwin Guthrie (1935) was a contiguity theorist who followed Watson in rejecting motivation and in other ways. He explained the great complexity and unpredictability of behavior in terms of the complexity of the stimulus situation. At any moment there are potentially millions of stimulus elements that one might respond to or have one's behavior conditioned to. Conditioning itself is simple and sudden, but the effective stimulus situation is impossible to control. So Guthrie's learning theory was forced to hypothesize unobservable little stimuli. The same problem in time caused the demise of Clark L. Hull's theory, which, in order to account for what looked like cognitive behavior, had to hypothesize unobservable little motivation terms, entities called r_G. The Skinnerians are no better off, for all their claims of objectivity and freedom from theory. They talk about self-reinforcement when the organism does something it is not supposed to, and they talk about conditioned (acquired) reinforcement when it does something that looks cognitive. Thus they are hypothesizing unobservable little reinforcers.

Ivan Pavlov and Edward Tolman

When Russian scientist Ivan Pavlov's work finally became available in English translation in 1927, it seemed vaguely familiar. It reminded readers of Watson's. They shared the same view of how important learning is and how it should be studied. The theory included no motivation, no reinforcement, no mind, and it was all very scientific. Pavlov emphasized inhibition, something that American psychologists had largely ignored but in time found fascinating. What was new was the procedure, the pairing of two stimuli; the bell and the food had to occur together. The critical contingency the experimenter had to control was the timing of the stimuli. With Thorndike's procedure the critical contingency was the relationship between the response and its "effect." The procedural contrast was called by different people Pavlovian versus trial and error, or classical conditioning versus instrumental, or respondent versus operant. There was always the uneasy feeling that while the two procedures were easily distinguished by their defining contingencies, perhaps there were not two separate underlying processes involved.

If there is a variable that one never varies, then one will never see its significance. Pavlov knew that his dogs had to be hungry or they would not salivate, so he always worked with hungry dogs. And so he never saw the significance of motivation. The first learning theorist to stress motivation was Edward Tolman (1932). He described a study by his student Tinklepaugh, who was studying monkeys and reinforcing their correct responses with pieces of banana. Occasionally Tinklepaugh would substitute lettuce for the banana; when this happened, the animals threw tantrums and became emotionally upset. Monkeys usually like lettuce and it can certainly be used as a reinforcer, so what had Tinklepaugh encountered here? First, he had the trivial finding that monkeys like bananas better than lettuce. Second, he had discovered that monkeys can anticipate receiving, or expect to receive, a particular kind of food. Thus, he had discovered what we call incentive motivation, motivation that depends upon the expected value of the outcome. Tolman's students also demonstrated effects of drive motivation, motivation that depends on the physiological state of the animal.

Thus, Tolman suddenly introduced two kinds of motivation, one psychological and one physiological, and he had abundant evidence for both kinds. He also challenged other conventional parts of Watsonian behaviorism, such as its mechanistic commitment. He introduced a cognitive language (e.g., *expectancies*) in place of connections and neurons. Tolman maintained that animals learn not S-R connections but the predictive significance and value of environmental stimuli, sequences of events (what leads to what), and where things are located in space (a "map" of a maze). In the 1940s Tolman developed the theme that animals learn places rather than responses (see, e.g., Tolman, Ritchie, and Kalish, 1946).

Those were exciting times. There were two paradigms, Pavlovian and Thorndikian, to be organized. One could explain all learning with this one, or that one, or with some of each (Mowrer, 1947). Mowrer attributed emotional and motivational learning to Pavlovian mechanisms, and most other learned behavior to reinforcement. There were contiguity theorists and reinforcement theorists. Some people studied motivation and others ignored it. Some were mechanists, and others appeared very cognitive. Some believed in tiny stimuli or responses, twinkles and twitches, and others looked at behavior globally. And new behavioral phenomena were being discovered at an accelerated rate.

Clark L. Hull

Could anyone put it all together? It seemed that Clark L. Hull and his dedicated followers might do it; they certainly tried. The great theory (Hull, 1943) was based on the reinforcement of S-R habits, but habits were only indirectly expressed in behavior. To be manifest, a habit had to be motivated by drive and/or incentive, and had to overcome the different kinds of inhibition that might be present. It was a very complex theory, but its virtue was that its complexity promised to match that of the empirical world. It was also a very explicit theory; everything was spelled out in detail. The theory even appeared to be able to explain away some of the mysterious things Tolman had reported. It was full of promise, and it gathered an enormous amount of attention.

Hull was fortunate to have a number of brilliant, energetic young associates who all agreed that this was the right kind of theory. Their disagreements were over details, and those differences called for further experiments to get everything straightened out. One could fuss over details, but all the Hullians endorsed the basic program. Miller and Dollard (1941) proposed a simpler model that anticipated many features of the great theory. Mowrer (1939) anticipated the all-important mechanism of reinforcement; he said a response is reinforced when it results in the reduction of some source of drive, such as fear. Kenneth Spence was another early associate of Hull's, and he had a multitude of graduate students who were proud to call themselves neo-Hullians and to work out different aspects of the theory. For them, the 1950s looked like the golden age because it was the time of awakening, the time of promise, and the time of payoff. Many of them moved away from animal learning and into human experimental, social, developmental, and clinical psychology. Learning was the center, but the time had come to apply the principles of behavior far and wide. Watson and Thorndike, the first learning theorists, had promised to build a better world with learning theory, and the neo-Hullians felt that the time had come to make good on that promise.

Two things went wrong. One, which should have been only a minor tactical setback, was that the drive-reduction hypothesis of reinforcement was wrong. That was discovered early on (Sheffield and Roby, 1950), and in his last written work Hull (1952) acknowledged the problem and said the hypothesis might have to be altered. The whole point of theory, according to Hull, is to use it to generate research and then use the research to modify the theory. So the loss of this particular hypothesis should not have hurt the basic Hullian program. But the neo-Hullians were severely wounded and badly discouraged. Furthermore, by about 1970, new difficulties had arisen with the concept of reinforcement itself (Bolles, 1975).

A second difficulty was that during the 1960s there were many problems with incentive motivation. It was based on the little response r_G, which had all the conceptual properties of a response (i.e., it was elicited by stimuli, it was conditionable, and it could be motivated). The problem was that it did not seem to be observable. The r_G concept was needed to account for Tolman's discovery that animals learn places (Hull held that it was elicited by spatial stimuli), and it was needed to explain a variety of other effects; but it was beginning to look like a fiction, a figment. The Hullians said that when the animal looks to the left, it encounters stimuli that elicit r_G and so it moves in that direction. Tolman said that the animal expects food to be off to the west, and since it is hungry and values food, it moves in that direction. If you cannot measure r_G, then you have no way to test Hull's view against Tolman's view of the situation. Eventually psychologists figured out that Tolman's theory is untestable because one cannot measure expectancies or values, and that Hull's theory is untestable because one cannot measure r_G. Learning theories are basically untestable. The great promise of Hull's theory was slipping away. The golden age was ending.

B. F. Skinner

Some found comfort in B. F. Skinner's approach. It could have been an alternative learning theory but chose to present itself as theoretically neutral. Certainly Skinnerians did not worry about theoretical matters as such. And they were eager to leave learning

behind and move into other areas of psychology and into applied problems. Others began to understand that there was something fundamentally flawed in the whole enterprise begun by Thorndike and Watson. Psychology did not become a science because it exorcised the mind and analyzed everything into atomic S-R units; it became a science as it looked systematically at psychological phenomena. If one wants to understand a social phenomenon, then one does not need a basic learning theory; one needs to look at social situations, social motivation, and social behavior strategies. And that is the sort of thing psychologists do now.

See also: GUTHRIE, EDWIN R.; HULL, CLARK L.; MATHEMATICAL LEARNING THEORY; PAVLOV, IVAN; THORNDIKE, EDWARD; TOLMAN, EDWARD C.; WATSON, JOHN B.

Bibliography

Bain, A. (1894). *The senses and the intellect,* 4th edition. London: Longmans, Green.

Bolles, R. C. (1975). *Learning theory.* New York: Holt.

Guthrie, E. R. (1935). *The psychology of learning.* New York: Harper's.

Hull, C. L. (1943). *Principles of behavior.* New York: Appleton.

—— (1952). *A behavior system.* New Haven, CT: Yale University Press.

Miller, N. E., and Dollard, J. (1941). *Social learning and imitation.* New Haven, CT: Yale University Press.

Morgan, C. L. (1894). *An introduction to comparative psychology.* London: Scott.

Mowrer, O. H. (1939). A stimulus-response analysis of anxiety and its role as a reinforcing agent. *Psychological Review 46,* 553–564.

—— (1947). On the dual nature of learning: A reinterpretation of "conditioning" and "problem-solving." *Harvard Educational Review 17,* 102–148.

Pavlov, I. P. (1927). *Conditioned reflexes,* trans. G. V. Anrep. London: Oxford University Press.

Sheffield, F. D., and Roby, T. B. (1950). Reward value of a nonnutritive sweet taste. *Journal of Comparative and Physiological Psychology 43,* 461–481.

Thorndike, E. L. (1898). Animal intelligence: An experimental study of the associative processes in animals. *Psychological Review Monograph Supplement 2* (8).

—— (1911). *Animal intelligence.* New York: Teachers College Press.

Tolman, E. C. (1932). *Purposive behavior in animals and men.* New York: Century.

Tolman, E. C., Ritchie, B. F., and Kalish, D. (1946). Studies in spatial learning: II. Place learning versus response learning. *Journal of Experimental Psychology 36,* 221–229.

Watson, J. B. (1914). *Behavior. An introduction to comparative psychology.* New York: Holt.

Watson, J. B., and Rayner, R. (1920). Conditioned emotional reactions. *Journal of Experimental Psychology 3,* 1–14.

Robert C. Bolles

LEARNING THEORY: CURRENT STATUS

When most students of psychology hear the term *learning theory*, they probably think about the history of psychology. After all, what comes to mind when you think about learning theory? Perhaps one thinks of the names of many great psychologists, such as Thorndike, Pavlov, Tolman, Hull, and Skinner. Perhaps you recall Skinner's pigeons pecking at lights in an operant chamber to obtain morsels of food. Or maybe you remember Pavlov's famous discovery that the sound of a metronome can be conditioned to make dogs salivate if it is presented together with powdered meat. But is learning theory a relic of psychology's past, as these vignettes might suggest? The answer is no. In fact, learning theory is an active and vibrant area of study in psychology, with a steady stream of fresh theories that are attempting to tacklelearning about complex stimuli, the involvement of context in memory retrieval, and the role of time in learning. Moreover, neuroscientists are increasingly relying on learning theory in the quest to dissect the brain systems involved in learning and memory. Learning theory is alive and well.

Modeling Learning

One of the most influential modern learning theories was crafted in the early 1970s by Robert A. Rescorla and Allan R. Wagner (Rescorla and Wagner, 1972). The Rescorla-Wagner model accounts for several features of a form of associative learning called Pavlovian conditioning. Pavlovian or classical conditioning is a type of learning in which "neutral" or conditional stimuli (CS), such as tones or lights, can predict the occurrence of biologically significant or unconditional stimuli (US), such as food or illness. After having been paired with a US, a CS elicits a learned or conditional response (CR) that often is similar to the unlearned or unconditional response (UR) elicited by the US.

Rescorla and Wagner used a simple mathematical formula to model Pavlovian conditioning:

$$\delta V_{CS} = \alpha(\lambda - \sigma V_T) \qquad (1)$$

The equation has three critical variables: α, the salience of the CS, λ, the magnitude of the US, and σV_T, the total amount of learning acquired by all of the CSs present on the trial (For simplicity, a fourth variable, β, describing the salience of the US has been omitted). According to this equation, the amount that is learned on a conditioning trial (δV_{CS}) is the product of the salience of the CS (α) and the difference between the magnitude of the US (λ) and the amount

Figure 1

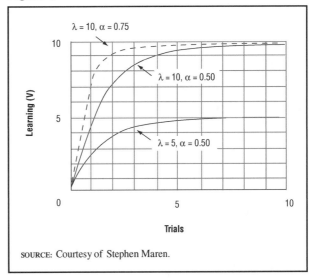

SOURCE: Courtesy of Stephen Maren.

Learning curves computed with the Rescorla-Wagner model. The asymptote of each curve (the point on the curve where learning is maximal) approaches λ, which represents the magnitude of the US. The rate at which learning occurs is determined by α, which represents CS salience. The values chosen for each variable are arbitrary. Note that the amount of learning on each trial (the change from one trial to the next) decreases over the course of training. In other words, learning is the greatest on the first trial.

of learning that has already accrued to all of the CSs presented on that trial (σV_T). A key feature of the model is that the amount that is learned on any given trial (CS, US, or CS-US presentation) is determined by how much the animal has already learned about all of the CSs present on that trial.

To illustrate some of the properties of the Rescorla-Wagner model, Figure 1 displays a family of learning curves computed with Equation 1. Note that the highest point on each learning curve (the asymptote) approaches the value of λ. The rate at which the asymptote is approached is determined by α. This means that the amount that is learned during classical conditioning is set by the strength of the US and the speed of that learning is set by the salience of the CS. For example, Pavlov's dogs learned to salivate profusely to a CS that was followed by a large quantity of powdered meat (the US). Similarly, the speed at which the dogs attained that profuse quantity of salivation was rapid when Pavlov used a salient CS, such as a loud metronome. The Rescorla-Wagner model predicts these features of Pavlovian conditioning.

Despite its simplicity, the Rescorla-Wagner model can account for a wide variety of interesting learning phenomena including extinction, blocking, and overshadowing. For example, in blocking conditioning, one CS (CS$_A$) prevents conditioning to another CS (CS$_B$) when the two are presented together during compound conditioning (CS$_A$/CS$_B$-US). Simply put, learning does not occur to CS$_B$ because the US is already perfectly predicted by CS$_A$-CS$_B$ doesn't tell the animal anything it doesn't already know. In terms of the Rescorla-Wagner model, the value of (λ-σV_T) is close to zero on the compound trial, because V$_{CSA}$ is close to 1 (CSA is already conditioned). The beauty of the Rescorla-Wagner model is that this simple mathematical equation can predict many complex learning phenomena.

Is the Whole More Than the Sum of Its Parts?

The Rescorla-Wagner model is an elemental model of conditioning because it makes predictions about learning based on the individual stimuli in a given trial. However, stimuli often occur together in complex combinations during classical conditioning. Consider, for example, the places where classical conditioning happens, such as a dentist's office. Here you learn to fear (CR) the sound of a dental drill (CS) that predicts tooth pain (UR). But you also learn that the dentist's office itself, which is composed of many unique stimuli (reclining chair, observation light, gurgling fountain, and the odor of the dentist's breath, to name a few), predict tooth pain and elicit learned fear. Rescorla and Wagner would argue that each of these contextual stimuli is an element, and that learning to these elements happens individually. According to their model, δV_{CS} is calculated for each element separately in order to determine the amount of learning that happens to these stimuli.

An alternative has been proposed by John M. Pearce at Cardiff University in the United Kingdom (Pearce, 1994). Pearce suggests that stimuli that co-occur should be treated as unique combinations or configurations of stimuli that are distinct from their elements. Hence, rather than break down the dentist's office into many individual elements (such as the gurgling sound and dentist's bad breath), Pearce argues that we form a configuration of stimuli, such as "dentist's office," that includes all of the individual stimuli and becomes associated with the US.

The power of this configural approach is apparent in a type of learning called negative patterning. In this form of learning, two different CSs (CS$_A$ and CS$_B$) are paired with a US, such as food. After several pairings, these CSs will elicit responses associated with food delivery, such as salivation. During this training, trials are interspersed in which CS$_A$ and CS$_B$ are presented together (a so-called compound trial) without food delivery. What happens in these compound trials? You might imagine that there is profuse salivation on these compound trials because both CS$_A$ and CS$_B$ predict food. But animals and people readily learn to withhold salivation on the compound trials because no food is delivered on these trials.

The Rescorla-Wagner model has trouble with this phenomenon because the compound stimulus CS$_A$/CS$_B$ is treated as the sum of two elements (CS$_A$ and CS$_B$), which strongly predict the US. Despite the fact that the US does not occur on compound trials, V$_{CSA/CSB}$ is always higher for the compound stimulus than the individual CSs. This incorrectly predicts that the compound stimulus will elicit a greater CR than the elements presented alone. However, Pearce's model can readily account for the fact that animals and people respond more on to the CS$_A$ and CS$_B$ compared to the compound stimulus. Pearce assumes that that compound stimulus is distinct from the elements that compose it—in effect, it is like a third CS. Using a computational formula much like the Rescorla-Wagner model, Pearce shows that animals rapidly learn to respond discriminatively on CS$_A$, CS$_B$, and CS$_A$/CS$_B$ trials. By considering stimuli as configurations that are more than the sum of their parts, Pearce has provided a new and powerful explanation for several forms of learning.

Retrieving the Meaning of an Event

Of course, stimuli, whether they are CSs or words, for that matter, often have ambiguous meanings. Consider, for example, the word *vessel*. This word has several different meanings; it may refer to a watercraft, a container, or a tube containing blood, for example. How do we interpret the meanings of such ambiguous stimuli? Recent studies indicate that the context within which the stimulus occurs is important for understanding its meaning. For instance, sentences such as "The *Titanic* was a grand vessel" or "The aorta is the largest vessel in the body" provide a context in which to understand the meaning of the word *vessel*.

Pavlovian conditioning experiments in animals indicate the importance of context in understanding the meaning of ambiguous CSs. For example, if a CS is first paired with food for several trials, but then presented by itself (without food), the ability of the CS to elicit a CR is weakened. This process is called extinction. Although one might imagine (as the Rescorla-Wagner model predicts) that presenting the CS by itself results in unlearning of the CS-US memory, considerable data suggest that extinction itself represents new learning. In this case, animals learn that the CS predicts the absence of the US. So how does the animal know how to respond to this ambiguous CS?

After all, the CS has predicted both the presence and absence of the US and various times.

Elegant work by Mark E. Bouton at the University of Vermont has solved this enigma (Bouton, 1993). Bouton has found that the context in which conditioning and extinction occur is critical for determining how animals respond to the CS. If animals are conditioned (i.e., receive CS-US pairings) in one context but are extinguished (i.e., receive the CS by itself) in a different context, then the context controls how the animals respond. If they are placed in the context where the CS was presented by itself, they retrieve a memory that the CS predicts the absence of the US and show little conditional responding. In contrast, if the animals are placed in the conditioning context, they retrieve a memory that the US will follow the CS and show high levels of learned behavior. Hence, Bouton argues that contexts—which include physical environments, internal states (such as hunger), and even time—regulate the ability of an ambiguous CS to evoke a learned response.

It's All in the Timing

The theories of Rescorla, Wagner, Pearce, and Bouton all assume that the foundation of learning is an association, a bond or link formed between two or more stimuli. Pavlovian conditioning, for example, assumes that an association forms between the CS and US, and that this association is necessary for the CS to elicit a learned response (CR). In a radical departure from this fundamental assumption of associative learning theory, Randy Gallistel and John Gibbon have argued that the time at which events occur, not associations between the events, is at the heart of learning and memory (Gallistel and Gibbon, 2000).

In any conditioning experiment, stimuli occur in a temporal as well as a physical context. Years of animal and human research have yielded important information about the influence of timing on Pavlovian conditioning. For example, conditioning is often optimal when the CS is turned on slightly before the US. Long intervals between the onset of the CS and US tend to produce weak learning; this is commonly called the delay of reinforcement gradient. However, conditioning is related to both the delay of reinforcement and the amount of time that elapses between CS-US trials (the intertrial interval or ITI). Learning rates are comparable across short and long delays of reinforcement long as the ITI is varied in accordance with the CS-US delay.

Gallistel and Gibbon's temporal model, which they call rate estimation theory, explains this and other properties of conditioning. In their model, animals compute the ratios between the temporal intervals associated with the delay of reinforcement and the ITI. These computations are then used to make decisions about how to respond to a particular stimulus. In general, conditioning improves when the ratio between the ITI and the delay of reinforcement is large. And, as mentioned before, increasing the duration of the delay and reinforcement gradient results in weaker conditioning unless the ITI increases as well. These predictions are made without any appeal to associations between the CS and US; in essence, the animals are just keeping time.

Despite the computational power of rate-estimation theory, the model faces with a fundamental challenge: Does the brain learn this way? The anatomical and physiological facts about brain function seem to be more consistent with associative models of learning and memory. For example, sensory pathways in the brain transmit information about CSs, USs, contexts, and other stimuli. There is considerable convergence among these pathways in several brain areas thought to be involved in learning and memory, such as the hippocampus and amygdala. Neurons in the brain exhibit changes in synaptic function after learning, and these changes are consistent with the associative nature of Pavlovian conditioning, for example (Maren, 1999).

One of the promises of associative learning theory is that it is stimulating and guiding neuroscientists in their quest for discovering the brain mechanisms of learning and memory. The continued elaboration and refinement of learning theories are an integral component of understanding both brain and behavior in humans and animals.

See also: LEARNING THEORY: A HISTORY

Bibliography

Bouton, M. E. (1993). Context, time, and memory retrieval in the interference paradigms of Pavlovian conditioning. *Psychological Bulletin 114,* 80–99.

Gallistel, C. R., and Gibbon, J. (2000). Time, rate, and conditioning. *Psychological Review 107,* 219–275.

Maren, S. (1999). Long-term potentiation in the amygdala: A mechanism for emotional learning and memory. *Trends in Neuroscience 22,* 561–567.

Pearce, J. M. (1994). Similarity and discrimination: A selective review and connectionist model. *Psychological Review,* 587–607.

Rescorla, R. A., and Wagner, A. R. (1972). A theory of Pavlovian conditioning: Variations in the effectiveness of reinforcement and nonreinforcement. In A. H. Black and W. F. Prokasy, eds., *Classical Conditioning II: Current Research and Theory.* New York: Appleton-Century-Crofts.

Steve Maren

LEFT HEMISPHERE

See: KNOWLEDGE SYSTEMS AND MATERIAL-SPECIFIC MEMORY DEFICITS

LOCALIZATION OF MEMORY TRACES

The brain consists of a vast number of individual cells called neurons. Individual neurons form highly complex patterns of interconnections with many other neurons. Each of these connections is called a *synapse* and a collection of interconnected neurons is called a *neural network*. It is within these networks of neurons and synapses that memories are formed and stored. The term *memory trace*, also called the *engram*, broadly refers to the change(s) in the brain that serves to store a memory. To fully understand the nature of a memory trace, at least three different but interrelated properties must be elucidated. First, the precise region within the brain where the memory dependent changes occur must be localized. This entails identifying the specific neural network (or neural circuit) that subserves the formation, storage, and retrieval of the particular memory and then localizing the site(s) of change(s) within that network that mediates storage of the memory. Second, once the site of memory storage has been identified, the biophysical properties of the changes that occurred within the neural network as a result of memory formation must be identified. For instance, these changes might involve strengthening synaptic connections between different neurons, a process that might entail expression of different, memory related genes. Finally, in addition to identifying the site of memory formation and the nature of the changes that occur, the memory specific pattern of neural activity within the network that occurs during recall of a memory must be delineated. This entry will focus primarily on the first step in understanding the nature of memory traces: localizing traces within the brain.

History of Memory Localization

In the early days of behaviorism, the observable, quantifiable study of behaviors, it was thought that each memory was represented as a change in the brain at one particular place. Karl Lashley began the search for the memory trace, stressing the now obvious point that in order to analyze the nature of memory traces, it is necessary to find them. In his classic 1929 monograph, *Brain Mechanisms and Intelligence*, he concluded that memories, at least memories for complex mazes in rats, did not have any particular locus in the cerebral cortex (equipotentiality); the more cortex removed, the more the impairment in memory (mass action). Walter Hunter was quick to point out that removing more cerebral cortex removed more sensory information (visual, auditory, kinesthetic), in effect reducing the number of available cues (e.g., animals that are blind do not learn mazes well). This issue has never really been resolved, at least for complex maze learning in the rat, although we now know that the hippocampus is important for such memories.

Following Lashley's failure to localize memory traces, some scientists adopted the view that they were distributed either widely throughout the brain or widely within certain brain structures like the cerebral cortex. But as more was learned about the anatomical and functional organization of the brain, it became clear that the brain does not have a diffusely distributed organization; instead, it has a highly structured organization. Donald Hebb, in his important and influential book *The Organization of Behavior* (1949), proposed a resolution of this dilemma by assuming that the organization of a memory trace can be complex and involve a number of brain areas but that the trace can involve specific connections in particular areas. This remains a common view. Hebb also proposed a possible mechanism of memory trace formation that has come to be known as the Hebb synapse. In brief, he argued that at neurons where traces are formed, there must be active input from a to-be-learned source (e.g., conditioned stimulus in Pavlovian terms) at the same time the neuron is firing action potentials. The Hebb synapse has come to be viewed more generally as a strengthening or weakening of one input (synapses) to a neuron if this input is active concurrent with activation from another input to the neuron.

By the end of the twentieth century, the focus had shifted away from memory traces in complex tasks to more specific and discrete learning and memory tasks, and research emphasized identifying the entire circuitries essential (necessary and sufficient) for particular forms of memory. Only after this has been accomplished can the memory traces be localized and analyzed. Well-established methods of lesions, electrical recording of neuronal activity, and electrical stimulation of brain tissue, together with anatomical tracing of pathways in the brain, have enabled much progress in the identification of essential memory circuits in the brain, at least for simpler forms of learning, although the experimental difficulties are formidable. Relatively new methods such as functional imaging, probes for genetic expression, or localized infusion of highly specific receptor antagonists or agonists have also become widely used tools in the search for essential memory circuits. Once the complete circuit for a particular form of learning has been identified, the next step of localizing the memory trace(s) within that circuit is orders of magnitude more difficult. Indeed, there are no universally agreed upon methods for doing so. This aspect of the search for memory traces has become the conceptual center of the field.

Localization of Different Types of Memories

There are many different types of learning and memory; for instance, learning to ride a bicycle differs from memorizing a list of facts. A distinction is often made between two general categories of memory: declarative (learning "what") and procedural (learning "how"). Many other terms have been suggested for this dichotomy; extreme examples of the two types of memory are one's memory of one's own recent experiences (declarative) and classical or Pavlovian conditioning, where a specific conditioned response like salivation or eye blink is learned to a particular conditioned stimulus (procedural). Although both types of memory formation involve many regions of the brain, the brain structures and systems essential for the two types of memories are quite different. Indeed, there are several different memory circuits and systems in the mammalian brain. Some of these will be noted here; each is treated in a separate article in this volume.

In humans and other mammals, the hippocampus appears to play a key role in recent experiential memory (declarative). Extensive damage to the hippocampus can markedly impair recent memory in humans and monkeys. Evidence suggests that the impairment is more in the establishing of memories—a process that appears to take weeks in monkeys and may take years in humans—than in their retrieval. In rodents, recent "working" memory and spatial memory are impaired by hippocampal lesions. Very recent or short-term memory in monkeys also involves the prefrontal areas of the cerebral cortex. The thalamus, the largest subdivision of the diencephalon, also plays a role in recent memory in humans. However, long-term permanent memories, representing our knowledge and our life experiences, are not stored in the hippocampus, prefrontal cortex, or thalamus—and thus are not impaired by damage to these structures. The cerebral cortex is often suggested as the storage site for these long-term memories, but definitive evidence is lacking.

In contrast, the clearest evidence for a high degree of localization of a memory trace exists for classical conditioning of discrete behavioral responses—for instance, the conditioned eyeblink response. This type of learning, which occurs in humans and other mammals, involves associating a neutral stimulus, such as a brief tone, with another stimulus, for instance an air puff to the eye, that evokes a specific movement such as an eye blink. After presenting the tone paired with the air puff, subjects are conditioned to blink their eye to the tone alone. Using the methods of stimulation, lesions, and recordings described above, the neural circuit that mediates this form of motor learning was found to critically involve the cerebellum and its associated brain-stem structures. Once this essential circuit was identified, the memory trace was localized within the circuit to a particular region of the interpositus nucleus in the cerebellum. In addition to the interpositus, there appear to be additional storage sites in the cerebellar cortex, and these sites certainly are distributed, in the sense that many thousands of neurons are involved. Localization of the memory trace for eyeblink conditioning is a critical first step toward elucidating the mechanisms of plasticity and the network-level properties mediating expression of the stored memory.

Unlike learned motor behaviors, such as eyeblink conditioning, that involve the cerebellum, fear conditioning, as in conditioned changes in heart rate and blood pressure following pairing of a tone or light with a painful electric shock, critically involves the hypothalamus and amygdala but not the cerebellum. As with eyeblink conditioning, much of the circuitry essential for conditioned fear has been identified. For this particular form of learning and memory, the amygdala is critically involved. In particular, the critical region for memory formation for conditioned fear appears to be localized to a region of the amygdala called the basolateral complex. However, it is uncertain whether the amygdala is the site of long-term storage of this type of memory. The amygdala is also critically involved in hormonal modulation of memory storage.

Because the memory traces for conditioned motor responses or conditioned fear are fairly localized, the memory traces for procedural learning tasks in general may also be relatively localized. In contrast, memory traces for declarative memories may be much more widely distributed. On the other hand, the fact that damage to speech areas in the human cerebral cortex appears to abolish memory for language suggests that this complex learning and memory process, perhaps the most complex yet evolved in nature, may have a considerable degree of localization.

A somewhat different approach has been taken in the study of "simplified" neuronal circuits in certain invertebrate preparations where the number of neurons is small, their sizes are large, and their interconnections are well specified. Here, simplified neural circuits containing only a few identified neurons can be isolated and particular training procedures, usually classical conditioning, can result in the circuits' showing changes in activity that can be long-lasting and can closely resemble similar associative learning in mammals. In these preparations it is possible to localize the learning-induced changes in the activities of the neurons and analyze the underlying mechanisms in some detail. These mechanisms can then provide models of putative mechanisms of memory storage in the mammalian brain.

Mechanisms of Memory Formation

As more and more memory traces are localized in the brain, understanding the biophysical properties of the changes that occur as a result of memory formation becomes possible. Theories abound regarding the nature of the mechanisms of memory trace formation. One early notion held that each memory was stored in a particular protein molecule. This view is no longer tenable, but proteins of course play key roles in the structure and functioning of nerve cells. Another early view was that the brain grew new pathways; thus, in Pavlovian conditioning a new pathway would grow to connect the conditioned stimulus region of the brain to the unconditioned stimulus or response region. This does not occur. Instead, evidence is uniformly consistent with the more modest view that there are changes in the actions of the synapses that are the sites of the interconnections and interactions among the neurons of the brain. Changes in synaptic actions can occur in many ways: changes in amount of neurotransmitter release, changes in receptor molecules, and a variety of other biochemical processes, ranging from calcium entry into neurons to second messenger systems (cyclic AMP, cyclic GNP, protein kinases, and so forth) to changes in gene expression.

Although the biophysical properties of synaptic plasticity have been extensively studied, definitive proof that these mechanisms actually mediate memory storage remains elusive. Perhaps the clearest evidence that synaptic plasticity is a mechanism of memory storage is in conditioned fear. Here, the evidence strongly indicates that a strengthening (potentiation) of synaptic transmission in the amygdala is critically involved in memory formation. However, whether this form of plasticity mediates long-term storage of the memory or whether it is simply an intermediate process in the long-term memory storage is unknown. The strongest evidence we have for a biological substrate of long-term memory storage concerns long-lasting structural changes in the synaptic interconnections among neurons. Enriched environments and even particular learning experiences can result in changes in the numbers and distributions of spine synapses on neuron dendrites, and even in changes in the number of dendritic branches in certain types of neurons. Possibly all these processes and many more are involved in memory formation. A great deal of progress has been achieved in the identification of essential memory circuits in the brain. The search for the memory trace has become one of the most active and exciting fields in neuroscience and psychology.

See also: AMNESIA, ORGANIC; CODING PROCESSES: ORGANIZATION OF MEMORY; EMOTION, MOOD, AND MEMORY; GENETIC SUBSTRATES OF MEMORY: CEREBELLUM; GUIDE TO THE ANATOMY OF THE BRAIN: AMYGDALA; GUIDE TO THE ANATOMY OF THE BRAIN: SYNAPSE; HEBB, DONALD; HORMONES AND MEMORY; INVERTEBRATE LEARNING; KNOWLEDGE SYSTEMS AND MATERIAL-SPECIFIC MEMORY DEFICITS; LASHLEY, KARL; LONG-TERM DEPRESSION IN THE CEREBELLUM, HIPPOCAMPUS, AND NEOCORTEX; LONG-TERM POTENTIATION; MEMORY CONSOLIDATION: MOLECULAR AND CELLULAR PROCESSES; MEMORY CONSOLIDATION: PROLONGED PROCESS OF REORGANIZATION; MORPHOLOGICAL BASIS OF LEARNING AND MEMORY; NEURAL SUBSTRATES OF CLASSICAL CONDITIONING; NEUROTRANSMITTER SYSTEMS AND MEMORY; PREFRONTAL CORTEX AND MEMORY IN PRIMATES; PROTEIN SYNTHESIS IN LONG-TERM MEMORY IN VERTEBRATES; SECOND MESSENGER SYSTEMS; SPATIAL LEARNING: ANIMALS; SPATIAL MEMORY; WORKING MEMORY: ANIMALS

Bibliography

Hebb, D. O. (1949). *The organization of behavior.* New York: Wiley.

Lashley, K. S. (1929). *Brain mechanisms and intelligence.* Chicago: University of Chicago Press.

LeDoux, J. E. (2000). Emotion circuits in the brain. *Annual Review of Neuroscience 23,* 155–184.

Maren, S. (2001). Neurobiology of Pavlovian fear conditioning. *Annual Review of Neuroscience 24,* 897–931.

Squire, L. R. (1986). Mechanisms of memory. *Science 232,* 1,612–1,619.

Squire, L. R., Knowlton, B., and Musen, G. (1993). The structure and organization of memory. *Annual Review of Psychology 44,* 453–495.

Thompson, R. F. (1990). The neurobiology of learning and memory. In K. L. Kelner and D. E. Koshland Jr., eds., *Molecules to models: Advances in neuroscience,* 219–234. Washington, DC: American Association for the Advancement of Science.

Thompson, R. F., and Kim, J. J. (1996). Memory systems in the brain and localization of a memory. *Proceedings of the National Academy of Sciences of the United States of America 93,* 13,438–13,444.

Thompson, R. F., and Krupa, D. J. (1994). Organization of memory traces in the mammalian brain. *Annual Review of Neuroscience 17,* 519–549.

Zola-Morgan, S., and Squire, L. R. (1993). Neuroanatomy of memory. *Annual Review of Neuroscience 16,* 547–563.

Richard F. Thompson
Revised by David J. Krupa

LONG-TERM DEPRESSION IN THE CEREBELLUM, HIPPOCAMPUS, AND NEOCORTEX

Long-term depression (LTD) is a type of synaptic plasticity in which the efficacy of signal transmission across a synapse is persistently reduced after a certain triggering activity. LTD in the cerebellum was proposed as a theoretical possibility around 1970 and was detected a decade later (Ito, Sakurai, and Tongroach, 1982). So far, several subtypes of LTD varying in cellular and molecular mechanisms have been found in the cerebellum, hippocampus, and neocortex. LTD occurs not only in excitatory synapses, but also in inhibitory ones. LTD may weaken or functionally interrupt useless or erroneous synaptic connections between neurons, providing an opposing mechanism against long-term potentiation (LTP) in various forms of learning and memory.

Induction and Observation of LTD

The various forms of LTD revealed to occur in the cerebellum, cerebellum-like structures in fish, hippocampus and neocortex have the following characteristic features. In this article, references for the cerebellum are largely omitted because they can be found in recent review articles (Ito, 2001; Hansel, Linden, and D'Angelo, 2001).

In the Cerebellum and Cerebellum-Like Structures

In the cerebellar cortex each Purkinje cell receives two distinct types of excitatory synapses, one from parallel fibers and the other from a (normally single) climbing fiber. LTD occurs when these two types of synapses are activated repeatedly in approximate synchrony, leading to an enduring decrease in synaptic strength of the parallel fibers. In in vitro cerebellar slices, LTD is typically induced by conjunctive stimulation at 1 hertz for five minutes (300 stimuli), which reduces the transmission efficacy by 30 to 40 percent (see Figure 1). To induce LTD, climbing fiber stimulation is often replaced by current-induced membrane depolarization that enhances entry of Ca^{2+} ions into Purkinje cell dendrites as in the case of climbing fiber stimulation (see below). Conjunctive LTD can be followed for one to three hours without sign of recovery. It is robust in the sense that its induction does not depend critically on the timing between climbing fiber and parallel fiber stimulations.

Strong stimulation of parallel fibers alone causes homosynaptic LTD. Conjunctive LTD is accompanied by LTD in the neighboring synapses located within a distance of 100 micrometers, which are not involved in conjunctive stimulation. Other types of LTD also occur in the cerebellum.

Brains of certain fish species contain a cerebellum-like structure that lacks climbing fibers. LTD occurs in parallel fiber-evoked excitatory postsynaptic potentials (EPSPs) in Purkinje cell–like neurons when EPSPs repeatedly precede postsynaptic spikes within 60 milliseconds (Bell, Han, Sugawara, and Grant, 1997).

In the Hippocampus

In a pyramidal cell of the hippocampal CA1 region, a low-frequency stimulation (LFS) of a bundle of presynaptic fibers (1 hertz for five to fifteen minutes) typically induces LTD, while a high-frequency stimulation (five stimuli at 100 hertz repeated at 200-millisecond intervals for two seconds) induces LTP. Associative stimulation of presynaptic fibers with postsynaptic membrane depolarization (5 hertz for sixteen seconds) also induces LTD or LTP depending on the time from pre- to postsynaptic activities (Nishiyama et al., 2000). While LTP is induced when presynaptic stimulation falls within the window from -2 to 12 milliseconds after postsynaptic spikes, LTD occurs when presynaptic stimulation either precedes the postsynaptic spikes by 16 to 28 milliseconds or follows with a delay of 15 to 20 milliseconds (see Figure 2). Associative LTD occurs in both stimulated (homosynaptic LTD) and unstimulated (heterosynaptic LTD) synapses, while LTP occurs only homosynaptically. As revealed in a triple chain of cultured hippocampal neurons, induction of associative LTD in a synapse is accompanied by back-propagated induction of LTD in a synapse on a presynaptic cell (Fitzsimonds, Song, and Poo, 1997). Through these LTD/LTP inductions, temporal information coded in the timing of individual spikes may be converted into spatially distributed patterns of persistent synaptic modifications in a neural network (Bi and Poo, 1999).

In the Neocortex

LFS-induced LTD occurs in layer III neurons of the visual cortex following stimulation of the white matter or layer IV (Kirkwood and Bear, 1994). Associative LTP or LTD is induced when presynaptic stimulation is paired with membrane depolarization. A relatively large membrane depolarization induces LTP, while a relatively small membrane depolarization causes LTD (Artola, Brocher, and Singer, 1990). This dichotomy depends on the amount of Ca^{2+} influx evoked by the depolarization (see below). LTD has also been observed in the sensorimotor (Bindman, Murphy, and Pockett, 1988) and prefrontal cortex (Hirsch and Crepel, 1990).

Signal Transduction Underlying LTD

Conjunctive LTD is a purely postsynaptic event, but in other LTD subtypes, the contribution of pre-

Figure 1

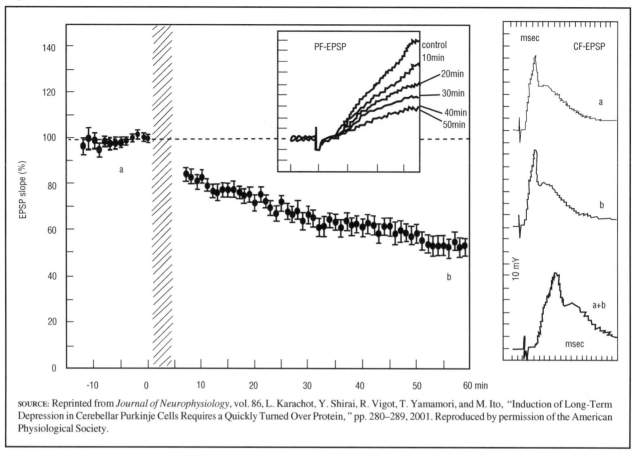

SOURCE: Reprinted from *Journal of Neurophysiology*, vol. 86, L. Karachot, Y. Shirai, R. Vigot, T. Yamamori, and M. Ito, "Induction of Long-Term Depression in Cerebellar Purkinje Cells Requires a Quickly Turned Over Protein," pp. 280–289, 2001. Reproduced by permission of the American Physiological Society.

LTD observed in Purkinje cells in cerebellar slices. Left, inset, EPSPs induced by stimulation of parallel fibers (PF-EPSP). Six traces of EPSPs recorded before (control) and 10 to 50 minutes after conjunctive stimulation of parallel fibers and a climbing fiber are superposed. Each trace indicates EPSPs averaged for 5 sweeps repeated every 5 seconds. The graph plots the rising slopes of the EPSPs against time. Shaded column indicates conjunctive stimulation. Right, a and b, climbing fiber-evoked EPSP superposed with Ca^{2+} spikes (CF-EPSP), recorded at the moments indicated in the graph. a+b, superposition of a and b on an expanded time scale.

synaptic factors is not excluded. The following post-synaptic signal transduction processes have been analyzed in synaptically induced as well as in various reduced forms of LTD induced with chemical or electrical stimulation of neurons in place of synaptic activation (Ito, 2001).

Receptors

LTD in excitatory synapses is, at least in part, due to a reduced number of functional AMPA receptor molecules in the postsynaptic membrane. Other types of receptors play roles in eventually inducing this change. Activation of NMDA receptors is required in LTD induction in excitatory synapses, but not in inhibitory synapses, of hippocampal neurons (Fitzsimonds, Song, and Poo, 1997). NMDA receptors are not functional in adult Purkinje cells. Parallel fiber synapses on Purkinje cells contain, besides AMPA receptors, type-1 metabotropic glutamate receptors (mGluR1s) and δ2 glutamate receptors, whereas

climbing fiber synapses contain AMPA receptors, type-1 corticotropin-releasing factor receptors (CRFR1s), and type-1 insulin-like growth factor receptors (IGF-1Rs). Inhibition of any of these receptors results in the blockage of LTD. The δ2 receptor is an orphan receptor with an unknown function. mGluR1s (see below), CRFR1s, and IGF-1Rs are associated with G-proteins which are coupled with certain second messenger processes.

Calcium Entry and Release from Intracellular Stores

Induction of conjunctive LTD requires enhancement of the intracellular Ca^{2+} concentration, for it is blocked by injection of a Ca^{2+} chelator, EGTA, into Purkinje cells. Climbing fiber impulses evoke Ca^{2+} influx into dendrites of Purkinje cells through voltage-sensitive Ca2+ channels. As underlying homosynaptic LTD, Ca^{2+} influx also occurs in association with parallel fiber-induced EPSPs, if the EPSPs are sufficiently large to activate voltage-sensitive Ca²⁺ channels. Ca²⁺ ions are also released from intracellular stores in endoplasmic reticula, when inositol trisphosphate (IP₃) receptors or ryanodine receptors on the reticula are activated. Inhibition of IP₃ receptors, depletion of Ca²⁺ stores, or genetically induced loss of endoplasmic reticulum in dendritic spines results in the blockage of conjunctive LTD. However, intracellular Ca²⁺ release is not required for the reduced form of LTD in isolated Purkinje cells.

In hippocampal and neocortical neurons, LTD induction depends on the membrane potential, which determines the entry of Ca²⁺ ions into neurons through cation channels associated with a NMDA receptors. These channels are normally blocked by Mg²⁺ ions that are removed at a depolarized membrane potential level. Modest and strong activations of NMDA receptors lead to LTD and LTP, respectively. Reduction of postsynaptic Ca²⁺ entry by partial blockage of NMDA receptors converts LTP to LTD (Nishiyama et al., 2000). LTP is also converted to LTD by injecting EGTA into neocortical neurons (Kimura, Tsumoto, Nishigori, and Yoshimura, 1990). Induction of homosynaptic and heterosynaptic LTD in the hippocampus requires functional ryanodine and IP₃ receptors, respectively. Functional blockade or genetic deletion of type-1 IP₃receptors leads to a conversion of LTD to LTP and elimination of heterosynaptic LTD, while blockage of ryanodine receptors eliminated only homosynaptic LTD (Nishiyama et al., 2000).

Metabotropic Glutamate Receptor-Driven Processes

Activation of mGluR1s in Purkinje cells results in activation of phopholipase C (PLC), which generates IP₃ (see above) and diacylglycerol (DAG) from membrane phospholipid. DAG activates PKC. mGluR1s could also be coupled with phospholipase A2 (PLA2), which produces arachidonic acid and oleic acid from membrane phospholipid. Inhibition of mGluR1s, PKC, PLA2 or receptors of IP₃ prevents LTD from induction, indicating that these are involved in LTD induction. Application of an mGluR5 agonist, DHPG, effectively induces LTD in hippocampal CA1 neurons (Fitzjohn, Kingston, Lodge, and Collingridge, 1999), which has been studied as a reduced form of hippocampal LTD.

Nitric Oxide and cGMP

Cerebellar granule cells contain a neuronal type of nitric oxide synthase (nNOS), and parallel fiber terminals release NO upon stimulation. NO, so released, diffuses into Purkinje cells, and activates guanylate cyclase to increase the level of cyclic GMP (cGMP). cGMP in turn activates cGMP-dependent

Figure 2

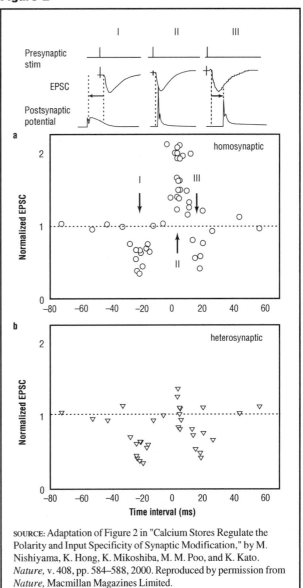

SOURCE: Adaptation of Figure 2 in "Calcium Stores Regulate the Polarity and Input Specificity of Synaptic Modification," by M. Nishiyama, K. Hong, K. Mikoshiba, M. M. Poo, and K. Kato. *Nature*, v. 408, pp. 584–588, 2000. Reproduced by permission from *Nature*, Macmillan Magazines Limited.

Critical time windows for the induction of LTP/LTD in the hippocampus by correlated pre- and postsynaptic activation. The pre-post time interval refers to the time between the onset of the EPSC and the peak of the postsynaptic action potential during each correlated activation as indicated by arrows in the records on the top. In a and b, normalized mean EPSC amplitudes measured at 30 to 40 minutes after correlated activation are plotted against the pre-post time intervals. a) Summary of changes in the homosynaptic pathway (n=50). b) Summary of changes in the heterosynaptic (unstimulated) pathway (n=34). Data are from a subset of experiments such as those shown in a, in which the control pathway was monitored throughout the experiment.

protein kinase (PKG). The role of NO in the induction of conjunctive LTD is evident because it is blocked when an inhibitor of NO synthase, L-NMMA, or hemoglobin (HB) which absorbs NO, is applied to cerebellar slices, or in those mice deficient of nNOS. Furthermore, sodium nitroprusside that releases NO or a membrane-soluble derivative of cGMP induces an LTD-like phenomenon when applied to cerebellar slices together with AMPA. However, there is no evidence that a reduced form of LTD in isolated Purkinje cells requires a NO-cGMP pathway.

Protein Kinases and Phosphatases

Induction of cerebellar conjunctive LTD requires activities of PKC, PKG, protein tyrosin kinase (PTK) and mitogen-activated protein kinase (MAPK) but not PKA. PKC phosphorylates serine-880 of AMPA receptors (see below), and PTK interacts with PKC. PKG acts on a PKG-specific substrate, G-substance, which is richly contained in Purkinje cells. The phosphorylated G-substrate was found to be a potent inhibitor of protein phosphatases, presumably type 2A. Inhibitors of PP1/2A induce LTD when combined with stimulation of AMPA receptors.

PKC and PTK, but not PKA, are involved in mGluR-induced LTD in neurons of hippocampal dentate gyrus (Camodeca, Breakwell, Rowan, and Anwyl, 1999). A Ca^{2+}/ Calmodulin-dependent protein phosphatase, calcineurin (or PP2B), mediates LTD induction in the hippocampus because a calcineurin inhibitor, FK506, blocks LFS induction of LTD in the visual cortex (Torii, Kamishita, Otsu, and Tsumoto, 1995). Mice deficient in the calcineurin catalytic unit B1 exhibited significantly diminished LFS-induced LTD in the hippocampus (Zeng et al., 2001). This is in contrast to the observation in Purkinje cells in which inhibition of PP2A facilitates conjunctive LTD. Calcineurin is also involved in LTD induction downregulating GABAA receptors in inhibitory synapses of the hippocampus (Lu, Mansuy, Kandel, and Roder, 2000).

Protein Synthesis

Translational inhibitors depressed the late phase of LTD in cultured Purkinje cells, but they abolished the entire LTD including its early phase in cerebellar slices. Studies using five-minute pulses of translational inhibitors revealed that a quickly turned over protein synthesis was required for LTD induction only during the fifteen-minute period from the onset of conjunctive stimulation (Karacho et al., 2001). A five-minute pulse application of transcriptional inhibitors also effectively blocked LTD induction with a delay of thirty minutes. Protein synthesis also plays roles in hippocampal neurons, in which a translational inhibitor blocked the late phase of LFS-induced LTD (Kauderer and Kandel, 2000) as well as the entire course of DHPG-induced LTD (Huber, Kayser, and Bear, 2000).

Phosphorylation and Inactivation of AMPA Receptors

Among subunits constituting AMPA receptors, the GluR2 subunits are dominant in parallel fiber-Purkinje cell synapses. Evidence suggests that at the end stage of cerebellar conjunctive LTD, GluR2 is phosphorylated at its serine-880 anchorage to GRIP, and freed AMPA receptors are removed from postsynaptic membrane by internalization via endocytosis. Similar consideration applies to associative LTD in hippocampal neurons (Luscher, Nicoli, Malenka, and Muller, 2000; Man et al., 2000).

Functional Roles of LTD

In the cerebellum-like structure of fish, LTD plays a clear role of lessening the effects of sensory inputs coinciding with command signals in order to allow only unpredicted sensory inputs to stand out, thus forming an adaptive sensory processor. Involvement of LTD in certain forms of cerebellar learning has been demonstrated using pharmacological or genetic means that impair LTD (Ito, 2001). Adaptation of reflexive eye movements was abolished by applying an NO scavenger or transfecting a pseudo inhibitor of PKC to the cerebellum. An NO scavenger or NOS inhibitor also blocked adaptation in smooth pursuit eye movement to repeated sudden increases in the velocity of the moving spotlight. Mice deficient in glial fibrillary acidic protein or phospholipase C β4 (Miyata et al., 2001) lacked LTD and did not exhibit the classical conditioning of eye blinking. A walking cat or mouse normally adapted to a sudden change in the running belt conditions, but not under the influences of NO scavenger or NOS inhibitor or mGluR1 deficiency, which block LTD.

Mice in which hippocampal LTD was diminished due to conditional knockout of calcineurin were specifically impaired in working memory and episodic-like memory tasks, including the delayed matching-to-place task and the radial maze task (Zeng et al., 2001).

Accumulating evidence indicates that LTD is a major type of synaptic plasticity that plays roles in various forms of learning and memory. It will be a future task to confirm whether LTD is converted to a permanent memory, and if so, by what mechanism is it converted. Researchers should also determine the specific functional roles of LTD in various forms of learning and memory.

See also: GLUTAMATE RECEPTORS AND THEIR CHARACTERIZATION; GUIDE TO THE ANATOMY OF THE BRAIN; NEURAL COMPUTATION: CEREBELLUM; NEURAL SUBSTRATES OF CLASSICAL CONDITIONING: DISCRETE

BEHAVIORAL RESPONSES; SECOND MESSENGER SYSTEMS; VESTIBULO-OCULAR REFLEX (VOR) PLASTICITY

Bibliography

Artola, A., Brocher, S., and Singer, W. (1990). Different voltage-dependent thresholds for inducing long-term depression and long-term potentiation in slices of rat visual cortex. *Nature* 347, 69–72.

Bell, C. C., Han, V. Z., Sugawara, Y., and Grant, K. (1997). Synaptic plasticity in a cerebellum-like structure depends on temporal order. *Nature* 387, 278–281.

Bi, G-Q., and Poo, M-m. (1999). Distributed synaptic modification in neural networks induced by patterned stimulation. *Nature* 401, 792–796.

Bindman, L. J., Murphy, K. P. S., and Pockett, S. (1988). Postsynaptic control of the induction of long-term changes in efficacy of transmission at neocortical synapses in slices of rat brain. *Journal of Neurophysiology* 60, 1,053–1,065.

Camodeca, N., Breakwell, N. A., Rowan, M. J., and Anwyl, R. (1999). Induction of LTD by activation of group I mGluR in the dentate gyrus in vitro. *Neuropharmacology* 38, 1,597–1,606.

Fitzjohn, S. M., Kingston, A. E., Lodge, D., and Collingridge, G. L. (1999). DHPG-induced LTD in area CA1 in juvenile rat hippocampus; characterization and sensitivity to novel mGlu receptor antagonists. *Neuropharamacology* 38, 1,577–1,583.

Fitzsimonds, R. M., Song, H-j., and Poo, M-m. (1997). Propagation of activity-dependent synaptic depression in simple neural networks. *Nature* 388, 439–448.

Hansel, C., Linden, D., and D'Angelo, E. (2001). Beyond parallel fiber LTD: The diversity of synaptic and non-synaptic plasticity in the cerebellum. *Nature Neuroscience* 4, 467–475.

Hirsch, J. C., and Crepel, F. (1990). Use-dependent changes in synaptic efficacy in rat prefrontal neurons in vitro. *Journal of Physiology (London)* 427, 31–49.

Huber, K. M., Kayser, M. S., and Bear, M. F. (2000). Role for rapid dendritic protein synthesis in hippocampal mGluR-dependent long-term depression. *Science* 288, 1,254–1,256.

Ito, M. (2001). Long-term depression: Characterization, signal transduction and functional roles. *Physiology Review* 81, 1,143–1,195.

Ito, M., Sakurai, M., and Tongroach, P. (1982). Climbing fibre induced depression of both mossy fibre responsiveness and glutamate sensitivity of cerebellar Purkinje cells. *Journal of Physiology (London)* 324, 113–134.

Karachot, L., Shirai, Y., Vigot, R., Yamamori, T., and Ito, M. (2001). Induction of long-term depression in cerebellar Purkinje cells requires a quickly turned over protein. *Journal of Neurophysiology* 86, 280–289.

Kauderer, B. S., and Kandel, E. R. (2000). Capture of a protein synthesis-dependent component of long-term depression. *Proceedings of the National Academy of Sciences of the United States of America* 97, 13,342–13,347.

Kimura, F., Tsumoto, T., Nishigori, A., and Yoshimura, Y. (1990). Long-term depression but not potentiation is induced in Ca^{2+}-chelated visual cortex neurons. *Neurological Report* 1, 65–68.

Kirkwood, A., and Bear, M. F. (1994). Homosynaptic long-term depression in the visual cortex. *Journal of Neuroscience* 14, 3,404–3,412.

Lu, Y. M., Mansuy, I. M., Kandel, E., and Roder, J. (2000). Calcineurin-mediated LTD of GABAergic inhibition underlies the increased excitability of CA1 neurons associated with LTP. *Neuron* 26, 197–205.

Luscher, C., Nicoli, R. A., Malenka, R. C., and Muller, D. (2000). Synaptic plasticity and dynamic modulation of the postsynaptic membrane. *Nature Neuroscience* 3, 545–550.

Man, H. Y., Lin, J. W., Ju, W. H., Ahmadian, G., Liu, L., Becker, L. E., Sheng, M., and Wang, Y. T. (2000). Regulation of AMPA receptor-mediated synaptic transmission by clathrin-dependent receptor internalization. *Neuron* 25, 649–662.

Miyata, M., Kim, H.-T., Hashimoto, K., Lee, T.-K., Cho, S.-Y., Jiang, H., Wu, Y., Jun, K., Kano, M., and Shin, H.-S. (2001). Deficient long-term synaptic depression in the rostral cerebellum correlated with impaired motor learning in phospholipase C b4 mutant mice. *European Journal of Neuroscience* 13, 1–11.

Nishiyama, M., Hong, K., Mikoshiba, K., Poo, M. M., and Kato, K. (2000). Calcium stores regulate the polarity and input specificity of synaptic modification. *Nature* 408, 584–588.

Torii, N., Kamishita, T., Otsu, Y., and Tsumoto, T. (1995). An inhibitor for calcineurin, FK506, blocks induction of long-term depression in rat visual cortex. *Neuroscience Letters* 185, 1–4.

Zeng, H., Chattarji, S., Barbarosie, M., Rondi-Reig, L., Philpot, B. D., Miyakawa, T., Bear, M. F., and Tonegawa, S. (2001). Forebrain-specific calcineurin knockout selectively impairs bidirectional synaptic plasticity and working/episodic-like memory. *Cell* 107, 617–629.

Masao Ito

LONG-TERM MEMORY

See: APLYSIA: MOLECULAR BASIS OF LONG-TERM SENSITIZATION; KNOWLEDGE SYSTEMS AND MATERIAL-SPECIFIC MEMORY DEFICITS; LONG-TERM DEPRESSION IN THE CEREBELLUM, HIPPOCAMPUS, AND NEOCORTEX; LONG-TERM POTENTIATION; PROTEIN SYNTHESIS IN LONG-TERM MEMORY IN VERTEBRATES

LONG-TERM POTENTIATION

[*Long-term potentiation (LTP) is defined as a persistent enhancement in the strength of a synaptic connection produced as a result of delivering a brief high frequency burst of neural activity (i.e., tetanus) to a presynaptic neuron or pathway. The enhanced synaptic efficacy can persist for hours, days, or even weeks, depending on the stimulus protocol. LTP is believed to be a prime candidate for a synaptic memory mechanism because of its persistence and the fact that it is found in brain regions that have been implicated in memory (e.g., the amygdala, hippocampus, cerebral cortex, and cerebellum). Five entries are devoted to this important mechanism. They include an* **OVERVIEW,** *discussions of the different forms and mechanisms of LTP in different brain regions, and* **BEHAVIORAL ROLES** *of LTP. The reader should also see the entry on the related phenomenon of* LONG-TERM DEPRESSION.]

OVERVIEW: COOPERATIVITY AND ASSOCIATIVITY

Long-term potentiation (LTP) is the collective name for synaptic plasticity processes in which brief (less than one second) episodes of intense synaptic activity lead to an enhancement of synaptic efficacy lasting hours to weeks, or longer. LTP in many regions has associative induction properties based on a requirement for coincident presynaptic and postsynaptic activity. This requirement is similar to that proposed on theoretical grounds by Donald Hebb in 1949 for a synaptic modification involved in learning and memory, known as the Hebb synapse. Because of its longevity and associative induction properties, scientists regard LTP as the prime neuronal model for learning and memory (see Figure 1).

Scientists first described LTP in the rabbit hippocampal formation, and later in the neocortex and a variety of other regions in the vertebrate (including human) nervous system. It has mostly been found for excitatory synapses in principal cells. These synapses are typically spine synapses; that is, located on small protuberances (spines) on the dendrite. Excitatory action in these synapses is mediated by glutamate acting on AMPA receptors located postsynaptically, and LTP is seen as an increase of this AMPA receptor-mediated transmission.

Associative LTP: A History

T. Lømo reported in a short note in 1966 that a few seconds of repetitive synaptic activation (10 to 15 hertz) led to a prolonged potentiation (LTP) of excitatory action on granule cells in the dentate gyrus of the hippocampus. In 1973, T. V. P. Bliss and A. R. Gardner-Medwin reported that LTP could last for weeks and that its induction appeared to depend on the number of activated presynaptic fibers, or rather the number of activated synapses. This dependence on the co-activation of many presynaptic fibers (cooperativity), and the restriction of LTP to the synapses of the activated fibers (input specificity), were demonstrated by several laboratories in the late 1970s. LTP induction was also found to be associative: A brief activation of a weak synaptic input that did not induce LTP by itself did so when occurring in close temporal contiguity with brief activation of a separate strong synaptic input to the same target neurons. Thus, LTP can form an associative connection between a weak input and a strong one or, alternatively seen, an association between a weak input and the response elicited by the strong one. In the mid-1980s several groups showed that LTP induction requires coincident spike activity of the presynaptic terminal and of the target postsynaptic neuron; that is, they demonstrated the existence of Hebb synapses. This requirement for postsynaptic depolarization of sufficient strength to evoke postsynaptic spike activity explains cooperativity. The requirement for coincident presynaptic activity explains associativity.

In 1983, G. L. Collingridge and colleagues showed that blocking another glutamate receptor, the NMDA receptor, prevented LTP induction. In the same year Dingledine described that NMDA channels permeate calcium ions, and G. Lynch and colleagues found that a rise in postsynaptic calcium was necessary for LTP induction. Moreover, several groups showed that the NMDA receptor was coupled to a voltage-sensitive channel; that is, it needed, in addition to glutamate, membrane depolarization to open. These results, together with the strict dependence of the induction on coincident presynaptic and postsynaptic activity, led H. Wigström and B. Gustafsson in 1985 to propose that LTP is initiated as a consequence of calcium influx through NMDA receptor channels co-localized with the AMPA receptors on the postsynaptic spine membrane. The NMDA receptor would act as a coincidence (and cooperativity) detector because of its need for both transmitter binding and membrane depolarization for activation. The co-localization of the NMDA and AMPA receptor channels on the subsynaptic spine membrane, together with a restricted localization of the rise in postsynaptic calcium due to the spine location of the synapse, would secure input specificity for LTP.

LTP Induction: Modulation of Threshold

Although many studies use unnatural stimulus conditions to induce LTP, such as a one-second synchronous activation of afferents at high frequency, physiological stimulus patterns have also been shown to be effective in inducing it. Brief burst stimulation that simulates the 5 to 7 hertz hippocampal EEG wave activity (theta rhythm) effectively produces LTP. This is because this stimulus pattern depresses inhibitory circuits and thereby enables a brief burst to produce substantial postsynaptic depolarization. High frequency presynaptic activation is not necessary for LTP induction. LTP can be induced in synapses activated by single stimuli at low frequency (such as 0.2 hertz) provided that this activation is associated with sufficient postsynaptic depolarization. Experimentally this depolarization can be provided by current-induced action potentials in the cell body that either passively spread or actively back-propagate into the dendritic tree where the synapses are located. Under physiological conditions when action potential activity is generated by synaptic excitation, the necessary depolarization will in addition be provided by the passive spread from active synapses. The synaptic excitation may actually play a triple role for generating the necessary conditions for LTP induction. First, by generating local depolarization in the synaptic region. Second, by generating action potentials in the cell body region that may back-propagate into the dendrite. Third, by its depolarization of the dendritic membrane facilitate back-propagation into the active dendritic region.

The threshold for inducing LTP is controlled by a number of factors. These include metaplasticity, neuromodulators, and pharmacological agents that all, directly or indirectly, interfere with the opening of NMDA receptor channels. Metaplasticity (plasticity of synaptic plasticity), a concept introduced by W. C. Abraham in 1995, is a change in induction threshold of LTP induced by prior synaptic, or cellular, activity, that is not necessarily expressed as change in efficacy of normal synaptic transmission. One possible mechanism would be a prolonged activity-dependent change in NMDA receptor-mediated signaling, such as a LTP of that signaling. In fact, such activity-dependent changes have been reported. Neuromodulators, such as norepinephrine, acetylcholine, serotonin, dopamine, glutamate (via its metabotropic receptors), and neuropeptides regulating attention, motivation, emotion, and wakefulness, will all modulate LTP induction. As these neuromodulators exert their neuromodulatory role by their action on synaptic transmission and on cellular excitability, the NMDA receptor dependent requirements for LTP induction will concurrently be affected. Similarly, pharmacological agents that affect excitatory or inhibitory synaptic transmission, or cellular excitability, will alter the threshold for LTP induction. For example, drugs that enhance inhibitory transmission such as ethanol and benzodiazepines will impair the generation of LTP.

LTP Expression

Independently of the induction intensity (above threshold) LTP is established with a similar time course and within less than a minute. Its duration is, however, variable, depending on the intensity and/or the repetition of the synaptic activity. Thus, following weak activation it may decay within minutes whereas an intense activation can lead to a LTP lasting weeks. The more prolonged LTP given by more intense synaptic activation may not only be explained by a greater extent of NMDA receptor activation but also by the concurrent activation of voltage-gated calcium channels and/or other receptor/channel systems. Based on the effect of protein synthesis inhibitors, LTP has been divided in an early phase (E-LTP, less than a few hours), and a late LTP (L-LTP). L-LTP is thus sup-

Figure 1

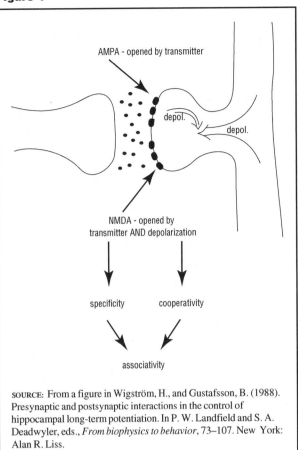

SOURCE: From a figure in Wigström, H., and Gustafsson, B. (1988). Presynaptic and postsynaptic interactions in the control of hippocampal long-term potentiation. In P. W. Landfield and S. A. Deadwyler, eds., *From biophysics to behavior*, 73–107. New York: Alan R. Liss.

Schematic representation of the model for associative LTP induction. A presynaptic terminal (left) releases the transmitter glutamate (dots) onto a spine of a pyramidal cell dendrite, on which AMPA and NMDA types of glutamate receptor channels are co-localized. Whereas AMPA receptor channels are opened by the transmitter alone, NMDA receptor channels require in addition coincident membrane depolarization. This dual requirement for the opening of NMDA receptor channels explains associative induction.

posed to rely on synthesis of new proteins whereas E-LTP relies on modification of pre-existing ones.

What aspect of synaptic transmission is actually modified in NMDA receptor-dependent LTP? This issue has been intensively debated since the mid-1980s. Despite numerous studies, the question of whether there is a more efficient release of glutamate, or an increase in AMPA receptor channel number or efficiency, is still unsettled. A complicating factor may be that NMDA receptor-dependent LTP is based on different expression mechanisms dependent on experimental conditions, for example cultured versus intact tissue, or on other factors such as brain region and animal age.

Nonassociative LTP

Long-term synaptic plasticity exists not only in the form of NMDA receptor-dependent LTP but also as nonassociative forms not relying on NMDA receptor activation. The foremost example of such NMDA receptor-independent LTP, first described by E. W. Harris and C. W. Cotman in 1986, is that in the synapse that connects granule cells in the dentate gyrus with CA3 pyramidal neurons in the hippocampus. In contrast to NMDA receptor-dependent LTP its expression appears undisputed whereas its induction mechanism is debated. A number of studies by R. A. Nicoll and colleagues in the 1990s have established that NMDA receptor-independent LTP is presynaptically expressed as an increased efficacy of transmitter release. These studies have also indicated its induction to be noncooperative, only related to presynaptic calcium accumulation. On the other hand, studies by D. Johnston and colleagues have indicated a cooperative induction, related to postsynaptic calcium influx via voltage-gated calcium channels and release from internal calcium stores. A similar NMDA receptor-independent LTP is also described for the synapse that connects granule cells and Purkinje cells in the cerebellum.

LTP on Interneurons

Glutamatergic afferent fibers do not only make excitatory synapses with principal cells, but also with interneurons. Scientists have debated whether these interneuronal synapses exhibit LTP. It would appear that LTP does not exist in most of these synapses. However, LTP with associative properties has been found in some interneuron types. Interestingly, this associative induction was found not to rely on NMDA receptor activation as in the principal cells, indicating the existence of other mechanisms for coincidence detection.

Conclusion

LTP denotes forms of synaptic plasticity with associative as well as nonassociative induction (i.e., they depend on temporal contiguity between activity in different pathways and on activity in a single pathway, respectively). Non-associative LTP will allow for a more efficient transmission in specific pathways that are intensely used, irrespective of activity in others. Associative LTP on the other hand strengthens synapses in a manner that relies on contiguity of activity in those neurons that are connected via the modifiable synapse. This Hebbian modification rule is a powerful device used in neural network models of nonsupervised learning to produce, for example, self-organizing capabilities.

See also: GLUTAMATE RECEPTORS AND THEIR CHARACTERIZATION; HEBB, DONALD

Bibliography

Abraham, W. C., and Bear, M. F. (1996). Metaplasticity: The plasticity of synaptic plasticity. *Trends in Neurosciences* 19 (4), 126–130.

Bailey, C. H., Giustetto, M., Huang, Y. Y., Hawkins, R. D., and Kandel, E. R. (2000). Is heterosynaptic modulation essential for stabilizing Hebbian plasticity and memory? *Nature Reviews Neuroscience* 1 (1), 11–20.

Gustafsson, B., and Wigstrom, H. (1988). Physiological mechanisms underlying long-term potentiation. *Trends in Neurosciences* 11 (4), 156–162.

Hanse, E., and Gustafsson, B. (1994). Onset and stabilization of NMDA receptor-dependent hippocampal long-term potentiation. *Neuroscience Research* 20 (1), 15–25.

Johnston, D., Williams, S., Jaffe, D., and Gray, R. (1992). NMDA-receptor-independent long-term potentiation. *Annual Review of Physiology* 54, 489–505.

Linden, D. J. (1999). The return of the spike: Postsynaptic action potentials and the induction of LTP and LTD. *Neuron* 22, 661–666.

Malenka, R. C., and Nicoll, R. A. (1999). Long-term potentiation—a decade of progress? *Science* 285, 1,870–1,874.

McBain, C.J., Freund, T. F., and Mody, I. (1999). Glutamatergic synapses onto hippocampal interneurons: Precision timing without lasting plasticity. *Trends in Neurosciences* 22 (5), 228–235.

Sanes, J. R., and Lichtman, J. W. (1999). Can molecules explain long-term potentiation? *Nature Neuroscience* 2 (7), 597–604.

Bengt Gustafsson
Eric Hanse

AMYGDALA

Long-term synaptic potentiation (LTP) has emerged as the likeliest synaptic substrate for rapid associative learning (Brown, Chapman, Kariss, and Keenan, 1988; Kelso and Brown, 1986). LTP has been reported in numerous brain structures, including the amygdala, where it may participate in emotional learning (Blair et al., 2001; Chapman, Kairiss, Keenan, and Brown, 1990). This article examines an unexpected property of LTP in synapses of the amygdala and the implications of this finding on attempts to link amygdalar LTP to emotional learning.

Amygdalar Neuroanatomy and Neurophysiology

Synaptic transmission and its plasticity seem to depend jointly on the identity of the presynaptic and postsynaptic neurons. A consideration of LTP in the amygdala thus requires some knowledge of the anatomy and physiology of the neurons in this brain region. The functional neuroanatomy is also important for interpreting electrophysiological recordings.

The amygdaloid nuclear complex is a collection of subnuclei that fall into two major classes based on cell morphology: those containing cortexlike neurons and those containing striatallike neurons (Swanson and Petrovich, 1998). The cortexlike group includes the lateral, basal, and basolateral nuclei, sometimes collectively termed the basolateral amygdaloid complex (BLA). The more medially located nuclei, including the central and medial nuclei, are part of the ventromedial expanse of the striatum.

At a circuit level, the functional neuroanatomy of the amygdala remains a mystery, but there have been a few studies of the anatomy and physiology of individual neurons (Chapman, Kairiss, Keenan, and Brown, 1990; Faulkner and Brown, 1999; Washburn and Moises, 1992). The organization of cells in BLA, although different from that of any other brain region, perhaps resembles most closely a combination of the adjacent perirhinal cortex and the CA3 region of the hippocampus. While the unusual cell-firing types are similar to those in the perirhinal cortex (Faulkner and Brown, 1999; McGann, Moyer, and Brown, 2001), the massive system of excitatory recurrents and consequent tendency toward epileptiform activity when pharmacologically disinhibited is reminiscent of the CA3 region of the hippocampus (Brown and Zador, 1990).

Combined studies of BLA by Brown and coworkers (Chapman, Kairiss, Keenan, and Brown, 1990; Faulkner and Brown, 1999) and Washburn and Moises (1992) suggest that there may be as many as seven firing patterns, including regular spiking, single spiking, late spiking, burst spiking, slow charging, irregular spiking, and fast spiking. Small, aspiny stellates tend to be fast-spiking cells, presumably inhibitory interneurons. Pyramids and large stellates can be regular spiking, single spiking, burst spiking, or late spiking. Little is known about other structure-function relationships.

Spontaneous postsynaptic potentials (PSPs) and postsynaptic conductances (PSCs) are commonly much larger than those of the CA1 region of the hippocampus but similar to those in CA3 pyramidal neurons (Faulkner and Brown, 1999; Johnston and Brown, 1984; Xiang and Brown, 1998). Electrical stimulation of the external capsule (EC) commonly elicits in BLA neurons an excitatory-inhibitory conductance sequence (Chapman, Kairiss, Keenan, and Brown, 1990), similar to that which Johnston and Brown and coworkers reported in hippocampal region CA3 (Barrionuevo, Kelso, Johnston, and Brown, 1986; Griffith, Brown, and Johnston, 1986; Johnston and Brown, 1983).

Discovery of LTP in the Amygdala

Brown's team looked for LTP elicited by EC stimulation in horizontal brain slices containing BLA (Chapman, Kairiss, Keenan, and Brown, 1990; Keenan, Chapman, Chang, and Brown, 1988). The gross cytoarchitecture of the slice was vividly revealed through the use of differential-interference contrast (DIC) optics and infrared (IR) illumination, which Brown and coworkers had been developing for this purpose (Keenan, Chapman, Chang, and Brown, 1988). At low magnification, IR-DIC optics sharply resolved the key landmarks needed to position the stimulating and recording electrodes to repeatable locations that can be reliably matched to corresponding plates of a rat brain atlas. Critically important were the borders of EC, the basolateral nucleus, the lateral nucleus, and the central nucleus (Chapman, Kairiss, Keenan, and Brown, 1990).

EC was selected as the placement site for the stimulation electrode for four reasons. First, it was the only visually discernible large population of known afferent inputs to BLA. Second, in contrast to other possible stimulation sites, this allowed a more homogeneous population of synapses, thus partaking of some of the virtues of studies of the Schaeffer collateral/commissural (Sch/com) inputs to pyramidal neurons in hippocampal region CA1. Third, because EC contains fast-conducting fibers, these were presumed to produce the earliest detectable postsynaptic responses. Fourth, neurophysiological results suggested that EC-elicited PSCs in BLA neurons contain monosynaptic responses from the stimulation site.

Regarding this last point, the critical question was not whether EC fibers project to BLA—they are known to do so. The question was whether the PSCs recorded in BLA neurons in response to EC stimulation reflected direct synaptic inputs from stimulated EC fibers. The obvious alternative was that PSCs recorded in response to EC stimulation were produced by inputs from other BLA neurons whose firing was caused by EC stimulation. The difference can be important for designing and interpreting neurophysiology experiments (Xiang and Brown, 1998).

To minimize activation of recurrent circuitry and to avoid epileptiform activity (Johnston and Brown, 1983; Xiang and Brown, 1998), the slices were not disinhibited pharmacologically. The excitatory component of the synaptic conductance waveform was first evaluated (Griffith, Brown, and Johnston, 1986) during baseline testing (thirty to ninety responses at 0.1 Hz). An attempt was then made to induce LTP by delivering three to ten trains (300 msec each) of high-frequency (100 Hz, "tetanic") electrical currents (each 0.1 msec) through the stimulation electrode that was positioned in EC. Following tetanic stimulation, testing was resumed at 0.1 Hz for as long as two hours.

The tetanic stimulation produced an early synaptic enhancement that relaxed back to a sustained level of synaptic potentiation. Because of posttetanic potentiation (PTP), the early enhancement lasted less than fifteen minutes, as in the hippocampus (Barrionuevo, Kelso, Johnston, and Brown, 1986; Kelso and Brown, 1986; Kelso, Ganong, and Brown, 1986). LTP was measured conventionally as the stable enhancement that clearly outlasted PTP. The tetanic stimulation protocol induced LTP in 80 percent of the neurons studied, which averaged a 46 percent increase.

Kinds of LTP in the Amygdala

Two obvious questions arise from the countless studies of LTP in the hippocampus. The first question is whether there is a kind of LTP in the amygdala whose induction depends on the activation of N-methyl-d-aspartate receptors (NMDARs). NMDAR-dependent LTP in the Sch/com input to CA1 is one of the most commonly studied forms of LTP. There is not much neurophysiological evidence for a similar kind of plasticity in the amygdala.

Chapman and Bellavance (1992) found that APV (50 µM), a competitive antagonist for glutamate at the NMDAR, did not block LTP induction produced by tetanic stimulation of EC. These investigators report that LTP induction could be inhibited by APV when the concentration was increased to 100 µM, but this concentration also strongly attenuated EC-evoked PSPs. The recording methods used by Chapman and Bellavance presumably tended to sample from a population of larger BLA neurons, but other researchers have reported similar results in BLA using selection criteria designed to sample small interneurons.

Mahanty and Sah (1998) examined LTP in a subset of cells that have fast-action potentials and that lack spike-frequency adaptation. EC stimulation (two trains of 100 stimuli presented at 30 Hz) resulted in LTP in seven of seven of these putative interneurons. Pharmacological and electrophysiological analysis suggested that NMDARs contribute relatively little to the EC-evoked PSCs. Application of APV (50 µM) had no effect on LTP induction in these putative interneurons.

LeDoux's team (Weisskopf, Bauer, and LeDoux, 1999) reported similar results in a previously unexplored synaptic circuit. They positioned a stimulating electrode in a region of the striatum immediately dorsal to the central nucleus and medial to the lateral nucleus, where they recorded evoked PSPs. LTP induction was unaffected when 50 µM APV was added to the bathing medium.

The second question to emerge from research on hippocampal LTP concerns the role of backpropagating dendritic Ca²⁺ spikes (Zador, Koch, and Brown, 1990). Research in Johnston's laboratory has shown that NMDARs are only part of the story behind LTP induction in the hippocampus (Magee, Hoffman, Colbert, and Johnston, 1998). Recent work by Johnston and coworkers (Magee and Johnston, 1997) demonstrated the critical importance of backpropagating Ca²⁺ spikes in controlling the induction of one form of LTP in the Sch/com synaptic input to CA1 pyramidal neurons. Blocking L-type Ca²⁺ channels prevented or greatly inhibited LTP induction in these pyramidal neurons (Magee and Johnston, 1997). In a parallel finding, Teyler and coworkers (Cavus and Teyler, 1996) have shown that the Sch/com synapses on CA1 pyramidal neurons can undergo two forms of LTP: one that is dependent on NMDARs and another that depends on L-type Ca²⁺ channels.

Teyler and coworkers noted that NMDAR-dependent LTP and Ca²⁺ channel-dependent LTP engage distinct signal transduction cascades and thus could have different functional significance for encoding (Cavus and Teyler, 1996; Morgan, Coussens, and Teyler, 2001). Teyler hypothesized that NMDAR-dependent LTP might be more critically involved in short-term memory, whereas Ca²⁺-channel-dependent LTP could be more important in long-term memory. This suggestion was based partly on findings by Teyler and coworkers (Morgan, Coussens, and Teyler, 2001) that Ca²⁺-channel-dependent LTP has a slower onset, it is more persistent, and it is less subject to elimination by long-term depression (LTD)—at least in brain slices.

Some additional findings from the previously mentioned study by LeDoux and coworkers (Weisskopf, Bauer, and LeDoux, 1999) are relevant to Teyler's hypothesis. Recall that LeDoux and coworkers examined LTP in a pathway to the lateral nucleus by stimulation of a region of the striatum that is near the central nucleus of the amygdala. Although they found no effect of bath application of 50 µM APV on LTP induction, bath application of the L-type Ca²⁺ channel blocker, Nifedipine (30 µM), prevented LTP.

Results from the handful of studies that have been done on the neuropharmacology of LTP in BLA neurons do not seem to fit the pattern seen in the most commonly studied form of LTP that can be induced in the Sch/com synaptic input to CA1 pyramids. With the Sch/com inputs, 100 µM APV effectively prevents LTP induction but has no detectable effect on evoked PSPs and no detectable effect on the expression of previously induced LTP (see Brown et al., 1989). NMDARs play a key role in inducing this form of LTP in Sch/com synapses (Brown, Chapman, Kairiss, and Keenan, 1988). However, under normal experimental conditions, NMDARs are not required for evoking PSPs or for expressing this form of LTP after it has been established.

Behavioral Implications of Amygdalar LTP

Information about amygdalar synapses has obvious implications for studies on the role of the amygdala in emotional learning. In one set of conditioning experiments, Davis and coworkers (Campeau, Miserendino, and Davis, 1992; Miserendino, Sananes, Melia, and Davis, 1990) perfused the amygdala with APV and claimed to have shown that the drug affects learning but not ordinary synaptic transmission nor the ability to recall previous learning. Direct studies of amygdalar synapses, however, predict that infusing BLA with APV at a concentration that blocks amygdala-dependent learning could also impair retrieval of previously established memories by interfering with synaptic signalling and therefore access to memory.

Other laboratories (Fendt, 2001; Lee, Choi, Brown, and Kim, 2001; Lindquist and Brown, 2002) convincingly demonstrated that APV infusion directly into the amygdala does impair its functioning in a more general manner than had been previously claimed by Davis and coworkers. As expected, infusing the amygdala with APV during the time of conditioning impaired learning (Lee, Choi, Brown, and Kim, 2001), as revealed by subsequent testing (done in the absence of APV). Contrary to claims by Davis and coworkers (Campeau, Miserendino, and Davis, 1992; Miserendino, Sananes, Melia, and Davis, 1990), these laboratories also found a profound memory impairment when the amygdala was perfused with APV at the time of testing (but not during the time of conditioning).

Multiple behavioral measures have shown that infusing BLA with APV profoundly impairs both the acquisition and expression of several classical, BLA-dependent, conditioned-fear responses (CRs). Perhaps even more surprising and dramatic was the finding that infusing BLA with APV also greatly attenuated or even eliminated unconditioned responses (URs) that are normally elicited during conditioning trials. UR reactivity during conditioning predicted CR production during subsequent testing (Lee, Choi, Brown, and Kim, 2001). The collective research on LTP in amygdalar neurons correctly anticipated that the effect of APV on amygdala function is much less specific than Davis and coworkers contended (Campeau, Miserendino, and Davis, 1992; Miserendino, Sananes, Melia, and Davis, 1990).

Conclusion

There are multiple forms of LTP/LTD that can be spatially segregated in different neurons or even colocalized in the same synapses. Since the discovery of amygdalar LTP by Brown and coworkers (Chapman, Kairiss, Keenan, and Brown, 1990) it has become clear that this form of LTP can be induced in the presence of APV unless the concentration is high enough to interfere with experimentally evoked PSPs. This form of LTP is especially interesting in the context of Teyler's hypothesis that APV-resistant LTP is preferentially involved in long-term memory, an idea that could be relevant to the persistence of emotional memory. Since1990, when LTP was first observed in amygdala brain slices, the reliability and resolution of in vitro technology has matured enough to hasten progress in subsequent research (Faulkner and Brown, 1999; Moyer and Brown, 2002).

See also: GUIDE TO THE ANATOMY OF THE BRAIN: AMYGDALA; NEURAL SUBSTRATES OF CLASSICAL CONDITIONING: FEAR-POTENTIATED STARTLE; NEURAL SUBSTRATES OF EMOTIONAL MEMORY

Bibliography

Barrionuevo, G., Kelso, S. R., Johnston, D., and Brown, T. H. (1986). Conductance mechanism responsible for long-term potentiation in monosynaptic and isolated excitatory synaptic inputs to hippocampus. *Journal of Neurophysiology 55,* 540–550.

Blair, H. T., Schafe, G. E., Bauer, E. P., Rodrigues, S. M., and LeDoux, J. E. (2001). Synaptic plasticity in the lateral amygdala: A cellular hypothesis of fear conditioning. *Learning and Memory 8,* 229–42.

Brown, T. H., Chapman, P. F., Kairiss, E. W., and Keenan, C. L. (1988). Long-term synaptic potentiation. *Science 242,* 724–728.

Brown, T. H., Ganong, A. H., Kairiss, E. W., Keenan, C. L., and Kelso, S. R. (1989). Long-term potentiation in two synaptic systems of the hippocampal brain slice. In J. H. Byrne and W. O. Berry, eds., *Neural models of plasticity.* San Diego: Academic Press.

Brown, T. H., and Zador, A. M. (1990). The hippocampus. In G. Shepherd, ed., *Synaptic organization of the brain.* New York: Oxford University Press.

Campeau, S., Miserendino, M. J., and Davis, M. (1992). Intra-amygdala infusion of the N-methyl-D-aspartate receptor antagonist AP5 blocks acquisition but not expression to an auditory conditioned stimulus. *Behavioral Neuroscience 106,* 569–574.

Cavus, I., and Teyler, T. J. (1996). Two forms of long-term potentiation in area CA1 activate different signal transduction pathways. *Journal of Neurophysiology 76,* 3,038–3,047.

Chapman, P. F., and Bellavance, L. L. (1992). Induction of long-term synaptic potentiation in the basolateral amygdala does not depend on NMDA receptor activation. *Synapse 11,* 310–318.

Chapman, P. F., Kairiss, E. W., Keenan, C. L., and Brown, T. H. (1990). Long-term synaptic potentiation in the amygdala. *Synapse 6,* 271–278.

Faulkner, B., and Brown, T. H. (1999). Morphology and physiology of neurons in the rat perirhinal-lateral amygdala area. *Journal of Comparative Neurology 411,* 613–642.

Fendt, M. (2001). Injections of the NMDA receptor antagonist aminophosphonopentanoic acid into the lateral nucleus of the amygdala block the expression of fear-potentiated startle and freezing. *The Journal of Neuroscience 21,* 4,111–4,115.

Griffith, W. H., Brown, T. H., and Johnston, D. (1986). Voltage-clamp analysis of synaptic inhibition during long-term potentiation in hippocampus. *Journal of Neurophysiology 55,* 767–775.

Johnston, D., and Brown, T. H. (1983). Voltage-clamp analysis of mossy fiber synaptic input to hippocampal neurons. *Journal of Neurophysiology 50,* 464–486.

——— (1984). Biophysics and microphysiology of synaptic transmission in hippocampus. In R. Dingledine, ed., *Brain slices.* New York: Plenum Press.

Keenan, C. L., Chapman, P. F., Chang, V., and Brown, T. H. (1988). Videomicroscopy of acute brain slices from hippocampus and amygdala. *Brain Research Bulletin 21,* 373–383.

Kelso, S. R., and Brown, T. H. (1986). Differential conditioning of associative synaptic enhancement in hippocampal brain slices. *Science 232,* 85–87.

Kelso, S. R., Ganong, A. H., and Brown, T. H. (1986). Hebbian synapses in hippocampus. *Proceedings of the National Academy of Sciences of the United States of America 83,* 5,326–5,330.

Lee, H. J., Choi, J.-S., Brown, T. H., and Kim, J. J. (2001). Amygdalar N-methyl-D-aspartate (NMDA) receptors are critical for the expression of multiple conditioned fear responses. *Journal of Neuroscience 21,* 4,116–4,124.

Lindquist, D. H., and Brown, T. H. (2001). Antagonizing NMDA receptors in the basolateral complex of the amygdala prevents conditioned enhancement of the rat eyeblink reflex. *Integrative Physiological and Behavioral Science 36,* 171.

Magee, J., Hoffman, D., Colbert, C., and Johnston, D. (1998). Electrical and calcium signaling in dendrites of hippocampal pyramidal neurons. *Annual Review of Physiology 60,* 327–346.

Magee, J. C., and Johnston, D. (1997). A synaptically controlled associative signal for Hebbian plasticity in hippocampal neurons. *Science 275,* 209–213.

Mahanty, N. K., and Sah, P. (1998). Calcium-permeable AMPA receptors mediate long-term potentiation in interneurons in the amygdala. *Nature 394,* 683–687.

McGann, J. P., Moyer, J. R., Jr., and Brown, T. H. (2001). Predominance of late-spiking neurons in layer VI of rat perirhinal cortex. *Journal of Neuroscience 21,* 4,969–4,976.

Miserendino, M. J. D., Sananes, C. B., Melia, K. R., and Davis, M. (1990). Blocking of acquisition but not expression of conditioned fear-potentiated startle by NMDA antagonists in the amygdala. *Nature 345,* 716–718.

Morgan, S. L., Coussens, C. M., and Teyler, T. J. (2001). Depotentiation of vdccLTP requires NMDAR activation. *Neurobiology of Learning and Memory 76,* 229–238.

Moyer, J. R., Jr., and Brown, T. H. (2002). Patch-clamp techniques applied to brain slices. In A. Walz, A. Boulton, and G. B. Baker, eds., *Advanced techniques for patch-clamp analysis.* Totowa, NJ: Humana Press.

Swanson, L. W., and Petrovich, G. D. (1998). What is the amygdala? *Trends in Neuroscience 21,* 323–331.

Washburn, M. S., and Moises, H. C. (1992). Electrophysiological and morphological properties of rat basolateral amygdaloid neurones in vitro. *Journal of Neuroscience 12,* 4,066–4,079.

Weisskopf, M. G., Bauer, E. P., and LeDoux, J. E. (1999). L-type voltage-gated calcium channels mediate NMDA-independent associative long-term potentiation at the thalamic input synapses to the amygdala. *Journal of Neuroscience 19,* 10,512–10,519.

Xiang, Z., and Brown, T. H. (1998). Complex synaptic current waveforms evoked in hippocampal pyramidal neurons by extracellular stimulation of dentate gyrus. *Journal of Neurophysiology 79,* 2,475–2,484.

Zador, A., Koch, C., and Brown, T. H. (1990). Biophysical model of a Hebbian synapse. *Proceedings of the National Academy of Sciences of the United States of America 87,* 6,718–6,722.

Thomas H. Brown
Derick H. Lindquist

BEHAVIORAL ROLES

Long-term potentiation (LTP) refers the enhanced ability of a neuron to excite a neuron with which it is connected as a result of previous successful activation in the same pathway. LTP is typically produced by electrically stimulating a group of input neurons in a way that produces simultaneous and repetitive activation of their target neurons. Following this high frequency repetitive activation, future stimulation of the input neurons produces larger and more rapid activation of the target neuron. The phenomenon of LTP has many of the features of memory, including a lasting change in the responsiveness of neurons following brief experience with specific inputs, suggesting that LTP may be the cellular basis of memory. At the same time, one should not confuse LTP with memory. LTP is a laboratory phenomenon that involves massive levels of activation never observed in nature. Thus, the best we can hope is that LTP and memory share a common basis in cellular mechanisms.

This section will summarize some of the recent research on the possible linkage between LTP and memory, using two main approaches: demonstrations of changes in synaptic efficacy consequent to a learning experience and attempts to prevent learning by pharmacological or genetic manipulation of the molecular mechanisms of LTP induction.

Do Conventional Learning Experiences Produce Changes in Synaptic Efficacy Similar to Those That Occur after LTP?

Tying changes in synaptic physiology to learning seems like a daunting task because of the expectation that the magnitude of such observable changes in gross field potentials would be vanishingly small following any normal learning experience. In addition, it is likely that learning involves both positive and negative changes in synaptic efficacy, that is, both LTP and long-term depression (LTD). Thus learning could result in changes in the distribution of potentiated and depressed synapses with little or no overall shift and consequently no change or even an overall reduction in the averaged evoked potentials commonly used to measure LTP.

Despite these concerns, an early study reported enhanced excitability of the hippocampal perforant pathway in rats who had been exposed for prolonged periods to an "enriched" environment (group housing with toys) as compared to "impoverished" environment (solitary housing without toys). Environmental enrichment resulted in an increased slope of the synaptic potential and larger population action potentials, consistent with the pattern of increased synaptic efficacy observed following. Perhaps the strong and long duration of learning involved in environmental enrichment overcame the "needle-in-the-haystack" problem by enhancing the excitability of many hippocampal neurons.

More recently, Joseph LeDoux and his colleagues demonstrated LTP-like changes in neural responses in the amygdala. They trained rats to fear tones by presenting repeated pairings of auditory stimuli and foot shocks. Subsequently, in trained rats, conditioned tones produced evoked potentials of greater slope and amplitude similar to the characteristics of LTP observed in the auditory pathway to the amygdala. There was no observable enhancement when the same tones and foot shocks arrived separately, and are therefore not associated with one another. Furthermore, the synaptic enhancements observed in trained rats were enduring, lasting as long as the behavioral response.

John Donoghue and his colleagues extended this approach to the motor cortex and another form of learning. They trained rats to reach with a paw through a small hole in a chamber to retrieve food pellets. Following the training, Donoghue and his colleagues removed the brain and measured the strength of connections between cells within the area of the motor cortex that controls hand movements. They used an in vitro preparation and evoked synaptic potentials (EPSPs) in a principal cell layer of the motor cortex by stimulating horizontal fibers that connect neighboring cells to one another. They found that for the same or lower intensity of input stimulation, the magnitude of the EPSPs on the side of the brain that controlled the trained paw (i.e., in the contralateral hemisphere) were consistently larger than those on the side of the brain that controlled the untrained paw. Furthermore, they found it difficult to induce LTP by electrical stimulation in the trained hemisphere but not in the untrained hemisphere. Thus, training produced an anatomically localized increase in synaptic efficacy that occluded the capacity for LTP. These observations show that synaptic potentiation results from motor learning and that the real plasticity phenomenon shares common resources with the artificial one. This study provides strong evidence for common cellular mechanisms of LTP and learning.

Do Treatments That Block LTP Prevent Memory?

The major limitation of the foregoing approach is that the experiments only provide *correlations* between aspects of LTP and memory. The converse approach is to establish *causal* links between the LTP and memory by seeing whether memory is disrupted by blocking LTP with drugs or genetic manipulations. This approach appeared fruitful because of the assumption that the manipulations would target plasticity, not normal information processing in the brain, and that they would knock out a critical kind of plasticity. This assumption arose from the observation that drugs such as D-2-amino-5-phosphonovalerate (AP5) selectively block the NMDA receptor and thus prevent hippocampal LTP while sparing normal synaptic transmission—hence the expectation that, to the extent that the role of the NMDA receptor is restricted to plasticity, these drugs would indeed block new learning without affecting nonlearning performance or retention of learning normally accomplished prior to drug treatment.

Some of the earliest and strongest evidence supporting a connection between LTP and memory came from studies on spatial learning by Richard Morris and his colleagues. These studies exploited a water-maze task in which rats learn to find an escape hidden in a pool. Initially Morris and his colleagues showed that AP5 prevented new spatial learning in the water maze. Drug-treated rats swam normally but did escape as rapidly as the normal rats did. To assess the rats' knowledge of the escape locus, the researchers used probe tests in which they removed the escape site and measured swimming near the location of the former escape site. Untreated rats showed a distinct preference for swimming in the vicinity of the former escape locus, but drug-treated rats showed little or no such bias, indicating the absence of memory of the escape location. Further experiments showed no effect of AP5 on memory when training was accomplished prior to drug treatment. This is the expected result, because NMDA receptors are necessary only for the induction of LTP, not for its maintenance.

In other research by Morris and his colleagues have shown how NMDA-receptor-dependent LTP might play a continuing role in updating memory. To this end they varied the water-maze task by changing the location of the escape platform every day. The rats consistently found the platform very rapidly on the second trial on a given day. The animals were then tested with different memory delays inserted between the first and second trial on each day. On some days, AP5 was infused into the hippocampus, and on other days a placebo was given. AP5 treatment resulted in a deficit on the second trial. Moreover, this deficit varied with the duration between the first and second trials: there was no impairment with a fifteen-second intertrial interval, but significant deficits ensued with a delay of at least twenty minutes. These data suggest that memory for specific episodes of spatial learning remains dependent on NMDA receptors and LTP, even after the animals have learned the environment and the general rules of the spatial task.

Other studies suggest that the cascade of molecular events occasioned by LTP may also mediate the cortical plasticity that underlies memory. Yadin Dudai and his colleagues have focused on taste learning mediated by the gustatory cortex of rats. When rats are exposed to a novel taste and subsequently become ill, they develop a conditioned aversion to that taste, and this learning is known to depend on the gustatory cortex. AP5 produced an impairment in taste-aversion learning, whereas the same injections given prior to retention testing or into an adjacent cortical area had no effect. It is likely, then, that modifications in cortical taste representations rely on NMDA-dependent LTP.

Furthermore, the blockade of protein synthesis in the gustatory cortex by infusion of an inhibitor prior to learning also prevents development of the conditioned-taste aversion. MAP kinase and a downstream protein kinase were activated selectively in the gustatory cortex within ten minutes of exposure to a novel taste; activation peaked at thirty minutes, whereas exposure to a familiar taste had no effect. Conversely, an MAP kinase inhibitor retarded conditioned-taste aversion. This combination of findings strongly implicate NMDA-mediated plasticity and subsequent specific protein synthesis as critical factors in the cortical modifications that mediate this type of learning.

Other research has used targeted genetic manipulations to show that blocking the cascade of molecular triggers for LTP also results in severe memory impairment. In one such early study, mice with a mutation of one form of CaMKII had deficient LTP and were selectively impaired in learning the Morris water maze. Manipulation of biochemical mechanisms by interference with specific genes has allowed a highly specific identification of some of the critical molecular events. One study by Alcino Silva and his colleagues showed that substituting a single amino acid in CaMKII that prevents its autophosphorylation resulted in a severe learning and memory deficit. Other new genetic approaches are providing a greater temporal- and region-specific blockade of gene activation. Susumu Tonegawa and his colleagues created a genetic block that was limited to postdevelopment activation of the genes for the NMDA receptor in the CA1 subfield of the hippocampus. This mutation selectively blocked LTP in that region. Despite these highly selective temporal and anatomical restrictions, the mice with this mutation were severely deficient in spatial learning and other types of memory dependent on hippocampal function. A complementary recent study showed that a mutation that results in overexpression of NMDA receptors can enhance several kinds of memory dependent on the hippocampus. Molecular genetic manipulations increasingly indicate that interference with other aspects of the LTP molecular cascade, specifically PKC and MAPK, also impair memory. Thus it seems likely that the full set of cellular events that mediate LTP play critical roles in memory.

Conclusion

LTP and memory are not the same thing, and there is no universal acceptance of evidence for shared mechanisms between LTP and memory. And, notwithstanding some contradictory evidence not covered in this article, there is, nevertheless, compelling evidence that learning enhances synaptic potentials in circuits relevant to memory. There is correspondingly strong evidence that blocking LTP with drugs or genetic manipulations can impair memory and destabilize relevant neural representations.

See also: GENETIC SUBSTRATES OF MEMORY: HIPPOCAMPUS; GLUTAMATE RECEPTORS AND THEIR CHARACTERIZATION; LONG-TERM POTENTIATION; NEURAL SUBSTRATES OF EMOTIONAL MEMORY; TASTE AVERSION AND PREFERENCE LEARNING IN ANIMALS

Bibliography

Green, E. J., and Greenough, W. T. (1986). Altered synaptic transmission in dentate gyrus of rats reared in complex environments. Evidence from hippocampal slices maintained in vitro. *Journal of Neurophysiology* 55, 739–750.

Martin, S. J., Grimwood, P. D., and Morris, R. G. M. (2000). Synaptic plasticity and memory: An evaluation of the hypothesis. *Annual Review of Neuroscience* 23, 649–711.

Rioult-Pedotti, M.-S., Friedman, D., Hess, G., and Donoghue, J. P. (1998). Strengthening of horizontal cortical connections following skill learning. *Nature Neuroscience* 1, 230–234.

Rogan, M. T., Staubli, U. V., and LeDoux, J. E. (1997). Fear conditioning induces associative long-term potentiation in the amygdala. *Nature* 390, 604–607.

Rosenblum, K., Berman, D.E., Hazvi, S., Lamprecht, R., and Dudai, Y. (1997). NMDA receptor and the tyrosine phosphorylation of its 2B subunit in taste learning in the rat insular cortex. *Journal of Neuroscience* 17, 5,129–5,135.

Silva, A. J., Smith, A. M., and Giese, K. P. (1997). Gene targeting and the biology of learning and memory. *Annual Review of Genetics* 31, 527–547.

Steele, R. J., and Morris, R. G. M. (1999). Delay dependent impairment in matching-to-place task with chronic and intrahippocampal infusion of the NMDA-antagonist D-AP5. *Hippocampus* 9, 118–136.

Stevens, C. F. (1998). A million dollar question: Does LTP = memory? *Neuron* 20, 1–2.

Tang, Y.-P., Shimizu, E., Dube, G. R., Rampson, C., Kerchner, G. A., Zhuo, M., Liu, G., and Tsien, J. Z. (1999). Genetic enhancement of learning and memory in mice. *Nature 401*, 63–69.

Tsien, J. Z., Huerta, P. T., Tonegawa, S. (1996). The essential role of hippocampal CA1 NMDA receptor-dependent synaptic plasticity in spatial memory. *Cell 87*, 1,327–1,338.

Howard Eichenbaum

MAINTENANCE

One of the most striking properties of memory is its extreme duration; people have memories dating as far back as twenty years or more. Similarly, one of the features of long-term potentiation or LTP (at least in certain brain structures) is its duration; it has been a major challenge for neurobiology to provide a cellular mechanism for long-lasting changes in synaptic transmission that outlast protein turnover. The discovery of the critical role of the NMDA receptors in triggering LTP indicated the existence of distinct stages in the establishment of LTP, which are generally defined as induction and maintenance (Bliss and Lynch, 1988). The former refers to events activated during the high-frequency stimulation, whereas the latter designates the processes that are responsible for the changes in synaptic transmission that underlie LTP and their long-term maintenance. In general, three types of mechanisms have been proposed as maintenance mechanisms: those producing increased transmitter release; those resulting in changes in spine electrical properties; and those implicated in regulating receptor properties (Landfield and Deadwyler, 1988). Since the 1980s evidence against and for each of these mechanisms has been obtained, and the most salient features of the arguments are presented in this entry.

Presynaptic Mechanisms

An increase in transmitter release could account for an increase in synaptic transmission; it is generally admitted, for instance, that short-term potentiation is due to increased transmitter release (Zucker, 1989). Biochemical and electrophysiological evidence has been obtained in support of the hypothesis that increased transmitter release accounts for LTP. Glutamate is likely to be the neurotransmitter used by synapses exhibiting LTP in various hippocampal pathways, and increased glutamate levels have been found after LTP induction in perfusates obtained with push-pull cannulas implanted in the dentate gyrus (Dolphin, Errington, and Bliss, 1982). Increased glutamate release was also found after LTP induction in hippocampal slices and in synaptosomes prepared from hippocampus of rats in which LTP

had been induced. Since the induction of LTP involves the postsynaptic activation of NMDA receptors, a retrograde signal has been postulated that relays the postsynaptic activation to the presynaptic terminal. Researchers initially proposed arachidonic acid to be such a retrograde signal, since activation of NMDA receptors stimulates phospholipase A2 (PLA2), and PLA2 inhibitors prevent LTP formation (Bliss and Lynch, 1988). Arachidonic acid could also provide a link with the presynaptic machinery involved in the regulation of transmitter release because it activates protein kinases that have been shown to participate in phosphorylation reactions important for transmitter release. Researchers later proposed that nitric oxide as well as carbon monoxide were retrograde signals, although the evidence for this conclusion remains highly controversial (Hawkins, Son, and Arancio, 1998; Malenka and Nicoll, 1999). While this mechanism could conceivably provide a satisfactory explanation for a short-lasting enhancement of transmitter release, in its present version it does not account for a long-lasting increase.

Quantal analysis of synaptic transmission (Martin, 1966) is an approach that, in principle, could provide an unambiguous answer to the question of the locus of the changes underlying LTP. It uses the intrinsic variability of transmitter release and statistical methods to determine the parameters generally thought to govern synaptic transmission; in effect, the probability of release, the number of release sites, and the elementary size of a postsynaptic response elicited by a quantum of neurotransmitter. Three groups have reported results obtained with quantal analysis in field CA1 before and after LTP induction in hippocampal slices. Two groups observed an increase in quantal content (Malinow and Tsien, 1990; Bekkers and Stevens, 1990), whereas one group observed an increase in quantal size (Foster and McNaughton, 1991). In addition to this ambiguity in the results, quantal analysis requires a number of assumptions that might not be satisfied at hippocampal synapses. In particular, several studies have indicated the existence of synapses with functional NMDA receptors but few, if any, functional AMPA receptors (the so-called silent synapses). Transformation of silent synapses into active synapses by LTP-inducing stimulation could account for the inconsistencies in results from quantal analysis (Malenka and Nicoll, 1999).

Finally, increased transmitter release could be accounted for by an increase in the number of synapses. Anatomical studies using quantitative electron microscopy have provided evidence that the number of certain categories of synapses, in particular sessile synapses, is increased in field CA1 following LTP induction (Lee, Schottler, Oliver, and Lynch, 1980;

Chang and Greenough, 1984). Although an increased number of synapses could explain the duration of LTP and account for its maintenance, it is not yet clear whether the increase in sessile synapses represents the formation of new synapses or the transformation of existing synapses by shape modifications (Toni et al., 1999).

Changes in Spine Electrical Properties

Since their discovery, there has been much speculation concerning the roles of dendritic spines in synaptic transmission and the possibilities that synaptic plasticity could be due to alterations in their electrical properties (Rall, 1978; Coss and Perkel, 1985). Because of their shape—large heads relative to long, narrow necks—they are considered to be high-resistance elements coupling voltage changes at the synapses with voltage changes in dendritic shafts. Based upon calculation and computer simulation, researchers have proposed that decreased neck resistance could account for increased synaptic responses (Wilson, 1988), which could affect the AMPA receptors more specifically than the NMDA receptors (Lynch and Baudry, 1991). Such a decrease in spine resistance could be due to an increase in neck dimension, and anatomical evidence indicates that LTP is accompanied by an increase in spines with wider and shorter necks. The recent discoveries of active elements (channels or pumps) in dendritic spines provide alternative means of modifying their electrical properties (Johnston, Magee, Colbert, and Cristie, 1996), although there is no evidence that these elements are modified following LTP induction.

Changes in Receptor Properties

One of the most important characteristics of LTP is that it is expressed by an increase in the component of the synaptic response resulting from the activation of the AMPA receptors with little changes in the component generated by the activation of NMDA receptors. Thus an alteration of the properties of the AMPA receptors has been proposed as a potential maintenance mechanism. Several studies have shown that both the ligand binding and the ionic conductance properties of the AMPA receptors are affected by a variety of manipulations. In particular, changes in the lipid environment of the AMPA receptors modify its affinity for agonists, an observation that could account for the involvement of PLA2 in LTP. Studies conducted in the 1990s on the molecular biology of the AMPA receptors have provided exciting results concerning the nature and properties of these receptors. AMPA receptors belong to a family of receptors encoded by at least four related genes, each existing

in two closely similar versions generated by alternative splicing of the genes, and designated flip and flop. Researchers have proposed that AMPA receptors exist as oligomers composed of a number of possible arrangements of flip and flop elements, with the flip elements providing larger currents than the flop (Sommer et al., 1990). Twenty-first-century research has suggested that LTP could result from a change in the composition of receptor subunits or in changes in the rates of receptor insertion or internalization in the synaptic membrane from a subsynaptic pool of receptors (Malinow, Mainen, and Hayashi, 2000). Another dimension related to the stabilization of the changes underlying LTP maintenance has recently been included to the search for the mechanisms of LTP. It is now apparent that LTP stabilization involves adhesion molecules and that there is a time window following LTP induction during which processes leading to LTP consolidation can be reversed, thus producing depotentiation (Lynch, 1998). There has been considerable discussion to determine whether depotentiation represents the same process as long-term depression of synaptic transmission. Although both processes share a number of features, there is not yet a general consensus as to the mechanisms and the significance of these forms of synaptic plasticity.

Conclusion

Although several mechanisms discussed in this entry could account for some characteristics of LTP, most of them run into difficulties when they have to explain its stability. This feature is almost certain to eliminate most mechanisms, however attractive they might appear, that are based solely on conformational or posttranslational changes in proteins. In particular, several speculative mechanisms of LTP maintenance have been based on the idea of biochemical switches, constituted of biochemical reactions involving positive feedback. The most popular of these biochemical switches is derived from the properties of autophosphorylation of calcium/calmodulin kinase type II, which is a very prominent protein in postsynaptic densities and especially in hippocampus (Crick, 1984; Lisman, 1994). The mechanism involved in LTP maintenance therefore will probably require structural modifications that can confer lasting stability to biochemical modifications responsible for changes in synaptic transmission. The coupling of these processes with those responsible for the maintenance of the adhesive properties of synaptic contacts represents a key feature in the evolution of adaptive properties of brain neuronal networks. Finally, the various mechanisms described above underline the richness of mechanisms that have evolved to produce synaptic plasticity and that are likely to contribute to the multiple forms of potentiation that are being uncovered at a variety of central synapses.

See also: GLUTAMATE RECEPTORS AND THEIR CHARACTERIZATION; GUIDE TO THE ANATOMY OF THE BRAIN: NEURON; MORPHOLOGICAL BASIS OF LEARNING AND MEMORY: VERTEBRATES

Bibliography

Bekkers, J. M., and Stevens, C. F. (1990). Presynaptic mechanism for long-term potentiation in the hippocampus. *Nature 346,* 724–729.

Bliss, T. V. P., and Lynch, M. A. (1988). Long-term potentiation: Mechanisms and properties. In P. W. Landfield and S. A. Deadwyler, eds., *Long-term potentiation: From biophysics to behavior.* New York: Liss.

Chang, F., and Greenough, W. T. (1984). Transient and enduring morphological correlates of synaptic activity and efficacy change in the rat hippocampal slice. *Brain Research 309,* 35–46.

Coss, R. G., and Perkel, D. H. (1985). The function of dendritic spines: A review of theoretical issues. *Behavior, Neurology, and Biology 44,* 151–185.

Crick, F. (1984). Memory and molecular turn-over. *Nature 312,* 101.

Dolphin, A. C., Errington, M. L., and Bliss, T. V. P. (1982). Long-term potentiation of the perforant path in vivo is associated with increased glutamate release. *Nature 297,* 496–498.

Foster, T. C., and McNaughton, B. L. (1991). Long-term synaptic enhancement in CA1 is due to increased quantal size, not quantal content. *Hippocampus 1,* 79–91.

Hawkins, R. D., Son, H., and Arancio, O. (1998). Nitric oxide as a retrograde messenger during long-term potentiation in hippocampus. *Progress in Brain Research 118,* 155–172.

Johnston, D., Magee, J. C., Colbert, C. M., and Cristie, B. R. (1996). Active properties of neuronal dendrites. *Annual Review of Neuroscience 19,* 165–186.

Landfield, P. W., and Deadwyler, S. A., eds. (1988). *Long-term potentiation: From biophysics to behavior.* New York: Liss.

Lee, K., Schottler, F., Oliver, M., and Lynch, G. (1980). Brief bursts of high frequency stimulation produce two types of structural changes in rat hippocampus. *Journal of Neurophysiology 44,* 247–258.

Lisman, J. (1994). The CaM kinase II hypothesis for the storage of synaptic memory. *Trends in Neurosciences 17,* 406–412.

Lynch, G. (1998). Memory and the brain: Unexpected chemistries and a new pharmacology. *Neurobiology of Learning and Memory 70,* 80–100.

Lynch, G., and Baudry, M. (1991). Re-evaluating the constraints on hypotheses regarding LTP expression. *Hippocampus 1,* 9–14.

Malenka, R. C., and Nicoll, R. A. (1999). Long-term potentiation—a decade of progress? *Science 285,* 1,870–1,874.

Malinow, R., Mainen, Z. F., and Hayashi, Y. (2000). LTP mechanisms: From silence to four-lane traffic. *Current Opinion in Neurobiology 3,* 352–357.

Malinow, R., and Tsien, R. W. (1990). Presynaptic enhancement shown by whole-cell recordings of long-term potentiation in hippocampal slices. *Nature 346,* 177–180.

Martin, A. R. (1966). Quantal nature of synaptic transmission. *Physiological Review 46,* 51–66.

Rall, W. (1978). Dendritic spines and synaptic potency. In R. Porter, ed., *Studies in Neurophysiology.* Cambridge, UK: Cambridge University Press.

Sommer, B., Keinanen, K., Verdoorn, T. A., Wisden, W., Burnashev, N., Herb, A., Kohler, M., Takagi, T., Sakmann, B., and Seeburg, P. H. (1990). Flip and flop: A cell-specific functional switch in glutamate-operated channels of the CNS. *Science 249,* 1,580–1,585.

Toni, N., Buchs, P.-A., Nikonenko, I., Bron, C. R., and Muller, D. (1999). LTP promotes formation of multiple spine synapses between an axon terminal and a dendrite. *Nature 401,* 421–425.

Wilson, C. J. (1988). Cellular mechanisms controlling the strength of synapses. *Journal of Electron Microscope Technology 10,* 293–313.

Zucker, R. S. (1989). Short-term synaptic plasticity. *Annual Review of Neuroscience 12,* 13–22.

Michel Baudry
Gary Lynch

SIGNAL TRANSDUCTION MECHANISMS AND EARLY EVENTS

Scientists believe that long-lasting changes in synaptic function are essential for learning and memory in the mammalian brain. A widely studied example of such synaptic plasticity is long-term potentiation (LTP). The remarkable feature of LTP is that a short burst of synaptic activity can trigger persistent enhancement of synaptic transmission lasting for at least several hours, and possibly weeks or longer. There is great interest in understanding the cellular and molecular mechanisms that underlie this form of synaptic plasticity. First found in the hippocampus, this phenomenon is now known to exist in cerebral cortex and other areas of the mammalian central nervous system (CNS). Indeed, damage to the hippocampus can result in certain defects in memory acquisition (see Milner, Squire, and Kandel, 1998).

Most studies on LTP focus on the synapse between Schaffer collaterals and hippocampal CA1 neurons. In this system, a brief burst of afferent stimulation leads to induction of LTP in postsynaptic CA1 cells through a combination of (1) membrane depolarization and (2) activation of glutamate receptors of the NMDA subtype (e.g., Collingridge, Kehl, and McLennan, 1983). Researchers generally agree that the depolarization relieves Mg^{2+} (magnesium ion) block of NMDA receptor channels and allows a Ca^{2+} (calcium ion) influx into dendritic spines that somehow triggers LTP (Nicoll, Kauer, and Malenka, 1988).

Back-Propagating Action Potentials

In hippocampal pyramidal neurons an important component of the membrane depolarization that allows opening of NMDA receptors is back-propagating action potentials. While action potentials are of course triggered in the active zone of the cell body, hippocampal pyramidal neurons along with many other types of CNS neurons can actively propagate action potentials into the dendritic regions. These dendritic action potentials are just like action potentials propagated down axons in that they are carried predominantly by voltage-dependent ion channels such as sodium channels. The penetration of the back-propagating action potential into the dendritic region provides a wave of membrane depolarization that allows for the opening of the voltage-dependent NMDA receptor/ion channels. In fact, the timing of the arrival of a dendritic action potential with synaptic glutamate input appears to play an important part in precise, timing-dependent triggering of synaptic plasticity in the hippocampus (Magee and Johnston, 1997). Moreover, modulatory neurotransmitter systems can regulate the likelihood of action potential back-propagation through controlling dendritic potassium channels, allowing for sophisticated information processing through an interplay of action potential propagation, glutamate release, and neuromodulation (Johnston, Hoffman, Colbert, and Magee, 1999).

Importance of a Rise in Postsynaptic $[Ca^{2+}]_i$

NMDA receptor activation leads to a transient $[Ca^{2+}]_i$ increase arising in the postsynaptic neuron, an effect that researchers have measured by the use of fluorescent Ca^{2+} indicator dyes in pyramidal cell dendrites within hippocampal slices (Regehr and Tank, 1990). A variety of experiments have demonstrated the importance of the rise in $[Ca^{2+}]_i$ for LTP. Ca^{2+} buffers such as EGTA or BAPTA have been introduced with the aim of suppressing the transient Ca^{2+} increase; such maneuvers are effective in preventing the induction of LTP (Lynch et al., 1983). Moreover, a rise in postsynaptic Ca^{2+}. independent of glutamate receptors, has been imposed by photoactivation of a caged Ca^{2+} compound, nitr-5; this method for Ca^{2+} delivery causes a sustained synaptic potentiation (Malenka, Kauer, Zucker, and Nicoll, 1988).

Involvement of Protein Kinases

The key question at this point is how a relatively brief rise in $[Ca^{2+}]_i$ can lead to a long-lasting enhancement of synaptic function. One popular hypothesis is that Ca^{2+} acts by activating signal transduction pathways sensitive to the elevation of postsynaptic Ca^{2+}. The pathways that have been implicated are quite varied and include: the Ca^{2+}-phospholipid dependent protein kinase (protein kinase C, PKC), multifunctional Ca/calmodulin-dependent protein kinase (CaMKII), calcium/calmodulin sensitive adenylyl cyclase and the PKA

pathway, the ras/ERK MAP kinase pathway, and calcium-responsive nitric oxide (NO) synthase (Adams and Sweatt, 2002; Lisman and Zhabotinsky, 2001; Lu, Kandel, and Hawkins, 1999; Sweatt, 1999; Hrabetova and Sacktor, 1996).

Involvement of Ca^{2+}-dependent protein kinases has been extensively tested and a wide variety of evidence is compatible with the general hypothesis of a necessity for postsynaptic protein kinase activation as being necessary for triggering LTP (see Figure 1). A necessity for PKC and CaMKII has been tested by intracellular injection of peptides that are potent and selective inhibitors of either PKC or CaMKII (Malinow, Schulman, and Tsien, 1989), and by characterization of kinase-deficient mice generated through gene knockout technology (Abielovich et al., 1993; Silva, Stevens, Tonegawa, and Wang, 1992). Pharmacologic inhibitors of MAP kinase activation have also been shown to block LTP induction (Adams and Sweatt, 2002). Involvement of the PKA pathway has been probed using pharmacologic and transgenic animal approaches, as has the involvement of the NO synthase/cGMP pathway (Lu, Kandel, and Hawkins, 1999; and Sweatt, 1999).

The results obtained with inhibition of PKC, CaMKII, PKA, MAP Kinase, and the NO/cGMP pathway can be interpreted in terms of a network of protein kinases, with protein phosphorylation as a link between the rise in $[Ca^{2+}]_i$ and the eventual expression of enhanced synaptic function. However, the topology of the network and the nature of the interactions remain undefined. Indeed, there is no evidence to date to exclude the idea that one or more of these enzymes act in a merely permissive way. At one extreme, background activity of a particular kinase might be necessary only prior to induction, to set the stage for some other signaling mechanism triggered by Ca^{2+}.

Evidence for Presynaptic Expression of LTP

The question of how the kinases act leads to consideration of ongoing debate about the nature of the maintained synaptic enhancement in LTP. There is a variety of evidence to support the view that both increased presynaptic transmitter release and enhanced glutamate receptor function postsynaptically are involved. The results indicating enhancement presynaptically support the idea of a retrograde signal that travels from the postsynaptic cell back to the presynaptic terminal. This line of reasoning has led to a search for specific compounds that might act as the retrograde messenger, with arachidonic acid, nitric oxide, and superoxide being the most widely con-

Figure 1

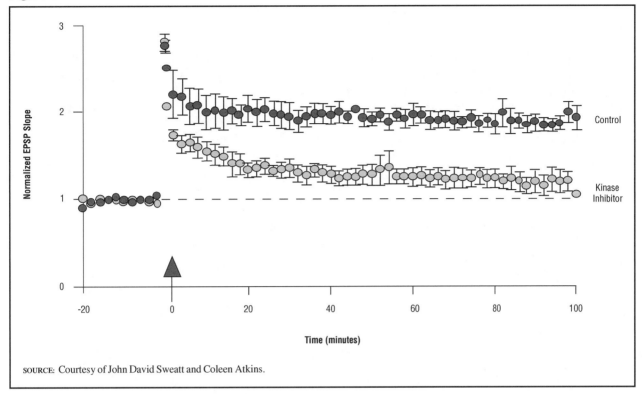

SOURCE: Courtesy of John David Sweatt and Coleen Atkins.

A typical LTP experiment and the effect of a protein kinase inhibitor on LTP. This plot shows the Excitatory Postsynaptic Potential (EPSP) magnitude, measured as the initial slope, over time. The arrow indicates a brief (2 seconds total) period of high-frequency synaptic stimulation. A fairly typical effect of application of a protein kinase inhibitor is shown—in this case the compound SL327, which inhibits activation of the ERK MAP Kinase cascade. The drug was present throughout the recording period.

sidered possibilities (Sweatt, 1999). The precise mechanisms by which these retrograde signals might affect neurotransmitter release are unclear, although presynaptic activation of PKC and the cGMP-dependent protein kinase are appealing possibilities.

Little is known for certain about possible presynaptic mechanisms that might be set in motion by putative retrograde messengers. A widely considered mechanism for synaptic potentiation involves a persistent enhancement of a presynaptic protein kinase, such as PKC (Linden and Routtenberg, 1989). The maintained expression of LTP can be reversibly blocked by bath application of a relatively nonspecific kinase inhibitor, H-7 (Malinow, Madison, and Tsien, 1988), and biochemical measurements show a sustained enhancement of PKC in hippocampal slices (Klann, Chen, and Sweatt, 1993; Hrabetova and Sacktor, 1996). PKC is known to increase the efficiency of excitation-secretion coupling in many systems, including chromaffin cells, motor nerve terminals, and cultured hippocampal neurons. Further exploration of presynaptic mechanisms is needed to determine which steps leading to exocytosis are enhanced in LTP.

Mechanisms of Postsynaptic Enhancement

In terms of mechanisms for enhancing postsynaptic responsiveness, two types of mechanisms are being actively pursued experimentally. One type of process is referred to as activation of "silent synapses" (Poncer and Malinow, 2001; Isaac, Nicoll, and Malenka, 1999). The concept is that some latent synapses have available only NMDA receptors and thus are inactive in terms of normal baseline synaptic transmission. Activation of NMDA receptors by the mechanisms described above leads to calcium influx and calcium-mediated insertion of AMPA receptors locally. Thus previously "silent" synapses become capable of baseline synaptic transmission and the net result is an increased efficacy of transmission.

A second mechanism under investigation is kinase-dependent regulation of AMPA receptors through direct phosphorylation. It is known that phosphorylation of AMPA receptors by PKC and CaMKII leads to increased conductance of ions through the AMPA channel, and evidence is available that phosphorylation at these regulatory sites increases with LTP-inducing stimulation (Lee et al.,

2000; Derkach, Barria, and Soderling, 1999; Barria et al., 1997). Thus it is hypothesized that through increased postsynaptic phosphorylation of AMPA receptors synaptic efficacy is increased by enhancement of AMPA receptor function. The "silent synapse" hypothesis and the enhanced AMPA receptor conductance hypothesis are not mutually exclusive; indeed both could be simultaneously occurring at different synapses between the same cells, or at the same synapses at different points in time.

Potential Roles for Protein Phosphatase Regulation

Finally, while increased protein phosphorylation has been hypothesized to play a key role in triggering LTP for quite some time, studies conducted since the turn of the century highlight a similar importance of tightly regulating protein dephosphorylation as one of the mechanisms controlling the induction of long-term synaptic change and lasting memory (Winder and Sweatt, 2001). In one series of studies, Isabel Mansui and her colleagues (Mallaret et al., 2001) engineered a mouse line in which the activity of the calcium-dependent phosphatase calcineurin (protein phosphatase 2B) could be regulated, in a reversible manner, by tetracycline administration to adult animals. In engineering their mouse they capitalized on the known mechanism of regulation of calcineurin; that is, its regulation by an intrinsic autoinhibitory domain. Mansui's group engineered a mouse in which they could regulate the expression of the isolated autoinhibitory domain of the calcineurin Aα subunit. In their mice, treatment of animals with tetracycline led to expression of the calcineurin autoinhibitory domain protein in several brain regions, including the hippocampus. They then investigated long-term potentiation in hippocampal slices, specifically in area CA1 where many of the earlier studies implicating kinases had been performed. Calcineurin inhibition enhanced the magnitude and duration of long-term potentiation in this region when LTP was triggered by high-frequency stimulation. These studies and a variety of others (Winder and Sweatt, 2001) suggest the possibility of an important role for calcium-dependent phosphatases in regulating the magnitude of LTP induction in the hippocampus.

Since the early 1990s, much progress has been made in scientific understanding of the mechanisms involved in LTP induction. A role for protein phosphorylation in LTP induction is clear. Dendritic action potentials were inconceivable in the early 1990s but in the twenty-first century are known to be critical components of information processing in neurons, through their contributions to LTP induction. Many questions remain concerning the targets of protein kinases in LTP, the role of morphological changes and local protein synthesis in early stages of LTP, and the seemingly perpetual question of pre- versus postsynaptic loci of LTP expression. Scientists are hopeful that continued research and progress will shed light on these topics.

See also: GLUTAMATE RECEPTORS AND THEIR CHARACTERIZATION; GUIDE TO THE ANATOMY OF THE BRAIN: HIPPOCAMPUS AND PARAHIPPOCAMPAL REGION; LONG-TERM POTENTIATION: OVERVIEW: COOPERATIVITY AND ASSOCIATIVITY; SECOND MESSENGER SYSTEMS

Bibliography

Abeliovich, A., Chen, C., Goda, Y., Silva, A. J., Stevens, C. F., and Tonegawa, S. (1993). Modified hippocampal long-term potentiation in PKC gamma-mutant mice. *Cell* 75 (7), 1,253–1,262.

Adams, J. P., and Sweatt, J. D. (2002). Molecular psychology: Roles for the ERK MAP kinase cascade in memory. *Annual Review of Pharmacology and Toxicology 42*, 135–163.

Barria, A., Muller, D., Derkach, V., Griffith, L. C., and Soderling, T. R. (1997). Regulatory phosphorylation of AMPA-type glutamate receptors by CaM-KII during long-term potentiation. *Science* 276 (5,321), 2,042–2,045.

Collingridge, G. L., Kehl, S. J., and McLennan, H. (1983). Excitatory amino acids in synaptic transmission in the Schaffer collateral-commissural pathway of the rat hippocampus. *Journal of Physiology 334*, 33–46.

Derkach, V., Barria, A., and Soderling, T. R. (1999). Ca^{2+}/calmodulin-kinase II enhances channel conductance of alpha-amino-3-hydroxy-5-methyl-4-isoxazolepropionate type glutamate receptors. *Proceedings of the National Academy of Sciences of the United States of America 96* (6), 3,269–3,274.

Hrabetova, S., and Sacktor, T. C. (1996). Bidirectional regulation of protein kinase M zeta in the maintenance of long-term potentiation and long-term depression. *Journal of Neuroscience 16* (17), 5,324–5,333.

Isaac, J. T., Nicoll, R. A., and Malenka, R. C. (1999). Silent glutamatergic synapses in the mammalian brain. *Canadian Journal of Physiology and Pharmacology 77* (9), 735–737.

Johnston D., Hoffman, D. A., Colbert, C. M., and Magee J. C. (1999). Regulation of back-propagating action potentials in hippocampal neurons. *Current Opinion in Neurobiology 9* (3), 288–292.

Klann, E., Chen, S.-J., and Sweatt, J. D. (1993). Mechanism of PKC activation during the induction and maintenance of LTP probed using a novel peptide substrate. *Proceedings of the National Academy of Sciences of the United States of America 90*, 8,337–8,341.

Lee, H. K., Barbarosie, M., Kameyama, K., Bear, M. F., and Huganir, R. L. (2000). Regulation of distinct AMPA receptor phosphorylation sites during bidirectional synaptic plasticity. *Nature 405* (6,789), 955–959.

Linden, D. J., and Routtenberg, A. (1989). The role of protein kinase C in long-term potentiation: A testable model. *Brain Research Reviews 14*, 279–296.

Lisman, J. E., and Zhabotinsky, A. M. (2001). A model of synaptic memory: A CaMKII/PP1 switch that potentiates transmission by organizing an AMPA receptor anchoring assembly. *Neuron 31* (2), 191–201.

Lu, Y. F., Kandel, E. R., and Hawkins, R. D. (1999). Nitric oxide signaling contributes to late-phase LTP and CREB phosphorylation in the hippocampus. *Journal of Neuroscience 19* (23), 10,250–10,261.

Lynch, G., Larson, J., Kelso, S., Barrionuevo, G., and Schottler, F. (1983). Intracellular injections of EGTA block induction of hippocampal long-term potentiation. *Nature 305*, 719–721.

Magee, J. C., and Johnston, D. (1997). A synaptically controlled, associative signal for Hebbian plasticity in hippocampal neurons. *Science 275* (5,297), 209–213.

Malenka, R. C., Kauer, J. A., Zucker, R. S., and Nicoll, R. A. (1988). Postsynaptic calcium is sufficient for potentiation of hippocampal synaptic transmission. *Science 242*, 81–84.

Malinow, R., Madison, D. V., and Tsien, R. W. (1988). Persistent protein kinase activity underlying long-term potentiation. *Nature 335*, 820–824.

Malinow, R., Schulman, H., and Tsien, R. W. (1989). Inhibition of postsynaptic PKC or CaMKII blocks induction but not expression of LTP. *Science 245*, 862–866.

Malleret, G., Haditsch, U., Genoux, D., Jones, M. W., Bliss, T. V., Vanhoose, A. M., Weitlauf, C., Kandel, E. R., Winder, D. G., and Mansuy, I. M. (2001). Inducible and reversible enhancement of learning, memory, and long-term potentiation by genetic inhibition of calcineurin. *Cell 104*, 675–686.

Milner, B., Squire, L. R., and Kandel, E. R. (1998). Cognitive neuroscience and the study of memory. *Neuron 20* (3), 445–468.

Nicoll, R. A., Kauer, J. A., and Malenka, R. C. (1988). The current excitement in long-term potentiation. *Neuron 1*, 97–103.

Poncer, J. C., and Malinow, R. (2001). Postsynaptic conversion of silent synapses during LTP affects synaptic gain and transmission dynamics. *Nature Neuroscience 4* (10), 989–996.

Regehr, W. G., and Tank, D. W. (1990). Postsynaptic NMDA receptor-mediated calcium accumulation in hippocampal CA1 pyramidal cell dendrites. *Nature 345*, 807–810.

Silva, A. J., Stevens, C. F., Tonegawa, S., and Wang, Y. (1992). Deficient hippocampal long-term potentiation in alpha-calcium-calmodulin kinase II mutant mice. *Science 257* (5,067), 201–206.

Sweatt, J. D. (1999). Toward a molecular explanation for long-term potentiation. *Learning and Memory 6*, 399–416.

Winder, D. G., and Sweatt, J. D. (2001). Roles of serine/threonine phosphatases in hippocampal synaptic plasticity. *Nature Reviews Neuroscience 2*, 461–474.

Richard W.Tsien
Revised by J. David Sweatt

Konrad Lorenz *(AP/WideWorld Photos)*

LORENZ, KONRAD (1903–1989)

The Austrian zoologist Konrad Lorenz was one of the pioneers of modern ethology, the comparative study of animal behavior. Also noted for his views on aggression, Lorenz was a corecipient of the Nobel Prize for physiology or medicine in 1973.

Konrad Zacharias Lorenz was born November 7, 1903, in Vienna, Austria. By his own account he was fascinated from an early age with keeping and observing animals. He attended Columbia University in New York for one term in 1922, received an M.D. from the University of Vienna in 1928, and was awarded a Ph.D. in zoology by the same university in 1933. His first professional appointment was at the Anatomical Institute in Vienna; he later became professor of psychology at the University of Königsberg.

Lorenz's flirtation with Nazi ideology after the German annexation of Austria in 1938 tarnished his scientific reputation, especially in the United States and Great Britain. In a 1940 paper he mixed Nazi jargon into a discussion of one of his favorite themes, the destructive effects of domestication on animals and humans. Lorenz's ideas sat well with Nazi theoreticians. He later repudiated this paper and acknowledged that it had brought him undeniable discredit.

During World War II Lorenz served as an army physician on the eastern front, where he was captured by Soviet troops. It was as a prisoner of war in Armenia from 1944 to 1948 that Lorenz wrote his first book. The Russian manuscript (published posthumously in 1996) anticipates many of his later ideas on animal behavior, evolution, instinct, and comparative methodology.

In 1958 Lorenz and Erich von Holst cofounded the Max-Planck-Institut für Verhaltensphysiologie at Seewiesen, Germany, where Lorenz remained as director until his retirement in 1973. Following his retirement, the Austrian Academy of Sciences created the Institute of Comparative Ethology, based at Lorenz's family home in Altenberg, where he served as director of the department of animal sociology until his death. In 1973 Lorenz, Niko Tinbergen, and Karl von Frisch shared the Nobel Prize in physiology or medicine for their pioneering work in ethology, the scientific study of animal behavior. In addition to his many scientific papers and books, Lorenz reached a wide audience with two popular books, *King Solomon's Ring* (1952), a reminiscence on the delights of animal study, and the more controversial *On Aggression* (1966), a discussion of the origins of animal and human aggression.

Lorenz was among the first to insist on the biological roots of animal behavior, asserting that behavior could be described with the same precision and scientific rigor as anatomy. Though this was probably his major contribution to the study of animal behavior, he always acknowledged his debt to two of his predecessors, Oskar Heinroth and Charles O. Whitman. Lorenz further argued that the comparative study of different species can reveal the effects of evolutionary adaptation on behavior. Behavior varies among species because it is shaped by natural selection and shows the influence of the animal's evolutionary history.

Behavior, Lorenz asserted, can be described with the same precision and scientific rigor as anatomy. He further argued that the comparative study of various species can reveal the effects of evolutionary adaptation on behavior, which varies among species because natural selection channels it to distinctive functions in the physical and social environments of different animals.

Lorenz's influence on contemporary research in learning and memory comes from two sources: his work on imprinting and his ideas about the interplay between learned and innate behavior. Imprinting is the formation of a powerful bond between young precocial birds and their parents. Research findings on imprinting, song-learning by birds, and other specialized forms of learning undermined the strict operant reinforcement theories of behaviorism, the school of thought that once dominated American psychology. Building upon Lorenz's pioneering work, later researchers have continued to do important work on the nature of imprinting, its neural basis, and the effects of imprinting on later mate choice.

The second source of Lorenz's influence on current research in learning and memory was his debate with the American psychologist Daniel S. Lehrman during the 1960s on the relative importance of nature and nurture in the development of behavior. Much of Lorenz's scientific work is an analysis of instinctive behavior, which he regarded as the expression of genetically accumulated information—hence animals' capacity for immediate, appropriate, unlearned responses to food, mates, offspring, or predators. Lorenz contrasted such genetically determined responses with learned behavior and regarded behavior as a sequence of learned and innate components. This view was criticized by Lehrman for ignoring important findings about the development of behavior. In his theory of instinct, Lorenz conflated a number of very different ideas about innate behavior, genetics, and evolution. The debate between Lorenz and Lehrman led to a clarification and revision of both positions.

The modern view of animal behavior preserves some of Lorenz's ideas, especially his insistence that functional behavior can occur in the absence of prior relevant experience. It is not correct, however, to regard such behavior as any more "genetic" than anything else that animals do, or to suppose that such behavior is developmentally inflexible. Both genes and the environment can account for differences in behavior, and these two influences interact in their effects on behavior. Less controversy surrounds another of Lorenz's theoretical contributions: his insistence that learning in not simply a matter of open-ended behavioral plasticity but rather consists of evolved rules for acquiring information and modifying behavior.

Lorenz performed little experimental work, preferring to draw on his enormous store of personal observation of animals. Many of his pronouncements on human behavior relied heavily on opinion and intuition. Nevertheless, his compelling insights and persuasive exposition of his ideas brought a new vigor to the scientific study of animal behavior.

Konrad Lorenz died on February 27, 1989, in Altenberg, Austria.

See also: IMPRINTING; OPERANT BEHAVIOR

Bibliography

Lorenz, K. (1940). Durch Domestikation verursachte Störungen arteigenen Verhalten. *Zeitschrift für angewandte Psychologie und Charakterkunde* 59, 1B81.

—— (1952). *King Solomon's ring.* London: Methuen.

—— (1965). *Evolution and modification of behavior.* Chicago: University of Chicago Press.

—— (1966). *On aggression.* London: Methuen.

—— (1996). *The natural science of the human species. An introduction to comparative behavioral research.* Cambridge, MA: MIT Press.

Nisbett, A. (1976). *Konrad Lorenz.* New York: Harcourt Brace Jovanovich.

David F. Sherry

LURIA, A. R. (1902–1977)

The Soviet psychologist Alexandr Romanovich Luria is best known for his work in neuropsychology but also contributed to developmental and crosscultural psychology. The son of a prominent physician, Luria graduated from the University of Kazan in 1921 and joined the staff of the Moscow Institute of Psychology in 1923. He tempered his early interest in psychoanalysis with a growing awareness of the need for objective methods. His attempts to study the unconscious by objective methods resulted in the book *The Nature of Human Conflicts* (1932). In 1924 Luria met Lev Vigotsky, and their subsequent collaboration—until Vigotsky's premature death in 1934— had a lifelong influence on Luria's work. Together they developed the concept of historicocultural psychology, advancing the thesis that higher cognitive functions result from the internalization of external cultural devices and codes.

Vigotsky and Luria embarked on two lines of research driven by the historicocultural theory: developmental studies of language acquisition and the regulatory role of language in behavior, and crosscultural studies of modes of inference among the tribes of Central Asia. Both lines of research ran afoul of the official Marxist dogma of Soviet authorities, who pressured Luria was to terminate his developmental and cross-cultural work.

Luria's scientific interests were gradually evolving toward more biological aspects of psychology and neuropsychology. In the early 1930s Luria turned his attention to the "nature-nurture" debate and embarked on a series of studies of cognitive processes in identical and fraternal twins. In the late 1930s, Luria, already a professor of psychology, earned a medical degree, perhaps because of an authentic intellectual evolution or perhaps because psychology had grown too ideologically parlous an endeavor amid the Stalinist strictures of Soviet academia. Luria's interest in neuropsychology intensified duringWorld War II, when he helped to develop remedial procedures for soldiers with head injuries.

Luria was more interested in developing a comprehensive theory of brain-behavioral relations rather than in describing clinical syndromes or developing diagnostic and remedial techniques. His early eclectic interests shaped his brand of neuropsychology. Luria entered the field at the time of the raging debate between "narrow localizationism" and "equipotentialism." He went beyond this simplistic dilemma and formulated his concept of "dynamic functional systems," which captures the relationship between the localizable dimensions of cognition and the complex traits, skills, and behaviors of everyday

A. R. Luria (*Dr. Lena Moskovich*)

life. Although Luria believed in the invariant localization of basic cognitive dimensions, he thought that cultural and developmental factors governed the dimensional composition of the "functional systems" corresponding to complex processes.

Given Luria's cultural-developmental interests, it is not surprising that the neuropsychology of language was foremost on his agenda in major works such as *Traumatic Aphasia* (1970), *The Role of Speech in the Regulation of Normal and Abnormal Behavior* (1961), and *The Higher Cortical Functions in Man* (1966). Luria's distinct taxonomy of aphasias reflects his interest in refined linguistic operational analysis. Luria's interest in the frontal lobes was a continuation of his earlier concern with self-regulation and consciousness. His emphasis on the hierarchic nature of cognitive control undoubtedly reflected his interactions with Nicholas Bernstein, a Soviet physiologist and mathematician who foreshadowed some of the basic concepts of cybernetics and who, like Vigotsky, suffered official ostracism for deviation from the Pavlovian doctrine.

In the later part of his career, Luria became deeply interested in memory. The monograph *Neuropsychology of Memory* (1976) describes his attempts to root amnesic syndromes in subcortical neuroanatomy. He distinguished the "midline" amnesic syndromes (curiously, without further distinguishing between the diencephalic and mesiotemporal variants) and pituitary, mesiofrontal, "massive prefrontal," and cortical memory deficits. He was particularly interested in the relationship between consolidation and executive functions.

Although Luria is widely known in the West for various adaptations of his diagnostic approaches, he never bothered to compile them into a battery. In fact, he abhorred the notion of a battery and always advocated a flexible, hypothesis-testing approach. He also disdained the notion of instrument standardization. Although Luria's bias against quantification is often cast in East-West terms, it is probably a generational phenomenon. After all, Luria the clinician descended from the the great turn-of-the-century European neurologist-phenomenologists. What makes his diagnostic approach singularly attractive is that every procedure targets a cognitive dimension accounted for in his brain-behavioral theory.

During the later part of his career, Luria was professor of psychology at Moscow State University, where he held the chair of neuropsychology, and director of the Neuropsychology Laboratory at the Bourdenko Institute of Neurosurgery in Moscow. He received numerous awards and was elected to various academies and learned societies in the Soviet Union and in the West.

The enduring influence of Luria's seminal work has been the subject of several books: *Contemporary Neuropsychology and the Legacy of Luria* (1990), *Hidden Histories of Science* (1996), and *The Executive Brain: Frontal Lobes and the Civilized Mind* (2001), to name a few. The centennial anniversary of his birth in 2002 has occasioned a number of scientific symposia worldwide.

See also: AMNESIA, ORGANIC; MEMORY CONSOLIDATION: MOLECULAR AND CELLULAR PROCESSES; MEMORY CONSOLIDATION: PROLONGED PROCESS OF REORGANIZATION; MNEMONISTS

Bibliography

Luria, A. R. (1932). *The nature of human conflicts*. New York: Liveright.

—— (1961). *The role of speech in the regulation of normal and abnormal behavior*, ed. J. Tizard, London: Pergamon.

—— (1966; reprint 1980). *The higher cortical functions in man*, trans. B. Haigh. New York: Basic Books.

—— (1970). *Traumatic aphasia*, trans. D. Bowden. The Hague: Mouton.

—— (1976). *Neuropsychology of memory*, trans. B. Haigh. Washington, DC: Winston.

Goldberg, E. (1990). *Contemporary neuropsychology and the legacy of Luria*. Hillsdale: Erlbaum.

—— (2001). *The executive brain: Frontal lobes and the civilized mind*. New York: Oxford University Press.

Sacks, O. W. (1996). Scotoma: Forgetting and neglect in science. In R. B. Silvers, ed., *Hidden histories of science*. New York: New York Review of Books.

Elkhonon Goldberg

M

MASSED TRAINING

See: DISTRIBUTED PRACTICE EFFECTS

MATHEMATICAL LEARNING THEORY

Theories of learning were enormously visible and influential in psychology from 1930 to 1950, but dropped precipitously from view during the next two decades while the information-processing approach to cognition based on a computer metaphor gained ascendancy. The groundwork for a resurgence of learning theory in the context of cognitive psychology was laid during the earlier period by the development of a subspecialty that may be termed *mathematical learning theory*.

In psychology, just as in physical and biological sciences, mathematical theories should be expected to aid in the analysis of complex systems whose behavior depends on many interacting factors and to bring out causal relationships that would not be apparent to unaided empirical observation. Mathematical reasoning was part and parcel of theory construction from the beginnings of experimental psychology in some research areas, notably the measurement of sensation, but came on the scene much later in the study of learning, and then got off to an inauspicious start. By the 1930s, laboratory investigation of conditioning and learning at both the animal and the human level had accumulated ample quantitative data to invite mathematical analysis. However, the early efforts were confined to the routine exercise of finding equations that could provide compact descriptions of the average course of improvement with practice in simple laboratory tasks (Gulliksen, 1934). Unfortunately, these efforts yielded no harvest of new insights into the nature of learning and did not enter into the design of research.

Clark L. Hull and Habit Strength

The agenda for a new approach that might more nearly justify the label *mathematical learning theory* was set by Clark L. Hull, who distilled much of the learning theory extant at the end of the 1930s into a system of axioms from which theorems might be derived to predict aspects of conditioning and simple learning in a wide variety of experimental situations (Hull, 1943). One of the central ideas was a hypothetical measure of the degree of learning of any stimulus-response relationship. This measure, termed *habit strength* (H), was assumed to grow during learning of the association between any stimulus and response according to the quantitative law

$$H = M \, (1 - e^{cN}) \tag{1}$$

where N denotes number of learning experiences, M is the maximum value of H, and c is a constant representing speed of learning. Thus, H should increase from an initial value of zero to its maximum as a smooth "diminishing returns" function of trials. However, knowing the value of H does not enable prediction of what the learner will do at any point in practice for two reasons. First, a test for learning may be given in a situation different from that in which practice occurred (as when a student studies at home but is tested in a classroom); according to Hull's principle of *stimulus generalization*, the effective habit strength on the test is assumed to be some reduced value H' that differs from H as a function of the difference between the two situations. Further, motivation must be taken into account. If the student in the example studies in a relaxed mood but arrives at the test situation in a state of anxiety, performance may be affected and fail to mirror the actual level of learning. In Hull's theory, it is assumed that the strength of the tendency to perform a learned act, termed *excitatory potential* (E), is determined by habit strength and level of motivation or emotion (denoted D) acting jointly according to the multiplicative relation

$$E = E \times D. \qquad (2)$$

These conceptions were implemented in vigorous research programs mounted by Kenneth W. Spence, one analyzing the relation between anxiety and learning in human beings and the other producing the first quantitative accounts of the ability of some animals to exhibit transposition (i.e., to generalize from learning experiences in terms of relationships such as brighter than or larger than, as distinguished from absolute values of stimulus magnitude).

The Law of Habit Growth

Hull's theory as a whole did not prove viable. It depended on too many assumptions and was too loose-jointed in structure to be readily testable, and its deterministic axioms lacked the flexibility needed to interpret varieties of learning more complex than simple conditioning. However, some components have survived to reappear as constituents of new theories. A notable instance is the law of habit growth. An implication of Equation 1 is that the change in habit strength, δH, on any trial can be expressed as

$$\delta H = c (M - H), \qquad (3)$$

in which form it is apparent that learning is fastest when the difference between current habit strength and its maximum is large, and slow when the difference is small. According to Hull's assumptions, and indeed nearly all learning theories of his time, the function should be applicable on any trial when the response undergoing learning occurs in temporal contiguity to reinforcement (that is, a positive incentive such as food for a hungry animal or a to-be-feared event such as an electric shock). In the course of re-

search over the next two decades, it became apparent that learning depends also on the degree to which an experience provides the learner with new information. If, for example, an animal has already learned that a particular stimulus, Sl, predicts the occurrence of shock, then on a trial when S1 and another stimulus, S2, precede shock in combination, the animal may learn nothing about S2 (Kamin, 1969). This observation and many related ones can be explained by a new theory, which can be viewed as a refinement and extension of one component of Hull's axiom about habit growth. In the new version, the change in habit strength on any learning trial is described by the function

$$\delta H = c (M - H_T), \qquad (4)$$

where H denotes strength of a particular habit undergoing acquisition—for example, the relation between S2 and shock in the illustration—and H_T denotes the sum of strengths of all habits active in the situation—for example, the habits relating both Sl and S2 to shock in the illustration (Rescorla and Wagner, 1972). Studying the new learning function, one can see that if habit strength for S1 is large enough so that H_T is equal to M, then there will be no increment in habit strength for S2. The prediction that learning about S2 is blocked by the previous learning about S1 has been borne out by many experiments. This success, and others like it, in dealing with novel and sometimes surprising findings has put the body of theory built by Rescorla and Wagner and others on the groundwork of Hull's system into a commanding position in present-day research on animal learning.

Probability Matching

At one time it appeared that the basic ingredients of Hull's theory could be adapted in a straightforward and simple way to apply to human learning. In the early 1950s, a physicist converted to mathematical psychology, in collaboration with an eminent statistician, arrived at the idea that the hypothetical notion of habit strength could be dispensed with so that learning functions like Equation 3 would be expressed in terms of changes in response probabilities (Bush and Mosteller, 1955). If, for example, a rat was learning to go to the correct (rewarded) side of a simple T maze, they assumed that when a choice of one side led to reward, the probability, p, of that choice would increase in accord with the function

$$\delta p = c (1 - p), \qquad (5)$$

and when it led to nonreward, p would decrease in accord with

$$\delta p = -cp \qquad (6)$$

where c is a constant reflecting speed of learning. By a simple derivation it can be shown that if reward on one side of the maze has some fixed probability (0, 1, or some intermediate value), Equations 5 and 6, taken together, imply a learning function of the same form as Hull's function for growth of habit strength. Also, the prediction can be derived that the final level of the learning function will be such that, on the average, the probability of choosing a given side is equal to the probability of reward on that side, as illustrated in Figure 1. This prediction of *probability matching* has been confirmed (under some especially simplified experimental conditions) in a number of studies. In an elegant series of elaborations and applications of this simple model, Bush and Mosteller (1955) showed that it could be carried over to human learning in situations requiring repeated choices between alternatives associated with different magnitudes and probabilities of reward, as in some forms of gambling.

However, only a few such applications appeared, and in time it became apparent that, although Bush and Mosteller's methods proved widely useful, neither their approach nor others building on Hull's system could be extended to account for many forms of human learning.

Figure 1

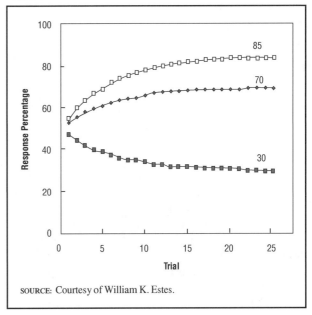

SOURCE: Courtesy of William K. Estes.

Theoretical predictions of percentages of responses to a given side of a choice point on each trial of an illustrative experiment for groups of learners who had different probabilities of reward (.85, .70, or .30) on that side. Details of the model are given in the text.

Statistical Learning Theory

The limitations of models based on conceptions of habit growth or similarly gradual changes in response probabilities were anticipated by the great pioneer of modern neuroscience, D. O. Hebb. In a seminal monograph, Hebb (1949) noted that, whereas slow and gradual learning characterizes animals low on the phylogenetic scale and immature organisms higher on the scale, the learning of the higher forms, most conspicuously human beings, as adults is normally much faster, and often takes the form of abrupt reorganizations of the products of previous learning (as when a person trying to master a technique of computer programming suddenly grasps a key relationship).

A theoretical approach that would prove more adaptable to the treatment of human learning appeared in the 1950s, contemporaneously with the work of Bush and Mosteller, in the development of statistical learning theory, also known as stimulus sampling theory (Estes, 1950). This approach is based on the ideas that even apparently simple forms of learning entail the formation of associations among representations in memory of many aspects of the situation confronting the learner, and that more complex forms are largely a matter of classifying or reclassifying already existing associations (now more often termed *memory elements*). In the earliest versions of the theory, the associations simply related stimuli and responses. If, say, a rat was learning the correct turn in a T maze, then on any trial associations would be formed between the response made, together with the ensuing reward or nonreward, and whatever aspects of the choice situation the animal happened to attend to (the notion of sampling).

An interesting mathematical property of this model is that for simple learning situations, if the total population of stimulus aspects available for sampling is large, the basic learning functions take a form identical to those of Bush and Mosteller's model (Equations 5 and 6), with the learning-rate parameter c interpreted as the proportion of stimulus aspects sampled on any trial. When the population is not large, however, the model is better treated as a type of probabilistic process (technically, a Markov chain) in which learning is conceived in terms of discrete transitions between states. A state is defined by the way the total set of memory elements is classified with respect to alternative responses. The model is thus able to handle the fact that learning is under some conditions slow and gradual but under other conditions fast and discontinuous. In a special case of the model, it is assumed that the learner perceives the entire stimulus pattern present on a trial as a unit, so that the system has only two states, one in which the unit is associated with the correct response and one in which it is not. Surprisingly at the time, this ultra-simplified model was found to account in detail for the data of experiments on the learning of elementary associations (as between faces and names) and concept identification, even for human learners (Bower, 1961).

The stimulus-sampling model automatically accounts for the phenomenon of generalization, which required a special postulate in Hull's system. If learning has occurred in one situation, the probability that the learned response will transfer to a new situation is equal to the proportion of aspects of the second situation that were sampled in the first. The sampling model has the serious limitation that it cannot explain how perfect discriminations can be learned between situations that have aspects in common. However, this deficiency was remedied in a new version formulated by Douglas L. Medin and his associates especially for the interpretation of discrimination and categorization (Medin and Schaffer, 1978). With a new rule for computing similarity between stimuli or situations, this formulation, generally known as the exemplar-memory model, has been shown to account for many properties of human category learning in simulated medical diagnosis and the like.

Connectionism

An interesting aspect of science is the way progress often occurs by seeing older theories in a new light. A striking instance is the observation that Rescorla and Wagner's extension of Hull's learning theory can be viewed as a special case of a type of adaptive network model that has been imported from engineering into the new branch of cognitive science known as *connectionism* (Rumelhart and McClelland, 1986). A connectionist network is composed of layers of elementary units (nodes) interconnected by pathways. When the network receives an input at the bottom layer, as from the stimulus display in a learning situation, activation is transmitted through the network to output nodes at the top layer that lead to response mechanisms. During learning, memories are stored not in individual units but as distributions of strengths of connections in groups of units. These strengths are modified during learning by a process that is driven by an overall tendency toward error correction. Connectionist models have been developed and applied for the most part in relation to complex cognitive activities such as speech perception and language acquisition (McClelland and Rumelhart, 1986), but it has also been discovered that the descendant of Hull's learning theory embodied in the Rescorla-Wagner model can be viewed as a special case of a connectionist network (Gluck and Bower, 1988). The consequence of this observation has been a wave of new work applying and extending what was originally conceived as a model of animal conditioning to a variety of work on human learning and categorization. Thus, by the recurring process of rediscovery and reinterpretation, mathematical learning theory has become active in a new guise as a component of the new discipline of cognitive science.

See also: DISCRIMINATION AND GENERALIZATION; HEBB, DONALD; HULL, CLARK L.; LEARNING THEORY: A HISTORY; LEARNING THEORY: CURRENT STATUS; SPENCE, KENNETH

Bibliography

Bower, G. H. (1961). Application of a model to paired-associate learning. *Psychometrika 26*, 255–280.

Bush, R. R., and Mosteller, F. (1955). *Stochastic models for learning.* New York: Wiley.

Estes, W. K. (1950). Toward a statistical theory of learning. *Psychological Review 57*, 94–107.

Gluck, M. A., and Bower, G. H. (1988). From conditioning to category learning: An adaptive network model. *Journal of Experimental Psychology: General 117*, 225–244.

Gulliksen, H. A. (1934). A rational equation of the learning curve based on Thorndike's law of effect. *Journal of General Psychology 11*, 395–434.

Hebb, D. O. (1949). *Organization of behavior: A neurophysiological theory.* New York: Wiley.

Hull, C. L. (1943). *Principles of behavior.* New York: Appleton.

Kamin, L. J. (1969). Predictability, surprise, attention, and conditioning. In B. A. Campbell and R. M. Church, eds., *Punishment and aversive behavior.* New York: Appleton-Century-Crofts.

McClelland, J. L., and Rumelhart, D. E. (1986). *Parallel distributed processing: Explorations in the microstructure of cognition,* Vol. 2. Cambridge, MA: MIT Press.

Medin, D. L., and Schaffer, M. M. (1978). Context theory of classification learning. *Psychological Review 85*, 207–238.

Rescorla, R. A., and Wagner, A. R. (1972). A theory of Pavlovian conditioning: Variations in the effectiveness of reinforcement and non-reinforcement. In A. H. Black and W. F. Prokasy, eds., *Classical conditioning,* Vol. 2: *Current research and theory.* New York: Appleton-Century-Crofts.

Rumelhart, D. E., and McClelland, J. L. (1986). *Parallel distributed processing,* Vol. 1. Cambridge, MA: MIT Press.

W. K. Estes

McGEOCH, JOHN A. (1897–1942)

John A. McGeoch (1897–1942) was the single most seminal figure in defining the research area known as verbal learning. Trained in the Chicago functionalist tradition by Harvey A. Carr, McGeoch received the Ph.D. in 1926 with a dissertation titled "A Study in the Psychology of Testimony." His professional career was notable for its meteoric advancement, its geographic mobility, and its massive research energy. After rising through the academic ranks at Washington University in St. Louis, he became professor at the University of Arkansas in 1928, at the age of 31. Two years later he went as chairman of the Psychology Department to the University of Missouri, a position he subsequently filled at Wesleyan University and at the University of Iowa (Pratt, 1943; Wolfle, 1943).

McGeoch's major work was *The Psychology of Human Learning: An Introduction* (1942). It was not intended as such: He had been at work, during the 1930s, with the collaboration of Carr, on a projected two-volume manual covering all published work on human learning. The first draft of the manual was about 80 percent complete in 1936, and had received chapter-by-chapter feedback from Carr (see Carr's introduction to McGeoch, 1942). After several years' delay, caused by ill health and frequent moves, McGeoch was persuaded by a publisher, on assuming the Iowa chairmanship, to write a digest of the manuscript, intended for use as a textbook. McGeoch's impact on the field has come through the comprehensiveness and authority of this book and its revision a decade later by his student Arthur L. Irion (McGeoch and Irion, 1952).

McGeoch's reputation rests additionally on a theoretical assertion and a related empirical corpus. The theoretical assertion is in a paper (McGeoch, 1932) that argues that the process of forgetting, which was by then his special commitment, could not in principle be explained by the mere passage of time, as was asserted by the decay theory of forgetting. Rather, he said, activities that occurred *during that time* must be responsible. It follows that to penetrate the mechanism of forgetting, one should study retroactive inhibition. McGeoch's most visible research activities respected that logical agenda.

His scientific style remained close to the data and was conservative with respect to theoretical leaps. McGeoch believed that the psychology of human learning and memory was in a basically pretheoretical phase, in which the field was responsible for determining, first of all, what the data *were* before proposing elaborate explanations of them. Postman (1972) has described this and other characteristics of the functionalist attitude McGeoch received from such predecessors as Carr and J. R. Angell and passed along to such students as A. W. Melton (an undergraduate at Washington University) and B. J. Underwood (a graduate student at Iowa). The austerity of his book, the programmatic drive of his experiments on retroactive inhibition, and his atheoretical bias established McGeoch as an archetype for the contrived laboratory approach to human learning and memory. In the more recent days of cognitive psychology, neither McGeoch's reputation nor the reputation of verbal learning has fared well. The latter tradition is held up as an example of the sterility into which orthodox science can pass.

John A. McGeoch *(Psychology Archives, University of Akron)*

In the context of McGeoch's total career, this reputation is largely erroneous: His dissertation was a series of field studies on memory as *testimony* in which McGeoch tested children (ages 9 to 14) in intact classrooms within the East St. Louis school system (McGeoch, 1928a, 1928b, 1928c). Among many other comparisons, he was interested in the relation between accuracy and intelligence, which he operationalized by contrasting normal and institutionalized children and by the administration to each group of the Army Alpha test (McGeoch, 1928b). An earlier publication (McGeoch, 1925a) had compared (1) the staged event (eyewitness reality) with (2) objects or (3) words as stimuli. Thus, McGeoch may be among a handful of pioneers in developing the study of eyewitness testimony in American psychology (all but one of the references he cited in this work were from German laboratories). Nor was this work on practical aspects of memory isolated: Others of his early publications concerned memory for poetry (Whitely and McGeoch, 1928), emotional measurement (McGeoch and Bunch, 1930), and the relation between suggestibility and juvenile delinquency (McGeoch, 1925b). The catholicism of his original research interests is solidly within the functionalist tradition. One speculation is that McGeoch later turned to the precision and control of experimental studies because of his commitment to finding answers for everyday problems in human life, not in order to escape from them.

See also: INTERFERENCE AND FORGETTING

Bibliography

McGeoch, J. A. (1925a). The fidelity of report of normal and subnormal children. *American Journal of Psychology 36,* 434–445.

———— (1925b). The relationship between suggestibility and intelligence in delinquents. *Psychological Clinic 6,* 133–134.

———— (1928a). The influence of sex and age upon the ability to report. *American Journal of Psychology 40,* 458–466.

———— (1928b). Intelligence and the ability to report. *American Journal of Psychology 40,* 596–599.

———— (1928c). The relation between different measures of the ability to report. *American Journal of Psychology 40,* 592–596.

———— (1932). Forgetting and the law of disuse. *Psychological Review 39,* 352–370.

———— (1942). *The psychology of human learning.* New York: Longmans, Green.

McGeoch, J. A., and Bunch, M. E. (1930). Scores in the Pressey X-O tests of emotion are influenced by courses in psychology. *Journal of Applied Psychology 14,* 150–159.

McGeoch, J. A., and Irion, A. L. (1952). *The psychology of human learning.* New York: Longmans, Green.

Postman, L. (1972). The experimental analysis of verbal learning and memory: Evolution and innovation. In C. P. Duncan, L. Seechrest, and A. W. Melton, eds., *Human memory: Festschrift for Benton J. Underwood,* pp. 1–23. New York: Appleton-Century-Crofts.

Pratt, C. C. (1943). John A. McGeoch: 1897–1942. *American Journal of Psychology 56,* 134–136.

Whitely, P. L., and McGeoch, J. (1928). The curve of retention for poetry. *Journal of Educational Psychology 19,* 471–479.

Wolfle, D. (1943). McGeoch's psychology of human learning: A special review. *Psychological Bulletin 40,* 350–353.

Robert G. Crowder

MEASUREMENT OF MEMORY

There are many techniques for measuring memory. Some methods are highly specialized, either for the purpose of addressing a particular research question or for diagnosing a specific memory dysfunction, but most measurement procedures are variants of the basic techniques described in this entry.

Measures of Recall

Immediate Serial Recall: Memory Span

In the most commonly used version of this task, a randomly ordered sequence of digits (e.g., 4-7-8-2-5-9) is read once to the participant, who is required to repeat them in the same order. The resulting measure is known as the digit span, defined as the number of digits that can be repeated in the correct order without error. An immediate difficulty is that an individual's performance may fluctuate slightly from one occasion to the next, six digits being correctly repeated on one occasion, for example, and seven on the next. The formal measurement of span is therefore usually taken as the number of digits that can be correctly recalled on 50 percent of occasions. The digit span test is found in such standard test batteries as the Wechsler Adult Intelligence Scale. Span can also be measured using items other than digits: letters or words, for example. However, it should be noted that the span measure obtained may vary with the kinds of items employed. Thus word span is typically somewhat shorter than digit span, and word span itself will vary depending on various features of the words, such as their length and familiarity.

Free Recall

In free recall, a list of items is presented and the task is to recall them in any order. The measure of memory is the number (or proportion) of these items recalled. If people are allowed to begin recalling immediately after the presentation of the last item, this simple measure is subject to a strong recency effect: The last few items in the list will be recalled very well (and usually recalled first). There is also a weaker primacy effect: The first few items in the list will be better recalled than those in the middle positions. In some applications these serial position effects are eliminated by inserting "buffer" items at the beginning and end of the list that are not counted as part of the recall measure.

Cued Recall

In cued recall, the task is to recall each item in response to a cue provided by the tester. This cue may have been presented along with the item at the time of study (an intra-list cue) or be an item not studied before (an extra-list cue). For example, a participant may study word pairs such as *dog-tail* and when tested be given the intralist cue *dog* and asked to recall the word with which it was paired. Alternatively, he or she may study a list of single words (including *tail* but not *dog*) and when tested be given the extra-list cue *dog* as a potential aid to recall. A special case of extra-list cuing is category cuing. If the list contained items from several different categories (fruits and animals), cued recall could take the form of providing the participant with the category labels as cues.

A potential difficulty in measuring cued recall is guessing. This problem arises when the items to be recalled have strong prior associations with the cue. For example, suppose the word *orange* was studied and at recall the extra-list cue *fruit* is provided. The participant may have forgotten the item *orange* but offer it merely because it is a plausible guess to the cue *fruit.* The usual solution to this difficulty is to obtain a baseline measure of how often the item is wrongly recalled in response to the cue when it was not on the study list. In this example, the control measure for the word *orange* would be its recall rate to the cue *fruit* when *orange* was not part of the study list.

Measures of Recognition Memory

Forced-Choice Recognition

In this procedure memory is measured by presenting each of the previously studied items (the "old" items) with one or more new items or "lures" and instructing the participant to choose which of these items is old. The measure is then the number or proportion of items correctly identified as old. There are two difficulties with this measure. Guessing poses an obvious problem because in the case of a two-alternative forced choice, someone who remembered nothing at all could guess correctly half the time. Increasing the number of lures reduces the expected rate of correct guessing but does not eliminate the problem entirely. Researchers have proposed various methods of "correcting for guessing," but they are often not used, partly because the problem of guessing is not as serious as it may seem. Normally one is interested not in the absolute number of items recognized but in the comparison of recognition rates across different occasions or conditions. If the influence of guessing is the same across these conditions, then the differences in the recognition rates between conditions will provide an adequate comparative measure.

A second potential source of difficulty is the nature of the lures. A recognition test can be made more or less difficult by altering the degree of similarity between the correct ("old") items and the lures. Thus errors are more likely if the lure is a synonym of the old item than if it is an unrelated word chosen at random.

Single-Item (Yes/No) Recognition Tests

In what may seem the simplest form of a recognition test, participants are shown each test item in turn and asked to respond "yes" if they have seen it before (an old item) and "no" if they have not (a new item). The test list contains a mixture of old and new items. A possible measure of memory would be the proportion of items correctly identified as old, a measure referred to as the hit rate. However, this measure has a serious shortcoming: It will be influenced by the participant's criterion for saying "yes." Adopting a lax criterion (that is, saying "old" even if the item is only faintly familiar) can yield a high hit rate, usually at the expense of mistakenly saying "old" to a large number of new items. Such errors are termed false positives or false alarms. Thus, from the participant's point of view, responding in a yes/no recognition test becomes a trade-off between hits and false alarms. The difficulty from a measurement point of view is that different participants may adopt different criteria, so that comparing hit rates alone can be very misleading.

Clearly what is needed is some way of adjusting the hit rate to take into account criterion differences reflected in the false alarm rate. One method is to take as a score the difference between hits and false alarms, a procedure that has little theoretical justification but offers a simple, and in many circumstances adequate, measure. A more sophisticated method is to make use of a model known as the theory of signal detection, a decision model taken from psychophysics. The model yields a measure, termed d (d-prime), that is independent of the participant's criterion and can be interpreted as a measure of the ability to discriminate difference in subjective familiarity between the old and the new items.

Other Measures of Memory

Measures of Prospective Memory

Prospective memory is remembering to perform an action at a future point in time: to follow an instruction to buy milk on the way home from work, for example. In order to measure prospective memory it is necessary to designate the point at which the future act of remembering is to be performed. In this regard it is possible to distinguish between time-based and event-based tasks. In time-based prospective remembering, an action must be performed at a specified time in the future, such as remembering to turn off the oven in ten minutes. In event-based prospective remembering, an action must be performed contingent on the occurrence of some other event, such as remembering to follow an instruction to lock the door on the way out.

Measures of Implicit Memory

Implicit measures are obtained through observing performance on a task that indirectly reveals the influence of past experience. A common example of an implicit memory test is word-fragment completion. Suppose a participant has seen a list that includes the word *assassin*. Some time later the participant is given a fragment completion test consisting of some but not all of the letters of the word (e.g., a—a—in) and asked to find the word that could be formed by filling in the blanks. No reference is made to the prior list. The essential aspect of an implicit memory test is that participants receive no instructions to remember items from the prior list, nor are they informed of the list's possible relevance. They may therefore be quite unaware that their performance is being influenced by a past experience. The measure of implicit memory is the improvement in performance on the word-fragment completion task. Improvement is measured relative to word-fragment performance obtained under control conditions in which the solution word (*assassin*) was not on the prior study list. Among the other tasks that can be used to measure implicit memory is stem completion. In this task participants are given the initial letters of a word and asked to add letters to complete a word. The major difficulty with implicit measures is to ensure that the participant is not making use of explicit memory strategies. One way to achieve this is to prevent participants from becoming aware of the relationship between the initial study and subsequent test phases of the procedure. Another is to instruct participants that they should avoid conscious strategies by responding with the first thing that comes to mind.

The Relationship among the Different Measures

The various measurement procedures described in this entry are not merely alternative ways of estimating a single "true" quantity that could be thought of as the "amount remembered." In this regard the measurement of memory is very different from the measurement of physical quantities such as length or weight. Various techniques for measuring the distance between two points should yield the same result, and any variation should be regarded as reflecting errors of measurement. The situation is quite different in the case of memory measurement. For example, in evaluating memory for an event, a recognition test and a recall test should not be thought of as alternative methods of measuring a single ideal quantity (the "amount" remembered) but as different measures of memory performance on two distinct, although possibly related, tasks. Much research suggests that under many circumstances different measures of memory are quite dissociated or uncorrelated, reflecting the fact that different measurement procedures tap different aspects of the memory system.

See also: IMPLICIT MEMORY; MEMORY SPAN

Bibliography

Tulving, E., and Craik, F. I. M., eds. (2000). *The Oxford handbook of memory.* New York: Oxford University Press.

Robert S. Lockhart

MEMORY CONSOLIDATION: MOLECULAR AND CELLULAR PROCESSES

Memory is a complex biological process involving multiple brain systems, each with a specialized function, and many molecular and cellular mechanisms that process and consolidate information in the brain. Although studies in recent years have made considerable inroads into the molecular and cellular mecha-

nisms required for triggering the intraneuronal synaptic processes underlying the initial stages of memory, little is known about the mechanisms that consolidate memories. Among the processes most intensively studied, mechanisms that regulate transcription seem to have a clear role in memory consolidation. Also, many studies have demonstrated that memory consolidation involves multiple brain systems. For example, while the hippocampus has a critical role in the initial stages of memory consolidation, remote memories seem to be dependent on cortical storage sites.

Memory and Protein Synthesis

Evidence from a variety of systems and organisms demonstrates that protein synthesis—during or shortly after training—is essential for the formation of long-term memory (LTM) (Davis and Squire, 1984). For example, the protein synthesis inhibitor anisomycin, given systemically before or immediately after training, blocks LTM (typically tested twenty-four hours after training) but not short-term memory (STM; 30–120 minutes after training) tested in a wide spectrum of behavioral tasks. Anisomycin can also block the later phases of long-term potentiation (LTP) without affecting its early stages (Frey et al., 1993). LTP is an experimental model of the synaptic plasticity mechanisms underlying learning and memory.

Unfortunately, most of the protein-synthesis inhibitor drugs have a variety of side effects that complicate the interpretation of the findings. Protein-synthesis inhibitors can make animals sick, and some of these inhibitors have nonspecific effects on the levels of "housekeeping" proteins necessary for cell health. Thus, the dramatic effects of protein-synthesis inhibitors on memory triggered a search for the transcription factors that direct the gene expression required for memory. Transcription factors bind to specific sequences in the promoters of genes and serve as attachment sites for the machinery that transcribes genes. Alterations of these transcription factors have far more specific biological effects than the transcription and translation inhibitors used to study memory.

CREB and Memory

Several lines of evidence from studies with multiple organisms and brain systems demonstrate that the cAMP Responsive Element Binding Protein (CREB) is one of the transcription factors regulating the synthesis of proteins necessary for the formation of LTM.

Learning activates several signaling pathways, including cAMP, CaMKIV and MAPK signaling cascades. Activation of these signaling cascades seems to lead to the phosphorylation and activation of CREB. Phosphorylated CREB bound to cAMP Responsive Elements (CRE sites) in the promoter of specific genes, such as *14-3-3 eta*, can then bind to a complex of proteins that transcribes those genes. Insights into the biochemistry of CREB directed the design of experiments that tested the impact on memory of both increases and decreases in CREB function.

In a wide range of species, including *Aplysia, Drosophila*, song birds, mice, and rats, CREB-dependent transcription has been demonstrated to be crucial for the formation of LTM. Furthermore, the levels of active CREB may also be an important determinant of the amount and schedule of training required for LTM. Higher levels of CREB facilitate LTM, while LTM formation in animals with lower CREB levels requires more training with longer intervals between trials. The involvement of CREB in memory formation does not seem to be restricted to certain forms of memory. Tests as diverse as olfactory conditioning in flies, fear conditioning, spatial memory, conditioned taste aversion, social recognition, and social transmission of food preferences in rodents demonstrate the involvement of CREB in memory formation. Similarly, CREB has a role in the stability of synaptic changes in a variety of species, including *Aplysia*, rats, and mice. Furthermore, CREB also has a role in other forms of plasticity, including topographical cortical reorganization and circadian rhythms (Silva et al., 1998)).

There is compelling evidence that cAMP-dependent signaling can activate CREB (Silva et al., 1998). Deleting both calcium/calmodulin induced adenyl cyclases (1 and 8), enzymes that generates cAMP, block the maintenance but not the induction of LTP in the CA1 region. Similarly, these genetic manipulations also cause deficits in hippocampal long-term memory. Pharmacological activation of adenyl cyclases turns on CREB and rescues the LTP and memory deficits of this mutant (Wong et al., 1999). Another kinase that can phosphorylate and activate CREB is calcium/calmodulin kinase IV (CaMKIV). Experiments with a dominant-negative form of CaMKIV (dnCaMKIV) expressed in the postnatal forebrain showed that this kinase has a role in the later stages of LTP. Similarly, behavioral tests indicated that this kinase modulates long-term memory formation: the dnCaMKIV mice showed specific long-term memory deficits in both spatial learning and contextual fear conditioning tasks. CREB activation was impaired by the dnCaMKIV transgene, confirming that this kinase activates CREB during learning (Kang et al., 2001).

Downstream Targets of CREB and Their Role on Memory

CREB controls the expression of other proteins that seem to regulate the complex molecular and cellular events underlying long-term memory. For example, multiple pulses of serotonin activate CREB in *Aplysia* and induce a set of genes, many of which may regulate synaptic plasticity and memory. Researchers have identified several synaptic plasticity candidate genes, including the CCAAT enhancer-binding protein, ApC/EBP. ApC/EBP contains CRE sites in the promoter region, is rapidly induced by cAMP, and exhibits properties consistent with an immediate early gene. Low levels of ApC/EBP are present in unstimulated sensory neurons, but there are higher levels during the initial phase of long-term facilitation (LTF), a synaptic model of LTM in *Aplysia*. Decreasing the expression of ApC/EBP selectively blocks the formation of LTF but not short term facilitation or STF (Alberini et al., 1994). Remarkably, inhibitory avoidance training in rats induces two homologs of ApC/EBP (C/EBP β and C/EBP α), and downregulation of C/EBP β with antisense oligonucleotides leads to deficits in long- but not in short-term memory in rats tested in this fear conditioning task (Taubenfeld et al., 2001).

C/EBP may regulate another transcription factor, ApAF (*Aplysia* Activating Factor) (Bartsch et al., 2000), which shares homology with the mammalian PAR family of transcription factors. Injection of recombinant ApAF into a cocultured *Aplysia* neuronal preparation converts the STF normally produced by one pulse of serotonin into LTF. Additionally, injection of antibodies against ApAF or injection of a dominant negative form of ApAF that contains only the bZIP domain blocks the LTF produced by five pulses of serotonin.

Zif268 is another transcription factor whose expression seems to be regulated by CREB. The promoter region of Zif268 contains two CRE sites and six SRE sites. The levels of Zif268 are upregulated shortly following LTP-inducing stimulation. Furthermore, mutant mice lacking Zif268 show specific deficits in the late phases of LTP. Similarly, LTM, but not STM tested with a variety of tasks, is abnormal in these mutants (Jones et al., 2001). Like the CREB$^{\alpha\delta-/-}$ mutant mice, the Zif268 mutants show deficits in spatial learning in the water maze following massed training, and these deficits are rescued by spaced training.

Hippocampal/Neocortical Interactions During Memory Consolidation

Memory consolidation involves the molecular cascades described above, but it also requires multiple brain regions. A number of studies have indicated that whereas memory is initially stored in the hippocampus, eventual storage takes place in cortical networks. Studies examining patients with hippocampal damage have found a loss of memory called temporally-graded retrograde amnesia (Squire, 1992): Patients with hippocampal damage suffer severe amnesia for memories that are a few years old at the time of injury (recent memory) but not for memories that are many years old (remote memory). Similar findings have been made in rodents. For example, contextual fear conditioning is severely disrupted by hippocampal lesions made one day, but not several weeks, after training. These studies suggest that the hippocampus processes new memories but that they are eventually stored elsewhere, presumably the cortex.

A study examining patients with cortical brain damage showed that they have recent but not remote memory, a result that is consistent with the theory that memory is only temporarily stored in the hippocampus and that it is eventually consolidated in the cortex. Interestingly, imaging brain function with the deoxyglucose technique showed that metabolic activity was high in the hippocampus when maze learning was recent, but relatively high in the cortex when maze learning was remote (Bontempi et al., 1999). Performance on the maze correlated only with hippocampal metabolism for recent memory and only with cortical metabolism for remote memory.

A study using molecular genetic techniques came to a strikingly similar conclusion (Frankland et al., 2001). In the mutants studied, LTP is normal in the hippocampus but deficient in the cortical regions thought to store memory. Remarkably, these mice showed normal memory for up to three days after training but dramatic forgetting over longer retention intervals (ten to fifty days). These data suggest that the abnormal LTP in the cortex interfered with the storage of memory there and that the normal LTP in the hippocampus may explain why memory was normal for up to three days after training. It is striking that a wide range of studies, ranging from genetic and imaging studies in mice to neuroanatomical lesions in rats, monkeys, and humans all demonstrate this striking interaction between the hippocampus and the neocortex in memory consolidation.

Editing Memory During Recall

Thus, memory goes through several stages where information is consolidated with different molecular mechanisms and in different brain structures. However, it would be misleading to think of animal memory as computer memory, a permanent etching of events and experiences. Instead, there is a overwhelming amount of data that show that memory is a constructive and dynamic process, designed to fine tune behavioral responses and not to faithfully record experiences. The very usefulness of memory has to do with this ability to extract and generalize from experience adaptive responses and rules that improve survival and fitness. It is not useful for the mouse to remember that a particular cat is dangerous. It is far more useful for it to learn that cats in general are dangerous. Moreover, a number of studies show that the very process of recall can bring memories to a labile state in which they can be edited or reconsolidated (Sara, 2000). Some of the very molecular mechanisms that lay down memories in the first place may be called upon during recall to edit these memory traces. Thus, blocking protein synthesis during recall interferes with memory just as dramatically as blocking it during training (Nader et al., 2000). Similarly, blocking CREB function during recall interferes with memory just as blocking it during training (Kida et al., 2002), an eloquent demonstration of the constructive essence of recall and of the fragile nature of memory.

See also: APLYSIA: MOLECULAR BASIS OF LONG-TERM SENSITIZATION; PROTEIN SYNTHESIS IN LONG-TERM MEMORY IN VERTEBRATES; SECOND MESSENGER SYSTEMS

Bibliography

Alberini, C. M., Ghirardi, M., Metz, R., and Kandel, E. R. (1994). C/EBP is an immediate-early gene required for the consolidation of long-term facilitation in *Aplysia. Cell 76*, 1,099–1,114.

Bartsch, D., Ghirardi, M., Casadio, A., Giustetto, M., Karl, K. A., Zhu, H., and Kandel, E. R. (2000). Enhancement of memory-related long-term facilitation by ApAF, a novel transcription factor that acts downstream from both CREB1 and CREB2. *Cell 103*, 595–608.

Bontempi, B., Laurent-Demir, C., Destrade, C., and Jaffard, R. (1999). Time-dependent reorganization of brain circuitry underlying long–term memory storage. *Nature 400*, 671–675.

Davis, H. P., and Squire, L. R. (1984). Protein synthesis and memory. *Psychology Bulletin 96*, 518–559.

Frankland, P., O'Brien, C., Ohno, M., Kirkwood, A., and Silva, A. (2001). CaMKII-dependent plasticity in the neocortex is required for remote memory. *Nature 411*, 309–313.

Frey, U., Huang, Y.-Y., and Kandel, E. R. (1993). Effects of cAMP simulate a late stage of LTP in hippocampal CA1 neurons. *Science 260*, 1,661–1,664.

Jones, M. W., Errington, M. L., French, P. J., Fine, A., Bliss, T. V., Garel, S., Charnay, P., Bozon, B., Laroche, S., and Davis, S. (2001). A requirement for the immediate early gene Zif268 in the expression of late LTP and long-term memories. *Nature Neuroscience 4*, 289–296.

Kang, H., Sun, L. D., Atkins, C. M., Soderling, T. R., Wilson, M. A., and Tonegawa, S. (2001). An important role of neural activity-dependent CaMKIV signaling in the consolidation of long-term memory. *Cell 106*, 771–783.

Kida, S., Josselyn, S., Ortiz, S., Kogan, J., Chevere I., Masushige, S., and Silva, A. (2002). CREB required for the stability of new and reactivated fear memories. *Nature Neuroscience 5*, 348–55.

Nader, K., Schafe, G. E., and LeDoux, J. E. (2000). The labile nature of consolidation theory. *Nature Reviews Neuroscience 1*, 216–219.

Sara, S. J. (2000). Retrieval and reconsolidation: Toward a neurobiology of remembering. *Learning and Memory 7*, 73–84.

Silva, A. J., Kogan, J. H., Frankland, P. W., and Kida, S. (1998). CREB and memory. *Annual Review of Neuroscience 21*, 127–148.

Squire, L. R. (1992). Memory and the hippocampus: A synthesis from findings with rat, monkeys, and humans. *Psychology Review 99*, 195–231.

Taubenfeld, S. M., Milekic, M. H., Monti, B., and Alberini, C. M. (2001). The consolidation of new but not reactivated memory requires hippocampal C/EBPbeta. *Nature Neuroscience 4*, 813–818.

Wong, S. T., Athos, J., Figueroa, X. A., Pineda, V. V., Schaefer, M. L., Chavkin, C. C., Muglia, L. J., and Storm, D. R. (1999). Calcium-stimulated adenylyl cyclase activity is critical for hippocampus-dependent long-term memory and late phase LTP. *Neuron 23*, 787–798.

Alcino Silva

MEMORY CONSOLIDATION: PROLONGED PROCESS OF REORGANIZATION

The origin of the concept of memory consolidation is generally credited to Georg Elias Müller and his student Alfons Pilzecker. Their 300-page monograph, published in 1900, proposed that memory is not formed instantaneously at the time of learning but takes time to be fixed (or consolidated). The studies involved lists of nonsense syllables and focused especially on retroactive inhibition, the finding that when two lists are learned in succession, learning the second list interferes with subsequent recall of the first list. On the basis of this finding, they suggested that the processes needed to form memory continue for a period of time after learning, during which time they are vulnerable to interference. While this origin of the consolidation concept is widely known, it is not generally known that the interval across which the putative consolidation process operated in these early experiments was less than ten minutes.

The consolidation concept subsequently came into widespread usage and found application in a number of contexts. The term is often used to refer to the cascade of molecular events, including protein synthesis, that unfolds during the hours after learning and ultimately results in morphological growth and change at synapses. The term is also used in the context of observations that damage to the hippocampus or related structures can produce temporally graded retrograde amnesia: impairment of memories that were acquired weeks, months, and even years earlier, despite sparing of more remote memories. There need be no confusion among these usages if one notes

that the former refers to molecular and cellular events within neurons and the latter to what retrograde amnesia has suggested about the brain systems involved in elaborating long-term memory. When one speaks about prolonged processes of reorganization (or prolonged consolidation), one is usually referring to this latter usage.

There are also other ways in which memory can undergo gradual change and reorganization across time that may be related to consolidation. For example, forgetting itself operates over a long period, with the result that details are lost and one is left with kernels of the past, the central meanings. One can forget the particulars while abstracting and retaining the main points. Thus, forgetting is not a passive process of progressive loss and dissolution but a dynamic process during which representations of the past within neocortex are continually reconstructed and reorganized. Events such as rehearsal and episodes of new learning also influence the structure of already established representations. These continuing influences on the structure of long-term memory are beyond the scope of this article.

A Brain System for Memory in the Temporal Lobe

In 1957 Scoville and Milner described the profound effects on memory following bilateral removal of the medial temporal lobe in a patient who became known as H.M. Comprehensive study of this patient established the fundamental principle that the ability to acquire new memories is a distinctly cerebral function, separable from other perceptual and intellectual functions. This discovery inspired efforts to develop an animal model of human memory impairment in the monkey and led eventually to the identification of the hippocampus and adjacent, anatomically related structures in the medial temporal lobe as components of a memory system important for the formation of long-term memory (Squire and Zola-Morgan, 1991). Disrupting the function of this system impairs the ability to form declarative memories (the ability to acquire new facts and events) while leaving intact a collection of nondeclarative memory abilities, including habits and skills, simple forms of conditioning, and other means by which experience can change how one interacts with the world. Disruption of medial temporal lobe function also causes retrograde amnesia—that is, the loss of memories that were acquired before the onset of amnesia. The finding that retrograde amnesia is typically temporally graded (most severe for recent events and less severe for remote events) suggested that medial temporal lobe structures are essential at the time of learning as well as after learning during a prolonged and gradual period of reorganization and consolidation. During consolidation, long-term memory is gradually stabilized within the neocortex.

Temporally Graded Retrograde Amnesia

The earliest evidence for temporally graded retrograde amnesia came from clinical observations of human patients recorded more than 100 years ago. Quantitative studies of retrograde amnesia began in the 1970s. For example, on a test of former one-season television programs, designed to permit the equivalent sampling of past time periods, psychiatric patients prescribed bilateral electroconvulsive therapy (ECT) for depressive illness exhibited temporally-graded retrograde amnesia covering about three years. Evidence relating temporally graded retrograde amnesia to the medial temporal lobe has come from patients for whom detailed neuropsychological information is available together with postmortem information about which structures were damaged. Such case material has shown that retrograde amnesia is brief when damage is limited to the CA1 field of the hippocampus (Zola-Morgan, Squire, and Amaral, 1986) and more extensive, covering fifteen years or more, when the damage is more extensive in this region (the CA fields, dentate gyrus, subiculum, and some cell loss in the entorhinal cortex) (Rempel-Clower, Zola, Squire, and Amaral, 1996). Despite reports of temporally graded retrograde amnesia in well-described patients, it is nevertheless the case that such studies depend on retrospective methods that make it difficult to document precisely the time course of the phenomenon. Accordingly, when prospective studies of retrograde amnesia in experimental animals began in the 1990s, the nature of retrograde amnesia, as well as the concept of consolidation, were placed on firmer ground.

Of more than ten studies that have been carried out in mice, rats, rabbits, and monkeys, most have found temporally graded retrograde amnesia following damage to the hippocampal region (Rempel-Clower, Zola, Squire, and Amaral, 1996; Squire, Clark, and Knowlton, 2001). The retrograde amnesia typically covers about one month. In addition, related work suggests that retrograde amnesia can become more extensive as damage extends beyond the hippocampus into adjacent medial temporal lobe structures. This pattern of findings implies that the hippocampus itself is important for memory for a relatively short period of time after learning and that the adjacent perirhinal and parahippocampal cortices remain important for a longer time. Ultimately, memory depends on widespread areas of the neocortex and is independent of the medial temporal lobe.

Uncertainties about Temporally Graded Retrograde Amnesia

Some uncertainties remain about temporally graded retrograde amnesia and its interpretation. First, there is not yet agreement as to whether spatial memories undergo the same kind of transition as nonspatial memories do—from a form that depends on the hippocampus and related structures to a form that is independent of these structures. On the one hand, the available data from humans suggest that spatial and nonspatial memory have the same status. For example, a profoundly amnesic patient with large medial temporal lobe lesions was able to recall the spatial layout of the neighborhood where he had lived as a child, and his memory in this respect was as good as the memory of healthy individuals who had lived as children in the same neighborhood (Teng and Squire, 1999). On the other hand, the findings from experimental animals are less clear. Some studies of rodents have found retrograde amnesia for spatial memory to be temporally graded after hippocampal lesions (Ramos, 1998; Squire, Clark, and Knowlton, 2001), but other studies have found memory to be affected similarly across past time periods (Sutherland et al., 2001).

A second uncertainty about temporally graded retrograde amnesia is whether episodic memory (that is, the recollection of autobiographical events) becomes independent of the medial temporal lobe in the same way that memory for general facts becomes independent. Some patients with medial temporal lobe lesions appear able to recollect specific events from their remote past as well as healthy individuals (Reed and Squire, 1997), whereas at least one patient with damage thought to be limited to the medial temporal lobe is described as quite incapable of remote episodic recollections (Cipolotti et al., 2001). A third source of uncertainty is that it is in principle possible to construct alternatives to a consolidation account of retrograde amnesia (Nadel and Moscovitch, 1997), although these ideas have difficulty accounting for the available facts (Knowlton and Fanselow, 1998).

Looking for Consolidation with Brain-Imaging Techniques

One difficulty with the concept of gradual memory consolidation is that this idea has depended largely on only one kind of evidence, namely, the evidence of temporally graded retrograde amnesia. Some efforts have been made to find direct evidence for memory consolidation in neuroimaging studies (functional magnetic resonance imaging [fMRI]) that assess medial temporal lobe activity while individuals recollect recent and more remote memories. These studies have yielded mixed results (Ryan et al., 2001; Niki and Luo, 2002; Haist, Bowden Gore, and Mao, 2001; Maguire, Henson, Mummery, and Frith, 2001). A difficulty in interpreting findings obtained with this technique is that the neuroimaging method provides information only about regions where activity correlates with a particular cognitive operation and does not provide information about which regions are essential. Perhaps the medial temporal lobe is very often engaged during memory retrieval but is essential only when recent memories are being retrieved. Or perhaps activation of the medial temporal lobe during recollection of recent and remote events is driven to a large extent by the encoding into long-term memory of the events of the test session, and by the re-encoding of the recollections themselves.

It is notable that work in experimental animals has found activity in the hippocampal region to differ depending on the length of the retention interval. Regional brain activity was mapped in mice tested five days or twenty-five days after learning. Increasing the retention interval from five to twenty-five days resulted in decreased hippocampal activity during retention testing (Bontempi, Laurent-Demir, and Jaffar, 1999). Additional studies in humans and experimental animals using neuroimaging techniques should be of value.

Gradual Memory Consolidation

Another reason that discussion continues about the concept of memory consolidation is that the idea itself is rather vague and depends on mechanisms not yet identified. The central idea is that medial temporal lobe structures direct the gradual establishment of memory representations in the neocortex, and this interaction between the medial temporal lobe and the neocortex embodies the consolidation process. Some researchers have proposed that the hippocampus can serve as a temporary memory store because hippocampal synapses change quickly. The neocortex can store information only gradually as an accumulation of small synaptic changes (McClelland, McNaughton, and O'Reilly, 1995). Consolidation occurs when the hippocampus (and the system to which it belongs) repeatedly activates representations in the neocortex, with the result that the neocortex can eventually support memory independently of the hippocampal system.

Computational considerations have suggested that consolidation is important precisely because it enables the neocortex to slowly incorporate into its representations the regularities of the environment, such as facts about the world (McClelland, McNaughton, and O'Reilly, 1995; O'Reilly and Rudy, 2001).

Figure 1

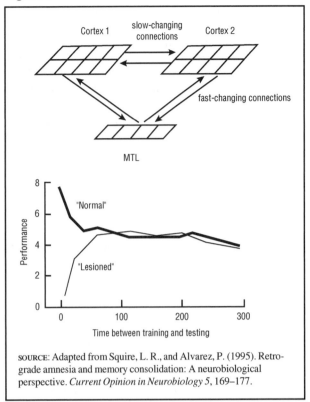

SOURCE: Adapted from Squire, L. R., and Alvarez, P. (1995). Retrograde amnesia and memory consolidation: A neurobiological perspective. *Current Opinion in Neurobiology 5*, 169–177.

A neural network model of memory consolidation. (top) Schematic diagram of the neural network model. Areas cortex 1 and cortex 2 represent association neocortex, and area MTL represents the medial temporal lobe memory system. Each unit in each area is reciprocally connected to all units in all other areas. A key feature of the model is that changes in the connections to and from the MTL area are fast and short-lasting, whereas changes in the connections between the neocortical areas are slow and long-lasting. Consolidation occurs when random activity in the MTL co-activates the stored patterns in cortex 1 and cortex 2, which results in strengthening of the cortico-cortical connections. (bottom) Performance of this model in a *retrograde amnesia* experiment. The network learned two different patterns concurrently, and was tested on how well it was able to reproduce the patterns after varying amounts of time, given presentation of a part of each pattern. The "Normal" curve (thick line) shows the performance the intact network. The "Lesioned" curve shows the performance of the network when the MTL area was inactivated immediately prior to testing.

Rapid modification of neocortical representations would lead to instability, for example, if one rapidly introduced into a network the fact that penguins are birds, but cannot fly, when birds are already represented in the network as animals that can fly. In such a case, McClelland and colleagues showed that the performance of the network would be markedly disrupted because the network begins to apply the characteristics of the penguin to other birds.

One proposal is that the hippocampal system stores only a compressed form of the memory but stores sufficient information to activate relevant sites in the neocortex. Consolidation occurs when the neocortex is repeatedly activated by the medial temporal lobe, either during rehearsal, reminiscence, or perhaps as a result of spontaneous reactivation during sleep. When activation occurs, gradual and long-lasting changes occur in the connections between the cortical sites. Eventually, these connections become so strong that the medial temporal lobe is not needed to recreate the original representation (see Figure 1).

Conclusion

The idea that memory can consolidate or reorganize after learning in a lengthy process rests largely on the phenomenon of temporally graded retrograde amnesia—namely, the finding in studies of both humans and experimental animals that damage to the medial temporal lobe can impair memories that were acquired recently while sparing more remote memories. These results have suggested that medial temporal lobe structures are required for a limited period after learning, during which time they direct a process of consolidation in the neocortex by gradually binding together the multiple, anatomically separate sites that together represent memory for a whole event.

Efforts to observe consolidation directly in neuroimaging studies have yielded mixed results. Uncertainties also remain concerning whether spatial memory operates by the same rules as nonspatial memory and whether memory for specific events that are unique to time and place consolidate in the same way as facts, which can be repeated in multiple contexts. Computational principles suggest that consolidation occurs because new information must be incorporated gradually into preexisting representations in the neocortex. Simple network models have been constructed that capture these ideas.

See also: GUIDE TO THE ANATOMY OF THE BRAIN: CEREBRAL CORTEX; GUIDE TO THE ANATOMY OF THE BRAIN: HIPPOCAMPUS AND PARAHIPPOCAMPAL REGION; MÜLLER, GEORG ELIAS

Bibliography

Bontempi, B., Laurent-Demir, C., and Jaffar, R. (1999). Time-dependent reorganization of brain circuitry underlying long-term memory storage. *Nature 400*, 671–675.

Cipolotti, L., Shallice T., Chan, D., Fox, N., Scahill, R., Harrison, G., Stevens, J., and Rudge, P. (2001). Long-term retrograde amnesia: The crucial role of the hippocampus. *Neuropsychologia 39*, 151–172.

Haist, F., Bowden Gore, J., and Mao, H. (2001). Consolidation of human memory over decades revealed by functional magnetic resonance imaging. *Nature Neuroscience 11*, 1,139–1,145.

Knowlton, B. J., and Fanselow, M. S. (1998). The hippocampus, consolidation and on-line memory. *Current Opinion in Neurobiology 8*, 293–296.

Maguire, E. A., Henson, R. N. A., Mummery, C. J., and Frith, C. D. (2001). Activity in prefrontal cortex, not hippocampus, varies parametrically with the increasing remoteness of memories. *NeuroReport 12*, 441–444.

McClelland, J. L., McNaughton, B. L., and O'Reilly, R. C. (1995). Why there are complementary learning systems in the hippocampus and neocortex: Insights from the successes and failures of connectionist models of learning and memory. *Psychological Review*, 419–437.

Müller, G. E., and Pilzecker, A. (1900). Experimentelle beitrage zur lehre vom Gedachtniss. *Zeitschrift fur Psychologie, Erganzungsband 1*, 1–300.

Nadel, L., and Moscovitch, M. (1997). Memory consolidation, retrograde amnesia and the hippocampal complex. *Current Opinion in Neurobiology 7*, 217–227.

Niki, K., and Luo, J. (2002). An fMRI study on the time-limited role of the medial temporal lobe in long-term topographical autobiographical memory. *Journal of Cognitive Neuroscience 14*, 500–507.

O'Reilly, R. C., and Rudy, J. W. (2001). Conjunctive representations in learning and memory: Principles of cortical and hippocampal function. *Psychology Review 108*, 311–345.

Ramos, J. M. J. (1998). Retrograde amnesia for spatial information: A dissociation between intra and extramaze cues following hippocampus lesions in rats. *European Journal of Neuroscience 10*, 3,295–3,301.

Reed, J. M., and Squire, L. R. (1997). Impaired recognition memory in patients with lesions limited to the hippocampal formation. *Behavioral Neuroscience 111*, 667–675.

Rempel-Clower, N., Zola, S. M., Squire L. R., and Amaral, D. G. (1996). Three cases of enduring memory impairment following bilateral damage limited to the hippocampal formation. *Journal of Neuroscience 16*, 5,233–5,255.

Ryan, L., Nadel L., Keil K., Putnam K., Schnyer D., Trouard T., and Moscovitch, M. (2001). Hippocampal complex and retrieval of recent and very remote autobiographical memories: Evidence from functional magnetic resonance imaging in neurologically intact people. *Hippocampus 11*, 707–714.

Scoville, W. B., and Milner, B. (1957). Loss of recent memory after bilateral hippocampal lesions. *Journal of Neurology, Neurosurgery, and Psychiatry 20*, 11–21.

Squire, L., and Kandel, E. R. (1999). *Memory: From mind to molecules.* New York: Scientific American Library.

Squire, L. R., and Alvarez, P. (1995). Retrograde amnesia and memory consolidation: A neurobiological perspective. *Current Opinion in Neurobiology 5*, 169–177.

Squire, L. R., Clark, R. E., and Knowlton, B. J. (2001). Retrograde amnesia. *Hippocampus 11*, 50–55.

Squire, L. R., and Zola-Morgan, S. (1991). The medial temporal lobe memory system. *Science 253*, 1,380–1,386.

Sutherland, R. J., Weisend, M. P., Mumby, D., Astur, R. S., Hanlon, F. M., Koerner, A., Thomas, M. J., Wu, Y., Moses, S. N., Cole, C., Hamilton, D. A., and Hoesing, J. M. (2001). Retrograde amnesia after hippocampal damage: Recent versus remote memories in two tasks. *Hippocampus 11*, 27–42.

Teng, E., and Squire, L. R. (1999). Memory for places learned long ago is intact after hippocampal damage. *Nature 400*, 675–677.

Zola-Morgan, S., Squire, L. R., and Amaral, D. G. (1986). Human amnesia and the medial temporal region: Enduring memory impairment following a bilateral lesion limited to field CA1 of the hippocampus. *Journal of Neuroscience 6*, 2,950–2,967.

Larry R. Squire

MEMORY DRUGS

See: COGNITIVE ENHANCERS; DRUGS AND
MEMORY; PHARMACOLOGICAL TREATMENT
OF MEMORY DEFICITS

MEMORY SEARCH

Encoding refers to the content or form in which information is stored in memory; *forgetting* is loss of the stored information with the passage of time or with exposure to interfering materials; and *retrieval* refers to accessing information from memory. Any observation of memory reflects all three components, but measurements of recognition time, reflecting memory search, emphasize retrieval. Recognition time is the time required to respond whether a visually presented test item was part of a previously studied list. For an example of a recognition test following a short-term memory list, see Figure 1. Recognition time and accuracy for individual items in both short-term and long-term memory are consistent with retrieval mechanisms involving parallel, or direct access, operations rather than unguided search through many memories. Some aspects of the increase in recognition time with the length of small short-term memory lists suggest a serial, or sequential, search of the list. However, when more detailed analysis of response times and accuracies is carried out, serial search is ruled out as the sole mechanism of retrieval of the prior experience of an item. Instead, response times inversely related to recency of items in particular list positions. Recency determines the efficiency of a simple, direct retrieval process. In contrast with the direct-access retrieval of item information, information about order generally reflects a slower, serial process of recovery from memory in which list items are searched in order.

Retrieval in Short-Term and Long-Term Memory

Primary, or short-term, memory (STM) for a few recently active concepts is distinct from secondary, or long-term, memory (LTM), which is the repository for all the varied information we retain over extended periods of time (James, 1890, 1950). Short-term memory has been described by some theorists as an active subset of long-term memory (Cowan, 1995). Retrieval from LTM during recognition (of a presented item) has many properties of direct access or content addressability (Gillund and Shiffrin, 1984; Murdock, 1971). Direct-access retrieval occurs when a cue or set of cues makes contact with memory in a unitary process without recourse to a sequence of

Figure 1

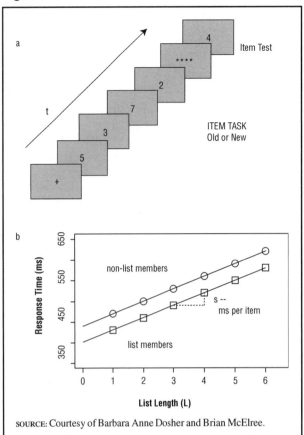

SOURCE: Courtesy of Barbara Anne Dosher and Brian McElree.

(a) A sample test sequence in an STM item-recognition experiment (see, e.g., Stemberg, S. [1966]. High speed scanning in human memory. *Science 153,* 652–654). In this sample, the items are digits presented visually over time (t) and the list length (4) is within the short-term range. Subjects press one of two keys to indicate whether or not the test item appeared on the current list. Time and accuracy of key presses are measured; (b) Typical results of the item-recognition experiments, graphing the average (correct) response time (RT) as a function of the length of the list for list members and nonmembers. RT increases approximately linearly with list length, with roughly equal slopes for list members and nonmembers (RT = bR + sL, R=Yes for list members or No for non-list members). The slope, s, has been used as a measure of retrieval efficiency.

searches through irrelevant memories. In contrast, recall or production (of a previously experienced but unpresented item) may involve a series of retrieval operations in which memory is successively sampled, using general list cues and previously retrieved items as retrieval cues (Raaijmakers and Shiffrin, 1981).

In the 1960s, strong claims were made that access to STM was fundamentally different from the direct-access retrieval from LTM. STM retrieval was asserted to involve a series of comparisons to all currently active concepts (Sternberg, 1966). Although this view fails to give a full account of memory search under all circumstances, it is a useful starting point.

Recognition Time and STM

Anecdotal information about human memory largely reflects memory failures. Scientists use both memory failures (errors) and measures of retrieval time to infer properties of memory. The ease of memory retrieval is often measured in terms of the average time to recognize (respond to) a test item (response time, RT). In S. Sternberg's (1966) classic short-term memory experiments, subjects decided whether a displayed digit (or, in other studies, letter, word, syllable, or outline shape) had appeared on a short study list of one to six items. One key-press indicated a yes response, another no (see Figure 1a). RT increased approximately linearly for each additional list item (see Figure 1b): mean $RT = b_R + sL$, $(R = Y$ or $N)$, where L is the list length, s is the additional average RT per list item, and b_R is a base time. This characteristic linear (or approximately linear) relationship holds for lists of up to six to nine items (Burrows and Okada, 1975), at which point the increment for additional items decreases sharply, possibly reflecting a transition from list lengths within the capacity of STM to those exceeding that capacity.

Underlying Retrieval Mechanisms

The linear relation of mean RT to list length, where both positive (yes) and negative (no) test items frequently yield approximately the same slope, was interpreted by Sternberg as evidence for a serial and exhaustive set of comparisons between the test item and all items in the list representation in short term memory (see Figure 2a). The slope s of the RT function (the added time for each additional list member) was identified as the time to compare the test item with each item on the list, one at a time, in series. The intercept b_R then reflects all the processing mechanisms (encoding of the test stimulus, organization and execution of the response) that do not depend on list length. If the list items were searched in series, equality of positive and negative slopes implies that the test item is compared exhaustively against all list items.

A search, or sequence of comparisons, that terminated upon finding a match would finish, on average, about halfway through the list when the item was positive, but would go through the list when the test item was negative. The slope of the negative tests would then be twice that of the positives; the 2:1 slope ratio is a property of some searches of items in visible displays but not of items in memory. Thus, parallel and linear list length functions are often thought to reflect exhaustive serial search in the retrieval of information from STM.

However, linear increases in mean RT with list length are also consistent with a parallel retrieval mechanism in which all comparisons take place at the same time, but with an efficiency that depends on the number of concurrent comparisons (see Figure 2b). This is called mechanism mimicry. Mimicry of serial mechanisms by parallel mechanisms occurs when only simple measures such as the average RT are available (see Townsend and Ashby, 1983, for a mathematical treatment of this mimicry). Hence, the regularities noted by Sternberg (1975; see Figure 1a) may result from exhaustive and serial comparisons, or from a set of parallel comparisons whose efficiency is affected by the number of comparisons, or by a direct-access process (see Figure 2c) whose efficiency is affected by other factors that covary with list length. More detailed analyses discriminate the serial and parallel mechanisms. In either case, time to retrieve information from STM depends on the number of items currently being remembered.

Direct-Access in Retrieval of Item Information

A serial exhaustive search mechanism has these properties: (1) linear increases in RT with list length where (2) slopes for positive and negative tests are equal; (3) RT should not depend on the position of a positive test item on the list; (4) the fastest (minimum) RTs should increase with the length of the list; and (5) the RT variance (a measure of variation from test to test) should increase linearly with list length for both positive and negative recognition tests. Over many variants of STM item recognition experiments, properties (1) and (2) hold approximately, although RT increases with list length may be more logarithmic than linear (Briggs, 1974). Properties (3) and (4), which require more detailed breakdowns of data, fail systematically. Retrieval of item information from STM, when considered in more detail, is inconsistent with serial exhaustive processing.

RT, the time to recognize an item from STM, depends strongly on its recency (property 3 fails). Test items experienced very recently yield fast RTs, with RT increases for each less recent item. There is also a small advantage for the first list item. Recency in the study list is the controlling factor whenever rehearsal is minimal or constrained to match study order. This is easily seen when the data are graphed appropriately (i.e., Monsell, 1978; see Figure 3a). Longer lists yield slower mean RTs because they include items of less recency. Averaging over list positions yields approximately linear (or logarithmic) increases in mean

Figure 2

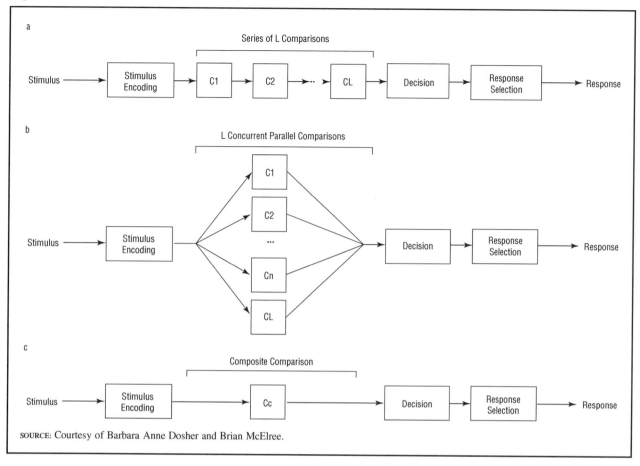

SOURCE: Courtesy of Barbara Anne Dosher and Brian McElree.

Schematics illustrating serial and parallel retrieval mechanisms for comparing a test item against the memory representation of the list. All these schematics distinguish nonretrieval processes (stimulus encoding, decision, response selection, and execution) from the retrieval processes or memory comparisons. Parallel retrieval mechanisms can mimic serial mechanisms in predicting average response time (RT; see Townsend, J. T., and Ashby, F. G. [1983]. *The stochastic modeling of elementary psychological processes*. New York: Cambridge University Press). a. Sternberg ([1966]. High speed scanning in human memory. *Science 153*, 652–654) proposed that recognition following short memory lists of length L consisted of a serial and exhaustive sequence of comparisons of the test item against a representation of each list item in memory. The test item is compared with all list items regardless of whether a match is found, and a new comparison does not begin until the preceding one has been completed; b. Recognition as a set of parallel, concurrent comparisons of the test item against representations of L list items. Efficiency depends on the number of concurrent comparisons; c. Recognition as direct access to a relevant list memory. Efficiency depends on familiarity (see McElree, B., and Dosher, B. [1989]. Serial position and set size in short-term memory: The time course of recognition. *Journal of Experimental Psychology: General 118*, 346–373).

RT with list length. Failure of the prediction that the minimum RT should depend fairly strongly on list length (property 4) is implied by the recency data (see Figure 3a): RT for the most recent items depends only weakly on the length of the list. Distributions of RTs from shortest to longest show only tiny shifts of the minimum with list length; average RT increases with list length largely reflect shifts in the longer RTs (see Figure 3b) (Hockley, 1984). Predictions of linear increases in variability (property 5) also fail. Other findings that contradict the exhaustive serial search mechanism are decreases in RT when a stimulus is repeated and decreased RT for stimuli with high test

probability, in situations where list items are the same over long sets of trials.

The list position effects and aspects of the RT distributions in item recognition tasks contradict properties 3, 4, and 5 of the serial exhaustive scan. The approximate equality of positive and negative slopes (property 2) contradicts terminating (nonexhaustive) scan. For item memory (as distinct from order memory see subsequent explanation), the data are consistent with a direct-access retrieval mechanism in which decreased availability of less recent items determines average RT for particular list positions and hence for different list lengths (McElree and Dosher, 1989).

Figure 3

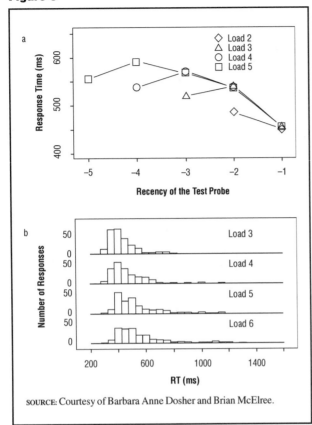

a

Load 2
Load 3
Load 4
Load 5

Response Time (ms)

600

500

400

−5   −4   −3   −2   −1

Recency of the Test Probe

b

Number of Responses

50
0
50
0
50
0
50
0

Load 3

Load 4

Load 5

Load 6

200   600   1000   1400

RT (ms)

SOURCE: Courtesy of Barbara Anne Dosher and Brian McElree.

(a) Recency and primacy in STM recognition. The response time (RT) is shown for each list position for each of several list lengths (list position is labeled in terms of recency, with -1 denoting the last item studied, -2 the next-to-last item studied, and so on). Recognition RT is fastest for items appearing closest to the end of short lists (right of graph), increasing as items become less recent, except for the first (primacy) item in each list (data from Monsell, S. [1978]. Recency, immediate recognition memory, and reaction time. *Cognitive Psychology 10*, 465–501). Recency effects on RT of both list members and nonmembers are not predicted by serial exhaustive mechanisms; (b) Distributions of RT (the number of responses in each RT band) for lists of length 3 to 6 (data from Hockley, W. E. [1984]. Analysis of response time distribution in the study of cognitive processes. *Journal of Experimental Psychology: Learning, Memory and Cognition 10*, 598–615). List length primarily affects the longest RTs. Serial mechanisms predict shifts in the entire distribution with list length.

Time Course of STM Retrieval for Item Information

A direct-access retrieval mechanism was directly confirmed by more detailed RT methods, which allow inferences about the full time course of retrieval. These methods interrupt retrieval at various times after onset of the test display and observe the rate of increase in correct responding with additional retrieval time. B. McElree and B. Dosher (1989) showed

that the rate of retrieval of items from lists of different length was fastest for the single most recent item—a case of an immediate match between the last item studied and the test item—but is otherwise unaffected by either list length or list position (see Figure 4). Retrieval from STM was parallel or direct access, yet the ultimate success of retrieval was limited by familiarity in memory. Recent items have been least affected by forgetting due to the passage of time or intervening items between study and test. The strength of items when measured by errors and the accessibility of items when measured by RT are both directly related to the recency of study, with a small additional advantage for the primacy or first item on the list.

LTM Retrieval

Recognition of items presented in longer lists that exceed estimates of STM capacity shows many of the same properties as recognition of items from short, recent lists. Recognition from longer lists leads to more errors than for STM lists, where the error rates may be less than 5 percent. However, as in STM, list position is an important factor in LTM, affecting both RT and accuracy. As in shorter lists, items near the end of the list are recognized more quickly and accurately. When longer lists are used, study is usually followed by many test trials, and location in the test protocol also has a powerful effect. Earlier tests yield faster RT and accuracy. Later in the test sequence, additional time and materials are interpolated between encoding and retrieval; this is another manipulation of recency. As with the STM data, study and test position effects on average RT primarily reflect shifts in the long tail of the RT distributions. Full time course of recognition is fastest for the single most recent item, and otherwise equivalent but limited by familiarity (Wickelgren, Corbett, and Dosher, 1980). These findings rule out recency-dependent serial comparisons that terminate on a match. The details of these data, when examined carefully, are accounted for by a parallel, direct-access retrieval process with shifts in estimated familiarity (Ratcliff, 1978).

Indeed, direct access appears to be a general property of item retrieval. The same time-course patterns are found in both supra- and sub-span lists (Wickelgren, Corbett, and Dosher, 1983; McElree, 2001), indicating that direct access is a property of both short- and long-term representations. Direct-access retrieval is also evident in the recovery of information from more complex representations and based on altered cues. For example, direct-access retrieval characterizes the recognition of an item that is part of a hierarchically coded group (McElree, 1998), as well as recognition that is based on component properties (e.g., phonological and semantic properties) of the memory representation. The latter finding in particular suggests that direct access arises from a content-addressable retrieval operation that may operate either on an exact representation or via reintegration of the studied item from related cues during retrieval.

Search Processes in Recovery of Order Information

Although item information appears to be recovered through a direct-access content-addressable retrieval process, this is not so for certain other forms of information. Studies indicate that the retrieval of relational information, including temporal order information in STM and positional information in LTM often require a slow serial search. For example, if information about the order of items in STM must be retrieved, both accuracy and retrieval speed depend strongly upon item recency (McElree and Dosher, 1993). Temporal order information in STM was examined with a judgment of recency task, in which subjects were presented two test probes from a short list of five or six items and asked to select the item that occurred more recently. The accuracy and speed of the order judgment, as measured either by mean RT or by time course analysis, was directly related to the recency of the most recent item. A related phenomenon occurs in n-back tasks, in which a positive response is restricted to a particular ordinal position (e.g., a 1-back match, a 2-back match) in a long ongoing sequence instead of an overt judgment of order (McElree, 2001). In both kinds of relational or order tasks, retrieval speed is directly controlled by the recency of the most recent relevant item, strongly implicating a memory search process that begins with the most recent item. One possibility is that ordered representations in memory are serially scanned from the most recent, moving backwards in time (for specific models see McElree and Dosher, 1993; McElree, 2001). Alternatively, order information may be reconstructed at retrieval by a serial chain process (Murdock, 1982), in which the last item on the list is used as a cue to recover the next item on the list from memory, and so on. In all cases in which the retrieval of relational or order information have been evaluated, some form of (terminating) successive or serial process operates. This stands in contrast to the direct-access recovery of item information from either STM or LTM.

Relation of STM Item and Order Retrieval to STM Recall

Another classic measure of STM is the ordered recall of all items on a short list. The list length at

Figure 4

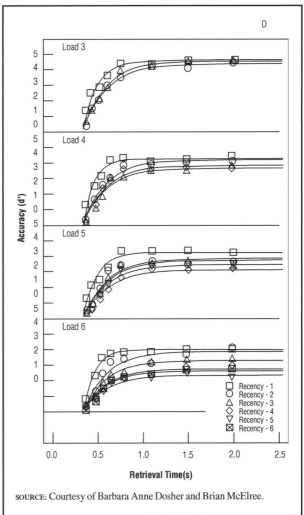

SOURCE: Courtesy of Barbara Anne Dosher and Brian McElree.

Full-time course of STM retrieval for list positions is consistent with parallel, direct-access mechanisms. Time course is measured by examining accuracy after allowed recognition times between 0.1 second and 2 seconds for list lengths of 3 to 6; d' is a bias-free measure of accuracy. Retrieval is fastest for the single most recent item in each list (labeled -1). Maximum accuracy late in retrieval varies with recency and primacy. Related effects on response times are shown in Figure 3a and Figure 3b. Data from McElree, B., and Dosher, B. (1989). Serial position and set size in short-term memory: The time course of recognition. *Journal of Experimental Psychology: General 118*, 346–373.

which ordered recall is perfect 50 percent of the time (usually an interpolated value) is called the memory span. Span and the RT and accuracy for recognizing a single list item both measure aspects of STM function. Historically, span has been taken as a measure of capacity (Miller, 1956; Baddeley, 1986), while recognition RT was taken as a measure of retrieval efficiency. Although the two measures do not strongly correlate with each other across individuals, they vary together across different to-be-remembered materi-

Figure 5

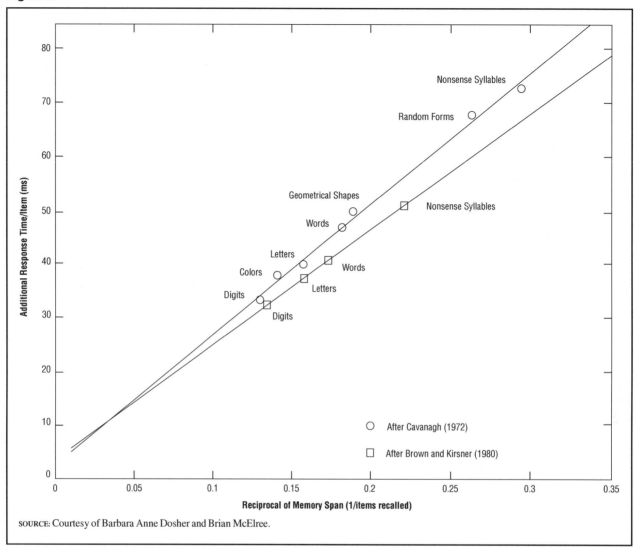

SOURCE: Courtesy of Barbara Anne Dosher and Brian McElree.

STM recognition and STM recall are strongly coupled over study material. The additional recognition response time (milliseconds) for each additional list member (s in Figure 1b) is correlated with the inverse of the longest list recalled in perfect order half the time, or memory span (items). Response time per item is a measure of STM retrieval efficiency and span is a measure of STM capacity. Familiar materials such as digits or letters yield larger measured capacity and more efficient retrieval than unfamiliar materials such as nonsense syllables or random shapes. Data from Cavanaugh, J. P. (1972). Relation between the immediate memory span and the memory search rate. *Psychological Review 79*, 525–530; and Brown, H. L., and Kirsner, K. (1980). A within-subjects analysis of the relationship between memory span and processing rate in short-term memory. *Cognitive Psychology 12*, 177–187.

als. J. P. Cavanaugh (1972) compared, via a survey of the research, the memory spans and the RT list-length slopes of digits, letters, words, shapes, and nonsense materials. Materials yielding higher spans (longer list lengths supporting 50% recall) exhibit relatively shallower slopes (less increase in average RT with increasing list length; see Figure 5). The primary factor producing differences in materials in both measures of STM may be overall familiarity (Puckett and Kausler, 1984).

The relationship between item recognition and memory span in ordered recall may reflect the differ-

ent retrieval demands of the two tasks. Item recognition reflects the strength of direct-access content addressable information in memory, while span, a measure of ordered recall, additionally requires the sequential access of ordered representations, either by sequential access of an intrinsically ordered representation, or by chained retrieval from a content-addressable store. In support of this view that STM recall is composed of a sequence of retrieval or scanning operations, the time to complete ordered recall of a span length list may be as long as 5 to 8 s (Dosher and Ma, 1998), generally compatible both with the time course of individual retrievals (see Figure 4) and with the time course of recovery of item information.

Relation to Other Abilities

The capacity of STM has been viewed as an elementary information-handling process, related to efficiency in a variety of mental tasks (Baddeley, 1986). The speed of access to information in STM, defined as the slope of the dependence of RT on list length (*s* in the linear equation above), has been tested as a correlate of the quality of performance on general cognitive indices such as aptitude scores. Correlations of capacity with psychometric measures are usually higher than those of retrieval time with psychometric measures (Sternberg, 1975). However, various special populations, such as the young and the elderly, have been shown to have characteristic increases in STM recognition times, either in base times or in slopes, compared with the performance of young adults (Sternberg, 1975). STM function is one of the important information-processing correlates with verbal intelligence (Palmer, MacLeod, Hunt, and Davidson, 1985). The concepts of STM and its close relative, working memory, have been central in recent years in the development of theories and predictive indices of general cognitive functions (Engle, Tuholski, and Kane, 1999).

See also: MEMORY SPAN; RETRIEVAL PROCESSES IN MEMORY; WORKING MEMORY: HUMANS

Bibliography

Baddeley, A. D. (1986). *Working memory*. New York: Oxford University Press.

Briggs, G. E. (1974). On the predictor variable for choice reaction time. *Memory & Cognition 2*, 575–580.

Burrows, D., and Okada, R. (1975). Memory retrieval from long and short lists. *Science 188*, 1,031–1,033.

Cavanaugh, J. P. (1972). Relation between the immediate memory span and the memory search rate. *Psychological Review 79*, 525–530.

Cowan, N. (1995). *Attention and memory: An integrated framework*. New York: Oxford University Press.

Dosher, B., and Ma, J. J. (1998). Output loss or rehearsal loop? Output time versus pronunciation time limits in immediate recall for forgetting matched material. *Journal of Experimental Psychology: Learning, Memory, and Cognition 24*, 316–335.

Engle, R. W., Tuholski, S., and Kane, M. (1999). Individual differences in working memory capacity and what they tell us about controlled attention, general fluid intelligence and functions of the prefrontal cortex. In A. Miyake and P. Shah, eds., *Models of working memory: Mechanisms of active maintenance and executive control*. Cambridge, MA: Cambridge University Press.

Gillund, G., and Shiffrin, R. M. (1984). A retrieval model for both recognition and recall. *Psychological Review 91*, 1–67.

Hockley, W. E. (1984). Analysis of response time distribution in the study of cognitive processes. *Journal of Experimental Psychology: Learning, Memory, and Cognition 10*, 598–615.

James, W. (1890; reprint 1950). *The principles of psychology*. New York: Dover.

McElree, B. (1998). Attended and non-attended states in working memory. *Journal of Memory and Language 38*, 225–252.

—— (2001). Working memory and focal attention. *Journal of Experimental Psychology: Learning, Memory, and Cognition 27*, 817–835.

McElree, B., and Dosher, B. (1989). Serial position and set size in short-term memory: The time course of recognition. *Journal of Experimental Psychology: General 118*, 346–373.

—— (1993). Serial retrieval processing in the recovery of order information. *Journal of Experimental Psychology: General 122*, 291–315.

Miller, G. E. (1956). The magic number seven, plus or minus two: Some limits of our capacity for processing information. *Psychological Review 63*, 81–97.

Monsell, S. (1978). Recency, immediate recognition memory, and reaction times. *Cognitive Psychology 10*, 465–501.

Murdock, B. B., Jr. (1971). A parallel processing model of scanning. *Perception and Psychophysics 10*, 289–291.

—— (1982). A theory for the storage and retrieval of item and associative information. *Psychological Review 89*, 609–626.

Palmer, J., MacLeod, C. M., Hunt, E., and Davidson, J. E. (1985). Information processing correlates of reading. *Journal of Memory and Language 24*, 59–88.

Puckett, J. M, and Kausler, D. H. (1984). Individual differences and models of memory span: A role for memory search rate? *Journal of Experimental Psychology: Learning, Memory, and Cognition 10*, 72–82.

Raaijmakers, J. G., and Shiffrin, R. M. (1981). Search of associative memory. *Psychological Review 88*, 93–134.

Ratcliff, R. (1978). A theory of memory retrieval. *Psychological Review 85*, 59–108.

Sternberg, S. (1966). High speed scanning in human memory. *Science 153*, 652–654.

—— (1975). Memory-scanning: New findings and current controversies. *Quarterly Journal of Experimental Psychology 27*, 1–32.

Townsend, J. T., and Ashby, F. G. (1983). *The stochastic modeling of elementary psychological processes*. New York: Cambridge University Press.

Wickelgren, W. A., Corbett, A. T, and Dosher, B. A. (1980). Priming and retrieval from short-term memory: A speed-accuracy tradeoff analysis. *Journal of Verbal Learning and Verbal Behavior 19*, 387–404.

Barbara Anne Dosher
Brian McElree

MEMORY SPAN

The term *memory span* refers to the maximum length of a sequence of items that can be reproduced from memory following a single presentation. Scientists have been interested in memory span since the publication of the first important study of memory, nineteenth-century German experimental psychologist Hermann Ebbinghaus's monograph in 1885. Using himself as his only subject, Ebbinghaus determined the number of presentations necessary for an error-free reproduction of a sequence of items; he found that this number decreased dramatically as the length of the sequence decreased until the sequence included only seven items, at which point only a single presentation was needed. Ebbinghaus showed no particular interest in this finding, but others did. Within two years, memory span was shown to increase systematically during childhood and to be appreciably shorter for the mentally impaired. Within a decade, memory span was firmly established in what was then an emerging field of mental abilities testing, where it has remained ever since.

Most often the procedure for testing memory span calls for the recall of the items in the order in which they were presented. Sometimes the order in which the items have to be recalled is entirely unconstrained; sometimes the items have to be recalled in their reverse order of presentation. But only rarely does the procedure call for more difficult transformations, such as recall of the items in alphabetical or numerical order. Such transformations would draw on what is often referred to as working memory and, interestingly, would probably provide a more valid measure of mental ability. Incidentally, the measure of choice for this ability has been a variant of memory span known as working memory span, which is the number of items that can be retained while performing some other cognitive task.

Measuring Memory Span

Order of reproduction aside, there has never been a fixed procedure by which memory span is measured. Most of the methods reviewed long ago by J. Paul Guilford and Karl Dallenbach (1925) are still extant. Sometimes the sequence of items is deliberately set somewhat too long for perfect reproduction, and memory span is defined as the number of items from this sequence that are recalled. This method is quick to administer but too problematic to be considered anything more than rough and ready. One problem is that the usual requirement that the items be recalled in their exact order of presentation has to be modified to allow for imperfect recall. Another is that, whatever the criterion regarding recall order, the number of items recalled is likely to vary according to the number presented, even in the supraspan range. For such reasons, memory span is usually determined by presenting lists of several different lengths and ascertaining the maximum length for which recall is perfect. In the procedure typical of most mental abilities tests, list length is at first so short that perfect reproduction is virtually certain, and then is gradually increased until errors are made.

Like any other psychological measure, memory span is not entirely reliable, and is therefore a statistical concept—the sequence length for which there is an even chance of perfect reproduction. For this reason, most tests include two or three lists of each length, a specific stopping rule, and a specific averag-

ing procedure. More precise estimates, as may be needed for certain research purposes, may be obtained with the staircase, or up-and-down, method. This involves the presentation of a series of lists, the length of any given list being one more than that of the immediately preceding list if the latter was correctly reproduced and one less if it was not. Memory span is given by averaging the list lengths. In determining this average the first few lists should be disregarded because they will reflect the arbitrary length of the first list. Also, the length of what would have been the next list in the series, as given by the length and outcome for the final presented list, should be included.

Ebbinghaus's finding of seven items as the maximum length for a reproducible list provides a first approximation of memory span. Closer approximations will vary with the age of the rememberer, for span increases through childhood and declines in old age. Moreover, span varies among individuals of the same age.

Factors in Memory Span

In addition to varying among individuals, memory span varies for a given individual according to a considerable number of factors. For example, span can be increased by presenting the items at an irregular rate, so that they appear temporally grouped. Also, span for verbal items tends to be slightly greater with auditory presentation than with visual presentation. Of particular interest is the effect of the nature of the list item. The most common kind of item, especially in mental abilities testing, is the digit. Digit span is roughly one item greater than letter span, which in turn is roughly one item greater than word span. Also used as list items have been nonsense syllables (which is what Ebbinghaus used), geometric designs, and pictures of objects. One finding that has emerged from a comparison of memory span for different kinds of items is an impressive linear relation between memory span and a hypothetical "search rate," operationalized in terms of the slope of the roughly linear function that relates the time to decide whether a test, or probe, item was included in a just-presented short sequence to the length of the sequence. Specifically, a relatively small increment in decision time is incurred by increasing the length of a sequence of items of the kind that yields a relatively large memory span. Although the significance of this finding remains uncertain, it clearly raises the question of how memory span should be conceptualized.

One way of conceptualizing memory span is as a measure of the capacity of what the American psychologist and philosopher William James called primary memory. In other words, memory span can be considered as the number of items that can be held in conscious mind at any given instance. Aside from its intuitive appeal, this interpretation is supported by evidence that memory span varies according to certain characteristics of the list items that are salient in conscious experience during performance of the task. In particular, the representation of the list items in mind usually takes the form of inner speech, and memory span has been found to depend on factors that can reasonably be regarded as relevant to the spoken form of the items. Thus, span is shorter when the list items are phonemically similar to one another than when they are phonemically dissimilar (e.g., shorter for *GBVDPTZ* than for *GMRKSQY*), when the list items are phonemically lengthy than when they are phonemically short (e.g., shorter for lists of polysyllabic words than for lists of monosyllabic words), and when subjects engage in irrelevant vocalization during list presentation—an activity that is likely to suppress covert naming of the items. Other support for the idea of memory span as the product of primary memory derives from evidence that memory span for one kind of item predicts fairly well memory span for another kind of item but is a poor predictor of performance on supraspan tasks that clearly cannot be performed on the basis of primary memory.

Such supportive evidence notwithstanding, the idea that memory span measures primary memory does little to shape twenty-first-century theorizing. One reason for this is that virtually all of today's memory theorists adopt an information-processing perspective, and they give little or no consideration to the conscious realization of the mechanisms they hypothesize. A more particular reason is that primary memory has been recast as a short-term store, the capacity of which has been estimated at three or four items. This estimate, which was based on the number of items recalled from toward the end of a supraspan sequence, is appreciably smaller than memory span. One way to account for the discrepancy is to make the plausible assumption that the capacity of primary memory varies with the nature of the task and that, unlike supraspan recall tasks, the memory span task stretches primary memory to its maximum. Another possibility, supported by recent evidence, is that memory span represents primary memory supplemented by secondary memory—that is, by items that have dropped out of conscious mind and have to be recollected.

A conception of memory span more in keeping with the zeitgeist, though not inherently incompatible with the primary memory interpretation, is that it represents the amount of information that can be articulated in a certain time, variously estimated as between 1.5 and 2.0 seconds. And, indeed, items that yield long spans, such as digits, tend to be those that are articulated relatively quickly. There are, however, exceptions to this rule, leaving memory span still without a satisfactory interpretation.

Bibliography

Brener, R. (1940). An experimental investigation of memory span. *Journal of Experimental Psychology 26*, 467–482.

Brooks, J. O., III, and Watkins, M. J. (1990). Further evidence of the intricacy of memory span. *Journal of Experimental Psychology: Learning, Memory, and Cognition 16*, 1,134–1,141.

Cavanaugh, J. P. (1972). Relation between immediate memory span and the memory search rate. *Psychological Review 79*, 525–530.

Cowan, N. (2001). The magical number 4 in short-term memory: A reconsideration of mental storage capacity. *Behavioral and Brain Sciences 24*, 87–114.

Dempster, F. N. (1981). Memory span: Sources of individual and developmental differences. *Psychological Bulletin 89*, 63–100.

Guilford, J. P., and Dallenbach, K. M. (1925). The determination of memory span by the method of constant stimuli. *American Journal of Psychology 36*, 621–628.

Miyake, A., ed. (2001). Individual differences in working memory. *Journal of Experimental Psychology: General 130*, 163–237.

Schiano, D. J., and Watkins, M. J. (1981). Speech-like coding of pictures in short-term memory. *Memory & Cognition 9*, 110–114.

Schweikert, R., and Boruff, B. (1986). Short-term memory capacity: Magic number or magic spell? *Journal of Experimental Psychology: Learning, Memory, and Cognition 12*, 419–425.

Underwood, B. J., Boruch, R. F., and Malmi, R. A. (1978). Composition of episodic memory. *Journal of Experimental Psychology: General 107*, 393–419.

Michael J. Watkins

MENTAL RETARDATION (INTELLECTUAL DISABILITIES)

In any society, certain individuals fail to make normal progress in intellectual, social, and linguistic growth and development, exhibiting marked difficulties in learning. The need to distinguish these individuals led the scientific community to develop intelligence tests, as well as to create an operational definition of *mental retardation*. Mental retardation (also called *intellectual disabilities*) is defined as significantly subaverage general intellectual functioning existing concurrently with deficits in adaptive behavior, and manifested during the developmental period. Clinicians typically interpret the condition to include those individuals who obtain an IQ (intelligence quotient) score two or more standard deviations below the mean (i.e., IQ less than 70) on an intelligence measure such as the Stanford-Binet or the Wechsler Adult Intelligence Scale. Clinicians usually include two other criteria—one including deficits in everyday functioning (so-called "adaptive behavior") and onset during the childhood years (i.e., before age eighteen)—in the three-criteria definitions of mental retardation.

Within the population with mental retardation itself, researchers and clinicians have further classified individuals due to the individual's degree of intellectual impairment. Thus, persons with mental retardation have often been described as having mild (IQ 55 to 69), moderate (40 to 54), severe (25 to 39), or profound (below 25) degrees of impairment. Especially for persons with severe or profound mental retardation, most individuals also show correspondingly lower levels of functioning on a wide variety of cognitive-linguistic and everyday tasks. For individuals with mild and moderate mental retardation, however, life success (e.g., performing well at work) seems much more determined by one's personality, perseverance, socialization skills, and lack of maladaptive behaviors.

IQ-related classifications have limited utility for understanding how different intellectual abilities may or may not be connected. In particular, an overreliance on an omnibus IQ score fails to acknowledge either the composite nature of this score or perspectives on the multidimensional nature of intelligence, such as those espoused by Howard Gardner (1983) and Jerry Fodor (1983). In fact, a single IQ score (e.g., 50) may be associated with markedly different patterns of development, with one child failing to make progress on language and performing near age level on visuospatial tasks and another showing the exact opposite pattern.

Another way to classify persons with mental retardation, then, relies on the cause or etiology of one's mental retardation. From the late 1960s until the early twenty-first century, several researchers have advocated what has been called the "two-group approach" to mental retardation (Hodapp, 1997). Adherents of this approach argue that the retarded population can be divided into those whose mental retardation is due to the same polygenetic and/or environmental factors causing IQ differences within typically developing individuals (cultural-familial mental retardation) versus those whose mental retardation is caused by a specific organic insult (organic mental retardation). This entry explores the cultural-familial and organic groups in turn.

Cultural-Familial Mental Retardation

The first group is comprised of those individuals whose mental retardation has no obvious organic etiology. Scientists do not know the cause of mental disability in approximately 50 percent of persons with mental retardation. One hypothesis is that this group simply forms the lower portion of the normal, Gaussian distribution of intelligence. Why such individuals are retarded remains unclear, but some (unspecified) interaction of biological, familial, psychological, social, and environmental risks seems likely. And, if (as in nonretarded persons) approximately half of the variation in IQ scores is due to the workings of many genes, such individuals may show their lower IQ scores from having received a poor "polygenetic draw." With the success of behavior geneticists, at least one of these polygenes for intelligence has been identified (Chorney et al., 1998). Future work will tease apart the effects of genetic and various environmental factors—working separately or in tandem over time—on one's overall IQ.

Organic Mental Retardation

Organic mental retardation includes all persons whose intellectual deficits can be attributed to one or more specific organic insults. Such insults can occur before birth (as in any of the 750-plus genetic disorders associated with mental retardation); at or around the time of birth (due to anoxia, prematurity); or in the years after birth (due to meningitis, head trauma).

Since the 1990s, scientists have made much progress in mental retardation by focusing on well-defined organic syndromes, particularly those related to such genetic disorders as Down syndrome, Prader-Willi syndrome, and Williams syndrome (Dykens and Hodapp, 2001). Such research ties these forms of mental retardation to particular patterns of cognitive, linguistic, adaptive, and maladaptive deficits. In examining functioning in persons with specific genetic etiologies of mental retardation, researchers also gain insights into the structure of human intelligence. Several of the major genetic forms of mental retardation are discussed in this entry, together with presenting symptoms, characteristic cognitive deficits, explorations of their neurobiological underpinnings, and attempts at treatment.

Down Syndrome

Down syndrome (DS), trisomy 21, is the best-known form of mental retardation and the most prevalent form known to be associated with a chromosomal abnormality, occurring once in every 800 to 1,000 live births. The syndrome was identified and described in 1866 by Langdon Down, and the extra twenty-first chromosome was discovered in 1959. Since that time, Down syndrome has been the focus of intensive genetic and behavioral research. Children with DS usually have characteristic physical features including the epicanthic fold (leading to its original label, "mongolism"), a protruding tongue, short stature, and hypotonia (weak muscle tone). DS often occurs together with such medical conditions as heart defects, leukemia, and gut atresia. Although in the past individuals with DS had a short life span and were often institutionalized, medical treatments have improved their life span and they are now typically raised at home. Persons with DS have received considerable attention for educational successes that have far outstripped earlier predictions. DS may be detected during pregnancy through chorionic villus sampling, or amniocentesis; this procedure is usually recommended in women above age thirty-five, who bear a substantially higher risk of carrying a Down syndrome baby (Pueschel, 2001).

Three behavioral characteristics appear in many (possibly most) individuals with Down syndrome (Rondal, Perera, and Nadel, 1999). The first involves a specific set of cognitive-linguistic strengths and weaknesses. In various studies, persons with Down syndrome appear particularly impaired in language. Such impairments, which are more pronounced than overall levels of mental age (MA) per se, occur in linguistic grammar, in expressive (as opposed to receptive) language, and in articulation. Conversely, persons with Down syndrome often show relatively higher performance on tasks of visual short-term memory.

A second behavioral issue involves the rate of development, with children with Down syndrome developing at slower rates as they get older. Such slowings of development may relate to age-related changes or to difficulties these children have in achieving certain cognitive tasks (e.g., language). A third, possibly related change concerns Alzheimer's disease. It is known that neuropathological signs of Alzheimer's disease appear to be universal in individuals with DS by age thirty-five or forty. Geneticists continue to explore the connection of DS with Alzheimer's, and continue to learn more about pathological segments of chromosome 21 involved in overlapping conditions.

Prader-Willi Syndrome

Prader-Willi syndrome is caused by missing genetic material from the chromosome 15 derived from the father—either a deletion on the paternally derived 15 or two chromosome 15s from the mother (so-called maternal disomy). Most individuals with Prader-Willi syndrome are short in stature (about 5 feet tall in adulthood) and show extreme hyperphagia (overeating). Indeed, hyperphagia and resultant obesity have long been considered the hallmarks of Prader-Willi syndrome, and most cases of early death in the syndrome relate to obesity and its related heart and circulatory problems (Dykens and Cassidy, 1999). In addition to hyperphagia, many individuals show obsessions and compulsions that are similar in level to those with clinically diagnosed obsessive-compulsive disorder.

Intellectually, most children with Prader-Willi syndrome show relative weaknesses on tasks involving consecutive, step-by-step order in problem solving, or sequential processing. In contrast, these children perform well on tasks requiring integration and synthesis of stimuli as a unified whole, or simultaneous processing. In addition to these more general cognitive profiles, research demonstrates that many individuals with Prader-Willi syndrome exhibit particularly high-level abilities in jigsaw puzzles. Such skills, which on average are way above typical children of comparable chronological ages, are especially shown in those having the deletion—as opposed to the maternal disomy—form of this disorder.

Williams Syndrome

Williams syndrome is caused by a micro-deletion on chromosome 7. Children with this syndrome generally show a characteristic, "elfin-like" facial appearance, along with heart and other health problems (Dykens, Hodapp, and Finucane, 2000). As many as 95 percent of these children suffer from hyperacusis, or a hypersensitivity to sound. Along with an almost overly social, outgoing style of personality, children with Williams syndrome also show a wide variety of anxieties and fears. Although not every child with Williams syndrome shows any or all of these fears, the vast majority do appear to be overly fearful compared to most children with mental retardation.

Apart from these medical and psychiatric issues, scientific attention has strongly focused on the interesting—possibly unique—cognitive-linguistic profile shown by most of these children. Children with Williams syndrome show relative strengths in language; for many years researchers thought that these children might even perform at chronological age levels on a variety of linguistic tasks. Although late-twentieth-century research has found that age-appropriate performance in language occurs in only small percentages of children with Williams syndrome (Mervis, Morris, Bertrand, and Robinson, 1999), these children nevertheless show relative strengths in language, as well as in auditory processing and in some areas of music. Conversely, many children with Williams syndrome perform especially poorly on a variety of visuo-spatial tasks.

Taken together, these patterns of strengths, weaknesses, and maladaptive behaviors have led to calls for interventions that might be tailored to different etiological groups. If, for example, persons with Williams syndrome are social and show relative strengths in language, they might benefit greatly from various group and "talk" therapies (Dykens and Hodapp, 1997). In Prader-Willi syndrome, strict supervision around food and eating has historically proven effective, but various drug regimens (mainly involving growth hormone) and clinical interventions (for obsessions and compulsions) are increasingly being tried. Educationally, too, calls have recently been made for etiology-based interventions (Hodapp and Fidler, 1999). In England, for example, S. Buckley (1999) has long advocated reading instruction for children with Down syndrome. The idea is that if for most of these children visual skills are relatively strong and language skills relatively weak, then reading may help them as an entryway into language. Although few such suggestions have so far been tested, future work promises to specify etiology-based intervention proposals and to evaluate if indeed such strategies are more effective than contemporary, more generic intervention approaches.

Developmental Accounts of Mental Retardation

Despite the extreme variability of cause in retardation, various researchers have for many years examined development in children with mental retardation (see articles in Burack, Hodapp, and Zigler, 1998). Such studies have generally focused on two related topics. In the first, studies examine the *sequences* or orderings in development. With only a few exceptions, most children develop in the universal orderings of development in most cognitive and linguistic domains.

A second developmental concern relates to the *structure* of development, or the ways in which developments in various domains go together. Although individuals with cultural-familial mental retardation likely show equal or near-equal levels of abilities across a variety of cognitive-linguistic domains, such does not appear to be the case in several genetic mental retardation disorders. Thus, children with Down syndrome show worse-than-MA-level performance in linguistic grammar, those with Prader-Willi syndrome show relative strengths in simultaneous processing (and weaknesses in sequential, step-by-step processing), and those with Williams syndrome display relatively strong language and weak visuo-spatial skills. Furthermore, in many cases, this pattern of strengths and weaknesses becomes more pronounced with age, such that children showing slight patterns of strength-over-weakness at early ages show more extreme patterns as they get older.

Until the mid-1990s, some researchers felt that such patterns provided evidence for "modular" skills in several genetic mental retardation disorders. In Williams syndrome, for example, some researchers held that language occurred at normal, age-equivalent levels and was separate from other areas of cognition. Later studies have generally proven such notions to be incorrect. Specifically, only about 5 percent of children with Williams syndrome show age-equivalent levels of language, and language, while a relative strength, appears connected to at least certain other cognitive abilities. Thus, in Williams syndrome (as with typically developing children), abilities in auditory short-term memory are strongly related with abilities in linguistic grammar. Such studies, which continue in many of these syndromes, promise to tell researchers both about strengths and weaknesses and inter-domain connections within each specific syndrome, as well how various aspects of cognition and language might be organized in nonretarded persons.

Bibliography

Buckley, S. (1999). Promoting the cognitive development of children with Down syndrome: The practical implications of recent psychological research. In J. A. Rondal, J. Perera, and L. Nadel, eds., *Down's syndrome: A review of current knowledge.* London: Whurr Publishers Ltd.

Burack, J. A., Hodapp, R. M., and Zigler, E., eds. (1998). *Handbook of mental retardation and development.* Cambridge, UK: Cambridge University Press.

Chorney, M. J., Chorney, K., Seese, N., Owen, M. J., Daniels, J., McGuffin, P., Thompson, L. A., Detterman, D. K., Benbow, C., Lubinski, D., Eley, T., and Plomin, R. (1998). A quantitative trait locus associated with cognitive ability in children. *Psychological Science 9*, 159–166.

Dykens, E. M., and Cassidy, S. B. (1999). Prader-Willi syndrome. In S. Goldstein and C. R. Reynolds, eds., *Handbook of neurodevelopmental and genetic disorders in children.* New York: Guilford Press.

Dykens, E. M., and Hodapp, R. M. (1997). Treatment issues in genetic mental retardation syndromes. *Professional Psychology: Research and Practice 28* (3), 263–270.

—— (2001). Research in mental retardation: Toward an etiologic approach. *Journal of Child Psychology and Psychiatry and Allied Disciplines 42*, 49–71.

Dykens, E. M., Hodapp, R. M., and Finucane, B. (2000). *Genetics and mental retardation syndromes: A new look at behavior and intervention.* Baltimore, MD: Paul H. Brookes Publishers.

Fodor, J. (1983). *Modularity of mind: An essay on faculty psychology.* Cambridge, MA: MIT Press.

Gardner, H. (1983). *Frames of mind.* New York: Basic Books.

Hodapp, R. M. (1997). Developmental approaches to children with disabilities: New perspectives, populations, prospects. In S. S. Luthar, J. A. Burack, D. Cicchetti, and J. R. Weisz, eds., *Developmental psychopathology: Perspectives on adjustment, risk and disorder.* Cambridge, UK: Cambridge University Press.

Hodapp, R. M., and Fidler, D. J. (1999). Special education and genetics: Connections for the 21st century. *Journal of Special Education 22*, 130–137.

Mervis, C. B., Morris, C. A., Bertrand, J. M., and Robinson, B. F. (1999). Williams syndrome: Findings from an integrated program of research. In H. Tager-Flusberg, ed., *Neurodevelopmental disorders: Contributions to a framework from the cognitive sciences.* Cambridge, MA: MIT Press.

Pueschel, S. M., ed. (2001). *A parent's guide to Down syndrome,* rev. edition. Baltimore, MD: Paul H. Brookes.

Rondal, J., Perera, J., and Nadel, L., eds. (1999). *Down syndrome: A review of current knowledge.* London: Whurr.

Robert M. Hodapp

METACOGNITION ABOUT MEMORY

Metacognition about memory, sometimes called metamemory, refers to the self-monitoring and self-control of one's own memory in the acquisition and retrieval of information. It is a relatively new topic, having been investigated by psychologists for approximately forty years. Before then, researchers viewed learners as passive, as blank slates onto which new ideas were etched through repetition. By contrast, subsequent researchers viewed the learner as an active controller of his or her learning, whether acquiring new or retrieving old information. Moreover, researchers now know that people can monitor their progress during both learning and retrieval.

For example, imagine a student who is studying for an examination that will occur tomorrow in French class, say on French-English vocabulary such as "*chateau*/castle" and "*rouge*/red." Let us keep that student in mind as we consider the monitoring and the control of the student's learning of the new vocabulary and his or her attempts to retrieve the answers during the test the next day.

A theoretical framework that integrates all of these processes into an overall system can be found in Nelson and Narens (1990).

Different kinds of monitoring processes can be distinguished in terms of when they occur in the learning/retrieval sequence and whether they pertain to the person's future performance (in which case the focus is said to be on prospective monitoring) or to the person's past performance (in which case the focus is said to be on retrospective monitoring).

Prospective Monitoring

Ease-of-Learning Judgment

The first metamemory judgment made by someone who is getting ready to learn new information occurs before learning begins. This ease-of-learning judgment is the person's evaluation of how easy or difficult the items will be to learn. For instance, the person might believe that the overall set of items will take a given amount of time to learn and that *chateau*/castle will be more difficult to learn that *rouge*/red. Underwood (1966) first showed that people are moderately accurate—not perfectly accurate but well above chance—at predicting which items will be easiest or hardest to learn. People's predictions of how easy it will be to learn each item, made in advance of learning, are moderately correlated (i.e., covaried) with their subsequent recall after a constant amount of study time on every item.

Judgments of Learning

The next kind of monitoring occurs during and/or at the end of learning. The person's judgment of learning is the evaluation of how well he or she has learned a given item; it is a prediction of the likelihood that the item will be recalled correctly on a future test. The psychologists Arbuckle and Cuddy (1969) first showed that the predictive accuracy of people's judgment of learning is above chance but far from perfect, like ease-of-learning judgments. Research by Leonesio and Nelson (1990) has shown, hwoever, that judgments of learning are more accurate than ease-of-learning judgments for predicting eventual recall; this is probably because the judgments of learning—but not ease-of-learning judgments—can be based in part on what the learner notices about how well he or she is mastering the items during learning.

Research by Nelson and Dunlosky (1991) showed a case in which judgments of learning are especially accurate: when they are made after a filled delay of at least thirty seconds following the offset of study of an item. This phenomenon, in which the accuracy of judgment of learning in predicting future recall is nearly perfect, is known as the delayed JOL effect.

Feeling-of-Knowing Judgments

These judgments are people's prediction of whether they will eventually remember an answer that they do not now recall. This was the first kind of metamemory judgment to be examined in the laboratory. The pioneering researcher, Hart (1965), found that these feeling-of-knowing judgments were somewhat accurate in predicting subsequent memory performance. The subsequent likelihood of correctly recognizing a nonrecalled answer was higher for nonrecalled items that people said were stored in their memory than for those reported as not stored in memory. However, as in the case of other metamemory judgments, the accuracy of this judgment was far from perfect; people often did not recognize answers they had claimed they would recognize, and they sometimes recognized those they thought they would not. The accuracy of predicting other kinds of memory performance (e.g., ease of relearning) on nonrecalled items was subsequently reviewed and investigated by Nelson, Gerler, and Narens (1984), who also offered several theoretical explanations for how people might make their feeling-of-knowing judgments.

Retrospective Confidence Judgments

In contrast to attempts by people to predict their future memory performance, retrospective confidence judgments occur after the venturing of the answer—whether correct or incorrect—and pertain to degrees of confidence in the correctness of the answer. For instance, if our hypothetical student were asked to recall the English equivalent of *chateau*, the person might say "castle" (correct answer) or might say "red" (incorrect answer); then he or she would make a confidence judgment about the likelihood that the recalled answer was correct. Fischhoff, Slovic, and Lichtenstein (1977) found that retrospective confidence judgments were substantially accurate but often marred by overconfidence. For instance, for those items to which people had given a confidence judgment of "80 percent likely to be correct," the actual percentage of correct recognition was much lower than 80 percent.

This overconfidence occurs primarily for confidence judgments made for individual items. Confidence judgments can also be made for a list of items (e.g., "How many of the fifty items on the test did you recall correctly?"), which is labeled an aggregate confidence judgment. Griffin and Tversky (1992) reported that aggregate confidence judgments are usually less overconfident (and sometimes even underconfident), a phenomenon known as the aggregation effect.

Control

Not only can people monitor their progress during learning and retrieval, but they can also control many aspects of their learning and retrieval. First, we will consider aspects they can control during self-paced learning, and then we will consider aspects they can control during retrieval.

Control During Self-Paced Learning

Allocation of Self-Paced Study Time During Learning. Our hypothetical student who is learning foreign-language vocabulary can choose to allocate large or small amounts of study time to each item and subsequently can allocate extra study time to some items. Moreover, as shown by Bisanz, Vesonder, and Voss (1978), the allocation of study time may be made in conjunction with the judgments of learning described above. In an investigation of learners of various ages, Bisanz and colleagues discovered that learners in the early years of primary school might make accurate judgments of learning but would not use those judgments when allocating additional study time across the items, whereas slightly older children would use those judgments when allocating additional study time. In particular, the older children allocated extra study time to items that they believed they had learned but not to those that they believed they had not learned. By contrast, the younger children were not systematic in allocating extra study time primarily to unlearned items.

Even adults do not always allocate more study time to more difficult items. Son and Metcalfe (2000) have shown that when there is insufficient time to study all items, subjects may allocate the most study time to easier items. For instance, if our hypothetical student judged his or her learning to be greater for *rouge*/red than for *chateau*/castle, then, if he or she had unlimited study time, that knowledge should result in extra study time for it than for *rouge*/red. If study time were limited, the student might allocate more time to *chateau*/castle than to *rouge*/red, perhaps reasoning that this strategy would enhance performance, though Son and Metcalfe's (2000) research shows no evidence that this strategy aids test performance.

Strategy Employed During Self-Paced Study. Not only can people control how much study time they allocate to various items (as discussed in the previous paragraph), but they can also control which strategy they employ during that study time. For many kinds of learning, there are strategies that are more effective than rote repetition. For instance, a mnemonic strategy for learning foreign-language vocabulary was investigated by Pressley, Levin, and Ghatala (1984). After people had learned some foreign-language vocabulary by rote and other foreign-language vocabulary by the mnemonic strategy, they were given a choice of using whichever strategy they wanted for a final trial of learning some additional foreign-language vocabulary. Only 12 percent of adults chose the mnemonic strategy if they had not received any test trial during the earlier learning phase, whereas 87 percent chose the mnemonic strategy if they had received test trials during the earlier learning phase. Apparently, people should have test trials to help them realize the effectiveness of different strategies for learning. Moreover, getting children to adopt the mnemonic strategy spontaneously required test trials during the earlier learning phase. The children also needed to have feedback after those test trials to tell them how well they had done on the rote-learned items versus the mnemonic-learned items.

Control During Retrieval

Control of Initiating One's Retrieval. Immediately after a questions is posed, before someone memory for the answer, he or she makes a metamemory decision about whether the answer is likely to be found in memory. For instance, if you were asked the telephone number of the president of the United States, you probably would decide immediately that the answer is not in your memory. Notice that you do not need to search through all the telephone numbers that you know, nor do you need to search through all the information you have stored in your memory about the president. You probably realize that the president does have a telephone number, but you know you don't know it, and therefore you don't initiate attempts to retrieve that answer. Consider how different that situation is from one in which you are asked the telephone number of one of your friends.

This initial feeling-of-knowing judgment that precedes an attempt to retrieve an answer was investigated by Reder (1987). She found that people were faster at making a feeling-of-knowing decision about whether they knew the answer to a general-information question (e.g., "What is the capital of Finland?") than they were at answering the question (e.g., saying "Helsinki"). This finding demonstrates that the metamemory decision is made before, not after, the retrieval of the answer. If and only if people feel that they know the answer will they initiate attempts to retrieve the answer from memory. When they feel that they do not know the answer, they don't even attempt to search memory (as in the example of the president's telephone number).

Control of the Termination of Extended Attempts at Retrieval. People may initially feel strongly enough that they know an answer to begin searching memory for it, but after fruitless extended attempts at retrieval, they will terminate the search. Nelson, Gerler, and Narens (1984) found that people would search longer for a sought-but-not-retrieved answer if they felt strongly that they knew the answer. Put differently, the amount of time that elapses before someone gives up searching memory for a nonretrieved answer tends to increase with the degree of the feeling that the person knows the answer.

For example, our hypothetical student mentioned above might spend a long time during the examination attempting to retrieve the English equivalent of *chateau* (which the person had studied the night before) but little or no time attempting to retrieve the English equivalent of *cheval* (which the person did not study previously). The metamemory decision to continue or terminate attempts at retrieving an answer from memory may also be affected by other factors, such as the total amount of time available during an examination.

Bibliography

Arbuckle, T. Y., and Cuddy, L. L. (1969). Discrimination of item strength at time of presentation. *Journal of Experimental Psychology 81*, 126–131.

Bisanz, G. L., Vesonder, G. T., and Voss, J. F. (1978). Knowledge of one's own responding and the relation of such knowledge to learning. *Journal of Experimental Child Psychology 25*, 116–128.

Fischhoff, B., Slovic, P., and Lichtenstein, S. (1977). Knowing with certainty: The appropriateness of extreme confidence. *Journal of Experimental Psychology: Human Perception and Performance 3*, 552–564.

Griffin, D., and Tversky, A. (1992). The weighing of evidence and the determinants of confidence. *Cognitive Psychology 24*, 411–435.

Hart, J. T. (1965). Memory and the feeling-of-knowing experience. *Journal of Educational Psychology 56*, 208–216.

Leonesio, R. J., and Nelson T. O. (1990). Do different measures of metamemory tap the same underlying aspects of memory? *Journal of Experimental Psychology: Learning, Memory, and Cognition 16*, 464–470.

Nelson, T. O., and Dunlosky, J. (1991). When people's judgments of learning (JOLs) are extremely accurate at predicting subsequent recall: The "Delayed-JOL Effect." *Psychological Science 2*, 267–270.

Nelson, T. O., Gerler, D., and Narens, L. (1984). Accuracy of feeling-of-knowing judgment for predicting perceptual identification and relearning. *Journal of Experimental Psychology: General 113*, 282–300.

Nelson, T. O., and Narens, L. (1984). Metamemory: A theoretical framework and some new findings. In G. H. Bower, ed., *The psychology of learning and motivation*. San Diego, CA: Academic Press.

Pressley, M., Levin, J. R., and Ghatala, E. (1984). Memory strategy monitoring in adults and children. *Journal of Verbal Learning and Verbal Behavior 23*, 270–288.

Reder, L. M. (1987). Strategy selection in question answering. *Cognitive Psychology 19*, 90–138.

Son, L. K., and Metcalfe, J. (2000). Metacognitive and control strategies in study-time allocation. *Journal of Experimental Psychology: Learning: Memory and Cognition 26*, 204–221.

Underwood, B. J. (1966). Individual and group predictions of item difficulty for free learning. *Journal of Experimental Psychology 71*, 673–679.

Thomas O. Nelson
Revised by Thomas O. Nelson and Petra Scheck

METAPLASTICITY

Most neural connections exhibit synaptic plasticity, increases or decreases in synaptic efficacy. Several distinct forms of synaptic plasticity exist, differing in both their induction requirements and time course of expression. Synaptic plasticity allows for dynamic modification of neural circuitry that can act on time scales ranging from milliseconds to potentially lifetimes, and has been implicated in a wide range of neural and behavioral phenomena including learning and memory. A body of literature has developed demonstrating that the ability to induce synaptic plasticity is itself modifiable; that is, plasticity is plastic. This is referred to as metaplasticity, a higher-order form of synaptic plasticity. Metaplasticity's critical feature is that, once instantiated, it modifies the ability of subsequent activity to alter synaptic efficacy, fundamentally altering the rules that govern when and how changes are expressed.

Metaplasticity has been observed in a variety of brain systems and across different species, suggesting that it may be a ubiquitous feature of synaptic operation. Of particular interest, metaplasticity is observed in brain structures that have been implicated in learning and memory (e.g., hippocampus, amygdala, cortex), suggesting that it may play a key role in the regulation of information processing. A state of metaplasticity can be created by the same factors that can induce plasticity itself: the intrinsic activity of a neuron (homosynaptic factors) as well as through the actions of hormones and neuromodulators (heterosynaptic factors). To distinguish between these two causal factors, a distinction can be made between activity-dependent metaplasticity, which refers to states created homosynaptically; and modulatory metaplasticity, which refers to states created heterosynaptically.

Activity-Dependent Metaplasticity

The intrinsic activity of a neuron has long been known to result in synaptic plasticity. The duration of the induced change, as well as the type of plasticity involved, depends upon the frequency, duration, and pattern of activity. For example, high frequency activation can produce long-term potentiation (LTP), an enhancement of synaptic strength that can last for hours. LTP has emerged as a leading cellular mechanism underlying learning, and is perhaps best characterized in the hippocampus. It is now understood that the ability to induce LTP is not a static feature of hippocampal neurons, but instead is strongly influenced by the recent activation history of the neuron. For example, a low frequency priming burst, which is insufficient for producing LTP, was found to increase the subsequent activity requirements for inducing LTP. This effect was transient, synapse-specific, and depended (as does LTP) on postsynaptic N-methyl-D-aspartate receptor (NMDAR) activation.

It is now understood that the induction of plasticity at hippocampal synapses is more complex than first appreciated. Depending upon the activity of the neuron, the expression of plasticity can be bidirectional, either exhibiting a long-term enhancement (LTP), or a long-term decrement (long-term depression; LTD). For example, 900 pulses at 1-3 Hz produces LTD, 900 pulses at 10 Hz results in no lasting change, and 900 pulses at 50 Hz produced LTP. These effects are blocked by the application of an NMDA receptor antagonist, suggesting a relatively straightforward relationship between the activity of a presynaptic neuron, postsynaptic Ca^{++} entry, and the direction of change. These data suggest the existence of a crossover point, where activity below this point produces LTD, activity at this point (e.g., 10 Hz) produces no change, and activity above this point produces LTP. This crossover point is represented as the modification threshold theta (θ_m) proposed as a theoretical neural plasticity algorithm in artificial neural networks in what is now commonly known as the *BCM rule*.

An important theoretical feature of θ_m is that it represents a sliding modification threshold, the level of which depends on the recent average activity of the synapse. This has been confirmed experimentally in the hippocampus, where prior activation of a synapse was found to modify activity thresholds for LTP and LTD (i.e., modify θ_m). For example, high frequency priming stimuli increases the threshold activity level required for LTP (modifies θ_m due to an increase in average activity), making it less likely that LTP will be induced and in parallel increasing the ability to induce LTD. Conversely, low frequency priming stimuli modifies θ_m to decrease the threshold activity requirement for LTP; thus reducing the probability of LTD. A behavioral means of altering θ_m was demonstrated in the developing visual cortex by Bear and Rittenhouse. In these experiments, early visual deprivation (which would decrease the average activity of cortical neurons) facilitated the induction of LTP compared to light-reared animals of similar age. These effects were reversed by as little as two days of visual experience, demonstrating the importance of neural activity in adjusting the modification threshold.

The underlying cellular mechanisms regulating plasticity are only partially understood. One possibility is that Ca^{++} entry during NMDAR activation may activate a molecular cascade leading to an alteration of the NMDAR itself. Because the NMDAR is a critical point of calcium entry into the postsynaptic neuron, these changes would significantly alter the properties of activity-dependent synaptic plasticity. In addition to signaling through the NMDAR, activation of *metabotropic glutamate receptors* (mGluRs) has also been shown to induce metaplasticity. For example, activation of group one mGluRs has been shown to facilitate LTP. The effects of group two mGluRs seem more complex, with reports of group two mGluR activation facilitating the induction of LTD in the dentate gyrus in vivo, but inhibiting LTD and facilitating LTP in area CA1 of the hippocampus in vitro. Thus, it appears that there are multiple regulatory mechanisms underlying activity-dependent metaplasticity, suggesting that there may be multiple modes of control over long-term synaptic plasticity.

Two possible functions for activity-dependent metaplasticity have been proposed. First, it may provide a mechanism to promote stability within a neural network by maintaining synaptic parameters within some optimal operating range. For example, increased levels of activity (which lead to enhanced synaptic efficacy) would concurrently raise the threshold for subsequent enhancement, thus applying a brake on facilitation. This would prevent saturation of the neural network at some ceiling level. Further, the sliding threshold would lead to the promotion of synaptic decrement, perhaps providing a means for resetting synaptic weights within a network. Conversely, low activity at a synapse would slide θ_m in the opposite direction, promoting synaptic enhancement and preventing saturation at some floor level. Second, metaplasticity may provide a functional means for integrating neural activity over extended periods of time. This function may have an especially important role in regulating synaptic connectivity in development, allowing experience occurring over extended periods of time to exert top-down control over the refinement of synaptic connectivity.

Modulatory Metaplasticity

Modulatory metaplasticity is the regulation of synaptic plasticity through the actions of extrinsic factors such as neuromodulators and hormones. It is important to distinguish modulatory metaplasticity from the myriad number of other effects that neuromodulators can have on the process of synaptic communication. Modulatory metaplasticity refers to the regulation of the induction of synaptic plasticity. It differs from a more generalized modulatory scaling of synaptic efficacy, which would affect all aspects of synaptic transmission and plasticity in equal fashion. A second characteristic of this form of metaplasticity is that it does not require the activity of the synapse whose plasticity is being regulated. This feature distinguishes modulatory metaplasticity from the activity-dependent forms described above.

A primary example of modulatory metaplasticity has been described in the synaptic regulation of the *defensive siphon withdrawal reflex* (SWR) in the marine invertebrate *Aplysia*. The SWR is subject to multiple forms of regulation including a dynamic form based upon the recent tactile experience of the animal. For example, a local water disturbance (turbulence) can produce a transient inhibition of the SWR that is a consequence of an elevation of reflex threshold, essentially increasing the signal requirement for reflex initiation in the face of greater environmental noise. This form of behavioral regulation can be mediated by an activity-dependent form of synaptic enhancement called short-term plasticity (STP) that is expressed by identified inhibitory interneurons in response to tactile stimulation. This transient elevation of inhibitory synaptic strength reduces the ability to activate excitatory interneurons in the SWR circuit; thus imposing a requirement for greater sensory input in order to activate these neurons (and subsequently the reflex). That specific forms of STP expressed by these inhibitory neurons could be significantly suppressed by tail shock and the subsequent release of serotonin was an important finding. This regulation of STP had direct behavioral consequences: Following tail shock, the same tactile experience that normally produced reflex inhibition instead resulted in either no change or a trend towards reflex enhancement. Thus modifying the capacity for STP fundamentally altered a basic regulatory response normally exhibited by the animal.

Stress and Metaplasticity

A rapidly growing body of literature demonstrates that behavioral stress can regulate LTP and serve as an example of modulatory metaplasticity in the mammalian brain. Studies have demonstrated that acute and severe behavioral stress (e.g., by restraining and shocking the animal) produces a marked impairment of LTP. Interestingly, the same stress that blocked the induction of LTP facilitates the induction of LTD, suggesting that stress may in fact be capable of modifying θ_m. Consistent with this, more mildly stressful situations can in fact produce a facilitation of LTP, suggesting that the level of stress is analogous to the level of average activity in determining the direction of θ_m modification. Prime candidates for mediating these effects of stress on synaptic plasticity are the corticosteroids released by the adrenal cortex in times of stress. The hippocampus contains an abundance of corticosteroid receptors which are of two types: (1) a high-affinity *mineralocorticoid receptor* (MR); and (2) a lower-affinity *glucocorticoid receptor* (GR). Differential binding to these receptor types may underlie the differential effects of mild and severe stress. MR agonists facilitate LTP, whereas GR agonists impair LTP and facilitate the induction of LTD. Therefore low levels of corticosteroids would primarily act through the high-affinity MR receptor and facilitate LTP, with higher levels leading to greater activation of the GR receptor leading to suppression of LTP.

The cellular mechanism underlying this form of modulatory metaplasticity may be similar to that of activity-dependent metaplasticity, in that both appear to involve Ca^{++} influx into the postsynaptic cell. Corticosteroids have been shown to induce a rise in Ca^{++} influx, the levels of which may depend upon levels of corticosteroids. In a similar fashion as proposed for activity-dependent metaplasticity, low levels of Ca^{++} entry produced by mild stress may lead to a functional shift in θ_m leading to a promotion of LTP, whereas more severe stress results in greater levels of Ca^{++} entry that shifts θ_m in the opposite direction, impairing LTP and promoting LTD. Thus an extrinsic modulator may regulate plasticity in fundamentally the same way as was observed with intrinsic activity. It is important to note that other factors besides the corticosteroids have been implicated in stress-induced regulation of LTP, including the cytokine inter-leukin-1beta and endogenous opioids.

Conclusion

It is now understood that the ability to induce many different forms of synaptic plasticity is not a static feature of a neuron, but is regulated both by the recent activity history of the synapse, as well as by the presence of a number of neuromodulators. While the detailed means by which regulation is achieved can be diverse, most seem to share a common feature in that they act through the same signaling pathways that induce plasticity, most notably through Ca++ signaling in the neuron. The apparent complexity of regulation poses a fundamental challenge in trying to relate synaptic events to behavioral output, because the direction of plasticity and even the capacity for induction may vary based upon a number of intervening factors. Clearly, metaplasticity endows the nervous system with additional degrees of freedom in the dynamic regulation of neural circuits and systems, adding yet another dimension to the already remarkable complexity of the brain.

See also: STRESS AND MEMORY

Bibliography

Abraham, W. C., and Bear, M. F. (1996). Metaplasticity: The plasticity of synaptic plasticity. *Trends in Neuroscience 19*, 126–130.

Bear, M. F., and Rittenhouse, C. D. (1999). Molecular basis for induction of ocular dominance plasticity. *Journal of Neurobiology 41*, 83–91.

Bienenstock, E. L., Cooper, L. N., and Munro, P. W. (1982). Theory for the development of neuron selectivity: Orientation specificity and binocular interaction in visual cortex. *Journal of Neuroscience 2*, 32–48.

de Kloet, E. R., Oitzl, M. S., and Joels, M. (1999). Stress and cognition: Are corticosteroids good or bad guys? *Trends in Neuroscience 22*, 422–426.

Dudek, S. M., and Bear, M. F. (1992). Homosynaptic long-term depression in area CA1 of hippocampus and effects of N-methyl-D-aspartate receptor blockade. *Proceedings of the National Academy of Sciences of the United States of America 89*, 4,363–4,367.

Fischer, T. M., Blazis, D. E., Priver, N. A., and Carew, T. J. (1997). Metaplasticity at identified inhibitory synapses in *Aplysia*. *Nature 389*, 860–865.

Huang, Y. Y., Colino, A., Selig, D. K., and Malenka, R. C. (1992). The influence of prior synaptic activity on the induction of long-term potentiation. *Science 255*, 730–733.

Kim, J. J., and Yoon, K. S. (1998). Stress: Metaplastic effects in the hippocampus. *Trends in Neuroscience 21*, 505–59.

Kirkwood, A., Rioult, M. C., and Bear, M. F. (1996). Experience-dependent modification of synaptic plasticity in visual cortex. *Nature 381*, 526–528.

Quinlan, E. M., Olstein, D. H., and Bear, M. F. (1999). Bidirectional, experience-dependent regulation of N-methyl-D-aspartate receptor subunit composition in the rat visual cortex during postnatal development. *Proceedings of the National Academy of Sciences of the United States of America 96*, 12,876–12,880.

Thomas J. Carew
Thomas M. Fischer

MIGRATION, NAVIGATION, AND HOMING

The prevailing view among behavioral biologists and ethologists of the 1950s was that the remarkable ability of migratory animals, especially birds, to return to the same breeding and wintering area year after year was based on innate mechanisms of orientation and navigation. Later this emphasis on hereditary control yielded to more dynamic conceptualizations of spatial-behavior mechanisms. The revised theory assigns a larger role to environmental influences and learning—experience-dependent change in behavior—in animal orientation and navigation.

Orientation

Orientation refers to a heading or directed movement that bears a specific spatial relationship to some environmental or proprioceptive reference. It is typically discussed metaphorically in terms of compass directions when the sun, stars, or the earth's magnetic field are used as orientation stimuli. Birds that migrate at night use all three of these environmental stimuli to orient their seasonal movements. Nocturnal migrants show an impressive ability to vary their response in accordance with changes of information from one orientation stimulus to another. For example, several species of birds have been shown to change their response based on experience with different ambient magnetic fields. Wiltschko and Wiltschko found that shifting the orientation of an ambient magnetic field resulted in birds' correspondingly shifting their migratory orientation. The birds likewise shifted their orientation with respect to the stars, which were not subjected to experimental shifting. This behavior suggests that birds could learn a new orientation response to the stars by using the magnetic field as a calibrating reference. Bingman and Wiltschko described similar results in birds of another species that learned a new orientation response to the setting sun based on their magnetic field experience.

But the earth's magnetic field is not always the primary calibrating orientation stimulus. Able and Able found that in one species orientation to the earth's magnetic field varied with information gleaned from celestial cues. These findings demonstrate that the migratory orientation of birds is modifiable by experience and hence, to that extent, learned.

The results described above were taken from experiments with birds that had already experienced at least one migration. Work with birds prior to their first migration has revealed that experience during their first summer may have an even larger effect on subsequent migratory behavior. Evidence suggests that migrant birds are born with an inherited disposition to orient in a particular direction with respect to the axis of celestial rotation and the earth's magnetic field. Emlen has shown that to learn a migratory-orientation response to specific star patterns, birds rely on the rotation of the night sky about its axis as a directional reference. Once directional information from celestial rotation is transferred to the star patterns during the birds' first summer, they can use the patterns as an independent source of directional information.

Surprisingly, the inherited migratory-orientation response to the earth's magnetic field can vary with a bird's first summer experience. Bingman (1983) found that varying magnetic-field experiences during the summer resulted in birds' learning different autumn migratory-orientation responses to the earth's magnetic field. The advantage of being able to change the innate orientation preference to the earth's magnetic field is that birds raised in areas of different magnetic field declination (the angular difference between magnetic north and geographic north) are still able to maintain both seasonally and geographically appropriate migratory orientation. Able and Able found that celestial rotation is the reference used by young birds to override their innate orientation response to the earth's magnetic field and learn a new response better suited to reaching their winter homes. Like experienced birds, young birds who have yet to engage in their first migration manifest learned changes in orientation behavior based on interpreting the directional relationships among a variety of environmental stimuli.

Birds are unique neither in their highly directed movements nor in their ability to learn new orientation responses. From its birth, the beachhopper (*Talitrus saltator*), a small crustacean that inhabits the shoreline of the Mediterranean, displays an orientation response to the sun that enables it to quickly move perpendicular to the shoreline axis in order to avoid danger. Ugolini and Macchi have shown that exposing young animals to a different environment can modify this innate orientation response. This is another example of altered orientation based on learning the spatial relationship among salient environmental stimuli, in this case sun and shoreline.

Navigation

Homing is the ability of an animal to return to some goal location or "home." *Navigation* is the range of spatial behavior mechanisms that facilitate homing. Traditionally, true navigation has encompassed both the ability to specify one's location in space relative to an undetectable goal location and the subsequent ability to determine a goal-oriented directional bearing.

The spatial orientation evinced by migratory birds does not necessarily involve true navigation, as was shown in Perdeck's experiments. Perdeck captured and marked thousands of starlings (*Sturnus vulgaris*) that were migrating through the Netherlands in autumn. The birds were then transported to Switzerland and released. An examination of the locations where the birds were subsequently recaptured revealed an important difference between adults that had already experienced one migration cycle and young birds that were migrating for the first time. Adult starlings were recovered primarily northwest of the release point. The northwesterly orientation corresponded to the direction needed to reach the birds' normal wintering homes near the northern coast of France. Therefore, the adults displayed true navigational behavior—they succeeded in determining a course from an unfamiliar location that brought them close to their traditional wintering quarters. Young birds, in contrast, were recovered primarily southwest of the release point. The southwesterly orientation corresponded to the direction required to reach the birds' winter homes from the area from which they were captured but not from the release location. Although displaying good orientation, the young birds failed to orient in a manner consistent with goal-directed, true navigation.

In addition to emphasizing the difference between orientation and navigation, Perdeck's results demonstrate the importance of experiential learning in at least some aspects of avian navigation toward a goal location. Young birds that had never been to the wintering area could not navigate a course to it. Young birds on their first migration appear to employ vector navigation, an innate disposition to fly in a certain direction for a fixed period of time in order to arrive in the general vicinity of their population's wintering range. However, it is only after experiencing their winter home that they develop the ability to navigate to it from unfamiliar locations. It appears that a similar learning process supports the ability of birds to navigate to and recognize the same breeding site year after year.

Salmon evince a similar aptitude for learning in returning to breed in their natal stream, as has been well documented by Cooper et al., who placed young coho salmon (*Oncorhynchus kisutch*) in a tank of water containing a specific odorant. They marked the fish and later released them into Lake Michigan. They then placed the odorant at the mouth of one stream that feeds into the lake. Sometime later, as the fish began to enter streams for breeding, the fish that had been exposed to the odorant in the tank were much more likely to enter the specially odorized stream. The fish apparently learned the characteristic odor of their stream during early development and used that information to guide their return home.

Perhaps the best-studied navigational system in animals is that of the homing pigeon. A number of distinct spatial-behavior mechanisms, nearly all of them influenced by environmental experience, govern pigeon homing. To orient in space, homing pigeons prefer to rely on the sun, but they can also have recourse to the earth's magnetic field. Wiltschko and Wiltschko have shown that sun orientation is not innate but depends on a young bird's learning the sun's path across the sky. Although they further reported that pigeons could learn to use the sun for orientation only during intervals of direct exposure to the sun, Budzynski et al. have shown that when young pigeons, like bees and other animal groups, are allowed to experience the sun for only one part of the day, that experience is sufficient for them to use the sun for orientation at any time of day.

Pigeons rely on at least two navigational mechanisms: a navigational map that they can use from distant locations where they have never been before, and landmark navigation, which they can use when they are in sensory contact with familiar environmental stimuli. In some young pigeons the ability to learn a navigational map depends on the opportunity to associate atmospheric odors with wind directions. Using fans to alter the relationship between wind direction and atmospheric odors experienced by different groups of young pigeons, Ioalé et al. raised pigeons that learned navigational maps that varied with the birds' experience of odors and wind direction.

Landmark navigation is similarly dependent on experience. Wallraff has shown that young birds confined to an outdoor aviary are able to learn a navigational map, as evidenced by their ability to orient toward home when released from a distant, unfamiliar location. Such birds are nonetheless impaired in returning home because of an inability to navigate in the vicinity of their home aviary. The lack of opportunity to fly outside their aviary rendered them unable to learn to navigate by familiar landmarks, which is important for navigation near home. Gagliardo et al. have shown that landmark navigation is at least partially based on visual information. Although the two

navigational systems seem to be parts of a single learning mechanism, Ioalé et al. (for the navigational map) and Gagliardo et al. (for landmark navigation) have shown that brain lesions to the hippocampus can impair navigational map and landmark navigation under some training conditions but not others. The implications of the hippocampus research is that there is more than one kind of navigational map and more than one type of landmark navigation differing at least in the neural mechanisms that support their acquisition.

Like orientation, learning in navigation is not unique to vertebrates. Gould has shown that honey bees (*Apis mellifera*) can learn a familiar landmark map in a manner similar to that of homing pigeons and that they are able to use this map from locations where they have never been before as long as they can maintain sensory contact with familiar landmarks.

What is remarkable about naturally occurring spatial learning is that it often occurs in the absence of any tangible external reward. For example, what is rewarding about associating atmospheric odors with wind direction to a young pigeon enclosed in an outdoor aviary? What is rewarding about learning the sun's path? It is difficult to explain such phenomena without assuming that animals are biologically predisposed to learn spatial relationships among environmental stimuli in a rapid and efficient way without dependence on environmental reinforcement. Natural selection has seemingly endowed animals with nervous systems that predispose intrinsic reinforcement of exploration. A spontaneous proclivity to explore, therefore, is a crucial element in most learned spatial behavior.

See also: SPATIAL LEARNING: ANIMALS

Bibliography

Able, K., and Able, M. (1990). Calibration of the magnetic compass of a migratory bird by celestial rotation. *Nature* 347, 378–380.
——— (1995). Interaction in the flexible orientation system of a migratory bird. *Nature* 364, 230–232.
Baker, R. (1984). *Bird navigation: The solution of a mystery*. London: Houder and Stoughton.
Berthold, P. (2001). *Bird migration: A general survey*. Oxford: Oxford University Press.
Bingman, V. (1983). Magnetic field orientation of migratory Savannah sparrows with different first summer experience. *Behaviour* 87, 43–53.
Bingman, V., and Wiltschko, W. (1988). Orientation of dunnocks (*Prunella modularis*) at sunset. *Ethology* 7, 1–9.
Budzynski, C., Dyer, F., and Bingman, V. (2000). Partial experience with the sun's arc is sufficient for all day sun compass orientation in homing pigeons, *Columba livia*. *Journal of Experimental Biology* 203, 2,341–2,348.
Cooper, J., Scholz, A., Horrall, R., Hasler, A., and Madison, D. (1976). Experimental confirmation of the olfactory hypothesis with artificially imprinted homing coho salmon (*Oncorhynchus kisutch*). *Journal of the Fisheries Resources Board of Canada* 33, 703–710.

Emlen, S. (1970). Celestial rotation: Its importance in the development of migratory orientation. *Science 170,* 1,198–1,201.

Gagliardo, A., Ioalé, P., and Bingman, V. (1999). Homing in pigeons: The role of the hippocampal formation in the representation of landmarks used for navigation. *Journal of Neuroscience 19,* 311–315.

Gagliardo, A., Odetti, F., and Ioalé, P. (2001). Relevance of visual cues for orientation at familiar sites by homing pigeons: An experiment in a circular arena. *Proceedings of the Royal Society of London. 268,* 2,065–2,070.

Gould, J. (1986). The local map of honeybees. Do insects have cognitive maps? *Science 232,* 861–863.

Healy, S. (1998). *Spatial representation in animals.* Oxford: Oxford University Press.

Ioalé, P., Gagliardo, A., and Bingman, V.P. (2000). Hippocampal participation in navigational map learning in young homing pigeons is dependent on training experience. *European Journal of Neuroscience 12,* 742–750.

Ioalé, P., Papi, F., Fiaschi, V., and Baldaccini, N. (1978). Pigeon navigation: Effects upon homing behavior by reversing wind direction at the loft. *Journal of Comparative Physiology 128,* 285–295.

Perdeck, A. (1958). Two types of orientation in migrating starlings, *Sturnus vulgaris* L., and chaffinches, *Fringilla coelebs* L., as revealed by displacement experiments. *Ardea 55,* 194–202.

Ugolini, A., and Macchi, T. (1988). Learned component in the solar orientation of *Talitrus saltator* Montagu (Amphipoda: Talitridae). *Journal of Experimental Marine Biology and Ecology 12,* 79–87.

Wallraff, H. (1966). Über die Heimfindeleistungen von Brieftauben nach Haltung in verschiedenartig abgeschirmten Volieren. *Zeitschrift für vergleichende Physiologie 52,* 215–259.

Wiltschko, R., and Wiltschko, W. (1980). The development of sun compass orientation in young homing pigeons. *Behavioral Ecology and Sociobiology 9,* 135–141.

Wiltschko, W., and Wiltschko, R. (1990). Magnetic orientation and celestial cues in migratory orientation. *Experimentia 46,* 343–351.

Verner P. Bingman

MISINFORMATION

See: RECONSTRUCTIVE MEMORY

MNEMONIC DEVICES

Mnemonic devices are methods for memorizing. The ancient Greek poet Simonides of Ceos is the legendary discoverer of mnemonic devices. Pleased by Simonides's praise, the twin gods Castor and Pollux called him from a banquet just before the hall collapsed. The other guests were mangled beyond recognition, but Simonides remembered the places they had been sitting and so was able to identify the dead. Such was the discovery of the method of loci (or locations). It became so much a part of the study of rhetoric that the most venerable of the Roman orators used the method of loci for memorizing their speeches. Their procedure was as follows: First, a series of loca-

tions (loci), such as those in a public building, were memorized. Second, some object was thought of to represent each important part of the oration, such as a spear to represent the tenth topic, war. Third, the image created for each topic was combined with the image of its corresponding location. The spear might be imaged as penetrating the tenth locus, a door. While making his speech, the orator thought of each location in turn and used the image seen in his mind's eye as the prompt for the next part of his address. After a few days, the images from the speech would fade from memory, but the more highly learned loci could be used to memorize a new speech.

During the Middle Ages and the Renaissance mnemonic devices were used not so much by orators for memorizing speeches as by scholars to classify and memorize all knowledge. This fascinating aspect of mnemonic devices is surveyed by Frances Yates (1966).

Principles of Mnemonic Learning

Most mnemonic procedures utilize the three memory processes of symbolizing, organizing, and associating. Symbolizing is finding a memorable, preferably imageable, representation for what is to be learned. In the aforementioned example, a spear represents war. Organizing involves activating a knowledge structure in memory, such as a set of loci, to which new information can be associated. The new information must then be associated to components of the knowledge structure. These knowledge-structure components, labeled mental cues, must have certain properties for mnemonic learning to be effective. Designing a mnemonic device must take into account how easily mental cues can be reconstructed, as well as how easily they can be associated with new information and how easily they can be discriminated from other mental cues (Bellezza, 1981). Visual imagery is often used by the learner to create the association between the mental cue and the symbol to be remembered.

Types of Mnemonic Devices

Higbee (1988) discusses the wide variety of mnemonic procedures and some of the research done on them. This entry attempts only a brief overview. Examples of some of the mnemonic devices mentioned appear in Table 1.

The process of organizing is particularly important when using a mnemonic technique such as the method of loci (see Figure 1), the story mnemonic, or the link mnemonic. When using the story mnemonic, a list of words is memorized by creating a story from them. The words become organized in memory by the

Table 1

Examples of Mnemonics

Mnemonic	Example
Story mnemonic	Make up a story to remember the following grocery list: bread, paper plates, apples, broom, hamburger. Example: "When I tried to walk into the grocery store, my way was blocked by a giant *loaf* of bread. I made a path of *paper plates* and climbed over the bread. A little boy then hit me with an *apple*. I chased him with a *broom*, and, when I caught him, he offered me a *hamburger*." Later, when one goes into the grocery store, the story made up about the grocery store will be recalled along with the items that should be purchased there.
Link mnemonic	You have to remember the following list of items to be purchased from the hardware store: hammer, red paint, rope, pliers, and glue. First form a visual image of a hardware store and the first word, *hammer*, interacting in some way. The *hardware* store window was smashed by a *hammer*. Do the same for the hammer and red paint. A *hammer* smashed the can of *red paint*. Next, *red paint* was poured over a coil of *rope*. Then, a *rope* was cut with a pair of *pliers*. Finally, the jaws of the *pliers* were stuck together with *glue*. To recall the list, first think of the hardware store, and the visual images should pull one another from memory like links in a chain.
Digit-consonant mnemonic	When trying to memorize a number, consonant sounds are substituted for digits, using the following rules: 0 → z, s, or soft c, 1 → t or d, 2 → n, 3 → m, 4 → r, 5 → 1, 6 → cj, j, sh, or soft g, 7 → k, hard c, hard g, or qu, 8 → f, v, or ph, 9 → p or b. The vowels, the letters w-h-y, and unpronounced consonants have no digit equivalents and can be used as fillers when creating the words. The number 0123456789 can be transformed into *Satan may hurl a huge coffee pie*. Later, to remember the number, first recall the sentence and then transform the sounds in the sentence back into digits using the digit-consonant rules.
Keyword mnemonic	Learn the meaning of the word *jejune* (pronounced gee, JUNE), which means not of interest, insipid. A keyword mnemonic could be as follows: Jejune → "Gee, June" (keyword) → Gee, June is not an interesting person (mnemonic image).
Face-name mnemonic	Associate the name *Ms. Flanagan* with her face or figure. Replace the name Flanagan with the more meaningful keyword *flannel gown*. Perhaps Ms. Flanagan's most noticeable feature is that she looks like a model. A visual image should be formed of Ms. Flanagan modeling a flannel nightgown to help associate her appearance with a symbol for her name. The next time one sees Ms. Flanagan, one will think of her as a model, think of her modeling a flannel nightgown, remember the keyword *flannel gown*, and remember her name as *Flanagan*.

SOURCE: Courtesy of Francis S. Bellezza.

theme and context of the story. When the list words later have to be recalled, the story can be reviewed by the learner and the list words recognized.

The link mnemonic is somewhat different from the method of loci or the story mnemonic: The successive words forming a pair in a list are associated using a visual image. Each image can be distinct and separate from the other images. All the words end up joined together in memory by visual images like links in a chain.

In other mnemonic devices the memory process of symbolizing is paramount. When memorizing numbers, a system that dates back to the seventeenth century, the digit-consonant mnemonic, can be used. In this system numbers are changed to words because words are more easily memorized than numbers. The words can then be recalled and changed back into the numbers they represent.

One of the most useful mnemonics has been the keyword mnemonic, in which symbolizing processes play an important role. The keyword mnemonic is particularly useful for learning the meanings of words. For example, when learning the word *hegemony*, meaning authority of one nation over others, the word must first be correctly pronounced (see Figure 2). It is pronounced something like he-GEM-oh-knee. Next, a keyword must be chosen that is familiar, meaningful, and sounds like the word to be learned.

The keyword for hegemony might be *gem*. Next, a visual image or sentence is formed that associates the key word with the meaning of the word to be learned. In this instance, the sentence might be *The nation with the most gems rules the others*. When coming across the word *hegemony* again, the learner must first think of the word *gem*, which then acts as a prompt for the mnemonic sentence containing the meaning of the word.

A useful but difficult variation of the keyword mnemonic is the face-name mnemonic used for associating names and faces. First, the person's name is transformed into a meaningful and concrete keyword, such as *Cushing* into *cushion*. The keyword then has to be associated to a salient bodily feature. In this example one might think of Mr. Cushing as having a cushion on his head because of his thick hair. When meeting Mr. Cushing again, one must recognize his hair as his critical physical feature. His hair should act as a cue for the word *cushion*, which in turn will act as a prompt for the name *Cushing*.

The mnemonic devices just reviewed are used to remember facts. Other less widely known mnemonic techniques—called process mnemonics—are designed to help remember rules, principles, and procedures. Process mnemonics have been used in Japan to help teach mathematical rules and computational skills and chemical formulas. Process mnemonics incorporate symbolizing, such as representing mathematical rules (e.g., "to divide fractions, multiply by a reciprocal") with more memorable and imageable phrases ("flip the fool into the pool," which refers to a jogger who is fooling around on a diving board by standing on his head). Association is used as well. In this example, the division sign between fractions (two joggers) is associated with a diving board. Higbee (1987) provides a more complete description of process mnemonics, which can be relatively complex.

Practical Applications

The more complicated mnemonic devices, such as the digit-consonant mnemonic, the keyword mnemonic, the face-name mnemonic, and process mnemonics require study and practice in order to be effective. But little research has been performed to determine if the investment in time and effort to become proficient in these mnemonics results in improved performance in the classroom, in the workplace, in situations in which many people's names have to be remembered, and so on. However, interest in this topic seems to be growing. The keyword mnemonic has been shown to be useful to students learning classroom-type materials. This is true for both average students and students with learning disabilities (Mastropieri et al., 1987). Using the "pool" process mnemonic described above, one researcher found that after three one-hour class sessions, third graders performed calculations with fractions as well as sixth graders and better than fourth and fifth graders (Higbee, 1987).

See also: MNEMONISTS

Bibliography

Bellezza, F. S. (1981). Mnemonic devices: Classification, characteristics, and criteria. *Review of Educational Research 51*, 247–275.

Higbee, K. L. (1987). Process mnemonics: Principles, prospects, and problems. In M. A. McDaniel and M. Pressley, eds., *Imagery and related mnemonic processes.* New York: Springer-Verlag.

—— (1988). *Your memory: How it works and how to improve it,* 2nd edition. New York: Prentice-Hall.

Mastropieri, M. A., Scruggs, T. E., and Levin, J. R. (1987). Mnemonic instruction in special education. In M. A. McDaniel and M. Pressley, eds., *Imagery and related and mnemonic processes.* New York: Springer-Verlag.

Yates, F. A. (1966). *The art of memory.* London: Routledge and Kegan Paul.

Francis S. Bellezza
Revised by Mark A. McDaniel

MNEMONISTS

The *Guinness Book of World Records* reports that in 1981 Rajan Srinavasen Mahadevan (known as Rajan)

Figure 1

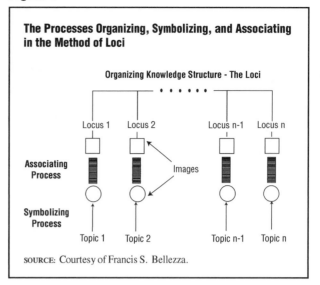

The Processes Organizing, Symbolizing, and Associating in the Method of Loci

SOURCE: Courtesy of Francis S. Bellezza.

recited the first 31,811 digits of pi from memory and that in 1987 Hideaki Tomoyori broke that record by reciting the first 40,000 digits. People performing such feats of memory are called mnemonists or memorists. Although feats like these are rare, since the 1890s there have been several scientific accounts of people with prodigious memories. Starting with the pioneering work of Alfred Binet, the scientific literature describes over a dozen people showing exceptional memory for verbal materials. Brown and Deffenbacher (1975) give a comprehensive review of these studies. Studies of exceptional memory performance contribute to our understanding of memory by describing the processes memorists use and by comparing them with processes used by people with ordinary memories.

Representative Case Studies

The studies on memorists have shown that they use a variety of techniques to remember material. Four memorists are presented here to demonstrate that variety: Shereshevskii, Alexander Craig Aitken, VP, and Rajan.

Shereshevskii

A. R. Luria (1968) has made Shereshevskii (S) the most famous mnemonist. (Luria referred to him only as S, but his real name later became known.) S was almost thirty when Luria began his studies, and the research continued for almost thirty years. Somewhat surprisingly, S was unaware that his memory was unusual until Luria began his investigations.

S used three basic processes, usually in combination, for remembering verbal material. The first was

Figure 2

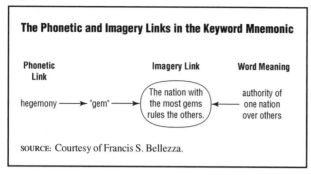

The Phonetic and Imagery Links in the Keyword Mnemonic

Phonetic Link | Imagery Link | Word Meaning

hegemony ⟶ "gem" → The nation with the most gems rules the others. ← authority of one nation over others

SOURCE: Courtesy of Francis S. Bellezza.

to generate rich visual images to represent information. When he became a stage performer, he trained himself to convert senseless words into meaningful images so that he could remember nonsense words or words from unfamiliar languages. The second process was to use familiar locations, such as stops on an oft-traveled street, to place the images mentally for later retrieval. This procedure is the method of locations (or loci) developed by the ancient Greek poet Simonides of Ceos in about 500 B.C. The method of locations has been discussed by authors as diverse as Aristotle and Thomas Aquinas. S apparently developed the technique independently. The third process was to create a story with appropriate images to retrieve the information.

With these techniques, S was able to remember any information presented. Luria was unable to find any limit to the amount of material S could recall in this fashion. More surprisingly, there appeared to be no limit to the duration of S's memory. Luria reports a request for recall of a fifty-word list given without warning sixteen years after presentation of the list. That request, like all the others Luria reports, resulted in successful retrieval of the list.

S had strong synesthesia, which appears to be unique among the memorists who have been investigated. Synesthesia is said to occur when information coming into one sensory system (e.g., audition) produces an effect in another sensory system (e.g., vision). S once said to the Russian psychologist Vygotsky, "What a crumbly, yellow voice you have" (Luria, 1968, p. 24). On another occasion, Luria was concerned that S might not remember his way in an unfamiliar location. S replied that he couldn't possibly forget because "here's this fence. It has such a salty taste and feels so rough; furthermore, it has such a sharp, piercing sound. . . ." (Luria, 1968, p. 38). Synesthesia interfered with the images S produced and presented an enduring problem for him. For example, S once noted that "Other times smoke or fog appears . . . and the more people talk, the harder it gets,

until . . . I can't make anything out" (Luria, 1968, p. 39).

Professor Aitken

Many psychologists think that Professor Aitken, who lived from 1895 to 1967, was the best all-around mnemonist. In a summary of the work on Aitken, Hunter (1977) points out that he was a brilliant mathematician, an excellent mental calculator, and an accomplished violinist with an extraordinary memory. His primary method for learning was to search out meaningful relationships within the material and with previously learned information. Hunter provides a quote from Aitken that best captures his approach:

> Musical memory can . . . be developed to a more remarkable degree than any other, for we have a metre and a rhythm, a tune, or more than one, the harmony, the instrumental color, a particular emotion or sequence of emotion, a meaning, . . . in the executant an auditory, a rhythmic and a muscular and functional memory; and secondarily in my case, a visual image of the page . . . perhaps also a human interest in the composer, with whom one may identify oneself . . . and an esthetic interest in the form of the piece. They are so many, and they are so cumulative, that the development of musical memory, and appreciation, has a multitude of supports. (1977, p. 157)

Although Aitken's memory was prodigious, it was not infallible. For example, in 1936 he correctly recalled sixteen three-digit numbers after four presentations. Two days later, he recalled all but one of the numbers and, after an additional presentation, he recalled them all. In 1960, without further study, he recalled twelve of the numbers but also produced eight incorrect numbers.

VP

VP (identified only by these initials in the published report) is an excellent chess player whose memory has been investigated by Hunt and Love (1972). VP has an exceptional memory but, like Aitken's, it is not infallible. For example, Hunt and Love reproduced VP's recall of an Indian story after intervals of 1 hour and 6 weeks. Although there were small changes in both recalls, his overall accuracy was remarkable.

VP learned material by relating it to prior information. For example, he knew several languages and could associate any three-letter string with a word. He learned number matrices by rows and sometimes recoded the row as a date. It is also clear that he spent a great deal of time practicing memorizing so that he became very adept at recoding information.

Rajan

Rajan has an exceptional memory for digits but not for other material. A group of researchers from Kansas State University (Thompson, Cowan, and Frieman, 1993) performed extensive tests on his memory. Their studies showed that Rajan learned sets of digits more rapidly than VP or S. He used a procedure pairing locations and digits to learn the material. He also encoded the digits in chunks (such as a row in a matrix). Thus, he learned that the fifth digit in the fourth row was 3 rather than using preexisting knowledge to encode the information. He explicitly attached cues to the chunks for retrieval. For example, he learned the first column in a matrix as a cue for retrieving each row of the matrix.

Once the material was learned, Rajan's procedure allowed for extremely effective retrieval of information. Working in the first 10,000 decimal digits of pi, he could retrieve a digit at a specified location (e.g., digit 4,765) in an average time of twelve seconds. He had the digits of pi chunked in groups of 10 digits. When he was given the first five digits of a ten-digit group in the first 10,000 digits of pi, he could give the next five digits in an average time of seven seconds.

The Memorists and a Theory of Skilled Memory

In several papers, Ericsson and his colleagues (e.g., Ericsson and Chase, 1982) suggest three general principles for skilled memory and illustrate these principles with people skilled at some aspect of memory. The three principles they propose are meaningful encoding (the use of preexisting knowledge to store the presented information in memory), retrieval structure (explicitly attaching cues to the encoded material to allow efficient retrieval), and speedup (a reduction in study time with further practice). They claim that ordinary subjects, as well as skilled memorists, show these principles.

Consistent with this theory, all four mnemonists described here attach retrieval cues when learning material to ensure accurate and fast retrieval. Further, three of them show a reduction in study time with practice. There is no clear evidence available on this point for Professor Aitken. However, it seems likely that he would show a similar effect.

The data from these memorists suggest that the skilled-memory theory founders on the third principle. All four memorists use procedures for encoding the material that are available to and used by people with ordinary memories. But, contrary to the theory, not all of them encode the material by relating it to preexisting knowledge. VP fits the theory because he encodes material by relating it to prior information.

Aitken uses that technique and also searches for relationships within the material to be learned. S uses imagery and the classic method of locations as his primary means for learning material. Because Ericsson and his colleagues clearly refer to relating the material to preexisting verbal knowledge, S's procedures do not conform to their theory. Rajan also does not fit the theory at all. His procedure, pairing locations and digits, cannot be construed as encoding by relation to preexisting knowledge.

Conclusion

The four memorists use quite different techniques to remember information, some of which call into question a portion of the theory of skilled memory. Their memories are unusually good, but the processes they use to remember can all be used by people with ordinary memories. In short, their memories are unusual in the amount they can remember but not in the processes they use to remember.

See also: MNEMONIC DEVICES

Bibliography

Brown, E. (1988). Superior memory performance and mnemonic encoding. In L. K. Obler and D. Fein, eds., *The exceptional brain.* New York: Guilford Press.

Brown, E., and Deffenbacher, K. (1975). Forgotten mnemonists. *Journal of the History of the Behavioral Sciences 11,* 342–349.

Ericsson, K. A., and Chase, W. G. (1982). Exceptional memory. *American Scientist 70,* 607–615.

Hunt, E., and Love, T. (1972). How good can memory be? In A. W. Melton and E. Martin, eds., *Coding processes in human memory.* Washington, DC: John Wiley.

Hunter, I. M. L. (1977). An exceptional memory. *British Journal of Psychology 68,* 155–164.

Luria, A. R. (1968). *The mind of a mnemonist.* New York: Basic Books.

Obler, L. K., and Fein, D. (1988). *The exceptional brain.* New York: Guilford Press.

Thompson, C. P., Cowan, T. M., and Frieman, J. (1993). *Memory search by a memorist.* Hillsdale, NJ: Erlbaum.

Charles P. Thompson

MODALITY EFFECTS

In the classic modality effect, immediate recall of the last few items from a verbal sequence is influenced by the presentation modality: Recall is more likely if the sequence is spoken aloud than if it is read silently. Most people are familiar with the experience of briefly retaining speech as if in a mental tape recorder and occasionally using this "echoic" memory to do a double take. An example is when one is asked the time while reading. The sounds linger in memory and one can recover them to get the meaning even if one was not paying attention at the exact moment when the question was asked. The auditory modality advantage

Figure 1

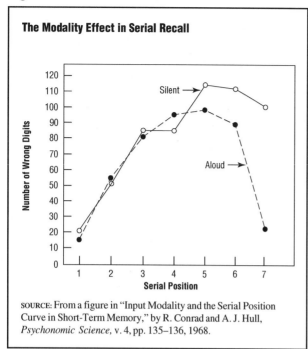

The Modality Effect in Serial Recall

SOURCE: From a figure in "Input Modality and the Serial Position Curve in Short-Term Memory," by R. Conrad and A. J. Hull, *Psychonomic Science*, v. 4, pp. 135–136, 1968.

has been widely attributed to an echoic memory system that stores raw acoustic information for at least several seconds no matter how one's attention is directed during stimulus presentation.

Evidence shows that modality effects can occur for sounds that were presented too long ago for echoic memory still to be used, and in situations in which there are no sounds. There is an advantage, for example, in recalling lip-read or signed words over silently read words. There are even certain circumstances that favor visual as opposed to auditory presentations. As a result, psychologists often use the term *modality effect* to refer to any differences in memory performance that are associated with differences in stimulus modality. Such modality effects are more pervasive, and of more fundamental importance, than researchers had previously thought. They show how various codes, or derived types of information, are used in memory. For example, when one hears a spoken word, one can reflect upon how it sounds (an acoustic code), how the word is formed from consonants and vowels (a phonological code), how one would pronounce it (an articulatory code), how the word would look if printed (an orthographic code), and what the word means (a semantic code). Such codes are preserved and processed to varying degrees and are used together as cues assisting the later recall of the word. The presentation modality influences how well or how easily various codes can be formed.

The Classic Effect

The classic modality effect occurs in comparing the immediate recall of sequences of verbal items that are presented in written or in spoken form. It does not matter much whether it is the experimenter or the subject who reads the spoken sequences aloud. Recall performance is usually plotted as a function of each item's serial position in the sequence. The modality effect occurs both when recall itself is serial—that is, when the items have to be recalled in their order of occurrence—and when recall is free, in the sense that subjects are free to choose any order of recall. Digit sequences are frequently used for serial recall; sometimes letters or syllables are used, sometimes unrelated words. In free recall, the sequences are almost always unrelated words. Two of the earliest demonstrations of this modality effect are reproduced in Figure 1 (serial recall) and Figure 2 (free recall).

The modality effect is intimately bound up with two other effects, the recency effect and the suffix effect. The recency effect is the finding that the last few (or most recent) items from a sequence are more likely to be recalled than the preceding items. As Figures 1 and 2 illustrate, in serial recall there is little recency effect for the silent sequences, but in free recall both input modes show a large recency effect and the modality effect appears as an enhanced recency effect. The suffix effect is the finding that in serial recall, a single spoken item at the end of the sequence, such as *zero* after the last to-be-recalled digit, essentially wipes out the modality effect. With the suffix, there is as little recency effect for spoken as for silent sequences.

The original explanation of the modality effect was the Precategorical Acoustic Storage (PAS) model described by Robert G. Crowder and John Morton in 1969. PAS is an auditory sensory memory store, the echoic counterpart of the visual sensory store (iconic memory). Its function is to retain speech input at precategorical level—that is, prior to analysis of meaning—for further processing. It was supposed to last about two seconds unless it was overwritten or erased by subsequent speech input. Thus, the modality effect presumably occurs because echoic memory of the last few items, unlike iconic memory, can persist long enough to contribute to immediate recall. This theory was useful in understanding modality, recency, and suffix effects as well as speech perception. The limitation in the PAS account is its inability to explain other modality effects that have been discovered since 1969.

Subsequent Developments

Three topics of special importance have led to modifications in scientific understanding since Crowder and Morton's PAS theory. They are modality effects in the absence of sound, long-term modality effects, and the role of stimulus timing in causing modality effects.

Modality Effects in the Absence of Sound

Modality and suffix effects in serial recall occur when the items are lip-read or mouthed silently instead of being spoken aloud, as was shown for example by Kathryn T. Spoehr and William J. Corin in 1978. These findings led to a revision of the PAS model and to several other theoretical developments. The revised PAS model, described by Crowder in 1983, assumes that information in PAS can also be activated by the facial-gestural features involved in lip-reading and mouthing, on the grounds that these features are involved in speech perception. Evidence of modality and suffix effects with American Sign Language in the congenitally deaf led Michael A. Shand and Edward S. Klima to propose a primary linguistic coding hypothesis, which assumes that such effects occur whenever the stimulus modality is compatible with the short-term memory code involved in a person's primary mode of communication. The revised hypotheses have merit but it is not clear if they can explain all modality effects. For instance, they cannot explain modality and suffix effects that have been discovered with tactile stimuli and with musical notes or rhythms.

Long-Term Modality Effects

There are various indications that auditory-modality-specific information persists longer than the two seconds that was originally assumed by the PAS theory. One is that modality effects have been shown to result largely from the ability of auditory information to survive in the presence of what is called output interference, or interference from the early part of the participant's own response. Several investigators (including Fergus I. M. Craik in 1969, C. Philip Beaman and John Morton in 2000, and Nelson Cowan and others in 2002) have found that when participants recall items from the end of the list first, lists in both modalities are recalled equally well. When participants recall items from the beginning of the list first, however, items from the end of the list are recalled much better for spoken lists than for printed lists. Part of these effects may occur because the written or typewritten responses that were used overwrite orthographic codes but Fergus Craik showed that much of the auditory advantage appears to persist even with spoken responses. Auditory codes are thus more likely to survive output interference.

Figure 2

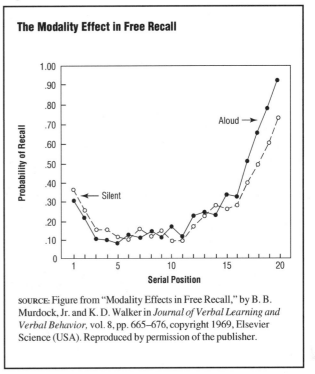

SOURCE: Figure from "Modality Effects in Free Recall," by B. B. Murdock, Jr. and K. D. Walker in *Journal of Verbal Learning and Verbal Behavior*, vol. 8, pp. 665–676, copyright 1969, Elsevier Science (USA). Reproduced by permission of the publisher.

There are also modality effects in long-term as well as short-term memory. For example, a spoken modality effect occurs in a free recall task, in which each word in the sequence is preceded and followed by lengthy periods of spoken distractor activity, as John M. Gardiner and Vernon H. Gregg showed in 1979. Such interference is assumed to eliminate any contribution from sensory or short-term memory because it wipes out modality and recency effects if it occurs only after the last word in the sequence.

A few modality effects have been discovered in other long-term memory tasks, including recognition memory, where Martin A. Conway and Susan E. Gathercole found an effect across all serial positions. Some of these effects are a reversal of the usual auditory superiority, and they seem to interact with other factors in ways that are as yet poorly understood. In long-term recall with written responses, either visual presentation or spoken presentation along with instructions to imagine how the word is printed help participants to avoid "false memories." In such studies, when numerous words from a semantic category are presented (e.g., *sleeve, button, collar,* and so on) there is a tendency to recall a central word that actually was not presented (e.g., *shirt*) and the availability of an orthographic code in memory appears to prevent that sort of mistake, as Ronald T. Kellogg showed in 2001.

Modality and Stimulus Timing

The long-term modality effect led Arthur M. Glenberg and Naomi G. Swanson in 1986 to propose a detailed model that assumes that temporal information is more finely represented in the auditory mode and that the modality effect reflects greater temporal distinctiveness. Because it is possible that temporal distinctiveness underlies the recency effect in both short-term and long-term memory, it can potentially provide a quite general account of modality and recency effects. A number of current studies have investigated temporal and ordinal factors. Though research indicates that serial-order information is better retained in the auditory mode, the evidence makes it less clear if the same is true for temporal information as such, as Ian Neath and Robert Crowder showed in 1990.

One indication that the temporal-information account has merit comes from studies of the grouping of items. In 1989 Clive Frankish showed that the benefit that comes from items in a list being separated by gaps into small groups is much greater for spoken lists than for printed lists. Nelson Cowan and others (2002) set up a situation in which lists of nine random digits were presented at a steady pace on some trials but, on other trials, were grouped into three sets of three with one-second gaps between groups. The response boxes to be filled in by the participant always appeared as three groups of three across the screen. This encouragement of grouping had a small benefit for the recall of printed lists, equivalently no matter whether the actual list was grouped or not. However, for spoken lists, there was a very large benefit of actual stimulus grouping—much larger than for visual lists—and no noticeable mental grouping for steadily paced lists. Thus, the mental representation of the list was much more dependent on the actual stimulus timing for spoken lists than for printed lists.

Modality effects have a broader empirical base than psychologists once realized, and late-twentieth-century discoveries have led to fresh theoretical approaches, among which temporal distinctiveness theory perhaps is the most influential. In addition to the alternative hypotheses already mentioned, there are other suggestions that there has been less time to evaluate. James S. Nairne suggested (in 1990) conceptualizing the memory trace in terms of modality-independent and modality-dependent features, which may or may not reflect sensory aspects of the stimulus. Catherine G. Penney (in 1989) developed a "separate streams" hypothesis, which assumes that modality separation of verbal items is inherent to the structure of short-term memory. All these ideas assign modality effects to more fundamental, less peripheral, aspects of memory function than originally envisaged in echoic memory theory.

See also: MEMORY SPAN

Bibliography

Beaman, C. P., and Morton, J. (2000). The separate but related origins of the recency effect and the modality effect in free recall. *Cognition 77*, B59–B65.

Conway, M. A., and Gathercole, S. E. (1987). Modality and long-term memory. *Journal of Memory and Language 26*, 341–361.

Cowan, N., Saults, J. S., Elliott, E. M., and Moreno, M. (2002). Deconfounding serial recall. *Journal of Memory and Language, 46,*153–177.

Crowder, R. G. (1983). The purity of auditory memory. *Philosophical Transactions of the Royal Society of London B302*, 251–265.

Crowder, R. G., and Morton, J. (1969). Precategorical acoustic storage (PAS). *Perception and Psychophysics 5*, 365–373.

Frankish, C. (1989). Perceptual organization and precategorical acoustic storage. *Journal of Experimental Psychology: Learning, Memory, and Cognition 15*, 469–479.

Gardiner, J. M. (1983). On recency and echoic memory. *Philosophical Transactions of the Royal Society of London B302*, 267–282.

Gardiner, J. M., and Gregg, V. H. (1979). When auditory memory is not overwritten. *Journal of Verbal Learning and Verbal Behavior 18*, 705–719.

Glenberg, A. M., and Swanson, N. G. (1986). A temporal distinctiveness theory of recency and modality effects. *Journal of Experimental Psychology: Learning, Memory, and Cognition 12*, 3–15.

Kellogg, R. T. (2001). Presentation modality and mode of recall in verbal false memory. *Journal of Experimental Psychology: Learning, Memory, and Cognition 27*, 913–919.

Morton, J., Crowder, R. G., and Prussin, H. A. (1971). Experiments with the stimulus suffix effect. *Journal of Experimental Psychology 91*, 169–190.

Nairne, J. S. (1990). A feature model of immediate memory. *Memory & Cognition 18*, 251–269.

Neath, I., and Crowder, R. G. (1990). Schedules of presentation and temporal distinctiveness in human memory. *Journal of Experimental Psychology: Learning, Memory, and Cognition 16*, 316–327.

Penney, C. G. (1989). Modality effects and the structure of short-term memory. *Memory & Cognition 17*, 398–422.

Shand, M. A., and Klima, E. S. (1981). Nonauditory suffix effects in congenitally deaf signers of American Sign Language. *Journal of Experimental Psychology: Human Learning and Memory 7*, 464–474.

Spoehr, K. T., and Corin, W. J. (1978). The stimulus suffix effect as a memory coding phenomenon. *Memory & Cognition 6*, 583–589.

John M. Gardiner
Nelson Cowan

MORPHOLOGICAL BASIS OF LEARNING AND MEMORY

[An increasing body of evidence indicates that learning and memory involve changes in the strength of the connections between neurons. However, changes in synaptic strength can be realized in many ways. One exciting possibility is that changes in strength are produced by growth of new synaptic contacts. This possibility was suggested more than a century

ago, but has received strong experimental support since the 1980s. These results are reviewed in the following two entries, which focus on studies in **INVERTEBRATE** *model systems and* **VERTEBRATE** *model systems respectively.*]

INVERTEBRATES

There is much evidence that learning and memory result from cellular changes occurring within individual neurons (Byrne, 1987), but the cellular mechanisms underlying these changes have resisted definitive elucidation. The mechanisms that produce a change in neuronal structure have received scant attention even though this class of mechanisms was first suggested more than a century ago (Ramón y Cajal, 1988). Researchers have observed morphological correlates of learning in several vertebrate and invertebrate model systems (Bailey and Kandel, 1993), but no one has proved that modifications of neuronal structure affect behavior. Nevertheless, the variety of model systems with morphological correlates suggests that this is one of the mechanisms that underlies learning.

An investigation of the morphological correlates of learning and memory should incorporate several features. First, there should be a readily observable behavior that can be modified by training. Second, the circuit mediating that behavior should be well known. Third, the morphology of the neurons in that circuit must be accessible to analysis. Although no real-world model system meets all of these criteria, a number of investigators have turned to invertebrates for model systems with few compromises.

The structural modifications vary among different systems. This is not surprising because morphological features may contribute to neuronal function in several ways. This article will focus on two broad classes of morphological changes: the large-scale remodeling of neuronal arborizations arising from outgrowth that seem to result in the formation of new synaptic connections and more localized structural changes that presumably affect preexisting connections.

Neurite Outgrowth

Cajal's original hypothesis suggested that learning is mediated by the outgrowth of new axons and the formation of new synaptic connections, a process that recapitulates brain development (Ramón y Cajal, 1988). This hypothesis has been tested in detail in the marine mollusk *Aplysia.* Two simple defensive reflexes in this animal have proved useful for studies of the cellular and molecular mechanisms of nonassociative learning: the siphon-gill withdrawal reflex and the tail-siphon withdrawal reflex.

Both withdrawal reflexes can be enhanced by sensitization, a form of nonassociative learning (Castellucci, Pinsker, Kupfermann, and Kandel, 1970; Walters, Byrne, Carew, and Kandel, 1983). Sensitization is the enhancement of a behavioral response resulting from the application of a novel or noxious stimulus to the animal. Sensitization in a variety of animals seems to be a short-lived phenomenon, recovering over the course of minutes to an hour. The long-term form of sensitization lasts from one day to roughly three weeks. Recent evidence suggests that the situation may be more complex. For example, there is a distinct form of sensitization with intermediate duration (Sutton and Carew, 2000). Investigators have identified several elements of the circuits mediating these reflexes. In both circuits, the sensory neurons are sites of short- and long-term plasticity. Neurite outgrowth followed long-term but not short-term sensitization.

Following sensitization of the siphon-gill withdrawal reflex, training increased the complexity of the axonal arbor of sensory neurons, as measured by total neurite length (Bailey and Chen, 1988a). In addition, the number of varicosities per neuron increased. These observations were consistent with enhanced convergence onto follower motor neurons. Tail sensory neurons yielded similar results (Wainwright, Zhang, Byrne, and Cleary, 2002). The effects of training, however, were limited to a region of the arborization in the pedal ganglion, which is where follower motor neurons are located. The total arborization length in this region was increased, as was the number of branch points and varicosities.

The honeybee is an interesting case because it has a powerful facility for learning the features and location of food. One of the most profound learning experiences for a foraging bee occurs on its first flight from the hive. Presumably, the animal learns navigational cues that the target reinforces, but the precise coding of the information remains unclear.

Given the complexity of learning, it likely draws on large portions of the brain. Some research has pointed to a correlation between learning and an increase in volume of two brain regions: the mushroom body and antennal lobe glomeruli (Farris, Robinson, and Fahrbach, 2001; Sigg, Thompson, and Mercer, 1997). In the mushroom body, the growth appears to be due at least in part to an increase in sprouting from Kenyon cell dendrites (Farris, Robinson, and Fahrbach, 2001). A form of olfactory learning in the fruit fly *Drosophila* yielded similar results (Balling et al., 1987).

A distinctive approach to morphological correlates has been taken with *Drosophila*. Rather than looking directly for correlates following a training session, investigators generate mutants that are deficient in learning and observe effects of the mutations on neuronal structure. In some cases these mutations have been found to affect the morphology of neurons in the central nervous system. Two commonly used mutations are *dnc* and *rut*. Both mutations impair a form of olfactory conditioning in which flies associate a particular odor with an electrical shock. Their critical effect is on the cAMP second-messenger pathway: *dnc* increases cAMP levels, and *rut* reduces them. Although they have opposite biochemical effects, both mutations result in larger numbers of spines and varicosities in a central process of the sensory neuron innervating the antero-notopleural thoracic bristle (Corfas and Dudai, 1991). More frequently, the effects of the mutations have been observed at the neuromuscular junctions of animals at the larval stage of development. In this preparation, the effects of the two mutations are different: *dnc* mutations increase motor neuron branching (Schuster et al., 1996), whereas *rut* mutations decrease branching (Cheung, Shayan, Boulianne, and Atwood, 1999).

The mollusk *Hermissenda* has been the subject of studies of associative conditioning between visual and rotational stimuli. A crucial site of plasticity is the photoreceptor. Following training, the arborization of the medial type B photoreceptor was reduced compared to controls (Alkon et al., 1990). This result is consistent with other biophysical and biochemical changes resulting in decreased synaptic strength to follower neurons.

In these model systems changes in the complexity of the arbor parallels the changes in synaptic efficacy. Neurite outgrowth presumably strengthens the behavioral response by forming new synapses to follower neurons. Neurite retraction presumably weakens the behavioral response by reducing the number of synapses. Because these changes appear to be associated only with long-lasting forms of learning, it seems that there is a high threshold for induction. Such changes would not seem to admit of easy reversal, but no testing has confirmed this hypothesis.

Modification of Synaptic Ultrastructure

Synaptic strength can be modulated by changes in neuronal structure that are more subtle than those outlined in the previous section. Usually such changes involve the structural modification of preexisting synapses. This possibility has been examined in great detail in *Aplysia*.

Following long-term sensitization training, the number of sensory neuron varicosities increases as does the size of the axonal arborization. This outgrowth results in an increase in the number of active zones, in the length of the active zone, and the number of vesicles in proximity to the release site (i.e., the vesicle complement; Bailey and Chen, 1983). These same features are smaller in animals subjected to long-term habituation. For example, sensory neurons from these animals had on average 35 percent fewer varicosities compared to controls. Quantitative analysis of the time course over which these anatomical changes occur during long-term sensitization suggests that alterations in the number of sensory neuron varicosities and active zones persist in parallel with the behavioral retention of the memory, whereas active zone length and vesicle complement do not (Bailey and Chen, 1989). Thus, there may be an overlapping cascade of mechanisms that sustain modifications in synaptic function.

In contrast with the extensive structural changes following long-term training, the morphological correlates of short-term memory in *Aplysia* (lasting minutes to hours rather than days to weeks) are far less pronounced and are primarily restricted to shifts in the proximity of synaptic vesicles adjacent to sensory neuron active zones, a phenomenon that may reflect altered levels of transmitter mobilization (Bailey and Chen, 1988b). These studies in *Aplysia* suggest a clear difference in the time course of structural events that underlie memories of differing durations. The transient duration of short-term memories probably involves the covalent modification of preexisting proteins and is accompanied by modest structural remodeling in the vicinity of the active zone, such as the translocation of synaptic vesicles to the release site.

Another model system in which synaptic structure seems correlated with function is the crayfish neuromuscular junction. This system does not permit an examination of the effects of a specific learning paradigm because the cellular plasticity underlying behavioral modifications does not occur at the neuromuscular junction. Instead, attention is focused on the effects of high-frequency stimulation, which produces both short- and long-term enhancements in synaptic strength.

In the crayfish preparation, a single axon makes numerous synaptic contacts with the muscle fiber. These synapses have different functional properties (Wojtowicz et al., 1994); some are affected by long-term facilitation, and some are not. Moreover, many synapses that release transmitter do not contribute to the EPSP, suggesting that changes in EPSP amplitude can be effected by modifying only a fraction of synapses.

Early ultrastructural studies supported the idea that high-frequency stimulation produced an increase in the percentage of synapses exhibiting presynaptic active zones. These observations suggest that alterations in neuronal activity can induce rapid structural transformations at the synapse, affecting primarily the active-zone. However, subsequent studies suggested that the effects of high-frequency stimulation were not persistent. Stimulation at 20 Hz for ten minutes produced an increase in the number of synapses per unit area of terminal membrane, a decrease in the synaptic area, and an increase in the number of dense bodies per unit of terminal membrane area or synapse area. Forty-five minutes later, however, the synapse was still facilitated, but these structural features were no longer different from control. Only one structural change was observed following long-term facilitation: In synapses that had more than one dense body, there was an increase in the number of synapses per unit area of terminal.

In *Drosophila,* mutants that interfere with learning also produce changes in the structure of the neuromuscular junction (Renger et al., 2000). For example, *dnc* mutations, which increase cAMP levels, produced relatively modest structural changes: the ratio of docked to undocked vesicles increased, and presynaptic and postsynaptic specializations became less densely stained. Structural changes following the *rut* mutation, which decreases cAMP levels, were more profound. The number of synapses per unit area of terminal decreased, but the size of each synapse increased. The ratio of docked to undocked vesicles decreased, and staining intensity of presynaptic and postsynaptic specializations was unaffected. If the structural changes at these peripheral synapses reflect similar changes within the central nervous system, then they could contribute to the learning deficits.

Causal Relationship Between Structure and Function

Notwithstanding the structural changes that seem to correlate with learning, the relationship between structure and function is not necessarily a simple one. For example, at the crayfish neuromuscular junction, muscle fibers are innervated by both tonic and phasic motor neurons. Tonic motor neurons are typically highly active, and their terminals typically evince large synaptic varicosities with large numbers of vesicles. Phasic motor neurons with low levels of impulse activity have thinner terminals with fewer vesicles. Aside from the greater number of tonic terminals, there are no marked differences in synaptic structure in the two populations of neurons (Msghina, Govind, and Atwood, 1998). Therefore other mechanisms, presumably biophysical or biochemical, are more im-

portant determinants of synaptic strength between the two different types of motor neurons.

In an elegant series of experiments at the developing neuromuscular junction of larval *Drosophila,* moderate underexpression of a cell adhesion molecule resulted in axonal outgrowth and varicosity formation (Schuster et al., 1996). More severe underexpression resulted in axonal retraction and decreased varicosity formation. These morphological changes did not by themselves produce changes in synaptic strength, however. Unknown intrinsic mechanisms maintained synaptic strength at an appropriate level by adjusting the number and size of active zones (Stewart, Schuster, Goodman, and Atwood, 1996). Enhancing synaptic strength required an activation of the cAMP second-messenger pathway and phosphorylation of the nuclear regulatory protein CREB. Thus, in addition to the difficulties of demonstrating the structural mechanisms of learning, there are the further challenges of demonstrating that those changes contribute to the modulated function of the neural circuit underlying the behavior.

In recent studies in *Aplysia* discussed earlier (Wainwright, Zhang, Byrne, and Cleary, 2002), the structural changes induced by four days of long-term sensitization training did not occur after only one day of long-term sensitization training. Moreover, the neurite outgrowth that accompanied four days of training occurred on both sides of the animal, even though the behavioral modification was limited to the trained side. These dissociations do not rule out the role of structural changes in learning but caution against the overinterpretion of results in the absence of appropriate controls.

It is difficult indeed to nail down the possible causal relationship between structural changes and behavioral changes. Structural changes require a large number of cellular processes, such as protein synthesis, cytoskeletal reorganization, organelle translocation, and membrane-membrane interactions. Therefore, in most model systems there is no single drug or manipulation that can block selected structural changes without affecting other normal cellular processes. Researchers are always seeking systems and control experiments that might permit a more precise determination of the possible causal role of structural changes.

Bibliography

Alkon, D. L., Ikeno, H., Dworkin, J., McPhie, D. L., Olds, J. L., Lederhendler, I., Matzel, L., Schreurs, B. G., Kuzirian, A., Collin, I., and Yamoah, E. (1990). Contraction of neuronal branching volume: An anatomical correlate of Pavlovian conditioning. *Proceedings of the National Academy of Sciences of the United States of America* 87, 1,611–1,614.

Bailey, C. H., and Chen, M. (1983). Morphological basis of long-term habituation and sensitization in *Aplysia*. *Science 220*, 9,193.

——— (1988a). Long-term memory in *Aplysia* modulates the total number of varicosities of single identified sensory neurons. *Proceedings of the National Academy of Sciences of the United States of America 85*, 2,373–2,377.

——— (1988b). Morphological basis of short-term habituation in *Aplysia*. *Journal of Neuroscience 8*, 2,452–2,459.

——— (1989). Time course of structural changes at identified sensory neuron synapses during long-term sensitization in *Aplysia*. *Journal of Neuroscience 9*, 1,774–1,780.

Bailey, C. H., and Kandel, E. R. (1993). Structural changes accompanying memory storage. *Annual Review of Physiology 55*, 397–426.

Balling, A., Technau, G. M., and Heisenberg, M. (1987). Are the structural changes in adult drosophila mushroom bodies memory traces? Studies on biochemical mutants. *Journal of Neurogenetics 4*, 65–73.

Byrne, J. H. (1987). Cellular analysis of associative learning. *Physiological Review 67*, 329–439.

Castellucci, V. F., Pinsker, H., Kupfermann, I., and Kandel, E. R. (1970). Neuronal mechanisms of habituation and dishabituation of the gill withdrawal reflex in *Aplysia*. *Science 167*, 1,745–1,748.

Cheung, U. S., Shayan, A. J., Boulianne, G. L., Atwood, H. L. (1999). *Drosophila* larval neuromuscular junction's responses to reduction of cAMP in the nervous system. *Journal of Neurobiology 40*, 1–13.

Corfas, G., and Dudai, Y. (1991). Morphology of a sensory neuron in *Drosophila* is abnormal in memory mutants and changes during aging. *Proceedings of the National Academy of Sciences of the United States of America 88*, 7,252–7,256.

Farris, S. M., Robinson, G. E., and Fahrbach, S. E. (2001). Experience- and age-related outgrowth of intrinsic neurons in the mushroom bodies of the adult worker honeybee. *Journal of Neuroscience 21*, 6,395–6,404.

Msghina, M., Govind, G. K., and Atwood, H. L. (1998). Synaptic structure and transmitter release in crustacean phasic and tonic motor neurons. *Journal of Neuroscience 18*, 1,374–1,382.

Ramón y Cajal, S. (1988). Anatomicophysiological considerations on the cerebrum. In J. DeFelipe and E. G. Gros, eds., *Cajal on the cerebral cortex*. New York: Oxford University Press.

Renger, J. J., Ueda, A., Atwood, H. L., Govind, C. K., and Wu, C.-F. (1996). Genetic dissection of structural and functional components of synaptic plasticity. II. Fasciclin II controls presynaptic structural plasticity. *Neuron 17*, 655–667.

——— (2000). Role of cAMP cascade in synaptic stability and plasticity: Ultrastructural and physiological analyses of individual synaptic boutons in *drosophila* memory mutants. *Journal of Neuroscience 20*, 3,980–3,992.

Schuster, C. M., Davis, G. W., Fetter, R. D., and Goodman, C. S. (1996). Genetic dissection of structural and functional components of synaptic plasticity. I. Fasciclin II controls synaptic stabilization and growth. *Neuron 17*, 641–654.

Sigg, D., Thompson, C. M., Mercer, A. R. (1997). Activity-dependent changes to the brain and behavior of the honey bee, *Apis mellifera* (L.). *Journal of Neuroscience 17*, 7,148–7,156.

Stewart, B. A., Schuster, C. M., Goodman, C. S. and Atwood, H. L. (1996). Homeostasis of synaptic transmission in *Drosophila* with genetically altered nerve terminal morphology. *Journal of Neuroscience 16*, 3,877–3,886.

Sutton, M. A. and Carew, T. J. (2000). Parallel molecular pathways mediate expression of distinct forms of intermediate-term facilitation at tail sensory-motor synapses in *Aplysia*. *Neuron 26*, 219–231.

Wainwright, M. L., Zhang, H., Byrne, J. H. and Cleary, L. J. (2002). Localized neuronal outgrowth induced by long-term sensitization training in *Aplysia*. *Journal of Neuroscience 20*, 4,132–4,141.

Walters, E. T., Byrne, J. H., Carew, T. J., and Kandel, E. R. (1983). Mechanoafferent neurons innervating tail of *Aplysia*. II. Modulation by sensitizing stimuli. *Journal of Neurophysiology 50*, 1,543–1,559.

Wojtowicz, J. M., Marin, L., and Atwood, H. L. (1994). Activity-induced changes in synaptic release sites at the crayfish neuromuscular junction. *Journal of Neuroscience 14*, 3,688–3,703.

Craig H. Bailey
Revised by Len Cleary

VERTEBRATES

The central issue in morphology of learning and memory is how such constructs are stored in the nervous system. The basic shape of neurons and synapses is illustrated in Figure 1. In the late nineteenth century, Santiago Ramón y Cajal (Spanish histologist, 1852–1934) suggested that learning might involve changes in the synaptic connections through which neurons communicate. Such synaptic change could take at least four possible forms. First, forming new synapses or removing existing synapses could alter the pattern of functional connections. Second, selectively strengthening or weakening some synapses could alter the pattern of functional connections. Very strong evidence exists for both of these possibilities during learning, and in models of learning such as *long-term potentiation* (LTP). Third, by forming new neurons (neurogenesis), neuronal circuits could be modified; there is increasing evidence that neurogenesis occurs in the mature brain. Fourth, changes could occur in both the nonsynaptic regions of neurons and in nonneural elements of the brain such as glial cells and the vascular system subserving the brain, for which evidence exists as well.

Changes in Synapse Number

Important roots of memory research lie in studies of the effects of experience upon brain development. For example, visual experience is necessary to develop normal visual ability in mammals. Searching for a basis for this in brain anatomy, Cragg (1975) and others, noted that animals deprived of visual experience had fewer synaptic connections per nerve cell in the visual cortex. These studies profoundly influenced thinking about the processes by which the brain stores information, because they showed that 1. brain structure is malleable; 2. synaptic organization can be orchestrated into different configurations by behavioral experience; 3. both forming new connections and pruning existing connections are involved in altering brain organization; and 4. differential experience can

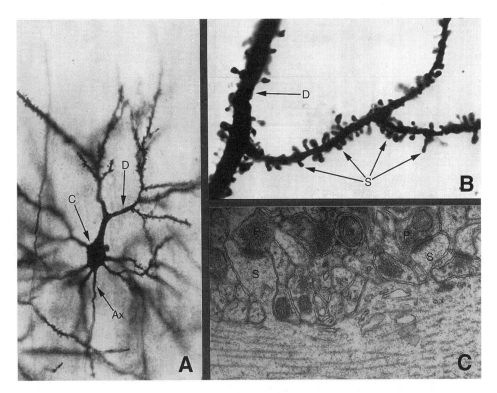

Figure 1. The nerve cell at three levels of magnification. A) Golgi-impregnated small pyramidal neuron from the upper visual cortex. C = soma or cell body, D = dendrites, Ax = axon. Input from other nerve cells arrives primarily on dendrites. Output of nerve cell is via the axon, to other neurons (original magnification 740x). B) Higher-magnification view of dendrite branches reveals fingerlike projections called spines (original magnification 2400x). C) Electron micrograph reveals that spines (S) are projections from dendrite (D) upon which presynaptic terminals (P) of axons terminate. The round, clear objects within the presynaptic terminal are vesicles, which are thought to contain the chemical neurotransmitter that is used for communication at the synapse (original magnification 28,000x). *(William T. Greenough and James D. Churchill)*

modify the structure of synapses, suggesting that synaptic efficacy (or strength) also can change. These effects of experience on synaptic connections during development led to proposals that such changes might underlie adult learning as well.

A separate developmental approach that was very fruitful in understanding brain substrates of learning and memory involved enriching the lives of young animals with additional stimulation. Donald Hebb (psychobiologist, 1904–1985) proposed ways in which synaptic change could be incorporated meaningfully into functional circuitry. With his students, he showed that enriching the rearing environment of rats with cagemates and toys improved the animals' ability to solve complex problems. Hebb concluded that behavior, and by implication brain organization, was permanently altered by this early experience. Subsequently, Rosenzweig, Bennett, and Diamond (1972) found that regions of the cerebral cortex were thicker and heavier in rats reared in enriched environments, compared with rats reared in solitary or group cages. Volkmar and Greenough (1972) followed up these

findings, reporting that visual cortical neurons of rats reared in enriched environments had larger dendritic fields than did those of cage-housed controls. Dendrites of neurons receive the bulk of the synaptic input (see Figure 1), so the implication was that new synapses formed. Similar findings were subsequently reported in other areas of the cerebral cortex and in brain regions such as the hippocampus, superior colliculus, and cerebellum. The enriched environment changed brain anatomy in adult rats, which is important evidence for involvement in learning and memory. Turner and Greenough (1985) found that rats reared in enriched environments had more synapses per neuron in the visual cortex, compared with rats reared alone or in pairs in standard laboratory cages. Moreover, similar changes occur in the striatum as well (Comery, Shah, and Greenough, 1995), suggesting that the experience-dependent changes in neuronal morphology influence multiple levels or systems in the brain. The general conclusion from these enriched environment studies is that when animals are placed in an environment in which they store information that affects later behavior, they form new synapses. (The term *enriched* is used in comparison with the typical laboratory environment and does not imply superiority to the natural environment.)

Follow-up studies have explored the effects of specific learning tasks upon these same measures. There is compelling evidence that many forms of learning change both the amount of dendrite per neuron and the number of synapses per neuron. For example, dendritic branching is increased in visual cortical neurons following twenty-five days of exposure to a series of maze problems (Greenough, Juraska, and Volkmar, 1979). Subsequent work used split-brain rats, severing the nerve fibers that allow the right and left hemispheres to communicate, and opaque contact lenses that restricted visual input from training to one eye. Neurons on the trained side of the brain selectively exhibited dendritic field size increases; thus these changes were not of the general sort that might be due to stress or arousal associated with the task, which should affect both sides of the brain equally. These studies, and others, indicated that the altered dendritic fields were associated with neural input and output related to the training.

Synaptogenesis is also implicated in associative learning. Tsukahara (1981) investigated associative limb flexion conditioning, using stimulation to the cerebral peduncle as the conditioned stimulus and electric shock to the forelimb as the unconditioned stimulus. In this paradigm, red nucleus lesions abolish the conditioned response, implicating the involvement of this structure. Electrophysiological studies following conditioning indicated enhanced input to the red nucleus from the cerebral cortex. Subsequently, Tsukahara's coworkers (Murakami, Higashi, Katsumaru, and Oda, 1987) reported morphological evidence for formation of new corticorubral synapses in conditioned animals.

Similar anatomical effects of training have been observed in other behavioral tasks. Stewart (1991) examined day-old chicks that learned to avoid pecking a bad tasting food particle and found an elevated number of synapses in a forebrain region previously shown to be involved in the learning. In another involved brain region there were also increases in the number of spines (see Figure l), the dendritic component of one type of synapse. Likewise, the density of spines was reported to be elevated in hippocampal area CA1 in adult rats following spatial learning (Moser, Trommald, and Andersen, 1994). Comparable changes have been observed in numerous other paradigms (e.g., bird song learning and imprinting in birds). Finally, while this discussion is confined to vertebrates, excellent evidence for comparable synaptic number changes in invertebrate plasticity paradigms also exists.

Neurogenesis presents yet another mechanism whereby brain organization could be modified in response to experience. For example, increased numbers of new neurons have been reported in the dentate gyrus of the hippocampus of animals exposed to a complex environment (Kempermann, Kuhn, and Gage, 1998) or permitted access to an exercise wheel (Van Praag, Christie, Sejnowski, and Gage, 1999). More specific to learning and memory, Gould et al. (1999a) reported that the number of new neurons in rat dentate gyrus dramatically increased following associative conditioning. While most reports of neurogenesis have been limited to rodents and to relatively unique areas in the brain such as the hippocampus or olfactory bulb, neurogenesis has been reported in the primate cortex (Gould, Reeves, Graziano, and Gross, 1999b) and disputed (Kornack and Rakic, 2001). While the issues of the extent, location, and functional relevance of neurogenesis has yet to be resolved, the mere possibility of such a mechanism in the mature central nervous system has spurred a great deal of excitement and hope for many areas of neural research.

Role of Synapse Formation in Plastic Neural Change

An issue that affects all of these studies is whether anatomical changes that are seen following training result merely from increased neural activity involved in performing the learned task. Muscles grow larger in response to exercise; perhaps neurons do too, such that these structural changes have nothing to do with learning or memory per se. (This issue is, of course, not unique to morphological studies; proposed molecular and other aspects of the cellular mechanisms of memory may similarly be artifacts of activity.)

There have been direct tests of the effects of neural activity versus learning on synapse change. For example, Black et al. (1990) compared a cerebellar cortical region in rats that had learned a complex series of motor tasks to that of rats that performed one of two forms of physical exertion involving little learning: running on a treadmill or in an activity wheel. Exercise alone had no effect on synapse number whereas rats that had learned increased the number of synapses per neuron in the cerebellar cortex. Similar effects have been observed in areas such as the motor cortex (Kleim et al., 1996). In contrast, blood vessel density was elevated in affected regions in rats that had exercised, whereas the motor learning rats had the same blood vessel density as control animals. These results indicate that activity and learning have very different effects on brain tissue.

Additional support for the role of synapse formation in plastic neural change has come from studies of long-term potentiation. LTP involves an increase in the response of postsynaptic neurons following high frequency bursts of presynaptic firing. LTP induction has been shown to increase spine density and modify dendritic morphology in the motor cortex (Ivanco, Racine, and Kolb, 2000) and in hippocampal subfield CA1 (Lee, Oliver, Schottler, and Lynch, 1981). Chang and Greenough (1984) included a type of high frequency stimulation that did not induce LTP, and subsequently did not alter synapse formation, suggesting that LTP-induced synaptogenesis was not caused by high frequency stimulation alone. In contrast to CA1, induction of LTP in the hippocampal dentate gyrus does not cause synapse formation but changes synapse structure (Geinisman, de Toledo-Morrell, and Morrell, 1991). Recent advances in microscopy have permitted near real time evaluation of changes in morphology of living neurons. Using these tools, Engert and Bonhoeffer (1999) reported that postsynaptic spines are formed de novo in response to stimulation. Taken together, these findings reinforce the view that numerous different cellular changes may be involved in learning, and other forms of neural plasticity as well.

Changes in Synapse Structure: Indications of Synapse Efficacy Change

Several structural features of synapses have been found to be altered by behavioral experience. One of the most obvious features is the size of synapses. Larger synapses may release more neurotransmitter or have more receptors, such that a size change could indicate a strength change. Early findings indicated smaller synapses in the visual cortex of animals visually deprived during development, and Tieman (1985) reported smaller geniculocortical synapses in monocularly deprived cats. Conversely, synapse size increased following imprinting in day-old chicks, and similar size changes were found after avoidance learning. Larger synapses were also observed in layer IV of the visual cortex of rats reared in enriched environments, compared with individually caged controls. Likewise, Van Harreveld and Fifkova (1975) described changes in the size of synaptic spine heads and necks (see Figure 1) following LTP induction in the dentate gyrus. Koch and Zador (1993) have suggested that larger spine components, and the associated spine neck restriction, may permit activation of focalized intracellular cascades and reduce electrical resistance, thereby facilitating the passage of synaptic current into the dendrite (Harris and Kater, 1994).

Synaptic vesicles are believed to contain neurotransmitters, and changes in their numbers could indicate changes in synapse strength. Synaptic vesicle numbers have been reported to decrease with visual deprivation (e.g., Tieman, 1985) and there are reports of both decreased vesicle density and altered vesicle location within the presynaptic terminal following LTP induction (e.g., Applegate, Kerr, and Landfield, 1987; Fifkova and Van Harreveld, 1977). In contrast, vesicle numbers have been shown to increase in rats reared in enriched environments (Nakamura, Kobayashi, Ohashi, and Ando, 1999; Sirevaag and Greenough, 1991).

At least three other synapse features appear to be sensitive to experience. First, small discontinuities in the postsynaptic density, termed *perforations*, have been found to increase in number following complex environment exposure and to decrease in affected synapses subsequent to sensory deprivation (Greenough, West, and DeVoogd, 1978). Moreover, Vrensen and Cardozo (1981) found that the number of perforated synapses increased in the visual cortex following visual discrimination learning. The function of these perforations is unknown. Second, the incidence of *multiple synaptic boutons* (presynaptic elements that synapse with multiple postsynaptic components) is elevated in numerous brain areas following exposure to a complex environment and in animals that have been trained in an associative learning paradigm (Geinisman et al., 2001; Jones et al., 1997). Third, the cellular organelles that synthesize protein, *polyribosomal aggregates*, are frequently found in the heads and necks of spines during periods of synapse formation (Steward and Falk, 1985). They are also found more frequently in spines of animals in complex environments, possibly reflecting greater rates of synapse formation. Protein synthesis at the synapse has been proposed as a memory mechanism (Steward and Schuman, 2001).

Changes in Nonneural Elements

The enriched environment work indicated from its earliest days that morphological changes were not restricted to neurons. Glial cells, supportive elements that maintain ionic, metabolic, and neurotransmitter homeostasis, respond similarly to environmental complexity. Sirevaag and Greenough (1991) reported that astrocytes grow larger and extend additional processes into the tissue during the first phase of their response to the animal's housing in an enriched environment. In a second phase, astrocytes divide, increasing their numbers, and shrink, on average, toward their preexposure size. These stages are qualitatively comparable with those of gliosis, the glial reaction to injury, yet protracted. Moreover, Anderson et al. (1994) have shown an increase in the volume of glia per Purkinje cell in the cerebellum of animals that learned a complex motor skill, but not those who simply exercised. Likewise, blood vessel density increased in rats placed in an enriched environment at the age of weaning. In animals that are older at the time they are first exposed to enrichment, this blood vessel response diminishes with increasing age.

Conclusion

Morphological research has provided strong evidence for both forms of synaptic change that have been proposed to underlie learning and memory. Formation, and occasionally loss, of synapses occurs both during periods of development when the brain is storing information and during exposure to specific learning tasks. Various control procedures have largely ruled out the possibility that these synaptic changes are artifactual results arising from factors other than learning. Changes in the structure of synapses, such as in the size or shape of synaptic components, also occur during learning and in other situations in which functional brain organization is altered, such as LTP. Many of these structural changes have been associated with synapse strength differences in other research. Developing research implicates addition of new neurons via neurogenesis and changes in nonneuronal elements of the brain. Thus the weight of the evidence indicates that both synapse formation/removal and synapse strength changes are involved in learning and memory, but additional mechanisms are also likely.

See also: MORPHOLOGICAL BASIS OF LEARNING AND MEMORY: INVERTEBRATES; PROTEIN SYNTHESIS IN LONG-TERM MEMORY IN VERTEBRATES

Bibilography

Andersen, B. J., Li, X., Alcantara, A. A., Isaacs, K. R., Black, J. E., and Greenough, W. T. (1994). Glial hypertrophy is associated with synaptogenesis following motor-skill learning, but not with angiogenesis following exercise. *Glia 11,*73–80.

Applegate, M. D., Kerr, D. S., and Landfield, P. W. (1987). Redistribution of synaptic vesicles during long-term potentiation in the hippocampus. *Brain Research 401,* 401–406.

Black, J. E., Isaacs, K. R., Anderson, B. J., Alcantara, A. A., and Greenough, W. T. (1990). Learning causes synaptogenesis, whereas motor activity causes angiogenesis, in cerebellar cortex of adult rats. *Proceedings of the National Academy of Sciences of the United States of America 87,* 5,568–5,572.

Chang, F.-L. F., and Greenough, W. T. (1984). Transient and enduring morphological correlates of synaptic activity and efficacy change in the rat hippocampal slice. *Brain Research 309,* 35–46.

Comery, T. A., Shah, R., and Greenough, W. T. (1995). Differential rearing alters spine density on medium-sized spiny neurons in the rat corpus striatum: Evidence for the association of morphological plasticity with early response gene expression. *Neurobiology of Learning and Memory 63,* 217–219.

Cragg, B. G. (1975). The development of synapses in kitten visual cortex during visual deprivation. *Experimental Neurology 46,* 445–451.

Engert, F., and Bonhoeffer, T. (1999). Dendritic spine changes associated with hippocampal long-term synaptic plasticity. *Nature 399,* 66–70.

Fifkova, E., and Van Harreveld, A. (1977). Long-lasting morphological changes in dendritic spines of dentate granular cells following stimulation of the entorhinal area. *Journal of Neurocytology 6,* 211–230.

Geinisman, Y., Berry, R. W., Disterhoft, J. F., Power, J. M., and Van der Zee, E. A. (2001). Associative learning elicits the formation of multiple-synapse boutons. *Journal of Neuroscience 21,* 5,568–5,573.

Geinisman, Y., de Toledo-Morrell, L., and Morrell, F. (1991). Induction of long-term potentiation is associated with an increase in the number of axospinous synapses with segmented postsynaptic densities. *Brain Research 566,* 77–88.

Gould, E., Beylin, A., Tanapat, P., Reeves, A., and Shors, T. J. (1999a). Learning enhances adult neurogenesis in the hippocampal formation. *Nature Neuroscience 2,* 260–265.

Gould, E., Reeves, A. J., Graziano, M. S., and Gross, C. G. (1999b). Neurogenesis in the neocortex of adult primates. *Science 286,* 548–552.

Greenough, W. T., Juraska, J. M., and Volkmar, F. R. (1979). Maze training effects on dendritic branching in occipital cortex of adult rats. *Behavioral and Neural Biology 26,* 287–297.

Greenough, W. T., West, R. W., and DeVoogd, T. J. (1978). Subsynaptic plate perforations: Changes with age and experience in the rat. *Science 202,* 1,096–1,098.

Harris, K. M., and Kater, S. B. (1994). Dendritic spines: Cellular specializations imparting both stability and flexibility to synaptic function. *Annual Review of Neuroscience 17,* 341–371.

Ivanco, T. L., Racine, R. J., and Kolb, B. (2000). Morphology of layer III pyramidal neurons is altered following induction of LTP in sensorimotor cortex of the freely moving rat. *Synapse 37,* 16–22.

Jones, T. A., Klintsova, A. Y., Kilman, V. L., Sirevaag, A. M., and Greenough, W. T. (1997). Induction of multiple synapses by experience in the visual cortex of adult rats. *Neurobiology of Learning and Memory 68,* 13–20.

Kempermann, G., Kuhn, H. G., and Gage, F. H. (1998). Experience-induced neurogenesis in the senescent dentate gyrus. *Journal of Neuroscience 18,* 3,206–3,212.

Kleim, J. A., Lussnig, E., Schwarz, E. R., Comery, T. A., and Greenough, W. T. (1996). Synaptogenesis and FOS expression in the motor cortex of the adult rat after motor skill learning. *Journal of Neuroscience 16,* 4,529–4,535.

Koch, C., and Zador, A. (1993). The function of dendritic spines: Devices subserving biochemical rather than electrical compartmentalization. *Journal of Neuroscience 13,* 413–422.

Kornack, D. R., and Rakic, P. (2001). Cell proliferation without neurogenesis in adult primate neocortex. *Science 294,* 2,127–2,130.

Lee, K. S., Oliver, M., Schottler, F., and Lynch, G. (1981). Electron microscopic studies of brain slices: The effects of high frequency stimulation on dendritic ultrastructure. In G. A. Kerkut, and H. V. Wheal, eds. *Electrophysiology of isolated mammalian CNS preparations.* New York: Academic Press.

Moser, M.-B., Trommald, M., and Andersen, P. (1994). An increase in dendritic spine density on hippocampal CA1 pyramidal cells following spatial learning in adult rats suggests the formation of new synapses. *Proceedings of the National Academy of Sciences of the United States of America 91,* 12,673–12,675.

Murakami, F., Higashi, S., Katsumaru, H., and Oda, Y. (1987). Formation of new corticorubral synapses as a mechanism for classical conditioning in the cat. *Brain Research 437,* 379–382.

Nakamura H., Kobayashi, S., Ohashi, Y., and Ando, S. (1999). Age-changes of brain synapses and synaptic plasticity in response to an enriched environment. *Journal of Neuroscience Research 56,* 307–315.

Rosenzweig, M. R., Bennett, E. L., and Diamond, M. C. (1972). Chemical and anatomical plasticity of brain: Replications and extensions. In J. Gaito, ed. *Macromolecules and behavior,* 2nd edition. New York: Appleton-Century-Crofts.

Sirevaag, A. M., and Greenough, W. T. (1991). Plasticity of GFAP-immunoreactive astrocyte size and number in visual cortex of rats reared in complex environments. *Brain Research 540,* 273–278.

Steward, O., and Falk, P. M. (1985). Polyribosomes under developing spine synapses: Growth specializations of dendrites at sites of synaptogenesis. *Journal of Neuroscience Research 13,* 75–88.

Steward O., and Schuman E. M. (2001). Protein synthesis at synaptic sites on dendrites. *Annual Review of Neuroscience 24,* 299–325.

Stewart, M. G. (1991). Changes in dendritic and synaptic structure in chick forebrain consequent on passive avoidance learning. In R. J. Andrew, ed. *Neural and behavioral plasticity.* London: Oxford University Press.

Tieman, S. B. (1985). The anatomy of geniculocortical connections in monocularly deprived cats. *Cellular and Molecular Neurobiology 5,* 35–45.

Tsukahara, N. (1981). Sprouting and the neuronal basis of learning. *Trends in Neurosciences 4,* 234–237.

Turner, A. M., and Greenough, W. T. (1985). Differential rearing effects on rat visual cortex synapses. I. Synaptic and neuronal density and synapses per neuron. *Brain Research 329,* 195–203.

Van Harreveld, A., and Fifkova, E. (1975). Swelling of dendritic spines in the fascia dentata after stimulation of the perforant fibers as a mechanism of post-tetanic potentiation. *Experimental Neurology 49,* 736–749.

Van Praag, H., Christie, B. R., Sejnowski, T. J., and Gage, F. H. (1999). Running enhances neurogenesis, learning, and long-term potentiation in mice. *Proceedings of the National Academy of Sciences of the United States of America 96,* 13,427–13,431.

Volkmar, F. R., and Greenough, W. T. (1972). Rearing complexity affects branching of dendrites in the visual cortex of the rat. *Science 176,* 1,445–1,447.

Vrensen, G., and Cardozo, J. N. (1981). Changes in size and shape of synaptic connections after visual training: An ultrastructural approach of synaptic plasticity. *Brain Research 218,* 79–97.

William T. Greenough
Revised by William T. Greenough and James D. Churchill

MOTOR SKILL LEARNING

A variety of motor skills occur in various forms of movement: work, play, sport, communication, dance, and so on. Psychophysical studies of the learning and retention of motor skills date from the 1890s, with neurophysiological studies coming later. Attempts to combine cognitive and neural approaches flourished in the twentieth century (Bernstein, 1967) and persist unabated, capitalizing on advances in technology.

The theoretical and operational emphases of this field parallel those in other subdomains of learning, in part because motor, perceptual, and cognitive skills are not mutually exclusive and in part because of anatomical advances that show the underlying modular architecture of the brain (Houk, 2001). Definitions of motor skills typically pertain to the movements of the limbs and torso as opposed to those of perceptions and the formulation of ideas, but the conceptual boundaries blur in the face of the planning that precedes elaborate motor acts.

How do people learn and remember how to dance, type, hop, play the piano, and tie their shoelaces? Bartlett (1932) said of the skilled tennis player, "When I make the stroke I do not, as a matter of fact, produce something absolutely new, and I never merely repeat something old." A central issue in the learning of motor skills is how the movement form is acquired through practice and retained over time. A related issue is the role that variations of movement form play in realizing the goal of the act. These two issues, movement invariance and motor equivalence, have been the focus of the theorizing about the acquisition and retention of motor skills.

Motor skills involve two distinctive operations: One is to select, recall, and initiate the movement segment required at each stage in a task; the other is to guide the trajectories of the movement segments so that they achieve the subgoals required to complete the task. Much of the work on skill learning and retention has emphasized the second operation, the refinement of trajectories based on the experience gained through the sensory consequences of the movement (Adams, 1971).

The emerging conceptions of cognitive psychology challenged the one-to-one memory accounts of movement representation. An outgrowth of this trend was Schmidt's (1975) schema theory of motor learning, which promoted a one-to-many representational construct for both recall and recognition processes of movement control. The representation for each memory state consisted of the relations between task, organism, and environmental variables rather than the absolute levels of the variables themselves. The schema was a generic rule for a given class of movements that allowed the generalization of movement outcome to a variety of task and environmental circumstances. Schema theory proposed that the more variable the practice within the potential class of movements (e.g., variations in the length, velocity, and/or angle of a forehand drive in tennis), the more general the schema rule would become for that activity. Neurobiologically based theories of movement control seem to be able to account for most of this framework (Bertier et al., 1993).

The schema theory seemed to provide a solution to two enduring problems in motor-skill acquisition and retention: novelty and the limited storage capacity. The novelty problem addresses the question of how the performer accommodates to novel tasks and environmental circumstances. The limited storage capacity of the CNS arises as a consequence of the many one-to-one representations that would be generated from an individual's lifetime movement experience, especially in the absence of schema theory. The Schmidt schema theory could not resolve the novelty problem because it did not explain the initial establishment of the movement class; it accounted only for changes in the scaling of force, velocity, or position of a given action pattern (such as a tennis forehand drive) rather than the generation of pattern of the forehand drive movement—perhaps because it did not interface with the emerging knowledge about the basal ganglia (Houk and Wise, 1995).

During the 1980s one-to-one and one-to-many prescriptive accounts of motor-skill learning were challenged by the tenets of the ecological approach to perception and action (Kugler and Turvey, 1987). The ecological approach seeks the solution to motor learning through the mapping of perception and action with minimal appeal to the representational processes typically posited by cognitive psychologists. A central concern has been the appropriateness of cognitive strategies proposed to map the emergent movement dynamics into a rule-based symbolic representation.

The emergent structure and variability of the movement sequence was subsequently analyzed in terms of physical-systems solutions to the mapping of the gradient and equilibrium regions of the perceptual and motor processes (Kugler and Turvey, 1987; Schoner and Kelso, 1988). A physical approach to the study of the learning and retention of motor skills must contend with the question of how information and dynamics relate to the intention of the performer. Learning can be viewed as an exploratory activity, with the performer searching for stable regions of the perceptual and motor dynamics that realize the goal of the act (Newell et al., 1989).

The 1990s saw a rising interest in understanding how the networks of the brain might learn to generate motor command signals capable of controlling skilled movements. Neural-network models of the cerebellum based on the anatomy and physiology of these circuits helped to relate skill acquisition and performance to many fundamental features of motor performance, such as the one-to-many representational construct for motor programs (Berthier et al., 1993) and the predictive capacity required to prevent instability caused by closed-loop control (Barto et al., 1999). Models of the interaction between the cerebellum and the cerebral cortex suggested the manner in which memories might be translocated to improve the speed and automaticity of practiced skills. New techniques such as transcranial magnetic stimulation

are shedding light on the changes in the motor cortex that occur with practice (Classen et al., 1998). Functional imaging of the brain is helping to define the networks that participate in motor programming (van Mier et al., 1998).

Conclusion

Traditional theories of motor learning and retention fail to capture many of the qualities of the progression from novice to expert in skill acquisition. The development of a skill is a continuous exploratory activity, not a replica of a static representation of action. Neurobiological cognitive models, based on new techniques for studying brain activation, combined with the ecological approach to perception and action, are beginning to capture some of the important qualities, both invariant and changing, of the dynamics of motorskill acquisition and retention.

Bibliography

Adams, J. A. (1971). A closed-loop theory of motor learning. *Journal of Motor Behavior 3*, 111–150.

Bartlett, F. C. (1932). *Remembering: A study of experimental and social psychology.* Cambridge: Cambridge University Press.

Barto, A. G., Fagg, A. H., Sitkoff, N., and Houk, J. C. (1999). A cerebellar model of timing and prediction in the control of reaching. *Neural Computation 11*, 565–594.

Bernstein, N. A. (1967). *The coordination and regulation of movements.* London: Pergamon.

Berthier, N. E., Singh, S. P., Barto, A. G., and Houk, J. C. (1993). Distributed representation of limb motor programs in arrays of adjustable pattern generators. *Journal of Cognitive Neuroscience 5*, 56–78.

Classen, J., Liepert, J., Wise, S. P., Hallett, M., and Cohen, L. G. (1998). Rapid plasticity of human cortical movement representation induced by practice. *Journal of Neurophysiology 79*, 1,117–1,123.

Fowler, C. A., and Turvey, M. T. (1978). Skill acquisition: An event approach with special reference to searching for the optimum of a function of several variables. In G. E. Stelmach, ed., *Information processing and motor control.* New York: Academic Press.

Houk, J. (2001). Neurophysiology of frontal-subcortical loops. In D. G. Lichter and J. L. Cummings, eds., *Frontal-subcortical circuits in psychiatry and neurology.* New York: Guilford Publications.

Houk, J. C., and Wise, S. P. (1995). Distributed modular architectures linking basal ganglia, cerebellum, and cerebral cortex: Their role in planning and controlling action. *Cerebral Cortex 5*, 95–110.

Hua, S. E., and Houk, J. C. (1997). Cerebellar guidance of premotor network development and sensorimotor learning. *Learning and Memory 4*, 63–76.

Kugler, P. N., and Turvey, M. T. (1987). *Information, natural law, and the self-assembly of rhythmic movement.* Hillsdale, NJ: Erlbaum.

Newell, K. M., Kugler, P. N., van Emmerik, R. E. A., and McDonald, P. V. (1989). Search strategies and the acquisition of coordination. In S. A. Wallace, ed., *Perspectives on the coordination of movement.* Amsterdam: North-Holland.

Schmidt, R.A. (1975). A schema theory of discrete motor skill learning. *Psychological Review 82*, 225–260.

Schoner, G., and Kelso, J. A. S. (1988). A dynamic theory of behavioral change. *Journal of Theoretical Biology 135*, 501–524.

van Mier, H., Tempel, L. W., Perlmutter, J. S., Raichle, M. E., and Petersen, S. E. (1998). Changes in brain activity during motor learning measured with PET: Effects of hand of performance and practice. *Journal of Neurophysiology 80,* 2,177–2,199.

Karl M. Newell
Revised by James C. Houk

MÜLLER, GEORG ELIAS (1850–1934)

During his tenure at the University of Göttingen from 1881 to 1921, the German psychologist Georg Elias Müller helped to spearhead major advances in theory and research into perception, learning, and memory.

Early Life and Career

Georg Elias Müller was born on July 20, 1850, into a clerical family in Grimma, Saxony, Germany. As a schoolboy he showed a precocious interest in natural science, philosophy, poetry, and history. In 1868 he began to study philosophy and history at the University of Leipzig and moved to the University of Berlin in 1869. In Berlin he became acquainted with Rudolph Hermann Lotze's writings, which shifted his focus from history to science as the subject closest to his principal interest, philosophy. After interrupting his studies to fight in the Franco-Prussian war of 1870–1871, he moved to Göttingen in 1872 to study with Lotze. The following year he submitted his doctoral dissertation on sensory attention (Müller, 1873) and he completed his postdoctoral dissertation on psychophysics (Müller, 1878) in 1876. Five years later he succeeded Lotze as chair of philosophy in Göttingen, a position he held for forty years, until his mandatory retirement in 1921.

By then Müller's institute had become one of the most important centers for experimental psychology in all of Europe, attracting students from all over the world. He also opened his laboratory to women at a time when research opportunities for women were nearly nonexistent. Among his students were Alfred Binet, E. R. Jaensch, Adolf Jost, David Katz, Oswald Kroh, Oswald Külpe, Lillian J. Martin, Eleanor McGamble, Alfons Pilzecker, Géza Révész, Edgar Rubin, and Friedrich Schumann. Müller, who was often described as a somewhat gruff character, was feared by his students as a relentless critic and a stickler for scientific rigor, but he was also cherished as a skillful listener and as an unfaltering supporter of their work. His meticulous, diligent, and innovative experimental approach earned his laboratory the reputation as the premier center for experimental psychology in all of Europe. Müller's pioneering vision also led to the formation of the "Society for Experimental Psychology," which he headed from 1904 to 1927.

Georg Elias Müller *(Georg-Elias-Müller Institute of Psychology)*

Main Work

Müller's main contributions to experimental psychology fall into three areas: psychophysics, visual perception, and memory.

Psychophysics

Working from the philosophical background of the mind-body problem, which energized his research all his life, Müller first directed his attention to psychophysics, the scientific discipline that spearheaded the establishment of psychology as an objective science. The Weber-Fechner law, which describes the relationship between physical and perceived stimulus intensity, had appeared in Gustav Fechner's groundbreaking work "Elements of Psychophysics" in 1860. While the idea of a lawful relationship between physical objects and perceived stimuli had been widely accepted, the experimental methods for obtaining measurements and the possibility of a mathematically precise treatment of subjective perceptions were the subject of extended scientific debate. Müller's postdoctoral dissertation, "On the Foundations of Psychophysics" (1878), and his paper on the method of right and wrong cases (later known as the method of constant stimuli) established Müller as an independent, critical thinker. His contributions were acknowledged in Fechner's "Revision of the Main Points of Psychophysics." His methods still are widely used in psychophysical experiments.

Visual Perception

Visual perception, especially color perception, occupied Müller in the late 1890s and led to his authoring four publications on this topic between 1896 and 1897. In these papers he argued that the three photochemical substances proposed by Ewald Hering as the basis of color vision were reversible by a chemical rather than a metabolic process. Moreover, he proposed that equal excitation by red/green, blue/yellow, and black/white resulted in the perception of "cortical gray" rather than the visual "silence" assumed by Hering. Müller returned to color perception after his retirement and remained with it until his final years, even at the expense of completing his autobiography. Instead, he summarized his observations and theories in two books: *On Sensations of Color: Psychophysical Investigations* (1930) and *Brief Contributions to the Psychophysics of Color Sensations* (1934).

Memory

Müller's work on memory is probably his best known. He inherited the topic from Hermann Ebbinghaus, whose monograph *On Memory* (1885) first demonstrated that even cognitive phenomena such as verbal memory could be successfully studied and quantified in the laboratory. When Ebbinghaus showed no further interest in memory research, Müller seized the opportunity. During the next thirty years Müller and his students made a number of seminal contributions. The most notable were "Experimental Contributions to the Investigation of Memory" (1894) and "Experimental Contributions to the Theory of Learning and Memory" (1900). Both articles describe sophisticated experimental methods for studying verbal memory, which were developed by Müller and his students Friedrich Schumann, Adolf Jost, and Alfons Pilzecker and became standard in experimental psychology for many decades.

Müller's first contribution was to recognize the importance of constructing lists of syllables that were equally difficulty to read and learn. To this end he tightened Ebbinghaus's rules for generating and selecting nonsense syllables. Müller's second contribution was to control the presentation of study material. Lists of syllables were mounted on a rotating cylinder, called a memory drum, and syllables were presented one at a time through a shutter behind which the memory drum was mounted. The subjects were instructed to respond by reading each syllable aloud with emphasis on every odd-numbered syllable, thus creating paired associates (pairs of emphasized and nonemphasized syllables, or trochees).

Müller and Schumann first adopted Ebbinghaus's method of determining how many trials were needed to memorize a list of twelve syllables (the method of complete mastery, or *Erlernungsmethode*). They then explored the conditions under which previously learned material facilitated the memorization of reorganized syllable lists (the method of savings, or *Ersparnismethode*). Using these methods, they determined that reading the pairs of syllables in trochaic style resulted in stronger associations between the syllables within the pair than between the adjacent syllables of two pairs. They also explored a number of conditions (e.g., retention delay) that either facilitated or weakened acquisition of the study material.

Müller and Pilzecker significantly improved on these early experiments by replacing the method of complete mastery with the method of right associates (*Treffermethode*), shifting the focus from acquisition to recall of learned material. In these experiments the number of learning trials for each list of syllable pairs was fixed. Then the subjects were cued with the first syllable of each pair and asked to recall the second syllable of each pair. This method, developed by Adolph Jost in Müller's laboratory, provided three ways to assess memory performance: correct answers, incorrect answers, and failures to recall. Moreover, the data could be supplemented by the subject's response times as measured by a novel apparatus. The shutter in front of the memory drum was now operated by an electromagnet. Opening the shutter exposed the cue syllable for each trial and triggered a chronometer. The subject's response was registered by a lip key or vibration-sensitive device that would stop the chronometer, close the shutter, and advance the memory drum to the next cue syllable. Armed with this methodology, Müller and Pilzecker began a series of experiments that quickly exceeded the scope of Ebbinghaus's original studies. After studying the effects of list repetition and retention interval on cued recall, they explored interference between associations. They first presented a pair of syllables (e.g., *ser-lad*) and in a later list used the same cue syllable (*ser*) in another association (e.g., *ser-kum*). Recall cued by ambiguous syllables was consistently lower than recall cued by unambiguous syllables.

These findings became fundamental to learning and memory research. Yet Müller's monograph with Pilzecker is probably best known for its novel proposal that learning does not induce instantaneous, permanent memories but that memory requires an interval of consolidation. He and Pilzecker arrived at that conclusion after a number of experiments on retroactive inhibition, a painstaking analysis of the types incorrect answers volunteers were prone to make, and a thoughtful consideration of a phenomenon they termed "perseveration" (i.e., the tendency of study material to inger in a subject's mind after learning). They wrote (Müller and Pilzecker, 1900, 196–197):

After all this, there is no alternative but to assume that, after a list of syllables has been read, certain physiological processes that serve to strengthen the associations induced during reading of that list continue with decreasing intensity for a period of time. These processes and their facilitating effects on these associations are being weakened to a greater or lesser extent if the experimental subject experiences further mental exhaustion immediately after reading a list. . . . It seems justified to suppose that the physiological processes mentioned her are the same that underlie perseverative tendencies. . . . Mental exertion in an experimental subject after reading a list of syllables has, first, the direct effect of weakening the perseverative tendencies of these syllables and, second, because the effect of these perseverative tendencies is to consolidate syllable associations, the additional effect of impairing these associations (retroactive interference).

Considering their observations on perseveration, Müller and Pilzecker proposed that consolidation occurred within about ten minutes. Yet their experiments did not systematically explore this time course. McDougall and Burnham quickly recognized the idea of memory consolidation because it provided a way to understand temporally graded retrograde amnesia that results from traumatic head injury. Later, Carl Duncan's experiments on ECS-induced retrograde amnesia in rats launched decades of research in many laboratories to study consolidation and its time course.

With the passing decades, awareness of Müller's importance to the field of experimental psychology, especially memory research, began to fade. But his groundbreaking experiments on memory still inspire productive research in cellular neurobiology and systems neuroscience.

An indefatigable scholar, Müller worked long after his retirement in 1921, producing important publications until his death, on December 23, 1934.

Bibliography

Boring, E. G. (1950). *History of experimental psychology.* New York: Appleton-Century-Crofts.

Burnham, W. H. (1903). Retroactive amnesia, illustrative cases and a tentative explanation. *American Journal of Psychology 14,* 382–396.

Duncan, C. P. (1949). The retroactive effect of electroshock on learning. *Journal of Comparative Physiological Psychology 42,* 32–44.

Ebbinghaus, H. (1885). *Über das Gedächtnis, Untersuchungen zur experimentellen Psychologie* [On memory, Investigations in experimental psychology]. Leipzig: Duncker and Humbolt.

Fechner, G. (1860). *Elemente der Psychophysik* [Elements of psychophysics], 2 vols. Leipzig: Breitkopf and Härtel.

——— (1882). *Revision der Hauptpuncte der Psychophysik* [Revision of the main points of psychophysics]. Leipzig: Breitkopf and Härtel.

Haupt, E. J. (1998). Origins of American psychology in the work of G. E. Müller, classical psychophysics and serial learning. In R. W. Rieber and K. Salzinger, eds., *Psychology Theoretical-Historical perspectives,* 2nd edition. Washington, DC: American Sociological Association.

Jost, A. (1897). Die Associationsfestigkeit in ihrer Abhängigkeit von der Verteilung der Wiederholungen [The strength of associations in relation to the distribution of repetitions]. *Zeitschrift für Psychologie 14,* 436–472.

Lechner, H. A., Squire, L. R., and Byrne, J. H. (1999). 100 years of consolidation—remembering Müller and Pilzecker. *Learning and Memory 6,* 77–87.

McDougall, W. (1901). Experimentelle Beitraege zur Lehre vom Gedaechtnis, von G. E. Mueller und A. Pilzecker [Experimental contributions to the theory of memory by G. E. Mueller and A. Pilzecker].*Mind 10,* 388–394.

Müller, G. E. (1873). *Zur Theorie der sinnlichen Aufmerksamkeit* [On the theory of sensory attention]. Ph.D. diss. Leipzig: Edelman.

——— (1878). *Zur Grundlegung der Psychophysik* [On the Foundations of Psychophysics], Vol. 4: *Kritische Beiträge. Bibliothek für Wissenschaft und Literatur.* 23 vols. Philosophische Abtheilung. Berlin: Greiben.

——— (1879). Über die Maasbestimmung des Ortsinnes der Haut mittels der Methode der richtigen und falschen Fälle [On the quantification of the location sense of the skin by way of the method of right and wrong cases]. *Pflüger's Archiv für die gesamte Physiologie 19,* 191–235.

——— (1930). Über die Farbenempfindungen, Psychophysische Untersuchungen. Band 1 und 2 [On Sensations of Color, Psychophysical Investigations]. *Zeitschrift für Psychologie, Ergänzungsband 17 and 18.* Leipzig: Barth.

——— (1934). *Kleine Beiträge zur Psychophysik der Farbempfindungen* [Brief Contributions to the Psychophysics of Color Sensations]. Leipzig: Barth.

Müller, G. E. and Pilzecker, A. (1900). Experimentelle Beiträge zur Lehre vom Gedächtnis [Experimental contributions to the theory of memory]. *Zeitschrift für Psychologie, Ergänzungsband 1,* 1–300.

Müller, G. E., and Schuman, F. (1894). Experimentelle Beiträge zur Lehre vom Gedächtnis [Experimental contributions to the investigation of memory]. *Zeitschrift für Psychologie 6,* 81–190, 257.

Sprung, L., and Sprung, H. (2000). Georg Elias Müller and the beginnings of modern psychology. In G. A. Kimble and M. Wertheimer, eds., *Portraits of pioneers in psychology,* Vol. 4. Mahwah, NJ: Erlbaum.

Hilde A. E. Lechner

MULTIPLE-MEMORY SYSTEMS

In 1950 Karl Lashley published his influential manuscript *In Search of the Engram,* in which he concluded that memory was widely distributed in the mammalian brain and that there is no apparent localization of mnemonic traces within specific brain structures. Five decades' worth of research since then suggests that his conclusion may have been partially incorrect. Whereas it is clear that distributed brain structures do indeed participate in mnemonic functions, it is also the case that there is some degree of neuroanatomical localization of learning and memory. There is extensive evidence that memory is organized in multiple systems that differ in terms of the type of memory they mediate. The multiple-memory-systems hypothesis is supported by findings of neuroscientific research in several mammalian species, including rats, monkeys, and humans (Hirsh, 1974; O'Keefe and Nadel, 1978; Olton, Becker and Handelmann, 1979; Packard, Hirsh, and White, 1989; Kesner, Bolland, and Dakis, 1993; Mishkin and Petri, 1984; Zola-Morgan, Squire, and Mishkin, 1982; Cohen and Squire, 1980; Warrington and Weiskrantz, 1982; Knowlton, Mangels, and Squire, 1996). In addition to providing neuroanatomical dissociations of the role of various brain structures in different memory tasks, an important goal of multiple-memory-systems research is elucidation of the psychological operating principles that distinguish different types of memory.

Early Evidence of Multiple-Memory Systems

W. B. Scoville and B. Milner (1957) provided early indirect evidence suggesting the existence of multiple-memory systems in the human brain. In an attempt to alleviate seizure activity in epilepsy and to develop possible alternatives to the practice of performing frontal lobotomies in treating psychosis, they excised large regions of the medial temporal lobe of the brain in a number of patients. The discovery that a severe anterograde human amnesic syndrome resulted from removal of temporal lobe neural tissue sparked immense interest in the role of this brain region in learning and memory. A process of elimination, in which mnemonic deficits were contrasted following varying degrees of damage to different temporal-lobe structures, led to the hypothesis that damage to the hippocampus was primarily responsible for the memory deficits observed in these patients. However, these so-called "temporal lobe amnesics" performed normally on some perceptual and motor-skill learning tasks (e.g. Milner, 1962; Corkin, 1968). These early discoveries of a pattern of spared and impaired learning abilities following temporal lobe damage was consistent with the hypothesis that memory is organized in multiple brain systems. However, the development of dual-memory theories, which might distinguish independent memory systems, did not begin in earnest for several more years.

Lower Animal Research and the Development of Dual-Memory Theories

The ability to produce localized brain damage in animals allowed experimental psychologists to pursue the development of an animal model of the human amnesic syndrome, and the mid-1960s saw several studies examining the effects of hippocampal system damage in various learning tasks. However, these early studies often failed to reveal memory deficits following lesions of the hippocampus, leading some investigators to conclude that this brain structure is not particularly important for mnemonic processes. One explanation for the failure of some animal studies to reveal memory deficits following hippocampal damage is that this structure mediates the acquisition of a specific type of memory. This latter view implies that evidence for a mnemonic role for the hippocampus would emerge only with the use of appropriate learning tasks, and this hypothesis became one of the primary tenets of several dual-memory theories abroad in the mid-1970s.

In an extensive early review of the effects of hippocampal system damage on performance of various learning and memory tasks in rats, R. Hirsh (1974) published perhaps the earliest example of a neurobiological-based dual-memory theory. Hirsh proposed that one way to describe the psychological operating principles that distinguished putative hippocampus-dependent and nonhippocampus-dependent memory systems involved consideration of the historic debate between cognitive (e.g. Tolman, 1932) and stimulus-response (e.g. Hull, 1943) learning theorists. In view of the extraordinary emphasis placed by early learning theorists on the question of *what* animals learn, it is not surprising that the debate between cognitive and S-R learning theorists was extremely influential. Hirsh suggested, "The behavior of hippocampally ablated animals is held to be everything for which early S-R theorists could have wished" (Hirsh, 1974, p. 439). That same year, J. O'Keefe and L. Nadel introduced a précis of their dual-memory theory, later elaborated on in their influential book *The Hippocampus as a Cognitive Map* (1978). Their remarkable discovery that hippocampal neurons fired in relationship to a rat's spatial location led O'Keefe and Nadel to suggest that the hippocampus is the neuroanatomical substrate of E. C. Tolman's (1932) cognitive spatial map. Expanding on these ideas, M. Mishkin and colleagues (1984) subsequently offered a distinction between a hippocampal-based cognitive memory system and a nonhippocampal based S-R habit memory system in the monkey brain.

Several other dual-memory theories have emerged based on research in rats, monkeys, and humans. One prominent theoretical distinction between different types of memory in humans is based on a pattern of spared and impaired learning in temporal lobe amnesia; it draws a distinction between hippocampus-dependent declarative memory and nonhippocampus-dependent procedural memory (Cohen and Squire, 1980). Declarative memory involves acquisition and expression of specific facts and events, whereas procedural memory involves acquisition of instrumental S-R habits and various forms of classically conditioned behaviors. A theoretical distinction between explicit and implicit memory processes in humans (Graf and Schacter, 1985) has also received extensive investigation and support. Explicit memory is held to involve the conscious recollection of facts and events, while implicit memory involves unconscious acquisition and expression of learned behavior. E. B Tulving's distinction between episodic and semantic memory represents an additional example of a multiple-memory-systems approach to memory organization in humans (Tulving, 1987).

Neuroanatomical Bases of Multiple-Memory Systems

Each dual-memory theory was developed from a consideration of the pattern of spared and impaired learning that follows damage to one particular brain region: the hippocampus. Thus, the existence of multiple-memory systems has often been suggested based on the observations of single dissociations—that is, damage to the hippocampus impairs performance of task X but not task Y. But, postulating functional independence of memory systems based on a single dissociation is difficult because of the potential existence of hierarchal relationships among the mnemonic role(s) of particular brain structures and task (Weiskrantz, 1989). A more compelling argument for the existence of multiple-memory systems in the brain requires the demonstration of a double dissociation, (a term coined by Teuber, 1955), in which damage to brain structure X impairs performance on task A but not task B, and damage to brain structure Y impairs performance on task B but not task A.

An early study in rats used two eight-arm radial-maze tasks to demonstrate a double dissociation between the mnemonic functions of the hippocampal system and caudate nucleus (Packard, Hirsh, and White, 1989). The radial maze consisted of a center platform with eight alley-shaped arms radiating away from the center and containing food cups at the distal end-points. In a standard win-shift version of the radial-maze task, rats obtained food rewards by visiting each arm of the radial maze once in a daily training session, and reentries into previously visited maze arms within a session were scored as errors. In a win-stay version of the radial-maze task, rats obtained food rewards by visiting four randomly selected and illuminated maze arms twice within a daily training session, and the spatial location of these maze arms varied by day. Two important features of these radial-maze tasks make them ideal for employing dissocia-

tion methodology to examine the hypothesis that the hippocampal system and caudate nucleus are parts of independent memory systems: 1. Performance in the win-shift task requires rats to remember those arms that have been previously visited, while performance in the win-stay task simply requires rats to learn to approach lit maze arms. Therefore, the win-shift task is often considered a prototypical test of spatial working memory and appears to involve the use of a cognitive mapping strategy. In contrast, the win-stay task is essentially a simultaneous visual discrimination and may involve acquisition of an S (light)-R (approach) habit; 2. The two tasks share the same motivational (appetitive), sensory (primarily visual), and motoric (maze running) characteristics; therefore, any differential effects of damage to separate brain areas on performance in the two tasks can be more readily ascribed to mnemonic processes.

When rats were tested in the acquisition of these two tasks following lesions of the hippocampal system and caudate nucleus, a double dissociation resulted: Hippocampal-system lesions selectively impaired acquisition of the win-shift task, while caudate-nucleus lesions selectively impaired acquisition of the win-stay task (Packard, Hirsh, and White, 1989). A double dissociation between the mnemonic functions of the hippocampus and caudate nucleus in these two radial maze tasks has also been demonstrated using post-training intracerebral infusions of memory-enhancing drugs (Packard and White, 1991). Evidence that the caudate nucleus is part of a memory system that mediates at least one form of nonhippocampal-dependent memory also comes from research in nonhuman primates and humans (Knowlton, Mangels, and Squire, 1996; Fernandez-Ruiz et al., 2001).

Besides the several studies that have dissociated the mnemonic functions of the mammalian hippocampus and caudate nucleus, other studies suggest that the cerebellum and amygdala mediate additional forms of learning and memory. R. Thompson and colleagues have described a role for the cerebellum in classically conditioned eyeblink behavior, providing a detailed analysis of the neural circuitry mediating the flow of information underlying the processing of unconditioned and conditioned stimuli in this form of Pavlovian conditioning (McCormick et al., 1981; Kim and Thompson, 1997). Other behavioral neuroscience research indicates that the mammalian amygdala mediates "stimulus-affect" memory, as evidence by a selective role for this brain region in fear conditioning (LeDoux, 1992; Davis, 1992), and stimulus-reward learning (e.g. Cador, Everitt, and Robbins, 1989; McDonald and White, 1993). Activation of efferent amygdala pathways by emotionally arousing events also modulates the distinct cognitive and S-R habit memory process subserved by the hippocampus and caudate nucleus (Packard, Cahill, and McGaugh, 1994).

Behavioral neuroscience research conducted largely over the last two decades has dramatically increased our understanding of neuroanatomical systems that mediate different types of memory in mammalian species ranging from the rat to the human. These findings suggest that elucidation of the neurobiological bases of memory organization will remain a complex task involving a consideration of patterns of spared *and* impaired memory function following various brain manipulations in lower animals, in neuropsychological studies of brain damaged humans, and in neuroimaging studies of memory processes in the intact human brain.

See also: AMNESIA, ORGANIC; DECLARATIVE MEMORY; EPISODIC MEMORY; IMPLICIT MEMORY; LOCALIZATION OF MEMORY TRACES; MEMORY CONSOLIDATION: PROLONGED PROCESS OF REORGANIZATION; NEURAL SUBSTRATES OF CLASSICAL CONDITIONING: DISCRETE BEHAVIORAL RESPONSES; NEURAL SUBSTRATES OF EMOTIONAL MEMORY

Bibliography

Cador, M., Robbins, T. W., and Everitt, B. J. (1989). Involvement of the amygdala in stimulus-reward associations: interaction with the ventral striatum. *Neuroscience 30,* 77–86.

Cohen, N. J., and Squire, L. R. (1980). Preserved learning and retention of pattern analyzing skill in amnesics: Dissociation of knowing how and knowing that. *Science 210,* 207–210.

Corkin, S. (1968). Acquisition of motor skill after bilateral medial temporal lobe excision. *Neuropsychologia 6,* 255–265.

Davis, M. (1992). The role of the amygdala in conditioned fear. In J. P. Aggleton ed., *The amygdala: Neurobiological aspects of emotion, memory, and mental dysfunction.* New York: Wiley-Liss.

Fernandez-Ruiz, J., Wang, J., Aigner, T. G., and Mishkin, M. (2001). Visual habit formation in monkeys with neurotoxic lesions of the ventrocaudal neostriatum. *Proceedings of the National Academy of Sciences of the United States of America 98,* 4,196–4,201.

Graf, P., and Schacter, D. L. (1985). Implicit and explicit memory for new associations and amnesic patients. *Journal of Experimental Psychology: Learning, Memory, and Cognition 11,* 501–518.

Hirsh, R. (1974). The hippocampus and contextual retrieval of information from memory: A theory. *Behavioral Biology 12,* 421–444.

Hull, C. L. (1943). *Principles of Behavior.* New York: Appleton-Century-Crofts.

Kesner, R. P., Bolland, B. L., and Dakis, M. (1993). Memory for spatial locations, motor responses, and objects: Triple dissociation among the hippocampus, caudate nucleus, and extrastriate visual cortex. *Experimental Brain Research 93,* 462–470.

Kim, J. J., and Thompson, R. F. (1997). Cerebellar circuits and synaptic mechanisms involved in classical eyeblink conditioning. *Trends in Neuroscience 20,* 177–181.

Knowlton, B. J., Mangels, J. A., and Squire, L. R. (1996). A neostriatal habit learning system in humans. *Science 273,* 1,399–1,402.

Lashley, K. S. (1950). In search of the engram. *Symposium of Society for Experimental Biology 4,* 454–482.

LeDoux, J. E. (1992). Emotion and the amygdala. In J. P. Aggleton, ed., *The amygdala: Neurobiological aspects of emotion, memory, and mental dysfunction.* New York: Wiley-Liss.

McCormick, D. A., Lavond, D. G., Clark, G., Kettner, R. E., Rising, C. E., and Thompson, R. F. (1981). The engram found? Role of the cerebellum in classical conditioning of nictitating membrane and eyelid responses. *Bulletin of the Psychonomic Society 18,* 103–105.

McDonald, R. J., and White, N. M. (1993). A triple dissociation of memory systems: Hippocampus, amygdala, and dorsal striatum. *Behavioral Neuroscience 107,* 3–22.

Milner, B. (1962). Les troubles de la memorie accompagnat des lesion hippocampiquesblilaterales. In P. Passant, ed., *Physiologie de l'Hippocampae.* Paris: Centre de la Recherche Scientifique.

Mishkin, M., and Petri, H. L. (1984). Memories and habits: Some implications for the analysis of learning and retention. In L. R. Squire and N. Butters, eds., *Neuropsychology of Memory.* New York: Guilford.

O'Keefe, J. and Nadel, L. (1978). *The hippocampus as a cognitive map.* Oxford, UK: Oxford University Press.

Olton, D. S., Becker, J. T., and Handelmann, G. E. (1979). Hippocampus, space, and memory. *Behavioral and Brain Sciences 2,* 313–365.

Packard, M. G., Cahill, L., and McGaugh, J. L. (1994). Amygdala modulation of hippocampal-dependent and caudate nucleus-dependent memory processes. *Proceedings of the National Academy of Sciences of the United States of America 91,* 8,477–8,481.

Packard, M. G., Hirsh, R, and White, N. M. (1989). Differential effects of fornix andcaudate nucleus lesions on two radial maze tasks: Evidence for multiple memory systems. *Journal of Neuroscience 9,* 1,465–1,472.

Packard, M. G., and White, N. M. (1991). Dissociation of hippocampus and caudate nucleus memory systems by posttraining intracerebral injection of dopamine nists. *Behavioral Neuroscience 105,* 295–306.

Scoville, W. B., and Milner, B. (1957). Loss of recent memory after bilateral hippocampal lesions. *Journal of Neurology, Neurosurgery, and Psychiatry 20,* 11–21.

Sutherland, R. J., and Rudy, J. W. (1989). Configural association theory: The role of the hippocampal formation in learning, memory, and amnesia. *Psychobiology 17,* 129–144.

Teuber, H. L. (1955). Physiological Psychology. *Annual Review of Psychology 6,* 267–296.

Tolman, E. C. (1932). *Purposive behavior in animals and men.* New York: Appleton-Century-Crofts.

Tulving, E. (1987). Multiple memory systems and consciousness. *Human Neurobiology 6,* 67–80.

Warrington, E. K, and Weiskrantz, L. (1982). Amnesia: A disconnection syndrome? *Neuropsychologia 20,* 233–247.

Weiskrantz, L. (1989). Remembering dissociations. In H. L. Roediger, and E. Tulving, eds., *Varieties of memory and consciousness: Essays in honour of Endel Tulving.* Hillsdale, NJ: Erlbaum.

Zola-Morgan, S., Squire, L., and Mishkin, M. (1982). The neuroanatomy of amnesia: Amygdala-hippocampus versus temporal stem. *Science 218,* 1,337–1,339.

Mark G. Packard

MULTIPLE PERSONALITY

See: AMNESIA, FUNCTIONAL

N

NATURAL SETTINGS, MEMORY IN

The study of memory as it is used in natural settings is now an accepted part of the scientific study of memory, engaging the attention of many researchers. This is a relatively new development; the classical study of memory took little interest in naturalistic studies. In the century between 1880 and 1980, an emphasis on experimental control led most experimenters to use specially prepared tasks and materials in their work, even if—as often happened—those tasks seemed meaningless to their subjects. The study of memory in natural settings was largely ignored.

Early Research

Two important exceptions to this trend are worth mentioning: eyewitness testimony and memory for stories. In the early 1900s, William Stern established a journal (*Beitrage zur Psychologie der Aussage*) devoted entirely to the study of testimony. In his experiments, Stern staged unexpected or dramatic events in the presence of groups of people who were then interrogated as if they had witnessed a real crime. Such testimony is surprisingly unreliable. Witnesses often give highly confabulated accounts of the event itself and are rarely able to describe the "criminals." Confidence is no guarantee of accuracy in such reports. Modern research confirms that eyewitnesses may be entirely wrong even when they are quite sure they are right. One documented way to improve eyewitness testimony is Edward Geiselman's "cognitive inter-

view," in which the witness is asked to recall events in different orders and from different perspectives.

F. C. Bartlett's 1932 book *Remembering* included the first systematic research on memory for stories, a field that was then largely neglected until the 1970s. Since that time, however, Bartlett's concept of "schema" has been widely adopted not only in the study of story recall but wherever memory is facilitated by preexisting mental structures.

A related subject is the study of memory as it appears in oral poetry and oral tradition—for example, in the preliterate heroic epics of ancient Greece. For decades this field was the province of humanistic scholars and classicists, but David Rubin's 1995 analysis based on the principles of cognitive psychology has been very successful.

Naturalistic versus Laboratory Methods

A 1978 conference at Cardiff, Wales, brought together many researchers with an interest in practical aspects of memory. In the opening address Ulric Neisser attacked the traditional study of memory as largely unproductive and called for a new emphasis on more naturalistic studies. Since that time many such studies have been conducted, and several related conferences have been held. This work is not without its critics. Some proponents of more traditional memory research believe that naturalistic studies have little value and that scientific progress can result only from controlled laboratory experiments. In an article titled "The Bankruptcy of Everyday Memory" Mahzarin Banaji and Robert Crowder asserted that a decade of naturalistic research had produced no important findings. A symposium incorporating nine replies to Banaji and Crowder appeared in the January 1991 *American Psychologist*. Since that time the controversy seems to have abated, with research on memory in natural settings now recognized as a significant component of the study of memory as a whole.

Long-Term Memories

Because laboratory experiments are necessarily limited in time, studies of very long-term memory almost always take advantage of natural settings. The most systematic studies of this kind have been conducted by Harry Bahrick and his associates, who have found that some forms of memory are very persistent. The ability to recognize yearbook photographs of one's high school classmates, for example, remains strong even thirty-five years after graduation. In contrast, recall of classmates' names declines steadily over the same period. Recall for the material actually learned in school (e.g., a foreign language) tends to drop off for the first five years, but after that there is little more forgetting over the next twenty-five. Interestingly, even very brief reminders may bring much of the apparently forgotten material to mind again.

Recall of Life Experiences

A number of psychologists have studied their own memories by making brief notes of one or more experiences each day for a prolonged period. Then, after a delay of months or years, they test their own recall of the recorded events. These "diary studies" have produced several clear results. For one thing, forgetting is not all-or-none: an event that seemed at first to be completely forgotten may be retrieved if more cues are provided. Another fairly obvious finding is that experiences rated as important are recalled somewhat better than unimportant ones. But importance turns out to be very difficult to rate: the true significance of an experience may depend on later developments and hence may not be apparent when it occurs.

Some scholars have suggested that memory is egotistically biased, that we recall our own actions as more praiseworthy (and perhaps our own experiences as more pleasant) than they really were. Such distortions certainly do happen and have been verified in research settings. Nevertheless, the diary studies confirm this tendency only in part. On the average, experiences rated as pleasant are indeed better remembered than unpleasant ones. But at least one study found that personally relevant unpleasant experiences were remembered best of all. There are probably individual differences in these types of bias.

In a different research tradition, Michael Ross has proposed a specific theory of the bias that appears when people try to remember their own past characteristics. (How severe were my headaches last month? How fast did I read before I took this study-skills course?) Such estimates are not so much recalled as deduced from the trait's current level (my headache today, my reading speed now) together with an implicit theory of its stability or tendency to change. When that implicit theory suggests that a trait is stable (my headaches are chronic, I always read this fast), its past value is "remembered" simply by reference to its present level. The situation is different when the implicit theory suggests that a change should have occurred. Thus people who have just been through a headache treatment program (or taken a study-skills course) will tend to "remember" their earlier pain levels as worse (or their earlier reading speed as slower) than they really were. After all, the treatment (or the course) must have done some good! This is only one of several possible sources of error in recalling medical information. Information that confirms patients' previous beliefs seems better remembered than information that gainsays those beliefs.

Memories Triggered by Cues

Another way to study memory for life events—pioneered by Francis Galton more than a century ago—is to provide random words as cues and ask subjects to report whatever personal experiences (if any) the cue brings to mind. When the number of memories retrieved is plotted on a log-log scale as a function of the time that has passed since the original event, an approximately linear forgetting function appears. There are, however, two significant departures from linearity in forgetting. One is that middle-aged and elderly individuals recall disproportionately many events from their years of adolescence and early adulthood (roughly from ages ten to twenty-five). This pattern is called the "reminiscence bump." The bump appears not only in memories of life experiences but also in the recall of music, books, and news events: apparently it is the most memorable period of life in every sense.

The other departure from linearity appears at the beginning of the forgetting function: few if any events are recalled from the first few years of life. The near absence of memories from early childhood, which Sigmund Freud called "infantile amnesia," has been the object of considerable interest in its own right. Current interpretations of this phenomenon have been much influenced by modern studies of young children's memory. Although children as young as two years have some ability to recall past experiences, memories at that age have little internal organization and require much cueing by adults. Perhaps it is because young children lack the narrative skills that are necessary to link individual memories to one another and to a develop life story that adults can recall so little from that period of life.

Flashbulb Memories

Some experiences are remembered so vividly and confidently that they seem unforgettable, almost as though the brain took a snapshot of the scene at that moment; such recollections are often called "flashbulb memories." Most "flashbulb memories" are of unique and personal experiences, but some are public (in a sense): they capture the moment when one first learned of some surprising and significant public event. Psychologists have studied the "flashbulb memories" created by hearing the news of the assassinations of President Lincoln, President Kennedy, and Martin Luther King Jr. (among others) as well as of other dramatic events such as the explosion of the space shuttle *Challenger,* the verdict in the O. J. Simpson trial, and so on. They have found that despite the strong subjective conviction that typically accompanies such memories, they are not neessarily accurate.

False memories can also occur in other contexts, often as a result of suggestion. Such suggestion can take many forms, but one particularly important context is psychotherapy. It is now well established that false memories of childhood sexual abuse can be produced by suggestion during therapy and that this can have serious consequences. To be sure, not all recollections of childhood abuse are false; many are all too valid. Unfortunately, valid and invalid memories are not distinguishable by any simple internal characteristic. The only way to establish the accuracy of a given recollection is with external evidence, which is not always available.

See also: AMNESIA, INFANTILE; EXPERTS' MEMORIES; FALSE MEMORIES; ORAL TRADITIONS

Bibliography

Bahrick, H. P. (1984). Semantic memory content in permastore: Fifty years of memory for Spanish learned in school. *Journal of Experimental Psychology: General 117,* 1–29.

Banaji, M. R., and Crowder, R. G. (1989). The bankruptcy of everyday memory. *American Psychologist 44,* 1,185–1,193.

Bartlett, F. C. (1932). *Remembering.* Cambridge, UK: Cambridge University Press.

Geiselman, R. E., Fisher, R. P., MacKinnon, D. P., and Holland, H. L. (1985). Eyewitness memory enhancement in the police interview: Cognitive retrieval mnemonics versus hypnosis. *Journal of Applied Psychology 70,* 401–412.

Gruneberg, M. M., Morris, P. E., and Syjes, R. N., eds. (1978). *Practical Aspects of Memory.* Chichester, UK: Wiley.

Ross, M. (1989). Relation of implicit theories to the construction of personal histories. *Psychological Review 96* 341–357.

Rubin, D. C., Rahhal, T. A., and Poon, L. W. (1998). Things learned early in adulthood are remembered best. *Memory & Cognition 26,* 3–19.

Ulric Neisser

NEOCORTICAL PLASTICITY

[A fundamental question in philosophy, psychology, and neuroscience concerns the development of our perceptions of the world. Are our perceptions completely determined by the intrinsic brain circuitry and its development, independent of experience (nativism), or are our perceptions and the underlying neural circuitry determined by experience (empiricism)? A truly major contribution of neuroscience in the twentieth century was the resolution of this issue, based largely on study of the development of the mammalian visual system. As might be expected the truth lies somewhere in between.

This extraordinary story is told in the third entry in this series, on the DEVELOPMENT OF THE VISUAL SYSTEM. *In brief, the basic wiring diagram of the mammalian visual system is specified by genetic and developmental factors. However, normal visual stimulation (i.e., experience) is necessary for the system to develop normally. Thus, occluding one eye in developing mammals (most work has been done on cats and monkeys) at a particular critical period markedly alters the normal wiring diagram in the primary visual system, resulting in markedly impaired vision. Patterned visual stimulation must be temporally synchronized (simultaneous) between the two eyes and must also be spatially synchronous for normal binocular vision to develop. This synchronized pattern leads to changes in the strength of the connections between active neurons, a phenomenon called synaptic plasticity.*

In addition to the extraordinary degree of plasticity seen in the development of the visual system, the ADULT VISUAL CORTEX *is also capable of a remarkable degree of adaptation and reorganization. Thus, infusing neuromodulatory and growth factors in the visual cortex of adult mammals can reinstate the plasticity in ocular dominance characteristics. Retinal lesions result in a wide range of biochemical changes in the deafferented visual cortex. Perhaps more important, the adult visual cortex exhibits marked synaptic plasticity: processes of* LONG-TERM POTENTIATION *(LTP) and* LONG-TERM DEPRESSION *(LTD). The Mc-Colloch effect is an example of perceptual plasticity that persists for up to twenty-four hours; after exposure to colored gratings, black and white gratings appear to be limited in complementary colors.*

Another system that exhibits dramatic neocortical plasticity is the SOMATOSENSORY CORTEX, *which consists of a number of processing areas with representations or "maps"*

of the body surface. Experience can alter the organization of these maps dramatically. Thus, amputation of digits or limbs in monkeys and humans results in marked changes in somatosensory cortex such that the maps of the adjacent intact body parts expand. Similarly, particular types of training (e.g., in tactile discriminations or motor skills) can result in expansion of the relevant regions of somatosensory cortex in both monkeys and humans. These experience-dependent alterations in somatosensory cortex appear to involve alterations in both the cortex itself and the relays of sensory information in the brain stem and thalamus.

The MOTOR CORTEX also exhibits marked plasticity. Training in particular motor skills can alter to some degree the organization of motor representation in the motor area of the neocortex. However extensive repetition of a particular movement does not necessarily result in expansion of representation of the movements in the motor cortex. There is evidence that processes of LTP and LTD are involved in motor learning. The cerebellum is also much involved in the learning of motor skills.]

ADULT VISUAL CORTEX—ADAPTATION AND REORGANIZATION

The adult visual cortex is capable of a remarkable degree of plasticity in the face of alterations of its normal pattern of input or in response to sensory adaptation or perceptual practice. This adult plasticity complements the use-dependent plasticity that plays an important role in the establishment of the normal organization during development.

Monocular Deprivation Plasticity in Adults

The shift in ocular dominance of cortical neurons as a consequence of monocular deprivation is one of the hallmarks of cortical plasticity during development. The potential for ocular dominance plasticity is greatest during a critical period of development, during which time thalamocortical axons segregate into ocular dominance columns. However, residual plasticity remains during later development even after this structural remodeling has occurred. However, later deprivation fails to induce plastic changes in ocular dominance to cortical neurons. Several lines of evidence suggest that ocular dominance plasticity can be restored to visual cortex through neuromodulators and growth factors. For example, modulation of cAMP activity through NA-beta adrenoreceptor activation, cholera A subunit, or forskolin produces a ocular dominance plasticity in adult cats that results in either a shift of ocular dominance or a reduction in binocularity. Cortical infusion of nerve growth factor, NGF, in adult cats, results in a paradoxical shift of ocular dominance toward the deprived eye.

Dark rearing tends to maintain the visual cortex in an immature, plastic state. This extended period of plasticity may be due to the prolonged expression of Cpg15, an activity-regulated gene that encodes a membrane-bound ligand that coordinates the growth of dendrites and axonal arbors and the maturation of their synapses. Normally, cpg15 levels decline during the critical period but dark-rearing results in the failure to down-regulate this gene and thus the cortex remains in a state of enhanced ability to form new synaptic connections.

Finally, the study of visual cortical development and plasticity has turned to mouse models, where despite the lack of ocular dominance segregation of thalamocortical afferents, knockouts of specific genes allows for the unprecedented ability to examine the role of receptors, ligands, and enzymes in the development and maintenance of visual cortical structure, function, and plasticity.

LTP and LTD in Visual Cortex

Adult visual cortex shows evidence for synaptic modifications in both in vitro and in vivo preparations. Tetanic stimulation of the LGN in adult rats leads to the induction of long-term potentiation (LTP) that is dependent on NMDA-receptor activation. The result is enhanced field potentials in layer 4 and deep layer 3 and increased visual evoked potentials to flash and grating stimulation. This LTP indication is paralleled by an increase in zif-268 expression in layers 2 and 3. In contrast, long-term depression, which has been hypothesized to underlie many plastic changes in development, has been inconsistently demonstrated in adult visual cortex. Consistent low-frequency stimulation (1 hertz) in cortical slices can induce LTD, but more physiologically based stimulation, based on a Poisson distribution of interpulse intervals, fails to produce LTD.

Plasticity Following Retinal and Cortical Lesions

Plastic changes in the topographic organization and receptive field properties have been reported in adult visual cortex following retinal and cortical lesions. Following binocular retinal lesions or monocular retinal lesions paired with enucleation of the other eye, researchers have observed a profound topographic reorganization of visual cortex. Immediately after the retinal lesion there is an unmasking of ectopic receptive fields in the deafferented cortical zone. These large, unmasked receptive fields can be displaced up to fifteen degrees, reflecting the unmasking of intrinsic horizontal connections that extend up to 5 millimeters. Over the following weeks to months, the cortical scotoma becomes nearly completely driven by receptive fields arising from non-lesioned portions of the retina. This reorganization is described by a progressive shift in the topographic map into the deafferented zone. Neurons within the reorganized zone demonstrate nearly normal orientation, direction, and spatial frequency tuning. However, the contrast thresholds of cells are markedly elevated. This second phase of cortical reorganization appears due in part to the growth of new cortical connections into the deafferented zone.

Retinal lesions in adults lead to a wide range of biochemical changes in the deafferented cortex. The growth factors BDNF, NT-3, and NGF are elevated from three days to two years post-lesion. Neurotrophin receptors p75, TrkB, and TrkC increase. The expression of CREB, CaMKII, and MAP2 are also increased. In contrast, zif268 is decreased at twenty hours and recovered by thirteen months, while synaptophysin and GAP-43 increased at six months post-lesion. Neurotransmitters also show changes in the deafferented zone. GABA and glutamic acid decarboxylase levels decrease within the deafferented zone while glutamate levels increase initially along the edge of the deafferented zone and this peak progressively shifts into the deafferented zone.

Similar to the plasticity evoked by retinal lesions in adults, a temporary artificial scotoma produces rapid increases in receptive field sizes of neurons along the border of the scotoma. Receptive fields increase nearly twofold in width during the scotoma and rapidly return to normal following removal of the scotoma. Similar results have been observed in areas V2 and V3 of macaque monkeys and may be related to perceptual filling-in and color-constancy phenomena.

There is evidence for functional reorganization after cortical lesions. In patients suffering from visual field defects due to cortical lesions, intensive visual training can lead to shrinkage of the scotoma. This phenomenon suggests that cortical tissue adjacent to the zone of destruction can recover functions in a use-dependent manner. Such an interpretation is supported by studies of cortical lesions in adult cats. Restricted lesions of visual cortex lead to plastic changes in visual field topography. Immediately after a cortical lesion, there is little if any change in visual topography, but there is some change in spontaneous activity and excitability of cells surrounding the lesion. Within two to three months, cells within this border region develop significantly larger receptive fields that result in a partial filling in of the cortical scotoma. This increase in RF size is limited to three to four degrees, which is approximately the same dimension reported for shifts in human cortical scotomas following extensive computer-based visual field training. In addition, there is functional MRI evidence for topographic reorganization extrastriate cortical areas following restricted lesions of primary visual cortex in adult humans.

Adaptation and Perceptual Learning

The perceptual phenomenon of adaptation aftereffects suggests the possibility of use-dependent and long-lasting (minutes to hours) modifications of responsiveness of feature-specific neurons in the visual cortex. Prolonged exposure to patterned stimuli leads to a feature-specific elevation of perceptual thresholds that lasts several minutes. Such adaptation has been shown for the movement and the orientation of contours, for the spatial frequency of gratings, and for color contrast. A related and very long-lasting (up to twenty-four hours) adaptation phenomenon is the McCulloch effect. After exposure to colored gratings of different orientation, black and white gratings appear to a subject to be tinted in complementary colors that remain associated with the respective orientations of the gratings. All these adaptation aftereffects show interocular transfer, indicating that adaptation has occurred at the cortical level. Recordings from single cells support the idea that adaptation occurs in visual cortex. Optical and single cell recordings in cat visual cortex demonstrate that adaptation to a given orientation produces a repulsive shift in the orientation tuning of single cells. This phenomenon is most pronounced at orientation singularities in visual cortex where the representations of the full range of orientations are brought into close physical proximity.

Perceptual learning refers to the increase in performance in discrimination tasks that results from practice. In general, this enhanced performance shows interocular transfer and is specific for the topographic location and specific stimulus features of the practiced task. These results have been interpreted as enhanced performance by task-specific cortical modules that receive retinotopic input and learn to solve a task after a short training phase.

In conclusion, behavioral, electrophysiological, and morphological evidence confirms the persistence of use-dependent plasticity in the striate cortex of adult mammals and humans. Furthermore, twenty-first century research has begun to uncover the biochemical mechanisms that support this cortical plasticity. This evidence supports the notion that adaptivity is a constituent property of cortical networks.

See also: GLUTAMATE RECEPTORS AND THEIR CHARACTERIZATION; GUIDE TO THE ANATOMY OF THE BRAIN: CEREBRAL CORTEX; LONG-TERM DEPRESSION IN THE CEREBELLUM,

HIPPOCAMPUS, AND NEOCORTEX; LONG-TERM POTENTIATION; SECOND MESSENGER SYSTEMS

Bibliography

Chino, Y., Smith, E. L., Whang, B., Matsuura, K., Mori, T., and Kaas, J. H. (2001). Recovery of binocular responses by cortical neurons after early monocular lesions. *Nature Neuroscience 4*, 689–690.

Crist, R. E., Li, W., and Gilbert, C. D. (2001). Learning to see: Experience and attention in primary visual cortex. *Nature Neuroscience 4*, 519–525.

Galuske, R. A., Kim, D-S., Castren, E., and Singer, W. (2000). Differential effects of neurotrophins on ocular dominance plasticity in developing and adult cat visual cortex. *European Journal of Neuroscience 12*, 3,315–3,330.

Gilbert, C. D. (1998). Adult cortical dynamics. *Physiological Reviews 78*, 467–485.

Heynen, A. J., and Bear, M. F. (2001). Long-term potentiation of thalamocortical transmission in adult visual cortex *in vivo*. *Journal of Neuroscience 21*, 9,801–9,813.

Imamura, K., Kasamatsu, T., Shirokawa, T., and Ohashi, T. (1999). Restoration of ocular dominance plasticity mediated by adenosine 3',5'-monophosphate in adult visual cortex. *Proceedings of the Royal Society of London 266*, 1,507–1,516.

Kirkwood, A., Lee, H-K., and Bear, M. (1995). Co-regulation of long-term potentiation and experience-dependent plasticity in visual cortex by age and experience. *Nature 375*, 328–331.

Nedivi, E., and Lee, W-C. A. (2002). Extended plasticity of visual cortex in dark-reared animals may result from prolonged expression of cpg15-like genes. *Journal of Neuroscience 22*, 1,807–1,815.

Obata, S., Obata, J., Das, A., and Gilbert, C. D. (1999). Molecular correlates of topographic reorganization in primary visual cortex following retinal lesions. *Cerebral Cortex 9*, 238–248.

Daniel J. Felleman

AUDITORY CORTEX

Learning is acquiring information and memory is storing it. A common belief is that sensory systems are only "sensory analyzers" that provide instantaneous knowledge of the world, but are not sites of information storage. However, during the last decade of the twentieth century, neurophysiological recordings in the auditory cortex revealed that learning and memory involve specific and enduring changes in the way that the brain analyzes and stores sound. This article covers the topic of neural plasticity in the auditory cortex (ACx) during learning and memory in adult animals and humans. As used here, the term "neural plasticity" refers to systematic, long-term (minutes to lifetimes) changes in the responses of neurons to the same physical stimulus (e.g, a tone) arising out of an experience.

Background

In 1955 Galambos and his colleagues performed a seminal experiment in which cats were classically conditioned by pairing an auditory conditioned stimulus (CS) with a puff of air (unconditioned stimulus, or US) to the face. Evoked potentials elicited by the CS in the ACx became larger during conditioning. This was soon followed by a two-tone discrimination study showing that the increased magnitude of response was caused by the specific association of a CS and US versus a second, unpaired tone. Many more studies in various animals and training situations also demonstrated that the responses of the auditory cortex to sounds were affected by the learned psychological importance of acoustic stimuli.

But these results had little effect on the neurobiology of learning/memory or auditory neurophysiology. Auditory physiologists took scant notice of learning studies that used only one or two tones because they shed little light on how the ACx processed the many acoustic frequencies to which it is sensitive. Learning/memory workers persisted in the shared assumption that the auditory cortex is a "sound analyzer" but not a "learning machine." But this assumption is not corroborated by the brain.

Receptive Field Plasticity in Learning and Memory

A solution to the impasse involved combining methods from auditory neurophysiology with those from learning and memory. Researchers determined the effects of classical conditioning on the receptive fields of neurons in the ACx. The receptive field (RF) of a cell is the part of the stimulus environment to which it is sensitive. Thus, the RF for frequency is described by a "tuning curve" that plots the number of cellular discharges as a function of acoustic frequency. The "best frequency" (BF) of a cell is the frequency that elicits the most discharges. Demonstrating that learning involves a systematic change in the processing of acoustic-frequency information involves showing an alteration in receptive fields when a subject learns that a particular frequency is behaviorally important.

This approach was first applied to the ACx in 1990 at the University of California at Irvine. RFs were obtained before and immediately after a single conditioning session in which a tone was paired with a mild shock. Behavioral conditioned responses developed. More importantly, the RFs developed systematic plasticity. Responses to the CS frequency increased, whereas responses to the best frequency and many other frequencies decreased. These opposing changes were often sufficient to shift frequency tuning toward or to the frequency of the CS so that it became the new BF (see Figure 1). Tuning shifts were caused only by association between a tonal CS and the shock US. Also, this plasticity was not caused by arousal to the CS frequency because RF shifts are still

Figure 1

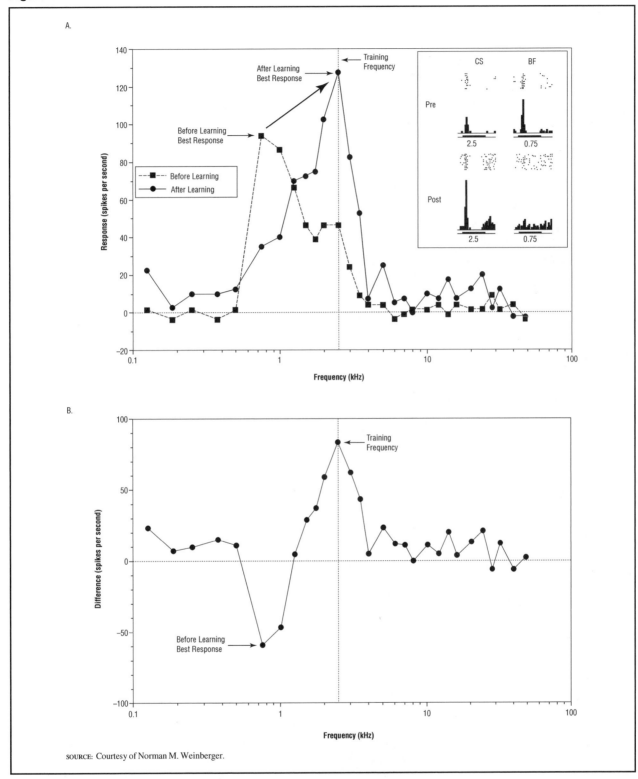

SOURCE: Courtesy of Norman M. Weinberger.

Learning shifts receptive field tuning to the frequency of the conditioned stimulus in tone-shock conditioning (30 trials). The best frequency before learning was 0.75 kHz. The subject was trained with a CS of 2.5 kHz. A. Pretraining and posttraining receptive fields. Note that tuning shifted so that 2.5 kHz became the best frequency. The inset shows the opposite changes of response in poststimulus time histograms for the pretraining BF and the CS frequency during the pre- and post-periods. B. Difference in receptive fields due to conditioning (Posttraining minus Pretraining RFs). Note that the maximum increase of response was at the CS frequency and the maximum decrease in response was at the pretraining best frequency.

Figure 2

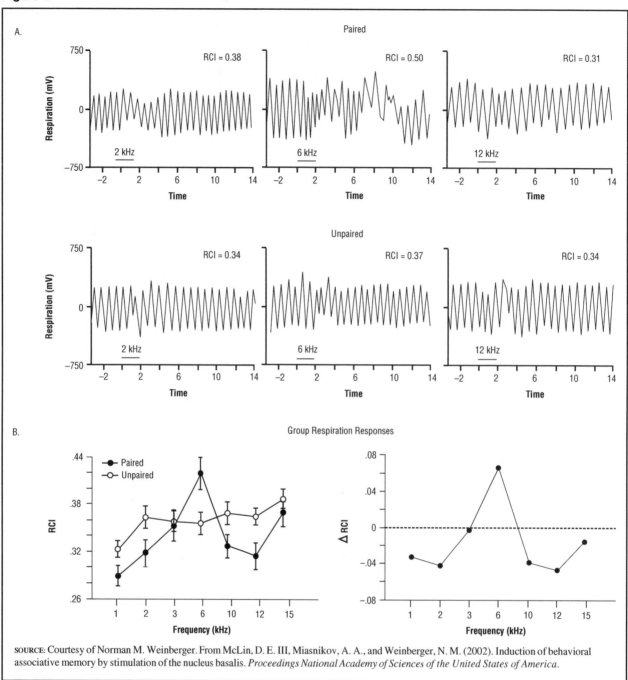

SOURCE: Courtesy of Norman M. Weinberger. From McLin, D. E. III, Miasnikov, A. A., and Weinberger, N. M. (2002). Induction of behavioral associative memory by stimulation of the nucleus basalis. *Proceedings National Academy of Sciences of the United States of America.*

CS-specific induction of behavioral memory (indexed by respiration changes) following pairing tone (6 kHz) with NB stimulation in another context. A) Examples of individual respiration records (with value of respiration change index, RCI) to three frequencies (2, 6, and 12 kHz) for one animal each from the paired and unpaired groups. The largest response was at 6 kHz for the paired animal (RCI = 0.50). Horizontal bar indicates tone duration. B) Frequency generalization functions. Left panel, group mean (± SE) change in respiration to all tones for both groups. The maximal response was at the CS frequency of 6 kHz for the paired group, but not for the unpaired group. Right panel, the group difference function (Paired minus Unpaired) shows a high degree of specificity of respiratory responses to 6 kHz.

observable after training when subjects are placed under general anesthesia and thus not aroused by stimuli.

RF plasticity possesses all of the major characteristics of memory. In addition to being associative, it is highly specific to the CS frequency, develops very rapidly (within five trials), exhibits consolidation (i.e., becomes stronger without additional training), and is retained indefinitely (tested to eight weeks). Moreover, RF plasticity exhibits generality across different types of training (e.g., one- and two-tone discrimination training, in both in classical and instrumental conditioning), and motivation (appetitive as well as aversive). RF plasticity also develops in humans and produces an expanded representation of the CS frequency in the ACx.

RF plasticity may provide a memory code for acquired stimulus importance: the greater the behavioral significance, the greater the number of cells that become tuned to that stimulus. Such a memory code could explain aspects of selective attention—for example, why one is more likely to hear one's own name in a noisy room than a random name. While background noise may control many neurons, the attunement of still more more networks of neurons to our names increases the probability that the name will engage some of these cells. This process could explain why the loss of memory in aging and brain degeneration take less of a toll on one's most important memories. If the memory is represented by more cells, then important information has a "safety factor" in numbers, which blunt the impact of cell loss.

Mechanisms and Functions

Subcortical neuromodulatory transmitter systems probably play a role in ACx plasticity in learning. The preponderance of evidence implicates the nucleus basalis cholinergic system (NB/ACh) in enabling the auditory cortex to store specific information. For example, RF plasticity induced in a variety of tasks, motivations, and species also can be induced by substituting NB stimulation for appetitive or aversive reinforcement. That this plasticity can be blocked by the administration of atropine directly to the ACx shows that the induced RF plasticity requires the engagement of cholinergic muscarinic receptors in the ACx. Moreover, pairing a tone with stimulation of the NB/ACh is sufficient to induce actual specific behavioral memory in the rat (see Figure 2). Although much more research is necessary, researchers have established the outlines of a reductionistic account of learning as the storage of specific information in the auditory cortex.

Bibliography

Bakin, J. S., and Weinberger, N. M. (1990). Classical conditioning induces CS-specific receptive field plasticity in the auditory cortex of the guinea pig. *Brain Research 536,* 271–286.

Galambos, R., Sheatz, G., and Vernier, V.G. (1955). Electrophysiological correlates of a conditioned response in cats. *Science 123,* 376–377.

Gonzalez-Lima, F., and Scheich, H. (1986). Neural substrates for tone-conditioned bradycardia demonstration with 2-deoxyglucose: II. Auditory cortex plasticity. *Behavioral Brain Research 20,* 281–293.

Gluck, H., and Rowland, V. (1957). Defensive conditioning of electrographic arousal with delayed and differentiated auditory stimuli. *Electroencephography and Clinical Neurophysiology 11,* 485–491.

McLin, D. E. III, Miasnikov, A. A., and Weinberger, N. M. (2002). Induction of behavioral associative memory by stimulation of the nucleus basalis. *Proceedings of the National Academy of Sciences of the United States of America.*

Morris, J. S., Friston, K. J., and Dolan, R. J. (1998). Experience-dependent modulation of tonotopic neural responses in human auditory cortex. *Proceedings of the Royal Society of London 265,* 649–657.

Recanzone, G. H., Schreiner, C. E., and Merzenich, M. (1993). Plasticity in the frequency representation of primary auditory cortex following discrimination training in adult owl monkeys. *Journal of Neuroscience 13,* 87–103.

Weinberger, N. M. (2002). Experience-dependent response plasticity in the auditory cortex: Issues, characteristics, mechanisms and functions. In T. Parks, ed., *Handbook of Auditory Research.* New York: Springer-Verlag.

Weinberger, N. M., and Diamond, D. M. (1987). Physiological plasticity of single neurons in auditory cortex: Rapid induction by learning. *Progress in Neurobiology 29,* 1–55.

Norman M. Weinberger

DEVELOPMENT OF THE VISUAL SYSTEM

The neocortex, or cerebral cortex, is a thick layer of cells (neurons) covering the outer surface of the forebrain. In humans and some other mammals it is wrinkled, with many folds separated by deep fissures. In humans 75 percent or more of the neurons in the forebrain are in the cerebral cortex, a much higher proportion than in for other animals. Partly for this reason, and also because of clinical observations on people with brain damage, most researchers believe that the cortex plays a significant role in uniquely human behaviors, such as highly complex learning and information processing.

Our knowledge of how the cortex works has grown enormously since the 1950s and 1960s, mostly through experiments in which the activity of cortical neurons is studied one neuron at a time. This procedure may seem paradoxical, since there is great redundancy in the brain and the activity of any particular neuron cannot be crucially important. But through painstaking studies of hundreds of thousands of neurons in different cortical regions, a picture has emerged that allows us to understand many basic operating principles of the cortex.

An important function of the cortex is perception. Just about all the information we receive from the world around us, through our senses, arrives eventually in the cortex. The visual cortex is one of the best-understood cortical regions. It has a complicated, elegant structural and functional organization that appears to underlie many processes of visual perception and recognition.

Researchers have devoted extensive experimentation to answering the intriguing question of how the brain develops these sophisticated mechanisms for analyzing and interpreting the visual world. It is now clear that visual experience early in life is extremely important: The system is highly malleable or plastic because its development depends on the type and amount of visual information the young, developing organism receives; this property may prefigure the kind of plasticity of the adult brain that enables humans and animals to learn new behaviors.

Basic Properties of Visual Cortical Neurons

Information from the two eyes converges on individual neurons in the visual cortex; most of these neurons can respond to visual stimuli presented in either eye and so are termed *binocular neurons*. Many cells, though, respond more strongly to stimulation of one eye than of the other; the term *ocular dominance* refers to the relative influence of the two eyes on a cell's response. Visual cortical neurons have another interesting property: They are feature detectors. Almost every neuron responds best to a specific stimulus: usually a line, bar, or straight edge having a particular orientation (e.g., horizontal, vertical, diagonal) and precise location in the visual field. A third principal characteristic of the responses of neurons in the visual cortex is the relationship between a binocular cell's preferred or optimal stimulus in each eye. Many cells show interocular matching; that is, the stimulus orientation that produces the best response is the same in both eyes and has the same location within the visual field. Many other cells have slightly different optimal stimulus orientations or locations in the two eyes. These small differences are called *interocular disparities*, and neurons that exhibit this property are termed *disparity detectors*.

Plasticity in Visual Development

The question of how this cortical system for the analysis of visual space develops early in life has been the subject of hundreds of experiments since the 1960s. An important overall conclusion is that many response characteristics of visual cortical neurons depend on early visual experience for their normal development; these include binocularity and ocular dominance, orientation selectivity, and interocular matching of cells' optimal stimulus requirements, especially location and orientation (i.e., disparity detection). Typically, experiments of this sort involve raising young animals (usually kittens or monkeys, whose visual systems resemble those of humans) for days or

weeks, controlling or manipulating their visual experience to depart from the norm in various ways. Ensuing microelectrode studies determine whether and how the abnormal experience has altered the activity of visual cortical cells.

During the first weeks or months of postnatal life, called the critical or sensitive period, the developing mammal's visual system undergoes a period of special vulnerability or susceptibility to the effects of many altered rearing conditions. As the critical period evolves into adulthood, the same manipulations of the animal's visual experience generally do not affect the physiological organization of the visual cortex in terms of neurons' response characteristics (although some kinds of plasticity persist).

For instance, early studies examined the effects of completely depriving kittens of experience with visual form or pattern by closing both eyelids during the first few postnatal weeks. Initially it appeared that this manipulation does not produce major changes: Visual cortical cells' binocularity and the distribution of ocular dominance are unaffected, and these kittens' cells also show orientation selectivity resembling that of normally reared kittens, although the precision of orientation detection is slightly reduced. Subsequently, more detailed experiments showed that the system of disparity-detecting neurons does not develop normally in binocularly deprived kittens.

By contrast, kittens raised with just one eyelid closed (monocular deprivation, or MD) show dramatic changes in their visual cortical organization. Nearly all the cells are responsive only to stimulation of the eye that was open, and almost none to stimulation of the formerly closed eye. As might be expected, behavioral tests of visual acuity reveal deficits in the deprived eye.

This cortical ocular dominance shift is not due simply to the presence or absence of patterned visual input but to the absence of simultaneous stimulation of both eyes, as shown by experiments in which kittens were raised with one eye closed for several days or a few weeks, after which that eye was opened and the opposite eye was closed for a comparable period (reverse suture), and also by experiments involving alternating daily MD. Kittens raised using these methods experience the same amount of patterned visual input through both eyes, but at any given moment only one eye is receiving stimulation. When cortical ocular dominance and binocularity are studied in these kittens, almost all neurons are visually responsive, but each responds only to stimulation of one eye; there are almost none of the binocular cells that make up 80 to 90 percent of the visual cortical neurons in normally reared kittens. Furthermore, if the relative amount (time) of stimulation given the two eyes is made unequal in these experiments, there is a corresponding change in the proportion of cells activated by stimulation of each eye.

Not only must patterned visual stimulation be temporally synchronized (simultaneous) between the two eyes in order for cortical binocularity to develop normally, it must also be spatially synchronous; that is, each part of the pattern must stimulate the same point on both retinas (corresponding points). Some humans exhibit an oculomotor disorder called strabismus, in which the two eyes are misaligned. People with this disorder often have poor visual acuity in one eye and almost always have deficient binocular depth perception. An animal model of strabismus, in which some of the muscles that control the position of the eyes are severed, has proved useful in studying the cortical effects of this disorder. Kittens raised with experimental strabismus show a marked loss of binocular neurons; in fact, the physiological organization of the visual cortex resembles that of kittens reared with alternating monocular deprivation.

The system of orientation-detecting neurons in the visual cortex is also susceptible to the effects of early visual experience. Kittens raised viewing contours or edges confined to a single orientation (e.g., vertical stripes) have a preponderance of visual cortical cells whose preferred receptive fields are at or near the experienced orientation; this finding is in marked contrast with the cortical organization of normally reared kittens, in which all possible orientations are represented about equally among cells' receptive fields.

In addition to the dramatic alterations in binocularity and orientation selectivity consequent upon experimental manipulations of early visual experience, there is also a degree of plasticity in the development of visual cortical cells specialized for disparity detection, especially interocular orientation disparity. For instance, there are changes in the visual cortices of kittens raised wearing prism goggles that introduce rotations of the images seen by the left and right eyes. These rotations are around the visual axis (line of sight), and are opposite in the two eyes, producing a controlled amount of interocular orientation disparity; that is, an edge or contour in the field of view does not give rise to parallel images on the two retinas, as is normally the case, but instead is displaced clockwise in one eye and counterclockwise in the other. If these rotations are small (e.g., eight degrees in each eye), there is a corresponding shift in the average disparity of cortical neurons' preferred receptive-field orientations between the two eyes: Most cells show an interocular orientation disparity that matches the experienced image rotation. On the other hand, if the rotations are large (e.g., sixteen degrees or more in

each eye), there is a disruption of binocularity: Most cells respond only to stimulation in one eye but not in both eyes. In this respect the effects of large interocular rotations are like those of strabismus or alternating monocular deprivation.

From an evolutionary standpoint, cortical plasticity in the development of interocular relationships has clear adaptive significance. The developing animal undergoes relatively rapid changes in height and in the lateral separation of the two eyes. There is thus a continually changing relation between the interocular image disparity of objects in the environment and the distance of those objects from the observer. The existence of neuronal disparity-detecting mechanisms able to adjust to these changes during early life provides an advantage in capturing prey, eluding predators, and so forth. Detailed reviews of the many studies on this issue have been written by Frégnac and Imbert (1984) and by Shinkman, Isley, and Rogers (1985).

Some Theoretical Considerations

A major problem is identifying underlying mechanisms responsible for plasticity in the developing visual system. One appealing idea involves binocular competition, in which fibers from the thalamus, some carrying information from one eye and some from the other, compete to form synapses on binocular cortical cells. Although the underlying competitive mechanism it is not yet clear, recent work points to a major role for nerve growth factor (NGF): rats with intraventricular injections of NGF fail to show the expected ocular dominance shift when subjected to MD during the critical period (Pizzorusso and Maffei, 1996). In any case, when researchers place one eye at a disadvantage during MD, fibers representing the other eye are more successful at making cortical connections.

At the same time, it is clear that neural activity originating in the deprived eye continues to play a role in animals subjected to MD. Some researchers have raised kittens with MD combined with damage to a small area of the retina in the open eye. Later, these kittens show the usual shift in ocular dominance toward the experienced eye, except that cortical cells that would otherwise have been responsive to stimulation of the damaged retinal area are instead responsive to stimulation of the deprived eye. The important role of intracortical inhibitory mechanisms is consistent with this finding. For example, if a drug that blocks the action of inhibitory neurotransmitters is administered to a previously monocularly deprived kitten while recordings from cells in the visual cortex are in progress, responsiveness to stimulation of the deprived eye increases immediately; this effect continues until the drug wears off and then disappears.

What, exactly, is the role of visual experience in neocortical development? Does it simply maintain the feature-detecting capabilities and the interocular relationships of visual cortical neurons, or does it sharpen and even alter these properties? Some researchers have related this question to the age-old philosophical issue of nature versus nurture; however, it is now clear that both genetic influences (nature) and the influences of the individual's unique visual environment (nurture) are crucial. The real question concerns the relative degree of these influences on the development of the organization of our visual system and of our perceptual capacities. Most researchers believe that early visual experience can, within limits, modify the formation of connections in the central nervous system, thereby exerting substantial control over the final outcome. This conclusion is borne out both by studies using experimental animals and by clinical observations on humans who have experienced visual disorders in early childhood.

Relation of Developmental Plasticity to Learning and Memory in Adults

Candidate Pharmacological and Neurochemical Mechanisms

We are now beginning to understand some mechanisms that may underlie both neural plasticity in early development and plasticity as manifested in adult learning and memory. These may include some dynamic aspects of the synaptic relations within neuronal networks of the cerebral cortex and some neurochemical, especially neurotransmitter, changes that accompany (and may ultimately be responsible for) some of the phenomena of neuronal plasticity described above. For instance, the neurotransmitters norepinephrine (NE) and acetylcholine (ACh) play a critical role in the formation and maintenance of adult memories, and visual cortical plasticity is reduced or abolished when levels of these neurotransmitters are substantially depleted experimentally.

Neurotransmitters exert many of their effects in the brain by acting on their receptors located on postsynaptic cells. There are numerous classes of receptors in the central nervous system; one notable type is *N*-methyl-D-aspartate (NMDA) receptor, whose action is voltage-dependent; its properties come into play only with some depolarization of the postsynaptic cell. It may therefore be a kind of gate, permitting additional excitation only atop some excitatory effects already present in the postsynaptic neuron. Activation of the NMDA receptor may thus be a neurochemical analogue of the behavioral excitation that

ensues from the combination of a conditioned stimulus and an unconditioned stimulus in a learning experiment. Indeed, drugs that block the NMDA receptor interfere with or even prevent the normal acquisition of learned responses in experimental animals. As with NA and ACh depletion, this effect has been obtained using several different kinds of conditioning procedures.

In kittens, the pharmacological blocking of NMDA receptors also blocks the neural plasticity shown in the loss of cortical binocular cells following monocular deprivation. NMDA receptors are composed of subunits that experimentation can selectively alter; recent studies have begun to delimit specific subunits responsible for various plastic changes in cortical neuronal function, both in vivo and also in vitro (Bear and Rittenhouse, 1999; Philpot et al., 2001). Furthermore, plasticity that arises from the actions of neurotransmitters and from the activation of NMDA receptors has been demonstrated at the cellular level through iontophoresis, recording from a single neuron while using minute electrical currents to eject small quantities of neurotransmitter substance or of NMDA from the electrode into the immediate vicinity of the neuron under study. The responses of many visual cortical cells to a visual stimulus presented to the nondominant eye, or at a nonoptimal orientation, show a substantial temporary increase in strength when these stimuli are repeatedly paired with the iontophoretic application of NA and ACh, or of NMDA and glutamate (an excitatory transmitter that acts upon NMDA receptors). This effect is evident in kittens but not in adult cats. Thus these neurotransmitter systems and the NMDA receptors have been clearly implicated in neuronal plasticity early in life and also in adult learning and memory.

Application of Transgenic Models

Some researchers have examined the visual cortical plasticity in genetically altered subjects. Gordon (1997) has provided an excellent review of results obtained using transgenic mice. For instance, ocular dominance shifts consequent upon MD occur in some mice bred to lack the gene encoding a particular form of calcium/calmodulin-dependent protein kinase II. Thus calcium, with its well-known role in presynaptic events, may help to signal activity-dependent plasticity using this particular protein. This novel line of research might yield major advances in our understanding of molecular mechanisms of both adult learning and memory and developmental plasticity.

Behavioral State

Various aspects of animal behavior that contribute to learning and memory appear to enable or enhance cortical plasticity. For instance, the well-studied effects of sleep upon memory consolidation apply in much the same fashion to MD-induced plasticity in visual cortex (Frank, Issa, and Stryker, 2001). Kittens that underwent anesthesia-induced sleep following MD exhibited more pronounced shifts in ocular dominance than kittens treated comparably but kept awake, either in a lighted environment or in darkness. Perhaps other behavioral-state variables can similarly affect cortical plasticity.

Conclusion

There has been a dramatic increase in experimental attention to the relation between brain mechanisms of developmental plasticity and of learning and memory. The search for general mechanisms of neural plasticity is likely to remain a central concern of neuroscience, which will benefit especially from studies of visual cortical neuronal networks.

See also: GLUTAMATE RECEPTORS AND THEIR CHARACTERIZATION

Bibliography

Bear, M. F., and Rittenhouse, C. D. (1999). Molecular basis for induction of ocular dominance plasticity. *Journal of Neurobiology 41,* 83–91.

Frank, M. G., Issa, N. P., and Stryker, M. P. (2001). Sleep enhances plasticity in the developing visual cortex. *Neuron 30,* 275–287.

Frégnac, Y., and Imbert, M. (1984). Development of neuronal selectivity in primary visual cortex of cat. *Physiological Reviews 64,* 325–434.

Gordon, J. A. (1997). Cellular mechanisms of visual cortical plasticity: A game of cat and mouse. *Learning and Memory 4,* 245–261.

Philpot, B. D., Weisberg, M. P., Ramos, M. S., Sawtell, N. B., Tang, Y.-P., Tsien, J. Z., and Bear, M. F. (2001). Effect of transgenic overexpression of NR2B on NMDA receptor function and synaptic plasticity in visual cortex. *Neuropharmacology 41,* 762–770.

Pizzorusso, T., and Maffei, L. (1996). Plasticity in the developing visual system. *Current Opinion in Neurology 9,* 122–125.

Shinkman, P. G., Isley, M. R., and Rogers, D. C. (1985). Development of interocular relationships in visual cortex. In R. N. Aslin, ed., *Advances in neural and behavioral development,* Vol. 1. Norwood, NJ: Ablex.

Paul G. Shinkman

MOTOR CORTEX

Nearly all adult behavior expresses an acquired motor skill. Because mammals have highly evolved motor regions of frontal cortex, including the primary motor cortex, they can acquire skilled motor behaviors involving a wide range of complex and adaptable movements. The remarkable adaptability of mammalian motor behavior suggests a high degree of functional flexibility in the motor cortex. There is now a large body of evidence demonstrating function-al plasticity within the motor cortex and that this plasticity represents the neural encoding of motor skill.

Motor Map Plasticity

More than a century ago Fritsch and Hitzig (1870) found that electrical stimulation applied to regions of frontal cortex could evoke movement and Hitzig. The subsequent refinements of intracortical microstimulation (Asanuma and Ward, 1971) have identified two basic principles of organization within the motor cortex. The first is that movements corresponding to body parts over which there is a high degree of control, such as the hand, are multiply represented over a larger area of cortex than those of less dexterous body parts such as the foot. The second is that, although the general location of the map within the cortex is constant, the particular organization of movement representations is dynamic and can change in response to a variety of manipulations (Sanes and Donoghue, 2000).

These two principles of cortical organization also appear to govern the encoding of skilled movement within the motor cortex. Motor-skill training leads to a reorganization of movement representations that expands the representations corresponding to trained movements. For example, squirrel monkeys trained to retrieve a food pellet from successively smaller food wells exhibit an expansion of wrist and digit representations into elbow and shoulder representations (Nudo, Milliken, Jenkins, and Merzenich, 1996). Rats trained to reach outside their cages to retrieve a food pellet show a comparable expansion of wrist and digit representations (Kleim, Barbay, and Nudo, 1998). There is also evidence for a similar reorganization following motor-skill learning in human subjects (Pascuel-Leoni et al., 1995).

Although these experiments show the concurrence of skill learning and map reorganization, they do not reveal whether these changes result from learning or drive the development of skill. A recent experiment examining the motor maps of rats at different times during skilled forelimb training suggests that reorganization occurs after the acquisition of motor skill. Significant expansion of wrist and digit movements requires ten days of skilled reach, training whereas significant improvements in reaching accuracy occurs after three days (Kleim et al., 2000). This temporal discrepancy seems to show that functional reorganization requires sufficient performance of the skilled movements once they have been acquired. Rats trained for three days followed by ten days without training do not exhibit any significant change in the distribution of movement representations (Hogg et al., 2001). However, simple movement repetition alone is not sufficient to drive changes in the motor maps. In one experiment, squirrel monkeys were trained daily to retrieve pellets from a large food well that does not require the development of skilled wrist movements but does involve extensive wrist and digit use; there was no significant map reorganization despite thousands of movement repetitions (Plautz, Milliken, and Nudo, 2000). Similarly, rats housed with running wheels for a month show no significant change in the distribution of forelimb movement representations (Kleim et al., 2002). Thus, motor map reorganization is dependent upon the acquisition and subsequent performance of novel skilled movements but does not occur in response to repetition of existing movements.

Neural Substrates of Motor Map Plasticity

In the microcircuitry of the motor cortex there are extensive recurrent axon collaterals that span several millimeters across the cortex (Huntley and Jones, 1991; Keller, 1993). Intracortical stimulation evokes movement by activating these horizontal afferents (Jankowska, Padel, and Tanaka, 1975). Hence changes in intracortical connectivity might mediate changes in the organization of movement representations. Several experiments have supported this hypothesis by demonstrating activity-dependent changes in synaptic efficacy within the horizontal connections of the motor cortex via differential patterns of electrical stimulation. Long-term potentiation (LTP) of synaptic responses occurs in response to high frequency stimulation (Hess and Donoghue, 1994), whereas lower frequency stimulation leads to long-term depression (LTD) of these same synapses (Hess and Donoghue, 1996). Although these changes are induced through artificial patterns of cortical stimulation, they demonstrate that the horizontal connections within the motor cortex are modifiable in response to differential motor experience.

More direct evidence for the role of horizontal afferent plasticity in motor learning has come from experiments showing that synaptic potentials following stimulation of intracortical afferents were significantly greater in the trained than in the untrained hemisphere (Rioult-Pedotti, Friedman, Hess, and Donoghue, 1998). Further, relative to the untrained hemisphere, LTP was reduced and LTD was enhanced in the trained hemisphere (Rioult-Pedotti, Friedman, Hess, and Donoghue, 2000). These results demonstrate that motor learning increases intracortical synaptic efficacy while maintaining the range within which synapses can be modified.

Changes in the efficacy of intracortical afferents may have an anatomical basis. Huntley (1997) has shown that the pattern of intracortical connections correlates with the functional reorganization that follows peripheral nerve lesions. Further, motor-skill training paradigms that induce motor map changes also cause changes in the morphology of cortical neurons. For example, cortical pyramidal neurons of rats trained on a skilled reaching task have a significantly increased dendritic arbor within the trained versus untrained motor cortex (Withers and Greenough, 1989; Greenough, Larson, and Withers, 1985). Further, rats trained daily to traverse a complex set of obstacles have significantly more synapses per neuron within the motor cortex than rats forced to run a flat, obstacle-free runway (Kleim, Lussnig, Schwarz, and Greenough, 1996). Finally, Kleim et al. (2002b) have shown that increases in synapse number within the rat motor cortex following skilled reach training is confined to those areas of cortex that also underwent reorganization of movement representations.

All of these data suggest that the development of skilled movement is encoded within the motor cortex through changes in the strength of intracortical afferents that may involve increases in synapse numbers. These adaptations of cortical circuitry then show up as changes in the distribution of cortical-movement representations. The coordinated anatomical and physiological plasticity thus represents a neural mechanism by which motor memories (engrams) are represented within the brain.

See also: MOTOR SKILL LEARNING

Bibliography

Asanuma, H., and Ward, J. E. (1971). Patterns of contraction of distal forelimb muscles produced by intracortical stimulation in cats. *Brain Research* 27, 97–109.

Fritsch, G., and Hitzig, E. (1870). On the electrical excitability of the cerebrum, trans. G. von Bonin. In *Some Papers on the Cerebral Cortex.* Springfield, MA: Thomas, 1960.

Greenough, W. T., Larson, J. R., and Withers, G. S. (1985). Effects of unilateral and bilateral training in a reaching task on dendritic branching of neurons in the rat sensory-motor forelimb cortex. *Behavioral and Neural Biology* 44, 301–314.

Hess, G., and Donoghue, J. P. (1994). Long-term potentiation of horizontal connections provides a mechanism to reorganize cortical motor maps. *The Journal of Neurophysiology* 71, 2,543–2,547.

—— (1996). Long-term potentiation and long term depression of horizontal connections in motor cortex. *Acta Neurobiologiae Experimentalis* 56, 397–405.

Hogg, T., Cooper, S., Vozar, D., VandenBerg, P. M., and Kleim, J. A. (2001). Expansion of distal forelimb representations within rat motor cortex is dependent upon performance and not acquisition of skilled forelimb movements. *Society for Neuroscience Abstracts* 27, 775.

Huntley, G. W. (1997). Correlation between patterns of horizontal connectivity and the extent of short–term representational plasticity in motor cortex. *Cerebral Cortex* 7, 143–156.

Huntley, G. W., and Jones, E. G. (1991). Relationship of intrinsic connections to forelimb movement representations in monkey motor cortex: A correlative anatomical and physiological study. *Journal of Neurophysiology 66*, 390–413.

Jankowska, E., Padel, Y., and Tanaka, R. (1975). The mode of activation of pyramidal tract cells by intracortical stimuli. *Journal of Physiology 249*, 617–636.

Keller, A. (1993). Intrinsic synaptic organization of the motor cortex. *Cerebral Cortex 3*, 430–441.

Kleim, J. A., Barbay, S., Cooper, N., Hogg, T., Reidel, C., Remple, M., and Nudo, R. J. (2002b). Motor-learning dependent synaptogenesis is localized to functionally reorganized motor cortex. *Neurobiology of Learning and Memory 77*, 63–77.

Kleim, J. A., Barbay, S., and Nudo, R. J. (1998). Functional reorganization of the rat motor cortex following motor skill learning. *The Journal of Neurophysiology 80*, 3,321–3,325.

Kleim, J. A., Cooper, N. R., and VandenBerg, P. (2002a). Exercise inducesangiogenesis but does not alter movement representations within rat motor cortex. *Brain Research, 934*, 1–6.

Kleim, J. A., Hogg, T., Whishaw, I. Q., Reidel, C., Cooper, N., and VandenBerg,P. (2000). Time course and persistence of motor learning-dependent changes in the functional organization of the motor cortex. *Society of Neuroscience Abstracts, 27*, 775.

Kleim, J. A., Lussnig, E., Schwarz, E. R., and Greenough, W. T. (1996). Synaptogenesis and fos expression in the motor cortex of the adult rat following motor skill learning. *The Journal of Neuroscience 16*, 4,529–4,535.

Nudo, R. J., Milliken, G. W., Jenkins, W. M., and Merzenich, M. M. (1996). Use-dependent alterations of movement representations in primary motor cortex of adult squirrel monkeys. *Journal of Neuroscience 16*, 785–807.

Pascual-Leone, A., Nguyet, D., Cohen, L. G., Brasil-Neto, J. P., Cammarota, A., and Hallett, M. (1995). Modulation of muscle responses evoked by transcranial magnetic stimulation during the acquisition of new fine motor skills. *Journal of Neurophysiology 74*, 1,037–1,045.

Plautz, E. J., Milliken, G. W., and Nudo, R. J. (2000). Effects of repetitive motortraining on movement representations in adult squirrel monkey: Role of use versus learning. *Neurobiology of Learning and Memory 74*, 27–55.

Rioult-Pedotti, M. S., Friedman, D., and Donoghue, J. P. (2000). Learning-induced LTP in neocortex. *Science 290*, 533–536.

Rioult-Pedotti, M. S., Friedman, D., Hess, G., and Donoghue, J. P. (1998). Strengthening of horizontal cortical connections following skill learning. *Nature Neuroscience 1*, 230–234.

Sanes, J. N., and Donoghue, J. P. (2000). Plasticity and primary motor cortex. *Annual Review of Neuroscience 23*, 393–415.

Withers, G. S., and Greenough, W. T. (1989). Reach training selectively alters dendritic branching in subpopulations of layer II/III pyramids in rat motor-somatosensory forelimb cortex. *Neuropsychologia 27*, 61–69.

Jeffrey A. Kleim

SOMATOSENSORY CORTEX

The somatosensory cortex of mammals has a number of subdivisions or processing areas. Although the number varies by species, each cerebral hemisphere in all mammals contains at least two systematic representations of the tactile receptors of the contralateral body surface, the primary somatic area SI, and the secondary somatic area SII. Neurons throughout these representations can be activated by stimuli on restricted portions of the body surface, the receptive fields of the neurons. These two representations have fairly consistent organizations from individual to individual within a species and conform to a general plan across species. Yet the organizations of the maps of the body surface can be altered in developing or adult mammals by removing or changing the significance of some of the inputs, or by damaging parts of maps. These changes in map organizations result from neurons losing their original receptive fields and acquiring new ones on different body parts. Thus, the organization of somatosensory cortex can change. Best documented in primates and rats, such changes have also been observed in humans.

Plasticity in the somatosensory cortex may be important in development by allowing the sensory systems of individuals to adjust to bodily growth through the use of information from the environment. Plasticity in adults may also be important in reassigning neurons to new roles after damage to the system in order to promote recovery. Following amputations, researchers have noted changes in patients' somatosensory cortex that often correlate with phantom pains. After a stroke, recovery of function is also related to changes in cortical organization.

The plasticity of the somatosensory cortex is probably most important for allowing adjustments in the neural network that may be critical in learning sensorimotor skills. Monkeys trained in various types of tactile discrimination tasks exhibit changes in the cortical organization of the trained skin surfaces that reflect the temporal and spatial structure of the trained stimuli. In humans, training for skilled motor behaviors evinces changes in SI. For example, trained violinists have larger SI representations of the hand used to finger the instrument than that used to bow it, and both representations are larger than in untrained subjects.

Researchers have used two dominant experimental methods to examine mechanisms underlying somatosensory plasticity. In one, they induce plasticity by cutting the sensory nerves to part of the skin or by dorsal rhizotomy. For example, over several weeks, neurons in the somatosensory cortex formerly activated by inputs from the denervated hand of a monkey acquire new receptive fields on adjoining parts of the hand that have intact sensory afferents. Some reactivation may occur sooner, within seconds or hours of the nerve section. In the other method, they induce plasticity by manipulating the patterns of use of the skin surface, thus obviating the need for a destructive lesion. For example, trimming all but two adjacent whiskers in a rat strengthens those whiskers' abilities to excite SI, both in their own somatotopic territory and in that of the other untrimmed whisker. Overall, there are likely to be several different cellular mechanisms of cortical plasticity with different intervals.

It is not clear how the cortex reorganizes, but there are several obvious possibilities. In both adult and developing brains, plasticity, particularly its initial stages, seems to result from alterations in the effectiveness of anatomical connections. Indeed, changes in synaptic efficacies of thalamocortical and intracortical projections have been detected after whisker pairing in intact animals and in brain slices. Such changes are likely based on Hebbian processes such as long-term potentiation (LTP) and depression (LTD), both of which can be elicited in SI. There is more evidence for these types of mechanisms: Blockade of the N-methyl-D-aspartate (NMDA) subtype of glutamate receptor, which is necessary for the induction of cortical LTP, can also block plasticity of SI.

In addition to Hebbian processes, some immediate recovery of cortical responsiveness might be due to a reduction in the lateral spread of inhibition of excitatory pathways, a result of removal of a source of activation for the inhibitory neurons. Other changes might be due to a reduction in the production of inhibitory or neuromodulatory (such as acetylcholine, norepinephrine, or serotonin) neurotransmitters in the deprived zones of cortex. Over longer times, new connections are likely to be formed, such as those observed in the hindbrain nuclei and cortex. Increases in the number, size, or strength of excitatory synaptic contacts probably play a major role, and this could involve the formation of new synapses and the elaboration of axon arbors, dendrites, and dendritic spines.

The changes in the cortex reflect, in part, adjustments made in the relays of sensory information in the brain stem and thalamus before they reach the cortex. There is evidence for changes in the receptive fields of spinal cord neurons after section or anesthetic block of peripheral nerves. Other changes, particularly sprouting of new connections after early lesions and transneuronal atrophy, have occurred in the hindbrain and thalamus and undoubtedly contribute to cortical reorganization. Probably all the mechanisms cited above underlie the plasticity in these subcortical somatosensory areas. There is evidence for purely cortical changes, however, including observations of receptive field changes in cortex that are not observed in thalamus, reorganization of SII after partial lesions of SI (which provides the only input to SII), and changes in isolated slices of cortex after reorganization. Interestingly, rats implanted with multielectrode arrays demonstrate rapid changes at all levels of the somatosensory pathway in response to anesthetic block of peripheral nerves; the dynamics of these changes suggest that the changes are relayed from the cortex to thalamus and hindbrain, not just in the ascending direction.

Plasticity of sensory representation in cortex has been most extensively studied for the somatosensory cortex, but reorganizations occur after partial removals of inputs for visual, auditory and motor areas as well. Thus, plasticity is a basic feature of important systems throughout the brain.

Bibliography

Buonomano, D. V., and Merzenich, M. M. (1998). Cortical plasticity: From synapses to maps. *Annual Review of Neuroscience 21*, 149–186.

Ebner, F. F., Rema, V., Sachdev, R., and Symons, F. J. (1997). Activity-dependent plasticity in adult somatic sensory cortex. *Seminars in Neuroscience 9*, 47–58.

Jones, E. G. (2000). Cortical and subcortical contributions to activity-dependent plasticity in primate somatosensory cortex. *Annual Review of Neuroscience 23*, 1–37.

Kaas, J. H. (1991). Plasticity of sensory and motor maps in adult mammals. *Annual Review of Neuroscience 14*, 137–167.

Jon H. Kaas
Revised by Peter W. Hickmott

NEURAL COMPUTATION

[Learning and memory emanate from the engagement of complex biochemical and molecular networks within neurons and complex interactions of neurons within neural networks. Neural computation seeks to understand the ways in which these various elements interact to process information and generate behavior in general; and, with respect to learning and memory, the ways in which these processes give rise to the encoding, storage, and retrieval of memories. Five entries on neural computation follow. The first, APPROACHES TO LEARNING, provides an overview of the field. This entry is followed by specific entries on the neural computations that occur in each of four selected brain regions that are involved in learning and memory: CEREBELLUM, HIPPOCAMPUS, NEOCORTEX, and OLFACTORY CORTEX.]

APPROACHES TO LEARNING

Nervous systems are capable of solving extraordinarily sophisticated computational problems. The visual or tactile recognition of an object in a cluttered scene is child's play, but well beyond the capability of the fastest digital computers. Most animals can navigate over rough surfaces with great agility, but present-day robots are limited in their movements to a very narrow range of terrains. We can learn to use language and to read and write well beyond anything so far accomplished by artificial intelligence. We take all of these abilities for granted because we are so good at them; trying to duplicate them with machines has made their great difficulty more apparent.

Neural computation is the systematic study of the computational principles underlying the function of neural systems, from the level of molecular mechanisms to the organization of brain systems (see Figure 1). This computational approach to neuroscience is still in its infancy (Sejnowski, Koch, and Churchland, 1988). There has been a recent emphasis on studying neural networks, small groups of highly connected neurons; however, as shown in Figure 1, neural networks are only one level of investigation in the nervous system, and neural computation depends on computational principles at each of these levels. A few general principles have emerged from the study of abstract models of neural systems that are likely to be important for the biological study of learning and memory.

Some Principles of Neural Computation

In the von Neumann architecture commonly used in digital computers, the memory and the processor are physically separated. This separation gives rise to a bottleneck in the flow of information between the two. In neural systems, memory and processing are intertwined; the same circuits that process sensory and motor information are involved in learning and the storage of new information. A unified processor-memory system allows many circuits to work together in parallel and, as a consequence, the solutions to many commonly occurring problems can be computed in only a few serial steps. The representation of sensations and memories in such an architecture is more difficult for us to imagine and to use than one in which the functions are segregated (Churchland and Sejnowski, 1992). The brain, however, did not evolve to make it easier for us to analyze.

Locality is an important constraint that arises when hardware for artificial neural networks is designed (Mead, 1989). Wires are expensive on computer chips, just as they are in the brain, so only limited connectivity is possible between processing elements. The organization of sensory processing into a hierarchy of maps and the laminar organization of cortical structures is wire-efficient. This also places constraints on the organization of learning systems, which share the same circuitry. In particular, the decision to store a piece of information at a particular location in the brain is a local one that depends on electrical and chemical signals that are spatially and temporally restricted. The Hebbian mechanism for synaptic plasticity that has been found in the hippocampus and neocortex obeys this principle of locality: The presynaptic release of neurotransmitter and the postsynaptic depolarization needed to trigger the long-term potentiation at these synapses are spatially contiguous, and there is a brief temporal window during which both signals must be present. Modulatory influences on learning may be more diffuse and widespread.

Neurons have limited dynamic range. Unlike digital systems, which are capable of accurately representing very large and very small numbers, the range of membrane potentials and firing rates found in neurons is limited. Also, the variability in the properties of neurons within the same population is significant, and the properties of the same neuron can vary with time. The same is true for analog VLSI (very-large-scale integration) circuits that are designed to mimic the processing that occurs in neurons (Mead, 1989). This variability and limited dynamical range have consequences for the way that information is coded and the way that neural circuits are designed. One way to preserve information is to process relative levels, or differences, rather than absolute levels. Thus, visual neurons are more sensitive to contrast (spatial differences) and changes (temporal differences) than to absolute intensity levels. Another mechanism for preserving information is dynamically altering baseline activity in neurons. Adaptive biochemical mechanisms inside cells, such as light adaptation in photoreceptors, allow neurons to remain in their most sensitive range. Adaptive mechanisms have been found for calibrating sensorimotor coordination, such as slow adaptation of the vestibulo-ocular reflex (VOR) to changes in the magnification of the lens (Lisberger, 1988).

Taxonomy of Learning Systems

Adaptation to ongoing sensory stimulation does not require an additional source of information outside the processing stream; this type of learning is called *unsupervised*. In contrast, the type of adaptation that occurs in response to sensorimotor mismatch does require an outside error signal; this is called *supervised* learning. In the case of VOR learning, the error signal is the slip of the image on the retina, and the gain of the reflex is changed to reduce the slip. The amount of supervision can vary from a crude good/bad reinforcement signal to very detailed feedback of information about complex sensory signals from the environment that might be termed a "teacher." Supervised learning is sometimes called *error-correction learning*.

It is not necessary for the error signal to come from outside the organism; important information about the proper operation of a circuit can be provided by another internal circuit, or even by internal consistency within the same circuit. For example, a sensory area that was trying to predict future inputs could compare its prediction against the next input to improve its performance. Such an unsupervised system with an internal measure of error is termed *monitored* (Churchland and Sejnowski, 1992). As shown in Fig-

Figure 1

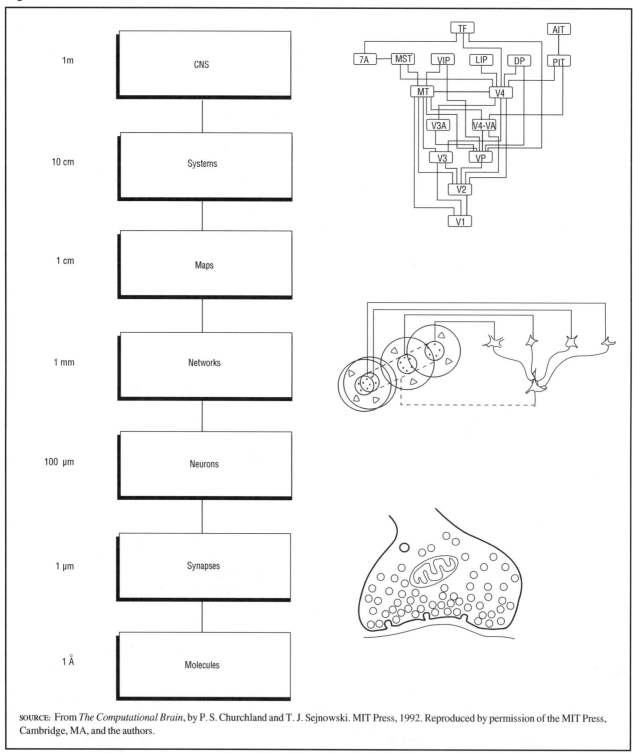

SOURCE: From *The Computational Brain*, by P. S. Churchland and T. J. Sejnowski. MIT Press, 1992. Reproduced by permission of the MIT Press, Cambridge, MA, and the authors.

Structural levels of organization in the nervous system. The spatial scale at which anatomical organizations can be identified varies over many orders of magnitude.

ure 2, all possible combinations of supervised and unsupervised, monitored and unmonitored, learning systems are possible.

Selected Examples

An interesting example of a monitored system is song learning in the white-crowned sparrow. In this species of songbird, the male hears the local dialect after hatching but does not produce the song until the next spring. At first the song is imperfect, but with each repetition the details improve until it is a good reproduction of the original song heard the previous year, even though there is no external "teacher" during the refinement. The internally stored template is compared with the imperfect song production; the error between them drives learning mechanisms to improve the song. This learning is monitored because the error is derived from an internal template of the desired sound. We may use a similar strategy when learning to produce new sounds in a foreign language.

Transformations between two populations of neurons can be learned with Hebbian mechanisms at the synapses between the input fibers and the output neurons. The pattern of activity on the input fibers is matched with the desired pattern on the output neurons. In some models of the cerebellum, for example, associative motor learning is mediated by climbing fibers, which provide a teaching signal to the output Purkinje cells. By including feedback projections of the output neurons back onto themselves, a partial input cue can regenerate the entire stored pattern. In this mode, the system is unsupervised because the desired output pattern of activity during learning is the same as the input pattern. Such content-addressable recurrent networks have been suggested as models for the piriform cortex and area CA3 of the hippocampus. Some properties such as memory capacity of associative networks of simplified processing units have been well studied; the analysis of networks based on model neurons with more complex properties is just beginning.

Learning mechanisms have also been used to model the development of cortical systems. One of the best-explored areas of unsupervised learning in artificial networks is competitive learning, in which incoming sensory information is used to organize the internal connections of a sensory map. For example, the formation of ocular dominance columns in visual cortex of cats and monkeys during development depends on competitive synaptic mechanisms. The development of ocular dominance columns can be mimicked in a computer model that uses Hebbian learning in the spatially restricted terminal arbors of axons projecting to the cortex from the lateral geniculate nucleus (Miller et al., 1989). Similar mechanisms can also be used in neural systems to learn more complex features that distinguish among different types of sensory inputs (Kohonen, 1984). It is also likely that other learning mechanisms are used to discover invariants of sensory patterns, which are often as important in pattern recognition as the distinctive

Figure 2

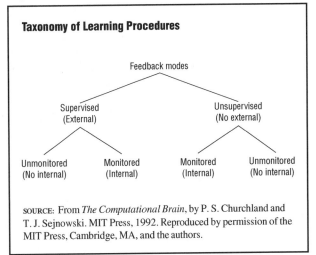

Taxonomy of Learning Procedures

SOURCE: From *The Computational Brain*, by P. S. Churchland and T. J. Sejnowski. MIT Press, 1992. Reproduced by permission of the MIT Press, Cambridge, MA, and the authors.

Supervised learning occurs when there is feedback on the performance of the system from the external environment. If the feedback is a scalar reward, it is called reinforcement learning. The learning is called monitored if the system has an internal measure of error.

features that separate classes (Churchland and Sejnowski, 1992).

As computers grow more powerful, it will become possible to simulate more complex models of neural systems; however, even these simulations will fall short of the richness of real neural systems and the complex environments that confront biological creatures. Hardware emulations that interact with the real world in real time would greatly improve our ability to test hypotheses about the organization of neural systems (Mead, 1989). Ultimately we will need to study complete model systems in order to understand the multiple levels of adaptation and learning that provide flexibility and stability in a changing world.

See also: BIRDSONG LEARNING; HEBB, DONALD; NEOCORTICAL PLASTICITY

Bibliography

Churchland, P. S., and Sejnowski, T. J. (1992). *The computational brain.* Cambridge, MA: MIT Press.

Kohonen, T. (1984). *Self-organization and associative memory.* Berlin: Springer-Verlag.

Lisberger, S. G. (1988). The neural basis for motor learning in the vestibulo-ocular reflex in monkeys. *Science 242,* 728.

Mead, C. (1989). *Analog VLSI and neural systems.* Reading, MA: Addison-Wesley.

Miller, K. D., Keller, J. B., and Stryker, M. P. (1989). Ocular dominance column development: Analysis and simulation. *Science 245,* 605–615.

Sejnowski, T. J., Koch, C., and Churchland, P. S. (1988). Computational neuroscience. *Science 241,* 1,299–1,306.

Terrence J. Sejnowski

CEREBELLUM

The cerebellum is located at the rear of the brain above the brain stem. It is connected to the spinal cord, brain stem, and cerebral cortex. The function of the cerebellum has been the topic of classic studies of the effects of lesions of the cerebellum—such as discoordination and dysmetria—in animals and human patients. These symptoms suggest that the cerebellum helps us to move precisely, smoothly, quickly, and even without visual feedback. Because learning is essential to the acquisition of such skills, one can infer that the cerebellum learns by itself, although it is possible it connects to a learning mechanism elsewhere in the brain.

A detailed analysis of neuronal circuits in and around the cerebellum (see Figure 1) has yielded network models, modular models, and control-system models of the cerebellum to represent its computational capabilities. The cerebellar cortex is modeled by the three-layered simple perceptron, which, in combination with nuclear structures, forms a functional module of the cerebellum, a cerebellar corticonuclear microcomplex. The microcomplex provides an adaptive control mechanism to a spinal-cord/brain-stem function. In cortical sensorimotor functions, it provides an internal model that helps feedforward control. In mental thought processes in the association cortex as well, it seemingly plays a similar role.

Neuronal Network in the Cerebellar Cortex

The cerebellar cortex is made up of five principal types of neurons (Purkinje, basket, stellate, Golgi, and granule cells) that are arranged in a very uniform pattern. The cerebellar cortex receives mossy fibers from various precerebellar nuclei, which also supply excitatory synapses to cerebellar nuclei by way of their collaterals. Input from the mossy fibers is relayed to the granule cells, which send out bifurcating axons, called parallel fibers, that run in beams. The axons of the granule cells supply excitatory synapses to Purkinje cells, which provide the sole output of the cerebellar cortex. Each Purkinje cell receives as many as 175,000 inputs from the granule cells. Thus, the connections from mossy fibers to granule cells to Purkinje cells are the major signal-flow pathway, allowing the distribution of input information received by mossy fibers to numerous granule cells from which Purkinje cells select information to generate their output signals. Normally, Purkinje cells fire simple spikes at approximately 50 hertz. The discharge frequency of simple spikes are modulated in response to mossy-fiber input.

Each Purkinje cell also normally receives a single climbing fiber exclusively from the inferior olive. Climbing fibers project to the cerebellar cortex, forming strong synaptic connections with Purkinje cells, and send collaterals to the cerebellar nuclei. Climbing-fiber input occurs at a relatively low frequency (around 1 hertz) and over a narrow dynamic range but powerfully excites Purkinje cells, causing them to generate bursts of three to four high-frequency spikes (complex spikes).

A theory propounded in 1970 indicated that conjunctive activation of a mossy-fiber/parallel-fiber pathway and a climbing fiber onto a Purkinje cell either strengthens or weakens the transmission from the parallel fiber to the Purkinje-cell synapse. Climbing-fiber signals will thus modify the signal flow through the cerebellar cortex. This operation is analogous to that in which all connections from the second to the third layer are strengthened or weakened by an outside teacher who recognizes correct or incorrect performance of the simple perceptron. Indeed, long-term depression (weakening) of synaptic strength (LTD) was discovered a decade later. The occurrence of LTD suggests that the cerebellar cortex learns by means of weakening connections responsible for erroneous performance.

In the simple-perceptron model, the cerebellum processes spatial information; in the adaptive-filter model, it processes temporal patterns. In the adaptive-filter model, the inhibitory connection between Golgi cells and granule cells constructs an integrator with a long time constant, which activates granule cells with varied latencies. A mossy-fiber signal would then be converted to time-scattered parallel-fiber signals from which Purkinje cells select an appropriate temporal pattern learned through climbing-fiber signals.

Functional Module of the Cerebellum: Microcomplex

The cerebellar cortex is organized into seven longitudinal (A, B, C1, C2, C3, D1, and D2) zones. Each zone sends Purkinje cell axons to a certain cerebellar or vestibular nucleus. Thus, zone A projects to fastigial and vestibular nuclei, zone B to vestibular nuclei, zones C1 and C3 to the rostral part of the interpositus nucleus and zone C2 to the caudal part of it, and zones D1 and D2 to the medial and lateral parts of the lateral (dentate) nucleus.

Each longitudinal zone of the cerebellar cortex is composed of a number of microzones. Each microzone projects to a small group of vestibular or cerebellar nuclear neurons and receives climbing fibers from a small group of inferior olive neurons, which project collaterals to a small group of nuclear neurons projected by the microzone. A microcomplex is an interconnected set of a microzone, a small group of nuclear neurons, and a small group of inferior olive neurons. The microzones defined in the paravermis and flocculus may measure about 10 mm2. In rats, one microzone of this size contains about 10,000 Purkinje cells and 2,740,000 granule cells. The human cerebellum is about 50,000 mm2 wide, so that it may contain as many as 5,000 microzones as its functional unit.

The microcomplex would function as a module of the cerebellum in the following manner. First, input signals from a precerebellar nucleus (except those from the inferior olive) drive the nuclear neurons, which generate output signals of the microcomplex under inhibitory influences of Purkinje cells. Second, the same input signals pass via mossy fibers to a microzone, where they are relayed by granule cells and in turn excite Purkinje cells and other cortical neurons, eventually evoking simple spikes in Purkinje cells. Simple spike discharges of Purkinje cells driven by moss-fiber signals produce a unique functional state of a microzone arising from concerted activities of excitatory and inhibitory synapses. Third, climbing fibers convey error signals pertaining to the operation of the neural system that includes the microcomplex, as generated by various neuronal mechanisms in diverse preolivary structures. Fourth, climbing-fiber error signals induce LTD in the conjointly activated parallel fiber-Purkinje cell synapses (learning rule) and thereby modify the operation of the microcomplex until the error signals are minimized. Climbing-fiber signals evoke complex spikes in Purkinje cells and thereby induce conducting impulses in Purkinje cell axons, which eventually evoke IPSPs in the nuclear neurons. However, the effects of the IPSPs on nuclear neurons are counteracted by the EPSPs evoked via collaterals of olivocerebellar fibers. The signal content of complex spikes has been analyzed in various motor behaviors and is related partly to consequence errors and partly to internally computed errors.

The postulated operation of the microcomplex, including inhibitory neurons in the cerebellar cortex, has been computer-simulated. However, since several forms of synaptic plasticity other than conjunctive LTD were observed in the cerebellum, further studies are needed to reproduce the performance of a microcomplex that incorporate these forms of synaptic plasticity.

Roles in Neural Control

The microcomplex gives an extracerebellar system an adaptive mechanism. Reflexes are classic con-

Figure 1

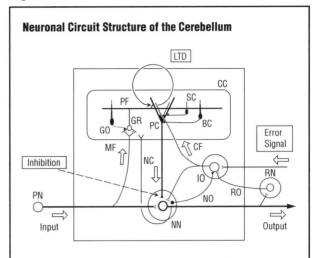

Abbreviations: CC, cerebellar cortex. NN, cerebellar and vestibular nuclei. IO, inferior olive. PN, precerebellar nucleus. RN, red nucleus (parvocellular part). MF, mossy fiber. CF, climbing fiber. PC, Purkinje cell. GR, granule cell. PF, parallel fiber. BC, basket cell. SC, stellate cell. GO, Golgi cell. IO, inferior olive. RN, red nucleus. RO, olivorubral projection. NO, nucleoolivary projection. NC, nucleocortical projection. Open triangle, excitatory synapse. Filled triangle, inhibitory synapse.

SOURCE: *Brain Research*, v. 886, pp. 237–245, 2000. From figure 1 in "Mechanisms of Motor Learning in the Cerebellum," by M. Ito. Reproduced by permission from Elsevier Science.

trol systems in the spinal cord and brain stem, which are converted to adaptive control systems by an attached microcomplex. Typical examples are the vestibuloocular reflex and eyeblink conditioning. Compound-movement systems such as those for locomotion or saccades are control systems equipped with a function generator. Innate behavior such as food intake, drinking, and reproductive activity is a form of control involving a motor program. The microcomplex introduces adaptability into these control systems.

When a sensorimotor cortex develops, the microcomplex forms a cerebrocerebellar communication loop, which may provide an internal model of the skeletomuscular system to be controlled by the motor cortex. Command signals generated by the motor cortex may perform precise control using an internal feedback through this internal model of the cerebellum even without referring to the external feedback (see Figure 2A). In the Smith predictor model, the internal model not only represents dynamics of the control object but also incorporates the delay time to be spent in the external feedback, so that it reproduces exactly the same effect as the external feedback. The microcomplex may also be attached parallel to the motor cortex and provides an inverse model of the skeletomuscular system, which also allows the control

Figure 2

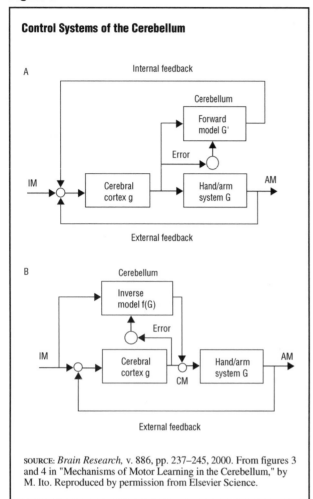

Control Systems of the Cerebellum

SOURCE: *Brain Research*, v. 886, pp. 237–245, 2000. From figures 3 and 4 in "Mechanisms of Motor Learning in the Cerebellum," by M. Ito. Reproduced by permission from Elsevier Science.

A. Seemingly feedforward control system with an internal feedback through a forward model. AM (actual movement) becomes equivalent to IM (instructed movement) if G' (signal transfer characteristics of the forward model) = G (that of the actual hand/arm system), even when the external feedback is interrupted. g is the signal transfer characteristics of the cerebral cortex. Originally proposed by Ito, M. (1984). *The cerebellum and neural control.* New York: Raven Press. B. Two-degrees-of-freedom control system. Originally proposed by Kawato, M., Furukawa, K., and Suzuki, R. (1987). A hierarchical neuronal network model for control and learning of voluntary movement. *Biological Cybernetics 57,* 169–185. f(G) represents the signal transfer characteristics of the inverse model. If f(G) = 1/G, AM=IM even when the external feedback is interrupted. CM, command signals.

to be performed without an external feedback (see Figure 2B).

The control with a forward or inverse model shown in Figure 2 can be generalized to the thought in which we move images, concepts, or ideas represented in the temporoparietal cortex by command signals generated by the prefrontal cortex. At the level of neuronal circuit, movement and thought could be controlled by the same mechanism. The thesis of the involvement of the cerebellum in mental activities was based on anatomical connections between the association cortex and cerebellar hemisphere. Brain-imaging studies have afforded evidence of an internal model.

See also: GUIDE TO THE ANATOMY OF THE BRAIN; LONG-TERM DEPRESSION IN THE CEREBELLUM, HIPPOCAMPUS, AND NEOCORTEX; NEURAL SUBSTRATES OF CLASSICAL CONDITIONING: DISCRETE BEHAVIORAL RESPONSES; VESTIBULO-OCULAR REFLEX (VOR) PLASTICITY

Bibliography

Albus, A. (1971). A theory of cerebellar function. *Mathematical Biosciences 10,* 25–61.

Blakemore, S. J., Frith, C. D., and Wolpert, D. M. (2001). The cerebellum is involved in predicting the sensory consequences of action. *NeuroReport 12,* 1,879–1,884.

Dow, R. S., and Moruzzi, G. (1958). *The physiology and pathology of the cerebellum.* Minneapolis: University of Minnesota Press.

Fujita, M. (1982). Adaptive filter model of the cerebellum. *Biological Cybernetics 45,* 195–206.

Groenewegen, H. J., and Voogd, J. (1977). The parasagittal zonation within the olivocerebellar projection. I. Climbing fiber distribution in the vermis of cat cerebellum. *Journal of Comparative Neurology 174,* 417–488.

Groenewegen, H. J., Voogd, J., Freedman, S. L. (1979). The parasagittal zonation within the olivocerebellar projection. II. Climbing fiber distribution in the intermediate and hemispheric parts of cat cerebellum. *Journal of Comparative Neurology 183,* 551–601.

Hansel, C., Linden, D., and D'Angelo, E. (2001). Beyond parallel fiber LTD: The diversity of synaptic and nonsynaptic plasticity in the cerebellum. *Nature Neuroscience 4,* 467–475.

Imamizu, H., Miyauchi, S., Tamada, T., Sasaki, Y., Takino, R., Futz, B. Yoshioka, T., and Kawato, M. (2000). Human cerebellar activity reflecting an acquired internal model of a new tool. *Nature 403,* 192–195.

Ito, M. (1984). *The cerebellum and neural control.* New York: Raven Press.

—— (1993). Movement and thought: Identical control mechanisms by the cerebellum. *Trends in Neuroscience 16,* 448–450.

—— (2001). Long-term depression: Characterization, signal transduction and functional roles. *Physiological Reviews 81,* 1,143–1,195.

Kawato, M., Furukawa, K., and Suzuki, R. (1987). A hierarchical neuronal network model for control and learning of voluntary movement. *Biological Cybernetics 57,* 169–185.

Leiner, H. C., Leiner, A. L., and. Dow, R. S. (1986). Does the cerebellum contribute to mental skill? *Behavioral Neuroscience 100,* 443–453.

Marr, D. (1969). A theory of cerebellar cortex. *Journal of Physiology 202,* 437–470.

Miall, R. C., Weir, D. J., Wolpert, D. M., and Stein, J. F. (1993). Is the cerebellum a Smith Predictor? *Journal of Motor Behavior 25,* 203–216.

Oscarsson, O. (1976). Spatial distribution of climbing and mossy fibre inputs into the cerebellar cortex. In O. Creutzfeldt, ed., *Afferent and intrinsic organization of laminated structures in the brain. Experimental Brain Research Supp. 1.* Berlin: Springer-Verlag.

Rosenblatt, F. (1962). *Principles of neurodynamics: Perceptron and the theory of brain mechanisms.* Washington, DC: Spartan Books.

Schweighofer, N., Arbib, M., and Dominey, P. F. (1996). A model of the cerebellum in adaptive control of saccadic gain. I. The model and its biological substrate. *Biological Cybernetics* 75, 19–28.

Schweighofer, N., Arbib, M. and Kawato, M. (1998). Role of the cerebellum in reaching movements in humans. I. Distributed inverse dynamics control. *European Journal of Neuroscience 10*, 86–94.

Nelson Donegan
Revised by Masao Ito

HIPPOCAMPUS

Both clinical neuropsychological studies and animal experiments involving damage to the hippocampal formation indicate that this structure plays a fundamental role in at least the initial establishment of long-term associative memory; however, the exact role of the hippocampus in associative memory, and the physiological and computational mechanisms by which this role is accomplished, remain subjects of intense study and debate. Although by no means proven, evidence favors the hypothesis that the hippocampus acts as a simple interim repository for memories of certain kinds of events, and that other (neocortical) circuitry draws on this repository during a process known as memory consolidation (e.g., Zola-Morgan and Squire, 1990). The following is a brief overview of some current ideas about how the unique circuitry of the hippocampal formation might enable rapid associative memory, and why such an interim repository might be necessary.

Specific events are generally represented in the nervous system as *distributed* patterns of activity within rather large populations of cells, and rarely by the activity of single cells. The activity pattern may be thought of as a *vector,* that is, a list of ones and zeros, indicating which neurons are firing and which are silent, or as a list of positive real numbers indicating the firing rates of the neurons over some short interval. Associative recall, by its most general definition, is the ability of the brain to reconstruct the vector corresponding to a stored event when presented with a vector that is missing some of the original information, has been corrupted somehow by noise, or merely bears some significant resemblance to the original. This ability is often called either *pattern completion* or *autoassociative recall.* Using the pre- and postsynaptic *conjunction* principle for modifying the connection strengths between neurons originally elaborated by Donald Hebb (1949), work in the 1960s and early 1970s by Kohonen (1972), Mart (1971), Steinbuch (1961), Willshaw and colleagues (1969), and others laid the theoretical foundations for how a simple pattern-completion network might operate. In particular, the work of Marr was seminal, because it outlined

several clear principles as to how actual neural circuits might accomplish this.

The essence of these principles is illustrated in Figure 1, which may be thought of as an incomplete and crude model for hippocampal regions CA3 and fascia dentata, and their neocortical inputs. The axons from the granule cells of the fascia dentata make sparse but strong contacts with the CA3 pyramidal cells. The axons of the pyramidal cells feed back into the pyramidal layer, making contacts that are initially ineffective but can be made effective by implementing "Hebbian" synaptic enhancement. That is, whenever a pyramidal cell is strongly activated by its granule cell input, those synapses that it receives from other pyramidal cells that have been activated by the same input become strengthened (in this illustration, the strength goes from 0 to 1). By strengthening the connections among neurons that have been active together during an event, it becomes possible later to recall that event in its entirety, given only a fragment of it. One of Marr's important contributions was the idea that a small population of inhibitory interneurons plays the crucial role of assessing the total number of active inputs and adjusting the threshold of the memory (pyramidal) cells such that only a fixed proportion of them are allowed to fire. This adjustment is accomplished essentially by dividing the total excitation of a given cell by the total number of active inputs. In this way, when an incomplete event is presented, the effective threshold of the pyramidal cells is lowered (because there is less inhibition). If the reduced input is part of a stored event, all of the corresponding synapses will have been strengthened and the correct cells will fire. Incorrect cells will not fire because they will, on average, not have as many enhanced inputs in that particular event. Thus, provided it is unique, even a small fragment of a stored event will cause activation of the full event. The reader unfamiliar with these principles might benefit by working through the example in Figure 1. For more detailed discussion, see McNaughton and Nadel (1989) or McNaughton and Barnes (1990).

There are, of course, constraints on the amount (and kinds) of information that can be stored by such a memory, as can readily be understood by imagining the consequences of attempting to store so much information that all of the synapses have been enhanced. At this point no information is recoverable. One solution is to encode an event with the minimum number of fibers necessary to capture its vital features (sometimes called *redundancy removal*). The hippocampus constitutes the highest level of association cortex in the nervous system, receiving its input from polymodal association cortex. Much of the processing that occurs in these areas can be thought of as redun-

Figure 1

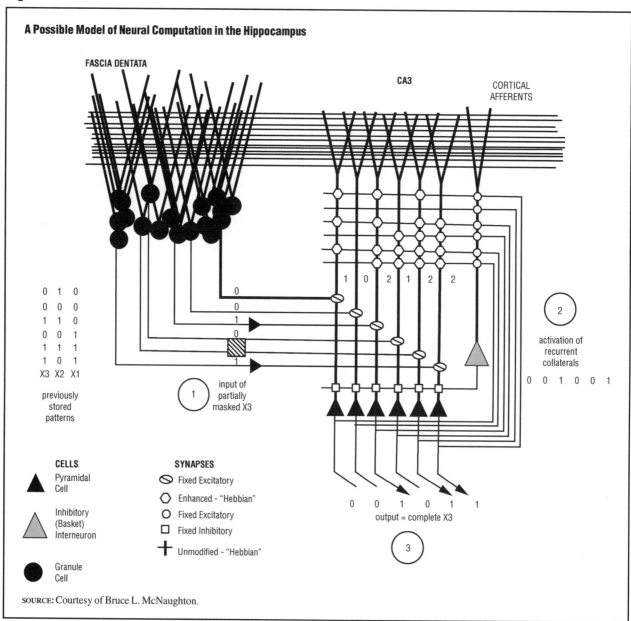

A Possible Model of Neural Computation in the Hippocampus

SOURCE: Courtesy of Bruce L. McNaughton.

dancy removal or *feature extraction.* Moreover, hippocampal cells are often silent for prolonged periods, suggesting that rather few of them are active at any one time. Another solution is to make the patterns to be stored as different from each other as possible, a process known as *orthogonalization,* because orthogonal vectors are uncorrelated.

Although feature extraction is itself an orthogonalization process, sometimes it is necessary to store as separate, one-time events that may differ only in some arbitrary but important way. Because feature detector formation requires "knowledge" of the long-term statistical regularities in the input, this solution

will not work. An alternative solution is to use an extra layer of very many cells between the input and the memory cells. By spreading the connections from the input to this layer more or less randomly, yet adjusting the thresholds so that about the *same total number* of intermediate cells as input cells are active, the degree of overlap between input events will be reduced. This is merely a consequence of the facts that, in the larger population, the probability that a given cell is active in any one event is reduced, and the probability of its being active in any two events is the square of the single-event probability. Marr called this solution *codon formation.* It is likely that the granule cells of the fascia dentata perform something like this function.

Although greatly oversimplified, models such as this go a long way toward accounting for the known anatomical and physiological organization of the hippocampal formation. Many theoretical and experimental neuroscientists believe that something like this process goes on in the hippocampus during the original encoding of long-term associative memory. One of the major outstanding questions in the field, however, is why the hippocampus, and presumably the information stored there, is necessary only for a limited period after the initial registration. Estimates of exactly how long vary from hours to years in different species, and for different kinds of memory. At present only educated guesses can be offered in answer to this question. The first is that it is probably both unnecessary and biologically expensive simply to store all experience; however, often it cannot be predicted at the time of an event whether the information is sufficiently important or reliable to be stored permanently. Second, if a set of events does contain some statistical regularity, it may be possible to generate a new "feature detector" for that regularity, and hence to achieve redundancy reduction in permanent memory. In order to assess this, however, some representation of the raw events must be stored for comparison. J. L. McClelland (personal communication) has proposed a somewhat related hypothesis, expressed in terms of the parallel distributed processing or connectionist models of cognitive psychology. Briefly, the argument is that learning appropriate and efficient internal representations for a particular problem or set of events generally requires multiple exposures to the events (at least with currently discovered algorithms). During these exposures a kind of global error term for the performance of the memory can be computed and used to correct (in small steps) the set of synaptic connection strengths *(weights)*. The argument, then, is that the hippocampus makes use of many cells to store a set of memories that later can be "played back" to the neocortex for the purpose of computing an appropriate set of connection weights to store the information with the minimal number of units. Ideas such as these, it is hoped, will eventually provide a firm computational explanation for the process of memory consolidation and the crucial role of the hippocampal formation.

A simple (and incomplete) model for the fascia dentata and CA3 subfields of the hippocampus illustrates how this system may implement *autoassociation*, using simple "Hebbian" synaptic enhancement. Inputs from fascia dentata essentially impose output patterns in CA3. The synapses of the activated recurrent collaterals that terminate on active pyramidal cells are enhanced (in this simple illustration, the weights go from 0 to 1). Later, input of some fragment of a stored pattern (1) activates a corresponding

subset of pyramidal cells and their recurrent collaterals (2). Each pyramidal cell then adds up how many of its currently active recurrent collateral synapses have previously been enhanced, and divides this by the total number of active inputs. If this is equal to or greater than threshold (i.e., 1), the unit fires. If not too many patterns are stored, the result will be the output of the complete original pattern (3). The inhibitory interneuron sums the total input and sets the divisor for the pyramidal cells accordingly. There is some evidence that something of this sort actually happens in the brain.

See also: PARALLEL DISTRIBUTED PROCESSING MODELS OF MEMORY

Bibliography

Hebb, D. O. (1949). *The organization of behavior.* New York: Wiley.

Kohonen, T. (1972). Correlation matrix memories. *IEEE Transactions on Computers C-21,* 353–359.

Marr, D. (1971). Simple memory: A theory for archicortex. *Philosophical Transactions of the Royal Society of London B262,* 23–81.

McNaughton, B. L., and Barnes, C. A. (1990). From cooperative synaptic enhancement to associative memory: Bridging the abyss. *Seminars in the Neurosciences 2,* 403–416.

McNaughton, B. L., and Nadel, L. (1989). Hebb-Marr networks and the neurobiological representation of action in space. In M. A. Gluck and D. E. Rumelhart, eds., *Neuroscience and connectionist theory.* Hillsdale, NJ: Erlbaum.

Steinbuch, K. (1961). Die Lernmatrix. *Kybernetik 1,* 36–45.

Willshaw, D. J., Buneman, O. P., and Longuet-Higgins, H. C. (1969). Nonholographic associative memory. *Nature 222,* 960–962.

Zola-Morgan, S. M., and Squire, L. R. (1990). The primate hippocampal formation: Evidence for a time-limited role in memory formation. *Science 250,* 288–289.

Bruce L. McNaughton

NEOCORTEX

One of the central goals of neuroscience research is to understand the nature of the computations carried out in the neocortex. The neocortex is a thin sheet of roughly 10^{10} neurons and fibers that forms the external surface of much of the brain. The neocortex arose recently in evolution, around the time that mammals branched off from reptiles. Yet over the past 60 million years, the neocortex has shown the most dramatic expansion and elaboration of any brain system. In fact, differences in the neocortex best distinguish the human brain from those of other mammals. The neocortex is involved in higher perceptual and cognitive processing and contains areas specialized for decision making, executive function, sensory perception (vision, hearing, touch, and smell), generating action, language, mathematics, and complex memory tasks.

The functional properties of neocortex depend upon its structure. There are four major principles of neocortical organization: First, the cortex is orga-

Figure 1

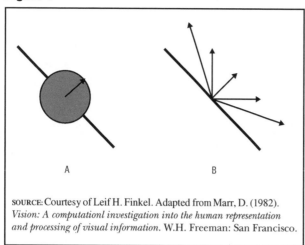

SOURCE: Courtesy of Leif H. Finkel. Adapted from Marr, D. (1982). *Vision: A computationl investigation into the human representation and processing of visual information.* W.H. Freeman: San Francisco.

Illustrations of the aperture problem. (A) Cortical neurons receive inputs from spatially restricted regions of the world, depicted in the figure as the shaded circular region. If a long line is viewed as it moves through this region, only the component of motion perpendicular to the line can be detected, since motion along the line's axis is undetectable. (B) This leads to an indeterminacy in detecting the true direction of motion of the line, since all motions sharing the same perpendicular component will be treated as equal.

nized vertically into six layers, each layer receiving from and sending connections to various brain sites. Second, there is a horizontal organization of the cortex into columns, such that neurons in a vertical column (of approximately 0.5 millimeter diameter) exhibit similar physiological properties. Third, most cortical areas contain one or more topographic maps. (In a topographic map, adjacent areas of the periphery are represented in adjacent areas of cortex. For example, in visual cortex, area Vl contains a map of the visual field; in somatosensory cortex, area SI contains four separate maps of the body surface.) Finally, cortical areas are functionally segregated—cells in each area are specialized for particular functional tasks. (For example, cells in visual area MT are specialized for motion detection, among other things, whereas those in visual area V4 are specialized for color and pattern analysis, among other things). The maps in different cortical areas are interconnected in a vast and intricate scheme.

In the somatosensory cortex (which mediates touch, temperature, and pain), maps are dynamically organized such that they change continuously in response to skin stimulation (Buonomano and Merzenich, 1998; Kaas, 2000). However, the visual neocortex has been the most intensively studied region and provides the clearest example of the kinds of computations the cortex must carry out.

Seeing is a complex act that requires a parallel analysis of shape, motion, depth, color, texture, and other attributes, all leading to the discrimination and recognition of an object. For example, a major cue to depth comes from stereopsis, a process of pattern matching in which the slightly disparate views of the world seen by the two eyes are compared; the distance of various objects is computed from the shift in view. Perception of depth thus results from a cortical computation.

Computations in another set of cortical areas result in perception of color. Contrary to the implications of simple optics, our perceptions of color are not solely determined by the wavelengths of light reflected from an object. As Edwin Land demonstrated, color perception is determined by the relative amount of light of different wavelengths reflected by an object as opposed to that reflected by its surrounding environment. Neurons in cortical area V4 have been found to respond to the color of an object as we perceive it; those in the lower-level area V1 respond to the wavelength of the light, not the color (Zeki, 1980); thus, the color computation probably depends on computations carried out in area V4.

The analysis of motion is similarly carried out in several stages and provides the best-investigated example of a cortical computation. In some species, such as the rabbit and the housefly, neurons in the retina are capable of detecting motion. In most mammals, however, sophisticated motion detection first arises in the cortex. Each cortical neuron receives visual inputs from only a small region of space—that is, it "sees" only a limited visual field. As Marr (1982) first pointed out, this leads to the so-called aperture problem (see Figure 1). If you look at a moving line through a small aperture, you can determine only the component of motion perpendicular to the line because it is impossible to tell whether the line is moving along its own axis. Each neuron faces essentially the same problem. Neurons in V1 are orientationally and directionally selective, which means that they respond only to lines and edges whose orientation falls within a certain narrow range (e.g., within ten degrees of vertical) and that are moving within a narrow range of directions (usually perpendicular to the preferred orientation). The only way around the aperture problem is to combine information from cells with different directional selectivities. This "neural synthesis" probably occurs in area MT (a small region of higher-level visual neocortex that receives input from area V1), as was shown in an ingenious experiment on monkey cortex by Movshon and colleagues (1985).

The key to Movshon's experiment is the visual stimulus presented to the monkey. The stimulus, as shown in Figure 2, consisted of two gratings (arrays of parallel, evenly spaced, lines), oriented at different angles, and each moving in a direction perpendicular to the orientation of their lines. If one draws two such gratings on transparent plastic sheets, superposes them, and moves them with respect to each other, then, instead of two sets of moving lines, one sees a checkerboard pattern moving in a third direction. This third direction is not the vector sum of the two component directions; rather, it is a more complicated function that reflects the intersection of the lines of uncertainty as specified by the constraints of the aperture problem (Movshon, Adelson, Grizzi, and Newsome, 1985).

Researchers presented this stimulus to alert monkeys and observed the responses of neurons in areas V1 and MT. In area MT, they found neurons that responded to the direction of motion of the checkerboard. In V1, they found no such neurons; rather, neurons responded to the direction of motion of either one grating or the other. Thus, to speak somewhat broadly, V1 "sees" only the component gratings, whereas MT "sees" the checkerboard. This is a situation analogous to color vision: A higher-level cortical area computes an object-related attribute based on information from lower cortical areas.

Taking this one step further, Bill Newsome and colleagues, in a remarkable series of experiments, demonstrated that the direction of motion of a stimulus, as viewed and reported by an awake, trained monkey, correlates precisely with the activation of individual neurons in area MT. By determining the selectivities of MT cells to various directions of motion, the experimenters could read off the neural response to any test stimulus. When the monkey occasionally made an error in judging the direction or velocity of the stimulus, it was correlated with a failure of the appropriate cells to fire. The investigators could even change the motion direction that the monkey perceived by stimulating particular cells to fire via implanted microelectrodes (Britten et al., 1992). A number of computational models have proposed mechanisms by which area MT may carry out these computations (Schrater, Knill, and Simoncelli, 2000).

Each area of the cortex is dedicated to particular computations; there are, however, similarities to the neuronal and architectural structure across the cortex. This suggests that a basic set of canonical computations may be carried out by all cortical regions and that differences in cortical computations may be largely due to the type of inputs received. It is not clear what the canonical cortical computations are, but researchers have suggested several candidate mechanisms.

Neurons in many regions of the neocortex and in phylogenetically older cortical regions such as the

Figure 2

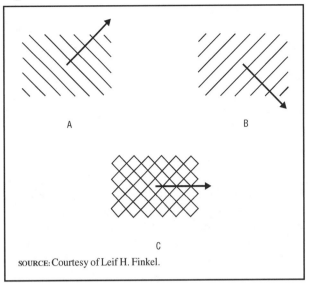

SOURCE: Courtesy of Leif H. Finkel.

The Movshon experiment (Movshon, J. A., Adelson, E. H., Grizzi, M. S., and Newsome, W. T. [1985]. The analysis of moving visual patterns. In C. Chagas, R. Gattass, and C. Gross, eds., *Pattern recognition mechanisms. Experimental Brain Research Supp.* 11, 117–151). A. Two gratings are shown, oriented at different angles. Each grating is moved in a direction perpendicular to the orientation of its lines, as indicated by the arrow. B. The two gratings are superposed and moved, as in (A). The resulting perception is of a checkerboard pattern moved in a third, unrelated direction (see text for details). This experiment illustrates how the cortex computes the direction of motion of an object from sets of indeterminate information (due to the aperture problem).

hippocampus can produce and maintain specific patterns of firing in response to a stimulus. As Earl Miller and colleagues have shown, if a monkey is shown a picture such as a photo of another monkey, specific recognition cells in high-level visual cortical areas (such as the inferotemporal IT cortex) will fire and continue to fire even after removal of the stimulus.

Neurons in areas of frontal cortex have an even more remarkable property. They can maintain a pattern of firing (in which certain neurons in the region continually fire while others are silent) even in the presence of distracting stimuli. The ability of a network to maintain a fixed pattern of activity in the absence of direct stimulus input is attractor behavior. Attractor states are stable and self-perpetuating because the inputs each cell receives via connections from other active neurons in the network are sufficient to maintain its firing. Based on theoretical considerations, John Hopfield (1982) proposed that attractor states might correspond to stored memories. Each attractor state (pattern of activity) has a "basin of attraction," a space of related activity patterns that transform into the attractor state, much like particles gravitationally attracted into a black hole. This confers on the network the property of auto-association or error-correction; if a noisy, corrupted or partial memory is used as input, the complete stored pattern can be retrieved.

The ability to stably maintain a piece of information in active or working memory is essential to any computational process. If we attempt to add two plus three, we have to store the first number while we fetch the second and perform the operation. Any type of matching process in recognition (e.g., "Wait a minute; I know that face!") requires holding a stimulus in working memory. Equally important is the ability to release the network from the memory or to use one memory as a prompt to the next associated memory in a sequence. In the frontal cortex, where neurons have the unique ability to hold on to the attractor state even in the face of distracting stimuli, the neuromodulator dopamine may control attractor stability (Durstewitz, Seamans, and Sejnowski, 2000). When dopamine levels are high, the attractors are robustly stable against distraction; when the dopamine level falls, distracting stimuli knock the system into a new pattern of activity corresponding to the novel stimulus. Some investigators have suggested that disorders of the dopamine system, such those typical of schizophrenia, may underlie the symptoms of perseveration (inability to get a thought out of one's head) and delusions/hallucinations (possibly the inappropriate linking of distracting stimuli or memories).

A cortical circuit can carry out different computations at different times. The system of neuromodulators, including acetylcholine, serotonin, noradrenaline, dopamine, and other agents are a control system regulating the kinds of computations and the flow of information between brain regions. For example, J. Lisman and N. A. Otmakhova (2001) have proposed that in the hippocampus bursts of dopamine may transiently switch a circuit into a learning mode (as opposed to an on-line information processing mode). Similarly, Michael Hasselmo (1999) has demonstrated that acetylcholine may switch between learning and recall, and may selectively suppress intrinsic as opposed to extrinsic inputs. The release of acetylcholine and noradrenaline correlate closely with visual attention, and both acetylcholine and dopamine are associated with inducing rapid changes in cortical connectivity. Disorders of the neuromodulatory system, coupled with structural damage to cells and synapses, are the hallmark of most of the neurodegenerative diseases with cognitive deficits (e.g., Alzheimer's disease).

Perhaps the greatest mystery in understanding cortical processing is the mechanism of integration.

A cortical hypercolumn integrates bottom-up, top-down, and horizontal (contextual) inputs. Taking our earlier example of color vision, the perceived color depends upon the incident wavelengths within the receptive field (bottom-up), the contextual inputs from neighboring regions of the visual field (horizontal), and top-down knowledge. Integration and inference are the central principles of cortical function, and mechanisms for these processes have been envisioned in several recent theories. Rajesh Rao and Dana Ballard (1999) have proposed that feedback loops between higher and lower areas carry out a kind of predictive coding. Higher areas "predict" the activity in the lower areas and send this prediction back via descending connections, and feedforward connections to the higher areas convey the residual errors in the prediction—a kind of neural Kalman filter. Several information-theory-based learning algorithms take a similar approach, in which the key operation is maximal compression of the represented information with the minimal loss of information about the inputs. Shimon Ullman has shown that a cortically inspired network based on maximizing mutual information can achieve remarkable image-recognition performance, including the ability to categorize novel objects into previously learned categories.

Cortical processing is extremely rapid. M. Fabre-Thorpe and colleagues (2001) have shown that well-known images can be recognized when presented at interstimulus intervals of fifty milliseconds. Given typical cortical firing rates, this result suggests that recognition and other higher processes require only one or two spikes from each cell—there is no time for any iterations of an algorithm. This harks back to a rule suggested by David Marr that a good neural algorithm operates in the time required for information to reach the relevant circuit but does not require any additional processing time. These timing constraints call for representations with fast dynamics. One likely candidate is the space-rate code (Maass, 2001) in which the degree of activation is represented by the fraction of neurons in a population that fire in a short (e.g., 5 ms) time window. Since, in each subsequent time window, the fraction firing can substantially change, information can be rapidly communicated.

How might recognition make use of spike-timing information? John Hopfield has demonstrated one possible mechanism using the example of speech recognition. Hopfield's network (2001) makes use of an array of feature detectors, each tuned to an onset or offset of sounds in a particular frequency range. Any speech stimulus (e.g., a speaker saying the word *one*) produces a spatiotemporal pattern of activation of the feature detectors. In Hopfield's network, the feature detectors activate cells in a second network whose firing fate adapts—that is, their firing rate slows with time after the stimulus. The rate of adaptation can be varied and is learned—it is set so that at some time point, all cells responding to the stimulus will have adapted to fire at the same rate. This common rate is transient—cells will continue to adapt, and their firing rates will diverge; except for a brief time window, all cells responding to the stimulus share a similar firing rate. Hopfield proposes that this situation, where a number of cells in a network fire at approximately the same rate, is statistically significant. It could be one of the fundamental kinds of computations carried out by cortical networks.

Understanding cortical computation remains a challenge. But advances in neuroscience, particularly the emergence of optical imaging techniques, coupled with the development of sophisticated information-theory models, offer the promise of new insights. Such advances promise a new era in artificial intelligence and the creation of information technologies powered by biology-based algorithms.

See also: GUIDE TO THE ANATOMY OF THE BRAIN: CEREBRAL CORTEX

Bibliography

Britten, K. H., Shadlen, M. N., Newsome, W. T., and Movshon, J. A. (1992). The analysis of visual motion: A comparison of neuronal and psychophysical performance. *Journal of Neuroscience 12*, 4,745–4,765.

Buonomano, D. V., and Merzenich, M. M. (1998). Cortical plasticity: From synapses to maps. *Annual Review of Neuroscience 21*, 149–186.

Durstewitz, D., Seamans, J. K., and Sejnowski, T. J. (2000). Neurocomputational models of working memory. *Nature Neuroscience 3*, 1,184–1,191.

Fabre-Thorpe, M., Delorme, A., Marlot, C., and Thorpe, S. (2001). A limit to the speed of processing in ultra-rapid visual categorization of novel natural scenes. *Journal of Cognitive Neuroscience 13*, 171–180.

Hasselmo, M. E. (1999). Neuromodulation: Acetylcholine and memory consolidation. *Trends in Cognitive Science 3*, 351–359.

Hopfield, J. J. (1982). Neural networks and physical systems with emergent collective computational abilities. *Proceedings of the National Academy of Sciences of the United States of America 79*, 2,554–2,558.

Hopfield, J. J., and Brody, C. D. (2001). What is a moment? Transient synchrony as a collective mechanism for spatiotemporal integration. *Proceedings of the National Academy of Sciences of the United States of America 98*, 1,282–1,287.

Kaas, J. H. (2000). The reorganization of somatosensory and motor cortex after peripheral nerve or spinal cord injury in primates. *Progress in Brain Research 128*, 173–179.

Land, E. H. (1983). Recent advances in retinex theory and some implications for cortical computations. *Proceedings of the National Academy of Sciences of the United States of America 80*, 5,163–5,169.

Lisman, J. E., and Otmakhova, N. A. (2001). Storage, recall, and novelty detection of sequences by the hippocampus: Elaborating on the Socratic model to account for normal and aberrant effects of dopamine. *Hippocampus 11*, 551–568.

Maass, W. (2001). Computation with spiking neurons. In M. A. Arbib, ed., *The handbook of brain theory and neural networks*. Cambridge, MA: MIT Press.

Marr, D. (1982). *Vision: A computational investigation into the human representation and processing of visual information*. San Francisco: W. H. Freeman.

Miller, E. K. (2000). The prefrontal cortex and cognitive control. *Nature Reviews Neuroscience 1*, 59–65.

Movshon, J. A., Adelson, E. H., Grizzi, M. S., and Newsome, W. T. (1985). The analysis of moving visual patterns. In C. Chagas, R. Gattass, and C. Gross, eds., *Pattern recognition mechanisms*. *Experimental Brain Research Supp. 11*, 117–151.

Rao, R. P., and Ballard, D. H. (1999). Predictive coding in the visual cortex: A functional interpretation of some extra-classical receptive-field effects. *Nature Neuroscience. 2*, 79–87.

Schrater, P. R., Knill, D. C., and Simoncelli, E. P. (2000). Mechanisms of visual motion detection. *Nature Neuroscience. 3*, 64–68.

Thorpe, S., Fize, D., and Marlot, C. (1996). Speed of processing in the human visual system. *Nature 381*, 520–522.

VanRullen, R., and Thorpe, S. J. (2001). The time course of visual processing: From early perception to decision-making. *Journal of Cognitive Neuroscience 13*, 454–461.

Zeki, S. M. (1980). The representation of colours in the cerebral cortex. *Nature 284*, 412–418.

Leif H. Finkel

OLFACTORY CORTEX AS A MODEL FOR TELENCEPHALIC PROCESSING

Changes to myriad synapses throughout the brain must be coordinated every time a memory is established, and these synapses must be appropriately reactivated every time the memory is retrieved. Once stored, memories can be recognized (as a re-experienced input) or recalled (via different input, such as a name evoking the memory of a face or a scene evoking memories of an experience) by many routes. We remember what tables are as well as we remember a specific table, and we recognize objects despite seeing them from quite different angles, under different lighting, in different settings. Computational simulations of synaptic modifications (e.g., long-term potentiation) in distinct brain-circuit architectures illustrate how these minute changes can give rise to coherent properties of memory; how analyses of different brain areas yield derivations of disparate memory functions; and how interactions among connected regions give rise to still new operating principles beyond those of their constituents.

The principal anatomical designs in mammalian brain are cortical: planar arrays of neurons, arranged with their cell bodies in sheets and their apical dendrites standing in parallel. This laminar pattern contrasts with that of most reptilian brain structures, in which neurons are grouped in globular clusters ("nuclei"); an exception is the cortically organized reptilian pallium. The phylogenetic origins of the mammalian neocortex (perhaps including transformed

Figure 1

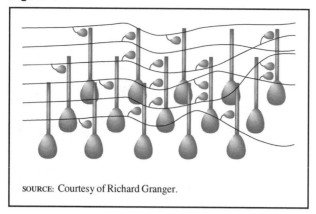

SOURCE: Courtesy of Richard Granger.

Characteristics of a cortical layer. Axons (horizontal lines) course through the apical dendrites of a layer of neurons making sparse, random synaptic contacts corresponding to entries in a matrix.

nonpallial precursors as well as pallium) are the subject of continuing controversy. The difference is one of function, not just form. With cells arrayed in a plane, the axons providing input to the structure pass through the dendritic field, making random and sparse synaptic contacts. This anatomical arrangement creates a biological version of a three-dimensional array or matrix in which the rows correspond to the input axons, the columns are the dendrites, and each matrix entry is a synaptic connection between an axon and dendrite (see Figure 1). The neocortex undergoes vast expansion with mammalian evolution, and as the cortex comes to dominate the brain, cortical computation comes to dominate behavior.

The Olfactory Bulb and Paleocortex

The olfactory paleocortex, one of the oldest relics in mammals of the reptilian pallium, is an apt starting point for evaluation of cortical computation. One reason is its relative simplicity (for instance, it has three primary layers instead of the six layers of the neocortex). Another is its relative proximity to its input environment. In other sensory systems, inputs typically proceed from a peripheral organ (e.g., cochlea) to one or more lower-brain structures (e.g., cochlear nucleus, colliculus), then to a noncortical (nuclear) structure in the thalamus (e.g., medial geniculate nucleus), and only then on to the primary cortex for the appropriate sense (e.g., auditory cortex). By comparison, olfactory receptors (activated by chemical odorants drawn in through the nose) project to the olfactory bulb and thence straight to olfactory cortex. (The structure is variously termed olfactory paleocortex, for its phylogenetic age; piriform, pyriform, or prepy-

riform cortex, for its pearlike shape; or primary olfactory cortex, for its placement as the first cortical structure to receive olfactory input relayed from the periphery.) Abstract models have been constructed based on four fundamentals of the olfactory system: its anatomical structure, its physiological operation during behavior, the characteristics of synaptic change caused by LTP, and the nature of the inputs that arrive naturally at the system during olfactory-related behaviors.

Figure 2 schematically illustrates the anatomical structure of a typical mammal's olfactory system (adapted from Shepard, 1991). In the figure the animal's nose is to the left, with the axons from the nose comprising the first cranial nerve (Nerve I) making synaptic contact (in the regions termed glomeruli) with the primary excitatory (mitral) cells of the olfactory bulb. Mitral cells are inhibited by granule cells via specialized synapses (see Haberly and Shepard, this volume), and mitral cell axons (comprising the lateral olfactory tract) project to cortex, where they form synaptic contacts with the apical dendrites of the primary cortical excitatory layer II and III cells. Those cells in turn project both forward, to provide the input to downstream brain structures (such as entorhinal cortex), and backward, to provide feedback to the bulb both directly and by way of the anterior olfactory cortex (often termed the anterior olfactory nucleus, despite its laminar rather than nuclear structure).

Simple Emergent Computations from Feedforward Operation of the Bulb-Cortex System

When an animal is actively engaged in olfactory learning behavior, the entire bulb-cortex system, its primary target output structures (entorhinal cortex and hippocampus), and even the overt behavioral sniffing activity of the animal operate in synchrony, at a rate of about four to eight cycles per second (Macrides, 1975; Macrides et al., 1982; Vanderwolf, 1992; Wiebe and Staubli, 2001). As the animal repeatedly samples or sniffs the olfactory environment, neurons through the entire "assembly line" of olfactory-hippocampal structures send spikes down their axons, in bursts occurring approximately every fourth to eighth of a second. Computer simulations of the resulting feedforward neuronal activity in the cortex have shown that LTP-like synaptic-change increments cause specific cortical target cells that initially responded to a particular odor to become increasingly responsive not only to that odor but also to a range of similar odors. Figure 3 uses broad simplifying assumptions to illustrate this straightforward principle.

Figure 2

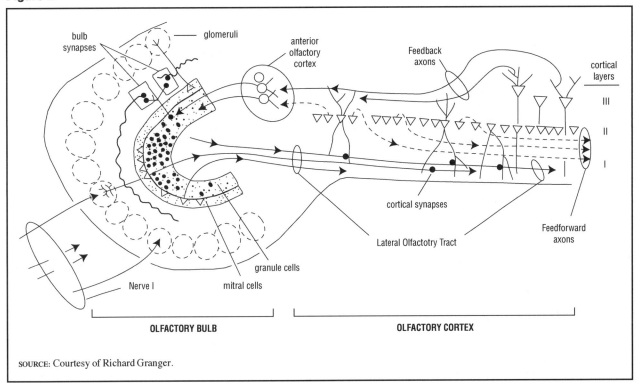

bulb synapses

glomeruli

anterior olfactory cortex

Feedback axons

cortical layers

III

II

I

bulb synapses

cortical synapses

Lateral Olfactotry Tract

Feedforward axons

granule cells

Nerve I

mitral cells

OLFACTORY BULB

OLFACTORY CORTEX

SOURCE: Courtesy of Richard Granger.

Schematic diagram of mammalian olfactory system anatomy. Input from receptor cells in the nose arrive via axons comprising the first cranial nerve, making synaptic contact with the dendrites of mitral cells in the olfactory bulb. Mitral cell axons in turn make synaptic contact with the apical dendrites (projecting downward, toward the cortical surface) of primary cells in the olfactory cortex. Cortical cell axons project forward to become input to successive anatomical structures (entorhinal cortex, hippocampus) as well as projecting backward to become feedback input to the inhibitory cells of the olfactory bulb.

(Models of the olfactory bulb [Anton et al., 1991; 1992] not discussed here are assumed).

In the left-hand panel of the diagram, input axons b, c, and d are active (arrows), and are assumed to be sufficient to elicit firing responses from three target cells (darkened). Synapses whose inputs and targets are coactive (highlighted) will potentiate. After potentiation, the enhanced synapses (enlarged, right panel) confer more voltage change than they did in their unpotentiated state, so fewer active inputs should suffice to elicit a target neuron response. Thus any of the depicted input patterns P, Q, and R may now suffice to activate the same three target cells, whereas none of these inputs would have activated these neurons prior to synaptic potentiation.

After potentiation episodes, inputs with highly overlapping activation patterns tend to educe identical neuronal response patterns in the cortex. The result is the mathematical operation of "clustering," in which sufficiently similar inputs are placed into a single category or cluster. The odor of a rose, a violet, or a lily might, after long-term potentiation, elicit only an undifferentiated response corresponding to

"flower scent" (and different odors elicit only their cluster responses—e.g., meat scent, smoke scent). This cluster responsecan give rise to useful "generalization" properties, informing the organism of the category of an otherwise unfamiliar odor, but, somewhat counterintuitively, it prevents the system from making fine distinctions among members of a cluster. These results are almost generic, as many computational frameworks with very different characteristics, including competitive networks (e.g., von der Malsburg, 1973; Grossberg, 1976; Rumelhart and Zipser, 1985; Coultrip et al., 1992); backpropagation (Rumelhart et al., 1986); and dynamical or excitatory feedback networks (e.g., Hopfield, 1982) can exhibit similar properties.

Complex Computations from Combined Feedforward and Feedback Olfactory Operation

Absent from the foregoing analysis is the extensive inhibitory feedback projection from cortical neurons to granule cells in the bulb. This pathway selectively inhibits those bulb inputs that generate cluster

Figure 3

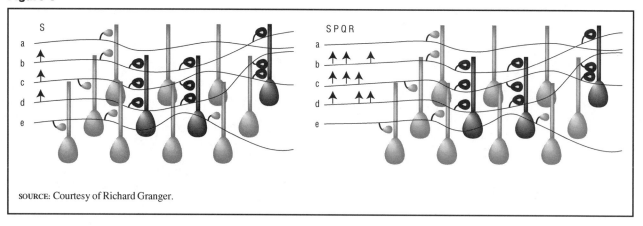

Simple effects of synaptic potentiation on cell response to feedforward inputs. (Left) Before potentiation, if three active synapses suffice to elicit a response from target cells, then the three darkened cells will respond to input S (the combined activation of axons b, c, and d), and their active synapses (highlighted) will potentiate. (Right) After potentiation, strengthened synapses (enlarged) contribute more voltage change to a cell whenever activated, so that the same three neurons may now fire in response to reduced inputs P, Q, and R, which would have been insufficient to elicit responses from these neurons before potentiation.

responses in the cortex, thereby unmasking the remainder of the bulb's activity. That remainder becomes the subsequent input to the cortex on the next activity cycle, whereupon the same cortical operations are performed. The result is that the second cortical response (one fourth to one eighth of a second later) will consist of a quite distinct set of neurons from the initial response, since most of the input components giving rise to that first response are now inhibited by the feedback from cortex to bulb. Analysis of the second (and ensuing) responses has shown successive subclustering of an input: the first cycle of response identifies the odor's membership in a particular cluster (e.g., floral), the next response (a fraction of a second later) identifies its membership in a particular subcluster (rose), then in a sub-subcluster (particular variety of rose), and so on. Roughly five "levels" of subclustering occur in the simulation before the inhibitory feedback to the bulb runs its course. That is, the system uses an unexpected type of temporal coding, using specific target neurons selectively activated at a series of different time points to discriminate among inputs.

This iterative subclustering activity turned out to be mathematically expressible as a novel algorithm for the well-studied statistical task of hierarchical clustering. All such algorithms have differential costs or complexity in terms of the time (number of mathematical steps) and space (amount of storage) required for each operation. Surprisingly, the derived olfactory algorithm exhibited computational costs that compared favorably with those in the (extensive) literature on such methods (Ambros-Ingerson et al., Kilborn et al., 1996). These studies represent an instance in which a novel and efficient algorithm for a well-studied computational problem emerged from simulation and analysis of a specific cortical network. The method was readily generalized to modalities other than olfaction. For instance, input patterns corresponding to speech sounds yielded naturally occurring clusters and subclusters on successive samples (see Figure 4). Elaboration of the algorithm gave rise to families of computational signal-processing methods whose performance on complex signal classification tasks has consistently equaled or outperformed those of competing methods (interested readers are referred to: Kowtha et al., 1994; Coultrip and Granger, 1994; Granger et al., 1997).

Biological Findings and Psychological Implications

If the olfactory system operates in this way, it should show striking behavioral and electrophysiological results. Behavioral experiments showed that rats recognized novel similar odors as members of a category yet also distinguished and recognized individual category members, providing evidence that animals build unsupervised similarity-based perceptual clusters (Granger et al., 1991). Individual olfactory cortical neurons, measured chronically in behaving animals, responded selectively when tested on very different odors. Moreover, responses were transient, corresponding to the interval of a specific sniff cycle but not to multiple cycles, a result a result that also corresponds with the computer simulations (McCollum et al., 1991). Findings arrived at under different experimental conditions have yielded various hy-

Figure 4

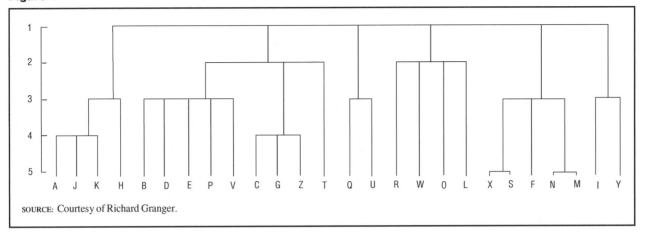

SOURCE: Courtesy of Richard Granger.

Hierarchy created by computer simulation of successive feedforward and feedback activity in an olfactory bulb-cortex-like structure, operating on spoken sounds rather than on olfactory input. Each sound is a letter of the alphabet. After simulated long-term potentiation, the initial simulated cortical response (1) does not differentiate among any letters, all of which are similar enough to each other (and different enough from other auditory inputs, from traffic noises to bird whistles) to belong to a single cluster. The next cortical response (2) differentiates "A, J, K" sounds from "B, C, T" sounds, and others. Successive responses (3–5) make iteratively finer distinctions. Eventually each letter belongs to its own sub-cluster.

potheses of olfactory function (e.g., Schoenbaum and Eichenbaum, 1995; Haberly, 2001). Further studies of unit neuron recordings in behaving animals will be needed to settle competing interpretations of the observed data.

The computational and neurobiological findings yield hypotheses about psychological function. Operations emerging from cortical circuits presumably constitute elemental psychological acts and contribute, through combination, to more complex mental processes in ways not yet understood. The evocation of successively finer-grained information about a stimulus via sequential cortical responses suggests a fundamental operation of repetitive perceptual sampling. Visual, auditory, and somatosensory cortices have anatomical architectures analogous to the olfactory bulb-cortex template, including excitatory feedforward and inhibitory feedback interactions with thalamic nuclei (see Herkenham, 1986; Jones, 1998, for reviews). Perhaps the second glance of a scene educes qualitatively different information from the first glance (even when such "glances" are covert cycles operating within these cortical structures, rather than behavioral eye movements). Humans exhibit synchronized rhythmic firing during learning and during complex sensory processing (Caplan et al., 2001; Sobotka and Ringo, 1997). And human subjects in perceptual and conceptual studies robustly recognize objects first at categorical levels and subsequently at successively subordinate levels (Mervis and Rosch, 1981; Schlaghecken, 1998; Kuhl et al., 2001), suggesting the presence of structured memories that are

hierarchically configured and sequentially traversed during recognition.

Modeling and analysis of other brain areas, including constituents of the hippocampal formation, auditory neocortex, the striatal complex, and thalamo-cortical loops, has yielded a range of additional, starkly different emergent fundamental computations for each structure, as well as novel complex operations from combinations of these (e.g., Lynch and Granger, 1992; Gluck and Granger, 1993; Granger et al., 1994; 1997; Myers et al., 1995; Kilborn et al., 1996; Aleksandrovsky et al., 1996; 1997). As in the case of the hierarchical clustering algorithm identified in the olfactory system, new functions derived from other brain regions exhibited computational characteristics comparable to algorithms of known power, often equaling or surpassing the best algorithms in cost and efficacy. Moreover, as in the case of the olfactory system, the results suggested new interpretations of both simple and complex psychological operations, intimating the development of more advanced hypotheses of human brain function.

See also: NEURAL COMPUTATION: APPROACHES TO LEARNING; NEURAL COMPUTATION: CEREBELLUM; NEURAL COMPUTATION: HIPPOCAMPUS; NEURAL COMPUTATION: NEOCORTEX

Bibliography

Aleksandrovsky, B., Brucher, F., Lynch, G., and Granger, R. (1997). Neural network model of striatal complex. In *Biological and Artificial Computation, from Neuroscience to Technology.*

IWANN'97 International Conference on Artificial and Natural Neural Networks. Berlin: Springer-Verlag, pp.104–115.

Aleksandrovsky, B., Whitson, J., Garzotto, A, Lynch, G., and Granger, R. (1996). An algorithm derived from thalamocortical circuitry stores and retrieves temporal sequences. *Proceedings of the International Conference on Pattern Recognition, IEEE Computer Society Press 4*, 550–554.

Ambros-Ingerson, J., Granger, R., and Lynch, G. (1990). Simulation of paleocortex performs hierarchical clustering. *Science 247*, 1,344–1,348.

Anton, P., Granger, R., and Lynch, G. (1993). Simulated dendritic spines influence reciprocal synaptic strengths and lateral inhibition in the olfactory bulb. *Brain Research 628*, 157–165.

Anton, P., Lynch, G., and Granger, R. (1991). Computation of frequency-to-spatial transform by olfactory bulb glomeruli. *Biological Cybernetics 65*, 407–414.

Bliss, T. V. P., and Lømo, T. (1973). Long-lasting potentiation of synaptic transmission in the dentate area of the anesthetized rabbit following stimulation of the perforant path. *Journal of Physiology 232*, 331–356.

Caplan, J., Madsen, J., Raghavachari, S., and Kahana, M. (2001). Distinct patterns of brain oscillations underlie two basic parameters of human maze learning. *Journal of Neurophysiology 86*, 368–380.

Coultrip, R., and Granger, R. (1994). LTP learning rules in sparse networks approximate Bayes classifiers via Parzen's method. *Neural Networks 7*, 463–476.

Coultrip, R., Granger, R., and Lynch, G. (1992). A cortical model of winner-take-all competition via lateral inhibition. *Neural Networks 5*, 47–54.

Gluck, M., and Granger, R. (1993). Computational models of the neural bases of learning and memory. *Annual Review of Neuroscience 16*, 667–706.

Granger, R., Staubli, U., Powers, H., Otto, T., Ambros-Ingerson, J., and Lynch, G. (1991). Behavioral tests of a prediction from a cortical network simulation. *Psychological Science 2*, 116–118.

Granger, R., Whitson, J., Larson, J., and Lynch, G. (1994). Non-Hebbian properties of LTP enable high-capacity encoding of temporal sequences. *Proceedings of the National Academy of Sciences of the United States of America 91*, 10,104–10,108.

Granger, R., Wiebe, S., Taketani, M., Ambros-Ingerson, J., and Lynch, G. (1997). Distinct memory circuits comprising the hippocampal region. *Hippocampus 6*, 567–578.

Grossberg, S. (1976). Adaptive pattern classification and universal recoding. I. Parallel development and coding of neural feature detectors. *Biological Cybernetics 23*, 121–134.

Haberly, L. (2001). Parallel-distributed processing in olfactory cortex, New insights from morphological and physiological analysis of neuronal circuitry. *Chemical Senses 26*, 551–576.

Herkenham, M. (1986). New perspectives on the organization and evolution of nonspecific thalamocortical projections. In E. Jones and A. Peters, eds., *Cerebral cortex*, Vol. 5. New York: Plenum Press.

Hopfield, J. (1982). Neural networks and physical systems with emergent collective computational abilities. *Proceedings of the National Academy of Sciences of the United States of America 79*, 2,554–2,558.

Jones, E. G.(1998). A new view of specific and nonspecific thalamocortical connections. *Advances in Neurology 77*, 49–71.

Karten, H. J. (1997). Evolutionary developmental biology meets the brain, the origins of mammalian neocortex. *Proceedings of the National Academy of Sciences of the United States of America 94*, 2,800–2,804.

Kilborn, K., Granger, R., and Lynch, G. (1996). Effects of LTP on response selectivity of simulated cortical neurons. *Journal of Cognitive Neuroscience 8*, 338–353.

Kowtha, V., Satyanarayana, P., Granger, R., and Stenger, D. (1994). Learning and classification in a noisy environment by a simulated cortical network. *Proceedings of the Third Annual Computer and Neural Systems Conference* Boston: Kluwer.

Kuhl, P., Tsao, F., Zhang, Y., DeBoer, B. (2001). Language, culture, mind, brain, Progress at the margins between disciplines. *Annals of the New York Academy of Science 935*, 136–174.

Lynch, G., and Granger, R. (1992). Variations in synaptic plasticity and types of memory in cortico–hippocampal networks. *Journal of Cognitive Neuroscience 4*, 189–199.

Macrides, F. (1975). Temporal relations between hippocampal slow waves and exploratory sniffing in hamsters. *Behavioral Biology 14*, 295–308.

Macrides, F., Eichenbaum, H. B., and Forbes, W. B. (1982). Temporal relationship between sniffing and the limbic (theta) rhythm during odor discrimination reversal learning. *Journal of Neuroscience 2*, 1,705–1,717.

McCollum, J., Larson, J., Otto, T., Schottler, F. Granger, R., and Lynch, G. (1991). Short-latency single-unit processing in olfactory cortex. *Journal of Cognitive Neuroscience 3*, 293–299.

Mervis, C., and Rosch, E. (1981). Categorization of natural objects. *Annual Review of Psychology 32*, 89–115.

Myers, C., Gluck, M., and Granger, R. (1995). Dissociation of hippocampal and entorhinal function in associative learning, A computational approach. *Psychobiology 23*, 116–138.

Puelles, L. (2001). Thoughts on the development, structure and evolution of the mammalian and avian telencephalic pallium. *Philosophical Transactions of the Royal Society of London 356, (Biol.)* 1,583–1,598.

Rosch, E., and Lloyd, B. B. (1978). *Cognition and categorization.* Hillsdale, NJ: Erlbaum.

Rumelhart, D., Hinton, G., and Williams, R. (1986). Learning representations by back-propagating errors. *Nature 323*, 533–536.

Rumelhart, D., and Zipser, D. (1985). Feature discovery by competitive learning. *Cognitive Science 9*, 75–112

Schlaghecken, F. (1998). On processing "beasts" and "birds," an event-related potential study on the representation of taxonomic structure. *Brain and Language 64*, 53–82.

Schoenbaum, G., and Eichenbaum, H. (1995). Information coding in the rodent prefrontal cortex. I. Single-neuron activity in orbitofrontal cortex compared with that in pyriform cortex. *Journal of Neurophysiology 74*, 733–750.

Shepherd, G. (1991). Computational structure of the olfactory system. In J. L. Davis and H. Eichenbaum, eds., *Olfaction, a model system for computational neuroscience*. Cambridge: MIT Press.

Sobotka, S., and Ringo, J. (1997). Saccadic eye movements, even in darkness, generate event–related potentials recorded in medial septum and medial temporal cortex. *Brain Research 756*, 168–173.

Vanderwolf, C. (1992). Hippocampal activity, olfaction, and sniffing: An olfactory input to the dentate gyrus. *Brain Research 593*, 197–208.

von der Malsburg, C. (1973). Self-organization of orientation sensitive cells in the striate cortex. *Kybernetik 14*, 85–100.

Wiebe, S., and Staubli, U. (2001). Recognition memory correlates of hippocampal theta cells. *Journal of Neuroscience 21*, 3,955–3,957.

Richard H. Granger, Jr.

NEURAL SUBSTRATES OF AVOIDANCE LEARNING

People and animals learn to avoid pain provided that warning stimuli are available to signal pain-inducing events. Such learning is generally of two types, active and inhibitory. *Active avoidance* refers to movements learned in response to warning stimuli for the purpose of avoiding pain. *Inhibitory avoidance* refers to inaction, learned because action in the presence of the warning stimuli has previously led to pain.

Limbic and Motor Systems

Research implicates the brain's limbic and motor systems in the mediation of avoidance learning. The limbic system is a vast network of interconnected regions including the amygdala, hippocampus, limbic thalamus and the cingulate area of the cerebral cortex. Relevant parts of the motor system include the striatum and the nucleus accumbens. Many laboratory studies of the neural substrates of avoidance learning involve locomotion (or its inhibition). Therefore, areas of the brain concerned with the initiation and maintenance of locomotion are also involved.

Theoretical Overview: WHAT and WHEN

Available data indicate that in avoidance learning the motor system acts as a WHAT system, and the limbic system acts as a WHEN system. The WHAT system determines what is to be done, that is, the particular behavior to be performed. Its functions include learning and remembering the response to be performed; making ready or *priming* the response when the avoidance situation is encountered; and executing the response. The WHAT system is relatively poor when it comes to remembering important signals in the environment, including the warning stimuli that call for avoidance behavior; the WHEN system is specialized to handle these functions. The WHEN system learns about and remembers warning stimuli, and issues *command volleys* of neuronal activity that tell the WHAT system precisely when to execute the avoidance response (see Figure 1).

Data supporting these ideas come from studies of the effects of experimentally induced brain damage (lesions) and from studies of the activity of brain neurons during avoidance learning. Gabriel (1993) reviewed much of the research data summarized below; citations of studies not included in the review are noted in the text that follows.

Active Avoidance Learning

Experimental lesions in the *medial dorsal* (MD) and *anterior* (AN) nuclei of the limbic thalamus, or lesions of the cingulate cortical areas that receive input from these thalamic nuclei, render rats, cats and rabbits incapable of active avoidance learning. Lesions in only one of the nuclei, or in the cingulate cortical projection field of a single nucleus, yield partial learning deficits. In addition, lesions of the amygdala block learning. In these studies laboratory tasks involve animals learning to jump over a barrier or learning to step in an activity wheel to avoid a mild electric shock signaled by tone or light warning stimuli. The deficit in animals with these lesions is a true learning deficit, not an inability to move or to perceive the warning stimuli.

The specific involvement of the limbic areas in avoidance learning receives further support from data indicating that cerebellar lesions, which block classical conditioning of eyeblink responses, do not affect avoidance learning in rabbits.

Studies of neuronal activity during active avoidance learning by rabbits in the activity wheel task have shown that amygdalar, limbic thalamic, and cingulate cortical neurons learn to produce impulses in response to the warning tone that signals shock. Impulse rate in trained rabbits increased just after the warning stimulus and reached its maximum rate just before the rabbits stepped, suggesting that stepping was triggered by the neuronal activity. That this activity is truly related to learning and not to generalized arousal is indicated by the fact that the activity is selective, for example, greater in response to the warning tone than to a second tone which is presented as often as the warning stimulus but is not predictive of shock.

Cingulate cortical neurons send axons to striatal motor areas such as the caudate nucleus. Active avoidance learning is impaired in animals with lesions in the caudate nucleus. Thus, the flow of nerve impulses from the cingulate cortex to the caudate nucleus and possibly to other motor areas is likely responsible for initiating active avoidance responses. Theoretically, the role of the caudate nucleus represents the function of the WHAT system, and the information flow from the limbic thalamus and the cingulate cortex to the caudate nucleus represents the command volley issued by the WHEN system.

During the acquisition of the stepping avoidance response by rabbits, two forms of neuronal learning have been noted in the limbic thalamus and in the cingulate cortex. One form is *discriminative* or *selective neuronal activity* (SA), as defined above, and the second form, *excitatory modulation* (EM), is a dramatic increase of impulse firing rate in trained rabbits in response to both warning and nonwarning tones. Two facts indicate that EM is, like SA, clearly a learning-related change and not merely a reflection of general arousal: 1. EM does not occur when rabbits experi-

Figure 1

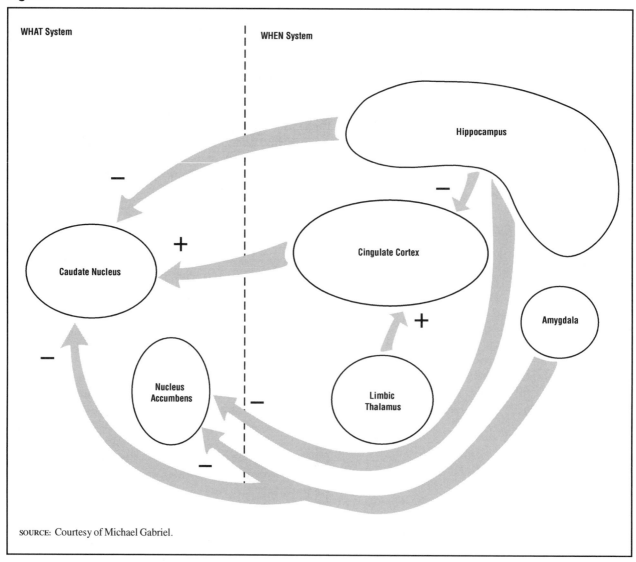

SOURCE: Courtesy of Michael Gabriel.

Schematic diagram of the information flows among brain structures involved in avoidance learning. The plus and minus signs represent, respectively, transmissions relevant to active and inhibitory avoidance behavior.

ence repeated sessions with shock and nonwarning tones, that is, tones that do not predict the occurrence of shock; and 2. EM occurs at different rates in different nuclei of the limbic thalamus. (General arousal or excitement would be expected to increase neuronal activity simultaneously in many brain areas.) Although they are combined in the limbic thalamus, EM and SA have different brain origins.

Origins of EM

Experimental lesions in the large fiber tract (the *mammillothalamic tract*) that runs from the hypothalamus to the AN block the development of EM in the AN; these lesions diminish performance efficiency of the avoidance response. Binding of the high-affinity ligand oxotremorine to muscarinic acetylcholine re-

ceptors increases in the AN during learning (Vogt et al., 1991), and scopolamine hydrobromide, which blocks these receptors, abolishes both the EM in the AN, as well as performance of the avoidance behavior. These results suggest that EM is due to stimulation by acetylcholine of the increased numbers of receptors in the AN. Acetylcholine is released by the terminals of brain stem tegmental neurons that project to the AN. Cholinergic stimulation may increase the excitation of AN neurons by enhancing the release of the mammillothalamic tract neurotransmitter or by increasing the excitability of AN neurons in response to that neurotransmitter. To summarize, EM originates in the limbic thalamus and has the function of amplifying the selective discharges as they are relayed to the cingulate cortex.

Selective Neuronal Activity in Two Functional Circuits

Immediately after the onset of training, SA in the anterior cingulate cortex develops very rapidly, whereas neurons of the posterior cingulate cortex and in the AN develop selective activity gradually. Separate lesions in these areas induced before training impair respectively, performance in the early and late stages of learning. These two circuits represent respectively the operations of an immediate or primary working memory circuit and a secondary or intermediate-term memory circuit. Development of SA in the secondary circuit is a result of short-term consolidation processes. SA also develops very rapidly in the parts of the ascending sensory (auditory) pathway for hearing, including the *medial geniculate nucleus* (MGN). Because MGN neurons project to the amygdala, it was believed that SA in the MGN engenders the SA in the amygdala. However, SA in the MGN was blocked during training of subjects with temporary amygdalar lesions, indicating that the amygdala engenders SA in the MGN.

Origins of Selective Activity

Additional studies have shown that the amygdala modulates the MGN by way of an amygdalar pathway to the auditory cortex and from there to the MGN. Auditory cortical lesions abolish the rapid SA in all areas, including the MGN, basolateral nucleus of the amygdala and the anterior cingulate cortex (Duvel et al., 2001). Subjects with these lesions make fewer learned responses than controls during the early sessions of discriminative avoidance learning, and they fail to discriminate between the CS+ and the CD- during the early sessions. However, the slower SA of the secondary circuit remains intact and these subjects eventually learn to normative levels of performance. Large permanent lesions of the amygdala block the development of gradual SA in the secondary memory circuit and neurons of the lateral anterior nucleus of the amygdala exhibited slow SA. These results indicate that 1. the amygdala initiates SA in the MGN and possibly in the auditory cortex; 2. the auditory cortex is the origin of SA in the remaining areas of the primary memory circuit; and 3. the lateral anterior area of the amygdala may initiate gradual SA of the secondary memory circuit.

Inhibitory Avoidance Learning

Experimental procedures used to study inhibitory avoidance learning include the delivery of shock after performance of an unlearned response by rats (moving from a lighted area to an innately preferred dark area), the delivery of shock after performance of a previously learned response (running in a maze alley for food or water reinforcement), or assessing choice behavior such as the relative amount of time spent in neutral areas compared with time spent in areas previously established as dangerous. The timing of avoidance responses is not greatly critical for learning of these tasks because subjects are not required, as they are in active avoidance tasks, to produce discrete behaviors at particular moments. Instead, behavior must be suppressed in response to configurations of static, continuously present environmental stimuli.

The hippocampus, a limbic area of the cerebral cortex, is important to complex memory functions. Hippocampal lesions are detrimental to inhibitory avoidance learning. Hippocampal involvement may reflect the fact that the warning stimuli in inhibitory avoidance tasks are often experimental environments or places, rather than discrete stimuli such as tones. Successful performance in such tasks depends on the cognitive mapping functions of the hippocampus, including remembering whether particular environments are dangerous or safe (see Nadel, O'Keefe, and Black, 1975).

As in active avoidance learning, outputs of the amygdala are be involved in initiating learning-related plasticity in other areas in response to aversive stimulation received during inhibitory avoidance training. Research of James L. McGaugh (2000) indicates that amygdalar outputs induce the hippocampus to store or consolidate memory underlying inhibitory avoidance learning. Hippocampal cognitive mapping operations could give rise to the suppression of movement toward dangerous environments as a result of information flow over a massive WHEN system pathway from the hippocampal formation to the nucleus accumbens. The latter area is a WHAT system component that has been implicated in the suppression of locomotion.

Finally, substantial evidence indicates that learning of immobility in response to discrete cues using Pavlovian training procedures appears to be mediated by plasticity that develops within the amygdala. In this instance, the amygdala is viewed as a site of memory storage rather than a plasticity-initiating agent.

See also: ACTIVE AND PASSIVE AVOIDANCE LEARNING: BEHAVIORAL PHENOMENA; GUIDE TO THE ANATOMY OF THE BRAIN: AMYGDALA; NEURAL SUBSTRATES OF CLASSICAL CONDITIONING: FEAR CONDITIONING, FREEZING; PASSIVE (INHIBITORY) AVOIDANCE, FEAR LEARNING

Bibliography

Duvel, A. D., Smith, D. M., Talk, A., and Gabriel, M. (2001). Medial geniculate, amygdalar and cingulate cortical training-induced neuronal activity during discriminative avoidance learning in rabbits with auditory cortical lesions. *Journal of Neuroscience 27*, 3,271–3,281.

Gabriel, M. (1993). Discriminative avoidance learning: A model system. In M. Gabriel and B. Vogt, eds. *Neurobiology of cingulate cortex and limbic thalamus*, 478–523. Toronto: Birkhauser.

McGaugh, J. L. (2000). Memory—a century of consolidation. *Science 287*, 248–251.

Nadel, L., O'Keefe, J., and Black, A. (1975). Slam on the brakes: A critique of Altman. Brunner and Bayer's response-inhibition model of hippocampal function. *Behavioral Biology 14*, 151–162.

Vogt, B. A., Gabriel, M., Vogt, L. J., Poremba, A., Jensen, E. L., Kubota, Y., and Kang, E. (1991). Muscarinic receptor binding increases in anterior thalamus and cingulate cortex during discriminative avoidance learning. *Journal of Neuroscience 11*, 1,508–1,514.

Michael Gabriel

NEURAL SUBSTRATES OF CLASSICAL CONDITIONING

[*Classical or Pavlovian conditioning, first described by Ivan Pavlov (see* PAVLOV, IVAN *), is a procedure where a neutral stimulus such as a light or sound (conditioned stimulus, CS) is presented together with an unconditioned stimulus (US) that elicits a behavioral response (UR). As a result of pairing, the CS comes to elicit a conditioned response (CR). In Pavlov's original experiments with dogs, a bell (CS) was paired with meat powder in the mouth (US). The salivation UR elicited by the meat powder came to be elicited by the bell, the CR. The CS must precede the US for learning to occur; in the* delay *procedure the CS and US co-terminate; in the* trace *procedure the CS offset occurs prior to the onset of the US. Although contiguity of the CS and US is necessary for learning, the contingency between them, the probability that the CS will predict the occurrence of the US, is critically important.*

The second entry in this section, on conditioning of **Discrete Behavioral Responses,** *uses eyeblink conditioning as the prototypic example (tone CS, corneal airpuff US). The cerebellum and its associated brainstem circuitry is the necessary and sufficient circuit for this form of learning; however, the hippocampus also becomes important in the trace procedure. Elsewhere in this book,* NEURAL SUBSTRATES OF EMOTIONAL MEMORY *provides an overview of fear learning, where a neutral CS is paired with an aversive, emotionally arousing US such as shock. The amygdala plays a key role in all aspects of fear conditioning. A major component of fear learning is classical conditioning of* **Cardiovascular Responses.** *Here, the amygdala, prefrontal cortex, and cerebellum are all involved. The most widely used behavioral index of* **Fear Conditioning** *is freezing. Here it appears that critical components of the fear memory are stored in a region of the amygdala. However the hippocampus also becomes critically important in learned freezing to context. Another productive method to study learned fear is* **Fear-Potentiated Startle.** *Here a light CS is paired with shock to establish conditioned fear to the light. This CS is then given together with a loud acoustic stimulus that elicits behavioral startle response. Presentation of the light CS enhances the startle response to the acoustic stimulus. Much of the circuitry for the startle response and fear potentiation of the response has been identified. As in freezing, the amygdala plays a critical role.*

The article on NEURAL SUBSTRATES OF AVOIDANCE LEARNING *is included in this book in part for contrast. It describes an example of instrumental learning, where the animal can influence the outcome, unlike classical conditioning. The focus in this entry is on active avoidance, where the animal can make a response (e.g., locomotion) when a CS occurs to avoid a shock US. But until the animal first moves to avoid the shock, the training is Pavlovian. Critical neural structures for this form of learning include the amygdala, certain nuclei of the thalamus, and the cingulated area of the cerebral cortex.*]

CARDIOVASCULAR RESPONSES

Learning is an enduring change in behavior arising from experience-induced structural changes in the brain. For example, during Pavlovian (classical) aversive learning, an organism learns that an auditory or visual stimulus (the conditioned stimulus, CS) that repeatedly precedes an electric shock (the unconditioned stimulus, UCS) predicts the occurrence of the shock. This learned association is reflected in a variety of adaptive cardiovascular responses to the CS and is a specific consequence of the associative relationship between the CS and UCS. The search for the structural changes of Pavlovian learning is governed by the assumption that an association between the CS and the UCS hinges on a convergence of information about both at a common brain structure or structures. It is this convergence that results in structural changes.

Researchers have used learned cardiovascular responses, particularly changes in heart rate (HR) in response to the CS during Pavlovian learning, as models for assessing learning and for identifying the brain regions in which learning-related structural changes occur. HR responses are especially useful because researchers have identified the location of the motor neurons that produce these responses and can thus identify the central brain structures that activate these neurons. This, then, sets the stage for determining the specific location(s) and nature of the structural changes.

The conditioned cardiovascular changes that occur during Pavlovian conditioning represent only one of a whole complex of nonspecific visceral responses that occur during classical conditioning. Acquisition of these learned autonomic adjustments occurs rapidly, often within just two to three CS/UCS presentations (Powell, McLaughlin, and Chachick, 2000). These changes may also accompany later-occurring specific learned somatomotor responses, such as the conditioned eye blink or the leg-flexion response. Learned autonomic changes are nonspecific responses because they occur regardless of the nature of the conditioning contingencies. A CS that signals an electric shock UCS delivered to either the orbital region or the footpad of animals, for example, results in a host of nonspecific CRs to the signals that are quite similar regardless of the application of the UCS. However, the learned somatomotor response is specific to the UCS, consisting of an eyeblink CR in the former case and leg-flexion CR in the latter. Hence such responses are usually referred to as specific conditioned responses.

There are many parametric differences between the acquisition of specific and nonspecific responses during classical conditioning. A wealth of research indicates that the the brain mechanisms responsible for the early-occuring heart rate and other nonspecific changes are quite different from those that mediate the later acquisition of somatomotor changes. We will concentrate on the former mechanisms, with specific reference to cardiovascular changes, although there is substantial evidence suggesting that there are interactions between the structures that mediate specific and nonspecific conditioning (Powell, McLaughlin, and Chachick, 2000).

Pathways Transmitting CS Information

Investigations of HR conditioning generally have used auditory CSs that precede an electric-shock UCS. Research by Joe LeDoux, using an auditory CS in the rat during Pavlovian aversive learning, has demonstrated that destruction of the inferior colliculus (a structure relaying auditory information from the most peripheral structures of the auditory system) blocks the expression of several nonspecific learned responses (LeDoux, Sakaguchi, and Reis, 1984). The inferior colliculus projects to the medial geniculate nucleus, and lesions of its magnocellular component (MGm) produce deficits in the acquisition of the learned bradycardiac responses (i.e., HR decreases) in the rabbit (McCabe, McEchron, Green, and Schneiderman, 1993). Destruction of the auditory cortex, which receives projections from the MGm, does not interfere with the initial acquisition of this learned response (Teich et al., 1988), suggesting that the auditory cortex is not necessary for learning the relationship between the CS and UCS. Thus, structures other than auditory cortex that receive MGm projections may be essential components of the circuit.

Central Structures Involved in Learned Bradycardia

There is substantial evidence that three separate but partially overlapping higher-level CNS structures mediate Pavlovian heart-rate conditioning; these include several subnuclei of the amygdala, the medial prefrontal cortex, and the cerebellar vermis. Interactions between these three structures are illustrated in Figure 1.

The work of David Cohen and associates (1984) on the pigeon, Bruce Kapp and colleagues on the rabbit (Kapp et al., 1991), and LeDoux and colleagues on the rat (LeDoux, 2000) have demonstrated a thalamic-amygdaloid circuit that is necessary for the elaboration of conditioned cardiovascular changes. These studies have shown that one recipient of projections from the MGm is the lateral nucleus of the amygdala (LeDoux, Farb, and Ruggiero, 1990), which projects to the amygdala central nucleus (Ace) and the basolateral (BL) nucleus. Cells in the somatic thalamus also project to the lateral nuclei. Since the UCS is electric shock, such inputs to the amygdala may well reflect UCS information; there is some evidence that the critical association between the CS and UCS takes place in this nucleus and is relayed to the ACe and BL nucleus.

The contribution of the ACe to learned bradycardia in the rabbit has been extensively investigated (Kapp et al., 1991). The ACe projects directly to the region of cardiodecelerative motor neurons within the medulla, and electrical stimulation of the ACe elicits vagal bradycardia and excitation of these neurons. Hence, the ACe is located between the CS pathway and the motor neurons that produce the response. Interference with its normal functioning markedly attenuates the learned response. Further, the activity of its neurons in response to the CS changes over repeated CS-UCS pairing; and, for some neurons, the greater the neuron's excitatory response to the CS, the greater the conditioned bradycardic response. These combined observations suggest the ACe excites motor neurons leading to response expression.

While the ACe may be a critical structure within the circuit, as noted above, other structures, including the cerebellar vermis and medial prefrontal cortex, also appear to be important (Supple and Kapp, 1989; Powell, McLaughlin, and Chachick, 2000). Lesions of either produce a marked attenuation of the response, and the activity of neurons to the CS in each region

Figure 1

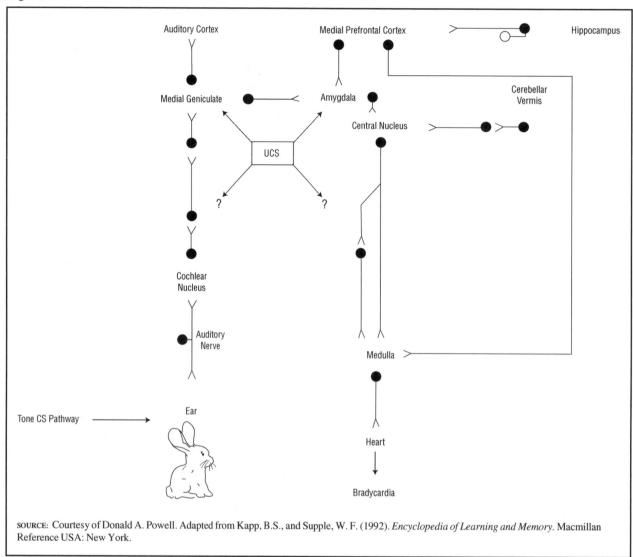

SOURCE: Courtesy of Donald A. Powell. Adapted from Kapp, B.S., and Supple, W. F. (1992). *Encyclopedia of Learning and Memory*. Macmillan Reference USA: New York.

A schematic diagram of the components of the putative neural circuit mediating learned bradycardia in the rabbit. The left side shows auditory structures that carry information about the tone CS. Components are believed to include primary auditory relay nuclei from the ear to the medial geniculate nucleus. CS information diverges from the primary auditory pathway at the level of the medial geniculate and is carried to the amygdala. From the amygdala, the central nucleus exerts both direct and indirect influences on motor neurons in the medulla that decrease heart rate when activated. The cerebellar vermis and medial prefrontal cortex, both important in learned bradycardia, may influence the central nucleus through indirect routes. The prefrontal cortex also projects directly to the medulla. Its control of learned HR adjustments may be influenced by neurons in the hippocampus. Evidence also suggest that information about the UCS may access the medial geniculate, the lateral nucleus of the amygdala, prefrontal cortex, cerebellar vermis, and perhaps other structures of the circuit. However, the pathways that transmit UCS information have not been extensively investigated. Nevertheless, there are multiple sites of CS and UCS convergence within the circuit, suggesting multiple potential sites of structural change.

changes as a function of repeated CS-UCS pairings. As with the ACe, in each region increased neuronal responses to the CS predicted greater CR response magnitude. Both regions are anatomically associated with the amygdala: the medial prefrontal cortex via a direct pathway to the BL and ACe, and the vermis via an indirect one. It has also been shown that effer-

ents from the prefrontal cortex project directly to the cardiac nuclei that control HR changes in the medulla (Buchanan et al., 1994). There is also considerable evidence that the hippocampus may be intimately involved in the stimulus processing associated with classical conditioning of HR responses. There is evidence that the ventral hippocampus, possibly via its efferents to the medial prefrontal cortex, plays a role in conditioning of nonspecific responses (Powell, McLaughlin, and Chachick, 2000). Information processed in the hippocampus may thus be responsible for the participation of the medial prefrontal cortex in HR conditioning.

Functional Considerations

Do these three different areas mediate nonspecific responses under different parametric and behavioral circumstances? LeDoux has pointed out that automatic subcortical processing of fearful stimuli by the amygdala offers the advantage of allowing the organism to a make a quick response to dangerous environmental stimuli (LeDoux, 2000). This subcortical circuit is thus important in the immediate response to environmental signs of danger. On the other hand, a host of studies in human subjects have revealed that an emotional component associated with prefrontal processing guides and affects complicated decision-making. The work of Damasio (1999), for example, indicates that the prefrontal cortex is important as an emotional component of memory selection, which guides response selection based upon its consequences. The role of the prefrontal cortex in conditioned HR responding may, therefore, be related to its integration with more complicated somatomotor response selection. Prefrontal projections bypass hypothalamic and brain-stem mechanisms, thus projecting directly to autonomic regulatory mechanisms in the medulla and spinal cord. Such processing by the prefrontal cortex may be related to integration of autonomic activity that is part of the emotional processing involved in normal adaptive behavior.

The role of the vermis in learned HR changes is unclear, although cerebellar control of HR changes in a number of situations is well established (Ghelarducci and Sebastiani, 1996). For example, pronounced bradycardia occurs during the diving reflex. Moreover, such learned HR changes may be related to the integration of autonomic activity with somatomotor learned responses, which are controlled by the cerebellum. These conclusions are, however, highly speculative at the present time.

Conclusion

So where is the occurrence, within the components of this circuit, of the convergence of CS and UCS information that is necessary for the structural changes responsible for HR learning? The research suggests that multiple components may represent sites of structural change that depend on continual cognitive and somatomotor behaviors. On the sensory side, neurons within the MGm are responsive to both the CS and UCS, and, like more central structures, neuronal activity changes as a function of repeated CS-UCS pairings (Supple and Kapp, 1989). Likewise, neurons in the amydala, cerebellar vermis, and medial prefrontal cortex are responsive to the UCS, although the pathways by which the UCS is transmitted to these structures are in need of further analysis. The evidence therefore suggests that structural changes may occur at multiple sites along this critical circuit.

See also: NEURAL SUBSTRATES OF EMOTIONAL MEMORY

Bibliography

Buchanan, S. L., Thompson, R. H., Maxwell, B. L., and Powell, D. A. (1994). Efferent connection of the medial prefrontal cortex in the rabbit. *Experimental Brain Research 100,* 469–483.

Cohen, D. H. (1984). Identification of vertebrate neurons modified during learning: An analysis of sensory pathways. In D. L. Alkon and J. Farley, eds., *Primary neural substrates of learning and behavioral change.* Cambridge, UK: Cambridge University Press.

Damasio, A. (1999). *The feeling of what happens: Body and emotion in the making of consciousness.* New York: Harvest/Harcourt.

Ghelarducci, B., and Sebastiani, L. (1996). Contribution of the cerebellar vermis to cardiovascular control. *Journal of the Autonomic Nervous System 56,* 149–156.

Kapp, B. S., Markgraf, C. G., Wilson, A., Pascoe, J. P., and Supple, W. F. (1991). Contributions of the amygdala and anatomically-related structures to the acquisition and expression of aversively conditioned responses. In L. Dachowski and C. F. Flaherty, eds., *Current topics in animal learning: Brain, emotion and cognition.* Hillsdale, NJ: Erlbaum.

LeDoux, J. E. (2000). Emotion circuits in the brain. *Annual Review of Neuroscience 23,* 155–184.

LeDoux, J. E., Farb, C., and Ruggiero, D. A. (1990). Topographic organization of neurons in the acoustic thalamus that project to the amygdala. *Journal of Neuroscience 10,* 43–54.

LeDoux, J. E., Sakaguchi, A., and Reis, D. J. (1984). Subcortical efferent projections of the medial geniculate nucleus mediate emotional responses conditioned to acoustic stimuli. *Journal of Neuroscience 4,* 683–698.

McCabe, P. M., McEchron, M. D., Green, E. J., and Schneiderman, N. (1993). Electrolytic and ibotenic acid lesions of the medial subnucleus of the medial geniculate prevent the acquisition of classically conditioned heart rate to a single acoustic stimulus in rabbits. *Brain Research 619,* 291–298.

Powell, D. A., McLaughlin, J., and Chachich, M. (2000). Classical conditioning of autonomic and somatomotor responses and their central nervous system substrates. In J. E. Steinmetz and D. S. Woodruff-Pak, eds., *Eyeblink classical conditioning,* Vol. 2: *Animal models.* Boston: Kluwer.

Supple, W. F., Jr., and Kapp, B. S. (1989). Response characteristics of neurons in the medial component of the medial geniculate nucleus during Pavlovian differential fear conditioning in rabbits. *Behavioral Neuroscience 103,* 1,276–1,286.

Teich, A. H., McCabe, P. M., Gentile, C. G., Jarrell, T. W., Winters, R. W., Liskowsky, D. R., and Schneiderman, N. (1988). Role of auditory cortex in the acquisition of differential heart rate conditioning. *Physiology and Behavior 44,* 405–412.

Bruce S. Kapp
William F. Supple
Revised by Donald A. Powell

DISCRETE BEHAVIORAL RESPONSES

Much of the research on how the brain codes and influences behavior has included studies of the neural bases of learning and memory. Physiological psychologists, neurophysiologists, neuroanatomists, and neuropsychologists have made major interdisciplinary contributions in this field, using a variety of experimental techniques.

One such productive research strategy in studying learning-related phenomena in the nervous system is the use of simple mammalian models. The model-systems approach assumes that the most promising path to an understanding of complex human learning and memory phenomena is the study of neural processes associated with simple learning and memory tasks in nonhumans. The governing assumption in such work is that the manner in which the brain codes learning and memory events is less complex in simple learning tasks than in more elaborate ones. This reduction in task complexity has made it possible to begin an analysis of the brain pathways and structures governing learning and memory processes.

Much useful data about brain substrates has emerged from classical conditioning of discrete behavioral responses. This approach involves presenting a conditioned stimulus (CS) just before a second, unconditioned stimulus (US). Before training, the CS typically elicits no overt response while the US reliably elicits a discrete, reflexive response called the unconditioned response (UR). After a number of CS-US pairings, however, the animal begins to execute the discrete response after presentation of the CS but before presentation of the US. This learned, anticipatory response is called the conditioned response (CR). Many investigations of the neural substrates of learning and memory have used this simple learning paradigm. The classical eyeblink-conditioning paradigm has significantly advanced the understanding of how the brain encodes learning processes. Two eyeblink-conditioning preparations are presented here: nictitating membrane/eyeblink conditioning in the rabbit and eyeblink conditioning in the freely moving rat.

Nictitating Membrane/Eyelid Conditioning in the Rabbit

In the early 1960s, Gormezano developed a classical conditioning preparation in rabbits that has proved valuable for the study of the neural bases of conditioning (see Gormezano, Kehoe, and Marshall, 1983 and Woodruff-Pak and Steinmetz, 2000). During simple classical delay conditioning, a tone or light CS is paired with a shock or air puff US. The CS initially causes no movement, while the US elicits movement of the nictitating membrane (the NM, a third eyelid found in some species) and closure of the outer eyelids. After 100 to 150 of these pairings, an NM or eyelid movement is elicited by the CS even in trials when the air puff or shock US is not presented. Because many of the parametric features of this behavioral paradigm have been well documented by Gormezano and associates, it has been adopted by a number of laboratories for use as a model system for the study of the neural substrates of learning (see Steinmetz, 2000 and Steinmetz et al., 2001, for reviews).

Data from a variety of animal preparations and from the human amnesia literature suggested that the hippocampus, a limbic system structure, was involved in coding learning and memory. Because of these observations, Thompson and associates attempted to assess hippocampal involvement in classical NM conditioning (e.g., Berger and Thompson, 1978). Recordings from the hippocampus revealed neurons that altered their firing patterns during paired but not unpaired presentations of the CS and US. Even before CRs were observed, neurons in the hippocampus began discharging in a pattern that preceded and "modeled" the amplitude and time course of the learned behavioral response (i.e., the unit activity looked as though it could be producing the behavioral response). But lesions of the hippocampus failed to abolish learning or retention of the simple motor response, even when the lesions included all of the neocortex as well as the hippocampus. These data indicated that the hippocampus was probably involved in coding the classically conditioned NM response but that it was not essential for producing CRs. More recent data suggest that in addition to possibly modulating the conditioning process during simple delay conditioning, an intact hippocampus may be necessary for more complex classical conditioning preparations like trace conditioning and discrimination-reversal conditioning. Furthermore, studies in humans suggest that awareness of the training contingencies may be an important determinant of the involvement of the hippocampus in conditioning (e.g., Manns, Clark, and Squire, 2000).

The interpositus nucleus of the cerebellum appears to be essential for classical conditioning (see Steinmetz, 2000 and Thompson, 1986, for reviews). The cerebellum is a structure that plays a major role in motor control. Recordings from the interpositus nucleus as well as portions of cerebellar cortex revealed populations of neurons that formed amplitude-time course models of the CR during paired CS-US presentations. Furthermore, electrolytic or chemical lesions of the interpositus nucleus (as small as one cubic millimeter) permanently abolished CRs in trained rabbits. Cerebellar lesions before training prevented the formation of CRs. The interpositus is known to output to the red nucleus, which in turn sends projections to brain-stem nuclei that control the musculature involved in generating NM movements and eyelid closure.

Brain stimulation, recording, and lesion methods have helped to delineate possible pathways involved in projecting the CS and US to the cerebellum. It appears that an acoustic CS may be projected to a number of primary brain-stem auditory nuclei that, in turn, relay parallel projections to lateral regions of the pontine nuclei. Cells in the lateral pontine nuclear regions may then project axons to the cerebellum. The air puff US appears to be projected from the cornea of the eye to the trigeminal nucleus in the brain stem to the inferior olivary complex (also in the brain stem). Cells in the inferior olive then appear to send axons to regions of the cerebellum. Data from temporary lesions (using the GABA agonist, muscimol, or brain cooling methods) and recording and stimulation studies have provided evidence that neuronal plasticity is established in cerebellar regions that receive convergent CS and US input and then relayed to brain-stem nuclei responsible for generating the motor response. Sites in the interpositus nucleus and discrete regions of the cerebellar cortex receive this convergent input; plasticity mechanisms at these sites are under investigation. Figure 1 shows a schematic diagram of neural circuitry that seems to play a role in classical eyelid conditioning.

The rabbit classical NM conditioning paradigm has produced a wealth of data concerning the neural substrates of a simple form of motor learning. The careful control over stimulus presentation and response elicitation afforded by this learning preparation has allowed the analysis of critical stimulus pathways and potential regions of stimulus convergence, thus advancing the study of the cellular bases of this form of learning.

Eyeblink Conditioning in the Freely Moving Rat

Rats have enjoyed a booming popularity as subjects in more recent classical eyeblink conditioning experiments. Several laboratories have begun using variations of a preparation described by Ronald Skelton (1988) to conduct classical eyeblink conditioning experiments in freely moving rats. This preparation uses tones or lights as CSs and periorbital stimulation as a US. Connections to the rat are made through a commutator that allows the rat free movement within the conditioning chamber.

Using rats instead of rabbits in eyeblink conditioning studies has some advantages: rats are less costly to purchase and maintain; more is known about the neuroanatomy of the rat; rats have a wider repertoire of other behaviors that can be studied at the same time as eyeblink conditioning; and the shorter lifespan of rats is better suited to developmental and aging studies.

Studies concerning the basic circuitry underlying eyeblink conditioning in the rat indicated that the basic neural substrates of this form of conditioning in rats are nearly identical to those of the rabbit. The cerebellum plays a critical role in encoding the learning and memory of the response. Other brain areas, like the hippocampus and neostriatum, are also involved in the conditioning process, and these regions seem to play a modulatory role in the learning and memory of this simple behavior.

The rat preparation has proved quite valuable for two lines of research. First, Stanton and colleagues have very successfully used the rat eyeblink conditioning preparation to study neural and behavioral correlates of development of this simple form of learning. For example, their elegant studies have shown that the development of conditioned responses parallels closely the development of the cerebellum and related brain circuits. Second, the rat eyeblink conditioning preparation has been used successfully to study the behavioral and neurological effects of early alcohol exposure, a model of the human condition known as fetal alcohol syndrome. In this model, neonatal rats are given binge levels of alcohol over a few days. Once the rats reach adulthood, researchers use eyeblink conditioning and neural recording and neuroanatomy methods to study the long-term effects of neonatal alcohol exposure on behavioral and neural function. Such studies indicate that neonatal alcohol exposure results in a permanent loss of neurons in the cerebellar cortex and the deep cerebellar nuclei and that that loss of these neurons, in turn, affects physiological and behavioral response during eyeblink conditioning, which requires the cerebellum.

Conclusion

The two different classical eyeblink conditioning discussed above have provided basic data on how the brain codes the learning of simple behavioral responses. Future work in this area will likely continue in two directions: further delineation of essential cellular processes that actually code the conditioning process (e.g., possible mechanisms in the cerebellum and brain stem that account for the conditioning);

Figure 1

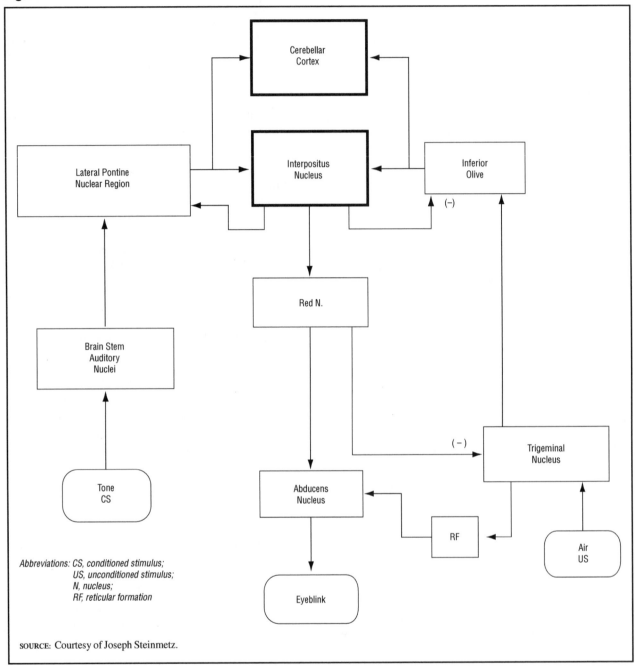

Abbreviations: CS, conditioned stimulus;
US, unconditioned stimulus;
N, nucleus;
RF, reticular formation

SOURCE: Courtesy of Joseph Steinmetz.

A schematic diagram depicting brain regions and circuitry proposed to be involved in classical eyeblink conditioning in rabbits and rats. The (-) depicts synapses where inhibition occurs. All other synapses are thought to be excitatory. Note the convergence of CS- and US-related information in the cerebellum.

and studies aimed at delineating the interactions between higher (e.g., cerebral cortex) and lower (e.g., brain stem and cerebellum) brain areas during classical conditioning. Genetic knockout and mutant preparations, reversible brain inactivation methods, basic molecular biology techniques, used in conjunction with eyeblink classical conditioning should advance our understanding of the neurobiology of learning and memory, especially by providing key data about how the brain codes simple learning tasks like classical conditioning of discrete responses.

See also: ACTIVE AND PASSIVE AVOIDANCE
LEARNING: BEHAVIORAL PHENOMENA;
CLASSICAL CONDITIONING: BEHAVIORAL
PHENOMENA; GUIDE TO THE ANATOMY OF THE
BRAIN: CEREBELLUM; NEURAL SUBSTRATES OF

CLASSICAL CONDITIONING: CARDIOVASCULAR RESPONSES; NEURAL SUBSTRATES OF CLASSICAL CONDITIONING: FEAR CONDITIONING, FREEZING; NEURAL SUBSTRATES OF CLASSICAL CONDITIONING: FEAR-POTENTIATED STARTLE

Bibliography

Berger, T. W., and Thompson, R. F. (1978). Neuronal plasticity in the limbic system during classical conditioning of the rabbit nictitating membrane response. I. The hippocampus. *Brain Research 145*, 323–346.

Gormezano, I., Kehoe, E. J., and Marshall, B. S. (1983). Twenty years of classical conditioning research with the rabbit. In J. M. Sprague and A. N. Epstein, eds., *Progress in physiological psychology*, Vol. 10, pp. 197–275. New York: Academic Press.

Green, J. T., Rogers, R. F., Goodlett, C. R. and Steinmetz, J. E. (2000). Impairment in eyeblink classical conditioning in adult rats exposed to ethanol as neonates. *Alcoholism: Clinical and Experimental Research 24*, 438–447.

Manns, J. R., Clark, R. E., and Squire, L. R. (2000). Parallel acquisition of awareness and trace eyeblink classical conditioning. *Learning and Memory 7*, 267–272.

Skelton, R. W. (1988). Bilateral cerebellar lesions disrupt conditioned eyelid responses in unrestrained rats. *Behavioral Neuroscience 102*, 586–590.

Stanton, M.A., and Freeman, Jr., J. H. (2000). Developmental studies of eyeblink conditioning in the rat. In D. S. Woodruff-Pak and J. E. Steinmetz, eds., *Eyeblink classical conditioning*, Vol. 2: *Animal models*. Boston: Kluwer.

Steinmetz, J. E. (2000). Brain substrates of classical eyeblink conditioning: A highly localized but also distributed system. *Behavioural Brain Research 110*, 13–24.

Steinmetz, J. E., Gluck, M. A., and Solomon, P. R., eds. (2001). *Model systems and the neurobiology of associative learning: A festschrift in honor of Richard F. Thompson*. Mahwah, NJ: Erlbaum.

Thompson, R. F. (1986). The neurobiology of learning and memory. *Science 233*, 941–947.

Woodruff-Pak, D. S., and Steinmetz, J. E., eds. (2000). *Eyeblink classical conditioning*, Vol. 2: *Animal models*. Boston: Kluwer.

Joseph E. Steinmetz

FEAR CONDITIONING, FREEZING

When threatened, some animals simply freeze. This defensive behavior has been studied in greatest detail in rats. Freezing behavior has been one index of fear in Pavlovian conditioning experiments investigating fear learning and memory. This article describes the adaptive value of freezing, its use in Pavlovian fear conditioning, and its neural substrates.

Freezing Behavior

Animals have developed numerous behaviors that help them avoid threats and danger. For example, when a deer mouse encounters a predator such as a snake, it may attempt to run away. Or it might try to fend off the predator by biting or fighting with it. When threatened by predators or dominant conspecifics, rats, mice, squirrels, and other prey species also freeze, often in a crouch, utterly devoid of movement except for breathing. Freezing is not passive, however; it is a coordinated, protective defense against danger.

Why should a rat freeze and not run away when threatened? The utility of freezing can be understood by observing the response of a cat to a ball suspended on a piece of string. The cat will likely ignore the ball if it is stationary. In contrast, if you wiggle the string, the cat becomes vigilant and vigorously pounces or paws the ball. This pouncing is predatory hunting behavior. The moving ball elicits this behavior for two reasons: the cat's visual system is very good at detecting movement, and movement triggers predatory attack. Freezing evolved to counter the predator's sensitivity to movement. Prey species freeze because many predators see stationary objects poorly, and they are less likely to detect immobile prey. Hence, in the vicinity of a predator, a still rat is a safer rat.

Animals typically spend more time freezing as the perceived danger increases. Therefore, freezing is a useful index of fear. For example, a rat will spend more time freezing in a chamber in which it received five aversive electric shocks than in a chamber in which it received one.

Freezing is best measured with time sampling. In this procedure, at regular intervals of a few seconds, a trained observer makes a judgment as to whether the animal is freezing or not at a given instant. The percentage of instantaneous samples scored as freezing provides a probability estimate of the behavior that is appropriate for statistical analysis. This sampling procedure is accurate, reliable, and reproducible.

Pavlovian Fear Conditioning

Fear is rapidly learned and measured in the laboratory with a procedure called Pavlovian fear conditioning. This method has become a standard means of exploring the behavioral processes and neural mechanisms of learning. In a typical Pavlovian fear-conditioning procedure, a rat is placed in a chamber where it is presented with a tone that is followed by a brief but mildly aversive foot shock. Later, during a test session, the rat is reexposed to either the chamber or the tone. During this reexposure the rat will display fear. With this preparation, the tone and the chamber serve as conditional stimuli (CS). They were originally neutral signals that did not predict danger, but after they were paired with an unconditional stimulus (US)—the foot shock—the animal responds fearfully to the CS. Such a response to the CS is called a conditional response (CR); freezing is an example of a CR. The shock-paired stimuli trigger CRs, which are measures of learning in Pavlovian experiments.

Brain Circuit of Fear Conditioning and Freezing

Scientists use several experimental techniques to characterize brain circuits. Lesion studies seek to damage a brain structure with surgical techniques. In this procedure a scientist may inject a neurotoxin into a specific target region to kill the cells there. After the animal recovers from surgery, it is tested to determine what effect the lesion has on its behavior. Infusion studies seek to temporarily alter function in a target brain structure through the injection of chemicals through surgically implanted injectors mounted to the animal's skull. Drugs can be infused before, during, or after a behavioral treatment. This technique has the advantage of being temporary and reversible. Electrophysiological studies seek to measure the electrical properties of targeted neurons associated with specific behaviors such as freezing.

Rat, humans, and other mammals share fundamentally similar brain circuits that underlie fear. Indeed, behavioral neuroscientists have described a set of interconnected brain regions that constitute a "fear circuit" that is similar in humans, rats, mice, rabbits, and monkeys. In all of these species a structure called the amygdala is a prominent component of the fear circuit

The amygdala is composed of a set of interconnected clusters of neurons called nuclei that lie in the interior portion of the temporal lobe. The Pavlovian fear-conditioning paradigm has shown that three nuclei within the amygdala make major contributions to fear behavior: the lateral (LA), basal (BA), and central nuclei (CEA). The LA and BA nuclei make up the frontotemporal amygdala (FTA). This part of the amygdala communicates most closely with the frontal and temporal lobes of the brain, and it is important for fear learning.

Moreover, critical components of the memory established during fear conditioning are located in the FTA. First, the FTA is connected to auditory, visual, olfactory, and brain regions that govern pain sensation. Thus, sensory information of the CS and pain information of the US converge in the FTA. Second, Pavlovian fear conditioning enhances the response of cells in the FTA that respond to tone CSs. Third, damage to the FTA produces a pronounced and often total loss of many Pavlovian fear responses such as freezing. Fourth, chemical inactivation of this structure disrupts fear learning. Thus, the FTA is critical for learning fear, and it may be the locus of the establishment of fear memory.

The CEA may be the output of the amygdala. It is closely tied with the striatum and specializes in modulating motor outflow. The FTA projects to the CEA, which in turn projects to a variety of structure that include the periaqueductal gray (PAG), the reticular formation, and the lateral hypothalamus. Damage to the CEA disrupts the expression of a wide range of defensive behaviors, including freezing.

The periaqueductal gray, or PAG, is highly interconnected with the CEA. This region coordinates defensive behaviors. Chemical or electrical stimulation of the dorsal-lateral PAG (dlPAG) triggers bursts of forward movements resembling flight. Damaging this region disrupts flightlike behavior. Consequently, the dlPAG seems to coordinate defensive reactions like flight. In contrast, chemical or electrical stimulation of the ventral PAG (vPAG) triggers freezing, and damage to this structure disrupts it. Interconnections between these areas may allow the animal to rapidly shift between freezing and flight.

The hippocampus is also plays a role in the expression of some types of fear behavior. When a rat is trained with a tone-shock pairing inside a chamber, the animals will later display fear of both the tone and chamber—the context. However, if the animal's dorsal hippocampus is damaged after training, it will freeze in response to the tone but not the context. Presumably the hippocampus plays a role in recognition of the chamber. An important aspect of context fear is that the effect of the hippocampal damage grades with time. That is, if the hippocampus is damaged one day after the training session, the amount of contextual fear disruption is large; if the damage occurs two months after the training session, the amount of contextual fear disruption is small. This property of contextual fear is similar to the retrograde amnesia seen in human patients who have hippocampal damage: these patients cannot recall events immediately before their brain damage, but they can recall events from years before.

Conclusion

Freezing, a defensive response common in rodents and other prey animals, has been employed as an index of fear in Pavlovian conditioning experiments that investigate fear learning and memory. The amygdala plays a role in fear responses in all mammalian species; contextual fear shares properties with human declarative memory. Thus, freezing behavior and Pavlovian fear conditioning provide a useful animal model of learning and memory.

See also: GUIDE TO THE ANATOMY OF THE BRAIN: AMYGDALA; GUIDE TO THE ANATOMY OF THE BRAIN: HIPPOCAMPUS AND PARAHIPPOCAMPAL REGION; NEURAL SUBSTRATES OF AVOIDANCE LEARNING; NEURAL SUBSTRATES OF CLASSICAL CONDITIONING: CARDIOVASCULAR RESPONSES;

NEURAL SUBSTRATES OF CLASSICAL
CONDITIONING: FEAR-POTENTIATED STARTLE;
NEURAL SUBSTRATES OF EMOTIONAL MEMORY

Bibliography

Edmunds, M. (1974). *Defence in animals: A survey of antipredator defences.* Burnt Mill, England: Longman.

Fanselow, M. S. (1994). Neural organization of the defensive behavior system responsible for fear. *Psychonomic Bulletin & Review 1*, 429–438.

—— (2000). Contextual fear, gestalt memories, and the hippocampus. *Behavioural Brain Research 110*, 73–81.

Fanselow, M. S., and LeDoux, J. E. (1999). Why we think plasticity underlying Pavlovian fear conditioning occurs in the basolateral amygdala. *Neuron 23*, 229–232.

Fendt, M., and Fanselow, M. S. (1999). The neuroanatomical and neurochemical basis of conditioned fear. *Neuroscience and Biobehavioral Reviews 23*, 743–760.

Squire, L. R., Clark, R. E., and Knowlton, B. J. (2001). Retrograde amnesia. *Hippocampus 11*, 50–55.

Swanson, L. W., and Petrovich, G. D. (1998). What is the amygdala? *Trends in Neurosciences 21*, 323–331.

Bill P. Godsil
Michael S. Fanselow

FEAR-POTENTIATED STARTLE

When a stimulus such as a light, which engenders little behavioral effect before pairing, is paired with an aversive stimulus such as a foot shock, the light (conditioned stimulus) can elicit seemingly fearful responses in animals: autonomic changes, freezing, and an increase in the amplitude of the startle reflex elicited by an auditory stimulus in the presence of the light. The last is called the *fear-potentiated startle effect* and can occur with an auditory, visual, tactile, or olfactory conditioned stimulus under conditions where startle is elicited by either a loud sound or an air puff.

Fear-potentiated startle is a valid measure of classical conditioning because it occurs only following paired rather than unpaired or "random" presentations of the conditioned stimulus. Potentiated startle shows considerable temporal specificity because its magnitude in testing is greatest at the interval after light onset that matches the light-shock interval in training. This paradigm offers a number of advantages as an alternative to most animal tests of fear or anxiety because it involves no operant and is reflected by an enhancement rather than a suppression of continuing behavior. Drugs like clonidine, morphine, diazepam, and buspirone, which differ in their mechanism of action yet all reduce fear or anxiety in humans, decrease potentiated startle in rats. Conversely, drugs like yohimbine, piperoxane, and B-carbolines, which induce anxiety in normal people and exaggerate it in anxious people, increase the magnitude of fear-potentiated startle in rats.

Neural Systems Involved in Fear-Potentiated Startle

A major advantage of the fear-potentiated startle paradigm is that fear is measured by a change in a simple reflex. Hence, with potentiated startle, fear is expressed through some neural pathway(s) activated by the conditioned stimulus that connects to the startle pathway. Figure 1 shows a schematic summary diagram of the neural pathways we believe are required for fear-potentiated startle, given a visual conditioned stimulus and foot shock as the unconditioned stimulus.

The Acoustic Startle Pathway

In the rat, the latency of acoustic startle is six milliseconds, recorded electromyographically in the foreleg, and eight milliseconds in the hind leg. This very short latency indicates that only a few synapses can be involved in mediating acoustic startle. Using a variety of techniques, we showed that acoustic startle was mediated by a pathway that includes auditory neurons embedded in the auditory nerve called cochlear root neurons, an area just dorsal to the superior olives in the nucleus reticularis pontis caudalis, and motoneurons in the spinal cord. Bilateral chemical lesions of these cell groups eliminate startle, whereas lesions in a variety of other auditory or motor areas do not. Startlelike responses can be elicited electrically from each of these nuclei, with progressively shorter latencies as the electrode is moved down the pathway.

Where Does Fear Activate the Startle Pathway?

By eliciting startlelike responses electrically from various points along the startle pathway in the presence and absence of a light previously paired with a shock, we concluded that fear ultimately alters transmission at the nucleus reticularis pontis caudalis. Injection of retrograde tracers into this part of the startle pathway indicated that it receives direct projections from the central nucleus of the amygdala, an area of the brain long implicated in fear, as well as from an area in the mesecenphalic reticular formation and deep layers of the superior colliculus.

Lesions of the Amygdala Block Fear-Potentiated Startle

Chemical lesions of either the basolateral or central nucleus of the amygdala following fear conditioning completely eliminate potentiated startle. In contrast, lesions of a variety of other brain areas, including the frontal cortex, insular cortex, visual cortex, hippocampus, septal nuclei, superior colliculus, red nucleus, and cerebellum, do not. Low-level electrical stimulation of the amygdala markedly increases acoustic startle amplitude at stimulus currents and durations that do not produce any other signs of behavioral activation.

Role of Different Amygdala Efferent Projections in Fear-Potentiated Startle

The pathway between the central nucleus of the amygdala and the part of the nucleus reticularis pontis caudalis that is critical for startle involves the caudal division of the ventral amygdalofugal pathway, which also sends collaterals to many brain-stem target areas involved in the somatic and autonomic symptoms of fear and anxiety. Lesions along this pathway completely block potentiated startle. In contrast, lesions of other major projections from the central nucleus of the amygdala do not. In addition to this direct pathway, an indirect pathway between the central nucleus of the amygdala and the deep superior colliculus/mesecephalic reticular formation is required for fear-potentiated startle because inactivation of this region completely blocked expression but not acquisition of fear-potentiated startle using a visual conditioned stimulus.

Convergence of Light and Shock Input at the Amygdala

Figure 1 shows that visual information reaches the amygdala by way of two parallel pathways. One involves direct retinal inputs to the lateral posterior nucleus of the thalamus, which projects directly to the basolateral amygdala and perirhinal cortex. The other involves retinal inputs to the dorsal lateral geniculate nucleus, which projects indirectly to the perirhinal cortex via the visual cortex. Lesions of both of these visual thalamic nuclei together, but not either one alone, blocked fear-potentiated startle when a visual, but not an olfactory, conditioned stimulus was used. When an auditory conditioned stimulus is used, this involves parallel inputs from the auditory thalamus to the perirhinal cortex either directly or indirectly via the auditory cortex. Pretraining or posttraining lesions of the entire auditory thalamus completely blocked fear-potentiated startle to an auditory but not to a visual conditioned stimulus. Posttraining lesions restricted to the main body of the medial geniculate, which projects to the perirhinal cortex via auditory cortex, also specifically blocked fear-potentiated startle to the auditory CS. Pain information reaches the amygdala via parallel pathways that include the caudal granular/dysgranular insular cortex and the posterior intralaminar nuclei of the thalamus. Pretraining lesions of both insular cortex

and the posterior intralaminar nuclei of the thalamus, but not lesions of either structure alone, blocked the acquisition of fear-potentiated startle. However, posttraining combined lesions of these areas together did not prevent expression of conditioned fear. These results suggest that parallel cortical and subcortical pathways are involved in relaying shock information during fear conditioning.

Role of the Anterior Perirhinal and Insular Cortex in Fear-Potentiated Startle

The perirhinal cortex, which receives either visual or auditory conditioned stimulus information, projects directly to the lateral and basolateral amygdala. Posttraining lesions of the anterior perirhinal cortex completely blocked the expression of fear-potentiated startle when a visual conditioned stimulus is used, provided the lesion destroyed both the dygranular and agranular portions of the perirhinal cortex. Posttraining lesions of the perirhinal area (including secondary auditory cortices) blocked fear-potentiated startle to both an auditory and visual conditioned stimulus. However, reliable potentiated startle was observed after retraining in animals sustaining main geniculate body lesions (which would destroy cortical connections between the thalamus and perirhinal cortex) or following pretraining lesions of the perirhinal area. These data suggest that cortical areas normally are used for the expression of fear conditioning but that subcortical areas can take over if the cortex is damaged. Finally, as mentioned before, shock information seems to require the insular cortex, which in turn projects directly to the lateral nucleus of the amygdala.

Glutamate Receptors in the Amygdala Are Critical for Fear-Potentiated Startle

Because conditioned and unconditioned stimulus information converge at the lateral and basolateral amygdala nuclei, this could be the site of plasticity for fear-potentiated startle. In fact, local infusion of NMDA antagonists into the amygdala blocked the acquisition but not the expression of fear-potentiated startle when a visual, auditory, or olfactory conditioned stimulus was used. This blockade of fear acquisition probably was not the result of preventing shock information from getting to the amygdala because this treatment also blocked the acquisition of second order fear-potentiated startle, which does not involve shock during second order training. Following conditioning, local infusion of non-NMDA antagonists block the expression of fear-potentiated startle.

Figure 1

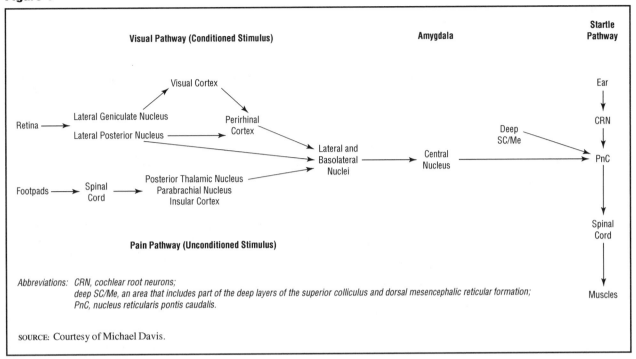

Schematic diagram of the neural pathways believed to be involved in the fear-potentiated startle effect using a visual conditioned stimulus and a footshock unconditioned stimulus.

Fear-Potentiated Startle in Humans

Fear-potentiated startle also can be measured in humans. In one test people are told that when a certain colored light comes on, they might get a shock on the wrist, whereas when a different-colored light comes on, they will not get a shock. Startle is elicited with bursts of noise through earphones, and the eye-blink component of startle is measured electromyographically from the obicularis oculi muscles. Startle amplitude was consistently higher in the presence of the light that signals shock. The size of this increase depended on when the subject expected the shock based on verbal instructions; the increase was also evident using conditioning procedures. Brain imaging studies show that the amygdala is activated during this verbally mediated fear-potentiated startle test and that patients with lesions of the amygdala failed to display fear-potentiated startle. People also show an increase in startle when they see scary pictures, such as a gun in the face, a dog about to bite, or mutilated bodies. The size of the increase in startle was directly related to the subjects' degree of negative valence and arousal.

Conclusion

The fear-potentiated startle paradigm has been useful for elucidating neural substrates of fear and anxiety. Conditioned fear appears to result when a formerly neutral stimulus comes to activate the amygdala after being paired with an aversive stimulus. Activation of the central nucleus of the amygdala increases startle via direct and indirect connections between the amygdala and a specific point in the acoustic startle pathway. More generally, the central nucleus of the amygdala and its efferent projections to the brain stem may constitute a central fear system that produces a constellation of fearlike behaviors in animals and people. Finally, the acquisition of conditioned fear may involve an NMDA-dependent process at the level of the amygdala.

See also: NEURAL SUBSTRATES OF CLASSICAL CONDITIONING: CARDIOVASCULAR RESPONSES; NEURAL SUBSTRATES OF CLASSICAL CONDITIONING: DISCRETE BEHAVIORAL RESPONSES; NEURAL SUBSTRATES OF CLASSICAL CONDITIONING: FEAR CONDITIONING, FREEZING; NEURAL SUBSTRATES OF EMOTIONAL MEMORY; PASSIVE (INHIBITORY) AVOIDANCE, FEAR LEARNING

Bibliography

Berg, W. K., and Davis, M. (1985). Associative learning modifies startle reflexes at the lateral lemniscus. *Behavioral Neuroscience* 99, 191–199.

Brown, J. S., Kalish, H. I., and Farber, I. E. (1951). Conditional fear as revealed by magnitude of startle response to an auditory stimulus. *Journal of Experimental Psychology* 41, 317–328.

Campeau, S., and Davis, M. (1995a). Involvement of subcortical and cortical afferents to the lateral nucleus of the amygdala in fear conditioning measured with fear-potentiated startle in rats trained concurrently with auditory and visual conditioned stimuli. *Journal of Neuroscience 15*, 2,312–2,327.

—— (1995b). Involvement of the central nucleus and basolateral complex of the amygdala in fear conditioning measured with fear–potentiated startle in rats trained concurrently with auditory and visual conditioned stimuli. *Journal of Neuroscience 15*, 2,301–2,311.

Davis, M. (2000). The role of the amygdala in conditioned and unconditioned fear and anxiety. In J. P. Aggleton, ed., *The amygdala*, Vol. 2. Oxford, UK: Oxford University Press.

Davis, M., and Astrachan, D. I. (1978). Conditioned fear and startle magnitude: Effects of different footshock or backshock intensities used in training. *Journal of Experimental Psychology: Animal Behavior Processes 4*, 95–103.

Davis, M., Falls, W. A., Campeau, S., and Kim, M. (1993). Fear-potentiated startle: A neural and pharmacological analysis. *Behavior Brain Research 58*, 175–198.

Davis, M., Gendelman, D. S., Tischler, M. D., and Gendelman, P. M. (1982). A primary acoustic startle circuit: Lesion and stimulation studies. *Journal of Neuroscience 6*, 791–805.

Davis, M., Schlesinger, L. S., and Sorenson, C. A. (1989). Temporal specificity of fear-conditioning: Effects of different conditioned stimulus-unconditioned stimulus intervals on the fear-potentiated startle effect. *Journal of Experimental Psychology: Animal Behavior Processes 15*, 295–310.

Falls, W. A., and Davis, M. (1994). Fear-potentiated startle using three conditioned stimulus modalities. *Animal Learning and Behavior 22*, 379–383.

Funayama, E. S., Grillon, C., Davis, M., and Phelps, E. A. (2001). A double dissociation in the affective modulation of startle in humans: Effects of unilateral temporal lobectomy. *Journal of Cognitive Neuroscience 13*, 721–729.

Gewirtz, J., and Davis, M. (1997). Second order fear conditioning prevented by blocking NMDA receptors in the amygdala. *Nature 388*, 471–474.

Grillon, C., Amelia, R., Merikangas, K., Woods, S. W., and Davis, M. (1993). Measuring the time course of anticipatory anxiety using the fear-potentiated startle reflex. *Psychophysiology 30*, 340–346.

Grillon, C., and Davis, M. (1997). Fear-potentiated startle conditioning in humans: Effects of explicit and contextual cue conditioning following paired versus unpaired training. *Psychophysiology 34*, 451–458.

Lang, P. J., Bradley, M. M., and Cuthbert, B. N. (1990). Emotion, attention, and the startle reflex. *Psychology Review 97*, 377–395.

Lee, Y., Lopez, D. E., Meloni, E. G., and Davis, M. (1996). A primary acoustic startle circuit: Obligatory role of cochlear root neurons and the nucleus reticularis pontis caudalis. *Journal of Neuroscience 16*, 3,775–3,789.

Meloni, E. G., and Davis, M. (1999). Muscimol in the deep layers of the superior colliculus/mesencephalic reticular formation blocks expression but not acquisition of fear–potentiated startle in rats. *Behavioral Neuroscience 113*, 1,152–1,160.

Paschall, G. Y., and Davis, M. (2002). Olfactory mediated fear potentiated startle. *Behavioral Neuroscience 116*, 4–12.

Phelps, E. A., O'Connor, K. J., Gatenby, J. C., Gore, J. C., Grillon, C., and Davis, M. (2001). Activation of the left amygdala to a cognitive representation of fear. *Natural Neuroscience 4*, 437–441.

Rosen, J. B., and Davis, M. (1988). Enhancement of acoustic startle by electrical stimulation of the amygdala. *Behavioral Neuroscience 102*, 195–202.

Rosen, J. B., Hitchcock, J. M., Miserendino, M. J. D., Falls, W. A., Campeau, S., and Davis, M. (1992). Lesions of the perirhinal cortex but not of the frontal, medial prefrontal, visual, or insular cortex block fear-potentiated startle using a visual conditioned stimulus. *Journal of Neuroscience 12*, 4,624–4,633.

Sananes, C. B., and Davis, M. (1992). N-Methyl-D-Aspartate lesions of the lateral and basolateral nuclei of the amygdala block fear-potentiated startle and shock sensitization of startle. *Behavioral Neuroscience 106*, 72–80.

Shi, C. J., and Davis, M. (1999). Pain pathways involved in fear conditioning measured with fear-potentiated startle: Lesion studies. *Journal of Neuroscience 19*, 420–430.

—— (2001). Visual pathways involved in fear conditioning measured with fear-potentiated startle: Behavior and anatomic studies. *Journal of Neuroscience 21*, 9,844–9,855.

Walker, D. L., and Davis, M. (2002). The role of glutamate receptors within the amygdala in fear learning, fear-potentiated startle, and extinction. *Pharmacology, Biochemistry, and Behavior 71*, 379–392.

Michael Davis

NEURAL SUBSTRATES OF EMOTIONAL MEMORY

Emotions are an integral part of our psychological life. For years, neuroscientists have largely ignored emotion, in part because it was believed that emotions were difficult to objectively define and measure, and therefore were outside the realm of legitimate scientific investigation. In recent years, however, great strides have been made in our understanding the brain pathways and structures underlying one especially important emotion: fear. In particular, much has been learned about how the brain learns to fear an object or situation, how learned fears can guide the acquisition of behaviors that are instrumental in avoiding danger, and how fear can augment the strength of memory formation of significant life events.

Classical Fear Conditioning

The fear learning system of the brain has been most extensively studied in the laboratory rat using a simple, robust form of associative learning known as classical or Pavlovian fear conditioning (LeDoux, 2000; 2002). In this behavioral paradigm, an animal learns to respond defensively to an initially neutral stimulus (the *conditioned stimulus*; CS) after it has been associated or paired with a noxious stimulus (the *unconditioned stimulus*; US). In rats, presentation of the CS after conditioning elicits defensive behavior (freezing) and supporting autonomic and endocrine adjustments. This is an implicit form of memory, which means that the brain system involved functions independently of conscious mediation (LeDoux, 2000, 2002). Nevertheless, conscious (or explicit) memories of the emotional experience can and often are formed in parallel.

In auditory fear conditioning, the most thoroughly studied form of implicit fear learning, a tone (CS) is paired with brief electrical shock to the feet (US). This form of fear conditioning involves transmission of auditory and somatic sensory information to the lateral nucleus of the amygdala (LA), an area that is critical for fear conditioning. During fear conditioning, individual neurons in the LA are well suited to integrate information about tone and foot shock. Cells in the LA, for example, receive direct projections from areas of the auditory thalamus and cortex. Inputs from each of these auditory areas converge onto single neurons in the LA, and these same cells are also responsive to the foot shock US. Further, auditory fear conditioning is disrupted either by permanent lesions or reversible functional inactivation targeted to the LA and adjacent areas (LeDoux, 2000; 2002; Maren, 2001).

The LA is not only the principle site of sensory input in the amygdala; it also appears to be an essential locus of plasticity during fear conditioning. For example, individual cells in the LA alter their response properties when CS and US are paired during fear conditioning; specifically, LA neurons that are initially weakly responsive to auditory input respond vigorously to the same input after fear conditioning (Quirk, Armony, Repa, Li, and LeDoux, 1997; Repa et al., 2001). Thus, a change occurs in the function of LA cells as the result of training, a finding that has contributed to the view that neural plasticity in the LA encodes key aspects of fear learning and memory storage (Blair et al., 2001; Fanselow and LeDoux, 1999; Maren, 1999; Quirk et al., 1997).

What mechanism may mediate the change that occurs in the LA as a result of conditioning? One of the leading candidates is *long-term potentiation* (LTP), an activity-dependent form of plasticity initially discovered in the hippocampus (Bliss and Lomø, 1973). LTP is an attractive candidate for a cellular mechanism of learning and memory during fear conditioning for several reasons. For one, LTP has been observed in each of the major sensory input pathways to the LA, including the thalamic and cortical auditory pathways (Maren, 1999, 2001). Second, fear conditioning itself has been shown to lead to electrophysiological changes in the LA similar to those observed following artificial LTP induction, and these changes persist over days (Maren, 1999). Third, associative LTP in the LA has been shown to be sensitive to the same contingencies as fear conditioning (Bauer, LeDoux, and Nader, 2001). That is, LTP in the LA appears to depend on the contingency between pre- and postsynaptic activity rather than simply on temporal contiguity, a hallmark of associative learning. Finally, amygdala LTP and fear conditioning have been shown to be subserved by similar biochemical or molecular mechanisms (Schafe, Nader, Blair, and LeDoux, 2001).

The LA is also critically involved in the expression of conditioned fear by way of its projections to the nearby central nucleus of the amygdala ([CE]; Amorapanth, LeDoux, and Nader, 2000; Nader, Majidishad, Amorapanth, and LeDoux, 2001; Pitkänen, Savander, and LeDoux, 1997). The CE is known to project to areas of the forebrain, hypothalamus, and brain stem that control behavioral, endocrine, and autonomic conditioned responses (CRs) associated with fear learning. Projections from the CE to the midbrain periacqueductal gray, for example, have been shown to be particularly important for mediating behavioral and endocrine responses such as freezing and hypoalgesia (De Oca, DeCola, Maren, and Fanselow, 1998; Helmstetter and Tershner, 1994), whereas projections to the lateral hypothalamus have been implicated in the control of conditioned cardiovascular responses (Iwata, LeDoux, and Reis, 1986). Importantly, while lesions of these individual areas can selectively impair expression of individual CRs, damage to the CE interferes with the expression of all fear CRs (LeDoux, 2000, 2002). Thus, the CE is typically thought of as the principal output nucleus of the fear system that acts to orchestrate the collection of hardwired, and typically species-specific, responses that underlie defensive behavior.

Instrumental Fear Learning

In addition to its role in Pavlovian fear conditioning, the amygdala contributes to other fear-related aspects of behavior. For example, Pavlovian fear conditioning is useful for learning to detect a dangerous object or situation, but the animal must also be able to use this information to guide ongoing behavior that is instrumental in avoiding that danger. In some situations, the animal must learn to make a response (i.e., move away, press a bar, or turn a wheel) that will allow it to avoid presentation of a shock or danger signal, a form of learning known as *active avoidance*. In other situations, the animal must learn not to respond, also known as *passive avoidance*. Both of these are examples of instrumental conditioning, and the amygdala plays a vital role in each.

The role of different amygdala nuclei, including the LA, CE, and the basal nucleus, in learning tasks that involve both classical and instrumental fear learning components has recently been examined (Amorapanth, LeDoux, and Nader, 2000; Killcross, Robbins, and Everitt, 1997). In one such study, for example, the animal was first trained to associate a tone with foot shock (the Pavlovian component). Next, the animal learned to move from one side of a two-compartment box to the other to avoid presentation of the tone (the instrumental component). In summary, while lesions of the LA appear to impair both the classical and instrumental aspects of fear learning, lesions of the CE impair only the Pavlovian component (i.e., the tone-shock association). Conversely, lesions of the basal nucleus impair only the instrumental component (learning to move to the second compartment). Thus, different outputs of the LA appear to mediate Pavlovian and instrumental behaviors elicited by a fear-arousing stimulus (Amorapanth, LeDoux, and Nader, 2000; Nader and LeDoux, 1998). This is not to say, however, that the basal nucleus is a site of motor control or a locus of memory storage for instrumental learning. Rather, it likely guides fear-related behavior and reinforcement via its projections to nearby striatal regions that are known to be necessary for reinforcement learning (Everitt, Cador, and Robbins, 1989; Everitt et al., 1999; Robbins, Cador, Taylor, and Everitt, 1989).

In spite of the fact that fear conditioning itself is an implicit form of learning and memory, during most emotional experiences explicit or conscious memories are also formed (LeDoux, 2000; 2002). These occur through the operation of the medial temporal lobe memory system involving the hippocampus and related cortical areas (Eichenbaum, 2000; Milner, Squire, and Kandel, 1998). The role of the hippocampus in the explicit memory of an emotional experience is similar to its role in other kinds of experiences, with one important exception. During fearful emotional experiences, the amygdala activates neuromodulatory systems in the brain and hormonal systems in the brain and body. Chemicals released by these systems modulate the function of forebrain areas such as the hippocampus and serve to enhance the storage of the memory in these areas (McGaugh, 2000). The primary support for this model comes from studies of inhibitory avoidance learning, where the animal must learn not to enter a chamber in which it has previously received shock. In this paradigm, various pharmacological manipulations of the amygdala that affect neurotransmitter or neurohormonal systems modulate the strength of the memory. For example, immediate posttraining blockade of adrenergic or glucocorticoid receptors in the amygdala impairs memory retention of inhibitory avoidance, while facilitation of these systems in the amygdala enhances acquisition and memory storage (McGaugh, 2000; McGaugh et al., 1993).

Thus, a picture has begun to emerge of the role of the amygdala and its different subnuclei in emo-

tional memory processes. The amygdala, and particularly the LA, participates both in reflexive or reactive forms of fear learning, where the animal learns to fear one stimulus that has been associated with another. However, the amygdala also appears to participate in instrumental or active forms of fear learning, where the animal must learn to cope behaviorally in the presence of fearful stimuli. In addition, the amygdala modulates the formation of memories in other systems of the brain, such as systems involved in explicit or conscious memory.

See also: GUIDE TO THE ANATOMY OF THE BRAIN; LONG-TERM POTENTIATION: AMYGDALA; NEURAL SUBSTRATES OF CLASSICAL CONDITIONING; PASSIVE (INHIBITORY) AVOIDANCE, FEAR LEARNING

Bibliography

Amorapanth, P., LeDoux, J. E., and Nader, K. (2000). Different lateral amygdala outputs mediate reactions and actions elicited by a fear-arousing stimulus. *Nature Neuroscience 3* (1), 74–79.

Bauer, E. P., LeDoux, J. E., and Nader, K. (2001). Fear conditioning and LTP in the lateral amygdala are sensitive to the same stimulus contingencies. *Nature Neuroscience 4*, 687–688.

Blair, H. T., Schafe, G. E., Bauer, E. P., Rodrigues, S. M., and LeDoux, J. E. (2001). Synaptic plasticity in the lateral amygdala: A cellular hypothesis of fear conditioning. *Learning and Memory 8*, 229–242.

Bliss, T. V. P., and Lomø, T. (1973). Long-lasting potentiation of synaptic transmission in the dentate area of the anesthetized rabbit following stimulation of the perforant path. *Journal of Psychology 232*, 331–356.

De Oca, B. M., DeCola, J. P., Maren, S., and Fanselow, M. S. (1998). Distinct regions of the periaqueductal gray are involved in the acquisition and expression of defensive responses. *Journal of Neuroscience 18* (9), 3,426–3,432.

Eichenbaum, H. (2000). A cortical-hippocampal system for declarative memory. *Nature Reviews Neuroscience 1*, 41–50.

Everitt, B. J., Cador, M., and Robbins, T. W. (1989). Interactions between the amygdala and ventral striatum in stimulus-reward associations: Studies using a second-order schedule of sexual reinforcement. *Neuroscience 30*, 63-75.

Everitt, B. J., Parkinson, J. A., Olmstead, M. C., Arroyo, M., Robledo, P., and Robbins, T. W. (1999). Associative processes in addiction and reward: The role of amygdala-ventral striatal subsystems. *Annual of the New York Academy of Science 877*, 412–438.

Fanselow, M. S., and LeDoux, J. E. (1999). Why we think plasticity underlying Pavlovian fear conditioning occurs in the basolateral amygdala. *Neuron 23* (2), 229–232.

Helmstetter, F. J., and Tershner, S. A. (1994). Lesions of the periaqueductal gray and rostral ventromedial medulla disrupt antinociceptive but not cardiovascular aversive conditional responses. *Journal of Neuroscience 14*, 7,099–7,108.

Iwata, J., LeDoux, J. E., and Reis, D. J., (1986). Destruction of intrinsic neurons in the lateral hypothalamus disrupts the classical conditioning of autonomic but not behavioral emotional responses in the rat. *Brain Research 368* (1), 161–166.

Killcross, S., Robbins, T. W., and Everitt, B. J. (1997). Different types of fear-conditioned behavior mediated by separate nuclei within amygdala. *Nature 388* (6,640), 377–380.

LeDoux, J. E. (2000). Emotion circuits in the brain. *Annual Review of Neuroscience 23*, 155–184.

—— (2002). *Synaptic self.* New York: Viking.

Maren, S. (1999). Long-term potentiation in the amygdala: A mechanism for emotional learning and memory. *Trends in Neuroscience 22* (12), 561–567.

—— (2000). Neurobiology of Pavlovian fear conditioning. *Annual Review of Neuroscience 24*, 897–931.

McGaugh, J. L. (2000). Memory—a century of consolidation. *Science 287* (5,451), 248–251.

McGaugh, J. L., Introini-Collison, I. B., Cahill, L. F., Castellano, C., Dalmaz, C., Parent, M. B., and Williams, C. L. (1993). Neuromodulatory systems and memory storage: Role of the amygdala. *Behavioural Brain Research 58*, 81–90.

Milner, B., Squire, L. R., and Kandel, E. R. (1998). Cognitive neuroscience and the study of memory. *Neuron 20*, 445–468.

Nader, K., Majidishad, P., Amorapanth, P., and LeDoux, J. E. (2001). Damage to the lateral and central, but not other, amygdaloid nuclei prevents the acquisition of auditory fear conditioning. *Learning and Memory 8*, 156–163.

Pitkänen, A., Savander, V., and LeDoux, J. E. (1997). Organization of intra-amygdaloid cicuitries in the rat: An emerging framework for understanding functions of the amygdala. *Trends in Neuroscience 10* (11), 517–523.

Quirk, G. J., Armony, J. L., Repa, J. C., Li, X.-F., and LeDoux, J. E. (1997). Emotional memory: A search for sites of plasticity. *Cold Spring Harbor Symposia on Biology 61*, 247–257.

Repa, J. C., Muller, J., Apergis, J., Desrochers, T. M., Zhou, Y., and LeDoux, J. E. (2001). Two different lateral amygdala cell populations contribute to the initiation and storage of memory. *Nature Neuroscience 4*, 724–731.

Robbins, T. W., Cador, M., Taylor, J. R., and Everitt, B. J. (1989). Limbic-striatal interactions in reward-related processes. *Neuroscience Biobehavioral Reviews 13*, 155–162.

Schafe, G. E., Nader, K., Blair, H. T., and LeDoux, J. E. (2001). Memory consolidation of Pavlovian fear conditioning: A cellular and molecular perspective. *Trends in Neuroscience 24*, 540–546.

Joseph E. LeDoux
Revised by Glenn E. Schafe and Joseph E. LeDoux

NEUROGENESIS

Contrary to a still widely held belief, the adult brain routinely generates new neurons. Strikingly, one of the two brain regions to which this adult neurogenesis is apparently restricted is the hippocampus. The hippocampus plays a key role in learning and memory, so the role that new neurons can contribute to its function is an inviting area for research. Most current theories on how the hippocampus processes information for storage consider the brain to be a network that is static at the level of neuronal numbers and plastic only at the level of neurites and synapses. However, mounting evidence indicates not only that the hippocampus produces new neurons but also that adult neurogenesis is tightly linked to hippocampal function. New neurons might contribute not only to hippocampal function, but they might also be indispensable to it.

What Is Adult Neurogenesis?

Neurogenesis is the development of neurons from neural stem or progenitor cells (see Figure 1). This developmental process begins with the division of the stem or progenitor cell and ends with a mature and functioning new neuron. Neurogenesis of the vast majority of neurons occurs during intrauterine development and ceases postnatally. In the hippocampus and the olfactory system, however, neurogenesis continues throughout life. Compared to the billions of neurons in the brain, the number of new neurons produced in the postnatal brain is very low and even decreases with age. In the hippocampus new neurons are generated only in the granule cell layer of the dentate gyrus, which increases in size with age. Under special circumstances single new neurons might be generated in brain regions outside the hippocampus or the olfactory system, most notably in the neocortex. It would be interesting to learn whether cortical neurogenesis under normal conditions would could contribute to learning and memory, because memory is stored in the neocortex. Elizabeth Gould from Princeton University has reported adult neurogenesis in the neocortex of primates, but Pasko Rakic and David Kornack from Yale University published a study in which they found no evidence of adult cortical neurogenesis. Although the function of neurogenesis in the olfactory system is not known, it appears that adult neurogenesis pertaining to learning processes occurs only in the hippocampal dentate gyrus.

Adult hippocampal neurogenesis in rats was first described by Josef Altman in 1965, but at that time the new neurons were considered to be a curiosity or an atavism. The methods then available did not allow a quantitative approach and a detailed phenotypic analysis. Consequently, adult hippocampal neurogenesis was "rediscovered" several times, most notably by Michael Kaplan in the late 1970s and in the early 1990s by Elizabeth Gould, then with Bruce McEwen at Rockefeller University in New York City. Georg Kuhn at the Salk Institute in La Jolla, California, was the first to use confocal microscopy in connection with immunofluorescent labeling techniques to investigate adult hippocampal neurogenesis. As a result, new cells could be unambiguously identified as neurons, and quantitative analyses became more feasible. In 1998 Peter Eriksson from Gothenborg, Sweden, used this technique to demonstrate that adult hippocampal neurogenesis occurs in humans.

In a parallel development, Fernando Nottebohm and his coworkers from Rockefeller University studied adult neurogenesis in birds. They were the first to add a strong functional context to this research. They found that song learning in adult canaries correlates

Figure 1

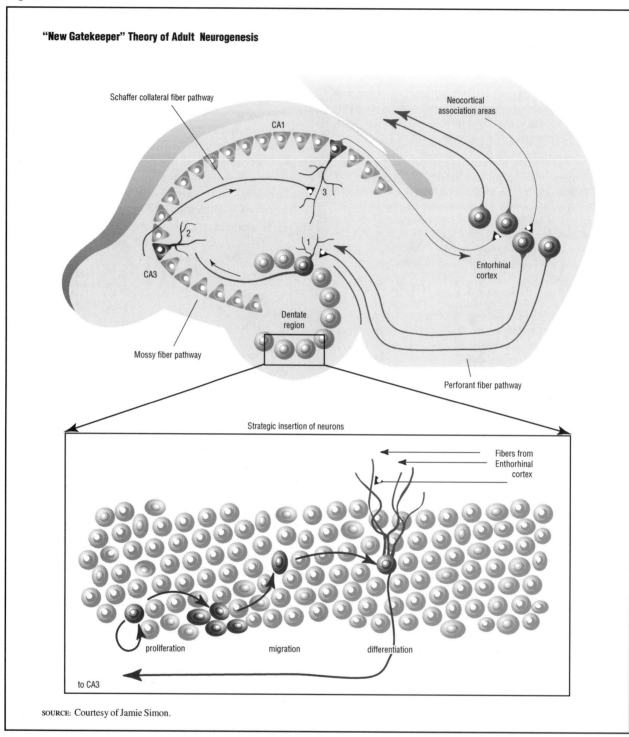

"New Gatekeeper" Theory of Adult Neurogenesis

SOURCE: Courtesy of Jamie Simon.

New neurons are strategically added to the narrowest stretch in the hippocampal three-synapse circuit. The hippocampus is the *gateway to memory* and its main function is to consolidate memory. Information is passed from cortical regions, including the entorhinal cortex, to the dentate gyrus (1). The axons of the granule cell neurons of the dentate gyrus project via the mossy fiber tract to area CA3 (2). The pyramidal neurons of CA3 connect to area CA1, from where the association cortex is reached. Long-term storage occurs in neocortical association areas. Information is processed in the hippocampus to allow long-term storage. It is not known in any detail how the hippocampus processes information; but new neurons might allow the hippocampus to modify the network at the point of greatest convergence and in the long run to adjust to altered functional needs. According to this theory, new neurons are not involved in the long-term storage of information. The bottom part of the figure illustrates the development of a proliferating neuronal stem or progenitor cell in the subgranular zone into a fully differentiated new granule cell.

strongly with adult neurogenesis in the brain center responsible for this behavior. They later showed that, in some food-storing bird species, neurogenesis is enhanced in those seasons in which the birds have to remember the location of their food caches.

How Is Adult Hippocampal Neurogenesis Regulated?

The development of a functional interpretation of adult hippocampal neurogenesis in mammals seemed more complex. Gould's early work emphasized a suppression of adult neurogenesis arising from chronic, severe stress and mediators of a stress reaction such as NMDA receptor activation and glucocorticoids; on this account adult hippocampal neurogenesis was due to stress-related damage to the hippocampus. Did this explanation imply that under normal conditions adult hippocampal neurogenesis contributes to hippocampal function? The late 1990s brought a wealth of studies showing the effects of numerous manipulations on adult hippocampal neurogenesis. While no conclusive theory of the regulation of adult hippocampal neurogenesis emerged from this research, it became apparent that adult neurogenesis reacts to a wide range of stimuli with great sensitivity but low specificity.

One solution to this puzzle lies in the definition of *neurogenesis*. The generation of a new neuron from a neuronal stem or progenitor cell entails a series of developmental steps. What is sometimes seems to be an effect on neurogenesis is often an impact on cell proliferation in which there is no certainty of a detectable change in the number of new mature neurons at a later time. Regulation of adult neurogenesis, however, occurs on several levels of neuronal development, including cell proliferation. Progenitor-cell proliferation might represent a rather nonspecific part in this regulation and can be influenced by many different factors.

Learning stimuli and experience, however, apparently do not influence progenitor-cell proliferation in the dentate gyrus but exert a survival-promoting effect on the progeny of the dividing cells. Animals that live in a so-called "enriched environment" (e.g., a cage providing much more sensory, physical, and social stimulation than the regular housing in laboratories) have a net increase in neurogenesis. This increase did not show a mandatory correlation with changes in cell proliferation, but was due to a survival-promoting effect on the progeny of the dividing cells. In old mice, no effect on the total number of surviving cells was detectable, but a phenotypic shift among these cells occurred toward more new neurons and at the expense of new glial cells.

Physical activity enhances adult neurogenesis. In addition to providing a hint of potential links between physical and mental activity and health, this finding suggests that active participation, in contrast to passive exposure to sensory stimuli, might affect adult neurogenesis. This finding dovetails with psychological learning theories that also emphasize active exploration and pursuit. Together these findings support the hypothesis that, in response to functional demand, new neurons can be recruited into hippocampal neuronal circuitry. The cellular machinery needed to achieve this goal goes far beyond a nonspecific mitogenic effect on the progenitor cells in the dentate gyrus.

Hippocampal Function and Adult Neurogenesis

The question of how the new neurons contribute to hippocampal function and thereby to learning and memory is linked to the more fundamental issue of the overall function of the hippocampus. Although the hippocampus is possibly the best-investigated structure in the brain, with a rich store of data available from researchers in anatomy, molecular biology, biochemistry, electrophysiology, and behavioral psychology, no "grand unifying theory" of hippocampal function has yet emerged. The hippocampus is classically characterized as "the gateway to memory" through which all information must pass to be remembered. Careful analysis of famous patient H.M. and animal research have indicated that bilateral hippocampal damage results in the inability to acquire new memory. Recall of older information, however, is spared. There is nonetheless a brief period of retrograde amnesia prior to the damage, indicating that a certain amount of time is needed for storage of information in cortical regions. During this time the hippocampus processes information for storage.

Not all kinds of information require hippocampal treatment. While declarative memory is considered hippocampus-dependent, procedural information, such as brushing your teeth (which is much more difficult to "declare" in words than to do), can be learned without hippocampal involvement. In the context of experimental research with animals, declarative memory is difficult to assess. Spatial navigation, however, is hippocampus-dependent and can be easily investigated in animals. Certain types of conditioning tasks are hippocampus-dependent, too, and therefore tests of spatial memory and conditioning tasks dominate animal experiments on hippocampal function.

In 2000 Tracey Shors, in collaboration with Elizabeth Gould, showed that the elimination of cell proliferation in the dentate gyrus by means of a cytostatic drug is followed by reduced performance on a hippocampus-dependent conditioning task, whereas performance on the hippocampus-independent form of the test was spared. While this result conforms well to theories linking adult hippocampal neurogenesis to hippocampal function, the study does not explain the function of the new neurons. This problem is similar to one faced in many knockout studies. Elimination of a particular gene often provides strong evidence that this gene is involved in a biological process, even that it is necessary for this process, but it rarely explains the specific nature of this involvement. One reason why the Shors study does not yet provide the full answer is that hippocampal function certainly goes beyond mediating eyeblink conditioning. In this sense the study even raises a new, puzzling question: Why would the hippocampus require new neurons for a task as simple and redundant as eyeblink conditioning?

Regarding spatial memory as an indicator of hippocampal function, our studies have shown that an increase in hippocampal neurogenesis correlates with an improvement on the Morris water maze task, a widely used test of hippocampal function in relation to spatial memory. However, this correlation never seemed to be linear. Levels of adult neurogenesis do not seem to be indicative of memory as storage capacity. Rather, adult hippocampal neurogenesis seems linked to the learning process itself; differences between animals living in an enriched environment emerged during the acquisition phase of the test. This makes sense if one considers the hippocampus as a gateway to memory, a processing unit that consolidates information for storage but not as the brain structure that provides long-term memory. But how can new neurons contribute function to this processing unit?

Joe Z. Tsien's group from Princeton University found that presenilin-1 knockout mice had reduced experience-induced neurogenesis without any signs of impaired memory formation. The group reasoned that new neurons might be necessary to "forget" old information, in the sense that the hippocampus would periodically need to clear the structure from "outdated hippocampal memory traces after cortical memory consolidation." This is a new twist on the idea that new neurons increase (or modify) the processor's working memory (RAM in a computer analogy). New neurons would allow the hippocampus to clear the structure for the processing of new information. Our own theory, explained below, is similar in emphasizing the modification of the processor network. In our view, however, cells need not be replaced to enable forgetting because information is not stored in single cells but is rather distributed over the synaptic weights in a network of neurons. Synaptic plasticity, which is essentially changing synaptic weights, is at the heart of the cellular mechanisms underlying memory. Moreover, synapses come and go. Altered connections cannot explain the recruitment of new neurons. But neurons are more than the sum of their connections. Neurons process information.

A Theory of New Neurons in Learning and Memory

If the hippocampus is the "gateway to memory," then adding new neurons in the hippocampus might amount to adding new gatekeepers to this portal (see Figure 1). The essentially three-synapse circuit within the hippocampal formation includes a bottleneck within the connection between the dentate gyrus and area CA3. The axons of granule cell neurons in the dentate gyrus form the mossy fiber tract, and adult neurogenesis adds new granule cells that rapidly seek connection to CA3.

Henriette van Praag and Alejandro Schinder at the Salk Institute in La Jolla studied the electrophysiological properties of newly generated granule cells and found that the new neurons are indeed functional. Information has to pass the narrows of the mossy fiber tract, and there appears to be a good reason for this forced concentration. A small network is fast and flexible. But the small network here has to cope with a huge range of input information. It has to adjust to novelty and complexity. If optimization here means having the smallest possible network that can handle the situation, and if single new neurons can be strategically introduced to the network, it becomes clearer how even a low rate of adult neurogenesis can be beneficial for the functional system. This view is also compatible with the fact that neurogenesis decreases in older age. If adult neurogenesis were to add units of memory to the hippocampus, old animals, who learn quite well, would have to rely on new neurons as much as younger animals. If the modification of the network were cumulative, however, older animals would require fewer new neurons because, given their greater experience, optimization of their network is already further advanced and requires fewer strategic additions.

The "new gatekeeper" theory might explain how the hippocampus could benefit from adult neurogenesis. It does not explain what the new neurons actually do. So far no conceptual links have been established between adult neurogenesis and existing theories about the many specialized hippocampal neurons, most notably place cells, with their response to a specific, recognized spatial pattern.

There is strong evidence that new neurons play a role in hippocampal function and thus in learning and memory. Their contribution most likely lies in a refinement of the processing unit, not in an extension of the storage capacity. But the precise manner in which this refinement takes place (and how a growing hippocampal network actually works) remains a question for current and future research.

See also: GUIDE TO THE ANATOMY OF THE BRAIN: HIPPOCAMPUS AND PARAHIPPOCAMPAL REGION

Bibliography

Altman, J., and Das, G. D. (1965). Autoradiographic and histologic evidence of postnatal neurogenesis in rats. *Journal of Comparative Neurology 124,* 319–335.

Feng, R., Rampon, C., Tang, Y. P., Shrom, D., Jin, J., Kyin, M., Sopher, B., Martin, G. M., Kim, S. H., Langdon, R. B., Sisodia, S. S., and Tsien, J. Z. (2001). Deficient neurogenesis in forebrain-specific presenilin-1 knockout mice is associated with reduced clearance of hippocampal memory traces. *Neuron 32,* 911–926.

Gould, E., Tanapat, P., Hastings, N. B. and Shors, T. J. (1999). Neurogenesis in adulthood: A possible role in learning. *Trends in Cognitive Science 3,* 186–192.

Greenough, W. T., Cohen, N. J., and Juraska, J. M. (1999). New neurons in old brains: Learning to survive? *Nature Neuroscience 2,* 203–205.

Kempermann, G., and Gage, F. H. (1999). New nerve cells for the adult brain. *Scientific American 280,* 48–53.

Kempermann, G., Kuhn, H. G., and Gage, F. H. (1997). More hippocampal neurons in adult mice living in an enriched environment. *Nature 386,* 493–495.

Rakic, P. (2002). Neurogenesis in adult primate neocortex: An evaluation of the evidence. *Nature Review Neuroscience 3,* 65–71.

Shors, T. J., Miesegaes, G., Beylin, A., Zhao, M., Rydel, T., and Gould, E. (2001). Neurogenesis in the adult is involved in the formation of trace memories. *Nature 410,* 372–376.

van Praag, H., Kempermann, G., and Gage, F. H. (2000). Neural consequences of environmental enrichment. *Nature Review Neuroscience 1,* 191–198.

van Praag, H., Schinder, A., Christie, B., Toni, N., Palmer, T. D., and Gage, F. H. (2002). Functional neurogenesis in the adult hippocampus. *Nature 415,* 1,030–1,034.

Gerd Kempermann
Fred H. Gage

NEUROIMAGING

Much of the cognitive neuroscience of memory has taken advantage of lesion-behavior studies, which assess behavioral deficits that ensue from damage to targeted parts of the brain. For example, lesions to the medial temporal lobe, buried deep in the brain, often produce profound anterograde amnesia.

In the mid-1980s functional neuroimaging began to play an increasingly important role in enhancing our understanding of the organization of memory in the human brain. Two of the main functional neuroimaging methods, positron emission tomography (PET) and functional magnetic resonance imaging (fMRI), measure signals related to blood flow or oxygenation. Both methods are based on the correlation of blood flow and neuronal activity: as is the case with muscles, blood flows more briskly in those parts of the brain that are the most active neuronally. PET can capture a single time-lapse image of forty seconds of blood flow. Methodological necessity dictated that PET studies of memory be done with blocked designs, which involve a comparison of the blood flow—and hence neuronal activity—resulting from several trials of a task performed in two separate blocks. fMRI can take images much more rapidly, usually producing a picture of the relative oxygenation level in blood vessels every two to three seconds. Although early fMRI studies still use blocked designs similar to those used in PET, the finer temporal capability of fMRI has also allowed event-related studies, in which trials of different types can be intermixed, much as in a standard cognitive psychological experiment. Researchers interested in the cognitive neuroscience of memory have developed ingenious applications of event-related designs for this technology. Although many imaging studies have confirmed the importance of medial temporal cortex to memory, the studies have also highlighted important contributions of other cortical areas, particularly the frontal cortex.

Encoding

A pair of papers, appearing in the same issue of the journal *Science,* highlighted the utility of event-related designs. In these studies participants were presented with either words (Wagner et al., 1998) or indoor/outdoor scenes (Brewer et al., 1998) and then were asked to make judgments about the items while undergoing imaging testing. These tasks were designed to be good incidental encoding tasks. Following the imaging sessions, the researchers administered recognition memory tasks for the studied items, noting which items the subjects remembered and which they forgot. They then sorted the images related to the encoding of the remembered or forgotten items. In both frontal and medial temporal regions, in the left hemisphere for the words and the right hemisphere for the scenes, activity was greater at encoding for the remembered than for the forgotten items. In other words, the level of activity at the time of encoding in these frontal and medial temporal regions predicted, on average, whether an item would be remembered or forgotten. Several further studies have replicated this "subsequent memory effect" in a number of encoding conditions.

Retrieval

Studies of memory retrieval have made several further associations between memory and cortical areas outside the medial temporal lobe. Starting with early PET studies of memory and continuing through many fMRI studies, right frontal activation was common when people retrieved information from episodic memory (Squire, 1992; Squire et al., 1992; Tulving et al., 1994). Considerable debate has focused on whether this right-frontal activation relates to the effortful state accompanying retrieval, to the successful retrieval of items or to postretrieval processes. Researchers are striving to develop new, more complex designs that aim to separate sustained, modelike processes from the transient processing of items (Donaldson, Petersen, Ollinger, and Buckner, 2001).

Other, left-lateralized cortical regions in parietal and frontal cortex have been more directly associated with retrieval success. Event-related studies, mainly of recognition memory tests, show greater activation in these regions for studied items than for previously unstudied, new words. Researchers have found these old-new effects in several kinds of experiments with different types of material, but always in similar regions (see Figure 1).

Finally, several studies (e.g., Nyberg, Habib, McIntosh, and Tulving, 2000) have suggested that recollection of, say, visual memories entails the reactivation of visual perceptual-processing mechanisms. In these studies, as people recall previously studied visual information, extra-primary visual regions are activated, even in the absence of a visual cue. It seems that some top-down process is reactivating perceptual mechanisms to retrieve specific perceptual content.

Other Studies

Other studies have focused on myriad other aspects of learning and memory, such as procedural learning (Karni et al., 1995), priming (Schacter and Buckner, 1998), and so on. Each of these lines of study seems to elucidate further neural mechanisms related to distinct memory processes. Such studies have yielded insights into cognitive architectures as well. For example, the earlier-noted right-prefrontal activation in many episodic retrieval tasks suggests the presence of a specific retrieval mode. Advancing neuroimaging technology promises to shed still more light on the neural mechanisms that underlie human memory and cognition.

See also: EPISODIC MEMORY; PROCEDURAL LEARNING

Bibliography

Brewer, J. B., Zhao, Z., Desmond, J. E., Glover, G. H., and Gabrieli, J. D. (1998). Making memories: Brain activity that predicts how well visual experience will be remembered. *Science 281,* 1,185–1,187.

Donaldson, D. I., Petersen, S. E., Ollinger, J. M., and Buckner, R. L. (2001). Dissociating state and item components of recognition memory using fMRI. *Neuroimage 13,* 129–142.

Karni, A., Meyer, G., Jezzard, P., Adams, M. M., Turner, R., and Ungerleider, L. G. (1995). Functional MRI evidence for adult motor cortex plasticity during motor skill learning. *Nature 377,* 155–158.

Nyberg, L., Habib, R., McIntosh, A. R., and Tulving, E. (2000). Reactivation of encoding-related brain activity during memory retrieval. *Proceedings of the National Academy of Sciences of the United States of America 97,* 11,120–11,124.

Schacter, D. L., and Buckner, R. L. (1998). Priming and the brain. *Neuron 20,* 185–195.

Squire, L. R. (1992). Memory and the hippocampus: A synthesis from findings with rats, monkeys, and humans. *Psychological Review 99,* 195–231.

Squire, L. R., Ojemann, J. G., Miezin, F. M., Petersen, S. E., Videen, T. O., and Raichle, M. E. (1992). Activation of the hippocampus in normal humans: A functional anatomical study of memory. *Proceedings of the National Academy of Sciences of the United States of America 89,* 1,837–1,841.

Tulving, E., Kapur, S., Markowitsch, H. J., Craik, F. I. M., and Habib, R. (1994). Neuroanatomical correlates of retrieval in episodic memory: Auditory sentence recognition. *Psychology 91,* 2,012–2,015.

Wagner, A. D., Schacter, D. L., Rotte, M., Koustaal, W., Maril, A., Dale, A. M., Rosen, B. R., and Buckner, R. L. (1998). Building memories: Remembering and forgetting of verbal experiences as predicted by brain activity. *Science 281,* 1,188–1,191.

Steven E. Petersen

NEURON

See: GUIDE TO THE ANATOMY OF THE BRAIN

NEUROTRANSMITTER SYSTEMS AND MEMORY

Ever since the discovery of the chemical nature of synaptic transmission, the role of neurotransmitters in the formation and retrieval of memories has been the subject of intense scientific investigation. As the number of both neurotransmitters and forms of memories has been steadily increasing over the years, the task of uncovering general principles describing the involvement of neurotransmitter systems in memory has become extremely difficult. Furthermore, the lack of understanding of the molecular and cellular mechanisms of learning and memory has limited the experimental approaches to two general strategies: (1) an interventional strategy using pharmacological tools or lesion/stimulation of specific neurotransmitter systems; and (2) a correlational strategy using "naturally" occurring conditions (neurological diseases, aging) affecting specific neurotransmitter systems, or genetically engineered mutant mice. Based

Figure 1

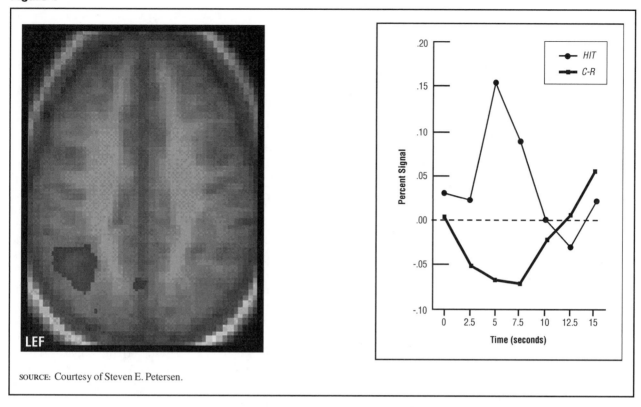

SOURCE: Courtesy of Steven E. Petersen.

The left panel shows the location of a parietal region in a horizontal slice from the brain. The right panel shows the difference in activation level between hits (correct identification of items that had been previously studied in a recognition test) and correct rejections (items correctly identified as being unstudied). This region shows a retrieval success effect in that the activity is much larger for hits and correct rejections.

on these studies, a number of neurotransmitters and neuronal pathways using these neurotransmitters have consistently demonstrated an important role in learning and memory (Chapoutier, 1989; Decker and McGaugh, 1991).

Glutamate

In early work using an avian retina preparation, proline was found to inhibit glutamate release; as proline had also been shown to inhibit learning and memory in chicks, researchers suggested that glutamate played a significant role in learning and memory. Building on these results, Cherkin and his colleagues (1976) published a series of articles demonstrating that various glutamate antagonists injected intracerebrally could retard memory consolidation in neonatal chicks, using a behavioral paradigm involving flavor aversion learning. In the 1990s, the role of glutamate in learning and memory received considerable support from two independent lines of research. First, the most studied cellular model of learning and memory is the long term potentiation (LTP) of synaptic transmission elicited by

brief bursts of high-frequency electrical stimulation of monosynaptic pathways using glutamate as a neurotransmitter (Malenka and Nicoll, 1999). The relationships among LTP, learning and memory, and glutamatergic systems have been further established by the use of specific antagonists of different subtypes of glutamate receptors (Morris et al., 1990), which clearly established that LTP induction is due to NMDA receptor activation while LTP maintenance involves modification of AMPA receptors. Manipulations affecting either type of receptors were found to have significant effect on learning and memory processes. For instance, positive modulators of AMPA receptors, the ampakines, have been shown to be cognitive enhancers (Ingvar et al., 1997), indicating that up-regulation of AMPA receptor-mediated synaptic responses facilitate LTP formation and AMPA LTP-mediated learning and memory processes. Likewise, overexpression of one subunit of NMDA receptors in mice, the NR2B subunit, resulted in increased LTP and learning and memory (Tsien, 2000). Second, various human conditions associated with major disturbances of memory exhibit marked degeneration of glutamatergic neurons. Thus, severe cases of amnesia are the result of loss of glutamatergic neurons in the hippocampal formation (Squire, 1986), and one of the hallmarks of Alzheimer's disease is a loss of glutamatergic neurons in entorhinal cortex and hippocampus (Hyman et al., 1987). All these studies point out to the critical role of glutamatergic pathways of the hippocampus in the formation of long-term memories.

GABA (γ-Aminobutyric Acid)

Historically, GABAergic neurons have been neglected as possible participants in memory processes. The discovery of the mode of action of benzodiazepines and the known effects of these compounds on memory renewed the interest in the possible role of GABA in memory. Thus benzodiazepines potentiate the effect of GABA at the GABA$_A$ receptors and generally produce an impairment of learning, whereas ligands acting at the benzodiazepine sites but producing an opposite effect (and therefore called reverse agonists) enhance learning in mice, chickens, and humans (Lister, 1985). Local administration of GABA agonists or antagonists in discrete brain regions have been effective in producing impairment or enhancement, respectively, in various learning tasks (McGaugh, 1989). In this case as well, the links between the GABAergic systems and LTP have been proposed to account for the role of GABA in learning and memory, as inhibition of GABA receptors generally facilitate LTP induction, while potentiation of GABA receptors prevent LTP induction.

Acetylcholine

Acetylcholine has long been involved in learning and memory (Deutsch, 1983). Pharmacological studies using both acetylcholinesterase inhibitors (producing increased levels of acetylcholine at synapses) and blockers of acetylcholine receptors have been performed in numerous learning tasks and animal species. The general conclusion is that impairment of cholinergic transmission produces cognitive impairment. This conclusion is also reinforced by studies in humans with pathological alterations in cholinergic function. Thus, Alzheimer's disease is associated with loss of cholinergic neurons in the nucleus basalis of Meynert (Coyle et al., 1983). In Parkinson's disease, memory impairment is correlated with a decrease in cholinergic function in the frontal cortex (Chapoutier, 1989). A possible unifying mechanism for a role of cholinergic neurons in memory processes has been ascribed to the participation of these neurons in the generation of rhythmical brain activity (θ and γ rhythms) directly involved in information storage and in LTP (Winson, 1990). In particular, acetylcholine-induced synchronization of neuronal firing in the theta range (5 to 7 hertz) produces optimal conditions for summation of excitatory depolarization, thereby facilitating activation of NMDA receptors, LTP induction, and ultimately memory formation.

Catecholamines, Serotonin, and Histamine

Although noradrenergic systems have often been implicated in learning and memory (Gold and Zornetser, 1983), studies using pharmacological blockade of norepinephrine receptors or destruction of noradrenergic neurons indicate that these neurons do not directly participate in the learning of a variety of tasks (Pontecorvo et al., 1988). However, the situation is probably more complicated, for noradrenergic, serotonergic, and histaminergic systems appear to participate in the modulation of some memory processes (D'Hooge and De Deyn, 2001). Depending on which subtype of receptors is activated under particular conditions, facilitation or inhibition or memory formation has been observed. In particular, it is now clear that spatial learning, which is often used to study mechanisms of learning and memory, depends upon the coordinated action of several brain regions and neurotransmitter systems. In addition, researchers have repeatedly argued that these modulatory systems are activated under numerous behavioral conditions (arousal and stress), which in turn affect information processing and storage in sensory and associational pathways.

Other Systems

Although not generally considered as neurotransmitters, a growing number of peptides have been found to be colocalized with traditional neurotransmitters and have been assigned the role of neuromodulators. Their role in synaptic function is still a matter of debate, but it is impossible not to mention the evidence implicating a number of neuropeptides in memory processes. In particular, ACTH and fragments of ACTH have repeatedly been shown to improve memory consolidation. Vasopressin has also been suggested as participating in memory formation, possibly through an interaction with noradrenergic systems (D'Hooge and De Deyn, 2001). Similarly, opioid peptides have been clearly implicated in memory processes, including the suggestion (Gallagher, 1985) that opioid peptide-containing neurons are part of a forgetting mechanism. Much attention has been devoted to the role of the steroid hormone estrogen in memory formation, as estrogen replacement therapy was found to alleviate cognitive deficits in postmenopausal women. The recent discovery that estrogen potentiates AMPA and NMDA receptor function and facilitates LTP induction provides a bridge between the cellular effects of estrogen and its behavioral effects. This finding also raises interesting questions related to the evolution of memory systems and of their relationships to reproductive and sexual behaviors.

Conclusion

As it becomes more and more widely accepted that learning and memory reflect the existence of a variety of synaptic plasticity mechanisms occurring at numerous stages of information processing and in different neuronal networks participating in information storage, it is not surprising that several neurotransmitter systems participate, directly or indirectly, in the processes of information storage and retrieval. The initial notion that one neurotransmitter was involved in one form of behavior has long been dismissed in favor of the idea that distributed and parallel neuronal networks participate in multiple sensory, motor, and cognitive operations. While the roles of glutamate and glutamatergic pathways as well as the functional significance of modifications of synaptic efficacy at glutamatergic synapses in this process are starting to be well established, leading to the development of the first "memory pill," the task of correlating the roles of other neurotransmitters and other neuronal pathways to specific forms of learning and memory still awaits the development of more specific pharmacological tools and behavioral tests. In particular, it is of crucial importance to define learning characteristics that are both species and time dependent as the demands on the learning and memory machinery are exquisitely sensitive to species requirements and time windows adapted to the particular species. It is clear, however, that this strategy will result in the development of more refined pharmacological treatments with potentials for alleviating more specific learning and memory disorders.

See also: COGNITIVE ENHANCERS; GLUTAMATE
RECEPTORS AND THEIR CHARACTERIZATION

Bibliography

Chapoutier, G. (1989). The search for a biochemistry of memory. *Archives of Gerontology and Geriatrics Supp. 1,* 7–19.

Cherkin, A., Eckardt, M. J., and Gerbrandt, L. D. (1976). Memory: Proline induces retrograde amnesia in chicks. *Science 193,* 242–244.

Coyle, J. T., Price, D. L., and DeLong, M. R. (1983). Alzheimer's disease: A disorder of cortical cholinergic innervation. *Science 219,* 1,184–1,190.

Decker, M. W., and McGaugh, J. L. (1991). The role of interactions between the cholinergic systems and other neuromodulatory systems in learning and memory. *Synapse 7,* 151–168.

Deutsch, J. A. (1983). The cholinergic synapse and the site of memory. In J. A. Deutsch, ed., *The physiological basis of memory.* New York: Academic Press.

D'Hooge, R., and De Deyn, P. P. (2001). Applications of the Morris water maze in the study of learning and memory. *Brain Research Reviews 36,* 60–90.

Gold, P. E., and Zornetser, S. F. (1983). The mnemon and its juices. *Behavioral and Neural Biology 38,* 151–189.

Hyman, B. T., Van, H. G. W., and Damasio, A. R. (1987). Alzheimer's disease: Glutamate depletion in the hippocampal perforant pathway zone. *Annals of Neurology 22* (1), 37–40.

Ingvar, M., et al. (1997). Enhancement by an ampakine of memory encoding in humans. *Experimental Neurology 146,* 553–559.

Lister, R. G. (1985). The amnesic action of benzodiazepines in man. *Neuroscience and Biobehavioral Review 9,* 87–94.

Malenka, R. C., and Nicoll, R. A. (1999). Long-term potentiation—a decade of progress? *Science 285,* 1,870–1,874.

McGaugh, J. L. (1989). Involvement of hormonal and neuromodulatory systems in the regulation of memory storage. *Annual Review of Neuroscience 12,* 255–287.

Morris, R. G. M., Davis, S., and Butcher, S. P. (1990). Hippocampal synaptic plasticity and NMDA receptors: A role in information storage. *Philosophical Transactions of the Royal Society of London B329,* 187–204.

Pontecorvo, M. J., Clissold, D. B., and Conti, L. H. (1988). Age-related cognitive impairments as assessed with an automated repeated measures memory task: Implications for the possible role of acetylcholine and norepinephrine in memory dysfunction. *Neurobiology of Aging 9,* 617–625.

Squire, L. R. (1986). Mechanisms of memory. *Science 232,* 1,612–1,619.

Tsien, J. Z. (2000). Building a brainier mouse. *Scientific American 282,* 62–68.

Winson, J. (1990). The meaning of dreams. *Scientific American 263,* 86–96.

Michel Baudry
Joel L. Davis

OBJECT CONCEPT, DEVELOPMENT OF

The object concept is the knowledge that objects are permanent, independent entities that exist in space and time even when one cannot perceive or act on them. Humans would be almost unable to function without this knowledge. Although children clearly acquire the object concept early in development, researchers disagree about exactly when and how they acquire it.

Piaget's Theory

The Swiss researcher Jean Piaget proposed the earliest comprehensive account of object concept development in the 1930s. Piaget believed that children gradually construct the concept over the first two years of life in a predictable and universal series of six stages. From birth to three or four months (Stages 1 and 2), infants do not truly perceive objects; they merely recognize stimulation associated with their own subjective experience, such as the reaction of pleasure connected with the sight of a caregiver or an attractive toy. By two months, infants turn to look at an object that makes a sound, demonstrating an integration of vision and hearing that gives objects greater solidity. Between four and eight months (Stage 3), infants noticeably progress toward acquiring the object concept. For example, infants visually or manually follow the path of an object that they drop and return to an object after dropping it out of sight. They also retrieve partially hidden objects and uncover

their own faces in order to see, as in games of peek-a-boo. From eight to twelve months (Stage 4), infants search for a completely hidden object and generalize their search to different objects and different covers or barriers. They do not, however, generalize to different locations. Infants who find a hidden toy in one location continue to search for it there even after seeing the toy hidden in a new location. Between twelve and eighteen months (Stage 5), infants incorporate location information into their object knowledge. They track the hidden object to its most recent hiding location, provided they see the toy hidden there (visible displacement). However, from eighteen to twenty-four months (Stage 6), infants find the hidden object in a new location even without seeing it hidden there (invisible displacement). According to Piaget, this behavior demonstrates that infants fully acquire the object concept between eighteen and twenty-four months.

Contradictory Evidence

Although the behaviors in Piaget's manual search tasks are highly replicable, many researchers disagree with his interpretations. When tasks are simplified, infants appear sensitive to hidden objects much earlier than Piaget proposed. Most research focuses on Stages 3 and 4, from four to twelve months. For example, in the violation-of-expectation method, infants simply watch events involving hidden objects while their looking times are measured. In one series of studies described by Renee Baillargeon in 1993, infants between four and seven months watched a barrier hide an object by rotating in front of it like a draw-bridge. In one event, the barrier bumped into the hidden object and then rotated back to its starting position (a possible event). In another event, the barrier rotated through the space occupied by the hidden object (an impossible event) before returning to its starting position. Infants looked significantly longer at the impossible event, suggesting they remembered the hidden object, expected the barrier to stop when it reached the object, and were surprised by the violation of this expectation. In many studies, described by Baillargeon in 1993 and 1998 and by others, infants between four and eight months looked longer at impossible than possible events across a range of objects, barriers, and displays. Such evidence suggests that infants in Piaget's Stage 3 not only mentally represent the existence of hidden objects but also other properties such as the location, height, and number of hidden objects, and even whether objects' behavior follows principles of gravity and inertia. These results suggest that infants understand the object concept earlier than Piaget proposed.

Why Do Looking and Reaching Differ?

Why do infants between four and eight months perform better on looking than reaching tasks? Researchers have proposed quite different explanations, resulting in considerable controversy. According to one account endorsed in 1993 by Baillargeon and by others, manual search tasks like those Piaget used may be inadequate for measuring infants' object knowledge; such tasks require infants to move a cover or barrier in order to retrieve an object. Infants may know the hidden object exists but are unable to demonstrate this knowledge by retrieving the object because of a secondary deficit in means-end ability. That is, infants may have difficulty planning a sequence of reaching for the cover and moving it out of the way (the means) in order to retrieve the object (the end). In contrast, infants can demonstrate their knowledge in violation-of-expectation studies because they do not require means-end skill. Other work has challenged this account. For instance, Yuko Munakata and colleagues in 1997 demonstrated that when means-end demands were equated for retrieving visible and hidden objects, infants succeeded more with visible objects. Thus, a means-end deficit cannot by itself account for infants' search problems. Whether the object is hidden or visible has a significant effect on infants' success.

According to other researchers, infants' longer looking at impossible than possible events may not reflect genuine object knowledge. Instead, infants' looking times may reflect simpler perceptual preferences for a familiar event or a novel event. According to researchers such as Richard Bogartz and others, interpretations that transcend perceptual explanations by appealing to mental representation may be too elaborate. Although this work has clearly demonstrated the importance of perceptual factors, such challenges cannot account for all violation-of-expectation results. Thus, cognitive factors also appear to affect infants' looking times, suggesting that infants may indeed have object knowledge early in development.

To explain the difference between looking and reaching performance, other accounts propose that the two tasks tap either different paths of knowledge or representations of different strengths. For example, according to Gavin Bremner, violation-of-expectation studies tap perceptual capacities that become gradually incorporated with development into infants' capacities for action in search tasks. Likewise, Munakata and colleagues in 1997 proposed that infants' object representations gradually become stronger with development. Infants may succeed in looking tasks with a weak representation of the hidden object but fail on reaching tasks because active search requires a stronger object representation.

Although researchers have fervently debated interpretation of violation-of-expectation studies, another line of research supports the position that infants have early sensitivity to hidden objects. In this approach, researchers present infants with a manual search task but hide the object in the dark instead of with a cover or barrier. The object becomes hidden when the lights go off, but infants can retrieve it with a simple direct reach instead of a means-end action. Using the reaching-in-the-dark method, researchers such as Rachel Clifton and colleagues found that infants between six and seven months reached for objects in the dark. In combination with violation-of-expectation results, these findings support the view that infants have object knowledge before they demonstrate it in means-end tasks.

Object Location

In addition to research on infants' object knowledge between four and eight months (Stage 3), infants' behavior with hidden objects from eight to twelve months (Stage 4) has also generated many studies. As described earlier, infants younger than twelve months have difficulty tracking a hidden object that changes location. For instance, infants who find a hidden toy in location A continue to search for it there, even after seeing the toy hidden in location B. Although this "A-not-B error" is easy to replicate in reaching versions of the task, researchers such as Ayesha Ahmed and others reported that infants erred less often in looking versions of the task. Like violation-of-expectation results with four- to eight-month-olds, this finding suggests that infants know more than they can demonstrate in manual search tasks.

Why then do infants make the A-not-B error in their manual search? Researchers disagree. Piaget originally proposed that infants cannot separate the object's existence from its location. In contrast, Esther Thelen and colleagues suggested the error results not from inadequate object knowledge but from the normal development of the dynamic processes of looking, remembering, planning for action, and reaching. This dynamic systems account proposes that these processes are continuously meshed or embodied such that knowledge cannot be separated from perception, memory, and reaching. Memory and reaching experience also play crucial roles in a different explanation of the A-not-B error that Adele Diamond reiterated in 1998. According to Diamond, the error results from a combination of limitations in both memory and inhibition. Infants' memory for the toy in location B fades quickly, and they have trouble inhibiting the previously reinforced reach to location A. This account shares some features with an alternative account of the A-not-B error that Munakata described in 1998. According to this account, competition between latent memory traces for location A and active memory traces for location B explains the error. Infants' repeated experience in finding the toy in location A results in a latent bias toward A. Infants also form active memory traces for location B, maintaining an accessible representation of the hidden toy at B. However, the strong latent memory traces for A override the weaker active memory for B, resulting in the error.

Alternatives to Piaget's Theory

Beyond these accounts, which address specific phenomena of object concept development (e.g., the A-not-B error or the difference between looking and reaching performance), researchers have proposed more comprehensive theories of the development of the object concept as a whole. Some accounts, like that posed by Elizabeth Spelke, propose that some degree of core object knowledge is present from birth. Other theories, like that described by Baillargeon in 1998, suggest that from birth there is a specialized learning mechanism that guides infants' acquisition of object knowledge. According to this account, infants initially form a broad category for events involving hidden objects and gradually expand their understanding of such events by identifying the important factors that affect it. In similar accounts, Fei Xu and others suggest that infants construct object representations from knowledge pathways that are initially separate. In particular, infants encode object motion and location information earlier in development than they encode object properties or features, only later incorporating both kinds of information in their object representations. Likewise, the 1997 account of Munakata and colleagues proposes that knowledge is graded, with object representations becoming stronger with development.

Conclusion

Piaget originally proposed that infants gradually develop the object concept from birth to age two. However, evidence collected from simplified tasks that measure looking suggests that infants have some object knowledge several months earlier than Piaget believed. Despite challenges to interpretations of looking studies and divergent explanations for why infants perform better in looking than reaching tasks, most researchers agree that looking studies demonstrate early sensitivity to hidden objects. Results from reaching-in-the-dark studies support this conclusion. Findings from looking versions of the A-not-B task likewise suggest that infants know more about objects than they demonstrate in their manual search, though researchers disagree about why infants err in the reaching version of the task. The goal for future research is to thoroughly test the predictions of these various accounts, with the hope of establishing a comprehensive framework for understanding infants' acquisition of the object concept.

Bibliography

Ahmed, A., and Ruffman, T. (1998). Why do infants make A not B errors in a search task, yet show memory for the location of hidden objects in a nonsearch task? *Developmental Psychology 34*, 441–453.

Baillargeon, R. (1993). The object concept revisited: New directions in the investigation of infants' physical knowledge. In C. Granrud, ed., *Visual perception and cognition in infancy: Carnegie-Mellon symposia on cognition.* Hillsdale, NJ: Erlbaum.

———— (1998). Infants' understanding of the physical world. In M. Sabourin, F. Craik, and M. Robert eds., *Advances in psychological science*, Vol. 2: *Biological and cognitive aspects.* East Sussex, UK: Psychology Press.

Bogartz, R. S., Shinskey, J. L., and Schilling, T. (2000). Object permanence in five-and-a-half month old infants? *Infancy 1*, 403–428.

Bremner, J. G. (1998). From perception to action: The early development of knowledge. In F. Simion and G. Butterworth, eds., *The development of sensory, motor and cognitive capacities in early infancy: From perception to cognition.* East Sussex, UK: Psychology Press.

Clifton, R. K., Rochat, P., Litovsky, R. Y., and Perris, E. E. (1991). Object representation guides infants' reaching in the dark. *Journal of Experimental Psychology 17*, 323–329.

Diamond, A. (1998). Understanding the A-not-B error: Working memory vs. reinforced response, or active versus latent trace. *Developmental Science 1*, 185–189.

Munakata, Y. (1998). Infant perseveration and implications for object permanence theories: A PDP model of the AB task. *Developmental Science 1*, 161–184.

Munakata, Y., McClelland, J. L., Johnson, M. H., and Siegler, R. (1997). Rethinking infant knowledge: Toward an adaptive process account of successes and failures in object permanence tasks. *Psychological Review 104*, 686–713.

Piaget, J. (1954). *The construction of reality in the child.* New York: Basic.

Spelke, E. (1995). Initial knowledge: Six suggestions. In J. Mehler and S. Franck, eds., *Cognition on cognition. Cognition special series.* Cambridge, MA: MIT Press.

Thelen, E., Schoner, G., Scheier, C., and Smith, L. B. (2001). The dynamics of embodiment: A field theory of infant perseverative reaching. *Behavioral and Brain Sciences 24*, 1–86.

Xu, F. (1999). Object individuation and object identity in infancy: The role of spatiotemporal information, object property information, and language. *Acta Psychologica 102*, 113–136.

Jeanne L. Shinskey

OBSERVATIONAL LEARNING

Psychological theories have traditionally emphasized learning from direct experience. If knowledge and skills could be acquired only by trial and error, human development would be greatly retarded, not to mention exceedingly tedious and hazardous. Moreover, limited time, resources, and mobility impose severe limits on the places and activities that people can directly explore to gain new knowledge and competencies. Nevertheless, humans have evolved an advanced cognitive capacity for observational learning that enables them to abbreviate knowledge acquisition by learning from the examples provided by others. Indeed, nearly all behavioral, cognitive and emotional learning that results from direct experience can be duplicated by observation of others' behavior.

A special power of social modeling is that it can transmit new ways of thinking and behaving to countless people in widely dispersed locales through symbolic modes of communication. By drawing on this symbolic modeling, observers can transcend the bounds of their immediate environment. With the advent of enormous advances in the technology of communication, observational learning from the symbolic environment is playing an increasingly powerful role in people's everyday lives.

Subfunctions Governing Observational Learning

Observational learning is governed by four subfunctions that are summarized in Figure 1. Attentional processes determine what people selectively observe in the profusion of modeling influences and what information they extract from modeled events. A number of factors influence what people choose to explore and how they perceive what is modeled in the social and symbolic environment, some pertaining to cognitive skills, preconceptions, and value preferences of the observers, and others to the conspicuousness, attractiveness, and functional value of the modeled activities themselves. Still other factors concern the structural arrangements of human interactions and social networks, which largely determine the types of models to which people have ready access.

People cannot be much influenced by observed events if they do not remember them. A second subfunction governing observational learning concerns centers on cognitive representational processes. Retention involves an active process of transforming and restructuring information about modeled events into rules and conceptions for generating new patterns of behavior. Preconceptions and emotional states can bias how observed information is transformed into memory codes. Similarly, recall involves reconstruction of past experiences rather than simple retrieval of registered past events.

In the third subfunction in observational learning—the production process—symbolic conceptions are transformed into appropriate courses of action. Conceptions are rarely translated into proficient action from the outset. Skills are usually perfected through a conception-matching process. Conceptions guide the construction and execution of behavior patterns. The behavior is modified as necessary to achieve close correspondence between conception and action. The richer the repertoire of subskills that people possess, the easier it is to integrate them to produce the new forms of behavior.

The fourth subfunction in observational learning concerns motivational processes. People do not perform everything they learn. Performance of observationally learned behavior is influenced by three major types of incentive motivators: direct, vicarious, and self-produced. People are more likely to perform observationally learned behavior if it is rewarding rather than punishing. The observed costs and benefits experienced by others influence the performance of modeled patterns as much as directly experienced consequences do. People are motivated by the successes of others who are similar to them but are discouraged their failures. Personal standards of conduct provide a further source of incentive motivation. People pursue activities that they find satisfying and that confer a sense of self-worth; they reject those of which they personally disapprove.

Abstract Observational Learning

Observational learning is not merely a process of behavioral mimicry. Highly functional patterns of behavior, which constitute the proven skills and estab-

Figure 1

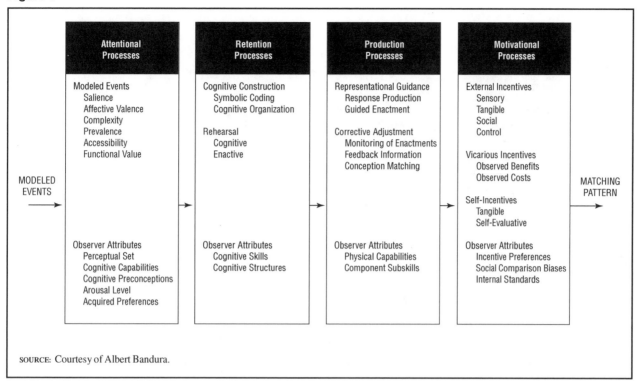

The four major subfunctions governing observational learning and the influential factors operating within each subfunction.

lished customs of a culture, may be adopted in essentially the same form as they are exemplified. There is little leeway for improvisation on how to drive automobiles or solve arithmetic problems. However, in many activities, subskills require improvisation in the mastery of varied challenges. Modeling influences can convey rules for generative and innovative behavior as well. For example, an individual may see others confront moral conflicts involving different matters but apply the same moral standard to them. In abstract observational learning, observers extract the rules or standards embodied in the specific judgments or actions exhibited by others. Once they learn a rule, they can use it to generate new instances of behavior that go beyond what they have seen or heard. Thus, on the basis of modeled information, people acquire standards for categorizing and judging events, linguistic rules of communication, thinking skills on how to gain and use knowledge, and personal standards for regulating motivation and conduct. Evidence that generative rules of thought and behavior can be created through abstract modeling attests to the broad scope of observational learning.

Multiple Effects of Observational Learning

So far the discussion has centered on the acquisition of knowledge, cognitive skills, and new styles of behavior through observational learning. In addition to creating new competencies, modeling influences have strong motivational effects. Seeing others gain desired outcomes by their actions can foster the incentives of positive expectations; observed adversities can serve as the disincentives of positive expectations. The motivational impact of modeled transactions depends on observers' outcome expectations, judgments of their ability to perform the modeled behavior, their perceptions of the likely success or failure of the modeled actions, and their expectation of similar results if they undertook comparable activities.

People are easily aroused by the emotional expressions of others. Therefore, observers can acquire lasting attitudes, values, and emotional dispositions toward persons, places, or things that they associate with modeled emotional experiences. They learn to fear the things that frightened others, to dislike what repulsed them, and to like what gratified them. Fears and intractable phobias can be weakened or eliminated by modeling coping strategies for exercising control over the things that are feared. Values can similarly be developed and altered vicariously by repeated exposure to the likes and dislikes of others.

During their daily lives, people have direct contact with only a small sector of the physical and social environment. They inhabit a limited locale, work in the same setting, travel the same routes, visit the same places, perform the same routines day in and day out, and interact with the same circle of friends and associates. Consequently, their conceptions of social reality with which they have little or no contact are greatly influenced by vicarious experiences—by what they see and hear—in the absence of direct experiential correctives. The more people's conceptions of reality depend upon the media's symbolic environment, the greater is its social impact. Many of the shared misconceptions about occupational pursuits, ethnic groups, minorities, the elderly, social and gender roles, and other aspects of life are at least partly engendered through symbolic modeling of stereotypes.

Social Diffusion Through Symbolic Modeling

Much of the preceding discussion has concerned observational learning at the individual level. Video systems feeding off telecommunications satellites have become the dominant vehicle for disseminating symbolic environments to vast populations. Social practices are being widely diffused within societies, and ideas, values, and styles of conduct are being modeled worldwide. Observational learning is thus coming to play an increasingly influential role in sociopolitical and transcultural change. In this broader function of social diffusion, modeling through the mass media instructs people in new ideas and social practices. Positive and negative incentives determine which of the modeled innovations will be adopted. People are linked together by networks of social relationships. Social networks provide diffusion paths for the spread of new ideas and behavior.

Observational learning takes many forms and produces diverse outcomes. The modeling influences on which it draws serve as instructors, motivators, inhibitors, disinhibitors, social facilitators, emotion arousers and modifiers, constructors of social realities, and transnational acculturators.

See also: LANGUAGE LEARNING: HUMANS

Bibliography

Bandura, A. (1986). *Social foundations of thought and action: A social cognitive theory.* Englewood Cliffs, NJ: Prentice-Hall.
—— (1997).*Self-efficacy: The exercise of control.* New York: Freeman.
—— (2002). Environmental sustainability through sociocognitive approaches to deceleration of population growth. In P. Schmuch and W. Schultz, eds., *The psychology of sustainable development.* Dordrecht, the Netherlands: Kluwer.
Braithwaite, J. (1994). A sociology of modelling and the politics of empowerment. *British Journal of Sociology* 45, 445–479.
Gerbner, G., Gross, L., Morgan, M., and Signorielli, N. (1994). Growing up with television: The cultivation perspective. In J. Bryant and D. Zillman, eds., *Media effects: Advances in theory and research.* Hillsdale, NJ: Erlbaum.
Rogers, E. M., and Kincaid, D. L. (1981). *Communication networks: Toward a new paradigm for research.* New York: Free Press.
Rosenthal, T. L., and Zimmerman, B. J. (1978). *Social learning and cognition.* New York: Academic Press.

Albert Bandura

OLDS, JAMES (1922–1973)

James Olds became a prominent figure in physiological psychology when he discovered, in 1953, that rats could be trained to perform a variety of experimental tasks, some at very high rates, in order to obtain a pleasurable electrical stimulus applied to a discrete central nervous system site. This procedure, often called self-stimulation or intracranial self-stimulation, is intimately related to the brain pathways that mediate positive reinforcement. At the time of his sudden death, Olds was Bing Professor of Behavioral Biology at the California Institute of Technology in Pasadena and a member of the National Academy of Sciences. The events leading up to the serendipitous discovery of pleasure centers in the brain were described both by Olds (1973b, 1975a, 1977) and others (Miller, 1980; Milner, 1989).

Early Life

Olds was born in Northbrook, Illinois, where his father, Leland, was industrial editor for the Federated Press. The family moved in 1931 to Nyack, New York, where Olds's father headed the New York State Power Commission. In 1939 the family moved to Washington, DC, where the elder Olds served as commissioner and then chairman of the Federal Power Commission until 1949. Olds began his college career as an undergraduate at the University of Wisconsin in Madison. He transferred to St. John's College in Annapolis, Maryland, and then worked briefly for the International News Service before being drafted into the army during World War II. Trained in Arabic, he spent most of his war service in Cairo, Egypt, with the Persian Gulf Command. After returning to the United States at the end of the war, Olds transferred to Amherst College, of which his grandfather had been president, to finish his undergraduate studies.

Olds received his doctoral training in the department of social relations at Harvard University. A relatively new department at that time, it included social, experimental, and clinical psychology and sociology. Olds's mentor was Richard Solomon, who gave him thorough training in experimental psychology and exposed him to the current literature on physiological psychology. Olds had a part-time job as editor of a book by Talcott Parsons, chairman of the department, to supplement his graduate fellowship. Olds's contributions were so substantial that Parsons made him a coauthor. This was an unusual intellectual apprenticeship for someone who later made major contributions to the understanding the neural substrates of reward learning. His contact with Olds during subsequent years provided the biological perspective for Parsons's sociological theorizing.

Olds's thesis dealt with motivation and was influenced by Donald Hebb's landmark book, *The Organization of Behavior* (1949). He planned to train under Hebb as a first step toward developing a neural realization of a model of Edward Tolman's sign-gestalt theory that ideas determine behavior (Olds, 1954). The basic conviction underlying Olds's career plans at this stage was that behavior had to be explained in terms of underlying brain activity. Olds felt that the two principal problems of physiological psychology were motivation and learning, that these two problems were closely intertwined, and that their solution depended on a detailed knowledge of the central nervous system. These basic ideas motivated Olds's entire professional career.

Professional Beginnings

After completing his doctoral thesis, Olds spent a year as a lecturer at Harvard and then moved on to McGill's psychology department to spend two years as a postdoctoral trainee under Hebb. During this period, Hebb's laboratory interacted extensively with the Wilder Penfield and Herbert Jasper groups at the Montreal Neurological Institute. When Olds arrived at McGill to begin his training, he was placed under the guidance of Peter Milner, who was then finishing his doctoral thesis. Milner taught him how to implant stimulating electrodes in the brain, and Olds prepared a rat with stimulating electrodes in what he assumed was the reticular formation, an area of considerable interest at that time. The hypothesis to be tested was that the animal would avoid stimulation in the reticular formation (assumed to be the source of neural activity to be reduced by behavior). But when the rat received stimulation through the implanted electrode, quite the opposite effect occurred. The rat actually was attracted to those locations that were associated with the stimulation. This observation in the very first rat he studied turned Olds's initial hypothesis on its head and also suggested that the brain contains reward or pleasure centers that mammals seek to activate during goal-seeking behaviors.

Some unsuccessful attempts to replicate the original electrode placement led to the determination that the hypothalamus and septal regions supported self-stimulation. Olds and Milner described their landmark discovery in a paper that appeared in 1954. It

James Olds *(California Institute of Technology)*

is interesting to note Milner's description of the energy and organizational ability that Olds showed in fleshing out their original observation (Milner, 1989). Olds went on to perform many systematic studies using a standard and sensitive technique to determine which portions of the brain supported self-stimulation. He also developed new technical approaches and took advantage of new developments in the brain/behavioral sciences. This approach also characterized the contributions he made to the study of learning and memory.

Mapping the Brain for Learning

Olds's laboratory at Caltech in the early 1970s was the scene of a unique series of studies designed to "map the brain for learning" (Disterhoft and Buchwald, 1980; Olds, 1973a). These studies used a technique he had perfected for recording small groups of neurons in the freely moving rat (Olds et al., 1972; Olds, 1975b). The basic objective was to determine how neurons in various brain regions in animals learning the same associative response compared over time. The regions that changed earliest, by definition, were especially notable in the formation and readout of the learned response.

Studies of how the auditory system might change its processing of the tone-conditioned stimulus demonstrated that neurons from the inferior colliculus up to the auditory cortex showed alterations in firing rate during differential auditory conditioning. The research focused intensively on the posterior nucleus of the thalamus, a region that receives multisensory afferent drive and showed large firing-rate changes very early in the learning process. The involvement of the hippocampus, a region that Olds sometimes referred to as the "Rosetta Stone of the brain," also received considerable attention. Olds's previous mapping of the brain for self-stimulation had demonstrated that widely spread brain regions supported this phenomenon. Studies of neurons in many other regions of the brain, including the nonspecific thalamus, the basal ganglia, the reticular formation, and the hypothalamus showed altered firing rates during an important behavioral event such as auditory learning.

The series of studies done by Olds's group yielded some additional general contributions to the study of learning and memory. First, they delineated the advantage of using an apparently simple task as a "model system" to study mechanisms of learning in the mammalian brain. Second, they clearly demonstrated that many neurons in many brain regions do change during acquisition of even a simple learning task. These data firmly supported the idea that learning is truly a distributed process in the brain. Third, they demonstrated the advantages of formulating temporal maps of alterations in the brain during learning as a way to determine where important alterations were occurring (Olds et al., 1972). The temporal maps were drawn in the two dimensions: from conditioned-stimulus onset through conditioned-response performance and from the first training trial through acquisition and overlearning of the conditioned response. This approach allowed a clear ranking of the relative importance of the many alterations in single-neuron activity observed during learning in widely scattered brain regions. Finally, the studies clearly emphasized the importance and strength of an approach that dissected individual subsystems for detailed analysis during learning of a common task. Subsystem analysis allows a more precise delineation of the total system interactions.

The approach Olds designed and that his group used to such obvious advantage was adapted by many laboratories and is still being profitably used in the continuing search for mechanisms of learning and memory. For example, Berger and Thompson (1978) used it in their analysis of hippocampal-system activity during learning of the nictitating membrane response in the rabbit. Woody (1974) had begun studies using temporal analysis of the motor side of the eyeblink pathways in overtrained cats at about the time the Olds group's mapping studies began. More recent approaches have combined in vitro analyses of hippocampal brain slices with in vivo recording to ensure precise study of localized cellular and subcellular alterations in the hippocampus during eyeblink conditioning (Disterhoft and McEchron, 2000).

Considerable progress has been made in the analysis of the mechanisms of fear conditioning over the past two decades. The most successful studies of this phenomenon have used and extended the approach pioneered by Olds and his colleagues in their mapping studies (Davis and Whalen, 2001; Schafe et al., 2001). These studies of emotional learning have resonated among nonneuroscientists interested in brain mechanisms of learning and behavior (Damasio, 1994; LeDoux, 1996), imparting renewed impetus to Olds's position that learning and motivation are pivotal problems in physiological psychology (now subsumed under the more encompassing term *neuroscience*).

Setting the Stage for Future Research

Olds spent considerable time and effort setting the stage for subsequent laboratory work; his colleagues were intimately involved in the daily sequence of events that led to the important observations that ensued. Olds's approach to postdoctoral training was modeled after that of Donald Hebb—learning by doing. His experience in Hebb's laboratory, where he discovered self-stimulation as a postdoctoral fellow, clearly impressed upon him the value of serendipity, personal effort, and scientific tinkering. The series of brain-mapping studies used that general approach and remain landmarks in the study of associative learning in mammalian brain.

Olds was passionately dedicated to studying the functioning of the brain. His one frustration was that he felt he had not devoted enough time to studying the brain. He felt that the more facts he had at his disposal, the more likely it was that he could assemble them into compelling insights. He spent a good deal of time thinking, talking, and writing about how the brain works (Olds, 1975a, 1977, 1980).

Olds was also fascinated with computers and electronics. Many of his ideas about brain function, such as his speculations about memory-storage function in the hippocampus, used computers and their memories as analogies (Olds, 1969). He expended much effort on developing and testing software and hardware for the abundant computer equipment in his laboratory. His studies of associative learning used a combined hardware-software system simultaneously to study a large number of brain regions in animals learning the same relatively simple associative task.

The technical problem of developing better ways to study single neurons in conscious animals was one to which Olds devoted considerable energy. One of the reasons he came to Caltech was to take advantage of the possibilities for developing electronic gadgetry for his experiments. He collaborated with an electrical engineer from the Jet Propulsion Laboratory in the design and building of what must have been one of the earliest telemetry systems for multiple single-neuron recording. The idea was to transmit signals from ten microwire electrodes simultaneously without incurring the danger of cable artifacts. The rat looked a little ungainly with the miniature transmitter on its head (considerably less miniature in 1971 than it would be today), but the system worked pretty well. Olds was always trying to come up with a better operational amplifier than the ones he was using, although the old standbys often worked better. He also was involved in troubleshooting things like electronic waveform identifiers; he wanted his to work more simply and efficiently. He would hook up a rat, sit down in front of an oscilloscope, and run a new waveform identifier through its paces by himself. He knew from experience that often the product did not work as precisely as the engineerintended.

The portion of the laboratory used for the mapping of learning was set up with four training stations. Olds used a recording station of his own and carried on a series of experiments separate from those of the postdoctoral fellows and graduate students. He traveled extensively, but when he was in town, he came in every morning to check the rat-in-training in his station and to check the setting of the waveform discriminators on the unit channels. Olds was very demanding about the quality of the data he and his group gathered. He was a firm believer that high-quality findings came from high-quality data. His system had numerous checks for electronic noise and other artifacts. He also took an intense interest in the experiments as they were being run. Those with freely moving rats ran from evening until early morning, the peak of the rats' diurnal cycle. A collaborator coming in during the evening to check experimental progress was likely to discover that Olds had been there shortly before. Olds was almost always in the laboratory early on Sunday to make notes on the printout or adjustments to the computer.

Olds and his collaborators met in his office every afternoon to discuss the data and their interpretation. These meetings often included theoretical discus-

sions that ranged far from the data at hand and discussions of appropriate strategies to use in current or future experiments. Descriptions of Olds's scientific activities by Neal Miller (1980) and Peter Milner (1989) confirm Old's lifelong eagerness to share ideas with colleagues and students and to approach brain function with novel perspectives.

Olds was a gracious, urbane man with a good sense of humor. He was also a family man. His wife, Marianne, worked closely with him in the lab. He also lavished considerable attention on his son, James, who was in high school during the time Olds was on the Caltech faculty.

See also: GUIDE TO THE ANATOMY OF THE BRAIN; LOCALIZATION OF MEMORY TRACES

Bibliography

Berger, T. W., and Thompson, R. F. (1978). Neuronal plasticity in the limbic system during classical conditioning of the rabbit nictitating membrane response. I. The hippocampus. *Brain Research 145*, 323–346.

Davis, M., and Whalen, P. J. (2001). The amygdala: Vigilance and emotion. *Molecular Psychiatry 6*, 13–34.

Damasio, A. R. (1996). *Descartes' error: Emotion, reason and the human brain.* New York: G. P. Putnam.

Disterhoft, J. F., and Buchwald, J. S. (1980). Mapping learning in the brain. In A. Routtenberg, ed., *Biology of reinforcement.* New York: Academic Press.

Disterhoft, J. F., and McEchron, M. D. (2000). Cellular alterations in hippocampus during acquisition and consolidation of hippocampus–dependent trace eyeblink conditioning. In D. Woodruff-Pak and J. E. Steinmetz, eds., *Eyeblink classical conditioning,* Vol. 2: *Animal models.* Norwell, MA: Kluwer.

Hebb, D. O. (1949). *The organization of behavior.* New York: John Wiley.

LeDoux, J. (1998). *The emotional brain: The mysterious underpinnings of emotional life.* New York: Simon and Schuster.

Miller, N. E. (1980). Introduction: Brain stimulation reward and theories of reinforcement. In A. Routtenberg, ed., *Biology of reinforcement.* New York: Academic Press.

Milner, P. M. (1989). The discovery of self-stimulation and other stories. *Neuroscience and Biobehavioral Reviews 13*, 61–67.

Olds, J. (1954). A neural model for sign-gestalt theory. *Psychological Review 61*, 59–72.

—— (1969). The central nervous system and the reinforcement of behavior. *American Psychologist 24*, 114–132.

—— (1973a). Brain mechanisms of reinforcement learning. In D. E. Berlyne and N. B. Madsen, eds., *Pleasure, reward, preference.* New York: Academic Press.

—— (1973b). Commentary on Olds and Milner's "Positive reinforcement produced by electrical stimulation of septal area and other regions of rat brain." In E. S. Valenstein, ed., *Brain stimulation and motivation: Research and commentary.* Glenview, IL: Scott, Foresman.

—— (1975a). Mapping the mind onto the brain. In F. G. Worden, J. P. Swazey, and G. Adelman, eds., *The neurosciences: Paths of discovery.* Cambridge, MA: MIT Press.

—— (1975b). Unit recordings during Pavlovian conditioning. In N. A. Buchwald and M. A. B. Brazier, eds., *Brain mechanisms in mental retardation.* New York: Academic Press.

—— (1977). *Drives and reinforcements: Behavioral studies of hypothalamic functions.* New York: Raven Press.

—— (1980). Thoughts on cerebral functions: The cortex as an action system. In A. Routtenberg, ed., *Biology of Reinforcement*. New York: Academic Press.

Olds, J., Disterhoft, J. F., Segal, M., Kornblith, C. L., and Hirsh, R. (1972). Learning centers of rat brain mapped by measuring latencies of conditioned unit responses. *Journal of Neurophysiology 35*, 202–219.

Olds, J., and Milner, P. M. (1954). Positive reinforcement produced by electrical stimulation of septal area and other regions of rat brain. *Journal of Comparative and Physiological Psychology 47*, 419–427.

Schafe, G. E., Nader, K., Blair, H. T., and LeDoux, J. E. (2001). Memory consolidation of Pavlovian fear conditioning: A cellular and molecular perspective. *Trends in Neuroscience 24*, 540–546.

Woody, C. D. (1974). Aspects of the electrophysiology of cortical processes related to the development and performance of learned motor responses. *The Physiologist 17*, 49–69.

John F. Disterhoft

OLFACTORY CORTEX

See: GUIDE TO THE ANATOMY OF THE BRAIN; NEURAL COMPUTATION

OLTON, DAVID (1943–1994)

David Olton was a psychologist who studied the neuroscience of memory and animal cognition. He discovered that rats not only learned and remembered places, but like humans, could keep lists of places in memory for hours. His work on memory in animals, aimed toward modeling human memory and amnesia, led to the discovery that remembering places required the same brain structures in rats and humans: the hippocampal system. These basic discoveries launched a research program into how the hippocampal system normally supported memory, how it was impaired by physical damage, aging, or by diseases such as Alzheimer's dementia, and how impaired memory might be restored.

David Olton was born in New Jersey and reared in Richmond, Virginia. He attended Haverford College, where he enjoyed the questions posed in philosophy classes, but he was more impressed with the surer methods of the natural sciences. After taking a course in psychophysics, he decided that the combination of psychological questions and empirical methods was the right fit. He earned a B.A. in psychology in 1964 and was awarded the Pennsylvania Psychological Association prize for the best undergraduate research project.

Olton's interest in behavioral neuroscience grew with his dissertation work at the University of Michigan, where he studied with Robert L. Isaacson. He wrote his doctoral thesis on the behavioral effects of penicillin injected into the hippocampus. He joined the faculty of Johns Hopkins University at the age of twenty-six in 1969, the same year he was awarded his Ph.D. Within ten years he was a full professor. He served as department chairman from 1982 to 1987 and remained a member of the Johns Hopkins faculty until he was struck down by pancreatic cancer at the age of fifty-one.

Scientific Context

Olton's central scientific interest was the brain mechanisms of memory. His career spanned the end of the behaviorist era, the emergence of modern neuroscience and cognitive science, and the widespread acceptance of animal cognition as a legitimate discipline. Some of the key influences on Olton's thinking were the ideas and findings of Scoville and Milner (1957) on case H.M., Tolman (1948) on cognitive maps, Mishkin and Delacour (1975) on primate models of amnesia, Tulving (1972) on episodic memory, Platt (1964) on strong inference, and Garner (1956) on converging operations. A thorough empiricist, Olton made his most important scientific contributions through his rigorous analytic studies of the contribution of the hippocampal system to memory and cognition in rats. He developed novel techniques and pioneered powerful combinations of converging methods. He was a master at translating abstract theoretical concepts into powerful experiments, and he was particularly ingenious when translating human neuropsychological findings into animal models.

The Radial Maze and Working Memory Theory

Olton's most prominent methodological contribution was the radial maze, and his best-known conceptual contribution was the idea that the hippocampus supported working memory. The method and the theory are linked historically and together constitute Olton's most influential work.

Olton and Samuelson introduced the radial maze in 1976. The paper described the maze, an elevated central platform with eight arms extending symmetrically "like spokes from a wheel." In the original task, the end of each arm had a food cup that was filled at the start of a daily trial, and rats learned to forage optimally—to enter each arm once to obtain food without reentering depleted arms. Probe experiments established that rats remembered the spatial location of the arms they had visited to get food and excluded alternative explanations such as scent marking, intramaze cues, and response chaining. This demonstration of spatial memory in rats was a new and important contribution to the emerging field of animal cognition. The result implied that rats represented a list of spatial locations—kept several places in mind—and, through a flexible memory process that was sensitive to interference, remembered which of those locations they visited on a given day. This finding was of such fundamental importance that the radial maze became a symbol of animal cognition.

After establishing these new facts on animal cognition, Olton pursued the neural bases of radial maze performance. Olton first demonstrated that performance depended upon the major extrinsic anatomical connections of the hippocampus (Olton, Walker, and Gage, 1978). Lesions of the entorhinal cortex, the fimbria-fornix, the septum, or the postcommissural fornix produced chance performance on the radial maze. Unilateral lesions of the fornix or entorhinal cortex did not impair performance, whereas crossed lesions that disconnected the hippocampus from cortical and subcortical throughput did. Lesions restricted to hippocampal neurons produced similar impairments to the disconnections (Handelmann and Olton, 1981; Jarrard, 1986). Together, the results were clear: lesions of the hippocampus, its extrinsic connections, or its intrinsic circuitry impaired performance in the radial maze. The task proved to be one of the most sensitive and selective measures of hippocampal function ever devised and is still in use. The basic cognitive requirements of the task—spatial discrimination, recent memory, flexible memory expression, and resistance to interference—influenced Olton's thinking about hippocampal function for his entire career.

Olton's initial analysis of the radial maze emphasized both spatial representation and flexible memory processing. His later work addressed how the hippocampus contributes to each of these two important task demands. He initially emphasized the importance of spatial representation and referred to converging evidence from lesion, stimulation, and recording studies. Thus, he showed that hippocampal seizures impaired radial maze performance (Olton and Wolf, 1982), and that neurons had place fields in the radial maze that, in principle, could represent the different arms as well as a rat's entrance into and exit from those arms (Olton, Branch, and Best, 1978). By the late 1970s, however, Olton became convinced that the hippocampus was crucial for recent memory for a wide range of stimuli aside from spatial ones. The evidence that swayed his view, together with the clarity of Olton's arguments, had a powerful and enduring influence on the neuroscience of memory and hippocampal function.

Olton assigned the arms of a seventeen-arm radial maze into either a "baited" or an "unbaited" set

David Olton (*Johns Hopkins University Department of Psychological and Brain Sciences*)

(Olton, 1978; Olton and Papas, 1978). Each arm in the baited set contained food at the start of a trial; the arms in the unbaited set never had food. For the baited set, the contingencies were the same as in the standard radial maze task: during a given trial, the rat had to choose each arm once and to avoid reentering that arm. In contrast, the rat always had to avoid entering the arms in the unbaited set to perform efficiently. The same spatial discrimination ability was required to distinguish arms in both sets, but flexible memory expression was required to remember which of the baited arms had been entered in a given trial. Normal rats entered each baited arm once during each trial and avoided unbaited arms altogether. In contrast, rats trained in the task and then given lesions of the hippocampal system repeatedly reentered baited arms within a trial but avoided entering unbaited arms. Thus, hippocampal lesions impaired flexible memory expression, but not spatial discrimination.

Around 1977, Olton adapted Honig's (1978) terms *working memory* to emphasize task components that required flexible memory for items within a trial and *reference memory* to describe task components that were unchanged across trials. Olton and Papas (1978) assembled these findings and concepts to claim that the hippocampus was required for working but not reference memory, even when the items to be remembered were spatial locations. After he investigated a nonspatial working memory task, Olton became more firmly convinced that memory processes better defined the unique contribution of the hippocampal system than spatial representation. Rats were trained to remember which of four visually and tactually distinct arms they had visited in a trial. The location of each of the four arms was changed after each choice, preventing rats from using a spatial representation of their locations. This nonspatial working memory task was severely impaired by lesions of the fimbria-fornix (Olton and Feustle, 1981).

The pattern of intact and impaired performance in the radial maze tasks culminated in Olton's working memory theory of hippocampal function, which informed his most-cited work, *Hippocampus, Space, and Memory* (Olton, Becker, and Handelmann, 1979). The theory claimed that the hippocampus is required for behaviors that demand working memory, independent of whether the material to be remembered was spatial. Working and reference memory were defined operationally, and testing procedures were explicitly distinguished from memory processes. Olton's working memory theory also addressed one of the two major deficits in amnesia associated with hippocampal damage: the inability of amnesic patients to remember recent events even (and perhaps especially) when those events are comprised of familiar items.

Working Memory: Cognitive Basis and Operational Definitions

Olton intended working-memory tasks to emphasize an event-based, trial-unique memory process (Olton et al., 1979). From the outset, however, the choice of the term *working memory* posed a problem for students. Cognitive neuroscientists had replaced *short-term memory* with *working memory* to describe a memory buffer that served as a representational workspace for manipulating items kept in mind (e.g., Baddeley, 1974). Although he did occasionally describe it as a memory buffer, Olton's working memory was not defined by duration, computational workspace, or consciousness. Rather, Olton used the term to operationalize a memory process described in ethology that was most similar to Tulving's (1972) description of episodic memory (Olton et al., 1979). From Olton's view, working memory entailed memory for events, items that occurred in a specific temporal and individual context. The distinct and varying significance of individual items, encoded as events within a temporal context, provided representations that guide responses more flexibly than their unvarying stimulus content.

Olton's working-memory theory made strong predictions through clear operational definitions.

The theory predicted that hippocampal lesions would impair working-memory tasks and spare reference-memory tasks. The clarity and simplicity of the ideas were compelling, and they inspired an international research effort that led to important advances in the neuroscience of memory, as described in detail below. Both of the predictions succeeded often, but not always. For example, some spatial-reference memory tasks did require the hippocampus, most notably in the water maze (Morris et al., 1982). The cumulative data refuted the strongest predictions of working-memory theory, and Olton conceded that this version of the theory was insufficient.

Although the distinction between working and reference memory did not account for the full range of effects of hippocampal system lesions, working memory procedures often required the septo-hippocampal system and differentially activated hippocampal neurons. In collaboration with Warren Meck, Gary Wenk, and Russ Church, Olton showed that hippocampal lesions impaired working memory for the duration of recently presented stimuli (Meck et al., 1984 ; Olton et al., 1988). In a double dissociation, prefrontal cortical circuits were shown to be crucial for attending to the duration of two simultaneously presented stimuli (Olton, Wenk, Church, and Meck, 1988). Single neurons in the hippocampus were more commonly and more strongly activated during performance of a nonspatial working memory task than during either a spatial or a cued reference-memory task that required the same perceptual discriminations and behaviors (Wible et al., 1986). Memory, rather than other task variables, strongly influenced hippocampal activity. The tasks required discrimination between cue boxes, and lesions of the hippocampal system impaired only the working-memory procedure (Raffaele and Olton, 1988). Seizure stimulation of the hippocampus completely reset working memory (Olton and Wolf, 1981; Knowlton et al., 1985) but had no effect on the learning of a spatial reference-memory discrimination (Knowlton et al., 1989). Spatial working-memory performance in a T-maze provided an especially sensitive, quantitative assay of septo-hippocampal function. Microinjections of GABA agonists or acetylcholine antagonists disrupted working memory performance, reduced acetylcholine release in the hippocampus, and suppressed hippocampal theta in tightly correlated patterns (Givens and Olton, 1990).

As the limitations of the original working-memory theory became clear, Olton sought to correct the principles, logic, and analytic approaches that misdirected the theory. Early in the 1990s he decided that his thinking had been too strongly influenced by categorical interpretations of dissociation experiments (the classic Olton model was a 2x2 table describing a double dissociation), and he began to consider quantitative, parametric experimental designs. His reading of the data had already convinced him that the spatial theory of hippocampal function was incomplete, that working-memory demand was a crucial variable in the extent to which tasks were impaired by hippocampal lesions, and that the categorical, operational definition of working memory limited its usefulness. He also began to reexamine the third cognitive requirement for performing the radial maze task to guide his thinking: resistance to interference (Olton and Shapiro, 1992; Shapiro and Olton, 1994).

Olton's new approach was fruitful. In a nonspatial, continuous, conditional-discrimination task, rats were trained to press one bar if two consecutive stimuli were the same and another bar if they were different (Wan, Pang, and Olton, 1994; see also Wible et al., 1992). By changing the frequency of stimulus repetition and delay interval, the experiment varied both proactive interference and working-memory demand. Even after months of training, high proactive interference and long delays revealed significant nonspatial working-memory impairments in rats with lesions of the hippocampus or fornix (Wan et al., 1994). His new approach to memory research had begun well when he became gravely ill.

Continuing Influence: Theory and Application

Working-Memory Theory

Olton's clear predictions and conceptual analyses posed a challenge that persists today: Can any current theory of hippocampal function accurately describe a priori, in operational terms, the full range of tasks that will be impaired or spared by damage to the hippocampal system? The varied-response strategies provided by multiple memory systems suggest that any particular task can be guided by more than one system. Even an operationally defined spatial working memory task in the radial maze can be solved, in principle, by response chaining and thus dispense with the hippocampus. So, operational distinctions aside, what remains of Olton's analysis of hippocampal function?

The conceptual core of working-memory theory emphasized important aspects of hippocampal function. Hindsight makes clear that the original operational definition Olton proposed for working memory did not distinguish between tasks that required memory for recent events (e.g., episodic memory) from those that could be solved by other mechanisms for maintaining short-term memory for recently ex-

perienced stimuli or behaviors. The potential complexity of the neural systems underlying operationally defined working memory tasks was known from cognitive neuropsychology, where different working memory systems were dissociated—compare H.M.'s short-term memory for verbal and nonverbal items—(Sidman, Stoddard, and Mohr, 1968), and from research on nonhuman primates (Fuster, 1995). Reference-memory tasks, defined operationally as trial-independent memory, can in principle depend upon memory for repeated episodes as well as those for the rules and procedures that were originally described to be the information-processing core of reference memory tasks (Olton et al., 1979). Subsequent research has revealed some of the complex circuitry underlying working and reference memory.

Research in Norman White's lab at McGill University used the radial maze to show that various operationally defined reference-memory tasks require distinct neural components that support independent memory strategies (e.g., McDonald and White, 1993). The hippocampus, the amygdala, and the caudate nucleus each support a different memory strategy for discriminating arms in the radial maze (Packard, Hirsh, and White, 1989; McDonald and White, 1983). In one such task, the hippocampal system was shown to be necessary for discriminating between adjacent but not separated arms of the maze. To learn this spatial reference memory discrimination, intact rats had to visit the two arms in succession during each daily trial, suggesting that learning the spatial discrimination depended upon comparisons supported by recent working memory (White and Oellet, 1997).

Working-memory mechanisms are also variable in rats, humans, and nonhuman primates. In rats the variety of brain substrates underlying working-memory tasks was shown by Kesner et al. (1993), who reported a triple dissociation among working-memory tasks. Lesions of the caudate, visual cortex, and hippocampus selectively impaired working memory for responses, visual objects, and locations, respectively (Kesner et al., 1993). Olton's latest ideas on hippocampal function, working memory, and interference also continue to influence memory research (e.g. Long and Kesner, 1998; Gilbert et al., 1998; Hampton et al., 1998; Fortin et al., 2002).

Spatial versus Nonspatial Memory

Olton's observations that the hippocampus is not required exclusively for spatial memory have been verified repeatedly. Many nonspatial memory tasks that require flexible responses to events have been shown to require the hippocampus in both rats and nonhuman primates. Lesions of the hippocampus impair social-recognition memory (Kogan et al., 2000), social transmission of food preference (Winocur,

1990; Bunsey and Eichenbaum, 1995), transitive inference (Bunsey and Eichenbaum, 1996; Dusek and Eichenbaum, 1997), DRL performance (Sinden et al., 1986), negative patterning (Sutherland and Rudy, 1989), trace eyelid conditioning (Solomon et al., 1986), and memory for olfactory sequences (Fortin, Agster, and Eichenbaum, 2002). Not all spatial discrimination tasks require the hippocampus. Thus, rats with fornix or hippocampal lesions not only learn to discriminate arms in a radial maze, but they can be trained to find a hidden platform in the Morris water maze using a reference-memory procedure, whereas they are unable to learn flexible responses such as a spatial-reversal learning in the same situation (Eichenbaum, Stewart, and Morris, 1990; Whishaw et al., 1995). Olton argued that by helping to encode the temporal context of events, the hippocampus contributes to behavioral flexibility. Thus, the same stimulus can be approached in one instance and avoided in a second instance because the unique sequence and the outcome of the behavioral interaction with that stimulus are remembered. A widespread view is that the hippocampus is indeed crucial for remembering items in their temporal context and that this memory provides the necessary representation for flexible memory expression. Empirical studies (Fortin et al., 2002) and theoretical reviews (Manns and Squire, 2001; Eichenbaum et al., 1999) emphasize this aspect of hippocampal function, which was the cognitive core of Olton's working memory theory.

Applications

Working memory procedures in general, and the radial maze in particular, remain in use in important studies to assess hippocampal function and memory in many species, including mice, nonhuman primates, and humans (Glassman et al., 1994). To cite only a few examples: The tight relationship between place field activity and spatial behavior in rats was first shown in a spatial-working memory task in a four-arm radial maze (O'Keefe and Speakman, 1987). Psychological stress and concomitant elevated corticosteroids were shown to selectively impair working memory in a radial maze (Diamond et al., 1996). Age-related memory deficits in nonhuman primates were examined using a formal variant of the radial-maze task (Rapp et al., 1997). A working-memory procedure in the water maze helped to clarify the importance of hippocampal NMDA receptors in memory (Steele and Morris, 1999). Finally, recent efforts to model Alzheimer's disease in transgenic mice have used a working-memory task in a radial water maze to track the progression of age-related memory deficits (e.g. Arandash et al., 2001). Olton's hypotheses, analyses, and approaches continue to influence memory science.

The Man

David Olton's contribution to science included far more than the sum of his research and ideas. Always serious about science, he was informal in his manner and had an ironic sense of humor about himself. These qualities made him a sought collaborator, a valued and respected colleague, and an outstanding mentor. Among his graduate, undergraduate, and postdoctoral students were Fred H. "Rusty" Gage of the Salk Institute, now president of the Society for Neuroscience; John Morrison, director of the Center for Neurobiology at Mount Sinai School of Medicine; and Gary Wenk, professor of psychology at the University of Arizona.

See also: SPATIAL MEMORY; WORKING MEMORY: ANIMALS

Bibliography

Arendash, G. W., King, D. L., Gordon, M. N., Morgan, D., Hatcher, J. M., Hope, C. E., and Diamond, D. M. (2001). Progressive, age-related behavioral impairments in transgenic mice carrying both mutant amyloid precursor protein and presenilin-1 transgenes. *Brain Research 891,* 42–53.

Baddeley, A. D., and Hitch, G. (1974). Working memory. In G. A. Bower, ed., *Recent advances in learning and motivation.* New York: Academic Press.

Bunsey, M., and Eichenbaum, H. (1996). Conservation of hippocampal memory function in rats and humans. *Nature 379* 255–257.

Diamond, D. M., Fleshner, M., Ingersoll, N., and Rose, G. M. (1996). Psychological stress impairs spatial working memory: Relevance to electrophysiological studies of hippocampal function. *Behavioral Neuroscience 110,* 661–672.

Eichenbaum, H., Stewart, C., and Morris, R. G. M. (1990). Hippocampal representation in place learning. *Journal of Neuroscience 10,* 3,531–3,542.

Garner, R. W., Hake, H. W., and Eriksen, C. W. (1956). Operationism and the concept of perception. *Psychological Review 63* (3), 149–159.

Givens, B. S., and Olton, D. S. (1990). Cholinergic and GABAergic modulation of medial septal area: Effect on working memory. *Behavioral Neuroscience 104,* 849–855.

Glassman, R. B., Garvey, K. J., Elkins, K. M., Kasal, K. L., and Couillard, N. L. (1994). Spatial working memory score of humans in a large radial maze, similar to published score of rats, implies capacity close to the magical number 7 ± 2. *Brain Research Bulletin 34,* 151–159.

Hampton, R. R., Shettleworth, S. J., and Westwood, R. P. (1998). Proactive interference, recency, and associative strength: Comparisons of black-capped chickadees and dark-eyed juncos. *Animal Learning and Behavior 26,* 475–485.

Handelmann, G. E., and Olton, D. S. (1981). Spatial memory following damage to hippocampal CA3 pyramidal cells with kainic acid: Impairment and recovery with preoperative training. *Brain Research 217,* 41–58.

Honig, W. K. (1978). Animal memory and animal learning. In H. L. Roitblat, T. G. Bever, and H. S. Terrace, eds., *Animal Cognition.* Hillsdale, NJ: Erlbaum.

Jarrard, L. E. (1986). Selective hippocampal lesions and behavior: Implications for current research and theorizing. In R. L. Isaacson and K. H. Pribram, eds., *The hippocampus,* Vol. 4. New York: Plenum.

Kesner, R. P., Bolland, B. L., and Dakis, M. (1993). Memory for spatial locations, motor responses, and objects: Triple dissociation among the hippocampus, caudate nucleus, and extrastriate visual cortex. *Experimental Brain Research 93,* 462–470.

Kogan, J. H., Frankland, P. W., and Silva, A. J. (2000). Long- term memory underlying hippocampus-dependent social recognition in mice. *Hippocampus 10,* 47–56.

McDonald, R. J., and White, N. M. (1993). A triple dissociation of memory systems: Hippocampus, amygdala, and dorsal striatum. *Behavioral Neuroscience 107,* 3–22.

Mishkin, M., and Delacour, J. (1975). An analysis of short-term visual memory in the monkey. *Journal of Experimental Psychology [Animal Behavior] 1,* 326–334.

Morris, R. G. M., Garrud, P., Rawlins, J. N. P., and O'Keefe, J. (1982). Place navigation impaired in rats with hippocampal lesions. *Nature 297,* 681–683.

O'Keefe, J., and Speakman, A. (1987). Single unit activity in the rat hippocampus during a spatial memory task. *Experimental Brain Research 68,* 1–27.

Olton, D. S., Becker, J. T., and Handelmann, G. H. (1979). Hippocampus, space and memory. *Behavioral and Brain Sciences 2,* 313–365.

Olton, D. S., Branch, M., and Best, P. J. (1978). Spatial correlates of hippocampal unit activity. *Experimental Neurology 58,* 387–409.

Olton, D. S., and Feustle, W. A. (1981). Hippocampal function required for nonspatial working memory. *Experimental Brain Research 41,* 380–389.

Olton, D. S., and Papas, B. C. (1979). Spatial memory and hippocampal function. *Neuropsychologia 17,* 669–682.

Olton, D. S., and Samuelson, R. J. (1976). Rememberance of places passed: Spatial memory in rats. *Journal of Experimental Psychology: Animal Behavior Processes 2,* 97–116.

Olton, D. S., and Shapiro, M. L. (1992). Mnemonic dissociations: The power of parameters. *Journal of Cognitive Neuroscience 4,* 200–207.

Olton, D. S., Walker, J. A., and Gage, F. H. (1978). Hippocampal connections and spatial discrimination. *Brain Research 139,* 295–308.

Olton, D. S., Wenk, G. L., Church, R. M., and Meck, W. H. (1988). Attention and the frontal cortex as examined by simultaneous temporal processing. *Neuropsychologia 26,* 307–318.

Olton, D. S., and Wolf, W. A. (1982). Hippocampal seizures produce retrograde amnesia without a temporal gradient when they reset working memory. *Behavioral and Neural Biology 33,* 437–452.

Platt, J. R. (1964). Strong inference. *Science 146,* 347–353.

Raffaele, K. C., and Olton, D. S. (1988). Hippocampal and amygdaloid involvement in working memory for nonspatial stimuli. *Behavioral Neuroscience 102,* 349–355.

Rapp, P. R., Kansky, M. T., and Roberts, J. A. (1997). Impaired spatial information processing in aged monkeys with preserved recognition memory. *NeuroReport 8,* 1,923–1,928.

Scoville, W. B., and Milner, B. (1957). Loss of recent memory after bilateral hippocampal lesions. *Journal of Neurology Neurosurgery and Psychiatry 20,* 11–21.

Sidman, M., Stoddard, L. T., and Mohr, J. P. (1968). Some additional quantiative observations of immediate memory in a patient with bilateral hippocampal lesions. *Neuropsychologia 6,* 245–254.

Steele, R. J., and Morris, R. G. M. (1999). Delay-dependent impairment of a matching–to–place task with chronic and intrahippocampal infusion of the NMDA-antagonist D-AP5. *Hippocampus 9,* 118–136.

Tolman, E. C. (1948). Cognitive maps in rats and men. *Psychological Review 56,* 144–155.

Tulving, E. (1972). Episodic and semantic memory. In E. Tulving and W. Donaldson, eds., *Organization of memory.* New York: Academic Press.

Wan, R. Q., Pang, K., and Olton, D. S. (1994). Hippocampal and amygdaloid involvement in nonspatial and spatial working memory in rats: Effects of delay and interference. *Behavioral Neuroscience 108,* 866–882.

White, N. M., and Oellet, M.–C. (1997). Roles of movement and temporal factors in spatial learning. *Hippocampus 7,* 501–510.

Wible, C. G., Findling, R. L., Shapiro, M., Lang, E. J., Crane, S., and Olton, D. S. (1986). Mnemonic correlates of unit activity in the hippocampus. *Brain Research 399,* 97–110.

Winocur, G. (1990). Anterograde and retrograde amnesia in rats with dorsal hippocampal or dorsomedial thalamic lesions. *Behavioural Brain Research 38,* 145–154.

Matthew L. Shapiro

OPERANT BEHAVIOR

In the 1930s B. F. Skinner developed a new methodology for the study of animal learning and behavior. He called it *operant behavior,* to reflect the fact that the animal "operated" on the environment to produce a reward, or *reinforcer. The Behavior of Organisms,* published in 1938, was the principal document in which he presented his findings and his conceptual approach to the study of animal learning and behavior.

In the method that Skinner developed, the animal (most often a rat, pigeon, or monkey) emits particular behaviors, called *instrumental responses* (or behaviors), to gain a reinforcer. Most often, these responses involve an operandum (formerly called manipulandum) that is suited to the subject's motor abilities. Rats, monkeys, and other mammals press a horizontal bar (or lever) in the experimental chamber (often called a *Skinner box*), while pigeons peck at a vertical disk (or key); fish can be taught to swim through a ring. Normally, the reinforcer immediately follows the response.

Animals learn to emit particular instrumental responses because the reinforcers *shape* behavior. Behaviors that are followed by a reinforcer increase in frequency, and behaviors that are not followed by a reinforcer decrease in frequency. For example, to train a rat to press a lever, the experimenter may first reinforce the animal every time it approaches the lever. When the rat is reliably approaching the lever, reinforcers are provided only if it actually touches the lever. Finally, only pressing the lever is reinforced. This shaping of behavior by progressively narrowing the range of behaviors that are reinforced (the *operant class*) is known as the method of *successive approximation.* If reinforcement for a behavior is discontinued, the behavior will decrease in frequency and may stop completely. This process is known as *extinction.*

Figure 1

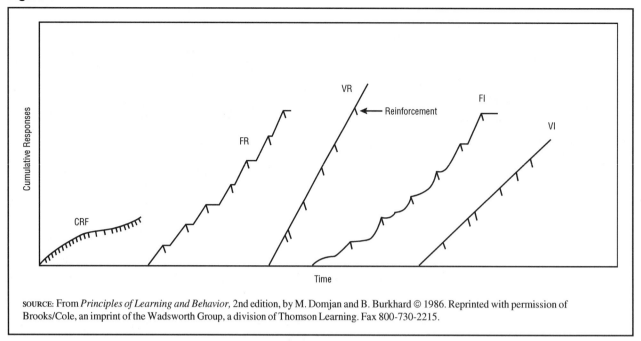

SOURCE: From *Principles of Learning and Behavior,* 2nd edition, by M. Domjan and B. Burkhard © 1986. Reprinted with permission of Brooks/Cole, an imprint of the Wadsworth Group, a division of Thomson Learning. Fax 800-730-2215.

Sample cumulative records of lever pressing on various simple reinforcement schedules. Horizontal displacements in the records indicate passage of time. Vertical displacements indicate cumulative responses. Hatch marks indicate times when the reinforcer is delivered. CRF is continuous reinforcement; FR, fixed ratio; VR, variable ratio; FI, fixed interval; and VI, variable interval. (Hypothetical data)

In *discrete-trial* procedures, the trial ends with a single response, and the probability, latency, or force of that response is recorded as the measure of behavior. Skinner developed another method of studying behavior that he called *free-operant* procedures. Here, the subject has access to the operandum for extended periods—sometimes an extended trial, on other occasions an entire experimental session—and can respond repeatedly during that period. Therefore, the *rate of responding* becomes the primary measure of behavior. Skinner developed an ingenious method for displaying the rate with a *cumulative record* (see Figure 1). Each response displaces a pen upward by a small amount on a moving strip of paper. This makes the rate of responding immediately visible as the measure of behavior. The higher the rate of responding, the steeper the slope of the cumulative record. However, in most current experimental applications, counters and computers are used to record and analyze response output. These measures allow for more quantitative analyses of behavior.

Schedules of Reinforcement

The designated instrumental response is followed on at least some occasions by a reinforcer such as a food pellet or liquid refreshment for the rat or monkey, grain for the bird, or money, tokens, or "points" for a human subject. Skinner designed *schedules of reinforcement* that provided reward only intermittently, in contrast with *continuous reinforcement,* where each response is reinforced. The subject may be reinforced only after emitting a number of responses, on a *ratio* schedule, or for a response after a period of time has elapsed, on an *interval* schedule. The required ratio may be constant on all occasions; this is a *fixed-ratio* schedule. Or it may vary from trial to trial; this is a *variable-ratio* schedule.

Likewise, in an interval schedule the interval may be fixed or variable. Skinner found that each of these schedules produced distinctive cumulative records. For example, in fixed-ratio schedules, animals frequently do not respond immediately after a reinforcer; this is called a *post-reinforcement pause.* Then they emit responses in a high-rate "burst" to obtain the reinforcer. In fixed-interval schedules, the subject typically does not respond immediately after the reinforcer, and the rate of responding steadily accelerates as the end of the interval approaches. Variable-interval and variable-ratio schedules usually generate steady rates of responding. Ratio schedules generally produce high rates of responding because the rate of reinforcement depends entirely on the rate of responding. However, ratio schedules requiring a large number of responses for each reinforcer may induce *ratio strain* in the form of extended periods of no responding.

These simple schedules of reinforcement can be combined into more complex schedules. One schedule may produce yet another schedule before a reinforcer is given, a *chain schedule,* or two schedules may regularly alternate on one operandum, a *multiple schedule.* In these schedules, distinctive stimuli signal which particular schedule is currently in effect. In a *mixed schedule,* the component schedules alternate, but they are not signaled by an external cue.

In *concurrent schedules,* two (or more) schedules are simultaneously in effect and the subject can choose between them. These schedules can be arranged on separate operanda or on one operandum. In the latter procedure the subject can choose between schedules by performing a switching response to a different operandum. It has been found that animals distribute the time spent responding to each schedule in proportion to the rate of reinforcement obtained from each. This relation is known as the *matching law.* Type of schedule, magnitude of the reinforcers, and type of reinforcement are also important determinants of choice. For example, studies of *self-control* have shown that animals are "impulsive"; they choose small, immediate reinforcers over delayed, but much larger, reinforcers.

Stimulus Control

Discriminative stimuli can signal the effective schedule of reinforcement. For rats, these can be different tones or the presence or absence of a "house light" in the chamber. For pigeons, different colors or patterns may be projected onto the response key. Monkeys are often presented with complex visual patterns. The discriminative stimuli come to control the rates of responding. For example, a pigeon will respond at the same rate to a key lit red or green if both colors signal a variable-interval (VI) schedule. However, if the VI schedule during the green-light component is removed, then the rate of responding to this negative stimulus rapidly decreases. The response rate to the red light, the positive stimulus, will actually increase over its previous level, a phenomenon called *behavioral contrast.* New stimuli from the same *stimulus dimension* can be presented in a *generalization test.* For example, if the discriminative stimuli used in training are two tones, then a rat may be tested with a range of tonal frequencies. *Gradients of generalization* (or discrimination) are readily obtained; that is, the amount of responding to each new stimulus is an orderly function of its similarity to the positive training stimulus.

If the stimuli are more complex, such as pictures, this provides an opportunity for the study of *concept attainment* when the stimuli belong to different classes. Pigeons, for example, readily learn to discriminate between pictures containing images of one or more people and pictures without a person.

Stimulus control is also studied using discrete-trial choice procedures. A stimulus is presented as a sample, and then the animal must choose which of two response alternatives is correct for that particular stimulus. Correct choices are reinforced. Such methods are analogous to *signal detection* experiments with human subjects and have provided precise measurements of animal perception. If a delay intervenes between the sample stimulus and the choice, the short-term memory or working memory of animals can be studied. Generally, the accuracy of choice decreases markedly with delays of even a few seconds.

Control with Aversive Stimuli

Positive reinforcers are normally *appetitive* stimuli. *Aversive* stimuli, such as electric shock or loud noise, are also effective in the control of behavior. If aversive stimuli are consequences for responding, they are *punishers,* and they reduce the rate of responding, which is otherwise maintained by positive reinforcement. Animals are very sensitive to both the strength and the frequency of the punishers. Aversive stimuli are also used in the study of *escape* and *avoidance.* The latter is most often studied in a free-operant situation. The subject, most often a rat, is subjected to brief, intermittent shocks. By emitting a required response, such as bar pressing or crossing a hurdle, the subject can postpone or cancel the shock. This procedure generates consistent rates of avoidance behavior in rats, monkeys, and other organisms, especially when each response guarantees a shock-free interval.

Summary

Operant methodology has shown that animal behavior is an orderly function of its antecedents (discriminative stimuli) and its consequences (reinforcement and punishment). It has also enabled experimenters to explore various areas of animal perception, cognition, and choice. Furthermore, the principles of operant behavior have application to humans. Operant techniques have been employed in personal instruction and in the treatment of dysfunctional human behavior.

See also: CONDITIONING, CLASSICAL AND INSTRUMENTAL; DISCRIMINATION AND GENERALIZATION; REINFORCEMENT

Bibliography
Catania, A. C. (1979). *Learning.* Englewood Cliffs, NJ: Prentice-Hall.

Domjan, M. P., and Burkhard, B. (1985). *The principles of learning and behavior*, 2nd edition. San Francisco: Brooks/Cole.

Flaherty, C. F. (1985). *Animal learning and cognition*. New York: Knopf.

Schwartz, B., and Reisberg, D. (1991). *Learning and memory*. New York: Norton.

Skinner, B. F. (1938). *The behavior of organisms*. New York: Appleton-Century.

W. K. Honig
Brent Alsop

ORAL TRADITIONS

Oral traditions depend on human memory for their preservation. Songs or stories from a tradition must be stored in one person's memory and passed to another person who can also remember and retell them. This process must occur over many generations. For example, verses from versions of ballads collected in the 1600s in Great Britain are similar to versions collected since the 1980s in North Carolina. Most of the words have changed, but the basic ideas and poetic structures have not. Similarly, the counting-out rhyme "Eenie meenie" has remained stable, though with much less change, for since the end of the nineteenth century. Rote memorization is not occurring. Rather there is evidence that poetic and meaning rules are being transmitted. Oral traditions must, therefore, have forms of organization and modes of transmission to decrease the changes that human memory usually imposes on verbal material (Rubin, 1995).

The major forms of organization that contribute to stability of oral traditions include imagery, gist, rhyme, alliteration, rhythm, and music.

Imagery is perhaps the most powerful and widespread factor in mnemonic systems. As Allen Paivio (1971) points out, imagery is most effective for concrete (versus abstract), parallel-spatial (versus sequential), and dynamic (versus static) processing. Oral traditions predominantly consist of sequences of concrete actions by active agents, not abstract principles (Havelock, 1978). In ballads, for example, verses that contain concrete, imageable actions are recalled better than ones that do not contain such actions (Wallace and Rubin, 1988).

Meaning or thematic organization plays a large role in adult oral traditions. The cognitive psychologists descriptions of such organization, including schemas, scripts, story grammars, and causal chains can all be used to quantify and describe thematic organization, although the rules for these vary from tradition to tradition. For instance, common scripts in epics include arming a hero or the hero's horse, assembling an army, and joining battle. The scripts are at least as well formed and strict as a college student's knowledge of going to the dentist's office or a fast-food restaurant. The forms of thematic organization allow singers to expand or contract their story at will, as is common in epic (Lord, 1960).

Poetics and music each add their own unique contribution. When two words in a ballad are linked by rhyme or alliteration, undergraduates have a higher recall for them than when the poetics are broken. Furthermore, when ballad singers perform the same ballad twice, they are less likely to change poetically linked words (Wallace and Rubin, 1988). Some genres, such as counting-out rhymes, have nearly all their words poetically linked (Rubin, Ciobanu, and Langston, 1997), whereas others have minimal poetics. Scientists know from the extensive research conducted by Douglas Nelson and Cathy McEvoy (Nelson, 1981) that rhyme cues function differently than meaning cues. It is as if rhyme cues a whole set, while meaning cues, when available, single out the target. Rhyme, as opposed to meaning cues, tends to work best with fast presentation rates, small set size, and strong cue strength—three conditions that tend to be present in the small world of oral traditions. Thus, rhymes have their own peculiar properties, which have been studied extensively and which are often well suited for oral traditions. This trait is true even with subjects not trained to attend to rhyme the way users of many oral traditions are.

Oral traditions are rhythmic. Rhythm functions in at least four ways: (1) rhythm is a constraint, like others, limiting word choice to words with the correct number of syllables or stress pattern; (2) rhythm creates slots that need to be filled, producing a demand characteristic to recall and thereby favors changes within a rhythmic unit rather than errors of omission; (3) rhythm, like meaning, provides an organization, allowing singers to select, substitute, add, or delete whole rhythmic units and continue, and such rhythmic units typically coincide with meaning units in oral traditions (Lord, 1960); and (4) rhythm emphasizes certain locations within lines, that facilitate other constraints, such as the placing of rhyme and alliteration on stressed syllables.

Imagery, meaning, poetics, and music all provide forms of organization or constraint. Once the properties of each form of organization are listed, it is easy to add the constraints together to produce an impressive total degree of constraint. However, more than additive effects are found. For example, although a rhyme or meaning cue by itself may not lead to recall of the last word of a line, when combined they can be effective because there is often only one word that fits them both.

Besides interaction effects that limit word choices, the specific properties of the various forms of organization complement each other. For instance, imagery leads to the original verbal stimulus being transformed into a nonverbal, atemporal representation. When a verbal output is needed, the original words and the order of presentation will not be available for retrieval and will be generated from the image, resulting in changes in wording and the order of ideas. Thematic organization, such as scripts, story grammars, and causal chains, however, function to preserve the temporal order lost by imagery. Even so, in most models of memory, words are translated to and from a more abstract representation that contains none of the sound pattern, allowing for the possibility of translation errors. This remaining lack is remedied by poetics and music, which preserve the sound pattern.

Many strategies of transmission add to the stability provided by the organizational constraints outlined. Songs in an oral tradition are recalled repeatedly after they have been mastered, that is they benefit from overlearning. Moreover, overlearning is usually spaced over time, in some cases once a year when the appropriate season arrives. Overlearning and spaced practice are two of the most powerful factors in maintaining material in memory for long periods. In addition, there are social supports aiding stability. In many genres, only experts who are suited by interest and ability are the active transmitters. They hear their songs from more than one source, which allows better variants to replace inferior ones. Their audience, though it may not be able to supply alternatives, can show approval or disapproval of what it hears.

Bibliography

Foley, J. M. (1988). *The theory of oral composition: History and methodology.* Bloomington: Indiana University Press.

Havelock, E. A. (1978). *The Greek concept of justice: From its shadow in Homer to its substance in Plato.* Cambridge, MA: Harvard University Press.

Kelly, M. H., and Rubin, D. C. (1988). Natural rhythmic patterns in English verse: Evidence from child counting-out rhymes. *Journal of Memory and Language* 27, 718–740.

Lord, A. B. (1960). *The singer of tales.* Cambridge, MA: Harvard University Press.

Nelson, D. L. (1981). Many are called but few are chosen: The influence of context on the effects of category size. In G. H. Bower, ed., *The psychology of learning and motivation,* Vol. 15. New York: Academic Press.

Paivio, A. (1971). *Imagery and verbal processes.* New York: Holt, Rinehart and Winston.

Rubin, D. C. (1995). *Memory in oral traditions: The cognitive psychology of epic, ballads, and counting-out rhymes.* New York: Oxford University Press.

Rubin, D. C., Ciobanu, V., and Langston, W. (1997). Children's memory for counting-out rhymes: A cross language comparison. *Psychonomic Bulletin & Review 4,* 421–424.

Wallace, W. T., and Rubin, D. C. (1988). "The wreck of the old 97": A real event remembered in song. In U. Neisser and E. Winograd, eds., *Remembering reconsidered: Ecological and traditional approaches to the study of memory.* Cambridge, UK: Cambridge University Press.

David C. Rubin

ORIENTING REFLEX HABITUATION

The orienting reflex (OR) is a complex response of the organism to a novel stimulus. It was discovered by Ivan Pavlov ([1927] 1960) as an interruption of ongoing activity by presentation of an unexpected stimulus (external inhibition). This inhibition of the ongoing activity, accompanied by somatic, vegetative, electroencephalographic, humoral, and sensory manifestations, was termed the "what-is-it reflex." The OR is a set of components contributing to optimize the conditions of stimulus perception. A sequence of ORs directed toward new aspects of the environment constitutes an exploratory behavior. The somatic components of the OR are represented by eye and head targeting movements, perking of ears, and sniffing. The vasoconstriction of peripheral vessels and vasodilation of vessels of the head, heart rate deceleration, and skin galvanic response (SGR) constitute vegetative OR components. Positron Emission Tomography has demonstrated enhancement of blood supply in different brain areas during sensory stimulation. The electroencephalographic manifestation of OR is characterized by negative steady potential shift that parallels a transition from slow-wave brain activity to high-frequency oscillations, demonstrating an enhancement of the arousal level (Lindsley, 1961). Humoral components of OR are represented by (-endorphin and acetylcholine released within brain tissues. The sensory components of OR are expressed in a lowering of sensory thresholds and increase of fusion frequency.

The repeated presentation of a stimulus results in a gradual decrement of OR components, called *habituation.* The process of habituation is stimulus-selective. That selectivity can be demonstrated with respect to elementary features (intensity, frequency, color, location, duration) as well as to complex aspects of stimuli (shape, accord, heteromodal structure). The habituation of the OR is also semantically selective, indicating a high level of abstraction in the OR control. In the process of habituation of OR, a neuronal model of the presented stimulus is elaborated in the brain. Any change of stimulus parameters with respect to the established neuronal model results in an elicitation of the OR. After a response to a novel stimulus, one sees the OR recover to a standard stimulus, a phenomenon called dishabituation. The OR is evoked by a mismatch signal resulting from the comparison of the presented stimulus with the established neuronal model. If the stimulus coincides with the neuronal model, no OR is generated. The neuronal model can be regarded as a multidimensional, self-adjustable filter shaped by a repeatedly presented stimulus. The magnitude of the OR depends on the degree of noncoincidence of the stimulus with the shape of the multidimensional filter. In accordance with the degree of spreading of excitation, local and generalized forms of ORs are distinguished. Short and long duration of excitation constitutes a basis for separation of phasic and tonic forms of ORs. In the process of habituation, tonic and generalized forms of OR are transformed into phasic and local ones (Sokolov, 1963).

The habituation of the OR can be studied using event-related potentials (ERPs) represented by a sequence of positive (P1, P2, P3) and negative (N1, N2) brain waves elicited by stimulus onset.

The computer-based isolation of separate ERPs evoked by rare stimuli demonstrates a partial habituation of vertex N1 that parallels the habituation of SGR. A novel stimulus results in an increase of N1 and evocation of SGR. Thus the stimulus deviating from the neuronal model triggers a modality-nonspecific negativity overlapping the stable part of N1 (Verbaten, 1988). The deviant stimuli following with short intervals among standard ones generate a modality-specific mismatch negativity overlapping N1-P2 components (Näätänen, 1990). The OR evoked by nonsignal stimuli is termed *involuntary OR*. It differs from an OR evoked by signal stimuli, which is termed *voluntary OR* (Maltzman, 1985). The OR habituated to a nonsignal stimulus is recovered under the influence of verbal instruction announcing that the stimulus is a target of the response. Such an enhancement of an OR due to verbal instruction is lacking in patients with frontal lobe lesions, whereas their ORs to nonsignal stimuli remain intact (Luria, 1973).

The verbal instruction actualizes a memory trace of the target stimulus. The presented stimuli are matched against the memory trace. The match signal is evident in brain ERPs as a processing negativity overlapping N1-N2. The processing negativity is the greater the more closely the stimulus matches the memory trace, which is activated by verbal instruction (Näätänen, 1990). Similar enhancement of OR can be observed in the process of elaboration of conditioned reflexes. The nonsignal stimulus evoking no OR after habituation produces an OR again after its reinforcement. During conditioned reflex stabilization, OR is gradually extinguished, but more slowly than in response to a nonsignal stimulus. When a new nonreinforced differential stimulus is introduced into the ex-

perimental procedure, the OR is reestablished. The more difficult is the differentiation of signals, the greater the OR. Thus the magnitude and stability of ORs depend on novelty, significance, and task difficulty. Involuntary and voluntary ORs can be integrated within a common attentional process: A novel nonsignal stimulus triggering an involuntary OR followed by a voluntary OR constitutes sustained attention.

The OR has its own reinforcement value and can be used as a reinforcement in the elaboration of conditioned ORs. The (-endorphin released by novel stimulus presentation plays a role of positive reinforcement in a search for novelty. The OR can contribute as an exploratory drive in selection of new combinations of memory traces during creative activity.

The OR at the neuronal level is represented by several populations of cells. The most important are novelty detectors, represented by pyramidal hippocampal cells characterized by universally extended receptive fields. Being activated by novel stimuli, these cells demonstrate stimulus-selective habituation that parallels the OR habituation at the macro level. Any change of input stimulus results in their spiking again. Thus a multidimensional neuronal model of a stimulus is formed at a single pyramidal neuron of the hippocampus. The selectivity of the neuronal model is determined by specific neocortical feature detectors extracting different properties of the input signal in parallel. The feature detectors characterized by stable responses converge on novelty detectors through plastic (modifiable) synapses. The plasticity of synapses on novelty detectors is dependent on hippocampal dentate granule cells. A set of excitations generated in selective feature detectors reach pyramidal and dentate cells in parallel. The dentate cells have synapses on pyramidal cells controlling the habituation process. The synapses of feature detectors constitute a map of features on a single novelty detector.

The neuronal model is represented on such a feature map by a specific pattern of synapses depressed by repeated stimulus presentations. The output signals of novelty detectors are fed to activating brainstem reticular formation neurons, generating an arousal reaction. The rest of the hippocampal pyramidal neurons are sameness detectors characterized by a background firing. A new stimulus results in an inhibition of their spiking. This inhibitory reaction is habituated by repeated stimulus presentation. The inhibitory response is evoked again by any stimulus change. The maximal firing rate is observed in sameness neurons under familiar surroundings. The output signals from sameness detectors are directed to inactivating reticular formation neurons, inducing drowsiness and sleep. The selective habituation of the

Figure 1

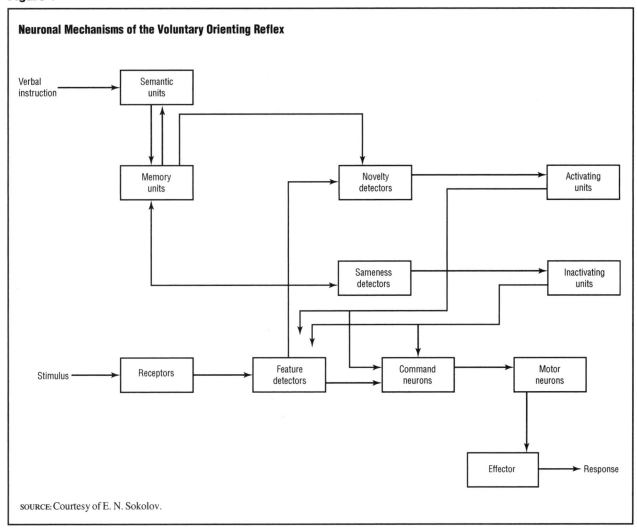

Neuronal Mechanisms of the Voluntary Orienting Reflex

SOURCE: Courtesy of E. N. Sokolov.

pyramidal cell responses is based on the potentiation of synapses of dentate cells on pyramidal neurons. Under such potentiation of dentate synapses, the pyramidal cells stop responding to afferent stimuli. The injection of antibodies against hippocampal granule cells results in elimination of pyramidal cell habituation (Vinogradova, 1970).

Such are the neuronal mechanisms of involuntary OR habituation. The neuronal mechanisms of voluntary OR are more complex (see Figure 1). The stimuli analyzed by feature detectors are recorded by memory units of the association cortex. The verbal instruction, through semantic units with the participation of frontal lobe mechanisms, selects a set of memory units as a template. The match signal generated by memory units of the template is recorded as processing negativity. The match signal is addressed to novelty detectors, resulting in an enhancement of OR to significant stimuli. Through novelty detectors and

sensitization of activating units, novel stimulus results in an electroencephalographic arousal correlated with sensitization of feature detectors and external inhibition of ongoing activity at the level of the command neurons. The repeated presentation of a stimulus switches on sameness neurons, which, with participation of inactivating units, induce lowering of the arousal level, expressed in drowsiness and sleep.

Bibliography

Lindsley, D. B. (1961). The reticular activating system and perceptual integration. In D. E. Sheer, ed., *Electrical stimulation of the brain.* Austin: University of Texas Press.

Luria, A. R. (1973). The frontal lobes and the regulation of behavior. In K. H. Pribram and A. R. Luria, eds., *Psychophysiology of the frontal lobes.* New York: Academic Press.

Maltzman, I. (1985). Some characteristics of orienting reflexes. *Psychiatry 2,* 913–916.

Näätänen, R. (1990). The role of attention in auditory information processing as revealed by event-related potentials and other brain measures of cognitive function. *Behavioral and Brain Sciences 13,* 201–288.

Pavlov, I. P. (1927; reprint 1960). *Conditioned reflexes: An investigation of the physiological activity of the cerebral cortex.*, trans. and ed. G. V. Anrep. New York: Dover.

Sokolov, E. N. (1963). Perception and conditioned reflex. Oxford: Pergamon Press.

——— (1975). The neuronal mechanisms of the orienting reflex. In E. N. Sokolov and O. S. Vinogradova, eds., *Neuronal mechanisms of the orienting reflex.* Hillsdale, NJ: Erlbaum.

Verbaten, M. N. (1988). A model for the orienting response and its habituation. *Psychophysiology 25*, 487–488.

Vinogradova, O. S. (1970). Registration of information and the limbic system. In G. Horn and R. Hind, eds., *Short-term changes in neuronal activity and behavior.* Cambridge, UK: Cambridge University Press.

E. N. Sokolov

OSCILLATIONS, SYNCHRONY, AND NEURONAL CODES

Cognitive systems have to explore a huge combinatorial space when searching for the consistent relations among features that define a perceptual object. Thus, mechanisms are required that permit rapid analysis and representation of relations between the responses of neurons whose activity signals the presence of particular features. A common and well-documented strategy for the binding of distributed responses is the implementation of conjunction-specific neurons that receive convergent input from elementary feature detectors and therefore respond selectively to the conjunctions of the respective features. This process is known as labeled *line coding*. However, this coding strategy, if not complemented by an additional binding mechanism, meets with a number of problems. First, large numbers of conjunction units are required for the exhaustive representation of the manifold intra- and cross-modal feature constellations of real-world objects. Second, it is hard to see how novel objects and hence entirely new relations among features can be recognized and represented because this would require rapid reconfiguration of input connections to previously uncommitted cells. Third, unresolved problems arise with the representation of the nested relations among the components of composite objects such as visual scenes or sentences (Singer, 1999; von der Malsburg, 1999).

A complementary strategy is needed, therefore, that permits a more flexible definition of relations than can be achieved with hard-wired conjunction units. As proposed by Donald Hebb (1949) and later elaborated by others, that complementary strategy is assembly coding. The assumption is that only components of objects—which may consist of rather complex conjunctions of elementary features but may be common to different objects—are represented by individual cells. The presence of the whole object seems to be signaled by the simultaneous responses of the ensemble of cells responding to the components. Thus, in ensemble coding individual neurons can contribute at different times to the representation of different objects by forming ensembles with varying partners. A neuron tuned to a particular component can then contribute to the representation of all objects containing this particular component and neurons representing elementary features can be recombined in ever-changing constellations to represent novel objects.

How to Tag Responses as Related?

Numerous theoretical studies have addressed the question how assemblies can organize themselves through cooperative interaction within associative neuronal networks. Here we focus on the problem of how cells can be tagged as related when they are grouped into an assembly. An unambiguous signature of relatedness is absolutely crucial for assembly codes because, in contrast to labeled line codes, the meaning of responses changes with the interpretive context, thus rendering false conjunctions deleterious for object recognition. The required mechanism must assure that the responses of the neurons that constitute an assembly are processed and evaluated together at subsequent processing stages and are not confounded with other, unrelated responses. In principle, such a process can be achieved by raising jointly and selectively the saliency of the responses belonging to an assembly.

There are three ways to achieve this goal: the inhibition and exclusion of responses from further processing, the enhancement of the discharge frequency of the selected responses, and the inducement of precise synchrony of the selected cells. All three mechanisms enhance the relative impact of the selected responses and can therefore be used to tag them as related. Single-cell studies have provided robust evidence that the first two mechanisms play a crucial role in the selection and grouping of responses.

The simultaneous organization of assemblies sharing common subsets of neurons is precluded by the impossibility of knowing which of the shared neurons would belong to which assembly. Hence, the frequent overlapping of assemblies necessitates a temporal segregation through multiplexing. Processing speed is then limited essentially by the rate at which different assemblies can follow one another and thus by the temporal resolution of the mechanism that labels responses as related. Through synchronization—the temporal regrouping of spikes—the saliency of responses can be modulated with higher temporal resolution than with tonic changes in the firing rate.

Synchronization exploits exclusively spatial and no additional temporal summation, and therefore this tagging mechanism can operate in principle with a temporal resolution at the level of individual spikes. Using synchronization as a complementary mechanism for the definition of relations also permits the possible advantage of specification of relations independently of the firing rate. The discharge rates of neurons depends on numerous variables such as the physical energy of stimuli or the match between stimulus and receptive field properties, and it may not always be obvious how these modulations of response amplitude can be distinguished from those signaling the relatedness of responses. Not all strong responses are necessarily related.

Synchrony as a Code for the Definition of Relations

Some researchers have suggested that the cerebral cortex imposes a temporal micro-structure on otherwise sustained responses and uses this temporal patterning to express through synchronization the degree of relatedness of the responses (Singer, 1999; Engel, Fries, and Singer, 2001). This suggestion ensued from the following discoveries: cortical neurons often engage in synchronous oscillatory activity that is not stimulus-locked but caused by internal interactions (Gray and Singer, 1989); neurons distributed both within and across cortical areas can synchronize their discharges within a millisecond; and synchronization probability reflects common Gestalt-criteria of perceptual grouping.

If internally generated synchronization were to serve as a signature of relatedness, it would need to meet several criteria: First, its precision should be in the millisecond range to match the temporal windows for effective spatial summation and Hebbian modifications. Second, it must be possible to generate and dissolve episodes of synchronous firing at a rate fast enough to be compatible with known processing speed. Third, synchronized activity must be more effective than nonsynchronized activity in driving cells in target structures because it can only serve as a tag of relatedness if it enhances the saliency of the synchronized responses. Fourth, there should be correlations between the occurrence of synchronization patterns and perceptual or motor processes. These predictions are supported by experimental evidence (Gray, 1999; Singer, 1999). Here we shall review only a selection of studies addressing the last postulate.

Attention and Response Selection

Spike synchronization and the often concomitant oscillatory patterning of responses in the β- and γ- frequency range are particularly well expressed when the brain is in an activated state—when the EEG is desynchronized and exhibits high power in the β- and γ-frequency range. Such EEG patterns are characteristic of the aroused, attentive brain, suggesting a role for synchronization in cognitive processes. This suggestion is supported by numerous observations in both animals and human subjects that synchronous oscillations in the γ-frequency range and their synchronization become more prominent during states of focused attention or when subjects are engaged in cognitive tasks that put strong demands on feature binding or short-term memory functions (Tallon-Baudry and Bertrand, 1999; Engel, Fries, and Singer, 2001). Multielectrode recordings from awake cats and monkeys trained to perform discrimination tasks indicate that attentional mechanisms enhance neuronal synchrony in anticipation of the expected task. There is an increase in oscillatory activity in the gamma-frequency range that is associated with increased coherence between the spontaneous discharges of cells and the oscillations of the local field potential (Roelfsema, Engel, König, and Singer, 1997). These attentional effects appear to be selective and confined to cortical areas and sites that need to be engaged for the execution of the anticipated tasks (Fries, Reynolds, Rorie, and Desimone, 2001).

A close correlation between response synchronization and stimulus selection has been found in experiments on binocular rivalry that were performed in strabismic animals (Fries, Schröder, Singer, and Engel, 2002). Because of experience-dependent modifications of processing circuitry, perception in strabismic subjects always alternates between the two eyes. We have exploited this phenomenon of rivalry to investigate how neuronal responses that are selected and perceived differ from those that are suppressed and excluded from supporting perception (see Figure 1). A close and highly significant correlation was observed between changes in the strength of response synchronization and the outcome of rivalry. Cells mediating responses of the eye that won in interocular competition increased the synchronicity of their responses upon presentation of the rivalrous stimulus to the other, losing eye, whereas the reverse was true for cells driven by the eye that became suppressed. Surprisingly, there were no consistent modifications of the amplitude of responses. It is only at later processing stages that the poorly synchronized responses to the suppressed stimuli fail to elicit suprathreshold responses and that cells respond only to the selected stimulus (Leopold and Logothetis, 1996).

Figure 1

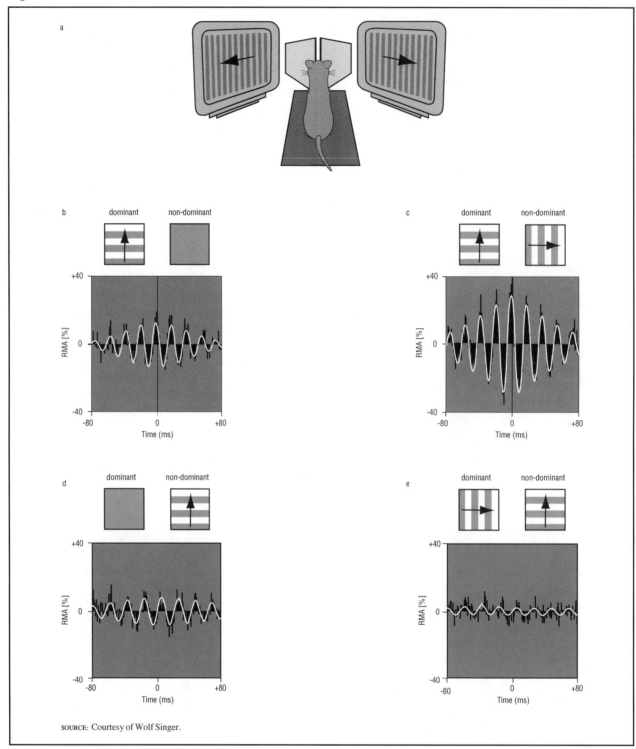

SOURCE: Courtesy of Wolf Singer.

Neuronal synchronization under conditions of binocular rivalry. (a) Using two mirrors, different patterns were presented to the two eyes of strabismic cats. Panels (b-e) show normalized cross-correlograms for two pairs of recording sites activated by the eye that won (b, c) and lost (d, e) in interocular competition, respectively. Insets above the correlograms indicate stimulation conditions. Under monocular stimulation (b), cells driven by the winning eye show a significant correlation, which is enhanced after introduction of the rivalrous stimulus to the other eye (c). The reverse is the case for cells driven by the losing eye (compare conditions d and e). The white continuous line superimposed on the correlograms represents a damped cosine function fitted to the data. RMA, relative modulation amplitude of the center peak in the correlogram, computed as the ration of peak amplitude over offset of correlogram modulation. This measure reflects the strength of synchrony.

Figure 2

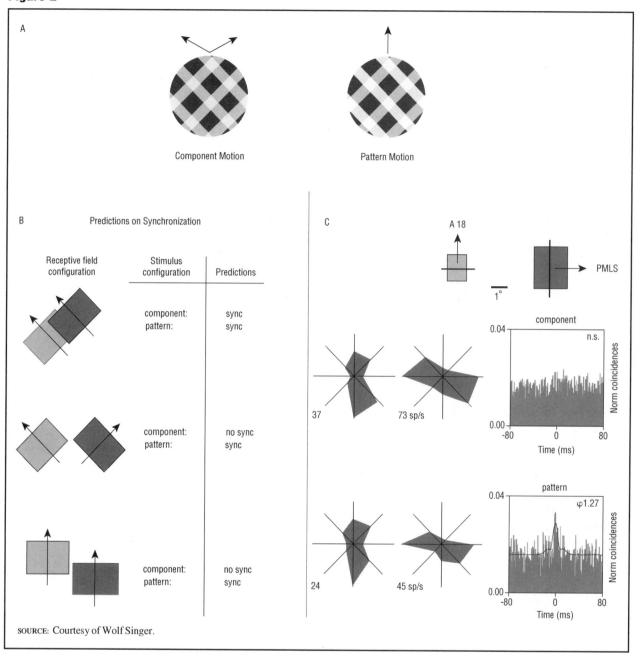

SOURCE: Courtesy of Wolf Singer.

A. Two superimposed gratings that differ in orientation and drift in different directions are perceived either as two independently moving gratings (component motion) or as a single pattern drifting in the intermediate direction (pattern motion), depending on whether the luminance conditions at the intersections are compatible with transparency. B. Predictions on the synchronization behavior of neurons as a function of their receptive field configuration (left) and stimulation conditions (right). C. Changes in synchronization behavior of two neurons recorded simultaneously from areas 18 and PMLS that were activated with a plaid stimulus under component (upper graph) and pattern motion conditions (lower graph). The two neurons preferred gratings with orthogonal orientation (see receptive field configuration, top, and tuning curves obtained with component and pattern, respectively) and synchronized their responses only when activated with the pattern stimulus (compare cross-correlograms on the right).

Synchronization and Feature Binding

The hypothesis that internal synchronization of discharges groups responses for joint processing predicts that synchronization probability should reflect some of the basic Gestalt criteria according to which the visual system groups related features during scene segmentation. A series of studies provided evidence that neurons distributed across different columns within the same or different visual areas and even across hemispheres synchronize their responses with almost no phase lag when activated with a single contour but fire independently when stimulated simultaneously with two different contours. This pattern suggests that synchronization results from a context-dependent selection and grouping process. The probability and strength of response synchronization reflect indeed some of the elementary Gestalt-criteria that underlie perceptual grouping. Stimulus configurations that comply with criteria such as continuity, proximity, and similarity in the orientation domain, colinearity, and common fate evoke synchronized responses with higher probability than configurations that are devoid of groupable features (Singer, 1999).

Researchers have observed an especially close correlation between neuronal synchrony and perceptual grouping in experiments with plaid stimuli. These stimuli are well suited for the study of dynamic binding mechanisms because minor changes of the stimulus cause a binary switch in perceptual grouping. Two superimposed gratings moving in different directions (plaid stimuli) may be perceived either as two surfaces, one being transparent and sliding on top of the other (component motion), or as a single surface, consisting of crossed bars that moves in a direction intermediate to the component vectors (pattern motion). If this grouping of responses is initiated by selective synchronization, three predictions must hold (see Figure 2): First, neurons that prefer the direction of motion of one of the two gratings and have colinearly aligned receptive fields should always synchronize their responses because they respond always to contours that belong to the same surface. Second, neurons that are tuned to the respective motion directions of the two gratings should synchronize their responses in case of pattern motion because they then respond to contours of the same surface, but they should not synchronize in case of component motion because their responses are then evoked by contours belonging to different surfaces. Third, neurons preferring the direction of pattern motion should also synchronize only in the pattern and not in the component motion condition.

Cross-correlation analysis of responses from cell pairs distributed either within or across areas 18 and the posterior medio-lateral suprasylvian sulcus (PMLS) of the cat visual cortex confirmed all three predictions. Cells synchronized their activity if they responded to contours that are perceived as belonging to the same surface (Castelo-Branco, Goebel, Neuenschwander, and Singer, 2000) (see Figure 2C). Dynamic changes in synchronization could, thus, serve to encode in a context-dependent way the relations among the simultaneous responses to spatially superimposed contours and thereby bias their association with distinct surfaces.

Conclusion

There is evidence that neuronal networks can synchronize neuronal discharges with a precision in the millisecond range and appear to exploit this ability for at least three purposes: first, for the precise signaling of temporal features across processing stages; second, for the selection of responses; and third, for the definition of relations among distributed responses with high temporal resolution. This selection and binding mechanism is best for ensemble coding because it meets the requirement for flexible and rapid binding of distributed responses in ever-changing constellations. Assembly coding, in turn, appears necessary in order to cope with the representation of the astronomical number of possible relations among features describing real-world objects.

It appears, then, as though the cerebral cortex applies two complementary coding strategies: an explicit representation of features and their conjunctions in the tuned responses of individual specialized neurons or populations of such neurons and an implicit representation of conjunctions of such explicitly coded contents in dynamically associated assemblies. The first strategy seems to apply to the representation of a limited set of features and some of their conjunctions and is in all likelihood reserved for items that occur very frequently and/or are of particular behavioral importance. The second strategy seems to be reserved for the representation of novel objects and of all those items for which an explicit representation cannot be realized, either because the explicit representation would require too many neurons or because the contents to be represented are too infrequent to warrant the implementation of specialized neurons.

See also: GUIDE TO THE ANATOMY OF THE BRAIN: CEREBRAL CORTEX

Bibliography

Castelo-Branco, M., Goebel, R., Neuenschwander, S., and Singer, W. (2000). Neural synchrony correlates with surface segregation rules. *Nature 405,* 685–689.

Engel, A. K., Fries, P., and Singer, W. (2001). Dynamic predictions: Oscillations and synchrony in top-down processing. *Nature Reviews Neuroscience 2,* 704–716.

Fries, P., Reynolds, J. H., Rorie, A., and Desimone, R. (2001). Modulation of oscillatory neuronal synchronization by selective visual attention. *Science 291,* 1,560–1,563.

Fries, P., Roelfsema, P. R., Engel, A. K., König, P., and Singer, W. (1997). Synchronization of oscillatory response in visual cortex correlates with perception in interocular rivalry. *Proceedings of the National Academy of Sciences of the United States of America 94,* 12,699–12,704.

Fries, P., Schröder, J.-H., Singer, W., and Engel, A. K. (2002). Oscillatory neuronal synchronization in primary visual cortex as a correlate of perceptual stimulus selection. *Journal of Neuroscience 22,* 3,739–3,754.

Gray, C. M. (1999). The temporal correlation hypothesis of visual feature integration: Still alive and well. *Neuron 24,* 31–47.

Gray, C. M., and Singer, W. (1989). Stimulus-specific neuronal oscillations in orientation columns of cat visual cortex. *Proceedings of the National Academy of Sciences of the United States of America 86,* 1,698–1,702.

Hebb, D. O. (1949). *The Organization of Behavior.* New York: John Wiley.

Leopold, D. A., and Logothetis, N. K. (1996). Activity changes in early visual cortex reflect monkeys' percepts during binocular rivalry. *Nature 379,* 549–553.

Roelfsema, P. R., Engel, A. K., König, P., and Singer, W. (1997). Visuomotor integration is associated with zero time-lag synchronization among cortical areas. *Nature 385,* 157–161.

Singer, W. (1999). Neuronal synchrony: A versatile code for the definition of relations? *Neuron 24,* 49–65.

Tallon-Baudry, C., and Bertrand, O. (1999). Oscillatory gamma activity in humans and its role in object representation. *Trends in Cognitive Sciences 3,* 151–162.

von der Malsburg, C. (1999). The what and why of binding: the modeler's perspective. *Neuron 24,* 95–104.

Wolf Singer

P

PARALLEL DISTRIBUTED PROCESSING MODELS OF MEMORY

This article describes a class of computational models that help us understand some of the most important characteristics of human memory. The computational models are called *parallel distributed processing* (PDP) models because memories are stored and retrieved in a system consisting of a large number of simple computational elements, all working at the same time and all contributing to the outcome. They are sometimes also called *connectionist* models because the knowledge that governs retrieval is stored in the strengths of the connections among the elements.

The article begins with a common metaphor for human memory, and shows why it fails to capture several key characteristics of memory that are captured by the PDP approach. Then a brief statement of the general characteristics of PDP systems is given. Following this, two specific models are presented that capture key characteristics of memory in slightly different ways. Strengths and weaknesses of the two approaches are considered, and a synthesis is presented. The article ends with a brief discussion of the techniques that have been developed for adjusting connection strengths in PDP systems.

Characteristics of Memory

A common metaphor for human memory might be called the "computer file" metaphor. On this metaphor, we store a copy of an idea or experience in a file, which we can later retrieve and reexamine. There are several problems with this view.

Memories are accessed by content. First of all, the natural way of accessing records in a computer is by their address in the computer. However, what actually happens in human memory is that we access memories by their contents. Any description that uniquely identifies a memory is likely to be sufficient for recall. Even more interesting, each individual element of the description may be nearly useless by itself, if it applies to many memories; only the combination needs to be unique. Thus

"He bet on sports. He played baseball."

is enough for many people to identify Pete Rose, even through the cues about baseball and betting on sports would not generally be sufficient as cues individually, since each matches too many memories.

Memory fills in gaps. The computer-file metaphor also misses the fact that when we recall, we often fill in information that could not have been part of the original record. Pieces of information that were not part of the original experience intrude on our recollections. Sometimes these intrusions are misleading, but often enough they are in fact helpful reconstructions based on things we know about similar memories. For example, if we are told that someone has been shot by someone else from a distance of 300 yards, we are likely to recall later that a rifle was used, even though this was not mentioned when we heard about the original event.

Memory generalizes over examples. A third crucial characteristic of memory is that it allows us to form generalizations. If every apricot we see is orange, we come to treat this as an inherent characteristic of apricots. But if cars come in many different colors, we come to treat the color as a freely varying property. So when we are asked to retrieve the common properties of apricots, the color is a prominent element of our recollection; but no color comes out when we are asked to retrieve the common properties of cars.

Proponents of the computer-file view of memory deal with these issues by adding special processes. Access by content is done by laborious sequential search. Reconstruction is done by applying inferential processes to the retrieved record. Generalization occurs through a process of forming explicit records for the category (e.g., *car* or *apricot*).

In PDP systems, these three characteristics of memory are intrinsic to the operation of the memory system.

Characteristics of PDP Systems

A PDP system consists of a large number of neuron-like computing elements called *units*. Each unit can take on an activation value between some maximum and minimum values, often 1 and 0. In such systems, the representation of something that we are currently thinking about is a pattern of activation over the computing elements. Processing occurs by the propagation of activation from one unit to another via connections among the units. A connection may be excitatory (positive-valued) or inhibitory (negative-valued). If the connection from one unit to another is excitatory, then the activation of the receiving unit tends to increase whenever the sending unit is active. If the connection is inhibitory, then the activation of the receiving unit tends to decrease. But note that each unit may receive connections from many other units. The actual change in activation, then, is based on the net input, aggregated over all of the excitatory and inhibitory connections.

In a system like this, the knowledge that governs processing is stored in the connections among the units, for it is these connections that determine what pattern will result from the presentation of an input. Learning occurs through adjustments of connection strengths. Memory storage is just a form of learning, and also occurs by connection weight adjustment.

To make these ideas concrete, we now examine two PDP models of memory. The models differ in a crucial way. In the first, each individual computing element (henceforth called a unit) represents a separate cognitive unit, be it a feature (for example, the color of something), or a whole object, or the object's name.

When we are remembering events, there is a unit for each event. Such models are called localist models. In the second type of model, cognitive units are not separately assigned to individual computing units. Rather, the representation of each cognitive unit is thought of as a pattern of activation over an ensemble of computing units. Alternative objects of thought are represented by alternative patterns of activation. This type of model is called a *distributed* model.

A Localist PDP Model of Memory

McClelland (1981) presented a PDP model that illustrates the properties of access by content, filling in of gaps, and generalization. The database for the model is shown in Figure 1. The network is shown in Figure 2.

The data base consists of descriptions of a group of people who are members of two gangs, the Jets and the Sharks. Each person has a name, and the list specifies the age, marital status, and education of each person. Perusal of the list reveals that the Jets are, by and large, younger and less well educated than the Sharks, and tend to be single rather than married. However, these tendencies are not absolute and, furthermore, there is no single Jet who has all of the properties that tend to be typical of Jets.

The goal of the network is to allow retrieval of general and specific information about individuals in the data base. The network consists of a unit for each person (in the center of Figure 2) and a unit for each property (name, age, educational level, occupation, gang) that a person can have. Units are grouped into pools by type as shown, so that all the name units are in one pool, for instance. There is a bidirectional excitatory connection between each person's unit and the units for each of his properties; and there are bidirectional inhibitory connections between units that can be thought of as incompatible alternatives. Thus there is inhibition between the different occupation units, between the different age units, and so on. There is also inhibition between the different name units and between the units for different individuals.

In this network, units take on activation values between 1 and -0.2. The output is equal to the activation, unless the activation is less than 0; then there is no output. In the absence of input, the activations of all the units are set to a resting value of -0.1.

Retrieval by Name

Retrieval begins with the presentation of a probe, in the form of externally supplied input to one or more of the property units. To retrieve the properties of Lance, for example, we need only turn on the name unit for Lance. The activation process is gradual and builds up over time, eventually resulting in a stable pattern that in this case represents the properties of Lance. Activation spreads from the name unit to the property units by way of the instance unit. Feedback from activated properties tends to activate the instance units for other individuals, but because of the mutual inhibition, these activators are kept relatively low.

Retrieval by Content

It should be clear how we can access an individual by properties, as well as by name. As long as we present a set of properties that uniquely matches a single individual, retrieval of the rest of what is known of properties of that individual is quite good. Other similar individuals may become partially active, but the correct person unit will dominate the person pool, and the correct properties will be activated.

Filling in Gaps

Suppose that we delete the connection between Lance and *burglar.* This creates a gap in the database. However, the model can fill in this gap, in the following way. As the other properties of Lance become active, they in turn feed back activation to units for other individuals similar to Lance. Because the instance unit for Lance himself is not specifying any activation for an occupation, the instance units for other, similar individuals conspire together to fill in the gap. In this case it turns out that there is a group of individuals who are very similar to Lance and who are all burglars. As a result, the network fills in *burglar* for Lance as well. One may view this as an example of guilt by association. In this case, it so happens that the model is correct in filling in *burglar,* but of course this kind of filling in is by no means guaranteed to be correct. Similarly, in human memory, our reconstructions of past events often blend in the contents of other, similar events.

Generalization

The model can be used to retrieve a generalization over a set of individuals who match a particular probe. For example, one can retrieve the typical properties of Jets simply by turning on the Jet unit and allowing the network to settle. The result is that the network activates *20s, junior high,* and *single* strongly. No name is strongly activated, and the three occupations are all activated about equally, reflecting the fact that all three occur with equal frequency among the Jets.

Figure 1

Name	Gang	Age status	Education	Marital	Occupation
Art	Jets	40s	JH	single	pusher
Al	Jets	30s	JH	married	burglar
Sam	Jets	20s	college	single	bookie
Clyde	Jets	40s	JH	single	bookie
Mike	Jets	30s	JH	single	bookie
Jim	Jets	20s	JH	divorced	burglar
Greg	Jets	20s	HS	married	pusher
John	Jets	20s	JH	married	burglar
Doug	Jets	30s	HS	single	bookie
Lance	Jets	20s	JH	married	burglar
George	Jets	20s	JH	divorced	burglar
Pete	Jets	20s	HS	single	bookie
Fred	Jets	20s	HS	single	pusher
Gene	Jets	20s	college	single	pusher
Ralph	Jets	30s	JH	single	pusher
Phil	Sharks	30s	college	married	pusher
Ike	Sharks	30s	JH	single	bookie
Nick	Sharks	30s	HS	single	pusher
Don	Sharks	30s	college	married	burglar
Ned	Sharks	30s	college	married	bookie
Karl	Sharks	40s	HS	married	bookie
Ken	Sharks	20s	HS	single	burglar
Earl	Sharks	40s	HS	married	burglar
Rick	Sharks	30s	HS	divorced	burglar
Ol	Sharks	30s	college	married	pusher
Neal	Sharks	30s	HS	single	bookie

Characteristics of a Number of Individuals Belonging to Two Gangs, the Jets and the Sharks

SOURCE: Courtesy of James L. McClelland.

In summary, this simple model shows how retrieval by content, filling in gaps, and generalization are intrinsic to the process of retrieval in the PDP approach to memory.

A Distributed PDP Model of Memory

The second model to be considered is a distributed model. Many authors (e.g., Kohonen, 1977; Anderson et al., 1977) have proposed variants of such models. The one shown in Figure 3 is from McClelland and Rumelhart (1985). The model is called *distributed* because there are no single units for individuals or for properties. Instead, the representation to be stored is a distributed pattern over the entire set of units. Similar memories are represented by similar patterns, as before; but now each unit need not correspond to a specific feature or property, and there are no separate units for the item as a whole. Again, the knowledge is stored in the connections among the units.

Methods for training such networks will be considered in more detail below. Suffice it to note one simple method, called the Hebbian method. According to this method, we increase the connection

Figure 2

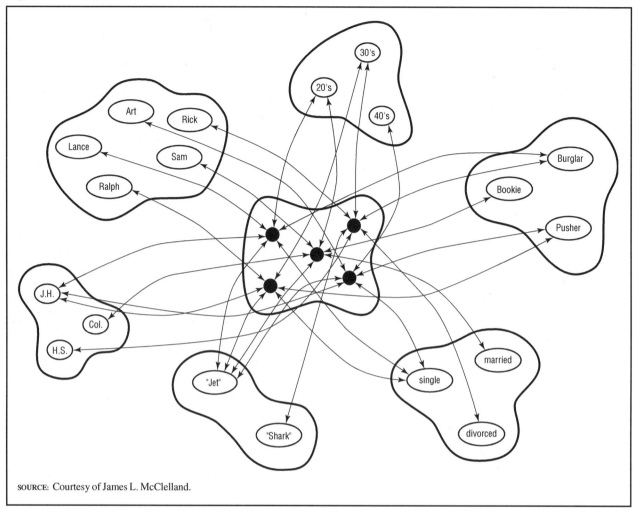

SOURCE: Courtesy of James L. McClelland.

Some of the units and interconnections needed to represent the individuals shown in Figure 1. The units connected with double-headed arrows are mutually excitatory. All the units within the same cloud are mutually inhibitory.

strength between two units if they are both active in a particular pattern at the same time.

Distributed networks trained with this Hebbian learning rule exhibit many of the properties of localist networks. They perform an operation, called *pattern completion*, that is similar to retrieval by content. In pattern completion, any part of the pattern can be used as a cue to retrieve the rest of the pattern, although there are limits to this that we will consider below. Because many memories are stored using the same connection weights, they have a very strong tendency to fill in gaps in one pattern with parts of other, similar patterns. These models also generalize. When similar patterns are stored, what is learned about one pattern will tend to transfer to those parts that it has in common with the other. When a set of similar patterns is stored, what is common to all of them will build up as each example is learned; what is different will cancel out.

There is a final important property of distributed memory models, and that is graceful degradation. The knowledge that governs the ability to reconstruct each pattern is distributed throughout the network, so if some of the connections are lost, it will not necessarily be catastrophic. In fact, the network can function quite well even when many of the units are destroyed, especially if it is relatively lightly loaded with memories.

A Synthesis

Each of the two models described above has some limitations. The localist model requires a special instance unit to be devoted to each memory trace; this is inefficient, especially when there is redundancy across different memories in terms of what properties tend to concur in the same memory. On the other hand, the distributed model is limited because only a few distinct patterns can be stored in the direct connections among the members of a set of units.

The best of both worlds can be obtained in a hybrid system, in which the various parts of the representation of a memory are bound together by a set of superordinate units, as in the localist model, but each superordinate unit participates in the representation of many different memories, as in the distributed model.

Learning Rules for PDP Systems

Several of the learning rules for PDP systems are reviewed in Rumelhart, Hinton, and McClelland (1986). Here we consider two main classes, Hebbian learning rules and *error-correcting* learning rules. We have already mentioned the Hebbian learning rule, which increases the strength of the connection between two units when both units are simultaneously active. In a common variant, the strength of the connection is decreased when one unit is active and the other is inactive.

These Hebbian learning rules are limited in what can be learned with them. Some of these limitations are overcome by what are called error-correcting learning rules. In such learning rules, the idea is that the pattern to be learned is treated not only as input but also as the target for learning. A pattern is presented, and the network is allowed to settle. Once it has done so, the discrepancies between the resulting pattern and the input pattern are used to determine what changes should be made in the connections. For example, if a unit is activated that should not be active, the connection weights coming into that unit from other active units will be reduced. Several very powerful learning procedures for adjusting connection weights that are based on the idea of reducing the discrepancy between output and target have been developed in recent years. The best-known is the back-propagation learning procedure (Rumelhart, Hinton, and Williams, 1986). Another important learning rule for PDP systems is the Boltzmann machine learning rule (Ackley, Hinton, and Sejnowski, 1985). Both work well in training the hybrid systems described above.

See also: LOCALIZATION OF MEMORY TRACES; NEURAL COMPUTATION; RECONSTRUCTIVE MEMORY

Bibliography

Ackley, D. H., Hinton, G. E., and Sejnowski, T. J. (1985). A learning algorithm for Boltzmann machines. *Cognitive Science 9*, 147–169.

Anderson, J. A., Silverstein, J. W., Ritz, S. A., and Jones, R. S. (1977). Distinctive features, categorical perception, and probability learning: Some applications of a neural model. *Psychological Review 84*, 413–451.

Figure 3

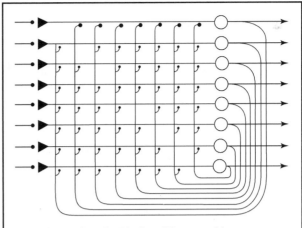

SOURCE: From a figure in "Distributed Memory and the Representation of General and Specific Information," by J. L. McClelland and D. E. Rumelhart. In *Journal of Experimental Psychology: General*, v. 114, pp. 159–188, 1985. Copyright © 1985 by the American Psychological Association. Reproduced by permission of the American Psychological Association.

A simple distributed memory, consisting of a small ensemble of eight processing units. Each unit receives input from the left and sends its output to the right. Each unit also has a modifiable connection to all the other units in the memory, as indicated by the branches of the output lines that loop back onto the input lines leading into each unit.

Hertz, J., Krogh, A., and Palmer, R. (1990). *Introduction to the theory of neural computation.* Redwood City, CA: Addison-Wesley.

Hinton, G. E., and Anderson J. A., eds. (1981). *Parallel models of associative memory.* Hillsdale, NJ: Erlbaum.

Kohonen, T. (1977). *Associative memory: A system theoretical approach.* New York: Springer-Verlag.

McClelland, J. L. (1981). Retrieving general and specific information from stored knowledge of specifics. Paper presented at the third annual meeting of the Cognitive Science Society. Berkeley, CA.

McClelland, J. L., and Rumelhart, D. E. (1985). Distributed memory and the representation of general and specific information. *Journal of Experimental Psychology: General 114*, 159–188.

Rumelhart, D. E., Hinton, G. E., and McClelland, J. L. (1986). A general framework for parallel distributed processing. In D. E. Rumelhart, J. L. McClelland, and the PDP Research Group, eds., *Parallel distributed processing: Explorations in the microstructures of cognition*, Vol. 1. Cambridge, MA: MIT Press.

Rumelhart, D. E., Hinton, G. E., and Williams, R. J. (1986). Learning internal representations by error propagation. In D. E. Rumelhart, J. L. McClelland, and the PDP Research Group, eds., *Parallel distributed processing: Explorations in the microstructures of cognition*, Vol. 1. Cambridge, MA: MIT Press.

Rumelhart, D. E., McClelland, J. L., and the PDP Research Group. (1986). *Parallel distributed processing: Explorations in the microstructure of cognition*, 2 vols. Cambridge, MA: MIT Press.

James L. McClelland

PASSIVE (INHIBITORY) AVOIDANCE, FEAR LEARNING

Fear learning is the process of gathering information about the internal and external environment in situations that evoke fear. Fear learning is the first step toward creating memories for fearful events (fear memories), which are robust and represent a long-lasting record of the acquired information that is capable of modifying behavior when retrieved. Like other forms of learning, fear learning (fear memory acquisition) is followed first by memory consolidation, a period of time when memories are still labile and can be modulated (enhanced or impaired), and then by memory storage (McGaugh, 2000).

Because memories cannot be directly observed and assayed, their existence is, by necessity, inferred from changes in behavior following an experience (Cahill, McGaugh, and Weinberger, 2001). Thus, to study learning and memory, subjects are interrogated by observing their performance in carefully designed behavioral tasks. In the study of fear learning and memory, the most widely used tasks are passive (inhibitory) avoidance and fear conditioning. This entry will focus on the former task and will discuss how its use has advanced the understanding of brain structures and neuromodulatory systems involved in consolidating and storing memories for fearful events. Although this presentation is based on findings obtained in rats and mice, passive avoidance has also been instrumental in understanding memory processes in chicks (Rose, 2000) and humans (Cahill and McGaugh, 1998).

Passive (Inhibitory) Avoidance

Memory in a passive avoidance task is inferred from the delay of a response that was readily made before the training. Because delaying a response is an active process, some investigators refer to the task as inhibitory, rather than passive, avoidance (Cahill and McGaugh, 1998; Izquierdo, Medina, and Barros, 1999). Passive (inhibitory) avoidance, or PA/IA, experiments are conducted in a two-compartment behavioral apparatus, where one compartment is designed to be naturally preferred by the animal (see Figure 1). During training, the animal is placed in the less-preferred compartment and the latency to enter the preferred compartment is noted. Upon completely entering the preferred compartment, the animal receives one or more inescapable foot shocks of a specified intensity and duration. The information the animal gathers during the training is fear learning. At a retention test, conducted hours, days, or months later, the animal is returned to the previously less-preferred compartment and the latency to enter the

shock compartment, which at this point is not electrified, is measured. This measure (retention latency) is used to infer the animal's memory for the fearful experience—the longer the retention latency, the better the memory. A long retention latency indicates a significant modification in the animal's behavior, as it contrasts with the animal's low initial entrance latency displayed before the training.

PA/IA testing has several features that make it a valuable tool for investigating brain systems involved in memory acquisition, consolidation, and retrieval. It is simple to administer and thus easy to replicate across laboratories, yet it is complex enough to engage multiple brain regions and neurotransmitter systems (Ambrogi Lorenzini et al., 1999; Izquierdo, Medina, and Barros, 1999; McGaugh, Ferry, Vazdarjanova, and Roozendaal, 2000). In addition, PA/IA is ethologically relevant in that it promotes fast learning, usually after one trial (in nature, an animal may not survive to pass on its genes if it does not learn to recognize and avoid a predator after a single encounter). One-trial learning provides a clear time stamp of when learning occurred. In combination with post-training manipulations, which selectively affect memory consolidation but not acquisition or retrieval (McGaugh, 1989), PA/IA training provides researchers the ability to study the brain mechanisms involved in consolidation of explicit-declarative memory for fearful events.

What Kind of Memory Does the Retention Latency Measure Represent?

Arguably, retention latency measured in PA/IA may reflect only a procedural memory (i.e., entering a place is aversive) (Wilensky, Schafe, and LeDoux, 2000). However, during PA/IA animals could acquire both explicit-declarative memories, such as those acquired during Pavlovian contextual fear conditioning ("I got shocked in this place"), and implicit-procedural memories that reflect a response-reinforcement contingency. Because acquiring procedural memories takes many more trials than acquiring explicit-declarative memories (Packard and McGaugh, 1996), measuring retention latencies after one-trial PA/IA most likely reflects explicit-declarative fear memories. Moreover, when the two types of memory were experimentally pitted against each other in a modified avoidance task, animals unambiguously expressed explicit-declarative fear memories. In this test, rats were trained on an active avoidance task by being repeatedly placed in the preferred compartment, each time shocked until they entered the less-preferred (light) compartment, and then tested by being placed in the light compartment. By showing high retention latencies, the rats indicated that they had learned where they had received foot shocks (explicit memory), rather than that they had to perform a response (procedural memory) (Parent, West, and McGaugh, 1994). Additionally, latencies to enter a compartment where foot shock was experienced can be successfully used to assess memory for contextual fear conditioning, a task in which receiving foot shocks is not contingent on any one particular response (Vazdarjanova and McGaugh, 1998).

Factors Involved in Consolidation of Memory for PA/IA

Stress hormones (adrenaline [or epinephrine] and glucocorticoids), when injected after training at the time when they are normally released by the adrenal glands following an emotional experience, can modulate the memory strength for one-trial PA/IA training. This modulation is dose-dependent (low to medium levels of stress hormones are memory enhancing, whereas high levels are memory impairing) and time-dependent (the effects are most pronounced when the treatments are administered immediately after training). Consistent with the idea that these hormones are endogenously released as a result of an emotional experience, memory is impaired by removing the adrenals, blocking peripheral β-adrenoceptors, or blocking the synthesis of glucocorticoids. Although their effects on memory consolidation are similar, adrenaline and glucocorticoids exert their effects via different pathways. Glucocorticoids are lipophilic and readily cross the blood-brain barrier, thus directly affecting memory consolidation in several brain regions by activating glucocorticoid receptors. When glucocorticoid receptor agonists are administered directly into the basolateral amygdala, hippocampus, or nucleus of the solitary tract (NTS), they enhance memory for PA/IA. The effects of glucocorticoids on memory appear to be mediated by the basolateral amygdala, as lesions of this region or inactivation of the amygdala's β-adrenoceptors block the memory-modulatory effects of peripheral and intrahippocampal or intra-NTS glucocorticoid treatments (Roozendaal, 2000).

Unlike glucocorticoids, adrenaline does not readily pass the blood-brain barrier and its effects on memory consolidation are mediated by β-adrenoceptors on the vagus nerve. Activation of the vagus nerve stimulates noradrenergic neurons in the NTS directly and noradrenergic neurons in the locus coeruleus indirectly. Thus, peripherally released adrenaline leads to centrally released noradrenaline. Although noradrenaline can modulate memory consolidation for PA/IA by acting directly on neurons in the basolateral amygdala, hippocampus, and entorhinal

Figure 1

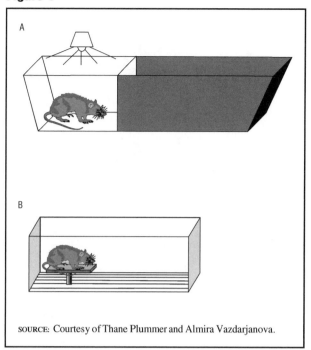

SOURCE: Courtesy of Thane Plummer and Almira Vazdarjanova.

A schematic representation of two versions of the passive (inhibitory) avoidance task (PA/IA) for rats and mice. A) In a "step-through PA/IA" task, the animal is placed in the light compartment of the two-compartment apparatus. Being nocturnal animals, rats and mice naturally prefer the dark compartment, so they enter it quickly. The sliding door between the two compartments is closed and the animal receives one or more inescapable footshocks. At the retention test, the animal is placed in the light compartment (the sliding door is open) and the latency to enter the dark compartment is recorded and used to infer the strength of the memory for the fearful experience. Higher footshock intensities, or more footshocks, lead to longer retention latencies. B) In the "step-down PA/IA" task, the initially less-preferred compartment is a small platform raised above a grid floor (rats and mice are afraid of heights). When the animal steps down with all four paws, it receives one or more footshocks. The retention latency is the latency to step down from the platform to the grid floor at the time of testing.

cortex (Izquierdo, Medina, and Barros, 1999), noradrenergic activation of the basolateral amygdala is of primary importance. Stress induces the release of noradrenaline in this region, and activation of the amygdala's β-adrenoceptors reverses the memory-impairing effects of GABAergic (gamma-aminobutyric acid) and opioid agonists, while blocking of the β-adrenoceptors blocks the memory enhancement produced by GABAergic and opioid antagonists. The effectiveness of the basolateral amygdala's β-adrenoceptors themselves depends on the activation of glucocorticoid receptors in this region (see Figure 2; also McGaugh, Ferry, Vazdarjanova, and Roozendaal, 2000).

Figure 2

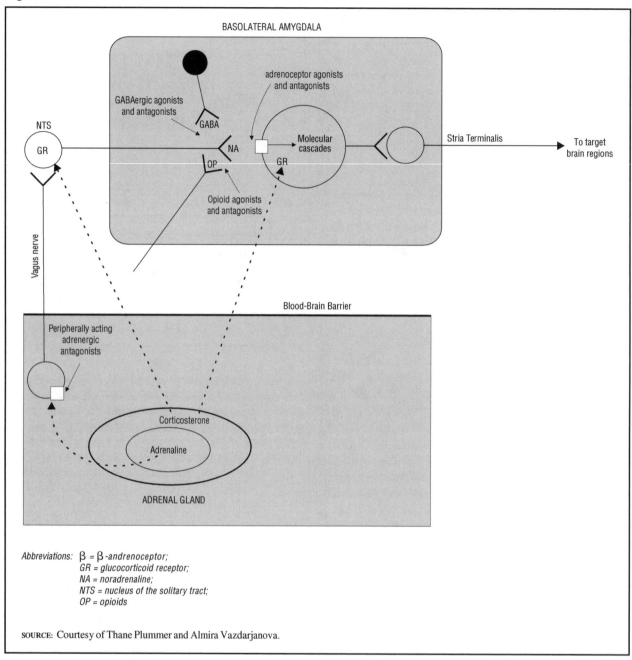

Abbreviations: β = β-adrenoceptor;
GR = glucocorticoid receptor;
NA = noradrenaline;
NTS = nucleus of the solitary tract;
OP = opioids

SOURCE: Courtesy of Thane Plummer and Almira Vazdarjanova.

A summary diagram of how stress hormones and other memory modulatory treatments interact in the basolateral amygdala to influence memory consolidation of emotional events, such as PA/IA, in other brain regions. During stress, the adrenal medulla releases adrenaline and the adrenal cortex releases corticosterone (cortisol in humans). Corticosterone freely passes the blood-brain barrier and acts on multiple brain regions. In the basolateral amygdala it modulates processes occurring downstream of activation of the β-adrenoceptors. Adrenaline, which does not pass the blood-brain barrier, activates the vagus nerve by acting on peripheral β-adrenoceptors. Vagus nerve afferents activate directly noradrenergic neurons in the nucleus of the solitary tract to release noradrenaline in the basolateral amygdala. Activation of β-adrenoceptors in the basolateral amygdala enhances memory by strengthening memory consolidation processes in target regions of the stria terminalis, and it supersedes the influences on memory of treatments acting on the GABAergic and opioid receptors in the basolateral amygdala.

Adrenergic, glucocorticoid, and cholinergic memory modulatory treatments produced by either systemic treatments or direct manipulations of the amygdala are reversed by lesions of the stria terminalis, one of the two major input-output pathway of the amygdala. Thus, the amygdala appears to modulate memory storage in target areas of the stria terminalis (McGaugh, Ferry, Vazdarjanova, and Roozendaal, 2000).

Memory for PA/IA is also modulated by glucose (the release of which is enhanced by adrenaline), vasopressin, and substance P, as well as cholinergic, GABA-ergic, dopaminergic, serotonergic, and opioid agents (Gold, 1995; Koob et al., 1991; McGaugh, 1989; Izquierdo, Medina, and Barros, 1999; Zhang, Berbos, and Wiley, 1996; Riekkinen, Kuitunen, and Riekkinen, 1995).

All neuromodulatory treatments discussed thus far appear to affect memory storage not only for PA/IA but for emotional experiences in general, as similar findings have been shown in other emotionally motivated tasks. Predictions based on the reported findings in rats and mice have been supported by results obtained in human subjects (Cahill and McGaugh, 1998).

Researchers debate whether the described mechanisms of memory consolidation for PA/IA, notably the role of the basolateral amygdala in memory storage, are the same as those for fear conditioning (Fanselow and LeDoux, 1999; Cahill, Weinberger, Roozendaal, and McGaugh, 1999; Maren, 1999; Vazdarjanova, 2000). Although the basolateral amygdala plays a modulatory role in memory consolidaton of PA/IA, it is probably also the site of memory storage for fear conditioning. This conclusion is based mainly on the observation that pretraining or pretest lesions or inactivation (both general and NMDA-receptor specific) of this brain region lead to decreased freezing behavior, a typical measure used to assess memory for fear conditioning. In addition, the basolateral amygdala develops LTP-like (long-term potentiation) plasticity as a result of auditory fear conditioning. However, both lines of evidence are also consistent with a modulatory role of the basolateral amygdala in fear conditioning. Thus, if disruption of activity in this region leads to decreased strength of memories for fear conditioning, animals will be less likely to display freezing, a behavior that indicates high levels of fear, while other measures of memory may be still evident. Consistent with this hypothesis are findings that following contextual fear conditioning, rats with complete lesions of the basolateral amygdala do not show freezing, but do display training-induced avoidance of the place where they had received foot shocks (Vazdarjanova and McGaugh, 1998). Furthermore, physiological plasticity following fear conditioning is not unique to the basolateral amygdala but is present in multiple brain regions (Mcintosh and Gonzalez-Lima, 1998; Poremba and Gabriel, 2001), suggesting that fear memories are likely encoded and stored in a distributed neural network across several brain regions.

Temporal Pattern of Memory Consolidation for PA/IA

Studies of functional inactivation of selective brain regions by anesthetics that block sodium channels, or by increasing inhibition through GABA-A receptors, have shown that memory consolidation for PA/IA occurs over a long period of time and involves sequentially a multitude of brain regions. Functional integrity of the hippocampus, medial septum, basolateral amygdala, nucleus of the solitary tract, and several cortical regions (insular, anterior prefrontal [Fr2], and posterior cingulated) is required during an early phase of memory consolidation (immediately and up to 1.5 hours after training), whereas that of the entorhinal and parietal cortecies is required during a later phase (0.5 to 3 hours or 1 to 3 hours, respectively). Finally, the functional integrity of brain regions that release neuromodulators in the hippocampus, amygdala, and cortex—such as the nucleus basalis, substantia nigra, and parabrachial nucleus—is required for a couple of days after training. The duration of memory consolidation appears to depend on the intensity of the training—the higher the footshock stimulus, the quicker the consolidation (Ambrogi Lorenzini et al., 1999; Bermúdez-Rattoni, Introini-Collison, and McGaugh, 1991; Izquierdo, Quillfeldt, and Medina, 1997; Mello e Souza, Vianna, and Izquierdo, 2000).

Conceptual Advances Facilitated by the Use of One-Trial PA/IA

The use of PA/IA and timed manipulations after training has helped identify the neuromodulatory systems and their interactions in brain regions, notably the basolateral amygdala, that modulate the consolidation of explicit memories for fearful events. PA/IA studies also revealed that memory consolidation is a dynamic process that occurs over hours to days and depends sequentially on networks of neurons distributed among several brain regions. The shift over time in the dependence of memory consolidation to cortical regions also indicates that, consistent with early predictions (Gerard, 1961), the cortex appears to be the ultimate repository for explicit-declarative long-term emotional memories. Finally, because PA/IA is useful in assessing both short-term memory (developing within seconds and lasting minutes to hours) and long-term memory (developing over time and lasting hours to years) (McGaugh, 2000) in the same subjects, it enabled the first demonstration in mammals that the processes underlying these two types of memory are independent. Fifteen different pharmacological manipulations that affect specific receptors or molecular cascades in the hippocampus, entorhinal, and parietal cortex impair short-term memory without affecting long-term memory (Izquierdo, Medina, and Barros, 1999). Thus, the development of long-term memory does not require intact short-term memory. The conceptual advances afforded by the use of PA/IA underscore the importance of this paradigm as a model system for studying emotional learning and memory processes.

See also: ACTIVE AND PASSIVE AVOIDANCE
   LEARNING: BEHAVORIAL PHENOMENA; NEURAL
   SUBSTRATES OF AVOIDANCE LEARNING; NEURAL
   SUBSTRATES OF CLASSICAL CONDITIONING;
   NEURAL SUBSTRATES OF EMOTIONAL MEMORY

Bibliography

Ambrogi Lorenzini, C., Baldi, E., Bucherelli, C., Sacchetti, B., and Tassoni, G. (1999). Neural topography and chronology of memory consolidation: A review of functional inactivation findings. *Neurobiology of Learning and Memory 71* (1), 1–18.

Bermúdez-Rattoni, F., Introini-Collison, I. B., and McGaugh, J. L. (1991). Reversible inactivation of the insular cortex by tetrodotoxin produces retrograde and anterograde amnesia for inhibitory avoidance and spatial learning. *Proceedings of the National Academy of Sciences of the United States of America 88,* 5,379–5,382.

Cahill, L., and McGaugh, J. L. (1998). Mechanisms of emotional arousal and lasting declarative memory. *Trends in Neuroscience 21* (7), 294–299.

Cahill, L., McGaugh, J. L., Weinberger, N. M. (2001). The neurobiology of learning and memory: Some reminders to remember. *Trends in Neurosciences 24* (10), 578–581.

Cahill, L., Weinberger, N. M., Roozendaal, B., and McGaugh, J. L. (1999). Is the amygdala a locus of "conditioned fear"? Some questions and caveats. *Neuron 23,* 227–228.

Fanselow, M., and LeDoux, J. (1999). Why we think plasticity underlying Pavlovian fear conditioning occurs in the basolateral amygdala. *Neuron 23,* 229–232.

Gerard, R. W. (1961). The fixation of experience. In A. Fessard, R. W. Gerard, and J. Konorski, eds., *Brain mechanisms and learning: A symposium.* Springfield, IL: Thomas.

Gold, P. E. (1995). Modulation of emotional and non-emotional memories: Same pharmacological systems, different neuroanatomical systems. In J. L. McGaugh, N. M. Weinberger, and G. Lynch, eds., *Brain and memory: Modulation and mediation of neuroplasticity.* New York: Oxford University Press.

Izquierdo, I., Medina, J. H., and Barros, D. M. (1999). Separate mechanisms for short- and long-term memory. *Behavioural Brain Research 103* (1), 1–11.

Izquierdo, I., Quillfeldt, J. A., and Medina, J. H. (1997). Sequential role of hippocampus and amygdala, entorhinal cortex and parietal cortex in formation and retrieval of memory for inhibitory avoidance in rats. *European Journal of Neuroscience 9* (4), 786–793.

Koob, G. F. et al. (1991). Vasopressin and learning: Peripheral and central mechanisms. In R. Frederickson, J. L. McGaugh, and D. L. Felten, eds., *Peripheral signaling of the brain: Role in neural-immune interactions, learning and memory.* Toronto: Hogrefe and Huber.

Maren, S. (1999). Long-term potentiation in the amygdala: A mechanism for emotional learning and memory. *Trends in Neurosciences 22* (12), 561–567.

McGaugh, J. L. (1989). Dissociating learning and performance: Drug and hormone enhancement of memory storage. *Brain Research Bulletin 23,* 339–345.

——— (2000). Neuroscience: Memory—a century of consolidation. *Science 287* (5,451), 248–251.

McGaugh, J. L., Ferry, B., Vazdarjanova, A., and Roozendaal, B. (2000). Amygdala: Role in modulation of memory storage. In John P. Aggleton, ed., *The Amygdala: A functional analysis,* 2nd edition. London: Oxford University Press.

Mcintosh, A., and Gonzalez-Lima, F. (1998). Large-scale functional connectivity in associative learning: Interactions of the rat auditory, visual, and limbic systems. *Journal of Neurophysiology 80,* 3,148–3,162.

Mello e Souza, T., Vianna, M. R. M., and Izquierdo, I. (2000). Involvement of the medial precentral prefrontal cortex in memory consolidation for inhibitory avoidance learning in rats. *Pharmacology, Biochemistry, and Behavior 66* (3), 615–622.

Packard, M. G., and McGaugh, J. L. (1996). Inactivation of hippocampus or caudate nucleus with lidocaine differentially affects expression of place and response learning. *Neurobiology of Learning and Memory 65,* 65–72.

Parent, M. B., West, M., and McGaugh, J. L. (1994). Memory of rats with amygdala lesions induced thirty days after footshock-motivated escape training reflects degree of original training. *Behavioral Neuroscience 108* (6), 1,080–1,087.

Poremba, A., and Gabriel, M. (2001). Amygdala efferents initiate auditory thalamic discriminative training-induced neuronal activity. *Journal of Neuroscience 21* (1), 270–278.

Riekkinen Jr., P., Kuitunen, J., and Riekkinen, M. (1995). Effects of scopolamine infusions into the anterior and posterior cingulate on passive avoidance and water maze navigation. *Brain Research 685* (1–2), 46–54.

Roozendaal, B. (2000). Glucocorticoids and the regulation of memory consolidation. *Psychoneuroendocrinology 25* (3), 213–238.

Rose, S. P. (2000). God's organism? The chick as a model system for memory studies. *Learning and Memory 7* (1), 1–17.

Vazdarjanova, A. (2000). Does the basolateral amygdala store memories for emotional events? *Trends in Neurosciences 23* (8), 345.

Vazdarjanova, A., and McGaugh, J. L. (1998). Basolateral amygdala is not critical for cognitive memory of contextual fear conditioning. *Proceedings of the National Academy of Sciences of the United States of America 95,* 15,003– 15,007.

Wilensky, A. E., Schafe, G. E., and LeDoux, J. E. (2000). The amygdala modulates memory consolidation of fear-motivated inhibitory avoidance learning but not classical fear conditioning. *Journal of Neuroscience 20* (18), 7,059–7,066.

Zhang, Z. J., Berbos, T. G., and Wiley, R. G. (1996). Loss of nucleus basalis magnocellularis, but not septal, cholinergic neurons correlates with passive avoidance impairment in rats treated with 192-saporin. *Neuroscience Letters 203* (3), 214–218.

Almira Vazdarjanova

PAVLOV, IVAN (1849–1936)

The Russian physiologist Ivan Petrovich Pavlov is best known as the discoverer of the conditioned reflex. The life and work of this Nobel laureate is encapsulated in his motto, "Observation and observation!" His work had an enormous influence on psychology in general and on the theory of learning and memory in particular.

Early Life and Work

Pavlov evolved from a religious to a scientific framework. His ancestry tracex to an illiterate eighteenth-century serf known only by his first name, Pavel (Anokhin, 1949). Pavel's son gained emancipation and became a member of the clerical estate. During the next two generations, the family head rose through the religious hierarchy from church sexton to deacon. The deacon was able to provide a seminary education for his sons, who became ordained priests. Pavlov's father, Petr Dmitrievich, the youngest of these sons, was a priest in Riazan, an ancient town about 120 miles south of Moscow.

Petr Pavlov, as Windholz notes (1991), had a library of his own and transmitted to his son a love of knowledge. His advice to his children was that any book should be read at least twice in order not to miss anything important and to recall it more accurately; Ivan took this advice to heart throughout his scientific career. But he could not accept his father's position on some fundamental issues, including religious ones. "I had heated arguments with my father," Ivan wrote later, "which, because of my position, led to strong words and ended in serious disagreements" (Pavlov, 1952, p. 447). Windholz suggests that the main sources of discord were Pavlov's loss of faith by the time he entered the seminary in Riazan in 1864; he left before completing his studies there.

When, in 1870, Pavlov enrolled in natural sciences in the Faculty of Physics and Mathematics at St. Petersburg University, his father refused to support him financially. Yet his family unwittingly supported this important change by providing an intellectual oasis during Pavlov's seminary period. Windholz notes that, unlike most seminary students, "Pavlov lived in his parents' home, which gave him considerable freedom to pursue his own intellectual interests" by being "able to avoid the discipline imposed upon seminarians living in the dormitory and enjoy[ing] uninhibited reading in a small room over the family living quarters" (Windholz, 1991, p. 58).

An important book that the young seminarian may have read in that small room was Ivan Sechenov's *Reflexes of the Brain* (1866). Sechenov had had a brush with the government censor, who forced him to change his original title—*An Attempt to Place Psychical Processes on a Physiological Basis*—to a less provocative one (Koshotiants, 1945). The idea that the study of behavior can yield an objective account of subjective processes is nevertheless evident in Sechenov's work. This assumption was the basis Pavlov's method in psychology: the objective study of mental processes. In this method, the only restriction on "the levels of explanatory constructs that are used [is] that the evi-

Ivan Pavlov *(Hulton-Deutsch Collection/Corbis-Bettmann)*

dence concerning those constructs be stated in an objective or scientifically communicable way" (Furedy, Heslegrave, and Scher, 1984, p. 182). Thus there are no Watsonian or Skinnerian restrictions on the nature of theoretical concepts; the only restrictions pertain to the mode of evaluation of the inferences about those concepts.

Like Sechenov, Pavlov was a revolutionary thinker who was able to finesse his encounters with authority without surrendering on vital points or courting personal ruin. The ultimate testament of his political skill was his ability to run an active laboratory during Stalin's regime. By this time, he had achieved the pinnacle of scientific status for his work on the physiology of digestion (the Nobel Prize, 1904), and had turned to the study of the "psychic" salivary (digestive) reflex (i.e., Pavlovian conditioning). Yet Pavlov also showed courage in challenging authority and asserting his intellectual integrity. Horsley Gantt, a young American scientist who was a visiting member of Pavlov's laboratory in the 1920s, recounts that when, in 1926, the minister of education and head of the department that supported Pavlov's laboratory visited the site, Pavlov refused even to meet with him, much less show him the laboratory. His stated reason was that he disapproved of the minister's recent book, *The ABC of Communism* (Gantt, 1991, p. 68). The survival and subsequent success of Pavlov's laboratory in the wake of this political insolence suggests that he knew just how far he could go in challenging authority.

One mark of Pavlov's fame is that his name is attached to key psychological ideas. The term "Pavlovian response" usually refers to automatic, nonreflective, reflexlike reactions. (The "brainwashing" activities of the Chinese and the North Koreans in the 1950s were considered to be "Pavlovian." Orthodox Marxist writings in psychology during the same period in the Soviet Union paid lip service to "Pavlovian principles").

The Pavlovian notion of differing strengths in the nervous system, a concept that arose from Pavlov's study of experimental neurosis occurring from the breakdown of conditional discrimination in dogs, is of general interest for personality theory. In the West, Hans Eysenck's work on extroversion and introversion drew heavily on these Pavlovian concepts. The theoretical ideas and concepts are complex and go well beyond the observable data that Watson (1913) argued were the only proper subject matter of psychology.

Classical Conditioning

Pavlov's most important conceptual contribution, however, was in experimental psychology. His most influential concept is that of the conditional reflex, which Pavlov examined in an experimental preparation now known as "classical" or "Pavlovian" conditioning. In studying this form of learning, he presented canine subjects with food (the unconditional stimulus or US) that unconditionally elicited salivation (the unconditional response or UR) and with a bell (the conditional stimulus or CS) that originally did not elicit salivation. The CS, conditional on being paired repeatedly with the US, came to elicit salivation—a response termed the conditional reflex or response (CR). In Pavlov's view, the classical conditioning preparation was contrary to "subjective psychology [which] held that saliva flowed because the dog wished to receive a choice bit of meat" (Grigorian, 1974, p. 433). This sort of cognitive and purposive formulation is akin to interpretations of the Skinner-box bar press, in which the rat is said to press a bar "in order to get the food."

While the classical conditioning preparation had been widely known in experimental psychology since the early twenties, no body of systematic reports of Pavlovian dog-salivary conditioning was published in the journal literature of experimental psychology. Pavlov's methods were based on single-case studies, and the dependent-variable differences were reported quasi-anecdotally rather than with specified reliability in terms of the rules of statistical inference. Furthermore, his preparation is extremely difficult to work with. For example, the typical canine subject requires some three months of adaptation to the holding harness before the food reliably (i.e., unconditionally) elicits salivation rather than competing struggling behavior.

The first set of systematic and extensive experimental explorations of the phenomenon of classical conditioning employed the human eyelid conditioning preparation. In this arrangement, an air puff to the eye (or, in later versions, an infra-orbital shock) served as the US, a blink as the UR and CR, and (usually) a tone as the CS (conditional stimulus). In the 1950s and 1960s many of the most rigorous of these studies were reported in *Journal of Experimental Psychology,* the leading experimental psychological journal of the period.

Most of the authors of these eyelid conditioning reports subscribed to the then dominant stimulus-response (S-R) approach to learning espoused by theorists like C. L. Hull (Hull, 1943) and K. W. Spence (Spence, 1956). According to the S-R approach, only stimulus-response associations were learned. This position contrasted with the position of the cognitive, stimulus-stimulus (S-S) theorists, led by R. C. Tolman, who argued that learning also involved both the acquisition of sign-signicate relationships such as "cognitive maps" as well as the teleological explanatory concept of purpose (e.g., Tolman, 1932).

Applied to the phenomenon of classical conditioning—widely considered to be the simplest form of learning—the S-R approach implies that conditioning is the learning of the association between a stimulus (the CS) and a specific response (the CR). Accordingly, most of these eyelid-conditioning experimenters (who produced a considerable volume of experimental evidence on the Pavlovian conditioning phenomenon) were sensitive to independent variables like the temporal contiguity between CS and US and to the dependent-variable distinction between responses that were CRs and those that were not. The contiguity independent variable was the period between CS and US onsets, or the CS-US interval. The optimal CS-US interval was found to be slightly less than a half second. In the eyelid-conditioning preparation, moreover, CS-US intervals of two seconds or more produced no conditioning at all (i.e., no increase in CS-elicited blinks as a function of paired CS-US trials), even though it could hardly be argued that the undergraduate subjects did not learn the (cognitive) "relation" between the tone and the puff that followed two seconds after the tone. Concerning the distinction between CRs and non-CRs, the CS-elicited response latency measurement was also crucial: shorter-latency blinks (occurring within 150 milliseconds following CS onset) were found to decrease rather than increase as a function of repeated CS-US pairings. Hence, as a routine matter of scoring the data, only longer-latency blinks (the frequency of occurrence of which did increase as a function of CS-US pairings) were classified as CRs.

Influence on Other Researchers

In addition to its role in generating a body of empirical knowledge about human classical eyelid conditioning in experimental psychology, Pavlov's CR concept was also influential as a theoretical construct. The originator of American S-R behaviorism, J. B. Watson (e.g., Watson, 1913) attempted to account for all psychological learning phenomena in terms of the Pavlovian CR, being attracted by the "observable" feature of this response, in contrast with "unobservable" mental events. As Watson tackled more complex psychological functions such as thinking, the "observable" status of his explanatory constructs became more dubious. For example, his explanation of thinking was that it was due to very slight movements of the tongue, but when experimenters looked and could not observe these tongue movements, Watsonian behaviorists retorted that the tongue movements were too small to be measured.

The theoretical Pavlovian conditional response concept reappeared in the guise of the fractional anticipatory goal response in the theorizing of the S-R learning theorist Hull (1935) and Spence (1956). This hypothetical response was said to be learned through classical conditioning. It was invoked by S-R theorists from the 1930s until the 1960s to account, in S-R terms, for experimental results (mainly from "latent learning" studies) that Tolman and his S-S learning followers put forward as evidence for cognitive, sign-significate, S-S learning. Like the earlier Watsonian slight-tongue-movements construct, the testable or "observable" status of the fractional anticipatory goal response was doubtful. It was even described by one Hull-Spence S-R proponent as "incorporeal" (Moltz, 1957). A few years before this metaphysical qualifier was issued for this hypothetical Pavlovian CR, proponents of Tolman's S-S expectancy-theory position presciently complained that the construct was a deus ex machina used by S-R theorists to "smuggle" the concept of cognition into their purportedly S-R accounts (Meehl and MacCorquodale, 1953).

The decline of the S-R approach in psychology and the "paradigm shift" to the cognitive, S-S approach (Segal and Lachman, 1972) resulted in a radical change in psychologists' theoretical perspective. Consistent with the continuing "cognitive revolution" that began in the late 1960s, Pavlovian conditioning, both as a phenomenon and as an explanatory concept, is conceived in Tolman-like cognitive and purposive terms. According to R. A. Rescorla (the S-S "contingency" approach's most eminent current exponent) Pavlovian conditioning is now not just interpreted but "*described* [author's emphasis] as the learning of relations among events so as to allow the organism to represent its environment" (Rescorla, 1988, p. 151). It is interesting to compare this Tolman-like cognitive ("relations between events") and purposive ("so as to allow") formulation with the "subjective psychology" account cited above—which Pavlov opposed and which is contrary to the mechanistic accounts of conditioning proposed by S-R theorists.

The 1970s and 1980s also saw the near abandonment of the eyelid preparation as a means of studying the Pavlovian (response) conditioning phenomenon. While a more reliable form of the preparation—the rabbit nictitating membrane preparation—was developed in the 1960s, it has been used mainly as a technique to study the effects of physiological manipulations rather than the phenomenon of conditioning itself. Consideration of the CS-US interval has essentially disappeared: indeed, in the currently dominant Rescorla-Wagner (1972) model of Pavlovian conditioning, the CS-US interval does not appear as a parameter. Considering the fact that, as indicated above, the CS-US interval is crucial in preparations such as eyelid conditioning, this omission may seem strange. However, most of the evidence and experimental work of current cognitive S-S Pavlovian conditioners is based on preparations where conditioning is not measured directly through assessing the CR but indirectly through assessing the effect of the CS on some instrumental indicator behavior, as in the conditioned emotional response preparation. Such indicator-behavior preparations are more likely to suggest that Pavlovian conditioning, in line with what Pavlov characterized as "subjective psychology," is the learning of "relations between events" (i.e., cognitive, S-S learning of CS/US contingency) rather than the learning of responding (i.e., the CR) to the CS. Still, the Pavlovian emphasis on using behavior as the objectively observed dependent variable has been retained by both the S-R experimentalists and their cognitive, S-S oriented successors.

The Pavlovian Society

Perhaps Pavlov's most important contribution to psychology was to encourage interdisciplinary research on the organism as an integrated whole. This legacy has been sustained by the Pavlovian Society, an international organization founded in the United States in 1955 by Horsley Gantt, who, as noted above, worked in Pavlov's laboratory. The official journal of this society is titled *Integrative Behavioral and Physiolog-*

ical Science. The focus "interdisciplinary research on the integrated organism" is central for the Pavlovian Society (Steinmetz, 2001). It is distinct from other contemporary scientific and scientific-professional societies in its thoroughly apolitical and unusual oess-penn to discussion and debate (Furedy, 2001). The society's motto is Pavlov's "Observation and observation!" To its members, the motto means that the issues should be debated in the light of the observed evidence, not the political loyalties of the interlocutors.

Thus, in addition to the emphasis on interdisciplinary, integrated research, Pavlov's influence today stands for open discussion and the resistance to political pressures on scientific research.

See also: CONDITIONING, CLASSICAL AND INSTRUMENTAL

Bibliography

Anokhin, P. K. (1949). *Ivan Petrovich Pavlov: Zhizn, deiatel'nost i nauchnaia shkola.* Moscow and Leningrad: Izdatel'stvo Akademii Nauk SSSR.

Furedy, J. J. (2001). An epistemologically arrogance community of contending scholars: A pre-Socratic perspective on the past, present, and future of the Pavlovian Society. (Gantt memorial Lecture, October, 2000 meeting of the Pavlovian Society, Annapolis). *Integrative Physiuological and Behavioral Science 36,* 5–14.

Furedy, J. J., Heslegrave, R. J., and Scher, H. (1984). Psychophysiological and physiological aspects of T-wave amplitude in the objective study of behavior. *Pavlovian Journal of Biological Science 19,* 182–194.

Gantt, W. H. (1991). Ideas are the golden coins of science. *Integrative Physiological and Behavioral Science 26,* 68–73.

Grigorian, N. A. (1974). Pavlov, Ivan Petrovich. In *Dictionary of scientific biography,* Vol. 10. New York: Scribner.

Hull, C. L. (1931). Goal attraction and directing ideas conceived as habit phenomenon. *Psychological Review 38,* 487–505.

—— (1943). *Principles of behavior: An introduction to behavior theory.* New York: Appleton-Century-Crofts.

Koshotiants, K. S. (1950). *I. M. Sechenov.* Moscow: Izdatel'stvo Akademii Nauk SSSR.

MacCorquodale, K., and Meehl, P. (1953) Preliminary suggestions as to a formalization of expectancy theory. *Psychological Review 60,* 55–63.

Moltz, H. (1957). Latent extinction and the fractional anticipatory goal response. *Psychological Review 64,* 229–241.

Pavlov, I. P. (1952). Ivan Petrovich Pavlov (avtobiografiia). In *Polnoe sobranie sochinenii,* Vol. 6. Moscow and Leningrad: Akademii Nauk SSSR.

Rescorla, R. A. (1988). Pavlovian conditioning: It's not what you think it is. *American Psychologist 43,* 151–160.

Rescorla, R. A., and Wagner, A. R. (1972). A theory of Pavlovian conditioning: Variations in the effectiveness of reinforcement and nonreinforcement. In A. H. Black and W. F. Prokasy, eds., *Classical conditioning: Current theory and research.* New York: Appleton-Century-Crofts.

Sechenov, I. (1866). *Refleksy golovnogo mozga.* St. Petersburg: Tipographiia A. Golovachova.

Segal, E. M., and Lachman, R. (1972). Complex behavior or higher mental process: Is there a paradigm shift? *American Psychologist 27,* 46–55.

Spence, K. W. (1956). *Behavior theory and conditioning.* New Haven, CT: Yale University Press.

Steinmetz, J. (2001). An editorial: A continuing commitment to the interdisciplinary research on the integrated organism. *Integrative Physiological and Behavioral Science 36,* 3–4.

Tolman, E. C. (1932). *Purposive behavior in animals and men.* New York: Appleton-Century.

Watson, J. B. (1913). Psychology as the behaviorist views it. *Psychological Review 20,* 158–177.

Windholz, G. (1991). I. P. Pavlov as a youth. *Integrative Physiological and Behavioral Science 26,* 51–67.

John J. Furedy

PERCEPTION

See: DISCRIMINATION AND GENERALIZATION

PHARMACOLOGICAL TREATMENT OF MEMORY DEFICITS

Everyone experiences occasional memory lapses, which are often termed *senior moments* by those older than they care to be. While a frequent source of complaint, such events are generally not cause for worry. However, there are diseases that can cause much more profound and debilitating memory impairment. The most commonly recognized illness that causes memory loss is Alzheimer's disease (AD). In addition, other neurodegenerative diseases, such as Parkinson's, Huntington's and Pick's disease, include memory problems among their symptoms. Vascular disorders and stroke are common causes of memory impairment in the elderly. There is also a rapidly growing population of otherwise healthy elderly people who develop memory problems that are severe enough to interfere with their everyday lives. While these conditions are most commonly seen in the aged, many young people with depression or schizophrenia, or who suffer from AIDS, also experience impaired memory. All of these people could potentially benefit from drug therapies that would relieve memory deficits.

Many treatments for ailing memory, both pharmacological and nonpharmacological have been described. However, no drug has been discovered that is overwhelmingly effective in improving memory. A major reason for this is that there are different types of memory, each of which engages, at least to some degree, different brain regions. Similarly, while the biochemical mechanisms required for memory formation are not completely understood, there is evidence indicating that more than one system is involved. This suggests that different drugs will be needed to treat the memory impairments that arise from different illnesses. In practice, the problem is compounded by the possibility that different stages of a disease may have different underlying causes, and by situations where more than one disease is present. For example, Alzheimer's disease can be categorized as mild, moderate, or severe, and some patients with AD also have Parkinson's disease or vascular dementia; each of these situations may require a different drug, or different amounts of the same drug, to be treated effectively. Thus, in order to show that a drug with only modest activity is effective, it is important to test the drug under controlled conditions that include a uniform patient population. In addition, double-blind trials comparing placebo against active drug are essential for objective evaluation of a drug candidate because placebo effects are relatively common in memory studies.

Prescription Drugs to Treat Memory Impairment

Drugs that are currently available to treat memory impairments can be divided into two broad classes, according to whether a physician's prescription is necessary to obtain them. Prescription drugs have had to meet defined standards of safety and must be shown to be effective to treat a particular condition. In the United States, the Food and Drug Administration (FDA) currently recognizes only AD and, more recently (summer of 2001), mild cognitive impairment as indications for memory enhancing treatment. All currently marketed prescription drugs for memory improvement have shown statistically significant results in AD patients. However, while the effects of these compounds were significant in controlled trials, in actual practice they have generally been meager. The disappointing results of these drugs could be because their mechanism of action is not an effective way to enhance memory. More likely, the poor outcome results from variability in the real-world patient population. An additional problem is that currently available drugs do not treat the cause of the illness, so memory in AD patients is continually getting worse. It may be that existing drugs would be more effective for treating people with less severe, or more slowly deteriorating, memory impairments.

Compounds that act to inhibit acetylcholinesterase dominate the group of currently available therapeutics to treat memory impairment in AD. This enzyme degrades acetylcholine, a neurotransmitter used by a population of neurons that degenerates in the early stages of the disease. The rationale for the development of acetylcholinesterase inhibitors is that they would strengthen and prolong the weakened signals sent by remaining cholinergic neurons in the brain of AD patients. A problem with this approach is that acetylcholine is also used as a neurotransmitter in the neuromuscular and autonomic nervous sys-

tems. Overactivation of these latter systems induces profound side effects, including nausea, vomiting, diarrhea and dizziness, and thus limiting the useful dose range of anticholinesterase drugs.

Cognex(r) (tacrine and tetrahydroacridine) became the first FDA-approved treatment for AD in 1993. Unfortunately, its mild memory enhancing properties were more than offset by the need to dose four times per day and problems with toxicity that required regular monitoring of liver function. When Aricept(r) (donepezil) became available in 1997, its superior safety margin and longer half-life (once-a-day dosing) allowed it to quickly supplant Cognex(r) as the preferred therapy for AD. At the beginning of 2002, Aricept(r) remains the most-used agent in its class. Two more recently available anticholinesterase compounds are Exelon(r) (rivastigmine; 1998) and Reminyl(r) (galanthamine; 2000). In addition to inhibiting acetylcholinesterase, Reminyl(r) is described as acting on brain nicotinic cholinergic receptor to enhance neurotransmitter release. It is not yet clear whether this action gives Reminyl(r) memory-improving properties that are superior to other acetylcholinesterase inhibitors.

Two other prescription drugs are marketed for the treatment of memory impairments, but these agents have not been approved by the FDA and so are not currently available in the United States. The first of these is Alcar(r) (acetyl-l-carnitine), which was first introduced in Italy in 1985; its mechanism of action seems, like that of the acetylcholinesterase inhibitors described above, also to involve enhancing cholinergic neurotransmission in the brain. However, the effect appears to be achieved by elevating levels of *nerve growth factor* (NGF), a neurotrophin that is critical to maintaining the survival and normal functioning of cholinergic neurons. (NGF administration is being explored as a therapy in its own right.) Akatinol(r) (memantine), first available in Germany in 1982, is different from all of the previously discussed drugs in that its primary action does not appear to involve cholinergic neurons. Akatinol(r) interacts in a complex way with glutamate-mediated neurotransmission, the most important excitatory system in the brain. Overactivation of glutamate receptors, particularly those of the NMDA (n-methyl-d-aspartate) type, leads to neuronal death. Akatinol(r) acts as an antagonist to prevent this overactivation, yet seems not to interfere with normal synaptic function. At this point it is not possible to compare the efficacy of Alcar(r) or Akatinol(r) to marketed anticholinesterase drugs, but observations based upon the long existing period of clinical experience suggest that neither drug will turn out to be a substantially better memory enhancer.

Nonprescription Drugs to Treat Memory Impairment

In addition to prescription drugs, a large number of over-the-counter agents are advertised as benefiting memory. Many nonprescription memory boosters are formulations containing several compounds. While it is not possible to discuss all of these compounds individually, some of them deserve mention. Huperzine A is a potent acetylcholinesterase inhibitor that is derived from a particular type of club moss and sold as a dietary supplement for memory loss and mental impairment. While Huperzine A has been shown to be an effective memory enhancer, its side effects are identical to other anticholinesterase drugs. In contrast to the agents that will be described in the remainder of this section, there are substantial risks associated with the use of Huperzine A.

Extracts from leaves of the *Ginkgo biloba* tree have been shown to improve memory in several studies of healthy volunteers and patients with dementia. How Ginkgo works is not entirely clear, but it seems to involve a combination of effects including increasing cerebral blood flow and antioxidant action. The latter reduces or prevents neuronal damage caused by the generation of chemical-free radical species. The active agents in Ginkgo extracts have not been completely characterized, and the extraction procedure is not standardized, so it is likely that currently marketed products have varying effectiveness. Two compounds derived from the ergot fungus, hydergine and nicergoline, share the enhancement of cerebral circulation that has been described for Ginkgo extracts. Both hydergine and nicergoline have shown some beneficial effects in treating memory impairments, but the compounds have not been evaluated as rigorously as Ginkgo.

Compounds that enhance learning and memory by an undefined mechanism are often termed *nootropics*. Although there are many agents that could be called nootropic, the name is most often applied to piracetam and its relatives: aniracetam, oxiracetam, and pramiracetam. Memory-enhancing effects of piracetam in animals were first described in the late 1960s. In the intervening years these drugs have been used to treat many conditions with memory impairment, including AD, but no convincing improvements have been described. Another nootropic, idebenone, shares a similar history.

A final compound of note is vitamin E. Low serum levels of vitamin E have been correlated with memory impairments. In addition, a high dose of vitamin E has been shown to be effective in slowing cognitive deterioration in AD patients. Vitamin E has antioxidant properties, so its beneficial properties are ascribed to reducing free radical damage. It is likely that vitamin E will not be shown to be particularly effective at improving memory; rather, its use seems better suited to protect against age- or disease-related memory impairments.

Conclusion

In the 1990s, a significant breakthrough in the treatment of memory disorders occurred with FDA approval of several acetylcholinesterase inhibitors for symptomatic treatment of AD. Although the currently marketed drugs are only modestly effective, they have refocused attention on the problem of memory impairment and the possibility that it can be treated. This, in turn, has provided a strong stimulus for research to develop more useful pharmacological treatments for memory impairment. Several promising drugs are currently undergoing clinical trials, and it is likely that substantial advances in the treatment of memory deficits will take place before 2010.

See also: ALZHEIMER'S DISEASE: BEHAVIORAL ASPECTS; ALZHEIMER'S DISEASE: HUMAN DISEASE AND THE GENETICALLY ENGINEERED ANIMAL MODELS; COGNITIVE ENHANCERS

Bibliography

Bai, D. L., Tang, X. C., and He, X. C. (2000). Huperzine A, a potential therapeutic agent for treatment of Alzheimer's disease. *Current Medicinal Chemistry* 7 (3), 355–374.

Fioravanti, M., and Flicker, L. (2001). Efficacy of nicergoline in dementia and other age associated forms of cognitive impairment (Cochrane Review). *Cochrane Database of Systematic Reviews 4*, CD003159.

Flicker, L., and Grimley Evans, G. (2001). Piracetam for dementia or cognitive impairment (Cochrane Review). *Cochrane Database of Systematic Reviews 2*, CD001011.

Gillis, J. C., Benefield, P., and McTavish, D. (1994). Idebenone. A review of its pharmacodynamic and pharmacokinetic properties, and therapeutic use in age-related cognitive disorders. *Drugs and Aging 5* (2), 133–152.

Giovanello, K. S., and Verfaellie, M. (2001). Memory systems of the brain: A cognitive neuropsychological analysis. *Seminars in Speech and Language 22* (2), 107–116.

Olin, J., Schneider, L., Novit, A., and Luczak, S. (2001). Hydergine for dementia (Cochrane Review). *Cochrane Database of Systematic Reviews 2*, CD000359.

Perkins, A. J., Hendrie, H. C., Callahan, C. M., Gao, S., Unverzagt, F. W., Xu, Y., Hall, K. S., and Hui, S. L. (1999). Association of antioxidants with memory in a multiethnic elderly sample using the third national health and nutrition examination survey. *American Journal of Epidemiology 150* (1), 37–44.

Salvioli, G., and Neri, M. (1994). L-acetylcarnitine treatment of mental decline in the elderly. *Drugs Under Experimental and Clinical Research 20* (4), 169–176.

Sano, M., Ernesto, C., Thomas, R. G., Klauber, M. R., Schafer, K., Grundman, M., Woodbury, P., Growdon, J., Cotman, C. W., Pfeiffer, E., Schneider, L. S., and Thal, L. J. (1997). A controlled trial of selegiline, alpha-tocopherol, or both as treatment for Alzheimer's disease. The Alzheimer's Disease Cooperative Study. *New England Journal of Medicine 336* (17), 1,216–1,222.

Sramek, J. J., Veroff, A. E., and Cutler, N. R. (2001). The status of ongoing trials for mild cognitive impairment. *Expert Opinion on Investigational Drugs 10* (4), 741–752.

Wettstein, A. (2000). Cholinesterase inhibitors and Ginkgo extracts—are they comparable in the treatment of dementia? Comparison of published placebo-controlled efficacy studies of at least six months' duration. *Phytomedicine 6* (6), 393–401.

Winblad, B., and Poritis, N. (1999). Memantine in severe dementia: Results of the 9M-Best Study (Benefit and efficacy in severely demented patients during treatment with memantine). *International Journal of Geriatric Psychiatry 14* (2), 135–146.

Zurad, E. G. (2001). New treatments for Alzheimer's disease: A review. *Drug Benefit Trends 13*, 27–40.

Gregory M. Rose

PHOBIAS

Phobias are intense, persistent, unadaptive fears that are irrational/excessive. They are commonly classified into three groups: *complex phobias*, including agoraphobia (fear of public places, travel); *social phobias* (fear of social situations/scrutiny); and *circumscribed phobias,* including intense fears of insects, animals, heights, and enclosed spaces.

There are biological contributions to the development of some phobias, but the main determinants appear to be learned. Three main pathways to the acquisition of phobias have been identified. The conditioning acquisition of a phobia results from exposure to a traumatic stimulation or from repeated exposures to aversive sensitizing conditions. The second pathway is vicarious acquisition: direct or indirect observations of people, or of other animals, displaying fear. Among humans the transmission of fear-inducing verbal information is the third pathway. For a considerable time, explanations of the acquisition of phobias were dominated by the conditioning theory, which emphasized the importance of exposure to traumatic stimulation; recognition that fears can be acquired vicariously and/or by the direct transmission of information has led to a fuller account of the causes of phobias.

Important advances have been made in our ability to reduce phobias. Under controlled conditions, it is now possible to produce substantial and lasting reductions of phobias within a few sessions. It requires greater effort and far more time to reduce the complex and intense phobias, such as agoraphobia, but even these respond moderately well to treatment programs. There have been several attempts to explain how and when these methods of fear reduction achieve their effects, but each explanation has limitations.

Despite the many opportunities and circumstances in which phobias might develop, people acquire comparatively few; a satisfactory explanation of phobias must accommodate this fact as well as the appearance of phobias in a significant minority of the human population. It has also become apparent that people are more resilient than most psychologists have implied. Phobic patients who behave courageously during the course of treatment and soldiers who perform dangerous acts are notable examples of resilience.

Causes

The major features of the conditioning theory of phobias are as follows. Fears are acquired by a process of conditioning. Neutral stimuli that often are associated with a fear-producing or pain-producing state of affairs develop fearful qualities. They become conditioned phobic stimuli. The strength of the phobia is determined by the number of repetitions of the association between the pain/fear experienced and the stimuli, and by the intensity of the pain or fear experienced in the presence of the stimuli. Stimuli that resemble the fear-evoking ones also acquire phobic properties; that is, they become secondary conditioned stimuli. The likelihood of a phobia's developing is increased by confinement, by exposure to intensely painful or frightening situations, and by frequent associations between the new conditioned stimulus and the pain/fear. In an important extension, it has also been proposed that once objects or situations acquire phobic qualities, they develop motivating properties. A secondary fear drive emerges. Behavior that successfully reduces fear, notably avoidance behavior, will increase in strength.

Supporting evidence for the theory was drawn from six sources: research on the induction of fear in laboratory animals, the development of anxiety states in combat soldiers, experiments on the induction of fear in a small number of children, clinical observations (e.g., dental phobias), incidental findings from the use of aversion therapy, and a few experiments on the effects of traumatic stimulation.

The strongest and most systematic evidence was drawn from a multitude of experiments on laboratory animals. It is easy to generate conditioned fear reactions in animals by exposing them to a conjunction of neutral and aversive stimuli, usually electric shock. These fear reactions can be intense and persistent. Phobias can result from traumatic experiences in combat. In clinical practice, it is not uncommon for patients to give an account of the development of their phobias that can be construed in conditioning terms, and sometimes they can date the onset of the phobias to a specific conditioning experience (e.g., Lautch, 1971, on thirty-four cases of dental phobia).

Di Nardo et al. (1988) found that nearly two-thirds of their subjects who were phobic toward dogs had experienced a conditioning event in which a dog featured, and in over half the dog had inflicted pain. It is important, however, that over two-thirds of a comparable group of subjects who were not frightened of dogs reported that they, too, had experienced a conditioning event, and that in over half of these instances the animal had inflicted pain.

These reports provide some support for the conditioning theory but also illustrate the fact that conditioning experiences, even those of a painful nature, do not necessarily give rise to a phobia or even to fear. Here, as in other instances, there was less fear than an unqualified conditioning theory would lead us to expect. Presumably the people who experienced conditioning events but failed to acquire a fear or phobia were "protected" by a history of harmless contacts with dogs. The roles that phobic patients attribute to direct and indirect experiences in generating their phobias differ with the content of the phobia, and of course the accuracy of their reports cannot be assured. In their analysis of 183 phobic patients, divided into six groups. Ost and Hugdahl (1985) found a range of attributions. For example, 88 percent of the agoraphobic patients attributed the onset of the phobia to a conditioning experience, but only 50 percent of those who were frightened of animals attributed the onset of their phobias to such an experience. Among the animal phobics, 40 percent traced the origin of the phobia to indirect experiences; such attribution was uncommon among the agoraphobics.

Although the importance of the phenomenon of acquired food aversions was not made evident until 1966, it is sometimes used to buttress the conditioning theory. The findings on this aversion also served to prompt radical rethinking of the concept of conditioning. Garcia and his colleagues were the first to demonstrate that strong and lasting aversive reactions can be acquired with ease when the appropriate food stimulus is associated with illness, even if the illness occurs many hours after eating (Garcia, Ervin, and Koelling, 1966). Given that the genesis of food aversions is a form of conditioning, if we also allow an equation between the acquisition of a food aversion and the acquisition of a fear, this phenomenon may have a bearing on the effect of the phobias.

If the acquisition of aversions is used to support the conditioning theory of phobias, it will have to take into account the temporal stretch of the phenomenon—that is, the delay that can intervene between the tasting of the food and the onset of the illness. Classical conditioning is expedited by temporal proximity between the stimuli, but food aversions can be easily and rapidly established even when there are long delays between the events. Hence, if the food aversion phenomenon provides support for a new or a revised conditioning theory of phobias, the temporal qualities of the conditioning processes must be deemphasized.

There are various arguments against acceptance of the conditioning theory of phobias as a comprehensive explanation. People fail to acquire phobias in what should be fear-conditioning situations, such as air raids. It is difficult to produce stable phobic or fear reactions in human subjects even under controlled laboratory conditions. The theory rests on the untenable equipotentiality premise (Seligman, 1972). The distribution of fears and phobias in normal and neurotic populations is difficult to reconcile with the theory. A significant number of people with phobias recount histories that cannot be accommodated by the theory. We also know that fears and phobias can be acquired vicariously, and that fears can be acquired by the reception of threatening verbal information. Fears, and possibly phobias as well, can be acquired even when the causal events are temporally separated (see Rachman, 1990).

Neoconditioning Concepts

The traditional insistence on the contiguity of the conditioned stimulus and the unconditioned stimulus as a necessary condition for the establishment of a conditioned response is mistaken. Rescorla has observed that "although conditioning can sometimes be slow, in fact most modern conditioning preparations routinely show rapid learning. One trial learning is not confined to flavor-aversion" (1988, p. 154). Apparently the associative span of animals "is capable of bridging long temporal intervals" (Mackintosh, 1983, p. 172). However, the learning must be selective; otherwise, animals would collect what Mackintosh has referred to as a "useless clutter of irrelevant associations." According to Mackintosh, the functioning of conditioning is to allow organisms to discover "probable causes of events of significance."

Given this new view, that conditioning is far more flexible and wide-ranging than was previously supposed, many of the objections to the conditioning theory of fear and phobias are weakened or eliminated. Although the application of neoconditioning concepts can shore up the conditioning theory, at the present stage the new view is too liberal. It lacks limits, and there is little left to disallow. In theory, almost any stimulus can become a conditioned signal for fear; but in practice people develop comparatively few phobias, and those we do acquire are confined to a limited range of stimuli. Phobias are not normally distributed.

Several sources of evidence suggest that phobias and fears can be acquired vicariously. Reports given by phobic patients, wartime observations, correlations between the phobias displayed by parents and children, laboratory demonstrations of conditioned fears, and research on animals have all provided some support for this view.

Verbal information can also generate a fear, and it is possible that in limited circumstances, it can even induce a phobia. Clinical evidence, especially that accumulating on the nature of panic disorders, suggests that phobias can be generated by information that is slightly or not at all threatening but is catastrophically misinterpreted by the recipient as being threatening.

Biological Determinants

The nonrandom distribution of human phobias, the high incidence of phobias of snakes and spiders and the low incidence of fears/phobias of motor travel, the remarkable speed with which certain objects can be transformed into objects of fear, and the common occurrence of irrational fears all point to the operation of nonlearned processes in the acquisition of fears and phobias. The main explanations fall into two classes: Some human fears and phobias are innately determined, or people are innately disposed rapidly to acquire phobias of certain specifiable objects or situations.

The most influential explanation is that set out by Martin Seligman, who argued, "The great majority of phobias are about objects of natural importance to the survival of the species . . . (human phobias are largely restricted to objects that have threatened survival, potential predators, unfamiliar places, and the dark)" (1972, p. 450). He postulates that certain kinds of fears are readily acquired because of an inherited biological preparedness. These phobias are highly prepared to be learned and, like other highly prepared relationships, "they are selective and resistant to extinction, and probably non-cognitive" (1972, p. 455).

The main features of prepared phobias are that they are very easily acquired (even by watered-down representations of the actual threat), selective, stable, biologically significant, and probably noncognitive. After some encouraging early laboratory demonstrations of fear preparedness in human subjects, subsequent research was disappointing because the phenomenon appeared to be too fragile. The laboratory effects appeared to be weak, transient, and difficult to reproduce. The plausibility of the concept has been weakened but not seriously damaged, and more powerful stimuli and more appropriate measures of fear responding are needed before the theory can be subjected to rigorous testing. The demonstration of preparedness in the development of phobias among laboratory monkeys encourages the belief that Seligman's theory retains considerable value. Mineka (1988) has shown that the fears induced in monkeys in laboratory conditions are intense, vivid, and lasting. The animals readily developed fears of snakes but showed little or no propensity to develop fears of biologically insignificant stimuli such as flowers.

Fear Reduction

Three powerful and dependable methods for reducing fear have been developed since the 1970s: desensitization, flooding, and therapeutic modeling. The common element in all three methods is the repeated and/or prolonged exposure of the fearful person to the stimulus or situation that provokes the fear (the exposure method). The selection of the appropriate fear-reducing technique depends on the nature of the phobia and the preference of the fearful subject, but all three methods are reliably robust. Fears of circumscribed stimuli, such as snakes or spiders, can be reduced fairly rapidly, even if they are intense and well established. The reduction or elimination of more complex fears, such as agoraphobia, requires greater effort and time. Despite these important practical advances, there still is no widely accepted explanation for the effects of these techniques.

See also: BEHAVIOR THERAPY; CONDITIONING, CLASSICAL AND INSTRUMENTAL; OBSERVATIONAL LEARNING; TASTE AVERSION AND PREFERENCE LEARNING IN ANIMALS

Bibliography

Di Nardo, P. A., Guzy, L. T., Jenkins, J. A., Bak, R. M., Tomasi, S. F., and Copland, M. (1988). Etiology and maintenance of dog fears. *Behaviour Research and Therapy 26*, 245–252.

Garcia, J., Ervin, F., and Koelling, R. (1966). Learning with prolonged delay of reinforcement. *Psychonomic Science 5*, 121–122.

Lautch, H. (1971). Dental phobia. *British Journal of Psychiatry 119*, 151–158.

Mackintosh, N. J. (1983). *Conditioning and associative learning.* New York: Oxford University Press.

Mineka, S. (1988). A primate model of phobic fears. In H. Eysenck and I. Martin, eds., *Theoretical foundations of behaviour therapy.* New York: Plenum Press.

Ost, L. G., and Hugdahl, K. (1985). Acquisition of blood and dental phobia and anxiety response patterns in clinical patients. *Behaviour Research and Therapy 23*, 27–34.

Rachman, S. J. (1990). *Fear and courage,* 2nd edition. New York: W. H. Freeman.

Rescorla, R. A. (1988). Pavlovian conditioning. *American Psychologist 43*, 151–160.

Seligman, M. E. P. (1972). Phobias and preparedness. *Behavior Therapy 2*, 307–320.

Stanley J. Rachman

Jean Piaget *(Psychology Archives, University of Akron)*

PHOTOGRAPHIC MEMORY

See: EIDETIC IMAGERY

PIAGET, JEAN (1896–1980)

Together with Sigmund Freud and B. F. Skinner, Jean Piaget (1896–1980) was one of the three most influential psychologists of the twentieth century. Among developmental psychologists he has had no equal or close second as to the volume, scope, and impact of his work. Yet he thought of his psychological work primarily as a tool for the creation of a new science, genetic epistemology—a new synthesis of logic, philosophy, history of science, biology, and psychology.

Life and Oeuvre

Piaget was born on August 9, 1896, in Neuchâtel, Switzerland, and died in Geneva, on September 17, 1980. His father, Arthur Piaget, was a historian. Jean's first publication, a paragraph about sighting an albino sparrow, appeared in 1907, when he was 11 years old. He was active until the end of his life, and posthumous monographs continued to appear until 1990. The total oeuvre comprises over sixty books and monographs plus nearly a thousand articles.

During his long life Piaget held professorships at the University of Paris and at the Swiss universities of Neuchâtel, Lausanne, and Geneva. The chairs he held were in psychology, sociology, and the history and philosophy of science. His longest association was with the University of Geneva. Among his many honors were over thirty honorary doctorates from major universities (the first from Harvard, 1936) in a dozen countries; numerous awards, including the Distinguished Scientific Contribution Award of the American Psychological Association (1970); and the presidency of various scientific associations. For many years he was director of the International Bureau of Education. His wife, Valentine Chatenay Piaget, was among his collaborators in the research for his first few books, and especially in the study of their three babies.

As an adolescent Piaget pursued malacology, the study of mollusks, and reached a professional level, publishing thirty-two papers in this field by 1916, his twentieth year. He continued this line of work in natural history for the rest of his life.

In 1918 Piaget received his doctorate in natural science from the University of Neuchâtel for a dissertation on the mollusks of the Valais, a region of Switzerland. By that time he had begun to move toward the study of psychology, which he pursued in Zurich and in Paris. In 1921 he published his first article on child logic and thought, a subject that grew to dominate his thinking throughout his later life.

Egocentrism

Piaget's first book in psychology, *The Language and Thought of the Child,* appeared in 1923. In it he introduced his conception of egocentrism, interpreting the world from one's own immediate perspective without adequately taking into account the existence of alternative perspectives. In three subsequent books during the 1920s Piaget showed how this egocentrism pervades the child's mentality from about the age of 5 to 10 in the domains of logic and reasoning, causal thinking, conceptions of the world, and (not published until 1932) moral judgment.

All of these works can be construed as studies of learning in a wide sense, since through its interaction with the world, the child's intelligence develops: Moving through several necessary stages, the child learns to think more and more like an adult. The same can be said of the trilogy Piaget wrote about his own three children in the first two years of life. These works, using the method of naturalistic observation, delineate the major stages in (a) the development of active, intelligent, inventive exploration of the world; (b) the child's own activity in the construction of reality (the permanent object, space, time, and causality); and (c) the emergence of language and the symbolic or representational function through play, dreams, and imitation.

Assimilation and Accommodation

In the course of his work on infant development, Piaget introduced the twin concepts of assimilation and accommodation as tools for understanding cognitive growth. The infant is born with a few basic reflexes. Through its own activity novelties arise (for example, through the chance coincidence of events) that are assimilated into these initial schemes, giving rise to changing schemes of action. These schemes can assimilate external events or stimuli and, equally important, they can assimilate each other, giving rise to new adaptive organizations. Paired with the process of assimilation is that of accommodation, the way in which the set of schemes or cognitive organizations must change in response to the new inputs ("aliments," as Piaget sometimes called them, emphasizing the digestion metaphor).

Toward the end of the first year of life, as the child repeats its actions in order to make interesting events recur (e.g., the noise of a rattle), it notices variations in its own actions and their consequences. These variations and their consequences are, in their turn, assimilated into existing schemes, and thus these schemes grow. Piaget considered this analysis of infant cognitive growth to be germane to his analysis and descriptions of the growth of thought at other levels, including the history of science.

Stages of Development

In the 1930s and 1940s Piaget's main focus was on the stagewise progression of intelligence in infancy and childhood. He elaborated his idea of three great periods of intellectual growth: sensorimotor (0–2 years), preoperational (2–6 or 7 years), and concrete operational (7–11 or 12 years). In the 1950s, this model was expanded to include adolescent cognitive development in the period of formal operations.

Genetic Epistemology

In the late 1940s Piaget displayed increasing preoccupation with the further elaboration of ideas long held, the approach that has become known as *genetic epistemology*. Some of the most important components of this approach had been sketched in his religious prose poem *La mission de l'idée* (1915) and in his philosophical novel *Recherche* (1918).

This phase was most fully expressed in Piaget's three-volume work *Introduction à l'epistémologie génétique* (1950). In 1956 he organized the Centre International de l'Epistémologie Génétique, an interdisciplinary center for research and reflection on questions concerning the intersection of the natural sciences, psychology (especially developmental), and philosophy (especially epistemology). Rather than becoming a philosopher, Piaget hoped to transform one branch of philosophy, epistemology, into a new science. In 1957, the Centre turned its attention to the study of learning—both logical models of the learning process and the learning and development of logical reasoning by the child. Piaget and his collaborators published their theoretical and empirical findings in four monographs (1959).

Equilibration Model

In the 1960s and 1970s, without dropping any of his previous concerns, Piaget turned his attention to elaborating the "equilibration model," an attempt to specify the actual mechanisms by which intellectual growth and change come about.

Alternative Theoretical Approaches

Throughout his life Piaget was interested in the contrast between his own theoretical approach and two others. He was quite drawn toward Gestalt psychology, especially its emphasis on holism and self-regulating systems; but in the end he rejected it as relying too heavily on the analogy between perception and thought, and being consequently nondevelopmental. He was never drawn toward behaviorism (or its antecedent, associationism); he objected to the lack of any intrinsic structure in knowledge accrued as an arbitrary collection of chance associations. He summed all this up in a favorite aphorism: Gestalt psychology speaks of structure without development; behaviorism, of development without structure.

Method

Piaget relied mainly on two related methods for the exploration of the child's intellect. For his trilogy on the origins of intellect in babies, and also for his earlier *Language and Thought in the Child*, he relied on naturalistic observation. For most of his work, however, he stuck to the "clinical method" of extended interaction between child and investigator, with searching analysis of the protocols (i.e., of what the child said and did in reaction to the problems posed by the adult). The clinical method evolved into something approaching naturalistic observation in problem-solving situations. The problems were not construed as tasks having definite solutions to be sought by the child, but as occasions to provoke thought in the child, thus permitting the experimenter to observe the child's way of thinking.

Using different age groups, these methods permitted the study of the broad trajectory of cognitive development. By avoiding narrower experimental approaches, Piaget sacrificed the opportunity for what might be called microscopic analysis of the effects of specifiable variables on cognitive functioning. What he gained was a better picture of child mentality as a whole—first as a system of beliefs and later as a structured group of operations.

Development, Learning, and Structure

Although the development of cognition as depicted by Piaget resembles what other psychologists might call "learning," there are a number of important differences. First, changes in performance are seen as a function of developmental stage, not of repeated exposures and responses to the same stimulus. Second, the investigator analyzes broad strategic changes in approach rather than the correctness and incorrectness of solutions or memories. Third, what accrues over time is not a sum of associations but operative structures; thus, for Piaget the older subject does not necessarily know "more" than the younger but knows differently.

For Piaget a structure is not the momentarily given perceptual configuration of interest to Gestalt psychologists. A mental structure is a set of logicomathematical operations or mental acts, permitting the decomposition of wholes into parts and the recomposition of wholes from parts. To take a very simple example, the idea of the permanent object entails the recognition of the continued existence of an object as it moves around in space—the movements AB + BC → AC, the movements AB + BA → 0. Thus, the idea of the permanent object is an embodiment of the group of displacements.

Conservation of Matter

In a key and famous illustration of the mentality of the concrete operational child, Piaget discovered that the young child does not understand that a given amount of matter remains the same under transformations of shape; thus, if water is poured from a short, wide vessel into a long, thin tube, the child may believe that as the water level mounts higher and higher, the amount of water increases. The weight of experimental evidence shows that the child is relatively unaffected by repeated exposures to this event, because it can always map the results of direct observations onto the preexisting schema. The argument

of reversibility—if the water is poured back into the first container, it regains the original level—will be a satisfying demonstration of conservation for the older child. The young child watching, or even pouring, the liquid can actually *see* the level mounting or falling but, because attention is centered on one dimension, does not yet grasp the idea of conservation that would lead to the coordination of changes of length and width.

In other words, direct teaching or learning is relatively ineffectual in modifying the growth of fundamental cognitive categories and operations, because these depend on the protracted, often slow, development of the knowing system as a whole through the self-regulated activity of that knowing system.

Memory

From 1921, when he published his first empirical study of child development, until the 1960s, Piaget did virtually no work on memory. A possible exception was his use of tasks involving memory but focusing on other problems. For example, in 1923, in *Language and Thought of the Child*, Piaget studied the way in which a child who has just been told a story repeats it to another child. This work could be considered a study of memory, but Piaget's interest was in the relation between the first child's comprehension of the story and the communication from the first child to the second. He was aware of the involvement of memory in this task but thought he could distinguish errors of memory from those of comprehension and communication. In his later work he took a very different tack, emphasizing the effect of changes in comprehension on memory.

For the most part, during a very long period Piaget's interest lay primarily in the general operations and structures of mental activity rather than in the contents of experience or the stuff of thought. But in a wider perspective Piaget believed that growth comes about through interaction with the world, and that this world must somehow be represented in the child's mind (and consequently in Piaget's theory). About 1942, Piaget began a systematic study of what he called the "figurative" aspects of thought—perception, imagery, and memory—was contrasted with the "operative" aspects of mental activity. By far the largest part of this effort was centered on the study of perception: some sixty experimental papers, brought together in *The Mechanisms of Perception* (1969). But he also studied mental imagery, which resulted in yet another volume, *Mental Imagery in the Child: A Study of the Development of Imaginal Representation* (Piaget and Inhelder, 1971).

The work on imagery led on to work on memory, resulting in the book *Memory and Intelligence* (Piaget,

Inhelder, and Sinclair-De Zwart, 1973). Perhaps the most striking finding of this work is that rather than remaining stable or decaying, a memory can actually improve with time because its evolving structure depends on the child's maturing operativity. For example, a young child shown a series of rods arranged from short to long may remember them 1 week later as a dichotomy, short rods and long rods. But 6 months later, reflecting the child's growing mastery of the scheme of seriation, the child may remember the series as it was originally presented. In contrast with his position in the 1920s, when he tried to separate memory from understanding, Piaget now concluded, "The structure of memory appears to be partly dependent on the structure of the operations" (Piaget, 1970, p. 719).

Collaborators

The work we call Piaget's was really teamwork. Its scope and volume are so vast that it cannot be imagined without the skillful leadership necessary to generate enthusiasm and maintain a sense of direction. Piaget had many collaborators, ranging from student assistants to distinguished scientists and scholars in various fields. Besides psychologists there were mathematicians, logicians, philosophers and historians of science, biologists, physicists, and linguists. Almost everyone he worked with called him patron (boss). His longest collaboration (50 years), and the most important, was with Bärbel Inhelder, who began as his student and became a distinguished scientist in her own right, almost always working together or in close proximity—both spatially and intellectually—with Piaget.

Conclusion

Since about 1970 there have been numerous critical studies of Piaget's empirical findings and of his theoretical approach. By about 1990, much of the anti-Piagetian criticism had ebbed and had given way to neo-Piagetian efforts to assimilate Piaget's findings, correct some of his errors, and synthesize his work with newer developments in cognitive and social psychology. Most of his empirical findings have been verified by studies in many countries. Perhaps his most important contribution to developmental psychology was to reveal the child as a thinking being, and the child's intellect as growing through its own efforts in interaction with the physical and social world.

See also: OBJECT CONCEPT, DEVELOPMENT OF

Bibliography

Chapman, M. (1988). *Constructive evolution, origins and development of Piaget's thought.* New York: Cambridge University Press.

Gruber, H. E., and Vonèche, J. J. (1977). *The essential Piaget.* New York: Basic Books.

Inhelder, B., Sinclair, H., and Bovet, M. (1974). *Learning and the development of cognition.* Cambridge, MA: Harvard University Press.

Kuhn, D., ed. (1989). *Human Development 32* (6), 325–387.

Piaget, J. (1921). Essai sur quelques aspects du développement de la notion de partie chez l'enfant. *Journal de psychologie normale et pathologique 18,* 449–480.

—— (1961; reprint 1969). *The mechanisms of perception,* trans. G. N. Seagrim. New York: Basic Books.

—— (1970). Piaget's theory. In P. H. Mussen, ed., *Carmichael's manual of child psychology.* New York: Wiley.

—— (1967; reprint 1971). *Biology and knowledge,* trans. B. Walsh. Chicago: University of Chicago Press.

Piaget, J., and Inhelder, B. (1966; reprint 1969). *The psychology of the child,* trans. H. Weaver. New York: Basic Books.

—— (1966; reprint 1971). *Mental imagery in the child: A study of the development of imaginal representation,* trans. P. A. Chilton. New York: Basic Books.

Piaget, J., Inhelder, B., and Sinclair-De Zwart, H. (1968; reprint 1973). *Memory and intelligence,* trans. A. J. Pomerans. New York: Basic Books.

Howard E. Gruber

PLACE CELLS

The hippocampus is a medial temporal lobe structure of critical importance for the encoding and retention of episodic memory in general and spatial memory in particular. A milestone in the detection of these hippocampal functions was the discovery that most of the pyramidal cells in the hippocampus exhibit location-specific activity (see Figure 1) and that the activity of such "place cells" is influenced by the training history of the animal. This chapter reviews place cells' governing mechanisms, their ensemble properties, and their possible contribution to spatial memory.

Historical Landmarks

Our understanding of hippocampal place cells rests on two important discoveries from the early 1970s. First, James B. Ranck reported that hippocampal neurones fall into two functionally different classes based on their firing patterns in freely moving rats. Complex-spike cells fired at low rates (normally < 1 Hz), but often in bursts of two to seven spikes at 150–200 Hz. These cells were likely to be pyramidal cells. Theta cells—the second class—had high spontaneous firing rates (normally > 10 Hz) and were probably inhibitory interneurons.

The second discovery was the observation by John O'Keefe and Jonathan Dostrovsky that a major proportion of complex-spike cells in the rat hippocampus had spatial correlates. These "place cells" fired when the rat was in a specific location (the "place field" of the cell) but were nearly silent in other posi-

Figure 1

SOURCE: Data recorded by Stig Hollup, May-Britt Moser, and Edvard Moser.

Place fields of 10 simultaneously recorded pyramidal cells and one interneuron (cell 10). Each diagram shows the path of the animal during foraging in a square open field (viewed from above). Locations of firing are shown for each cell. Each dot indicates the position of a spike. Note that pyramidal cells fire at distinct locations, whereas the interneuron fires throughout the environment.

tions (see Figure 1). Firing rates in the field were often ten to twenty times higher than the background rate. Place fields reflected location as such and not behavior emitted at specific locations. Different cells had place fields at different places, and collectively they covered the entire test environment (see Figure 1). Unlike the sensory cortices, firing correlates in the hippocampus were strongly nontopographic: place fields of neighboring cells in the hippocampus were not closer than those of distant cells.

These discoveries led to the suggestion that place cells form a distributed, maplike representation of the spatial environment that the animal can use for efficient navigation (O'Keefe and Nadel, 1978). These findings and the accompanying theory have strongly stimulated research on hippocampal function. New technology has expanded the study of place cells to neuronal ensembles (Wilson and McNaughton, 1993) and has the power to reveal how cognitive functions arise from complex interactions in defined neuronal networks.

What Factors Determine a Place Field?

Hippocampal place cells respond to multiple sources of sensory information (Best et al., 2001). Under most conditions, distal visual landmarks exert the strongest influence. When such landmarks are rotated in concert, place fields frequently follow the landmarks. When the test environment is stretched or truncated, there is often a corresponding change in the shape of the place field. Proximal landmarks such as surfaces usually exert weaker control over the place field. Place fields are also controlled by other sensory modalities. Many hippocampal neurons respond to distinct odors and are influenced by kinesthetic and vestibular cues generated by the rat's own movement. These influences are particularly powerful when visual input is unavailable or less reliable. When a rat is released from a closed start box at an unpredictable location, for example, place fields are controlled by the amount of movement for the first few seconds, before external visual landmarks take over.

Place cells, however, do not passively mirror the sensory input that the animal receives. First, place fields develop slowly. When a rat enters a new environment for the first time, place fields are weak and dispersed. Sharp and distinct place fields develop only after five to ten minutes, at a much slower rate than that at which sensory information passes to the hippocampus. Second, changes in place fields are not predictable from the amount of change in sensory input. Place fields often remain in place after significant landmarks are removed from the environment. At other times, two apparently identical environ-

ments may give rise to very different place representations, and subtle changes in sensory input may completely change the spatial firing correlates of a set of hippocampal neurons. Third, not all locations in an environment are represented by an equal number of place cells. In enclosed chambers, place fields appear to be more common near edges and walls than in the center; in environments with distinct reward locations, a larger number of cells may have place fields at the goal location than at other locations. All these observations suggest that the relation between the structure of the environment and the firing fields of hippocampal neurons is nonlinear.

Place Cells, Spatial Memory, and Synaptic Plasticity

Place cells appear to be responsible for some of the underlying memory computations of the hippocampus (Moser and Paulsen, 2001; Eichenbaum, 2001). Several observations suggest that individual hippocampal pyramidal cells express information retrieved from the animal's memory. First, as long as a rat remains in its recording apparatus, there is often no change in the location-specific firing of hippocampal place cells after the removal of surrounding landmarks or the switching off of lights. That this persistence of firing obtains even in cells that were originally under strong visual control suggests that recent experience influences firing patterns. Second, because a cell's firing or not at a given location may depend on where the animal comes from and where it is going next, it appears that recent memory can influence the activity of a place cell. Third, hippocampal area CA1 contains cells that apparently respond when experience is incongruent with predictions from memory, such as when a salient stimulus suddenly appears or disappears at a particular location. The existence of these mismatch-responsive cells means that CA1 cells may simultaneously receive information from the senses and from memory.

Once a place cell has developed a localized firing pattern in a new environment, the place field remains stable for weeks or more, as predicted if the cell contributes to a particular spatial memory. Some researchers have suggested that the formation of place fields, like spatial memory, depends on long-term potentiation (LTP) in hippocampal excitatory synapses. Blockade of the NMDA receptor abolishes both associative LTP and overnight stability of new place fields in a new environment. However, the development of place fields is not disrupted, and new place fields can be maintained for at least one to two hours in the absence of NMDA receptors, suggesting that LTP-independent mechanisms may be essential only for the long-term maintenance of place fields.

Place Cell Ensembles

Memory operations are reflected in the firing properties of individual hippocampal neurons; a more complete understanding of how place cells contribute to spatial memory requires insight into the constantly changing interaction between large numbers of place cells. Two phenomena—remapping and reactivation—illustrate the dynamic organization of place cells at the ensemble level.

Place fields of simultaneously recorded pyramidal cells exhibit all-or-none remapping. The entire population of recorded neurons may adopt new firing correlates after a change in a single but defining feature of an environment, such as the conversion of a square environment to a circular one while all other landmarks remain fixed. Some place cells start to fire at new locations, others become silent, and previously silent cells become active. The original map of place fields is accurately reinstated when the original environment is restored. This pattern suggests a linkage of place cells in functional ensembles that correspond to distinguishable test environments or test conditions. Each place cell is likely to participate in multiple ensembles that are active at different times.

A second example of ensemble coding is the striking observation that cells with overlapping place fields persist in correlated firing during sleep episodes subsequent to the behavioral session (Sutherland and McNaughton, 2000). Not only the pattern of coactivity, but also temporal firing sequences resemble those recorded during preceding behavior. This form of reactivation is temporally specific. It is strongest shortly after the behavioral session and decays with time. Reactivation is particularly associated with sharp waves, which are bursts of synchronous activity in hippocampal pyramidal cells during slow-wave sleep and awake rest. These bursts have the capacity to induce plasticity in downstream areas and may be involved in the consolidation of long-term memory in the neocortex (Buzsaki, 1989). Reactivation occurs during REM sleep, too.

There is also temporal organization of pyramidal-cell activity in the hippocampus. Hippocampal networks display characteristic oscillatory activity during spatial learning, and the timing of spikes relative to oscillations in the theta and gamma frequency bands may carry significant information. Such oscillations occur during memory processing, but the exact significance of temporal firing patterns for memory formation in the hippocampus is not yet understood.

Place Fields and Hippocampal Circuitry

Place cells exist in all subfields of the hippocampus and in the dentate gyrus, subiculum, and entorhinal cortex. The sharpest fields are in the hippocampus proper; firing fields in the subiculum and entorhinal cortex are more dispersed. Place-related activity in the hippocampus may result from sequential processing along the trisynaptic circuit of the hippocampus (dentate gyrus, CA3, CA1), or the relevant information is carried by the direct excitatory input from entorhinal cortex to each subfield. Disruption of the trisynaptic circuit by selective lesions in the dentate gyrus or CA3 does not abolish place fields in CA1, suggesting that the direct input is sufficient for establishing and maintaining spatial activity in hippocampal pyramidal neurons (Moser and Paulsen, 2001).

If place cells participate in neuronal ensembles that collectively contribute to memory of location and other episodic information, these ensembles must somehow be tied together. It has been suggested that place cells are organized as continuous attractor networks where neurons with firing fields at the current or nearby locations are mutually excited, whereas those with fields at other locations are inhibited in a distance-dependent manner. Distance between place fields of two pyramidal neurons may be encoded by the strength of the connecting synapses. Some researchers have suggested that the recurrent network of area CA3 has attractor properties, but recurrent networks in afferent structures such as the entorhinal cortex may have similar capacity. The CA1 lacks the internal excitatory connections needed to maintain ensemble structure.

Conclusion

Place cells carry strong signals that are expressed reliably in large proportions of the hippocampal neuronal population, and they are found in a part of the brain that plays clear roles in specific memory operations. With new powerful techniques that allow the study of neuronal computation at the ensemble level, the study of place cells can contribute to our understanding of the workings of memory and cognition.

Bibliography

Best, P. J., White, A. M., and Minai, A. (2001). Spatial processing in the brain: The activity of hippocampal place cells. *Annual Review of Neuroscience 24*, 459–486.

Buzsaki, G. (1989). Two-stage model of memory trace formation: A role for "noisy" brain states. *Neuroscience 31*, 551–570.

Eichenbaum, H. (2001). A cortical-hippocampal system for declarative memory. *Nature Reviews Neuroscience 1*, 41–50.

Moser, E. I., and Paulsen, O. (2001). New excitement in cognitive space: Between place cells and spatial memory. *Current Opinion in Neurobiology 11*, 745–751.

O'Keefe J., and Dostrovsky, J. (1971). The hippocampus as a spatial map. Preliminary evidence from unit activity in the freely moving rat. *Brain Research 34*, 171–175.

O'Keefe, J., and Nadel, L. (1978). *The hippocampus as a cognitive map*. Oxford: Clarendon Press.

Ranck, J.B., Jr. (1973). Studies on single neurons in dorsal hippo-campal formation and septum in unrestrained rats. I. Behav-ioral correlates and firing repertoires. *Experimental Neurology 41*, 461–531.

Sutherland, G. R., and McNaughton, B.L. (2000). Memory trace reactivation in hippocampal and neocortical neuronal ensem-bles. *Current Opinion in Neurobiology 10*, 180–186.

Wilson, M. A., and McNaughton, B. L. (1993). Dynamics of the hippocampal ensemble code for space. *Science 261*, 1,055–1,058.

Edvard I. Moser

PLACE VERSUS RESPONSE LEARNING REVISITED IN THE BRAIN

A chief concern of learning and memory researchers involves determining *what* is learned in a given situa-tion. Edward L. Thorndike (1933) was an early pro-ponent of the view that animals learn associations be-tween stimuli and responses (i.e., S-R learning), and in his influential *law of effect*, Thorndike essentially proposed that S-R associations were strengthened by reinforcement (a satisfying event) and weakened by nonreinforcement (an annoying event). In Thorn-dike's laboratory investigation of the learning abilities of several animal species, the learning curves that he observed were gradual; he therefore argued that learning was not akin to intuition or the sudden illu-mination of a light bulb. Rather, learning appeared to be an incremental process of trial-and-error, re-sulting in the eventual acquisition of S-R associations. Thorndike's early S-R learning theory and the rise of James B. Watson's psychological behaviorism influ-enced the subsequent work of the psychologist Clark L. Hull, who introduced fairly elaborate mathemati-cal formulas in his description of a S-R habit learning theory (Hull, 1943).

Edward C. Tolman was an early proponent of a different theoretical approach to understanding learned behavior. Tolman (1932) argued that S-R theory did not adequately explain all learning phe-nomena; he suggested instead that animals acquire expectations about how various behaviors would lead to a desired goal. Tolman used terms such as *inference*, *intention*, and *purpose* to explain learned behavior. His views on animal learning were perhaps most clearly defined in his hypothesis that animals form a cogni-tive map of the environment in which spatial relation-ships among multiple stimuli are represented in memory and could be used to guide goal-directed be-havior.

The Plus-Maze Task and the Behaviorist versus Cognitivist Debate

A significant empirical battle flared between S-R behaviorist and cognitive-learning theorists, and in-volved the investigation of behavior in several learn-ing tasks. One task that employed a plus-maze appa-ratus can illustrate these two approaches to understanding what animals learn (Tolman, Ritchie, and Kalish, 1946). The plus-maze is essentially two T-mazes arranged so that a goal box (e.g., east or west), can be approached from one of two start boxes (e.g., north or south). In one version of the task, rats are trained over trials to obtain food from a consistently baited goal box (e.g., west), from the same start box (e.g., south). According to S-R learning theory, rats can learn to approach the baited goal box by acquir-ing a response tendency (i.e., a specific body turn at the choice point). In contrast, according to cognitive learning theory, rats trained in this task learn the place or spatial location of the reinforcer, and this ex-pectation can guide an approach response to the bait-ed goal box.

Both behaviorist and cognitive learning theories can adequately explain the acquisition of this version of the plus-maze task. However, a probe trial in which trained rats are given a trial starting from the oppo-site start box (e.g., north) can assess the type of infor-mation acquired. Rats with knowledge of the spatial location of the reinforcer should continue to ap-proach the baited goal box on the probe trial (i.e., place learning), whereas rats that have learned a spe-cific body turn should choose the opposite goal box on the probe trial (i.e., response learning). In their early research, Tolman and colleagues demonstrated that rats trained in a plus-maze to approach a goal box from the same start point on each trial could in-deed display place learning when probe trial behavior was later assessed. In addition, rats can acquire place learning in a version of the plus-maze task in which they are trained to approach the same goal arm (e.g., west) from two different starting points (e.g., north and south). In this version of the task, rats are re-quired to make a different body turn at the maze choice point (i.e., left or right), depending on the start position; therefore response learning would be ineffective for acquiring the task.

Taken together, these demonstrations of place learning in the plus-maze suggest that S-R theories may not adequately explain all types of learning. However, subsequent research revealed that in addi-tion to place learning, rats could also use response learning in acquiring plus-maze behavior. For exam-ple, under some experimental conditions, rats trained to approach the same goal arm (e.g., west) from a consistent starting point (e.g., south), tended to display response learning on a subsequent probe trial. Moreover, rats can acquire response learning in a version of the plus-maze task in which they are trained from two different starting points (e.g., north and south) and are required to make a consistent body turn response (e.g., turn left) at the maze choice point. In an influential review of the plus-maze literature, Restle suggested that the relative use of place and response learning depends on various experimental factors, most critically the availability of intra- and extra-maze cues (Restle, 1957). For example, environments in which various distal extra-maze cues are present favor place learning, whereas the use of sparsely cued extra-maze environments favor response learning.

Neurobiology of Memory Organization and the Behaviorist versus Cognitivist Debate

Although the plus-maze task appeared to hold early promise for resolving the dispute between behaviorists and cognitive theorists in favor of one theoretical viewpoint, the findings of various plus-maze studies clearly indicated that brain-intact rats are capable of both place and response learning. However, contemporary behavioral neuroscience research suggests a possible resolution of this debate. Research has revealed that mammalian memory is organized in relatively independent brain systems that differ in the types of memory they mediate (Hirsh, 1974; O'Keefe and Nadel, 1978; Cohen and Squire, 1980; Mishkin and Petri, 1984; Eichenbaum and Cohen, 2001). There is evidence that the hippocampus is part of a memory system that mediates cognitive memory, whereas the caudate-putamen is part of a memory system that mediates stimulus-response or habit memory (e.g., Packard, Hirsh, and White, 1989; Fernandez-Ruiz et al., 2001). The multiple-memory-systems hypothesis raises the interesting possibility that place and response learning may in fact have distinct neural substrates, suggesting that a neurobiologically based approach may help to address the differing viewpoints of S-R and cognitive-learning theorists (Mishkin and Petri, 1984).

Multiple Memory Systems and the Place versus Response Learning Debate

A plus-maze study was designed to differentiate the mnemonic roles of the hippocampus and caudate-putamen (Packard and McGaugh, 1996). In this study rats were trained in a daily session to obtain food from a consistently baited goal box and were allowed to approach this maze arm from the same starting box on each trial. Following seven days of training, rats were given a probe trial to determine whether they had ac-

quired the task using place information or had learned a specific body-turn response. Prior to the probe trial, rats received intrahippocampal or intracaudate infusions of a vehicle solution or lidocaine, an anesthetic that produces a temporary inactivation of neural function in the affected brain region. On the probe trial, rats receiving vehicle infusions into the hippocampus or caudate-putamen were predominantly place learners. Lidocaine infused into the hippocampus blocked expression of place learning, whereas similar infusions into the caudate-putamen did not. Therefore, the functional integrity of the hippocampus but not caudate-putamen is necessary for the expression of place learning. Following extended training in the plus-maze, rats given a second probe trial switch from place learning to response learning (Ritchie, Aeschliman, and Pierce, 1950; Hicks, 1964). Therefore, in the study by Packard and McGaugh (1996), the rats were trained for an additional seven days, given a second probe trial on the sixteenth day, and again received intracerebral infusions of lidocaine prior to the probe trial. On this second probe trial rats receiving vehicle infusions into either the hippocampus or caudate-putamen were predominantly response learners, providing evidence of a switch from place to response learning tendencies with extended training.

On the second probe trial, intrahippocampal infusions of lidocaine did not block the expression of response learning. However, rats receiving intracaudate infusions of lidocaine prior to the second probe trial exhibited place learning, demonstrating a blockade of the expression of response learning. Taken together, these findings demonstrate a double dissociation between the roles of the hippocampus and caudate-putamen in place and response learning, respectively. Moreover, when the shift from the use of place to response learning occurs, the hippocampus-dependent place representation is not extinguished or forgotten. Rather, at a time in training in which animals predominantly use response learning, the place representation can be brought back into use or "unmasked" by a blockade of the caudate-putamen response learning system.

The shift in the use of a hippocampus-dependent place strategy to a caudate-dependent response strategy suggests that in a learning task in which both memory systems can provide an adequate solution, the hippocampal system mediates a rapid cognitive form of learning that initially guides behavior, whereas the caudate-putamen mediates a more slowly developing S-R or habit form of learning that eventually guides learned behavior. This raises the intriguing possibility that infusions of memory-enhancing drugs into these two brain structures during early training might influence the time-course of this shift. In an experiment designed to address this possibility, rats received posttraining intrahippocampal or intracaudate infusions of the amino acid neurotransmitter glutamate during early time points in cross-maze training (Packard, 1999). As observed previously, rats receiving saline control injections predominantly displayed place learning on an early (day eight) probe trial, and response learning on a later (day sixteen) probe trial. However, rats receiving posttraining intrahippocampal infusions of glutamate predominantly displayed place learning on both the early and late probe trials, suggesting that infusion of glutamate into the hippocampus strengthened a place learning representation and prevented the shift to response learning that occurs with extended training. In contrast, rats given posttraining glutamate infusions into the caudate-putamen predominantly displayed response learning on both the early and late probe trials, suggesting that infusion of glutamate into the caudate-putamen accelerated the shift to response learning that is normally observed with extended behavioral training.

The findings from behavioral neuroscience research employing brain lesion and intracerebral drug infusion techniques provide a partial neurobiological resolution of the place versus response learning debate. Whereas previous research clearly demonstrates that brain-intact animals are capable of both place and response learning (Restle, 1957), such behaviors do not reflect a single learning and memory system. Rather, distinct neuroanatomical substrates that include the hippocampus and caudate-putamen mediate the acquisition of place and response learning, respectively. Thus, four decades after the introduction of the plus-maze task as a means of addressing the fundamental question of what animals learn in a given situation, the mammalian brain appears to have spoken in favor of the viewpoint that the historic debate between S-R and cognitive learning theorists may in part have been misguided in to impose a single theoretical viewpoint on all types of learning.

See also: GUIDE TO THE ANATOMY OF THE BRAIN: HIPPOCAMPUS AND PARAHIPPOCAMPAL REGION

Bibliography

Blodgett, H. C., and McCutchan, K. (1947). Place versus response learning in the T-maze. *Journal of Experimental Psychology 37,* 412–422.

Cohen, N. J., and Eichenbaum, H. (1993). *Memory, amnesia, and the hippocampal system.* Cambridge, MA: MIT Press.

Cohen, N. J., and Squire, L. R. (1980). Preserved learning and retention of pattern analyzing skill in amnesics: Dissociation of knowing how and knowing that. *Science 210,* 207–210.

Fernandez-Ruiz, J., Wang, J., Aigner, T. G., and Mishkin, M. (2001). Visual habit formation in monkeys with neurotoxic lesions of the ventrocaudal neostriatum. *Proceedings of the National Academy of Sciences of the United States of America 98,* 4,196–4,201.

Hull, C. L. (1943). *Principles of behavior.* New York: Appleton-Century-Crofts.

Mishkin, M., and Petri, H. L. (1984). Memories and habits: Some implications for the analysis of learning and retention. In L. R. Squire and N. Butters, eds., *Neuropsychology of memory.* New York: Guilford.

O'Keefe, J., and Nadel, L. (1978). *The hippocampus as a cognitive map.* Oxford: Oxford University Press.

Packard, M. G. (1999). Glutamate infused posttraining into the hippocampus or caudate-putamen differentially strengthens place and response learning. *Proceedings of the National Academy of Sciences of the United States of America 96,* 12,881–12,886.

Packard, M. G., Hirsh, R., and White, N. M. (1989). Differential effects of fornix and caudate nucleus lesions on two radial maze tasks: Evidence for multiple memory systems. *Journal of Neuroscience 9,* 1,465–1,472.

Packard, M. G., and McGaugh, J. L. (1996). Inactivation of the hippocampus or caudate nucleus with lidocaine differentially affects expression of place and response learning. *Neurobiology of Learning and Memory 65,* 65–72.

Restle, F. (1957). Discrimination of cues in mazes: A resolution of the place versus response controversy. *Psychological Review 64,* 217–228.

Ritchie, B. F., Aeschliman, B., and Pierce, P. (1950). Studies in spatial learning: VIII. Place performance and acquisition of place dispositions. *Journal of Comparative and Physiological Psychology 43,* 73–85.

Thorndike, E. L. (1933). A proof of the law of effect. *Science 77,* 173–175.

Tolman, E. C. (1932). *Purposive behavior in animals and men.* New York: Appleton-Century-Crofts.

Mark G. Packard

PREFRONTAL CORTEX AND MEMORY IN PRIMATES

A primate needs its prefrontal cortex for behavior based on information accumulated before the moment of action. The prefrontal cortex is especially important if the information is new to the organism or conflicts with prior cues or memories that call for different actions. Whether the information is new or old, it must be retained in memory until the moment it can inform an act. It is the prefrontal cortex that supports this short-term memory (also called working memory) that subserves behavior.

Prefrontal memory is a matter not of content or duration but of context, the context of action. Short-term memory is not the only function of the prefrontal cortex, nor is it exclusively the role of the prefrontal cortex. But, insofar as action requires short-term memory, it also needs the prefrontal cortex. It follows that this part of the cortex is essential for the construction of sequential behaviors, especially if they are novel or require choices. It is needed for the syntax of the action, including, of course, the syntax of the spoken language, particularly creative speech.

The prefrontal cortex is the cortex of the pole of the frontal lobe. It is that part of the cerebral cortex to which the nucleus mediodorsalis of the thalamus projects. Phylogenetically, it is the neocortical region that undergoes the greatest and latest expansion (see Figure 1). It reaches maximum development in the brain of the human, where it occupies almost one-third of the totality of the neocortex. In the course of evolution, its dorsolateral aspect, that is, the cortex of the external convexity of the frontal lobe, develops relatively more than its medial and inferior aspects. This is an important consideration because the dorsolateral prefrontal cortex supports mainly cognitive functions, whereas the orbitomedial prefrontal cortex mostly pertains to emotional and visceral functions.

Cytoarchitectonically, the prefrontal cortex of the primate (area FD of Von Bonin and Bailey, 1947) includes areas 9, 10, 11, 12, and 13 of Brodmann (1909). It is one of the best-connected of all neocortical regions; it is directly and reciprocally connected to the anterior and dorsal thalamus, the hypothalamus, and limbic structures, especially the amygdala and the hippocampus. It sends profuse efferent fibers to the basal ganglia. Dorsolateral prefrontal areas have rich reciprocal connections with many other neocortical areas of the frontal lobe and of the temporal and parietal lobes. The first clear indication of the involvement of the prefrontal cortex in short-term memory was provided by Jacobsen in the early 1930s (Jacobsen, 1935). He showed that monkeys with lesions of the dorsolateral prefrontal cortex are impaired in the learning and performance of delayed response (DR) and delayed alternation (DA) tasks. These tasks fall within a general category of behavioral tasks—delay tasks—that demand from the animal the performance of motor acts in accord with sensory information presented a few seconds or minutes earlier. In other words, delay tasks demand short-term memory for the logical and consequent bridging of temporal gaps between perception and action, the mediation of cross-temporal contingencies of behavior. Primates deprived of substantial portions of dorsolateral prefrontal cortex cannot properly perform delay tasks, regardless of the nature of the sensory information that guides them, especially if after a long delay between sensory cue and motor response.

There appears, however, to be some specificity of prefrontal areas with regard to the type of sensory information they help retain. Lesions of the cortex of the sulcus principalis are most detrimental to performance of delay tasks with spatially defined sensory cues, such as DR and DA. However, time seems to override space on this matter. Those spatial tasks are impaired only when a delay occurs between cue and response. The critical factor is the time during which the cue must be retained. Furthermore, dorsolateral prefrontal lesions also impair performance of delay tasks in which the sensory cue is not spatially defined, a correlation that has been demonstrated by local cortical cooling. The cryogenic depression of a large portion of dorsolateral cortex (area 9), including the sulcus principalis, induces a reversible deficit in performance of delay tasks, whether the cue is visual and spatially defined (as in DR) or not (as in delayed matching to sample). Furthermore, the cryogenic deficit also affects delayed matching tasks in which the cue (sample) is perceived by active touch (haptically).

Humans with dorsolateral prefrontal lesions also show impairments in delay tasks. Tasks in which the material to be retained can be verbally encoded are affected more by lesions of the left than of the right prefrontal cortex. They are impaired most of all by bilateral lesions. The human prefrontal syndrome usually involves disorders of attention, planning, and language. Prefrontal patients have difficulty maintaining attention on internal cues or short-term retention of mental material. Their planning is poor for both the short and the long term; it is as if they lacked "memory of the future" in addition to memory of the recent past. Both retrospective and prospective representations are needed for the sequential construction not only of external motor action but also of "internal action," such as sequential logical thinking—hence the trouble the patients have in this kind of activity, whether expressed in spoken language or not. Speech is most impaired if it requires the bridging of long intervals (cross-temporal contingencies) between subjects and verbs, subjects and predicates, or logically interdependent sentences. The trouble is extreme in lesions of Broca's area, which is a part of the prefrontal cortex specialized in the most elementary aspects of linguistic syntax. Animal and human neuropsychology thus suggests that the prefrontal cortex is essential for bridging cross-temporal contingencies of behavior, and that this is so at least in part because of its role in short-term memory.

Microelectrode recording in the monkey has corroborated the role of the prefrontal cortex in short-term memory. Prefrontal neurons show sustained activation of firing during the delay periods of delay tasks (see Figure 2). Statistical analysis and control experiments indicate that this activation is

- a result of learning the task;
- dependent on the presence of a cross-temporal contingency between cue and motor response;
- related in some cells to the property of the cue on which the response depends;
- related in some cells to the response that the animal has to execute at the end of the delay;

Figure 1

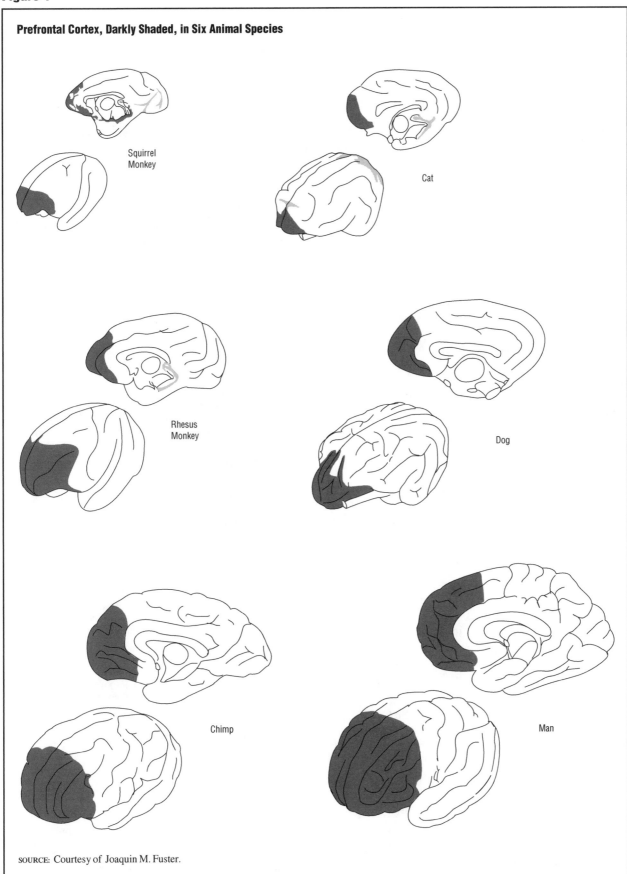

Prefrontal Cortex, Darkly Shaded, in Six Animal Species

Squirrel Monkey

Cat

Rhesus Monkey

Dog

Chimp

Man

SOURCE: Courtesy of Joaquin M. Fuster.

Figure 2

Discharge of a neuron in the prefrontal cortex of a monkey during five delayed-response trials. The cue period is marked by a horizontal bar and the response of the animal by an arrow. Note the sustained activation of the cell during the delay (the memory retention period, about 60 seconds long in the last two trials); note also that the cell reverts to the lower level of spontaneous discharge immediately after every trial. *(Joaquin M. Fuster)*

- directly related to the efficacy with which the animal performs the task.

All these indications are consistent with the assumption that prefrontal neurons participate in cortical networks that, by their sustained activation, retain sensory information as long as needed for prospective action.

The analysis of single-unit discharge in other areas of association cortex (inferotemporal and posterior parietal) during visual and haptic delay tasks has revealed sustained neuronal activations in those areas. This observation, in addition to the study of the effects of local cortical cooling on remote cortical cell discharge and delay-task performance, has led to the following inference: The prefrontal cortex exerts its role in short-term memory and preparation for action through close functional interplay with areas of posterior association cortex with which it is intimately and reciprocally connected. Thus, the activated cortical network that retains sensory information during behavior has several components in short-term memory. Posterior areas are involved in the network inasmuch as the information falls within their special modality (vision, audition, somesthesis, and so on). The prefrontal cortex is involved inasmuch as the information calls for prospective goal-directed action. The maintenance of activity in the network is assured by the continuous circulation of excitatory impulses within and between all contributing areas, including the prefrontal cortex if the outcome is to be a goal-directed action in accord with the sensory information.

The prefrontal cortex of the primate is a large and phylogenetically new part of the cerebral cortex that performs a critical function in short-term memory that subserves action. Thus, it is critically important for sequential behaviors with cross-temporal contingencies. In the human, such behaviors include the spoken language and logical thought, which is a form of sequential "inner action." The memory function of the prefrontal cortex is one of several functions that this cortex supports in cooperation with other associative cortical areas. These functions are essential for the syntax of action—for organization of behavior in the time domain.

See also: GUIDE TO THE ANATOMY OF THE BRAIN; WORKING MEMORY: HUMANS

Bibliography

Bauer, R. H., and Fuster, J. M. (1976). Delayed-matching and delayed-response deficit from cooling dorsolateral prefrontal cortex in monkeys. *Journal of Comparative Physiology and Psychology 90,* 293–302.

Bonin, G. von, and Bailey, P. (1947). *The neocortex of Macaca mulatta.* Urbana: University of Illinois Press.

Brodmann, K. (1909). *Vergleichende Lokalisationslehre der Grosshirnrinde in ihren Prinzipien dargestellt auf Grund des Zellenbaues.* Leipzig: Barth.

Fuster, J. M. (1973). Unit activity in prefrontal cortex during delayed-response performance: Neuronal correlates of transient memory. *Journal of Neurophysiology 36,* 61–78.

——— (1985). The prefrontal cortex, mediator of cross-temporal contingencies. *Human Neurobiology 4,* 169–179.

——— (1997). *The prefrontal cortex, anatomy, physiology, and neuropsychology of the frontal lobe.* 3rd edition. Philadelphia: Lippincott-Raven.

——— (2001). The prefrontal cortex—an update: Time is of the essence. *Neuron 2,* 319–333.

Fuster, J. M., Bodner, M., and Kroger, J. K. (2000). Cross-modal and cross-temporal association in neurons of frontal cortex. *Nature 405,* 347–351.

Goldman-Rakic, P. S. (1987). Circuitry of primate prefrontal cortex and regulation of behavior by representational memory. In F. Plum, ed., *Handbook of physiology, Section 1: The Nervous System,* Vol. 5. Bethesda, MD: American Physiological Association.

Jacobsen, C. F. (1935). Functions of the frontal association area in primates. *Archives of Neurology and Psychiatry 33*, 558–569.

Joaquin M. Fuster

PRIMATES, VISUAL ATTENTION IN

The neural mechanisms for visual attention intervene between sensation and action. Neither strictly sensory nor motor, they constitute the neural filters that select certain aspects of visual information for greater attention and influence over action. Visual attention includes mechanisms for arousal, alerting, vigilance, and selective attention for spatial location or visual features. Of these, the ones that most directly affect visual processing are selective attention to a location in space or to a visual feature of an object. These latter mechanisms help route selected visual inputs to visual-processing structures in the brain and also to motor control systems, usually at the expense of nonselected inputs. Behavioral examinations of visual processing, functional-imaging studies in humans, and single-unit studies in the nonhuman primate indicate that selection mechanisms are in play. These experiments aim to understand the influence of attention on the processing of information and the neural signals that underlie selective attention.

Behavioral Experiments

Behavioral experiments show that individuals cannot and do not process all the information present in complex visual scenes. It is not possible, for example, to recognize within the same instant more than one or two objects in a typical complex scene. When subjects are asked to report different attributes of simultaneously presented images, they nearly always perform worse than when asked to report the attributes of the objects separately. In certain conditions, major changes in scenes go undetected because the capacity of the brain's limited capacity to code and process complex information. But, when subjects are told to attend to only one of two simultaneously presented objects, or to a particular location in a scene, their performance returns to the levels expected for only one object. Selective attention provides a mechanism for choosing which information is noticed and which is ignored, thus ensuring that unimportant information does not crowd out important information. Moreover, since visual acuity is poor outside of the center of gaze, the eyes must be moved to scan and process visual scenes. Selective attention provides a method for selecting single targets for the neural system that controls the eyes (oculomotor system).

Control of Attention

The selective filters that underlie selective attention operate in space and on features of objects, selecting locations and features of visual stimuli for heightened processing. The neurobiology underlying this process lends itself to separation into two parts: the mechanisms that control attention and the mechanisms that are, in turn, influenced by attention. In some cases, attention is controlled by features intrinsic to a stimulus. Some objects attract attention to themselves, an automatic process that occurs because of separation of figures from their background resulting from differences in color, contrast, motion ("pop-out"). Yet, even after automatic figure-ground separation, a typical visual scene will still contain many different figures of equal salience that are nevertheless of different behavioral relevance. In this case, attention can be actively wielded to filter information in the scene; a neural signal that reflects this active process is a "top-down" signal that controls attention.

Studies using functional imaging in human subjects have identified several target structures that may provide the signals that control selective visual attention in humans. The control system for spatially directed attention, identified by functional imaging, is both widely distributed and closely associated with the oculomotor system; it involves the posterior parietal cortex, parts of the frontal cortex, the pulvinar nucleus of the thalamus, and possibly the superior colliculus. The close association with the oculomotor system accords with the principle that an important role for selective attention is the direction of the eyes to the behaviorally relevant stimuli in complicated visual scenes. Neurophysiology in nonhuman primates performing attention tasks indicates a neural mechanism for the operation of attention in some of these structures. In these structures, a given neuron responds to stimuli in a limited region of space (i.e., its receptive field), and this response is enhanced whenever the animal directs its attention into the region. This response enhancement may provide the "top-down" signal that potentiates the processing of visual stimuli that appear in that location. When these signals are absent because of damage or dysfunction within any of these structures, particularly if the damage is unilateral, subjects suffer a variety of attentional disorders. One such attentional disorder is extinction, a difficulty in detecting or perceiving objects within the affected portion of the visual field when a competing object is located in intact portions of the field.

Influence of Attention

The neural signals derived from these brain areas influence the processing of visual stimuli in the sensory areas that process visual information. Functional imaging studies show that attention influences the processing of visual information in all visual areas, from the earliest visual area, primary visual cortex to the last visual areas, in both the ventral and dorsal visual processing streams. In these imaging studies, the instruction to attend to a stimulus can modulate the response to visual stimuli, altering the response to a visual stimulus by 10 to 30 percent. This effect is larger in later stages of visual processing, raising the possibility that the smaller modulations in primary visual cortex result from feedback from higher areas. The results in human imaging replicate those in neurophysiological recordings of behaving primates, although the influence of attention on responses in early visual areas in primates has not been demonstrated in single-unit studies. But extrastriate visual cortical areas that process information about object features such as color and shape (such as Visual Area 4), receive attentional control signals, and act as the local attentional filters. The properties of the neurons' responses to visual stimuli and the effect of attention reflect both behavior in the absence of attention and the influence of attention on that behavior. When more than one stimulus is placed in the receptive field of a single neuron, the neuron's activity reflects an averaging of the response to both of the stimuli.

The presence of more than one stimulus in the receptive field interferes with that neuron's ability to carry information about the stimulus. Behaviorally, this interference is mirrored in poor performance with simultaneously presented objects. But when an animal is instructed to attend to a single stimulus within the receptive field of the neuron, the response of the neuron will be determined almost solely by the color, shape, or orientation of the attended stimulus. In presence of the top-down signal wielded by attention, neurons communicate little information about the features of ignored stimuli, and the interference is filtered out of the signal. Thus, the neurons that process the visual information are influenced by the control signals for attention to act as filters of information that select relevant information and discard irrelevant information, providing a mechanism for sorting out the complexity of the visual world.

Bibliography

Kanwisher, N., and Wojciulik, E. (2000). Visual attention: Insights from brain imaging. *Nature Reviews Neuroscience 1*, 91–100.

Kastner, S., and Ungerleider, L. G. (2000). Mechanisms of visual attention in the human cortex. *Annual Review of Neuroscience 23*, 315–341.

Olson, C. R. (2001). Object-based vision and attention in primates. *Current Opinion in Neurobiology 11*, 171–179.

Rensink, R. A. (2002). Change detection. *Annual Review of Psychology 53*, 245–277.

Reynolds, J. H., and Desimone, R. (1999). The role of neural mechanisms of attention in solving the binding problem. *Neuron 24*, 19–29, 111–25.

Robert Desimone
Revised by Bharathi Jagadeesh

PRIMATES, VISUAL PERCEPTION AND MEMORY IN NONHUMAN

Anatomical and physiological studies have revealed at least thirty separate areas with visual functions in the cortex of monkeys, and there could be even more visual areas in the cortex of humans. One view of the division of labor among the visual areas holds that there are two main processing systems: one devoted to identifying *what* an object is and the other devoted to identifying *where* an object is (Ungerleider and Mishkin, 1982). On this view, the occipitotemporal cortex is mainly the province of the former system, known as the ventral stream because of the idea that visual information *flows*, in some sense, from occipital cortex forward and ventrally toward the temporal cortex (see Figure 1). The other system, known as the dorsal stream because information is held to flow from occipital to parietal cortex, seems to play a role in either spatial perception, as noted above, or alternatively, in the guidance of movements to spatial targets (Milner and Goodale, 1996). This article will focus on the ventrally directed, occipitotemporal processing stream and its role in object perception and memory.

Anatomy of the Occipitotemporal Pathway for Object Identification

The occipitotemporal pathway begins with the projection from the striate cortex (the primary visual cortex, V1) to the second and third visual areas, V2 and V3, which in turn project to area V4 (see Figure 1). These prestriate visual areas are arranged in adjacent cortical belts that nearly surround the striate cortex. The major output of area V4 is to a widespread region within the inferior temporal cortex, including area TEO posteriorly and area TE anteriorly. The inferior temporal cortex is in receipt of highly processed visual information arising not only from lower-order visual areas but also from subcortical structures, including the thalamus and basal ganglia. Area TE is often considered to be the last, or *highest-order,* visual area in the cortical system for object identification because its principal cortical outputs are to areas in the temporal and frontal lobes that are not exclusively concerned with vision.

Murray and Bussey (1999) have argued that perirhinal cortex, a multimodal region that lies adjacent to area TE, should be considered a ventral extension of the ventral visual stream. The perirhinal cortex receives anatomical connections not only from area TE but also from brain areas that process auditory, somatic sensory, and visuospatial information. Although perirhinal cortex is not solely dedicated to the processing of visual sensory inputs, it may nevertheless carry out a higher-order level of visual processing than TE, perhaps by representing even more complex conjunctions of stimulus features than area TE, together with other kinds of sensory inputs. In this way, the perirhinal cortex may bring together disparate pieces of information about objects, including their associated attributes.

Neurons in the visual cortex *see*, or represent, pieces of our visual world. The amount of visual space that a neuron represents, or is responsive to, is the visual receptive field. In striate and prestriate areas the representation in the cortex is maplike or *visuotopic*; that is, nearby parts of visual space are represented in nearby parts of a cortical area in a systematic mapping. The representations in these fields are also restricted to the contralateral visual field. In area TEO of inferior temporal cortex, this visuotopic organization seems to be coarser than that in earlier fields; in area TE it may be nonexistent. In area TE, in contrast to other visual fields, neurons have large receptive fields that often cross the midline. Thus, neurons in area TE can *see* an object regardless of its position in the visual field.

Also in the temporal cortex are at least two areas involved in processing motion vision: the middle temporal and middle-superior temporal areas, abbreviated as MT and MST, respectively (not illustrated). These areas are in the depths of the superior temporal sulcus, near the temporal-parietal-occipital junction, and are often considered a third visual stream, contrasting motion vision with the object vision of the ventral stream and the spatial vision of the dorsal stream.

Although much of the neural mechanism for object identification can be viewed as a bottom-up process, in which low-level inputs are transformed into a more useful representation through successive stages of processing, anatomical studies have shown that each of the feedforward projections between successive pairs of areas in the occipitotemporal pathway is reciprocated by a feedback projection. Such projections from higher-order processing stations back to lower-order ones could mediate some top-down aspects of visual processing, such as the influence of selective attention.

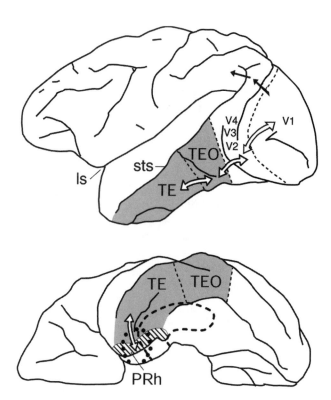

Figure 1. Location of inferior temporal cortex (gray shading) in macaque monkey brain, shown on a schematic drawing of the lateral view (top) and ventral view (bottom) of the left hemisphere of the brain. The inferior temporal cortical fields related solely to vision are areas TE and TEO. The perirhinal cortex (oblique hatching) is a multimodal region that is ventrally adjacent to area TE. White arrows indicate flow of information from striate cortex (V1) to prestriate (V2, V3, V4) areas into inferior temporal cortex, which in turn projects to perirhinal cortex. These areas together constitute the *ventral visual stream*. Black arrows suggest flow of information from striate to prestriate to parietal cortex, the *dorsal stream*. In the schematic of the ventral view (bottom), heavy dotted and dashed lines show approximate locations of the amygdala and hippocampus, respectively; the amygdala and hippocampus are limbic structures buried deep in the temporal lobe. Abbreviations: ls, lateral sulcus (also known as the Sylvian fissure); PRh, perirhinal cortex; sts, superior temporal sulcus; V1, striate cortex or primary visual cortex; V2-4, prestriate cortical areas. *(Elisabeth A. Murray)*

Neuronal Properties in the Visual Areas of the Occipitotemporal Pathway

Given the nearly sequential anatomical route to the inferior temporal cortex from V1, one would expect many types of visual information relevant to object identification to be processed within each area along the route. Indeed, physiological studies have shown that neurons in V1, V2, and V3 are sensitive to one or (usually) more stimulus qualities that we perceive, such as size, orientation, spatial frequency, texture, color, direction of motion, and binocular disparity. Neurons in the motion pathway reflect precisely the judgements reported by monkeys about the direction in which a field of light spots is moving on average. Furthermore, exciting cells by passing electrical current through an electrode near them systematically affects a monkey's perceptual judgement. For example, if a group of neurons represents upward motion, then stimulating these cells during a period when the light spots are tending to move to the left will induce the illusion that they are moving slightly up as well as left. Finally, in the perirhinal cortex and in the neighboring area TE, neurons respond less to familiar than to novel visual stimuli. Thus, these neurons carry signals about whether objects have been seen before (recognition memory). In addition, neurons in this region also reflect the relative recency of viewing of objects.

It is possible to view the areas along the occipitotemporal pathway as forming a processing hierarchy. As one moves along the pathway from V1 to perirhinal cortex, both neuronal response latencies and average receptive field size increase steadily, which is consistent with the notion that neuronal responses in later areas are built up from those in earlier areas. A hierarchical model further predicts that the product of visual processing will become more complex at each successive stage in the pathway. So far, the results of anatomical and physiological studies support this idea.

Although early findings led some theorists to propose that neurons in the anterior ventral temporal cortex code specific objects within their large, bilateral receptive fields, there is overwhelming evidence that neurons in this region, especially in area TE and perirhinal cortex, respond selectively to object features such as shape, color, and texture rather than to specific objects. Thus, the neural code for object recognition and identification must be a population code based on stimulus features. The only exception appears to be the small proportion of neurons selective for faces and, more rarely, hands. Why should the coding of faces be treated differently from the coding of other objects? One possibility is that faces are extremely important to primates not only for the recognition of individuals in the social group but also for social communication by facial expression. Thus, there may have been selective pressure to evolve specialized neural mechanisms for the analysis of faces and facial expression.

Effects of Lesions in the Visual Areas of the Occipitotemporal Pathway

Numerous studies have shown that lesions of V1 produce a scotoma, or blind spot, that corresponds to the part of the visual field represented in the damaged area. The effects of selective lesions of V2 and V3 on visual perception and memory have not yet been investigated. As described below, the impairments that follow lesions of areas V4, TEO, TE, and perirhinal cortex are consistent with a contribution from these areas to the object-identification process.

Lesions of Area V4

Several studies in monkeys have examined the contribution of V4 lesions to color and form vision. Although one reported that the lesion impaired color constancy but not hue or form discrimination, subsequent studies found impairments in both hue and form discrimination, which is consistent with the notion that V4 processes both color and form information and relays this information to the inferior temporal cortex.

Lesions of Areas TEO, TE, and Perirhinal Cortex

Damage to the inferior temporal cortex, including areas TEO, TE, and the perirhinal cortex, leads to deficits in the identification of objects through vision. Behavioral tasks designed to test visual abilities in monkeys indicate that inferior temporal cortical damage produces difficulties in discriminating and in matching objects on the basis of vision. If the damage is restricted to areas TE and TEO, objects can still be identified by touch. Because basic sensory capacities such as acuity and color vision are largely intact after inferior temporal cortical damage, the difficulty is considered to be one of higher-order vision. The nature of the impairment caused by inferior temporal cortex lesions is controversial. One idea is that damage to this region results in a loss of the ability to represent features (e.g. the color red), in such a way that the greater the damage, the fewer visual features that can be represented. Another idea is that it is not the ability to represent features that is lost, but, rather, the ability to represent conjunctions of features. Both these ideas emphasize the role of inferior temporal cortex in visual perception, that is, its role in representing visual features. On either view, damage to inferior temporal cortex will lead to disruption of stored representations of features, resulting in a loss of long-term visual memory. At the same time, this damage would result in an impaired ability to represent features, a perceptual deficit. Thus, it appears that neurons in the inferior temporal cortex contribute to both perception and memory and that perceptual and mnemonic functions are anatomically inseparable in this part of the brain.

Visual Attention

Contributions of ventral stream areas to object identification typically are examined by presenting objects against a blank background. In a naturalistic visual scene, however, the visual system must identify and select objects from a multitude of objects, a process termed attention. Attention appears subject to at least two influences: the strength of the sensory signals processed by the ventral stream areas and the (learned) relevance of a particular object. Monkeys with combined lesions of V4 and area TEO are deficient in directing attention to objects in the visual field when there are multiple, distracting objects, and their difficulty increases when the distracting stimuli are made more salient by increasing their contrast (De Weerd, Peralto, Desimone, and Ungerleider, 1999).

Visual-Recognition Memory

In monkeys the delayed nonmatching-to-sample (DNMS) task has proved a reliable measure of visual recognition memory for objects. On each trial the animal is shown a sample object, which it displaces in order to find a food reward underneath; then, about ten seconds later, the animal is shown both the sample and a novel object for choice. The monkey can obtain another food reward by choosing the novel object. When the animal has learned the nonmatching rule, the task is made more difficult—either by increasing the delay between the sample presentation and the choice test or by increasing the number of items to be remembered—to tax the monkey's memory.

Lesions of area TE together with much of the ventrally adjacent perirhinal cortex lead to severe deficits on DNMS (Mishkin, 1982). More recent work suggests that area TE, at least dorsal portions of it, is not as important for visual-recognition memory as the perirhinal cortex. Indeed, lesions restricted to the perirhinal cortex lead to more severe impairments in recognition memory than do lesions to any other part of the inferior temporal cortex yet investigated.

The multimodal nature of the sensory inputs to this region is shown by the deficits in tactile and visual-recognition memory that result from lesions of the perirhinal cortex. Monkeys with lesions of perirhinal cortex can usually perform the nonmatching task if the delay between the sample and the choice is short, but their performance falls nearly to chance levels when the delays are as long as a minute or two; hence, the deficit seems to be one of memory. However, it is clear that the role of perirhinal cortex on visual processing extends beyond recognition memory and includes a role for representing conjunctions of features. Some accounts have questioned the memory interpretation and have argued instead for a unified theory of the contribution of the inferior temporal cortex to perception and memory.

Interactions of the Occipitotemporal Pathway with the Limbic System

In some instances, storage of visual memories must occur through the interaction of the visual cortex with medial temporal-lobe limbic structures (see Figure 1). It appears that the inferior temporal cortex is critical for storing knowledge about objects, the hippocampus for knowledge about places and events, and the amygdala for linking object, event, or place information with affective valence. Thus, the system might be organized in a hierarchical fashion with the inferior temporal cortex providing an initial stage of processing involving object recognition, association, and identification. In later stages, already-processed information about objects would be linked with events or affective valences by the hippocampus and amygdala, respectively. If so, we might expect that, to the extent that the later stages of processing require knowledge about objects, damage to the inferior temporal cortex, including the perirhinal cortex, would disrupt storage of information linking objects with events and affective valence.

See also: DISCRIMINATION AND GENERALIZATION

Bibliography

Dean, P. (1982). Visual behavior in monkeys with inferotemporal lesions. In D. J. Ingle, M. A. Goodale, and R. J. W. Mansfield, eds., *Analysis of visual behavior.* Cambridge, MA: MIT Press.

Desimone, R., and Ungerleider, L. G. (1989). Neural mechanisms of visual perception in monkeys. In F. Boller and J. Grafman, eds., *Handbook of neuropsychology,* Vol. 2. Amsterdam: Elsevier.

De Weerd P., Peralto, M. R. III, Desimone, R., and Ungerleider, L. G. (1999). Loss of attentional stimulus selection after extrastriate cortical lesions in macaques. *Nature Neuroscience 2,* 753–758.

Gaffan, D., Harrison, S., and Gaffan, E. A. (1986). Visual identification following inferotemporal ablation in the monkey. *Quarterly Journal of Experimental Psychology 38B,* 5–30.

Milner, A. D., and Goodale, M. A. (1996). *The visual brain in action.* Oxford: Oxford University Press.

Mishkin, M. (1982). A memory system in the monkey. *Philosophical Transactions of the Royal Society of London B298,* 85–95.

Murray, E. A. (2000). Memory for objects in nonhuman primates. In M. Gazzaniga, ed., *The Cognitive Neurosciences,* 2nd edition. Cambridge, MA: MIT Press.

Murray, E. A., and Bussey, T. J. (1999). Perceptual-mnemonic functions of the perirhinal cortex. *Trends in Cognitive Sciences 3,* 142–151.

Newsome, W. T. (1997). The King Solomon lectures in neuroethology. Deciding about motion: Linking perception to action. *Journal of Comparative Physiology A 181,* 5–12.

Squire, L. R. (1987). *Memory and brain.* New York: Oxford University Press.

Tanaka, K. (1996). Inferotemporal cortex and object vision. *Annual Review of Neuroscience 19,* 109–139.

Ungerleider, L. G., and Mishkin, M. (1982). Two cortical visual systems. In D. J. Ingle, M. A. Goodale, and R. J. W. Mansfield, eds., *Analysis of visual behavior.* Cambridge, MA: MIT Press.

Leslie G. Ungerleider
Elisabeth A. Murray
Revised by Elisabeth A. Murray

PROCEDURAL LEARNING

[*Procedural learning or procedural memory refers to retention of motor skills. The distinction between procedural memory and declarative memory is usually framed between* knowing how *and* knowing that, *with the first phrase referring to procedural knowledge (knowing how to do something) and the second phrase to declarative knowledge (knowing the nature of events or the world). People know how to ride a bicycle, how to type, or how to find their way by using a map. On the other hand, people know that Rome is the capital of Italy, that the attack on Pearl Harbor occurred on December 7, 1941, and that Winston Churchill was prime minister of England.*

The two entries on procedural learning that follow are devoted to research conducted in two different but overlapping traditions, one with animal models and the other with human subjects. The former is concentrated on research on the neural substrates of several conditioning paradigms used to study learning in ANIMALS. *The work with* HUMANS *is concerned with how patients with various types of brain damage learn new skills. Although the experimental traditions are different, the overarching aim of both is to characterize the neural processes underlying procedural learning and memory.*]

ANIMALS

Neurobehavioral research conducted primarily between 1980 and 2000 employed dissociation methodology to provide compelling evidence for the existence of multiple memory systems in the mammalian brain. Although evidence of neuroanatomical dissociations of the role of various brain structures in different memory tasks is a critical step in advancing the multiple-memory systems hypothesis, a full understanding of memory organization involves elucidation of the psychological operating principles that distinguish different types of memory. One putative form of memory present in the mammalian brain is declarative memory and involves the acquisition, consolidation, and retrieval of cognitive information for facts and events (Cohen and Squire, 1980; Eichenbaum and Cohen, 2001). Declarative memory appears to rely on a neuoranatomical system composed of various structures in the medial temporal lobe, most notably the hippocampus. In contrast, procedural memory involves the acquisition, consolidation, and retrieval of information acquired in tasks involving various types of Pavlovian classical conditioning and instrumental/operant learning paradigms. This article describes evidence indicating that procedural memory involves several, largely separable neuroanatomical systems, including the cerebellum, basal ganglia, and amygdala.

Cerebellum and the Classically Conditioned Eyeblink Response

In the early 1980s Richard Thompson and his colleagues (McCormick et al., 1981) demonstrated a critical role for the cerebellum in the classically conditioned eyeblink response in the rabbit. In this paradigm animals receive pairings of an auditory conditioned stimulus (CS—a tone), and an unconditioned stimulus (UCS—an air puff delivered to the eye). The naturally occurring rabbit eyeblink response is a defensive mechanism initially emitted in response to unconditioned stimulus. However, following several presentations of the tone-air puff contingency, the animal learns to produce the eye blink (i.e., a conditioned response) in the absence of the air puff. A series of elegant studies employing irreversible and reversible lesions, neuroanatomical tracing, and electrophysiological techniques have mapped out the neural circuitry underlying the processing of unconditioned and conditioned stimuli in eyeblink conditioning (Kim and Thompson, 1997). This circuitry includes an unconditioned stimulus pathway in which the dorsal accessory olive projects through the inferior cerebellar penduncle and a conditioned stimulus pathway involving mossy-fiber projections to the cerebellum via the pontine nuclei. The interpositus nucleus of the cerebellum receives converging CS-US information, and this deep cerebellar nuclei plays a critical role in both the acquisition and expression of the classically conditioned eyeblink response. The lack of impairment of performance of unconditioned eyeblink behavior following lesions of the interpositus nucleus provides critical evidence of a selective role for this nucleus in learned or conditioned eyeblink behavior. Study of the role of cerebellar circuitry in the acquisition and expression of conditioned eyeblink behavior represents perhaps the best example of a model approach to understanding the neurobiological bases of a form of procedural learning in the mammalian brain.

The Basal Ganglia and Stimulus-Response Habit Learning

In a multiple-memory systems approach to memory organization, there is evidence that components of the basal ganglia (specifically the caudate-putamen or dorsal striatum) mediate the acquisition of tasks that involve the formation of stimulus-response habits (Mishkin and Petri, 1984; Packard, Hirsh, and White, 1989). In several studies, the role of the rodent basal ganglia in procedural/habit learning has been dissociated from the role of the hippocampal system in cognitive/declarative memory. An early study examining the selective role of the basal dorsal striatum in S-R habit learning involved an experiment using two food-rewarded, eight-arm radial maze tasks; a cognitive/declarative win-shift task that required rats to remember the arms they had visited earlier in a daily training session; and a procedural/S-R habit win-stay task that required rats to acquire a simultaneous visual (light-dark) discrimination. Lesions of the dorsal striatum impair acquisition of the win-stay task and do not affect acquisition of the win-shift task, whereas lesions of the hippocampal system produce the opposite dissociation (Packard, Hirsh, and White, 1989).

An additional study used two water-maze tasks to investigate the selective role of the basal ganglia in S-R memory (Packard and McGaugh, 1992). In these tasks two rubber balls protruding above the water surface served as cues. One ball (correct) was on top of a platform that could be used to escape from the water, and the other ball (incorrect) was on top of a thin rod and thus did not provide escape. The two balls also differed in visual appearance (i.e., vertical versus horizontal black/white stripes). In a cognitive/declarative version of the task, the correct platform was in the same spatial location on every trial, but the appearance of the ball varied. Therefore, this version of the task requires rats to learn to approach the correct ball on the basis of spatial location, not visual pattern. In a procedural/S-R habit version of the task, the rats located the correct platform in different spatial locations across trials, but the visual pattern was consistent. Therefore, this task could be acquired by learning an approach response to the visual cue. Lesions of the dorsal striatum impair acquisition of the S-R habit task without affecting acquisition of the spatial task (Packard and McGaugh, 1992). Other findings indicating that lesions of the rodent dorsal striatum impair two-way active avoidance behavior, simultaneous tactile discriminations, egocentric response learning, and conditional visual and auditory conditioning also support a role for the dorsal striatum in S-R habit learning and memory (Kirkby and Kimble, 1968; Colombo, Davis, and Volpe, 1989; Reading, Dunnett, and Robbins, 1991; Adams, Kesner, and Raggozino, 2001; Kesner, Bolland, and Dakis, 1993).

The Amygdala and Stimulus-Affect Conditioning

The mammalian amygdala has long been implicated in the neurobiology of emotional behavior; this function of the amygdala seems to extend to emotional learning. Bruce S. Kapp and his colleagues provided some of the early evidence of a role for the amygdala in conditioned fear learning (Kapp, Frysinger, Gallagher, and Haselton, 1979). Joseph E. LeDoux's team has extensively investigated the role of the amygdala in a fear-conditioning paradigm in rats in which brief electrical shock is paired with exposure to either a discrete auditory cue or a specific environmental context (LeDoux, 1992; Fendt and Fanselow, 1999). In a series of anatomical, lesion, and pharmacological studies these investigators have mapped out a potential neural circuit in which conditioned stimulus (e.g., tone) and unconditioned stimulus (e.g., shock) information converge in the basolateral amygdala. Projections from the basolateral nucleus to the central nucleus of the amygdala and subsequent downstream projections to various brain-stem regions allow for the expression of various autonomic and behavioral responses (e.g., freezing behavior, heart-rate and blood-pressure changes) in response to discrete and contextual conditioned stimuli. The auditory cortex is not necessary for the acquisition of discrete auditory cue fear conditioning. Rather, auditory information projected to the amygdala from the medial geniculate nucleus of the thalamus is apparently sufficient to support this form of fear conditioning. These findings suggest a rapid-response procedural learning system that can bypass neocortical involvement in cognitive assessment of threatening stimuli.

Further evidence of a role for the amygdala in learned fear responses in the rat emerged from an investigation of the fear-potentiated startle response by Michael Davis and his colleagues (e.g. Davis, 1992). In these experiments, rats initially receive pairings of a light or tone with foot shock. During subsequent training, the normal startle response that results from exposure to a loud noise is potentiated by concurrent presentation of the light or tone conditioned stimulus. Findings from lesion, pharmacological, and anatomical studies converge to indicate a role for the amygdala in the acquisition and expression of fear-potentiated startle.

Aside from its involvement in aversively motivated learning, evidence indicates a role for the amygdala in the acquisition and expression of appetitively motivated stimulus-affect learning tasks. For example, pretraining and posttraining basolateral amygdala lesions in rats impair acquisition and expression of conditioned place preference behavior for both natural rewards such as food and sex (Cador, Robbins, and Everitt, 1989) and addictive drugs such as amphetamines (Hiroi and White, 1991; Hsu, Schroeder, and Packard, 2002). In this task, rats are confined in contrasting environments that alternate daily: on one day in an environmental context paired with natural or drug rewards and on the next day in a second context that is not paired with the rewarding treatment. On a reward-free test session given following training, the amount of time spent in the two environments is measured, and rats demonstrate a reliable conditioned place preference for—that is, spend longer amounts of time in—the environment previously paired with the rewarding stimulus. Investigators interested in the neurobiological bases of addiction have traditionally used this task. However, animals display approach behavior to specific environmental stimuli in a drug-free state on the test day, and therefore expression of a conditioned place preference requires memory for an association between previously neutral stimuli and the rewarding affective consequences of the treatment.

It should be noted that not all investigators agree that the mnemonic function of the amygdala involves a long-term role in memory storage. James L. McGaugh and his colleagues argue that amygdala damage impairs unconditioned fear responses (specifically freezing behavior), and therefore suggest caution in proposing a role for the amygdala role in learned fear responses (Cahill, Weinberger, Roozendaal, and McGaugh, 1999; Fanselow and LeDoux, 1999). In addition, evidence indicates that the amygdala (specifically the basolateral nucleus) modulates memory processes occurring in other brain structures, including declarative memory processes mediated by the hippocampus and stimulus-response habit learning mediated by the basal ganglia (Packard, Cahill, and McGaugh, 1994). However, a modulatory role for the amygdala in some types of learning does not itself rule out a possible long-term role in memory storage in stimulus-affect conditioning. There is a need for further task-specific analysis of the potential short-term versus long-term roles of the amygdala in memory and for consideration of the role of separate amygdala nuclei in different types of learning and memory.

There has been significant progress in identifying neuroanatomical components of separable procedural memory systems in the mammalian brain, including the cerebellum, basal ganglia, and amygdala. Although this article has focused on studies of lower animals, there is similar evidence for the role of these various structures in some of these forms of procedural memory in nonhuman primates (Zola-Morgan, Squire, and Mishkin, 1982; Fernandez-Ruiz, Wang, Aigner, and Mishkin, 2001;) and humans (Knowlton, Mangels, and Squire, 1996; Cohen and Squire, 1980; Johnsrude et al., 2000).

See also: DECLARATIVE MEMORY; NEURAL SUBSTRATES OF CLASSICAL CONDITIONING; NEURAL SUBSTRATES OF EMOTIONAL MEMORY

Bibliography

Adams, S., Kesner, R. P., and Ragozzino, M. E. (2001). Role of the medial and lateral caudate-putamen in mediating an auditory conditional response association. *Neurobiology of Learning and Memory* 76, 106–116.

Cador, M., Robbins, T. W., and Everitt, B. J. (1989). Involvement of the amygdala in stimulus-reward associations: Interaction with the ventral striatum. *Neuroscience* 30, 77–86.

Cahill, L., Weinberger, N. M., Roozendaal, B., and McGaugh, J. L. (1999). Is the amygdala a locus of "conditioned fear"? Some questions and caveats. *Neuron* 23, 227–228.

Cohen, N. J., and Squire, L. R. (1980). Preserved learning and retention of pattern analyzing skill in amnesics: Dissociation of knowing how and knowing that. *Science* 210, 207–210.

Colombo, P. J., Davis, H. P., and Volpe, B. T. (1989). Allocentric spatial and tactile memory impairments in rats with dorsal caudate lesions are affected by preoperative training. *Behavioral Neuroscience* 103, 242–250.

Davis, M. (1992). The role of the amygdala in conditioned fear. In J. P. Aggleton, ed., *The amygdala: Neurobiological aspects of emotion, memory, and mental dysfunction.* New York: Wiley-Liss.

Fanselow, M. S., and LeDoux, J. E. (1999). Why we think plasticity underlying Pavlovian fear conditioning occurs in the basolateral amygdala. *Neuron* 23, 229–232.

Fendt, M., and Fanselow, M. S. (1999). The neuroanatomical and neurochemical basis of conditioned fear. *Neuroscience and Biobehavioral Reviews* 23, 743–760.

Fernandez-Ruiz, J., Wang, J., Aigner, T. G., and Mishkin, M. (2001). Visual habit formation in monkeys with neurotoxic lesions of the ventrocaudal neostriatum. *Proceedings of the National Academy of Sciences of the United States of America* 984, 4,196–4,201.

Hiroi, N., and White, N. M. (1991). The lateral nucleus of the amygdala mediates expression of the amphetamine conditioned place preference. *Journal of Neuroscience* 11, 2,107–2,176.

Johnsrude, I. S., Owen, A. M., White, N. M., Zhao, W. V., and Bohbot, V. (2000). Impaired preference conditioning after anterior temporal lobe resection in humans. *Journal of Neuroscience* 20, 2,649–2,656.

Kapp, B. S., Frysinger, R. C., Gallagher, M., and Haselton, J. R. (1979). Amygdala central nucleus lesions: Effects on heart rate conditioning in the rabbit. *Physiology and Behavior* 23, 1,109–1,117.

Kesner, R. P., Bolland, B. L., and Dakis, M. (1993). Memory for spatial locations, motor responses, and objects: Triple dissociation among the hippocampus, caudate nucleus, and extrastriate visual cortex. *Experimental Brain Research* 93, 462–470.

Kim, J. J., and Thompson, R. F. (1997). Cerebellar circuits and synaptic mechanisms involved in classical eyeblink conditioning. *Trends in Neuroscience* 20, 177–181.

Kirkby, R. J., and Kimble, D. P. (1968). Avoidance and escape behavior following striatal lesions in the rat. *Experimental Neurology* 20, 215–227.

Knowlton, B. J., Mangels, J. A., and Squire, L. R. (1996). A neostriatal habit learning system in humans. *Science* 273, 1,399–1,402.

LeDoux, J. E. (1992). Emotion and the amygdala. In J. P. Aggleton, ed., *The amygdala: Neurobiological aspects of emotion, memory, and mental dysfunction.* New York: Wiley-Liss.

McCormick, D. A., Lavond, D. G., Clark, G., Kettner, R. E., Rising, C. E., and Thompson, R. F. (1981). The engram found? Role of the cerebellum in classical conditioning of nictitating membrane and eyelid responses. *Bulletin of the Psychonomic Society 18,* 103–105.

Mishkin, M., and Petri, H. L. (1984). Memories and habits: Some implications for the analysis of learning and retention. In L. R. Squire and N. Butters, eds., *Neuropsychology of memory.* New York: Guilford.

Packard, M. G., Cahill, L., and McGaugh, J. L. (1994). Amygdala modulation of hippocampal-dependent and caudate nucleus-dependent memory processes. *Proceedings of the National Academy of Sciences of the United States of America 91,* 8,477–8,481.

Packard, M. G., Hirsh, R, and White, N. M. (1989). Differential effects of fornix and caudate nucleus lesions on two radial maze tasks: Evidence for multiple memory systems. *Journal of Neuroscience 9,* 1,465–1,472.

Packard, M. G., and McGaugh, J. L. (1992). Double dissociation of fornix and caudate nucleus lesions on acquisition of two water maze tasks: Further evidence for multiple memory systems. *Behavioral Neuroscience 106,* 439–446.

Reading, P. J., Dunnett, S. B., and Robbins, T. W. (1991). Dissociable roles of the ventral, medial, and lateral striatum on the acquisition and performance of a complex visual stimulus response habit. *Behavioral Brain Research 45,* 147–161.

Zola-Morgan, S., Squire, L., and Mishkin, M. (1982). The neuroanatomy of amnesia: Amygdala-hippocampus versus temporal stem. *Science 218,* 1,337–1,339.

Mark G. Packard

HUMANS

In discussing long-term memory, scientists have found it useful to distinguish between several kinds of memory that rely on different brain systems. The major distinction is between declarative memory, which refers to the conscious memory of facts and events, and nondeclarative memory, which refers to nonconscious memory of skills, habits, or other modes of learning that proceed beneath the surface of conscious awareness. Declarative memory is what most people call memory. It depends on the integrity of the hippocampus and related structures of the medial temporal lobe. Nondeclarative memory affects our behavior without our explicit knowledge. It is a heterogeneous collection of nonconscious memory abilities that depend on various other structures within the brain (Squire et al., 1993; see Figure 1).

One well-studied component of nondeclarative memory is procedural memory. The difference between declarative memory and procedural memory is the difference between "knowing that" and "knowing how." Procedural learning describes the formation of skills and habits. It is the most primitive form of learning, the first to develop in infancy (Tulving and Schacter, 1990). Because it requires extensive practice, it is a slow and inflexible learning system that

eventually takes on an automatic or reflexive quality. It is, however, long-lasting and reliable, as any bike rider knows—even after years of absence from a bicycle, one never loses the skill. While most declarative learning is not impaired by rapid-eye-movement (REM) sleep deprivation, procedural learning is (Stickgold et al., 2001).

Skills, the procedures that allow us to function in the world, include motor, perceptual, and cognitive processes. Examples of learned skills are driving a car with a manual transmission (motor), a parent's attentiveness to his or her baby's cry in a distant room (perceptual), and increasing alacrity in solving a Rubik's Cube with practice (cognitive). Habits are a form of gradual, incremental learning, a settled pattern of responses toward repeated stimuli. An example of a habit is a person regularly opening the refrigerator door when he or she walks into the kitchen. Like skills, habits allow us to function efficiently in the world by responding to stimuli with minimal cognitive effort. While declarative memory can, in some cases, enhance or hasten the acquisition of skills and habits, usually conscious awareness of learning is not necessary; once the information is acquired, it often becomes difficult to verbalize it. This is why procedural learning is called "nondeclarative."

The Case of Patient H.M.

By far the most famous example of a patient who has retained procedural learning in the absence of declarative memory is the case of H.M., a patient with severe intractable epilepsy who underwent surgery as a last attempt at correcting his condition. Surgeons removed most of his medial temporal lobe structures bilaterally and left him devoid of declarative memory, and therefore suffering from amnesia. Brenda Milner (1962) later showed that he was capable of improving his performance on a mirror-drawing task in which participants trace the outline of a figure with a stylus (e.g., a star) while watching the reflection of their efforts in a mirror. While initially challenging, the task becomes easier with practice. Despite not having any recollection of ever performing the task, H.M. became more accurate across sessions, demonstrating that he had acquired this skill. This was the earliest evidence that skill-learning can occur without declarative memory. There is evidence that not only motor-skill learning (as tested by the mirror drawing task) but also perceptual and cognitive-skill learning can also proceed in the absence of declarative memory.

Motor-Skill Learning

Motor-skill learning is tested primarily by three tasks: the mirror drawing described above, rotary

Figure 1

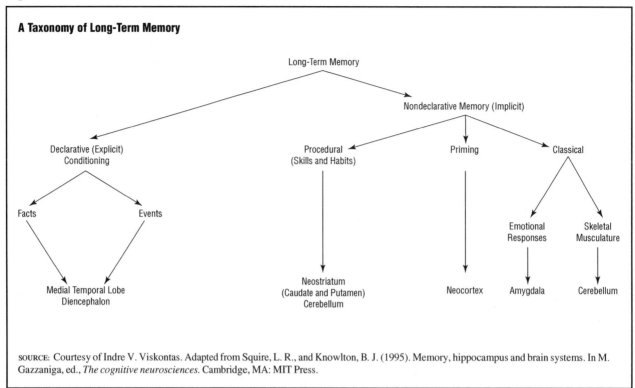

A Taxonomy of Long-Term Memory

SOURCE: Courtesy of Indre V. Viskontas. Adapted from Squire, L. R., and Knowlton, B. J. (1995). Memory, hippocampus and brain systems. In M. Gazzaniga, ed., *The cognitive neurosciences.* Cambridge, MA: MIT Press.

pursuit, and serial reaction time (SRT). In rotary pursuit, participants try to keep a hand-held stylus in contact with a nickel-sized metal disk that rotates on a table. With practice, participants are able to maintain this contact for longer periods of time. Suzanne Corkin (1968) has shown that patients with declarative memory deficits (i.e., amnesics) are able to improve their performance on this task. In the SRT task, participants press the corresponding button when a target item appears in one of four locations on a screen. The appearance of the target follows a ten-to-twelve trial sequence that the participants eventually learn implicitly. SRT learning remains intact in amnesics (Nissen and Bullemer, 1987).

Furthermore, both the basal ganglia and the cerebellum play a role in motor-skill learning (Gabrieli, 1998). The basal ganglia are a group of subcortical structures that surround the thalamus and include the caudate, putamen, and globus pallidus. Neuroimaging techniques have shown that SRT skill learning activates the basal ganglia (Karni et al., 1995). Lesions to the cerebellum, a structure at the base of the brain, can impair mirror-tracing skills (Sanes et al., 1990). Many scientists believe that the acquisition of motor skills depends on the basal ganglia, while the association of visual cues with motor actions depends on the cerebellum (Willingham et al., 1996).

Perceptual-Skill Learning

In addition to having intact motor-skill learning, patients with amnesia also have intact perceptual-skill learning. One of the most popular tests of perceptual-skill learning is reading mirror-reversed text. While people with declarative memory problems show improved mirror-reading with practice, patients with basal ganglia damage (e.g., people with Huntington's disease) evince mildly impaired learning (Martone et al., 1984).

Learning Cognitive Skills and Habits

Cognitive-skill learning has also been tested using several tasks, the most common of which are the tower tasks and the artificial grammar learning task. Habit learning in humans has been measured using a probabilistic classification task. The tower tasks require planning and problem solving: participants are asked to change the location of objects according to certain rules. For example, in the tower of Hanoi task, the subject is presented with three pegs with a set of disks on the leftmost peg. The goal is to move all the disks to the rightmost peg, with the disks piled in order from largest to smallest. The subject may move a disk to an adjacent peg on each move and may not put a larger disk on top of a smaller disk. The tower tasks have yielded mixed results: some researchers have found normal learning in amnesic patients under some circumstances (Cohen et al., 1985) but not others (Butters et al., 1985). It is likely that the tower tasks draw on both procedural memory and declarative memory for the consequences of particular moves that one has already tried.

The artificial grammar task requires the abstraction of rules and regularities underlying seemingly random strings of letters. The rules allow only certain letter strings to follow other letter strings. After viewing a series of these "grammatical" letter strings without being told about the rules, people are able to classify new strings as either "grammatical" or "nongrammatical" fairly accurately. However, they are not able to report much about the rules and generally feel that they had simply been guessing. Again, amnesic patients cannot remember individual training letter strings very well but perform as well as normal people when classifying new strings (Knowlton, Ramus, and Squire, 1992; Knowlton and Squire, 1996).

The probabilistic classification task that has been used to test habit learning is the "weather prediction" task, which involves a series of cues that are probabilistically associated with either a "sunny" or "rainy" outcome. On each trial participants try to guess which outcome will occur for the cues presented. Because the cues are associated with a particular outcome on only 60 to 90 percent of the trials, memorizing individual trials is not as helpful as accruing knowledge across many trials. Patients with amnesia perform normally on the probabilistic classification task, even in the absence of conscious recollection of the training episode (Knowlton et al, 1994; 1996).

Neural Substrates of Habit Learning in Humans

In neuropsychology, the best evidence for a brain region's involvement in a cognitive process is a double dissociation, in which patients with a particular lesion are impaired at task A but intact at task B, while patients with a different lesion show the opposite pattern. In humans, such a double dissociation was found by Knowlton and colleagues (1996) among amnesic patients and those with Parkinson's disease (PD). Both groups of patients were asked to perform the weather prediction task described above. Both groups were also asked some multiple-choice questions designed to investigate whether they remembered the learning situation. Patients with amnesia were able to learn the classification task but showed almost no declarative memory for the learning episode. In contrast, PD patients were able to remember details of the learning episode but showed no learning in the probabilistic classification task. Since the brain regions damaged by PD include the neostriatum (caudate and putamen structures that are part of the basal ganglia) but not the medial temporal lobes, the experimenters concluded that the neostriatum is responsible for habit learning.

The ultimate output of the basal ganglia is the frontal cortex. In turn, the frontal cortex sends a major projection to the neostriatum. This corticostriatal loop appears to be important for procedural learning. This finding is supported by reports that patients with striatal damage exhibit deficits in skill learning as well as habit learning. Furthermore, a recent neuroimaging study by Poldrack and colleagues (2001) has shown the medial temporal lobe-based declarative memory system and the cortico-striatal based procedural memory system may have a reciprocal relationship during learning. They administered the probabilistic classification (weather prediction) task to healthy young people and designed two conditions, one emphasizing the declarative aspects of the task and the other the nondeclarative aspects. The investigators found that the declarative version elicited medial temporal lobe activity, while the nondeclarative version elicited activity in the basal ganglia and other subcortical structures. Also, activity in the basal ganglia was negatively correlated with activity in the medial temporal lobes.

Conclusion

Procedural learning involves skill and habit learning, both of which are spared in the abolition of declarative memory. While declarative memory depends on medial temporal lobe structures (e.g, the hippocampus), skill and habit learning depend on the basal ganglia. Other structures, such as the cerebellum, may also play a role in some forms of procedural learning. The development of new procedural learning tasks that can be used with brain-injured patients or in neuroimaging studies will help elucidate the neural substrates of this form of learning.

See also: DECLARATIVE MEMORY

Bibliography

Butters, N., Wolfe, J., Martone, M., Granholm, E., and Cermak, L. S. (1985). Memory disorders associated with Huntington's disease: verbal recall, verbal recognition, and procedural memory. *Neuropsychologia 6*, 729–744.

Cohen, N. J., Eichembaum, H., Deacedo, B. S., and Corkin, S. (1985). Different memory systems underlying acquisition of procedural and declarative knowledge. *Annals of the New York Academy of Sciences 444*, 54–71.

Corkin, S. (1968). Acquisition of a motor skill after bilateral medial temporal–lobe excision. *Neuropsychologia 6*, 255–265.

Gabrieli, J. D. E. (1998). Cognitive Neuroscience of human memory. *Annual Review of Psychology 49*, 87–115.

Karni, A., Meyer, G., Jezzard, P., Adams, M. M., Turner, R., and Ungerleider, L. G. (1995). Functional MRI evidence for adult motor cortex plasticity during motor skill learning. *Nature* 377, 155–158.

Knowlton, B. J., Ramus, S. J., and Squire, L. R. (1992). Intact artificial grammar learning in amnesia: Dissociation of classification learning and explicit memory for specific instances. *Psychological Science 3*, 177–179.

Knowlton, B. J., and Squire, L. R. (1996). Artificial grammar learning depends on implicit acquisition of both abstract and exemplar-specific information. *Journal of Experimental Psychology: Learning, Memory, and Cognition 22*, 169–181.

Knowlton, B. J., Squire, L. R., and Gluck, M.A. (1994). Probabilistic classification in amnesia. *Learning, Memory, and Cognition 21*, 699–710.

Martone, M., Butters, N., Payne, M., Becker, J. T., and Sax, D. S. (1984). Dissociations between skill learning and verbal recognition in amnesia and dementia. *Archives of Neurology 41*, 965–970.

Milner, B. (1962). Les troubles de la mémoire accompagnant des lesions hippocampiques bilatérales. In P. Passouant, ed., *Physiologie de l'hippocampe*. Paris: Centre de la Recherche Scientifique.

Nissen, M. J., and Bullemer, P. (1987). Attentional requirements of learning: Evidence from performance measures. *Cognitive Psychology 19*, 1–32.

Poldrack, R. A., Clark, J, Pare-Blagoev, E. J., Shohamy, D., Creso Moyano, J., Myers, C., and Gluck, M. A. (2001). Interactive memory systems in the human brain. *Nature 414*, 546–550.

Sanes, J., Dimitrov, B., and Hallett, M. (1990). Motor learning in patients with cerebellar dysfunction. *Brain 113*, 103–120.

Squire, L. R., and Knowlton, B. J. (1995). Memory, hippocampus and brain systems. In M. Gazzaniga, ed., *The cognitive neurosciences*. Cambridge, MA: MIT Press.

Squire, L. R., Knowlton, B., and Musen, G. (1993). The structure and organization of memory. *Annual Review of Psychology 44*, 453–495.

Stickgold, R., Hobson, J. A., Fosse, R., and Fosse M. (2001). Sleep, learning, and dreams: Off-line memory reprocessing. *Science 294*, 1,052–1,057.

Tulving, E., and Schacter, D. L. (1990). Priming and human memory systems. *Science 247*, 301–306.

Willingham, D. B., Koroshetz, W. J., and Peterson, E. W. (1996). Motor skills have diverse neural bases: Spared and impaired skill acquisition in Huntington's disease. *Neuropsychology 10*, 315–321.

Indre V. Viskontas
Barbara J. Knowlton

PROSE RETENTION

As with memory for other kinds of verbal material, memory for prose is a complex function of various factors. Some of the more important factors include 1. the kind of reading or studying activity in which the learner engages while processing a text; 2. the particular type of prose that is being remembered; 3. the kinds of information and events that intervene between the initial reading of the text and when remembering is attempted; and 4. the way in which memory is assessed (e.g., through recall, short-answer, multiple-choice, or true/false tests; see Figure 1). For clarity of presentation, this entry considers each of these factors separately. In reality, however, each of these factors does not operate in isolation; instead, they work together to influence memory for prose.

Influences of Encoding and Reading Processes

One of the dominant themes in contemporary memory research is that memory benefits to the extent that the material is processed for meaning. The same holds true for prose. For example, research has shown that readers who have been instructed to count the number of four-letter words in a passage do not remember the passage as well as readers who have been instructed to rate the paragraphs for ambiguity (Schallert, 1976). Similarly, if a text is written so that its topic is obfuscated, the degree to which meaningful processing can take place decreases, and this text is recalled less well than a text in which the topic is clearly stated (e.g., through an informative title or by reference to the topic throughout the text; Bransford and Johnson, 1972). The lesson here is straightforward: A prerequisite for remembering prose is extracting the meaning that is being conveyed.

On the assumption that readers typically are extracting meaning as they read, one can further analyze the components of that meaning which are retained. It is typically the case that people do not remember prose verbatim (except with concerted effort, and even then it is difficult; Sachs, 1967). Instead, prose retention is characterized by *memory for the ideas* that are captured by the particular words used. Further, memory for the ideas in a text generally conforms to the following function. The main or most important ideas are recalled best, followed by ideas of intermediate importance, with unimportant details usually recalled least well.

The reader's point of view or frame of reference partly determines the importance of the ideas contained in the text. Because an idea's level of importance determines its memorability, very different patterns of memory for the same text can be observed across readers who adopt different points of view. For example, a prose passage about a household and its daily activities will be remembered differently by a reader who adopts the perspective of a prospective home buyer compared with a reader who adopts the perspective of a burglar appraising particular properties for a clandestine visit (Fass and Schumacher, 1981). The differences in recall for these two readers will directly reflect the fact that the particular ideas in the passage differ in importance, depending on the perspective adopted while reading the passage.

Figure 1

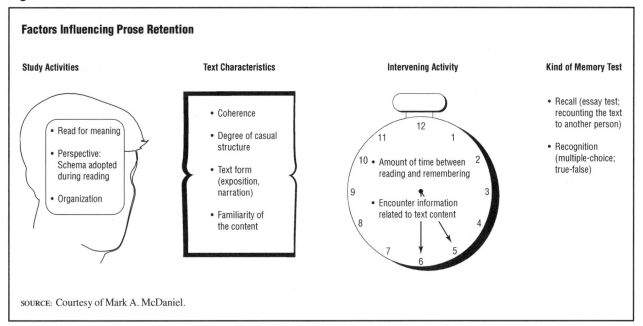

Factors Influencing Prose Retention

Study Activities

- Read for meaning
- Perspective: Schema adopted during reading
- Organization

Text Characteristics

- Coherence
- Degree of casual structure
- Text form (exposition, narration)
- Familiarity of the content

Intervening Activity

12 1 2 3 4 5 6 7 8 9 10 11

- Amount of time between reading and remembering
- Encounter information related to text content

Kind of Memory Test

- Recall (essay test; recounting the text to another person)
- Recognition (multiple-choice; true-false)

SOURCE: Courtesy of Mark A. McDaniel.

Consistent with findings for other types of verbal material, good prose retention depends on reading activities that engage attention toward understanding the individual ideas in a text and how these ideas are organized or interrelated. Such activities can include trying to explain the information to oneself, thinking about causes or results, relating the information to prior knowledge, and creating linkages between the presented ideas. Numerous factors influence the degree to which such reading activities will be engaged. Not surprisingly, readers seem to become more engaged for text rated as more interesting than for less interesting text, with more interesting text being better remembered (Son and Metcalf, 2000). Individual readers vary as well, with some readers spontaneously engaging in more active processing of the text than others, thereby increasing retention for the prose material. Individuals can be instructed or encouraged to use selected reading or study strategies (e.g., self-explanation, outlining) designed to stimulate greater comprehension and organization of the information in the text. These reading strategies generally improve overall recall of factual (expository) text (McDaniel and Donnelly, 1996; Slater, Graves, and Piche, 1985).

One difference between prose memory and memory for word lists is that prose allows special forms of organization that are not operative with simpler materials. The varied kinds of organizational factors that can be influential in prose memory are best revealed by considering how the genre of the prose affects remembering.

Prose Organization and Prose Type

Generally, narrative prose (e.g., a story) is better remembered than expository prose (e.g., an essay or article). The superior memorability of narratives relative to expositions is probably due in large part to readers' better ability to organize and interrelate the ideas expressed in a narrative. There are a number of differentiating factors between narratives and expository prose that could underlie the extent to which the ideas expressed in the text are organized by the reader. Though it may ultimately turn out that not all of these factors are important in accounting specifically for the memory differences between narratives and expository text, these factors do seem to play a role in prose memory.

One factor is that readers presumably activate relevant structures of world knowledge when attempting to understand a text. These structures are usually called schemata (singular, schema). In general, schemata are believed to influence the degree to which incoming text information is organized. Text content for which readers have a schema is believed to be better organized and elaborated, and thus better remembered, than text content for which readers have a poorly articulated or sketchy schema. For instance, researchers have shown that a narrative about a fictitious baseball game is better recalled by readers knowledgeable about baseball (i.e., readers who have a baseball schema) than readers who are not knowledgeable about baseball (Spilich et al., 1979).

In contrasting narratives and expository text, it is arguably the case that narratives have content for which most of the readers in the culture have relevant schemata, whereas for expository texts, the content articulates with schemata that only a subset of readers might possess. Narratives are about people or other animate objects, their goals and conflicts, and their other activities—concepts for which readers have schemata. Narratives frequently entail events that, if not directly experienced by the reader, relate to basic cultural values and goals (e.g., finding happiness, wealth, and love). The influence of schemata in organizing and guiding memory of narratives can be observed when readers try to recall narratives from a culture with which they have little familiarity. Recall of such narratives is characterized by the omission and transformation of ideas and details in the narrative that do not fit with the conventional schema of the reader's culture (Bartlett, 1932).

Prose can also be organized by linking the elements in terms of causal relations. Causal relations capture relations between events (described in a text) that involve motivation, psychological causation (e.g., greed causes certain behaviors), and physical causation (e.g., rain causes things to become slippery). Understanding a narrative seems to involve the formation of a sequence of causal relations into a chain that links the opening of the narrative to its outcome. In remembering a narrative, people tend to remember those parts of a narrative which fit into the causal chain and forget the parts which are not incorporated into it (Fletcher and Bloom, 1988). More generally, better memory for narrative prose may occur because causal sequences are more clearly defined in narratives than in expository passages.

A third factor that contributes to prose organization is the reader's knowledge about the structure of conventional text forms. That is, when reading a fairy tale, regardless of the particular content, one expects to see certain components: a setting, an initiating event posing a problem, an attempt at its solution by the protagonist, and a consequence. This knowledge presumably allows the reader to better organize the information found in the passage.

In contrast, expository prose does not seem to entail a consistent structure, thereby reducing the extent to which the reader has a prestored structure that facilitates organization. Late-twentieth-century research indicates, however, that if readers are explicitly trained to notice and utilize some conventional expository forms (e.g., argumentative structures), then memory for such material is improved. Further, this positive effect is obtained for older as well as younger adults (Meyer, Young, and Bartlett, 1990).

Remembering Prose over Time

The organizational processes outlined previously exert greater influence as the interval between reading and attempted remembering increases. If recall is attempted within minutes after reading, then information that does not fit an initial perspective or schema can be recovered. If recall is delayed for at least one day, however, then recall of information that does not fit the schema may drop substantially, whereas information that fits the schema will still be well recalled (Fass and Schumacher, 1981). Similarly, in some cases study strategies designed to increase organizational processing of a text (e.g., outlining) will not improve memory for a text (relative to reading alone, with no studying) when recall is tested immediately, but will increase recall when testing is delayed for several days (Einstein et al., 1990). This increasingly beneficial mnemonic effect of organization with longer retention intervals is another aspect of prose memory that parallels memory for simpler verbal material.

Another factor that affects memory for prose is information that the learner encounters between reading a text and trying to remember it. Such intervening information can have facilitative as well as interfering effects on retention. To illustrate both kinds of effects, consider a biography about a poet named Susan. In the biography it is stated that Susan's father was a servant who died of diphtheria when Susan was five years old. After reading this biography, another biography is encountered in which Ann's blacksmith father dies of lung cancer when Ann is two years old. Research has shown that readers who are given the two biographies and are then asked to recall the first biography, recall the theme of the first biography (e.g., "the main character's father died when she was young") better than readers who are not given the second biography. But readers given the second biography do *not* recall the specific details of the first biography (the father's occupation, what he died of, and when) as well as the readers not given the second biography (Bower, 1974).

Perhaps one of the more interesting features of prose recall is that intervening information, or even a long retention interval, can promote reconstruction in remembering. Reconstruction refers to the finding that memory of a text can be distorted by the inclusion of information consistent with the theme of the text but not actually mentioned in it. Reconstruction also includes alteration of information that was in the text to bring it more in line with information encountered subsequent to the text or with readers' schemata that were activated in comprehending the text. For instance, in one study (Spiro, 1980) participants read a narrative about two college students who started dating seriously but disagreed about their desires to have children. After the participants read the text, the experimenter casually mentioned that the students had ended up getting married. Several weeks later, the participants attempted to recall the narrative. Their recall included reconstructions and distortions consistent with the new information mentioned by the experimenter but not actually in the narrative (e.g., "The students underwent counseling to correct the major discrepancy").

Prose recall need not always be reconstructive. If the reader expects a memory test on what has been read, then recall is more reproductive. That is, details are recalled more accurately, and there is very little inclusion of extra information not actually in the text. Also, in situations in which the reader's initial interpretative schema is invalidated at the time of recall, recall becomes more reproductive (Hasher and Griffin, 1978).

Assessing Prose Retention

In discussing prose retention, much of the focus has been on remembering as evidenced in recall. The influence of many of the aforementioned factors changes, however, if remembering is assessed with recognition memory tests. In recognition tests, the learner is presented with facts stated in the text and facts not stated in the text, and must determine which facts were presented and which were not. Common kinds of recognition tests include true/false and multiple-choice tests. In general, if prose memory is tested with recognition tests, the robust influence of organizational factors like those discussed earlier can be mitigated or eliminated. Thus, recognition is the same regardless of whether the text is written so that its overall theme can be clearly identified. Further, information that does not fit an encoding schema is recognized as well as information that does fit it, even if memory is tested one week after the text was read (McDaniel and Kerwin, 1987). Thus, as is the case with simple verbal materials, organizational factors play a more prominent role when prose retention is measured with recall than when measured with recognition.

See also: CODING PROCESSES: LEVELS OF PROCESSING; CODING PROCESSES: ORGANIZATION OF MEMORY; EXPERTS' MEMORIES; ORAL TRADITIONS; RECONSTRUCTIVE MEMORY

Bibliography

Bartlett, F. C. (1932). *Remembering*. Cambridge, UK: Cambridge University Press.

Bower, G. H. (1974). Selective facilitation and interference in retention of prose. *Journal of Educational Psychology 66*, 1–8.

Bransford, J. D., and Johnson, M. K. (1972). Contextual prerequisites for understanding: Some investigations of comprehension and recall. *Journal of Verbal Learning and Verbal Behavior 11*, 717–726.

Einstein, G. O., McDaniel, M. A., Owen, P. D., and Coté, N. C. (1990). Encoding and recall of texts: The importance of material appropriate processing. *Journal of Memory and Language 29*, 566–581.

Fass, W., and Schumacher, G. M. (1981). Schema theory and prose retention: Boundary conditions for encoding and retrieval effects. *Discourse Processes 4*, 17–26.

Fletcher, C. R., and Bloom, C. P. (1988). Causal reasoning in the comprehension of simple narrative texts. *Journal of Memory and Language 27*, 235–244.

Hasher, L., and Griffin, M. (1978). Reconstructive and reproductive processes in memory. *Journal of Experimental Psychology: Human Learning and Memory 4*, 318–330.

McDaniel, M. A., and Donnelly, C. M. (1996). Learning with analogy and elaborative interrogation. *Journal of Educational Psychology 88*, 508–519.

McDaniel, M. A., and Kerwin, M. L. E. (1987). Long-term prose retention: Is an organizational schema sufficient? *Discourse Processes 10*, 237–252.

Meyer, B. J. F., Young, C. J., and Bartlett, B. J. (1989). *Memory improved: Reading and memory enhancement across the life span through strategic text structures*. Hillsdale, NJ: Erlbaum.

Sachs, J. (1967). Recognition memory for syntactic and semantic aspects of connected discourse. *Perception and Psychophysics 2*, 437–442.

Schallert, D. L. (1976). Improving memory for prose: The relationship between depth of processing and context. *Journal of Verbal Learning and Verbal Behavior 15*, 621–632.

Slater, W. H., Graves, M. F., and Piche, G. L. (1985). Effects of structural organizers on ninth-grade students' comprehension and recall of four patterns of expository text. *Reading Research Quarterly 20*, 189–202.

Son, L. K., and Metcalfe, J. (2000). Metacognitive and control strategies in study-time allocation. *Journal of Experimental Psychology: Learning, Memory, and Cognition 26*, 204–221.

Spilich, G. J., Vesonder, G. T., Chiesi, H. L., and Voss, J. F. (1979). Text processing of domain-related information for individuals with high and low domain knowledge. *Journal of Verbal Learning and Verbal Behavior 18*, 275–290.

Spiro, R. J. (1980). Accommodative reconstruction in prose recall. *Journal of Verbal Learning and Verbal Behavior 19*, 84–95.

Mark A. McDaniel

PROTEIN SYNTHESIS IN LONG-TERM MEMORY IN VERTEBRATES

Most modern theories assume that memories are stored in the brain in the form of changed patterns of synaptic connections within ensembles of neurons, although it remains debated whether such patterns are stable once formed or subject to dynamic change. Any such growth or reorganization of synapses requires the synthesis of the molecules comprising them, especially the proteins and lipids of the synaptic and dendritic membranes. The idea that memory formation involves protein synthesis has been around for a long time—certainly since the days of Santiago Ramón y Cajal (Spanish histologist, 1852–1934) at the beginning of the twentieth century—but serious experimental tests of the idea became possible only with techniques available beginning in the 1960s. The adult brain has one of the highest rates of protein synthesis of any body organ, and also shows the greatest diversity of protein molecules. Some 30,000 different proteins are synthesized in the primate brain, only a small fraction of which have been characterized or ascribed functional roles. Many protein species are likely to be involved in memory consolidation, and it is unlikely that any of them are uniquely required; what provides the specificity for the memory trace is not the particular protein but the new pattern of synapses it helps to construct.

Two general approaches, sometimes described as *interventive* and *correlative,* have been used to identify these proteins. In the first, the behavioral consequences of either blocking protein function or preventing protein synthesis from occurring during or after training an animal on a particular task have been studied. If protein synthesis is necessary for memory formation, animals in which the synthesis has been blocked at the time of training should be amnesic for the task when subsequently tested. The second approach attempts to measure an increase in the synthesis or turnover of particular proteins as a result of the training experience. Both approaches have methodological pitfalls. Preventing protein expression or blocking function may have general effects on behavior, sensory or motor performance, or arousal, and therefore exert an effect on memory nonspecifically. Similarly, increases in protein synthesis following training could be the consequence of nonspecific behaviors such as the motor activity involved in carrying out the training task. Ruling out such alternative explanations requires devising careful control experiments.

Interventive Strategies

Proteins are synthesized in a series of steps beginning with the copying (transcribing) of strands of DNA into messenger RNA (mRNA), after which the mRNA is translated into the sequence of amino acids that constitutes the protein. Many proteins, especially those of the cell and synaptic membranes, are further modified posttranslationally. For instance, to synthesize glycoproteins, which are key constituents of the cell membrane, it is necessary to add sugar molecules to the protein chains before transporting them to the cellular sites at which they will function. Inhibiting any one of the steps in this synthetic sequence from the DNA to the finished molecule may block the synthesis of a protein or render it nonfunctional, and hence interfere with memory formation. The first experiment of this sort was made in the mid-1960s,

using an inhibitor of RNA synthesis, 8-azaguanine. Rats were trained to swim a water maze and then injected with the inhibitor. It had no effect on the performance of animals that had already learned the maze, or on their ability to swim in general. However, if the inhibitor was injected during the training trials, and the rats were tested the following day, they showed impaired memory for the maze.

In the decades that followed, experimenters employed various antibiotics that interfere with particular steps in protein synthesis: puromycin, cycloheximide, acetoxycycloheximide, and anisomycin. The consensus observation, in a variety of appetitive and aversive paradigms and with several species including rodents, birds, fish, molluscs and insects, is that concentrations of antibiotic sufficient to inhibit more than eighty percent (e.g., 80%) of all protein synthesis in the brain for several hours are, perhaps surprisingly, without effect on performance of already-learned tasks or other aspects of behavior. However, if the inhibitors are injected within specific time windows relative to the time of training (or testing), they will produce amnesia in animals tested twenty-four hours or more later. Behavioral controls rule out the possibility that these amnestic effects are due to some form of state dependency, and although the inhibitors have a variety of less specific biochemical effects (notably increasing the concentrations of intracellular amino acids, including several that are neurotransmitters and can be neurotoxic), it is generally agreed that they do indeed exert their amnestic effect by preventing the synthesis of proteins necessary for memory formation. More recently attention has turned to the blockade of specific proteins or protein classes. Glycoprotein synthesis can be blocked with the metabolic analogue 2-deoxygalactose. The expression of specific proteins can be prevented in mice or fruit flies by transgenic techniques such as the use of inducible knockouts, and in many species by antisense RNAs targeted against the specific transcribed RNA sequences coding for a particular protein. Appropriate antibodies can also functionally block proteins, especially membrane proteins, whose structure makes them accessible in vivo. Thus a monoclonal antibody raised against a key synaptic membrane constituent, the neural cell adhesion molecule N-CAM, a central player in the processes of cell-cell recognition, is amnestic if injected into rats trained in a passive avoidance task some six to eight hours after training. Antisense molecules that prevent the synthesis of the amyloid precursor protein, APP, or N-CAM, are also amnestic. Mouse knockouts lacking the cyclic AMP response element binding protein (CREB) also show characteristic learning deficits.

Correlative Studies

Like the interventive approach, correlative studies began in the 1960s. Because it is unlikely that there will be measurable increases in the total amount of proteins in general or of specific proteins in particular during memory formation, the initial approach was to measure the rate of protein synthesis during training by the use of a radioactive precursor. A radioactively labeled amino acid, injected into the bloodstream, is taken into the brain and there becomes incorporated into protein. The amount of radioactivity found in the protein after a fixed time interval then depends, among other factors (which need to be controlled for), on the rate of synthesis of the protein. If more radioactivity is found in brains of trained than of control animals, this is assumed to indicate that the training procedure has resulted in enhanced synthesis (or turnover), and the behavioral question then becomes that of ensuring that it is memory formation rather than some other aspect of the task that has increased the synthesis.

Some of the clearest evidence for enhanced protein synthesis using this approach came from studies of early learning in the chick, especially imprinting and one-trial passive avoidance training. These tasks involve strong and biologically programmed learning in an otherwise naive animal, and therefore maximize the chance of finding changes. For example, training on the passive avoidance task results in a long lasting increase in incorporation of radioactive amino acids into the proteins of specific brain regions.

To study such increases in more detail, it is necessary to know which brain regions might be involved. Here, an autoradiographic mapping technique can be employed in which, after incorporation of the radioactivity, the brains are sectioned and apposed to X-ray film, and the specific regions showing training-related increases identified by image analysis. Such techniques have been used to show enhanced protein synthesis in the rat hippocampus during a variety of learning paradigms.

The next task becomes that of identifying which of the many proteins are involved. Various approaches are possible. Subcellular fractionation can show in which cellular compartments the new proteins are most concentrated. In both rat and chick there are increases both in soluble proteins such as tubulin and in synaptic membrane constituents such as N-CAM. In an unusual training task in goldfish—in which the animal has a float attached to its belly that inverts it, so that it has to learn to swim correctly once more—a different class of low-molecular weight soluble glycoproteins, named *ependymins*, has been identified by similar techniques. This class of molecules has also been shown to be relevant in mammalian learning. Other imaging techniques, such as in situ hybridization or immunocytochemistry, can define specific cellular regions, such as dendritic spines, as showing increased levels of particular messenger RNAs or proteins.

Memory Consolidation and Memory Phases

The demonstration of the time windows during which protein synthesis inhibitors are amnestic has been an important piece of evidence in developing stage theories of time-dependent processes in memory formation. Thus it was early demonstrated that if protein synthesis inhibitors were administered around the time of training in, for instance rodents or chicks, then animals could learn and show memory retention for periods of an hour or so, after which a progressive amnesia set in. This was taken to indicate a distinction between short-term memory, not requiring new protein synthesis, and long-term memory, for which such synthesis was necessary. Giving the inhibitor one to two hour posttraining no longer results in amnesia and hence memory was said to be now stable and protein synthesis independent. However, this proved to be simplistic; a second time window four to six hours downstream of the training experience was found in a number of paradigms during which memory consolidation once more becomes sensitive to protein synthesis inhibitors.

The current working hypothesis is that the initial stages of memory formation involve transient synaptic membrane events. These events include the phosphorylation of membrane proteins (including the presynaptic protein known as B50 or GAP43) by a membrane-bound enzyme, protein kinase C. This phosphorylation step activates a cycle of intracellular second messengers, including calcium ions, and transcription factors, such as CREB, which in turn trigger a genomic response in the neuronal cell nucleus. The initial genomic response is to switch on a family of specific immediate early genes whose protein products include in particular c-fos, c-jun, and zif. These proteins are expressed only during the early phases of neuronal plasticity, when neurons are growing or actively differentiating, and they have been shown to increase dramatically in concentration in a number of learning tasks, including brightness discrimination in the rat and passive avoidance in the chick, as well as hippocampal long-term potentiation. But c-fos and c-jun, although they are excellent markers to show where in the brain neural plasticity is occurring, are themselves only intermediates; their production acts as a trigger for the activation of further genes (late genes) whose products include the proteins and glycoproteins already mentioned. It is the enhanced synthesis of these proteins, in the so-called second synthetic wave, four to six hours downstream of training, which makes consolidation once more sensitive to the general synthesis inhibitors as well as to specific antisense or antibodies against, for instance, the families of cell adhesion molecules such as N-CAM. These adhesion molecules have sticky glycosylated extracellular domains. Projecting both from pre- and postsynaptic sides, they can bind together rather like a molecular form of Velcro, holding the synaptic junction in a specific configuration. It is therefore assumed that these are the ultimate effector proteins required for lasting remodelling of synapses.

Consolidation and Reconsolidation

Recently even this conclusion concerning stable memory has been called into question. If an animal is trained on a task, and some time—hours to days later—given a reminder by being exposed once more to the original training situation, then the previously stable memory again becomes labile and sensitive to protein synthesis inhibitors. For some researchers, reminder plus inhibitor results in lasting amnesia, implying that in some way reactivating a memory requires retraversing the same biochemical pathway that was initially engaged. Others find that the effect of the inhibitors is transient, suggesting a temporary blockade of access to an otherwise unimpaired memory. The phenomenon is intriguing but its interpretation remains an arena of active debate.

Conclusion

Protein synthesis is universally necessary for the formation of long-term memory, although some forms of newly acquired memory may persist for long periods in the absence of such synthesis. The proteins involved are synthesized in increased amounts in specific cells in the hours following a training experience and during the period of memory consolidation. Different proteins are synthesized at different times after training in a time- and space-dependent sequence; in the first phase they include members of the immediate-early family, such as c-fos and c-jun. Later stages involve the synthesis of the microtubular protein tubulin and glycoprotein components of synaptic and dendritic membranes, including members of the cell adhesion family. Others certainly remain to be identified. If their expression or function is prevented, amnesia results. Some may also be required for the expression of old but newly activated memories. These proteins are not, however, in themselves specific to the particular memory. What conveys specificity is the pattern of neurons whose connections are modified by the learning experience; the proteins are part of the housekeeping processes involved in modifying those connections. Identifying more precisely the proteins involved, their locations, and their functions will help substantially in the development of theories of memory formation, in addition to being of major intrinsic neurobiological interest, and of potential relevance to the treatment of such conditions as Alzheimer's disease.

See also: MEMORY CONSOLIDATION: MOLECULAR AND CELLULAR PROCESSES; MEMORY CONSOLIDATION: PROLONGED PROCESS OF REORGANIZATION

Bibliography

Davis, H. P., and Squire, L. R. (1984). Protein synthesis and memory: A review. *Psychological Bulletin 96,* 518–559.

DeZazzo, J., and Tully, T. (1995). Dissection of memory formation: From behavioral pharmacology to molecular genetics. *Trends in Neuroscience 18,* 212–217.

Dudai, Y. (1989). *Neurobiology of memory.* Oxford: Oxford University Press.

Goelet, P., Castelluci, S., Schachner, S., and Kandel, E. R. (1986). The long and the short of long-term memory—a molecular framework. *Nature 322,* 19–423.

Izquierdo, I., and Medina, J. H. (1997). Memory formation: The sequence of biochemical events in the hippocampus and its connection to activity in other brain structures. *Neurobiology of Learning and Memory 68,* 285–316.

Mileusnic, R., Lancashire, C., and Rose, S. P. R. (1999). Sequence specific impairment of memory formation by NCAM antisense oligonucleotides. *Learning and Memory 6,* 120–127.

Nader, K., Schafe, G. E., and LeDoux, J. E. (2000). Fear memories require protein synthesis in the amygdala for reconsolidation after retrieval. *Nature 406,* 722–726.

Radyushkin, K. A., and Anokhin, K. V. (1999). Recovery of memory in chicks after disruption during learning: The reversibility of amnesia induced by protein synthesis inhibitors. *Neuroscience and Behavioral Physiology 29* (1), 31–36.

Rose, S. P. R. (1992). *The making of memory.* London: Bantam.

—— (2000). God's organism? The chick as a model system for memory studies. *Learning and Memory 7,* 1–17.

Steven P. R. Rose

PSYCHOPHARMACOLOGY

See: COGNITIVE ENHANCERS; DRUGS AND MEMORY; PHARMACOLOGICAL TREATMENT OF MEMORY DISORDERS

R

RAMÓN Y CAJAL, SANTIAGO (1852–1934)

Santiago Ramón y Cajal, born in the small Spanish town of Petilla de Aragón on May 1, 1852, was a major figure in the history of neuroanatomy. As related in his delightful autobiography, he was somewhat mischievous as a child and determined to become an artist, much to the consternation of his father, a respected local physician. Eventually, however, Ramón y Cajal entered the University of Zaragoza, and received a degree in medicine in 1873. As a professor of anatomy at Zaragoza, his interests were mostly in bacteriology until 1887, when he visited Madrid and first saw through the microscope histological sections of brain tissue treated with the Golgi method, which had been introduced in 1873.

Although few workers had employed this technique, Ramón y Cajal immediately saw that it offered great hope in solving one of the most vexing and fundamental problems in morphology: How do nerve cells interact with each other? This realization galvanized and directed the rest of his scientific life, which was extremely productive in originality, scope, and accuracy.

To place Ramón y Cajal's work in historical perspective, one must recall that, while studies of the gross anatomy of the brain can be traced back as far as Greek philosopher Aristotle, the first real insight into the disposition of its major fiber tracts was not gained until the middle of the nineteenth century, and even then the interpretation of this information was subject to great controversy. Shortly after the German botanist Jacob Schleiden, the German naturalist Theodor Schwann, and the German pathologist Rudolf Virchow proposed the cell theory in the 1830s, Joseph von Gerlach, Sr., and Otto Friedrich Karl Dieters suggested that nerve tissue was special in the sense that nerve cells are not independent units but instead form a continuous syncytium or reticular net. This concept was later refined by the Italian physician Camillo Golgi, who concluded that the axons of nerve cells form a continuous reticular net, whereas their dendrites serve a nutritive role, much like the roots of a tree.

Using Golgi's technique, Ramón y Cajal almost immediately arrived at the opposite conclusion, from his examination first of the cerebellum, and then of a wide variety of other sensory and motor systems. In short, he proposed that neurons interact by way of contact rather than continuity. His work on both the mature and the developing nervous system (he discovered the growth cone in 1890) provided the best evidence for the neuron doctrine (that neurons are independent units or cells, as in other tissues) until the introduction of the electron microscope in the 1950s.

Important as this evidence was, Ramón y Cajal's greatest conceptual achievement was the law of dynamic polarity. Based on his analysis of Golgi-impregnated neurons in the retina and other sensory systems, where the direction of information flow from the periphery to the central nervous system seems obvious, Ramón y Cajal concluded that, in general, the

Santiago Ramón y Cajal *(Library of Congress)*

dendrites and perikaryon of a neuron receive information, whereas its axon transmits information. This brilliant generalization allowed him to lay out the basic organization of circuitry throughout the nervous system. This research was summarized in the monumental three-volume work *Textura del sistema nervioso del hombre y de los vertebrados*, published between 1899 and 1904, then expanded and translated into the definitive French edition, *Histologie du système nerveux de l'homme et des vertébrés* (1909–1911). This account deals systematically with all parts of the mammalian nervous system and many aspects of its development, and provides a great deal of information on the organization of the nervous system in fish, amphibians, reptiles, and birds.

Ramón y Cajal next examined in great detail the histological changes that can be observed during the degeneration and regeneration of neural tissue following damage. The results of this work were summarized in another monumental work that is still well worth reading, the two-volume *Degeneration and Regeneration of the Nervous System*, first published in Spanish in 1913–1914.

Ramón y Cajal received many honors, including the Nobel Prize, which he shared with a contentious Golgi in 1906. By the time Ramón y Cajal died, at the age of eighty-two in 1934, he had become one of the most famous and revered Spaniards of the twentieth century. In addition to the neurohistological work outlined herein, he wrote widely appreciated books on color photography, advice to young investigators, and well-known Spanish aphorisms.

Ramón y Cajal's description of the organization of cerebral cortical circuitry is unparalleled in depth and breadth. As early as 1894 he advanced the hypothesis that the remarkable intellectual growth seen in people who engage in continuous mental exercise is due to an enhanced elaboration of axon collaterals and dendritic processes within cortical circuitry.

See also: GUIDE TO THE ANATOMY OF THE BRAIN: NEURON; GUIDE TO THE ANATOMY OF THE BRAIN: SYNAPSE

Bibliography

De Filipe, J., and E. G. Jones. (1988). *Cajal on the cerebral cortex.* New York: Oxford University Press.

Ramón y Cajal, S. (1899–1904). *Textura del sistema nervioso del hombre y de los vertebrados,* 3 vols. Madrid: N. Moya.

—— (1909–1911). *Histologie du système nerveux de l'homme et des vertébrés,* trans. L. Azoulay. 2 vols. Paris: Norbert Maloine.

—— (1928). *Degeneration and regeneration of the nervous system.* trans. and ed. R. M. May. 2 vols. London: Oxford University Press.

—— (1989). *Recollections of my life,* trans. E. H. Craigie with J. Cano. Cambridge, MA: MIT Press.

—— (1990). *New ideas on the structure of the nervous system in man and vertebrates,* trans. N. Swanson and L. W. Swanson. Cambridge, MA: MIT Press.

Larry W. Swanson

RECONSTRUCTIVE MEMORY

Subjectively, memory feels like a camera that faithfully records and replays details of our past. In fact, memory is a reconstructive process prone to systematic biases and errors—reliable at times, and unreliable at others. Memories are a combination of new and old knowledge, personal beliefs, and one's own and others' expectations. We blend these ingredients in forming a past that conforms to one's haphazardly accurate view of oneself and the world.

Reconstructing the Past

Traditionally, psychologists were interested in the temporal retention of information. Since the early 1930s, many psychologists have shifted their focus from the quantity of memory to its accuracy (Koriat, Goldsmith, and Pansky, 2000). The British psychologist Frederic C. Bartlett (1932) conducted one of the first systematic investigations of memory accuracy. He asked subjects to read a legend about Indian hunters called "The War of the Ghosts" and then to retell it to another subject who had not read it. The second subject then told the story to another subject, and so on, until ten subjects had heard it. The story involves two young Indian hunters who meet a group of men in a canoe, who, in turn, invite the hunters to join them in battle upriver. One young Indian accepts and the other declines. During battle, the young Indian is wounded and realizes that the men of the war party are ghosts. He returns home, recounts his tale, and dies the next morning.

Bartlett found that subjects retained the overall gist of the story but that they also revised the story, systematically omitting and modifying details. For example, subjects omitted mystical references, such as ghosts, which are not part of Westerners' worldview; they embellished other details. In the original story, the second Indian declined to join the party because his relatives would not know his whereabouts. By the tenth retelling, one subject explained that this Indian refused because his elderly mother was dependent on him, a revision that manifests Western concepts of a son's responsibilities in general and perhaps that subject's family ties in particular. Another common change was that subjects tended to add a moral, possibly because stories in Western culture often have morals. Bartlett concluded, "Remembering . . . is an imaginative reconstruction, or construction, built out of the relation of our attitude towards a whole mass of organized past reactions or experiences" (p. 213).

Bartlett's study exemplifies how time and retelling distort the memory of stories. Another study conducted in the early 1930s using ambiguous drawings showed that what we are told that we are viewing easily distorts visual material. If people are shown two circles and a line and are told that the picture represents either glasses or dumbbells, subjects' later drawings of the original picture will assume the suggested appearance (Carmichael, Hogan, and Walter, 1932).

There are many other studies that demonstrate the malleability of memory for words, stories, and pictures. For example, Henry Roediger and Kathleen McDermott (1995) altered a procedure originally developed by James Deese in which people study lists of closely related words like *bed, pillow, tired,* and *dream*. When later asked to recall studied words, subjects frequently claim that they saw other words like *sleep* that were not presented but are related to those that were. Subjects often assert these "false memories" with a high degree of confidence and detail (e.g., that a male as opposed to a female voice spoke the word). There is some debate about whether subjects generate the word *sleep* while studying the word list or later, when asked to recall the entire word list. In either case, peo-

ple draw inferences—not necessarily accurate—about their present and past experiences.

Yet another way to demonstrate memory's attempt at synthesis is to present subjects with successive, thematically related slides depicting common routines like going grocery shopping. One slide shows a woman putting a box of items into her shopping cart. The next slide shows several oranges on the ground. When subjects are asked later to recognize slides that had previously been shown, they mistakenly say that they saw a slide depicting the woman removing an orange from the bottom of a pile of oranges (Hannigan and Tippens-Reinitz, 2001). They make this causal inference because people naturally attempt to piece together the fragments of their past in order to make memory as coherent as possible.

Misinformation

Work on the "misinformation effect" further demonstrates the ease with which accumulated information skews memory (Loftus, 1979). In the misinformation effect, misleading information about an event from one's past reduces the accuracy of the memory of an event. In one study, Elizabeth Loftus and colleagues showed subjects a simulated automobile-pedestrian accident (Loftus, Miller, and Burns, 1978): a vehicle stops at an intersection, turns right, and then hits a pedestrian. Half the subjects viewed a stop sign at the intersection. After viewing the scene, these subjects were asked a question that mentioned either a stop sign or a yield sign. In a final memory test, these subjects were asked whether they saw a stop sign or a yield sign. When the subjects were asked a question consistent with what they had seen, they chose the correct sign 75 percent of the time. However, when the question was inconsistent with what they had seen, they chose the correct sign only 41 percent of the time. These investigators concluded that some subjects had initially encoded a stop sign in memory but that the subsequent mention of a yield sign altered their memory.

Does the new information alter the original memory trace, or does it coexist with the original information in memory (Ayers and Reder, 1999)? According to the altered-trace view, the original memory is changed permanently and is inaccessible to recollection. According to the coexistence view, the original information is still accessible with the right retrieval cues. The issue of memory's permanence remains a fundamental, unresolved question in memory research. But whatever your view about the underlying memory traces, it is clear that the memory reports of subjects are changed, and many subjects appear to believe strongly in their misinformation memories.

Figure 1

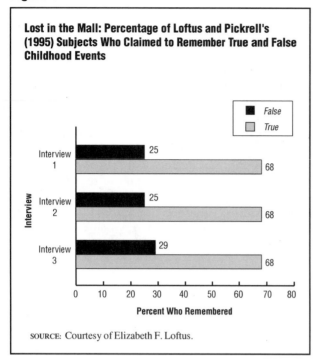

Lost in the Mall: Percentage of Loftus and Pickrell's (1995) Subjects Who Claimed to Remember True and False Childhood Events

SOURCE: Courtesy of Elizabeth F. Loftus.

Although the evidence indicates that our memories are malleable and easily manipulated, there are circumstances in which memory is relatively resistant to change. For example, if people publicly state that they remember a detail, subsequent suggestions are less likely to induce a change of mind. There is also resistance to changed recollection in the face of gross disparities between clearly perceived details and contradicting misinformation. It is also possible to reduce misinformation effects by warning people about misleading messages or by requiring subjects to determine the precise source of the misinformation—for example, "Did I see the flat tire in the film, or did I hear or read about it after I saw the film?" (Loftus, 1997). Thus, memory is reconstructive, and reconstructions are susceptible to—but not powerless against—subsequent misleading information.

Implanted Memories

The previous examples demonstrate the disturbing ease with which the details of memory can be manipulated. But it doesn't stop there—it is also possible to implant entire false memories. People can be led to believe that, as children, they were lost in a shopping mall or that they had knocked over a punch bowl at a wedding and spilled punch on the bride's parents (Hyman, Husband, and Billings, 1995; Loftus and Pickrell, 1995). In a series of interviews, Loftus and

Pickrell asked subjects to recall as much as possible about four childhood event descriptions that a relative had provided. Three of these events were true, and one was false: that the subject had been lost in a shopping mall at the age of five for an extended time and had been rescued by an elderly woman and reunited with the family. In three suggestive interviews, during which subjects were led to believe all the events occurred, subjects remembered the real events about 70 percent of the time and the false ones about 25 percent of the time (see Figure 1).

Imagination offers another way to implant false memories. Subjects are asked to imagine in detail an event that never occurred. Later, they are asked to rate their confidence that the event truly happened. The act of imagination typically causes subjects to increase their confidence in the reality of these events. Although some researchers argue that certain memories are highly resistant to suggestion and imagination, others have shown that it is even possible to increase people's confidence that they had witnessed demonic possession as a child (Mazzoni, Loftus, and Kirsch, 2001). These studies indicate that implantation of entirely false memories is possible.

Once implanted, the false memory is often barely distinguishable from real ones. Research has shown that there can be statistical differences between a group of real memories and a group of false ones: For example, the real memories possessing more sensory detail (Heaps and Nash, 2001; Schooler, Gerhard, and Loftus, 1986). But people can give detailed descriptions of their false memories that sometimes lead them and others to regard the memories as real. Moreover, it is difficult to determine the truth or falsity of a single memory report.

Another line of research aims to determine whether true and false memories elicit different brain activity. In such work, subjects read a list of closely related words and later try to recognize whether or not they had previously seen those words and other novel but related words. During the recognition phase of the experiment, subjects' brain activity is monitored by sophisticated neuroimaging tools like magnetic resonance imaging (MRI) or event-related potentials (ERPs). There is some preliminary evidence that neuroimaging may permit scientists to glimpse the neural signatures of true and false memories (Fabiani, Stadler, and Wessels, 2000); however, more work is needed to confirm the utility of this approach.

Evaluation and Attribution

It is clear that memory can fail in a variety of ways. However, the precise reason why memory fails is less clear. Larry Jacoby and others have shown that the manner in which people evaluate their present processing in light of the past may explain in part both how and why memory fails. For example, the ease with which a memory comes to mind after exposure to misinformation or after imagining the memory in question may rightly or wrongly lead the person to believe that the memory is real. In fact, unless there is another, more likely, reason or source to explain why a memory or experience currently feels familiar, people will typically attribute feelings of familiarity to past experience (Jacoby, Kelley, and Dywan, 1989; Whittlesea and Williams, 2001). Thus, it is possible to influence memory by changing the way in which the present experience is processed, evaluated, and then attributed to the past.

Conclusion

Far from a reliably faithful rendering of the past, memory is a reconstruction that usually retains the gist but not the details of bygone experiences. The recounting of one's past, the exposure to misleading postevent information and suggestion, integration of thematically related material, and imagination are several of the means by which memory is constructed—or misconstructed. Once reconstructed, the original memory may prove elusive. Given the potential fallibility of our recollections, it is surprising that memory functions as well as it does.

See also: FALSE MEMORIES

Bibliography

Ayers, M. S., and Reder, L. M. (1999). A theoretical review of the misinformation effect: Predictions from an activation-based memory model. *Psychonomic Bulletin & Review 5,* 1–21.

Bartlett, F. C. (1932). *Remembering: A study in experimental and social psychology.* New York: Macmillan.

Carmichael, L., Hogan, H. P., and Walter, A. A. (1932). An experimental study of the effect of language on the reproduction of visually perceived form. *Journal of Experimental Psychology 15,* 73–86.

Fabiani, M., Stadler, M. A., and Wessels, P. M. (2000). True but not false memories produce a sensory signature in human lateralized brain potentials. *Journal of Cognitive Neuroscience 12,* 941–949.

Hannigan, S. L., and Tippens-Reinitz, M. T. (2001). A demonstration and comparison of two types of inference-based memory errors. *Journal of Experimental Psychology: Learning, Memory, and Cognition 27,* 931–940.

Heaps, C. M., and Nash, M. (2001). Comparing recollective experience in true and false autobiographical memories. *Journal of Experimental Psychology: Learning, Memory, and Cognition 27,* 920–930.

Hyman, I. E., Jr., Husband, T. H., and Billings, F. J. (1995). False memories of childhood experiences. *Applied Cognitive Psychology 9,* 181–197.

Jacoby, L. L., Kelley, C. M., and Dywan, J. (1989). Memory attributions. In H. L. Roediger III, and F. I. M. Craik, eds., *Varieties of memory and consciousness: Essays in honour of Endel Tulving.* Hillsdale, NJ: Erlbaum.

Koriat, A., Goldsmith, M., and Pansky, A. (2000). Toward a psychology of memory accuracy. *Annual Review of Psychology 51,* 481–537.

Loftus, E. F. (1979). *Eyewitness testimony.* Cambridge, MA: Harvard University Press.

—— (1997). Creating false memories. *Scientific American 277,* 70–75.

Loftus, E. F., Miller, D. G., and Burns, H. J. (1978). Semantic integration of verbal information into a visual memory. *Journal of Experimental Psychology 4,* 19–31.

Loftus, E. F., and Pickrell, J. E. (1995). The formation of false memories. *Psychiatric Annals 25,* 720–725.

Mazzoni, G. A. L., Loftus, E. F., and Kirsch, I. (2001). Changing beliefs about implausible autobiographical events: A little plausibility goes a long way. *Journal of Experimental Psychology: Applied 7,* 51–59.

Roediger, H. L., III, and McDermott, K. B. (1995). Creating false memories: Remembering words not presented in lists. *Journal of Experimental Psychology: Learning, Memory, and Cognition 21,* 803–814.

Schooler, J. W., Gerhard, D., and Loftus, E. F. (1986). Qualities of the unreal. *Journal of Experimental Psychology: Learning Memory, and Cognition 12,* 171–181.

Whittlesea, B. W. A., and Williams, L. D. (2001). The discrepancy-attribution hypothesis: II. Expectation, uncertainty, surprise, and feelings of familiarity. *Journal of Experimental Psychology: Learning, Memory, and Cognition 27,* 14–33.

Elizabeth F. Loftus
Rick L. Leitner
Revised by Daniel M. Bernstein and Elizabeth F. Loftus

REHABILITATION

See: ELECTROCONVULSIVE THERAPY AND MEMORY LOSS; HEAD INJURY; PHARMACOLOGICAL TREATMENT OF MEMORY DEFICITS; REHABILITATION OF MEMORY DISORDERS

REHABILITATION OF MEMORY DISORDERS

Memory impairment is one of the most pervasive and debilitating consequences of a range of neurological conditions, including closed-head injury, aneurysm, stroke, encephalitis, tumor, anoxia, Korsakoff's syndrome, and dementia. This inability to remember recent experiences or to acquire any new long-term memories is frequently resistant to rehabilitation. Recent empirical and theoretical advances in psychology and neuroscience, however, have broadened understanding of the cognitive and neural mechanisms of memory and have provided a new perspective on memory rehabilitation. It is now apparent that memory is not a unitary entity; it can break down in a variety of ways, and although some aspects of memory are seriously compromised, others remain unaffected. For rehabilitation to be successful, it must take account of the spared as well as the impaired cognitive and neural processes. Finding ways to tap into intact processes to accomplish the kinds of memory tasks that are impaired, however, has not been easy, and so this approach to rehabilitation remains only one of several.

Approaches to rehabilitation fall into two broad categories: those that attempt to remediate the underlying impairment and achieve broad improvements in memory and those that intervene at a behavioral level and try to achieve specific functional outcomes. The second approach has been more fruitful: patients have been able to take advantage of ways to bypass or compensate for their deficits and thus attain some level of independence in their everyday lives. But general mnemonic improvements, which might apply broadly across a range of memory situations, have proved elusive.

Practice and Rehearsal Techniques

Extensive practice or rehearsal is essential for the acquisition and retention of information by memory-impaired individuals. The effects of practice, however, are highly specific and tend not to generalize beyond the trained materials. It is, therefore, important that practice be directed towards information that is useful in everyday life. Simple repetitive exercise or rote rehearsal, however, is unlikely to achieve long-term retention. Instead, short periods of distributed practice are more effective. One such method, spaced retrieval, involves repeated practice at retrieving to-be-learned information at gradually increasing retention intervals. This technique has been successful in teaching memory-impaired patients, including those with Alzheimer's disease, various kinds of information important in their daily lives, including name-face associations, locations of objects, and aspects of orientation (Camp and McKitrick, 1992). The method may rely on residual memory function or tap into other preserved memory processes.

Mnemonic Strategies

Teaching a variety of mnemonic strategies, including visual imagery and verbal elaboration, has achieved only spotty success with neurologically impaired patients. For many patients, the techniques are too demanding and difficult. They are often effective, however, for individuals with unilateral lesions and material-specific deficits. People with left-hemisphere lesions and problems in verbal memory may benefit from visual-imagery strategies, whereas those with right-hemisphere lesions and difficulties in visuo-spatial memory may find verbal methods, such as first-letter cuing, more useful. Like rehearsal strat-

egies, mnemonic techniques can be used to help people acquire specific pieces of new information important in their daily lives, but they do not provide broad-based memory improvements because of their lack of applicability to new materials and contexts. Because mnemonic strategies are useful only for mildly impaired patients, these strategies likely rely on residual memory function (Glisky and Glisky, 2002).

External Aids and Environmental Supports

Compensating for memory impairments has often involved providing external aids for remembering, such as notebooks and diaries; bell timers and alarm watches; environmental restructurings such as labels and directions; and, most recently, microcomputers, recorders, pagers, and electronic organizers. Although the simplest of these—labels and signage—can be used effectively by even the most severely impaired individuals, aids such as notebooks, computers, and electronic organizers require training and extensive practice and may be beneficial only for mildly impaired individuals; more severely impaired patients may be unable to learn how to use these devices. Barbara Wilson and her colleagues (2001) have reported considerable success with a simple paging device that requires little learning, can be used effectively by even very severely impaired patients, and can be programmed to meet the needs of individual patients. The device provides people with needed information at various times of the day, enabling them to perform important daily functions that they would otherwise be unable to remember.

Vanishing Cues

The method of vanishing cues was developed expressly to take advantage of the implicit learning and memory abilities that are spared in amnesic patients in order to teach them useful information and skills. This technique, which involves the gradual withdrawal of cues across learning trials, was thought to capitalize on patients' preserved abilities to retrieve recently presented information in response to fragment cues. Using this method, Glisky and colleagues (1994) demonstrated that even people with serious memory impairments could acquire a variety of domain-specific skills and knowledge, including computer procedures, data entry, database management, and word-processing. Patients learned this information despite having little or no memory of the occasions of learning and were later able to use it in the workplace or in the home.

Errorless Learning

Wilson and colleagues (Evans et al., 2000) showed that preventing errors during learning facilitates the acquisition of new information in people with memory disorders. Errorless learning has been effective in teaching memory-impaired patients a range of useful information, including names, the use of a memory notebook and an electronic memory aid, and items of general knowledge. Other methods, such as vanishing cues and spaced retrieval in combination with errorless learning, may prove beneficial, particularly for very severely impaired patients, who have to rely on preserved implicit memory.

Conclusion

Current understanding of memory disorders favors a rehabilitation strategy that focuses on achieving improved functioning rather than on treating underlying impairment. Because the benefits are specific and limited, it is important to ensure that rehabilitation is directed towards solving real-world problems. The finding of preserved-memory abilities in amnesic patients suggests that there may be alternative routes to usable memory if ways could be found to recruit these intact cognitive and neural structures. Although relatively little is known about the reorganization of brain function after damage, recent neuroimaging studies have suggested that such reorganization is possible and may have functional consequences (Grady and Kapur, 1999). Finding ways to encourage reorganization and to tap into preserved functions will be important tasks for future research in memory rehabilitation.

See also: MNEMONIC DEVICES; PHARMACOLOGICAL TREATMENT OF MEMORY DEFICITS

Bibliography

Baddeley, A. D., Wilson, B. A., and Watts, F. N. (1995). *Handbook of memory disorders.* Chichester, UK: John Wiley.

Camp, C. J., and McKitrick, L. A. (1992). Memory interventions in Alzheimer's-type dementia populations: Methodological and theoretical issues. In R. L. West and J. D. Sinnott, eds., *Everyday memory and aging: Current research and methodology.* New York: Springer-Verlag.

Evans, J. J., Wilson, B. A., Schuri, U., Andrade, J., Baddeley, A., Bruna, O., Canavan, T., Della Sala, S., Green, R., Laaksonen, R., Lorenzi, L., and Taussik, I. (2000). A comparison of "errorless" and "trial-and-error" learning methods for teaching individuals with acquired memory deficits. *Neuropsychological Rehabilitation 10,* 67–101.

Glisky, E. L., and Glisky, M. L. (2002). Learning and memory impairments. In P. J. Eslinger, ed., *Neuropsychological interventions.* New York: Guilford Press.

Glisky, E. L., Schacter, D. L., and Butters, M. A. (1994). Domain-specific learning and remediation of memory disorders. In M. J. Riddoch and G. W. Humphreys, eds., *Cognitive neuropsychology and cognitive rehabilitation.* Hove, UK: Erlbaum.

Grady, C. L., and Kapur, S. (1999). The use of neuroimaging in neurorehabilitative research. In D. T. Stuss, G. Winocur, and I. H. Robertson, eds., *Cognitive Neurorehabilitation.* Cambridge UK: Cambridge University Press.

Wilson, B. A., Emslie, H., Quirk, K., and Evans, J. (2001). Reducing everyday memory and planning problems by means of a paging system: A randomized control crossover study. *Journal of Neurology, Neurosurgery, and Psychiatry 70,* 477–482.

Elizabeth L. Glisky

REINFORCEMENT

In its earliest technical usages, the term *reinforcement* implied strengthening, echoing its colloquial usage. It has been applied to a broad range of phenomena in learning, including the operant or instrumental behavior studied by B. F. Skinner and the respondent or classical conditioning procedures of Ivan Pavlov. The term, which also applies to certain types of machine learning procedures studied by computer scientists and engineers, now refers mostly to cases in which behavior has some consequences and, by virtue of these consequences, comes to occur more often. The term *reward*, sometimes used as a nontechnical synonym, is not equivalent. For example, one can speak of delivering a reward even without evidence that the reward has an effect on behavior.

As a classical example of reinforcement, imagine a rat in a chamber with a lever and a cup into which food pellets can be delivered. If pressing the lever does nothing, the rat presses only occasionally. If each press produces a food pellet, however, the rat presses the lever more often. The food is called a reinforcer, and the rat's lever press is said to have been reinforced. The response that increases must be the one that produced the consequence. For example, if lever presses produce shock and only the rat's jumping increases, it would be inappropriate to speak of either lever pressing or jumping as reinforced. An ambiguity of usage is that *reinforcement* sometimes refers to delivery of the reinforcer ("the lever press was reinforced" means that lever presses produced food) and sometimes to the resulting behavior change ("the lever press was reinforced" means that lever presses occurred more often because they produced food). The sense is usually clear from the context.

The Operant Nature of Reinforcement

Edward Thorndike's experiments with animals in problem boxes were early examples of studies of reinforcement. Typically, a food-deprived animal was placed inside a box with food available outside. Sooner or later, typically by chance, the animal operated a device that released the door and freed it from the box. With repetition it operated the device more and more rapidly upon being placed in the box. To describe his findings, Thorndike formulated his law of effect. The law went through many revisions, but its essence was that responses can be made more probable by some consequences and less probable by others; in language closer to Thorndike's, responses with satisfying effects are stamped in, whereas those with annoying effects are stamped out.

Behavior that is modified by its consequences is called operant behavior or, in older and less common usages, instrumental behavior, which is behavior that operates on its environment. It is said to be emitted because it is primarily determined by its consequences; it does not require an eliciting stimulus, as in reflex relations (e.g., as when a puff of air to the eye produces a blink). Operants are classes of responses defined by their environmental effects rather than by their topography (their form or the particular muscle groups involved). For example, a rat might press a lever with its left paw, its right paw, or both paws; it might even depress the lever by biting or sitting on it. But similar movements at the other end of the chamber, far from the lever, would not be lever presses no matter how closely they resembled the responses that operated the lever.

Skinner significantly extended the analysis of reinforcement. One of his critical contributions was to clarify the difference between operant learning and the classical or respondent learning that had been studied by Pavlov (in Pavlov's experiments, the organism's responses had no effect on the stimuli that were presented).

Consider the relation between a red traffic light and a driver's stepping on the brakes. The red light sets the occasion for stepping on the brakes; this response occurs at a red light and not at a green light because it has different consequences in the presence of each stimulus. A stimulus that signals or sets the occasion for different consequences of responding is discriminative. Three terms are involved: the discriminative stimulus, the response, and the consequences of the response in the presence of that stimulus.

For example, imagine a pigeon in a chamber with a feeder; above the feeder is a small disk or key that can be lit from behind with lights of different colors. Suppose that reinforcement of the pigeon's key peck depends on the presence of a green or a red light. If the peck produces food only when the key is green, the pigeon will come to peck in the presence of green but not red. Its pecking in the presence of green is a discriminated operant. Discriminative stimuli correspond to the stimuli colloquially called signals or cues. They do not elicit responses; instead, they set the occasions on which responses have consequences.

Positive and Negative Reinforcement

A variety of consequences can serve as reinforcers, ranging from those of obvious biological significance, such as food or water or a sexual partner, to minor changes in things seen or heard or touched. Consequences are not restricted merely to the production of stimuli. Responses can remove stimuli, as when operating a switch turns off a light; responses can prevent stimuli from occurring, as when unplugging a lamp before repairing it eliminates the possibility of a shock; and responses can even change the consequences of other responses, as when replacing a burned-out light bulb makes the previously ineffective response of operating the light switch an effective response again. Each type of consequence may affect later behavior.

A stimulus is a positive reinforcer if its presentation increases the likelihood of responses that produce it and a negative reinforcer if its removal increases the likelihood of responses that terminate or prevent or postpone it. Negative reinforcers are sometimes called aversive stimuli. Responding that turns off an aversive stimulus (e.g., when a rat turns off a loud noise by pressing a lever) is escape responding. Responding that prevents or postpones an aversive stimulus (e.g., when a rat's lever press prevents or postpones the delivery of an electric shock) is avoidance responding.

Reinforcement and Punishment

Consequences can reduce responding instead of increasing it. For example, if shock is delivered whenever a rat grooms its tail, the rat may groom its tail less often. Responding reduced by its consequences is therefore punished. Punishment, simply the inverse of reinforcement, has had a more controversial history. Thorndike's early versions of the law of effect argued that behavior could be stamped out by annoyers as well as stamped in by satisfiers, but he later withdrew the part that dealt with the stamping out of behavior.

A rat's reinforced lever pressing can be reduced when presses are punished by shock, but the responding recovers to earlier levels once punishment is discontinued. Because punishment suppresses responding only temporarily, some have argued that it is ineffective. Yet reinforcement would also have to be judged ineffective by this criterion. In early studies standards for the effectiveness of punishment were different from those for the effectiveness of reinforcement. Investigations tended to concentrate on the recovery of responding after punishment was discontinued rather than on the reduction of responding during punishment.

Punishment is effective, but that does not recommend it. It is usually an undesirable method for eliminating behavior. Thorndike and his successors were probably right for the wrong reasons. For example, one major problem is that aversive stimuli used as punishers have side effects, such as eliciting aggressive behavior.

Shaping and the Selection of Behavior

Reinforcement does not establish connections or associations between responses and stimuli. Rather, it changes the probability of classes of responses. Some responses become more likely and others less likely. In other words, some responses survive in the organism's behavior, whereas others do not. In this respect, reinforcement works by selection. It operates on populations of responses within the lifetime of the individual organism much as evolutionary selection operates on populations of organisms over successive generations.

The selective nature of reinforcement is best illustrated by shaping, a procedure that creates new responses through the successive reinforcement of other responses that more and more closely approximate it. For example, a rat may rarely if ever press a lever with a force that approximates its own body weight, but it can be induced to do so by selective reinforcement of stronger and stronger presses. Shaping begins with whatever behavior is available. At the start, most presses will probably be weak; but with reinforcement of the strongest ones, the force of pressing will increase a little, and the criterion for reinforcement then moves up to the strongest of the new population of responses. This step in turn produces another increase in force and another change in criterion, and so on, until the rat is pressing with a force that might never have occurred in the absence of the shaping procedure. Reinforcement has had many useful applications, and shaping has figured in a significant way in many of them, including the training of animals and the production of speech in autistic children.

Computational Reinforcement

Learning through reinforcement is studied in computer science and engineering, where the term *reinforcement learning* is applied to learning algorithms that include some of the principles of reinforcement observed in animal behavior. However, a different type of learning is most commonly studied in these fields. This is called supervised learning (or sometimes "learning by example" or "learning with a teacher") in which a system learns from a collection of examples, where each example consists of an input,

usually is a list of numbers, together with a desired, or target, output specifying the response that the system should produce when given that input. The object of the task is for the system to learn a response rule that produces the desired responses for the example inputs and also for novel inputs it may receive in the future.

A reinforcement learning system, in contrast, learns from signals that evaluate the quality of the learning system's behavior without explicitly telling the system what its behavior should be. Evaluative feedback tells the learning system whether or not, and possibly by how much, its behavior has improved or deteriorated; or it provides a measure of the "goodness" of the behavior; or it just provides an indication of success or failure. Evaluative feedback does not directly tell the learner what it should have done or how it should change its behavior. Instead of trying to match a standard of correctness (i.e., match desired outputs), a reinforcement learning system tries to maximize the goodness of behavior as indicated by evaluative feedback. To do this, it has to actively try alternatives, compare the resulting evaluations, and use some kind of selection mechanism to guide behavior toward the better alternatives. Whereas supervised learning is instructional, reinforcement learning is selectional, like reinforcement in animal learning.

Reinforcement learning is useful from a computational perspective because the evaluation component, sometimes called a "critic," requires much less information and knowledge than the "teacher" in a supervised learning system. It is possible to evaluate a system's behavior without knowing what the correct behavior would be. In fact, a critic does not even need access to the learning system's actions; it can evaluate their consequences on some complex process. It does not need to know anything about the mechanism by which the actions produce these consequences. A complication is that actions can have delayed as well as immediate consequences; evaluative feedback generally evaluates the consequences of all of the system's past behavior. Researchers have developed a number of methods enabling a system to learn efficiently under these conditions.

Several technologies have benefited from applications of reinforcement learning. Although inspired by reinforcement phenomena in animal behavior, research in computational reinforcement learning seeks mainly to create learning methods that can make artificial systems more autonomous and adaptable; it does attempt to create accurate models of animal learning.

Conclusion

The principle of reinforcement emerged in experimental psychology to account for increases in an animal's responding that are due to its consequences. Computer scientists and engineers have adapted this principle to create systems that improve their behavior over time by learning from their own experiences.

See also: ALGORITHMS, LEARNING; OPERANT BEHAVIOR

Bibliography

Estes, W. K. (1944). An experimental study of punishment. *Psychological Monographs 57*, 263.

Pavlov, I. P. (1927). *Conditioned reflexes*, trans. G. V. Anrep. London: Oxford University Press.

Skinner, B. F. (1938). *The behavior of organisms*. New York: Appleton-Century-Crofts.

—— (1969). *Contingencies of reinforcement*. New York: Appleton-Century-Crofts.

—— (1981). Selection by consequences. *Science 213*, 501–504.

Sutton, R. S., and Barto, A. G. (1998). *Reinforcement learning: An introduction*. Cambridge, MA: MIT Press.

Thorndike, E. L. (1898). Animal intelligence: An experimental study of the associative processes in animals. *Psychological Review Monograph Supplements 2*, 109.

A. Charles Catania
Revised by Andrew G. Barto

REINFORCEMENT OR REWARD IN LEARNING

[Reinforcements and rewards drive learning. They can add effect to otherwise neutral percepts with which they coincide. They can alter the probability of behaviors that precede them, as Thorndike captured in his Law of Effect. How reinforcers and rewards exert these effects is the topic considered in the following four sections.

The first section considers the **ANATOMICAL** *pathways of the brain that mediate reinforcement. This section takes the perspective that pathways for reinforcement are part of a larger brain system that supports adaptive, goal-directed behaviors, including feeding, drinking, and reproduction. From this perspective, reinforcement-driven learning and memory are major influences on the likelihood of production of goal-directed behaviors. The pathways that mediate reinforcement have been delineated by a combination of traditional anatomical tracing techniques and the use of electrical stimulation to identify areas where neuronal activation substitutes for natural reinforcements.*

A brain system in which reinforcement learning plays a strong role involves pathways through the cerebellum that mediate classical conditioned motor responses. As summarized in **CEREBELLUM**, *conditioned stimuli and reinforcement signals critical to classical motor conditioning converge in the cerebellar cortex and deep nuclei, and compose the memory trace that mediates this form of learning. In this situation, the reinforcing stimulus is viewed as a "teaching" input that directly elicits the motor response and, when paired with a neutral stimulus, confirms the predictive relationship between the two stimuli. Multiple lines of evidence have been brought to bear on the nature of this interaction and its pathways. These studies have revealed that the dorsal olivary nucleus is the source of the reinforcing input to the cerebellar cortex in support of conditioned motor responses.*

The section on **ELECTRICAL SELF-STIMULATION** *focuses on the use of electrical stimulation to identify brain areas and pathways that mediate reinforcement. These studies have revealed that brief trains of electrical stimulation at specific sites serve as reinforcements for goal-directed behaviors. This artificial activation of the reinforcement pathway is perceived as intensely rewarding, and can support a variety of behaviors. Studies using this technique, combined with other approaches, have been used to characterize a widespread brain system that supports reinforced behaviors. This pathway involves the mesolimbic dopamine system that arises in the ventral tegmental area and projects to the forebrain in the nucleus accumbens. The outputs of this system strongly influence the extrapyramidal motor system, as well as limbic cortical and subcortical areas involved in the assessment of stimulus contingencies and emotional behavior.*

Another brain system in which reinforcement learning plays a critical role is the extrapyramidal motor system, and the **STRIATUM** *is a major component of that system. Neurons in the striatum detect both the delivery of rewards and the presentation of stimuli that predict rewards. Some cells fire at specific steps in a sequence of events leading to rewards. In addition, the activity of striatal neurons can reflect general states of expectation of rewards predicted by previous experience. The striatum receives signals from the orbitofrontal cortex about reward preferences, and receives global reinforcement signals from the mesolimbic dopamine system. How the striatum integrates this information to make predictions about future rewarding events constitutes a major area of study on reinforcement mechanisms.*

Together these sections provide an overview of different aspects of reinforcement and reward as a major influence in the formation of memory traces that support acquired behavioral responses.]

ANATOMICAL SUBSTRATES

The relationship of reinforcement to behavior is a useful prologue to a discussion of the brain circuits that mediate reinforcement (see Figure 1). Reinforcement and reward are parts of a larger system that mediates adaptive behavior that ensures the survival of the animal and the species. Adaptive behaviors, often called goal-directed or appetitive behaviors, include feeding, drinking, and reproduction. Goal-directed behavior can be divided into three phases: initiation, procurement, and consummatory (Watts and Swanson, 2002). In the initiation phase, there is a need or desire for the goal and a decision to fulfill it. For example, when you realize you are hungry, you first make the decision to eat. The consummatory phase involves fulfillment of the goal—in this case, eating. In between is the procurement phase where the goal is sought out. In reinforcement, a part of the procurement phase, the goal or reward increases the probability of occurrence of the behavior used to obtain it.

There are many factors that influence reinforcement: learning, memory, motivation, emotion, and locomotion. There must be a memory of previous experience with the goal to adopt the best strategy to obtain it. Learning occurs when the animal (or person) adapts its previous experience to the current circumstances. This may involve a Pavlovian associative mechanism, through which environmental stimuli that signal reward availability become conditioned stimuli, or instrumental learning, to determine which actions are effective in obtaining the goal, or an interaction between the two (Parkinson, Cardinal, and Everitt, 2000). Motivation is how hard one is willing to work to obtain a goal. Put another way, motivation energizes the response needed to obtain the goal. Emotion is very difficult to define precisely. However, by introspection we know that events with a high emotional impact profoundly affect our ability to learn and remember. Once the associations have been formed and the strategies selected, any attempt to reach the goal requires the skeletomotor system. If the response requires locomotion, then it also requires spatial or contextual learning to navigate through the environment to a remembered location of the reward. However, the response may require other forms of motor output instead, such as reaching and grasping, or pressing a lever, as in the classic laboratory experiment.

Historical Perspective

The first evidence that reinforcement is mediated by dissociable brain pathways came from studies of intracranial self-stimulation. This research demonstrated that focal electrical stimulation of various sites in the brain could be reinforcing events (Wise, 1998). Identifying sites involved in self-stimulation made it possible to ask questions about the systems with which these sites interact and how they ultimately interact with motor systems to influence behavior. Mappings of the most sensitive reinforcing sites implicated a variety of structures in the limbic system, including the nucleus accumbens, limbic cortex, amygdala, hippocampus, and dopaminergic pathways originating in

Figure 1

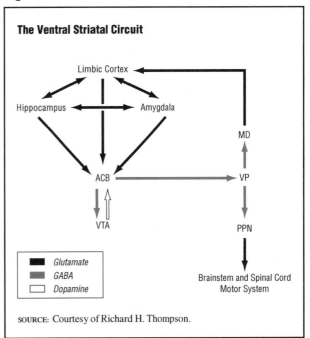

SOURCE: Courtesy of Richard H. Thompson.

A schematic representation of the ventral striatal circuit mediating adaptive motor responding for reward. The three major transmitters used in this circuit are indicated. The nucleus accumbens (ACB) is viewed as a ventral part of a larger striatal system and a primary anatomical region for integrating glutamatergic inputs from the limbic cortex (a general term for areas in the medial [e.g., prelimbic and anterior cingulate] and lateral [e.g., insular] prefrontal cortices that share many structural and functional aspects), hippocampus, and amygdala with the dopaminergic input originating in the ventral tegmental area (VTA). Activation of the nucleus accumbens is thought to inhibit the ventral pallidum (VP), the major output structure of the ventral striatal circuit. Inhibition of the ventral pallidum would then disinhibit its downstream targets in the mediodorsal nucleus of the thalamus (MD) and pedunculopontine tegmental nucleus (PPN) in the caudal brainstem. The mediodorsal nucleus provides feedback related to ventral striatal output via projections to the same areas of limbic cortex that project to the nucleus accumbens. The pedunculopontine nucleus sends descending projections to the reticular formation and spinal cord to initiate locomotion and other motor responses.

the brain stem (Wise, 1998; Ikemoto and Panksepp, 1999). Subsequently, the emphasis shifted to the mesolimbic dopamine system that arises in the ventral tegmental area and projects densely to the nucleus accumbens. Research showed that systemic administration of dopamine antagonists, which block or inactivate dopamine receptors, decrease rates of spontaneous locomotion; rates of self-stimulation, regardless of the site of stimulation; and rates of instrumental responding for both natural (e.g., food or water) and drug reward (e.g., cocaine or heroin)

(Salamone, Cousins, and Snyder, 1997; Ikemoto and Panksepp, 1999). The latter observation is important because it implies that drug abuse involves the same reinforcement mechanisms in the brain as natural rewards (Wise, 1997). While these observations are compelling, it should be noted that dopamine antagonists decrease responding but do not abolish it; therefore, the learned response is intact. In addition, dopamine-depleted rats always choose a less preferred but freely available reward, whereas intact animals always do the opposite. These observations suggest that dopamine is more involved in the arousal or motivational aspects of reward than in the informational aspects of stimulus-reward association formation (Salamone, Cousins, and Snyder, 1997; Parkinson, Cardinal, and Everitt, 2000).

The nucleus accumbens is a major site at which dopamine exerts its effects, in part because dopamine levels in the nucleus accumbens increase in response to the presentation of natural reward, the self-administration of most drugs of abuse, or in response to conditioned stimuli that predict their availability (Di Chiara, 1998). Moreover, microinjection of dopamine antagonists directly into this structure had much the same effect on the above responses as did systemic administration (Salamone, Cousins, and Snyder, 1997; Ikemoto and Panksepp, 1999).

The Nucleus Accumbens

A major advance in understanding the circuits that mediate reinforcement came with the realization that the nucleus accumbens was the ventral component of a larger striatal system. The dorsal striatum is part of the basal ganglia or extrapyramidal motor system and has been studied extensively for its role in initiating or coordinating movements of individual joints and limbs (Mink). The advantage of viewing the nucleus accumbens as part of this system is that it generates predictions of its anatomical organization and provides insights into the functional organization of behavior. Thus, the close relationship between the nucleus accumbens, or ventral striatum, and motor systems was fully appreciated only after recognition of its striatal nature.

Anatomically, this organization has several consequences. One is the appreciation of the predominance of inputs from the cortical mantle. Whereas the cortical inputs to the dorsal striatum arise primarily from somatosensory and motor-cortex and other isocortcal (i.e., neocortex, or six-layered cortex) regions, the inputs to the ventral striatum originate in allocortical (a general term for cortex with less than six layers) regions such as the limbic cortex, amygdala, and hippocampus (Groenewegen, Wright, and Beijer,

1996). A second consequence is the realization that, like the dorsal striatum, most of the output of the nucleus accumbens is to nigral- and pallidal-like structures (Groenewegen, Wright, and Beijer, 1996). Projections to nigral-like structures are inputs to the ventral tegmental area and to the substantia nigra that provide the dopaminergic input to the ventral and dorsal striata, respectively (Redgrave, Prescott, and Gurney, 1999). The nucleus accumbens also projects to a ventral pallidum, whose output is organized in a manner similar to that of the globus pallidus of the dorsal basal ganglia; its major projections are to the thalamus and brain stem (Groenewegen, Wright, and Beijer, 1996).

The thalamic projection of the ventral pallidum is to the mediodorsal nucleus. This nucleus is reciprocally connected with the limbic cortex. Thus, the same cortical regions that project to the nucleus accumbens receive feedback related to nucleus accumbens output. This pallidothalamocortical loop may have a cognitive function through its influence on the planning of subsequent actions (Floresco, Braaksma, and Phillips, 1999). These limbic cortical regions also project to the (pre) motor cortex, providing yet another avenue through which the ventral striatal system can influence the extrapyramidal motor system (Groenewegen and Uylings, 2000).

The projection from the ventral pallidum to the brain stem is primarily to the pedunculopontine tegmental nucleus, an interdigitated population of neurons with ascending and descending projections (Winn, Brown, and Inglis, 1997). The region of descending projections is sometimes called the mesencephalic locomotor region because of its projections to the spinal cord and to reticulospinal neurons and because electrical stimulation of this region elicits locomotion that varies with the intensity of stimulation. Thus, low-intensity stimulation elicits walking, whereas increasing levels elicit first a trot and then a gallop in four-legged animals. The region of ascending projections is sometimes called the midbrain extrapyramidal area because of its projections to the dorsal basal ganglia, which include an input to the dopaminergic neurons of the substantia nigra.

Thus, the ventral striatal circuit has two major routes to gain access to the motor system and influence behavioral output: directly, via projections to the brain stem, and indirectly, via interactions with the basal ganglia. Influences on the dorsal basal ganglia primarily involve modulation of its dopaminergic input but also include those mediated by the more extensive projections of the midbrain extrapyramidal area and those transmitted via the thalamocortical loop.

Cortical Contributions to Reinforcement

The major inputs to the nucleus accumbens (other than dopamine) originate in the limbic cortex, amygdala, and hippocampus. In addition to dense, convergent inputs to the nucleus accumbens, each of these structures is reciprocally connected with the other (Groenewegen and Uylings, 2000). Although a selective role in reinforcement has been shown for each, these interconnections illustrate the interdependent nature of the various aspects of reinforcement. For example, learning about the contingency of reward, to some degree depends on the context in which it is learned, whereas the reverse holds true for contextual learning.

The functions attributed to each of these regions have been based primarily on lesion studies, wherein a nucleus or a region is inactivated to allow an assessment of its contribution to behavior. From these studies, the limbic cortex has been implicated in forming the neural representations that underlie assessment of contingency (determining the relation between response and outcome) and goal status (the current value of the reward) (Balleine and Dickinson, 1998). The amygdala has been implicated in the process whereby affective value is attributed to events. The amygdala is actually composed of many nuclei, each implicated in its own set of emotional responses (Aggleton, 1992). In terms of appetitive behavior, the basolateral nucleus of the amygdala has received the most extensive study. The basolateral nucleus mediates the ability of conditioned stimuli to influence behavior (Parkinson, Cardinal, and Everitt, 2000). This is especially relevant in the context of drug abuse, wherein conditioned stimuli that predict drug availability can elicit craving and precipitate relapse, even after long periods of abstinence (Shalev, Grimm, and Shaham, 2002). The hippocampus has long been implicated in spatial and contextual learning. Lesions of this structure decrease exploratory locomotion and impair the ability of animals to navigate through the environment while searching for food and other rewards (Mogenson et al., 1993).

Thus, the allocortical inputs to nucleus accumbens are collectively involved in assessing the relevance of primary and conditioned stimuli and their relation to the required response. These are essential contributions to Pavlovian, instrumental, and contextual learning. Therefore, these inputs to the nucleus accumbens transmit the informational content relevant to reinforcement learning (Parkinson, Cardinal, and Everitt, 2000).

Information Flow Through the Nucleus Accumbens

Information flow through the nucleus accumbens appears to operate on the principle of disinhibition. The GABA neurons in the ventral pallidum have high rates of spontaneous activity that tonically inhibit their downstream targets in the mediodorsal nucleus and brainstem (Mogenson et al., 1993). The projection neurons in the nucleus accumbens are GABAergic but have very low rates of spontaneous activity. Thus, glutamatergic inputs from the allocortex excite nucleus accumbens neurons, causing them to fire and inhibit the pallidal neurons, which, in turn, disinhibit the projections from the thalamus and brain stem. An important aspect of this disinhibitory process is that it permits or releases behavior rather than initiating it directly. This process is consistent with the idea that the command is for a general direction or plan of behavior, rather than dictating the individual components.

Accordingly, the nucleus accumbens may serve as a selection filter, first matching the information about the nature of the stimulus and the response requirements from the allocortex with the motivational, or arousing, effects mediated by dopaminergic projections from the brain stem and then selecting the appropriate response strategy (Redgrave, Prescott, and Gurney, 1999). The ventral striatal circuit is well-suited to this task. The projection neurons in the nucleus accumbens are bistable—they exhibit two relatively stable states: a hyperpolarized "down" state that results in low levels of spontaneous activity and a more depolarized "up" state in which synaptic inputs easily trigger bursts of action potentials (O'Donnell et al., 1999).

The cellular function of dopamine varies with the state of the nucleus accumbens neuron such that dopamine may act as an excitatory, or facility, neurotransmitter when the neuron is in the up state or may exert an inhibitory effect when they are in the down state (O'Donnell et al., 1999). Such a mechanism would increase the output of the most active nucleus accumbens neurons and suppress activity in the remaining neurons. The effect would create a "winner-take-all" system where only one functionally related ensemble of neurons is active at a time. This can be conceptualized as different patterns of allocortical activity selecting or disinhibiting different channels that are maintained as they pass through the nucleus accumbens circuit on their way to the motor system to influence specific sets of behaviors.

Conclusion

We can now more precisely define reinforcement as a process that selectively potentiates goal-directed behavior, the form and direction of which depends upon learned associations relating the significance of predictive stimuli and environmental conditions. In terms of the neural circuits mediating reinforcement (see Figure 1), information about stimulus-reward associations is generated in the allocortex, where each part mediates a specific set of functions: The limbic cortex evaluates goal status and its relation to predictive cues, the amygdala generates the emotional value attached to primary reward and conditioned stimuli, whereas the hippocampus generates contextual representations of the environment. In the nucleus accumbens, these inputs are integrated with the arousing or motivational input subserved by dopaminergic neurons in the midbrain. The nucleus accumbens then selects the appropriate channel before transmitting its output to motor systems. Thus, reinforcement occurs when the nucleus accumbens integrates informational aspects of stimulus-reward associations with motivational arousal to select and initiate the behavioral strategy best suited to obtaining the goal.

See also: REINFORCEMENT

Bibliography

Aggleton, J. P. (1992). *The amygdala: Neurobiological aspects of emotion, memory, and mental dysfunction.* New York: Wiley-Liss.

Balleine, B. W., and Dickinson, A. (1998). Goal-directed instrumental action: contingency and incentive learning and their cortical substrates. *Neuropharmacology 37,* 407–419.

Di Chiara, G. (1998). A motivational learning hypothesis of the role of mesolimbic dopamine in compulsive drug use. *Journal of Psychopharmacology 12,* 54–67.

Floresco, S. B., Braaksma, D. N., and Phillips, A. G. (1999). Thalamic-cortical-striatal circuitry subserves working memory during delayed responding on a radial arm maze. *Journal of Neuroscience 19,* 11,061–11,071.

Groenewegen, H. J., and Uylings, H. B. (2000). The prefrontal cortex and the integration of sensory, limbic and autonomic information. *Progress in Brain Research 126,* 3–28.

Groenewegen, H. J., Wright, C. I., and Beijer, A. V. (1996). The nucleus accumbens: Gateway for limbic structures to reach the motor system? *Progress in Brain Research 107,* 485–511.

Ikemoto, S., and Panksepp, J. (1999). The role of nucleus accumbens dopamine in motivated behavior: A unifying interpretation with special reference to reward-seeking. *Brain Research Reviews 31,* 6–41.

Mink, J. W. (1996). The basal ganglia: Focused selection and inhibition of competing motor programs. *Progress in Neurobiology 50,* 381–425.

Mogenson, G. J., Brudzynski, S. M., Wu, M., Yang, C. R., and Yim, C. C. Y. (1993). From motivation to action: A review of dopaminergic regulation of limbic→nucleus accumbens→ventral pallidum→pedunculopontine nucleus circuitries involved in limbic motor integration. In P. W. Kalivas and C. D. Barnes, eds., *Limbic motor circuits and neuropsychiatry.* Boca Raton, FL: CRC Press.

O'Donnell, P., Greene, J., Pabello, N., Lewis, B. L., and Grace, A. A. (1999). Modulation of cell firing in the nucleus accumbens. *Annals of the New York Academy of Sciences 877,* 157–175.

Parkinson, J. A., Cardinal, R. N., and Everitt, B. J. (2000). Limbic cortical-ventral striatal systems underlying appetitive conditioning. *Progress in Brain Research 126,* 263–285.

Redgrave, P., Prescott, T. J., and Gurney, K. (1999). The basal ganglia: A vertebrate solution to the selection problem? *Neuroscience 89,* 1,009–1,023.

Salamone, J. D., Cousins, M. S., and Snyder, B. J. (1997). Behavioral functions of nucleus accumbens dopamine: Empirical and conceptual problems with the anhedonia hypothesis. *Neuroscience and Biobehavioral Reviews 21,* 341–359.

Shalev, U., Grimm, J. W., and Shaham, Y. (2002). Neurobiology of relapse to heroin and cocaine seeking: A review. *Pharmacological Reviews 54,* 1–42.

Watts, A. G., and Swanson, L. W. (2002). Anatomy of motivational systems. In H. Pashler and R. Gallistell, eds., *Stevens's handbook of experimental psychology.* New York: John Wiley.

Winn, P., Brown, V. J., and Inglis, W. L. (1997). On the relationships between the striatum and the pedunculopontine tegmental nucleus. *Critical Reviews in Neurobiology 11,* 241–261.

Wise, R. A. (1997). Drug self-administration viewed as ingestive behaviour. *Appetite 28,* 1–5.

—— (1998). Drug-activation of brain reward pathways. *Drug and Alcohol Dependence 51,* 13–22.

Richard H. Thompson

CEREBELLUM

Researchers have extensively studied the neural substrates mediating reinforcement during classical conditioning of discrete motor responses. In a seminal *Science* (1986) paper, Richard F. Thompson proposed a cerebellar model of associative learning in which the convergence of conditioned stimulus (CS) and unconditioned stimulus (UCS) information at cerebellar cortex and the cerebellar deep nuclei form the basis of the memory trace in classical conditioning. One of the central tenets of this model—which is based on electrophysiological, lesion, and stimulation data—is that reinforcement in the form of the UCS is conveyed to the cerebellum via climbing fibers originating in the inferior olive.

The Nature of Reinforcement

In its simplest and most widely accepted definition, the term *reinforcement* applies to any stimulus or consequence that increases the likelihood that the immediately antecedent behavior will occur again in an operant learning task. As regards classical conditioning, however, the term is often applied to the UCS, which elicits a reflex (unconditioned response, or UCR) and, when paired with a neutral CS, strengthens or confirms the predictive relationship between the two stimuli. Conceptually, the UCS may be thought of as a teaching input.

Electrophysiology of the Inferior Olive

Rescorla and Wagner have proposed a behavioral model of classical conditioning (1972; Rescorla, 1988) in which associative strength is greatest early in training and declines with each stimulus pairing. If that model is true, then neural activity within the reinforcement pathway ought to decrease across training. In 1991 Sears and Steinmetz tested this hypothesis and reported that UCS-evoked activity in the rabbit dorsal accessory olive was large during the initial training trials but decreased concomitantly with the development of conditioned responses (CRs) later in training. On exclusively UCS trials or on a paired trial in which the rabbit failed to give a CR, evoked activity within the olive was again apparent, suggesting that olivary activity may be an error-detection signal. Sears and Steinmetz proposed that such a partial reinforcement mechanism maintains continued CR expression. Single-unit recordings of Purkinje cells conducted by Foy and Thompson in 1986 indicated that the decrement in olivary activity with continued training was reflected in cerebellar cortical activity. At the beginning of training, 61 percent of 118 studied neurons displayed complex spikes in response to UCS onset. At the end of training, only 27 percent of the Purkinje cells displayed complex spikes evoked by UCS onset.

The foregoing data indicate that once the association between the CS and UCS has been formed, no further activity in the UCS pathway is necessary except in the case of a performance error. A significant body of behavioral data supports this view. For example, Kamin (1968) has demonstrated that once a CS-UCS association has been formed, insertion of a second CS immediately after the first yields no behavioral learning to the new CS. Kamin calls this process blocking. No new information is added by the second CS, so the animal essentially ignores it. If continued activity were to occur in the UCS pathway, then the animal should attach the same associative properties to the second CS. Kim, Krupa, and Thompson (1998) demonstrated exactly this phenomenon by injecting the GABA antagonist picrotoxin into the olivary complex after acquisition of the first CS-UCS (tone-air puff) association. The antagonist prevented the normal diminution of olivary activity that occurs with training. Subsequent training with both the original and a second CS (light) was accompanied by evoked complex spike activity in the cerebellar cortex to both CSs. Exclusively CS test trials indicated that the animal acquired comparable associations between both CSs and the UCS.

Inferior Olive Lesions

If the inferior olive is the source of reinforcing input to the cerebellum, then destruction of this nucleus should produce behavioral phenomena that are identical to those observed when the exteroceptive UCS is omitted from training trials. Lesions of the rostromedial portions of the inferior olive block CR acquisition in rabbit training using paired-tone (CS) and air-puff (UCS) presentations in a standard delay-conditioning procedure (McCormick, Steinmetz, and Thompson, 1985). Further, in experienced animals, lesions of this nucleus gradually abolished learned responses in a manner that was similar to that observed in intact control animals undergoing extinction (i.e., exclusively CS trials).

Electrical Stimulation of the Inferior Olive

Substitution of an exteroceptive UCS with electrical stimulation of the inferior olive or climbing fiber afferents to the cerebellum provides, perhaps, the most stringent test of whether this structure is the locus of reinforcement during classical conditioning. Electrical stimulation must be able to recreate all of the behavioral phenomena normally associated with peripheral UCS presentations during conditioning.

Stimulation of the inferior olive produces a variety of movements, depending on the location of the stimulating electrode. These movements may include eye blinks; movement of the head, neck, facial muscles; or limbs. Pairings of a tone CS and electrical stimulation of the dorsal accessory nucleus of the inferior olive as the UCS produces normal rates of eye-blink conditioning (Mauk, Steinmetz, and Thompson, 1986). Furthermore, the range of interstimulus intervals (ISI) with UCS electrical stimulation was identical to that of peripheral UCSs. Conditioning was maximal when the CS-UCS interval was held at 150 or 250 msec. Shorter intervals of 50 msec prevented acquisition.

Electrical Stimulation of Cerebellar White Matter

One criticism leveled against the preceding experiments is that eye blinks elicited by stimulation of the inferior olive as the UCS might reflect antidromic activation of spinal trigeminal neurons and spread of activation to mossy-fiber collaterals that project to rabbit lobule HVI (site of facial map) (Moore and Blazis, 1989). To explore this issue, Swain, Shinkman, Nordholm, and Thompson performed a parametric investigation of cerebellar white-matter stimulation in 1992. They chose as the site of stimulation the white matter immediately underlying cerebellar lobule HVI because it is remote from brain stem and spinal-reflex pathways. Stimulation at this site would activate climbing fibers and other cerebellar afferents. In their study, white-matter stimulation elicited eye blinks as well as movements of the face or neck and, when paired with a tone, CS produced learning comparable to that seen with peripheral UCSs or with olivary stimulation. No significant differences were noted in learning rate for the various movements evoked by stimulation. When switched to CS alone presentations, the animals extinguished rapidly and upon reinstatement of paired training showed reacquisition with substantial savings. Similar findings have been reported by Gormezano and colleagues (1983) in paradigms using a peripheral UCS. The correspondence between learning in their experiment and conditioning with a peripheral UCS was remarkable even upon examination of the small details. For example, researchers found that the percentage of CRs on the last day of reacquisition training was smaller than that of the last day of acquisition training. While this difference was not significant, it is consistent with reports by several investigators that the CS may acquire inhibitory properties during extinction training that become evident upon retraining.

The experiment included control rabbits that received either randomly or explicitly unpaired presentations of the tone CS and white-matter stimulation as the UCS. Animals that received explicitly unpaired presentations of the conditioning stimuli were profoundly impaired when they were subsequently switched to a paired CS-UCS training procedure. Previous behavioral work by Rescorla (1969) has demonstrated that the explicitly unpaired control procedure may result in the CS acquiring inhibitory properties such that subsequent acquisition training is retarded.

A subsequent study by the group (Swain et al., 1999) found that exposure to as few as 108 exclusively UCS trials was sufficient to produce a potent UCS preexposure effect. Animals exposed to the UCS prior to training typically required more than 600 trials to learn. Animals that received no preexposure learned at a normal rate (100–200 trials). Exposure to UCSs of fixed duration also promoted an increase in the amplitude and a decrease in the latency of the stimulus-evoked reflex as trial presentations progressed. There have been similar findings for UCS preexposure and reflex augmentation with exteroceptive UCSs (Mis and Moore, 1973).

The authors (Swain et al., 1992) also reported anecdotal observations that further support the hypothesis that cerebellar white-matter stimulation as a UCS results in normal behavioral learning. After an animal that exhibited an ipsilateral lip movement to cerebellar stimulation had been trained and completed the experiment, an impromptu experiment was conducted. While the animal was in its home cage, if a whistle at about 1kHz (CS-tone frequency) was presented, the rabbit responded with a conditioned lip movement. If a whistle of a different pitch was presented, the rabbit did not respond. These observations suggest that conditioning was specific to the tone CS and not to context and that the CR exhibited a stimulus generalization gradient to the frequency of the whistle.

Conclusion

Destruction of the olive or its efferent climbing fibers blocks learning in naïve animals and extinguishes it in the experienced ones. Physiological records indicate that olivary neurons respond strongly to UCS presentation at the beginning of training but subside as learning occurs. Stimulation or suppression of activity within the olivary climbing-fiber system can recreate a host of behavioral phenomena, including conditioned inhibition, the UCS preexposure effect, UR augmentation, and blocking. Together these data indicate that the inferior olive and its efferent axons, the climbing fibers, are the neural pathway that conveys information about reinforcement to the cerebellum.

See also: CONDITIONING, CELLULAR AND NETWORK SCHEMES FOR HIGHER-ORDER FEATURES OF; GUIDE TO THE ANATOMY OF THE BRAIN: CEREBELLUM; KAMIN'S BLOCKING EFFECT: NEURONAL SUBSTRATES; REINFORCEMENT

Bibliography

Foy, M. R., and Thompson, R. F. (1986). Single unit analysis of Purkinje cell discharge in classically conditioned and untrained rabbits. *Society for Neuroscience Abstracts 12*, 518.

Gormezano, I., Kehoe, E. J., and Marshall, B. S. (1983). Twenty years of classical conditioning research with the rabbit. In J. M. Sprague and A. N. Epstein, eds., *Progress in psychobiology and physiological psychology*, Vol. 10. New York: Academic Press.

Kamin, L. J. (1968). Attention-like processes in classical conditioning. In M. R. Jones, ed., *Miami symposium on the prediction of behavior: Aversive stimulation*. Miami: University of Miami Press.

Kim, J. J., Krupa, D. J., and Thompson, R. F. (1998). Inhibitory cerebello–olivary projections and blocking effect in classical conditioning. *Science 279*, 570–573.

Mauk, M. D., Steinmetz, J. E., and Thompson, R. F. (1986). Classical conditioning using stimulation of the inferior olive as the unbconditioned stimulus. *Proceedings of the National Academy of Sciences of the United States of America 83*, 5,349–5,353.

McCormick, D. A., Steinmetz, J. E., and Thompson, R. F. (1985). Lesions of the inferior olivary complex cause extinction of the classically conditioned eyelid response. *Brain Research 359*, 120–130.

Mis, R. W., and Moore, J. W. (1973). Effects of preacquisition US exposure on classical conditioning of the rabbit's nictitating membrane response. *Learning and Motivation 4*, 108–114.

Moore, J. W., and Blazis, D. E. J. (1989). Stimulation of a classically conditioned response: A cerebellar network implementation of the Sutton-Barto-Desmond model. In J. H. Byrne and W.

O. Berry, eds., *Neural models of plasticity.* New York: Academic Press.

Rescorla, R. A. (1969). Pavlovian conditioned inhibition. *Psychological Bulletin 72,* 77–94.

———— (1988). Behavioral studies of Pavlovian conditioning. *Annual Review of Neuroscience 11,* 329–352.

Rescorla, R. A., and Wagner, A. R. (1972). A theory of Pavlovian conditioning: Variations in the effectiveness of reinforcement and nonreinforcement. In A. H. Black and W. F. Prokasy, eds., *Classical conditioning II: Current research theory.* New York: Appleton-Century-Crofts.

Sears, L. L. and Steinmetz, J. E. (1991). Dorsal accessory inferior olive activity diminishes during acquisition of the rabbit classically conditioned eyelid response. *Brain Research 545,* 114–122.

Swain, R. A., Shinkman, P. G., Nordholm, A. F., and Thompson, R. F. (1992). Cerebellar stimulation as an unconditioned stimulus in classical conditioning. *Behavioral Neuroscience 106,* 739–750.

Swain, R. A., Shinkman, P. G., Thompson, J. K., Grethe, J. S., and Thompson, R. F. (1999). Essential neuronal pathways for reflex and conditioned response initiation in an intracerebellar stimulation paradigm and the impact of unconditioned stimulus preexposure on learning rate. *Neurobiology of Learning and Memory 71,* 167–193.

Thompson, R. F. (1986). The neurobiology of learning and memory. *Science 233,* 941–947.

Rodney A. Swain

ELECTRICAL SELF-STIMULATION, BRAIN

For physiological psychology, the discovery that electrical stimulation of certain brain regions is so powerfully rewarding that laboratory rats eagerly self-administer it was an earthquake, the shock waves of which rippled through the popular press in hyperbolic recountings. "It may prove the key to human behavior," trumpeted a Montreal newspaper. Some reports even went so far as to fuel fears that brain stimulation reward (BSR) could be used as an agent for social control. However amusing in retrospect, much of this hype was an understandable reflection of the amazement, shared by scientists and laypeople alike, of the powerful and immediate impact of electrical stimulation on behavior. The stimulation electrode, injecting a meaningful signal into the neural circuitry mediating goal-directed behavior, can turn the average lab rat into a craven voluptuary, willing to press a lever to the point of starvation or exhaustion.

Even though the initial hype has subsided (Talwar et al., 2002), BSR has become a model system for the study of positive reinforcement. Because organisms acquire new responses to obtain electrical stimulation, the effect qualifies as reinforcement according to the law of effect. Early evidence suggested that brain stimulation reward differs in some respects from conventional rewards such as food and water, whereas later research emphasized their similarities.

Researchers have linked the rewarding effect of electrical stimulation to the mechanisms governing choice between competing goals and activities.

The Relationship Between BSR and Natural Rewards

Researchers explored the relationship between BSR and gustatory rewards in an extensive series of experiments whereby, under various physiological states, rats had to choose between lateral hypothalamic (LH) stimulation varying in strength and either gustatory reward alone or a compound reward consisting of a gustatory reward plus fixed BSR. The researchers estimated preference by varying the strength of the stimulation triggered by one spout while holding constant the reward triggered by a second spout. They measured the stimulation strength required to produce isopreference. The experimental protocol sought to minimize the difference between the gustatory reward and the BSR. Thus, the gustatory reward was intraorally infused in small volumes via a catheter, while an intragastric cannula minimized the accumulation of gustatory reward in the gut to simulate the instantaneous and insatiating nature of BSR.

Initially, when given a choice between a gustatory stimulus (an intraoral infusion of sucrose) and LH stimulation, the rats choose the sucrose infusion if the brain stimulation was weak; but they shifted their preference as the LH stimulation became stronger. With sucrose availability, rats eschew suprathreshold levels of brain stimulation in favor of the sucrose reward. Clearly, the availability of sucrose alters the preference for BSR when the two rewards are evaluated in a common system of measurement wherein the larger reward is selected. In a subsequent experiment, researchers pitted LH stimulation against a compound reward consisting of sucrose and an equi-preferred train of brain stimulation to determine whether the results of the common evaluation can summate. Indeed, the rats assigned a higher value to the compound reward than to its sucrose component alone. The strength of LH stimulation required to balance the compound reward exceeded the stimulation strength required to balance the sucrose reward alone. The finding that BSR and sucrose reward can be combined lends further support to the idea of evaluation in a common system of measurement.

The competition and summation experiments confirm the hypothesis that BSR and natural rewards have something important in common: they are evaluated on a common currency scale. As McFarland and Sibley pointed out (1975), orderly choice between mutually exclusive behaviours must be based on a common currency; the influences contributing to the choice of each activity seem to converge on a "behavioural final common path" (p. 265). There is considerable evidence that thresholds for BSR remain remarkably stable across a variety of states that are associated with changes in choice of goal object. Prominent among these states are changes in energy balance or nutrient requirements. For example, neither the increase in salt appetite that accompanies sodium depletion nor the suppression of appetite that accompanies postingestive feedback is associated with substantial changes in BSR. These findings suggest that BSR mimics a global currency of goal evaluation.

In contrast to these findings, other research has shown that BSR is sensitive to changes in energy balance when the electrode is in a specific region of the LH (perifornical LH). Moreover, leptin, a hormone that communicates the state of the fat stores to the brain, exerts opposite influences on the rewarding effect of stimulating food restriction-sensitive and -insensitive sites. These results suggest that functionally distinct pathways, differentially responsive to the state of the organism, exist within the neural substrate for BSR. One way of interpreting the contrast between the results obtained at different stimulation sites is to propose that stimulation at the restriction-insensitive sites mimics a global currency, whereas stimulation at restriction-sensitive sites mimics a local one, a currency related to long-term energy stores.

The Neural Circuitry Subserving Reward: Lessons from Studies on BSR

The Directly Stimulated Stage

Electrical stimulation provides the most effective means of introducing a reward signal into the brain. The strength of the electrically induced rewarding effect and the ease with which it can be controlled render electrical stimulation a powerful tool for studying the reward substrate. Consider the task of linking BSR to the activity of identified neurons. The first step toward accomplishing this task is to identify the neurons in the immediate vicinity of the electrode tip whose direct activation gives rise to the rewarding effect of the stimulation. Finding these cells and tracing their inputs and outputs is likely to shed light on the mechanisms in the brain that underlie the behavioral effects of positive reinforcement.

The initial strategy employed to investigate the BSR system was to map the brain sites that support self-stimulation. Stimulation of numerous regions evokes BSR. An especially effective site is the medial forebrain bundle (MFB), which allows easy shaping of self-stimulation behavior. Accordingly, finding the directly stimulated stage (first stage) of MFB self-stimulation has been the focus of intensive research. For decades researchers sought the quantitative characteristics of the first-stage neurons through psychophysical techniques. Behavioral measurements of recovery from refractoriness, collision block, and anodal hyperpolarization block have led to the idea that the directly stimulated neurons subserving the powerfully rewarding effect produced by electrical stimulation of the MFB originate in the basal forebrain and give rise to fine, myelinated axons that descend through the MFB toward the tegmentum. Further research has supported this idea. Excitotoxic lesions of a region in the lateral basal forebrain that includes the lateral preoptic area, the substantia innominata, and parts of the bed nucleus of the stria terminalis increase the threshold for self-stimulation of more caudal sites along the MFB. Fos immunostaining has shown that rewarding stimulation of the MFB activates neurons in the region of the effective lesions.

The Role of Dopamine Neurons

BSR is similar in certain respects to the self-administration of psychomotor stimulants. Both are self-administered in a compulsive fashion, both may activate the same brain circuitry, and both are dopamine-dependent. Microdialysis and voltametry studies indicate that both psychomotor stimulant reward and BSR elevate dopamine levels in the nucleus accumbens. But the most compelling evidence suggesting dopaminergic involvement in BSR comes from pharmacological studies. Dopamine receptor blockers increase self-stimulation thresholds, whereas dopamine agonists have the opposite effect.

Researchers believed that direct activation of MFB dopamine fibers initiated rewarding signals in this region until psychophysical and electrophysiological findings ruled out this possibility. Dopamine neurons are not myelinated, and their thresholds of activation are above the level of the stimulation parameters commonly used in BSR studies. The question then arises: What place does the dopamine system occupy in the neural substrate of the rewarding effect?

According to the simplest hypothesis, the dopamine neurons are in series with the first-stage ones and thus carry the reward signal. An alternative hypothesis is that the dopamine neurons do not actually relay the reward signal but rather play a permissive role at some stage of the BSR substrate. One example of a permissive role would be to gate signal processing in the pathway responsible for the rewarding effect. Perhaps increased activity in the dopamine neurons enhances transmission of the reward signal, whereas decreased activity reduces or even blocks its transmission.

The permissive-role hypothesis finds substantial corroboration in a microdialysis study designed to measure the levels of dopamine released in the nucleus accumbens during self-stimulation for equi-rewarding pulses that consisted of different combinations of stimulus parameters of the electrical stimulation. Some had argued that if the reward signal travels along dopamine neurons, the release of dopamine should not depend on the stimulus parameters because equi-rewarding stimuli should produce a constant output in all neural stages carrying the reward signal, irrespective of the spatio-temporal nature of the signal. However, the results showed that the magnitude of dopamine release differed between sets of self-stimulation parameters that, nevertheless, produced the same rewarding effect. The finding that the rewarding effect of the stimulation is not mirrored in the magnitude of dopamine release as measured by microdialysis contravenes the hypothesis that the reward signal elicited by MFB stimulation is relayed by the mesolimbic dopamine neurons.

Another study measuring dopamine release from dopamine terminals in the nucleus accumbens by voltametry provided additional evidence that dopamine is not a neural substrate for reward per se. The study showed that although dopamine release correlated with the ability of animals to learn the self-stimulation behavior, extracellular dopamine was nonetheless absent during self-stimulation itself. These results are consistent with two hypotheses: that dopamine is related to the novelty and predictability of rewards and that dopamine neurons provide teaching signals for appetitive learning and reinforcement. Dopamine could thus mediate plasticity changes at sites in the brain that subserve the learning of the self-stimulation behavior. Indeed, there appears to be a correlation between dopamine-dependent potentiation in corticostriatal circuits and the rate of acquisition of lever-pressing behavior.

Future studies might clarify the relationship between the first stage of the BSR substrate and dopamine neurons while shedding light on circuitry involved in both the processing of reward information and the reinforcement learning.

See also: GUIDE TO THE ANATOMY OF THE BRAIN

Bibliography

Arvanitogiannis, A., Flores, C., Pfaus, J. G., and Shizgal, P. (1996). Increased ipsilateral expression of Fos following lateral hypothalamic self-stimulation. *Brain Research* 720, 148–154.

Arvanitogiannis, A., Tzschentke, T. M., Riscaldino, L., Wise, R. A., and Shizgal, P. (2000). Fos expression following self-stimulation of the medial prefrontal cortex. *Behavioural Brain Research* 107, 123–132.

Arvanitogiannis, A., Waraczynski, M., and Shizgal, P. (1996). Effects of excitotoxic lesions of the basal forebrain on MFB self-stimulation. *Physiology and Behavior* 59, 795–806.

Carr, K. D. (1996). Feeding, drug abuse, and the sensitization of reward by metabolic need. *Neurochemistry Research* 21, 1,455–1,467.

Fulton, S., Woodside, B., and Shizgal, P. (2000). Modulation of brain reward circuitry by leptin. *Science* 287, 125–128.

Gallistel, C. R., Shizgal, P., and Yeomans, J. S. (1981). A portrait of the substrate for self-stimulation. *Psychological Review* 88, 228–273.

Garris, P. A., Kilpatrick, M., Bunin, M. A., Michael, D., Walker, Q. D., and Wightman, R. M. (1999). Dissociation of dopamine release in the nucleus accumbens from intracranial self-stimulation. *Nature* 398, 67–69.

McFarland, D. J., and Sibley, R. M. (1975). The behavioural final common path. *Philosophical Transactions of the Royal Society of London B* 270, 265–293.

Miliaressis, E., Emond, C., and Merali, Z. (1991). Re-evaluation of the role of dopamine in intracranial self-stimulation using in vivo microdialysis. *Behavioural Brain Research* 46, 43–48.

Olds, J., and Milner, P. M. (1954). Positive reinforcement produced by electrical stimulation of septal area and other regions of rat brain. *Journal of Comparative and Physiological Psychology* 47, 419–427.

Reynolds, J. N. J., Hyland, B. I., and Wickens J. R. (2001). A cellular mechanism of reward-related learning. *Nature* 413, 67–70.

Shizgal, P. (1997). Neural basis of utility estimation. *Current Opinion in Neurobiology* 7, 198–208.

—— (1999). On the neural computation of utility: Implications from studies of brain stimulation reward. In D. Kahneman, E. Diener, and N. Shwarz, eds., *Well-being: The foundations of hedonic psychology.* New York: Russell Sage Foundation.

Talwar, S. K., Xu, S., Hawley, E. S., Weiss, S. A., Moxon, K. A., and Chapin, J. K. (2002). Rat navigation guided by remote control. *Nature* 417, 37–38.

Wise, R. A. (1996). Addictive drugs and brain stimulation reward. *Annual Review of Neuroscience* 19, 319–340.

Andreas Arvanitogiannis

STRIATUM

The role of rewards in the survival and well-being of biological agents ranges from the control of vegetative functions to the organization of voluntary, goal-directed behavior. The brain extracts the reward information from a large variety of stimuli and events for appropriate use in the control of behavior. Recent studies revealed that neurons in a limited number of brain structures carry specific signals about past and future rewards. The neurophysiological study of reward processing within the framework of goal-directed behavior may contribute to a basic understanding of mechanisms of drug abuse and could thus have a strong medical and social impact. This article concerns the reward signals in the striatum and describes how its neurons detect rewards, learn to predict future rewards from past experience, and use reward information for learning, choosing, preparing and executing goal-directed behavior.

Behavioral Functions of Rewards

Biological agents need to acquire nutrional substances from the environment and interact with sexual partners for reproduction. The brain controls the contact with foods, fluids, and sexual partners and mediates the adaptation of behavior to novel or changed situations. Neuronal mechanisms not only detect rewards but also predict them on the basis of representations formed by past experience. Through these mechanisms rewards serve as goals for voluntary and intentional forms of behavior.

Rewards have several basic functions. A popular view holds that rewards induce subjective feelings of pleasure and contribute to positive emotions. Rewards act as positive reinforcers by increasing the frequency and intensity of behavior leading to the acquisition of goal objects in classical and instrumental conditioning procedures. The learning function is based on the discrepancy between the prediction and occurrence of rewards (reward-prediction error).

Rewards are goals that elicit approach and consummatory behavior. Reward objects have positive motivational value because they elicit effortful behavioral reactions. The values arise either through innate mechanisms or, in most cases, learning. In this way rewards help to establish value systems for behavior and serve as key references for behavioral decisions. Differences in perceived reward values in individual agents and situations may help to explain variations in behavioral choices.

A Case for the Striatum in Reward Mechanisms

The basal ganglia are composed of the striatum (caudate nucleus, putamen, and ventral striatum, including nucleus accumbens), dopamine neurons of the substantia nigra and ventral tegmental area (groups A8, A9, and A10), and a number of other structures. Current evidence suggests that the basal ganglia are important for control of voluntary, goal-directed behavior and the processing of rewarding outcomes. Human diseases involving these structures lead to deficits in voluntary behavior and movements (Parkinsonism, schizophrenia, and Huntington's chorea). Lesioning and psychopharmacological and electrical self-stimulation experiments strongly indicate that dopamine neurons and the ventral striatum serve prime motivational functions (Robbins and Everitt 1996). Major addictive substances, such as cocaine and heroin, increase the dopamine concentration in the ventral striatum, and animals try to receive injections of dopamine or opiates into the ventral striatum (Wise, 1996). Single neurons in the basal ganglia pre-

parate and initate movements and process information about rewarding outcomes (Schultz, 2000).

Neurophysiology of Reward Mechanisms in the Striatum

Neurons in the striatum detect the delivery of rewards and discriminate among them. Other striatal neurons detect conditioned, reward-predicting visual stimuli and discriminate reward-predicting from nonpredicting stimuli. Many natural situations involve sequences of individual movements that lead to a final reward. Neurons in the ventral striatum respond differentially to sequential cues at different steps away from the reward. It appears that these neurons report the positions of individual stimuli within a behavioral sequence and thus signal the progress towards the reward.

A well learned reward-predicting stimulus evokes a state of expectation. Striatal neurons are active during several seconds of expectation of predictable rewards. Their activity follows a reward-predicting stimulus and persists for several seconds until the reward is delivered. Such neurons discriminate between different future rewards and other, nonrewarding predictable task events, such as movement-eliciting stimuli or instructions cues. The activity may reflect a neuronal representation of reward established through previous experience. Reward-detecting and reward-expecting neurons are found about twice as often in the ventral striatum as in the caudate and putamen. These findings may provide neurophysiological correlates for the known motivational functions of the ventral striatum.

Expectations change with experience. Animals expect reward initially on all trials when learning to discriminate rewarded from nonrewarded stimuli. Similarly, neurons in the striatum show reward expectation activity during initial trials with novel stimuli, and this activity is progressively restricted to rewarded rather than unrewarded trials. These adaptations are reflected in the activity of neurons in the striatum.

Expected rewards may serve as goals for voluntary behavior if information about the reward is present while behavioral reactions toward the reward are being prepared and executed (Dickinson and Balleine, 1994). Neuronal mechanisms in the striatum may integrate reward information into processes mediating the behavior leading to the reward. Some neurons in the anterior striatum show sustained activity for a few seconds during the preparation of a movement. These activations occur much more commonly in rewarded than unrewarded trials and vary with the type of reward expected for the movement. Thus both the future reward and the movement toward the reward are represented by these neurons. The reward-dependent activity may be a way in which the expected reward is represented by neurons and can influence neuronal processes underlying the behavior toward that reward.

Reward Information Arriving at the Striatum

The striatum is a part of a limited network of brain structures involved in the processing of reward information. Although it is difficult at the moment to assess the different functions of each of these structures, we can describe the neuronal activities in some of the structures sending information to the striatum.

The orbitofrontal cortex, the ventral part of the frontal lobe, is a part of the limbic system involved in motivation and emotions. Some of its neurons project to the striatum, in particular its ventral part, including nucleus accumbens. Orbitofrontal neurons discriminate between different rewards on the basis of the subject's preferences (Tremblay and Schultz, 1999). For example, a neuron is more active when a preferred rather than a nonpreferred reward is expected. But when the initially nonpreferred reward occurs in trials alternating with an even less preferred reward, the nonpreferred award will become the preferred one and the neuron will be activated predominantly by this reward. These neurons do not code rewards on the basis of their physical properties. Rather, they code the relative preference of the reward. Neurons coding the relative preference for rewards might provide important information to neuronal mechanism in the frontal lobe underlying goal-directed behavioral choices.

Dopamine neurons in the substantia nigra and the ventral tegmental area project to the dorsal and ventral striatum, respectively. Most dopamine neurons show short, phasic activations following the presentation of liquid and food rewards and conditioned visual and auditory reward-predicting stimuli. However, dopamine neurons do not respond to rewards unconditionally but code them relative to what is predicted, suggesting that they code a reward-prediction error (Waelti et al., 2001). The dopamine response may be a global reinforcement signal sent in parallel to all neurons in the striatum. Learning theory suggests that prediction errors play a crucial role in learning and that the phasic dopamine response may be an ideal teaching signal for approach learning. This signal strongly resembles the teaching signal used by effective temporal-difference reinforcement models (Montague et al., 1996). Indeed, artificial neuronal networks that use this type of teaching signal learn to play world-class backgammon.

Less is known about reward processing in other brain structures. Neurons in the amygdala, which projects to the ventral striatum, react to the occurrence of rewards and discriminate between different liquid and food rewards. Neurons in the dorsolateral prefrontal cortex show reward-discriminating activity during the preparation of movements and may thus be involved in the organisation of behavior directed towards rewarding goals (Watanabe, 1996).

Conclusion

The striatum processes reward information in different ways. Neurons in the striatum detect and discriminate between among rewards and may play a role in assessing the nature and identity of individual rewards. However, the striatum not only detects and analyses past events, but it also constructs and dynamically modifies predictions based on past experience. Striatal neurons respond to learned stimuli that predict rewards and show sustained activity during periods pr reward expectations. They even take guesses about future rewards and adapt their activity to experience.

Once we understand more about how the brain treats rewards, we can investigate how reward information produces motivated behavior. Neurons in structures that control behavior seem to incorporate information about upcoming rewards when coding reward-seeking behavior. Future research may permit us to understand how such activity may lead to choices and decisions incorporating both the cost and the benefit of behavior. We should also investigate neuronal mechanisms behind higher, more cognitive rewards typical for human behavior. Such research would help us to understand further how brains control important characteristics of voluntary and motivated behavior of complex organisms, possibly to the extent that individual differences in brain function explain variations in basic traits of personality.

Bibliography

Dickinson, A., and Balleine, B. (1994). Motivational control of goal-directed action. *Animal Learning and Behavior 22*, 1–18.

Montague, P. R., Dayan, P., and Sejnowski, T. J. (1996). A framework for mesencephalic dopamine systems based on predictive Hebbian learning. *Journal of Neuroscience 16*, 1,936–1,947.

Robbins, T. W., and Everitt, B. J. (1996). Neurobehavioral mechanisms of reward and motivation. *Current Opinion in Neurobiology 6*, 228–236.

Robinson, T. E., and Berridge, K. C. (1993). The neural basis for drug craving: An incentive-sensitization theory of addiction. *Brain Research Reviews 18*, 247–291.

Schultz, W. (2000). Multiple reward systems in the brain. *Nature Reviews Neuroscience 1*, 199–207.

Waelti, P., Dickinson, A., and Schultz, W. (2001). Dopamine responses comply with basic assumptions of formal learning theory. *Nature 412*, 43–48.

Watanabe, M. (1996). Reward expectancy in primate prefrontal neurons. *Nature 382,* 629–632.

Wise, R. A. (1996). Neurobiology of addiction. *Current Opinion in Neurobiology 6,* 243–251.

Wolfram Schultz

REPETITION AND LEARNING

Sayings such as "Practice makes perfect" illustrate the well-known fact that repetition improves learning. This was discussed by numerous ancient and medieval thinkers and was demonstrated empirically by Hermann Ebbinghaus, the first researcher to carry out a prolonged series of experiments on human memory. In a classic 1885 book, Ebbinghaus showed that retention of information improves as a function of the number of times the information has been studied. Since the time of Ebbinghaus, countless investigators have used repetition to study learning and memory.

Although experimenters typically find a consistent relationship between repetition and learning, numerous authors (Guthrie, 1935) have pointed out that this does not necessarily mean that the learning process itself has to be either gradual or continuous. Most learning situations contain a number of smaller facets or subproblems that must be mastered before learning is complete. It is possible that each of these subproblems is mastered suddenly, perhaps through insight. However, the subproblems are learned at different times, with more and more of them mastered as the number of trials increases. This analysis proposes that a gradual improvement in learning as a result of repetition may reflect the accumulation of subproblems that have been mastered in a sudden fashion. Distinguishing between a truly continuous learning process and the accumulation of small, sudden insights is difficult. A common assumption is that learning may be either gradual or sudden, depending on the background of the learner and the nature of the information to be learned. For example, Harry Harlow (1949) showed that learning to novel situations may occur slowly and continuously but may appear in sudden flashes of insight when the organism has had experience in a number of similar situations. Thus, although the amount of learning may appear to grow gradually and continuously as a result of repetition, determination of whether subcomponents of the task are learned gradually or suddenly is more difficult and requires careful analysis.

Although the total amount learned increases as a function of repetition, the amount learned on each trial will not be constant. Repetition effects exhibit negative acceleration: The most learning occurs in the first exposure to a stimulus or situation, and the amount learned in each subsequent exposure continually declines until further improvement is too small to be detected. The rate of learning is negatively related to the amount already learned. Hintzman and Curran (1995) have shown that people can register the occurrence of a repeated stimulus while failing to learn more about its specific details. First impressions of a repeated stimulus are particularly important, as people may show little evidence for having noticed subtle changes that are introduced to a stimulus after its first presentation (DiGirolamo and Hintzman, 1997).

Why Does Repetition Improve Learning?

Anderson and Schooler (1991) have pointed out that the sensitivity of learning to repetition is evidence for its efficiency and adaptiveness because the frequency with which information has been used in the past is a very good predictor of whether it will be needed in the future. Still, although repetition has been intensively studied, the mechanisms underlying its effects are still poorly understood. Moreover, there is no reason to believe that a single explanation could apply to all situations where repetition facilitates learning.

Of particular interest to many researchers has been the effect of repeated study on human memory, and the two dominant explanations of these repetition effects were both discussed by Ward (1893). One class of explanations (called a functional approach by Ward but more commonly known as strength theory in twenty-first-century scientific circles) claims that there is a single location in memory storage that corresponds to an event. Every time the event is repeated, that location (known as the memory trace) increases in effectiveness or strength. It is also assumed that stronger traces are easier to retrieve from memory than are weaker traces. Repetition thus improves learning by increasing the strength of a single memory trace. A second class of explanation for the effects of repetition on memory was called an atomistic approach by Ward but is now known as multiple-trace theory. This approach assumes that every occurrence of an event is a unique episode. Every time an event occurs, a separate, independent memory trace is formed. This trace contains information about the time and situation in which that occurrence happened. The more times an event occurs, the more traces of that event are placed in memory. According to this multiple-trace theory, repetition improves learning because finding at least one trace of an event becomes easier when there are more traces of that event in memory.

A fundamental difference between these two accounts concerns the representation of the individual occurrences of a repeated item. The strength theory claims that each occurrence of an event strengthens a single memory trace. Since each occurrence has the same effect, the specific details of individual occurrences are lost. In contrast, the multiple-trace theory claims that every occurrence produces its own trace. The individuality of specific occurrences is maintained.

Experiments distinguishing between these two accounts have often required participants to remember a list of words. A word on the list may occur once or a varying number of times. After seeing the list, participants are shown the list items again and asked to make a judgment regarding how often each item occurred on the list. Even when they do not expect to be tested on the frequencies of the items, people are typically able to perform this task with considerable (but not perfect) accuracy. However, strength theory and multiple-trace theory make different proposals as to how participants are able to make judgments about the frequency of occurrence of list items. Strength theory claims that participants retrieve the memory trace corresponding to a test item and evaluate that trace's strength. They then use the strength to make a judgment of frequency. For example, if a memory trace is very strong, participants will guess that the item occurred many times on the list. If a memory trace is weak, they may decide that the item occurred once (or possibly not at all) on the list. In contrast, the multiple-trace theory claims that participants make judgments of frequency by retrieving as many traces as possible of that item occurring in the context of the list. They then base their judgments on a count of the traces they found.

Numerous experiments have investigated whether a frequency judgment is based on a single trace or on the retrieval of many different traces. For example, Hintzman and Block (1971) showed participants two lists of words, five minutes apart. Some words occurred on both lists. Each word occurred zero, two, or five times on List 1 and zero, two, or five times on List 2. After seeing both lists, participants were asked to estimate frequency of occurrence separately for each list. They were quite accurate at this task; their estimates were chiefly influenced by the frequency of the item on the list being judged and were influenced little by the item's frequency on the other list. Such a finding is difficult for a strength theory to explain: If judgments of frequency were based simply on the overall strength of the trace of the word, people would not be able to make separate estimates for the frequency of an item on two lists. However, a multiple-trace theory would predict this finding because frequency judgments are seen as being based on a count of individual traces, each carrying information about its time of formation.

Subsequent studies have found further evidence in favor of a multiple-trace theory. For example, when some words are presented visually and others auditorily, participants are able to give separate frequency judgments for each kind of presentation. Also, they are able to judge how often a word followed another word on a list. Such findings suggest that the individual identities of the occurrences of a repeated event are maintained in memory, as assumed by the multiple-trace theory (Greene, 1992).

Studies such as these suggest that a multiple-trace theory is necessary to account for the effects of repetition on memory. They do not show that such a theory is sufficient to account for all the effects of repetition. The question of whether repetition has other effects in addition to the creation of multiple memory traces has not been resolved, although there is some evidence that repeated events are remembered better than would be expected on the basis of memory for specific presentations (Watkins and LeCompte, 1991). Moreover, there is little evidence that would allow one to determine whether the multiple-trace approach can be applied to all of the situations in which learning is improved by repetition.

When Is Repetition Ineffective in Increasing Learning?

Although the emphasis in this entry has necessarily been on the mechanisms through which repetition improves learning, one should not assume that repetition alone is always sufficient. For example, consider a common coin, such as the American penny. Although people have seen such coins countless times, as Nickerson and Adams (1979) showed, people can have quite poor memory for the details of a penny. They are often unable to remember exactly where such features as the date and the words "In God We Trust" are located. There is no need for people to attend to these features of a penny because pennies can easily be distinguished from other coins on the basis of their size and color. This suggests that attention to an event may be necessary before repetition of that event leads to noticeable improvements in memory. The generality of this claim has been established by studies demonstrating poor memory for other currencies, for the details of telephone dials, and for the messages of common advertisements.

Additional examples of ineffective repetition have come from experiments on rote rehearsal (Glenberg, Smith, and Green, 1977; Rundus, 1977). In these studies, participants read repeated words aloud over and over. An unexpected memory test on the words is later given. Memory performance is usually only slightly affected by the number of times that a person read each word aloud. On the other hand, if people are encouraged to carry out more active, effortful processing on the words, memory improves dramatically as study time is increased.

One situation in which repetition impairs memory is when people have to recall a short series of digits or letters in order. Recall is impaired if one of the items is repeated in the series. This phenomenon, known as the Ranschburg effect, was introduced into the modern psychological literature by Crowder and Melton (1965). Critical to understanding this negative effect of repetition is the fact that people have to remember that an item was repeated and the locations of each occurrence in the series. The Ranschburg effect occurs because recall of the first occurrence of the repeated item inhibits accurate recall of the second occurrence (Greene, 2001).

Thus, repetition need not lead to improved learning. Rather, repetition leads to increased opportunities for learning to occur. Whether learning takes place will depend on the type of information that has to be remembered and the amount and nature of processing that a person carries out.

See also: DISTRIBUTED PRACTICE EFFECTS

Bibliography

Anderson, J. R., and Schooler, L. J. (1991). Reflections of the environment in memory. *Psychological Science 2*, 396–408.

Crowder, R. G., and Melton, A. W. (1965). The Ranschburg phenomenon: Failures of immediate recall correlated with repetition of elements within a stimulus. *Psychonomic Science 2*, 295–296.

DiGirolamo, G. J., and Hintzman, D. L. (1997). First impressions are lasting impressions: A primacy effect in memory for repetitions. *Psychonomic Bulletin & Review 4*, 121–124.

Ebbinghaus, H. (1885; reprint 1964). *Memory: A contribution to experimental psychology.* New York: Dover.

Glenberg, A., Smith, S. M., and Green, C. (1977). Type 1 rehearsal: Maintenance and more. *Journal of Verbal Learning and Verbal Behavior 16*, 339–359.

Greene, R. L. (1992). *Human memory: Paradigms and paradoxes.* Hillsdale, NJ: Erlbaum.

——— (2001). Repetition effects in immediate memory in the absence of repetition. In H. L. Roediger III, J. S. Nairne, I. Neath, and A. M. Surprenant, eds., *The nature of remembering: Essays in honor of Robert G. Crowder.* Washington, DC: American Psychological Association.

Guthrie, E. R. (1935). *The psychology of learning.* New York: Harper.

Harlow, H. F. (1949). The formation of learning sets. *Psychological Review 56*, 51–65.

Hintzman, D. L., and Block, R. A. (1971). Repetition and memory: Evidence for a multiple-trace hypothesis. *Journal of Experimental Psychology 88*, 297–306.

Hintzman, D. L., and Curran, T. (1995). When encoding fails: Instructions, feedback, and registration without learning. *Memory & Cognition 23*, 213–226.

Nickerson, R. S., and Adams, M. J. (1979). Long-term memory for a common object. *Cognitive Psychology 11*, 287–307.

Rundus, D. (1977). Maintenance rehearsal and single-level processing. *Journal of Verbal Learning and Verbal Behavior 16*, 665–681.

Ward, J. (1893). Assimilation and association. *Mind 2*, 347–362.

Watkins, M. J., and LeCompte, D. C. (1991). The inadequacy of recall as a basis for frequency knowledge. *Journal of Experimental Psychology: Learning, Memory, and Cognition 17*, 1,161–1,176.

Robert L. Greene

RESCORLA-WAGNER MODEL

See: KAMIN'S BLOCKING EFFECT: NEURONAL SUBSTRATES; LEARNING THEORY: CURRENT STATUS; MATHEMATICAL LEARNING THEORY; SOMETIMES OPPONENT PROCESS (SOP) MODEL, IN CONDITIONING

RETRIEVAL PROCESSES IN MEMORY

The processes of learning and memory are often subdivided into stages of *encoding* (initial learning of information), *storage* (maintaining information over time), and *retrieval* (using stored information). Processes of encoding establish some representation of experience in the nervous system, which is referred to as an engram or memory trace. Memory traces certainly have physiological underpinnings, but cognitive psychologists use the construct as an abstraction to refer to the changed state of the cognitive system before and after some experience. Retrieval processes refer to the means of accessing stored information and can be affected by a variety of factors.

Retrieval is the key process in the act of remembering (Roediger, 2000). Most experiences of life are encoded and stored (at least briefly) but will never be retrieved and thus will have no real consequence for the individual. Encoding and storage are cheap, in the sense that all events leave their traces. Retrieval is the process by which latent information is actualized in ongoing behavior. A person may or may not realize that past events are being retrieved and are affecting current behavior. Explicit retrieval is referred to as remembering; when previous behavior affects ongoing performance outside of awareness, psychologists refer to it as priming of the behavior. The distinction corresponds roughly to the contrast between explicit and implicit memory processes (McDermott, 2000).

The division of processes into those affecting encoding, storage, or retrieval seems simple in concept but cannot be completely defended in practice. One reason is that it is impossible to distinguish cleanly between encoding and storage processes, because the two are inextricably connected. When does initial learning (encoding) end and maintenance of information over time (storage) begin? There is no clear answer to this question; suggestions provided by some theorists to cut this Gordian knot are relatively arbitrary. However, separation between the bundle of processes referred to as encoding and storage, on the one hand, and those involving retrieval, on the other, can be accomplished more directly.

The general logic of this separation is to hold conditions of encoding and storage constant and to manipulate only conditions of retrieval. For example, two groups of people could be presented with material (lists of words or sets of stories) to remember and could be treated identically until the time they are tested. Then one group of people might simply be given a blank sheet of paper and asked to recall all that they can of the material. Imagine that they recall 40 percent of the materials under these free recall conditions (so called because they are given no external cues to aid recall and are free to recall material in any order). This measure might be thought to reflect the amount of information that people have encoded and stored—the amount they know—but this conclusion would ignore the possibility that the bottleneck in performance is at the retrieval stage. Perhaps the people really have encoded and stored much more, but have simply failed to retrieve the extra material. This possibility can be examined by testing another group of subjects who are given retrieval cues to prompt recall of the material. Often appropriate cues can produce great benefits relative to free recall (Mantylä, 1986).

The advantage of cued recall over free recall indicates that more information is available (or is stored) in memory than is accessible (retrievable) on a particular test such as free recall (Tulving and Pearlstone, 1966). More generally, no test of memory provides a perfect measure of information stored in memory; the retrieval processes involved in any test filter the information. At best, people assess the information that can be produced under a particular set of retrieval conditions. Although no test or set of retrieval conditions can ever provide a perfect window on the contents of memory, study of retrieval processes can proceed meaningfully in many different ways.

Repeated Testing

One straightforward way to study retrieval processes is to test people repeatedly on the same material, under the same or differing conditions. For example, people might study sixty pictures of easily named objects and then be tested on the names of those objects under conditions of free recall for seven minutes (that is, with a large amount of time so they are not

rushed). After a first test, they would be given a second and then a third test under identical conditions without intervening study of the material. An almost universal finding in such experiments is that people will recall items on the second and third tests that they did not recall on the earlier tests, a phenomenon called reminiscence (Ballard, 1913). Of course, some pictures recalled on the first test might be forgotten on later tests, but surprisingly the reminiscence or recovery between tests often outweighs the inter-test forgetting. When total recall improves over tests, this phenomenon is called hypermnesia (Erdelyi and Becker, 1974). Whereas reminiscence (recall of items on a later test that could not be recalled on an earlier test) almost always occurs in experiments, hypermnesia is observed more rarely and usually under free recall conditions (i.e., without retrieval cues). Under certain conditions the phenomenon is quite reliable, so the challenge is to specify the necessary conditions for its observation. One idea is that relational processing (associating the materials with one another) protects against forgetting across repeated tests whereas processing of individual items (providing features that distinguish them from others) leads to recovery of new items across tests (Burns, 1993). Whichever is the case—and some argue for a hybrid theory—the phenomena of reminiscence and hypermnesia point up again that a single test of retention provides a faulty assessment of the amount of information stored in memory (Roediger and Challis, 1989).

Testing with Retrieval Cues

The most popular method of studying retrieval processes is by manipulating the nature of the testing conditions, particularly the types of cues given to aid recollection. One precondition for studying explicit retrieval with cues is that the rememberer must be placed in what E. Tulving (1983) has called the retrieval mode. That is, the individual must be attempting to retrieve from his or her past. For example, you might see a ladder in your environment as you walk to work and it does not cue any memories; however, if you are asked, "Tell me about an experience from your past that involves a ladder," the query will catapult you into the retrieval mode and you will probably come up with a relevant memory. In studies of cued recall the retrieval mode is assumed by giving people explicit instructions to remember, which has led some theorists to ignore the concept (because it is a constant condition). However, retrieval mode is critical to understanding remembering.

In a typical cued recall paradigm, people are given a list of words to remember that belong to common categories. The list might be composed of words such as *hawk, crow, goose, woodpecker, desk, dresser, couch,* and *footstool,* representing *birds* and *articles of furniture.* After receiving a long list with many words and categories, some people are tested under conditions of free recall (recall the words in any order) and some under conditions of cued recall (the same instruction, but now the names of the categories are provided as retrieval cues). The typical finding is that people tested with category names as retrieval cues recall many more items than those tested without cues, showing again the disparity between information that is available in memory and that accessible on a particular test. The gains from cues are genuine and not due merely to guessing items belonging to the categories, because the items used are typically not the most likely to be guessed (*robin* and *sparrow* are avoided as study materials in favor of *crow* and *woodpecker*).

What causes retrieval cues to be effective? A primary consideration is what type of information was learned and how it was encoded—what information is stored in memory. The general principle governing retrieval of such stored information is called the encoding specificity principle: Retrieval cues are effective to the extent that they help reinstate or recreate processes involved in original learning (Tulving, 1983). The idea is that events are encoded in specific ways—people retain specific coded features of their experiences that may comprise the memory traces of these experiences. Retrieval cues are then effective to the extent that they match or overlap the specific encoded features. In addition, the match between cues and traces must be distinctive for provoking a specific memory; the cue should specify one event and not many events. A cue such as "remember the lecture" is ineffective in aiding recollection of a particular lecture because it is too general. You have been to many lectures.

Numerous laboratory experiments have confirmed the essence of the encoding specificity principle. If people are in the retrieval mode, retrieval cues that more precisely match, or recreate, the original features of the learning experience (and not other experiences) promote better recall (see Roediger and Guynn, 1996, for numerous examples). This is not to say that all retrieval phenomena are well accounted for, because empirical problems exist. For example, certain types of cues that seem as if they should be effective are not; in some cases, seemingly "good" retrieval cues actually hinder rather than help recall. One example is part-list cuing inhibition, wherein giving people part of a list of studied items hurts recall relative to control conditions (Slamecka, 1968). For example, if people are given lists of words belonging to common categories (such as the aforementioned examples) and then at test time either are given only category names as cues or are given category names plus two items from the categories, recall of the remaining items from the categories will be better when only category names are given as cues. Providing some items from the category in addition to the category names will recreate the learning situation better than just giving the category names, but in fact such item cues hurt recall.

Explaining this retrieval inhibition has proved to be a challenge; much research has established the validity of the finding and eliminated many artifactual possibilities for the results (Nickerson, 1984). One interpretation links the part-list cuing effect to a cue-overload principle, an idea embedded in the foregoing paragraphs but not named. The cue-overload principle states that a retrieval cue becomes less effective as more events are subsumed under the cue (Watkins, 1975) because each extra event makes the cue less distinctive with regard to any particular event. So, for example, a category name retrieval cue provides better recall of the studied members of a category if two items were given in each category of the list rather than six items. In the case of part-list cues, it may be assumed that presentation of the category members at test somehow adds to the number of items subsumed under the category name cue and thereby reduces recall. Numerous observations accord with the cue overload principle's interpretation of the part-list cuing effect, although other theories exist as well.

The cue overload principle complements the encoding specificity principle in making sense of the variable effectiveness of retrieval cues. Further, the cue-overload idea shows that both the compatibility of cue to the encoded trace and the distinctiveness of the process matters. That is, if one has had many experiences that leave similar traces, a retrieval cue may match too many of the traces to be effective.

State-Dependent Retrieval

Alcohol and other drugs having a depressing effect on the central nervous system are known to impair retention of information. The usual interpretation is that alcohol interferes with the neural processes that underlie encoding and storage of information, or the consolidation of information. This is likely true, but may not represent the whole story of drug-induced amnesia. Retrieval factors are at work, too. Clinicians working with alcoholic patients have observed that the patient may, for instance, hide a paycheck while drunk and then not be able to remember where it is hidden when sober. However, the next time the patient gets drunk, the check may be recovered. The phenomenon suggests that successful retrieval of memories may depend on matching the pharmacological states in which information is learned and used.

This phenomenon of state-dependent retrieval (better recall when pharmacological states of learning and testing match rather than mismatch) has been verified in laboratory experiments. In one case (Eich, Weingartner, Stillman, and Gillin, 1975) volunteer students smoked marijuana or a placebo cigarette before being exposed to a categorized word list. Four hours later the subjects again smoked either a marijuana cigarette or a placebo and then were tested on the material, first by free recall and then by cued recall in which category names served as the retrieval cues.

The results are shown in Table 1; first consider the free recall results, where the number of words recalled from the set of 48 is shown. If people were sober both when they studied the words and when they were tested on them, they performed best (11.5 words recalled). If they were under the influence of marijuana at study but sober at test time, they recalled fewest (6.7). This condition represents the usual case of drug-induced amnesia, when people experience events under the drug but are sober when tested. Is this effect due only to encoding and storage factors, or are retrieval factors at work, too? This question can be answered by examining the last row: When people were drugged at both study and test time, they recalled more words (10.5) than when they were drugged only during study time (6.7). Just as in the anecdote about the alcoholics related above, retention improved when the pharmacological state at test time matched that at study time. Do not conclude from this experiment that drugs improve memory, because they usually do not. (When people learned the information sober but were tested under marijuana, they performed worse than when tested sober.)

Although state-dependent retrieval is a real phenomenon, it usually occurs only under free recall conditions, as can be verified by examining the cued recall results. The category names served as good retrieval cues, because cued recall was better than free recall in all four conditions. However, the state-dependent retrieval effect (better recall in the drug-drug study and test condition compared with the drug-sober condition) has vanished. These results are broadly consistent with the encoding specificity hypothesis. Under conditions of free recall, a person's pharmacological state can serve as a retrieval cue, and if the cues match between study and test conditions, performance is enhanced. However, when powerful external retrieval cues are provided, they overshadow the weak "state" cues and render them ineffective. This account explains the common finding that state-dependent retrieval effects are rarely found on tests employing cued recall (Eich, 1989).

Table 1

Results of the Experiment on State-Dependent Retrieval

Condition		Average Number of Words Recalled	
Study	Test	Free Recall	Cued Recall
Placebo	Placebo	11.5	24.0
Placebo	Drug	9.9	23.7
Drug	Placebo	6.7	22.6
Drug	Drug	10.5	22.3

SOURCE: Courtesy of Henry L. Roediger III and Michelle L. Meade. Adapted from Eich, J. E., Weingartner, H., Stillman, R. C., and Gillin, J. C. (1975). State dependent accessibility of retrieval cues in the retention of a categorized list. *Journal of Verbal Learning and Verbal Behavior 14*, 408-417.

Do state-dependent retrieval phenomena exist with states other than drug states? The conditions most often investigated are moods, in studies where researchers induce happy or depressed moods in people by various means prior to study or test of material. The expected finding is that congruence of mood at study and test should produce better retention than when moods mismatch. This result has been reported in some studies, but there have been numerous failures to replicate it and the reasons for this state of affairs are not well understood at this point.

Transfer-Appropriate Processing

A viewpoint related to the encoding specificity hypothesis is transfer-appropriate processing, which emphasizes that all retention tests can be considered as cases of transfer of prior experience to the test situation. Depending on the nature of the task used to assess memory, some experiences will provide good transfer and others will provide poor transfer. Further, this approach emphasizes the relativity of memory tests: Some methods of learning may prove superior for one type of test but disastrous for another. The phrase transfer-appropriate processing was first used to explain some puzzling results obtained in the levels of processing tradition (Morris, Bransford, and Franks, 1977). Under many conditions, if people study events while focusing on their meaning, they retain the events better later than if they had focused on other aspects of the events, such as what they look or sound like, while studying them (Craik and Tulving, 1975). For words, retention is better on many tests after people have generated meaningful associations for the words (thus forcing attention to their meaning) than when rhyming words have been generated (causing attention to sounds or phonemes).

Most of the tests showing the superiority of meaningful encodings have been those, such as recall or recognition, that are thought to rely heavily on meaning (Roediger and Guynn, 1996). But suppose a test were given for the sound of words following study experiences encouraging attention to either the meaning or the sound of words; e.g., the word *beagle* was studied in a long list and the retrieval cue is, "Recall a word on the list that rhymed with legal." When such tests were constructed, the results came out largely as expected: Having people think about the rhyming aspects of words during study produced better performance on tests requiring knowledge of the sound of the words than did study experiences emphasizing the meaning of words (Morris, Bransford, and Franks, 1977). Therefore, the ways in which one studies events are not inherently good or bad for later retention; instead, whether study strategies are good or bad depends on their relation to the nature of the test. Learning experiences transfer well or poorly depending on the nature of the test and the type of knowledge it requires. The same idea is inherent in the encoding specificity principle.

The concept of transfer-appropriate processing has been applied to several different problems. One is the explanation of differences between explicit tests of memory (those in which people are told that their memories are being tested) and implicit tests of memory (those in which people are simply given a new task and retention is measured by how prior experiences transfer to the new task). Many implicit memory tests seem to involve perceptual components and to benefit from appropriate perceptual processing, whereas many explicit tests depend upon meaningful processing. Numerous experiments have confirmed that these two broad areas of experience (perceptual, conceptual) differentially affect certain tests in the predicted manner (Roediger, 1990).

Related Topics

Retrieval processes play a role in all memory phenomena, so the coverage in this entry has perforce been selective. For example, the fact that distinctive events are well remembered may be interpreted in terms of the cue overload principle; similarly, the inhibition from part-list cues may be related to the tip-of-the-tongue phenomenon wherein people are blocked from recalling well-known information by intrusion of related information. All memories depend not just on conditions of encoding and storage, but also on myriad retrieval factors.

See also: CODING PROCESSES; DRUGS AND MEMORY; EMOTION, MOOD, AND MEMORY; IMPLICIT MEMORY

Bibliography

Ballard, P. B. (1913). Oblivescence and reminiscence. *British Journal of Psychology Monograph Supplements 1*, 1–82.

Burns, D. J. (1993). Item gains and losses during hypermnesic recall: Implications for the item-specificelational information distinction. *Journal of Experimental Psychology: Learning, Memory, and Cognition 19*, 163–173.

Craik, F. I. M., and Tulving, E. (1975). Depth of processing and the retention of words in episodic memory. *Journal of Experimental Psychology: General 104*, 268–294.

Eich, E. (1989). Theoretical issues in state-dependent memory. In H. L. Roediger, III, and F. I. M. Craik, eds., *Varieties of memory and consciousness: Essays in honour of Endel Tulving*. Hillsdale, NJ: Erlbaum.

Eich, J. E., Weingartner, H., Stillman, R. C., and Gillin, J. C. (1975). State dependent accessibility of retrieval cues in the retention of a categorized list. *Journal of Verbal Learning and Verbal Behavior 14*, 408–417.

Erdelyi, M. H., and Becker, J. (1974). Hypermnesia for pictures: Incremental memory for pictures but not for words in multiple recall trials. *Cognitive Psychology 6*, 159–171.

Mantylä, T. (1986). Optimizing cue effectiveness: Recall of 500 and 600 incidentally learned words. *Journal of Experimental Psychology: Learning, Memory, and Cognition 12*, 66–71.

McDermott, K. B. (2000). Implicit memory. In A. E. Kazdin, ed., *The encyclopedia of psychology*. New York: American Psychological Association and Oxford University Press.

Morris, C. D., Bransford, J. D., and Franks, J. J. (1977). Levels of processing versus transfer appropriate processing. *Journal of Verbal Learning and Verbal Behavior 16*, 519–533.

Nickerson, R. S. (1984). Retrieval inhibition from part-set cuing: A persisting enigma in memory research. *Memory & Cognition 12*, 531–552.

Roediger, H. L. (1990). Implicit memory: Retention without remembering. *American Psychology 45*, 1,043–1,056.

——— (2000). Why retrieval is the key process in understanding human memory. In E. Tulving, ed., *Memory, consciousness, and the brain: The Tallinn conference*. Philadelphia: Psychology Press.

Roediger, H. L., and Challis, B. H. (1989). Hypermnesia: Increased recall with repeated tests. In C. Izawa, ed., *Current issues in cognitive processes: The Tulane-Floweree symposium on cognition*. Hillsdale, NJ: Lawrence Erlbaum Associates.

Roediger, H. L., and Guynn, M. J. (1996). Retrieval Processes. In E. L. Bjork and R. A. Bjork, eds., *Memory: Handbook of perception and cognition*. San Diego, CA: Academic Press.

Slamecka, N. J. (1968). An examination of trace storage in free recall. *Journal of Experimental Psychology 76*, 504–513.

Tulving, E. (1983). *Elements of episodic memory*. New York: Oxford University Press.

Tulving, E., and Pearlstone, Z. (1966). Availability versus accessibility of information in memory for words. *Journal of Verbal Learning and Verbal Behavior 5*, 381–391.

Watkins, M. J. (1975). Inhibition in recall with extralist "cues." *Journal of Verbal Learning and Verbal Behavior 14*, 294–303.

Henry L. Roediger III
Michelle L. Meade

REWARD LEARNING

See: REINFORCEMENT OR REWARD IN LEARNING

RIBOT, THÉODULE (1839–1916)

Théodule Armand Ribot (1839–1916) was born in Guingamp, Brittany. After attending lycée in Saint-Brieuc, he entered the École Normale Supéricure at Paris in 1862. He received his degree in philosophy in 1865, and until 1872 he taught philosophy in the secondary schools of Vesoul and Laval. In 1870 Ribot published his first work, *La psychologie anglaise contemporaine*. Seven years later he gave up teaching so that he could concentrate on writing. He also attended clinical courses in psychiatry given by Valentin Magnan, Benjamin Ball, Jules Luys, Félix Voisin, and Jean-Martin Charcot, then defended his thesis, "L'hérédité psychologique." In 1876 Ribot and Hippolyte Taine founded the journal *Revue Philosophique*, which is still published.

In 1885, Ribot started a course in experimental psychology at the Sorbonne; in 1888, through the influence of Ernest Renan, a chair of experimental and comparative psychology was created at the Collège de France that Ribot occupied until he retired in 1901. He was elected to the Académie des Sciences Morales et Politiques (Section of Philosophy) in 1899.

Ribot was responsible for creating in France "scientific" psychology, rejecting a psychology that depended on spiritualism and introspection in favor of one that depends on facts and must agree with known physiological and biological data. Ribot was interested in pathological psychology because it enabled one to understand normal psychological mechanisms by discovering the laws that govern facts. Influenced by Herbert Spencer's evolutionism, Ribot described, as did Hughlings Jackson, the law of regression (or of dissolution) that controls pathological mental phenomena, such as the amnesias. Importantly, Ribot's contributions were purely intellectual, the result of personal reflection upon events reported by others, which he categorized and regrouped. He never tried to construct models. His work was empirical and rational rather than experimental.

Ribot is probably best known today for his law of regression in the amnesias, Ribot's Law. The law outlines in a logical fashion the progressive dysfunction of memory in disease. First to be affected are recent memories. Second, personal memories disappear, "going downward to the past." Third, things acquired intellectually are lost bit by bit; last to disappear are habits and emotional memories. Thus, Ribot's Law refers to progressive amnesia as a temporal gradient going from the most recent to the oldest memories. For Ribot this law implied that memory depends upon permanent modifications and organization of neurons, and it is their disorganization that leads to amnesia. Ribot's Law considers only one type of memory, defined by a double capacity of conservation and of reproduction of certain states (for example, a skill); the recognition and localization in the past that are carried by consciousness are exclusively psychological and do not constitute memory. Ribot applied his law to aphasias, which he regarded as partial amnesias.

Théodule Ribot (*Psychology Archives, University of Akron*)

Ribot's influence was significant because it represented the beginnings of pathological psychology, which included neuropsychology. Two of his students influenced psychology: Pierre Janet, who succeeded him at the Collège de France, and Alfred Binet. Ribot's biological concepts led the philosopher Henri Bergson to write *Matière et mémoire* (1896).

Bibliography

Centenaire de Th. Ribot. Jubilé de la psychologie scientifique française 1839–1889–1939 (1939). Agen: Imprimerie Moderne.

Dugas, L. (1924). *Le philosophe Théodule Ribot*. Paris: Payot.

Gasser, J. (1988). La notion de mémoire organique dans l'oeuvre de T. Ribot. *History and Philosophy in Life Sciences 10*, 293–313.

Ribot, T. (1881). *Les maladies de la mémoire*. Paris: Baillière.

—— (1883). *Les maladies de la volonté*. Paris: Baillière.

—— (1885). *Les maladies de la personnalité*. Paris: Alcan.

—— (1889). *La psychologie de l'attention*. Paris: Alcan.

—— (1896). *La psychologie des sentiments*. Paris: Alcan.

—— (1897). *L'évolution des idées générales*. Paris: Alcan.

—— (1900). *L'imagination créatrice*. Paris: Alcan.

—— (1905). *La logique des sentiments*. Paris: Alcan.

—— (1907). *Essai sur les passions*. Paris: Alcan.

—— (1910). *Problèmes de psychologie affective.* Paris: Alcan.
—— (1914). *La vie inconsciente et les mouvements.* Paris: Alcan.

Jean-Louis Signoret

RIGHT HEMISPHERE

See: KNOWLEDGE SYSTEMS AND MATERIAL-
SPECIFIC MEMORY DEFICITS

S

SAVANT SYNDROME

Savant syndrome (formerly called idiot savant syndrome) refers to an exceedingly rare but remarkable condition in which persons with severe mental handicaps have some isolated but spectacular islands of genius or brilliance that stand in stark, incongruous contrast with the serious limitations of the overall handicaps. The mental handicap can be either autism or mental retardation. The skills, remarkable as they are, exist within a very narrow range of human abilities. They include music (usually piano); art (drawing or sculpting); calendar calculating (the ability to give the day of the week for any past or future date); lightning calculating (the ability to add, multiply, subtract, or divide complex numbers with lightning rapidity); and mechanical or spatial skills including map memorizing, visual measurement, unusual sensory discrimination such as enchanced sense of touch and smell, or perfect appreciation of time without knowledge of a clock. These skills, within these very narrow bands, are always linked to a spectacular memory.

In some persons *(talented savants)* the skills are remarkable simply in contrast with the handicap; in others *(prodigious savants)* the abilities are spectacular in contrast with the handicap and would be spectacular even if they occurred in normal persons. Savant syndrome can be hereditary or it can be acquired following central nervous system injury before, during, or after birth. It occurs in males approximately six times more frequently than in females. The skills can appear suddenly, without explanation, and can disappear just as suddenly.

The condition was first described in 1887 by J. Langdon Down (better known for having described Down syndrome). He was struck by the paradox of deficiency and superiority in a number of cases he saw as superintendent of a hospital in England. At that time in Britain the word *idiot* was an accepted legal classification for a *severe* degree of mental retardation and did not have the pejorative, comical connotation the term now has. Down combined that word with the term *savant*—knowledgeable person—derived from the French word *savoir* (to know), to denote these fascinating persons. The term is a misnomer in that almost all cases have an IQ of 40 or above, and thus have moderate rather than the severe mental retardation that now-archaic legal term *idiot* once defined.

Superior memory is a trait all savants share. It is a particular type of memory, however: very deep but within a very narrow area; concrete and not richly associative; direct and nonsymbolic; nonemotional and seemingly automatic or unconscious. This "memory without reckoning" may be akin to what Mishkin, Malamut, and Bachevalier (1984) refer to as "habit" memory, as opposed to "cognitive" memory; it relies on a brain circuitry that is more primitive and lower than the later-developed, higher brain circuitry of cognitive or associative memory. In the savant this unconscious memory presumably is relied upon as an alternative pathway to damaged higher-level cognitive memory circuitry.

There has been no well-designed study of the prevalence of savant syndrome, but it has been reported to occur in 1 out of 2,000 in an institutionalized mentally retarded population and in as many as 1 out of 10 autistic persons. Mental retardation and autism are both developmental disabilities, but since autism is so much less common than mental retardation, the number of savants is generally evenly divided between those with autism and those with mental retardation. In the movie *Rain Man*, the character Raymond Babbit (played by Dustin Hoffman) is the best-known portrayal of a savant, in that instance an autistic savant. It is important to remember, however, that not all autistic persons are savants and not all savants are autistic. The number of prodigious savants worldwide is estimated to be less than fifty as of 1991. Talented savants are, of course, more common; but the savant syndrome overall is still a rare condition.

Bibliography

Mishkin, M., Malamut, B., and Bachevalier, J. (1984). Memories and habits: Two neural systems. In G. K. Lynch, J. L. McGaugh, and N. M. Weinberger, eds., *Neurobiology of learning and memory.* New York: Guilford Press.

Treffert, D. A. (1988). The idiot savant: A review of the syndrome. *American Journal of Psychiatry 145* (5), 563–572.

—— (1989). *Extraordinary people: Redefining the "idiot savant."* New York: Harper & Row.

—— (1990). *Extraordinary people: Understanding savant syndrome.* New York: Ballantine Books.

Darold A. Treffert

SCHIZOPHRENIA AND MEMORY

Schizophrenia affects approximately 1 percent of the population worldwide. It typically involves hallucinations and delusions, also known as psychotic or positive symptoms. Markedly impaired social skills and cognitive deficits, also known as negative symptoms, are also core features. In fact, schizophrenia was originally called dementia praecox (i.e., early onset dementia, to highlight the impairment of cognition. The cognitive domains most often affected by schizophrenia include attention, memory, and language. These deficits are evident even before the onset of positive symptoms (during the so-called "prodrome") and in untreated schizophrenic patients. It is therefore unlikely that the cognitive features of schizophrenia result simply from chronic illness, institutionalization, or medication side effects. Most important, the degree of cognitive decline is the best predictor of functional outcome: that is, how the patient will do in the community once the most severe psychotic features have abated. Here we will focus on abnormalities of memory, describing the type of memory impairment typical of schizophrenia and the cerebral abnormalities that may account for this impairment.

Memory Deficits in Schizophrenia

Despite variable methods and the inherent heterogeneity of schizophrenia, a number of consistent findings appear throughout the literature (Aleman et al., 1999). Here we highlight some of the patterns of memory deficits in schizophrenia:

- While schizophrenia is associated with a wide range of cognitive difficulties, deficits in memory are particularly pronounced.

- The memory impairment is selective, affecting primarily explicit memory. Implicit memory, including perceptual priming and procedural memory, appears to be relatively intact.

- Even within explicit memory, tests of recall ("Tell me everything you saw") are affected more than recognition ("Did you see this before?"). Patients with schizophrenia have difficulty forming associations between items during the encoding (study) period, and do not show the normal pattern of heightened recall after studying words that have common features (i.e., words that are easily associable). Defective recall may therefore be attributable to both poor organization of related items at encoding, and poor search strategies at retrieval.

- Further examination of the explicit memory deficit indicates a specific impairment in memory that requires conscious recollection of the study episode (i.e., episodic memory) as compared to simple recognition or familiarity-based memory processes. Patients with schizophrenia are less likely to state that they clearly "remember" an event, more often saying that they simply "know" that the event has occurred. Word frequency modulation, which leads to a greater degree of conscious recollection in healthy adults, has no such effect on patients with schizophrenia. Finally, while healthy subjects use both personally relevant and inter-item associations to recollect words, patients with schizophrenia are less likely to do so, relying instead on bizarre and ineffectual linkages.

- These deficits are not due solely to poor concentration, lack of motivation, distracting positive symptoms, or a medication side effect.

Patients with schizophrenia often suffer from selective impairment of memory that requires the conscious recollection of the study episode, but they retain implicit (and other automatic) memory. Given the recognized abnormality in creating effectual associations, a primary role of impaired "feature-binding" seems to account for the episodic memory impairment in schizophrenia. That is, patients with schizophrenia do not appear to bind together the multifold features of everyday events and therefore find it hard to remember them in detail. Because the ability to place memories in the detailed context of the initial experience is critical for a continued sense of self and the maintenance of a personal history, abnormalities in this realm may relate to the aberrant conscious experiences of schizophrenia.

Neuroimaging of Memory Function in Schizophrenia

Uncovering the neural basis for these deficits in memory is an area of intensive research. Given the role of the hippocampus and the prefrontal cortex (PFC) in normal memory, these regions are the primary focus of this pursuit. Scientists are using both structural neuroimaging techniques (e.g., magnetic resonance imaging [MRI]) and functional neuroimaging techniques (e.g., positron emission tomography [PET] and functional magnetic resonance imaging [fMRI]). In the following section we will briefly summarize the major findings as they apply to schizophrenia (Weiss and Heckers, 2001).

Structural Neuroimaging Studies

The spatial resolution afforded by MRI allows investigators to correlate performance on cognitive tasks with the volume of specific brain regions, including the hippocampus and subdivisions of the PFC. Some evidence suggests just such a link in schizophrenia, with memory performance correlating with the integrity of these two regions. Overall, however, it has been difficult to link memory performance to cerebral structure in schizophrenia, perhaps because the structural changes associated with schizophrenia are subtle. Indeed, the neuropathology of schizophrenia may not involve overt neuronal loss or marked tissue atrophy but rather decreases in the number of only a subset of neurons or deficient connections. These subtle changes may lead to disturbances of cognitive performance without gross morphologic abnormality and therefore would be undetectable with structural neuroimaging. To evaluate the possibility of a functional abnormality within the frontal lobes, the hippocampus, or both, researchers must use methods that allow visualization of cerebral activity.

Functional Neuroimaging Studies

Functional neuroimaging proceeds from the premise that focal neuronal activity relates either to regional cerebral blood flow (rCBF) or to the local degree of glucose metabolism. There are two major classes of functional imaging paradigms: those that examine the resting pattern of activity in a target population (e.g., schizophrenic patients with poor memory) and those that assess changes in cerebral activity during the performance of a task. There are several studies of baseline cerebral activity during memory performance in schizophrenia, but they have yielded discrepant results. Hence, the exact relation between resting cerebral activity and memory performance in schizophrenia remains unclear. Because measures of baseline cerebral activity may not adequately represent the fleeting changes of neuronal activity associated with mental processes, research has shifted to the study of cerebral activity during the performance of memory tasks.

These "cognitive activation" studies attempt to capture the "neural signature" of memory processing—to identify those structures involved at the time of task performance. Researchers obtain images during the performance of a memory task (encoding or retrieval) and during a baseline state. The subtraction of baseline activity from that demonstrated during memory processing allows researchers to infer which regions are "activated" during the memory. Thus it is the change in activity associated with task performance, sometimes called "recruitment," that is commonly reported. Using this type of neuroimaging paradigm, schizophrenic subjects (when compared to controls) appear to show a relative lack of task-related activation in regions known to play a role in normal memory (e.g., PFC and hippocampus).

Frontal Lobe Abnormalities

Patients with schizophrenia commonly demonstrate diminished frontal lobe activation (particularly in the left hemisphere) during memory task performance. Fletcher and colleagues (1998) found that schizophrenic subjects recalled brief word lists (fewer than four words) as well as controls but that they showed a dramatic drop-off in performance with longer lists, a result that suggests a deficit in explicit memory. As word-list lengths increased, both groups initially showed increasing left PFC activation in response. With longer word lists, however, the patients were unable to sustain the degree of prefrontal activation displayed by the normal subjects. These results indicate that schizophrenic subjects are unable to maintain necessary levels of PFC activation in response to increasing task demands.

The relative lack of memory-task-related frontal activation is not a universal finding. Some investigators have demonstrated task-related *hyperactivity* of the DLPFC in schizophrenic subjects, possibly indicating impaired efficiency of DLPFC function during the performance of a memory task. Task-related hypoactivity may depend on disease-specific characteristics, particularly the degree of negative symptoms.

Deficient frontal activity has been linked to "dysexecutive" features of memory; the inability to organize information for optimal performance. While control subjects use the implicit semantic associations between words to facilitate encoding and support subsequent retrieval, schizophrenic subjects do not use this strategy. Instead, patients tend to use ineffectual or bizarre associations, leading to poorer recall. The inability to use the "normal" associative mechanisms that take advantage of inherent properties of the items to be remembered correlates with a lack of activation in the inferior frontal lobes bilaterally. Difficulty in organizing encoding and retrieval strategies in schizophrenia therefore appear to be associated with lower memory task-related metabolism in regions of prefrontal cortex.

Temporal-Lobe Abnormalities

Recent studies in patients with schizophrenia demonstrate abnormal baselin levels of activity in the temporal lobe and memory task-related *hypoactivity* of the hippocampus. Heckers and colleagues (1998) studied subjects after they learned words using a deep semantic encoding strategy or a shallow perceptual one. During scanning, subjects were asked to complete three-letter word stems of the target words. Normal subjects recalled more words after deep semantic encoding, which was associated with a recruitment of the hippocampus; the attempt to retrieve the words encoded using the shallow perceptual strategy resulted in bilateral activation of the prefrontal cortex. Schizophrenic subjects recalled fewer words after deep semantic encoding, which was associated with an impaired recruitment of the hippocampus. Increased hippocampal activity at baseline and impaired recruitment during episodic memory retrieval might represent the functional correlate of an abnormal cortico-hippocampal interaction in schizophrenia. These findings complement the studies of abnormal frontal cortex activity in schizophrenia. A frontal-hippocampal disconnection in schizophrenia may involve temporal-lobe circuits that play a role in the processing of language, pathways to and from the hippocampal formation, or both.

As with the findings of frontal hypoactivity, abnormalities in temporal lobe activation are not universal. Several studies, despite showing impairments of explicit memory in the schizophrenic cohort, have failed to demonstrate functional abnormalities in the temporal lobe. It is unclear whether this is due to differences in experimental design, image acquisition, disease characteristics, or other as yet unknown factors.

Conclusion

The results reviewed here suggest an abnormality of hippocampal and prefrontal cortex function during memory in schizophrenia. The pace of discovery in this area has been quite rapid. The next major strides in the understanding of the neural basis of schizophrenia await the advent of even better technology that would allow more precise temporal and spatial assessment of neural functions.

See also: BEHAVIOR THERAPY

Bibliography

Aleman, A., Hijman R., de Haan, E. H. F., and Kahn, R. S. (1999). Memory impairment in schizophrenia: A meta-analysis. *American Journal of Psychiatry 156,* 1,358–1,366.

Fletcher, P. C., McKenna, P. J., Frith, C. D., Grasby, P. M., Friston, K. J., and Dolan, R. J. (1998). Brain activations in schizophrenia during a graded memory task studied with functional neuroimaging. *Archives of General Psychiatry 55,* 1,001–1,008.

Heckers, S. (2001). Neuroimaging studies of the hippocampus in schizophrenia. *Hippocampus 11,* 520–528.

Heckers, S., Rauch, S. L., Goff, D., Savage, C. R., Schacter, D. L., Fischman, A. J., and Alpert, N. M. (1998). Impaired recruitment of the hippocampus during conscious recollection in schizophrenia. *Nature Neuroscience 1,* 1,318–1,323.

Weiss, A. P., and Heckers, S. (2001). Neuroimaging of declarative memory in schizophrenia. *Scandinavian Journal of Psychology 42,* 239–250.

Stephan Heckers
Anthony P. Weiss

SCHOOL LEARNING

School learning is the acquisition of knowledge, subject matter, information, understanding, and skill from teaching. Research on learning and memory provides teachers with essential scientific knowledge that is useful for understanding and improving school learning.

What Can Be Learned from Teachers?

Schools and teachers have made much progress in the teaching of complex subject matter. Today teachers teach difficult subjects, such as calculus in high school, that were previously thought to be impossible for students of that age to learn. Even the learning of expert performance involves intensive work with teachers. See Ericsson and Charness (1994) and Ericsson, Krampe, and Tesch-Romer (1993) for discussions of expert performance.

Ancient and Modern Conceptions of Learning

Modern conceptions of learning originated in ancient Greece and Rome. Since Socrates tried to teach a slave boy the Pythagorean theorem in the *Meno* by having him construct the theorem from innate ideas rather than by telling him the theorem, teachers and researchers have studied how students acquire, remember, and use knowledge. Plato's emphasis on constructive learning resembles modern conceptions of school learning that emphasize the importance of having students construct meaning by relating new concepts to familiar ideas called schemata or to memories of experience called scripts.

Aristotle wrote that students learn information by forming relations or associations between new information and previously learned information or concepts that are stored in memory as images. He believed that subject matter and other abstract information are logically organized in memory into hierarchies that consist of classes, or general concepts, divided into species, or smaller groups. His ideas about hierarchically organized abstract verbal information resemble modern understanding of the organization of semantic memory (Kintsch, 1980). Aristotle's ideas about associations underlie much of modern thinking about how to enhance learning, retention, and understanding in schools by teaching students to associate new information and prior knowledge through the use of imagery and verbal processes.

Aristotle influenced school learning in ancient times, when memory-training systems (mnemonics)—many of them similar to present-day techniques—were taught to students, orators, and statesmen (Cicero, 1967). In the Middle Ages, Aristotle's ideas about forming associations between new and familiar concepts influenced the widespread use of statues, paintings, mosaics, and murals to relate various abstract moral concepts to familiar contexts. Modern conceptions—of school learning as association building and knowledge acquisition as the construction of hierarchically organized relations between new and old information—still reflect these ancient ideas of Plato and Aristotle.

How Students Learn Individually and in Groups

Recent research in educational psychology, cognitive psychology, and neuropsychology helps us to understand how memory, knowledge acquisition, attention, learning strategies, and metacognition (self-control of learning) influence school learning. This research shows the importance of getting students to attend to the information to be learned, to relate it actively to their knowledge and experience, and to use it to solve problems. The research also shows that students can learn "how to learn" (learning strategies) and can learn to control and to monitor their own learning (metacognition).

Most such research focuses on how students learn when they work individually with teachers, mentors, and coaches. However, recent research on situative learning emphasizes social context, viewing learning as the product of systems of group interaction (Greeno, Collins, and Resnick, 1996). Research on group learning in schools has begun to identify the conditions best suited to conceptual learning by cooperative groups. Cohen (1994) finds that cooperative groups interact well in tasks that require cooperation, present loosely structured problems, provide pretraining in group work, and impose little direct teacher supervison. Cooperative group learning can play an important role in achievement in concept learning. For example, Kourilsky and Wittrock (1992) found that by working in cooperative groups, high school students increased their learning of concepts in economics by 30 percent when they generated relations between their experience and the abstract subject matter.

Memory

The information students have organized into schemata in their semantic (abstract and verbal) memory and into scripts in their episodic (concrete and imaginal) memory influences their learning and comprehension. In schools, teaching procedures focus on building relations between these semantic and episodic types of information in memory and the new information to be learned. Mining these relations boosts memory or comprehension or both.

Learning to Remember Facts

Factual information—dates, names, places, and so on—is often difficult to remember because it seems to bear little relation to other information of interest or importance to students. Memory for factual information improves when learners construct relations, even arbitrary ones, between their semantic or episodic memories and the facts to be learned. Mnemonic systems are built on that principle. For example, lists of words can be remembered in order by forming images between the words on the list and mnemonic words organized into a series (e.g., *one* is a bun, *two* is a shoe). Capitals of states can be remembered by forming colorful or comic associations between the name of the state and its capital city (Levin, 1985). The objective of this procedure is to make the learning of facts meaningful in some way, much as Aristotle and Cicero did with mnemonic devices.

Acquiring Knowledge in School

Knowledge acquisition requires understanding and comprehension of what one has learned. Research on reading comprehension and science learning shows the importance of schemata (Rumelhart, 1980) and student preconceptions (Wittrock, 1994) in determining what students will understand and how their comprehension can be improved. For example, when students read a passage from a new perspective, they can comprehend it differently.

Elementary school students' preconceptions about concepts in science influence their comprehension in school. Students who have unscientific conceptions of electricity often have difficulty in learning how it functions. Students in elementary school and in high school also differ in their understanding of the composition of matter, such as gases. Benson, Wittrock, and Baur (1993) found that many students, even in high school, do not understand that gases are made of particles (molecules). It is important that teachers take into account such student preconceptions.

Research on the teaching of comprehension and the acquisition of knowledge in schools shows that students in schools acquire knowledge and increase their comprehension when they generate meanings for information, such as subject matter, stories, and concepts (Wittrock, 1998). The generation of summaries, pictures, inferences, applications, and examples is an effective way to organize information and to relate it to experience and knowledge stored in memory. Comprehension and understanding function best when students construct two types of relations: among the parts of the subject matter and between the subject matter and the learner's knowledge and experience (Wittrock, 1990). Both verbal processes (e.g., summaries and inferences) and imagery (pictures, graphs, and diagrams) enhance comprehension when students use them to construct these two types of relations.

Concise summaries that contain appropriate verbal and visual components (words and pictures), as opposed to mere written summaries, improve explanations and foster comprehension (Mayer et al., 1996). Student generation of summaries or of analogies as they read a text also can significantly increase comprehension without increasing the time needed to learn (Wittrock and Alesandrini, 1990). As with the facilitation of memory of factual information, the student's building of relations between memory and new information enhances school learning. However, with comprehension and understanding, these relations are less arbitrary, more organized, more meaningful, and more integrated with schemata and scripts (Grabowski, 1996).

Attention

Research in neuropsychology and in cognitive psychology shows the importance of attention in learning in schools. Long-term, voluntary attention (i.e., ability to focus one's thoughts on themes or concepts rather than classroom distractions) is especially important. Mentally retarded or learning-disabled children and some hyperactive children have trouble maintaining needed levels of attention in school. These children often can be taught to control their voluntary attention by learning "self-talk" strategies that emphasize the relevant learning task. Research on divided attention shows that learners can process two different tasks, especially familiar ones, at the same time if each of the tasks comes from a different sensory mode. But when both tasks simultaneously enter the same sensory register, e. g. the ears, only one message will receive much attention (Anderson, 1990).

In classrooms teachers can apply knowledge from research on attention to understand how objectives and questions enhance learning. Objectives and questions direct student attention in productive ways designed to stimulate learning. Clark and Wittrock (2000) discuss methods to facilitate attention. These methods include increasing motivation to attend, avoiding divided attention, directing attention by cueing important concepts, and providing advance organizers (coherent introductions).

Learning Strategies and Metacognition

Learning strategies are procedures for constructing relations across concepts and between new information and experience and knowledge (e.g., constructing summaries, inferences, and pictures). Metacognition is awareness of and control over one's thoughts (e.g., planning to use a comprehension strategy). Learning strategies and metacognition often produce large increases in comprehension and knowledge acquisition when students learn to plan and to monitor their thinking and studying, to control their attention, and to use comprehension strategies such as analogy building and summarizing. Studies on teaching thinking skills, learning strategies, and metacognition show large gains—around 50 percent—in comprehension when students use learning strategies or metacognition in school (Mayer and Wittrock, 1996; Lambert and McCombs, 1998).

Conclusion

Modern research on learning and memory has greatly enhanced the understanding of school learning and its improvement. Unfortunately, the power and the utility of these research findings has only begun to affect teaching in the schools. There is a useful convergence between the ancient writings of Plato and Aristotle about constructive learning and association building and modern scientific research on learning and knowledge acquisition; both the ancient and modern precepts indicate that school learning involves the construction of meaning for new information by attending to it, organizing it, and relating it to one's knowledge and experience.

See also: ARISTOTLE; MNEMONIC DEVICES; PROSE RETENTION

Bibliography

Anderson, J. R. (1990). *Cognitive psychology and its implications*. New York: W. H. Freeman and Company.

Aristotle (1928). *The works of Aristotle*. Vol. 1, ed. W. D. Ross. Oxford: Clarendon Press.

—— (1964). On memory and recollection. In *On the soul (De anima); Parva naturalia; and on breath*, trans. W. S. Hett. Cambridge, MA: Harvard University Press.

Benson, D. L., Wittrock, M. C., and Baur, M. E. (1993). Students' preconceptions of the nature of gases. *Journal of Research in Science Teaching 30*, 587–597.

Cicero. (1967). *De oratore*, ed. E. W. Sutton, Cambridge, MA: Harvard University Press.

Clark, R., and Wittrock, M. C. (2000). Psychological principles in training. In S. Tobias and J. D. Fletcher, eds., *Training and retraining*. New York: Macmillan.

Cohen, E. G. (1994). Restructuring the classroom: Conditions of productive small groups. *Review of Educational Research 64*, 1–35.

Ericsson, K. A., and Charness, N. (1994). Expert performance, its structure and acquisition. *American Psychologist 49*, 725–747.

Ericsson, K. A., Krampe, R. T., and Tesch-Romer, C. (1993). The role of deliberate practice in the acquisition of expert performance. *Psychological Review 100*, 363–406.

Grabowski, B. L. (1996). Generative learning. In D. H. Jonassen, ed., *Handbook for Research on Educational Communications and Technology*. New York: Macmillan.

Greeno, J. G., Collins, A. M., and Resnick, L. B. (1996). Cognition and learning. In D. C. Berliner and R. C. Calfee, eds., *Handbook of educational psychology*. New York: Simon & Schuster.

Kintsch, W. (1980). Semantic memory: A tutorial. In R. S. Nickerson, ed., *Attention and performance*, Vol. 8. Hillsdale, NJ: Erlbaum.

Kourilsky, M., and Wittrock, M. C. (1992). Generative teaching: An enhancement strategy for the learning of economics in cooperative groups. *American Educational Research Journal 29*, 861–876.

Lambert, N. M., and McCombs. B. L., eds. (1998). *How students learn*. Washington, DC: American Psychological Association.

Levin, J. R. (1985). Educational applications of mnemonic pictures: Possibilities beyond your wildest imagination. In A. A. Sheikh and K. S. Sheikh, eds., *Imagery in education*. Farmingdale, NY: Baywood.

Mayer, R. E., Bover, W., Bryman, A., Mars., R., and Tapangco, L. (1996). When less is more: Meaningful learning from visual and verbal summaries of science textbook lessons. *Journal of Educational Psychology 88*, 64–73.

Mayer, R. E., and Wittrock, M. C. (1996). Problem-solving transfer. In D. C.. Berliner and R. C. Calfee, eds., *Handbook of educational psychology*. New York: Simon & Schuster.

Plato. *Meno*. Loeb Classical Library. Cambridge, MA: Harvard University Press.

Rumelhart, D. E. (1980). Schemata: The building blocks of cognition. In R. J. Spiro, B. C. Bruce, and W. F. Brewer, eds., *Theoretical issues in reading comprehension*. Hillsdale, NJ: Erlbaum.

Wittrock, M. C. (1990). Generative processes of comprehension. *Educational Psychologist 24*, 345–376.

—— (1994). Generative science teaching. In P. J. Fensham, R. F. Gunstone, and R. T. White, eds., *The content of science: A constructivist approach to its teaching and learning*. London: Falmer Press.

—— (1998). Cognition and subject matter learning. In B. L. McCombs and N. Lambert, eds., *How students learn*. Washington, DC: American Psychological Association.

Wittrock, M. C., and Alesandrini, K. (1990). Generation of summaries and analogies and analytic and holistic abilities. *American Educational Research Journal 27*, 489–502.

M. C. Wittrock

SECOND MESSENGER SYSTEMS

All cells of the body respond to their environment. For most cell types, the responses can be both general and be related to the cell's particular function. An example of a general response is the regulation of sugar utilization: When sugar is plentiful, glucose is polymerized to glycogen, a storage form. When sugar is scarce, the biochemistry of the cells will be adjusted so that glycogen is broken down to make sugar available. Stimulation of gland cells to release their secretion is a specialized response. In neurons the regulated specialized functions include properties of ion channels; availability of synaptic vesicles for exocytosis (a process called mobilization); and responsiveness of postsynaptic receptors. These functions can be altered transiently (in a time frame of minutes to hours) or for much longer periods, if not permanently. Short-term changes are produced by modifying existing proteins in the cell, modifications that are rapidly reversed when the second-messenger is removed. Long-term changes result when the second-messenger pathway changes transcription, ultimately producing a change in gene expression and the production of new proteins.

Many of these responses, both general and specialized, are produced by signal transduction, a process in which an extracellular stimulus activates a specific receptor on the surface of the responding cell. As a result, the receptor initiates changes in the biochemical state of the cell through the production of a substance that, in turn, alters the cell's responsiveness. This modulating substance is called a second messenger because it is evoked by an environmental cue (the "first messenger"). The process is called signal transduction because the external stimulus is recoded (transduced) into the change in biochemical state. Although ionized calcium (Ca^{2+}) is often thought of as a second messenger, it may be more instructive to call it a primary regulator. Along with membrane potential, it is the ultimate governor of excitability and synaptic transmission in nerve cells.

Historically, formulation of the concepts and principles for understanding second messenger systems arose from studies of two physiological processes: regulation of sugar metabolism in muscle and fat cells (adipocytes), and the conversion of light energy into nerve impulses in the rod cells of the retina. In the 1950s, Sutherland and Rall (1957) discovered the first second messenger, cyclic adenosine monophosphate (cAMP), and Sutherland and his coworkers identified the enzymatic pathway by which cAMP is synthesized and showed how it brings about the changes in sugar metabolism. At about the same time, Wald (1959) investigated how rhodopsin converts the energy of a photon into a chemical signal; the enzymatic and electrophysiological events in phototransduction were thus identified. We now know that both of these processes are mediated by sets of proteins encoded by genes that are closely related phylogenetically and that operate by similar mechanisms.

Production of Second Messenger Molecules

Most second messenger systems follow a similar molecular strategy. The pathway is initiated when an external cue—most often a neurotransmitter, a hormone, an odorant, a physical stimulus such as light, or a mechanical force—activates a receptor. These receptors, which are single polypeptide chains, have seven membrane-spanning ("serpentine") domains. Although these molecules have several domains exposed on the external surface of the responding cell, the actual binding site for the first messenger is slightly buried within the membrane. Some of the receptor is also situated on the intracellular side of the membrane; a part of this intracellular domain associates with another protein, called a G-protein because it binds a guanosine nucleotide (GDP or GTP).

The receptors that usually mediate signal transduction are closely related members of a large gene family that, in addition to rhodopsin, contains adrenergic receptors, muscarinic acetylcholine receptors, and receptors for serotonin, dopamine, histamine, and all neuropeptides. The trimeric G-proteins belong to another large gene family. They are made up of three subunits ($\alpha\beta\gamma$). The α subunit binds GDP when associated with an inactive receptor—a receptor that has not been activated by an external stimulus; it binds GTP when the receptor is activated. More than a dozen isoforms of α subunits have been identified, each of which interacts with different receptors. There are fewer types of the β and γ subunits.

When the α subunit binds GTP because of receptor activation, it dissociates from the $\beta\gamma$ portion of the complex. Nevertheless, it retains its association with the inner surface of the cell's external membrane. Depending on the particular combination of receptor and G-protein, the dissociated α subunit either activates or inhibits the next component of the second messenger system, which can be called a primary effector. If the α subunit is stimulatory, its interaction with the primary effector results in synthesis of a second messenger.

The cAMP system is the best-understood intracellular signaling pathway. Binding of a neurotransmitter—such as norepinephrine to the β_1-adrenergic receptor—activates a stimulatory G-protein (G_s), which promotes the synthesis of cAMP from adenosine triphosphate (ATP) by adenylyl cyclase. This primary effector enzyme, which is a twelve-membrane-spanning protein, operates only when it is associated with an α_s subunit with bound GTP. The α_s-cyclase complex also acts as a GTPase, an enzymatic activity that hydrolyzes bound GTP to GDP and P_i. When GTP is replaced by GDP, the α_s subunit dissociates from the cyclase and reassociates with the receptor, to be activated again. Some receptors—for example, the muscarinic acetylcholine receptor—interact with an inhibitory G-protein (G_i). The $\alpha_i\alpha$ subunit, when activated by the muscarinic receptor, associates with adenylyl cyclase to block the synthesis of cAMP. The opposing actions of norepinephrine and acetylcholine on the cyclase through G_s and G_i represent one form of second messenger interaction called cross-talk.

An important functional aspect of signal transduction pathways, inherent in the arithmetic of the relationships among these components (receptor/G-protein/primary effector), is amplification of the external stimulus. A neuron has far fewer receptor molecules than G-proteins and primary effectors. Amplification occurs when the relatively few stimulated receptors activate many primary effectors. Moreover, since primary effectors are enzymes that produce the second messenger catalytically, this step amplifies the signal even further.

What Second Messengers Do

Second messengers activate secondary effectors, enzymes that are protein kinases in most instances. Typically these enzymes, which catalyze the transfer of the terminal (γ) phosphoryl group of ATP to hydroxyl groups of serine or threonine residues in proteins, are multifunctional: They can phosphorylate many different protein substrates. Secondary effector enzymes include the cAMP-dependent protein kinases (PKA), protein kinase C (PKC), and the

Ca^{2+}/calmodulin-dependent protein kinases. Phosphorylation of substrate proteins, which can be called secondary regulators, changes their properties either to stimulate or to inhibit their function. These changes in the activity of substrate proteins by phosphorylation are the means by which the responses to the environmental stimulus are produced. For example, phosphorylation of a channel protein can alter the flux of ions into the neuron to raise or lower the membrane potential. Another example is the phosphorylation of transcription activators, which promotes their binding to DNA. An example important to the neurobiology of memory is the cAMP response element binding protein (CREB). When phosphorylated by cAMP, CREB joins with other proteins to form a complex that binds to the promoter region of genes whose transcription is stimulated by cAMP.

Whether a substrate can be phosphorylated depends on the amino acid sequences around the serine and threonine residues in the substrate protein: Each type of kinase prefers special sequences. Often more than one type of protein kinase can phosphorylate the same protein. The phosphorylations then occur at different sites in the substrate molecule, however.

A serine/threonine protein kinase can exist in several isoforms in the same neuron. The isoforms of each type of kinase are closely related, some encoded by the same genes with diversity produced by alternative RNA splicing and others encoded by distinct but closely related genes. Most protein kinases are related phylogenetically, including tyrosine-specific kinases that phosphorylate proteins on the hydroxyl group of tyrosine residues. Protein kinases that can phosphorylate a variety of substrates are called multifunctional. There are also dedicated kinases that phosphorylate only a special protein substrate (for example, the β-adrenergic receptor kinase) or kinases that are present in only a few kinds of neurons (for example, the cGMP-dependent protein kinase).

PKA was the first protein kinase to be described. This enzyme consists of two regulatory (R) subunits and two catalytic (C) subunits. (There are two major types of R subunits, R^I and R^{II}, and several isoforms of C.) The PKAs illustrate how second messenger kinases are regulated: The common mechanism of activation is through binding of the second messenger to release the catalytic center from inhibition. With PKA, the inactive (inhibited) kinase is activated when the concentration of cAMP is elevated within the cell according to the reaction

$$R_2C_2 + 4 \text{ cAMP} + 2(R - 2\text{cAMP}) + 2C.$$

The two R subunits each bind two molecules of cAMP and dissociate from the C subunits, which, when released, are then free to phosphorylate protein substrates. The free C subunits remain enzymatically active until the concentration of cAMP within the cell falls, which results in the dissociation of the cAMP bound to the R subunits. Lacking cAMP, R subunits reassociate with C subunits, thereby inhibiting the enzyme.

Inositol Polyphosphates, Diacylglycerol and Arachidonic acid

Many receptors activate phospholipase C (PLC) through other G-proteins. PLC catalyzes the hydrolysis of phospholipids in the external membrane of the responding cell. Phospholipids consist of a glycerol moiety esterified at the first (sn 1 position) and second (sn 2) hydroxyl groups to fatty acids, and, at its third, to a diester of phosphoric acid and one of four special alcohols (inositol in phosphatidylinositol, PI; choline in PC; ethanolamine in PE; and serine in PS). In the PI of nervous tissue, the fatty acid at the sn 1 position is usually stearic (an eighteen-carbon saturated fatty acid); the second hydroxyl is usually esterified to arachidonic acid, an unsaturated twenty-carbon fatty acid. The PLC activated in this second messenger system is a diesterase that hydrolyzes PI to an inositol phosphate and diacylglycerol (DAG). Inositol is an unsaturated six-membered cyclic polyalcohol that, in addition to the phosphoryl linkage, can be phosphorylated at hydroxyl groups on the other five carbons. Most often the fourth and fifth hydroxyl groups are phosphorylated in the inositol moiety of nerve cells (PIP_2). When hydrolyzed by PLC, it is therefore called inositol 1,4,5-trisphosphate (IP_3), a water-soluble second messenger. Other inositol polyphosphates exist, but it is not yet certain whether they, too, act as second messengers. Diacylglycerol, which is soluble only in lipid, remains within the membrane and also serves as a second messenger. PLA_2, which hydrolyzes PI at the sn 2 position to release arachidonic acid, also is activated by a G-protein-coupled receptor for histamine and other neurotransmitters. The arachidonic acid produced by receptor-mediated activation of PLA_2 can serve as a second messenger itself or it can be converted into many metabolites, some of which alter synaptic transmission and neuronal excitability.

PKC, another multifunctional enzyme, is activated by DAG. (Phorbol esters, tumor-promoting substances from plants, act as potent pharmacological analogues of DAG.) There now are fourteen isoforms of PKC known. All require the presence of membrane lipid, notably PS, to be active. The PKCs fall into four groups (classical, novel, atypical and μ-like), whose enzymatic properties reflect the presence or absence of various functional domains. For example classical PKCs which require CaM^{2+}-ion for enzymatic activity, have a C2 consensus sequence that is responsible for binding Ca^{2+}. Other PKCs lack the sequence and are active independently of Ca^{2+}. The functional significance of this variety of isoforms is not yet known, but structural diversity is presumed to cause differences in substrate specificity and subcellular localization. Unlike PKA, the regulatory and catalytic regions of the PKCs are both parts of a single polypeptide chain. The catalytic part is masked by the regulatory domain. When a lipid activator and membrane (and Ca^{2+} for the classical forms) bind to the regulatory domain of the enzyme, its conformation changes, exposing the catalytic part of the kinase for action. The dependence of the PKC isoforms on Ca^{2+} is an important instance of the complexity of regulation by second messengers. In the pathway involving PLC, both DAG and IP_3 are formed. The function of IP_3 as a second messenger is to bind an intracellular receptor that is located on the cytoplasmic surface of the endoplasmic reticulum. When this receptor is activated, stored Ca^{2+} is released, thereby raising the intracellular concentration of the free ion.

Ca^{2+} is required for the action of many enzymes in neurons, either as the free ion or often complexed to calmodulin, a small protein that can bind four Ca^{2+} ions. In addition to the major forms of PKC, Ca^{2+} is required by some forms of adenylyl cyclase, guanylyl cyclase, PLC, phospholipase A_2 (PLA_2), 5-lipoxygenase, some protein phosphatases, and one other kinase, Ca^{2+}/calmodulin-dependent protein kinase II. This multifunctional kinase, like the PKCs, is a single polypeptide chain containing both regulatory and catalytic domains. Unlike either of the other kinases, however, it exists in the cell as a complex of several individual kinase molecules, the exact number varying with the type of cell and with the location within the neuron. This enzyme is quite abundant but is highly concentrated in dendritic spines of neurons where it is the most abundant protein in the postsynaptic density.

MAP Kinases

There are three families of MAP (mitogen activated protein) kinases: kinases of the ERK type, p38 MAP kinases, and JUN kinases. These enzymes are all activated through cascades of kinase kinases, each one specific to the MAP kinase to be activated. The first kinase kinase in a cascade typically is activated by the receptor-mediated mobilization of a small (MW 20,000–40,000) G-protein (Ras, Raf, Rho, Ran, which are distantly related to the α-subunits of the trimeric G-proteins.) This mobilization, which initiates the second-messenger pathway, results in the phosphorylation of the first "upstream" kinase, which then goes on to phosphorylate the next. Finally the last upstream kinase (a MAP kinase kinase, or MAPKK) is a distinctive enzyme that phosphorylates the MAP kinase at two adjacent, amino acid residues, one a threonine, the other a tyrosine.

The activated MAP kinase is imported into the nucleus, where it phosphorylates (and activates) specific transcription factors. Thus, even though MAP kinases do phosphorylate proteins in the cytoplasm (for example, p38 kinase phosphorylates and activates PLA_2), their most characteristic function appears to be the second-messenger mediation of changes in gene expression.

Degradation of Second Messengers

cAMP and cGMP are rapidly degraded by several different phosphodiesterases. There are many phosphodiesterase inhibitors that prolong the action of these cyclic nucleotides, including caffeine and theophylline, which occur naturally. Some of these degradative enzymes can also be secondary effectors—for example, in rod cells, where receptor-activated G-proteins activate a cGMP-phosphodiesterase. The second messengers derived from membrane phospholipids are inactivated by being reincorporated into the membrane. IP_3 is dephosphorylated by several phosphatases, one of which is blocked by Li^+ ion. (This inhibition may be important for the effectiveness of Li^+ in the treatment of bipolar depression.)

Although individual protein substrates phosphorylated by the various protein kinases are discussed elsewhere, it is important to point out here that they exist only transiently because of the rapidity with which protein phosphatases remove phosphoryl groups from the proteins. Phosphoryl groups from proteins phosphorylated at serine/threonine residues are removed by one class of protein phosphatases, phosphate on tyrosine residues, by another. With MAP kinases, the phosphoryl groups on both serine/threonine and tyrosine are removed by a specific class of phosphatase.

Variations of Signal Transduction Pathways

Although the typical second messenger system consists of all of the components described, there are examples in which one or more of them is absent. In some instances the receptor-activated G-protein itself acts directly on a secondary regulator—for example, in heart muscle cells, where the G-protein modulates an ion channel without any intervening constituents. Some ion channels are gated directly by cyclic nucleosides, thereby circumventing the need for protein phosphorylation. Guanylyl cyclase can be activated by nitric oxide (NO), a short-lived gas that passes through membranes, bypassing a receptor/G-protein complex. NO is formed in neurons from the amino acid arginine as a consequence of the activation of the enzyme NO synthetase (which requires reduced nicotinamide adenine dinucleotide phosphate and Ca^{2+} ions) through a second messenger pathway. NO is unusual because it does not act as a second messenger in the neuron in which it is synthesized, but in a neighboring nerve cell. It is possible that arachidonic acid and its metabolites also may act transcellularly as second messengers; in this way they also would bypass receptor, G-protein, and primary effector enzyme. Finally, some secondary effector enzymes are linked directly to their own special receptor through the membrane; important examples of this kind of signaling are the so-called receptor tyrosine protein kinases.

See also: APLYSIA: CLASSICAL CONDITIONING AND OPERANT CONDITIONING; APLYSIA: MOLECULAR BASIS OF LONG-TERM SENSITIZATION; GENETIC SUBSTRATES OF MEMORY: HIPPOCAMPUS; HORMONES AND MEMORY; INVERTEBRATE LEARNING; LONG-TERM DEPRESSION IN THE CEREBELLUM, HIPPOCAMPUS, AND NEOCORTEX; LONG-TERM POTENTIATION: SIGNAL TRANSDUCTION MECHANISMS AND EARLY EVENTS; NEUROTRANSMITTER SYSTEMS AND MEMORY

Bibliography

Caron, M. G., and Lefkowitz, R. J. (1993). Catecholamine receptors: Structure, function, and regulation. *Recent Progress in Hormone Research 48*, 277–290.

Cobb, M. H. (1999). MAP kinase pathways. *Progress in Biophysics and Molecular Biology 71*, 479–500.

Dekker, L. V., Palmer, R. H., and Parker, P. J. (1995). The protein kinase C related gene families. *Current Opinion in Structural Biology 5*, 396–402.

Greengard, P. (2001). The neurobiology of slow synaptic transmission. *Science 294*, 1,024–1,030.

Kennedy, M. B. (2000). Signal-processing machines at the postsynaptic density. *Science 290*, 750–754.

Nishizuka, Y. (1995). Protein kinase C and lipid signaling for sustained cellular responses. *FASEB Journal 9*, 484–496.

Schulman, H., and Hyman, S. E. (1999). Intracellular signaling. In M. J. Zigmond, F. E. Bloom, S. C. Landis, and L. R. Squire, eds., *Fundamental neuroscience.* San Diego: Academic Press.

Schwartz, J. H. (2001). The many dimensions of cAMP signaling. *Proceedings of the National Academy of Sciences of the United States of America 98*, 13,483–13,484.

Siegelbaum, S. A., Schwartz, J. H., and Kandel, E. R. (2000). Modulation of synaptic transmission: Second messengers. In E. R. Kandel, J. H. Schwartz, and T. M. Jessell, eds., *Principles of Neuroscience*, 4th edition. New York: McGraw-Hill.

Soderling, T. R. (2000). CaM-kinase: Modulators of synaptic plasticity. *Current Opinion in Neurobiology 10*, 375–380.

Sutherland, E., and Rall, T. W. (1957). Isolation of cyclic AMP. *Journal of the American Chemical Society 79*, 3,608.

Takai, Y., Takuya, S., and Takahashi, M. (2001). Small GTP binding proteins. *Physiology Review 81*, 153–208.

Taylor, S. S., Buechler, J. A., and Yonemoto, W. (1990). cAMP–dependent protein kinase: Framework for a diverse family of regulatory enzymes. *Annual Review of Biochemistry 59*, 971–1,005.

Wald, G. (1959). Life and light. *Scientific American 201*, 92–108.

Zang, X., and Majerus, P. W. (1998). Phosphatidylinositol signaling reactions. *Seminars in Cell Development and Biology 9*, 153–160.

James H. Schwartz

SEMANTIC MEMORY

[*Semantic memory is our acquired knowledge about the everyday world. The following two sections characterize our current understanding about semantic memory from the cognitive and the neurbiological perspectives. In both sections, two common themes in research on semantic memory are discussed: whether semantic memory is fundamentally distinct from memory for personal experiences (episodic memory) and how to characterize the organization of semantic knowledge in terms of its cognitive dimensions and its representation in the brain.*

Semantic memory is often distinguished from episodic memory as what one "knows" independent of what one "remembers," that is, consciously recollects learning in a particular personal episode. Endel Tulving, who introduced the distinction between semantic and episodic memory, has argued that semantic memory is a distinct memory system, independent from that of episodic memory. Yet, all of our conscious learning experiences are initially a part of episodic memory, consistent with a common alternative view that semantic memory is knowledge abstracted from the information common to many episodes. One central question in research on semantic memory is whether and how episodic memory and semantic memory are mediated by different neural structures or brain systems. Several lines of evidence suggest semantic memory is mediated by cerebral cortical areas without involvement of the hippocampus, whereas episodic memory relies critically on hippocampal function.

As yet we have only a preliminary understanding of the cognitive dimensions of semantic memory. **COGNITIVE EFFECTS** *outlines research suggesting three principal cognitive dimensions: categorization of objects by their features, judgments about relationships between concepts, and the capacity to combine multiple elementary concepts into distinct and more complex concepts.*

It is generally viewed that semantic memory is mediated by the cerebral cortex, as best demonstrated in cases of semantic dementia, a selective loss of semantic memory, consequent to cortical deterioration. However, there is considerable controversy over whether separate areas of the cerebral cortex process specific domains of semantic memory, and about the nature of the functional distinctions. There have now been several observations of deficits in specific domains of semantic knowledge following damage to particular areas of the cerebral cortex, as well as observations of activation of particular cortical areas during naming in specific domains of objects. It is not clear whether these selectivities reflect specif-

ic categories of semantic knowledge or distinct types of cognitive or perceptual processing associated with particular categories of information. **NEUROBIOLOGICAL PERSPECTIVE** *outlines this issue.*]

COGNITIVE EFFECTS

Researchers originally conceptualized semantic memory as human knowledge of language (Tulving, 1972). The term now generally refers to one's everyday knowledge of the world, as contrasted with episodic memory, one's knowledge of personal experience. Semantic memory includes such facts as, "Robins are birds," "Chairs have legs," and "Fireworks are dangerous." Semantic memory has been thought by some researchers (Tulving and Schacter, 1990) to be a functionally separate memory system, distinct from episodic memory. Neuroimaging techniques implicate differential brain region activity in semantic and episodic tasks (Wheeler, Suss, and Tulving, 1997; Knowlton, 1998). There is some suggestion in scalp-based recordings of electrical brain activity following stimulus presentation (event related potentials) that a wave of negative amplitude may accompany. Nevertheless, the interdependence of semantic and episodic information (McKoon, Ratcliff, and Dell, 1986; Shoben and Ross, 1986) urges caution in accepting the claim that these are separate systems. Indeed, the best-known computational model of memory continues to treat the two as part of the same (declarative) memory system (Anderson, and Lebiere, 1998).

Semantic and episodic recall may be distinguished by whether one believes one knows something, or whether one personally remembers it (Knowlton and Squire, 1995). Mark Wheeler and colleagues (1997) proposed that semantic memory is associated with the absence of the phenomenological experience of remembering, a distinction that may prove more relevant than one based on content. Thus, semantic memory may include autobiographical content that is known, but not remembered.

Research in semantic memory can be divided into three categories concerning human knowledge of concepts: First, one knows that concepts belong to various categories. Second, one knows that concepts have certain properties and bear certain relations to other concepts. Third, one knows that concepts can be combined with other concepts.

Categorical Knowledge

Categorical knowledge is the most studied area in semantic memory. One of the robust findings in this area is the typicality effect (Rosch, 1975). Items that are good examples of a category are more readily verified as members than are poor examples. For example, people decide that "Robins are birds" more rapidly than "Chickens are birds."

The typicality effect has its counterpart for false statements (the relatedness effect: Smith, Shoben, and Rips, 1974). These are easier to disconfirm if subject and predicate are unrelated. For example, "A goose is a mammal" is more difficult to disconfirm than "A goose is a tool."

There are many proposed explanations of the typicality effect. It has been ascribed to computing similarity to a prototype or to multiple members of a category, and to feature overlap between an item and a category description. Other factors such as frequency (Barsalou, 1985; Heit and Barsalou, 1996) appear to moderate typicality, although twenty-first-century evidence does not strongly support an earlier claim that familiarity is one of these (Hampton, 1997). While typicality is often discussed in terms of similarity of semantic memory representations, there is a growing acknowledgment among the scientific community that the notion of similarity is itself a complex construct requiring some basis for comparison (Medin, Goldstone, and Gentner, 1993). For example, similarity may sometimes involve abstract decisions based on common goals or instrumentalities. Typical items to bring to school (books, a calculator, a pen) may be similar by virtue of accomplishing related goals, but will be unlikely to share much physical resemblance.

Context effects are common in semantic memory research. For example, early findings indicated that the size of the typicality effect varies as a function of the proportion of related false statements among the test stimuli (McCloskey and Glucksberg, 1979). Other studies have shown that the same categories may exhibit different typicality and similarity relationships in different contexts. Thus, what is a typical bird in southern Florida may depend in part upon whether the informant is Hispanic (Schwanenflugel and Rey, 1986). Similarly, North Americans will alter their judgments of the typicality of various birds when asked to take the perspective of a South American (Barsalou, 1987). These effects extend to similarity. Black and grey will be more similar than grey and white in the context of cloud color, but not in the context of hair color (Medin and Shoben, 1988).

Other effects are more controversial (see Chang, 1986, for a review). For example, it has often been argued that there is a category size effect in semantic memory in which it is harder to confirm membership in a large category than it is in a smaller one. However, reversals of this finding do occur. The finding may in part be confounded with the fact that larger categories tend to be at a higher level of abstraction than smaller categories (for example, "tool" and "implement").

Theoretical Concerns

The question of how categorical information is represented in memory remains unresolved. Some early theorists suggested that semantic memory could be viewed as a hierarchical tree or semantic network (Collins and Quillian, 1969; Holyoak and Glass, 1975) in which concepts such as "robin" and "canary" would be represented at the bottom of the tree with links from both extending up to "bird." Others espoused a componential approach in which concepts were represented as sets of properties or semantic features. Semantic decisions were made by a comparison of these features or properties (Smith et al., 1974; McCloskey and Glucksberg, 1979). Yet other representations and mechanisms have been proposed to account for categorical knowledge. A partial listing of representations includes prototypes, images, exemplars, schemas, situational models, and hyperdimensional vectors that represent semantic similarity by tracking the contexts in which different concepts may be found. None of these approaches by itself is likely to account for all of the available data, and different semantic units subject to different processes may be required (Brewer, 1993). For example, production frequency (the frequency with which an item is generated as an example of a category) and typicality ratings appear to provide different contributions to classification times. The suggestion has been made that the former relies on retrieval of network links whereas the latter involves a similarity computation operating over features (Hampton, 1997). Sophisticated techniques suggest that retrieval of information occurs continuously in time as opposed to in discrete quanta (Kounios, 1997), but whether such results are inconsistent with network models, as researchers sometimes claim, will be sensitive to the specific structural and processing assumptions adopted by such models.

Judgments of Relative Magnitude

Although there have been some direct investigations of how people process information about properties of concepts, most of the work on this question has concerned how people make judgments of relative magnitude such as, "Are rabbits larger than mice?"

Empirical Findings

The oldest and most robust finding in the literature is the symbolic distance effect. Objects that are further apart on some dimension are more readily discriminated than objects that are closer together (Moyer, 1973). For example, it is easier to determine that "Desks are larger than strawberries" than "Desks are larger than dogs."

A second finding, the congruity effect, is that judgments are easier when the question matches the magnitude of the objects, small or large (Banks, 1977). If one asks which is larger, a person's response will be faster with large than with small things. But if one asks which is smaller, a person's response will be faster with small things.

A third finding is the bowed serial position effect: Holding symbolic distance constant, objects of intermediate magnitude are more difficult to discriminate than objects of extreme magnitude (Shoben, Čech, Schwanenflugel, and Sailor, 1989). For example, it is more difficult for a person to select the larger of "wolf" and "pig" than to select the larger of either "toad" and "snail" or of "bull" and "elephant."

Like decisions about categorical information, judgments of relative magnitude are subject to context effects. Whether pairs such as "rabbit-beaver" are discriminated more readily under the instruction to select the smaller or the larger item will depend on the presence of large pairs. If there are no larger pairs, then "rabbit" and "beaver" suddenly behave as if they are large items (Čech and Shoben, 2001). Moreover, in appropriate contexts, multiple congruity effects may ensue, each corresponding to a different group of items.

There are also effects of categorization difficulty. Some items are difficult to classify as large or small, and others are relatively easy. In general, items of extreme magnitude are more readily classified than items of intermediate magnitude. This finding helps explain the serial position effect. When items across the magnitude scale are equated for categorization difficulty, no bowed serial position effect occurs (Shoben and Wilson, 1998).

Finally, there are reference point effects. If people are asked to determine which of two objects is closer to a third, the task is harder if the items are far from the reference point (Holyoak, 1978). Thus, for example, it is easier to determine whether 4 or 5 is closer to 3 than whether 6 or 7 is closer to 3.

Theories of Relational Information

Many theories have been proposed to account for relational judgments, although most have problems explaining at least some of the findings. Priming or expectancy-based theories claim that asking which is larger or smaller will bias people toward the specified size. However, there appear to be congruity effects that are not due to such priming; moreover, these models wrongly predict that congruity should occur early in processing, rather than late (Čech, 1995). Traditionally, theories fall into two broad camps: those like the discrete code model (Banks, 1977), which posit comparison of discrete, propositional information, and analogical models like the reference point model (Holyoak, 1978), which posit direct comparison of stored analogical magnitude information. Models used by twenty-first-century researchers include the recoding model (Čech and Shoben, 2001), evidence accrual models (Petrusic, 1992; Birnbaum and Jou, 1990), and the connectionist model of Leth-Steensen and Marley (2002).

The recoding model claims that people use range and co-occurrence information to cluster items into groups. People assign relative, contrastive magnitude codes to items within a group ("this is large," "that is small") to facilitate comparison. Comparison thus necessarily relies on attentional and categorization processes. However, in evidence accrual models, item magnitudes are sampled until there is sufficient evidence regarding relative size. Finally, the Leth-Steensen and Marley model also includes an evidence accrual component, but enables responding on the basis of positional information (whether an item is fourth or third largest, for example). This latter model employs learned associations and effectively combines aspects of the other approaches. William Petrusic has suggested that models under which people operate may differ: Some people seem to act in accord with the recoding model, and others seem to use evidence accrual.

A domain of particular interest concerns numerosity judgments. Researchers in this area study the relative merits of the single-format and the multiple-format assumptions (Blankenberger and Vorberg, 1997). The single-format assumption asserts that different number representations ("4," "four," "IV") project onto the same semantic representations, whereas the multiformat assumption claims multiple semantic representations for numbers (Dehaene, 1997). Some numerical comparison studies examine these positions by focusing on the brain regions active during the comparison of different number types, and others study how format influences the distance effect. For example, is the average time required to determine the larger of the pairs "two-four" and "2-4" the same as the time required to compare "two-4" and "2-four"? The answer appears to be no: Different distance effects are found with mixed-format numbers (Vorberg and Blankenberger, 1993). Although it is premature to favor the multiple-format assumption from results such as these, the domain of numerical comparisons does hold out the promise of helping scientists determine how rich semantic representations are.

Conceptual Combinations

A problem in categorization concerns how concepts are combined. Some of these combinations appear superficially simple, while others are clearly more complex. For example, "red ball" can readily be paraphrased as "a ball that is red," but "malarial mosquitoes" must instead be paraphrased as "mosquitoes that cause malaria." "Red ball" uses a predicating adjective, "red," in which a property of the modifier is ascribed to the head noun, while "malarial mosquitoes" employs the nonpredicating adjective "malarial." Phrases involving nonpredicating adjectives are sometimes more difficult to comprehend (Murphy, 1990), although faster comprehension times have also been reported for nonpredicating nominal compounds (Gagné, 2000). In nonpredicating compounds, the interpretation appears to rely on establishing some relationship between the two components (a relational interpretation).

Most research on conceptual combinations has used predicating adjectives. One fundamental question is how people determine membership in combined categories. For example, "A cardinal is a red bird" is clearly true, because a cardinal is clearly both a red thing and a bird. At the same time, "A female cardinal is a red bird" is only partly true, because female cardinals are only somewhat red. Such concerns might lead researchers to propose a min rule: An exemplar is a member of a combined category only to the minimum degree that it is a member of the category defined by the adjective and the category specified by the noun. Despite the intuitive appeal of such a rule, it cannot handle many cases: Guppies are perhaps the paradigmatic example of the category "pet fish," but they are good examples of neither pets nor fish. Empirical judgments of subjects show clear violations of the min rule (Smith and Osherson, 1984).

In natural language corpora, conceptual combinations that involve an initial predicating noun are less frequent than combinations that require a relational interpretation, although there is disagreement about the exact disproportion in the two types. Most contemporary work in conceptual combination centers around the dual-process model (Wisniewski, 1997) and the CARIN model (Gagné and Shoben, 1997). In the dual-process model, relational interpretations require a process of scenario construction in which specified roles may be assigned the two concepts. Property interpretations, in contrast, arise from a process of alignment in which alignable differences (differing values on a common dimension) help drive the decision regarding which property to move to the complex conceptual schema of the head noun. An alignable difference between "dog" and "man," for example, is that each locomotes using legs, although a dog moves on four legs. Thus, a potential interpretation of "dog man" is a man who travels on all fours, whereas a potential interpretation of "man dog" is a dog walking upright. By way of contrast, a relational interpretation of "dog man" might include some scenario in which an individual prefers dogs to cats. This model has recently been extended to include nonalignable differences that display spatial correspondences (Wisniewski and Middleton, 2002): Kangaroos and dogs do not have a readily retrievable common dimension on which "pouch" can serve as a contrasting value that helps distinguish the two, but the presence of equivalent spatial areas on dogs and kangaroos may allow the interpretation that a "kangaroo dog" is a dog with a pouch on the lower front of its body.

CARIN does not rely on an alignment process, or a privileged attempt to modify the representation of the head noun. Instead, the model posits that the repertoire of relations associated with the modifier will guide finding an appropriate interpretation. For example, because "mountain" has a high frequency of relations involving location, "mountain man" will likely be interpreted as a man who lives on a mountain. Accordingly, the relative rarity of property interpretations ought to result in long interpretation times.

The interpretation process for conceptual combinations has also been modeled as a constraint satisfaction process that requires simultaneous solutions to the constraints of diagnosticity, plausibility, and informativeness (Costello and Keane, 2000). Moreover, like categorization and magnitude comparisons, conceptual combinations are also subject to context effects (Gerrig and Bortfeld, 1999). The work on conceptual combinations illustrates the reliance on a much richer and more complex semantic memory than researchers assumed in the early work on network and feature models.

Broader Issues

This review has necessarily been selective, with many topics omitted. In closing, however, it should be noted that one's knowledge of the world will influence most of the cognitive things that one does. Solving a problem, following directions, or simply reading involves one's semantic memory. Semantic memory is fundamental to cognition.

See also: CONCEPTS AND CATEGORIES, LEARNING OF; DRUGS AND MEMORY; SEMANTIC MEMORY: NEUROBIOLOGICAL PERSPECTIVE

Bibliography

Anderson, J. R., and Lebiere, C. (1998). *The atomic components of thought.* Mahwah, NJ: Erlbaum.

Banks, W. P. (1977). Encoding and processing of symbolic information in comparative judgments. In G. H. Bower, ed., *The psychology of learning and motivation,* Vol. 11. New York: Academic Press.

Barsalou, L. W. (1985). Ideals, central tendency, and frequency of instantiation as determinants of graded structure in categories. *Journal of Experimental Psychology: Learning, Memory, and Cognition 11* (4), 629–654.

—— (1987). The instability of graded structure: Implications for the nature of concepts. In U. Neisser, ed., *Concepts and conceptual development: Ecological and intellectual factors in categorization.* Cambridge, UK: Cambridge University Press.

Birnbaum, M. H., and Jou, J. (1990). A theory of comparative response times and "difference" judgments. *Cognitive Psychology 22* (2), 184–210.

Blankenberger, S., and Vorberg, D. (1997). The single-format assumption in arithmetic fact retrieval. *Journal of Experimental Psychology: Learning, Memory, and Cognition 23* (3), 721–738.

Brewer, W. F. (1993). What are concepts? Issues of representation and ontology. In G. V. Nakamura, R. M. Taraban, and D. L. Medin, eds., *The psychology of learning and motivation,* Vol. 29: *Categorization by humans and machines.* San Diego, CA: Academic Press.

Čech, C. G. (1995). Is congruity due to encoding? *Journal of Experimental Psychology: Learning, Memory, and Cognition 21* (5), 1,275–1,288.

Čech, C. G., and Shoben, E. J. (2001). Categorization processes in mental comparisons. *Journal of Experimental Psychology: Learning, Memory, and Cognition 27* (3), 800–816.

Chang, T. M. (1986). Semantic memory: Facts and models. *Psychological Bulletin 99* (2), 199–220.

Collins, A., and Quillian, M. R. (1969). Retrieval time from semantic memory. *Journal of Verbal Learning and Verbal Behavior 8,* 240–247.

Costello, F. J., and Keane, M. T. (2000). Efficient creativity: Constraint-guided conceptual combination. *Cognitive Science 24* (2), 299–349.

Dehaene, S. (1997). *The number sense: How the mind creates mathematics.* New York: Oxford University Press.

Gagné, C. L. (2000). Relation-based combinations versus property-based combinations: A test of the CARIN theory and the dual-process theory of conceptual combination. *Journal of Memory and Language 42* (3), 365–389.

Gagné, C. L., and Shoben, E. J. (1997). Influence of thematic relations on the comprehension of modifier-noun combinations. *Journal of Experimental Psychology: Learning, Memory, and Cognition 23* (1), 71–87.

Gerrig, R. J., and Bortfeld, H. (1999). Sense creation in and out of discourse contexts. *Journal of Memory and Language 41* (4), 457–468.

Hampton, J. A. (1997). Associative and similarity-based processes in categorization decisions. *Memory & Cognition 25* (5), 625–640.

Heit, E., and Barsalou, L. W. (1996). The instantiation principle in natural categories. *Memory 4* (4), 413–451.

Holyoak, K. J. (1978). Comparative judgments with numerical reference points. *Cognitive Psychology 10* (2), 203–243.

Holyoak, K. J., and Glass, A. L. (1975). The role of contradictions and counterexamples in the rejection of false sentences. *Journal of Verbal Learning and Verbal Behavior 14* (2), 215–239.

Knowlton, B. J. (1998). The relationship between remembering and knowing: A cognitive neuroscience perspective. *Acta Psychologica 98* (2–3), 253–265.

Knowlton, B. J., and Squire, L. R. (1995). Remembering and knowing: Two different expressions of declarative memory. *Journal of Experimental Psychology: Learning, Memory, and Cognition 21* (3), 699–710.

Kounios, J. (1996). On the continuity of thought and the representation of knowledge: Electrophysiological and behavioral time-course measures reveal levels of structure in semantic memory. *Psychonomic Bulletin & Review 3* (3), 265–286.

Leth-Steensen, C., and Marley, A. A. J. (2000). A model of response time effects in symbolic comparison. *Psychological Review 107* (1), 62–100.

McCloskey, M., and Glucksberg, S. (1979). Decision processes in verifying category membership statements: Implications for models of semantic memory. *Cognitive Psychology 11* (1), 1–37.

McKoon, G., Ratcliff, R., and Dell, G. S. (1986). A critical evaluation of the semantic-episodic distinction. *Journal of Experimental Psychology: Learning, Memory, and Cognition 12* (2), 295–306.

Medin, D. L., Goldstone, R. L., and Gentner, D. (1993). Respects for similarity. *Psychological Review 100* (2), 278.

Medin, D. L., and Shoben, E. J. (1988). Context and structure in conceptual combination. *Cognitive Psychology 20* (2), 158–190.

Moyer, R. S. (1973). Comparing objects in memory: Evidence suggesting an internal psychophysics. *Perception and Psychophysics 13* (2), 180–184.

Murphy, G. L. (1990). Noun phrase interpretation and conceptual combination. *Journal of Memory and Language 29* (3), 259–288.

Petrusic, W. M. (1992). Semantic congruity effects and theories of the comparison process. *Journal of Experimental Psychology: Human Perception and Performance 18* (4), 962–986.

Rosch, E. H. (1975). Cognitive representations of semantic categories. *Journal of Experimental Psychology: General 104* (3), 192–233.

Schwanenflugel, P. J., and Rey, M. (1986). The relationship between category typicality and concept familiarity: Evidence from Spanish- and English-speaking monolinguals. *Memory & Cognition 14* (2), 150–163.

Shoben, E. J., Čech, C. G., Schwanenflugel, P. J., and Sailor, K. M. (1989). Serial position effects in comparative judgments. *Journal of Experimental Psychology: Human Perception and Performance 15* (2), 273–286.

Shoben, E. J., and Ross, B. H. (1986). The crucial role of dissociations. *Behavioral and Brain Sciences 9* (3), 568–571.

Shoben, E. J., and Wilson, T. L. (1998). Categorization in judgments of relative magnitude. *Journal of Memory and Language 38* (1), 94–111.

Smith, E. E., and Osherson, D. N. (1984). Conceptual combination with prototype concepts. *Cognitive Science 12* (4), 485–527.

Smith, E. E., Shoben, E. J., and Rips, L. J. (1974). Structure and process in semantic memory: A featural model for semantic decisions. *Psychological Review 81* (3), 214–241.

Tulving, E. (1972). Episodic and semantic memory. In E. Tulving and W. Donaldson, eds., *Organization of memory.* New York: Academic Press.

Tulving, E., and Schacter, D. L. (1990). Priming and human memory systems. *Science 247,* 301–306.

Vorberg, D., and Blankenberger, S. (1993). Mentale repräsentation von zahlen. *Sprache and Kognition 12* (2), 98–114.

Wheeler, M. A., Suss, D. T., and Tulving, E. (1997). Toward a theory of episodic memory: The frontal lobes and autonoetic consciousness. *Psychological Bulletin 121* (3), 331–354.

Wisniewski, E. J. (1997). When concepts combine. *Psychonomic Bulletin & Review 4* (2), 167–183.

Wisniewski, E. J., and Middleton, E. L. (2002). Of bucket bowls and coffee cup bowls: Spatial alignment in conceptual combination. *Journal of Memory and Language 46* (1), 1–23.

Edward J. Shoben
Revised by Claude G. Čech

NEUROBIOLOGICAL PERSPECTIVE

Consider the following questions: Do acorns have stems? Do you tune a guitar by tightening and loosening the strings? Do deer have white noses? If you were able to answer these questions correctly (yes, yes, no), then you were using semantic memory. Much of semantic memory relates to the brain systems that enable us to store and retrieve semantic knowledge. This article explores the neurobiology of this process.

Multiple Long-Term Memory Systems

When you remember that acorns have stems, you are using your semantic memory. When you remember the time you gathered acorns with your father in fifth grade, you are using your episodic memory. In both cases you are retrieving information from long-term memory. Are there, in fact, two separate memory systems for these two types of memories?

In 1972, the psychologist Endel Tulving first argued that there are two separate memory systems. Tulving distinguished between memories that have an autobiographical reference (i.e., episodic memories) and memories that do not (i.e., semantic memories). Cognitive psychologists have disagreed about whether episodic and semantic memories reflect two distinct systems or whether they are part of a common long-term memory system. However, neuropsychologists have provided compelling evidence that there are two distinct systems: one for our knowledge of events and one for our knowledge of facts. This evidence comes from patients who have selective impairments of semantic memory.

Impairments if semantic memory correlate with several etiologies of brain damage. The most common cause of semantic-memory impairments is Alzheimer's disease, a progressive dementia that causes widespread cortical degeneration. Semantic memory impairments also attend acute illnesses such as stroke or infection. These conditions, however, commonly involve both episodic and semantic memory impairments. Yet there is one condition, semantic dementia, in which patients exhibit a progressive loss of semantic memory (Hodges, Patterson, Oxbury, and Funnell, 1992). By definition, patients with semantic dementia have an impairment in semantic memory but normal episodic memory.

One of the earliest symptoms of semantic dementia is anomia, an impairment in the ability to find words when speaking or writing. Patients with this disorder also have problems with semantic memory tasks that do not require language at all. The pyramids and palm trees test is a common test of nonverbal knowledge that requires the patient to identify semantic relationships between pictures (Howard and Patterson, 1992). For example, the patient might be asked to indicate which picture belongs with a pyramid: a palm tree or a fir tree. This task does not require language comprehension or production (i.e., the patient is simply pointing at pairs of pictures), but it does require semantic memory. Patients with semantic dementia are unable to answer simple questions of this type. The selective loss of semantic memory in semantic dementia may indicate idea that semantic memory and episodic memory are two distinct long term memory systems.

In all of the etiologies of brain damage associated with semantic memory loss, there is widespread and often bilateral damage to the temporal lobes. Semantic dementia may result from a variant of Alzheimer's disease in which degeneration is initially restricted to the temporal lobes. Semantic dementia may also result from Pick's disease, another degenerative disease that is associated with temporal lobe atrophy. Pick's disease does not affect the medial temporal lobes, including the hippocampus, which is a part of the brain associated with episodic memory.

Separate or Unitary Semantic Stores

When Tulving first defined semantic memory, he described it as a "mental thesaurus" that supported language use. Since that time, many investigators of semantic memory have broadened their definitions of semantic memory to include both verbal and nonverbal knowledge. Clearly, semantic memory can be accessed from both verbal labels and visual depictions. Many psychologists, however, have questioned whether there is a unitary semantic memory store or whether there are separate stores for verbal and nonverbal memory.

We have already seen one piece of evidence for a unitary semantic memory store: As mentioned above, patients with semantic dementia have impairments of both verbal and nonverbal tests of semantic knowledge. Curiously, a few patients have deficits that seem restricted to a single test modality (e.g., Beauvois, 1982). But it is unclear whether this pattern reflects a true loss of semantic memory or merely an impairment in accessing semantic memory from one kind of input.

Another method for investigating questions about semantic memory is to noninvasively measure regional changes in metabolism or blood flow in the brain of a healthy subject who is performing a cognitive task (e.g., functional magnetic-resonance imaging). Several neuroimaging studies have tested the existence of a unitary semantic store. In one such study (Vandenberghe et al., 1996), brain imaging was conducted during either a verbal semantic task (word matching) or a visual semantic task (similar to the pyramids and palm trees test). The activation of many common regions of the brain in these tests is consistent with the theory that there is a unitary semantic memory store for both verbal and nonverbal retrieval.

Categories of Semantic Memory

For decades cognitive psychologists have been debating the two issues discussed above: whether semantic memory is distinct from episodic memory and whether there is a unitary semantic store. The evidence reviewed above simply fuels the controversy with evidence from neurobiology. There is, however, another question about semantic memory that originated with neuropsychologists: Are there separate stores of semantic memory for different taxonomic categories, such as animals and tools?

This might seem like a strange hypothesis, but the evidence for it is very compelling. Imagine administering a simple picture-naming task to a brain-damaged patient. You show the patient pictures of all sorts of objects, such as a trellis, a compass, and an abacus, and the patient can name them with little difficulty. However, when you show the patient a picture of something as simple as a duck or a bee, the patient struggles and fails to come up with the name. This very pattern of behavior has been reported in dozens of patients, most of them afflicted with herpes simplex encephalitis (a brain infection), who have semantic memory impairments restricted to categories of natural items (Warrington and Shallice, 1984).

One hypothesis for this peculiar pattern of impairments is that natural items (e.g., plants and animals) are more difficult to identify because they are less familiar or more visually complex (Funnell and Sheridan, 1992). Carefully controlled studies have largely ruled out this supposition, however (Farah, McMullen, and Meyer, 1991). There have been a few cases of the reverse pattern: patients with impaired knowledge of man-made objects but with relatively well-preserved knowledge of natural objects (Warrington and McCarthy, 1987). Although rare, this disorder provides stronger evidence for the hypothesis that there are separate memory stores for natural objects and human-made objects. Some researchers (Caramazza and Shelton, 1998) have argued that separate stores have developed for categories for which there is some evolutionary significance (e.g., plants, animals, and tools).

Domains of Semantic Memory

In the preceding section, the evidence for separate semantic memory stores for different categories seemed clear-cut. However, many investigators believe that there is another, more plausible, interpretation of these category-specific deficits. The following two questions illustrate an important difference between our knowledge of natural objects and our knowledge of human-made objects: How would you define *tiger* so that someone could distinguish it from similar concepts (e.g., leopards, lions, and bobcats)? You would probably mention something about the color and size of tigers. In contrast, how would you define a clock (as distinct from a radio or a lamp)? In this case, you are probably less likely to talk about color or size or even shape, because clocks come in all varieties. Instead, you would probably talk about the function of clocks. Hence the defining attributes of natural items are more likely to be visual than those of human-made items.

This distinction leads to another hypothesis about a distinction within semantic memory: there may be different memory stores for different kinds, or domains, of semantic knowledge. Knowledge of any concept may be distributed across a variety of distinct memory stores that are tied to sensorimotor systems (Allport, 1985). According to this hypothesis, patients who appear to have a deficit pertaining to natural objects in fact have a visual-knowledge deficit that is most evident when tested on items defined by visual attributes (i.e., natural objects). The difficulty of distinguishing absolutely between object category and knowledge domain makes it is hard to experimentally distinguish between these two hypotheses. Some investigators have pointed to interesting exceptions to the natural/man-made distinction that are more consistent with a visual/functional dichotomy. For example, patients described as having a deficit pertaining to natural objects may also have impairments with musical instruments, which are largely defined by visual attributes (Warrington and Shallice, 1984).

Neuroimaging studies have also been used to test this hypothesis (e.g., Thompson-Schill, Aguirre, D'Esposito, and Farah, 1999). For example, when subjects are asked to name natural objects (e.g., animals), brain activation is observed in areas associated with vision; in contrast, when subjects are asked to name human-made objects (e.g., tools), brain activation is observed in areas concerned with motor control (Martin et al., 1995). Results of this sort have been taken as evidence that the fundamental distinction within semantic memory is one of domain of knowledge and not taxonomic category.

There are other sources of evidence that semantic memory is organized according to domain. Recall that patients with semantic dementia have global deficits in semantic memory when tested either verbally or visually. However, there is one domain in which these patients show preserved semantic knowledge: Patients with semantic dementia often continue to demonstrate normal use of objects long after they fail to identify these objects correctly on other tests of semantic memory. This pattern of behavior stands in stark contrast to another disorder, ideational apraxia, an impairment in object use in patients who test normally for traditional semantic memory (Ochipa, Rothi, and Heilman, 1989). Thus, there may be a semantic memory store for object use that is distinct from other domains of semantic memory.

Conclusion

Neurobiological studies of semantic memory have addressed some fundamental questions of semantic memory and have raised a few new questions as well. Disorders that selectively impair semantic memory provide evidence that semantic memory is a memory system that is distinct from episodic memory. Neuroimaging studies have indicated that verbal and nonverbal semantic retrieval depends on a common memory store. Within this semantic store, however, there appear to be distinctions based either on taxonomic category or type of knowledge. Neuroimaging and neuropsychological studies support the theory that semantic memory is distributed across different sensorimotor systems, such as object appearance and object use.

See also: EPISODIC MEMORY; SEMANTIC MEMORY: COGNITIVE ASPECTS

Bibliography

Allport, D. A. (1985). Distributed memory, modular subsystems and dysphasia. In S. K. Newman and R. Epstein, eds., *Current perspectives in dysphasia.* Edinburgh: Churchill Livingstone.

Beauvois, M. F. (1982). Optic aphasia: A process of interaction between vision and language. *Philosophical Transactions of the Royal Society of London, 298,* 35–47.

Caramazza, A., and Shelton, J. R. (1998). Domain-specific knowledge systems in the brain the animate-inanimate distinction. *Journal of Cognitive Neuroscience 10,* 1–34.

Farah, M. J., McMullen, P. A., and Meyer, M. M. (1991). Can recognition of living things be selectively impaired? *Neuropsychologia, 29,* 185–193.

Funnell, E., and Sheridan, J. (1992). Categories of knowledge? Unfamiliar aspects of living and nonliving things. *Cognitive Neuropsychology 9,* 135–153.

Hodges, J. R., Patterson, K., Oxbury, S., and Funnell, E. (1992). Semantic dementia. Progressive fluent aphasia with temporal lobe atrophy. *Brain 115,* 1,783–1,806.

Howard, D., and Patterson, K. (1992). *Pyraminds and palm trees: A test of semantic access from pictures and words.* Bury St. Edmunds: Thames Valley Test Company.

Martin, A., Haxby, J. V., Lalonde, F. M., Wiggs, C. L., and Ungerleider, L. G. (1995). Discrete cortical regions associated with knowledge of color and knowledge of action. *Science 270,* 102–105.

Ochipa, C., Rothi, L. J., and Heilman, K. M. (1989). Ideational apraxia: A deficit in tool selection and use. *Annals of Neurology 25,* 190–193.

Thompson–Schill, S. L., Aguirre, G. K., D'Esposito, M., and Farah, M. J. (1999). A neural basis for category and modality specificity of semantic knowledge. *Neuropsychologia 37,* 671–676.

Tulving, E. (1972). Episodic and semantic memory. In E. Tulving and W. Donaldson, eds., *Organization of memory.* New York: Academic Press.

Vandenberghe, R., Price, C., Wise, R., Josephs, O., and Frackowiak, R. S. (1996). Functional anatomy of a common semantic system for words and pictures. *Nature 383,* 254–256.

Warrington, E. K., and McCarthy, R. A. (1987). Categories of knowledge. Further fractionations and an attempted integration. *Brain 110,* 1,273–1,296.

Warrington, E. K., and Shallice, T. (1984). Category specific semantic impairments. *Brain 107,* 829–854.

Edward J. Shoben
Revised by Sharon L. Thompson-Schill

Richard Semon *(Source unknown)*

SEMON, RICHARD (1859–1918)

Richard Wolfgang Semon is a relatively unknown but nevertheless important figure in the history of research on learning and memory. Although little noticed by both his contemporaries and memory researchers today, Semon anticipated numerous modern theories and, perhaps ironically, created one of the best known terms in the memory literature, *engram.*

Semon was born in Berlin on August 22, 1859. His father, Simon, was a stockbroker, and the Semon family became part of the upper echelon of Berlin Jewish society during Richard's childhood. Simon's severe losses in the stock market crash of 1873 imposed a much humbler lifestyle on the family. Semon's older brother, Felix, left Germany after receiving a medical degree and practiced in England, where he became a historic pioneer of clinical and scientific laryngology.

As a child, Richard Semon expressed a strong interest in biology and zoology. He attended the University of Jena—a major European center of biological research—and received a doctorate in zoological studies in 1883 and a medical degree in 1886. While at Jena, Semon was influenced heavily by the famous evolutionary biologist Ernst Haeckel, whose monistic philosophy stressed the importance of attempting to unify diverse biological phenomena within a single set of theoretical principles.

Semon's career as an evolutionary biologist developed rapidly during the 1890s. Shortly after assuming an associate professorship at Jena in 1891, he led a major expedition to Australia in search of the "missing link." The expedition was responsible for the discovery of 207 new species and twenty-four new genera. When he returned from Australia in 1893, Semon continued his research at Jena until 1897, when his life changed dramatically. He became involved with Maria Krehl, then wife of an eminent professor of pathology at Jena, Ludolph Krehl. The ensuing scandal in Jena led to Semon's resignation. He and Maria moved to Munich, where he began working as a private scholar, and the pair eventually married.

Semon wrote two major books on memory during the next twenty years: *Die mneme* (1904), translated as *The Mneme* (1921), and *Die mnemischen Empfindungen* (1909), translated as *Mnemic Psychology* (1923). His work attracted little attention, and Semon's acute dismay about his lack of recognition is evident in letters written to his colleague and ally, the Swiss psychiatrist August Forel (Schacter, 1982). Depressed over the neglect of his work, troubled by Germany's role in World War I, and shattered by his wife's death from cancer, Semon took his own life on December 27, 1918.

Theory of Memory

A full appreciation of Semon's ideas about human memory requires a look at the biological context from which they emerged. His first book, *Die mneme*, embedded human memory a more global theory that broadened the construct of memory to include more than simple remembering of facts, events, and the like. Semon argued for viewing heredity and reproduction as forms of memory that preserved the effects of experience across generations. He referred to the fundamental process that subserved both heredity and everyday memory with a term of his own creation, "Mneme." According to Semon, Mneme is a fundamental organic plasticity that allows the preservation of effects of experience; it is Mneme "which in the organic world links the past and present in a living bond" (1921, p.12).

Semon distinguished among three aspects of the mnemic process that he believed are crucial to the analysis of both everyday memory and of hereditary memory, and he described them with additional terms of his own invention in order to avoid the potentially misleading connotations of ordinary language: *engraphy*, *engram*, and *ecphory*. *Engraphy* refers to the encoding of information into memory; *engram* refers to the change in the nervous system—the "memory trace"—that preserves the effects of experience; and *ecphory* refers to a retrieval process, or "the influences which awaken the mnemic trace or engram out of its latent state into one of manifested activity" (Semon, 1921, p.12). In attempting to apply these constructs to the analysis of hereditary memory— that is, to understanding how the experiences of one organism could somehow influence its progeny— Semon encountered a variety of biological phenomena that led him to place great emphasis on ecphory as a crucial determinant of memory.

Semon's speculative ideas on hereditary memory met with severe criticism because they relied heavily on the discredited doctrine of the inheritance of acquired characteristics, which had been developed by the French biologist Lamarck (Schacter, 2001). Nevertheless, the concern with ecphoric processes that emerged from this analysis enabled Semon to develop new perspectives on human memory that elaborated without any reference to hereditary phenomena in his second book, *Die mnemischen empfindungen*. At the time that Semon wrote this book, memory researchers paid almost no attention to the ecphoric or retrieval stage of memory; they were caught up almost entirely with processes occurring at the time of encoding or

engraphy (Schacter, 2001; Schacter, Eich, and Tulving, 1978). By contrast, Semon developed a detailed theory of ecphoric processes and argued that succssful ecphory requires that the conditions prevailing at the time of engraphy (i.e., encoding) are partially reinstated at the time of ecphory. He laid great emphasis on this latter idea, elevating it to a "Law of Ecphory." This concern with the relation between conditions of engraphy and ecphory anticipated rather closely such modern notions as the encoding-specificity principle and transfer-appropriate processing.

Semon also developed novel ideas about the beneficial effects of repetition on memory. In contrast to the then widely accepted idea that repetition of a stimulus improves memory by strengthening the pre-existing engram of that stimulus, Semon argued that each repetition of a stimulus creates a unique, context-specific engram; at the time of ecphory, the multiple, separate engrams are combined by a resonance process that Semon termed *homophony*. This multiple-engram approach to repetition effects, with its strong emphasis on ecphoric processes, anticipated a number of recently influential conceptualizations, such as the multiple-trace model developed by Hintzman and colleagues (Schacter et al., 1978).

Notwithstanding the prescience of many of Semon's ideas, his contemporaries ignored his contributions. This neglect may be due to several factors: his theoretical emphasis on ecphoric processes at a time when few were interested, his social isolation as a private scholar without institutional affiliation, and his discredited Lamarckian approach to hereditary memory. Curiously, the one construct developed by Semon that appropriated by subsequent researchers—the engram—did not represent a novel contribution and was one of the less interesting parts of his otherwise innovative theoretical approach.

See also: EPISODIC MEMORY; REPETITION AND LEARNING; RETRIEVAL PROCESSES IN MEMORY

Bibliography

Schacter, D. L. (2001). *Forgotten ideas, neglected pioneers: Richard Semon and the story of memory*. Philadelphia: Psychology Press.

Schacter, D. L., Eich, J. E., and Tulving, E. (1978). Richard Semon's theory of memory. *Journal of Verbal Learning and Verbal Behavior 17*, 721–743.

Semon, R. (1904). *Die Mneme*. Leipzig: W. Engelmann.

—— (1909). *Die mnemischen empfindungen*. Leipzig: W. Engelmann, Leipzig.

—— (1921). *The mneme*. London: Allen and Unwin.

—— (1923). *Mnemic psychology*. London: Allen and Unwin.

Daniel L. Schacter

SENILITY

See: AGING AND MEMORY IN HUMANS;
ALZHEIMER'S DISEASE: BEHAVIORAL ASPECTS;
ALZHEIMER'S DISEASE: HUMAN DISEASE AND
THE GENETICALLY ENGINEERED ANIMAL
MODELS; PHARMACOLOGICAL TREATMENT
OF MEMORY DEFICITS

SENSORY MEMORY

Sensory memory is an agency of information storage that not only carries the mark of the sense modality in which the information originally arrived—imagery is the more general term for that—but also carries traces of the sensory processing that was engaged by the experience. Sensory memory is the brain's detailed record of a sensory experience. Thus, we can generate a visual image of an object without actually seeing it, but we cannot thereby have a sensory memory of it. Although auditory and visual verbal stimuli have received the most attention, there are other forms of sensory memory (e.g., for nonverbal shapes, touch, and smell).

Visual Sensory Memory

Research on visual sensory memory has focused on two phenomena: iconic memory and subjective persistence, descriptions of which follow below.

Iconic Memory

A single monograph by George Sperling, *The Information Available in Brief Visual Presentations* (1960), abruptly brought both the concept and the methods of visual sensory memory to modern attention. The subjects in Sperling's experiment saw twelve letters (three rows of four) in a brief flash. In a whole-report control condition, the subject was asked to report all twelve of the letters presented; in the partial-report conditions, a tone indicated which row was to be reported, the pitch of the tone corresponding to the row tested (high, medium, and low tones for first, second, and third rows, respectively). The results showed that subjects had about nine letters available to the visual system if the tone indicating which row to report sounded just as the display went off. People could report an average of three out of the four letters on any row. However, partial-report scores dropped to half that figure, almost exactly the level of whole report, if the cue tone was delayed by one second.

Subjective Persistence

Ralph N. Haber and Lionel Standing briefly showed subjects a three-by-three array much like those used in Sperling's experiments. However, the task was to adjust the timing of two auditory clicks to coincide with the apparent onset and offset of the display. The duration of the display varied from 100 to 1,000 milliseconds. By turning a knob, subjects could control the occurrences of two clicks relative to the visual exposure of the display. For a given objective duration, the mean onset adjustment can be subtracted from the mean offset adjustment to arrive at an estimate of how long the display seemed to last. Haber and Standing found that these subjective durations were longer than the objective durations. This is consistent with the suggestion that some form of visual storage follows the termination of the external display. Various procedures have been used to examine subjective persistence and have arrived at estimates of about 100 to 200 milliseconds.

Max Coltheart distinguished two sorts of memory. One type, visible persistence, refers to the subjective experience that the stimulus remains available to the visual system after stimulus offset, much in the manner of an afterimage. A second type, termed iconic memory by Coltheart, refers to the formal availability of information from the stimulus as measured in Sperling's partial-report technique. The main support for Coltheart's distinction between visible persistence and iconic memory is that the two obey different empirical laws. Experiments on iconic memory (for example, the study by Sperling) show essentially no effect of initial stimulus duration within a reasonable range during the first few hundred milliseconds. Likewise, in iconic memory experiments, the effect of stimulus luminance on performance is either positive or negligible. When techniques measuring visible persistence—subjective duration—are used, however, both display duration and luminance show an inverse effect on the length of persistence. That is, brighter and briefer displays seem to last longer than dimmer and longer ones.

Auditory Sensory Memory

Different aspects of auditory sensory memory have been clarified through work on precategorical acoustic storage and on recognition masking, discussed below in turn.

Precategorical Acoustic Storage

Robert G. Crowder and John Morton proposed in 1969 that auditory sensory (that is, precategorical) memory lies behind the consistent advantage of auditory over visual presentation in serial, immediate recall situations. They suggested that following a spoken stream of characters or words, people have access not only to the interpretations they have made of these items (categorical memory) but also to the actual sounds of the most recent item or items. This is why in modality comparisons the auditory presentation resulted in superior performance, but only for the last few positions in the list. Presentation of an extra item called a stimulus suffix, posing no additional load on memory, erased most or all of this auditory advantage. Subsequent experiments showed that the meaning of this suffix item had no effect on its tendency to reduce performance on the recency portion of an auditory list. However, differences between the list to be remembered and the redundant suffix had a large effect if they were changes in physical properties, such as spatial location or voice quality (male versus female). This sensitivity to physical attributes, along with the insensitivity to conceptual attributes, would be expected of a precategorical memory store.

The modality-suffix findings on immediate memory were confidently attributed to precategorical acoustic storage until experiments by Kathryn T. Spoehr and William J. Corin (1978) and by Ruth Campbell and Barbara Dodd (1980) showed that the original hypothesis had been too simple. These authors demonstrated that silent lipreading and related procedures produced results in immediate memory that were almost indistinguishable from auditory presentation and were readily distinguishable from visual presentation.

Recognition Masking

In 1972 Dominic W. Massaro delivered to subjects one of two possible pure tones, twenty milliseconds long and pitched at either 770 or 870 Hz. The main task was to identify which of the two tones had been presented. After this target, and at delays of from 0 to 500 milliseconds, a masking tone (820 Hz) was presented. In general, presentation of the masking tone reduced subjects' abilities to identify correctly or to recognize which of the two tones had come before, especially if the mask came within about 250 milliseconds of the target. The logic of this experiment is that if the original target tone had been fully processed before the mask arrived, there would have been no decrement in its identification. But if the target was still being processed when the mask arrived, there must have been a sensory trace of it still available somewhere in the auditory system. Comparable experiments with speech have given much the same result.

From a detailed review of results and models of auditory integration and auditory persistence, Nelson Cowan (1984) distinguished two types of auditory sensory memory: short and long. The short auditory store is believed to have a useful life of about 250 milliseconds and is represented in the experiments on recognition masking and related techniques. The long auditory store may last as long as two to ten sec-

onds, roughly a logarithmic step longer, and underlies the suffix and modality comparisons.

Developments since 1990

Research since 1990 has addressed the mechanisms of sensory memory. In the previous edition of this volume, storage and proceduralist views of sensory memory were compared. The storage view suggests that there are dedicated storage repositories in the brain for sensory information, whereas the proceduralist view states instead that retention is a natural consequence of the information processing that was originally aroused by the experience in question. There are still puzzles that remain to be sorted out for each view. If there are dedicated storage repositories, they must be complex enough to explain why sensory memory of a stimulus seems to be influenced by the context of preceding stimuli in that modality. If retention is a consequence of processing, though, it must be complex enough to explain why there can be brain damage that interferes with the memory for short lists of spoken words while leaving the ability to perceive spoken words intact (as discussed, for example, by Alan D. Baddeley and Robert H. Logie).

The truth may lie in between these views. In a 1995 book, *Attention and Memory: An Integrated Framework*, Nelson Cowan argued that there actually are short and long sensory stores in all modalities, not just the auditory modality. If so, it may be that a proceduralist view is more suitable for the short store, which is intricately tied to perception and is experienced as continuing sensation, than for the long store, which is experienced as memory.

The contradiction between visual information persistence and subjective persistence has been addressed, for example by Dominic W. Massaro and Geoffrey R. Loftus (1996), with the idea that both could result from a single underlying process, with properties that seem to match Cowan's (1995) short store. The change in the intensity of the process over time would determine the subjective experience of the iconic image, whereas the accumulation or integration of this process over time would determine the available information about the visual stimulus. In 1987, Cowan proposed something similar for sounds.

Sensory memory is interesting as a bridge between what we experience and what we remember. A simple view in which sensory memory fades inevitably in a few seconds, like a fizzling sparkler, has proved to be too simplistic. Sensory memory rides upon perceptual processing but then seems to outlast it in a weakened form. Some residue even seems permanent, as in the memory that allows recognition of the voices of one's close friends.

See also: MODALITY EFFECTS

Bibliography

Baddeley, A. D., and Logie, R. H. (1999). Working memory: The multiple-component model. In A. Miyake and P. Shah, eds., *Models of working memory: Mechanisms of active maintenance and executive control.* Cambridge, UK: Cambridge University Press.

Campbell, R., and Dodd, B. (1980). Hearing by eye. *Quarterly Journal of Experimental Psychology 32,* 85–99.

Coltheart, M. (1980). Iconic memory and visible persistence. *Perception and Psychophysics 27,* 183–228.

Cowan, N. (1984). On short and long auditory stores. *Psychological Bulletin 96,* 341–370.

—— (1987). Auditory sensory storage in relation to the growth of sensation and acoustic information extraction. *Journal of Experimental Psychology: Human Perception and Performance 13,* 204–215.

—— (1995). *Attention and memory: An integrated framework.* Oxford Psychology Series, No. 26. New York: Oxford University Press.

Cowan, N., Saults, S., and Nugent, L. (2001). The ravages of absolute and relative amounts of time on memory. In H. L. Roediger III, J. S. Nairne, I. Neath, and A. Surprenant, eds., *The nature of remembering: Essays in honor of Robert G. Crowder.* Washington, DC: American Psychological Association.

Crowder, R. G. (1976). *Principles of learning and memory.* Hillsdale, NJ : Erlbaum.

—— (1978). Sensory memory systems. In E. C. Carterette and M. P. Friedman, eds., *Handbook of perception,* Vol. 9. New York: Academic Press.

—— (1983). Iconic memory. *Philosophical Transactions of the Royal Society of London B302,* 283–294.

—— (1989). Modularity and dissociations of memory systems. In H. L. Roediger III and F. I. M. Craik, eds., *Varieties of memory and consciousness: Essays in honor of Endel Tulving,* pp. 271–294. Hillsdale, NJ: Erlbaum.

Crowder, R, G., and Morton, J. (1969). Precategorical acoustic storage (PAS). *Perception and Psychophysics 5,* 365–373.

Dixon, P., and Di Lollo, V. (1994). Beyond visible persistence: An alternative account of temporal integration and segregation in visual processing. *Cognitive Psychology 26,* 33–63.

Efron, R. (1970). The minimum duration of a perception. *Neuropsychologia 8,* 57–63.

Haber, R. N., and Standing, L. (1970). Direct estimates of the apparent duration of a flash. *Canadian Journal of Psychology 24,* 216–229.

Kolers, P. A., and Roediger, H. L. III (1984). Procedures of mind. *Journal of Verbal Learning and Verbal Behavior 23,* 425–449.

Massaro, D. W. (1972). Preperceptual images, processing time, and perceptual units in auditory perception. *Psychological Review 79,* 124–145.

Massaro, D. W., and Loftus, G. R. (1996). Sensory and perceptual storage: Data and theory. In E. L. Bjork and R. A. Bjork, eds., *Memory.* San Diego: Academic Press.

Sakitt, B. (1976). Iconic memory. *Psychological Review 83,* 257–276.

Sperling, G. (1960). The information available in brief visual presentations. *Psychological Monographs 74* (498).

Spoehr, K. T., and Corin, W. J. (1978). The stimulus suffix effect as a memory coding phenomenon. *Memory & Cognition 6,* 583–589.

Robert G. Crowder
Revised by Nelson Cowan

SERIAL ORGANIZATION

A critical form of memory organization, and one people frequently use, is retention of events in the temporal order in which they occurred. Consider, for example, your memory for the events that occurred last summer. If someone asked you what you did during your summer vacation, most likely you would discuss the events in the sequence in which they occurred, beginning with those that occurred at the start of the summer and concluding with those that occurred at the summer's end. Alternatively, you could report together all the parties you attended and report as another group all the times you went hiking or swimming. However, retention in terms of temporal sequence, or serial order, is most common.

Definitions and Distinctions

To study the retention of serial order in the laboratory, the information pertaining to temporal sequence must be distinguished and isolated from other types of related information. The relevant distinctions can be made clear by considering the following hypothetical situation: Imagine a waiter in a restaurant who is taking dinner orders from the people sitting around a table. Usually in such a situation the individuals make their requests in a temporal sequence that follows the spatial arrangement of the seats around the table. However, in the present situation this ordinary practice is not observed. Instead, the waiter takes the requests in an order determined by the individuals' ages and genders, starting with the oldest woman and ending with the youngest man. This situation is illustrated in Figure 1. The first order is for ham, the second for liver, the third for steak, and the fourth for chicken. The temporal sequence of the requests is thus ham, liver, steak, and chicken, a sequence that does not correspond to the spatial arrangement around the table. Hence, the temporal and spatial orders are not the same. When the waiter returns to deliver the dinners, he serves the first person liver, the second turkey, the third steak, and the last chicken. The waiter thus makes two mistakes. In the case of the turkey, he brings a dinner requested by nobody, and in the case of the liver, he gives a dinner ordered by one person to another. The first type of mistake is an item error because the identity of the dinner item is incorrect. The second type is an order error because a correct item is brought but is placed in the wrong position in the temporal sequence. For a discussion of laboratory methods used to distinguish between the retention of item, temporal order, and spatial order information, see Alice F. Healy et al. (1991).

Figure 1

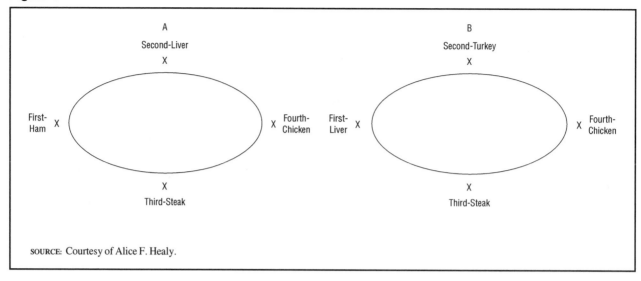

SOURCE: Courtesy of Alice F. Healy.

Arrangement of table when waiter takes dinner orders (A) and when dinner is served (B) in hypothetical restaurant situation.

Another important distinction that must be made is the difference between the order of the items and their positions in the sequence. (Some researchers refer to this same distinction as involving relative versus absolute positions.) This distinction can be clarified by considering a related hypothetical situation with the same waiter and diners. In this case, the waiter returns to take the requests for dessert. The first person orders ice cream, the second nothing, the third cake, and the last pudding. The waiter correctly brings the first person ice cream and the last pudding, but he gives the cake to the second person instead of the third. The waiter, therefore, correctly remembers the order of desserts—cake between ice cream and pudding—but he confuses the second and third temporal positions.

Empirical Results

Although a number of techniques have been used to study retention of serial order (see Cowan, Saults, Elliott, and Moreno, 2002, for a novel set of techniques), two procedures have been most popular. Much of the early work on this topic used serial learning with the method of anticipation, and many subsequent studies used short-term serial recall with the distractor paradigm. In both methods, the results of primary interest have focused on the serial position curve, which reveals the proportion of correct responses as a function of the position of each item on the list.

Serial Learning Method of Anticipation

In serial learning, subjects attempt to learn an ordered list of items (often nonsense syllables or words)

across a number of successive trials. On each trial the list is presented and the subject tries to recall it. With the method of anticipation, the subjects are not required to recite the entire list at one time. Rather, each list item is presented in turn, and the subjects are required to anticipate (i.e., recall) each item before it is presented, in response to the item immediately preceding it on the list. A correct response is scored whenever the subject correctly anticipates an item, and the subject receives feedback (i.e., the subject is told the next item in the sequence) regardless of whether a correct response is made. Usually the experimental trials are continued until the subjects are able to anticipate every item with no errors. At that point, the investigator counts the number of correct responses made at each position in the list, and it becomes evident that the items in the different ordinal positions in the list are not learned with the same ease. Rather, items at the beginning and end of the list yield more correct responses than those in the middle. The point of maximum difficulty is somewhat beyond the center of the list.

Although the total number of correct responses on the list may decrease when the items are more difficult, as when nonsense syllables are used instead of words or when the rate of list presentation is faster, the serial position curve remains constant across such changes in the learning situation when it is plotted as the proportion of the total number of correct responses made at each position in the list. The constancy of the serial position curve when plotted in this manner is known as the Hunter-McCrary law (McCrary and Hunter, 1953). A typical serial position curve for an eight-item list is shown in Figure 2, which presents data reported by Bennett B. Murdock (1960) in an important article relating the serial position function to results of experiments in domains of psychology outside of verbal learning. The serial position function is described as bow shaped because it resembles a bow used in archery. The large relative advantage for the items from the beginning of the list is known as the primacy effect, and the smaller relative advantage for the items from the end of the list is known as the recency effect.

Short-Term Serial Recall with the Distractor Paradigm

On a trial in the distractor paradigm used to study serial recall over a short time interval, subjects are given a short list of items to remember (typically three to five letters), then are required to participate in an interpolated distractor task that is meant to prevent them from rehearsing the list (e.g., they may be told to count backward from a random number), and finally they are asked to recall the list of items according to the order of presentation. The duration of the distractor task, or the length of the retention interval, varies from trial to trial but is usually quite short (no longer than twenty seconds). Also, the list of items to be recalled changes from one trial to the next. A correct response is scored whenever the subject recalls an item that was shown and places it in the ordinal position in which it occurred on the list. The time course of forgetting the serial list is revealed by comparing the proportion of correct responses at each retention interval. The resulting retention function is usually very steep; forgetting is very rapid in this paradigm. A plot of the proportion of trials on which correct responses are made at each ordinal position in the list reveals a serial position curve that is usually bow shaped and nearly symmetrical; the primacy effect is approximately equal in magnitude to the recency effect. Typical serial position curves for three different retention intervals are shown in Figure 3, which presents data reported by Healy (1974). In Healy's study, order information was isolated from item information because the same four items were shown on every trial of the experiment; the subjects knew the identity of the items in advance and had only to reconstruct the order in which they were shown on a particular trial.

Theoretical Models

A number of theoretical models have been proposed to account for serial organization. Classic models have included simple associative mechanisms, which were elaborated by contemporary models.

Figure 2

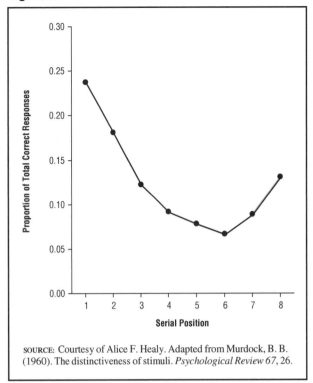

SOURCE: Courtesy of Alice F. Healy. Adapted from Murdock, B. B. (1960). The distinctiveness of stimuli. *Psychological Review 67*, 26.

Typical serial position curve for an eight-item list learned under the serial method of anticipation. The data are plotted as the proportion of the total number of correct responses made at each serial position of the list.

Classic Models

Although researchers have proposed many models of serial order retention, two simple opposing models dominated the early research on this topic. Both models include associative mechanisms as the basis for retaining serial order information. According to the associative chaining model, item-to-item associations are constructed so that the first item in a serial list is linked to the second item as a stimulus-response pair, the second item is linked in the same way to the third item, and so on to form an associative stimulus-response chain of items (Crowder, 1968). For example, given the list of dinner orders ham, liver, steak, and chicken in the hypothetical restaurant example discussed earlier, ham would be associated with liver, liver with steak, and steak with chicken. The second model to account for serial order retention involves positional associations. By this account, each item on the list is associated with the ordinal number corresponding to its serial position in the list (Young, Hakes, and Hicks, 1967). In the example described earlier, ham would be associated with the number 1, liver with 2, steak with 3, and chicken with 4. Experimental evidence has refuted both of these simple explanations for serial order retention.

Figure 3

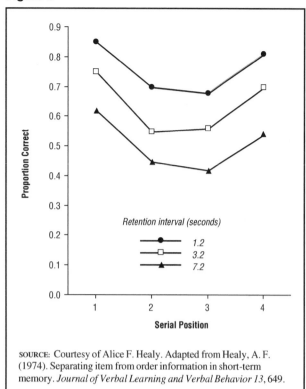

SOURCE: Courtesy of Alice F. Healy. Adapted from Healy, A. F. (1974). Separating item from order information in short-term memory. *Journal of Verbal Learning and Verbal Behavior 13*, 649.

Typical serial position curves for a four-item list recalled under the distractor paradigm. The data are plotted as the proportion of trials on which correct responses were made at each retention interval and serial position of the list.

Contemporary Models

Despite the problems with the simple associative models, two more complex contemporary models have been proposed that can be viewed as extensions of the earlier models. Both models have derived support from a wide range of experimental investigations and observations, including the pervasive serial position functions. According to the theory of distributed associative memory (TODAM), serial order information is represented in memory as a series of pairwise associations linking successively presented items. TODAM resembles the traditional chaining approach except that the items in the list and their associations are stored together in memory. Each item is represented as a list of features or a vector of numbers. Rather than simple links connecting the two items in a pair, the items are connected by means of "convolution," which is a mathematical operation that merges the separate vectors for the items into a single composite vector. The vectors for all the items in the list and for all the pairwise associations are added to a common memory vector. The mathematical details of TODAM and its ability to account for data from many serial order tasks are described in the work of Ste-

phan Lewandowsky and Bennett B. Murdock (1989) and Murdock (1995).

In contrast with TODAM, a second influential model of serial order retention emphasizes positional information. According to this perturbation model, the representation of order information derives from the representation of position information, so that subjects can recall items in the temporal sequence exactly to the extent that the positional information they have stored in memory can adequately prescribe the order. Associations are included in the perturbation model. However, instead of associative bonds linking successive items on the list, there are associative bonds between each item and a single control element, which represents some aspect of the current context in which the list is presented. For example, given two successively presented items X and Y, rather than an association of the form X-Y, the perturbation model includes associations of the form X-C-Y, where C represents the control element. This new associative mechanism has allowed for an elegant description of both short-term and long-term serial order recall. For lucid discussions of the perturbation model, see William K. Estes (1972, 1997).

Late-twentieth-century models have either refined the associative mechanisms (Henson, 1998) or introduced new nonassociative mechanisms for explaining serial recall. For example, the primacy model of Michael P. A. Page and Dennis Norris (1998) is centered on the notion of a primacy gradient of activations reflecting the strength with which the start of the list is associated with each successive list item. According to this model, there is a repeating cycle in which the item with the greatest activation is selected for recall and then suppressed.

Clearly much progress has been made in understanding the processes underlying serial organization in memory, but there is still considerable controversy among researchers because the processes appear to be more complex than originally envisioned.

See also: MEMORY SPAN

Bibliography

Cowan, N., Saults, J. S., Elliott, E. M., and Moreno, M. V. (2002). Deconfounding serial recall. *Journal of Memory and Language 46*, 153–177.

Crowder, R. G. (1968). Evidence for the chaining hypothesis of serial verbal learning. *Journal of Experimental Psychology 76*, 497-500.

Estes, W. K. (1972). An associative basis for coding and organization in memory. In A. W. Melton and E. Martin, eds., *Coding processes in human memory*. Washington, DC: Winston.

——— (1997). Processes of memory loss, recovery, and distortion. *Psychological Review 104*, 148–169.

Healy, A. F. (1974). Separating item from order information in short-term memory. *Journal of Verbal Learning and Verbal Behavior 13*, 644–655.

Healy, A. F., Cunningham, T. F., Gesi, A. T., Till, R. E., and Bourne, L. E. (1991). Comparing short-term recall of item, temporal, and spatial information in children and adults. In W. E. Hockley and S. Lewandowsky, eds., *Relating theory and data: Essays on human memory, in honor of Bennet B. Murdock.* Hillsdale, NJ: Erlbaum.

Henson, R. N. A. (1998). Short-term memory for serial order: The start-end model. *Cognitive Psychology 36*, 73-137.

Lewandowsky, S., and Murdock, B. B. (1989). Memory for serial order. *Psychological Review 96*, 25–57.

McCrary, J. W., and Hunter, W. S. (1953). Serial position curves in verbal learning. *Science 117*, 131-134.

Murdock, B. B. (1960). The distinctiveness of stimuli. *Psychological Review 67*, 16–31.

—— (1995). Developing TODAM: Three models for serial-order information. *Memory & Cognition 23*, 631–645.

Page, M. P. A., and Norris, D. (1998). The primacy model: A new model of immediate serial recall. *Psychological Review 105*, 761–781.

Young, R. K., Hakes, D. T., and Hicks, R. Y. (1967). Ordinal position number as a cue in serial learning. *Journal of Experimental Psychology, 73*, 427–438.

Alice F. Healy

SEX DIFFERENCES IN LEARNING

Findings in the field of neuroendocrinology, which explores the functional relationships between hormones and the brain, have indicated that the release of testicular (androgens) and ovarian (estrogens) hormones during critical periods of brain development exert a profound effect on the genesis and survival of neurons in specific brain areas, resulting in sex differences in reproductive behaviors. Sex differences are not restricted to the reproductive sphere, however. They are found in a broad range of nonreproductive behaviors such as aggression, locomotor activity, play behavior, and learning abilities. While the debate on whether sex differences in cognition are determined by biological or sociocultural factors is long lasting, increasing experimental evidence indicates that sex differences could be determined by genetic or hormonal factors. Support for this conclusion is of four kinds. First, sex differences have been reported in various learning abilities that depend on neural structures other than those involved in reproductive functions. Second, there are sex differences in the morphology of neural structures mediating learning abilities. Third, lesions of neural structures underlying learning abilities can affect males and females differently. Finally, sex differences in learning abilities, brain morphology, and/or in the effects of brain lesions can be reversed by manipulations of gonadal steroid hormones in animals or by normal fluctuation of sex hormones across the life span in humans.

Sexual Dimorphism in Learning Abilities

Although the majority of data pertaining to the effects of gonadal steroid hormones on learning abilities have been gathered in rodents, there is growing evidence for similar effects in primates, including humans. In rodents (Beatty, 1979), mature male rats make fewer errors than females in learning complex mazes, and are faster learners in appetitive learning. Conversely, female rats outperform males in discrimination reversal learning and in the acquisition of active avoidance. This pattern of male and female performance in avoidance learning can be reversed by treating ovariectomized female rats with androgens (testosterone) and male rats with antiandrogens from birth to adulthood. Finally, lesions of brain areas known to be functionally involved in avoidance learning, such as the basal ganglia, do not impair performance of males and females equally. For example, small lesions of the globus pallidus impair acquisition of active avoidance in males but not in females. This sex difference in the effects of pallidal lesions can be reversed by androgenization of female rats and feminization of male rats. These data in rodents suggest that androgens are, at least in part, responsible for the sex differences in learning abilities.

In nonhuman primates (Mitchell, 1977), adult female rhesus monkeys outperform males in spatial memory, as measured by the delayed-response task. Similarly, adult female chimpanzees exhibit significantly superior short-term stimulus memory, as measured by the delayed matching-to-sample task. Finally, although male and female rhesus monkeys perform similarly on tasks of object memory and executive function, young males outperform young females on a spatial memory task (Lacreuse et al., 1999). This superior level of spatial ability in young males declined sharply with age, and, at older age, males do not perform significantly better than females. These studies in adult primates did not examine whether the sex differences in learning abilities could be reversed by perinatal gonadal steroid hormone treatments, but such evidence has been obtained in studies of infant primates.

Acquisition of an object discrimination reversal task, known to depend on the integrity of the orbital prefrontal cortex in the adult monkey, is significantly more rapid in male infant monkeys than in females (Clark and Goldman-Rakic, 1989). Postnatal injections of testosterone propionate in the females enhances their performance to the level of the normal infant males. When orbital prefrontal cortex is removed in infancy, intact male monkeys and androgenized female monkeys are as impaired as adult monkeys with the same lesions, whereas untreated infant females do not differ from untreated age-matched females. The data suggest that the orbital prefrontal cortex matures earlier in male than in female monkeys. Conversely, acquisition of a concurrent visual discrimination learning task, known to depend on the integrity of the inferior temporal cortex, is significantly more rapid in female infant monkeys than in males (Bachevalier and Hagger, 1991) and this sex difference is positively correlated in three-month-old male animals with circulating levels of testosterone (the higher the level of testosterone, the poorer the score), but not with estradiol levels. Neonatal orchiectomy, which reduced plasma testosterone levels, hastens performance on visual discrimination learning in male infant monkeys, whereas treatment of androgens (dihydrotestosterone) in neonatally ovariectomized female infant monkeys delays their performance. Finally, early postnatal inferior temporal cortex lesions affect performance of female but not of male infant monkeys, though male and female adults with the same lesions are impaired equally. The data suggest that this temporal cortical area is functionally more mature in female infant monkeys than in males. Thus, gonadal steroid hormones appear to play an inductive role in the postnatal differentiation of cortical mechanisms.

For humans, many studies have reported that women excel in verbal abilities, perceptual speed, articulation, and fine motor skills, whereas men generally excel in tasks measuring visuospatial abilities, particularly those requiring mental rotation of objects and imagining what an object would look like from a different vantage point (Halpern, 1992). Although direct manipulation of gonadal hormones is not possible in humans, the organizational and activational effects of the hormones on cognitive functions have usually been inferred from the studies of different populations of individuals. They include boys and girls suffering from long-standing prenatal hormonal anomalies or that have been exposed to exogenous hormones in utero, women during regular fluctuations of estrogen and progesterone throughout the menstrual cycle or postmenopausal women receiving hormone replacement therapy, and elderly individuals showing a decline in cognitive functions. Thus, girls with congenital adrenal hyperplasia (CAH) who are genetically masculinized and prenatally exposed to excessive androgens show significant enhancement of visuospatial ability as compared to unaffected females. Also, boys exposed prenatally with DES (a synthetic estrogen) show poorer performance on several spatial tasks than males who suffer from low testosterone due to post puberty pathology (Reisnich et al., 1991). In addition, when performance on several visuospatial tasks is compared at different phases of the menstrual cycle, women perform significantly more poorly during the estrogen surge just prior to ovula-

tion than at other points in the cycle. Conversely, higher levels of estrogen during the cycle are associated with better performance on many tasks in which women typically excel. When postmenopausal women are tested either when receiving their estrogen therapy or when they are off their medication for at least four days, performance on fine motor and spatial tasks tends to be faster and more accurate during the testosterone treatment compared with the off-treatment phase (Hampson and Kimura, 1992). Finally, estrogen deficiency in menopausal women is associated with memory impairments that are reversible by estrogen replacement therapy, whereas testosterone replacement therapy in elderly men enhances spatial performance (Janowsky et al., 1994).

The double dissociation found in infant monkeys with the object discrimination reversal and concurrent discrimination tasks have been replicated in very young children using almost identical cognitive tasks and nonverbal procedures (Overman et al., 1997). Boys under the age of twenty-nine months significantly outperform girls on the object reversal task, but girls outperform boys on the concurrent discrimination task. Given the close parallel in learning behavior in human infants and infant monkeys, it is reasonable to propose that the gender differences are mediated by similar biological mechanisms in both species. Therefore, in children, as in infant monkeys, there may be a more rapid maturation of orbital prefrontal circuits in boys and a more rapid maturation of inferior temporal circuits in girls.

Sex Differences in Brain Areas Related to Learning Abilities

Although no direct correlation has been established between sex differences in learning abilities and morphology of brain areas, sex differences in numerous neural structures related to learning abilities are well documented in rodents (Beatty, 1979; Juraska, 1991). In the limbic system (bed nucleus of the stria terminalis and hippocampus), the number and volume of neurons differ in male and female rats. These morphological differences are reversed after postnatal treatment with gonadal steroid hormones. The rate of neonatal cell proliferation has been shown to be slower in male than in female rats, indicating a delayed maturation of the neocortex in males compared with that of females. Similarly, the neurons in the somatosensory cortex of young male rats are larger than those of females, reflecting a cortical immaturity and, possibly, a less developed synaptic network in males than in females. In research conducted in the 1990s, sex differences in humans have also been found for functional asymmetry (Voyer, 1996), brain morphology, metabolism, weigh, volume, and neocortical neuron number (Gur et al., 1995; Pakkenberg and Gundersen, 1997; Hampson and Kimura, 1992).

Mechanisms of Action

The question of precisely how gonadal hormones exert their organizational and activational influence on brain areas related to learning abilities remains to be answered. There is, however, indirect evidence regarding the mechanism of their action on brain areas mediating learning abilities (Luine and McEwen, 1985). For example, gonadal steroid hormones are known to act via intracellular receptors located in limbic structures and some parts of the neocortex. In the developing rhesus monkey, androgen metabolism has been observed in all cortical areas; this activity declines from prenatal to early postnatal life. Also, the presence of sex differences in neurochemical concentrations and regulatory processes suggests an influence of gonadal steroid hormones on the differentiation of neurochemical features of neurons. Finally, gonadal steroid hormones stimulate neurite outgrowth during the sensitive period of brain differentiation, presumably by increasing the competitive advantage of neurons to make connections with other neurons. The perinatal androgen surge seen in infant males could therefore affect the rate of brain maturation by influencing neuronal connectivity at the cortical level.

There are also several possible mechanisms by which gonadal steroids may exert more transient, or activational, effects on central nervous system during adulthood. Estradiol as well as other gonadal hormones can regulate the concentrations of specific enzymes involved in neurotransmitter synthesis and breakdown (McEwen et al., 1984). This action may offer a way by which a single hormone can simultaneously exert different effects on different behavioral systems.

Conclusion

Although sex differences in cognitive and learning abilities are presently widely acknowledged, the basis for these differences remains controversial. The data reviewed in this entry suggest that androgens organize the brain pre- and perinatally for all sexually dimorphic behaviors, including problem-solving behaviors, and this appears to be true in mammals, nonhuman primates, and humans. Moreover, the pattern of variation in learning abilities documented over the menstrual cycle and during aging processes raises the possibility that sex differences in cognitive abilities in humans may also at least be partly due to an activational influence of sex hormones on the brain throughout life. Thus, it is becoming clear that sex differences in structure and function are likely to be a pervasive characteristic of brain organization and mediated by gonadal steroid hormones. Nevertheless, the challenge is to precisely specify biological mechanisms by which these differences occur and to take into consideration the circular interactions between biological factors and socioenvironmental factors. Ultimately, the understanding of cognitive sex differences will necessarily depend upon converging evidence from many different disciplines, including endocrinology, animal and human behavior, neurobiology, electrophysiology, and brain imaging.

See also: DISCRIMINATION AND GENERALIZATION; NEURAL SUBSTRATES OF AVOIDANCE LEARNING

Bibliography

Bachevalier, J., and Hagger, C. (1991). Sex differences in the development of learning abilities in primates. *Psychoneuroendocrinology 16*, 179–190.

Beatty, W. W. (1979). Gonadal hormones and sex differences in nonreproductive behaviors in rodents: Organizational and activational influences. *Hormones and Behavior 12*, 112–163.

Clark, A. S., and Goldman-Rakic, P. S. (1989). Gonadal hormones influence the emergence of cortical function in nonhuman primates. *Behavioral Neuroscience 103*, 1,287–1,295.

Gur, R. C., et al. (1995). Sex differences in regional glucose metabolism during a resting state. *Science 267*, 528–531.

Halpern, D. F. (2000). *Sex differences in cognitive abilities*, 3rd edition. Mahwah, NJ: Erlbaum.

Hampson, E., and Kimura, D. (1992). Sex differences and hormonal influences on cognitive function in humans. In J. B. Becker, S. M. Breedlove, and D. Crews, eds, *Behavioral Endocrinology*. Cambridge, MA: MIT Press.

Janowsky, J. S., Oviatt, S. K., and Orwoll, E. S. (1994). Testosterone influences spatial cognition in older men. *Behavioral Neuroscience 108*, 325–332.

Juraska, J. M. (1991). Sex differences in "cognitive" regions of the rat brain. *Psychoneuroendocrinology 16*, 105–119.

Lacreuse, A., et al. (1999). Spatial cognition in rhesus monkeys: Male superiority declines with age. *Hormones and Behavior 36*, 70–76.

Luine, V. N., and McEwen, B. S. (1985). Steroid hormone receptors in brain and pituitary. In N. Adler, D. Pfaff, and R. W. Goy, eds., *Handbook of behavioral neurobiology*, Vol. 7: *Reproduction*. New York: Plenum Press.

McEwen, B. C., et al. (1984). Towards a neurochemical basis of steroid hormone action. In L. Martini, and W. F. Ganong, eds., *Frontiers in Neuroendocrinology*, Vol. 8. New York: Raven Press.

Mitchell, G. (1977). A note on sex differences in learning or motivation in nonhuman primates. *Laboratory Primate Newsletter 16*, 1–5.

Overman, W. H., Bachevalier, J., Schumann, E., and McDonough-Ryan, P. (1997). Sexually dimorphic brain-behavior development: A comparative perspective. In N. A. Krasnegor, G. R. Lyon, and P. S. Goldman-Rakic, eds., *Development of the prefrontal cortex: Evolution, neurobiology, and behavior*. Baltimore, MD: Brookes Publishing Company.

Pakkenberg, B., and Gundersen, H. J. (1997). Neocortical neuron number in humans: Effects of sex and age. *Journal of Comparative Neurology 384*, 312–320.

Reinisch, J. M., Ziemba-Davis, M., and Sanders, S. A. (1991). Hormonal contributions to sexually dimorphic behavioral development in humans. *Psychoneuroendocrinology 16*, 213–278.

Voyer, D. (1996). On the magnitude of laterality effects and sex differences in functional literalities. *Laterality 1*, 51–83.

Jocelyne B. Bachevalier

SKINNER, B. F. (1904–1990)

The American psychologist B. F. Skinner was renowned for his pioneering work in behaviorism. Born on March 20, 1904, in Susquehanna, Pennsylvania, Burrhus Frederic Skinner was the older son of Grace Madge Burrhus Skinner and William Arthur Skinner, an attorney with some political aspirations. Skinner's younger brother died suddenly of a cerebral aneurysm at the age of sixteen. Skinner did his undergraduate work at Hamilton College in Clinton, New York, where he majored in English. During the summer before his senior year, he studied at the Bread Loaf School of English at Middlebury, Vermont. There he met Robert Frost, who asked Skinner to send him some of his work. Frost's comments encouraged Skinner to try writing, at first in his parents' home and later in New York City's Greenwich Village. He discovered that "I had nothing important to say" (Skinner, 1970, p. 7). He then turned to psychology and graduate work at Harvard University.

Several factors drew Skinner to psychology. First, his biology teacher directed him to Jacques Loeb's *Physiology of the Brain and Comparative Psychology* (1900) and Pavlov's *Conditioned Reflexes* (1927). Then the writings of Bertrand Russell, in *The Dial*, a literary magazine, and in the book *Philosophy* (1927), which he read while writing in Greenwich Village, led him to J. B. Watson's *Behaviorism* (1924). Harvard's department of psychology did not strengthen his interest in behaviorism, but Fred S. Keller, then a graduate student in the department, did. Skinner described Keller as "a sophisticated behaviorist in every sense of the word" (1970, p. 9) and his thesis as having "only the vaguest of Harvard connections" (1970, p. 10). It included his study of eating rate in the rat (which came to be the response rate of later work), two brief papers on the reflex and drive, and his paper on the concept of the reflex in psychology. That concept was based on an operational analysis in which he insisted on defining it as an observed correlation of stimulus and response. He used the equation $R = f(S, A)$, where R stood for reflex strength, S for stimulus, and A for any condition affecting reflex strength, such as drive, which was specified in terms of the deprivation operation (Skinner, 1977).

After receiving his Ph.D., Skinner served as a junior fellow in the Harvard Society of Fellows for three years; then he moved to the University of Minnesota where, during World War II, he embarked on a project to train pigeons to guide missiles. While at the University of Minnesota, he married Yvonne (Eve) Blue, with whom he had two children, Julie and Deborah. In 1945 he moved to Indiana University, where he remained until 1947, when he returned to Harvard University. During that same year, he delivered his William James Lectures on Verbal Behavior, which evolved into his book on that subject in 1957.

As he himself implied, Skinner held on to the concept of "reflex" beyond its usefulness when he wrote his book *The Behavior of Organisms* in 1938. Not long after that, he gave up the concept because operant behavior not elicited but emitted; he thus ceased to be a stimulus-response psychologist. This means that Skinner did not conceive of human beings, or any organisms, as automatons waiting to have some behavior elicited. Rather, he viewed them as emitting behavior upon which the environment acts by selecting some of it through the provision of consequences. Also important in this context is the concept of classes of behavior and classes of stimuli—Skinner referred to this as the generic nature of stimulus and response (1935). Even though *behavior analysis*, a term now used to describe Skinner's concepts of learning, refers to classes, not some hyperspecified atomistic stimulus and response, uninformed people still characterize Skinner's approach incorrectly as atomistic.

The difficulty of eliciting operant behavior necessitated the invention of a special procedure to produce "new" behavior—hence the concept of "shaping." Skinner's approach to learning emphasized the three-part reinforcement contingency. Behavior occurring on particular occasions and followed by certain consequences (reinforcers) will be strengthened by those consequences; that is, other members of the same response class will have a higher probability of occurring on similar occasions. There are positive and negative reinforcers. The former strengthens the behavior that produces it and the latter strengthens the behavior that avoids or eliminates it. Reinforcers are also divided into unconditioned (primary) and conditioned (secondary). The former act as reinforcers without any learning history, whereas the latter act as reinforcers because of their association with the unconditioned reinforcers. Skinner distinguished reinforcers from punishing stimuli, which weaken the behavior they produce.

Skinner's concept of operant behavior has generated many experiments, including those on schedules of reinforcement in which the different intermittent patterns of reinforcement give rise to characteristic patterns of response rates (Ferster and Skinner, 1957). The concept of intermittent reinforcement was significant in a variety of ways, notably in its resemblance to the conditions of the natural environment, which brought basic learning research closer to the "real" world. The number of different kinds of intermittent schedules that can be generated is limited only by the experimenter's imagination, but they generally fall into two broad classes: one in which reinforcement depends on the frequency or type of behavior and the other in which it depends on the occurrence of a response following the passage of a certain interval or various intervals.

Intermittent schedules of reinforcement produced behavior that is particularly resistant to extinction and thus gave rise to the study of maintenance of behavior, to which other learning approaches gave scant attention. Maintenance of behavior is like memory, a concept Skinner avoided. Instead of viewing recall as "searching a storehouse of memory," he considered the conditions, both external and response-produced, that increase "the probability of responses" (Skinner, 1974, pp. 109–210). Interestingly, Skinner did not limit his work to basic research. With respect to memory, he wrote a charming and informative book (Skinner and Vaughn, 1983) outlining a program of self-management in old age.

Skinner's book on verbal behavior (1957) appeared in the same year as his work on intermittent reinforcement (Ferster and Skinner, 1957). He considered the former to be his most important contribution to psychology and viewed verbal behavior as he did other behavior, not as standing for something else (Skinner, 1945) but as constituting the subject matter of interest. In contrast with methodological behaviorists, who must restrict their studies to currently measurable phenomena, Skinner the radical behaviorist was able to extend his analysis to private events that cannot yet be measured. In his book on verbal behavior and later in his *Contingencies of Reinforcement* (Skinner, 1969), Skinner explicitly recognized that not all behavior is produced through conditioning; rule-governed behavior is produced not through exposure to the actual contingencies of reinforcement but to a verbal description of those contingencies. In one of his last papers, Skinner (1990) suggested that such rule-governed behavior might, as "knowledge by description," postpone the destruction of the earth.

Skinner applied his principles of behavior to many areas of functioning. In education, he invented programmed instruction, a form of learning in which students always make the "correct" response, thus having their correct responses immediately reinforced (Skinner, 1954a; 1968). He used the methods of shaping and stimulus fading to make that possible. In abnormal psychology, he first talked about behavior modification by applying reinforcement to psychotic patients' behavior (Skinner, 1954b). He applied behavior analysis to the study of drugs (Skinner

B. F. Skinner *(The Library of Congress)*

and Heron, 1937), thereby initiating an area still practiced and useful; and, as already mentioned, he applied it to old age.

Skinner's first excursion into the study of culture and how to improve took the form of a novel, *Walden Two* (Skinner, 1948). He returned to that theme in *Science and Human Behavior* (Skinner, 1953) and in *Beyond Freedom and Dignity* (Skinner, 1971). He always remained close to the principles of behavior analysis that he had discovered in his basic research. Skinner was undoubtedly one of the most influential psychologists of the twentieth century. His systematization of behavior was never limited to learning as such. Rather, he and others applied his approach to all areas of psychology. A reconsideration of his basic papers, complete with comments by his supporters and critics—along with his response to those comments—appeared in Catania and Harnad (1984).

B. F. Skinner died in 1990.

See also: BEHAVIORISM; OPERANT BEHAVIOR; PAVLOV, IVAN; WATSON, JOHN B.

Bibliography

Catania, A. C., and Harnad, S., eds. (1984). Canonical papers of B. F. Skinner. *The Behavioral and Brain Sciences 7*, 473–724.

Ferster, C. F., and Skinner, B. F. (1957). *Schedules of reinforcement.* New York: Appleton-Century-Crofts.

Loeb, J. (1900). *Physiology of the brain and comparative psychology.* New York: Putnam.

Pavlov, I. (1927). *Conditioned reflexes.* London: Oxford University Press.

Russell, B. (1927). *Philosophy.* New York: W. W. Norton.

Skinner, B. F. (1935). The generic nature of the concepts of stimulus and response. *Journal of General Psychology 12,* 40–65.

——— (1938). *The behavior of organisms.* New York Appleton-Century-Crofts.

——— (1945). The operational analysis of psychological terms. *Psychological Review 52,* 270–277.

——— (1948). *Walden two.* New York: Macmillan.

——— (1953). *Science and human behavior.* New York: Macmillan.

——— (1954a). The science of learning and the art of teaching. *Harvard Educational Review 24,* 86–97.

——— (1954b). A new method for the experimental analysis of the behavior of psychotic patients. *Journal of Nervous and Mental Diseases 120,* 403–406.

——— (1957). *Verbal behavior.* New York: Appleton-Century-Crofts.

——— (1968). *The technology of teaching.* New York: Appleton-Century-Crofts.

——— (1969). *Contingencies of reinforcement.* New York: Appleton-Century-Crofts.

——— (1970). B. F. Skinner: An autobiography. In P. B. Dews, ed., *Festschrift for B. F. Skinner.* New York: Appleton-Century-Crofts.

——— (1971). *Beyond freedom and dignity.* New York: Alfred A. Knopf.

——— (1974). *About behaviorism.* New York. Alfred A. Knopf.

——— (1976). *Particulars of my life.* New York: Alfred A Knopf.

——— (1977). The experimental analysis of operant behavior. In R. W. Rieber and K. Salzinger, eds., The roots of American psychology: Historical influences and implications for the future. *Annals of the New York Academy of Sciences 291,* 374–385.

——— (1979). *The shaping of a behaviorist.* New York: Alfred A. Knopf.

——— (1983). *A matter of consequences.* New York: Alfred A. Knopf.

——— (1990). To know the future. *The Behavior Analyst 13,* 103–106.

Skinner, B. F., and Heron, W. T. (1937). Effects of caffeine and benzedrine upon conditioning and extinction. *Psychological Record 1,* 340–346.

Skinner, B. F., and Vaughn, M. E. (1983). *Enjoy old age.* New York: W. W. Norton.

Watson, J. B. (1924). *Behaviorism.* New York: W. W. Norton.

Kurt Salzinger

SLEEP AND MEMORY CONSOLIDATION

More than two hundred years have passed since David Hartley (English psychologist and philosopher, 1705–1757) first proposed that dreaming might alter the strength of associative links between memories, and more than one hundred years since Sigmund Freud (Austrian neurologist and founder of psychoanalysis, 1856–1939) suggested that dreaming served to process traumatic memories. But it has only been since 1953, with the discovery of rapid eye movement (REM) sleep by Eugene Aserinsky and Nathaniel Kleitman, that studies of sleep's role in memory processing began in earnest. Since then, a wide range of studies have provided converging evidence on the important role sleep plays in the off-line reprocessing of waking memories. Whether dreaming plays a similar role remains unclear.

Sleep's complex role in memory consolidation makes our understanding of that role more difficult. Multiple memory systems exist within the brain store and process different types of information in separate anatomical regions. For example, episodic memory recall in humans is dependent on the hippocampus, whereas access to procedural memories is not. Numerous mechanisms can contribute to memory consolidation. Consolidation can refer to the simple strengthening of a memory, its movement from one memory system to another, or its functional linking to other, associated memories. As a result, sleep's contribution to memory consolidation depends on the precise memory system involved and the form of consolidation being considered. Sleep represents a similarly complex phenomenon because it consists of a series of brain states with different neurophysiological and neurochemical properties. This deceptively simple question of sleep's role in memory reprocessing must be expanded to address the contribution of specific stages of sleep to various mechanisms involved in the consolidation of several distinct forms of memory.

The REM Sleep Cycle

Sleep in mammals follows a rhythmic pattern of alternating REM and nonREM (NREM) sleep. In humans, this cycle has a period of approximately ninety minutes, and continues throughout the night (see Figure 1, top panel). NREM sleep is divided into four stages, ranging from very light (stage I) sleep onset to deep slow wave sleep (SWS; stages III and IV), so named because of its characteristic electroencephalographic (EEG) pattern (see Figure 1, second panel). Throughout the night this ninety-minute period remains relatively constant, but a slow shift from a preponderance of SWS early in the night toward a preponderance of REM sleep at the end of the night occurs.

Several physiological parameters vary across the REM cycle. As sleep progresses from stage I to stage IV, EEG patterns show progressively slower and higher amplitude waves, whereas REM sleep shows a high frequency low amplitude EEG pattern. Thus, REM sleep has been given the alternate name of paradoxical sleep, based on the similarity between its EEG pattern and the pattern seen in waking. These distinct EEG waveforms seen in different sleep stages may contribute differentially to various aspects of memory consolidation. Tonic muscle activity, measured by the electromyogram (EMG), decreases with descent through light NREM sleep into SWS, but is at its lowest level in REM sleep (see Figure 1, third panel). During REM, a descending spinal path from the brainstem bulbar reticular formation actively inhibits the voluntary muscles. The resulting atonia produces a functional paralysis during REM sleep, which is necessary to prevent the physical acting out of dreams. Spontaneous eye movements, recorded in the electrooculogram (EOG) also show distinct stage-dependent patterns (see Figure 1, bottom panel). While NREM sleep stages II through IV show little or no eye movements, both sleep onset (stage I) and REM sleep show stereotypical patterns of movements. During sleep onset, slow rolling eye movements, lasting one to three seconds are observed, whereas during REM sleep phasic bursts of rapid eye movements are seen. These bursts correlate with times of peak dream recall.

The shift from NREM to REM sleep is accompanied by an increase in release of acetylcholine in the brain and a simultaneous near-cessation of release of norepinephrine and serotonin. Brain imaging studies show that most brain regions become less active during NREM sleep; several distinct regions, including the anterior cingulate and medial orbitofrontal cortices and the amygdala become more active in REM sleep. Together, these changes are thought to control the variations in memory reprocessing and dreaming seen across the sleep cycle.

Human Procedural Skill Consolidation

The clearest evidence of the important role sleep plays in human memory reprocessing comes from studies of the consolidation of procedural learning. Posttraining sleep can improve both perceptual and motor skill learning.

In visual texture discrimination tasks, training only leads to improved performance after a night's sleep (see Figure 2). Subjects trained and then retested the same day show no improvement, whereas subjects retested after a night's sleep show significant improvement. Similarly, subjects that are sleep deprived the night after training and then retested two days later, also show no improvement. Thus, sleep the night after training appears critical for the consolidation of this learning. Those stages of sleep that are most important remain unclear. Studies have found that selectively decreasing either REM or SWS can block improvement, and overnight improvement correlates both with the amount of SWS early in the night and the amount of REM sleep late in the night. These findings in humans match findings in rats, suggesting that a two-step process of sleep-dependent memory

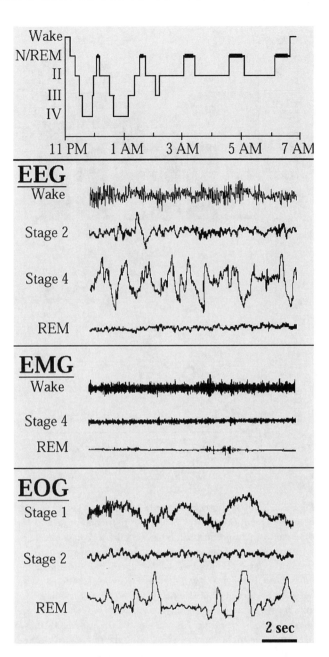

Figure 1. The human REM sleep cycle. Top panel: The 90-minute REM cycle shifts from SWS early in the night toward REM sleep late in the night. Second panel: EEG waves become slower and larger in SWS, but rapid and small in REM sleep. Third panel: Muscle tone (EMG) decreases with deeper NREM sleep, but is actively inhibited in REM sleep. Bottom panel: Eye movements (EOG) show slow-rolling eye movements in Stage 1 and rapid-eye movements in REM sleep. *(Robert Stickgold)*

consolidation requiring SWS followed by REM sleep occurs.

In contrast to these findings with perceptual skill tasks, motor skill tasks can show dependence on stage II NREM sleep. Individuals show a twenty percent increase in speed on a finger-tapping task after a night's sleep, correlating with the amount of stage II sleep

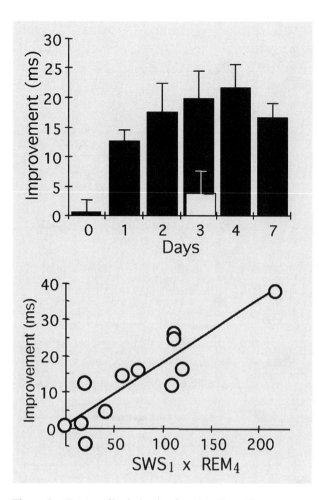

Figure 2. Texture discrimination learning. Top: Time course of improvement over 7 days. Subjects were trained at various times between 1 and 6 P.M. and then tested 1 to 7 days later. Testing was carried out at the same time of day as training, except for day 0, when subjects were trained and retested on the same day. Open bar at day 3 - Subjects were tested after 3 days, but were prevented from sleeping from the time of training until 9 P.M. on the following night. Error bars = s.e.m. Bottom: Two-step model of memory consolidation. The product of the percent of the night spent in SWS during the first quarter of the night (SWS1) and in REM sleep during the last quarter of the night (REM4) is plotted against improved performance for each subject. *(Robert Stickgold)*

obtained, especially late in the night. These differences between perceptual and motor skill learning may reflect the fact that different brain regions are involved in each of these forms of learning.

Human Declarative Memory Consolidation

Less convincing evidence exists for sleep's role in the consolidation of declarative memories. Sleep deprivation, particularly REM sleep deprivation, has little or no effect on the retention of simple declarative memories such as paired word associates, but may in-

terfere with the retention or consolidation of more complex declarative memories, such as recall of lists of words grouped into categories, or the acquisition of such complex skills at BASIC computer programming, foreign languages, or Morse code. It is, however, unclear whether it is the specifically declarative portion of such learning or more subtle, nondeclarative components that are being affected. Nevertheless, these results suggest that some aspects of complex declarative memories are supported by sleep.

Animal Memory Consolidation

Because the classification of a memory as declarative requires a verbal statement of recall, it is impossible to know whether animals possess such memories. However, many forms of animal learning are clearly impaired by subsequent REM sleep deprivation, indicating that the role of sleep in memory consolidation is not uniquely human. In rats, posttraining REM deprivation impairs both aversive and appetitive tasks, although simpler tasks may not share this property. Thus, simple shock avoidance training is unaffected by subsequent REM sleep deprivation, whereas a more complex, shuttle box avoidance task is REM sleep dependent. Memory consolidation appears to be sensitive to REM deprivation only during specific REM windows (Carlyle Smith, 1985), often occurring hours to days after the initial training. These REM windows are further characterized by increased REM sleep following training. During periods when REM-dependent memory consolidation is occurring, the brain appears to produce more REM sleep.

In humans, declarative memories are dependent on the hippocampus for their encoding and initial recall, whereas procedural skill learning is largely independent of this structure. In rats, spatial learning tasks are hippocampally mediated, and it is possible to look at the role of sleep in consolidating hippocampally mediated memories in rats by comparing spatial and non-spatial tasks. Surprisingly, both types of tasks are found to be sleep dependent; posttraining REM deprivation impairs performance on both the Morris water maze and the eight-arm radial arm maze. Thus, these tasks may correspond to the complex declarative memory tasks in humans, which show a similar REM dependency.

Memory Reactivation in Sleep

Studies showing that patterns of brain activation seen during learning are reactivated during sleep provide additional support for sleep dependent memory processing. Evidence for this comes from both animal and human experiments. Recordings from the rat hippocampus show the most direct evidence, revealing that the rat hippocampus, during both REM and NREM sleep, activates patterns of neuronal activity that mimic patterns seen earlier when the rat was navigating a maze. The patterns are sufficiently complex that one can visualize the virtual maze running activity of the sleeping rat. Interestingly, this repetition is seen during NREM sleep only in the first thirty minutes after maze running, while the REM reactivation is seen twenty-four hours later. Thus, as has been suggested from behavioral studies, memory processing might occur first during NREM sleep and only subsequently during REM sleep. Similar patterns of reactivation have been seen in the neocortex. Unfortunately, no behavioral studies exist to show that this replay of patterns of either hippocampal or neocortical neuronal activity during sleep are actually associated with memory consolidation.

Less direct evidence of the reactivation of neuronal ensembles coding memory traces is found in dream reports collected during the sleep onset period following intense video game play. Sixty to ninety percent of subjects that played either the video game *Tetris*, or the arcade game *Alpine Racer II*, reported dreamlike images from the game when awakened during the first few minutes of sleep following several hours of intensive game play. In most cases, the images were accurate copies of game elements, suggesting that memory traces were being reactivated during the sleep onset period. Subjects playing *Alpine Racer* reported both visual and kinesthetic imagery, indicating that coordinated multimodal replay is occurring. Surprisingly, the reactivation is not hippocampally mediated, since amnesic patients with extensive damage to both hippocampi produce similar *Tetris* images despite being unable to identify the source of the images or to recall playing the game.

Some researchers continue to question sleep's role in memory consolidation, but the findings reviewed here point toward an important and complex role for sleep in the off-line reprocessing of learning and memory. The evidence is clearest for the role of REM sleep in the consolidation of procedural learning. The possible roles of deep sleep in consolidating procedural memories and of stage II NREM sleep in consolidating motor skill learning are less clear, as is sleep's role in consolidating and integrating declarative memories. There is mixed evidence of roles for both SWS and REM sleep in these processes. Taken together with evidence for patterns of neuronal replay during REM, NREM, and even sleep onset, a picture begins to emerge in which each stage of sleep makes a unique contribution to off-line memory reprocessing. Further work is needed to permit the unequivocal identification of these contributions.

See also: MEMORY CONSOLIDATION: MOLECULAR AND CELLULAR PROCESSES; MEMORY CONSOLIDATION: PROLONGED PROCESS OF REORGANIZATION; MOTOR SKILL LEARNING

Bibliography

Aserinsky, E., and Kleitman, N. (1953). Regularly occurring periods of ocular motility and concomitant phenomena during sleep. *Science 118*, 361–375.

Freud, S. (1900). *The interpretation of dreams.* New York: Basic Books.

Hartley, D. (1791). *Observations on man, his frame, his duty and his expectations.* London: Johnson.

Hennevin, E., Hars, B., Maho, C., and Bloch, V. (1995). Processing of learned information in paradoxical sleep: Relevance for memory. *Behavioural Brain Research 69*, 125–135.

Peigneux, P., Laureys, S., Delbeuck, X., and Maquet, P. (2001). Sleeping brain, learning brain. The role of sleep for memory systems. *Neuroreport 12* (18), A111–124.

Siegel, J. M. (2001). The REM sleep-memory consolidation hypothesis. *Science 294*, 1,058–1,063.

Smith, C. (1985). Sleep states and learning: A review of the animal literature. *Neuroscience and Biobehavioral Reviews 9,* 157–168.

—— (1995). Sleep states and memory processes. *Behavioural Brain Research 69*, 137–145.

Stickgold, R. (1998). Sleep: Off-line memory reprocessing. *Trends in Cognitive Sciences 2* (12), 484–492.

Stickgold, R., Hobson, J. A., Fosse, R., and Fosse, M. (2001). Sleep, learning and dreams: Off-line memory reprocessing. *Science 294*, 1,052–1,057.

Vertes, R. P., and Eastman, K. E. (2000). The case against memory consolidation in REM sleep. *Behavioral and Brain Sciences 23*, 867–876.

Robert Stickgold

SOCIAL MEMORY PROCESSES

Studies of social memory support the trite adage, "Two heads are better than one." But there is more to this story. When recalling meaningful materials such as stories, word lists, and criminal acts, groups remember more than individuals. But in the recall of meaningless materials such as nonsense syllables, group and individual recall do not differ. However, even with meaningful materials, collaborative memory typically falls short of performance predicted by combining individual output (Clark and Stephenson, 1989). To determine if social interaction influences group recall, students of social memory have turned to comparisons between collaborative and nominal groups (see Figure 1).

Collaboration in Recall

In 1997, Weldon and Bellinger advocated testing nominal groups. In nominal groups participants actually recall separately, and the sum of their nonoverlapping output is calculated. For example, if Tom, Susan, and Hugh are members of a three-person

Figure 1

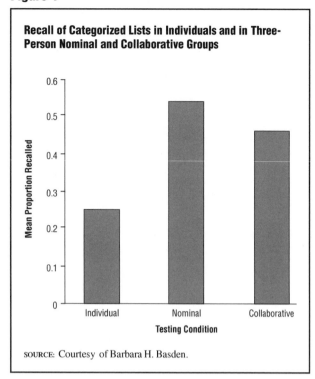

Recall of Categorized Lists in Individuals and in Three-Person Nominal and Collaborative Groups

SOURCE: Courtesy of Barbara H. Basden.

nominal group and both Tom and Susan recall the word *puma,* that word would be counted as being recalled only once. The advantage of using nominal groups is that the effect of social interaction on group productivity can be determined; the recall of *n* persons recalling collaboratively is compared to the recall of *n* persons recalling individually. From the results of experiments that tested recall in three-person nominal and collaborative groups, Weldon and Bellinger as well as Basden, Basden, Bryner, and Thomas (1997) concluded that nominal groups recall more material than collaborative groups, a phenomenon they label collaborative inhibition. Thus, social interaction hurts rather than helps recall. To rephrase the adage: "Two heads apart are better than two heads together."

There is an interesting addendum to this research. Basden, Henry, and Basden (2001) gave both collaborative and nominal groups a second individual recall test. Understandably, the average recall of collaborating subjects was higher than that of nominal subjects on this final individual test. After all, collaborating subjects have the benefit of hearing the recall of others in their group on the initial recall test. When the nonoverlapping recall of the subjects in former nominal or collaborative groups was examined, former nominal group subjects outperformed former collaborative group subjects. In other words, collabo-

ration enhanced the recall of individual subjects but reduced the output of the group as a whole.

Interpretations of Collaborative Inhibition

Contrary to popular intuition, collaborative inhibition does not result from social loafing. (Social loafing refers to motor tasks such as tug-of-war in which a person working with others exerts less effort than a person working alone.) Weldon, Blair, and Huebsch (2000) tested the effect of motivational variables on collaborative inhibition. When they paid collaborative groups to recall more words, collaborative-group recall still fell short of nominal-group recall. Basden, Basden, Bryner, and Thomas (1997) proposed an alternative interpretation of collaborative inhibition. They argued that individual retrieval strategies are disrupted during collaborative recall. For example, suppose Susan's retrieval strategy involved recalling *puma, lion,* and *tiger,* in that order. Hearing Tom recall *puma* and Hugh recall *orange* leads Susan toward recalling fruits and away from recalling *lion* and *tiger,* which she would have normally retrieved after recalling *puma.*

Several lines of evidence support the strategy-disruption interpretation of collaborative inhibition. For one, organization as measured by clustering (the tendency to recall exemplars of taxonomic categories together) is greater in the recall protocols of nominal subjects than those of collaborative groups, and forcing groups to organize their recall by category eliminates collaborative inhibition (Basden, Bryner, and Thomas, 1997). Furthermore, providing retrieval cues at the time of the test reduces or eliminates collaborative inhibition, as does having group members study items in the same rather than in different orders (Finlay, Hitch, and Meudell, 2000). Alternative interpretations are that waiting one's turn to recall and/or coordinating one's efforts with others may block production (Weldon, Blair, and Huebsch, 2000) and that the specificity of retrieval cues is greater for individual recall than for collaborative recall—that is, the encoding context originally experienced by the individual is diluted during collaborative tests (Andersson and Rönnberg, 1996).

Errors and Social Contagion

Group recall is usually more complete and more accurate than individual recall when groups discuss the events to which they were exposed and strive to reach consensus before recording their joint recall (e.g., Yarmey and Morris, 1998). When recall is collected without prior discussion and ensuing arrival at consensus, collaborative groups may produce more errors than nominal groups. Basden, Basden, Thomas, and Soupasith (1998) tested false memory in groups by omitting the most common examples (e.g., *apple*), from lists made up of common taxonomic categories (e.g., *fruit*.) Collaborative groups falsely recalled more critical omitted items than did nominal groups. Furthermore, members of collaborative groups who had not recalled a given critical item often did so on a subsequent individual-recall test, indicating that memory errors may spread from one group member to another.

Roediger, Meade, and Bergman (2001) studied the spread of memory errors within groups. After briefly studying an everyday scene, such as a bathroom, two undergraduates alternated in recalling objects from that scene. Unbeknownst to the true subject in the experiment, the other undergraduate was a confederate of the experimenter. The confederate recalled a nonpresented critical object—a toothbrush, for example—in the course of recalling objects that were actually present in the scene. On a subsequent individual recall test, true subjects often falsely recalled the toothbrush, the critical object. Roediger and colleagues referred to the spread of false information from person to person as social contagion. In subsequent research, social contagion was induced by an implied presence—a bogus confederate, for example. Social contagion is greater when the presentation is brief, when false information is introduced more than once, and when a live rather than a simulated confederate provides the misinformation.

Characteristics of Group Members

People who are familiar with the memory abilities of others in their group may show less collaborative inhibition than people who are unfamiliar with others in the group. Collaborative inhibition is less evident in dyads composed of friends than in dyads composed of nonfriends (Andersson and Rönnberg, 1996). Johannsen, Andersson, and Rönnberg (2000) found that prospective memory in older couples was influenced by reliance on one another's memory. Couples who reported using transactive memory (Wegner, Giuliano, and Hertel, 1985)—knowledge of their partner's memory—showed less collaborative inhibition than older couples who did not. To illustrate transactive memory, a husband may not attempt to remember proper names that he knows his wife will remember, so he instead concentrates on remembering dates and times. Dixon and Gould (1998) studied story recall in young and old participants (older than sixty-five) tested either individually, in two-person groups, or in four-person groups. Collaboration had similar effects on the recall of younger and older participants. As group size increased, recall increased as much for older as for younger participants. Recall at each group size was greater for younger than for older participants. In a second experiment, Dixon and Gould tested story recall in older and younger married couples. Somewhat surprisingly, older couples did not differ from younger couples. Older couples appear to profit more from transactive memory than do younger couples.

Collaboration in Recognition Tests

In tests of recognition memory, groups outperform individuals. As before, "Two heads are better than one." However, as with recall tests, it is important to know if group members effectively share information. Clark, Hori, Putnam, and Martin (2000) found that both two- and three-person groups produced hits more often than individuals but that collaboration did not reduce false-alarm rates. Clark et al. argued that a recall-to-reject strategy underlies group superiority in hits. When a group member can recall an item's occurrence or the circumstances surrounding the item's occurrence, he/she may convince others that the item was actually presented. According to Clark et al., collaboration facilitates recognition performance beyond levels expected from simple rules such as "majority wins" or "follow the leader." As in collaborative-recall tests, performance on collaborative-recognition tests may be influenced by the responses of others in the group. Schneider and Watkins (1996) found that true subjects who made their recognition choices after false responses were given by the experimenter's confederate often conformed to the confederate's choices.

Collective Memory

As illustrated by collaborative memory of long-married couples, memory for events may be distributed among the members of a group (Wegner et al., 1985). Acquiring a complete account of an event—a collective memory—may require obtaining contributions from all members of the group. To study memory distribution in groups, Weldon (2000) proposed a social-network analysis of collective memory. However, the concept of collective memory goes beyond the idea that memory for events is dispersed among members of a group. Memory both emerges from and supports social interaction (Halbwachs, 1980). For example, the growth of autobiographical memory in children depends upon collaborative recall of parent and child (Farrant and Reese, 2000); researchers have studied collective memories of cultures by obtaining memory reports from people of different nationalities. A full understanding of collective memory may require interdisciplinary efforts.

See also: COLLECTIVE MEMORY

Bibliography

Andersson, J., and Rönnberg, J. (1996). Collaboration and memory: Effects of dyadic retrieval on different memory tasks. *Applied Cognitive Psychology 10*, 171–181.

Basden, B. H., Basden, D. R., Bryner, S., and Thomas, Robert L. III (1997). A comparison of group and individual remembering: Does collaboration disrupt retrieval strategies? *Journal of Experimental Psychology: Learning, Memory, and Cognition 23*, 1,176–1,189.

Basden, B. H., Basden, D. R., Thomas, R. L., III, and Souphasith, S. (1998). Memory distortions in collaborative recall. *Current Psychology 16*, 225–246.

Basden, B. H., Henry, S., and Basden, D. R. (2001). Costs and benefits of collaborative remembering. *Applied Cognitive Psychology 14*, 497–507.

Clark, N. K., and Stephenson, G. M. (1989). Group remembering. In P. B. Paulus, ed., *Psychology of Group Influence*, 3rd edition. Hillsdale, NJ: Erlbaum.

Clark, S. E., Hori, A., Putnam, A., and Martin, T. P. (2000). Group collaboration in recognition memory. *Journal of Experimental Psychology: Learning, Memory, and Cognition 26*, 1,578–1,588.

Dixon, R. A., and Gould, O. N. (1998). Younger and older adults collaborating on retelling everyday stories. *Applied Developmental Science 2*, 160–171.

Farrant, K., and Reese, E. (2000). Maternal style and children's participation in reminiscing: Stepping stones in children's autobiographical memory development. *Journal of Cognition and Development 1*, 193–225.

Finlay, F., Hitch, G. J., and Meudell, P. R. (2000). Mutual inhibition in collaborative recall: Evidence for a retrieval-based account. *Journal of Experimental Psychology: Learning, Memory, and Cognition 26*, 1,556–1,567.

Halbwachs, M. (1950; reprint 1980). *The collective memory*, trans. F. J. Ditter, Jr., and V. Y. Ditter. New York: Harper and Row.

Johansson, O., Andersson, J., and Rönnberg, J. (2000). Do elderly couples have a better prospective memory than other elderly people when they collaborate? *Applied Cognitive Psychology 14*, 121–133.

Roediger, H. L., Meade, M. L., and Bergman, E. T. (2001). Social contagion of memory. *Psychological Bulletin and Review 8*, 365–371.

Schneider, D. M., and Watkins, M. J. (1996). Response conformity in recognition testing. *Psychonomic Bulletin & Review 3*, 481–483.

Wegner, D. M., Giuliano, T., and Hertel, P. T. (1985). Cognitive interdependence in close relationships. In W. Ickes, ed., *Compatible and incompatible*. New York: Springer-Verlag.

Weldon, M. S. (2000). Remembering as a social process. In Medin, D. L., ed., *Psychology of Learning and Motivation*, Vol. 40. San Diego: Academic Press.

Weldon, M. S., and Bellinger, K. D. (1997). Collective memory: Collaborative and individual processes in remembering. *Journal of Experimental Psychology: Learning, Memory, and Cognition 23*, 1,160–1,175.

Weldon, M. S., Blair, C., and Huebsch, P. D. (2000). Group remembering: Does social loafing underlie collaborative inhibition? *Journal of Experimental Psychology: Learning, Memory, and Cognition 26*, 1,568–1,577.

Yarmey, A. D., and Morris, S. (1998). The effects of discussion on eyewitness memory. *Journal of Applied Social Psychology 28*, 1,637–1,648.

Barbara H. Basden

SOMETIMES OPPONENT PROCESS (SOP) MODEL, IN CONDITIONING

Sometimes opponent process (SOP) is an associative, real-time, quantitative theory of Pavlovian conditioning. As such, it describes basic principles from which the behavioral regularities of Pavlonian conditioning can be deduced, and it makes predictions about yet-to-be observed Pavlovian phenomena. It specifies rules for stimulus representation, how learning occurs, and how learning that cannot be observed directly in translated into performance. This article does not present the equations that describe these principles, but they are available in related articles (Mazur and Wagner, 1982; Wagner, 1981).

SOP's Basic Principles

Theories of learning assume that experiences are recorded in a theoretical memory system. They describe how that memory system is conceptualized, how experiences come to be represented, and how memories affect behavior. As for any theory, these basic principles are the assumptions the theory makes from which the predictions will follow. A good theory strives to explain the observable phenomena through a priori assumptions that are as few and as simple as possible.

SOP assumes that experiences activate corresponding theoretical representations in the memory system. For example, a cat hears the sound of a can opener and then is fed; these events may activate corresponding sound and food representations. The cat does not have to learn how to represent these incoming events. What it does learn is how to associate one event with another; that is, the cat may learn to associate the sound of the can opener with the food, as a function of experiencing that sound and the food together in time and space. As is common in psychological theories, SOP assumes that memories—or, representations—become associated with each other as a function of their temporal and spatial contiguity, and that what is learned are changes in connections (associations) among representations. SOP further proposes that observable behavior reflects which representations are being processed, and how strong their processing is.

The central principle of SOP is that stimulus representation consists of a large but finite set of theoretical elements that are in one of three dynamic states. This is illustrated in Figure 1a. To use the cat-food example: When the cat encounters the food, elements in the corresponding cat-food representation are activated. The course of activation is determined: there is a brief period of focal processing during which the elements are in a state designated A1. These elements do not stay long in this focal activation state, however, but decay passively into a secondary, more peripheral state designated A2. Eventually, when the food is no longer present, the elements passively decay further into inactivity (I). How long an element might be in each dynamic state depends on three parameters: p_1, which reflects the perceived salience of the incoming stimulus and is assumed to increase monotonically with the intensity of the stimulus; p_{d1}, which determines how likely an element is to go from A1 to A2; and p_{d2}, which determines how likely an element is to go from A2 to I. It is assumed that $p_{d1}p_{d2}$.

Stimulus Representation

Figure 2 depicts the application of these rules for elemental dynamics to the instance of exposure to a stimulus that occurs in real time. The figure shows the proportion of total stimulus representation elements that are active across time. In each moment in which the stimulus is presented, p1 of the inactive elements are activated to the A1 state. However, pd1 of those elements in A1 also decay to A2. The result is an A1 function that shows an increase followed by a decrease and relative flattening, until the stimulus is withdrawn and there is decay to inactivity. The form of the A1 function, which is SOP's stimulus representation, is similar to that which has been observed in psychophysical experiments with human subjects who are asked to estimate the perceived intensity of a stimulus (e.g., light, sound, or smell) across time. They report an initial growth in the intensity of sensation followed by a decrease—an adaptation to the stimulus—before it is turned off (Marks, 1974).

Rules for Learning

In SOP, learning—the acquisition of associations between stimulus representations—is determined by the conjunction of active A1 and A2 elements. If the sound of the can opener is considered a conditioned stimulus (CS), and the food an unconditioned stimulus (US), then an excitatory association between that CS and US will come about to the extent that the elements that represent the CS and the elements that represent the US are currently in the A1 state. The likelihood of such concurrent CS_{A1} and US_{A1} activation increases with the degree of contiguity of the two events. An excitatory association is one that may activate the representations that are linked; hearing the opener now may elicit a memory of food.

SOP captures the difference between the experience of an event and its memory by assuming that associatively activated representations reach only the A2 processing level. Thus, once an association be-

Figure 1

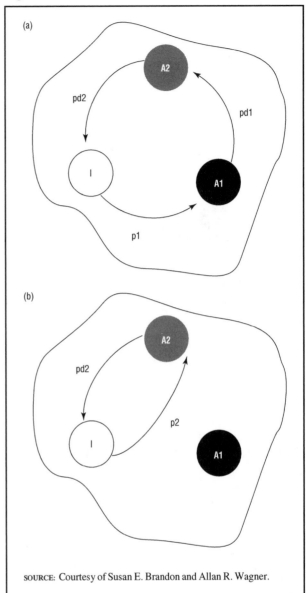

(a) A depiction of a node in the memory system of SOP, presumed to be activated by a peripheral stimulus in a Pavlovian conditioning situation. The connected circles within each node represent the three activity states in which nodal elements may reside, and the connecting paths show the allowable state transitions. (b) The dynamic states (circles) and the allowable course of activation (paths) for an SOP node that is activated by another, associated node.

tween a CS and US is established, a CS may activate its associated US representation to its A2 processing state, i.e., US_{A2}. This is shown in Figure 1b as the direct link from I to A2. The likelihood of such activation is determined by the parameter p2, which is a function of the strength of the CS trace and the strength of the association.

Figure 2

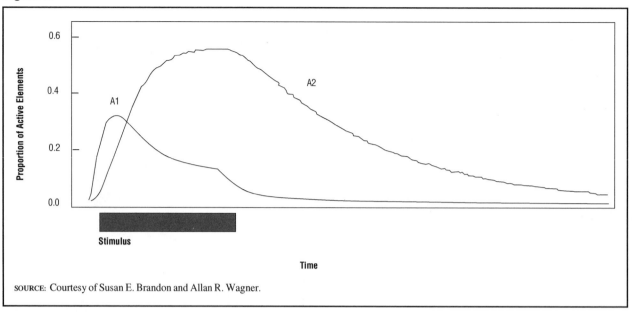

SOURCE: Courtesy of Susan E. Brandon and Allan R. Wagner.

The proportion of total elements that are in A1 and A2 across time with the presentation of a peripheral stimulus.

Associative strength can also be inhibitory, where an inhibitory association may make it harder for one representation to activate another to which it is linked. Inhibitory associative strength grows when the elements of one representation are in A1 and elements of another are in A2. An effective way to produce an inhibitory CS-US association is to present the US first and then the CS. This should be effective to the extent that it ensures the concurrent processing of CS_{A1} with US_{A2}. Excitatory tendencies (V^+) and inhibitory tendencies (V^-) are assumed to summate in a single associative connection (σV) that may have a net excitatory or net inhibitory strength.

Rules for Performance

The performance rule in SOP follows from its assumptions about dynamic states and the nature of the learned associations: a conditioned response (CR) is functionally the same as the behavior that is elicited by the A2 processing state of the stimulus with which it is associated. The behavior that is identified as a CR, therefore, can be elicited by presenting the associated US and looking for its secondary (A2) response.

Acquisition and Extinction

Figure 3a shows the expected change in net associative strength and the corresponding stimulus traces and increments in V^+ and V^- for a first CS-US pairing, a fiftieth CS-US pairing when learning is as-

ymptotic, and an initial extinction trial (Figure 3b). On Acquisition, Trial 1, there is a considerable overlap of CS_{A1} and US_{A1}, along with smaller overlap of CS_{A1} and US_{A2}. (There is overlap of CS_{A2} and US_{A1} and US_{A2} also, but the associations thus formed are presumed to have little behavioral effect.) The contiguous CS_{A1}/US_{A1} processing produces a relatively large increase in V^+, and the smaller CS_{A1} and US_{A2} overlap produces relatively little V^-, resulting in a relatively large gain in σV_{CS-US}. After many pairings (Acquisition, Trial 50), the onset of the CS elicits US_{A2} processing as a function of the associative connection that is established; that is, the CS now results in a CR (recall that the CR reflects US_{A2} processing). There also is a reduction in US_{A1} when the US is presented because of the effect of the CS to put elements into US_{A2}, making these elements unavailable for activation to US_{A1}. This reduction in US_{A1} processing can be seen in a reduced unconditioned response (UR) to the US, where the primary UR is assumed to reflect US_{A1} processing. Finally, because the US is not present until the end of the CS period, there also is considerable overlap of CS_{A1} and US_{A2}, which results in an increment in V^-. At asymptote, the V^+ and V^- cancel each other out, and there is no net change in associative strength. The negatively accelerated course of learning, the elicitation of a CR by a CS, and the so-called conditioned diminution of the UR to that US, are fundamental behavioral characteristics of Pavlovian conditioning.

Figure 3

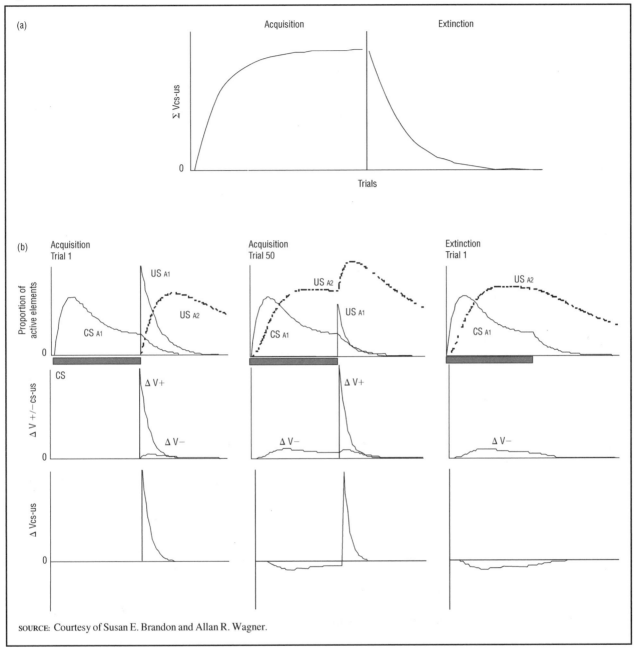

SOURCE: Courtesy of Susan E. Brandon and Allan R. Wagner.

(a) Predicted $\sigma V_{CS\text{-}US}$ for a series of acquisition trials followed by a series of extinction trials. (b) Simulated activity in CS and US nodes and resulting changes in $V^+_{CS\text{-}US}$, $V^-_{CS\text{-}US}$, and $\delta V_{CS\text{-}US}$ are shown for the first acquisition trial, the fiftieth acquisition trial, and the first extinction trial.

Extinction occurs (Extinction, Trial 1) with CS-alone trials. Now, because the CS has the capacity to elicit US_{A2} processing, there is an increment in V^- and no counteracting increment in V^+, since the US is not presented. With continued presentations of the CS alone, there is a gradual decrease in $\sigma V_{CS\text{-}US}$ and less and less of a tendency for the CR to be elicited. The latter also is a behavioral characteristic of Pavlovian conditioning.

Cue-Competition Effects

SOP explains cue-competition effects in Pavlovian conditioning with the same principles as those that explain acquisition and extinction. One powerful cue competition effect is blocking, a condition in which learning a CS-US association fails in spite of the good temporal contiguity of the two stimuli. For example, suppose that the cat of our previous example had previously learned to associate the turning on of the kitchen light with food and that only then did we present the sound of the can opener and the light together preceding the food. Now the cat would be unlikely to learn to make a conditioned response to the sound. It appears that previously learning to associate the light with food makes the normally effective pairing of sound and food ineffective for association.

The blocking effect can be understood with reference to the functions in Figure 3 for Acquisition Trial 50. Here, the previously trained CS (the light) regularly elicits a CR, reflecting the US_{A2} processing elicited by that CS. The addition of the novel CS (the sound), will result in the overlap of $CS_{A1-sound}$ with the same US_{A1} and subsequent US_{A2} processing that is elicited already by the conjunction of $CS_{A1-light}$ and the US. That is, there will be an initial increment in V^-, followed by a comparable increment in V^+, that will accrue equally for both CSs. Since V^- and V^+ balance out, there is no net increment in either association. The CS_{sound} US association, starting at 0, thereby fails to acquire any σV. That is, the cat will not learn a sound-food association.

Conclusion

SOP is able to explain much of what is known about Pavlovian conditioning, including cue-competition effects. By rationalizing excitatory and inhibitory learning in terms of A1/A1 and A1/A2 conjunctions in time, it allows us to understand how the outcome of a conditioning trial depends on the order of the CS and US and the difference between simple conditioning and conditioned inhibition training. By rationalizing priming effects in terms of A1 and A2 effects over time, it allows us to understand blocking (as shown above), as well as short-term habituation and pre-trial CS and US exposure effects. By rationalizing the relationship of a CR and UR as the CR reflecting only US_{A2} processing, without the US_{A1} processing additionally elicited by the US, we can understand why the CR sometimes mimics the UR and sometimes does not.

Extensions of the SOP model have been developed to increase its theoretical power, to allow for an understanding of occasion setting (Brandon and Wagner, 1998), CR timing (Brandon, Vogel, and Wagner, 2002), and various differences in Pavlovian conditioning involving skeletal versus emotional responses (Wagner and Brandon, 1989). Wagner and Donegan (1989) have further indicated how it may relate to the known neural circuitry for eyeblink conditioning.

See also: ALGORITHMS, LEARNING; CONDITIONING, CELLULAR AND NETWORK SCHEMES FOR HIGHER-ORDER FEATURES OF; KAMIN'S BLOCKING EFFECT: NEURONAL SUBSTRATES; LEARNING THEORY: A HISTORY; LEARNING THEORY: CURRENT STATUS; MATHEMATICAL LEARNING THEORY; NEURAL COMPUTATION: APPROACHES TO LEARNING

Bibliography

Brandon, S. E., Vogel, E. H., and Wagner, A. R. (2002). Computational theories of classical conditioning. In J. W. Moore, ed., *A neuroscientist's guide to classical conditioning.* London: Cambridge University Press.

Brandon, S. E., and Wagner, A. R. (1998). Occasion setting: Influences of conditioned emotional responses and configural cues. In N. Schmajuk and P. Holland, eds., *Occasion setting: Associative learning and cognition in animals.* Washington, DC: American Psychological Association

Marks, L. E. (1964). *Sensory processes.* New York: Academic Press.

Mazur, J. E., and Wagner, A. R. (1982). An episodic model of associative learning, in M. L. Commons, R. J. Herrnstein, and A. R. Wagner, eds., *Quantitative analyses of behavior*, Vol. 3: *Acquisition.* Cambridge, MA: Ballinger.

Wagner, A. R. (1981). SOP: A model of automatic memory processing in animal behavior. In N. E. Spear and R. R. Miller, eds., *Information processing in animals: Memory mechanisms.* Hillsdale, NJ: Erlbaum.

Wagner, A. R., and Brandon, S. E. (1989). Evolution of a structured connectionist model of Pavlovian conditioning (AESOP). In S. B. Klein and R. R. Mowrer, eds., *Contemporay learning theories: Pavlovian conditioning and the status of traditional learning theory.* Hillsdale, NJ: Erlbaum.

——— (2001). A componential theory of Pavlovian conditioning. In R. R. Mowrer and S. B. Klein, eds., *Handbook of contemporary Learning Theory.* Mahway, NJ: Erlbaum.

Wagner, A. R., and Donegan, N. H. (1989). Some relationships between a computational model (SOP) and an essential neural circuit for Pavlovian (rabbit eyeblink) conditioning. In R. D. Hawkins and G. H. Bower, eds., *The psychology lf learning and motivation*, Vol. 23: *Computational models of learning in simple neural systems.* Orlando, FL: Academic Press.

Susan E. Brandon
Allan R. Wagner

SOURCE MONITORING

Source monitoring refers to cognitive processes involved in making attributions about the origins of mental experiences; for example, attributing a mental experience to something dreamed, something imagined, or a perceived event. The concept of source memory overlaps with, but is more general than, the idea of memory for context. Source monitoring is an important aspect of everyday cognition, for example, in deciding whether one took one's medication or just thought about taking it, read about a space alien invasion in a tabloid or a news magazine, or really saw the defendant at the crime scene with a knife or just heard about the knife later. Errors in source monitoring range from the trivial (telling a joke to the same person you heard it from) to the egregious (mistaking a memory of a dream of being sexually abused for a memory of a real event from childhood).

Marcia Johnson and her colleagues (1993) have detailed a theoretical framework for understanding the cognitive processes and factors that influence source memory. According to the source monitoring framework, any given mental experience typically does not include a single feature or tag or label specifying what it is (e.g., a memory of a dream, an imagination, a perception). Rather, people attribute some mental experiences to memories based on the experience's features. Events have many features (objects, location, people, color, taste, emotions, ongoing thoughts), some of which are encoded in memory; a few or many of these features may be brought to mind (reactivated) after only a few minutes or years later. What a person calls that later mental experience depends on what features it includes and on the person's beliefs about the differences between mental experiences from different sources. For example, people usually expect memories for events (sometimes called episodic memory) to contain details reflecting such aspects as the who, what, when, where, why, and how of the event. A mental experience that does not have such details might be attributed to, for example, inference, general knowledge, or belief, depending on the particular features it does have.

Different types of encoding processes (e.g., seeing, hearing, thinking, dreaming) and different types of events (e.g., movie, telephone call) tend to produce memorial representations that are characteristically different from each other. For example, memories of imagined events typically have less vivid perceptual, temporal, and spatial information than perceived events and more information about intentional cognitive operations (e.g., actively generating images while thinking). Therefore, if a mental experience had substantial perceptual detail, one would tend to attribute it to a perceived event (e.g., something one saw). However, there is variability among memories from any particular source, and the distributions of features from different sources overlap. For example, some dreams are more vivid or plausible than some waking events. Thus, remembering always involves evaluating the quality and quantity of activated characteristics in light of expectations about typical characteristics of mental experiences from various sources.

Source attributions are often made rapidly and without deliberation based on heuristic judgments about activated features. However, source monitoring sometimes entails more systematic processes that are typically slower and more deliberate, including retrieving additional information, extended reasoning, and so on. For example, a vivid memory of Frank talking to Paul at a party might be contradicted by retrieving additional information that places Frank out of town at the time of the party. Similar distinctions between relatively automatic and more controlled processes of remembering have been made by L. Hasher and R. Zacks (1979), L. Jacoby and C. Kelley (1989), and other researchers. Both heuristic and systematic source attributions are affected by a rememberer's biases, goals, agendas, and meta-memory beliefs. For example, one will usually engage more systematic source monitoring processes if the cost of a mistake is high, but engage only relatively automatic, heuristic processes for most everyday remembering.

Historical Context

The concept of reality monitoring was introduced in the early 1980s by M. K. Johnson and C. L. Raye (1981) to explain how memories for internal events (e.g., thoughts, imaginations) are discriminated from memories for external, perceived events, and why they are sometimes confused. This concept was subsumed by the more general source monitoring framework in the early 1990s. The theoretical ideas incorporated in the source monitoring framework were proposed to help organize and understand diverse findings and guide additional research. For example, studies in the 1950s and 1960s showed that people falsely recall (Deese, 1959) or falsely recognize (Underwood, 1965) associates of presented words: Hearing *thread, haystack, sharp,* and so on, can lead people to misremember hearing *needle,* presumably because they thought of *needle* during study and later mistake the thought for an actual presentation of the word. In the 1970s, M. K. Johnson and J. D. Bransford and colleagues (1973) showed that people falsely recognize ideas that were only implied in sentences. For example, after hearing, "The man *dropped* the delicate glass pitcher on the floor" people often remember hearing, "The man *broke* the delicate glass pitcher on the floor." The 1970s and 1980s produced many studies showing that people's memory for experiences tends to be shaped by their expectations or schemas (see Alba and Hasher, 1983, for a review). For example, W. F. Brewer and J. C. Treyens (1981) showed that people who had briefly waited in an office were likely to falsely remember items such as books, which were not in the office but might be expected to be, and to not remember unexpected items that were there (e.g., a skull). E. F. Loftus and colleagues (1978) showed that information introduced when people were questioned about an event was later sometimes (mis)remembered as part of the original event.

Such findings illustrate that people confuse information from different sources. For example, as part of their normal comprehension processes, people think of related information during encoding or remembering (or both) and misattribute this information to the actual event. Other times, they confuse what they saw with what they heard or read, or confuse two similar experiences. Yet, sometimes memory is quite accurate. The source monitoring framework specifies the factors that influence the likelihood that memory will be accurate or distorted.

Factors Affecting Source Monitoring

Source monitoring depends on the type, amount, and quality of activated information, the extent to which the active information helps uniquely specify the source, the judgment processes engaged, the weights assigned to different features, and the criteria used when making the source attribution. Neither the activated features (representations) nor the processes that act on them are perfect, and thus errors occur. A basic tenet of the source monitoring framework is that inaccurate source monitoring (sometimes called source confusions, source misattributions, source errors, source amnesia, source forgetting, memory distortions, or false memories) and accurate source monitoring arise via the same mechanisms.

Anything that disrupts the encoding, consolidation, or retention of the features of events will negatively affect source monitoring. For example, at encoding, divided attention or focusing on one's own emotions rather than event details can increase source monitoring errors, presumably because useful source-specifying information fails to be, or is weakly, bound to other features of the event. Errors increase when the diagnosticity of available source information is reduced, for example, when semantic or perceptual similarity between events from different sources is increased. Errors also increase when more lax criteria are used to evaluate mental experiences, features are weighted inappropriately, attention is divided at test, or the time that is available to make a source judgment is limited. Individual motives and the social/cultural context can influence all of these factors.

The general view that remembering is not a simple matter of "retrieving" memory traces but rather a subjective experience with phenomenal qualities that differ in important ways has generated new interest in assessing the subjective qualities of memories. One approach asks people to distinguish between items they *know* and items they *remember*; another uses memory characteristics questionnaires to elicit more detailed ratings of features of memories. For example, such studies have shown that, on average, false memories tend to be rated as having less perceptual detail than true memories.

Brain Regions Involved in Source Monitoring

Neuroimaging data (e.g., from functional magnetic resonance imaging) together with neuropsychological studies of brain damaged patients with amnesia indicate that the hippocampus plays a central role in the binding of features into complex representations—a process critical for later source monitoring. Profound disruptions in source monitoring, such as delusions, hallucinations, and confabulations, can arise from damage to frontal brain regions, indicating that these regions are critical for source monitoring. Neuroimaging studies that show activation of frontal regions during source monitoring in healthy individuals provide converging evidence. Children and older adults have more difficulty with source monitoring than do college-aged adults, particularly as the similarity of the sources increases. Researchers have suggested that such findings may reflect the relatively late maturation of frontal functions in children and the increased probability of pathology in frontal regions associated with aging. One goal of current neuroimaging work is to more clearly delineate the brain circuits underlying the encoding, revival, and evaluation of memories.

Bibliography

Alba, J. W., and Hasher, L. (1983). Is memory schematic? *Psychological Bulletin 93*, 203–231.

Belli, R. F., and Loftus, E. F. (1994). Recovered memories of childhood abuse: A source monitoring perspective. In S. J. Lynn and J. W. Rhue, eds., *Dissociation: Clinical and theoretical perspectives*. New York: Guilford Press.

Brewer, W. F., and Treyens, J. C. (1981). Role of schemata in memory for places. *Cognitive Psychology 13*, 207–230.

Deese, J. (1959). On the prediction of occurrence of particular verbal intrusions in immediate recall. *Journal of Experimental Psychology 58*, 17–22.

Gardiner, J. M., and Richardson-Klavehn, A. (2000). Remembering and knowing. In E. Tulving and F. I. M. Craik, eds., *The Oxford handbook of memory*. New York: Oxford University Press.

Hasher, L., and Zacks, R. T. (1979). Automatic and effortful processes in memory. *Journal of Experimental Psychology: General 108*, 356–388.

Hintzman, D. L. (2000). Memory judgments. In E. Tulving and F.I. M. Craik, eds., *The Oxford handbook of memory*. New York: Oxford University Press.

Jacoby, L. L., Kelley, C. M., and Dywan, J. (1989). Memory attributions. In H. L. Roediger, III, and F. I. M. Craik, eds., *Varieties of memory and consciousness: Essays in honour of Endel Tulving*. Hillsdale, NJ: Erlbaum.

Johnson, M. K. (1997). Source monitoring and memory distortion. *Philosophical Transactions of the Royal Society of London 352*, 1,733–1,745.

Johnson, M. K., Bransford, J. D., and Solomon, S. K. (1973). Memory for tacit implications of sentences. *Journal of Experimental Psychology 98*, 203–204.

Johnson, M. K., Hashtroudi, S., and Lindsay, D. S. (1993). Source monitoring. *Psychological Bulletin 114*, 3–28.

Johnson, M. K., Hayes, S. M., D'Esposito, M., and Raye, C. L. (2000). Confabulation. In J. Grafman and F. Boller, eds.,

Handbook of neuropsychology, 2nd edition. Amsterdam, Netherlands: Elservier Science.

Johnson, M. K., and Raye, C. L. (1981). Reality monitoring. *Psychological Review* 88, 67–85.

——— (1998). False memories and confabulation. *Trends in Cognitive Sciences* 2, 137–145.

Loftus, E. F., Miller, D. G., and Burns, H. J. (1978). Semantic integration of verbal information into a visual memory. *Journal of Experimental Psychology: Human Learning and Memory* 4, 19–31.

Mitchell, K. J., and Johnson, M. K. (2000). Source monitoring: Attributing mental experiences. In E. Tulving and F. I. M. Craik, eds., *The Oxford handbook of memory.* New York: Oxford University Press.

Roberts, K. P., and Blades, M., eds. (2000). *Children's source monitoring.* Mahwah, NJ: Erlbaum.

Roediger, H. L., III (1996). Memory illusions. *Journal of Memory and Language* 35, 76–100.

Schacter, D. L., Norman, K. A., and Koutstaal, W. (1998). The cognitive neuroscience of constructive memory. *Annual Review of Psychology* 49, 289–318.

Spencer, W. D., and Raz, N. (1995). Differential effects of aging on memory for content and context: A meta-analysis. *Psychology and Aging* 10, 527–539.

Underwood, B. J. (1965). False recognition produced by implicit verbal responses. *Journal of Experimental Psychology* 70, 122–129.

Marcia K. Johnson
Karen J. Mitchell

SPACED TRAINING

See: DISTRIBUTED PRACTICE EFFECTS

SPATIAL LEARNING: ANIMALS

Resources that animals need are usually distributed patchily within their home range, and many animals learn where they are and how to reach them. Stuart Altman describes how one troop of baboons responded to ripe berries on an isolated bush in the center of their home range as a sign of their availability elsewhere and trekked to a remote patch of bushes bearing the same fruit.

Some animals cache food when it is abundant, remember the precise locations of the caches for long periods, and return to empty the caches when food is scarce. Clark's nutcracker provides a dramatic example. The birds collect tens of thousands of pine seeds in the autumn for recovery during the subsequent winter and spring. Scrub jays caching food in the laboratory remember not only where they have cached it but also which items they have stored in which locations. Proof came from an experiment by Nicola Clayton and Anthony Dickinson in which birds were given two different foods to cache. Before the birds were allowed to recover either food, they were prefed with one. Prefeeding caused the birds to focus their search on sites containing the other untasted and so more appealing food—a result that implies that birds know where they have hidden particular food items. By using food that rapidly rots, the same experimenters showed that scrub jays also know when they made the cache. Lastly, birds remember that they have emptied a cache, and they avoid revisiting empty sites. Other resources that animals remember include watering sites, nests, places where mates are to be encountered, shelters, and bolt holes. Spatial knowledge is closely integrated with other forms of knowledge that may influence what spatial information is stored, when it is retrieved, and how long it is remembered.

Some animals have evolved set procedures for acquiring needed navigational information. Indigo buntings learn the constellations of stars around the North Star, and they use that constellation for guidance in their migration. The birds are preprogrammed to learn the unique pattern of stationary stars that lies close to the Earth's axis of rotation and so do not move across the night sky. Wasps and bees perform highly structured learning or orientation flights when first leaving a new feeding site or their nest. The flight is designed to emphasise landmarks that are close to the goal and that can thus provide precise navigational information. In a single such flight, they learn enough about the arrangement of landmarks to be able to return there. Rats explore a new environment and reexplore a familiar one when changes occur. During exploration they learn the layout of the environment without the benefit of any immediate reward. In one experiment to demonstrate such learning, rats explored a T-maze with two visually distinct goal boxes and with all extra-maze cues screened off. After the rats had explored the empty maze several times, they were placed singly in one of the goal boxes and allowed to eat there. When re-placed at the entrance, most rats returned directly to the box where they had been fed. A control group fed in one goal box without prior exploration of that particular maze showed no tendency to return to the same box. Exploration allows the rats to learn the paths to different recognized locations that only later come to be associated with a valued resource.

It is remarkable that a wide array of animals, from insects to primates, acquire and store the same two distinct types of spatial information. One kind is derived from dead reckoning, also known as path integration. An animal leaving its home base continuously monitors the direction and distance of the path that it takes and uses this path-derived information to keep an updated record of its direction and distance from home. Consequently, it is always able to take a direct path home, even after a circuitous outward journey. On finding a good source of food, both insects and mammals store the path integration coordinates of the food site. Equipped with these stored coordinates, they can later return to that site by subtracting the coordinates of the site from their current coordinates as given by path integration.

The second kind of stored spatial information does not have positional coordinates attached to it. It comes from memories of visual landmarks that can indicate a site or a route or signal what kind of action the animal ought to perform there. It is still unclear whether there exists in any animal an intimate connection between memories of landmarks and their positional coordinates. In insects the available evidence suggests that memories of landmarks and of positional coordinates are kept separate.

Some insects, birds, and possibly mammals learn the position of a site in terms of the distance and direction of one or more visual landmarks from it. They then return to the site by moving until their current distances and directions from those landmarks match the stored ones. Precision in locating the site is enhanced by learning the distances and directions of several landmarks and by emphasizing information that comes from landmarks that are nearer to the site. It is likely that mammals also learn the spatial relationships between landmarks, but experimental corroboration has proved elusive.

The richness of animals' memories of the arrangement of landmarks is illustrated by an experiment by David Brodbeck on chickadees. It showed that these birds learn a caching site in terms of several potential retrieval cues. Birds were trained to find seeds in one wooden block in an array of four differently decorated blocks that were attached to a wall in a large aviary. The site is thus specified by room cues, position in the array, and the appearance of the baited block. On test trials the array was shifted as a group, so that one block was moved to the location occupied by the baited block, and the other blocks in the array were rearranged. Birds in these tests looked for their seeds following a consistent order. They first searched at the site that was specified by the landmarks in the room, then at the site defined by position within the array of blocks, and lastly in the block that was correctly decorated. Birds had thus learned all these properties of the caching site and were guided by them in a set hierarchy.

A similar example of a predisposition to learn multiple features of the surroundings of a significant site comes from insects. Honeybees learn both the local landmarks that pinpoint a site and the panoramic context within which the local landmarks are set. As a bee flies within the vicinity of the site, the appearance of the distant panorama changes less with the bee's movements than does the appearance of local landmarks. Consequently the distant panorama can be recognized more reliably than the local landmarks. Insects exploit this piece of ecological geometry and use their memory of the panorama to prime the recall of local landmarks, which can thus be identified when viewed from unusual viewpoints or under unusual lighting conditions.

To reach a desired goal animals either follow familiar paths or, more rarely, plan a new route from an arbitrary starting point to a goal that is not visible from the starting point. Evidence for such route planning comes from a study by Charles Menzel and colleagues on a young Bonobo chimpanzee, Kanzi. Kanzi could be told through lexigrams which out of several goals in a familiar wooded area he should head for. The chimpanzee was led to an arbitrary starting point and then given a lexigram signaling a familiar location that was out of sight and that harbored food or some other desirable item. On all occasions Kanzi led a human companion to the correct location. Sometimes Kanzi took direct trails, and sometimes he followed a more indirect path. There is as yet little understanding of the behavioral mechanisms underlying route planning.

Although ants and bees can reach a familiar feeding site solely by means of path integration, they notice and approach prominent objects on the route and rapidly come to learn the appearance of these landmarks. The landmarks are used to segment the route, and insects learn vectors of the appropriate direction and distance to take them from one landmark to the next. The division of a route into sections increases the insect's chances of reaching its goal. First, prominent beacons that attract the insect at the end of each segment make it easy to correct for inaccurate vectors or crosswinds that deflect the insect from its proper path. Second, the precision with which the insect is delivered to its goal depends on the accuracy of the vector from the final beacon rather than on a vector covering the whole path from start to finish. Again we see that animals are naturally biased to learn features of their environment that improve navigational accuracy. Spatial learning is strongly guided by built-in mechanisms and strategies that predispose animals to learn about navigationally useful features of their environment, often in anticipation of their need for later guidance.

See also: FORAGING; MIGRATION, NAVIGATION, AND HOMING; PLACE CELLS; SPATIAL MEMORY

Bibliography

Healy, S. D., ed. (1998). *Spatial representation in animals.* Oxford: Oxford University Press.

Pearce, J. M. (1997). *Animal learning and cognition,* 2nd edition. Hove, UK: Psychology Press.

Shettleworth, S. J. (1998). *Cognition, evolution, and behavior*. New York: Oxford University Press.

Lynn Nadel
Revised by Thomas S. Collett

SPATIAL MEMORY

Spatial memory pertains to the spatial structure of outdoor spaces, buildings, rooms, and maps; it includes knowledge of where objects are, of routes from place to place, and of distances and directions between locations. The evolutionary success of humans has depended, in part, on abilities to navigate in unfamiliar territory, to locate sources of food and water, and to be able to return to those sources and to home at a later time. In contemporary societies, people rely on their spatial memories for activities as mundane as reaching out in the morning darkness to shut off an alarm and as consequential as escaping from an office building during a raging fire. The spatial memories of insects, rodents, and nonhuman primates have been investigated extensively (Gallistel, 1990), but this chapter will focus on aspects of human spatial memory.

Route versus Survey Knowledge

Large-scale environments cannot be viewed in their entirety from a single vantage point and therefore can only be learned via navigation. When people learn a large-scale environment without the aid of a map, their knowledge initially consists of routes from place to place. With sufficient experience, people may learn the straight-line (Euclidean) distances and directions between locations and perhaps gain maplike or survey knowledge of the environment (Thorndyke and Hayes Roth, 1982). At one time researchers thought that route knowledge had to precede survey knowledge (Siegel and White, 1975). Recent studies have shown that the type of knowledge acquired depends on the goals of the learner, irrespective of the learning experience. For example, people perform better on survey knowledge tasks (e.g., drawing a map) when their goal is to learn the overall layout of an environment than when their goal is to learn routes, regardless of whether they learn the environment from a map or from navigation (Taylor, Naylor, and Chechile, 1999).

Orientation Dependence

An important property of spatial memories is that information is easier to retrieve from some perspectives than from others. Commit Figure 1 to memory. Then make the following judgments without looking

Figure 1

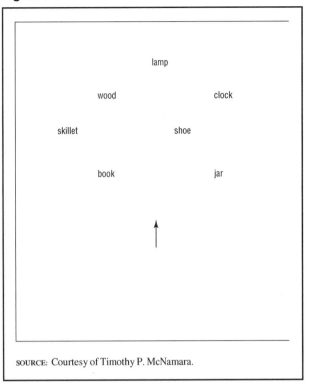

SOURCE: Courtesy of Timothy P. McNamara.

An example of the types of layouts used to investigate the orientation dependence of spatial memory. Objects are placed on the floor of a large room. Participants memorize the layout from one or more study views, and then make judgments of relative direction using their memories (e.g., Imagine you are standing at the clock and facing the shoe. Point to the skillet). The arrow indicates a possible viewing position.

at the figure: (a) Imagine you are standing at the book and facing the wood. Point to the clock. (b) Imagine you are standing at the wood and facing the shoe. Point to the book. Problem (a) is easier than (b), even though the pointing direction is the same. This phenomenon is an example of orientation dependence, and it is observed in many tasks and in memories of maps, rooms, and large-scale environments, even when several views are learned (Shelton and McNamara, 2001). Although there may be situations in which spatial memories are orientation independent, such that familiar and unfamiliar views are retrieved and recognized equally efficiently (Evans and Pezdek, 1980), these situations are the exception.

Orientation dependence has typically taken the form of better performance on familiar views and perspectives, as in (a), than on unfamiliar views and perspectives, as in (b), but other patterns have also been observed (Mou and McNamara, 2002). An important consequence of the orientation dependence of spatial memories is that people sometimes get lost when returning from a destination. The environment looks different coming and going.

Spatial Reference Systems

The concept of location is inherently relative. One cannot describe or specify the location of an object without providing a frame of reference. The location of a chair in a classroom, for example, can be specified in terms of the room itself (e.g., the chair is in the corner by the door), other chairs in the room (e.g., the chair is in the first row and second column), or an observer (e.g., the chair is in front of me). The primate brain represents spatial information using many types of spatial reference systems (Anderson, Snyder, Bradley, and Xiang, 1997).

Spatial reference systems fall into two categories: egocentric reference systems, which specify location and orientation with respect to the observer (as in, the chair is in front of me); and environmental reference systems, which define spatial relations with respect to elements of the environment, such as the perceived direction of gravity, landmarks, or the floor, ceiling, and walls of a room (as in, the chair is in the corner by the door).

Human spatial memories rely primarily on environmental reference systems (Shelton and McNamara, 2001). When people learn a map, locations of objects in a room, or even larger spaces, they select a reference system in the environment for representing its spatial structure. The particular reference system that is selected depends on the person's experiences, the structure of the environment itself, and spatial and nonspatial properties of objects in the environment. This process is similar to determining the "top" of a figure or an object (Rock, 1973; Tversky, 1981); in effect, conceptual "north" (and perhaps, south, east, and west) is assigned to the layout, creating privileged directions in memory of the environment (conceptual north need not correspond to true or magnetic north or any other cardinal direction). Retrieval of spatial relations is more efficient in directions aligned with this reference axis than in other directions. In Figure 1, for instance, an observer viewing the space from the position of the arrow might use the axes defined by the walls of the room and the intrinsic structure of the layout (the objects can be grouped into rows and columns parallel to the walls) to construct a reference system for remembering the locations of objects in the room. Egocentric spatial relations must be represented at the perceptual level for the purpose of guiding action in the environment (Sholl and Nolin, 1997). It is an open question whether egocentric spatial relations are represented in long-term spatial memories.

Hierarchical Representations

Spatial knowledge is stored in the brain hierarchically (Stevens and Coupe, 1978). When people learn the locations of objects in an environment, they group the objects into ever larger clusters. For example, a hierarchical representation of an office may specify that the telephone and coffee cup are on the desk, that the desk is next to the chair, and that the desk and chair are in the office. Objects are grouped on the basis of their properties (e.g., the functional relation between a chair and a desk), aspects of the environment (e.g., barriers), and even organizational strategies unique to a particular person (McNamara, 1986; McNamara, Hardy, and Hirtle, 1989).

One way to interpret these findings is that people represent spatial relations in locally defined reference systems and these reference systems are then related to one another in higher-order reference systems (Poucet, 1993). For example, locations of objects in a room might be represented by a reference system local to the room. Such a reference system could then serve as an "object" in a reference system defining the spatial relations among the rooms on the same floor of a house; these could then serve as "objects" in a reference system relating floors of the house to one another.

Spatial Memory and the Brain

Functional neuroimaging using PET (positron emission tomography) and fMRI (functional magnetic resonance imaging) are proving to be powerful methods for investigating areas of the brain involved in spatial learning and navigation. This research is new, but consistent findings are emerging. The parahippocampal gyrus seems to be involved in a variety of spatial tasks (Epstein and Kanwisher, 1998). The hippocampus, predominantly on the right, is associated with the recollection of familiar routes (Maguire, Frackowiak, and Frith, 1997). Dorsal areas of the brain (e.g., the posterior parietal cortex) seem to be recruited for processing the locations of objects, whereas ventral areas (e.g., the lingual and fusiform gyri) seem to be recruited for processing the appearance of objects and scenes (Aguirre and D'Esposito, 1997). This dorsal-ventral dissociation is analogous to that observed in vision (Mishkin, Ungerleider, and Macko, 1983). Recent evidence indicates that route and survey learning recruit a common cortical network in the brain and that survey learning recruits a subset of the route-learning areas (Mellet et al., 2000; Shelton and Gabrieli, 2002).

Figure 2

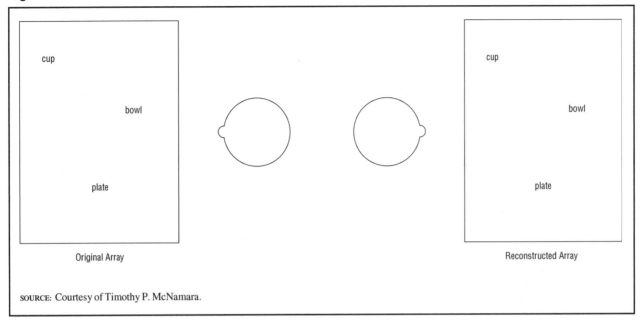

cup

bowl

plate

Original Array

cup

bowl

plate

Reconstructed Array

SOURCE: Courtesy of Timothy P. McNamara.

Testing situation used to investigate spatial reference systems. The participant viewed a layout of objects on a table, and then turned halfway around to reconstruct the layout on another table. Tenejapan participants preserved the orientation of the layout with respect to the environment, as illustrated.

Language and Culture

Spatial memories are not insulated from language and culture. The Mayan language Tzeltal uses an environmental reference system to describe the spatial relations among objects. This reference system corresponds to cardinal directions established by the mountainous terrain in which the speakers live (e.g., downhill = north, uphill = south, across = east or west). Tzeltal does not have the egocentric spatial terms *left* and *right*. When shown an array of objects on a table and asked to reconstruct the array on another table behind them after turning 180 degrees (see Figure 2), Tzeltal speakers reconstruct the array preserving its orientation with respect to the environmental reference system, not with respect to their egocentric perspective (Levinson, 1996). In contrast, speakers of Dutch (and presumably speakers of most Western languages) preserve egocentric, not environmental, spatial relations (e.g., plate to the left in the reconstructed array). Almost superhuman navigational abilities have been documented in several cultures, including those of the Australian Aborigines (Lewis, 1976) and Puluwat Islanders (Gladwin, 1970); experiments have shown that Aboriginal children perform substantially better than white children on tests requiring the children to remember the locations of objects (Kearins, 1981).

Gender Differences

There is a long history of research on gender differences in spatial ability (Maccoby and Jacklin, 1974) but relatively few studies have examined spatial learning and memory of room-sized and larger spaces. Those studies have shown that males perform better than females or that the genders do not differ (Montello, Lovelace, Golledge, and Self, 1999). Recent experiments have documented an intriguing dissociation between females and males in spatial abilities. Females perform better than males on tasks that require memory of the locations and identities of objects, whereas males perform better than females on tasks that require keeping track of orientation in large-scale environments (Montello et al., 1999; Silverman et al., 2000). (There is, of course, large variability within genders, with some men performing better than some women on object-location tasks, and some women performing better than some men on orientation tasks.) How can this dissociation be explained? According to the hunter-gatherer theory, spatial sex differences arise from a sexual division of labor between hunting and gathering during human evolution (Silverman and Eals, 1992). Tracking and killing animals, a predominately male activity, required monitoring one's location and orientation over large distances, whereas foraging for edible plants, a predominately female activity, required memory of the locations of plants and other immobile foods and then relocating them in subsequent growing seasons.

Conclusion

Spatial memories of large environments are composed of route knowledge and survey knowledge. Route knowledge is usually acquired before survey knowledge, but the learner's goals affect what is learned. Some perspectives of a familiar environment can be retrieved more efficiently than others. This orientation dependence arises because people store knowledge about location and orientation in terms of reference directions or axes. The use of different reference directions or axes in different locales may explain why spatial memories are hierarchical. Emerging evidence indicates that different areas of the brain specialize in representing and processing specific kinds of spatial memories. Gender, language, and culture influence the development and pattern of spatial capabilities.

See also: SPATIAL LEARNING: ANIMALS

Bibliography

Aguirre, G. K., and D'Esposito, M. (1997). Environmental knowledge is subserved by separable dorsal/ventral neural areas. *Journal of Neuroscience* 17, 2,512–2,518.

Anderson, R. A., Snyder, L. H., Bradley, D. C., and Xiang, J. (1997). Multimodal representation of space in the posterior parietal cortex and its use in planning movements. *Annual Review of Neuroscience 20*, 303–330.

Epstein, R., and Kanwisher, N. (1998). A cortical representation of the local visual environment. *Nature 392*, 598–601.

Evans, G. W., and Pezdek, K. (1980). Cognitive mapping: Knowledge of real-world distance and location information. *Journal of Experimental Psychology: Human Learning and Memory 6*, 13–24.

Gallistel, C. R. (1990). *The organization of learning*. Cambridge, MA: MIT Press.

Gladwin, T. (1970). *East is a big bird*. Cambridge, MA: Harvard University Press.

Kearins, J. M. (1981). Visual spatial memory in Australian Aboriginal children of desert regions. *Cognitive Psychology 13*, 434–460.

Levinson, S. C. (1996). Frames of reference and Molyneaux's question: Crosslinguistic evidence. In P. Bloom, M. A. Peterson, L. Nadel, and M. F. Garrett, eds., *Language and space*. Cambridge, MA: MIT Press.

Lewis, D. (1976). Observations on route finding and spatial orientation among the Aboriginal peoples of the western desert region of central Australia. *Oceania 46*, 249–282.

Maccoby, E. E., and Jacklin, C. N. (1974). *The psychology of sex differences*. Stanford, CA: Stanford University Press.

Maguire, E. A., Frackowiak, R. S. J., and Frith, C. D. (1997). Recalling routes around London: Activation of the right hippocampus in taxi drivers. *Journal of Neuroscience 17*, 7,103–7,110.

McNamara, T. P. (1986). Mental representations of spatial relations. *Cognitive Psychology 18*, 87–121.

McNamara, T. P., Hardy, J. K., and Hirtle, S. C. (1989). Subjective hierarchies in spatial memory. *Journal of Experimental Psychology: Learning, Memory, and Cognition 15*, 211–227.

Mellet, E., Bricogne, S., Tzourio-Mazoyer, N., Ghaëm, O., Petit, L., Zago, L., Etard, O., Berthoz, A., Mazoyer, B., and Denis, M. (2000). Neural correlates of topographic mental exploration: The impact of route versus survey perspective learning. *NeuroImage 12*, 588–600.

Mishkin, M., Ungerleider, L. G., and Macko, K. A. (1983). Object vision and spatial vision: Two cortical pathways. *Trends in Neurosciences 6*, 414–417.

Montello, D. R., Lovelace, K. L., Golledge, R. G., and Self, C. M. (1999). Sex-related differences and similarities in geographic and environmental spatial abilities. *Annals of the Association of American Geographers 89*, 515–534.

Mou, W., and McNamara, T. P. (2002). Intrinsic frames of reference in spatial memory. *Journal of Experimental Psychology: Learning, Memory, and Cognition 28*, 162–170

Poucet, B. (1993). Spatial cognitive maps in animals: New hypotheses on their structure and neural mechanisms. *Psychological Review 100*, 163–182.

Rock, I. (1973). *Orientation and form*. New York: Academic Press.

Shelton, A. L., and Gabrieli, J. D. E. (2002). Neural correlates of encoding space from route and survey perspective. *Journal of Neuroscience 22*, 2,711–2,717

Shelton, A. L., and McNamara, T. P. (2001). Systems of spatial reference in human memory. *Cognitive Psychology 43*, 274–310.

Sholl, M. J., and Nolin, T. L. (1997). Orientation specificity in representations of place. *Journal of Experimental Psychology: Learning, Memory, and Cognition 23*, 1,494–1,507.

Siegel, A. W., and White, S. H. (1975). The development of spatial representations of large-scale environments. In H. W. Reese, ed., *Advances in child development and behavior*. San Diego: Academic Press.

Silverman, I., Choi, J., Mackewn, A., Fisher, M., Moro, J., and Olshansky, E. (2000). Evolved mechanisms underlying wayfinding: Further studies on the hunter-gatherer theory of spatial sex differences. *Evolution and Human Behavior 21*, 201–213.

Silverman, I., and Eals, M. (1992). Sex differences in spatial abilities: Evolutionary theory and data. In J. H. Barkow, L. Cosmides et al., eds., *The adapted mind: Evolutionary psychology and the generation of culture*. New York: Oxford University Press.

Stevens, A., and Coupe, P. (1978). Distortions in judged spatial relations. *Cognitive Psychology 10*, 422–437.

Taylor, H. A., Naylor, S. J., and Chechile, N. A. (1999). Goal-specific influences on the representation of spatial perspective. *Memory & Cognition 27*, 309–319.

Thorndyke, P. W., and Hayes Roth, B. (1982). Differences in spatial knowledge acquired from maps and navigation. *Cognitive Psychology 14*, 560–589.

Tversky, B. (1981). Distortions in memory for maps. *Cognitive Psychology 13*, 407–433.

Timothy P. McNamara

SPENCE, KENNETH (1907–1967)

Kenneth W. Spence (1907–1967) played a major role in psychology from the early 1930s until his untimely death. His impact is illustrated by the fact that from 1962 to 1967, he was the most cited author in a survey of the fourteen most prestigious psychological journals (Myers, 1970). Spence's influence resulted from achievements as experimentalist, theorist, methodologist, and teacher. In all of these roles, he operated as a natural science psychologist, one who believed that the science of psychology can employ the same methods of empirical inquiry and theory construction as physics, chemistry, and biology. In essence, he was asserting that psychology, in principle, is capable of producing a body of reliable scientific knowledge. To achieve this goal he deemed it necessary to conceptualize psychology as the science of behavior, not of the mind. That is, the basic observations of the science of psychology are the behavior of organisms, not the direct examination of conscious experience. This methodological position, Behaviorism, was initially expressed, in a radical form, by John B. Watson (Kendler, 1987), but since has matured into a more sophisticated version known as *neobehaviorism*.

Early Life

Spence was born May 6, 1907, in Chicago. When he was 4, Western Electric transferred his father, an electrical engineer, to Montreal. He majored in psychology at McGill University, receiving a B.A. in 1929 and an M.A. in 1930. His Ph.D. was granted in 1933 by Yale University, where he served as a research assistant to Robert M. Yerkes, under whose direction he completed a dissertation on the visual acuity of chimpanzees. The dominant intellectual influence during his Yale days evolved from the inspirational ideas of Clark L. Hull, who set as his goal the formulation of a theoretical interpretation of behavior that emulated the conceptual structure of Newtonian physics.

Hull's general approach was shaped by both Ivan Pavlov and Edward Thorndike. Pavlovian conditioning, for Hull, was the simplest form of learning, and hence principles of conditioning could provide the premises from which more complex forms of behavior could be deduced (explained). Thorndike's *law of effect* represented, for Hull, another fundamental principle of behavior; rewards, technically known as *reinforcements,* are necessary for the formation and strengthening of a connection between a situation and behavior, or what became to be known as a *stimulus-response association* (e.g., in Pavlovian conditioning the sound of a tone became connected with salivation because it was reinforced by food).

While a graduate student, Spence prepared a paper (Spence, 1932) that illustrated Hull's general strategy. Based on assumptions about the effect of delayed reinforcement in conditioning, Spence predicted that in a complex maze, one with several successive choice points, entrances into blind alleys would be eliminated in a backward order, that is, the blinds are more difficult the farther they are from the goal. After completing his graduate work at Yale, Spence accepted a National Research Council fellowship to the Yale Laboratories of Primate Biology at Orange Park,

Kenneth Spence *(Psychology Archives, University of Akron)*

Florida, where he published his classical theory of animal discrimination learning (Spence, 1936), a conception that is still influential (Kendler, 1992). In 1937 he moved to the University of Virginia as an assistant professor of psychology. The following year he was appointed associate professor at the University of Iowa, where, in 1942, he became professor and head of the Department of Psychology, a position he occupied until 1964, when he moved to the University of Texas.

Spence's Work

Kenneth Spence's efforts in theoretical psychology are characterized by a consistent direction and a close relationship between facts and theory. He had (a) an ability to express ideas in a lucid prose that resulted from clear thinking and hard work; (b) a flair for designing clever experimental tests of competing hypotheses; (c) a knack for analyzing data so that their theoretical implications would become fully apparent; (d) an ingenious talent for theoretically integrating a range of experimental results with the added, and unusual, feature of being able to offer possible alternative explanations, even some from competing theories; and (e) a special aptitude, in spite of limited mathematical training, to coordinate his theoretical interpretation with a quantitative model that structured an empirical problem so that further theoretical clarification and empirical development could occur.

One excellent example of Spence's style of theoretical and empirical structuring is exhibited in his influential analysis of discrimination learning of animals (Spence, 1936), which contained one of the first mathematical simulations (without the aid of a computer!) of a theory. The model, which seeks to identify the psychological processes involved in how animals learn to choose between two stimuli when one is followed by reward and the other is not, postulates two basic theoretical mechanisms that Hull had employed in interpreting conditioning phenomena: excitation and inhibition. When the animal is reinforced for selecting one stimulus, that habit (stimulus-response association) is gradually strengthened; when a response to the other cue is not reinforced, that habit is gradually weakened. When the difference in strengths between the two competing habits reaches a certain value, the subject consistently chooses the reinforced stimulus. Spence had no illusion that his formulation represented a complete interpretation of the discrimination learning process. He readily acknowledged that certain fundamental processes, such as complex perceptual mechanisms, were ignored but insisted, as a matter of strategy, that discrimination learning, as well as all psychological problems, must be broken down into bare essentials to be investigated fruitfully. Reducing discrimination learning to the analysis of competing habits in a simple experimental situation was a fruitful strategy for dealing with fundamental principles of behavior.

Spence's theory of discrimination learning had many ramifications, including the formulation of an ingenious stimulus-response explanation (Spence, 1937) of the transposition phenomenon, the tendency for nonverbal organisms to transfer a relational choice from one problem to a subsequent one (e.g., after learning to choose a medium gray in preference to a lighter one, a rat will probably select a darker gray rather than the previously rewarded medium gray). In addition, his theory initiated a crucial controversy as to whether discrimination learning was a continuous or noncontinuous process, occurring gradually or suddenly (Kendler, 1987).

Although Spence's discrimination learning theory was designed for nonverbal organisms, he sought to discover how the acquisition of symbolic skills would influence discrimination learning. He encouraged a doctoral student, Margaret Kuenne (1946), to investigate this problem; she found that in a transposition problem the behavior of inarticulate youngsters was similar to that of rats, in that simple stimulus-response associations were formed but the acquisition of symbolic skills introduced a more complex pattern of stimulation and associative connections that enhanced relational responding. This led to a two-stage theory of discrimination learning (Kendler and Kendler, 1962, 1975) in which the lower stage (single-unit), based upon Spence's continuity model, hypothesized that the responses of subhuman animals were directly linked (associated) to stimuli (e.g., black, white), whereas higher-level functioning (mediational model) suggested that incoming stimulation is transformed into some internal conceptual representation (e.g., brightness) that guides subsequent behavior. This model, which had its origins in Spence's discrimination learning theory, could account for developmental changes in the discrimination learning exhibited by humans.

From 1950 to the end of his life, classical (Pavlovian) eyeblink conditioning with human subjects occupied Spence's interest. His efforts revealed basic principles of habit formation and the interaction effects between habits and drives. With the collaboration of Janet A. Taylor, who later became his wife, the role of anxiety as a motivational mechanism was empirically and theoretically analyzed (e.g., Spence and Taylor, 1951; Spence, 1956). Spence (1966) was able, by clever experimental manipulations, to get human subjects to respond either in a simple associative manner analogous to subhuman behavior or in a cognitive (mediational) manner. This was another example of his effort, as well as that of several of his students, to gain an experimental grip on evolutionary processes in behavior theory.

Groundbreaking Psychologist

In 1955, Spence was invited to deliver the Silliman Lectures at Yale, a prestigious series that until then had been given by distinguished physical and biological scientists such as Ernest Rutherford, Enrico Fermi, and Charles Sherrington. The lectures, published under the title *Behavior Theory and Conditioning* (1956), can be characterized as a realistic and reasonable theoretical interpretation of a wide range of experimental data. Unlike many of the theoretical messiahs who have dotted the psychological landscape with grandiose theories, Spence's formulation was never far removed from experimental evidence. In essence, Spence was an experimental psychologist's theorist because his hypotheses were clearly testable.

Spence's skills as an experimentalist and theorist were matched by his talents as a methodologist. With the collaboration of the philosopher of science Gustav Bergmann, Spence contributed to the clarification of the meaning of psychological concepts and the logic of psychological measurement (Bergmann and Spence, 1941, 1944). His greatest contribution as a methodologist was his clarification of issues in theoretical psychology, particularly in relation to the comparative analysis of competing learning theories. The competing theory to the Hull-Spence model that interested Spence the most was Edward Tolman's cognitive theory of animal learning. This formulation generated much confusion among both behaviorists and antibehaviorists; the former could not reconcile Tolman's hypothesized mentalistic processes with methodological behaviorism, and the latter denied that Tolman could be labeled a behaviorist if he employed phenomenological experience as a metaphor for his theoretical constructs. Spence clearly distinguished between the strategies employed for conceptualizing theoretical processes—mechanistic, phenomenological, mathematical, or some other—and the theory's deductive, empirical consequences. Unfortunately this distinction between a theorist's thinking style and the explicit theory with its deductive empirical implications was not fully appreciated at the time of the cognitive revolution, and as a result needless disputation and misunderstanding were encouraged. Many segments of the psychological community failed to appreciate the linkage between neobehaviorism in general, and Spence's theoretical efforts in particular, in attempting to understand the relationship between associative and cognitive processes (Kendler, 1984).

Spence's contributions to psychology cannot be limited to his own publications. His inspired teaching must also be considered. Many of his seventy-five doctoral students, too many to mention, made solid contributions to the science of psychology: "All of his doctoral students carry with them some of Spence's ideas and commitments and a desire to achieve a level of quality in their own work that would be acceptable to their Professor" (Kendler, 1967, p. 341).

In addition to being the first and only psychologist to give the Silliman Lectures, Spence received many other honors, including membership in the National Academy of Sciences, the Howard Crosby Warren Medal of the Society of Experimental Psychologists in 1953, and the American Psychological Association's Scientific Contribution Award in 1956, the first year that it was presented. But perhaps the greatest honor Spence aspired to was a place in the history of psychology. Although it is difficult to penetrate the haze of the future, especially in relation to psychology, a discipline that is conceptualized in many antithetical ways, it is likely that Spence will be remembered as a clear and sophisticated exponent of natural science psychology and as a theorist and empiricist who, while appreciating the immaturity of the science of psychology, was nevertheless able to advance it with fruitful conceptions of learning and motivation.

See also: DISCRIMINATION AND GENERALIZATION; EVOLUTION AND LEARNING

Bibliography

Bergmann, G., and Spence, K. W. (1941). Operationism and theory construction. *Psychological Review 48,* 1–14.
—— (1944). The logic of psychological measurement. *Psychological Review 51,* 1–24.
Kendler, H. H. (1967). Kenneth W. Spence: 1907–1967. *Psychological Review 74,* 335–341.
—— (1984). Evolutions or revolutions? In K. M. B. Lagerspetz and P. Niemi, eds., *Psychology in the 1990's.* Amsterdam: North Holland.
—— (1987). *Historical foundations of modern psychology.* Pacific Grove, CA: Brooks/Cole.
Kendler, H. H., and Kendler, T. S. (1962). Vertical and horizontal processes in problem solving. *Psychological Review 69,* 1–16.
—— (1975). From discrimination learning to cognitive development: A neobehavioristic odyssey. In W. K. Estes, ed., *Handbook of learning and cognitive processes,* Vol. 1. Hillsdale, NJ: Erlbaum.
Kendler, T. S. (1992). *Levels of cognitive development.* Hillsdale, NJ: Erlbaum.
Kuenne, M. R. (1946). Experimental investigation of the relation of language to transposition behavior in young children. *Journal of Experimental Psychology 36,* 471–490.
Myers, C. R. (1970). Journal citations and scientific eminence in contemporary psychology. *American Psychologist 25,* 1,041–1,048.
Spence, K. W. (1932). The order of eliminating blinds in maze learning by the rat. *Journal of Comparative Psychology 14,* 9–27.
—— (1936). The nature of discrimination learning in animals. *Psychological Review 43,* 427–429.
—— (1937). The differential response in animals to stimuli varying within a single dimension. *Psychological Review 44,* 430–444.
—— (1956). *Behavior theory and conditioning.* New Haven, CT: Yale University Press.
—— (1966). Cognitive and drive factors in the extinction of the conditioned eye blink in human subjects. *Psychological Review 73,* 445–451.
Spence, K. W., and Taylor, J. A. (1951). Anxiety and strength of the UCS as determiners of the amount of eyelid conditioning. *Journal of Experimental Psychology 42,* 183–186.

Howard H. Kendler

SPINAL PLASTICITY

Spinal plasticity refers to short- or long-term alterations of the excitability of the spine's neural pathways. Although the mammalian spinal cord is a unique part of the central nervous system, it is most commonly identified as a transmitter of information to and from the brain and as a repository of various reflex functions that allow an automatic response to external stimuli. But spinal cord pathways are dynamic and continuously changing systems, not static, hard-wired entities simply transmitting information from the body to the brain and back.

Spinal reflexes appear to be hard-wired functional circuits whose excitability temporarily varies with descending activity from the brain or with repeated sensory input. In the 1930s, however, work began to show that the spinal reflex pathways might be altered in ways that have many characteristics of learning and memory in the intact mammal.

Nonassociative Excitability Changes

Researchers have long been aware of memory-like but temporary alterations of spinal reflex excitability. Short-term decreases in excitability were studied in the early 1900s and termed reflex fatigue. However, since about 1975, researchers have learned about both decreases and increases in spinal reflex excitability; they now know that there are essentially four overlapping phases of spinal reflex alterations, mainly representing increased excitability caused by sensory inputs to the cord.

The most rapidly developing and rapidly lost changes are habituation and sensitization. Habituation is a decrease in spinal reflex excitability caused by repeated stimulation; it results in decreased response to a sustained stimulus. Once the stimulus is removed, excitability returns to normal in seconds or minutes. Sensitization (sometimes known as windup) is an increased excitability to a sustained stimulus that is also rapidly lost, usually within 90 to 120 seconds after stimulus cessation. Either habituation or sensitization may occur with as little as one or two stimulus applications; both seem to be due to altered neurotransmitter release from either incoming sensory nerve terminals or from interneurons within the reflex pathways.

The second stage of excitability alteration is termed long-term sensitization and occurs with longer and/or more intense stimulus inputs. Long-term sensitization, once established, decreases for hours or even for a day with no further stimulation to the reflex circuit. This excitability increase is likely due to an alteration of cell membrane receptor sensitivity of the secondary interneurons of the reflex pathways.

The third stage of excitability alterations is spinal fixation. Here, a fairly intense, thirty-to-fifty-minute stimulus to the spinal cord can increase the excitability of the activated reflex pathways for as long as several days and is essentially a memory trace in the spinal cord. The excitability increase may be strong enough to produce continuing motoneuron output after removal of the initiating stimulus. Fixation can be produced by stimulation or lesions of various brain regions, or by stimulation of peripheral skin or a sensory nerve. Inflammation of a peripheral area such as a knee joint can also produce increases in spinal reflex excitability that are similar to fixation. Fixation seems similar to long-term potentiation (LTP), which may be a part of learning and memory in intact animals. Fixation and other long-term excitability increases are likely due to alterations in interneuron cell membrane receptors produced by upregulation of genes controlling membrane function.

The fourth stage of nonassociative excitability alterations may be permanent. With prolonged stimulus input into the reflex paths of the cord, inhibitory interneurons regulating excitability balance may be destroyed. In addition, some evidence points to an increase in excitatory synapse formation in these circumstances. The loss of inhibitory control and increased numbers of excitatory synapses would lead to a permanent excitability increase.

Associative Changes

Initial research on learning in the spinal cord began with attempts to determine the simplest part of the nervous system that could support learning. Researchers used classical conditioning operations, following a conditioned stimulus with an unconditioned stimulus to the hind limb of an anesthetized, spinally transected subject (usually a dog). Although the early studies were inconclusive, later studies using well-established control group technology proved that spinal reflex excitability could be altered by classical conditioning procedures. Spinal conditioning shows many features of classical conditioning in the intact animal, although the spinal reflex system apparently cannot learn to respond differentially. The learned changes do not spontaneously decay but show the extinction decreases typical of classical conditioning. Reflex excitability alterations induced by classical conditioning procedures occur in the interneurons of the reflex pathways rather than in the initial synapses of the sensory fibers into the cord or in the motoneurons. In addition to excitability alterations arising from classical conditioning, spinal reflexes respond to instrumental conditioning operations, which can drive spinal reflex excitability either up or down, depending on the conditioning situation.

While most studies of classical and instrumental learning in the spinal cord have used painful or nociceptive stimuli, a similar alteration of spinal reflex excitability has been demonstrated in intact monkeys taught to increase leg muscle tone over many days. The change was gradual but also enduring, occurring in the spinal reflexes but involving nonnociceptive inputs.

Conclusion

The major spinal reflex excitability changes shown by associative and nonassociative procedures indicate that spinal reflexes play a vital role in sensory information processing. The major impact of spinal reflex excitability changes may be in chronic pain. Increased spinal-pathway excitability is probably a factor in many of the most intractable chronic-pain syndromes. Understanding the cellular basis of spinal reflex and spinal pathway excitability alterations might offer breakthroughs in the treatment of some of these debilitating conditions. In addition, the increased understanding of spinal pathway plasticity is leading to advances in the rehabilitation of spinal cord injuries and in the technological means of increasing the mobility of patients with incomplete or even complete spinal transections.

See also: CONDITIONING, CLASSICAL AND INSTRUMENTAL; HABITUATION AND SENSITIZATION IN VERTEBRATES; NEURAL SUBSTRATES OF CLASSICAL CONDITIONING: DISCRETE BEHAVIORAL RESPONSES

Bibliography

Coderre, T. J. (2001). Noxious stimulus-induced plasticity in spinal cord dorsal horn: Evidence and insights on mechanisms obtained using the formalin test. In M. M. Patterson and J. W. Grau, eds., *Spinal cord plasticity: Alterations in reflex function.* Boston: Kluwer Academic Press.

Groves, P., and Thompson, R. (1970). Habituation: A dual-process theory. *Psychological Review* 77(5) 419–450.

Patterson, M. M. (1976). Mechanisms of classical conditioning and fixation in spinal mammals. In A. H. Reisen and R. F. Thompson, eds., *Advances in psychobiology.* New York: Wiley.

—— (2001). Spinal conditioning: The first seventy years. In J. E. Steinmetz, M. A. Gluck, and G. D. Solomon, eds., *Model systems and the neurobiology of learning.* Mahwah, NJ: Erlbaum.

—— (2001). Spinal fixation: Long-term alterations in spinal reflex excitability. In M. M. Patterson and J. W. Grau, eds., *Spinal cord plasticity: Alterations in reflex function.* Boston: Kluwer Academic Publishers.

M. M. Patterson, and J. W. Grau, eds. (2001). *Spinal cord plasticity.* Boston: Kluwer Academic Publishers.

Wernig, A., Nanassy, A. et al. (2001). Laufband (treadmill) therapy in incomplete para- and tetraplegia. In M. M. Patterson and J. W. Grau, eds., *Spinal cord plasticity: Alterations in reflex function.* Boston: Kluwer Academic Publishers.

Willis, W. D. (2001). Mechanisms of central sensitization of nociceptive dorsal horn neurons. In M. M. Patterson and J. W. Grau, eds., *Spinal cord plasticity: Alterations in reflex function.* Boston: Kluwer Academic Publishers.

Wolpaw, J. R. (2001). Spinal cord plasticity in the acquisition of a simple motor skill. In M. M. Patterson and J. W. Grau, eds., *Spinal cord plasticity: Alterations in reflex function.* Boston: Kluwer Academic Publishers.

Michael M. Patterson
Michael J. Bartelt
Revised by Michael M. Patterson

STIMULUS CONTROL

See: DISCRIMINATION AND GENERALIZATION

STRESS AND MEMORY

Stressful and emotional events can promote or impair the acquisition of new memories, depending on the type of stressful experience, the type of learning—even the sex of the animal. Stress is the external condition that places demands on the organism, and the stress response is the organism's adaptive response to the stressor, typically measured as changes in performance or physiological or biochemical states.

Most adaptive responses are crucial to an organism's capacity for survival and are easily reconcilable with theories of natural selection. For instance, the release of glucocorticoids from the adrenal glands directs glucose to the brain and musculature in preparation for "fight or flight," thereby eliminating unnecessary processing of ongoing vegetative functions such as digestion. These physiological responses to stress in turn affect cognitive processes such as learning and memory, thereby allowing the animal to prepare for or avoid subsequent sources of stress. The interaction between stress and memory is a complex one that does not always serve the best interests of the animal.

At first it seems reasonable to assume that there is a direct correlation between degree of stress and degree of detriment. In reality, animals (including humans) perform optimally at moderate levels of demand, and performance is compromised at the extremes. Hence, the relationship between stress and performance is an inverted U-shaped function: Performance is impaired equally at high levels of stress and at low levels (boredom or drowsiness); moderate levels, performance is enhanced. For example, exposure to a moderate stressor such as background noise can facilitate performance of a prolonged vigilance task. Substituting arousal for stress, Donald Hebb (1955) suggested that continuing neural activity could provide a physiological means of describing such self-motivating phenomena as curiosity and exploration and their obvious contribution to learning. Moreover, he emphasized that without such an arousal foundation, no learning would occur. This relationship, in combination with the inverted-U relationship proposed between stress and performance, predicts a linear relationship between stress and arousal. Others, however, have reported an upright U-shaped correlation between stress and arousal, which forecasts a monotonic relationship between stress and performance. Still others report that stress and arousal are independent variables.

Exactly how stressful experience will affect memory formation depends, presumably, on the significance of the information to be remembered and therefore on the type of learning that is being tapped. Under most circumstances, an animal will remember an aversive event for most of its life. But subsequent experience can change these memories. Autonomic tasks entailing a high degree of preparedness are less likely to be adversely affected than tasks requiring high cognitive capacity and concentration. These two extremes can be viewed as the ends of a continuum, with stress impairing performance as task difficulty increases. This relationship is exemplified by the intense training and practice required of highly skilled professionals such as military personnel, who must perform optimally under high levels of stress and uncertainty.

The degree to which stress impinges on performance is highly susceptible to individual differences. Although there is a limit to the attentive capacity that can be allocated to a particular task, this capacity is not fixed and will vary from individual to individual and from day to day. On the evidence of human self-report scales, high-anxiety subjects tend to perform optimally on easy tasks, and low-anxiety subjects perform optimally under more demanding circumstances; within tasks, low-anxiety subjects perform better during early stages of learning, and high anxiety facilitates the later stages. Other variables include social factors, age, and disease. But the most significant is past memories. The animal must not only calculate the imbalance between the perceived demand and the ability to cope with that demand but must also incorporate this information into its previous experience.

In the early 1960s J. B. Overmier and M. E. P. Seligman noticed that dogs exposed to inescapable shock were later impaired in their ability to perform a task where escape was possible. They suggested that the animals became helpless after learning that the aversive event and the ability to cope with that event were not contingent; they termed the phenomenon learned helplessness. Because the secondary characteristics that accompany helplessness—weight loss, sleep disturbances, decreased activity, and so on—resemble characteristics of depressed humans, the phenomenon evolved into one of the first experimental models of depression. It has helped to demonstrate stress-induced effects on immune function, ulcer development, tumor growth, analgesia, aggression, and status within a dominance hierarchy. But impairment in performance remains the most notable result.

However intuitively appealing, this paradigm of helplessness is constrained by more general theories

of stress and learning and, in fact, depends on individual sex, species, and strain differences as well as the nature and difficulty of the task. For example, prior exposure to inescapable stresses such as tail shocks or swim stress facilitates classical conditioning of the eyeblink response in male rats, whereas exposure to the same stresses impairs conditioning in female rats. Recent studies in humans have suggested that males and females also differ in the ways in which they deal with stress; males tend to isolate themselves, whereas females tend to befriend others and seek comfort. These differences can affect what types of learning opportunities arise after stressful experience.

One of the first scientists to define stress and its adaptive utility and underlying mechanisms was the eminent physiologist Hans Seyle. Dr. Seyle defined the stress response as the nonspecific response of the body to any demand placed upon it. In general, Seyle was referring to activation of the hypothalamic-pituitary-adrenal (HPA) axis. In this axis, hypothalamic peptides activate adrenocorticotropin (ACTH) secretion from the anterior pituitary. ACTH induces the release of glucocorticoids from the adrenal cortex, and glucocorticoids, in turn, inhibit the release of pituitary ACTH. Glucocorticoids are released peripherally into the blood upon most stressful encounters and are potentially damaging, especially in high concentrations and/or chronic conditions. There are numerous reports that they can impair later learning; however, there are also reports that they can enhance it. As with exposure to a stressful event, the degree and direction of the effect depends on the amount of glucocorticoids that are released and the time of exposure.

In addition to glucocorticoids, many other stress-related neuromodulators can affect mnemonic processes. The catecholamines have been implicated in learning, as are the dopaminergic systems. Along with ACTH, β-endorphin is released from the pituitary in response to stress. Peptides such as the opioids (the enkephalins), vasopressin, and neuropeptide Y can be affected by exposure to a stressful experience and can thereby influence memory processes. One of more ubiquitous substrates affected by stress is the glutamatergic system, including the corresponding receptors, n-methyl-d-aspartate (NMDA) and α-amino-3-methylsoxazole-4-propionic acid (AMPA). Glutamate is the primary excitatory neurotransmitter in the brain, and activation of its receptors is critical to many types of learning. The dramatic extent to which stress affects this system affords ample opportunity for stressful experiences to affect processes of learning and memory.

Exposure to acute or chronic stressor experiences induces a variety of effects on neuronal plasticity, affecting synaptic morphology, receptor affinity and number, gene expression, and electrophysiological responsiveness. For example, exposure to an acute stressor of inescapable tail shocks induces immediate early gene (IEG) expression, impairs long-term potentiation (LTP), and can enhance the density of dendritic spines; research has identified all of these factors as possible biological substrates for learning in the mammalian brain. Many of these effects unfold in the hippocampal formation, a part of the brain that plays a critical role in some types of memory formation. In addition, the amygdala is a critically factor in many defensive and affective responses to stress or danger. This limbic structure integrates information from numerous sources and sensory systems and participates in the formation of memories about those experiences that are necessary for ensuring an appropriate response to future danger.

Many of the foregoing neuromodulatory systems are colocalized, and the brain regions are highly interconnected, making it difficult to interfere experimentally with one without affecting another. Furthermore, given the wide diversity of stressors and the inherent variance in individual responsiveness to the same stressor, it is probable that specific but overlapping circuits contribute to stress effects on learning. Finally, these stress-induced responses are not necessarily detrimental to the physical and psychological well-being of the organism; in the aftermath of the stressful encounter, they contribute to the reestablishment of homeostasis and an appropriate consolidation of the experience.

See also: HORMONES AND MEMORY; LEARNED HELPLESSNESS; NEURAL COMPUTATION: HIPPOCAMPUS; NEURAL SUBSTRATES OF CLASSICAL CONDITIONING: DISCRETE BEHAVIORAL RESPONSES; NEURAL SUBSTRATES OF EMOTIONAL MEMORY

Bibliography

Blanchard, D. C., and Blanchard, R. J. (1988). Ethoexperimental approaches to the biology of emotion. *Annual Review of Psychology 39*, 43–68.

Cox, T. (1980). *Stress.* Baltimore: University Park Press.

Lupien, S. J., and Lepage, M. (2001). Stress, memory, and the hippocampus: Can't live with it, can't live without it. *Behavioral Brain Research 14*, 137–158.

Shors, T. J. (1998). Sex and stress effects on learning and memory: For better or for worse. *The Neuroscientist 4*, 353–364.

Taylor, S. E., Klein, L. C., Lewis, B. P., Gruenewald, T. L., Gurang, R. A., and Updegraff, J. A. (2000). Biobehavioral responses to stress in females: Tend-and-befriend, not fight-or-flight. *Psychological Review 107*, 411–429.

Tracey J. Shors

STROKE

See: AMNESIA, ORGANIC; FRONTAL LOBES AND EPISODIC MEMORY; KNOWLEDGE SYSTEMS AND MATERIAL-SPECIFIC MEMORY DEFICITS; REHABILITATION OF MEMORY DISORDERS

SYNAPSE

See: GUIDE TO THE ANATOMY OF THE BRAIN

STRUCTURAL CHANGES AND MEMORY

See: MORPHOLOGICAL BASIS OF LEARNING AND MEMORY

T

TASTE AVERSION AND PREFERENCE LEARNING IN ANIMALS

Historically taste aversion learning arose as a problem in evolutionary biology. The English naturalist Charles Darwin was puzzled by an incongruity: Some tender caterpillars were brightly colored and exposed themselves so that they caught the eye of every passing bird. Such behavior appeared maladaptive. Years later, the English anthropologist and naturalist Alfred Russell Wallace suggested that brightly colored butterfly larva probably tasted bitter and might be poisonous; therefore the colors served to deter birds and other predators. Subsequent research supported Wallace's hypothesis. Consumption of the colorful insects causes gastric nausea and emesis, and after one or two trials birds and other predators learn to avoid them. As larva, these insects feed on plants that evolved the bitter toxins as a defense against herbivores; the insects turned that defense to their own advantage.

Taste aversion learning proved to be widespread in phylogeny and ontogeny. Taste-toxin conditioned aversions have been observed in snails, insects, fish, frogs, salamanders, lizards, snakes, domestic and wild birds, and in mammals, ranging from fetal and neonate rats, to young children and adult humans. Even protozoans reject bitter, the natural taste of plant poisons. The ubiquity of the phenomenon indicates that this mechanism to protect the gut must have evolved many millions of years ago.

In the mid-1960s taste aversion learning caught the attention of experimental psychologists. They observed that when an animal drinks a tasty solution marked by a bright-noisy signal, and is later injected with a mild toxin, the animal will develop an aversion to the taste but not to the bright-noisy signal. Conversely, if the animal is mildly shocked on the feet, it will avoid the bright-noisy signal but not the tasty solution. Second, and more important, the shock must be applied immediately after the signal for effective learning, but the toxin injection can be delayed for several hours after the consumption of the tasty solution. Moreover, a one trial situation, that is, a single pairing of the taste with the toxin injection, is sufficient to elicit a strong aversion to that particular taste. These factors, known as (1) selective association and (2) long-delay learning, are the major behavioral characteristics of taste aversion learning. This type of behavioral paradigm, that came to be known later as conditioned taste aversion (CTA), can tolerate an interstimulus interval of up to six to eight hours between the taste (the conditioned stimulus, CS) and the malaise inducing agent (the unconditioned stimulus, US) during the training session. After consumption, the internal representation of the taste would probably be encoded in an "on-hold" position over hours before a decision is being made of whether the food is safe or not. This long interstimulus interval enables the dissociation in time of neuronal events that generate the memory of the sensory stimulus from those that subserve the association of the memory of the CS with the US, that is, the negative reinforcer.

Since the 1980s, the ecological paradigm of CTA, by virtue of its aforementioned experimental advantages, has been adopted by several research groups in the study of the behavioral, pharmacological, cellular, and molecular aspects of learning and memory in mammals. In the laboratory, a routine CTA protocol is composed of the following steps: (1) the preconditioning session (three to four days), in which rats learn to drink water from the liquid container (usually the liquid is supplied in glass pipettes); (2) the conditioning session (a single day), where rats sample the taste (usually a solution of saccharin, but many other tastes can be used) and around thirty to sixty minutes later administered with the transient malaise-inducing agent (an intraperitoneal injection of a solution of lithium chloride is used as the standard US, but the US can range from rotation and irradiation to drugs and poisons); and (3) the testing session, which can vary between one and six days. Rejection of the conditioned taste can be easily monitored by measuring the amount of the taste consumed by the animal on the day of the test (a single-bottle test), and comparing this volume to that consumed on the day of conditioning. Another way of quantifying aversion to a specific taste is to calculate a so-called "aversion index," based on the total amount of water consumed compared to the taste in a multiple-choice situation.

The neurobiological mechanisms of the CS-US association in CTA are known only in broad outline. In the rat, the processing of gustatory information begins with transduction of chemical stimuli which reach the oral cavity. The taste receptors send afferents via the facial and glossopharyngeal nerves to the nucleus of the solitary tract in the brainstem. The receptors in the viscera also send vagal fibers converging to the same nucleus. The blood carries absorbed food products to the area postrema, where blood monitors report to the solitari nucleus. The CS-US routes then proceed to the parabrachial nucleus (PBN) located in the pons, the more anterior region of the brainstem. Neurophysiological experiments indicate that a complex series of looping circuits interconnect these nuclei in the brainstem with higher brain areas such as the gustatory cortex, located in the insular cortex (IC). Although the IC is unnecessary for simple reflex responses to gustatory stimulus, anatomical and metabolic lesion experiments have shown that the IC is required for the retention of learned taste aversion. The amygdala, another region interconnected with the PBN and the IC, is believed to play an important role is assessing the hedonic value of the consumed taste (i.e., the emotional aspect of the taste learning experience). All in all, the behavioral, anatomical, and pharmacological data accumulated to date suggest that the IC is the area of the brain involved in the encoding of the memory of the taste and in the processing the detection of taste unfamiliarity (see below); the amygdala as the region responsible for the evaluation of the hedonic value of the taste as well as the expression of CTA; and the PBN as the locus of the CS-US association.

An important element in CTA is the novelty, or unfamiliarity, of the taste stimulus. Sampling of any kind of a novel tastant by the rat, even in the absence of the negative reinforcer, will result in the formation of a memory to that specific taste. However, if these same animals are then subjected to CTA training (now in the presence of the malaise-inducing compound), they will show a poorer aversion to the taste compared to animals that were not pre-exposed to it. The CS in CTA is most effective in rendering a strong aversion response if it is unfamiliar to the organism at the time of conditioning, A major question is, How does the brain "know" when a taste is familiar or unfamiliar? Taste novelty detection is expected to require some type of fast internal comparator that matches the on-line (sensory) information with off-line (memory) information. A potential candidate for this comparator is a corticothalamo-brainstem system. The thalamus may compare the on-line sensory information coming from the brainstem with previous taste memory representations retained in the IC, and when a mismatch is identified (if the on-line taste information is novel), it triggers the behavioral response on the one hand, and initiates memory encoding in the IC on the other.

By using the advantage of a single conditioning trial, investigators have examined the role of several biochemical and molecular processes involved in the discrete phases of acquisition, consolidation, and extinction of CTA memory. For example, the microinfusion of a protein synthesis inhibitor into the IC blocks CTA learning when administered before the exposure to the taste, but not before the testing trial, indicating that the synthesis of new proteins in the cortex is a critical step for the formation, but not for the retrieval, of the taste memory. Along this line of experimentation, researchers have found that the cellular and molecular mechanisms that subserve CTA are similar to those that subserve other forms of learning. These specific molecular devices ("switches") are turned on/off in different brain regions during CTA (e.g., activation of cholinergic receptors and phosphorylation of glutamate NMDA receptors in the IC, and activation of specific intracellular signaling cascades together with modulation of gene expression in the IC and in the central nucleus of the amygdala). These essential molecular entities are also differentially activated in the brain according to the stimulus dimension and context. For example, muscarinic receptors and activation of members of the mitogen-activated protein kinase (MAPK) signaling cascade are necessary for the acquisition of CTA to a novel taste but not to a familiar one.

As mentioned, CTA results in a robust learning, but yet, this behavior is very plastic. The aversive memory can last for several months without significant decay. However, if after conditioning animals are subsequently exposed to the taste in the absence of the negative reinforcer (as in a test situation), and provided that they sample even a tiny amount of the taste, the aversive memory will commence to decay. This phenomenon, first described by the Russian physiologist Ivan Pavlov as experimental extinction, does not result in the erasure of the original aversive memory, but rather reflects a relearning process in which now the new CS-NoUS association comes to control behavior.

See also: FOOD AVERSION AND PREFERENCE LEARNING IN HUMANS

Bibliography

Berman, D. E., and Dudai, Y. (2001). Memory extinction, learning anew, and learning the new: Dissociations in the molecular machinery of learning in cortex. *Science 291*, 2,417–2,419.

Berman, D. E., Hazvi, S., Neduva, V., and Dudai, Y. (2000). The role of identified neurotransmitter systems in the response of insular cortex to unfamiliar taste: Activation of ERK1-2 and formation of a memory trace. *Journal of Neuroscience 20*, 7,017–7,023.

Berman, D. E., Hazvi, S., Rosenblum, K., Seger, R., and Dudai, Y. (1998). Specific and differential activation of mitogen-activated protein kinase cascades by unfamiliar taste in the insular cortex of the behaving rat. *Journal of Neuroscience 18*, 10,037–10,044.

Bures, J., Bermudez-Rattoni, F., and Yamamoto, T. (1998). *Conditioned taste aversion: Memory of a special kind.* New York: Oxford University Press.

Bures, J., Buresova, O., and Krivanek, J. (1988). *Brain and behavior: Paradigms for research in neural mechanisms.* New York: Wiley.

Garcia, J., Ervin, F. R., and Koeling, R. A. (1966). Learning with prolonged delay of reinforcement. *Psychonomic Science 5*, 121–122.

Garcia, J., Kimmeldorf, D. J., and Koelling, R. A. (1955). Conditioned aversion to saccharin resulting from exposure to gamma radiation. *Science 122*, 157–158.

Garcia, J., McGowan, B. K., Ervin, F. R., and Koelling, R. A. (1968). Cues: Their relative effectiveness as a function of the reinforcer. *Science 160*, 794–795.

Lamprecht, R., and Dudai, Y. (2000). The amygdala in conditioned taste aversion: It's there, but where. In J. Aggleton, ed., *The amygdala: A functional analysis*, 2nd edition. Oxford: Oxford University Press.

Rosenblum, K., Berman, D. E., Hazvi, S., Lamprecht, R., and Dudai, Y. (1997). NMDA receptors and the tyrosine phosphorylation of its 2B subunit in taste learning in the rat insular cortex. *The Journal of Neuroscience 17*, 5,129–5,135.

Schafe, G. E., Sollars, S. I., and Bernstein, I. L. (1995). The CS-US interval and taste aversion learning: A brief look. *Behavioral Neuroscience 109*, 799–802.

Yamamoto, Y., et al. (1994). Neural substrates for conditioned taste aversion in the rat. *Behavioral Brain Research 65*, 123–137.

Diego E. Berman

Edward Thorndike *(Psychology Archives, University of Akron)*

THORNDIKE, EDWARD (1874–1949)

Edward Lee Thorndike was born on August 31, 1874, in Williamsburg, Massachusetts. He died on August 9, 1949, in Montrose, New York. Thorndike proceeded very rapidly through his graduate education. After receiving a B.A. at Wesleyan University in 1895, he transferred to Harvard University, where he received a second B.A. in 1896 and his M.A. the following year. In 1898, Thorndike completed his Ph.D. at Columbia University, where he spent virtually his entire academic career as a professor at Teachers College (1899–1940). While this article will not dwell on Thorndike's achievements in the applied area that came to be called *educational psychology*, it should be noted that he created that field and developed it during his entire career at Columbia.

Thorndike's experimental studies of learning in monkeys brought him his first position at Teachers College as an instructor in genetic psychology. The dean of Teachers College, James E. Russell, hired Thorndike because he thought those studies to be "a pretty good stepping stone to a study of the nature and behavior of children" (*Current Biography*, 1941, p. 857). The ingenuity of Thorndike's animal experiments had made a very favorable impression on William James at Harvard, as well as on his major professors at Columbia, each of whom would have strongly endorsed him for the position in Teachers College. Thorndike's contributions to the fledgling science of psychology are of the highest importance and come down to us well into the end of the twentieth century.

The Study of Animal Intelligence

To Thorndike goes the credit for putting what was to become the experimental psychology of animal learning (the study of animal intelligence) on a sound laboratory and theoretical footing. Thorndike's studies (1911), which began around 1896 at Harvard and continued at Columbia University, were much more controlled than those of any of his predecessors. He employed a variety of vertebrate species (fish, chicks, dogs, cats, monkeys) and typically placed them in a problem situation, such as a puzzle box or a maze, from which they had to escape in order to get food and/or join companions. He observed the number of errors or latency to escape across trials and generally published quantitative information on the behavior of his experimental subjects. He attempted to control the life history or extra-experimental experiences of his animals and also kept the problem situation standard.

General Learning Theory

From his experimental observations, Thorndike proposed a general theory of learning that held that the animal learned the association between an act and a situation on the basis of the success of the act in bringing about a "satisfying" state of affairs. He proposed that it is through the Law of Effect that acts that bring about a satisfying state of affairs are gradually "stamped-in" the nervous system and those that lead to an annoying or discomforting state of affairs are gradually "stamped-out." Thorndike believed the animal had to behave actively to learn in the problem situation and that the animal's particular movements in the particular situation are validated or made invalid depending on whether they lead to satisfying or annoying consequences. Learning was thus the gradual association of particular movements in particular situations leading to certain ends. Thorndike believed that the actual connections between nerve cells in the brain underlying situation-response (S-R) associations were strengthened by reward ("satisfaction") and weakened by punishment ("annoyance").

To better appreciate Thorndike's theoretical contribution, it is necessary to briefly recall the history of thought about learning. The dominant theme of the psychological process involved in learning has always been some sort of associationism, so that was not Thorndike's particular contribution. The change that Thorndike injected into the concept of associationism concerned the nature of the association: It was not ideas that animals associated, it was movements (R) in a given situation (S) that led to satisfying consequences. Thorndike spoke of neuronal connections in the brain and hypothesized that the synaptic links between them were gradually made more traversable by use and by satisfactory consequences, whereas disuse or annoying consequences made the neuronal connections underlying other S-R associations less traversable. This was Thorndike's neurological account of trial-and-error learning, later reintroduced and expanded in a significant way by Donald O. Hebb (1949).

The foregoing represents Thorndike's bequest to what became "general behavior (learning) theory" in the field of psychological science in the 1940s. Today, general behavior theory no longer holds such a central place in psychological science.

Contributions to Animal Psychology

Thorndike also made three influential contributions to comparative (animal) psychology. First, by the introduction of the puzzle box and other standard testing situations, and the careful quantification of his observations, he set the comparative psychology of learning on an objective course from which it has rarely deviated. Thorndike also incidentally helped pave the way for the methodological and theoretical Behaviorism of John B. Watson a decade later, but it is clear that a number of other significant intellectual threads were tending in that same direction around (and even before) the turn of the century: Ivan Sechenov's "reflexes of the brain" (1863), Ivan Pavlov's highly quantitative conditioning procedures (Yerkes and Morgulis, 1909), Jacques Loeb's (1912) physico-chemical reductionism and his tropistic theory of psychology (movements are "forced" by external stimuli), and especially H. S. Jennings's (1906) objective experimental approach to behavioral adaptation in single-celled paramecia, among other protozoan and lower metazoan organisms. In fact, with the publication of Watson's *Behavior: An Introduction to Comparative Psychology* (1914) and *Psychology from the Standpoint of a Behaviorist* (1919), virtually all of the general psychology became objective in methodology. Psychology became the study of behavior (instead of the mind), with the conditioned response (reflex) as its primary unit of analysis and conditioning as its tool. (Not all would agree that psychology should be limited to the study of reflexes or conditioning, so cognitive psychology has become quite popular in the late 1900s.)

Second, Thorndike postulated that *all* learning involved the Law of Exercise (use and disuse) and the

Law of Effect. Therefore, from the comparative-psychological viewpoint, according to Thorndike, animals differed merely in "the delicacy, number, complexity, and permanence of associations." On these measures, dogs were somewhat more intelligent than cats, dogs and cats exceeded fish, monkeys exceeded dogs and cats, and humankind exceeded monkeys. (However, a real "gauge" of intelligence or learning ability—or a genuine application of a gauge—was still lacking.) According to Thorndike, nonhuman animals did not have ideas: *Homo sapiens* had ideas but these were derived from learning via exercise and effect.

These issues (S-R association and the roles of behavioral activity and reinforcement) have remained prominent to this day in general learning (behavior) theory, which one might define somewhat mischievously as the noncomparative approach to animal intelligence—if we understand by "comparative" the search for species *differences* as well as similarities not only in behavioral adjustment per se but also in the psychological processes mediating these adjustments. General behavior theory holds that principles of conditioning are applicable across all vertebrate species, including humans, and that cognitive psychology will one day be explicable in terms of principles of conditioning. The power or influence of conditioning theory has waned considerably in the final decades of the 1900s, whereas cognitive psychology is in the ascendancy.

Third, one of Thorndike's least appreciated contributions to comparative psychology is embodied in his notion that as we "ascend" the vertebrate series of animals, we likely have the possibility for the learning of more associations more quickly and lastingly because the trend is for the brain to be larger and thus to have more connections (synapses) in it. Thorndike does not give us his authority for this generalization about the evolution of the brain, but likely he was following Herbert Spencer and the writings of more contemporaneous, neurologically well-versed writers such as the Herrick brothers (Clarence Luther, the originator of psychobiology, and his younger brother C. Judson). In any event, this grand generalization resurfaced, with new trappings, in Hebb's (1949) concept of the A/S ratio: the ratio of association area to sensory projection area of the brain. Although there are no exact figures available, the ratio of association to primary sensory areas increases rather remarkably from the "lower" vertebrates (fishes, amphibians, reptiles) to the "higher" ones (birds and mammals).

By inference, Hebb (1949) assumed this ratio to be relevant "to the greater speed with which the 'lower' species can learn to respond selectively to the environment, and to the comparative simplicity of the behavior when it is fully developed" (p. 126). He also predicted the relevance of the ratio to the slow initial or primary learning of higher vertebrates (especially primates), in which the sensory projections are small relative to the size of the association areas: "If the sensory projection is small, association cortex large, the [environmental] control will take longer; the period of 'primary learning,' that is, will be long" (p. 124). Finally, the larger association area of the higher vertebrates (birds and mammals) would account for their greater efficiency at maturity. For Hebb, the learning capacity of higher species at maturity is not merely the capacity for a greater number of associations (Thorndike); it also reflects an emancipation from direct control by the stimulus of the moment from the immediate environment (i.e., an evolutionary difference in central or psychological mediation).

In recent years, an important tome has appeared to put some meat on the bare bones of Thorndike's and Hebb's speculations on the increase in the size of the brain in the vertebrate lineage: Harry Jerison's *Evolution of the Brain and Intelligence* (1973). There has indeed been a progressive enlargement of the brain even when the general increase in body size in higher versus lower vertebrates is calculated in the equation. Birds and mammals stand out conspicuously in "encephalization quotient" when compared with lower vertebrates of the same body size: Birds and mammals have "extra neurons" when their brain size is compared to the size it ought to be, given a high correlation between brain and body size across species (not, however, across individuals *within* a species). The conventional explanation for the increase in brain size in birds and mammals is "that they had invaded new niches in which there was an adaptive advantage for enlarged brains" (Jerison, 1973, p. 16).

With Jerison's elegant statistical formulas we at last have a metric or gauge (however gross it may be) for the evolution of the brain. But what of the evolution of intelligence? Is it valid to continue to ask whether intelligence (learning ability) has evolved in the usual sense that transcends ecological niches and ecological considerations? If so, can it be meaningfully and validly measured in the laboratory? What is the psychological gauge? These issues bedevil us to the present day with supporters on both sides of the controversy.

[*Some material for this entry was excerpted, with permission, from G. Gottlieb (1979), Comparative psychology and ethology, in E. Hearst, ed., The first century of experimental psychology. Hillsdale, NJ: Erlbaum.*]

Bibliography

Bitterman, M. E. (1965). Phyletic differences in learning. *American Psychologist 20*, 396–410.

Gottlieb, G. (1984). Evolutionary trends and evolutionary origins: Relevance to theory in comparative psychology. *Psychological Review 91*, 448–456.

Hebb, D. O. (1949). *The organization of behavior.* New York: Wiley.

Hodos, W., and Campbell, C. B. G. (1969). Scala naturae: Why there is no theory in comparative psychology. *Psychological Review 76*, 337–350.

Jennings, H. S. (1906). *The behavior of lower organisms.* New York: Macmillan.

Jerison, H. (1973). *Evolution of the brain and intelligence.* New York: Academic Press.

Loeb, J. (1912; reprint 1964). *The mechanistic conception of life*, ed. D. Fleming. Cambridge, MA: Harvard University Press.

Sechenov, I. M. (1863; reprint 1965). *Reflexes of the brain*, trans. S. Belsky. Cambridge, MA: MIT Press.

Thorndike, E. L. (1911; reprint 1965). *Animal intelligence.* New York: Hafner.

Watson, J. B. (1914). *Behavior: An introduction to comparative psychology.* New York: Henry Holt.

—— (1919). *Psychology from the standpoint of a behaviorist.* Philadelphia: Lippincott.

Yerkes, R. M., and Morgulis, S. (1909). The method of Pawlow in animal psychology. *Psychological Bulletin 6*, 257–273.

Gilbert Gottlieb

TIP-OF-THE-TONGUE PHENOMENON

The tip-of-the-tongue (TOT) phenomenon refers to the experience of feeling confident that one knows an answer, yet is unable to produce the word. For example, in conversation or writing most people have had the occasional experience of trying, but failing to retrieve someone's name or a word from memory. This type of memory retrieval has been referred to as a tip-of-the-tongue (TOT) state because one experiences the frustrating feeling that the retrieval of the word is imminent and on the "tip of the tongue." Although psychologists have long been aware of this phenomenon, Roger Brown and David McNeill (1966) conducted one of the first experimental studies of TOT states. In this study, they attempted to experimentally induce TOT states in college students by presenting definitions of relatively rare words (e.g., *to give up the throne*). The subjects' task was to name the word for the definition (e.g., *abdicate*). Brown and McNeill found that they could induce a TOT state on approximately 10 percent of trials.

Subsequent research on TOT states has been conducted by experimentally inducing TOT states in the laboratory or asking subjects to keep diaries of everyday occurrences of TOTs (Brown, 1991). These studies have yielded varied characteristics of TOT states. For example, TOTs are more likely to occur for infrequently used words. Interestingly, when experiencing a TOT state, subjects are often able to accurately retrieve information about the non-recalled word (e.g., the first letter of the word or the number of syllables). Thus, subjects seem to have partial information available about the target word, yet cannot retrieve the word. Also, subjects sometimes report an alternate word that comes to mind and seems to "block" the retrieval of the target word. These "blockers" often share semantic (i.e., meaning) or phonological (i.e., sound) features with the target word (e.g., *abide* for the word *abdicate*). Diary studies of naturally occurring TOTs have revealed that most often TOTs are resolved spontaneously, such that the target word seems to simply "pop into mind" *after* previous retrieval attempts have been abandoned (Burke, MacKay, Worthley, and Wade, 1991; Heine, Ober, and Shenaut, 1999).

There have been two competing theoretical explanations for why TOT states occur during memory retrieval. The blocking hypothesis states that TOTs are caused by an alternate, more accessible word that first comes to mind that then serves to block or inhibit the retrieval of the correct target word. Support for the blocking explanation comes from the experimental finding that presenting a phonologically related cue word with a definition for a target word resulted in *more* TOTs than when an unrelated cue word was presented (Jones, 1989; Jones and Langford, 1987). Similar results have been found by presenting cues that share orthography (letters) with the target word (Smith and Tindell, 1997). Also, it appears that TOTs are more difficult to resolve when an alternate word has come to mind than when there is no alternate word (Burke et al., 1991), possibly suggesting that the alternate word blocks the target word and thus causes the TOT.

On the other hand, the incomplete activation hypothesis states that "blocker" words are merely the consequence, not the cause of TOTs. According to this explanation, TOTs are caused by the weak or incomplete activation of the target word. Semantic information about the target word may be activated, but the corresponding phonological representation may be only partially activated. A more accessible, phonologically similar alternate word may become activated and at first appear to "block" the target word. Based on the incomplete activation hypothesis, one would expect that providing a phonologically related cue word with the definition should actually facilitate target retrieval, rather than produce a TOT state. Meyer and Bock (1992) provided initial evidence for the incomplete activation hypothesis. In three experiments that were designed to address these competing explanations (blocking versus incomplete activation), Meyer and Bock reported (1) semantically and phonologically related cue words facilitated rather than hindered target word retrieval (contrary to Jones's findings); (2) phonological cues facilitated retrieval more than semantic cues; and (3) these related cues facilitated retrieval even after an initial unsuccessful target retrieval attempt. Subsequent studies also have provided evidence that processing phonologically related words decreases TOT states and increases correct target responses (James and Burke, 2000), lending further support to the incomplete activation explanation of TOTs.

Although most people experience TOTs occasionally, there is evidence that TOTs may increase with age. TOT experiences represent a common memory complaint of older adults and thus have been extensively studied in the older adult population. Indeed, both laboratory and diary studies indicate that older adults report more TOT experiences and have less partial information available about target words than younger adults (Brown and Nix, 1996; Burke et al., 1991; Heine et al., 1999). The literature has been somewhat inconsistent regarding whether older adults report more or fewer alternate words (i.e., blockers) that come to mind while in a TOT state. There appears to be no age differences in terms of the percentage of TOTs resolved or the time to resolution. As might be expected, theoretical accounts for the increase in TOTs as a function of old age have focused on age-related deficits in word-retrieval due to (1) the interfering effects of related words that act as blockers that inhibit the retrieval of the target words; or (2) incomplete activation of the target due to degraded connections between the semantic representation and the phonological representation of the word (Burke et al., 1991; James and Burke, 2000).

There also has been an interest in the neural correlates of TOTs as a reflection of memory retrieval failure. Using neuroimaging techniques (event-related fMRI), Maril, Wagner, and Schacter (2001) scanned subjects while answering general knowledge questions. Subjects indicated whether they knew the answer (successful retrieval), did not know the answer (unsuccessful retrieval), or were in a TOT state. The results indicated that there was a selective response in anterior cingulate-prefrontal cortices of the brain during a TOT state, relative to successful and unsuccessful retrievals. This is interesting because this area of the brain has been associated with the control and resolution of cognitive conflict. Thus, these neuroimaging results seem to correspond with the behavioral experience of TOT states.

The experimental study of TOTs has provided psychologists with valuable information on the process of memory retrieval. Neuroimaging data may further delineate the neural underpinnings of this everyday memory phenomenon.

Bibliography

Brown, A. S. (1991). A review of the tip-of-the-tongue experience. *Psychological Bulletin 109,* 204–223.

Brown, A. S., and Nix, L. A. (1996). Age-related changes in the tip-of-the-tongue experience. *American Journal of Psychology 109,* 79–91.

Brown, R., and McNeill, D. (1966). The "tip of the tongue" phenomenon. *Journal of Verbal Learning and Verbal Behavior 5,* 325–337.

Burke, D., MacKay, D. G., Worthley, J., and Wade, E. (1991). On the tip of the tongue: What causes word finding failures in young and older adults? *Journal of Memory and Language 30,* 542–579.

Heine, M. K., Ober, B. A., and Shenaut, G. K. (1999). Naturally occurring and experimentally induced tip-of-the-tongue experiences in three adult age groups. *Psychology and Aging 14,* 445–457.

James, L. E., and Burke, D. M. (2000). Phonological priming effects on word retrieval and tip-of-the-tongue experiences in young and older adults. *Journal of Experimental Psychology: Learning, Memory, and Cognition 26,* 1,378–1,391.

Jones, G. V. (1989). Back to Woodworth: Role of interlopers in the tip-of-the-tongue phenomenon. *Memory & Cognition 17,* 69–76.

Jones, G. V., and Langford, S. (1987). Phonological blocking in the tip of the tongue state. *Cognition 26,* 115–122.

Maril, A., Wagner, A. D., and Schacter, D. L. (2001). On the tip of the tongue: An event-related fMRI study of semantic retrieval failure and cognitive conflict. *Neuron 31,* 653–660.

Meyer, A. S., and Bock, K. (1992). The tip-of-the-tongue phenomenon: Blocking or partial activation. *Memory & Cognition 20,* 715–726.

Smith, S. M., and Tindell, D. R. (1997). Memory blocks in word fragment completion caused by involuntary retrieval of orthographically related primes. *Journal of Experimental Psychology: Learning, Memory, and Cognition 23,* 355–370.

Janet M. Duchek
Jessica M. Logan

TOLMAN, EDWARD C. (1886–1959)

The American psychologist Edward Chace Tolman was a forerunner of modern cognitive psychology; he showed that animals in learning mazes acquire organized spatial and temporal information about the maze and about the consequences of various alternative behaviors. In developing this approach, he was combating the dominant views of his time, which emphasized the acquisition of conditioned reflexes rather than knowledge about environmental events. Although several short biographies or reviews of Tolman's contributions are available (Crutchfield, 1961; Crutchfield et al., 1960; Hilgard, 1980; Innes, 1999, 2000; McFarland, 1993; Ritchie, 1964; Tolman, 1952), it is especially appropriate that one be included in an encyclopedia of learning and memory because workers in this field today are using ideas that were initiated and often developed by Tolman, although they do not necessarily recognize the source. Tolman's concepts and findings have helped to shape modern understanding of learning, memory, and cognition.

Edward C. Tolman *(Psychology Archives, University of Akron)*

Early Life

Tolman was born in Newton, Massachusetts, on April 14, 1886, into a prosperous family that valued hard work, high thinking, and social responsibility. After high school he attended the Massachusetts Institute of Technology, where his father served on the board of trustees. In his autobiography Tolman comments, "I went to MIT not because I wanted to be an engineer but because I had been good at mathematics and physics in high school and because of family pressure. After graduating from Technology (in electrochemistry), I became more certain of my own wants and transferred to Harvard for graduate work in philosophy and psychology" (1952, p. 323).

Among the experiences at Harvard that Tolman mentions as having influenced his later life were Ralph Barton Perry's course in ethics, which, he wrote, "laid the basis for my later interest in motivation and indeed gave me the main concepts (reinforced by a reading of McDougall's *Social Psychology* as part of the requirement of the course) which I have retained ever since; . . . Holt's seminar in epistemology in which I was introduced to and excited by the 'New Realism'; and Yerkes' course in comparative, using Watson's *Behavior: An Introduction to Comparative Psychology*, which was just out, as a text" (p. 325). Tolman also spent the summer of 1912 at the University

of Giessen in Germany, where he studied with Kurt Koffka, one of the founders of Gestalt psychology.

In 1915 Tolman married Kathleen Drew and received his Ph.D. He then spent three years as an instructor at Northwestern University before accepting a position at the University of California at Berkeley in 1918. Except for brief periods, Tolman spent the rest of his life at Berkeley, where he had a distinguished scientific career and was an intellectual leader in the university community.

Early Experiments in Animal Learning

The line of research that occupied most of Tolman's life started when, on arriving in Berkeley, he found, he later wrote, that "it was up to me to suggest a new course. Remembering Yerkes' course and Watson's textbook, I proposed 'Comparative Psychology,' and it was this that finally launched me down the behaviorist slope" (1952, p. 329). This slope may have been behaviorist, but it was of a new and unusual kind that reflected Tolman's education at Harvard.

In his early experiments and papers, Tolman focused on the the rat's behavior in the maze to the exclusion of other types of apparatuses because it gave opportunities for observing the animal's solution to problems in space, in getting from here to there. He believed that when a rat ran from the start of a maze to the goal, its behavior reflected a purpose—getting to the goal *in order to* get something—and knowledge about the spatial layout. In referring to such knowledge, Tolman used terms such as *sign-gestalt-expectation*, which referred to his assumption that if, in the presence of a certain sign (that is, the events at the start box and on into the maze), the rat behaved in a particular way, it would achieve certain goals. The term *gestalt* referred to Tolman's assumption that the rat was acquiring a "cognitive map" that would allow it to use its organized information in getting to the goal.

In Tolman's early writings, including his major book, *Purposive Behavior in Animals and Men* (1932), he maintained the neorealist argument that knowledge and purpose could be directly observed in the behavior of the rat in the maze. But by 1932 he was also working with a different idea: that knowledge and purpose were inferences from behavior rather than characteristics of behavior. These inferences Tolman came to call "intervening variables" to convey the idea that knowledge and purpose intervene between the stimulus and behavior and guide the behavior (Tolman, 1938). In his autobiography Tolman (1952) takes the position that such intervening variables not only serve as summary statements that bring together data but also refer to real, presumably causal events.

Latent Learning Experiments

Tolman and his students conducted a vigorous, broad program of research on learning and problem solving in rats that served both to test his ideas and to change them in the light of new data. Two lines of research will be mentioned briefly here. The first, latent learning experiments, showed that rats learn about the layout of a complex maze even though, in the absence of reward, they show little or no evidence of such learning. When, after some trials, they are first rewarded in the goal box, they show almost error-free behavior on the next trial. These latent learning experiments demonstrated several points. First, learning is different from performance and is occurring even when there is no clear evidence for it. Current reviews show that research of this sort continues to grow and prove fruitful. Second, the latent learning experiments showed that rats gain organized knowledge of the maze that transcended the conceptual framework of stimulus-response. Third, animals learn *about* rewards. This conclusion was inconsistent with the dominant view of the era: that rewards determine which behaviors are learned. Tolman's conclusion is consistent with much later research in Pavlovian conditioning (Rescorla, 1978).

Groundbreaking Research

A second line of research, closely related to the first, directed a variety of cleverly constructed experiments to the problem of whether the animal could use its knowledge of the maze to make inferences about what to do in new situations. Tolman's team guided rats to the goal along a circuitous route for a number of trial, then deprived it of that route, and then exposed it to a variety of alternatives, one of which would lead more directly to the goal. The results showed that the animal was able to use its knowledge about the spatial arrangements in the room to make the appropriate inference and take the direct route. Other research by Tolman and his students aimed at control processes such as selective testing of alternative possible solutions ("hypotheses" and "vicarious trial and error").

At a time when learning theorists were still trying to establish *the* theory of learning, Tolman (1949) published an article entitled "There Is More than One Kind of Learning." In it he proposed that some of the basic disputes about learning might be resolved if investigators agreed that there are a number of kinds of learning: "The theory and laws appropriate to one kind may well be different to those appropriate to other kinds" (p. 144). Some of the types of learning that Tolman proposed are still under investigation.

Although Tolman, like his contemporaries, thought mostly in terms of the plasticity of behavior, he did not ignore genetic influences. In fact, in 1924 he was the first to apply the technique of selective breeding to the study of genetics of behavior, obtaining "maze-bright" and "maze-dull" strains of rats. His student Robert Tryon then carried out a successful program of selective breeding for maze ability over several generations. This was replicated in other laboratories and extended to other kinds of behavior. This clear evidence for the influence of genes on behaviors was important in holding a place for behavior genetics during the period when environmentalism was dominant (McClearn and Foch, 1988).

All of Tolman's research showed a remarkably coherent but nevertheless broad-ranging character. Although he dissented from the animal-learning orthodoxy from the 1930s through 1950s, Tolman's position had become a dominant one in animal learning by the 1980s and 1990s.

Later Accomplishments

Tolman received many honors, including election to the Society of Experimental Psychologists, the National Academy of Sciences, the American Philosophical Society, and the American Academy of Arts and Sciences. He was an honorary fellow of the British Psychological Society and was awarded honorary degrees by a number of universities. Tolman was president of the American Psychological Association in 1937, president of the Society for the Psychological Study of Social Issues in 1940, and vice president of the American Association for the Advancement of Science in 1942. The Fourteenth International Congress of Psychology was scheduled to be held in the United States in 1954, and Tolman was to be its president. When it became apparent that the United States, because of its anticommunist policy, was likely to refuse admission to many participants from abroad, the venue was changed to Canada, and Tolman became copresident along with Canadian psychologist Edward A. Bott.

In 1949, Tolman took a leadership role in the Berkeley faculty's resistance to the imposition of a loyalty oath by the university. Prevented from teaching, he spent the academic year of 1949–1950 away from Berkeley. The nonsigners finally won their case in court in 1953, gaining recognition of tenure at the university, and Tolman's professorship was restored.

See also: LEARNING THEORY: A HISTORY

Bibliography

Crutchfield, R. S. (1961). Edward Chace Tolman. *American Journal of Psychology* 74, 135–141.

Crutchfield, R. S., Krech, D., and Tryon, R. C. (1960). Edward Chace Tolman: A life of scientific and social purpose. *Science 131* 714–716.

Hilgard, E. R. (1980). Edward Chace Tolman. *Dictionary of American Biography*, Supp. 6. New York: Scribners.

Innis, N. K. (1999). Edward Chace Tolman. In J. A. Garraty and M. C. Carnes, eds., *American national biography*, Vol. 21. New York: Oxford University Press.

—— (2000). Edward Chace Tolman. In A. E. Kazdin, ed., *Encyclopedia of psychology*, Vol. 8. Washington, DC: American Psychological Association.

McClearn, G. E., and Foch, T. T. (1988). Behavioral genetics. In R. C. Atkinson, R. J. Herrnstein, G. Lindzey, and R. D. Luce, eds., *Steven's handbook of experimental psychology*, 2nd edition, Vol. 1. New York: Wiley.

McFarland, D. (1993). Animal behaviour: Psychobiology, ethology, and evolution. New York: Wiley.

Rescorla, R. A. (1978). Some implications of a cognitive perspective on Pavlovian conditioning. In S. H. Hulse, H. Fowler, and W. K. Honig, eds., *Cognitive processes in animal behavior*. Hillsdale, NJ: Erlbaum.

Ritchie, B. F. (1964). Edward Chace Tolman. *Biographical Memoirs, National Academy of Sciences*, Vol. 37. New York: Columbia University Press.

Tolman, E. C. (1920). Instinct and purpose. *Psychological Review 27*, 217–233.

—— (1924). The inheritance of maze-learning ability in rats. *Journal of Comparative Psychology 4*, 1–18.

—— (1932). *Purposive behavior in animals and men*. New York: Century.

—— (1938). The determiners of behavior at a choice point. *Psychological Review 45*, 1–41.

—— (1949). There is more than one kind of learning. *Psychological Review 27*, 217–233.

—— (1952). Autobiography. In E. G. Boring et al., eds., *A history of psychology in autobiography*, Vol. 4. Worcester, MA: Clark University Press.

Mark R. Rosenzweig
Donald A. Riley

U

UNDERWOOD, BENTON (1915–1994)

Benton J. Underwood was one of the preeminent leaders in the postwar development of research on the acquisition and retention of verbal materials (Keppel, 1997, p. 469). He studied verbal learning and memory in the 1940s at the University of Missouri, then later at the University of Iowa, under such important figures as Arthur W. Melton (Missouri), John A. McGeoch, and Kenneth W. Spence (both at Iowa). In 1946, Underwood took a teaching position at Northwestern University in Evanston, Illinois, where he remained until his retirement in 1983. Over four decades he did groundbreaking work in associative learning, verbal discrimination, transfer of training, distribution of practice, interference and forgetting, and the composition of memory.

Antecedents

Hermann Ebbinghaus carried out the first systematic study of verbal learning and memory in 1885. Acting as both experimenter and subject, he learned lists of nonsense syllables (e.g., *cak, roq*) and then tested his retention of them. His efforts provide our first picture of an empirically generated forgetting curve. Ebbinghaus's curve revealed substantial forgetting in the hours immediately following original learning. Why was there so much forgetting so soon after learning? This puzzle Underwood later helped to solve.

At the start of the twentieth century, William James's work was the chief influence on American psychology. Unlike German psychologists, who em-phasized the mind's structure and had given birth to a scientific psychology, James stressed the mind's activity. His ideas, combined with those of British philosophers and the American spirit of doing and acting, created a movement called American Functionalism. A student of Underwood's once commented: "To my mind, the term *functionalist* and the name Underwood are synonymous" (Freund, 1998, p. 318).

The functionalist perspective within the newly developing field of psychology approached problems of learning and memory in associationistic terms. How are associations between verbal items learned and remembered? As Underwood commented, "I am an incurable associationist" (1982, p. 8). It seemed obvious to him that in innumerable instances associations played a dominant role in our learning and retention of verbal material: When did Christopher Columbus discover the new world? Who is the current vice president? Clearly, to answer such questions we must learn an association between initially unrelated facts (e.g., between a name and date). The experimental task given to subjects typically involved paired-associate learning: the presentation of pairs of items to a subject charged with learning an association between the members of each pair to facilitate the recall of the second item upon presentation of the first.

Another important characteristic of the functionalist perspective was its use of stimulus-response (S-R) language borrowed from behaviorism, which dominated American psychology until the 1950s. Paired-associate learning, for example, was described as

Benton Underwood (*Northwestern University Archives*)

learning an association between a stimulus (the first member of the pair) and a response (the second member). Principles of classical conditioning were incorporated into explanations of human learning and retention of verbal material. Forgetting of verbal material, for example, was discussed in terms of extinction and spontaneous recovery of associations, a language perfectly in tune with that of the behaviorists. Other salient characteristics of the functionalist orientation to psychology include an insistence on modest theory building, a close interplay between theory and data, and an interest in analyzing phenomena in terms of their component processes or parts.

Learning and Memory

In 1932 McGeoch argued that forgetting was due to the intervention of events that occured after the acquisition of information and was not simply a matter of decay or disuse. Forgetting caused by a learner's activities in the interval between original learning and a test of retention is called retroactive inhibition. Its primary mechanism was thought to be response competition. On this view, forgetting occurs when new learning competes with the original learning. In 1959, Underwood provided evidence for an additional mechanism, that of unlearning. He showed that original learning actually became unavailable for recall as new learning proceeded.

Nevertheless, additional research suggested that the more powerful factor producing forgetting was proactive inhibition. Proactive inhibition occurs when information learned before the target material interferes with retention (e.g., an old telephone number intrudes on your attempt to recall a more recent number). Because memory researchers often had their subjects learn and remember many lists, there was an opportunity to examine forgetting as a function of the number of prior lists acquired by subjects in the learning laboratory. In 1957, in a classic piece of detective work, Underwood showed that retention of a single list of items after twenty-four hours decreased as a function of the number of prior lists that had been learned (see Figure 1). Retention of a single list without prior learning was about 75 percent, not just 25 percent, which had been a conclusion drawn from Ebbinghaus's forgetting curve. Ebbinghaus was affected by the proactive inhibition resulting from learning and recalling many, many lists. In later years Underwood and his students demonstrated how proactive interference operates even in very short-term memory situations and provide further accounts of possible sources of proactive interference in long-term retention of verbal material.

An associationistic perspective led Underwood to conclude that associations of common words will likely occur implicitly during a learning task. An adult learning a list of words such as *sugar, bitter,* and *candy* will likely implicitly think of the word *sweet*. In 1965, Underwood showed that these implicit associative responses, or IARs, played a role in producing false recognition. For example, learners who experience words related to *sweet*, such as the above, later come to falsely state that they had actually experienced the word *sweet*. Underwood demonstrated a role for IARs in many different learning and memory tasks.

Attributes of Memory

Consider a simple learning task. A list of word pairs is presented. Your task is simply to remember which word in each pair is the right one (for example, as designated by the experimenter by underlining). When the word pairs are shown again (with no identification of right items) can you remember which is the right one? Of course you can, at least after a few learning trials. But how do you do it? In 1966, Underwood and his students presented a frequency theory of verbal discrimination learning. It is a beautiful example of the functionalist approach. The theory is modest in scope (accounting mainly for verbal discrimination decisions), closely tied to the data (making clear, easily tested predictions), and permits analysis of a larger phenomenon (verbal discrimination) into its constituent processes. The theory posits that subjects make decisions in verbal discrimination tasks based on a subjective frequency differential between right and wrong members. This situational frequency differential is built up through representational responses (a perceptual processing of the item), rehearsal responses, and implicit associative responses.

This theory has survived many tests and has been extended to other situations, accounting, for example, for our ability to perform on a recognition memory test. Consider what sometimes happens on a multiple-choice exam. Initially, one alternative looks right (familiar), but as we consider the other alternatives, our confidence decreases. Frequency theory suggests that the initial verbal discrimination is based on a subjective difference in frequency that arises from our prior study of the right item; but that differential is lost as we raise the frequency (familiarity) of other alternatives.

Underwood's thinking about frequency as an attribute of memory led to a consideration of the composition of memory. Or, as Underwood asked in 1969, "Of what does a memory consist?" (p. 559). His answer was that memory, our record of an event, is a collection of attributes. There is no corpus or body of memory that can be recalled directly. Memory attributes both aid discrimination (e.g., frequency) and retrieval (e.g., IARs). Many everyday experiences provide evidence of such a conceptualization. Tip-of-the-tongue experiences, for example, sometimes involve an ability to remember letters of a word (orthographic attribute) when we can't remember the whole word. Many students have had the experience of being able to remember where on a textbook page an answer was studied but not being able to remember the item itself (spatial attribute). Underwood's attribute theory helps to explain learners' performance in many tasks and, along with other multidimensional theories, has enhanced our understanding of memory.

Underwood published more than 200 scientific articles, books, chapters, and monographs, and his work elicited a plethora of awards and honors, including election, in 1970, to the National Academy of Sciences. He was a distinguished teacher and superb methodologist whose research and textbooks inspired the work of countless students and colleagues.

Figure 1

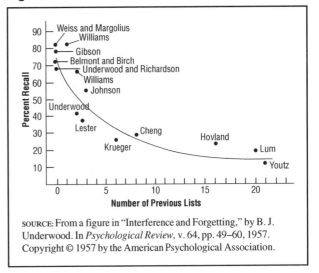

SOURCE: From a figure in "Interference and Forgetting," by B. J. Underwood. In *Psychological Review*, v. 64, pp. 49–60, 1957. Copyright © 1957 by the American Psychological Association.

Percent recall of a single list as a function of the number of previous lists learned in the experiment.

See also: EBBINGHAUS, HERMANN

Bibliography

Barnes, J. M., and Underwood, B. J. (1959). "Fate" of first-list associations in transfer theory. *Journal of Experimental Psychology 58*, 97–105.

Duncan, C. P., Sechrest, L., and Melton, A. W., eds. (1972). *Human memory: Festschrift in honor of Benton J. Underwood*. New York: Appleton-Century-Crofts.

Ekstrand, B. R., Wallace, W. P., and Underwood, B. J. (1966). A frequency theory of verbal discrimination learning. *Psychological Review 73*, 566–578.

Freund, J. S. (1998). Benton J. Underwood: A tribute of memories. In G. A. Kimble and M. Wertheimer, eds., *Portraits of pioneers in psychology*, Vol. 3. Mahweh, NJ: Erlbaum.

Keppel, G. (1997). Benton J. Underwood (1915–1994). *American Psychologist 52*, 469–470.

McGeoch, J. A. (1932). Forgetting and the law of disuse. *Psychological Review 39*, 352–370.

Postman, L. (1972). The experimental analysis of verbal learning and memory: Evolution and innovation. In C. P. Duncan, L. Sechrest, and A. W. Melton, eds., *Human memory: Festschrift in honor of Benton J. Underwood*. New York: Appleton-Century-Crofts.

Underwood, B. J. (1949). *Experimental psychology*. New York: Appleton-Century-Crofts.

—— (1957). Interference and forgetting. *Psychological Review 64*.

—— (1957). *Psychological research*. New York: Appleton-Century-Crofts.

—— (1965). False recognition produced by implicit verbal responses. *Journal of Experimental Psychology 70*, 122–129.

—— (1969). Attributes of memory. *Psychological Review 76*, 559–573.

—— (1982). *Studies in learning and memory: Selected papers*. New York: Praeger.

Zechmeister, E. B., and Nyberg, S. E. (1982). *Human memory: An introduction to research and theory*. Belmont, CA: Wadsworth.

Eugene B. Zechmeister

V

VESTIBULO-OCULAR REFLEX (VOR) PLASTICITY

The vestibulo-ocular reflex (VOR) is driven by head movement and moves the eyes in the direction opposite to the head movement, automatically stabilizing vision relative to space. The VOR is mediated by a trineuronal arc composed of the primary vestibular neurons, relay neurons in vestibular nuclei, and motoneurons for the extraocular muscles. The optokinetic eye-movement response (OKR) is another ocular reflex induced by optokinetic stimuli generated by movements of the visual field relative to the head. VOR and OKR share the same vestibular nuclear neurons and oculomotor neurons, and synergistically stabilize vision. The VOR/OKR pathways are attached with commissural connections between the bilateral vestibular nuclei, internuclear connections between motor nuclei, and other connections with the tegmentum and the cerebellum.

Two types of plasticity have been recognized in the VOR/OKR. The first is gradual recovery of the heavy nystagmus induced by unilateral labyrinthectomy (vestibular compensation) (Magnus, 1924; Vidal et al., 1998). A lesion to the cerebellum retards the onset of recovery, and, when made after recovery, it transiently removes the compensation. Hence, the cerebellum may play a role in initiating this type of plasticity (Courjon et al., 1982). The second is gradual changes of the VOR and OKR gain (amplitude ratio of eye rotation versus head or visual-field rotation) in altered visuovestibular environments (VOR/PKR ad-

aptation) (Gonshor and Melvill-Jones, 1974; Ito et al., 1974; Robinson, 1976). Since the flocculus, an evolutionarily old part of the cerebellum, sends inhibitory axons of Purkinje cells directly to the VOR relay neurons (Fukuda et al., 1972), the flocculus may be the center for the adaptation of VOR/OKR (Ito, 1982). The compensation and adaptation in the VOR/OKR provide simple model systems representing learning capabilities of neuronal circuits (Ito, 1984, 1998; Raymond et al., 1996).

Neuronal Circuit for the VOR and OKR

The VOR contains a number of component reflexes. They arise from the three semicircular canals (horizontal, anterior, and posterior) and two otolith organs (utricle and saccule) in each labyrinth and act on six extraocular muscles (medial and lateral rectus, superior and inferior rectus, superior and inferior oblique) in each eye. In experiments, the VOR is usually divisible into horizontal, vertical, or torsional components through the application of yaw, pitch, roll, linear motion or static tilt to the head. When moving freely, the VOR is mediated via the concerted operation of numerous parallel pathways linking the ten sensors in two labyrinths with the twelve muscles in two eyes (Ezure and Graf, 1984).

In the horizontal VOR, horizontal semicircular canals are stimulated by ipsilateral head rotations that result in transmission of neural signals via the primary vestibular nerve fibers to relay cells of the VOR in the vestibular nuclei. The VOR relay cells, in turn, transmit either excitatory or inhibitory signals to motoneurons in the abducens and oculomotor nuclei. Rotation of the head to one side induces contraction of the ipsilateral medial rectus and contralateral lateral rectus muscles, and relaxation of the ipsilateral lateral rectus and contralateral medial rectus muscles, so that both eyes move in a direction opposite to that of the head rotation. Optokinetic signals arising from the retina are sent to VOR relay neurons, inducing the OKR.

Cerebellar Connections to VOR/OKR Pathways

The flocculus in rabbits and cats has five to six major folia and in rats only one. The classic anatomy of the monkey cerebellum shows ten folia in the flocculus, but recent studies on neuronal connectivity have revealed that the rostrally located five folia belong to the ventral paraflocculus and not to the flocculus (Gerrits and Voogd, 1989). Purkinje cells, which are localized to a narrow zone (H zone, about one mm across) extending across the folia of the flocculus, supply inhibitory synapses to the horizontal VOR-relay neurons. Other zones related to the vertical or torsional VOR flank the H zone (Nagao et al., 1985; Sato and Kawasaki, 1991; Van der Steen et al., 1994). Physiological experiments detect these zones by local electrical stimulation, which induces distinct horizontal, vertical, or rotatory eye movements. The flocculus receives vestibular, optokinetic, and neck afferent signals via mossy fibers, and optokinetic and vestibular signals via climbing fibers (Ito, 1984).

The nodulus and uvula, other phylogenically old parts of the cerebellum, receive vestibular mossy fiber inputs through certain vestibular nuclear neurons, which receive Purkinje cell axons from the nodulus and uvula (Xiong and Matushita, 2000). The nodulus and uvula receive optokinetic signals via climbing fibers.

Velocity Storage and Neural Integrator

Head rotation in darkness at a constant velocity induces nystagmus, which consists of alternating slow phases representing the VOR and quick phases resetting the eye position. Under this condition impulses evoked in the first-order vestibular afferents decline rapidly, within five seconds. Yet the slow-phase velocity of the nystagmus decays slowly, with a time constant of about twenty seconds. There must be a brain-stem mechanism, a velocity storage that stores the initial head velocity as transduced by the canals and maintains it despite the decay in the firing rate of the canal afferents (Raphan et al., 1979). Since electrical stimulation of the nodulus and uvula induces a rapid de-

cline in the horizontal slow-phase velocity, these cerebellar regions may control the velocity storage (Solomon and Cohen, 1994). The same system is responsible for optokinetic after-nystagmus (OKAN).

In the VOR, the head velocity signals generated by the labyrinth are converted to eye position signals for the extraocular muscles. In the OKR, the retinal slip velocity signals are also integrated to eye position signals. Hence, the VOR/OKR pathways must contain a neural integrator mechanism (Robinson, 1975). The integrator for the horizontal VOR/OKR may involve the nucleus prepositus hypoglossi and/or the commissural inhibitory projections between bilateral vestibular nuclei (Arnold and Robinson, 1997). The integrator for the vertical VOR is provided by the interstitial nucleus of Cajal in the midbrain (Fukushima et al., 1992). The velocity storage and neural integrator may represent functions of the same neuronal circuit, but their identity remains unclear.

Compensation for Unilateral Labyrinthectomy

The behavioral recovery from unilateral labyrinthectomy in rats was accompanied by asymmetric expression of isoforms of protein kinase C (PKC α, γ, and δ) in the flocculonodular lobe, with a regionally selective increase in the number of PKC-immunopositive Purkinje cells contralateral to the lesion (Goto et al., 1997). This asymmetry occurred within six hours after the labyrinthectomy and was resolved to the control, symmetric pattern within twenty-four hours. The compensation was retarded in rats after intracerebroventricular application of PKC inhibitors (Balaban et al., 1999). Since PKC is required for induction of long-term depression (LTD) in Purkinje cells, these observations suggests that LTD plays a role in vestibular compensation. But because slow recovery of compensation still occurs after lesioning the cerebellum, plastic changes should occur also outside the cerebellum. Reserachers have found an increase in GABAergic neurons in cat vestibular nuclei after unilateral labyrinthectomy (Tighilet and Lacour, 2001); a neuronal network simulation suggests a change in the commissural inhibitory connections (Graham and Dutia, 2001).

VOR/OKR Adaptation

In laboratory experiments, sinusoidal or velocity-step, whole-body rotation in darkness induces the horizontal VOR; the VOR gain is the ratio of the attained eye velocity vs. the applied head velocity. The sinusoidal rotation is convenient for measuring the gain and phase of the VOR separately, whereas velocity steps enable us to separate components of VOR responses, which arise with different latencies.

The VOR exhibits marked adaptive changes in gain under sustained mismatching between movement of the head in space and movement of the visual surroundings. Long-term visuovestibular mismatching of days or months can be generated using prism or lens goggles (Gonshor and Melvill-Jones, 1974; Robinson, 1976). However, for short-term mismatching of one to four hours, it is convenient to use the combined rotation of the turntable on which the animal is mounted and a screen representing the visual surroundings (Ito et al., 1974; Nagao, 1989). Both the wearing of Dove prism goggles, which reverse the right-left axis of the visual field, and the in-phase rotation of the turntable and screen in the same direction cause adaptive reduction of horizontal VOR gain. Both the wearing of magnifying lenses (2x) and the out-of-phase rotation of the turntable and screen in opposite directions cause an adaptive increase in horizontal VOR gain. The OKR gain adaptively increases during sustained rotation of the visual field around a stationary animal.

The view that the flocculus is the center for the VOR/OKR adaptation gains support from the observation that the adaptation no longer occurs after lesioning the flocculus, interruption of the climbing fiber input to the interruption of the climbing fiber input to the flocculus, or deprivation of NO that is required for induction of LTD, as tested in various animals. Subdural application of a NO scavenger to the rabbit and monkey flocculus blocked VOR adaptation (Nagao and Ito, 1991). Injection of a NO scavenger or a NOS inhibitor into the goldfish cerebellum (Li et al., 1995) inhibited adaptive increase in VOR gain. NO synthase (NOS)-deficient mutant mice lacked OKR adaptation (Katoh et al., 2000). Induction of LTD also requires activation of PKC; accordingly, transgenic mice that selectively express the pseudosubstrate PKC inhibitor, PKC [19-31], in Purkinje cells lacked VOR adaptation (De Zeeuw et al., 1998).

Researchers have studied the effects of the acute removal of flocculus functions after the development of the VOR adaptation to determine whether or not the once-established VOR adaptation is retained in the flocculus. Microdialysis of lidocaine into the goldfish cerebellum abolished both induction and retention of the VOR adaptation (McElligot et al., 1998), suggesting that the memory for the VOR adaptation is retained, probably entirely, in the cerebellum. In another experiment on goldfish, however, no less than 30 percent of the altered VOR gain was retained after ablation of the cerebellum (Pastor et al., 1994), a result that favors the view that the memory is partly stored outside the cerebellum. A system identification

study on the monkey vertical VOR (Hirata and Highstein, 2001) suggests that adaptive changes occur in both the flocculus and nonflocculus pathways.

Neuronal Mechanisms of VOR Adaptation

The major signals of Purkinje cells are simple spikes, elicited by mossy-fiber inputs. In rabbits, ipsilateral horizontal head rotation causes either an increase (in-phase type) or decrease (out-of-phase type) in the simple spike discharges from H-zone Purkinje cells. During sustained visuovestibular mismatching, the simple spike modulation of H-zone Purkinje cells becomes predominantly out-of-phase or in-phase, corresponding to the increase or decrease in the VOR gain, respectively (Ito, 1984, 1998). Complex spikes representing climbing fiber signals are evoked by optokinetic stimuli. Researchers have assumed that these complex spikes encode retinal slips, but a study by Frens and colleagues suggests that they encode the eye-movement performance error rather than retinal slip (2001). The changes in simple spike-response patterns are supposed to result from LTD induced by error signals of climbing fibers and to cause the VOR gain changes (Ito 1982, 1998). Nevertheless, studies of the monkey flocculus/paraflocculus suggest that VOR adaptation is the cause, not the consequence, of the simple spike modulation in Purkinje cells that reflect eye velocity changes (Miles and Lisberger, 1981; Hirata and Highstein, 2001).

Comments

Although there is a scholarly consensus about the important roles of the cerebellum in the VOR plasticity, its mechanisms remain unclear, partly because of the use of different animal species and different types of VOR. The sampling of Purkinje cells from both the flocculus and ventral paraflocculus also complicate interpretation because these areas have substantially different input and output connections (Gerrits and Voogd, 1989; Nagao et al., 1997a, b). It should be noted that these areas have different functional assignments: The flocculus plays a role in the control of VOR and OKR, whereas the ventral paraflocculus plays roles in ocular following movement (Shidara et al., 1993) and in the smooth pursuit of a moving target (Stone and Lisberger, 1990). These complications pose the need for further research.

See also: GUIDE TO THE ANATOMY OF THE BRAIN: CEREBELLUM; LONG-TERM DEPRESSION IN THE CEREBELLUM, HIPPOCAMPUS, AND NEOCORTEX

Bibliography

Arnold, D. B., and Robinson, D. A. (1997). The oculomotor integrator: Testing of a neural network model. *Experimental Brain Research 113,* 57–74.

Balaban, C. D., Preilino, M., and Romero, G. G. (1999). Protein kinase C inhibition blocks the early appearance of vestibular compensation. *Brain Research 845*, 97–101.

Courjon, J. H., Flandrin, J. M., Jeannerod, M., and Schmid, R. (1982). The role of the flocculus in vestibular compensation after hemilabyrinthectomy. *Brain Research 239*, 251–257.

De Zeeuw, C. I., Hansel, C., Bian, F., Koekkoek, S. K. E., Van Alphen, A. M., Linden, D. J., and Oberdick. J. (1998). Expression of a protein kinase C inhibitor in Purkinje cells blocks cerebellar LTD and adaptation of the vestibulo-ocular reflex. *Neuron 20*, 495–508.

Ezure, K., and Graf, W. (1984). A quantitative analysis of the spatial organization of the vestibulo-ocular reflexes in lateral- and frontal-eyed animals. II. Neuronal networks underlying vestibulo-oculomotor coordination. *Neuroscience 12*, 95–109

Frens, M. A., Mathoera, A. L., and van der Steen, J. (2001). Floccular complex spike response to transparent retinal slip. *Neuron 30*, 796–801.

Fukuda, J., Highstein, S. M., and Ito, M. (1972). Cerebellar inhibitory control of the vestibulo-ocular reflex investigated in rabbit's IIIrd nucleus. *Experimental Brain Research 14*, 511–526.

Fukushima, K., Kaneko, C. R. S., and Fuchs, A. F. (1992). The neuronal substrate of integration in the oculomotor system. *Progress in Neurobiology 39*, 609–639.

Gerrits, N. M., and Voogd, J. (1989). The topographical organization of climbing and mossy fiber afferents in the flocculus and the ventral paraflocculus in rabbit, cat and monkey. *Experimental Brain Research Series 17*, 26–29.

Gonshor, A., and Melvill-Jones, G. M. (1974). Extreme vestibulo-ocular adaptation induced by prolonged optical reversal of vision. *Journal of Physiology, London 256*, 381–414.

Goto, M. M., Romero, G. G., and Balaban, C. D. (1997). Transient changes in flocculonodular lobe protein kinase C expression during vestibular compensation. *Journal of Neuroscience 17*, 4,367–4,381.

Graham, B. P., and Dutia M. B. (2001). Cellular basis of vestibular compensation: Analysis and modeling of the role of the commissural inhibitory system. *Experimental Brain Research 137*, 387–396.

Hirata, Y., and Highstein, S. M. (2001). Acute adaptation of the vestibuloocular reflex: signal processing by fluccular and ventral parafloccular Purkinje cells. *Journal of Neurophysiology 85*, 2,267–2,288.

Ito, M. (1982). Cerebellar control of the vestibulo-ocular reflex-around the flocculus hypothesis. *Annual Review of Neuroscience 5*, 275–296.

——— (1984). *The Cerebellum and Neural Control*. Raven Press: New York.

——— (1998). Cerebellar learning in the vestibulo-ocular reflex. *Trends in Cognitive Science 2*, 313–321.

Ito, M., Shiida, N. Yagi, N., and Yamamoto, M. (1974). The cerebellar modification of rabbit's horizontal vestibulo-ocular reflex induced by sustained head rotation combined with visual stimulation. *Proceedings of Japan Academy 50*, 85–89.

Katoh, A., Kitazawa, H., Itohara, S., and Nagao, S. (2000). Inhibition of nitric oxide synthesis and gene-knockout of neuronal nitric oxide synthase impaired adaptation of mouse optokinetic response eye movements. *Learning and Memory 7*, 220–226.

Li, J., Smith S. S., and McElligott, J. G. (1995). Cerebellar nitric oxide is necessary for vestibulo-ocular reflex adaptation, a sensorimotor model of learning. *Journal of Neurophysiology 74*, 489–494.

Magnus, R. (1924). *Korperstellung*. Berlin: Springer.

McElligot, J. D., Beeton, P., and Polk, J. (1998). Effect of cerebellar inactivation by lidocaine microdialysis on the vestibuloocular reflex in goldfish. *Journal of Neurophysiology 79*, 1,286–1,294.

Miles, F. A., and Lisberger, S. G. (1981). Plasticity in the vestibuloocular reflex: A new hypothesis. *Annual Review of Neuroscience 4*, 273–299.

Nagao, S. (1989). Behavior of floccular Purkinje cells correlated with adaptation of vestibulo–ocular reflex in pigmented rabbits. *Experimental Brain Research 77*, 531–540.

Nagao, S., and Ito, M. (1991). Subdural application of hemoglobin to the cerebellum blocks vestibuloocular reflex adaptation. *NeuroReport 2*, 193–196.

Nagao, S., Ito, M., and Karachot, L. (1985). Eye field in the cerebellar flocculus of pigmented rabbit determined with local electrical stimulation. *Neuroscience Research 3*, 39–51.

Nagao, S., Kitamura, T., Nakamura, N., Hiramatsu, T., and Yamada, J. (1997a). Differences of the primate flocculus and ventral paraflocculus in the mossy and climbing fiber input organization. *Journal of Comparative Neurology 382*, 480–498.

——— (1997b). Location of efferent terminals of the primate flocculus and ventral paraflocculus revealed by anterograde axonal transport methods. *Neuroscience Research 27*, 257–269.

Pastor A. M., De Cruz, R. R., and Baker, R. (1994). Cerebellar role in adaptation of the goldfish vestibuloocular reflex. *Journal of Neurophysiology 72*, 1,383–1,394.

Raphan, T., Matsuo, V., and Cohen, B. (1979). Velocity storage in the vestibulo-ocular reflex arc (VOR). *Experimental Brain Research 35*, 229–248.

Raymond, J. L., Lisberger, S. G., and Mauk, M. D. (1996). The cerebellum: A neuronal learning machine? *Science 272*, 1,126–1,131.

Robinson, D. A. (1975). Oculomotor control signal. In G. Lennerstrand and P. Bach-y-Rita, eds., *Basic mechanisms of ocular motility and their clinical implications*. Pergamon: Oxford.

——— (1976). Adaptive gain control of vestibuloocular reflex by the cerebellum. *Journal of Neurophysiology 39*, 954–969.

Sato, Y., and Kawasaki, T. (1991). Identification of the Purkinje cell/ climbing fiber zone and its target neurons responsible for eye movement control by the cerebellar flocculus. *Brain Research Review 16*, 39–64.

Shidara, M., Kawano, M., Gomi, H., and Kawato, M. (1993). Inverse-dynamics model eye movement control by Purkinje cells in the cerebellum. *Nature 365*, 50–52.

Solomon, D. and Cohen, B. (1994). Stimulation of the nodulus and uvula discharges velocity storage in the vestibulo-ocular reflex. *Experimental Brain Research 102*, 57–68.

Stone, L. S., and Lisberger, S. G. (1990). Visual responses of Purkinje cells in the cerebellar flocculus during smooth–pursuit eye movements in monkeys. I. Simple spikes. *Journal of Neurophysiology 63*, 1,241–1,261.

Tighilet, B., and Lacour, M. (2001). Gamma amino butyric acid (GABA) immunoreactivity in the vestibular nuclei of normal and uynilateral vestibular neurectoimized cats. *European Journal of Neuroscience 13*, 2,255–2,267.

Van der Steen, J., Simpson, J. I., and Tan, J. (1994). Functional and anatomic organization of three-dimensional eye movements in rabbit cerebellar flocculus. *Journal of Neurophysiology 72*, 31–46.

Vidal, P.-P., de Waele, C., Vibert, N., and Muhlethaler, M. (1998). Vestibular compensation revisited. *Otolaryngology-Head and Neck Surgery*, *119*, 34–42.

Xiong, G., and Matushita, M. (2000). Connections of Purkinje cell axons of lobule X with vestibulocerebellar neurons projecting to lobule X or IX in the cat. *Experimental Brain Research 133*, 219–228.

Masao Ito

VISUAL MEMORY

See: MODALITY EFFECTS; PRIMATES, VISUAL
PERCEPTION AND MEMORY IN NONHUMAN;
VISUAL MEMORY, BRIGHTNESS AND FLUX IN

VISUAL MEMORY, BRIGHTNESS AND FLUX IN

The study of simple visual discriminations reveals fundamental properties of learning and memory in the nervous system. Physical measures of the light source include energy emitted (*flux*) or reflected (*reflectance*) from the stimulus per unit area. Heinrich Klüver (1942) called it *brightness* if the total amount of light was measured over the whole stimulus source (including contours and edges), and *density of luminous flux* if measured over a unit area of the stimulus. He concluded that visually decorticated monkeys could solve a luminous-flux problem but not a brightness problem.

Using this definition, a brightness discrimination includes both light intensity and light contrast on edges that contribute to pattern perception. A flux discrimination, on the other hand, pertains to differences in light intensity per unit area. This intensity can be for the whole stimulus (total flux) or for parts of the stimulus (local flux). For example, a horizontal-versus-vertical-stripes pattern problem can be equated for total flux and for total brightness (same number of contrasting contours) and yet the edges of the stimulus cards have differences in local flux. Discrimination tasks for intensity that are used for testing animals, whether black and white cards with edges or black and white alleys with an edge that creates a contrast (the wall separating the alleys), normally are not purely flux discriminations but are brightness discriminations that include elements of pattern discrimination. Discriminations more purely restricted to flux can be achieved by use of contact lenses that diffuse light and obscure edges, by successive discrimination problems in which both alleys being lit means to go one way or both alleys being dark means to go the other way, or by a shuttle box in which the subject sits in the middle of the apparatus, one alley is lit, and the alley 180 degrees away is not. The distinguishing feature between a flux and a brightness discrimination is that the latter has contours created by contrasting levels of flux within the same stimulus.

In the simplest visual discrimination a subject distinguishes between a black and a white stimulus card. With this task Karl Lashley (1935) studied the role of cerebral neocortex in his search for the physical manifestation of memory, for the *engram*. Rats without any neocortex cannot discriminate visual patterns (Lavond and Dewberry, 1980). However, rudimentary visual functions remain in that decorticated rats can see moving objects, can detect the deep side of a visual cliff, and can learn or relearn the brightness discrimination.

Importantly, the results of brightness discrimination training illustrate the property of behavioral *recovery of function* following brain injury. Lashley trained rats on a brightness discrimination and then systematically removed fractions of the cerebral neocortex. After removal of visual neocortex there was no evidence for retention of the brightness discrimination. With continued training, however, the rats reacquired the discrimination, taking as many trials as initially required to learn. One possible conclusion would be that the lesion destroyed the memory and, once it was removed, a new memory could be reestablished with the same effort. However, this is a somewhat fortuitous result in that it is an outcome of the training criterion used, because posteriorly decorticated subjects perform better when trained with less stringent criteria and worse when trained to successively more stringent criteria (Spear and Braun, 1969). This indicates that normal learning and learning by posteriorly decorticated subjects are by different mechanisms.

The recovery of brightness discriminations is consistent with Lashley's previous observations on maze learning (1929) where he found *equipotentiality* (all parts of the neocortex have the same capacity for supporting memory) and *mass action* (large areas of neocortex contribute to the memory). There is one caveat, however, in that he confined these properties to visual cortex for visual discriminations. Lashley did not think that the anterior neocortex participated in visual discriminations as it does for maze learning. However, more recent work supports the generalization of visual function to the entire neocortex (Cloud, Meyer, and Meyer, 1982).

Bauer and Cooper (1964) suggested that memory was not stored in the neocortex at all, but that visual cortex was necessary for seeing the stimulus as a pattern discrimination (a brightness discrimination). They suggested that learning after a visual cortical lesion was by using a different stimulus feature (i.e., a flux discrimination). However, there is evidence that both brightness and flux are learned simultaneously. Meyer and Meyer showed that a neural stimulant facilitates recovery of the flux discrimination but not a pattern discrimination (see Meyer and Meyer, 1977, for review). They suggest that the role of the neocortex is to add context in facilitating access to subcortically established engrams rather than to act as a store for memories. LeVere and Morlock supported this conclusion using a behavioral interference test, a simultaneous brightness discrimination (lit versus dark alleys, 1973), and a successive flux discrimination (both alleys lit means go one way, both dark means go the other way, 1974). Rats were initially trained to one habit, then had the visual neocortex removed. If the cortical lesion actually destroyed the memory, then it should not matter whether the subjects were trained to the same habit or to the opposite habit (go the other way). LeVere and Morlock found that training to the opposite habit took substantially longer to learn, indicating that the old memory still existed and interfered with learning the opposite habit.

As was true in Lashley's time, no one has yet localized the memory for a flux discrimination. Lesions of visual subcortical structures (superior colliculus, lateral geniculate, pretectal area, accessory optic nuclei) or of the limbic system (septum, hippocampus, amygdala), in combination with visual decortication, do not prevent relearning. The fault probably lies within Walter Hunter's criticisms (1930) that there is not enough experimental control over the instrumental training task used in this research. The more general question is whether the neocortex is involved in any memory. Squire (1987) reviews the best evidence for cortical memory, which can also be interpreted as suggesting that the cortex is necessary for perception of the stimuli but not for memory itself. Clearly, these are issues that are not resolved and continue to be of interest.

Bibliography

Bauer, J. H., and Cooper, R. M. (1964). Effects of posterior cortical lesions on performance of a brightness discrimination task. *Journal of Comparative and Physiological Psychology 58*, 84–93.

Cloud, M. D., Meyer, D. R., and Meyer, P. M. (1982). Induction of recoveries from injuries to the cortex: Dissociation of equipotential and regionally specific mechanisms. *Physiological Psychology 10*, 66–73.

Hunter, W. S. (1930). A consideration of Lashley's theory of the equipotentiality of cerebral action. *Journal of Genetic Psychology 3*, 455–468.

Klüver, H. (1942). Functional significance of the geniculo-striate system. In H. Klüver, ed., *Visual mechanisms*. Lancaster, PA: Jaques Cattell Press.

Lashley, K. S. (1929). *Brain mechanisms and intelligence: A quantitative study of injuries to the brain*. Chicago: University of Chicago Press.

——— (1935). The mechanism of vision: XII. Nervous structures concerned in the acquisition and retention of habits based on reactions to light. *Comparative Psychology Monographs 11*, 43–79.

Lavond, D. G., and Dewberry, R. G. (1980). Visual form perception is a function of the visual cortex: II. The rotated horizontal-vertical and oblique-stripes pattern problems. *Physiological Psychology 8*, 1–8.

LeVere, T. E., and Morlock, G. W. (1973). Nature of visual recovery following posterior neodecortication in the hooded rat. *Journal of Comparative and Physiological Psychology 83*, 62–67.

Meyer, D. R., and Meyer, P. M. (1977). Dynamics and bases of recoveries of functions after injuries to the cerebral cortex. *Physiological Psychology 5*, 133–165.

Spear, P. D., and Braun, J. J. (1969). Nonequivalence of normal and posteriorly neodecorticated rats on two brightness discrimination problems. *Journal of Comparative and Physiological Psychology 67*, 235–239.

Squire, L. R. (1987). *Memory and the brain*. New York: Oxford University Press.

David Lavond

W

WATSON, JOHN B. (1878–1958)

John Broadus Watson (1878–1958), the founder of behaviorism, was born January 9, 1878, near Greenville, South Carolina. He spent his preadolescent years in a farm community, where he acquired numerous manual skills and an affectionate familiarity with the behavior of many animals. At about the time his father deserted the family, the Watsons moved into the cotton-mill town of Greenville, which his mother thought would provide a better educational and religious atmosphere for the children. Watson later characterized himself as a mediocre student and a lazy, rebellious teenager (with a couple of arrests to brag about). Nevertheless, he managed to persuade officials at Furman University in Greenville to admit him. An average student at Furman from 1894 to 1899, Watson graduated with an A.M. degree; only philosophy and psychology had interested him at all. His mother's death in 1900 removed any remaining pressure to pursue a career in theology; by then, in any case, he had become antagonistic to established religion. Gordon Moore, his professor in philosophy and psychology, had attended and favorably described the University of Chicago, so Watson wrote to its president about his ambitions to attend a "real university" and "amount to" something professionally. Persuasive once again, he started graduate work there in 1900.

Watson had expected to concentrate on philosophy, with the eminent John Dewey as his mentor. However, he "never knew what Dewey was talking about" and, despite taking a variety of philosophy courses to fulfill a minor-area requirement, he later confessed that only some of the British empiricists (who emphasized past experience and principles of association as the crucial sources of human knowledge) aroused his interest. Typically for the turn of the century, psychology was part of the philosophy department, and Watson soon gravitated toward James R. Angell as his major professor. Angell was experimentally oriented and a leader of the burgeoning school of functionalism, which tolerated differing conceptions of the field of psychology but stressed the role of evolutionary factors, environmental adaptation, objectivity, and practical matters. This outlook contrasted with that of experimental introspectionists (e.g., the "structuralists"), who used human observers reporting on their private conscious experience, without regard for biological or practical implications.

Watson felt uncomfortable when asked to introspect in the standard ways, and he did not produce consistent reports under those conditions; but he said he felt at home with animals. Working under Angell and Henry Donaldson (who along with Jacques Loeb, an extremely mechanistic and materialistic biologist, handled Watson's other minor area, neurology), he studied possible correlations between problem-solving skills and the degree of medullation (myelination) in the brains of white rats at various ages. After three years of intense dedication to university duties and various odd jobs that he took to support himself—overwork that presumably caused the relatively brief breakdown he suffered during his final year—in

665

John B. Watson *(Library of Congress)*

1903 Watson received the first Ph.D. in psychology to be awarded by Chicago. His dissertation, *Animal Education,* was published in the same year.

Early Career

Watson remained at Chicago until 1908, first as Angell's assistant and then as an instructor. Even though he taught his students about orthodox introspective methods with human observers, his own research involved only animals. With Harvey Carr he carried out influential work on the sensory basis of maze learning in rats (neither vision nor audition nor smell was presumably crucial; rather, what was important was feedback stimulation from the animal's own movements: kinesthesis or the "muscle sense"); with Robert Yerkes he began studies of color vision that eventually involved several nonhuman species; and he failed to find good evidence for learning by imitation in monkeys. In addition, Watson spent the first of several summers on an island near Florida, observing the natural, instinctive behavior of birds (noddy terns and sooty terns), some of which he isolated at birth. His bird studies were thoughtful and creative; besides homing behavior, he investigated what today we would call Imprinting, instinctive drift, territoriality, and egg, mate, and nest recognition. This nonla-

boratory work is particularly noteworthy because, somewhat ironically, B. F. Skinner later assessed it as Watson's best research, and the ethologist Konrad Lorenz falsely concluded that "if J. B. Watson had only once reared a young bird in isolation," he would never have stressed conditioning as much as he did.

As early as 1903–1904 Watson confided to some Chicago colleagues his growing belief that psychology could become an objective and practical science only if it rid itself of unverifiable, unreliable introspective methods and focused instead on the study of observable behavior—events that could be recorded by an outsider—rather than on inferred, private states of consciousness or experience. Associates like Angell argued that his suggestion might be appropriate for animal research but would hardly be satisfactory for human beings. Another 10 years passed before Watson publicly proposed such ideas as the main bases for the approach he called behaviorism.

In 1908 Watson became full professor of experimental and comparative psychology at Johns Hopkins University in Baltimore. He continued his animal research, and soon assumed the leadership of the Johns Hopkins psychology program and the editorship of several important journals in experimental psychology. With the encouragement and stimulation of Knight Dunlap and Karl Lashley, he began to concentrate on developing his behavioristic psychology, first presented to a large audience in a landmark *Psychological Review* article in 1913. In a radical redefinition of psychology, Watson claimed that his field, animal learning and behavior—which had generally been relegated to a minor position in psychology or had not been viewed as part of psychology at all—was the one truly objective, scientific area of psychology. Furthermore, he maintained that the techniques used in the animal laboratory could be profitably, objectively, and practically applied to human beings; the goal of psychology was to predict and control behavior, not to analyze consciousness into its elements or to study vague "functions" or processes like perception, imagery, and volition. According to Watson, psychology had not yet emancipated itself from philosophy and religion, which it must do to become a true science—the science of behavior, of stimulus (S) and response (R: movements and secretions).

Historians of psychology have had no difficulty tracing possible antecedents for virtually all of Watson's specific ideas and arguments. Among others, they have cited views of philosophers (empiricists-associationists, materialists, positivists, pragmatists), biologists (evolutionary theorists, naturalists, objectivists, reflexologists), and early psychologists (nonmentalistic students of animal and human sensation, learning, memory, and intelligence—as well as functionalists like Angell). However, the direct influence on Watson of most of these views is unclear. In any event, his approach was original because of how it combined a variety of emphases, dissatisfactions, and opinions in a unique, revolutionary way. He offered a straightforward, bold program that was easy to understand (and easy to attack).

Generally favorable opinions about Watson's approach (as well as his established reputation as a researcher, administrator, and editor) led to his election as president of the American Psychological Association (APA) 2 years after the publication of his behaviorist manifesto. Many psychologists correctly believed that institutional and societal support for independent departments of psychology and new research facilities would be increased by redefining psychology along practical and objective lines like those offered by Watson.

Human Learning Research

In his APA presidential address (1915) Watson described research with both animals and humans, but for the first time in his career he stressed the latter. The talk offered a specific positive alternative to the techniques for studying human psychology that he had condemned in print two years before. Such an extension of his approach would presumably help convert to behaviorism those psychologists who believed that animal studies could not be of great significance for human affairs. The new method was essentially the conditioned-reflex procedure of Ivan Pavlov and Vladimir Bekhterev, which Watson had only recently begun to examine and appreciate. (Previously he had stressed the associationist laws of frequency and recency; he frowned on Edward L. Thorndike's law of effect because the notion of strengthening or weakening S-R bonds by means of subsequent satisfaction or discomfort seemed subjective to him, although it is the forerunner of Skinner's law of operant reinforcement.) From his own studies with human beings Watson illustrated a variety of Pavlovian conditioning phenomena that seemed relevant for everyday human behavior. He boasted, "We give no more instruction to our human subjects than we give to our animal subjects."

Except for a minor study with rats, the rest of Watson's academic career (suddenly aborted within 5 years) involved work with humans, especially young infants in the Phipps Psychiatric Clinic directed by Adolf Meyer. There was one brief interruption, when Watson served in the army during World War I (1917–1918) as a psychologist concerned mainly with aviation skills. Despite his irritation with the military establishment, Watson's views on the technological potential of psychology were bolstered.

Immediately after the war, Watson worked with a graduate student, Rosalie Rayner, on his most famous single study. It originated from his claim that emotional behavior in human infants was based on three fundamental types of unlearned, well-defined stimulus-response (S-R) patterns: fear, rage, and love. More complex emotional reactions, to specific objects and situations, arose through associative learning and transfer—and supposedly could not be attributed to hereditary predispositions. Primarily by means of Pavlovian procedures adopted directly from animal research, 11-month-old Albert B. was conditioned to fear a white rat by associating presentations of the rat with a very loud noise. Soon the mere sight of the rat caused Albert to whimper, cry, and move as far away as he could. This fear reaction transferred to other furry objects, like a rabbit or a Santa Claus mask. Unfortunately, Albert left the nursery too soon for Watson to attempt to eliminate the child's newly acquired habits. A few years later, Mary Cover Jones, whose research at Columbia University was unofficially supervised by Watson, compared various methods for removing children's fears of animals. Some treatments worked better than others. This research, along with Watson's and Jones's comments about its practical implications, marks the beginning of the fields of behavior modification and behavior therapy.

Watson denied any significant initiating or mediating role for the brain, and he would not consider possible cognitive processes intervening between the external S and the subject's R. His approach was thus peripheralistic in its focus on movements and secretions, and not on changes in the central nervous system. He worried that serious consideration of the existence of such intervening, unobservable processes would be subjective and unscientific; in any case it was unnecessary for behavioral prediction and control. But Watson did include implicit or covert behavior and "verbal reports" within his behaviorism. For example, he viewed thinking as basically silent speech, talking to yourself, that was potentially measurable by means of sensitive recording instruments attached to appropriate muscles (of the lips, tongue, larynx)—a general idea, not really original with Watson, that stimulated much research. Also, a person's regular, overt utterances could be objectively recorded as a form of behavior. Still, Watson was accused of making an alarming concession: of retaining introspection under another guise, the verbal report.

In 1920, while engrossed in his work with infants and other experiments involving adult human learning, Watson was faced with divorce proceedings initiated by his wife, who had discovered his love affair with Rayner. The participants were so well known (the Rayner family was politically and socially prominent in Maryland) that the case became a local and national sensation. Although Watson had probably believed that he was too important a figure at Johns Hopkins and in American psychology to lose his job over such a personal matter, he was forced to resign from the university in 1920. He never again held any official academic position. He and Rayner were married as soon as the divorce was final.

From Science to Advertising

Resilient and self-reliant, Watson began an entirely new career at the J. Walter Thompson Agency, viewed by its president, Stanley Resor, as a "university of advertising." Watson started at the bottom, surveying the demand for different kinds of rubber boots along the Mississippi River and acting as a salesman in Macy's department store to observe consumer reactions. He eventually became a vice president and was directly involved in many campaigns for specific products. He favored emotional over rational appeals but contributed no strikingly novel methods to the field of advertising, as some writers have claimed. Financially successful compared with his academic years, he asserted, "It can be just as thrilling to watch the growth of a sales curve of a new product as to watch the learning curve of animals or men."

After his dismissal from Johns Hopkins, Watson continued to write and lecture about behaviorism, but the books, radio broadcasts, and magazine articles were directed mainly at a popular audience. Aside from Freud, he was probably the psychologist best known to the American public in the first half of the twentieth century. Unfortunately, his views became progressively more simplistic, dogmatic, brash, and extreme. Still, his book *Behaviorism* (1924), though hastily written, was favorably received; a *New York Times* reviewer said it marked a new "epoch in the intellectual history of man," and the *New York Herald-Tribune* declared that "perhaps this is the most important book ever written." Even Bertrand Russell said it was "massively impressive."

In this and later writings Watson repudiated his earlier acceptance of the existence of certain human instincts and instead presented an extremely environmentalist, learning-based point of view. A widely cited passage, usually quoted without some qualifications that he did add, claimed that with the right kind of early experience and training, one could make any healthy infant into a "doctor, lawyer, artist . . . even beggar-man and thief, regardless of the talents . . . abilities, vocations, and race of his ancestors." Such a democratic view, combined with Watson's optimistic vision of psychology's general role in transforming society, was attractive to the American public, which

was becoming more urbanized and seemed to recognize the need for an effective technology of behavior (for example, in education and retraining). Interestingly, behaviorism never gained strong support in Europe, perhaps because traditional values there were more intellectual, philosophical, and abstract; democratic, practical ideals were not so prevalent.

Watson's popular book *Psychological Care of Infant and Child* (1928), dedicated to "the first mother who brings up a happy child," had a definite influence on American child-rearing practices in the 1930s. Some writers have described Watson as the Dr. Spock of his day, but unlike Spock he maintained that the upbringing of children should be quite objective and routinized, with minimal affection and sentimentality. His own children said that he was "all business," believing that tenderness would have a harmful effect on their independence and emotional control. In Watson's autobiographical sketch (1936) he apologized for the infant-care book, admitting that he had insufficient knowledge to write it. He did not, however, retract any of its specific advice.

Different varieties of behaviorism had emerged almost as soon as Watson proposed his own brand, but in the 1930s to 1960s more sophisticated "neobehaviorists" (e.g., Edwin Guthrie, Clark Hull, B. F. Skinner, and Edward Tolman) flourished during the so-called golden age of learning theory. These persons and their current impact are discussed elsewhere in this volume, along with views of contemporary cognitive psychologists, who generally reject many of behaviorism's assumptions and emphases—but not its objective methodology.

Rosalie Watson's death in 1936 left her husband depressed for a long time. Although he worked at an advertising firm for another decade, he preferred the isolation of his rural Connecticut home and farm, part of which he had built himself, to social and intellectual activities. The APA presented Watson with a special award in 1957, the year before his death on September 25, 1958, and almost 40 years after he left academia. He was honored as the initiator of a "revolution in psychological thought" and a person whose work was a vital determinant of "the form and substance of modern psychology."

See also: BEHAVIORISM; CONDITIONING, CLASSICAL AND INSTRUMENTAL; GUTHRIE, EDWIN R.; HULL, CLARK L.; LEARNING THEORY: A HISTORY; LEARNING THEORY: CURRENT STATUS; PAVLOV, IVAN; SKINNER, B. F.; THORNDIKE, EDWARD; TOLMAN, EDWARD C.

Bibliography

Boakes, R. A. (1984). *From Darwin to behaviourism: Psychology and the minds of animals.* Cambridge, UK: Cambridge University Press.

Buckley, K. W. (1989). *Mechanical man: John Broadus Watson and the beginnings of behaviorism.* New York: Guilford Press.

Cohen, D. (1979). *J. B. Watson: The founder of behaviourism.* London: Routledge and Kegan Paul.

Harrell, W., and Harrison, R. (1938). The rise and fall of behaviorism. *Journal of General Psychology* 18, 367–421.

O'Donnell, J. M. (1985). *The origins of behaviorism: American psychology, 1870–1920.* New York: New York University Press.

Watson, J. B. (1913). Psychology as the behaviorist views it. *Psychological Review* 20, 158–177.

——— (1914). *Behavior: An introduction to comparative psychology.* New York: Henry Holt.

——— (1919). *Psychology from the standpoint of a behaviorist.* Philadelphia: Lippincott.

——— (1924). *Behaviorism.* New York: W. W. Norton.

——— (1928). *Psychological care of infant and child.* New York: W. W. Norton.

——— (1936). John Broadus Watson (autobiographical sketch). In C. Murchison, ed., *A history of psychology in autobiography*, Vol. 3, pp. 271–281. Worcester, MA: Clark University Press.

Eliot Hearst

WORKING MEMORY

[*Working memory refers to the ability to hold a small amount of information in mind and work with it, often in the face of distraction. One aspect of working memory is the straightforward ability to retain information over short intervals— or short-term memory—a topic studied both in nonhuman animals and in humans. The paradigms used are necessarily different in the two cases, but the intent is to study how information is retained over short time periods. Working memory in humans is believed to involve verbal and nonverbal processes, perhaps with two types of capacity for working memory. Working memory capacity in humans seems to be related to general intelligence; some propose that the capacity to hold information in mind in spite of interference may underlie the concept of general intelligence.*

The two sections here review work on the topic of working memory both in **ANIMALS** *and in* **HUMANS**. *Various species of animal show remarkable mnemonic abilities that are quite specialized. However, when experiments are conducted that compare as directly as possible animals with humans, often many features of performance (such as serial position curves) are similar. The first section covers such research with animal subjects; the second provides information conducted in both a behavioral and a neuroimaging tradition with human subjects.*]

ANIMALS

Animals have good memories. There are anecdotal reports of dogs greeting their masters after years of absence and of bears and elephants squaring old scores after many years. Birds, too, can have remarkable recall. The Clark's nutcracker recovers more than 30,000 pine seeds buried in some 3,000 cache sites in the forest (Vander Wall, 1982). It must remember site locations after snow covers the forest and even burrow at an angle through the snow to arrive at the location. They use new cache sites each year and must overcome potential confusion (i.e., interference) over current and previous sites.

The recall of cache sites for six months certainly qualifies as long-term memory (LTM). But the borderline between long- and short-term memory (STM) is far from clear; in fact, the distinction between STM and LTM may have outlived its usefulness for behavioral analyses of memory (Crowder, 1993). Perhaps a more useful distinction is that between "working" and "reference" memory (Honig, 1978). These terms are free of the theoretical baggage carried by the terms STM/LTM or the similar primary/secondary memory. In the nutcracker example, reference memory would be the skill-learning involved in storing and retrieving seeds (Balda and Kamil, 1992). Working memory would apply to this year's cache sites.

Remarkable though the capacity and duration of nutcracker may be, the underlying processes and mechanisms are what compel the attention of researchers who seek to understand how memory works. Such insight requires laboratory investigations that manipulate independent variables critical to memory. Such work is proceeding briskly along two avenues of research: neurobiological and behavioral.

Investigations of neural mechanisms of memory use simple, quick—almost instantaneous—learning procedures. A repeated application of a stimulus (e.g., tactile) to an organism (e.g., sea slug) can produce habituation—a diminished response (e.g., siphon withdrawal)—or sensitization—a heightened response. This is a primitive form of learning: modification of a response through experience. Since all learning depends on memory, tests of learning are also tests of memory. Neuroplasticity studies have shown changes in cellular mechanisms, membrane channels, second-messengers, and protein syntheses related to memory (Squire and Kandel, 2001).

Another nearly instantaneous learning procedure is fear conditioning, a pairing of two stimuli (classical or Pavlovian conditioning). Rats learn to freeze (remain immobile) when encountering a stimulus paired with electric shock. Fear conditioning has shown that dorsal hippocampal lesions disrupt recent memories of the conditioning context (e.g., test chamber) but not those of the conditioned stimuli (e.g., tones) themselves (Anagnostaras et al., 2001).

Other neurobiological memory procedures require instrumental responses to escape unpleasant situations or to obtain rewards. Rats readily learn the location of a hidden platform in order to rest from swimming in a Morris water maze. Water maze studies have shown that LTP, NMDA receptors, and the dorsal (but not ventral) hippocampus are related to memory (Morris et al., 1986). Rats also readily learn the locations of food in radial-arm mazes. They are very good at remembering, for example, which arms have not been visited on a particular trial and thus still contain rewards. Four-arm "plus" mazes have played a key role in revealing the mnemonic components of the place cells of rats (O'Keefe and Speakman, 1987). Strategies used to solve water and radial-arm maze tasks occasionally make interpretation of results complex, and such strategies (i.e., reference memory) can confound measures of working memory. Other memory results raise questions about the universality of the hippocampus in rats' place memory. In delayed nonmatching to sample (DNMS), monkeys choose a stimulus that does not match a previously seen sample. DNMS in monkeys depends less on the hippocampus than place memory in rats. Some researchers are trying to determine whether the hippocampus will prove necessary for general "relational" memory (Cohen and Eichenbaum, 1994) or just place memory. A newer, more sensitive procedure for identifying the role of the hippocampus in nonplace memory is a habituation procedure called preferential viewing (Alvarado and Bachevalier, 2000). Monkeys (or children) view and habituate to a picture, then are tested with that picture presented with a novel picture. The subject viewing mainly the novel picture shows good memory of habituation.

Investigations of behavioral mechanisms of animal memory have traditionally used single-memory items on each trial. Single-memory-item tests may be well suited to neurobiological investigations (e.g., treatment versus normal groups) but by themselves do not reveal much about memory mechanisms (Shettleworth, 1998, p. 257; Olson et al., 1995; Kamil, 1988). Explorations of human memory mechanisms have used list-memory procedures for a long time (Ebbinghaus, 1902). Memory is typically best for items at the beginning (primacy effect) and at the end (recency effect) of each list, producing a U-shaped serial-position function (SPF). Delaying recall (or recognition) eliminates the recency effect. This selective elimination supported the hypothesis that the recency effect represented STM (Glanzer and Cunitz, 1966), and helped stimulate the cognitive revolution of the 1960s. The degree to which animals share similar STM processes with humans became testable only in the 1990s because of the extreme difficulty of training animals in list-memory tasks. Nevertheless, the list memory of rats, pigeons, dolphins, squirrel monkeys, capuchin monkeys, rhesus monkeys, and chimpanzees has been tested.

Two experiments with rhesus monkeys show similarities to human memory processing and expand upon these findings. In a visual-memory experiment, monkeys saw lists of four different "travel-slide" pictures. After a delay (0, 1, 2, 10, 20, or 30 seconds later) following each list, the monkeys indicated whether a test picture presented in a different location was or was not in the list (Wright et al., 1985). Figure 1 (upper portion) shows the changes in the monkeys' four-item serial-position functions for three of the retention delays. Like humans, the monkeys' recency effect dissipated with retention delay. A new finding was the gradual appearance of the primacy effect with delay, and this finding was made possible by using much shorter lists than those used with humans. The primacy and recency effects were separately manipulated and dissociated by retention interval, and the benchmark U-shaped function emerged as a transitional function. Similar changes have been shown for humans (e.g., using four- or five-item lists of snowflake or kaleidoscope patterns), capuchin monkeys, and pigeons (Korsnes, 1995; Neath, 1993; Wright, 1999a; Wright et al., 1985). One issue was whether SPFs for other types of memory (e.g., auditory) would change with delay like those for visual memory.

In an auditory memory experiment, monkeys heard lists of four natural/environmental sounds. After a delay (0, 1, 2, 10, 20, or 30 seconds later) following each list, they had to touch one of two side speakers to indicate whether or not a test sound was in the list (Wright, 1998). As in the visual memory experiment, researchers drew from a large pool of sounds (520 in this case), each one unique to each day's trials. The most striking feature of the auditory memory SPFs (see Figure 1) is that their shape is opposite to that of the visual memory results. Initially, there was no recency effect. The recency effect appeared to lengthen with delay, and the primacy effect dissipated. Thus, evidence about how one memory system works may not reveal much about the workings of other memory systems: vision, auditory, taste, smell, and touch.

Another finding is the counterintuitive one that memory—specifically, visual primacy and auditory recency—can improve with time. Thus, mechanisms other than memory decay must be responsible for the SPFs. To explore possible mechanisms, researchers manipulated interference among auditory list items. The first list items were shown to interfere (proactively, i.e., forward in time) with the monkey's memory of the last list items (Wright, 1999b). Diminishing or eliminating this interference greatly enhanced memory for the last items, a result that ruled out lack of consolidation as an explanation of poor memory of the last list items. With long delays, the last list items

Figure 1

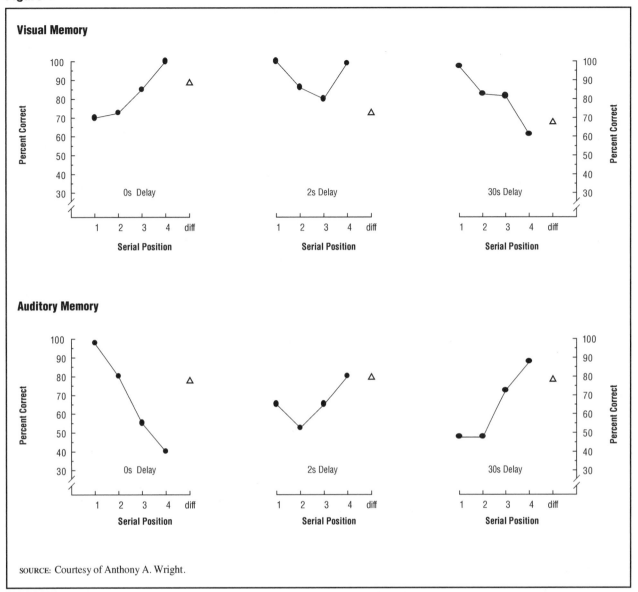

SOURCE: Courtesy of Anthony A. Wright.

Average serial position functions for different groups of monkeys tested in a 4-item visual memory task (top) or a 4-item auditory memory task (bottom). The parameter delay is the retention interval between list and test. Serial position 1 is the first list item. Unfilled points (Diff) are from trials in which the test matched no list item.

interfered (retroactively, i.e., backward in time) with the monkey's memory of the first list items. Diminishing or eliminating this interference greatly improved memory of the first item, a result that ruled out forgetting (i.e., memory decay) as an explanation for poor memory of the first list items.

Researchers face the challenge of closing the gaps between neurobiological and behavioral approaches to animal and human memory. This interdisciplinary approach will require a blend of molecular, cellular, neurochemical, anatomical, imaging, behavioral, and computational techniques.

See also: APLYSIA: MOLECULAR BASIS OF LONG-TERM SENSITIZATION; NEURAL SUBSTRATES OF EMOTIONAL MEMORY

Bibliography

Alvarado, M. C., and Bachevalier, J. (2000). Revisiting the maturation of medial temporal lobe memory functions in primates. *Learning and Memory* 7, 244–256.

Anagnostaras, S. G., Gale, G. D., and Fanselow, M. S. (2001). Hippocampus and contextual fear conditioning: Recent controversies and advances. *Hippocampus* 11, 8–17.

Balda, R. P., and Kamil, A. C. (1992). Long-term spatial memory in Clark's nutcracker, *Nucifraga columbiana. Animal Behaviour* 44, 761–769.

Cohen, N. J., and Eichenbaum, H. (1994). *Memory, amnesia, and the hippocampal system.* Cambridge, MA: MIT Press.

Crowder, R. G. (1993). Short-term memory: Where do we stand? *Memory & Cognition 21,* 142–145.

Ebbinghaus, H. E. (1902). *Grundzuge der Psychologie.* Leipzig: Von Veit.

Glanzer, M., and Cunitz, A. R. (1966). Two storage mechanisms in free recall. *Journal of Verbal Learning and Verbal Behavior 5,* 351–360.

Honig, W. K. (1978). Studies of working memory in the pigeon. In S. H. Hulse, H. Fowler, and W. K. Honig, eds., *Cognitive processes in animal behavior.* Hillsdale, NJ: Erlbaum.

Kamil, A. C. (1988). A synthetic approach to the study of animal intelligence. In D. W. Leger, ed., *Nebraska Symposium on Motivation,* Vol. 35. Lincoln: University of Nebraska Press.

Korsnes, M. S. (1995). Retention intervals and serial list memory. *Perceptual and Motor Skills 80,* 723–731.

Morris, R. G. M., Anderson, E., Lynch, G. S., and Baudry, M. (1986). Selective impairment of learning and blockade of long-term potentiation by an N-methyl-D-aspartate receptor antagonist, AP5. *Nature 319,* 774–776.

Neath, I. (1993). Distinctiveness and serial position effects in recognition. *Memory & Cognition 21,* 689–698.

O'Keefe, J., and Speakman, A. (1987). Single unit activity in the rat hippocampus during a spatial memory task. *Experimental Brain Research 68,* 1–27.

Olson, D. J., Kamil, A. C., Balda, R. P., and Mims, P. J. (1995). Performance of four-seed caching corvid species in operant tests of nonspatial and spatial memory. *Journal of Comparative Psychology 109,*173–181.

Shettleworth, S. J. (1998). *Cognition, evolution, and behavior.* New York: Oxford University Press.

Squire, L. R., and Kandel, E. R. (1998). *Memory from mind to molecules.* New York: W. H. Freeman and Co.

Vander Wall, S. B. (1982). An experimental analysis of cache recovery in Clark's nutcracker. *Animal Behaviour 30,* 84–94.

Wright, A. A. (1998). Auditory list memory in rhesus monkeys. *Psychological Science 9,* 91–98.

—— (1999a). Visual list memory in capuchin monkeys (*Cebus apella*). *Journal of Comparative Psychology 113,* 74–80.

—— (1999b). Auditory list memory and interference in monkeys. *Journal of Experimental Psychology: Animal Behavior Processes 25,* 284–296.

Wright, A. A., Santiago, H. C., Sands, S. F., Kendrick, D. F., and Cook, R. G. (1985). Memory processing of serial lists by pigeons, monkeys, and people. *Science 229,* 287–289.

Anthony A. Wright

HUMANS

Working memory is a system that provides short-term storage of information used in complex cognitive activities such as planning, reasoning, problem-solving, and language. This mental blackboard is a temporary workspace that makes possible the examination, manipulation, and tranformation of internally represented information during these cognitive activities—and also allows its subsequent erasure.

Suppose you ordered three bottles of mineral water at $1.80 a bottle and gave the waiter ten dollars. How much change would you expect? Working this out would likely involve retaining the results of your initial calculations while performing other operations, storing interim results for which you would have no need after arriving at the answer and the details of which would likely escape you upon subsequent inquiry. The temporary storage and manipulation of information required to perform this and many similar tasks is working memory.

Short-Term versus Working Memory

Researchers have long accepted this idea of a form of separate, temporary memory storage—one quite distinct from the system of long-term storage—for many years. In the nineteenth century William James (1890) proposed the term *primary memory* for a form of temporary storage that was at least partly responsible for the experience of what he termed "the specious present," the experience that time is continuous, extending beyond the consciousness of the currently encountered microsecond.

Despite the theorizing of James, the twentieth century saw little interest in the mental capacity for short-term storage until the 1950s, which saw the rise of a "cognitive revolution," a surge of interest in the information-processing approach to the analysis of human cognition that used the newly developed digital computer as a basis for new theories of the workings of the mind. This sea change, coupled with some of the practical problems that had arisen from the attempt to apply psychology to wartime issues, led to renewed interest in both attention and short-term storage, thanks in good measure to the work of Broadbent (1958).

By the late 1960s a general consensus emerged in favor of the separation of memory into at least two systems: a short-term, limited-capacity store that can hold information for a matter of seconds and that feeds a far more capacious and durable long-term store. The dominant model of this period was that proposed by Atkinson and Shiffrin, in which information passes through a series of brief sensory registers that are part of the processes of perception and then moves into a limited-capacity short-term store. The latter acts as a working memory, with a series of strategies or controls that organize and maintain incoming material to optimize learning and subsequent recall. This model gives a good account of the available data and is still portrayed as the dominant view of memory in many introductory textbooks.

Nevertheless, despite its attractive simplicity, the model soon began to encounter problems. One difficulty was its learning assumption: the longer an item is held in short-term storage (STS), the greater is its probability of transfer into long-term memory. Evidence conflicting with this assumption came from data that initially seemed to support the two-store model. Patients suffering from amnesia following brain damage appeared to show drastic impairment of long-term learning but retained their short-term store (Baddeley and Warrington, 1970). Conversely, Shallice and Warrington (1970) identified other patients showing exactly the opposite pattern: normal long-term learning but problems on short-term memory tasks. The double dissociation found in such patients conformed to the Atkinson and Shiffrin model quite nicely, except for one crucial point: If, as the model proposed, short-term storage was a crucial working memory that made learning and long-term storage possible, then how could patients with a gross disruption of the short-term store learn and recall normally? A defective short-term store should have led to massive problems in learning, memory, and general cognition if this system indeed served as a working memory.

The Baddeley and Hitch Model

Baddeley and Hitch (1974) tried to clarify the problems in the Atkinson and Shiffrin model by attempting to simulate in normal subjects the deficits suffered by patients with short-term memory problems. They attempted to disrupt short-term memory function by requiring the subject to perform a memory-span task while attempting to learn, reason, or comprehend. The two-store model should predict that requiring the subject to maintain a string of, say, six digits would nearly fill the limited-capacity short-term store. If the latter acts as a crucial working memory, then the subject's capacity for other tasks should be almost totally disrupted. The pattern of results obtained across a range of activities was quite consistent. While there was indeed some impairment, even a concurrent load of six numbers produced only modest disruption, even in the capacity to perform quite demanding reasoning tasks. Baddeley and Hitch (1974) concluded that these results were inconsistent with the Atkinson and Shiffrin model (1968), and proposed an alternative multicomponent model to replace the unitary short-term store.

The Baddeley and Hitch working memory model consisted of three components: an attentional control system they termed the central executive and two subsidiary slave systems, the phonological loop which maintains and manipulates speech-based information, and the visuospatial sketchpad which provides a temporary storage system for visuospatial information (see Figure 1). This model still remains as the most widely accepted account of the function and organization of working memory, and as such merits further description.

Figure 1

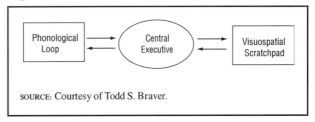

SOURCE: Courtesy of Todd S. Braver.

The structure of working memory proposed by Baddeley and Hitch. The boxes labeled phonological loop, central executive, and visuospatial scratchpad represent the proposed components or subsystems of working memory.

The phonological-loop component seems to be made up of two subcomponents, a store that will hold auditory-verbal memory traces for about two seconds and a subvocal rehearsal process. This process can both maintain the items within the store by recycling them subvocally and register visually presented items in the store by means of subvocalization. The short-term phonological storage system seems specially adapted to language learning since it provides critical mechanisms for keeping novel phonological strings active and in the correct serial order that allows their binding to appropriate meanings. Evidence supporting this hypothesis comes from studies of vocabulary acquisition in children, in whom the functioning of the phonological store predicts individual differences in language-learning skills (Baddeley, Gathercole, and Papagno, 1998).

The visuospatial sketchpad may represent a separate system specializes in the maintenance of information using visuospatial rather than linguistic codes (i.e., mental images). There is evidence that it may constitute two subsystems, one concerned with spatial information and the relative location of objects and the with pattern information. Patients with a disruption to the operation of the spatial system may have difficulty in finding their way around but have no problem in recalling or using information concerning the visual characteristics of objects, such as the color of a banana or the shape of a dachshund's ears. Other patients show the opposite pattern of deficits (Farah, 1988). Some research suggests that rehearsal of information in the sketch pad might be similar to shifting spatial attention, and as such appears to be linked to the brain system that controls eye movements (Awh and Jonides, 2001).

The central executive, the most complex and least understood component of working memory, at first seemed to operate along the lines of the model of attentional control proposed by Norman and Shallice (1986). This model assumes that continual activity is controlled in two major ways: by the running off of existing programs or scripts, or by the intervention of the supervisory attentional system (SAS). The latter is capable of interrupting continual semiautomatic programs when they reach an impasse or when longer-term goals demand a departure from the continual activity. A secondary function proposed for the central executive was to coordinate and integrate the operation of the two buffer systems in tasks requiring either simultaneous or alternating storage of both verbal and visuospatial information.

The influential Baddeley and Hitch model spawned a great deal of research in the 1970s and 1980s, much of it geared toward the study of the properties of the two slave storage systems, especially that of the phonological loop. A second theme of research on working memory during this period was an examination of its role in individual differences in higher-level cognitive abilities. In 1980, Daneman and Carpenter suggested that verbal working memory capacity could predict abilities in a range of general language skills, such as reading comprehension and verbal SAT scores (Daneman and Carpenter, 1980). Verbal working memory capacity was measured using a task called the reading span, which determines how many words the subject can retain in short-term memory while simultaneously performing intervening language-processing tasks (reading sentences out loud). Subsequent studies have validated and replicated the original findings using a variety of similar span tasks and cognitive predictors. Many theorists now believe that working-memory capacity might serve as a strong analogue to the notion of a domain-general intelligence factor (Engle, Tuholski, Laughlin, and Conway, 1999). Other studies have supported the notion of the Baddeley and Hitch model that there are two separate working-memory capacities, with one predicting verbal abilities and the other predicting visuospatial ones (Shah and Miyake, 1996).

Mechanisms of Working Memory

Since 1990, the focus of research on working memory has shifted to a more thorough study of its critical psychological and biological mechanisms: How do the components of working memory "work" and how does the brain implement them? This trend has been driven by the rise of cognitive neuroscience as a discipline and also by the development of new experimental methods such as human brain imaging for studying working memory. For example, nonhuman primate research has suggested that active maintenance of information through the sustained firing of neuronal populations provides a cellular mechanism of working memory (Goldman-Rakic, 1995). This short-term storage mechanism contrasts sharply with the cellular mechanisms that seem to underlie long-term memory—the strengthening of (synaptic) connections between neurons.

A primary focus of both the animal and human brain imaging studies of working memory has been the prefrontal cortex. For example, when humans perform working memory tasks, there is a reliable sustained increase in activity within the prefrontal cortex during maintenance periods, with the magnitude of increase related to working memory load. This finding has been demonstrated using a number of simple task paradigms, including the N-back (Cohen et al., 1997) and Sternberg item-recognition task (Jha and McCarthy, 2000). Both tasks are delayed-response paradigms in which the information to be stored in working memory must be matched against a subsequent probe item, changes from trial to trial, and can vary in the number of items that must be held and in the delay period of maintenance. In the N-back a continuous sequence of items is presented one at a time, each requiring a determination whether it matches an item presented a specified number (N) of trials back (e.g., in a three-back condition the last A in the sequence ABCA would be considered a match). Thus, the task requires that a previous item must be maintained in its appropriate sequence and stored over intervening items. The Sternberg task is similar but typically presents the memory set simultaneously followed by an unfilled delay interval. Figure 2 shows data on the time course of prefrontal cortex activity as a function of working-memory load in both the N-back and Sternberg tasks.

Other brain-imaging research on working memory has provided converging support for the Baddeley and Hitch model by suggesting that there is a neuroanatomical segregation of verbal and visuospatial short-term storage, of storage and rehearsal in verbal working memory, and of maintenance and manipulation (e.g., central executive) functions (Smith and Jonides, 1999). These findings remain controversial because not all studies have observed such distinctions. One possibility is that the components of the model do not cleanly map on to the brain, especially as regards the relationship between the maintenance and control functions of working memory.

As a consequence, attention has turned toward gaining a better understanding the nature of the executive-control functions needed for successful working memory during complex cognition. A first critical question is whether separable control functions play different roles within working memory. A number of possible control operations have been suggested, such as the following: shifting or switching attention between the mental sets needed to perform different tasks; inhibition or suppression of inappropriate response tendencies or irrelevant information; moni-

Figure 2

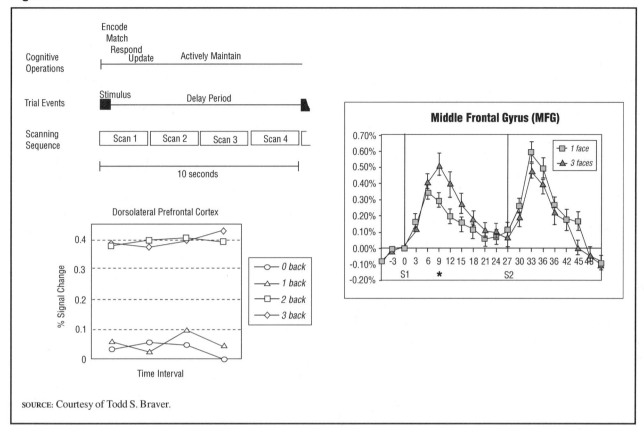

SOURCE: Courtesy of Todd S. Braver.

(Left) Activation of prefrontal cortex (dorsolateral region) during performance of the N-back task. The upper panel refers to the experimental design of the study, in which four brain imaging scans were acquired during the course of each trial. Because of the long delay interval (10 seconds) between trials, activity reflecting active maintenance should be present during the later scans of each trial (scans 3 and 4). The lower panel shows the average activity level in this prefrontal cortex region across four different N-back conditions (0-back through 3-back) during the course of a trial. The greater activity for 2-back and 3-back conditions relative to 0-back and 1-back conditions reflects sensitivity to working memory load. The constant level of activity across the trial suggests a sustained response reflecting active maintenance. Adapted from Cohen, J. D., Perstein, W. M., Braver, T. S., Nystrom, L. E., Noll, D. C., Jonides, J., and Smith, E. E. (1997). Temporal dynamics of brain activation during a working memory task. *Nature 386*, 604–608. (Right) Activation of prefrontal cortex (same dorsolateral region) during performance of Sternberg task using faces as stimulus items. Activation is plotted from the time of the presentation of the memory set (S1) to the time of the subsequent probe item (S2), which occurred 27 seconds later. The increased activation for the 3-face condition reflects a sensitivity to working memory load. The increased activity (relative to the pretrial baseline) throughout the delay interval suggests that the response reflects active maintenance. Adapted from Jha, A. P., and McCarthy, G. (2000). The influence of memory load on delay-interval in a working-memory task: An event-related functional MRI study. *Journal of Cognitive Neuroscience 12*, 90–105.

toring and updating the contents of working memory; temporal tagging or contextual coding of incoming information; and planning or sequencing intended actions (Smith and Jonides, 1999). Some evidence suggests the statistical independence of these functions (Miyake et al., 2000); but it is unclear whether these functions are instantiated by truly separable systems or might be further reducible to a more fundamental, unitary set of mechanisms.

A second central issue is the exact relationship between the mechanisms supporting active maintenance and those that control this process. Models such as that of Baddeley and Hitch suggest a strict segregation between maintenance and control functions. Yet other models suggest that these functions are more tightly intertwined, with active maintenance of goal representations serving as a primary means of control (O'Reilly, Braver, and Cohen, 1999). One view argues for a distinction between two types of maintenance mechanisms: goal-related information maintained in the focus of attention that is robustly protected from interference and transiently activated (via spreading associative processes) information from long-term memory that decays over brief intervals (Cowan, 1995). The first mechanism seems more domain-general and may reflect the functions of the prefrontal cortex; the second mechanism likely reflects more domain-specific maintenance operations that are widely distributed across different brain regions. However, the two sources of working memory seem to be interdependent, with actively maintained goal information biasing the time course of activated long-term memory (through refreshment or suppression). Conversely, spreading activation of long-term memory elements might drive the activation or updating of goal representations.

Many studies have suggested that the individual differences in working-memory capacity most strongly related to skill in complex cognitive tasks (and constructs of fluid intelligence) are those pertaining to goal-maintenance mechanisms rather than to the activation of long-term memory elements (Kane, Bleckley, Conway, and Engle, 2001). Thus, the notion of working-memory capacity may be a misnomer, referring not to the number of items that can be maintained simultaneously but rather to the efficacy with which an individual can represent and maintain even a single goal within the focus of attention in the face of interference and distraction.

There is much still to be understood about the nature and mechanisms of working memory. Progress in understanding working memory will likely come from the further specification of mechanisms that arise both from direct comparisons between models and from their implementation in explicit computational formalisms (Miyake and Shah, 1999). Nevertheless, the general concept of a working memory system that provides temporary storage for a wide range of cognitive activities has proved to be a useful one, and is likely to remain so. While theoretical models of working memory are likely to change and become more complex, the study of working memory is likely to significantly inform such diverse cognitive domains as attention, reasoning, language, individual difference, and the executive control of behavior.

See also: JAMES, WILLIAM; LONG-TERM POTENTIATION; PREFRONTAL CORTEX AND MEMORY IN PRIMATES; SENSORY MEMORY

Bibliography

Atkinson, R. C., and Shiffrin, R. M. (1968). Human memory: A proposed system and its control processes. In K. W. Spence, ed., *The psychology of learning and motivation: Advances in research and theory.* New York: Academic Press.

Awh, E., and Jonides, J. (2001). Overlapping mechanisms of attention and spatial working memory. *Trends in Cognitive Sciences 5,* 119–126.

Baddeley, A., Gathercole, S., and Papagno, C. (1998). The phonological loop as a language learning device. *Psychological Review 105,* 158–173.

Baddeley, A. D., and Hitch, G. J. (1974). Working memory. In G. Bower, ed., *The psychology of learning and motivation,* Vol. 8. New York: Academic Press.

Baddeley, A. D., and Warrington, E. K. (1970). Amnesia and the distinction between long- and short-term memory. *Journal of Verbal Learning and Verbal Behaviour 9,* 176–189.

Broadbent, D. E. (1958). *Perception and communication.* Oxford: Pergamon.

Cohen, J. D., Perstein, W. M., Braver, T. S., Nystrom, L. E., Noll, D. C., Jonides, J., and Smith, E. E. (1997). Temporal dynamics of brain activation during a working memory task. *Nature 386,* 604–608.

Cowan, N. (1995). *Attention and memory.* Oxford: Oxford University Press.

Daneman, M., and Carpenter, P. A. (1980). Individual differences in working memory and reading. *Journal of Verbal Learning and Verbal Behavior 19,* 450–466.

Engle, R. W., Tuholski, S. W., Laughlin, J. E., and Conway, A. R. A. (1999). Working memory, short-term memory, and general fluid intelligence: A latent-variable approach. *Journal of Experimental Psychology: General 128,* 309–331.

Farah, M. J. (1988). Is visual imagery really visual? Overlooked evidence from neuropsychology. *Psychological Review 95,* 307–317.

Goldman-Rakic, P. S. (1995). Cellular basis of working memory. *Neuron 14,* 477–485.

James, W. (1890). *Principles of psychology.* New York: Holt, Rinehart, and Winston.

Jha, A. P., and McCarthy, G. (2000). The influence of memory load on delay-interval in a working-memory task: An event-related functional MRI study. *Journal of Cognitive Neuroscience 12,* 90–105.

Kane, M. J., Bleckley, M. K., Conway, A. R. A., and Engle, R. W. (2001). A controlled-attention view of WM capacity. *Journal of Experimental Psychology: General 130,* 169–183.

Miyake, A., Friedman, N. P., Emerson, M. J., Witzki, A. H., Howerter, A., and Wager, T. D. (2000). The unity and diversity of executive functions and their contributions to complex "frontal lobe" tasks: A latent variable analysis. *Cognitive Psychology 41,* 49–100.

Miyake, A., and Shah, P., eds. (1999). *Models of working memory: Mechanisms of active maintenance and executive control.* New York: Cambridge University Press.

Norman, D. A., and Shallice, T. (1986). Attention to action: Willed and automatic control of behavior. In R. J. Davidson, G. E. Schwartz, and D. Shapiro, eds., *Consciousness and self-regulation,* Vol. 4. New York: Plenum Press.

O'Reilly, R. C., Braver, T. S., and Cohen, J. D. (1999). A biologically based computational model of working memory. In A. Miyake and P. Shah, eds., *Models of working memory: Mechanisms of active maintenance and executive control.* New York: Cambridge University Press.

Shah, P., and Miyake, A. (1996). The separability of working memory resources for spatial thinking and language processing: An individual differences approach. *Journal of Experimental Psychology 125,* 4–27.

Shallice, T., and Warrington, E. K. (1970). Independent functioning of verbal memory stores: A neuropsychological study. *Quarterly Journal of Experimental Psychology 22,* 261–273.

Smith, E. E., and Jonides, J. (1999). Storage and executive processes in the frontal lobes. *Science 283,* 1,657–1,661.

Alan D. Baddeley
Revised by Todd S. Braver

GENERAL INDEX

Page references to entire articles are in **boldface.** Illustrations are indicated by page references in *italics.* Persons are indexed only when there is a substantial reference to them or a substantial quotation by them. In references to research work by three or more authors, as a rule only the first author is indexed.

A

Ablation, in hypnotic age regression, 240–241
Abraham, W. C., 341
Abstractions, comparative learning studies, 91–92
Accessory olfactory bulb (AOB), 210
Access to memory. *See* Cues, retrieval; Recall; Retrieval processes in memory
Accommodation and assimilation, Piaget on, 527
Acetylcholine
    activity-dependent regulation of synthesis of, 4
    decrease of, in Alzheimer's disease, 18, 85
    decrease of, in cognitive impairment, 476
    as excitatory neuromodulator, 189–190
    memory and, 476
    neural computation and, 444
    pregnenolone enhancement of, 86
    visual cortical plasticity and, 428
Acetylcholinesterase inhibitors. *See* Cholinesterase inhibitors
Acetylcoenzyme A, 4
Acetyl-l-carnitine (Alcar), 521
Acoustic startle reflex. *See* Startle reflex

Acquired distinctiveness, in discrimination, 114
ACTH (adrenocorticotropin)
    memory effects, 233
    memory modulation, 476
    in stress response, 642
Actin
    filaments, in synapse structure, 215
    in neurons, 205
Actinomycin-D, for transcription prevention, 167
Action potentials
    back-propagating, in LTP signal transduction, 351–352
    dendritic, and long-term potentiation, 352, 354
    generated by neurons, 204
Activation view, of implicit memory, 245
Active avoidance learning. *See* Avoidance learning, active and passive
Activity-dependent regulation of neurotransmitter synthesis, **4–6**
    acetylcholine, 4
    catecholamines, 4–6
    defined, 4
    See also Protein synthesis
Adaptation aftereffects, in visual cortex, 421
Adaptive behavior, 566–567
Adenylyl cyclase
    in *Aplysia* sensitization, 34
    in memory consolidation, 367
Ader, R., 122
ADHD (attentional deficits/ hyperactivity disorder), 320
Adolescents, development of memory in, 71–74
Adrenal hyperplasia, congenital, learning and, 614
Adrenalin. *See* Epinephrine

Adrenal medulla, tyrosine hydroxylase modulation, 5
Adrenocorticotropin (ACTH), 233, 476, 642
β-Adrenoreceptor antagonists, injection into amygdala, 234
β-Adrenoreceptors, epinephrine's effect on, 232
Affective responses. *See* Emotion, mood, and memory; Emotions
Africanized honeybees, 262
Age
    eidetic imagery and, 131
    infant memory and, 254, 255
    See also Aging and memory in animals; Aging and memory in humans
Age regression, hypnotic, 240–241
Aging and memory in animals, **7–10**
    eyeblink classical conditioning, 7–9, *8*
    spatial learning and memory, 9
    transgenic mouse models of Alzheimer's disease, 9–10
Aging and memory in humans, **10–13**
    cross-sectional methods of age comparison, 10
    episodic memory changes, 11–12
    indirect memory tests of, 11
    prospective memory failure, 13
    semantic memory changes, 11
    short-term and working memory changes, 12–13
    underlying changes affecting, 10–11
Agnosia
    associative, 306
    hypnotic, 240
    modality-specific associative, 306–307
    selective, 307

Hemispheres of brain. *See* Left hemisphere of brain
Hereditary memory, 606
Hermissenda, **277–280**
associative learning in, 277–280, 402
cellular and synaptic plasticity, 278, *279*
memory consolidation mechanisms, 278, 280
Pavlovian conditioning of, 277–278, *279*
Hertel, P. T., 134
Heterosynaptic neurons, modulation of, in *Aplysia*, 43
Hewes, A. K., 264
The Higher Cortical Functions in Man (Luria), 357
Higher-order classical conditioning, 98–100
experimental models, 98
theoretical models, 98, *99*
High vocal center (HVc) in birdsong learning, 64, 66, *66*, 68, *68*, 69
Hilgard, E. R., 2
Hindbrain (rhombencephalon), 180, 187
Hintzman, D. L., 237
Hippocampal amnesia. *See* Amnesia, organic
Hippocampal damage
blocking eliminated by, 304
deficient memory for targets or facts, 159
organic amnesia related to, 29
recent memory impairment in, 333
temporally-graded amnesia in, 368, 369, 370
Hippocampus, **171–175, 202–204**
adult neurogenesis, 469, *470*, 471–473
Alzheimer's disease impairment of, 9, 10, 18
anatomy, 202–204
associative memory and, 439–441
birds, size and role of, 139
blocking and, 304
aCaMKII, LTP, and learning, 172–173
CA1 neurons, 203–204
CA3 neurons, 203
corticosteroid receptors, 389
declarative memory and, 107
disruption of LTP and learning, 174–175
early experience and learning, 123
entorhinal cortex connections, 214

eyeblink classical conditioning and, 8–9
in fear behavior, 462
fornix, as connection to hypothalamus, 204
functions, 471–472
as "gateway to memory," *470*, 472
general features, 202
genetic substrates of memory, 171–175
gradual memory consolidation in, 371
inhibitory avoidance learning, 453
learned bradycardia, 456–457
long-term depression in, 335, *337*, 388
long-term potentiation in, 172–173, 388
LTP enhancement and learning, 174, 347
memory consolidation and, 367–368, 369, 371, 372
metaplasticity, 388
multiple memory systems and, 414–415, 534
neocortical interaction with, during memory consolidation, 367–368, 371
neural computation, 439–441, *440*
neurogenesis, 469, *470*, 471–473
neuroimaging, in memory consolidation, 371
neuron structure, 181
nictitating membrane classical conditioning, 458
NMDA receptor function and learning, 173
perforant pathway, 203, 214
perirhinal cortex connections, 214
place cells, **529–532**, *530*
recent memory and, 333
in reinforcement, 569
in schizophrenia, 590
signaling pathways and synaptic plasticity, 173
sleep and, 620–621
spatial learning and, 9, 472, 489, 529, 531
transcription, translation, and long-term memory, 173–174
trisynaptic organization, 203
voles, 139
wiring, 202–204
working memory and, 489–491
See also Hippocampal damage

Hippocampus, Space, and Memory (Olton et al.), 489
The Hippocampus as a Cognitive Map (O'Keefe and Nadel), 414
Hirsh, R., 414
Histamine, memory modulation, 476
Histologie du système nerveux de l'homme et des vertébrés (Ramón y Cajal), 558
Historia animalium (Aristotle), 47
Historicocultural psychology, 55, 357
Hitch, G. J., 264, 673–675
Hoff, M., 15
Hoffman, Dustin, 588
Holst, Erich von, 355
Homing. *See* Migration, navigation, and homing
Homing pigeons, 392
Homology, defined, 258
Homophony, 606
Honeybee. *See* Bees
Hopfield, John, 444–445
Hormones, **232–234**
birdsong learning and, 67–69
gonadal, 67–69, 234, 615
interaction among hormonal systems, 234
memory effects, 232–234
neonatal disturbance of, behavioral effects, 121
stress hormones, 513, *514*
See also specific hormone
Horridge, G. A., 259
5-HT. *See* Serotonin
Hull, Clark L., **234–237**, *235*
early career and honors, 234–235
habit strength measure of, 359–360
influence on Spence, 637
learning theory of, 235–237, 327–328
neobehaviorism, 57
on Pavlovian conditioned response, 519, 637
stimulus generalization principle of, 360
Thorndike's influence on, 533, 637
Hummingbirds, song learning in, 64
Hunt, J. McV., 239
Hunter, Walter S., **237–239**, *238*, 332
Hunter-McCrary law, 610
Hunting behavior, predatory, 461
Huntington's disease
basal ganglia involvement, 191
dorsal striatum abnormality in, 192
episodic memory and, 111
memory impairment, 520